Mexico

Baja
Peninsula
p719

Copper Canyon &
Northern Mexico
p765

Northern
Central
Highlands
p659

Central
Pacific
Coast
p509

Western
Central
Highlands
p597

Around Mexico
City p151

Mexico
City p69

Veracruz
p219

Yucatán
Peninsula
p269

Oaxaca
p437

Chiapas &
Tabasco
p369

Kate Armstrong, Ray Bartlett, Stuart Butler, Ashley Harrell,
John Hecht, Anna Kaminski, Tom Masters, Liza Prado,
Simon Richmond, Regis St Louis, Phillip Tang

Contents

PLAN YOUR TRIP

ON THE ROAD

SURASEK / SHUTTERSTOCK ©

Contents

PALACIO DE BELLAS ARTES,
MEXICO CITY P135

CAROLINA ARROYO / SHUTTERSTOCK ©

TORTA AHOGADA (DROWNED
SANDWICH) P613

Contents

COVID-19

We have re-checked every business in this book before publication to ensure that it is still open after the COVID-19 outbreak. However, the economic and social impacts of COVID-19 will continue to be felt long after the outbreak has been contained, and many businesses, services and events referenced in this guide may experience ongoing restrictions. Some businesses may be temporarily closed, have changed their opening hours and services, or require bookings; some unfortunately could have closed permanently. We suggest you check with venues before visiting for the latest information.

MARCOS BOTELHO JR/SHUTTERSTOCK ©

Right: Hierve El
Agua (p467)

WELCOME TO
Mexico

It has taken me more than 50 years to tick Mexico off my bucket list, and I'm left wondering why it took me so long. For starters, the country's diversity – its terrain, cuisine, culture and the arts – is simply astounding. It is impossible not to find your perfect holiday location here, be it at a balmy beach resort, a charming pueblo mágico, or the big daddy of all metropolises, Mexico City. Everywhere you look are brilliant colors, everywhere you go there's music – what's not to love about that?

By Simon Richmond, Writer
🐦 @simonrichmond 📷 simonrichmond
For more about our writers, see p896

Mexico

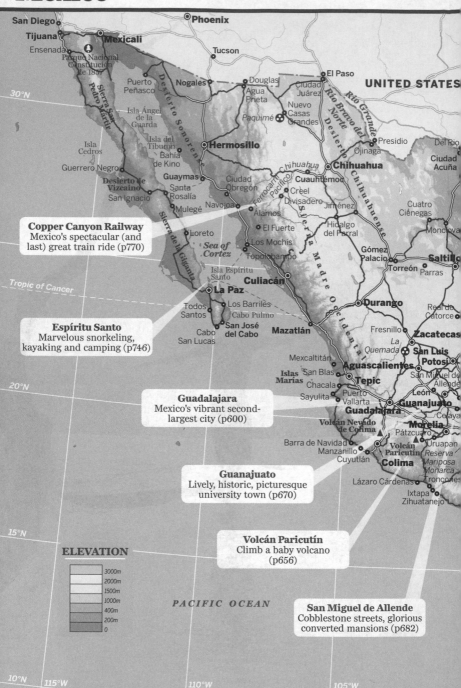

Copper Canyon Railway
Mexico's spectacular (and last) great train ride (p770)

Espíritu Santo
Marvelous snorkeling, kayaking and camping (p746)

Guadalajara
Mexico's vibrant second-largest city (p600)

Guanajuato
Lively, historic, picturesque university town (p670)

Volcán Paricutín
Climb a baby volcano (p656)

San Miguel de Allende
Cobblestone streets, glorious converted mansions (p682)

UNITED STATES

San Diego
Tijuana
Ensenada
Mexicali
Phoenix
Tucson
Nogales
Douglas
Agua Prieta
Ciudad Juárez
El Paso
Presidio
Del Rio
Ciudad Acuña
Parque Nacional Constitución de 1857
Puerto Peñasco
Desierto Sonoren
Nuevo Casas Grandes
Paquimé
Ojinaga
Isla Ángel de la Guarda
Isla Cedros
Isla del Tiburón
Bahía de Kino
Hermosillo
Chihuahua
Cuauhtémoc
Creel
Divisadero
Jiménez
Cuatro Ciénegas
Monclova
Guerrero Negro
Desierto de Vizcaíno
San Ignacio
Guaymas
Santa Rosalía
Ciudad Obregón
Navojoa
Alamos
El Fuerte
Hidalgo del Parral
Gómez Palacio
Torreón
Parras
Saltillo
Mulegé
Loreto
Los Mochis
Topolobampo
Durango
Real de Catorce
Sierra de la Giganta
Sea of Cortez
Isla Espíritu Santo
Culiacán
La Paz
Todos Santos
Los Barriles
Cabo Pulmo
San José del Cabo
Mazatlán
Fresnillo
La Quemada
Zacatecas
San Luis Potosí
Cabo San Lucas
Mexcaltitán
San Blas
Aguascalientes
San Miguel de Allende
Islas Marías
Chacala
Sayulita
Puerto Vallarta
Tepic
León
Guanajuato
Celaya
Guadalajara
Volcán Nevado de Colima
Morelia
Pátzcuaro
Barra de Navidad
Manzanillo
Cuyutlán
Volcán Paricutín
Uruapan
Reserva Mariposa Monarca
Troncones
Colima
Lázaro Cárdenas
Ixtapa
Zihuatanejo

ELEVATION
3000m
2000m
1500m
1000m
400m
200m
0

PACIFIC OCEAN

Río Bravo del Norte
Río Grande
Desierto Chihuahuense
Chihuahua
Ferrocarril Pacifico
Sierra Madre Occidental
Sierra San Pedro Mártir

30°N
Tropic of Cancer
20°N
15°N
10°N
115°W
110°W
105°W

N 0 ⎯⎯⎯⎯⎯ 500 km
0 ⎯⎯⎯⎯⎯ 250 miles

Fort Worth ● Dallas

OF AMERICA

Jackson ◉

Montgomery ●

Tallahassee ●

Mississippi River

Austin ◉
Houston ●
San Antonio ●

Baton Rouge ◉

Eagle Pass
Piedras Negras

Nuevo Laredo ● Laredo

Gulf of Mexico

McAllen
Reynosa ● Brownsville
Monterrey ● Matamoros
Padre Island

Teotihuacán
The awesome Pyramids of
the Sun and the Moon (p157)

Chichén Itzá
Simply breathtaking ancient
Maya ruins (p342)

25°N

Sierra Madre
Matehuala ● Ciudad Victoria

Reserva de la Biosfera El Cielo

Mexico City
Mammoth, fascinating,
cultured metropolis (p69)

Tropic of Cancer

Reserva de la Biosfera Sierra Gorda

Tampico ●

Mérida
Beautiful, cultured
colonial city (p320)

CUBA

Ek' Balam
Parque Nacional
Isla Contoy

Progreso Río Isla Mujeres
Izamal Lagartos
Querétaro ● Tuxpan Tizimín ● Cancún
Pachuca Poza Rica Mérida Puerto Morelos
Papantla Valladolid Playa del Carmen
MEXICO El Tajín Chichén Isla Cozumel
CITY ● Teotihuacán Uxmal Itzá
Tlaxcala Campeche ● Felipe Carrillo Puerto
Toluca Xalapa Tulum 20°N
Cardel Reserva de la
Cuernavaca Puebla Veracruz Ciudad del Biosfera Reserva de la
Córdoba Tlacotalpan Carmen Calakmul Biosfera
Orizaba Escárcega Sian Ka'an
Chilpancingo Tehuacán Coatzacoalcos Chetumal ●

San Cristóbal de las Casas
Colonial charm and
Maya culture (p379)

Caribbean Sea

Xpujil
Calakmul

Belize City ◉

BELIZE

Sierra Madre del Sur
Monte Albán Villahermosa
Acapulco Istmo de Palenque
Pie de la Tehuantepec Tuxtla Ocosingo Yaxchilán
Cuesta Oaxaca Gutiérrez San Cristóbal
Juchitán de las Casas
Puerto Pochutla Tehuantepec Tonalá
Escondido Puerto Comitán
Ángel Bahías de **GUATEMALA**
Huatulco Volcán
Reserva de la Tacaná
Biosfera La (4100m) **HONDURAS**
Encrucijada Tapachula TEGUCIGALPA
SAN

Palenque
Exquisite Maya architecture
in jungle setting (p398)

Reserva Mariposa Monarca
Monarch butterflies in
their millions (p644)

GUATEMALA SALVADOR
CITY

EL SALVADOR

NICARAGUA

Oaxaca
Gorgeous handicrafts,
unique cuisine (p440)

Oaxaca Coast
Blissed-out beach-lovers'
nirvana (p473)

100°W

95°W

90°W

Mexico's Top Experiences

1 ANCIENT RUINS

Exploring Mexico's ancient ruins is an unmissable experience and one that leaves an unforgettable impression as you stand before towering pyramids and intricately designed temples, some of which are thousands of years old. As you'll appreciate, not only did these ancient civilizations pull off very sophisticated architecture but they also knew a thing or two about mathematics, astronomy and art. The cities they left behind remind us of this brilliant legacy. Above: Palenque (p399)

ANTON_IVANOV/SHUTTERSTOCK ©

JUSTIN FOULKES/LONELY PLANET ©

Juggle Ruins and Wildlife-Watching

Not only will you find Palenque's exquisite Maya temples (pictured left) fascinating but you get the added plus of spotting wildlife in a surrounding jungle habitat that's home to black howler monkeys (pictured right) and colorful scarlet macaws. p398

ANNA OMELCHENKO/SHUTTERSTOCK ©

MATTEO COLOMBO/GETTY IMAGES ©

Gaze at Supersized Pyramids

When in Mexico City take a detour to Mexico's biggest ancient city, Teotihuacán, to check out some of the world's tallest pyramids. A common misconception is that these astonishing structures are Aztec, but they were actually built by the earlier Teotihuacan. p157

Drive the Ruta Puuc

Feast your eyes on some of Mexico's most sophisticated ancient architecture as you tour spectacular Uxmal (pictured; p333) and the Ruta Puuc region. The road along the Puuc Route traverses hilly countryside dotted with seldom-visited Maya ruins. p337

2 FEAST ON FAB FOOD

How prolific is Mexican cuisine? Unesco awarded it 'Cultural Heritage' status, so yeah, it's that good. Whether you're delving into scrumptious street eats, experimenting with the unique flavors of the highly diverse regional cuisine or dining in refined contemporary fusion restaurants, you'll soon realize that eating can easily become both a highlight and an obsession, and that's especially true when you find yourself in some of Mexico's top foodie destinations

Munch on *Mole* and Bugs

For the quintessential Oaxacan eating experience, hit the capital's bustling food markets for exquisite homemade *moles* (dishes prepared with thick chili-based sauces; pictured above) and crunchy fried grasshoppers. p454

Eat Your Way Through the Capital

Mexico City boasts the most diverse food scene in Mexico and there's no better place for a taco crawl. *Tacos al pastor*, anyone? For something more upscale, the tasting menu at Pujol offers a meal of a lifetime. p115

Savor Yucatecan Flavor

Family-run restaurants, markets and street stalls all take food seriously in the Yucatán and you'll understand why after trying classics such as *panuchos* (fried tortillas stuffed with refried beans) and *cochinita pibil* (achiote-rubbed, slow-cooked pork). p326

3 INTO THE BLUE

With thousands of kilometers of coastline and the world's second-largest barrier reef, Mexico is a dream come true for divers and snorkelers. Plunge into the translucent waters of the Mexican Caribbean and you'll feel like you're floating in space as you drift dive among soaring walls. Or head for the wildlife-rich waters of the Sea of Cortez and explore colorful reefs in some of the most biologically diverse waters on the planet.

Dive at World-Famous Sites

It's hard to imagine a more exhilarating experience than what awaits you in Cozumel's national marine park, one of the planet's top dive destinations for its abundant marine life, primo drift diving, steep walls and cerulean waters with excellent visibility. p295

LEONARDO GONZALEZ/SHUTTERSTOCK ©

Discover Southern Baja

Dive the only coral reef on the west coast of North America, in one of Mexico's most extraordinary marine parks, at Cabo Pulmo (pictured above). p752

Plunge into the Pacific

From the Pacific coast's Bahía de Banderas (pictured right) to the Bahías de Huatulco, there's no shortage of hotspots to explore in a region teeming with marine life. p54

4 RIDING THE COPPER CANYON TRAIN

MANFRED GOTTSCHALK/GETTY IMAGES ©

J.S. LAMY/SHUTTERSTOCK ©

WESTEND61/GETTY IMAGES ©

You've probably heard of Mexico's astonishing Copper Canyon, a canyon system four times larger than Arizona's Grand Canyon. Take in the breathtaking scenery as you chug along on a train to picturesque small towns where you can hop off for a hike or bike ride and admire the region's towering high-walled canyons, hot springs and cascading waterfalls.

Hiking to Towering Waterfalls

Hike out to the nation's highest year-round waterfall and walk along an extensive off-the-beaten-path trail network at Cascada de Basaseachi. p780

Zip-lining over Deep Canyons

Parque de Aventura Barrancas del Cobre allows you to appreciate Copper Canyon's astonishing vistas with the added rush of rock climbing and zip-lining. p777

Cycling and Soaking

The highlands town of Creel provides many opportunities to venture out on bike or foot. Explore the area on your own or hook up a tour that takes you to hot springs. p778

5 UNFORGETTABLE BEACH ADVENTURES

Beach life in Mexico is pretty rewarding in and of itself, so imagine just how sweet it is when you add some epic activities into the mix. Whether you're getting barreled in pounding surf, spying enormous whales in the Sea of Cortez or witnessing armies of sea turtles coming ashore for nesting season, you'll never cease to be amazed by the natural wonders of Mexico's glorious coast.

Witness a Turtle Invasion

Watching turtles come ashore by the thousands to lay their eggs in the soft sands of Playa Escobilla (pictured below right) will leave you completely in awe. p485

ALYSSA QUINN/SHUTTERSTOCK ©

Surfing the Pacific Coast

From the Baja Peninsula to the southern Pacific coast, Mexico is full of awesome surf spots such as Todos Santos and the Mexican Pipeline in Puerto Escondido (pictured above; p475).

Watching Gentle Giants

Head to Loreto in February and March to experience one of the best places in Mexico to spot the blue whale (pictured bottom right), the largest animal on the planet. p743

6 CULTURAL CITIES

Even if you don't consider yourself much of an architecture buff, the regional cities in Mexico will wow you with their palatial buildings, and their vibrant nightlife scenes are nothing to sneeze at either. These places have long been regarded as their regions' cultural capitals, meaning they also have a vast offering of cool museums, art galleries and tasty regional cuisine.

Yucatán's Cultural Mecca

Admire a cathedral that's nearly as old the city itself and stay in old *henequén* haciendas that have been converted into gorgeous hotels in Mérida. p320

Soak Up University Life

Roam the winding streets and hills of Guanajuato (pictured) and rejoice in its university town vibe and its many cultural offerings, especially the world-class Cervantino Festival. p670

Heartbeat of Jalisco

Embrace the Mexican heartland while knocking back tequilas in mansions and belting out ballads with the mariachis. The food scene in Guadalajara never disappoints. p600

7 HITTING THE ROAD

There are more ways than one to fuel your wanderlust in Mexico: buckle up for some epic drives to ancient ruins, turquoise coasts and splendid cities; cruise past mesmerizing desert-meets-sea landscapes, stop at majestic swimming holes and wind through misty mountains en route to beautiful beach towns.

GREY82/SHUTTERSTOCK ©
JOSÉ IGNACIO SOTO/SHUTTERSTOCK ©

JORGE MALO PHOTOGRAPHY/GETTY IMAGES ©

Baja California Dreaming

Start with some wine-tasting in Valle de Guadalupe before cruising all the way down the scenic peninsula to the lovely beaches of Los Cabos. p729

Above: Playa del Amor, Cabo San Lucas (p756); Left: Valle de Guadalupe (p729)

JAKUB ZAJIC/SHUTTERSTOCK ©

Journey to Oaxaca

The road from Mexico City to the Oaxaca coast is a feast for the senses as you eat exquisite *moles*, explore mountaintop Zapotec ruins and linger on sublime beaches. p437

Playa Carrizalillo, Puerto Escondido (p474)

Maya Ruins and Caribbean Blue

A loop route around the Yucatán leads to one surprise after another as you stop at ancient Maya ruins, precious cenotes (limestone sinkholes) and white-sand beaches along the Mexican Caribbean. p269

Cenote X'Kekén, Valladolid (p351)

Need to Know

For more information, see Survival Guide (p853)

Currency
Mexican peso (M$)

Language
Spanish, 68 other national languages

Visas
All tourists must have a tourist permit, available on arrival. Some nationalities also need visas.

Money
Mexico is largely a cash economy. ATMs and exchange offices are widely available. Credit cards are accepted in many midrange and top-end hotels, restaurants and stores.

Cell Phones
Many US and Canadian carriers offer Mexico roaming deals. Mexican SIM cards can be used in unlocked phones.

Time
Most of Mexico is on Hora del Centro (GMT/UTC minus six hours). Six northern and western states are on GMT/UTC minus seven or eight hours; one eastern state is on GMT/UTC minus five hours.

When to Go

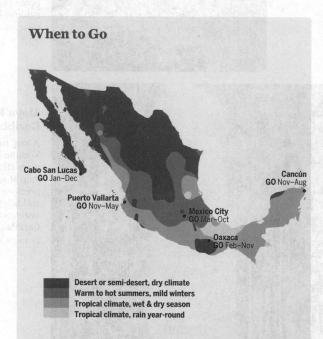

Cabo San Lucas
GO Jan–Dec

Puerto Vallarta
GO Nov–May

Mexico City
GO Mar–Oct

Oaxaca
GO Feb–Nov

Cancún
GO Nov–Aug

Desert or semi-desert, dry climate
Warm to hot summers, mild winters
Tropical climate, wet & dry season
Tropical climate, rain year-round

High Season
(Dec–Apr)

➡ The driest months across most of Mexico, bringing winter escapees from colder countries.

➡ Christmas and Easter are Mexican holiday times, with transportation and coastal accommodations very busy.

Shoulder Season
(Jul & Aug)

➡ Hot almost everywhere and very wet on the Pacific coast.

➡ Vacation time for many Mexicans and foreigners. Accommodations prices go up in some popular areas.

Low Season
(May & Jun, Sep–Nov)

➡ May and June see peak temperatures in many areas.

➡ September is the heart of the hurricane season, which doesn't always bring hurricanes but does bring wind and heavy rains on the Gulf and Pacific coasts.

Useful Websites

Lonely Planet (www.lonely planet.com/mexico) Destination information, hotel bookings, traveler forum, videos and more.

Mexico Cooks! (www.mexico cooks.typepad.com) Excellent blog on Mexican life.

Visit México (www.visitmexico. com) Official tourism site with plenty of helpful ideas.

Planeta.com (www.planeta. com) Articles, listings, links, photos and more.

Expats in Mexico (www. expatsinmexico.com) Online magazine packed with info about living in the country.

Mexperience (www.mexper ience.com) Features on all things Mexico.

Important Numbers

Country code	☑52
Emergency	☑911
International access code	☑00

Exchange Rates

Australia	A$1	M$15
Belize	BZ$1	M$10
Canada	C$1	M$16
Eurozone	€1	M$24
Guatemala	Q1	M$2.5
Japan	¥100	M$18
New Zealand	NZ$1	M$14
UK	UK£1	M$27
USA	US$1	M$20

For current exchange rates, see www.xe.com.

Daily Costs

Budget: Less than M$800

➡ Hostel dorm bed: M$160–280; double room in budget hotel: M$300–650

➡ *Comida corrida* (fixed-price lunch) in low-budget restaurant: M$60–90

➡ 2hr (150km) bus trip: M$200–230

Midrange: M$800–M$2500

➡ Double room in midrange hotel: M$700–1500

➡ Two-course meal with drinks: M$400–600

➡ Museum entry: M$10–70

➡ City taxi ride: M$35–65

➡ Hiking/rafting/mountain-biking day trip: M$900–2000

Top End: More than M$2500

➡ Double room in top-end hotel: M$1600–5000

➡ Dinner with drinks: over M$600

➡ Personalized day tour: M$1500–2000

➡ 1-tank dive: M$1700–2200

Opening Hours

Where there are significant seasonal variations in opening hours, we provide hours for high season. Some hours may be shorter in shoulder and low seasons. Hours vary widely but the following are fairly typical.

Banks 9am–4pm Monday to Friday

Bars and clubs 1pm–midnight

Cafes 8am–10pm

Restaurants 9am–11pm

Shops 9am–8pm Monday to Saturday

Supermarkets and department stores 9am–10pm daily

Arriving in Mexico

Aeropuerto Internacional Benito Juárez (Mexico City; p142) Authorized taxis, with ticket offices inside the airport, cost M$245 to central areas. Metrobús buses (M$30, plus M$10 for a smart card sold by machines inside the airport) serve some central areas. The metro (subway; M$5) operates from 5am (6am Saturday, 7am Sunday) to midnight; its Terminal Aérea station is 200m from the airport's Terminal 1.

Aeropuerto Internacional de Cancún (p280) Airport shuttles to downtown or the hotel zone cost around M$110 per person for shared rides; taxis cost up to M$650. ADO buses run to downtown Cancún (M$88, frequent).

Getting Around

Bus Mexico's efficient, comfortable and reasonably priced bus network is generally the best option for moving around the country. Services are frequent on main routes.

Air Over 60 cities are served by domestic flights, which are well worth considering for longer intercity trips. Fares vary widely depending on the airline and how far in advance you pay.

Car A convenient option giving maximum independence. Roads are serviceable, with speeds generally slower than north of the border or in Europe. Rental rates start around M$700 per day, including basic insurance.

Train Train travel is limited to one spectacularly scenic train route in northern Mexico.

For much more on **getting around**, see p865

First Time Mexico

For more information, see Survival Guide (p853)

Checklist

➡ Check that your passport is valid for at least six months beyond your stay

➡ Get necessary immunizations well in advance

➡ Check your government's Mexico travel information

➡ Organize travel insurance

➡ Make bookings (for accommodations, travel, restaurants)

➡ Inform your credit- or debit-card company

➡ Check if you can use your cell phone in Mexico

What to Pack

➡ International electrical adaptor (for non–North Americans)

➡ Flashlight (torch)

➡ Driver's license (if driving)

➡ Sun hat and sunglasses

➡ Waterproof jacket

➡ Sturdy footwear

➡ Warm clothing

➡ Charcoal tablets to treat Montezuma's revenge

➡ Mexican Spanish phrasebook

Top Tips for Your Trip

➡ Try not to worry too much about crime. Mexico's much-reported drug-gang violence happens mostly in a small number of places and the country's most-visited areas are little touched by it.

➡ Get out of the cities and coastal resorts into the countryside and smaller towns and villages, where you'll see a side of Mexican life that many tourists miss.

➡ Get used to 'Mexico time' – things won't run like clockwork.

➡ Pick a region that you particularly want to explore rather than trying to cover the whole country.

What to Wear

In beach towns, shorts and short skirts are common; sleeveless tops are fine. Take some sleeved tops and long pants or skirts to protect against sun and mosquitoes, and for wearing beyond the beach – more conservative dress should be observed when visiting inland cities and towns, as well as churches everywhere. Pack a sweater or a warm jacket for cooler inland areas and for Mexico's notoriously frosty air-conditioned buses. A sun hat is essential; good, inexpensive options are sold throughout Mexico.

Sleeping

In popular destinations, book a couple of months in advance for Christmas, Easter, Semana Santa and July/August.

Hostels Found largely in backpacker-heavy destinations, hostels are inexpensive, and are often run by savvy travelers.

Hotels Hotels range from nondescript to sensitively renovated historic residences.

Guesthouses Typically good value and family-run, guesthouses offer a great taste of local life.

Cabañas Cabins and huts, mostly found at beach destinations, range from basic to luxurious.

Camping and hammocks In more budget-oriented beach spots, you can often sleep in a hammock or pitch a tent cheaply.

Money

Plan on making cash purchases with pesos. A few businesses accept US dollars. It's easy to get pesos from ATMs using a major credit or debit card. You can pay with major credit and debit cards at most midrange and all top-end restaurants, shops and hotels.

For more information, see p858.

Bargaining

It's worth asking if a discount is available on room rates, especially if it's low season or you're staying more than two nights. In markets some haggling is expected. Unmetered taxis will often shave some pesos off the initial asking price.

Tipping

Many service workers depend on tips to supplement miserable wages.

Attendants Car-parking and gas-station attendants expect M$5 to M$10.

Hotels It's nice (though optional) to leave 5% to 10% of your room costs for those who keep it clean and tidy.

Porters Airport and hotel porters usually get M$50 to M$100.

Restaurants Tip 10% to 15% unless service is included in the check.

Taxis Drivers don't expect tips unless they provide some extra service.

Language

Mexico's main language is Spanish. Many Mexicans working in the tourism industry also speak some English, often good English. In any accommodations catering to international travelers, you can get by with English. Still, it's useful and polite to know at least a few words of Spanish – Mexicans appreciate you making the effort to greet with *'Buenos días'*, even if they break into fluent English.

❶ Where can I buy handicrafts?
¿Dónde se puede comprar artesanías?
don·de se pwe·de kom·prar ar·te·sa·nee·as

Star buys in Mexico are the regional handicrafts produced all over the country, mainly by the indigenous people.

❷ Which *antojitos* do you have?
¿Qué antojitos tiene? ke an·to·khee·tos tye·ne

'Little whimsies' (snacks) can encompass anything – have an entire meal of them, eat a few as appetisers, or get one on the street for a quick bite.

❸ Not too spicy, please.
No muy picoso, por favor. no mooy pee·ko·so por fa·vor

Not all food in Mexico is spicy, but beware – many dishes can be fierce indeed, so it may be a good idea to play it safe.

❹ Where can I find a *cantina* nearby?
¿Dónde hay una cantina cerca de aquí?
don·de ai oo·na kan·tee·na ser·ka de a·kee

Ask locals about the classical Mexican venue for endless snacks, and often dancing as well.

❺ How do you say ... in your language?
¿Cómo se dice ... en su lengua?
ko·mo se dee·se ... en su len·gwa

Numerous indigenous languages are spoken around Mexico, primarily Mayan languages and Náhuatl. People will appreciate it if you try to use their local language.

Etiquette

Mexicans are not huge sticklers for etiquette. Their natural warmth takes precedence.

Greetings 'Mucho gusto' (roughly 'A great pleasure') is a polite thing to say when you're introduced to someone, accompanied by a handshake. If it's a woman and a man, the woman offers her hand first.

Pleasing people Mexicans love to hear that you're enjoying their country. They are slow to criticize or argue, expressing disagreement more by nuance than by blunt contradiction.

Visiting homes An invitation to a Mexican home is an honor for an outsider; you will be treated very hospitably. Take a small gift, such as flowers or something for the children. Be at least 30 minutes late; being on time is considered rude.

What's New

Sporadic violence from the ongoing drugs war continues to put a dent in Mexico's image, but with more than 41 million international visitors in 2018 adding around US$22 billion to the economy, the country remains a popular vacation destination.

Sunrise at Chichén Itzá

Avoid the fearsome crowds at Mexico's most famous Maya sight (p342) by booking a pricey but unforgettable private tour, which will allow you to enter the ruins before dawn. You'll have the chance to watch the sunrise over El Castillo and then a further two hours to explore the grounds before the bus tours and general punters arrive at 8am.

The Chepe Express

Ride the new luxury train (p770) along the famous Copper Canyon route between Los Mochis and Creel. The vintage-inspired carriages serve up grand views, and there's an excellent restaurant and stylish lounge-bar on board.

Centro Cultural Juan Beckman Gallardo

Opened in 2018, this beautifully designed cultural center (p625) houses a fascinating museum on the Tequila region's history and culture, from pre-Hispanic times to the present.

Museo Leonora Carrington

This new gallery (p709) in Xilitla is dedicated to the surreal artistic work of the British-born but Mexican at heart Leonora Carrington, who was also a women's rights campaigner.

Museo del Café Córdoba

In the city where Mexico's coffee industry started, this new museum (p246) explains all about the bean, with admission including guided tastings of premium coffees.

LOCAL KNOWLEDGE

WHAT'S HAPPENING IN MEXICO

•••

Simon Richmond & John Hecht, Lonely Planet writers

Sick of corruption and drug-related crime, voters elected left-wing politician Andrés Manuel López Obrador as president in 2018. Among his administration's sweeping economic changes, funding for the national tourism promotion board was reallocated for construction of the Tren Maya, an ambitious 1525km intercity railway connecting numerous tourist hotspots across the Yucatán Peninsula, including Palenque and Cancún. AMLO, as López Obrador is known, vowed to complete the train line by 2023; however, environmentalists and Maya rights activists have criticized the project, saying it will impinge on the Calakmul Biosphere Reserve, the second-largest tropical forest in the Americas after the Amazon. The president also promised to complete a long-delayed highway in 2022 that will link Oaxaca City with Puerto Escondido as it cuts travel time in half between the capital and the coast. Meanwhile, Mexico is moving to legalize marijuana for recreational use, which would make it one of only a handful of countries to do so on a national level.

Telefónica Gastro Park

Food-truck heaven (p723) comes to Tijuana in an industrial zone of the city, where up-and-coming chefs and entrepreneurs turn out everything from tacos and ramen to craft beer and gourmet coffee.

Museo Juan Soriano

This sleek new museum (p198) in Cuernavaca brings big names in Mexican contemporary art to its temporary exhibitions, along with a sculpture garden and a library for perusing art, design and architecture tomes.

Casa Guillermo Tovar de Teresa

The complete collection of poet Sor Juana Inés de la Cruz is among the artistic treasures, including paintings, sculptures, furniture and rugs, at this sumptuous new Mexico City museum (p90).

Metrobús Línea 7

Take in Mexico City's major sights from the top deck of this comfortable London-like double-decker bus (p148) which connects many major sights along the Paseo de la Reforma.

Flavor Teller

A longtime Dutch resident of Mazatlán draws on a decade's worth of street-food exploration to bring you the best of the city's typical eats during her fun food tours (p515).

Kokoyome

This remote and rustic lodge (p784) is tucked in Copper Canyon country with its own waterfalls, sweeping vistas and a green ethos few can match (including a spring-fed water source and delicious food grown on-site).

LISTEN, WATCH & FOLLOW

For inspiration and up-to-date news, visit www.lonelyplanet.com/mexico/articles.

Roma (2018) Tenderly observed tale of an upper-middle-class family in Mexico City in the early 1970s, directed by Alfonso Cuarón.

On the Plain of Snakes (Paul Theroux, 2019) The travel-writing titan gets under the skin of contemporary Mexico.

The Mexico Podcast: History & Present Nothing is off limits in Brandon Springer's podcast on all things Mexico.

Pati Jinich (https://patijinich.com) James Beard Award–winning, Mexican-born chef of a US public TV show on Mexican cuisine.

FAST FACTS

Food trend Plant-based swaps in traditional dishes

Active volcanos 48

Population below poverty line 40%

Population 128 million

MEXICO   USA   UK

≈ 35 people per sq mile

Coffee, Chiapas

Fabulous cafes, part of the third-wave coffee trend, are starting to spring up in Chiapas, a historic coffee plantation region – including Café Pillangó (Comitán; p418), Cafeología (San Cristóbal de las Casas; p391) and Buenos Diaz Cafe (Tapachula; p427).

Accommodations

Find more accommodations reviews throughout the On the Road chapters (from p67)

Accommodations Types

B&Bs & Casas de Huéspedes Usually small, comfortable, midrange or top-end guesthouses, often family-run, beautifully designed and offering friendly, personal attention.

Cabañas Cabins or huts (of wood, brick, adobe or stone), often with a palm-thatched roof, and most often found at beach destinations. They range from basic with dirt floors, to the positively deluxe with rates of over M$2000.

Campgrounds & Trailer Parks Most organized campgrounds are actually trailer parks set up for RVs (recreational vehicles, campers) and trailers (caravans) that are also open to tent campers at lower rates.

Hammocks Hammock space is available in many of the more low-key beach spots. A hammock can be a very comfortable and cheap place to sleep in hot areas (keep mosquito repellent handy).

Hostels Budget accommodations, always with shared dorms, sometimes with private rooms. Cleanliness and security vary, but popular hostels are great places for meeting fellow travelers.

Posadas Covering anything from basic budget hotels to tastefully designed, small, midrange places.

PRICE RANGES

The following price ranges refer to accommodations for two people in high season, including any taxes charged.

$ less than M$800

$$ M$800–1600

$$$ more than M$1600

Best Places to Stay

Best in Mexico

This is your chance to stay in some beautifully designed and incredibly historic hotels, inns and resorts. Alternatively, choose to experience some amazing nature locations in rustic sleeping bliss.

➡ La Casona (p113), Mexico City

➡ Hotel Hacienda de Cortés (p200), Cuernavaca

➡ Del Carmen Concept Hotel, (p611) Guadalajara

➡ Hotel Casa Eugenia (p640), Morelia

➡ Le Blanc (p276), Cancún

➡ Encanto Acapulco (p588), Acapulco

Best on a Budget

A hostel dorm is the obvious budget choice with the best backpacker places offering private rooms, too, alongside a pool, bar or cafe, gardens and sundecks. There are good-value hotels, as well – often with bags of character.

➡ Casa San Ildefonso (p110), Mexico City

➡ Nómadas Hostel (p325), Mérida

➡ Mayan Monkey (p305), Tulum

➡ Casa Ángel (p449), Oaxaca City

➡ Casa Maricela (p688), San Miguel de Allende

➡ Hostal Tres Central (p374), Tuxtla Gutiérrez

Best for Families

Beachside resorts and hotels are the ideal choice for family vacations and Mexico has no shortage of excellent options to suit all budgets here. Also think about staying close to major archaeological sites and in rural, national park areas where everyone can connect with ancient culture and nature.

→ Hacienda Chichén (p348), Chichén Itzá

→ Las Palmas (p501), Bahías de Huatulco

→ Casamar (p479), Puerto Escondido

→ Inn at Mazatlán Resort & Spa (p518), Mazatlán

→ Gran Sueño (p751), La Ventana

→ El Pedregal (p793), Álamos

Best for Solo Travelers

Major cities and mid-sized towns work well for solo travelers either looking to blend into the crowd or connect with locals through a range of activities. Also consider hostels and places that run cultural and social events.

→ Luz en Yucatán (p325), Mérida

→ Posada Yolihuani (p650), Pátzcuaro

→ Hostal Casa los Abuelos (p813), Cuatro Ciénegas

→ Hostal Casa Balché (p358), Campeche

→ El Ángel Azul (p747), La Paz

→ La Betulia (p450), Oaxaca City

Best Sustainable Stays

Caring for the environment and finding excellent accommodations in Mexico are not mutually exclusive. Among our top sustainable picks are places that recycle, grow their own food, use solar energy and collect rainwater in cisterns.

→ Adele's Ranch Bus (p728), Northern Baja

→ Campo Archelon (p738), Bahía de los Ángeles

→ Acre (p753), San José del Cabo

→ Centro Ecoturístico Ayutl Maruata (p564), Michoacán coast

→ Hotel El Rey del Caribe (p276), Cancún

→ La Posada del Sol (p306), Tulum

Booking

Book well ahead if you plan to travel during Semana Santa (Easter), which often coincides with Spring Break in the US and Christmas–New Year holidays, as well as for local festivals such as Día de Muertos. Many midrange and top-end establishments in tourist destinations will raise

Casa San Ildefonso (p110), Mexico City

their rates during these busy periods. Budget accommodations are more likely to keep the same rates all year. You can find self-catering places to stay through Airbnb and other room-sharing and short-term rentals websites.

Lonely Planet (www.lonelyplanet.com/mexico/hotels) independent reviews, as well as recommendations on the best places to stay.

Hostelworld (www.hostelworld.com) Provides plentiful hostel listings and online reservations.

Taxes

Accommodations rates are subject to two taxes:

IVA (value-added tax; 16%)

ISH (lodging tax; 2% or 3% depending on the state)

Many budget establishments only charge you these taxes if you require a receipt, and they quote room rates accordingly (ie not including taxes).

INSPIRED BY MAPS / SHUTTERSTOCK ©

Month by Month

January

It's warm in coastal and lowland areas, cool in the highlands and dry everywhere, attracting flocks of foreign tourists. The first week is holiday season, with transportation booked up and coastal resorts very busy.

🎭 Día de los Santos Reyes

January 6 (Three Kings' Day or Epiphany), rather than Christmas, is the day when Mexican children traditionally receive presents, commemorating the Three Kings' gifts for the baby Jesus. Mexicans eat *rosca de reyes*, a large oval sweetbread decorated with candied fruit.

🎭 Mérida Fest

Throughout most of the month, Mérida celebrates its diverse culture with dance, music, theater, art, acrobatic shows and other cultural events. (p325)

🎭 Festival Alfonso Ortíz Tirado

In late January, tens of thousands descend upon tiny Álamos for this multiday festival featuring some of the world's top musicians playing classical and chamber music, blues, bossa nova and *trova* (troubadour-type music). (p792)

🐦 Migratory Bird Season

January is the peak season for migratory birds along Mexico's Pacific coast. Lagoons and rivers at places such as Laguna Manialtepec and Lagunas de Chacahua are packed with fowl, and San Blas even holds an International Migratory Bird Festival. (p527)

February

Temperatures are marginally higher than in January, but it remains dry, making this a great month to be in much of Mexico, though it can still be cold in the north and at high altitudes.

🎭 Día de la Candelaría

Candlemas (February 2), commemorating the infant Jesus's presentation in the temple, is widely celebrated. In Tlacotalpan several days of festivities feature bull-running in the streets, and a flotilla of boats following an image of the Virgin down the Río Papaloapan. (p260)

🎭 Carnaval

A big bash preceding the 47-day penance of Lent, Carnaval happens during the week leading up to Ash Wednesday (March 2, 2022). It's wildest in Veracruz, La Paz and Mazatlán, with parades, music, drinking, dancing, fireworks and fun.

🐦 Whale-Watching Season

Magnificent gray whales calve in bays and lagoons around the Baja Peninsula from mid-December to mid-April. Whales can also be spotted along the whole Pacific coast during this period. Best months for Baja whale-watching are February and March. (p740)

March

It's getting steadily warmer all over Mexico, but it's

still dry and the winter season for foreign tourism continues.

☆ Spring Break

US students get a week's break in late February or March (dates vary between colleges) and many head to Mexican resort towns such as Cancún, Puerto Vallarta or Cabo San Lucas for days of over-the-top partying.

🏃 Ultra Caballo Blanco

Started by American runner Micah True, this 82km ultramarathon near Urique follows tough but gorgeous canyon trails, at altitude. The race pays homage to the native Tarahumara, who have a centuries-old tradition of long-distance running and whose very name means 'the running people'. (p775)

🎇 Chacala Music & Arts Festival

The small Pacific coast fishing town of Chacala celebrates everything from music and dance to regional cuisine and local art at beachside venues. (p532)

🎇 Festival Internacional del Cine

Mexico's biggest film event of the year draws top international actors and directors to Guadalajara for a week each March, with more than 250 films screened before over 100,000 viewers. (p610)

🎇 Vernal Equinox

Visitors mob Chichén Itzá for the spring (March 20 to 21) and autumnal (September 21 to 22) equinoxes, when shadows resemble a serpent ascending or descending El Castillo pyramid. Almost the same effect happens for a week preceding and following each equinox. (p342)

🎇 Festival del Centro Histórico de CDMX

Mexico City's historic center hosts music, theater, dance and literary events featuring talent from Mexico and abroad – the capital's biggest cultural bash of the year. (p109)

April

Temperatures continue to increase, but it stays dry. Semana Santa (Easter Week), which can be in March or April, is Mexico's major holiday week of the year, with tourist accommodations and transportation packed.

🎇 Semana Santa

Semana Santa is the week from Palm Sunday to Easter Sunday (April 10, 2022). Good Friday sees solemn processions in many places, and enormous crowds attend a re-enactment of the Crucifixion in Iztapalapa, Mexico City. (p109)

🛍 Tianguis Artesanal de Uruapan

Semana Santa kicks off with a major crafts competition and Uruapan's main square is then filled with exhibitions and sales of Michoacán handicrafts for the following two weeks. (p657)

🎇 Feria de Morelia

This three-week fair which starts in late April and runs into May, sees regional dance performances, bullfights, agricultural and handicraft exhibitions, plenty of partying and (at the end) fireworks in Michoacán's capital. (p635)

May

Temperatures reach annual peaks in cities such as Mérida (average daily high 35°C), Guadalajara (31°C), Oaxaca (30°C) and Mexico City (26°C). It's low season for tourism, meaning cheaper accommodations prices.

🎇 Cinco de Mayo

Celebrating the battle (May 5) in 1862 when Mexican forces defeated French troops, the streets of Puebla, where the fighting happened, close for a huge parade of floats with the military, performers and dancers entertaining more than 20,000 people. The following two weeks feature other events. (p167)

June

The rainy season begins, bringing heavy downpours in the southeast, in some places along the Pacific coast and in the central highlands. June to August is brutally hot in the north. Tourist numbers and hotel prices remain low.

🍴 Festival del Mole Poblano

Puebla celebrates its most famous contribution to Mexican cuisine, the chocolatey *mole poblano* sauce, in early June. (p167)

Feria de Corpus Christi

Papantla's big bash features spectacular *voladores* performances (where men suspended by their ankles whirl around a tall pole) and indigenous dances, plus *charreadas* (Mexican rodeos) and parades. (p253)

Surf's Up

Countless spots along the Pacific coast, including Puerto Escondido with its legendary Mexican Pipeline, enjoy superb swells from April/May to October/November. June to August generally sees the biggest waves. Beginners can learn to surf almost year-round. (p475)

Whale Shark–Watching

Massive whale sharks congregate to feed on plankton off Isla Contoy, north of Cancún, between mid-May and mid-September. (p273)

July

It's rainy in the southeast, central highlands and along the Pacific coast, but this is a summer vacation month for both foreigners and Mexicans, bringing busy times and higher prices at many tourist destinations.

La Feria de las Flores

This week-long, major flower festival in Mexico City includes the display of myriad varieties of plants, family activities, performances, and botany-related paintings and sculpture. The festival has pre-Hispanic

origins, when followers of Xiuhtecuhtli, Lord of Flowers, would make floral offerings in return for abundant crops. (p109)

Guelaguetza

Oaxaca is thronged for this fantastically colorful feast of regional dance on the first two Mondays after July 16, with plenty of other celebratory events accompanying it. (p449)

Fiesta de Santa Magdalena

Xico, Veracruz, is abuzz with processions involving elaborate costumes and dance for much of July in celebration of the town's patron saint. A running of the bulls takes place through the streets on July 22. (p242)

August

The summer holiday season continues, as do the rains, although they're less intense in most areas.

Feria de la Uva

The Coahuila city of Parras celebrates wine every August. Think parades, live-music performances, sporting events, religious ceremonies, and thousands and thousands of glasses of wine. The climax? A dance party at Casa Madero, the oldest winery in the Americas. (p812)

Feria de Huamantla

Huamantla, east of Mexico City, lets rip over a few days and nights during its mid-August fair. On August 14 the streets are carpeted with flowers and colored

sawdust. A few days later there's a Pamplona-esque running of the bulls (www.facebook.com/LaFeriaDe-Huamantla). (p185)

La Morisma

Zacatecas stages a spectacular mock battle with 10,000 participants, commemorating the Christians' win over the Moors in old Spain, usually on the last weekend of August. (p714)

September

It's the height of the hurricane season on the Yucatán Peninsula and Mexico's coasts. It's also rainy in most places, with poor visibility for Caribbean divers.

Día de la Independencia

On Independence Day (September 16) patriotic celebrations mark the anniversary of Miguel Hidalgo's 1810 call to rebellion against Spain, the Grito de Dolores. On the 15th, the Grito is repeated from every Mexican town hall, followed by fireworks. The biggest celebrations are in Mexico City. (p109)

October

Low season for tourism, with the possibility of hurricanes, but the rains ease off everywhere except the Yucatán Peninsula.

Copper Canyon Season

October, along with November and March, is one of the best months to visit northwest Mexico's spectacular canyon country, with temperatures not too hot at the bottom of the canyons, nor too cold at the top. (p765)

✹ Festival Internacional Cervantino

Guanajuato's two- to three-week arts festival, dedicated to Spanish writer Miguel de Cervantes, is one of the biggest cultural happenings in Latin America, with performances by worldwide music, dance and theater groups. (p675)

✹ Festival de las Ánimas

A new tradition in Mérida, this seven-day festival preceding Día de Muertos culminates in the Paseo de Ánimas (the Parade of Souls) – a procession of participants dressed in traditional Yucatecan clothes, with skulls painted on faces, from the graveyard to Parque San Juan. (p325)

November

The weather is mostly dry and hot temperatures are subsiding. Snow tops the high peaks of the central volcanic belt.

✹ Día de Muertos

On the Día de Muertos (November 2) cemeteries come alive as families deco-

rate graves and commune with their dead, some holding all-night vigils. Special altars appear in homes and public buildings. Associated events start days before, notably around Pátzcuaro, Uruapan, Mexico City and Oaxaca.

✹ Festival de Música de Morelia

This classical-music festival takes place in Morelia and is befitting of a city that is home to the oldest music conservatory in the Americas. Performances are held in various plazas, churches and theaters. (p640)

✖ Festival Gourmet International

Guest chefs from around Mexico and the world descend on the Pacific resort of Puerto Vallarta for this 10-day feast of the culinary arts. (p541)

🔒 Expo Artesanal

Taking place at the Centro Cultural Tijuana, this superb arts-and-crafts festival features handicrafts for sale from all over Mexico. (p726)

December

A dry month almost everywhere, and as cool as it gets. International winter tourism gets going

and the Christmas–New Year period is Mexican holiday time, with accommodations busy and prices high.

✹ Día de Nuestra Señora de Guadalupe

Several days of festivities throughout Mexico lead up to the feast day of the Virgin, the country's religious patron – the Day of Our Lady of Guadalupe (December 12). Millions converge on Mexico City's Basílica de Guadalupe. (p106)

✹ Christmas

Christmas is traditionally celebrated with a feast in the early hours of December 25, after midnight mass. Pre- or post-Christmas events in some towns include *pastorelas* (nativity plays), as in Tepotzotlán and Pátzcuaro, and *posadas* (candlelit processions), as in Taxco.

🦋 Monarch Butterfly Season

From late October to mid-March the forests of the Reserva de la Biosfera Santuario Mariposa Monarca (Monarch Butterfly Biosphere Reserve) turn orange as millions of large monarch butterflies winter here. The best time to watch them is on a warm, sunny afternoon. (p644)

Plan Your Trip
Itineraries

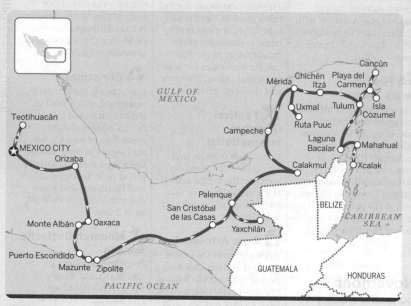

ARTUROGI / GETTY IMAGES ©

Beaches, Cities & Temples of Mexico's South

This classic journey leads south from Mexico's central heartland to its glorious Caribbean coast, and gives a superb sampling of the ruins, jungle, cities and beaches that make the country so fascinating.

Start by exploring the exciting megalopolis of **Mexico City**, key to any understanding of the country. Take a side trip to the awesome pyramids at **Teotihuacán**, capital of ancient Mexico's biggest empire. Then head east to charming **Orizaba**, close by the country's tallest peak Pico de Orizaba,

before crossing the mountains southward to **Oaxaca**. This cultured colonial city, with Mexico's finest handicrafts, sits at the heart of a beautiful region with a large indigenous population. Give yourself a day to explore the ancient Zapotec capital, **Monte Albán**, nearby.

Head to one of the relaxed beach spots on the Oaxaca coast, such as **Puerto Escondido**, **Mazunte** or **Zipolite**, for a few days of sun, surf and sand, before continuing east to **San Cristóbal de las Casas**, a beautiful highland town surrounded by intriguing indigenous villages. Move on to

Mansión Carvajal (p355), Campeche

Palenque, perhaps the most stunning of all ancient Maya cities, with its backdrop of emerald-green jungle, and **Yaxchilán**, another marvelous Maya city, accessible only by river.

Head northeast to **Campeche**, an attractive mix of colonial city and bustling modern town, detouring to the remote and ancient Maya city of **Calakmul** en route – this may add a couple of days to the itinerary but is worth every kilometer, we promise. Move on to colonial **Mérida**, the Yucatán Peninsula's lively cultural capital and the base for visiting the superb ruins of **Uxmal** and the **Ruta Puuc**. Next stop:

Chichén Itzá, the most celebrated of all the Yucatán's Maya sites. From here it's on to **Tulum** on the Caribbean coast, another spectacular Maya site set beside a glorious beach. If it's too busy for you, opt for the quiet, laid-back vibe of **Laguna Bacalar**, or if you want to go diving, head to the coast and stay in **Mahahual** or remote **Xcalak**. Finally, make your way northward along the Riviera Maya to the resort town of **Playa del Carmen**, with a side trip to **Isla Cozumel** for excellent snorkeling and diving. End at Mexico's most popular and unabashed coastal resort, **Cancún**.

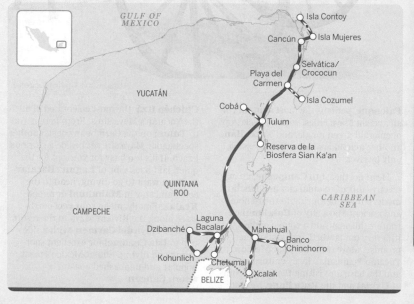

Riviera Maya & Costa Maya Getaway

12 DAYS

This journey showcases the best of Mexico's Caribbean coast, from the bustling beaches and frenetic nightlife of the Riviera Maya to the soporific charm of seaside villages along the Costa Maya. Some wonderfully scenic Maya ruins and terrific diving and snorkeling add a bit of action to a beach vacation.

Fly into **Cancún** and head straight for relaxed **Isla Mujeres** for beaches and snorkeling, taking a side trip to **Isla Contoy**, a national park with superlative bird-watching.

Alternatively, opt for hip **Playa del Carmen** with its own fine beaches, underwater activities and lively nightlife. 'Playa' is also the jumping-off point for the dive sites of **Isla Cozumel**. If you have kids, spend a day at the turtle farm on Isla Mujeres, one of the nearby 'ecoparks' such as **Selvática** with its 12 jungle zip-lines, or **Crococun** in Puerto Morelos, an interactive zoo with crocodiles and monkeys. Next stop: **Tulum**, with one of Mexico's most perfect beaches and its most spectacularly located Maya site. Nearby are the pyramids and temples of **Cobá**, as well as the wildlife-rich **Reserva de la Biosfera Sian Ka'an**. South of Tulum the Costa Maya is less developed and less touristed than the Riviera Maya. Head to **Mahahual**, a laid-back village with snorkeling and diving at the coral atoll **Banco Chinchorro**, or the tiny fishing town of **Xcalak**, another excellent water-sports base.

After three nights' chilling in these towns, backtrack to the northern end of Chetumal Bay before heading south to the tranquil **Laguna Bacalar**, where you can bask in the sun and bathe in the cenote-clear water that is painted unreal shades of blue, turquoise and green. For a diversion, head into the jungle and find yourself exploring the ruins of **Kohunlich** and **Dzibanché**, where you're likely to have the places to yourself.

Finish your trip in the relaxed, low-key city of **Chetumal**, where you can either travel onwards to Belize or turn around and, if you're worried that you missed out on Cancún's nightlife, spend your last night there and paint the town red.

Top: Tulum (p302)
Bottom: Templo de los Mascarones (p318), Kohunlich

18 DAYS · Baja from Tip to Toe

PLAN YOUR TRIP ITINERARIES

The world's second-longest peninsula seems tailor-made for road tripping, with 1200km of road snaking through picturesque villages, along dramatic coastline and past otherworldly rock canyons. Baja's charms are further enhanced by its appealing colonial towns, world-class diving and some of the best fish tacos you'll ever taste.

Enjoy a full-on day of Mexican life on the streets in **Tijuana** before taking the **Valle de Guadalupe** winery route, stopping for a day or two to tour the vineyards and taste the terrific tipples. Make a stop in **Ensenada** for great fish tacos and a stroll through the shopping streets, then head south via the Carretera Transpeninsular's spectacular desert scenery. If it's migration season (December to April), book a whale-watching tour at **Guerrero Negro**. Or, continue south and detour to **Sierra de San Francisco** to view ancient petroglyphs in the local caves.

Further south, pass through **San Ignacio** for a look at the most beautiful colonial church in Baja, and some sea-dwelling leviathans during whale-watching season. Stop in **Mulegé** for a tranquil paddle in the cerulean **Sea of Cortez**. The highway then hugs the coast en route to **Loreto**, where you can spend a day or two discovering the artisan shops, great restaurants, historic architecture and a 17th-century mission. Heading south again, the road passes several stunning beaches before ducking inland and back toward the unspoiled charms of **La Paz**. Spend a day kayaking and snorkeling off the island of **Espíritu Santo**.

Next, stop at **Todos Santos**, a gorgeous little town with galleries, sea-turtle nesting grounds and beautiful historical buildings, en route to wild **Cabo San Lucas**. Indulge in banana-boating, parasailing and other beach activities before hitting the bars, and take a boat to **Land's End** for a glimpse of the magical stone arch. If you need a respite, head for **San José del Cabo**, Cabo's tamer twin, with its appealing colonial church, art galleries and a clutch of good restaurants. Or, go underwater for a closer glimpse of the reef at **Cabo Pulmo** – the only living reef in the Sea of Cortez, teeming with schooling big-eyed jacks, whale sharks and more.

Top: Tijuana (p722)
Bottom: Sea lion off Espíritu Santo (p746), La Paz

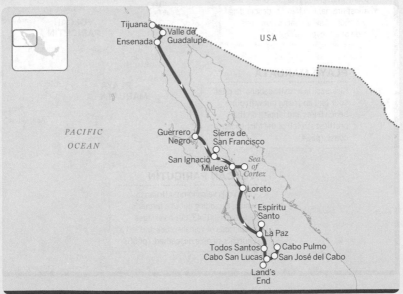

Off the Beaten Track: Mexico

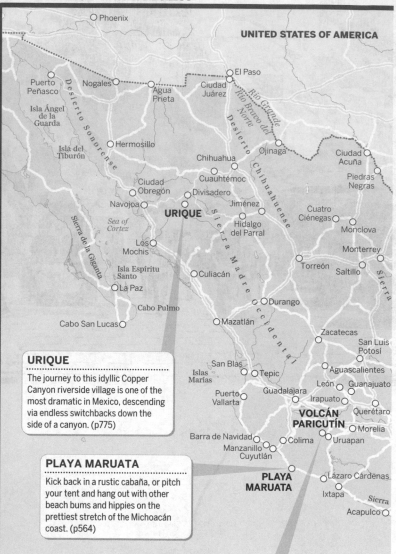

UNITED STATES OF AMERICA

Phoenix

El Paso

Puerto Peñasco
Nogales
Agua Prieta
Ciudad Juárez
Desierto Sonorense
Isla Ángel de la Guarda
Isla del Tiburón
Hermosillo
Chihuahua
Ojinaga
Ciudad Acuña
Piedras Negras
Cuauhtémoc
Ciudad Obregón
Divisadero
Jiménez
Cuatro Ciénegas
Monclova
Navojoa
URIQUE
Hidalgo del Parral
Sierra Madre Occidental
Desierto Chihuahuense
Río Grande
Río Bravo del Norte
Monterrey
Los Mochis
Torreón
Saltillo
Sea of Cortez
Isla Espíritu Santo
Culiacán
Sierra de la Giganta
La Paz
Durango
Cabo Pulmo
Mazatlán
Zacatecas
Cabo San Lucas
San Luis Potosí
San Blas
Aguascalientes
Islas Marías
Tepic
León
Guanajuato
Puerto Vallarta
Guadalajara
Irapuato
VOLCÁN PARICUTÍN
Querétaro
Barra de Navidad
Colima
Uruapan
Morelia
Manzanillo
Cuyutlán
PLAYA MARUATA
Lázaro Cárdenas
Ixtapa
Sierra
Acapulco

PACIFIC OCEAN

URIQUE

The journey to this idyllic Copper Canyon riverside village is one of the most dramatic in Mexico, descending via endless switchbacks down the side of a canyon. (p775)

PLAYA MARUATA

Kick back in a rustic cabaña, or pitch your tent and hang out with other beach bums and hippies on the prettiest stretch of the Michoacán coast. (p564)

VOLCÁN PARICUTÍN

Climb this volcano near Uruapan, which, exploding out of a farmer's field back in 1943, buried villages under tons of volcanic rock, but left a church's steeple unscathed. (p656)

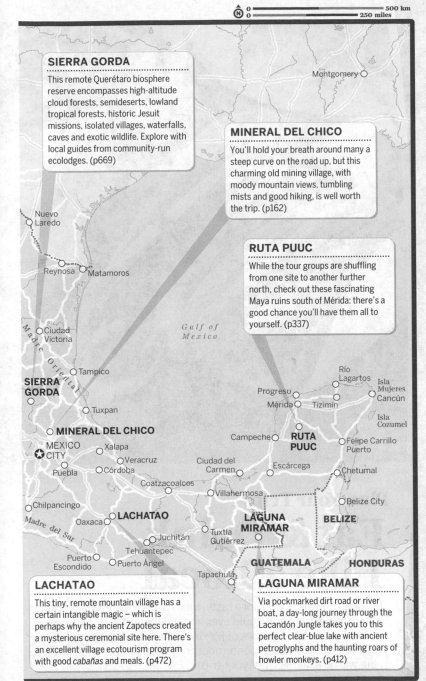

500 km
250 miles

SIERRA GORDA

This remote Querétaro biosphere reserve encompasses high-altitude cloud forests, semideserts, lowland tropical forests, historic Jesuit missions, isolated villages, waterfalls, caves and exotic wildlife. Explore with local guides from community-run ecolodges. (p669)

MINERAL DEL CHICO

You'll hold your breath around many a steep curve on the road up, but this charming old mining village, with moody mountain views, tumbling mists and good hiking, is well worth the trip. (p162)

RUTA PUUC

While the tour groups are shuffling from one site to another further north, check out these fascinating Maya ruins south of Mérida: there's a good chance you'll have them all to yourself. (p337)

LACHATAO

This tiny, remote mountain village has a certain intangible magic – which is perhaps why the ancient Zapotecs created a mysterious ceremonial site here. There's an excellent village ecotourism program with good *cabañas* and meals. (p472)

LAGUNA MIRAMAR

Via pockmarked dirt road or river boat, a day-long journey through the Lacandón Jungle takes you to this perfect clear-blue lake with ancient petroglyphs and the haunting roars of howler monkeys. (p412)

Montgomery

Nuevo Laredo

Reynosa Matamoros

Ciudad Victoria

Madre Oriental

Tampico

SIERRA GORDA

Tuxpan

MINERAL DEL CHICO

MEXICO CITY

Xalapa

Puebla Córdoba Veracruz

Coatzacoalcos

Chilpancingo

Oaxaca LACHATAO

Madre del Sur

Juchitán

Tehuantepec

Puerto Escondido Puerto Ángel

Tapachula

Gulf of Mexico

Progreso

Mérida Tizimín

Río Lagartos

Isla Mujeres Cancún

Isla Cozumel

Campeche RUTA PUUC

Félipe Carrillo Puerto

Ciudad del Carmen

Escárcega

Chetumal

Villahermosa

Belize City

Tuxtla Gutiérrez

LAGUNA MIRAMAR

BELIZE

GUATEMALA

HONDURAS

Tacos de pescado (fish tacos)

Plan Your Trip

Eat & Drink Like a Local

Mexican cuisine is far more tasty, fresh, varied, carefully prepared and creative than you could ever imagine before you start trying it. Venture into the flavors of Mexico, anywhere from simple street taco stands to refined contemporary fusion restaurants, and eating will be a highlight of your trip.

A Year In Food

With food festivals happening year-round and many ingredients available throughout the year, there's never a bad time for foodies to visit Mexico. However, some dishes are only available at certain times of the year.

March–April

Meatless dishes such as *romeritos* (seepweed, a wild plant that resembles rosemary, boiled and served in a *mole* sauce) show up on most vegetarian Lent menus.

May–Oct

Huitlacoche, the tar-like, black corn fungus used as a tortilla filling, follows the corn season.

Oct–Nov

Pan de muertos (bread of the dead), *calaveras de azúcar* (sugar skulls) and *calabaza en dulce* (candied pumpkin) are just some of the festive treats consumed on and in the lead-up to Día de Muertos (Day of the Dead, November 1 and 2).

Dec

A traditional Mexican Christmas menu includes turkey and *bacalao* (dried codfish cooked with olives, capers, onions and tomatoes).

Food Experiences

Meals of a Lifetime

Expendio de Maíz, **Mexico City** (p123) No menu or official name (apart from the 'corn dealer' description), just a communal table with food straight from the *comal* hot plate.

El Mural de los Poblanos, **Puebla** (p170) Enjoy excellent, traditional *poblano* dishes in an elegant setting. The house specialty is five kinds of *mole* (a type of chili sauce).

Dos, **Veracruz City** (p228) The six-course tasting menu brings creativity to simple things such as a taco or enchilada.

Sunset Bar & Grill, **San Carlos** (p790) Feast on mouthwatering seafood and creative cocktails tinged with *bacanora* (the Sonoran version of tequila).

Tintoque, **Puerto Vallarta** (p548) Chef Joel Ornelas impresses diners with creative, beautiful reimagining of classic flavors.

Alcalde, **Guadalajara** (p616) Superb seasonal menus from a chef who worked at Copenhagen's famed Noma restaurant.

Casa Oaxaca, **Oaxaca City** (p455) Magically combines Oaxacan and other flavors in delectably original ways.

Áperi, **San Miguel de Allende** (p690) A cutting-edge, anything-goes experience enjoyed at the kitchen table.

Ku'uk, **Mérida** (p327) A modern take on Yucatecan cuisine, with gorgeous presentation on slate, leaves and shells.

El Secreto, **San Cristóbal de las Casas** (p391) High-end gourmet cuisine in a rich color palette and equally stunning presentation.

Cheap Treats

Mexico has one of the world's great street-food cultures. All over the country, street stands, markets and small restaurants dole out endless supplies of filling and nutritious snacks and light meals, morning, noon and night. The busiest stands usually have the tastiest offerings and freshest ingredients.

Foremost are the many varieties of *antojitos* ('little whims'), light dishes using *masa* (corn dough). The quintessential *antojito* is the taco – meat, fish or vegetables served atop a tortilla (Mexico's ubiquitous corn- or wheat-flour flatbread). Delicious varieties include *tacos al pastor* (with spit-cooked pork), *tacos de carne asada* (with grilled beef) and *tacos de pescado* (fish tacos, a favorite on the Pacific coast). There are many more types of *antojito* and an infinite variety of ingredients that can go into them. The most popular types include:

Quesadillas A tortilla folded in half with a filling of cheese and/or other ingredients.

Enchiladas Lightly fried tortillas with fillings, covered in a chili sauce.

Tamales A wodge of *masa* mixed with lard, with stewed meat, fish or veggies in the middle, steamed in corn husks or banana leaf.

PAUL BRIGHTON / SHUTTERSTOCK ©

Other common street foods:

Tortas Sandwiches (hot or cold) using a white-bread roll.

Elotes Freshly steamed or grilled corn on the cob, usually coated in mayonnaise and often sprinkled with chili powder.

Dare to Try

Grasshoppers (*chapulines*) Fried with chili powder and garlic; they make a surprisingly munchable snack, especially accompanying a glass of mezcal. Plentiful in Oaxaca.

Corn fungus (*huitlacoche*) The black mold that grows on some cobs of corn (maize) has a truffle-like texture and has been considered a delicacy since pre-Hispanic times. Available during the mid-year rainy season at Mexico City's Mercado San Juan (p138).

Cow's-eye tacos (*tacos de ojos*) Yes, that's right. Cow's eyes chopped up, steamed and put in tacos. Soft enough but not especially flavorsome and can be a bit greasy. Found at taco stands around the country, including Los Cocuyos (p115), in Mexico City.

Grubs and worms *Escamoles* (ant larvae) and *gusanos de maguey* (maguey worms) are seasonal fare from about March to June in the Puebla–Tlaxcala area. In Morelia, you can also wrap your tongue around *alacranes* (scorpions).

Local Specialties

Mexico City

The great melting pot of Mexican people and food, the capital has a vibrant street-food culture, with *antojitos* everywhere – at street stands, markets and thousands of taco stands. At the other end of the culinary scale, top chefs create fantastic fusion dishes in ultra-contemporary restaurants melding haute-cuisine techniques with traditional Mexican ingredients, especially in the neighborhoods of Condesa, Roma and Polanco.

Veracruz

Two main factors strongly influence Veracruz cooking: its proximity to the ocean (and abundance of seafood), and centuries of Spanish and Afro-Caribbean influence. Standout dishes include *huachinango a la veracruzana* (red snapper in a spicy tomato sauce), *arroz a la tumbada* (a seafood-and-rice soup), *camarones enchipotlados* (shrimp in a *chipotle* sauce) and *pollo encacahuatado* (chicken in a peanut sauce).

Yucatán Peninsula

Caribbean flavors and indigenous Maya recipes influence the cuisine of Mexico's southeast corner. The most famous dish is *cochinita pibil* – slow-cooked pork marinated in citrus juices and *achiote* (a spice made from red seeds) and traditionally roasted in a pit in the ground. A staple is the fiery *chile habanero* – habanero sauce goes well on *papadzules* (tacos stuffed with hard-boiled eggs and pumpkin-seed sauce). Don't miss *sopa de lima,* a soup made from turkey, lime and tortilla pieces.

Oaxaca

This southern state is famed for its unique dishes. Greatest renown belongs to its

---

VEGETARIANS & VEGANS

In many parts of Mexico, 'vegetarian' is not a word in the local lexicon. Many Mexicans still think of a vegetarian as a person who doesn't eat red meat. Many more have never even heard the word *veganista* (vegan), though this is changing, particularly in Mexico City, where 'vegan food' is now a byword for hipness. The good news is that almost every city, large or small, has real vegetarian restaurants (some even have vegan ones) and their popularity is increasing. Also, many traditional Mexican dishes are vegetarian: *ensalada de nopales* (cactus-leaf salad); quesadillas made with *huitlacoche*, cheeses and even flowers such as zucchini flowers; *chiles rellenos de queso* (cheese-stuffed *poblano* chilies); and *arroz a la mexicana* (Mexican-style rice). Be warned, however, that many dishes are prepared using chicken or beef broth, or some kind of animal fat, such as *manteca* (lard).

Yellow chili pepper with *escamoles* (ant larvae), tortilla and black refried beans

many *moles*. Oaxaca is also the world capital of mezcal, a potent sipping liquor made from agave plants which is enjoying an upsurge in popularity. *Tlayudas* (crunchy grilled tortillas topped with cheese, lettuce and refried beans) are also known as 'Mexican pizzas'. A more unconventional local specialty is *chapulines* (grasshoppers), which are far tastier than they sound.

Central Mexico

Guadalajara is famed for its *birria* (chili-spiced goat or lamb stew, eaten with tortillas, pickled onions, cilantro and salsa) and *tortas ahogadas* (sandwiches of chopped fried pork soaked in a spicy sauce). In Tequila, the town that gave Mexico its most famous drink, you can visit distilleries, or even take one of several express excursion trains from Guadalajara. The city of Puebla has a proudly distinctive cuisine including perhaps Mexico's single-most-famous dish – *mole poblano,* a thick sauce of chilies, fruits, nuts, spices and chocolate, usually served over chicken.

How to Eat & Drink
When to Eat

Desayuno (breakfast) Usually served from 8:30am to 11am, it tends to be on the hearty side. Egg dishes are popular and some Mexicans down serious meaty platefuls.

Comida (lunch) The main meal of the day, usually served between 2pm and 4:30pm and comprising a soup or other starter, main course (typically meat, fish or seafood) and a small dessert. *Comida corrida,* also known as *menú del día,* is an inexpensive fixed-price lunch menu.

Cena (dinner) For Mexicans, dinner is a lighter meal than lunch and often not eaten till 9pm. Nearly all restaurants serving dinner open from as early as 7pm, though, offering full menus for those who want them.

Snacks At almost any time of day you can grab an *antojito* or *torta* at a cafe or street market stall. You can also get sandwiches (toasted) in some cafes.

COOKING CLASSES

To learn more about Mexican cuisine, consider signing up for a class at one of the following:

➡ Estela Silva's Mexican Home Cooking School (p183), Tlaxcala

➡ Casa de los Sabores (p447), Oaxaca City

➡ Patio Mexica Cooking School (p571), Zihuatanejo

➡ Los Dos (p324), Mérida

➡ Cooking with Juan Pablo (p817), Monterrey

➡ La Piña Azul Escuela de Cocina (p686), San Miguel de Allende

Where to Eat

In general, *restaurantes* (restaurants) have full, multicourse menus and a range of drinks to accompany meals, while *cafés* and *cafeterías* offer shorter menus of lighter dishes and their drinks may focus on coffee, tea and soft drinks. Other types of eatery:

Cantina Traditional Mexican watering hole. Beer, tequila and *cubas* (rum and coke) are served alongside *botanas* (snacks) such as *quesadillas de papa con guacamole* (potato quesadillas with guacamole) or snails in *chipotle* sauce.

Comedor 'Eating room'; usually refers to low-budget restaurants serving simple, straightforward meals.

Fonda Small, frequently family-run eatery, often serving *comidas corridas*.

Mercado (market) Many Mexican markets have *comedor* sections where you sit on benches eating economical, home-style food cooked up on the spot.

Taquería Stall or small eatery specializing in tacos.

What to Drink

Tequila & Mezcal

Both tequila and mezcal are spirits distilled from agave plants, but – legally – tequila has to be made from blue agave grown in the state of Jalisco, or specifically designated areas of Guanajuato, Michoacán, Nayarit and Tamaulipas. Methods of production and quantities of agave involved vary widely from place to place, which means no two spirits will taste the same. With hundreds of different brands, *mezcalerías* (bars specializing in mezcal) are thriving, especially in cities.

Beer

Two major breweries dominate Mexico's beer market. Grupo Modelo makes the brands Corona, Victoria, Modelo Especial, Pacífico, Montejo and Negra Modelo. Cervecería Cuauhtémoc Moctezuma produces Sol, Carta Blanca, Dos Equis, Superior, Tecate and Bohemia, among others.

In the last few years, however, *cervezas artesanales* (microbrews) have exploded onto Mexico's beer scene. Good ones to look out for include Baja Brewing Company (www.bajabrewingcompany.com), Cerveza Minerva (www.cervezaminerva.mx) from Jalisco, Aguamala (p734) in Ensenada, Cerveza Rrëy (www.cervezarreyusa.com) in Monterrey, and Cervecería de Colima (https://cerveceriadecolima.com) in, of course, Colima.

Super refreshing are *micheladas* (beer cocktails). The basic recipe adds lime juice, ice and a dash of salt to cold beer. They are

THE TRUTH ABOUT *MOLE*

Mexican chef and author Zarela Martínez once told me that in *mole* the sauce is the dish. What she meant was that when we eat *mole* we eat it because we want the sauce. The meat – whether it be chicken, turkey or pork – plays a secondary role. A complex sauce made with nuts, chilies and spices, *mole* defines Mexican cuisine. Although *mole* is often called chocolate sauce, only a very small percentage of *moles* include this ingredient. The confusion is understandable since the recipe for *mole poblano* (mole from the state of Puebla), the most widely known *mole* in the country, includes a small amount of chocolate. But most Mexicans would agree that when it comes to *mole*, Oaxaca is the place to go. It's known as 'The Land of Seven Moles' (p454).

Mauricio Velázquez de León, Food Writer

Top: Market snacks, Mexico City (p138)

Bottom: Tacos in *mole* sauce

ARIADNA126 / GETTY IMAGES ©

PULQUE *MAURICIO VELÁZQUEZ DE LEÓN*

If tequila and mezcal are brothers, then *pulque* would be the father of Mexican spirits. Two thousand years ago, ancient Mexicans started to extract the juice of agave plants to produce a milky, slightly alcoholic drink that the Aztecs called *octli poliqhui*. When the Spanish arrived in Mexico, they renamed the drink *pulque*. Even though *pulque* has a lower alcohol content than tequila or mezcal, it is much harder on the palate. Because it is not distilled, it retains an earthy, vegetal taste and has a thick, foamy consistency that some people find unpleasant. In some places it is mixed with fruit juices, such as mango or strawberry, to make it more palatable. When *pulque* is mixed with juices, it is called *curado*.

Mauricio Velázquez de León, Food Writer

often served with Clamato juice and other spicy seasonings, too.

Wine

The first vineyards in North America were planted in Mexico by the Spanish in the 16th century, but it is only in the last 20 years or so that the industry has started to make wines that have caught international attention. There are seven main regions where vines are grown; it's generally agreed that Mexico's best vintages come from Valle de Guadalupe, in the north of the Baja Peninsula (the area even boasts a wine route). The main types of wine are *varietales* (single varietals), *combinadas* (blends) and *vinos espumosos* (sparkling wines).

Nonalcoholic Drinks

Across Mexico you will find *juguerías*, street stalls or small establishments selling fresh-squeezed fruit and vegetable juices. These places also sell *licuados,* a Mexican version of a milkshake that normally includes banana, milk, honey and fruit. There are some creative combinations, too, with ingredients such as *nopal* (cactus leaves), pineapple, lemon and orange, or vanilla, banana and avocado.

In *taquerías* and most restaurants you will find *aguas frescas*, juices diluted with water and sugar. Some of them resemble iced teas. In *agua de tamarindo*, the tamarind pods are boiled then mixed with sugar before being chilled, while *agua de jamaica* is made with dried hibiscus leaves. Others such as *horchata* are made with melon seeds and/or rice.

Menu Decoder

This food glossary explains dishes you'll find on Mexican menus and the names of basic foods.

a la parrilla grilled on a barbecue grill

a la plancha grilled on a metal plate

al carbón cooked over open coals

aves poultry

bebidas drinks

carnes meats

empanizado fried in breadcrumbs

ensalada salad

entradas starters

filete fillet

frito fried

huevos eggs

jugo juice

legumbres pulses

mariscos seafood (not fish)

menú degustación tasting menu

mole rich, complex sauce, sometimes including chocolate, poured over meats

pescado fish

plato fuerte main dish

postre dessert

salsa sauce

sopa soup

verduras vegetables

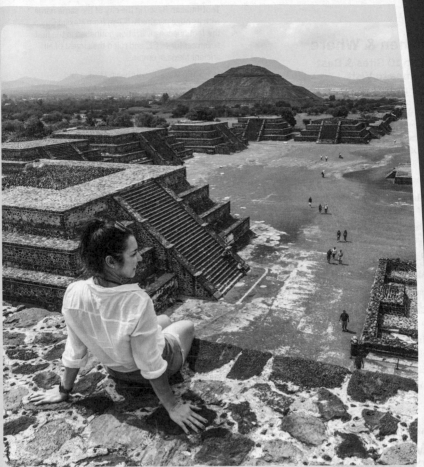

Teotihuacán (p157)

Plan Your Trip

Exploring Mexico's Ancient Ruins

Mexico's ancient civilizations were the most sophisticated and formidable in North and Central America. These often highly organized societies didn't just build towering pyramids and sculpt beautiful temples; they could also read the heavens, do complicated mathematics and invent writing systems. Exploring their sites is an unmissable Mexico travel experience.

When & Where

Top 10 Sites & Best Times to Visit

Most of Mexico's major pre-Hispanic sites are scattered around the center, south and southeast of the country. Here's our top 10, along with the best time of year to visit them. Most sites open daily 9am to 5pm (some close Monday). Arriving early means fewer visitors and lower temperatures.

Teotihuacán, central Mexico Year-round

Chichén Itzá, Yucatán Peninsula September to November

Uxmal, Yucatán Peninsula September to November

Palenque, Chiapas October to May

Monte Albán, Oaxaca October to May

Yaxchilán, Chiapas October to May

Calakmul, Yucatán Peninsula November to May

Tulum, Yucatán Peninsula November to June

El Tajín, Veracruz October to May

Templo Mayor, Mexico City Year-round

Mexico's Ancient Civilizations

Archaeologists have been uncovering Mexico's ancient ruins since the 19th century. Many impressive sites have been restored and made accessible to visitors, others have been explored in part, and thousands more remain untouched, buried beneath the earth or hidden in forests. The major civilizations were these:

Olmec Mexico's 'mother culture' was centered on the Gulf coast, from about 1200 BCE to 400 BCE. It's famed for the giant stone sculptures known as Olmec heads.

Teotihuacán Based in the city of the same name with its huge pyramids, 50km from Mexico City, the Teotihuacán civilization flourished in the first seven centuries CE, and ruled the largest of all ancient Mexican empires.

Maya The Maya, in southeast Mexico and neighboring Guatemala and Belize, flowered most brilliantly in numerous city-states between 250 CE and 900 CE. They're famed for their exquisitely beautiful temples and stone sculptures. Maya culture lives on today among the indigenous populations of these regions.

Toltec A name for the culture of a number of central Mexican city-states, from around 750 CE to 1150 CE. The warrior sculptures of Tula are the most celebrated monuments.

Aztec With their capital at Tenochtitlán (now Mexico City) from 1325 CE to 1521 CE, the Aztecs came to rule most of central Mexico from the Gulf coast to the Pacific. The best known Aztec site is the Templo Mayor in Mexico City (p73).

Site Practicalities

➡ The most famous sites are often thronged with large numbers of visitors (arrive early). Others are hidden away on remote hilltops or shrouded in thick jungle, and can be the most exciting and rewarding to visit for those with an adventurous spirit.

➡ Admission to archaeological sites costs from nothing up to M$481, depending on the site (only a handful of places, all in Yucatán state, cost more than M$90).

➡ Go protected against the sun and, at jungle sites, mosquitoes.

➡ Popular sites have facilities such as cafes or restaurants, bookstores, souvenir stores, audio guides in various languages and authorized (but not fixed-price) human guides.

➡ Little-visited sites may have no food or water available and may have poor road access.

➡ Guided tours to many sites are available from nearby towns, but public transportation is usually available, too.

➡ Major sites are usually wheelchair accessible.

➡ Explanatory signs may be in Spanish only, or in Spanish and English, or in Spanish, English and a local indigenous language.

Mexico's Ruins

MAIN PRE-HISPANIC SITES

REGION	SITE	PERIOD	DESCRIPTION
CENTRAL MEXICO	Teotihuacán (p157)	0-700 CE	Mexico's biggest ancient city, capital of the Teotihuacán empire
	Templo Mayor (p73)	1375-1521 CE	Ceremonial center of the Aztec capital, Tenochtitlán
	Cholula (p174)	0-1521 CE	City & religious center
	Tula (p156)	900-1150 CE	Major Toltec city
	Cantona (p188)	600-1000 CE	Huge, well-preserved, little-visited city
	Tlatelolco (p105)	12th century - 1521 CE	Site of main Aztec market & defeat of last Aztec emperor Cuauhtémoc
	Xochicalco (p199)	600-1200 CE	Large, hilltop religious & commercial center
CHIAPAS	Palenque (p398)	100 BCE-740 CE	Beautiful major Maya city
	Yaxchilán (p414)	7th-9th centuries CE	Maya city
	Toniná (p396)	c 600-900 CE	Maya temple complex
	Bonampak (p411)	8th century CE	Maya site
NORTHERN MEXICO	Paquimé (p802)	900-1340 CE	Trading center linking central Mexico with northern desert cultures
OAXACA	Monte Albán (p461)	500 BCE-900 CE	Hilltop ceremonial center of Zapotec civilization
	Mitla (p466)	c 1300-1520 CE	Zapotec religious center
	Yagul (p463)	900-1400 CE	Zapotec & Mixtec ceremonial center
VERACRUZ	El Tajín (p254)	600-1200 CE	Town & ceremonial center of Classic Veracruz civilization
	Quiahuiztlán (p231)	600-1300 CE	Totonac town & necropolis
	El Cuajilote (p244) & Vega de la Peña (p245)	600-1400 CE	Towns of unidentified civilization
	Cempoala (p232)	approx 1200 BCE	Totonac town
YUCATÁN PENINSULA	Chichén Itzá (p342)	2nd-14th centuries CE	Large, well-restored Maya/Toltec city
	Uxmal (p333)	600-900 CE	Maya city
	Tulum (p302)	c 1200-1600 CE	Late Maya town & ceremonial center
	Calakmul (p363)	Approx 1st-9th centuries CE	Huge, once-very-powerful Maya city, little restored
	Cobá (p308)	600-1100 CE	Maya city
	Kabah (p337)	750-950 CE	Maya city
	Ruta Puuc (p337)	750-950 CE	Three Puuc Maya sites (Sayil, Xlapak, Labná)
	Edzná (p362)	600 BCE-1500 CE	Maya city
	Becán (p365)	550 BCE-1000 CE	Large Maya site
	Xpuhil (p366)	Flourished 8th century CE	Maya settlement
	Ek' Balam (p353)	Approx 600-800 CE	Maya city
	Dzibanché (p318)	Approx 200 BCE-1200 CE	Maya city
	Kohunlich (p318)	100-600 CE	Maya city

HIGHLIGHTS	LOCATION/TRANSPORTATION
Pyramids of Sun and Moon, Calzada de los Muertos, palace murals	50km northeast of Mexico City; frequent buses
Ceremonial pyramid	Downtown Mexico City
World's widest pyramid	8km west of Puebla; frequent buses
Stone pillars carved as warriors	80km north of CDMX; 1km walk or taxi from Tula bus station
24 ball courts, unique street system	90km northeast of Puebla; taxi or *colectivo* from Oriental
Aztec temple-pyramid	Northern Mexico City; trolleybus or metro
Pyramid of Quetzalcóatl	35km southwest of Cuernavaca; bus
Exquisite temples with jungle backdrop	7km west of Palenque town; frequent combis
Temples & other buildings in riverside jungle setting	Beside Río Usumacinta, 15km northwest of Frontera Corozal; boat from Frontera Corozal
Temples & pyramids on hillside	14km east of Ocosingo; combis from Ocosingo
Superb, if weathered, frescoes	150km southeast of Palenque; van or bus to San Javier (140km), then taxi and van
Adobe walls & buildings, clay macaw cages, rare geometric pottery	Casas Grandes village; bus or taxi from Nuevo Casas Grandes, 7km north
Pyramids, observatory, panoramas	6km west of Oaxaca; bus
Unique stone mosaics	46km southeast of Oaxaca; bus or *colectivo*
Large ball court, rock 'fortress'	35km southeast of Oaxaca; bus or *colectivo* then 1.5km walk
Rare niched pyramids, 17 ball courts, *voladores* ('fliers') performances	6km west of Papantla; bus or taxi
Unique temple-like tombs, lofty viewpoint	3km walk up from Hwy 180, opposite Villa Rica village
Remote jungle setting	17km south of Tlapacoyan; take *colectivo* or taxi then walk
11m-high pyramid Templo Mayor	49km northwest of Veracruz City; car, taxi or tour from Veracruz City
El Castillo 'calendar temple', Mexico's biggest ball court, El Caracol observatory, Platform of Skulls	117km east of Mérida, 2km east of Pisté village; buses from Mérida, Pisté & Valladolid
Pyramids, palaces, riotous sculpture featuring masks of rain god Chaac	80km south of Mérida; buses from Mérida
Temples & towers on superb Caribbean-side site	130km south of Cancún; taxi, walk or cycle from Tulum town
High pyramids with views over rainforest	60km south of Escárcega-Chetumal road; car, tour from Xpujil, Chicanná or Campeche, taxi from Xpujil or Escárcega
Towering pyramids in jungle setting	50km northwest of Tulum; bus or *colectivo* from Tulum, or bus from Valladolid
Palace of Masks, with 300 Chaac masks	104km south of Mérida; car, bus or tour from Mérida
Palaces with elaborate columns & sculptures, including Chaac masks	120km south of Mérida; car, bus or tour from Mérida
Five-story pyramid-palace, Temple of Masks	53km southeast of Campeche; minibuses & shuttle service from Campeche
Towered temples	8km west of Xpujil; taxi, tour or car
Three-towered ancient 'skyscraper'	Xpujil town, 123km west of Chetumal; buses from Campeche & Escárcega, buses & *colectivos* from Chetumal
Huge Acrópolis; high pyramid with unusual carving	23km north of Valladolid; taxi or *colectivo*
Semi-wild site with palaces & pyramids	68km west of Chetumal; car, taxi or tour from Chetumal or Xpujil
Temple of the Masks	56km west of Chetumal; car, taxi, or bus & 9km walk

Resources

Colecciones Especiales Street View (www.inah. gob.mx/es/inah/322-colecciones-especiales -street-view) Take virtual tours of 27 sites in Google Street View.

Instituto Nacional de Antropología e Historia (www.inah.gob.mx) Mexico's National Institute of Anthropology and History administers 187 archaeological sites and 120 museums.

Mesoweb (www.mesoweb.com) A great, diverse resource on ancient Mexico, especially the Maya.

An Archaeological Guide to Central and Southern Mexico Joyce Kelly's book was published in 2001 and is still the best of its kind, covering 70 sites.

Top Museums

Some archaeological sites have their own museums, but there are also important city and regional museums that hold many of the most valuable and impressive pre-Hispanic artifacts and provide fascinating background on ancient Mexico.

Museo Nacional de Antropología (p91) The superb National Museum of Anthropology in Mexico City has sections devoted to all the important ancient civilizations, and includes such treasures as the famous Aztec sun stone and a replica of King Pakal's treasure-laden tomb from Palenque.

Museo de Antropología (p233) Mainly devoted to Gulf coast cultures, this excellent museum in Xalapa contains seven Olmec heads and other masterly sculptures among its 25,000-piece collection.

Parque-Museo La Venta (p431) This outdoor museum-cum-zoo in Villahermosa holds several Olmec heads and other fine sculptures from the site of La Venta, moved here in the 1950s when La Venta was under threat from petroleum exploration.

Museo Maya de Cancún (p272) One of Mexico's most important collections of Maya artifacts, assembled from sites around the Yucatán Peninsula.

BURUMBO / SHUTTERSTOCK ©

Parque-Museo La Venta (p431)

PRE-HISPANIC NUMBERS

Ancient Mexicans loved numbers. We've assembled some of our own:

8km of tunnels dug by archaeologists beneath Cholula's Tepanapa Pyramid

70m – the height of Teotihuacán's Pyramid of the Sun

100km – the length of the *sacbé* (stone-paved avenue) from Cobá to Yaxuna

120 mural-covered walls in Teotihuacán's Tetitla Palace

300 masks of Chaac, the rain god, at Kabah's Palace of Masks

15,000 ritual ball-game courts found in Mexico (so far)

20,000 human hearts ripped out for the re-dedication of Tenochtitlán's Templo Mayor in 1487

25 million – estimated population of Mexico at the time of the Spanish conquest (1521)

Plan Your Trip

Outdoor Activities

Mexico is a tremendous destination for fresh-air fiends. Whether you're looking to conquer some tall peaks, ride some serious waves or white water, or explore bottomless sinkholes and world-class reefs in a scuba suit, there are plenty of options to keep you occupied. Bird-watchers will also be happy here.

Surfing

Mexicos's best surfing is found primarily along the Pacific coast, with Puerto Escondido, Mazatlán, Sayulita, La Ticla and Troncones among the hot spots. There's also surfing along the Baja Peninsula, with relatively uncrowded waves in north Baja, around Ensenada, and more consistent (but crowded) waves around Cabo San Lucas.

Puerto Escondido (p475) The Mexican Pipeline beach break is world-famous, but Escondido has mellower waves, too.

Troncones (p566) A long, strong, world-class left point break and some excellent beach breaks.

Sayulita (p535) Dependable, medium-sized waves, good for practicing or learning, with a mellow party vibe.

Ensenada (p734) There's a perfect point break at San Miguel.

Barra de Nexpa (p564) One of several spots with healthy waves along the little-touched Michoacán coast.

San Blas (p527) For intermediates and beginners, with many beach and point breaks, and one of the world's longest waves.

Todos Santos (p761) The beaches surrounding this town offer some of the best swells in Baja.

Zipolite (p487) Nude beach on Oaxaca's unsullied coast that's also known for its big waves.

A Year in Activities

Diving & Snorkeling
Humpback whales and whale sharks are seen off the Pacific coast and the Baja Peninsula from December to February, while September and October are best for spotting hammerheads in the Sea of Cortez. Visibility is best off the Caribbean coast in August and September.

White-Water Rafting
October is considered the best month, though rafting is possible year-round.

Surfing & Kitesurfing
April to October is the best season for surfing in the Baja Peninsula and along the Pacific coast.

Hiking & Trekking
December to April, when there is virtually no rain in upland areas, is good for walking. Note that temperatures can still reach averages of 28°C.

Bird-Watching
Possible year-round.

Kitesurfing

Kitesurfing has taken off as a sport in all the main coastal regions. Top locations include Cozumel, Isla Blanca and Playa del Carmen in the Yucatán, the Pacific Coast's Bucerías, La Ventosa and Puerto Vallarta, Baja's La Ventana and Punta San Carlos, and the Costa Esmeralda in Veracruz.

El Cuyo Kite School (www.elcuyokiteschool.com) Great instructors and a superb place for catching the northern winds in Yucatán.

Isla Holbox (p286) Sandy streets, few visitors, reliable winds and glorious, empty waters.

Sian Kite Watersports (www.facebook.com/siankitetulum) Whiz along the waves by the Tulum ruins.

La Ventana (p751) Small fishing town, great kitesurfing community and reliable winds from October to April.

Hiking & Trekking

Mexico's lofty volcanoes provide the country's most challenging trekking; you'll need plenty of stamina and a head for heights if planning on summiting the 5636m Pico de Orizaba in Veracruz state. Less demanding are the Nevado de Toluca, El Malinche and Iztaccíhuatl peaks. Hiking trails run through the Copper Canyon and between the Zapotec villages of Oaxaca's Sierra Norte, among other places.

3 Amigos (p780) Explore Copper Canyon with this top-tier outfit or take one of its self-guided hikes.

Expediciones Sierra Norte (p446) Organizes one- to four-day hiking trips to the Pueblos Mancomunados, a pioneering community tourism project.

Pico de Orizaba (p250) Climbing Mexico's tallest mountain is a week-long endeavor once you take acclimatizing to the altitude into account. Treks around lower levels of the dormant volcano are an easier alternative.

Popocatépetl & Iztaccíhuatl (p180) Private hikes up dormant volcano Iztaccíhuatl for panoramic views across to recently explosive volcano Popocatépetl.

Parque Ecológico Chipinque (p815) Just 12km from Monterrey, this park offers excellent hiking and mountain biking on well-marked trails, including up Copete de Águilas (2200m).

Reserva de la Biosfera Los Tuxtlas (p266) The volcanic region above the steamy coastal plains of southern Veracruz includes lakes, nature reserves and the 1748m Volcán San Martín.

Nevado de Toluca (p213) Mexico's fourth-tallest peak, Nevado has two summits on the crater rim, with fantastic views across two snow-fringed crater lakes.

Admire Mexico (p633) Take on the magnificent Volcán Nevado de Colima (4260m) with this top-notch outfit.

Diving & Snorkeling

Mexico has numerous great diving and snorkeling spots. The best diving conditions are found in the warm, clear waters of the Caribbean coast, off Quintana Roo and along the Yucatán Peninsula's Riviera Maya and Costa Maya. Additionally, advanced divers can explore the Yucatán's many cenotes (sinkholes).

Yucatán Peninsula (p269) With the world's second-largest barrier reef, it's world-famous for its abundant coral and tropical fish.

Isla Mujeres (p282) Snorkeling trips with whale sharks and a dive around an underwater sculpture museum await.

Banco Chinchorro (p312) Wreck-studded coral atoll off the southern end of the Caribbean coast.

Bahías de Huatulco (p495) A string of beautiful Pacific bays with several coral plates and more than 100 dive sites.

Xel-Há (p291) This ecopark on the Riviera Maya offers snorkeling in a beautiful natural aquarium.

Laguna de la Media Luna (p706) Has an underwater cave ideal for advanced diving.

Cabo Pulmo (p753) A magnificent coral reef and spectacular diving and snorkeling experiences.

Veracruz (p225) Excellent wreck diving, plus beautiful reeds around Isla de Sacrificios and, in the north of the state, Isla Lobos.

White-Water Rafting & Kayaking

The three main regions for rafting are Veracruz, San Luis Potosí and Morelos. Veracruz' Río Filobobos, near Tlapacoyan, and

Top: Nevado de Toluca (p213)

Bottom: Surfing at Sayulita (p535)

SOLLINA IMAGES / GETTY IMAGES ©

SAFETY GUIDELINES FOR DIVING

Before embarking on a scuba-diving, free-diving or snorkeling trip, consider the following to ensure a safe and enjoyable experience:

➡ Possess a current diving-certification card from a recognized scuba-diving instruction agency.

➡ Be sure you are healthy and feel comfortable diving.

➡ If you don't have your own equipment, ask to see the dive shop's before you commit. Make sure you feel comfortable with your dive master: after all, it's your life.

➡ Obtain reliable information about physical and environmental conditions at the dive site from a reputable local dive operation, and ask how local trained divers deal with these considerations.

➡ Be aware of local laws, regulations and etiquette about marine life and the environment.

➡ Dive only at sites within your level of experience. Engage the services of a competent, professionally trained dive instructor or dive master.

➡ Find out if your dive shop has up-to-date certification from **PADI** (www.padi. com), **NAUI** (www.naui.org) or the internationally recognized Mexican diving organization **FMAS** (www.facebook.com/FMAS.org.mx).

➡ Know the locations of the nearest decompression chambers and the emergency telephone numbers.

➡ Avoid diving less than 18 hours before a high-altitude flight.

Río Antigua, accessed from Jalcomulco, vary from mild to wild (Class II-IV), Santa Maria's Class III rapids in San Luis Potosí are suitable for beginners, while Morelos' Río Amacuzac is Class III-IV on the lower rapids.

Expediciones México Verde (p244) Ride the churning rapids of the Río Antigua, then relax in a temascal (pre-Hispanic steam bath).

Aventurec (p245) Combine wet and wild adventure on the Río Filobobos with visiting two beautiful, barely discovered archaeological sites.

MS Xpediciones (p708) Recommended whitewater adventures on the Río Santa Maria.

Bird-Watching

Given the diversity of Mexico's ecosystems, it's little wonder that the country is an excellent destination for birders. The Copper Canyon has over 400 resident, migrating and wintering species, Oaxaca's Sierra Norte is home to over 500 species, while Reserve de la Biosfera Sian Ka'an is great for spotting endemic species. For organized trips, contact **Mexico-Birding Tours** (www.mexico-birding.com) and Xalapa-based Robert Straub (p236).

La Tovara (p527) Spy a variety of bird species on a boat tour through the San Blas mangroves.

Laguna Manialtepec (p483) Coastal lagoon just north of Puerto Escondido chock-a-block with colorful waterfowl.

Laguna Catemaco (p263) Dozens of species of native and migrating waterfowl, including herons and cormorants.

Reserva de la Biosfera Calakmul (p363) Over 350 bird species reside or fly through here.

Plan Your Trip

Mexico's Día de Muertos

Few festivals reveal more about Mexican spirituality than Día de Muertos (Day of the Dead), the remembrance of departed loved ones on November 1 and 2. You may think you know something about this colorful fiesta from movies such as *Coco* and *Spectre*, but nothing can really prepare you for the full emotional punch and fun of experiencing the celebrations in Mexico itself.

Origins of the Festival

The tradition, which commemorates departed relatives and loved ones, is a mash-up of pre-Hispanic beliefs dating back 3000 years and Catholicism. According to Aztec lore, the dead reside in an underworld called Mictlán; on Día de Muertos, which was originally celebrated in August, the dead can return to their homes. The Catholic conquistadors, hoping to assimilate the holiday through their favored tactic of cultural *mestizaje* (mixing), moved it to coincide with All Saints' Day (November 1) and All Souls' Day (November 2).

How It's Celebrated

By celebrating death, Mexicans salute life and they do it the way they celebrate everything else – with food, drinks, music and much colorful decoration. In 2008, Unesco recognized the importance of Día de Muertos by adding the holiday to its list of Intangible Cultural Heritage of humanity.

Among many indigenous communities, Día de Muertos is still very much a religious and spiritual event. For them, the observance might more appropriately be called Noche de Muertos (Night of the Dead), because families actually spend

Best Places to Celebrate

Mexico City

Festivities in the capital include several major parades, the construction of giant public *ofrendas* (altars) to deceased celebrities and worthies, the decoration and display of giant skulls and *alebrijes* (colorful wooden animal figures) and face-painting events.

Oaxaca City

See flower-decorated *ofrendas* and lit-up niches at the Panteón General and visit the cemeteries in the villages surrounding the city, such as Santa Cruz Xoxocotlán.

Lago de Pátzcuaro

Parades, crafts markets, exhibitions and concerts are held in the Lago de Pátzcuaro area, and cemeteries are packed with visitors throughout the festivities.

La Huasteca

Dubbed *Xantolo*, the local Day of the Dead celebration is a dynamic and traditional affair where people take to the streets in costume to perform dances in groups called *comparsas*.

PARTICIPATION TIPS

➜ Major parades and festivities, such as the ones in Mexico City and Pátzcuaro, attract huge crowds. For a chance of getting a good view of the celebrations, stake out your spot on the parade route early and book accommodations in such areas well in advance.

➜ It's still rainy season in areas such as Mexico City during Día de Muertos – dress appropriately for (almost certain) late-afternoon and evening showers.

➜ Consider joining a guided tour such as the ones offered by Mexico City–based **Aztec Explorers** (https://aztecexplorers.com) to gain a greater insight into the nuances and traditions of the festival.

➜ Watch the animated movies *Coco* and *Book of Life*.

➜ Read *The Skeleton at the Feast* by Elizabeth Carmichael and Chloë Sayer.

➜ Have your face painted in traditional skeletal designs and wear Halloween-style costumes, by all means. But also recognize the deep spiritual element of the festival, especially when visiting cemeteries. Be respectful of local customs and the way each family chooses to remember its departed loved ones.

whole nights at the graveyard communing with the dear departed. It's a joyous affair involving much drinking, dancing and live mariachi-band music.

Ofrenda

The centrepiece of Día de Muertos celebrations is the *ofrenda* which is set up in a house or, as some families prefer, in the graveyard. It is decorated with vivid orange and yellow *cempasuchil* (marigold) flowers, plates of *tamales* (stuffed, steamed corn dough), sugar-shaped skulls and *pan de muerto* ('bread of the dead': a loaf made with egg yolks, mezcal and dried fruits). There's always a container of water (spirits arrive thirsty after their journey) as well as the favorite foods of the deceased, so that they feel welcomed upon their return. Marigold petals are scattered from altar to gravesite to guide the dead back to their place of rest. Copal (tree-resin) incense is burnt to purify the area around the altar.

Calaveras

Skeletons and *calaveras* (models of skulls) are other essential elements of Día de Muertos. Sugar skulls, chocolate coffins, papier-mâché skeletons and *papel picado* ('perforated paper') decorations in all the colors of the rainbow are sold in markets and shops everywhere. They make for wonderful souvenirs of the event.

The designs of many decorative items are inspired by the images of artist José Guadalupe Posada (1852–1913), who was renowned for his satirical figures of a skeletal Death cheerfully engaging in everyday life: working, dancing, courting, drinking and riding horses into battle. Posada's most famous deathly creation is Catrina, who always wears a feathery hat, fancy shoes and a long dress – she is considered the personification of Día de Muertos. Diego Rivera immortalized La Catrina as the centre point of his giant mural *Sueño de una tarde dominical en la Alameda Central* (Dream of a Sunday Afternoon in the Alameda Central) on display in Mexico City's Museo Mural Diego Rivera (p85).

Where It's Celebrated

Día de Muertos is a Mexico-wide event, but there are some places where the festivities are on a major scale or involve unique traditions.

Mexico City

It may have taken James Bond to kick-start the grand parade through the heart of the capital in the 2015 movie *Spectre*, but since then the city authorities have embraced public celebrations with enthusiasm.

Elaborate *ofrendas* show up across the city – some of the best can be seen at Anahuacalli (p104), Museo Dolores Olmedo (p97), the Zócalo (p78), Plaza Santo Domingo in El Centro and in the ancient Aztec neighborhood of San Andrés Mixquic in the extreme southeast of the Distrito Federal. Also worth checking out are the giant skulls and papier-mâché *alebrijes*, each decorated by different artists, that are displayed along Reforma around Monumento a la Independencia.

The climax of over a week of events is the street parade Desfile de Día de Muertos with hundreds of costumed dancers and performers joining giant *calavera* puppets along Reforma to the Zócalo. Websites with details on all the city's events include http://festivaldemuertos.cdmx.gob.mx and the English-language section of news website **El Universal** (www.eluniversal.com.mx/english).

Michoacán

The villages around Pátzcuaro (p647), most notably Tzintzuntzan (p654), and the Isla Janitzio (p652) stage some of the most popular (and crowded!) Día de Muertos celebrations in Mexico. Parades, crafts markets, dancing, ceremonies, exhibitions and concerts are held in the area on both November 1 and 2. Also worth considering is Uruapan (p655) where Día de Muertos is also very colorful and enthusiastically celebrated.

Oaxaca

The Día de Muertos celebrations in Oaxaca City (p449) are among Mexico's most vibrant, with concerts, exhibitions and other special goings-on starting days beforehand. Homes, cemeteries and some public buildings are decorated with fantastically crafted altars; streets and plazas are decked with *tapetes de arena* (colored sand patterns and sculptures); and *comparsas* parade the streets.

Oaxaca's main cemetery, the **Panteón General**, 1km east of downtown, is the scene of concerts in the evenings of October 31 and November 1. Many villages, too, stage special events, with some Oaxaca accommodations and agencies arranging visits: the candlelit graveyard vigil through the October 31–November 1 night in **Santa Cruz Xoxocotlán**, a few kilometers south of the city, is particularly beautiful.

Yucatán

A big player in Día de Muertos celebrations is Mérida (p320), where it's known as *Hanal Pixan* (Feast of the Souls) in Maya. Families gather to eat *pibipollo* (chicken *tamales* cooked in banana skins), which they believe are shared with them by their ancestors. Don't miss the Paseo de Ánimas (p325), when locals flaunt their skeleton-style and parade through the altar-lined streets. Musical renditions, artist performances and local food carts add to the festivities.

On the Riviera Maya, 6km south of Playa del Carmen, the theme park Xcaret (p291) hosts a Day of the Dead festival, from October 31 to November 2, with dance, theater, music and colorful altars.

La Huasteca

In this region, which covers parts of the states of Tamaulipas, Veracruz, Puebla, Hidalgo, San Luis Potosí, Querétaro and Guanajuato, Día de Muertos is better known as *Xantolo*. Pronounced 'shantolo', the word is derived from Castilian *xanto* (holy) and from Náhuatl *olo* (abundance). The parades here are noisy, day-long affairs with participants wearing handmade wood-carved masks and local traditional dress. Zone in on the atmospheric colonial town of Xilitla (p708) or contact local guides **Auténtico San Luis** (http://autenticosanluis.com), who can arrange a tour that takes you to several celebrations across the region.

Elsewhere in Mexico

The cultural program devoted to the Day of the Dead in Puebla (p167) starts in late October and includes nighttime museum visits and viewings of *ofrendas*. By local tradition on October 28, those who lost their lives in a road accident are remembered; on October 29, those who died in a violent event; on October 30, those who drowned; on October 31, children who died; and on November 1 and 2, the deceased in general.

If you're after a less commercially hyped Día de Muertos experience, head away from the major cities to smaller villages and towns such as the *pueblos mágicos* of Naolinco (p236) and Xico (p242) in Veracruz state.

Plan Your Trip
Family Travel

The sights, sounds and colors of Mexico excite kids, and Mexicans love children, who are part and parcel of most aspects of life here. There are many child-friendly attractions and activities for kids of all ages, and with very few exceptions, children are welcomed at all accommodations and at almost any cafe or restaurant.

Keeping Costs Down

Accommodations

Beach hotels and *cabañas* (cabins) countrywide are geared to families. Family rooms and accommodations with kitchens are widely available, and most hotels will put an extra bed or two in a room at little extra charge. Renting an apartment can also be great value, as you'll be able to self-cater.

Eating

Inexpensive Mexican snacks such as quesadillas, burritos and tacos, or *elotes* (steaming corn cob) s straight from a street cart, are good options for introducing kids to local flavors. In many cities and towns there are plenty of budget places serving up familiar international fare. Fresh fruit is abundant and cheap.

Activities

Some attractions have children's admission prices and/or family-ticket deals.

Transport

Major international rental firms should all be able to provide cars with child seats. Also worth considering is traveling by bus: the deluxe, executive and 1st-class services all are very comfortable with toilets on board, and extras such as drinks, snacks, wi-fi and movies screened on board – a good distraction on long journeys.

Children Will Love...

On & In the Water

Learn to surf Kids as young as five can take classes at many spots with gentler waves along the Pacific coast, including Mazatlán, Sayulita, Ixtapa, Puerto Escondido and San Agustinillo.

Spot turtles, dolphins and whales Boat trips head out from many places along the Pacific coast and in the Baja Peninsula.

Snorkel tropical seas Many beaches on the Caribbean coast and islands, and some on the Pacific, provide calm waters and colorful marine life for beginners.

Ride a gondola Cruise ancient Aztec canals at Xochimilco (p107) in Mexico City.

Uyo Ochel Maya (p303) Float down centuries-old, Maya-built canals through mangrove swamps filled with flowers and tropical fish.

Multi-Adventure

Creel (p778) A fine base for exploring the wonders of Copper Canyon, with horseback rides, waterfall walks, lakeside boating, dramatic zip-lines, indigenous villages, and a world-famous train ride.

Selvática (p291) Award-winning zip-line circuit through the jungle near Puerto Morelos, with its own cenote (limestone sinkhole) for swimming.

Cobá (p308) This jungle-surrounded ancient Maya site near Tulum has pyramids, a zip-line and bicycles for pedaling around the network of trails.

Cuajimoloyas (p472) Horseback riding, mountain biking, hiking and a spectacular 1km zip-line in the mountains near Oaxaca.

Cable car Enjoy the views from the *teleférico* in Durango (p806), Orizaba (p248), Taxco (p206) and Zacatecas (p711).

Wildlife

Acuario Inbursa (p96) This world-class mega-aquarium in Mexico City wows kids with manta rays, piranhas and crocodiles, while the Soumaya (p96) and Jumex (p96) museums just across the road will entertain the parents.

Baja whale-watching (p740) See massive gray whales and their calves off the coasts of the Baja Peninsula between December and February – usually requires several hours in a boat, so best for older kids.

Zoomat (p373) The zoo at Tuxtla Gutiérrez has 180 animal species, all from the state of Chiapas, including several types of big cat.

Playa Escobilla (p485) See thousands of turtles crawl out of the ocean in a single night to lay eggs on this Oaxaca beach.

Crococun (p288) Interactive zoo in Puerto Morelos with crocodiles and wild monkeys.

Reserva de la Biosfera Santuario Mariposa Monarca (p644) Be wowed by millions of fluttering monarch butterflies in this forest reserve, accessible on horseback or by foot.

Museums

Museo Nacional de Antropología (p91) The carvings, statues and skulls inside Mexico's best museum are a huge hit with kids.

Papalote Museo del Niño There are two of these fun, hands-on children's museums – one in Mexico City (p95), one in Cuernavaca (p198). Good for kids up to about 11.

La Esquina: Museo del Juguete Popular Mexicano (p683) Stunning museum in San Miguel de Allende where kids can see what toys were like before the digital revolution.

Museo Nacional del Títere (p184) The national puppet museum in Huamantla displays dolls and marionettes from all around the world.

Museo Amparo (p164) There are often free art workshops for children on Saturday and Sunday at this Puebla museum loaded with pre-Hispanic artifacts.

Spectacles

Voladores This indigenous Totonac rite involves men ('fliers') climbing up a 30m-high pole then casting themselves off backward, attached only by ropes. Performed regularly at El Tajín (p254), in Papantla (p253) and at Mexico City's Museo Nacional de Antropología (p91).

Folk dance Highly colorful, entertaining shows are given regularly by the Ballet Folklórico de México (p135) in Mexico City and Guelaguetza groups in Oaxaca, and at Mérida's Parque Santa Lucía (p321).

Encendido de Catedral (p639) Every Saturday night, Morelia lights up with fireworks over its magnificent cathedral, lively music and cheering crowds.

Ferrocarril Chihuahua Pacífico (p770) One of the world's most incredible rail journeys.

Region by Region
Mexico City

The capital keeps kids happy with a world-class aquarium, a hands-on children's museum, a first-rate zoo, dedicated kids' entertainment and activities, and parks and plazas full of space and fun.

Central Pacific Coast

The Pacific coast offers all conceivable types of fun in, on and under the ocean and lagoons. There's a vast range of places to base yourself, from sophisticated Puerto Vallarta to easygoing Zihuatanejo and countless smaller spots.

Yucatán Peninsula

Cancún, the Riviera Maya and nearby islands are geared for vacation fun. The area is full of great beaches offering every imaginable aquatic activity, hotels designed to make life easy and attractions from jungle zip-lines to swimming in cenotes. Other parts of the peninsula are great if your kids will enjoy exploring Maya ruins.

Good to Know

Look out for the icon (🏠) for family-friendly suggestions throughout this guide.

Documents for under-18 travelers Carrying notarized written permission from a parent or guardian is required by Mexican law for Mexican minors (under-18-year-olds, including those with dual nationality) or foreign minors residing in Mexico, if departing from Mexico without a parent or legal guardian. Check with a Mexican consulate well in advance of travel on what needs to be done.

Health Children are more easily affected than adults by heat, disrupted sleep patterns, changes in altitude and foreign food. Take care that they don't drink tap water, be careful to avoid sunburn, cover them up against insect bites and ensure you replace fluids if a child gets diarrhea.

Medical care See a doctor about vaccinations at least one month – preferably two – before your trip. In Mexico, privately run hospitals and clinics offer better facilities and care than public ones. Adequate travel insurance will cover the cost of private medical care.

Babies Mexican women are unlikely to breastfeed in public: you might want to do likewise. Diapers (nappies) and sunscreen are widely available, but you may not easily find wet wipes, other creams, baby foods or familiar medicines outside larger cities and tourist towns.

Useful Resources

Lonely Planet Kids (www.lonelyplanetkids.com) Loads of activities and great family-travel blog content.

First Words Spanish (shop.lonelyplanet.com) A beautifully illustrated book that introduces the Spanish language for ages five to eight.

Mexico Cassie (https://mexicocassie.com) Features and tips on family travel in Mexico from an expat British mum based in Mérida.

Kids' Corner

Say What?

Hello.	Hola. *o·la*
Goodbye.	Adiós. *a·dyos*
Thank you.	Gracias. *gra·syas*
My name is ...	Me llamo ... *me ya·mo ...*

Did You Know?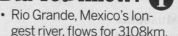

- Rio Grande, Mexico's longest river, flows for 3108km.
- Popocatépetl is one of the world's most active volcanoes.

Have You Tried?

Chapulines
(fried grasshoppers)

WENDY CONNETT / GETTY IMAGES ©

Regions at a Glance

Mexico City

Museums
Nightlife
Food

Museums Galore

You name it, Mexico City probably has a museum for it: from avant-garde art to pre-Hispanic artifacts and antique toys. Don't miss the world-class Museo Nacional de Antropología and Frida Kahlo's famed blue house.

Enter the Night

Mexico City is the country's party capital, where old-world cantinas moonlight as hip bars or queer cabaret spaces. Learn salsa in a plaza by day, sip top mezcal on an exclusive rooftop bar at sundown, then let loose on the dance floor of a megaclub until the wee hours.

Culinary Melting Pot

The capital has fabulous restaurants of many kinds and regional Mexican cuisine gets top billing. Everyone here seems to have an opinion on where you can find, say, the best Guerrero-style *pozole* (a hearty hominy, meat and veg soup) or the tastiest Yucatecan *cochinita pibil* (slow-roasted marinated pork).

p69

Around Mexico City

Archaeological Sites
Small-Town Escapes
Food

Ancient Architecture

Some of Mexico's most awe-inspiring ruins stand within a few hours' drive of the capital. Teotihuacán, with its stunning Pyramids of the Sun and the Moon, is the most famous, but fascinating sites such as Cacaxtla, Xochitécatl, Xochicalco and Cantona can be explored in virtual solitude.

Pueblos Mágicos

With their leafy plazas, traditional crafts and gorgeous colonial edifices, remarkably well-preserved 'magical towns' such as Cuetzalan, Tepoztlán, Malinalco and Valle de Bravo provide a perfect escape from the thick air and crowds of the capital.

Regional Specialties

An incredible variety of indigenous ingredients and imported culinary influences combine in complex regional cuisines. Many towns have their own specialty, such as the pasties from the mining villages above Pachuca, or Puebla's famed *mole poblano*.

p151

Veracruz

Archaeological Sites
Food
Outdoor Adventure

Ancient Cultures

Several distinct pre-Hispanic cultures graced Mexico's Gulf coast, and all have left a weighty legacy. Examine the Classic Veracruz ruins of El Tajín with its curious niched pyramid and the magnificence of Totonac Cempoala, and see the genius of ancient sculptors in Xalapa's Museo de Antropología.

Fish, Glorious Fish

Thanks to the state's 690km-long coastline, fish (and seafood) headlines most menus, in particular the spicy mélange known as *huachinango a la veracruzana* (Veracruz-style snapper). Lining up behind it are the distinctive *moles* of Xico and the gourmet coffee of Coatepec and Córdoba.

River Deep, Mountain High

Mexico's highest mountain, the snow-tipped Pico de Orizaba, towers over central Veracruz and presents the country's toughest trekking challenge. Down in the valleys, Río Antigua and Río Filobobos attract white-water daredevils.

p219

Yucatán Peninsula

Beaches
Diving & Snorkeling
Maya Ruins

A Day at the Beach

Finding your ideal beach is simply a matter of hopping on a bus (or boat). From the debauchery of Cancún to lonely Costa Maya beaches such as Xcalak, the bleached-white sands and beautiful warm waters mustn't be missed.

Into the Blue

With hundreds of kilometers of Caribbean coastline and the world's second-largest barrier reef, the region is a diver's and snorkeler's dream. Banco Chinchorro and Isla Cozumel are the superstars and Cancún's underwater sculpture garden provides another unique experience.

Oldies but Goodies

From world-famous Chichén Itzá to virtually unheard-of sites such as Ek' Balam, the Yucatán is dotted with spectacular pyramids and temples. Many have a resonating atmosphere that even the loudest tour groups can't diminish.

p269

Chiapas & Tabasco

Nature
Outdoor Adventure
Indigenous Culture

Birds & Beasts

Nesting turtles, roaring monkeys and flashes of rainbow plumage are standard fare in the jungles and on the misty mountains and sandy beaches of this biodiverse region that's full of rare and endangered wildlife.

In Motion

Whether you're rappelling into a jungle sinkhole, bouncing over a stretch of white water in a rubber raft, or climbing a 4000m volcano, Chiapas has multiple ways to raise your adrenaline levels.

Temples & Tradition

The world of the Maya lives on everywhere you turn here, from the preserved stone temples of Classic Maya civilization to the persistence of dramatic pre-Hispanic religious rituals and the intricate handwoven textiles and clothing still worn by many.

p369

Oaxaca

Beaches
Outdoor Activities
Culture

Coast of Dreams

With 550km of sandy Pacific strands and wildlife-rich lagoons, Oaxaca's coastline has it all – the pumping surf of Puerto Escondido, the blissed-out traveler scene of San Agustinillo and Mazunte, and the resort attractions of low-key Bahías de Huatulco.

The Great Outdoors

Hike through the Sierra Norte's mountain forests, surf the Pacific swells, raft rivers from the hills to the sea, snorkel or dive the beautiful Huatulco bays, and spot whales, dolphins and turtles off the Pacific coast.

Traditional & Cutting Edge

Oaxaca state is a cultural hub in so many senses, from Oaxaca City's vibrant arts scene to the distinctive Oaxacan cuisine and endlessly inventive handicrafts of the state's indigenous peoples. It all wraps up in a unique and proud Oaxacan regional identity.

p437

Central Pacific Coast

Outdoor Activities
Food
Beaches

Natural Highs

Kayak across a lagoon at dawn, ride horses into the Sierra Madre, swim among flitting butterflies in a boulder-strewn river, watch pelicans and whales parade through the waves, or scan the nighttime sands for nesting mama turtles.

Seafood Heaven

Sidle up to a beachside table at sunset, grab a cold beer and a fresh-cut lime and settle into a plateful of *pescado zarandeado* (grilled fish), *tiritas* (citrus-and-chili-marinated raw-fish slivers) or shrimp and red snapper cooked a dozen different ways.

Surf & Sand

Conjure up the beach of your dreams and you'll find it here, whether wiggling your toes in the sand with margarita in hand, or chasing perfect waves along an endless ultramarine horizon.

p509

Western Central Highlands

Culture
Food
Scenery

Art & Crafts

The highlands heave with indigenous culture, most notably that of the thriving Purépecha people, whose arts and crafts are sold around Pátzcuaro and Uruapan. You'll find superb art galleries and shopping in Guadalajara and its suburbs of Tlaquepaque and Tonalá.

Culinary Feast

When Unesco listed Mexican cuisine as Intangible Cultural Heritage in 2010, it made special mention of Michoacán, whose edibles are often termed the 'soul food' of Mexico. Throw in *birria* (a spicy goat or lamb stew) from Jalisco washed down with local tequila, and you've got a veritable feast.

Volcanic Drama

Tiny Colima state packs a scenic punch with its dramatic twin volcanoes. For equally glorious scenery, don't miss the modern marvel of Volcán Paricutín in Michoacán.

p597

Northern Central Highlands

Museums
Outdoor Adventures
Colonial Cities

Historic & Contemporary

Home to fascinating indigenous cultures and most of the silver that brought opulence to Mexico's colonial grandees, this region was also the birthplace of Mexican independence. Excellent museums highlight everything from historical heroes to contemporary art.

Natural Playground

This adventure playground region offers the chance to rappel into giant sinkholes and snorkel inland lakes in the Huasteca Potosina, ride into deserts around Real de Catorce and search for macaws in Sierra Gorda caves.

Pedestrian Paradise

Cobblestone streets lined by gorgeous colonial stone mansions and churches make for fascinating exploration on foot. Towns and cities here are made for getting lost in – up narrow *callejones* (alleys) or down steep steps. You'll eventually end up on a pretty, laurel-tree-filled plaza.

p659

Baja Peninsula

Scenery
Wine
Water Sports

Majestic Mountains, Tropical Paradise

Few places in the world have deserts just steps away from turquoise lagoons and high, pine-forested mountains just a couple of hours' drive inland. At every corner there are vistas that seem pulled from the pages of a vacation calendar.

Ruta del Vino

The Valle de Guadalupe is producing the best wines in Mexico and this 'Napa Sur' is garnering international acclaim. Its Wine Route makes for a great day (or two) out.

Surfing & Diving

Baja is a paradise for surfers of all levels, with beach, point and reef breaks up and down the Pacific coastline. Divers can do a two-tank dive in the Pacific and be in the natural aquarium of the Sea of Cortez in time for a night dive.

p719

Copper Canyon & Northern Mexico

Colonial Towns
Museums
Outdoor Adventures

Charming Continuity

The gorgeous old towns of Álamos with its wonderful hotels and restaurants, Durango with its expansive plazas and museum offerings, and Parras with its long-standing viticultural tradition, seduce visitors with the pull of bygone centuries.

Marvelous Museums

Monterrey's spectacular Parque Fundidora includes the Horno3 museum devoted to steelmaking. In Saltillo you'll find museums focusing on the desert environment, *sarape* textiles and birdlife, while Durango's and Chihuahua's impressive offerings include museums dedicated to Pancho Villa.

Great Outdoors

An idyllic coastline, vast deserts, dramatic canyons and climates from alpine to subtropical all contribute to a wealth of wildlife and superb hiking and biking options.

p765

On the Road

AT A GLANCE

POPULATION
9.03 million

ELEVATION
2240m

BEST B&B
Red Tree House
(p113)

BEST CANTINA
Cantina Tío Pepe
(p127)

**BEST
TACOS AL PASTOR**
El Huequito (p117)

WHEN TO GO
Mar–May
Catch the last of the
warm, dry weather
before the hot, rainy
season begins.

Sep–Oct
Spots of rain but
without the heat for
European-type mild
weather.

Nov–Feb
Rainy season ends
and the month
begins with colorful
Día de Muertos
festivities.

Palacio de Bellas Artes (p84)
LEILA ASHTARI/LONELY PLANET

Mexico City

Mexico City has always been the sun in the Mexican solar system. Though maligned in the past, the city is cleaning up its act, with revamped public spaces springing back to life, the culinary scene exploding and a cultural renaissance flourishing. By largely managing to distance itself from the drug war, the nation's capital also remains a relative safe haven.

The buzzing downtown area reveals the capital's storied history, from pre-Hispanic splendor to the contemporary megalopolis; while time slows to village pace at its edges on boating excursions along ancient canals, and in opulent neighborhoods with inspired dining and drinking, where old-school cantinas and intriguing museums sit alongside edgy contemporary galleries and glamorous plazas.

INCLUDES

History

Driving over the sea of asphalt that now overlays this highland basin, you'd be hard-pressed to imagine that, a mere five centuries ago, it was filled by a chain of lakes. It would further stretch your powers to imagine that today's downtown was on an islet criss-crossed by canals, or that the communities who inhabited the island and the banks of Lago de Texcoco spoke a patchwork of languages that had as little to do with Spanish as Malay or Urdu. As their chronicles related, the Spaniards who arrived at the shores of that lake in the early 16th century were just as amazed to witness such a scene.

A loose federation of farming villages had evolved around Lago de Texcoco by approximately 200 BC. The biggest, Cuicuilco, was destroyed by a volcanic eruption three centuries later.

Breakthroughs in irrigation techniques and the development of a maize-based economy contributed to the rise of a civilization at Teotihuacán, 40km northeast of the lake. For centuries Teotihuacán was the capital of an empire whose influence extended as far as Guatemala. It was unable to sustain its burgeoning population, however, and fell in the 8th century to internal divisions; it was abandoned and left in ruins. Details are scarce as no written records were kept. Over the following centuries, power in central Mexico came to be divided between varying locally important cities, including Xochicalco to the south and Tula to the north. The latter's culture is known as Toltec (Artificers), a name coined by the later Aztecs, who looked back to the Toltec rulers with awe.

Aztec Mexico City

The Aztec, or Mexica (meh-*shee*-kah), probably arrived in the Valle de México in the 13th century. A wandering tribe that claimed to have come from Aztlán, a mythical region in northwest Mexico, they acted as mercenary fighters for the Tepanecas, who resided on the lake's southern shore and were allowed to settle on the inhospitable terrain of Chapultepec.

The tribe roamed the swampy fringes of the lake, finally reaching an island near the western shore around 1325. There, according to legend, they witnessed an eagle standing atop a cactus and devouring a snake (an image today seen on the Mexican flag), which they interpreted as a sign, as seen in a prophecy, to stop and build a city, Tenochtitlán.

Tenochtitlán rapidly became a sophisticated city-state whose empire would, by the early 16th century, span most of modern-day central Mexico from the Pacific to the Gulf of Mexico and into far southern Mexico. The Aztec built their city on a grid plan, with canals as thoroughfares and causeways to the lakeshore. In the marshier parts they created raised gardens by piling up vegetation and mud and planting willows. These *chinampas* (versions of which still exist at Xochimilco in southern Mexico City) gave three or four harvests yearly.

The Spanish arrived in 1519, fracturing Mexican civilization and turning native people into second-class citizens in just two years. When these invaders arrived, Tenochtitlán's population was between 200,000 and 300,000, while the entire Valle de México had perhaps 1.5 million inhabitants, making it one of the world's densest urban areas.

Capital of Nueva España

So assiduously did the Spanish raze Tenochtitlán that only a handful of structures from the Aztec period remain visible today. Having wrecked the Aztec capital, they set about rebuilding it as their own. Conquistador Hernán Cortés hoped to preserve the arrangement whereby Tenochtitlán siphoned off the bounty of its vassal states.

Ravaged by disease, the Valle de México's population shrank drastically – from 1.5 million to under 100,000 within a century of the conquest. But the city emerged as the prosperous, elegant capital of Nueva España, with broad streets laid over the Aztec causeways and canals.

Building continued through the 17th century, but problems arose as the weighty colonial structures began sinking into the squishy lake bed. Furthermore, lacking natural drainage, the city suffered floods caused by the partial destruction in the 1520s of the Aztec's canals. One torrential rain in 1629 left the city submerged for five years.

Urban conditions improved in the 18th century as new plazas and avenues were installed, along with sewerage and garbage-collection systems. This was Mexico City's gilded age.

Independence

On October 30, 1810, some 80,000 independence rebels, fresh from victory at Guanajuato, overpowered Spanish loyalist forces west of the capital. Unfortunately they were ill equipped to capitalize on this triumph

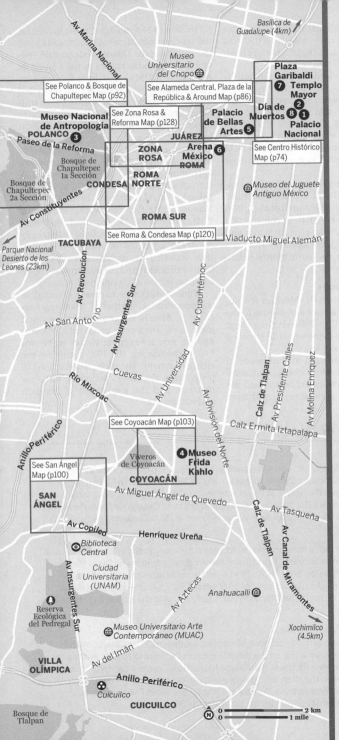

Mexico City Highlights

❶ Palacio Nacional (p77) Studying Diego Rivera's tableau of Mexican history.

❷ Templo Mayor (p73) Marveling at Aztec ruins in the heart of downtown.

❸ Museo Nacional de Antropología (p91) Gazing upon the Aztec sun stone and other superb pre-Hispanic relics.

❹ Museo Frida Kahlo (p102) Sharing Frida's style at her birthplace, Casa Azul in Coyoacán, now home to a museum.

❺ Palacio de Bellas Artes (p84) Feasting your eyes on colorful murals and folkloric dance performances in an art deco theater.

❻ Lucha Libre (p136) Cheering on the masked heroes at the *lucha libre* (Mexican wrestling) bouts.

❼ Plaza Garibaldi (p81) Singing along to mariachi ballads in this soulful plaza.

❽ Día de Muertos (p109) Celebrating the dearly departed while watching giant skeletons dance toward the Zócalo.

and their leader, Miguel Hidalgo, chose not to advance on the city – a decision that cost Mexico 11 more years of fighting before independence was achieved.

Following the reform laws established by President Benito Juárez in 1859, monasteries and churches were appropriated by the government, then sold off, subdivided and put to other uses. During his brief reign (1864–67), Emperor Maximilian laid out the Calzada del Emperador (today's Paseo de la Reforma) to connect Bosque de Chapultepec with the center.

Mexico City entered the modern age under the despotic Porfirio Díaz, who ruled Mexico for most of the years between 1876 and 1911. Díaz ushered in a construction boom, building Parisian-style mansions and theaters, while the city's wealthier residents escaped the center for newly minted neighborhoods to the west.

Modern Megalopolis

After Díaz fell in 1911, the Mexican Revolution brought war, hunger and disease to the streets of Mexico City. Following the Great Depression, a drive to industrialize attracted more money and people.

Mexico City continued to mushroom in the 1970s, as the rural poor sought economic refuge in its thriving industries, and the metropolitan-area population surged from 8.7 million to 14.5 million. Unable to contain the new arrivals, Mexico City spread beyond the bounds of the Distrito Federal (DF; Federal District; today known as the Ciudad de México, or CDMX) and into the adjacent state of México. The result of such unbridled growth was some of the world's worst traffic and pollution. At last count, the Greater Mexico City area had more than 22 million inhabitants.

For seven decades, the federal government ruled DF directly, with presidents appointing 'regents' to head notoriously corrupt administrations. Finally, in 1997, DF gained political autonomy. In 2000 Andrés Manuel López Obrador, of the left-leaning PRD (Party of the Democratic Revolution), was elected mayor. *Capitalinos* (capital-city residents) approved of 'AMLO.' His initiatives included an ambitious makeover of Centro Histórico and the construction of an overpass for the city's ring road.

While AMLO was narrowly defeated in the presidential election of 2006 (an outcome he fiercely contested based on fraud allegations), his former police chief, Marcelo Ebrard, won a sweeping victory in Mexico City, consolidating the PRD's grip on the city government. The PRD passed a flood of progressive initiatives, including same-sex marriage and the legalization of abortion and euthanasia.

MEXICO CITY IN...

Two Days

Day one dawns and you find yourself standing in the Zócalo (p78), once the center of the Aztec universe. Explore the pre-Hispanic ruins at Templo Mayor (p73) then admire Diego Rivera's cinematic murals at Palacio Nacional (p77). On day two delve into Mexico's past at Museo Nacional de Antropología (p91) and Castillo de Chapultepec (p94). Come nightfall, sip mezcal over mariachi music at Plaza Garibaldi (p81).

Four Days

Greet the new day with a stroll around the fountains and leafy paths of Alameda Central (p85), making time to acquaint yourself with the art deco splendor and Diego Rivera mural of Palacio de Bellas Artes (p84). Next head for some *artesanías* (handicrafts) shopping at La Ciudadela (p138) and designer gifts at Barrio Alameda (p138). If it's Saturday, spend the rest of the afternoon learning to dance at the adjacent Plaza de Danzón (p108).

One Week

Get to know the southern districts: visit Museo Frida Kahlo (p102) in Coyoacán and do dinner and mezcal sampling on the delightful Jardín Centenario (p102), or shop for quality crafts at San Ángel's Bazar Sábado (p140) market. Devote a day further south in Xochimilco and spend the afternoon gliding along ancient canals (p97) on a *trajinera* (gondola). Reserve Wednesday or Sunday evening for the Ballet Folklórico de México (p135), or Tuesday, Friday or Sunday for lucha libre (p136).

In December 2018 AMLO finally became President with a landslide victory on the back of a promise to root out corruption. One of his first actions was to cancel the construction of a multibillion-peso airport on the pretext of a vote where only 1% of the population participated. The airport was already one-third constructed and cancellation fees amounted to billions of pesos. It alarmed investors in the city and the country teetered towards recession. In 2019 the city's first female mayor, Claudia Sheinbaum, an environmental engineer, announced a million-peso investment in the transport system over decades. Sheinbaum also had to deal with the fallout of feminist protests that resulted in graffiti damage to El Ángel (p89; Monumento a la Independencia) that polarised Mexicans – was it too extreme or was it a needed wake-up call to the femicide and gender inequalities in the country?

Insecurity remains the greatest challenge for Sheinbaum, and with her approval rating continuing to slide, she, and Mexico City, need a meaningful accomplishment quickly.

◉ Sights

You could spend months exploring all the museums, monuments, plazas, colonial-era buildings, monasteries, murals, galleries, archaeological finds, shrines and religious relics that this encyclopedia of a city has to offer – Mexico City shares billing with London for having the most museums of any city in the world.

Plan ahead, as most museums (including Frida Kahlo's house; p102) and parks close on Monday, while most waive their admission fees to residents on Sunday, thus attracting crowds. Many museums will accept student IDs from abroad for discounts. If you plan on visiting Teotihuacan, Monday can be a time-efficient day.

CDMX (as metropolitan Mexico City is now officially known) comprises 16 *delegaciones* (boroughs), which are in turn subdivided into around 1800 *colonias* (neighborhoods). Though the vast urban expanse appears daunting, the main areas of interest to visitors are fairly well defined and easy to traverse, contained mainly within the *colonias* of Roma, Condesa, Polanco, Centro Histórico, Alameda Central, Coyoacán and San Ángel.

Note that some major streets, such as Avenida Insurgentes, keep the same name for many kilometers, but the names (and numbering) of many lesser streets may switch every 10 blocks or so.

Often the easiest way to find an address is by asking for the nearest metro station.

Besides their regular names, many major streets are termed Eje (axis). The Eje system establishes a grid of priority roads across the city.

◉ Centro Histórico

Packed with magnificent buildings and absorbing museums, the 668-block area defined as the Centro Histórico is the obvious place to start your explorations. More than 1500 of its buildings are classified as historic or artistic monuments and it is on the Unesco World Heritage list. It also vibrates with modern-day street life and nightlife, and is a convenient area to stay.

Since 2000, money has been poured into upgrading the image and infrastructure of the Centro. Streets have been repaved, buildings refurbished, lighting and traffic flow improved and security bolstered. New museums, restaurants and clubs have moved into the renovated structures, and festivals and cultural events are staged in the plazas, spurring a continued downtown revival.

At the center of it all lies the massive Zócalo, downtown's main square, where pre-Hispanic ruins, imposing colonial-era buildings and large-scale murals convey Mexico City's storied past.

In true forward-looking, *chilango* (Mexico City inhabitants) style, the Zócalo, Plaza Tolsá (p79) and Gran Hotel Ciudad de México (p111) opened themselves to international audiences when heavily featured in the James Bond *Spectre* film (2015).

Metro station Zócalo is conveniently in the heart of the Centro, but the area can also be approached from the west from metro Allende, or even metro Bellas Artes at Alameda Central if you wish to experience the crowds of Calle Madero. In the far southern edge of the Centro, metro Isabel La Católica allows you to cross the student bars on and around Calle Regina.

★ **Templo Mayor**   ARCHAEOLOGICAL SITE
(Map p74; ☑ 55-4040-5600; www.templomayor. inah.gob.mx; Seminario 8; adult/student M$75/ free; ☺ 9am-5pm Tue-Sun; Ⓜ Zócalo) Before the Spaniards demolished it, the Aztec 'Great Temple' Teocalli of Tenochtitlán covered the site where the cathedral now stands, as

Centro Histórico

Ê N
0 — 400 m
0 — 0.2 miles

Salón Los Ángeles (660m)

Garibaldi M

Garibaldi M

Lerdo

Paseo de la Reforma

Tianguis Dominical de Antigüedades la Lagunilla (270m)

Rayón

Centro Cultural Universitario Tlatelolco (800m); Plaza de las Tres Culturas (890m)

Libertad

Mercado Tepito

Lagunilla M

Santa Muerte Altar (900m)

Héroe de Granaditas

República de Ecuador

República de Paraguay

República de Brasil

República de Nicaragua

República de Costa Rica

Florida

Aztecas

República de Bolivia

República de Colombia

República de Venezuela

Rodríguez Puebla

Santísima

Calle del Carmen

Plaza de Loreto

San Ildefonso

Justo Sierra

36

6

República de Argentina

Mundo Joven - Zócalo

42

Secretaría de Educación Pública

3

República de Brasil

47

La Palma

Plaza Santo Domingo

71

56

Altuna

Comonfort

República de Honduras

Incas

República de Perú

Belisario Domínguez

República de Chile

República de Cuba

Donceles

73

75

49

Allende M

Allende

19

68

70

15

Plaza Tolsá

59

Condesa

Tacuba

22

29

26

Plaza Garibaldi

Plaza Montero

Plaza de la Concepción

74

28

18

Eje Central Lázaro Cárdenas

27

Allende

79

2 de Abril

Santa Veracruz

23

Palacio de Bellas Artes

1

Bellas Artes M

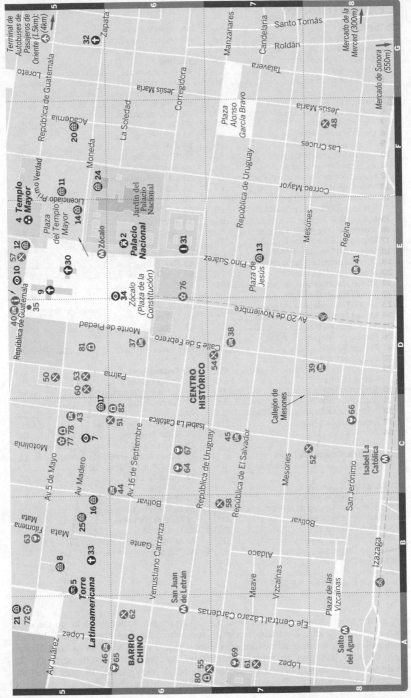

Terminal de Autobuses de Pasajeros de Oriente (1.5km); (4km)

Mercado de la Merced (300m)

Mercado de Sonora (550m)

Loreto

Zapata

32

Zapata

República de Guatemala

Academia

20

Manzanares

Candelaria

Santo Tomás

Roldán

Talavera

Jesús María

Corregidora

La Soledad

Plaza Alonso García Bravo

Jesús María

48

Moneda

24

Las Cruces

Primo Verdad

11

Licenciado

14

Jardín del Palacio Nacional

República de Uruguay

Correo Mayor

4 Templo Mayor

Plaza del Templo Mayor

2 Palacio Nacional

Mesones

Regina

12

M Zócalo

57

10

30

9

35

República de Guatemala

40

31

Pino Suárez

13

Plaza de Jesús

41

E

76

Zócalo (Plaza de la Constitución)

34

Monte de Piedad

37

Calle 5 de Febrero

38

Av 20 de Noviembre

Oxo

D

81

Palma

CENTRO HISTÓRICO

54

39

50

53

60

43

17

82

51

Isabel La Católica

45

Callejón de Mesones

66

Motolinía

77 78

7

República de Uruguay

64 67

República de El Salvador

52

Mesones

Av 5 de Mayo

Av Madero

Av 16 de Septiembre

44

Bolívar

58

Bolívar

San Jerónimo

Isabel La Católica M

16

25

Mata

Gante

Venustiano Carranza

Aldaco

Meave

Vizcaínas

Plaza de las Vizcaínas

Salto del Agua M

Filomena Mata

63

8

33

San Juan de Letrán M

Izazaga

Torre Latinoamericana

5

62

Eje Central Lázaro Cárdenas

69

61

80 55

López

Av Juárez

BARRIO CHINO

21

72

46

65

López

Centro Histórico

well as the blocks to its north and east. It wasn't until 1978, after electricity workers happened on an 8-tonne stone-disc carving of the Aztec goddess Coyolxauhqui, that the decision was taken to demolish colonial buildings and excavate the Templo Mayor.

The temple is thought to be on the exact spot where the Aztec saw the symbolic eagle on a cactus with a snake in its beak (though some say Spaniards added the serpent) – the symbol of Mexico today. In Aztec belief this was, literally, the center of the universe.

Like other sacred buildings in Tenochtitlán, the temple was enlarged several times, with each rebuilding accompanied by the sacrifice of captured warriors. What we see today are sections of the temple's seven different phases. At the center is a platform dating from about 1400. On its southern half, a sacrificial stone stands in front of a shrine to Huitzilopochtli, the Aztec war god. On the northern half is a chac-mool (a Maya reclining figure) before a shrine to the water god, Tláloc. By the time the Spanish arrived, a 40m-high double pyramid towered above this spot, with steep twin stairways climbing to shrines of the two gods.

The entrance to the temple site and museum is east of the cathedral, across the hectic **Plaza del Templo Mayor**, where it's possible to see much of the exterior of the Templo without entering. Authorized tour guides (with Sectur ID) offer their services by the entrance.

The onsite **Museo del Templo Mayor** (included in the site's admission price) houses a model of Tenochtitlán and artifacts from the site, and gives a good overview of Aztec, aka Mexica, civilization, though it has little signage in English, unlike the ruins. Pride of place is given to the great wheel-like stone of Coyolxauhqui (She of Bells on Her Cheek), best viewed from the top-floor vantage point. She is shown decapitated, the result of her murder by Huitzilopochtli (her brother, the hummingbird god of war, the sun and human sacrifice), who also killed his 400 brothers en route to becoming top god.

Ongoing excavation continues to turn up major pieces. Just west of the temple, a monolithic stone carved with the image of Tlaltecuhtli, the goddess of earth fertility, was unearthed in October 2006 and is now prominently displayed on the museum's 1st floor.

Another key find was made in 2011 when a ceremonial platform dating from 1469 was uncovered. Based on historical documents, archaeologists believe the 15m structure was used to cremate Aztec rulers. A dig also turned up what archaeologists believe is the trunk of a sacred tree found at a newly discovered burial site at the foot of the temple. In 2017 a tower 6m in diameter made from over 650 human skulls was found nearby, believed to be Huey Tzompantli, mentioned by Spanish conquistadors but undiscovered until now. Most surprisingly, the remains of the sacrificed included women and children.

Then in 2019, two sacrificial burial sites were uncovered – a boy dressed as Huitzilopochtli, and a jaguar in warrior-garb – giving hope to finding royal Aztec tombs, which have yet to be found despite decades of excavation.

A newer entrance hall open to the public displays objects discovered over four years of the hall's excavation – funerary objects, bones, colonial-era fine china and pre-Hispanic structures of Cuauhxicalco (the place of the eagle vessel) – keeping Templo Mayor continually intriguing even for return visitors.

★**Palacio Nacional** PALACE
(National Palace; Map p74; ☑55-3688-1255; www.historia.palacionacional.info; Plaza de la Constitución; ⊘9am-5pm Tue-Sun; ⓂZócalo) ꜰʀᴇᴇ Inside this grandiose colonial palace you'll see Diego Rivera murals (painted between 1929 and 1951) that depict Mexican civilization from the arrival of Quetzalcóatl (the Aztec plumed serpent god) to the post-revolutionary period. The nine murals covering the north and east walls of the 1st level above the patio chronicle indigenous life before the Spanish conquest.

The Palacio Nacional is also home to the offices of the president of Mexico and the Federal Treasury.

The first palace on this spot was built by Aztec emperor Moctezuma II in the early 16th century. Cortés destroyed the palace in 1521, rebuilding it as a fortress with three interior courtyards. In 1562 the crown purchased the building from Cortés' family to house the viceroys of Nueva España, a function it served until Mexican independence.

As you face the palace, high above the center door hangs the **Campana de Dolores**, the bell rung in the town of Dolores Hidalgo by Padre Miguel Hidalgo in 1810 at the start of the War of Independence. From the balcony underneath it, the president delivers the *grito* (cry) – *¡Viva México!* – on the evening of September 15 to commemorate independence.

Catedral Metropolitana CATHEDRAL
(Metropolitan Cathedral; Map p74; ☑55-5510-0440; http://catedralmetropolitanacdmx.org; Zócalo; ⊘8am-8pm; ⓂZócalo) ꜰʀᴇᴇ One of Mexico City's most iconic structures, this cathedral is a monumental edifice: 109m long, 59m wide and 65m high. Started in 1573, it remained a work in progress during the entire colonial period, thus displaying a catalog of architectural styles, with successive generations of builders striving to incorporate the

innovations of the day. The conquistadors ordered the cathedral built atop the Templo Mayor and, as a further show of domination at a key historical moment, used most of the templo's Aztec stones in its construction.

The first thing you notice upon entering is the elaborately carved and gilded **Altar de Perdón** (Altar of Forgiveness). There's invariably a line of worshippers at the foot of the **Señor del Veneno** (Lord of the Poison), the dusky Christ figure on the right. Legend has it that the figure attained its color when it miraculously absorbed a dose of poison through its feet from the lips of a clergyman to whom an enemy had administered the lethal substance.

The cathedral's chief artistic treasure is the gilded 18th-century **Altar de los Reyes** (Altar of the Kings), behind the main altar. Fourteen richly decorated chapels line the two sides of the building, while intricately carved, late-17th-century wooden choir stalls by Juan de Rojas occupy the central nave. Enormous painted panels by colonial masters Juan Correa and Cristóbal de Villalpando cover the walls of the sacristy, the first component of the cathedral to be built.

Visitors may wander freely, though you're asked not to do so during Mass. A donation is requested to enter the golden **Sacristía Mayor** (⊙ 2-4:45pm) and the **crypt** (⊙ 11am-5pm Fri-Wed), where guides provide commentary. You can also climb the **campanario** (bell tower; M$20; ⊙ 10:30am-6pm), but it was closed for repairs without an end date at the time of writing. Mexico City's archbishop conducts Mass at noon on Sunday.

Zócalo
PLAZA

(Map p74; Plaza de la Constitución; M Zócalo) The heart of Mexico City is the Plaza de la Constitución. Residents began calling it the Zócalo, meaning 'base,' in the 19th century, when plans for a major monument to independence went unrealized, leaving only the pedestal. Measuring 220m from north to south, and 240m from east to west, it's one of the world's largest city squares.

The ceremonial center of Aztec Tenochtitlán, known as the Teocalli, lay immediately northeast of the Zócalo. Today the Zócalo is home to the powers that be. On its east side is the Palacio Nacional (the presidential palace), on the north is the Catedral Metropolitana, and on the south are the city government offices. Jewelry shops and extravagant hotels line the arcade known

as the Portal de Mercaderes on the plaza's west side.

The **Danzantes Aztecas** dance daily in the plaza, wearing snakeskin loincloths and shell ankle bracelets and chanting in Náhuatl. Drummers bang on the conga-like *huehuetl* (indigenous drum) and barrel-shaped *teponaztli* (slit drum). It is meant to evoke the Aztec *mitote*, a frenzied ceremony performed by preconquest Mexicans at harvest times, although scant evidence exists of the actual dance moves.

The square has variously served as a forum for mass protests, free concerts, a human chessboard, a regular gallery of Día de Muertos (Day of the Dead) altars and an ice-skating rink. It's even been a canvas for photo artist Spencer Tunick, who filled the square with 18,000 nude Mexicans in May 2007.

The huge Mexican flag flying in the middle of the Zócalo is ceremonially raised at 8am by soldiers of the Mexican army, then lowered at 6pm.

Sagrario Metropolitano
CHURCH

(Map p74; Plaza de la Constitución s/n; ⊙ 8am-6:30pm; M Zócalo) **FREE** Adjoining the east side of the Catedral Metropolitana is the 18th-century Sagrario Metropolitano. Originally built to house the archives and vestments of the archbishop, it is now the city's main parish church. Its front entrance and mirror-image eastern portal are superb examples of the ultradecorative Churrigueresque style.

Centro Cultural de España
CULTURAL CENTER

(Spanish Cultural Center; Map p74; ☑ 55-5521-1925; www.ccemx.org; República de Guatemala 18; ⊙ 11am-9pm Tue-Fri, 10am-9pm Sat, 10am-4pm Sun; M Zócalo) **FREE** The Centro Cultural de España always has a variety of cutting-edge art exhibitions going on, such as 'Vibraciones' where visitors 'listened' to music resonating through their skin. In the basement you'll find the **Museo de Sitio**, an interesting museum with the remains of 'El Calmécac,' a school where children of Aztec nobility received religious and military training during the reigns of emperors Ahuízotl and Moctezuma II. It was built between 1486 and 1502.

Also in the museum are various artifacts unearthed as the cultural center was being expanded between 2006 and 2008, including several 2.4m-tall pre-Hispanic *almenas* (spiral-shaped decorative pieces), colonial-era ceramic objects and a weathered 20th-century handgun.

DON'T MISS

MEXICO CITY'S QUIRKY SIGHTS

Mundo Chocolate Museum (MUCHO; Map p128; www.mucho.org.mx; Milán 45, Colonia Juárez; adult/child M$75/50; ⊙11am-5pm, cafe 9am-7pm; ⊡Reforma) A beautifully restored 1909 building houses Mundo Chocolate, a museum and store known as MUCHO that celebrates all things chocolate. The permanent exhibit includes an enclosed room of 2981 chocolate discs covering four walls, and you'll also find various sculptures made of, you guessed it, chocolate. *Xico*, a local artist's take on a Mexican hairless dog, watches over the museum courtyard.

Museo del Calzado El Borceguí (El Borceguí Shoe Museum; Map p74; ☑55-5510-0627; 2nd fl, Bolívar 27, Centro Histórico; ⊙10am-2pm & 3-6pm Mon-Sat; Ⓜ Zócalo) At this shoe museum – and the oldest shoemaker in Mexico, operating since 1865 – there are over 2000 pieces of footwear on show, many from famous feet such as Mexican authors Carlos Fuentes and Elena Poniatowska, *fútbol* (soccer) players, Louis XIV of France and Queen Elizabeth II, plus Magic Johnson's size 14½ basketball shoes, and Neil Armstrong's lunar boots. Fashionistas and fetishists will delight at the styles organized by decades. Who doesn't want to see Japanese sandals made of rice hay?

Museo del Juguete Antiguo México (MUJAM, Antique Toy Museum; ☑55-5588-2100; www.museodeljuguete.mx; Dr Olvera 15, cnr Eje Central Lázaro Cárdenas; adult/child M$75/50; ⊙9am-6pm Mon-Fri, to 4pm Sat, 10am-4pm Sun; Ⓟ ⊞; Ⓜ Obrera) Mexican-born Japanese collector Roberto Shimizu has amassed more than a million toys in his lifetime, and this jumbled four-floor museum showcases about 60,000 pieces, ranging from life-size robots to dusty, tiny action figures. Shimizu himself designed many of the unique display cases from recycled objects. Sadly there is no explanatory text, which makes many objects difficult to identify.

Santa Muerte Altar (Altar de La Santa Muerte en Tepito; www.facebook.com/santamuertetk; Alfarería 12, north of Mineros, Tepito; ⊙rosary service 5pm, 1st day of the month; Ⓜ Tepito) Often garbed in a sequined white gown, wig and clutching a scythe in her bony hand, the Saint Death figure is the object of a fast-growing cult in Mexico, particularly in Tepito, where many have lost faith in Catholicism. Visiting *creyentes* (believers) often include criminals, the poor, transgender-identifying people and those on the fringes of society. Enter the notoriously dangerous Tepito 'hood at your own risk; there was a shooting here in 2016. The busy rosary service is a safer time to visit. It's three blocks north of metro Tepito.

Museo de la Tortura (Museum of Torture; Map p74; ☑55-5521-4651; Tacuba 15, Centro Histórico; adult/student/child under 6yr M$60/45/free; ⊙10am-6pm; Ⓜ Allende) Displaying European torture instruments from the 14th to 19th centuries, including a metal-spiked interrogation chair and the menacing skull splitter, this museum has surefire appeal for the morbidly curious. Explanatory English text is a little short. Although kids get free entry, they might find the displays distressing. No photography allowed.

The cultural center's splendidly restored colonial-era building, which conquistador Hernán Cortés once awarded to his butler, has a cool terrace bar (p136) that stages live music and DJ sets. There are great views of the cathedral from here.

Museo Archivo de la Fotografía MUSEUM (Photographic Archive Museum; Map p74; ☑17-19-30-00; www.cultura.cdmx.gob.mx/recintos/maf; República de Guatemala 34; ⊙10am-6pm Tue-Sun; Ⓜ Zócalo) **FREE** Occupying a 16th-century colonial-era building, the city's photo museum hosts changing exhibits focusing on all things Mexico City. Additionally, the museum has amassed a vast archive comprising a century's worth of urban images. Explanations in Spanish.

Plaza Tolsá PLAZA (Map p74; Ⓜ Bellas Artes) Several blocks west of the Zócalo near Alameda Central is this handsome square, named after Manuel Tolsá, the illustrious late-18th-century sculptor and architect who completed the Catedral Metropolitana (p77). He also created the bronze equestrian statue of the Spanish king Carlos IV (r 1788–1808), which is the plaza's centerpiece in front of the Museo Nacional de Arte; it originally stood in the Zócalo.

MEXICO CITY FOR CHILDREN
•••
As with elsewhere in Mexico, kids take center stage in the capital.

Museums

Museums frequently organize hands-on activities for kids. The Museo de la Secretaría de Hacienda y Crédito Público (p81) often stages puppet shows on Sunday. For something that both adults and kids can love, the colorful Museo de Arte Popular (p85) tends to win over most children. Another great option is the Museo del Juguete Antiguo México (p79), a fascinating toy museum with more than 60,000 collectibles on display. Universum (p101) is a science museum with a planetarium and interactive exhibits for kids on biodiversity and more.

In Xochimilco is the Museo Dolores Olmedo (p97), where peacocks and pre-Hispanic dogs occupy the gardens. Children's shows are performed in the patio (museum ticket required) on Saturday and Sunday at 1pm, and the museum offers workshops for children.

Parks & Plazas

Mexico City's numerous parks and plazas are usually buzzing with kids' voices. Bosque de Chapultepec (p91) is the obvious destination, as it contains the Papalote Museo del Niño (p95) and several lakes such as the large Lago de Chapultepec with paddle-boat rentals. Across the avenue, 100m in front of the Museo Nacional de Antropología (p91) entrance, older kids might get into the death defying *voladores* rite – 'flying' from a 20m-high pole – every 30 minutes. In Xochimilco (p96) kids will find riding the gondolas through the canals as magical as any theme park.

In Polanco is the world-class aquarium Acuario Inbursa (p96). Also consider Condesa's Parque México, where kids can rent bikes and where Sunday is family-activity day in the elaborate fenced-in play area. Plaza Hidalgo (p102) in Coyoacán is another fun-filled spot with balloons, street mimes, cotton candy, plentiful ice cream and churros, though there is barely room to move on weekends. Further south, the university sculpture garden (p101) has a trail leading through volcanic fields past a dozen-or-so innovative pieces. The most formidable work is an enormous ring of concrete blocks by sculptor Mathias Goeritz.

Shows & Books

Many theaters, including the **Centro Cultural del Bosque** (Map p92; ☑ 55-5283-4600, ext 4408; www.ccb.bellasartes.gob.mx; Campo Marte, cnr Paseo de la Reforma, Bosque de Chapultepec; ☺ box office noon-3pm & 5-7pm Mon-Fri & prior to events; ⋆; Ⓜ Auditorio), and **Centro Cultural Helénico** (Map p100; ☑ 55-4155-0919; www.helenico.gob.mx; Av Revolución 1500, Colonia Guadalupe Inn; ☺ box office 3pm-8:45pm Mon-Fri, from 11am Sat & Sun; ⋆; Ⓜ Altavista), stage children's plays and puppet shows on weekends and during school holidays. Animated movies are a staple at cinemas around town, though keep in mind that children's films are usually dubbed in Spanish. The city's main library **Biblioteca de México** (National Library; Map p86; ☑ 55-4155-0830; www.bibliotecademexico.gob.mx; Plaza de la Ciudadela 4, Alameda Central; ☺ 8:30am-7:30pm, kids; Ⓜ Balderas) 𝐅𝐑𝐄𝐄 houses the adorably named Bebeteca and Ludoteca spaces to encourage babies and kids to play and read amongst the cushions. It's also a useful rest stop for parents to plonk down after shopping at the adjacent Centro de Artesanías La Ciudadela (p138).

In late October look out for the parade and display of giant *alebrijes* (painted wooden carvings), and the Día de Muertos (p109) parade, both along Reforma to the Zócalo.

Information

For more on activities for children, see the 'Infantiles' section at **Conaculta** (www.mexicoescultura.com); or the 'Family' events on **CDMX Travel** (www.cdmxtravel.com) in English.

Most metro stations and trains are too cramped and hot for prams and lack elevators. Baby-change facilities are available at most museums, but only in larger restaurants. Even without children, walking through crowds in Centro Histórico can be a tiring experience; while the leafy, compact centers at the heart of colonias Roma, Condesa and Coyoacán allow for a little more freedom of movement without having to constantly hand-hold.

Museo Nacional de Arte MUSEUM
(National Art Museum; Map p74; ☑55-8647-5430; www.munal.mx; Tacuba 8; M$70, Sun free, camera/video use M$5/30; ⊙10am-5:30pm Tue-Sun; ✚; M Bellas Artes) Built around 1900 in the style of an Italian Renaissance palace, this museum holds collections representing every school of Mexican art until the early 20th century. A highlight is the work of José María Velasco, depicting the Valle de México in the late 19th century. Free guided tours in English are available at noon and 2pm.

Free loan of strollers and wheelchairs with photo ID.

Antiguo Colegio de San Ildefonso MUSEUM
(Map p74; ☑55-3602-0035; www.sanildefonso.org.mx; Justo Sierra 16; adult/student/child under 12yr M$50/25/free, Sun free; ⊙10am-6pm Tue-Sun; M Zócalo) Diego Rivera, José Clemente Orozco and David Siqueiros painted murals here in the 1920s. Most of the work on the main patio is by Orozco; look for the portrait of Hernán Cortés and his concubine La Malinche underneath the staircase. The amphitheater, off the lobby, holds Rivera's first mural, *La creación*, undertaken on his return from Europe in 1923. Built in the 16th century, the former Jesuit college today hosts outstanding temporary art exhibitions.

Palacio de Minería HISTORIC BUILDING
(Palace of Mining; Map p74; ☑55-5623-2982; www.palaciomineria.unam.mx; Tacuba 5; tours M$30; ⊙tours 11am & 1pm Sat & Sun; M Bellas Artes) The Palacio de Minería was where mining engineers trained in the 19th century. A neoclassical masterpiece, the palace was designed by Manuel Tolsá and built between 1797 and 1813. Today it houses a branch of the national university's engineering department. Visits are by 50-minute guided tour only.

Since 1893 the palace has displayed four restored meteorites that struck northern Mexico 50,000 years ago, one weighing more than 14 tons. There's also a small museum on Tolsá's life and work.

Palacio Postal HISTORIC BUILDING
(Correo Mayor; Map p74; ☑55-5512-0091; 1st fl, Tacuba 1; ⊙8:30am-7:30pm Mon-Fri, 10am-4pm Sat, 10am-2pm Sun; ✚; M Bellas Artes) FREE More than just Mexico City's central post office, this golden palace built in 1907 is an Italianate confection designed by the Palacio de Bellas Artes' original architect, Adamo Boari. Flourishes of art nouveau, art deco, rococo, neoclassical and Moorish styles are incorporated into the building. The beige stone facade features baroque columns and carved filigree around the windows. The bronze railings on the monumental staircase inside were cast in Florence.

The small **Postal Museum** (Map p74; ☑55-5510-2999; Tacuba 1; ⊙8.30am-7.30pm Mon-Fri, 10am-2pm Sun; M Bellas Artes) FREE on the 1st floor is where philatelists can ogle a design of the first stamp ever issued in Mexico.

Museo Interactivo de Economía MUSEUM
(MIDE, Interactive Museum of Economics; Map p74; ☑55-5130-4600; www.mide.org.mx; Tacuba 17; adult/student M$95/75; ⊙9am-6pm Tue-Sun; M Allende) The former hospital of the Bethlehemite religious order has been the home of this economics museum since 2006. A slew of hands-on exhibits is aimed at breaking down financial concepts. For coin connoisseurs, the highlight is the Banco de México's numismatic collection.

Museo de la Secretaría de Hacienda y Crédito Público MUSEUM
(Finance Secretariat Museum; Map p74; ☑55-3668-1657; Moneda 4; ⊙10am-5pm Tue-Sun; M Zócalo) FREE Sure, the name is a tough sell (yay, let's go to the Finance Secretariat Museum!), but it's actually a very interesting place. The museum shows off works from its collection of more than 30,000 pieces of Mexican art, much of it contributed by painters and sculptors in lieu of paying taxes. Built in the 16th century, the former colonial archbishop's palace also hosts a full program of cultural events (many free), from *funciones de títeres* (puppet shows) to chamber music recitals.

The building sits atop the Templo de Tezcatlipoca, a temple dedicated to an Aztec god often associated with night, death and change through conflict. You'll see the temple's stairs just off the renovated main patio.

Plaza Garibaldi PLAZA
(Map p74; Eje Central Lázaro Cárdenas, cnr República de Honduras; mariachi song M$130-150; P; M Garibaldi) Every night the city's mariachi bands belt out heartfelt ballads in this festive square. Wearing silver-studded outfits, they toot their trumpets and tune their guitars until approached by someone who'll pay for a song. Also roaming Garibaldi are white-clad *son jarocho* groups, hailing from Veracruz, and *norteño* combos, who bang out northern-style folk tunes. The notoriously seedy Garibaldi continues to undergo a makeover that includes heightened security,

but caution is still sensible. Check restaurant bills and avoid withdrawing money from the ATMs here.

The latest addition to the plaza is the **Museo del Tequila y el Mezcal** (Map p74; www.mutemgaribaldi.mx; Plaza Garibaldi; M$70; ☺11am-10pm Sun-Wed, to midnight Thu-Sat; Ⓜ Garibaldi), which has exhibits explaining the origins and production processes of Mexico's two most popular distilled-agave drinks.

Metrobús línea 7 runs along Reforma from Chapultepec and El Ángel, passing here at the 'Plaza Garibaldi' stop.

Avenida Madero   STREET
(Map p74) This stately pedestrianized shopping avenue west of the Zócalo, linking Bellas Artes and the Zócalo, boasts a veritable catalog of architectural styles and some small museums. Expect slow-moving throngs of families, teens, tourists, the occasional pickpocket, and street performers on weekends.

Housed in a gorgeous neoclassical building two blocks from the square, **Museo del Estanquillo** (Map p74; ☑55-5521-3052; www.museodelestanquillo.cdmx.gob.mx; Isabel La Católica 26; ☺10am-6pm Wed-Mon; Ⓜ Allende) FREE contains the vast pop-culture collection amassed over the decades by CDMX essayist and pack rat Carlos Monsiváis. The museum illustrates various phases in the capital's development by means of the numerous photos, paintings and movie posters from the collection.

Palacio de Iturbide (Palacio de Cultura Banamex; Map p74; ☑55-1226-0004; www.fomento culturalbanamex.org; Av Madero 17; ☺10am-7pm; Ⓜ Allende) FREE, with its late-18th-century baroque facade, is a few blocks west. Built for colonial nobility, in 1821 it became the residence of General Agustín Iturbide, a Mexican independence hero who was proclaimed emperor here in 1822. (He abdicated less than a year later, after General Santa Anna announced the birth of a republic.) It hosts exhibits drawn from the bank's extensive art collection, enhanced by the building's atrium.

Half a block past the pedestrian corridor Gante stands the amazing **Casa de los Azulejos** (House of Tiles; Map p74; ☑55-5512-1331; Av Madero 4; ☺7am-1am; Ⓜ Allende) FREE. Dating from 1596, it was built for the Condes (Counts) del Valle de Orizaba. Most of the tiles that adorn the outside walls were produced in China and shipped to Mexico

on the Manila *naos* (Spanish galleons used until the early 19th century). The building now houses a Sanborns restaurant in a covered courtyard around a Moorish fountain. You are free to enter and climb the staircase, which has a 1925 mural by Orozco.

Across the way, the **Templo de San Francisco** (Map p74; ☑55-5521-7331; Av Madero 7; ☺8am-8pm; Ⓜ Allende) is a remnant of the vast Franciscan monastery erected in the early 16th century over the site of Moctezuma's private zoo. In its heyday it extended two blocks south and east. The monastic complex was divvied up under the post-independence reform laws, and in 1949 it was returned to the Franciscan order in a deplorable state and subsequently restored. The elaborately carved doorway is a shining example of 18th-century baroque. Popular open-air art exhibitions are held in the adjoining atrium.

Rising alongside the monastery, the **Torre Latinoamericana** (Latin American Tower; Map p74; ☑55-5518-7423; www.miradorlatino. com; Eje Central Lázaro Cárdenas 2; adult/child M$120/80; ☺9am-10pm; Ⓜ Bellas Artes) was Latin America's tallest building when constructed in 1956. Thanks to the deep-seated pylons that anchor the building, it has withstood several major earthquakes. If you want to learn more about the construction of the tower and downtown's centuries-long development, a **museum** on the 38th floor houses a permanent photo exhibition. Up above, **views** from the 41st-floor lounge bar and the 44th-floor observation deck are spectacular, smog permitting. Admission is free if you're just visiting the bar.

Ex Teresa Arte Actual   MUSEUM
(Map p74; ☑55-4122-8020; www.exteresa. bellasartes.gob.mx; Licenciado Primo Verdad 8; ☺10am-6pm Tue-Sun; Ⓜ Zócalo) FREE Mexico City was built atop a sloshy lake bed and it's sinking fast, as evidenced by this teetering former convent. The 17th-century building now serves as a museum for performance art, contemporary art exhibits, concerts and the occasional movie screening. Be sure to gaze up at the dual dome.

Museo Nacional de las Culturas   MUSEUM
(National Museum of Cultures; Map p74; ☑55-5542-0484; www.museodelasculturas.mx; Moneda 13; ☺10am-5pm Tue-Sun; Ⓜ Zócalo) FREE Constructed in 1567 as the colonial mint, this renovated museum exhibits the art, dress and handicrafts of Mexico's and the world's cultures. Mixed in for good measure are natural

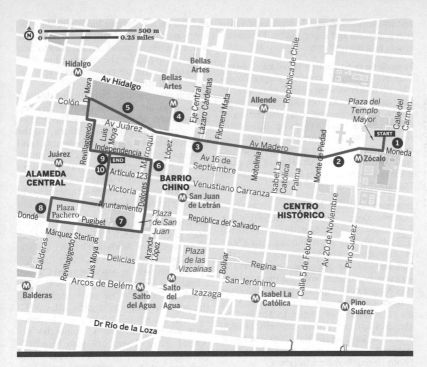

🏃 City Walk
Goin' Downtown

START EX TERESA ARTE ACTUAL
END ALAMEDA CENTRAL
LENGTH 5KM; THREE HOURS

Nothing beats wandering to fully appreciate the rich history of the *centro*.

Kick things off in the slanted, 17th-century **① Ex Teresa Arte Actual** (p82) building. If there's one place that can put into perspective the sinking-city phenomenon, it's here.

As you cross the **② Zócalo** (p78), one of the world's largest squares, stop and contemplate that the surrounding buildings sit atop Aztec temples. Some of the imposing colonial-era structures were built with materials from the pre-Hispanic ruins.

Continue west along bustling Avenida Madero to reach the **③ Torre Latinoamericana** (p82) skyscraper. To get a feel for just how far Mexico City's concave valley spans, take in the view from the observation deck.

Next drift by the art nouveau majesty of **④ Palacio de Bellas Artes** (p84) to

spend time strolling the adjacent **⑤ Alameda Central** (p85), downtown's orderly park with fun fountains and a famous Diego Rivera mural at the west end.

Cut across Avenida Juárez to Calle Dolores and drop by the **⑥ Cantina Tío Pepe** (p127), one of the city's oldest cantinas, for a beer or tequila.

Head south on Dolores to **⑦ Mercado San Juan** (p138), a 60-year-old market frequented by chefs and devout foodies. Look for Gastronómico San Juan for wonderful deli treats and complimentary wine.

Exit the market on Pugibet and go west to Balderas to find **⑧ Centro de Artesanías la Ciudadela** (p138), a large crafts market with decent prices and great variety.

Return to the Alameda Central for a meal of Oaxacan slow food at **⑨ Sin Nombre** (p118), the restaurant with no name. Cap off the evening at the convivial *mezcalería* (mezcal bar) next door, **⑩ Bósforo** (p130). *¡Salud!*

history elements alongside replicas of Egyptian sculptures and K-pop outfits. Explanatory text is in Spanish only.

Templo de la Santísima Trinidad CHURCH
(Map p74; Zapata 60, cnr Santísima; M Zócalo) The profusion of ornamental sculpture on the baroque facade, including ghostly busts of the 12 apostles and a representation of Christ with his head in God's lap, is the main reason to visit the Church of the Holy Sacrament, five blocks east of the Zócalo as you walk along Calle Moneda. Most of the carving was done by Lorenzo Rodríguez between 1755 and 1783.

Suprema Corte de Justicia PUBLIC ART
(Supreme Court; Map p74; 55-4113-1000; Pino Suárez 2; ⊙9am-5pm Mon-Fri; M Zócalo) **FREE** In 1940 Mexican muralist José Clemente Orozco painted four panels around the 2nd level of the Supreme Court's central stairway, two dealing with the theme of justice. A more contemporary take on the same subject, *La historia de la justicia en México* (The History of Justice in Mexico), by Mexico City–born Rafael Cauduro, unfolds over three levels of the building's southwest stairwell. Free audioguides available to 4pm. Photo ID required for admission.

Museo de la Ciudad de México MUSEUM
(Museum of Mexico City; Map p74; 55-5522-9936; www.cultura.cdmx.gob.mx/recintos/mcm; Pino Suárez 30; adult/student M$34/17, Sun free; ⊙10am-6pm Tue-Sun; M Pino Suárez) **FREE** Formerly a palace of the Counts of Santiago de Calimaya, this 18th-century baroque edifice now houses a museum with extensive exhibits focusing on the city's history and culture. Past exhibits include the history of the water issues in CDMX and protest-placard graphic design. Upstairs is the former studio of Joaquín Clausell, considered Mexico's foremost impressionist. The artist used the walls as a sketchbook during the three decades he worked here until his death in 1935.

★Secretaría de Educación Pública PUBLIC ART
(Secretariat of Education; Map p74; 55-3601-1000; República de Brasil 31; ⊙8am-4pm Mon-Fri; República de Argentina) **FREE** The two front courtyards here are lined with 120 fresco panels painted by Diego Rivera in the 1920s. Together they form a tableau of 'the very life of the people,' in the artist's words. Uniquely, the murals are open-air and not in a museum, but along the passageways lining the working offices of the education department, which means you are likely to ponder the murals all to yourself and can get up close to see every detailed brushstroke.

Each courtyard is thematically distinct: the one on the east end deals with labor, industry and agriculture, while the interior one depicts traditions and festivals. On the latter's top level is a series on proletarian and agrarian revolution, underneath a continuous red banner emblazoned with a Mexican *corrido* (folk song). A likeness of Frida Kahlo appears in the first panel as an arsenal worker. Bring photo ID to enter.

Museo José Luis Cuevas MUSEUM
(Map p74; 55-5522-0156; www.museojose luiscuevas.com.mx; Academia 13; M$30, Sun free; ⊙9:30am-5:30pm Tue-Sun; M Zócalo) This museum showcases the works of artist Cuevas, a leader of the 1950s Ruptura movement, which broke with the politicized art of the post-revolutionary regime. Cuevas' *La giganta*, an 8m-tall bronze female figure with some male features, dominates the central patio. There are also hundreds of pieces by other Latin American artists such as Guatemalan geometric artist Carlos Mérida and Uruguayan painter Ignacio Iturria.

⊙ Alameda Central & Around

Emblematic of the downtown renaissance, the rectangular park at the northwest of the Centro Histórico holds a vital place in Mexico City's cultural life. Surrounded by historically significant buildings, Alameda Central has been the focus of ambitious redevelopment over the past decade. In particular, the high-rise towers on the Plaza Juárez, adjacent new restaurants and the revamp of art deco buildings such as Barrio Alameda have transformed the zone south of the park, much of which was destroyed in the 1985 earthquake. Metro stations Bellas Artes and Hidalgo are located on the Alameda's east and west sides, respectively. The north–south Eje Central Lázaro Cárdenas passes just east of the park.

★Palacio de Bellas Artes ARTS CENTER
(Palace of Fine Arts; Map p74; 55-4040-5300; http://museopalaciodebellasartes.gob.mx; Av Juárez; museum M$70, Sun free; ⊙10am-6pm Tue-Sun; P; M Bellas Artes) Immense murals

by world-famous Mexican artists dominate the top floors of this splendid white-marble palace – a concert hall and arts center commissioned by President Porfirio Díaz. Construction on the iconic building began in 1905 under Italian architect Adamo Boari, who favored neoclassical and art nouveau styles.

Complications arose as the heavy marble shell sank into the spongy subsoil, then the Mexican Revolution intervened. Architect Federico Mariscal eventually finished the interior in the 1930s, utilizing the more modern art-deco style.

On the 2nd floor are two early 1950s works by Zapotec-heritage painter Rufino Tamayo: *México de hoy* (Mexico Today) and *Nacimiento de la nacionalidad* (Birth of Nationality), a symbolic depiction of the creation of the *mestizo* (mixed-ancestry) identity.

At the west end of the 3rd floor is Diego Rivera's famous *El hombre en el cruce de caminos* (Man at the Crossroads), originally commissioned for New York's Rockefeller Center. The Rockefellers had the original destroyed because of its anti-capitalist themes, but Rivera re-created it here in 1934.

On the north side are David Alfaro Siqueiros' three-part *La nueva democracia* (New Democracy) and Rivera's four-part *Carnaval de la vida mexicana* (Carnival of Mexican Life). To the east is José Clemente Orozco's *La katharsis* (Catharsis), depicting the conflict between humankind's 'social' and 'natural' aspects.

The 4th-floor **Museo Nacional de Arquitectura** (MUNARQ; Map p74; ☑55-8658-1100; https://munarq.inba.gob.mx; Av Juárez s/n; M$50, Sun free; ◎10am-6pm Tue-Sun; ⓜBellas Artes) features changing exhibits on contemporary architecture. In addition, the palace stages outstanding temporary art exhibitions.

The renovated Bellas Artes theater (p135) is itself a masterpiece (though only viewable during performances), with a stained-glass curtain depicting the Valle de México. Based on a design by Mexican painter Gerardo Murillo (aka Dr Atl), it was assembled by New York jeweler Tiffany & Co from almost a million pieces of colored glass. The theater is the stage for seasonal opera and symphony performances and the Ballet Folklórico de México (p135).

There are lofty views of the Palacio from the cafe terrace of the Sears building across the road.

★**Museo Mural Diego Rivera** MUSEUM
(Diego Rivera Mural Museum; Map p86; ☑55-5512-0754; https://museomuraldiegorivera.inba.gob.mx; cnr Balderas & Colón; adult/student M$35/free, Sun free; ◎10am-6pm Tue-Sun, to 9pm last Wed of month; ⓜHidalgo) This museum is home to one of Diego Rivera's most famous works, *Sueño de una tarde dominical en la Alameda Central* (Dream of a Sunday Afternoon in the Alameda Central), a 15m-long mural painted in 1947. Rivera imagined many of the figures who walked in the city from colonial times onward, among them Hernán Cortés, Benito Juárez, Porfirio Díaz and Francisco Madero.

All are grouped around a *Catrina* (skeleton in pre-revolutionary women's garb). Rivera himself, as a pug-faced child, and Frida Kahlo stand beside the skeleton. Charts identify all the characters. The museum was built in 1986 to house the mural, after its original location, the Hotel del Prado, was wrecked by the 1985 earthquake.

Camera (M$5) and video (M$30) use both cost extra.

★**Museo de Arte Popular** MUSEUM
(Museum of Popular Art; Map p86; ☑55-5510-2201; www.map.cdmx.gob.mx; Revillagigedo 11; adult/child & student M$60/free, Sun free; ◎10am-6pm Tue & Thu-Sun, to 9pm Wed; ⓕ; ⓜJuárez) A major showcase for folk art, this is a colorful museum that even kids love. Crafts are thematically displayed from all over Mexico, including carnival masks from Chiapas, *alebrijes* (colorful wooden animal figures) from Oaxaca and a whole section dedicated to Day of the Dead. An illustrated wall map provides an overview of Mexico's regions and their traditions.

The museum occupies the former fire department headquarters, itself an outstanding example of 1920s art deco by architect Vicente Mendiola. The ground-level **shop** sells quality, unique handicrafts.

Alameda Central PARK
(Map p86; Av Juárez; ⓕ; ⓜBellas Artes) Created in the late 1500s by mandate of then-viceroy Luis de Velasco, the Alameda took its name from the *álamos* (poplars) planted over its rectangular expanse. By the late 19th century the park was graced with European-style statuary and lit by gas lamps. It became the place to be seen for the city's elite. Today the Alameda is a popular refuge, particularly on Sunday when families stroll its pathways and lovers snuggle on benches.

Alameda Central, Plaza de la República & Around

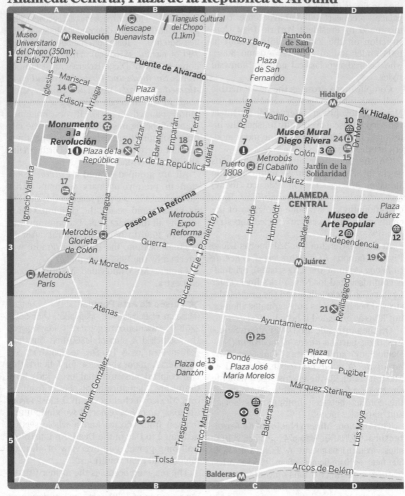

The park is fitted out with dancing fountains, free wi-fi and well-manicured gardens rife with fragrant lavender plants; it's relatively safe and pleasant even on weekend nights. Don't expect to find any street food here – it's banned.

Laboratorio de Arte Alameda   MUSEUM
(Alameda Art Laboratory; Map p86; ☑55-8647-5660; www.artealameda.bellasartes.gob.mx; Dr Mora 7; adult/student M$35/free, Sun free; ☺9am-5pm Tue-Sun; Ⓜ Hidalgo) As is often the case with museums in the *centro,* the 17th-century former convent building that contains the Laboratorio de Arte Alameda

is at least as interesting as its contents. Here you can catch installations by leading experimental artists from Mexico and abroad, with an emphasis on electronic and interactive media. Past exhibits include 'Tecno-Pop' examining design and technology in the era of the meme.

Museo Memoria y Tolerancia   MUSEUM
(Memory & Tolerance Museum; Map p86; ☑55-5130-5555; www.myt.org.mx; Plaza Juárez 12; adult/student M$90/70, audioguide M$20, temporary exhibitions M$30; ☺9am-6pm Tue-Fri, 10am-7pm Sat & Sun; Ⓜ Bellas Artes) A mazelike, unique museum of 55 halls dedicated to preserving the

memory of genocide victims. The multimedia exhibit chronicles crimes committed against humanity in Cambodia, Guatemala, Sudan, Rwanda and the former Yugoslavia, as well as those perpetrated during the Holocaust. Recent temporary exhibitions have focused on migration, misogyny, LGBTIQ+ identity, and Chinese genocide in Mexico. Permanent exhibitions educate on all these themes.

Museo Franz Mayer   MUSEUM
(Map p86; ☎ 55-5518-2266; https://franzmayer. org.mx; Av Hidalgo 45; M$60, cloister only M$10; ⏰ 10am-5pm Tue-Sun; Ⓜ Bellas Artes) This museum is the fruit of the efforts of German-born Franz Mayer. Prospering as a financier in his adopted Mexico, Mayer amassed the collection of Mexican silver, ceramics, textiles and furniture now on display. Look out for the annual World Press Photo (www.worldpress photo.org) exhibition held here between late July and late September.

The exhibit halls open onto a sumptuous colonial-era patio where you can grab a bite at the excellent **Cloister Café**.

The museum occupies the old church and hospice of the San Juan de Dios order, which under the brief reign of Maximilian became a halfway house for prostitutes.

Iglesia de la Santa Veracruz   CHURCH
(Map p86; ☑55-5512-3841; Plaza de Santa Veracruz, Av Hidalgo; Ⓜ Bellas Artes) Originally constructed in 1586, this church was rebuilt in the 18th century and now houses the Museo Franz Mayer (p87). It features two doors in Mexican baroque style.

Museo Nacional de la Estampa   MUSEUM
(MUNAE; Map p74; ☑55-5521-2244; https://museonacionaldelaestampa.inba.gob.mx; Av Hidalgo 39; adult/student M$50/free, Sun free; ☺10am-6pm Tue-Sun; Ⓜ Bellas Artes) Devoted to the graphic arts, this museum has thematic exhibits, such as Zapata through contemporary images, from its collection of more than 12,000 prints. The museum also does interesting temporary expositions that showcase works from Mexico and abroad.

La Ciudadela   CULTURAL CENTER
(Map p86; Balderas; Ⓜ Balderas) The formidable compound now known as 'The Citadel' started off as a tobacco factory in the late 18th century, though it's best known as the scene of the Decena Trágica (Tragic Ten Days), the coup that brought down the Madero government in 1913. Today it's home to the Biblioteca de México (p80). Locals use its name interchangeably for the Centro de Artesanías La Ciudadela (p138) across the plaza, where vendors sell a wide array of crafts from around Mexico.

Centro de la Imagen (Map p86; ☑55-4155-0850; http://centrodelaimagen.cultura.gob.mx; Plaza de la Ciudadela 2; ☺10am-7pm Wed-Sun; Ⓜ Balderas) FREE, the city's photography museum, is at the Calle Balderas entrance.

◉ Plaza de la República & Around

★**Monumento a la Revolución**   MONUMENT
(Map p86; www.mrm.mx; Plaza de la República; all access adult/child M$90/70, 360 observation deck only M$60; ☺noon-8pm Mon-Thu, to 10pm Fri & Sat, 10am-8pm Sun; ꤉Plaza de la República) Unveiled in 1938, this monument contains the tombs of the revolutionary and post-revolutionary heroes Pancho Villa, Francisco Madero, Venustiano Carranza, Plutarco Elías Calles and Lázaro Cárdenas. The star today is the 65m-high summit **paseo linternilla** (Map p86; all access adult/child M$90/70) accessed by glass elevator and opening to a spiraling staircase that ascends to a round terrace with a panoramic view of the city. Below it is the equally impressive, though not as tall, **360 observation deck** (Map p86; ☑55-5592-2038; www.mrm.mx; included in all access ticket, observation deck only M$60; ☺noon-8pm Mon-Thu, to 10pm Fri & Sat, 10am-8pm Sun; ꤉Plaza de la República), which is as high as you can go without the all-access pass.

You can also access the skeleton of the structure in the **1910 Structure Galleries**, and there is an interesting basement art gallery, the **Paseo Cimentación** (Map p86; ☑55-5592-2038; all access adult/child M$90/70; ☺noon-8pm Mon-Thu, to 10pm Fri & Sat, 10am-8pm Sun; ꤉Plaza de la República), where you can check out temporary art exhibitions amid a labyrinth of gigantic steel beams that serve as the structure's foundation.

Underlying the plaza and monument, the spruced-up **Museo Nacional de la Revolución** (National Museum of the Revolution; Map p86; ☑55-5546-2115; www.cultura.cdmx.gob.mx/recintos/mnr; Plaza de la República; adult/student M$34/17, Sun free; ☺9am-5pm Tue-Fri, to 6:30pm Sat & Sun; ꤉Plaza de la República) covers a 63-year period, from the implementation of the constitution guaranteeing human rights in 1857 to the installation of the post-revolutionary government in 1920. Explanatory text is in Spanish only.

Originally meant to be a legislative chamber, construction of the current Monumento a la Revolución was interrupted by the Revolution itself, and there was talk of demolishing the building, but instead it was modified and given a new role.

Kids love frolicking in the plaza's fountains, while at night the monument's renovated architectural features are highlighted by colorful lights.

Museo Universitario del Chopo   MUSEUM
(☑55-5546-8490; www.chopo.unam.mx; González Martínez 10; adult/student M$30/15, Wed free; ☺11.30am-7pm Wed-Sun; Ⓜ San Cosme) You can't miss the prominent spires of this university-run museum. Parts of the old building, made of forged iron from Düsseldorf, were brought over in pieces and assembled in Mexico City around the turn of the 20th century. Chopo boasts wide, open spaces in which ramps serve as showroom floors and

high ceilings permit larger-than-life exhibits for contemporary artworks. The museum also hosts modern dance performances and screens international and Mexican indie movies.

◉ Zona Rosa & Reforma

Wedged between Paseo de la Reforma and Avenida Chapultepec, the 'Pink Zone' was developed as an international playground and shopping district during the 1950s, when it enjoyed a cosmopolitan panache. Since then, however, Zona Rosa and Reforma has lost ground to more fashionable neighborhoods such as Condesa and Roma. It's now a diverse hodgepodge.

Zona Rosa is one of the country's largest gay and lesbian districts and an expat magnet, with a significant Korean population (and associated Korean, Japanese and Chinese restaurants that outshine Chinatown). Touristy stores, sports bars and fast-food outlets line busy pedestrianised Calle Génova; high-end hotels tower along Paseo de la Reforma; and Calle Amberes (and around) has the greatest concentration of LGBTIQ+ clubs. Contrastingly, the area north of Paseo de la Reforma is landmarked by the US embassy and the restaurants and bars to cater to its business clientele. Although technically named **Colonia Cuauhtémoc**, most locals know the embassy area near El Ángel as 'Reforma', and it is fast becoming also known as 'Little Tokyo' for the Japanese restaurants, bars and hotels there.

To the east crossing Avenida Insurgentes Norte, the neighbourhood including Zona Rosa is technically **Colonia Juárez** but is also referred to as 'Reforma' (many Mexicans won't have heard of 'Juárez', and will confuse 'Cuauhtémoc' with the identical borough name for Roma and Condesa). This part of Reforma is emerging as a new hip enclave. The tranquil **Plaza Washington** on the corner of Calles Londres and Dinamarca is the latest pocket to flourish with boutique businesses in an attempt to keep the zone in the pink.

El Ángel   MONUMENT
(Monumento a la Independencia; Map p128; Paseo de la Reforma; Ⓜ Insurgentes) FREE The symbol of Mexico City, known as 'El Ángel' (The Angel), this gilded Winged Victory on a 45m-high pillar was sculpted for the independence centennial of 1910. Inside the monument are the remains of Miguel Hidalgo, José María Morelos, Ignacio Allende and nine other notables. Thousands of people congregate around the monument on Independence Day, New Year's Eve, for victory celebrations following important Mexican *fútbol* matches, and occasional free concerts.

PASEO DE LA REFORMA

Mexico City's grandest thoroughfare, Paseo de la Reforma, often referred to as 'Reforma' (giving the Zona Rosa and Reforma area its name), traces a bold southwestern path from Tlatelolco to Bosque de Chapultepec, skirting Alameda Central and crossing the Zona Rosa and Reforma neighborhood. Emperor Maximilian of Hapsburg laid out the boulevard to connect his castle on Chapultepec Hill with the old city center. After his execution, it was given its current name to commemorate the reform laws instituted by President Benito Juárez. In recent years the pleasantly walkable avenue has become smartly refurbished and its broad, statue-studded medians stage book fairs and art exhibits.

Paseo de la Reforma links a series of monumental *glorietas* (traffic circles) starting near Alameda Central with **El Caballito** (Map p86; Ⓜ Hidalgo), a yellow representation of a horse's head by the sculptor Sebastián. It continues by the **Centro Bursátil** (Map p128; Ⓜ Insurgentes), an angular tower and mirror-ball ensemble housing the nation's Bolsa (stock exchange), before arriving at the golden icon of Mexico City, Monumento a la Independencia, known as **El Ángel**.

At Paseo de la Reforma's intersection with Sevilla is the monument commonly known as **La Diana Cazadora** (Diana the Huntress; Map p128), a 1942 bronze sculpture actually meant to represent the *Archer of the North Star*. The Paseo becomes leafier at the Bosque de Chapultepec with the lofty Castillo de Chapultepec (p94) inside, plus top museums Museo de Arte Moderno (p95), Museo Tamayo (p95) and Museo Nacional de Antropología (p91), before finishing at **Auditorio Nacional** (Map p92; ☑ 55-9138-1350; www.auditorio.com.mx; Paseo de la Reforma 50; ☺ box office 10am-7pm Mon-Sat, 11am-6pm Sun; Ⓜ Auditorio).

It's also a magnet for political demonstrations, and in August 2019 a protest against femicide ended in graffiti on El Ángel to draw attention to the problems of inequality in the country. The site remains boarded up for years-long repairs at the time of writing.

⊙ Condesa

Colonia Condesa's striking architecture, palm-lined esplanades and joyful parks echo its origins as a haven for a newly emerging elite in the early 20th century. Mention 'Condesa' today and most people think of it as a trendy area of attractive restaurants, stylish boutiques and hot nightspots. Fortunately much of the neighborhood's old flavor remains, especially for those willing to wander outside the valet-parking zones. Stroll the pedestrian medians along Ámsterdam, Avenida Tamaulipas or Avenida Mazatlán to admire art deco and California colonial-style buildings. The focus is the peaceful **Parque México**, the oval shape of which reflects its earlier use as a horse-racing track and today attracts professional dog walkers, dancers practicing their moves, lovers whispering on the benches, and families in the children's play area. Two blocks northwest is **Parque España**, which has another kids' zone.

Casa Guillermo Tovar de Teresa   MUSEUM
(Map p120; ☑55-1103-9800; www.museosouma ya.org; Valladolid 52; ⊙10.30am-6.30pm) FREE
The converted art storehouse of historian and bibliophile Guillermo Tovar de Teresa opened its doors in 2018 as a sumptuous museum of the Museo Soumaya (p96) family. On display are over 1000 artworks including paintings, sculptures, furniture, rugs and the complete collection of poet Sor Juana Inés de la Cruz.

The small museum opens 365 days a year, useful for Mondays when most other sights close.

⊙ Roma

Northeast of Condesa and south of Zona Rosa and Reforma, Roma is a hip enclave in the rapid process of gentrification. Once inhabited by artists and writers, it's now also the home of designer labels and international dining, while still retaining its slower pace in the backstreets. This is where Beat writers William S Burroughs and Jack Kerouac nat-urally gravitated during their 1950s sojourn in Mexico City. Built at the turn of the 20th century, the neighborhood is a showcase for Parisian-influenced architecture, which was favored by the Porfirio Díaz regime. Some of the most outstanding examples stand along Colima and Tabasco. When in Roma, linger in the cafes and check out the art galleries and specialty shops along Colima. A stroll down Orizaba passes two lovely plazas – Río de Janeiro, with a statue replica of Michelangelo's *David*, and Luis Cabrera, which has beautiful fountains (Beat writers once posed for a photo here).

On weekends inspect the **Bazar de Cuauhtémoc** (Tianguis de Antigüedades; Map p120; Jardín Dr Chávez, Colonia Doctores; ⊙10am-5pm Sat & Sun; 🚇Jardín Pushkin), an antique market in a small park – walk to the eastern end of Álvaro Obregón, Roma's main thoroughfare, then one block north along Avenida Cuauhtémoc.

Small, independent art galleries and museums are scattered around Roma.

Museo del Objeto del Objeto   MUSEUM
(Museum of Objects; Map p120; ☑55-5533-9637; www.elmodo.mx; Colima 145; adult/student/child under 12yr M$50/25/free; ⊙10am-6pm Tue-Sun; 🚇Durango) Packing a collection of nearly 100,000 pieces, some as old as the Mexican War of Independence (1810), this two-story design museum tells unique versions of Mexican history by compiling objects for thematic exhibits such as *fútbol* in Mexico. The permanent collection groups together items such as matchboxes, printing stamps and plenty of tins – for tobacco, shoe polish and gramophone needles. Many of the items are viewable on the website.

Centro de Cultura Casa Lamm   ARTS CENTER
(Map p120; ☑55-5525-1332; www.galeria casalamm.com.mx; Álvaro Obregón 99; ⊙10am-7pm Mon-Sat, to 5pm Sun; 🚇Álvaro Obregón) FREE This cultural complex contains a gallery for contemporary Mexican painting and photography as well as an excellent art library.

MUCA Roma   MUSEUM
(Map p120; ☑55-5511-0925; www.muca roma.unam.mx; Tonalá 51; ⊙10am-7pm Tue-Sun; 🚇Durango) FREE Sponsored by the Universidad Nacional Autónoma de México (UNAM), this small university museum exhibits Mexican and international contemporary art with ties to science or new technology.

◉ Bosque de Chapultepec

Chapultepec (Náhuatl for 'Hill of Grasshoppers') served as a refuge for the wandering Aztec before becoming a summer residence for their noble class. It was the nearest freshwater supply for Tenochtitlán. In the 15th century Nezahualcóyotl, ruler of nearby Texcoco, oversaw the construction of an aqueduct to channel its waters over Lago de Texcoco to the pre-Hispanic capital.

Today Mexico City's largest park, the Bosque de Chapultepec, covers more than 4 sq km, with lakes and several excellent museums. Up until recently, it also has been an abode of Mexico's high and mighty, containing the former presidential residence, Los Pinos (p95), and a former imperial palace with a view, Castillo de Chapultepec (p94).

Sunday is the park's big day, as vendors line the main paths and throngs of families come to picnic, navigate the lake on rowboats and crowd into the museums with free Sunday admission. Most of the major attractions are in or near the eastern **1a Sección** (1st Section; Map p92; https://chapultepec.org.mx; ⊙5am-6pm Tue-Sun; Ⓜ Chapultepec), while a children's museum dominates the 2da Sección. The whole park is closed on Mondays, unless it is a public holiday.

A pair of bronze lions overlooks the main gate at Paseo de la Reforma and Lieja. Other access points are opposite the Museo Tamayo, Museo Nacional de Antropología and by metro Chapultepec. The fence along Paseo de la Reforma serves as the **Galería Abierta de las Rejas de Chapultepec** (Map p92; Paseo de la Reforma; ⊙24hr) FREE, an outdoor photo gallery.

Chapultepec metro station is at the east end of the Bosque de Chapultepec, near the Monumento a los Niños Héroes and Castillo de Chapultepec. Auditorio metro station is on the north side of the park, 500m west of the Museo Nacional de Antropología. The comfortable Línea 7 metrobús rides along Paseo de la Reforma from Plaza Garibaldi and El Ángel, passing Bosque de Chapultepec (except Sundays from 6:30am to 2pm), and terminating at Auditorio Nacional.

The 2da Sección of the Bosque de Chapultepec lies west of the Periférico. To get to the 2da Sección from metro Chapultepec, find the 'Paradero' exit and catch a 'Feria' bus at the top of the stairs. These depart continuously and travel nonstop to the 2da Sección, dropping off riders at the Papalote Museo del Niño (p95). In addition to this family attraction, there's a pair of upscale lake-view restaurants on Lago Mayor and Lago Menor.

★ Museo Nacional de Antropología
MUSEUM

(National Museum of Anthropology; Map p92; ☑55-5553-6266; www.mna.inah.gob.mx; cnr Paseo de la Reforma & Calz Gandhi; adult/child under 13yr M$75/free, video recording M$45, parking M$20; ⊙9am-5pm Tue-Sun; Ⓟ; ☐Antropología) This world-class museum stands in an extension of the Bosque de Chapultepec and is a highlight of visiting CDMX. Its long, rectangular courtyard is surrounded on three sides by two-level display halls. The 12 ground-floor *salas* (halls) are dedicated to pre-Hispanic Mexico, while upper-level *salas* show how Mexico's indigenous people live today, with the contemporary cultures located directly above their ancestral civilizations. The vast museum offers more than most people can absorb in a single visit.

Everything is superbly displayed, with much explanatory text translated into English. At the entrance, you will find the starting point for free one-hour guided tours (four daily except Sunday, 10:30am to 5pm; reservation recommended) in English, which are very worthwhile to make sense of Mexico's complicated history.

The giant column fountain in the courtyard is known as *el paraguas* (the umbrella) and acts as a reminder of the connection to nature. Each side depicts a different sculpture – east showing the integration of Mexico; west, outward-looking Mexico; and north and south, the fight for liberty in Mexico's villages.

The best place to start is the Introducción a la Antropología and work counterclockwise from there. The first few halls are introductions to anthropology in general, and demonstrate how the hemisphere's earliest settlers got here and developed from nomadic hunting life to a more settled farming existence in Mexico's central highlands.

Many short-on-time visitors jump straight into the Teotihuacán hall displaying models and objects from the Americas' first great and powerful state. This then moves into the Los Toltecas, which displays one of the four basalt warrior columns from Tula's Temple of Tlahuizcalpantecuhtli.

The next hall is devoted to the Mexica, aka Aztec. Come here to see the famous sun stone, unearthed beneath the Zócalo in 1790,

Polanco & Bosque de Chapultepec

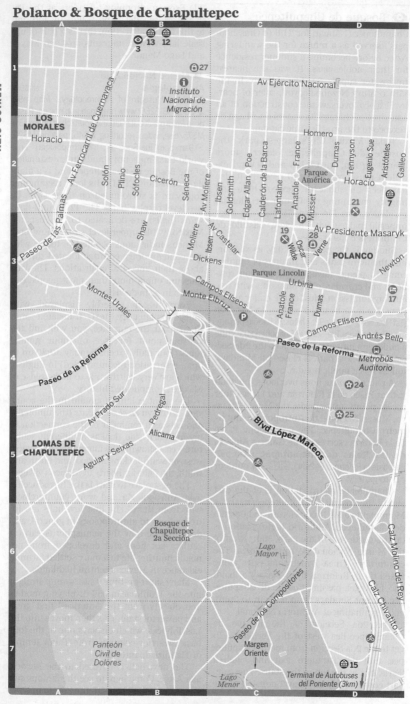

MEXICO CITY

LOS MORALES

Horacio

Instituto Nacional de Migración

Av Ejército Nacional

Homero

Parque América

Horacio

POLANCO

Av Presidente Masaryk

Parque Lincoln

Urbina

Campos Elíseos

Monte Elbruz

Paseo de la Reforma

Andrés Bello

Metrobús Auditorio

Blvd López Mateos

Montes Urales

Paseo de la Reforma

Av Prado Sur

Alicama

Aguiar y Seixas

LOMAS DE CHAPULTEPEC

Bosque de Chapultepec 2a Sección

Lago Mayor

Paseo de los Compositores

Calz Molino del Rey

Calz Chivatito

Panteón Civil de Dolores

Margen Oriente

Lago Menor

Terminal de Autobuses del Poniente (3km)

Av Ferrocarril de Cuernavaca

Paseo de las Palmas

Solón

Plinio

Sófocles

Cicerón

Séneca

Shaw

Moliere

Ibsen

Av Castelar

Dickens

Campos Elíseos

Av Moliere

Ibsen

Goldsmith

Edgar Allan

Calderón de la Barca

Poe

Lafontaine

Anatole

France

Musset

Dumas

Tennyson

Eugenio Sue

Aristóteles

Galileo

Wilde

Oscar

Verne

Newton

Anatole France

Dumas

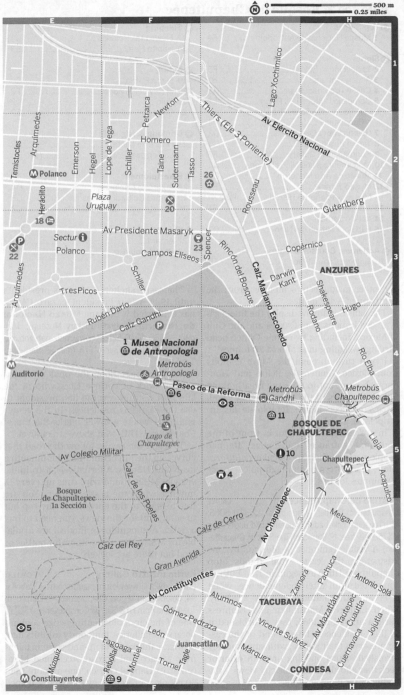

MEXICO CITY SIGHTS

Polanco & Bosque de Chapultepec

and other magnificent sculptures from the pantheon of Aztec deities.

The halls that follow display the fine legacy of civilizations from Oaxaca and the Gulf of Mexico, including two stone Olmec head carvings weighing in at almost 20 tonnes.

If you rush through the Maya exhibits from Mexico, Guatemala, Belize and Honduras, be sure not to miss the breathtaking full-scale replica of the tomb of King Pakal, discovered deep in the Templo de las Inscripciones at Palenque.

In a clearing about 100m in front of the museum's entrance, indigenous Totonac people perform their spectacular *voladores* rite – 'flying' from a 20m-high pole – every 30 minutes for tips.

Castillo de Chapultepec CASTLE
(Chapultepec Castle; Map p92; ☑5211-5066; with museum ticket adult/student/child under 13yr M$75/free/free; ◷9am-5pm Tue-Sun; Ⓜ Chapultepec) A visible reminder of Mexico's bygone aristocracy, the 'castle' that stands atop Chapultepec Hill was begun in 1785 but not completed until after independence, when it became the national military academy. When Emperor Maximilian and Empress Carlota arrived in 1864, they refurbished it as their residence. The east end of the castle preserves their palace, with sumptuously furnished salons opening onto an exterior deck that affords panoramic city views – the highlight for many visitors.

The castle sheltered Mexico's presidents until 1939, when President Lázaro Cárdenas converted it into the **Museo Nacional de Historia** (National History Museum; Map p92; ☑55-4040-5215; www.mnh.inah.gob.mx; adult/child under 13yr M$75/free; ◷9am-5pm Tue-Sun).

On the upper floor, the opulent rooms are the work of Porfirio Díaz, who in the late 19th century was the first president to use the castle as residences. In the center is a patio where a tower marks the top of Chapultepec Hill, 45m above street level.

To reach the castle, follow the road that curves up the hill behind the Monumento a los Niños Héroes. Alternatively, a trainlike vehicle (M$25 round-trip) runs up every 15 minutes when the castle is open. You are free to walk to the entrance at the top but to enter, and for the views, you need to buy a ticket. Audioguides in English are available for M$75. No entry with water bottles or food but there are lockers.

Kurimanzutto Gallery GALLERY
(Map p92; www.kurimanzutto.com; Rebollar 94, Colonia San Miguel Chapultepec; ◷11am-6pm Tue-Thu, to 4pm Fri & Sat; Ⓜ Constituyentes) **FREE** One of the city's most cutting-edge contemporary art galleries, temporary exhibits here showcase the works of up-and-coming talent from Mexico and abroad. Acclaimed Mexican artist Gabriel Orozco, one of more than 30 people represented by the gallery, helped

to conceive the concept of Kurimanzutto with co-founders Jose Kuri and Monica Manzutto. The pleasant 1949 building was converted from an industrial patisserie and features exposed wooden beams and lots of natural light.

Museo de Arte Moderno MUSEUM
(Museum of Modern Art; Map p92; 55-5211-8331; https://mam.inba.gob.mx; cnr Paseo de la Reforma & Calz Gandhi; adult/student M$70/free, Sun free; 10:15am-5:30pm Tue-Sun; P; Chapultepec) The collection here exhibits work by noteworthy 20th-century and contemporary Mexican artists, including canvases by Dr Atl, Rivera, Siqueiros, Orozco, Tamayo and O'Gorman, and Frida Kahlo's *Las dos Fridas,* possibly her best-known painting. It also has good temporary expositions with a focus on Mexican artists.

Free-admission Sundays are very busy as families spill in from the Bosque de Chapultepec.

Museo Tamayo MUSEUM
(Map p92; 55-4122-8200; www.museotamayo.org; Paseo de la Reforma 51; M$70, Sun free; 10am-6pm Tue-Sun, also 6pm-9:30pm last Wed of month; P; Antropología) A multilevel structure built to house international contemporary art, donated by Oaxaca-born painter Rufino Tamayo to the people of Mexico. The small museum exhibits one main cutting-edge work from around the globe at a time, which is thematically arranged with shows from the Tamayo collection and one or two other tiny shows. There's a rustic-chic **restaurant** overlooking the park, an ideal breakfast stop before exploring Chapultepec's sights.

Jardín Botánico GARDENS
(Botanical Garden; Map p92; 55-5553-8114; 1a Seccion, Bosque de Chapultepec, Paseo de la Reforma; 10am-6pm Tue-Sun; Chapultepec) FREE Highlighting Mexico's plant diversity, this 4-hectare complex in Chapultepec is divided into sections that reflect the country's varied climatic zones. There are plenty of cacti and agave, a wonderful greenhouse full of rare orchids, and straw creepy-crawly statues that kids might enjoy. The Jardín underwent a major revamp in 2018, bringing a new garden highlighting Mexico's chilies, and a grasshopper space stocked with plants that they love.

The nearest Chapultepec entrance to the garden is across from Museo Tamayo.

Monumento a Los Niños Héroes MONUMENT
(Map p92; Tue-Sun; Chapultepec) The six marble columns marking Chapultepec park's eastern entrance commemorate the 'boy heroes,' six young cadets who perished in battle. On September 13, 1847, 8000 US troops stormed Castillo de Chapultepec, which then housed the national military academy. Mexican General Santa Anna retreated before the onslaught, but the youths, aged 13 to 20, chose to defend the castle. Legend has it one of them, Juan Escutia, wrapped himself in a Mexican flag and leaped to his death rather than surrender.

The event is commemorated each year on Día de los Niños Héroes, September 13.

Papalote Museo del Niño MUSEUM
(Map p92; 55-5237-1773; www.papalote.org.mx; 2da Sección, Bosque de Chapultepec; museum/IMAX/planetarium M$199/99/99, museum + IMAX or planetarium M$249, family of 4 all access M$949; 9am-6pm Mon-Fri, 10am-7pm Sat & Sun, also 6-11pm Thu for adults only; P; Constituyentes) Your children won't want to leave this innovative, hands-on museum. Here kids can put together a radio program, channel their inner mad scientist, join an archaeological dig and try out all kinds of technological gadgets and games. Little ones also get a kick out of the planetarium's 'domodigital' and IMAX theater. Parking is M$20 per hour.

Complejo Cultural Los Pinos NOTABLE BUILDING
(Former Presidential Residence; Map p92; 55-5093-53-00; https://lospinos.cultura.gob.mx; Parque Lira s/n; 10am-5pm Tue-Sun; Constituyentes) The former official residence of Mexican presidents is a white mansion built in 1853 and known simply as 'Los Pinos.' When President López Obrador (AMLO) came to power in 2018, he transformed Los Pinos into a museum open to the public. There is little on display and little explanatory text, so you have to use your imagination to enjoy the architecture and garden.

Polanco

The affluent neighborhood of Polanco, north of Bosque de Chapultepec, arose in the 1940s as a residential alternative for a burgeoning middle class anxious to escape the overcrowded *centro.* Metro Polanco is in the center of the neighborhood, while metro Auditorio lies at its southern edge.

Polanco is known as a Jewish enclave and also for its exclusive hotels, fine restaurants, sky-high apartment rents (the most expensive in the city and Latin America), international companies, and designer clothing stores along Avenida Presidente Masaryk. For visitors the biggest draw is that some of the city's most prestigious museums and art galleries are here or in nearby Bosque de Chapultepec (p91).

Museo Jumex   MUSEUM
(Map p92; www.fundacionjumex.org; Blvd Miguel de Cervantes Saavedra 303, Colonia Ampliación Granada; adult/student/child M$50/free/free, Sun free; ⏱10am-7pm Tue-Sun; Ⓟ) Museo Jumex was built to house one of Latin America's leading contemporary art collections. Temporary exhibits draw on a collection of around 2600 pieces from renowned Mexican and international artists previously including Gabriel Orozco, Fernanda Gomez, Andy Warhol and Jeff Koons.

Free guided tours are available in English by reservation (check the website) or in Spanish four times a day. The terrace on the 1st level has excellent views of Museo Soumaya next door.

'Ejército Defensa' buses departing from metro Chapultepec leave you one block south of the museum at the corner of Avenida Ejército Nacional and Avenida Ferrocarril de Cuernavaca.

Another Jumex branch, in the museum's original location north of Mexico City in sketchy Ecatepec, focuses on more experimental art. It's a bit of a trek from the city, but one that many art lovers have been willing to make over the years. See the website for directions.

Museo Soumaya   MUSEUM
(Map p92; www.museosoumaya.org; Blvd Miguel de Cervantes Saavedra 303, Colonia Ampliación Granada; ⏱10:30am-6:30pm; Ⓜ Polanco) FREE Someone ought to tell Mexican billionaire Carlos Slim that bigger isn't always better. Named after his late wife, this six-story behemoth (plated with 16,000 aluminum hexagons; designed by son-in-law architect Fernando Romero with guidance by Frank Gehry) holds a large collection of sculptures by Frenchman Auguste Rodin, including his *Thinker*, and Catalan surrealist Salvador Dalí. The museum also contains worthy Rivera and Siqueiros murals and paintings by French impressionists, but there's too much filler.

Acuario Inbursa   AQUARIUM
(Map p92; ☎55-5395-4586; www.acuario inbursa.com.mx; Av Miguel de Cervantes Saavedra 386; adult/child under 3yr M$215/free; ⏱10am-6pm; Ⓜ Polanco) Mexico's largest aquarium holds 1.6 million liters of water and 280 well-cared-for marine species, including barracuda, manta rays and five types of sharks. Four of the aquarium's five stories lie underground, with the ground level home to the star attraction: a colony of Gentoo and chinstrap penguins. The tanks were built to withstand a large-scale temblor in earthquake-prone Mexico City.

It's about a 2km walk or taxi ride from metro Polanco.

Galería López Quiroga   GALLERY
(Map p92; ☎55-5280-1710; www.lopezquiroga. com; Aristóteles 169; ⏱10am-7pm Mon-Fri, to 2pm Sat; Ⓜ Polanco) FREE Specializes in sculptures, paintings and photography by contemporary Latin American and Mexican artists, including works by Francisco Toledo, Rufino Tamayo and José Luis Cuevas.

⊙ Xochimilco & Around

Almost at the southern edge of CDMX, a network of canals flanked by gardens is a vivid reminder of the city's pre-Hispanic legacy. Remnants of the *chinampas* (raised fertile land where indigenous inhabitants grew their food), these 'floating gardens' are still in use today. Gliding along the canals in a fancifully decorated *trajinera* is an alternately tranquil and festive experience. On weekends a fiesta atmosphere takes over as the waterways become jammed with boats carrying groups of families and friends. Local vendors and musicians hover alongside the partygoers, serving food and drink (now with alcohol limits). Midweek, the mood is much calmer.

Xochimilco (Náhuatl for 'Place where Flowers Grow') was an early target of Aztec hegemony, probably due to its inhabitants' farming skills. The Xochimilca piled up vegetation and mud in the shallow waters of Lake Xochimilco, a southern offshoot of Lago de Texcoco, to make the *chinampas,* which later became an economic base of the Aztec empire. As the *chinampas* proliferated, much of the lake was transformed into a series of canals. Approximately 180km of these waterways remain today. The *chinampas* are still under cultivation, mainly for garden plants and flowers such as poinsettias and

PARQUE NACIONAL DESIERTO DE LOS LEONES

Cool, fragrant pine and oak forests dominate this 20-sq-km **national park** (☑55-5814-1171; http://cdmxtravel.com/en/attractions/desierto-de-los-leones-national-park.html; M$17; ⊙9am-5pm Tue-Sun; P) in the hills surrounding the Valle de México. Around 23km southwest of Mexico City and 800m higher, it makes for a fine escape from the carbon monoxide and concrete.

The name derives from the **Ex-Convento Santo Desierto del Carmen** (Ex-Convento del Desierto de los Leones; ☑714-144-0257; Camino al Desierto de los Leones; M$14; ⊙10am-5pm Tue-Sun; P), the 17th-century former Carmelite monastery within the park. The Carmelites called their isolated monasteries 'deserts' to commemorate Elijah, who lived as a recluse in the desert near Mt Carmel. The 'Leones' in the name may stem from the presence of wild cats in the area, but more likely it refers to José and Manuel de León, who once administered the monastery's finances.

The restored monastery has exhibition halls and a restaurant. Tours in Spanish are run by guides (garbed in cassock and sandals) who lead you through expansive gardens around the buildings and the patios within, as well as some underground passageways.

The rest of the park has extensive walking trails. Note that robberies have been reported, so stick to the main paths; the safest times are the busy weekend mornings. Next to El León Dorado restaurant, stairs lead down to a gorgeous picnic area with several small waterfalls and a duck pond.

Most visitors arrive in a car, but rickety *camiones* (trucks or buses) head to the *ex-convento* hourly from metro Viveros (in front of the 7-Eleven), or from **Paradero las Palmas** (Map p100) in San Ángel, on Saturday and Sunday from 8am to 3:30pm. Monday to Friday there are departures every half hour from outside Metro Barranca del Muerto or Mixcoac on *camiones* with 'Santa Rosa' on their windshield, terminating two hours later in a mountain town called Santa Rosa, from where you need to take a 20-minute taxi for the last 8km.

---

marigolds. Owing to its cultural and historical significance, Xochimilco was designated a Unesco World Heritage site in 1987.

Though the canals are definitely the main attraction, Xochimilco has plenty to see. East of **Jardín Juárez** (Xochimilco *centro's* main square) is the 16th-century **Parroquia de San Bernardino de Siena**, with elaborate gold-painted *retablos* (altarpieces) and a tree-studded atrium. South of the plaza, the bustling **Mercado de Xochimilco** covers two vast buildings: the one nearer the Jardín Juárez has fresh produce and an eating 'annex' for *tamales* (stuffed, steamed corn-based snacks with various fillings) and various prepared food; the other sells flowers, *chapulines* (grasshoppers), sweets and excellent *barbacoa* (savory barbecued mutton).

Xochimilco also boasts several friendly *pulquerías* (bars serving *pulque,* a low-alcohol brew); and about 3km west of Jardín Juárez is one of the city's best collection of Diego Rivera works, **Museo Dolores Olmedo** (☑55-5555-1221; www.museodoloresolmedo.org.mx; Av México 5843; M$100, Tue free; ⊙10am-6pm Tue-Sun, kids'

shows 1pm Sat & Sun; 🛈; 🚇La Noria), which also exhibits paintings by Frida Kahlo.

To reach Xochimilco, take metro line 2 to the Tasqueña station then follow the signs inside the station to the transfer point for the *tren ligero,* a light-rail system that extends to neighborhoods not reachable by metro. Xochimilco is the last stop. Upon exiting the station, turn left (north) and follow Avenida Morelos to the market, Jardín Juárez and the church. If you don't feel like walking, bicycle taxis will shuttle you to the *embarcaderos* (boat landings) for M$30.

Xochimilco Canals　　　　　CANAL
(boats per hour M$500, boat taxis one-way per person M$30; P🛈; 🚇Xochimilco) Hundreds of colorful *trajineras* await passengers at the village's 10 *embarcaderos* to paddle you through the waterways dotted with birdlife and hedged by patchy trees. The tranquil city escape is only broken by the odd party boat or food and drink touts gliding up alongside. Nearest to the center are Belem, Salitre and San Cristóbal, about 400m east of the plaza, and Fernando Celada, 400m west of the plaza on Avenida Guadalupe Ramírez.

On Saturday and Sunday, 60-person *lanchas colectivas* (boat taxis) run between the Salitre *embarcadero* and the Nativitas *embarcadero* (near the corner of Avenida Hermenegildo Galeana and Calle del Mercado) 1.4km southeast along the canal.

Boats seat from one to 20 people, making large group outings relatively cheap. Before boarding the *trajinera*, you can buy soft drinks and food from vendors at the *embarcaderos* if you fancy an onboard picnic while cruising.

Since a tragedy in late 2019 when an intoxicated young man drowned, alcohol sales are now very restricted and life jackets are available for passengers, though there's only about two or three per gondola. If you are willing to board without a life jacket, you are technically required to sign a release form, though this is rarely enforced. Other new rules forbid climbing from one boat to another. Visitor numbers have taken a beating, so you might find the canals very quiet.

The official hourly price is fixed and per boat, not per person, so beware of markups.

◉ San Ángel

Settled by the Dominican order soon after the Spanish conquest, San Ángel, 12km southwest of the center, maintains its colonial splendor despite being engulfed by the metropolis. It's often associated with the big Saturday crafts market (p140) held alongside the Plaza San Jacinto. Though the main approach via Avenida Insurgentes is typically chaotic, wander westward to experience the old village's cobblestoned soul – it's a tranquil enclave of colonial-era mansions with massive wooden doors, potted geraniums behind window grills and bougainvillea spilling over stone walls. It's easy to feel like you aren't in a city at all.

La Bombilla station of the Avenida Insurgentes metrobús is about 500m east of the Plaza San Jacinto. Otherwise catch a bus from metro Miguel Ángel de Quevedo, 1km east, or from metro Barranca del Muerto, 1.5km north along Avenida Revolución.

Plaza San Jacinto   PLAZA
(Map p100; San Ángel Centro; 🚌 La Bombilla) Every Saturday the Bazaar Sábado (p140) brings masses of color and crowds of people to this San Ángel square, 500m west of Avenida Insurgentes. **Museo Casa del Risco** (Map p100; 🖉55-5550-9286; www.museocasadelrisco.

org.mx; Plaza San Jacinto 15; ⊘10am-5pm Tue-Sun) **FREE** is midway along the plaza's north side. The elaborate fountain in the courtyard is a mad mosaic of Talavera tile and Chinese porcelain. Upstairs is a treasure trove of Mexican baroque and medieval European paintings. About 50m west of the plaza is the 16th-century **Parroquia de San Jacinto** (Map p100; 🖉55-5616-2059; Plaza San Jacinto 18-Bis; ⊘8am-8pm) and its peaceful gardens.

★ Museo Casa Estudio Diego Rivera y Frida Kahlo   MUSEUM
(Diego Rivera & Frida Kahlo Studio Museum; Map p100; 🖉55-5550-1518; https://estudiodiegorivera. inba.gob.mx; Diego Rivera, cnr Av Altavista; adult/student M$30/free, Sun free, camera use M$30; ⊘10am-5:30pm Tue-Sun; 🚌 La Bombilla) If you saw the movie *Frida* (2002), you'll recognize this museum, designed by Frida Kahlo and Diego Rivera's friend, the architect and painter Juan O'Gorman. The artistic couple called this place home from 1934 to 1940. Frida, Diego and O'Gorman each had their own separate house: Rivera's abode preserves his upstairs studio with art tools and papier-mâché figures, while Frida's (the blue one) and O'Gorman's have been cleared for temporary exhibits.

The houses are linked by a walkway, visually reflecting their joined but separate lives. It's a 15- to 20-minute secure taxi or Uber ride to Kahlo's other blue house, Museo Frida Kahlo (p102).

Across the street is the San Ángel Inn (p125). Now housing a prestigious restaurant, the former *pulque* hacienda is historically significant as the place where Pancho Villa and Emiliano Zapata agreed to divide control of the country in 1914.

It's a pleasant 2km walk or taxi ride from *metrobús* La Bombilla.

Museo de El Carmen   MUSEUM
(Map p100; 🖉55-5616-1504; http://elcarmen. inah.gob.mx; Av Revolución 4; adult/child under 13yr M$55/free, Sun free; ⊘10am-5pm Tue-Sun; ♿; 🚌 La Bombilla) A storehouse of magnificent sacred art in a former school run by the Carmelite order. The collection includes oils by Mexican master Cristóbal de Villalpando, though the big draw is the collection of mummies in the crypt. Thought to be the bodies of 17th-century benefactors of the order, they were uncovered during the revolution by Zapatistas looking for buried treasure.

FRIDA & DIEGO

A century after Frida Kahlo's birth, and more than 50 years after Diego Rivera's death, the pair's fame and recognition are stronger than ever. In 2016, Kahlo's painting *Dos desnudos en el bosque (La tierra misma)* sold at auction in New York for US$8 million, the highest amount ever paid for a Latin American artwork. In 2007 a retrospective of Kahlo's work at the Palacio de Bellas Artes attracted more than 440,000 visitors. Though attendance at the Rivera survey that followed was not so phenomenal, the show reminded visitors that the prolific muralist had been an international star in his own lifetime. The artists are inseparably linked in memory, and both artists were frequent subjects in each other's work.

Rivera first met Kahlo, 21 years his junior, while painting at the Escuela Nacional Preparatoria, where she was a student in the early 1920s. Rivera was already at the forefront of Mexican art, and his commission at the school was the first of many semi-propaganda murals on public buildings that he was to execute over three decades. He had already fathered children by two Russian women in Europe, and in 1922 he married 'Lupe' Marín in Mexico. She bore him two more children before their marriage broke up in 1928.

Kahlo was born in Coyoacán in 1907 to a Hungarian-Jewish father and Oaxacan mother. She contracted polio at age six, leaving her right leg permanently thinner than her left. In 1925 she was horribly injured in a trolley accident that broke her right leg, collarbone, pelvis and ribs. She made a miraculous recovery but suffered much pain thereafter. It was during convalescence that she began painting. Pain – physical and emotional – was to be a dominating theme of her art.

Kahlo and Rivera both moved in left-wing artistic circles, and they met again in 1928. They married the following year. Frida's mother thought Diego was too old, fat, communist and atheist for her daughter, describing the liaison as 'a union between an elephant and a dove.' Their relationship was definitely always a passionate love-hate affair. Rivera wrote: 'If I ever loved a woman, the more I loved her, the more I wanted to hurt her. Frida was only the most obvious victim of this disgusting trait.'

In 1934, after a spell in the USA, the pair moved into a new home in San Ángel, now the Museo Casa Estudio Diego Rivera y Frida Kahlo (p98), with separate houses linked by an aerial walkway. After Kahlo discovered that Rivera had had an affair with her sister, Cristina, she divorced him in 1939, but they remarried the following year. She moved back into her childhood home, the Casa Azul (p102) in Coyoacán, and he stayed at San Ángel – a state of affairs that endured for the rest of their lives. Their relationship endured, too.

Despite the worldwide wave of Fridamania that followed the hit biopic *Frida* in 2002, Kahlo had only one exhibition in Mexico in her lifetime, in 1953. She arrived at the opening on a stretcher. Rivera said of the exhibition: 'Anyone who attended it could not but marvel at her great talent.' She died at the Blue House the following year. Rivera called it 'the most tragic day of my life... Too late I realized that the most wonderful part of my life had been my love for Frida.'

Museo de Arte Carrillo Gil MUSEUM
(Map p100; ☎ 55-8647-5450; www.museo deartecarrillogil.com; Av Revolución 1608, cnr Pabellón Altavista; adult/student M$50/free, Sun free; ☺ 10am-6pm Tue-Sun; ℗; 🚇 Altavista) One of the city's first contemporary-art spaces, this San Ángel museum was founded by Yucatecan businessman Álvaro Carrillo Gil to store a large collection he had amassed over many years. Long ramps in the building lead up to cutting-edge temporary exhibits and some lesser-known works by Diego Rivera, José Clemente Orozco and David Alfaro Siqueiros.

Jardín de la Bombilla PARK
(Map p100; btwn Av de la Paz & Josefina Prior; 🚇 La Bombilla) FREE In this tropically abundant, pruned park spreading east of Avenida Insurgentes, paths encircle the **Monumento a Álvaro Obregón** (Map p100), a monolithic shrine to the post-revolutionary Mexican president. The monument was built to house the revolutionary general's arm, lost

MEXICO CITY SIGHTS

San Ángel

San Ángel

in the 1915 Battle of Celaya, but the limb was cremated in 1989.

'La Bombilla' was the name of the restaurant where Obregón was assassinated in 1928. The killer, José de León Toral, was involved in the Cristero rebellion against the government's anti-church policies.

In July the park explodes with color as the main venue for La Feria de las Flores (p109), a major flower festival.

◎ Ciudad Universitaria

Two kilometers south of San Ángel, the **Ciudad Universitaria** (University City; www.unam.mx; ▣ Centro Cultural Universitario) is the main campus of the UNAM. With about 330,000 students and 38,000 teachers, it's Latin America's largest university. Five former Mexican presidents are among its alumni, as is Carlos Slim, ranked the world's second-richest person in 2015, and Alfonso Cuarón, the first Latin American to win a director's Oscar (for *Gravity*).

Founded in 1551 as the Royal and Papal University of Mexico, UNAM is the second-oldest university in the Americas. It occupied various buildings in the center of town until the campus was transferred to its current location in the 1950s. Although it is a public university open to all, UNAM remains 'autonomous,' meaning the government may not interfere in its academic policies. It is Mexico's leading research institute and has long been a center of political dissent.

An architectural showpiece, UNAM was placed on Unesco's list of World Heritage sites in 2007. Most of the faculty buildings are scattered at the north end. As you enter from Avenida Insurgentes, it's easy to spot the **Biblioteca Central** (Central Library), 10 stories high and covered with mosaics by Juan O'Gorman. The south wall, with two prominent zodiac wheels, covers colonial times, while the north wall deals with Aztec culture. **La Rectoría**, the administration building at the west end of the vast central lawn, has a vivid, three-dimensional Siqueiros mosaic on its south wall, showing students urged on by the people.

Across Avenida Insurgentes stands the **Estadio Olímpico** (☑ 55-5325-9000; https://pumas.mx/estadio; Av Insurgentes Sur 3000, Ciudad Universitaria; ▣ Ciudad Universitaria), built from volcanic stone for the 1968 Olympics. With seating for over 72,000, it's home to UNAM's Pumas *fútbol* club, which competes in the national league's Primera División. Over the main entrance is Diego Rivera's sculpted mural on the theme of sports in Mexican history.

East of the university's main esplanade, the **Facultad de Medicina** (Faculty of Medicine) features an intriguing mosaic mural by Francisco Eppens on the theme of Mexico's *mestizaje* (blending of indigenous and European races).

A second section of the campus, about 2km south, contains the **Centro Cultural Universitario** (☑ 55-5622-7003; www.cultura.unam.mx; Av Insurgentes Sur 3000; ▣ Centro Cultural Universitario), a cultural center with five theaters, two cinemas, the delightful Azul y Oro restaurant (p126) and two excellent museums.

To get to University City, take *metrobús* Línea 1 to the Centro Cultural Universitario (CCU) station, or go to metro Universidad and hop on the 'Pumabús,' a free on-campus bus. The Pumabús has limited service on weekends and holidays.

MUAC   MUSEUM
(Museo Universitario Arte Contemporáneo; ☑ 55-5622-6972; www.muac.unam.mx; Av Insurgentes Sur 3000, Centro Cultural Universitario; Sun & Wed M$20, Thu-Sat M$40, Thu & Sat 6-8pm free; ☉ 10am-6pm Wed, Fri & Sun, to 8pm Thu & Sat; ℗; ▣ Centro Cultural Universitario) Designed by veteran architect Teodoro González de León, the contemporary art museum's sloping, minimalist-style glass facade stands in stark contrast to the surrounding 1970s buildings. Inside you'll find cutting-edge temporary exhibitions occupying nine spacious halls with impressive lighting and high ceilings. The modern works include paintings, audio installations, sculptures and multimedia art from Mexico and abroad. Past exhibitions include works by Chinese artist Ai Wei Wei.

Universum   MUSEUM
(Museo Universitario de Ciencias; ☑ 55-5424-0694; www.universum.unam.mx; Circuito Cultural de Ciudad Universitaria s/n; adult/child M$90/80; ☉ 9am-6pm Tue-Fri, from 10am Sat & Sun; ♿; ▣ Centro Cultural Universitario) A huge science museum offering fun-filled attractions for kids, such as a planetarium and permanent exhibits that explore biodiversity, the human brain and much more. Nearby is the university **sculpture garden**, with a trail leading through volcanic fields past a dozen-or-so innovative pieces. The most formidable work is an enormous ring of concrete blocks by sculptor Mathias Goeritz.

◎ Coyoacán

Coyoacán ('Place of Coyotes' in the Náhuatl language), about 10km south of downtown, was Cortés' base after the fall of Tenochtitlán. Only in recent decades has urban sprawl overtaken the outlying village. Coyoacán retains its restful identity, with narrow colonial-era streets, cafes and a lively atmosphere. Once home to Leon Trotsky and Frida Kahlo (whose houses are now fascinating museums), it has a decidedly countercultural vibe, most evident on weekends, when assorted musicians, mimes and crafts markets draw large but relaxed crowds to Coyoacán's central plazas.

The nearest metro stations to central Coyoacán, 1.5km to 2km away, are Viveros, Coyoacán and General Anaya. The stroll from metro Coyoacán is pleasant, but if you don't fancy a walk, get off at Viveros station, walk south to Avenida Progreso and catch a rickety eastbound 'Metro Gral Anaya' pesero (Mexico City name for a *colectivo*) to the market. Returning, 'Metro Viveros' peseros go west on Malintzin. 'Metro Coyoacán' and 'Metro Gral Anaya' peseros depart from the west side of Plaza Hidalgo. A secure taxi or Uber is about M$120 and takes 35 minutes from Roma.

San Ángel–bound peseros and buses head west on Avenida Miguel Ángel de Quevedo, five blocks south of Plaza Hidalgo.

★ **Museo Frida Kahlo** MUSEUM
(Casa Azul; Map p103; ☑55-5554-5999; www.museofridakahlo.org.mx; Londres 247; adult Tue-Fri M$230, Sat & Sun M$250, student M$45, video guide M$80, camera use M$30; ⊙10am-5:45pm Tue & Thu-Sun, from 11am Wed; Ⓜ Coyoacán) Renowned Mexican artist Frida Kahlo was born in, and lived and died in, Casa Azul (Blue House), now a museum. Almost every visitor to Mexico City makes a pilgrimage here to gain a deeper understanding of the painter (and maybe to pick up a Frida handbag). Arrive early to avoid the crowds, especially on weekends; book tickets online to jump the queue.

Built by Frida's father Guillermo three years before her birth, the house is littered with mementos and personal belongings that evoke her long, often tempestuous relationship with husband Diego Rivera and the leftist intellectual circle they often entertained here. Kitchen implements, jewelry, photos and other objects from the artist's everyday life are interspersed with art, as well as a variety of pre-Hispanic pieces and Mexican crafts. The collection was greatly expanded in 2007 after the discovery of a cache of previously unseen items that had been stashed in the attic. Since 2012 the exhibition Appearances Can Be Deceiving: The Dresses of Frida Kahlo places the focus on

Kahlo's image and famous style, displaying many of the dresses uncovered in her bathroom, alongside her spine-straightening corsets. The intersection of her disability, fashion sense, artistic themes and fame is a worthy exploration. In fact, a version of this exhibition toured to the V&A Museum in London in 2018.

Kahlo's art expresses the anguish of her existence as well as her flirtation with socialist icons: portraits of Lenin and Mao hang around her bed and, in another painting, *Retrato de la familia* (Family Portrait), the artist's Hungarian-Oaxacan roots are fancifully entangled.

It's a pleasant 1.5km walk here from metro Coyoacán.

★ **Museo Casa de León Trotsky** MUSEUM
(Map p103; ☑55-5658-8732; http://museocasadeleontrotsky.blogspot.com; Av Río Churubusco 410; adult/student M$40/20, camera use M$15; ⊙10am-5pm Tue-Sun; Ⓜ Coyoacán) The Trotsky home, now a museum, remains much as it was on the day when one of Stalin's agents, a Catalan named Ramón Mercader, caught up with the revolutionary and smashed an ice axe into his skull. Memorabilia and biographical notes are displayed in buildings off the patio, where a tomb engraved with a hammer and sickle contains Trotsky's ashes.

Having come second to Stalin in the power struggle in the Soviet Union, Trotsky was expelled in 1929 and condemned to death in absentia. In 1937 he found refuge in Mexico. At first Trotsky and his wife Natalia lived in Frida Kahlo's Blue House, but after falling out with Kahlo and Rivera they moved a few streets northeast. Bullet holes remain in the bedroom, the markings of a failed assassination attempt.

The entrance is at the rear of the old residence, facing Avenida Río Churubusco. Ask about free guided tours in English at the entrance.

Plaza Hidalgo & Jardín Centenario PLAZA
(Map p103) The focus of Coyoacán life is its central plaza – actually two adjacent plazas: the **Jardín Centenario**, with the village's iconic coyotes frolicking in its central fountain; and the larger, cobblestoned **Plaza Hidalgo**, with a statue of the eponymous independence hero. It's the scene of most of the weekend fun when people congregate on its benches and in surrounding bars, restaurants, cafes, ice-cream parlours and *churro* joints.

Coyoacán

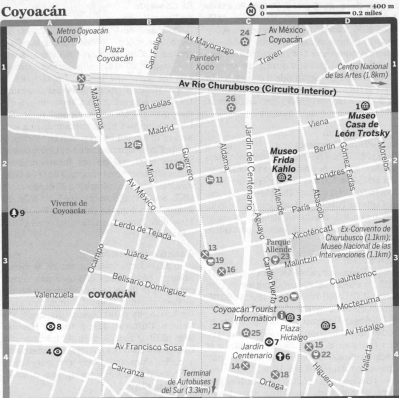

Coyoacán

The **Casa de Cortés** (Antiguo Palacio del Ayuntamiento de Coyoacán; Map p103; ☑55-5484-4500; Jardín Hidalgo 1; ⊙8am-9pm; Ⓜ Coyoacán), on the north side of Plaza Hidalgo, is where conquistador Cortés established Mexico's first municipal seat during the siege of Tenochtitlán. The south side is dominated by the **Parroquia de San Juan Bautista** (Map p103; Plaza Hidalgo; ⊙8am-7pm; Ⓜ Coyoacán) and its adjacent former monastery.

Museo Nacional de Culturas Populares
MUSEUM

(Map p103; ☑55-4155-0920; http://museoculturas populares.gob.mx; Av Hidalgo 289; adult/child under 12yr M$15/free, Sun free; ⊙10am-6pm Tue-Thu, to 8pm Fri-Sun; Ⓜ Coyoacán) The Museo Nacional de Culturas Populares stages innovative exhibitions on folk traditions, indigenous crafts and celebrations in its various courtyards and galleries.

Anahuacalli
MUSEUM

(Diego Rivera Anahuacalli Museum; ☑55-5617-4310; www.museoanahuacalli.org.mx; Calle Museo 150; adult/child under 16yr M$90/15, camera use M$30; ⊙11am-5:30pm Tue-Sun; Ⓟ; Ⓡ Xotepingo) Designed by Diego Rivera to house his collection of pre-Hispanic art, this museum is a templelike structure of volcanic stone. The 'House of Anáhuac' (the Aztec name for the Valle de México) also contains one of Rivera's studios and some of his work, including a study for *Man at the Crossroads,* the mural whose original version was commissioned and destroyed by the Rockefeller Center in 1934, which Rivera later reproduced in the Palacio de Bellas Artes (p84).

In November elaborate Day of the Dead offerings pay homage to the painter, and from April to early December the museum hosts free concerts at 1pm on Sunday, which range from classical to regional folk music.

Anahuacalli is 5km south of Coyoacán. The Fridabus travels here from Museo Frida Kahlo (p102) on weekends at 12.30pm, 2pm and 3.30pm for adult/child M$150/75. Tickets can only be bought from Museo Frida Kahlo and are return tickets, but only start from Museo Frida Kahlo (there are no ticket sales at Anahuacalli).

You can also take the *tren ligero* from metro Tasqueña to the Xotepingo station. Exit on the west side and walk 200m to División del Norte. Cross and continue 600m along Calle Museo.

Ex-Convento de Churubusco
HISTORIC BUILDING

(☑55-5688-2088; 20 de Agosto 127, Colonia San Diego Churubusco; ⊙Mass 7:30am Mon-Fri, 5 services 8:30am-7pm Sun; Ⓜ General Anaya) On August 20, 1847, this former convent was the scene of a historic military defeat, when Mexican troops defended it against US forces advancing from Veracruz in a dispute over the US annexation of Texas. The US invasion was but one example in a long history of foreign intervention in Mexico, as compellingly demonstrated in Churubusco's **Museo Nacional de las Intervenciones** (National Interventions Museum; ☑55-5604-0699; www.intervenciones.inah.gob.mx; 20 de Agosto s/n; M$75, Sun free; ⊙9am-6pm Tue-Sun; Ⓜ General Anaya). Entry into the church itself is during Mass only. From metro General Anaya, it's a 500m walk west.

Plaza Santa Catarina
PLAZA

(Map p103; Jardín Santa Catarina 10; Ⓜ Viveros) About a block south of Coyoacán's *vivero* (nursery) is Plaza Santa Catarina, with the modest, mustard-colored church that gives the square its name. Across the street, the **Centro Cultural Jesús Reyes Heroles** (Map p103; ☑55-5554-5324; Av Francisco Sosa 202; ⊙8am-6pm) is a colonial-era estate with a coffee shop and lovely grounds, where yuccas and jacarandas spring from carefully tended gardens.

Viveros de Coyoacán
PARK

(Map p103; ☑55-5484-3524; www.viveros coyoacan.gob.mx; Av Progreso 1; ⊙6am-6pm; Ⓜ Viveros) FREE A pleasant approach to Coyoacán's central plazas is through the Viveros de Coyoacán, the principal nurseries for Mexico City's parks and gardens. The 38.9-hectare swath of greenery, 1km west of central Coyoacán, is popular with joggers and great for a stroll, but watch out for belligerent squirrels!

From metro Viveros, walk south (right, as you face the fence) along Avenida Universidad and take the first left, Avenida Progreso.

⊙ Cuicuilco

One of the oldest significant remnants of pre-Hispanic settlement within the CDMX, Cuicuilco echoes a civilization that stood on the shores of Lago de Xochimilco as far back as 800 BCE. In its heyday in the 2nd century BCE, the 'place of singing and dancing' counted as many as 40,000 inhabitants – at that time the Teotihuacán civilization was only just beginning to rise to importance. The site was abandoned a couple of centuries later, however, after an eruption of the nearby Xitle volcano covered most of the community in lava.

Today archaeological works continue to reveal new sections, with an investment package of M$36.5 million announced in 2019 to improve facilities and expand the onsite museum. The area is overgrown with grass in large areas, creating a real sense of discovery. The highlight is a 23m-tall, circular, pyramid-like mound.

Zona Arqueológica Cuicuilco
ARCHAEOLOGICAL SITE

(www.inah.gob.mx; Av Insurgentes Sur s/n; ⏱9am-5pm; 🅿; 🚇Villa Olímpica) FREE The principal structure here is a huge circular platform of four levels, faced with volcanic stone blocks, which probably functioned as a ceremonial center. Set amid a park with sweeping views of the area and studded with cacti and shade trees, it makes a nice picnic spot. The site has a small museum (earmarked for expansion) containing skulls and artifacts discovered during excavations.

◉ Tlalpan

Tlalpan today is what Coyoacán used to be – an outlying village with a bohemian atmosphere coupled with some impressive colonial-era architecture. The municipal seat of Mexico City's largest *delegación,* Tlalpan sits at the foot of the southern Ajusco range and enjoys a cooler, moister climate. There are some fine restaurants along the arcades of the charismatic plaza. To get here take metrobús Línea 1 to Fuentes Brotantes and walk four blocks east to the main square.

Museo de Historia de Tlalpán
MUSEUM

(🗷55-5485-6036; Plaza de la Constitución 10; ⏱10am-6pm Tue-Sun; 🚇Fuentes Brotantes) FREE This museum hosts compelling contemporary art and historical exhibits in naturally lit galleries off the courtyard. In 2019, archeological pieces from Cuicuilco were displayed here for the first time and are likely to be exhibited again.

Casa Frisaac
CULTURAL CENTER

(🗷55-5485-3266; https://casafrissac-blog.tumblr.com; Plaza de la Constitución 1; ⏱8am-8pm; 🚇Fuentes Brotantes) FREE This 19th-century estate, once the property of President Adolfo López Mateos, houses an art gallery with temporary exhibits, and a small auditorium for concerts and dance performances.

Capilla de las Capuchinas Sacramentarias
CHAPEL

(🗷55-5573-2395; Av Hidalgo 43; per person M$200; ⏱visiting hours 10am, 11am & 4pm Tue-Thu; 🚇Fuentes Brotantes) There's a sublime simplicity about this chapel, located inside a convent for Capuchin nuns. Designed by modernist architect Luis Barragán in 1952, the austere altar, free of the usual iconography, consists only of a trio of gold panels. In the morning, light streams through a stained-glass window made by German-Mexican artist Mathias Goeritz. Visits of 30 to 40 minutes by appointment only; cash only.

◉ Tlatelolco & Guadalupe

Plaza de las Tres Culturas
HISTORIC SITE

(Plaza of the Three Cultures; 🗷55-5583-0295; www.tlatelolco.inah.gob.mx; Eje Central Lázaro Cárdenas, cnr Flores Magón; ⏱8am-6pm; 🅿; Ⓜ Tlatelolco) FREE So named because it symbolizes the fusion of pre-Hispanic and Spanish roots into the Mexican *mestizo* identity, this plaza displays the architectural legacy of three cultural facets: the Aztec pyramids of Tlatelolco, the 17th-century Spanish Templo de Santiago and the modern tower that houses the Centro Cultural Universitario (p106). You can view the remains of Tlatelolco's **main pyramid-temple** and other Aztec buildings. The double pyramid on view has twin staircases that once supposedly ascended to temples dedicated to Tláloc and Huitzilopochtli.

Tlatelolco was previously believed to be founded by an Aztec faction on a separate island in Lago de Texcoco in the 14th century and later conquered by the Aztec of Tenochtitlán. But a pyramid excavated on the site in late 2007 actually predates the establishment of Tenochtitlán by as much as 200 years. All agree, however, that Tlatelolco was the scene of the largest public market in the Valle de México, connected by a causeway to Tenochtitlán's ceremonial center.

During the siege of the Aztec capital, Cortés defeated Tlatelolco's defenders, led by Cuauhtémoc. An inscription about the battle in the plaza translates as, 'This was neither victory nor defeat. It was the sad birth of the *mestizo* people that is Mexico today.' Recognizing the significance of the site, the Spanish erected the **Templo de Santiago** here in 1609, using stones from

TLATELOLCO MASSACRE OF 1968

The Plaza de las Tres Culturas (p105) in Tlatelolco is a symbol of modern troubles. On October 2, 1968, hundreds of student protesters were massacred here by government troops on the eve of the Mexico City Olympic Games. The weeks before the Olympics had been marked by a wave of protests against political corruption and authoritarianism, and President Gustavo Díaz Ordaz, anxious to present an image of stability to the world, was employing heavy-handed tactics to stop the unrest.

On that October day, helicopters hovered over the plaza and a massive police contingent cordoned off the protest zone. Suddenly shots rang out, apparently from the balcony that served as a speakers' platform. Police then opened fire on the demonstrators and mayhem ensued. A government-authorized account reported 20 protesters killed, though researchers and media reports estimate the real number is closer to 300.

The generally accepted theory, though there are many, is that the government staged the massacre, planting snipers on the balcony. To this day the incident still generates a massive annual protest march from Tlatelolco to the Zócalo on October 2.

Aztec structures as building materials. Just inside the main doors of this church is the **baptismal font of Saint Juan Diego**.

Along Eje Central Lázaro Cárdenas, northbound trolleybuses pass right by the Plaza de las Tres Culturas. Metrobús Línea 7 runs along Reforma from Chapultepec and El Ángel passing here at the 'Tres Culturas' stop.

**Centro Cultural
Universitario Tlatelolco**　MUSEUM
(✆ ext 49646, 55-5117-2818; www.tlatelolco.unam.mx; Flores Magón 1; adult/student M$30/15, Sun free; ◷ 10am-6pm Tue-Sun; Ⓜ Tlatelolco) The events that occurred before, during and after the 1968 massacre on Plaza de las Tres Culturas are chronicled in Memorial del 68, a compelling multimedia exhibit in the Centro Cultural Universitario Tlatelolco. The cultural center has two other outstanding permanent exhibits in the Museo de Sitio.

The latter shiny museum houses more than 400 objects unearthed at the archaeological site, such as pre-Hispanic offerings and ceramic artifacts. The interactive museum continues on the 2nd floor in the tower building across the way, where you can learn about colonial-era Tlatelolco and the area's flora and fauna. The tower's 3rd floor is home to the **Colección Stavenhagen**, an extraordinary collection of more than 500 pre-Hispanic clay and stone sculptures, including amusing animal figures and phallic works.

Basílica de Guadalupe　SHRINE
(www.virgendeguadalupe.org.mx; Plaza de las Américas 1, Colonia Villa de Guadalupe; ◷ 6am-9pm; Ⓜ La Villa-Basílica) FREE A cult developed around this site after a Christian convert named Juan Diego claimed in December 1531 that the Virgin Mary appeared before him on the Cerro del Tepeyac (Tepeyac Hill). After numerous sightings, so the story goes, the lady's image was miraculously emblazoned on Diego's cloak, causing a bishop to believe the story and build a shrine in her honor. To this day the *basílica* remains a place of pilgrimage and worship.

Over the centuries Nuestra Señora de Guadalupe came to receive credit for all manner of miracles, hugely aiding the acceptance of Catholicism by native Mexicans, helped greatly by presenting her with Mexican facial features. Despite the protests of some clergy, who saw the cult as a form of idolatry (with the Virgin as a Christianized version of the Aztec goddess Tonantzin), in 1737 the Virgin was officially declared the patron of Mexico. Two centuries later she was named celestial patron of Latin America and empress of the Americas, and in 2002 Juan Diego was canonized by Pope John Paul II.

Today the Virgin's shrines around the Cerro del Tepeyac (formerly an Aztec shrine site) are the most revered in Mexico, attracting thousands of pilgrims daily and hundreds of thousands on the days leading up to her feast day, December 12. Some pilgrims travel the last meters to the shrine on their knees.

Around 1700, to accommodate the faithful flock, the four-towered Basílica de Guadalupe was erected at the site of an earlier shrine. But by the 1970s, the old yellow-domed building (now called the Antigua Basílica) proved inadequate to the task, so the new blue-roofed Basílica de Nuestra Señora de Guadalupe was built next door. Designed by Pedro Ramírez Vázquez, it is a vast, round, open-plan structure with a capacity of more than 40,000 people. The image of the Virgin, dressed in a green mantle trimmed with gold, hangs above and behind the main altar of the basílica, where moving walkways bring visitors as close as possible. Mass is performed hourly.

The rear of the Antigua Basílica is now the **Museo de la Basílica de Guadalupe** (☑55-5577-6022; Plaza Hidalgo; adult/child under 12yr M$5/free; ◷10am-6pm Tue-Sun; Ⓜ La Villa-Basílica), which houses a fine collection of colonial art interpreting the miraculous vision.

Stairs behind the Antigua Basílica climb about 100m to the hilltop **Capilla del Cerrito** (Hill Chapel), where Juan Diego had his vision, then lead down the east side of the hill to the Parque de la Ofrenda, with gardens and waterfalls around a sculpted scene of the apparition. Continue on down to the baroque **Templo del Pocito**, a circular structure with a trio of tiled cupolas, built in 1787 to commemorate the miraculous appearance of a spring where the Virgen de Guadalupe stood. From there the route leads back to the main plaza, re-entering it beside the 17th-century **Antigua Parroquia de Indios** (Parish of Indians).

To reach the Basílica de Guadalupe, take the metro to La Villa–Basílica station, then walk two blocks north along Calzada de Guadalupe. Both Capital Bus (p108) and Turibús (p108) hop-on, hop-off tourist buses make a stop near the Basílica.

🏃 Activities

Boating

Isla de las Muñecas BOATING
(Island of the Dolls; Embarcadero Cuemanco, Xochimilco; boat per hour M$500) For a truly sur-

real experience, head for Xochimilco and hire a gondola to the Island of the Dolls, where hundreds of creepy, decomposed dolls hang from trees. An island resident fished the playthings from the canals to mollify the spirit of a girl who had drowned nearby.

The best departure point for the four-hour round trip is Cuemanco *embarcadero*. To get here, go to metro General Anaya and exit the station on the east side of Calzada de Tlalpan, then walk 50m north to catch a 'Tláhuac Paradero' pesero. Get off at the Embarcadero Cuemanco entrance.

Cycling

On Sunday mornings (8am to 2pm; except the last Sunday of the month) Paseo de la Reforma is closed to auto traffic from Bosque de Chapultepec to the Alameda Central for El Paseo Dominical, and you can join the legions of *chilangos* who happily skate, cycle or scoot down the avenue. An ever-changing roster of bike- and scooter-sharing apps are used in CDMX.

Ecobici CYCLING
(Map p128; ☑55-5005-2424; www.ecobici.cdmx. gob.mx; Oaxaca 7, Roma Norte; rentals 1/3/7 days M$104/208/346; ◷11am-7pm Mon-Fri, 11am-3pm Sat & Sun; Ⓜ Insurgentes) The Mexico City government rents commuter bikes to visitors on a daily and weekly basis. You'll need a Visa or MasterCard for the deposit and a passport or driver's license for ID (you don't need to give it over). The bicycle-share program works with smart cards and allows you to ride for up to 45 minutes between docking stations.

To avoid paying a fine for exceeding 45 minutes, simply exchange the bike at a different

---

BIKE TRAILS

The *ciclovía* is an extensive bike trail that follows the old bed of the Cuernavaca railroad as far as the Morelos border. It extends from Avenida Ejército Nacional in Polanco through the Bosque de Chapultepec, skirting the Periférico freeway from near Papalote Museo del Niño to Avenida San Antonio, with several steep bridges passing over the freeways.

Another path follows Avenida Chapultepec along a protected median from Bosque de Chapultepec to Centro Histórico, though a detour through the streets of Roma is ignored by motorists. A third route runs along Paseo de la Reforma from the Auditorio Nacional to downtown.

The CDMX-created Ecobici app and website are useful for routing along *ciclovías*, even if you aren't an Ecobici user.

Every Sunday (except the last Sunday of the month) Paseo de la Reforma and several main downtown streets are closed off to traffic from 8am to 2pm and riders can enjoy a 26km 'ciclotón' route from Auditorio Nacional to the Basílica de Guadalupe.

station. Ecobici is a great option for exploring the Centro, Roma, Condesa, and Zona Rosa and Reforma neighborhoods, which have the greatest concentration of stations. You can also register in front of the plaza Reforma 222 at a booth with the same hours on Paseo de la Reforma 222.

Kayaking

Michmani KAYAKING
(☑55-2039-0377; Embarcadero Cuemanco, Xochimilco, off Anillo Periférico Sur; per hour M$50; ☺10am-6pm) Take in some of the quieter parts of the Xochimilco canals while kayaking, and do some bird-watching while you're at it within this ecotourism park. You'll spot ducks, egrets and herons, among many other migratory and endemic species. You can also visit the many nurseries along the shores.

To get here, go to metro General Anaya and exit the station on the east side of Calzada de Tlalpan, then walk 50m north to catch a 'Tláhuac Paradero' pesero. Get off at the Embarcadero Cuemanco entrance and walk about 1km to Michmani, just beyond the *embarcadero.*

Lago de Chapultepec KAYAKING
(Chapultepec Lake; Map p92; www.chapultepec. com.mx/agendaVer/2142; Bosque de Chapultepec; 2-person kayak/paddleboat/rowboat per hour M$60/50/60; ☺9am-4:30pm Tue-Sun; Ⓜ Auditorio) Take a kayak, paddleboat or rowboat out for a spin with the ducks on Chapultepec Lake. The nearest park entrance is opposite the Museo Nacional de Antropología. Click on *lanchas* (boats) on the website.

☕ Courses

Plaza de Danzón DANCING
(Map p86; lessons M$20-50; ☺10am-2:30pm & 4:30-6pm Sat; Ⓜ Balderas) If you like to dance, learn a few steps at the Plaza de Danzón, northwest of La Ciudadela, near metro Balderas. Couples of all ages (but especially mature dancers) crowd the plaza every Saturday afternoon to do the *danzón,* an elegant and complicated Cuban step that infiltrated Mexico in the 19th century. Lessons in *danzón* and other styles are given.

Mama Rumba DANCING
(Map p120; ☑55-5564-6920; www.facebook. com/mamarumba.rl; Querétaro 230, Roma; Fri & Sat M$120, Wed & Thu women/men M$50/100; ☺9pm-3am Wed-Sat; ☐ Sonora) Managed by a Havana native, Mama Rumba in Roma features contemporary salsa, with music by the house big band. If you'd like to take a 1½-hour class (free with entrance fee), dance instructors will get you started Wednesday and Thursday at 9pm; while weekends get packed.

Mama Rumba has a larger branch in San Ángel at Plaza Loreto.

Centro de Enseñanza Para Extranjeros LANGUAGE
(Foreigners' Teaching Center; ☑55-5622-2470; www.cepe.unam.mx; Av Universidad 3002, Ciudad Universitaria; 6-week course M$12,000; ☐ Ciudad Universitaria) The national university offers six-week intensive language classes, meeting for three hours daily from Monday through Friday. Students who already speak Spanish can take courses on Mexican art and culture.

☞ Tours

Capital Bus TOURS
(Map p128; www.capitalbus.mx; Liverpool 155, Zona Rosa; day pass adult M$160-250, child M$90, Teotihuacán day tour adult/child M$750/600; ☺ticket office 8:30am-6:30pm; Ⓜ Insurgentes) Take a day trip to the Teotihuacán pyramids (includes bilingual guide and entrance fees) and the Basílica de Guadalupe, or tour Mexico City with a hop-on, hop-off day pass (see website for ticket-booth locations). Capital Bus also runs outings to nearby colonial towns, such as silver-making center Taxco and culinary-capital Puebla.

Day passes can be bought from the main stops such as Fuente de Cibeles and to the left of Catedral Metropolitana (p77) at the Zócalo.

Turibús BUS
(Map p74; ☑55-5141-1360; www.turibus.com.mx; adult M$160-180, child 4-12yr M$80-90, Teotihuacán M$700-950; ☺9am-9pm; ⊞) Red double-decker buses run four *circuitos* (routes) across the city on the one ticket: Centro (downtown), Sur (south, including Frida Kahlo museum), Hippódromo (Polanco and Chapultepec) and Basílica (north). Buses pass every 15 to 60 minutes and you can hop off and on at any designated stop. All routes coincide on the west side of Catedral Metropolitana (p77).

Buy ticket-wristbands on board or at major stops such as El Ángel (p89) or Mercado Roma (p123).

Turibús also offers day trips to Teotihuacán (includes admission fee and bilingual guide), and themed tours (M$100 to M$970), including mezcal, cantinas, *lucha libre,* palaces, museums and food tasting. See the website for times.

Journeys Beyond the Surface   TOURS
(☑ cell 55-1745 2380; www.travelmexicocity.com.
mx; group tours per person with/without car
US$290/225) Personalized eight-hour walk-
ing tours (with breaks!) on aspects of the
CDMX experience, with an off-the-beaten-
track attitude. See murals and graffiti
street art, or three-hour night tours of *lucha libre* and plazas for example. Guides
are well versed in history and anthropology if you choose to visit pre-Hispanic and
colonial-era sites. All entrance fees are extra and tours including Teotihuacán cost
M$300.

Mexico Soul & Essence   FOOD & DRINK
(Alegría in Mexico; ☑ cell 55-2917-5408; http://
ruthincondechi.wordpress.com; tours US$100-175,
cooking courses US$300) Ruth Alegría, one of
the city's foremost food experts, runs customized culinary and cultural excursions.
Ruth can arrange dining outings, market
tours or specialized trips. She also offers an
entertaining Mexican cooking course.

🎆 Festivals & Events

**Festival del Centro Histórico
de CDMX**   CULTURAL
(www.festival.org.mx; ⊙ Mar/Apr) Across two
weeks Centro Histórico hosts music, theater,
dance and culinary events featuring talent
from Mexico and abroad – it's the city's biggest cultural bash of the year.

Semana Santa   RELIGIOUS
(⊙ Mar/Apr) The most evocative events of
Holy Week, the week before Easter, are in
the Iztapalapa district, 9km southeast of the
Zócalo, where a gruesomely realistic passion
play is enacted on Good Friday, culminating
with a faux crucifixion outside Museo del
Fuego up the Cerro de la Estrella.

Hordes of people escape the city, leaving
the streets eerily, or wonderfully, quiet and
many businesses closed.

La Feria de las Flores   FERIA
(Jardín de la Bombilla; ⊙ Jul; 🚇) **FREE** This
major flower festival explodes with color
in the Jardín de la Bombilla. The weeklong
cultural festivities include the display and
sale of myriad varieties of plants, family activities, performances, and botany-
related painting and sculpture. The festival
has pre-Hispanic origins, when followers
of Xiuhtecuhtli (Lord of Flowers) would
make floral offerings in return for abundant crops.

Foundation of Tenochtitlán   DANCE
(Plaza de las Tres Culturas, Tlatelolco; ⊙ Aug 13;
Ⓜ Tlatelolco) Held to celebrate the foundation
of the Mexican capital, this is a major summit for Concheros (Aztec dancers) on Plaza
de las Tres Culturas in Tlatelolco.

Grito de la Independencia   FIREWORKS
(Palacio Nacional, Colonia Centro; ⊙ Sep 15; Ⓜ Zócalo) On September 15, the eve of Independence
Day, thousands gather in the Zócalo to hear
the Mexican president's version of the *Grito
de Dolores* (Cry of Dolores), Hidalgo's famous
call to rebellion against the Spanish in 1810,
from the central balcony of the Palacio Nacional at 11pm. Afterward there's a fireworks
display.

On the night, and those leading up to the
date, plenty of Mexican dishes and alcohol
are consumed in a show of patriotism, and
as an excuse to celebrate!

★ **Día de Muertos**   CULTURAL
(Day of the Dead; http://festivaldemuertos.cdmx.
gob.mx; ⊙ Nov) In the lead-up to Day of the
Dead (November 1 and 2), elaborate *ofrendas* (altars) show up everywhere. The
huge annual street parade, Desfile de Día
de Muertos, has been held since 2016 (initially in response to the faux parade in
James Bond film *Spectre*) with over 1000
costumed dancers and performers joining
giant *calavera* (skeleton) puppets along
Reforma to the Zócalo.

Some of the best *ofrendas* can be seen
at Anahuacalli (p104), Museo Dolores
Olmedo (p97), the Zócalo (p78), Plaza
Santo Domingo in el Centro (replacing Ciudad Universitaria since 2016), and in the
neighborhood of San Andrés Mixquic in the
extreme southeast of the CDMX. Check the
official government website for a program of
the city's main events.

Traditionally families and friends remember the lives of those who have passed away
and it is believed that their spirits are able to
revisit the earthly plane for a night, attracted
by the *ofrendas*, to join in the celebrations.

**Día de Nuestra Señora de
Guadalupe**   RELIGIOUS
(Day of Our Lady of Guadalupe; Basílica de Gua-
dalupe; ⊙ Dec 12; Ⓜ La Villa-Basílica) At the
Basílica de Guadalupe (p106), the Day of
Our Lady of Guadalupe caps 10 days of fes-
tivities that honor Mexico's religious patron.
The number of pilgrims reaches millions by
December 12, the main day, when groups of

indigenous dancers perform nonstop on the basilica's broad plaza.

🛏 Sleeping

Mexico City is brimming with sleeping options. Trendy **Roma** makes an excellent base, especially near Avenida Álvaro Obregón, with plenty of restaurants and bars. Gorgeous **Condesa** is conveniently nearby with mostly chic boutique hotels and guesthouses, and a smattering of budget hostels.

Some of the most reasonably priced lodgings are in **Centro Histórico**. Hostels ring the **Zócalo**. Midrange, though characterless, hotels abound in the **Alameda** area. After the shoppers leave the city centre on weeknights, it can feel unnervingly quiet in the backstreets.

The **Plaza de la República** area around the Monumento a la Revolución is awash with hotels, with a number of dives interspersed amid the business-class establishments in this semiresidential zone.

Luxurious accommodations and international chains tower nearby in **Polanco** and **Zona Rosa and Reforma**. North of Bosque de Chapultepec, upmarket Polanco has excellent business- and boutique-hotel accommodations, but very little for peso-counters. It also can also feel generic and little like Mexico.

Cultural **Coyoacán** in the south is a wonderfully tranquil, isolated escape. The artist-friendly community has limited budget options but several appealing guesthouses. Check with **Coyoacán tourist information** (Map p103; ☑55-5658-0221; Jardín Hidalgo 1, Coyoacán; ⊙10am-8pm; Ⓜ Coyoacán) office about short-term homestays.

🛏 Centro Histórico

★ Casa San Ildefonso HOSTEL $
(Map p74; ☑55-5789-1999; www.casasanildefonso.com; San Ildefonso 38; incl breakfast dm/d M$400/1020, s/tw without bathroom M$550/850; ⊜@🛜; Ⓜ Zócalo) A 19th-century building that most recently served as a storage facility for street vendors has been transformed into a cheerful hostel off a pedestrian thoroughfare. Unlike most downtown hostels, the high-ceiling dorms, private rooms and common areas here get wonderful sunlight. Guests have breakfast in a tranquil courtyard with a fountain, singing canaries and the gremlin-esque mascot Delfina.

Hotel Castropol BUSINESS HOTEL $
(Map p74; ☑55-5522-1920; http://hotelcastropol.com; Av Pino Suárez 58; s/tw/tr M$550/600/660; ⊜🛜; Ⓜ Pino Suárez) Minimalist, spacious rooms for peso-watchers are hard to come by when the Zócalo is in sight at the end of the street. Here you not only get loads of cleanliness, marble and a flat-screen TV, but also a handy budget restaurant and the bar-filled Regina corridor kicking it nearby.

Hotel Isabel HOTEL $
(Map p74; ☑55-5518-1213; www.hotel-isabel.com.mx; Isabel La Católica 63; s/d/tr M$480/690/990, r without bathrooms/d M$330/500; ⊜@🛜; 🚇 República del Salvador) A longtime budget-traveler's favorite, the Isabel offers large, well-scrubbed rooms with old but sturdy furniture, high ceilings and great (if noisy) balconies, plus a hostel-like social scene. Remodeled rooms cost a touch more. Single rooms with shared bathrooms are good value for the area.

Hostal Regina HOSTEL $
(Map p74; ☑55-5434-5817; www.hostalreginacentrohistorico.com; Calle 5 de Febrero 53; incl breakfast dm/d/q without bathroom M$280/550/1300; ⊜@🛜; Ⓜ Isabel La Católica) Off the lively Regina corridor, this 18th-century historic building makes a great base to explore downtown. On offer are dark, chic private rooms with wooden floors, high ceilings and shared bathrooms. The rooftop and ground-level bars of this self-professed *party hostal* stay noisy until about 2am many nights. Free pizza on weeknights helps guests mingle. Prices are about 10% cheaper Sunday to Thursday.

Mexico City Hostel HOSTEL $
(Map p74; ☑55-5512-3666; www.mexicocityhostel.com; República de Brasil 8; incl breakfast dm M$200, tw with/without bathroom M$660/520; ⊜@🛜; Ⓜ Zócalo) Steps from the Zócalo, this colonial-era structure has been artfully restored, with original wood beams and stone walls as a backdrop for modern, energy-efficient facilities. Small rooms have basic beds on terracotta floors. Immaculate bathrooms trimmed with *azulejos* (painted ceramic tiles) amply serve around 100 occupants. Nearby bars get noisy on weekends.

Hostel Mundo Joven Catedral HOSTEL $
(Map p74; ☑55-5518-1726; http://mundojovenhostels.com; República de Guatemala 4; incl breakfast dm M$230, d with/without bathroom M$740/560; ⊜@🛜; Ⓜ Zócalo) Backpacker central, this HI affiliate is abuzz with a global rainbow of

young travelers. Low-ceilinged dorms and private rooms are cramped but tidy and guests love the rooftop bar, though it's not the quietest of hostels. 'Quirky' bonuses include a free 10-minute massage.

Hotel Gillow
HOTEL $$

(Map p74; ☑55-5518-1440; www.hotel gillow.com; Isabel La Católica 17; s/d/tw/ste M$1090/1320/1500/1910; ⊜@🛜; Ⓜ Allende) In a historic building, Hotel Gillow has friendly, old-fashioned service and remodeled rooms done up with faux-wood floors and flat-screen TVs. If available, request a double room with a private terrace.

★Gran Hotel Ciudad de México
HOTEL $$$

(Map p74; ☑55-1083-7700; www.granhoteldela ciudaddemexico.com.mx; Av 16 de Sepiembre 82; r/ ste incl breakfast from M$3548/5555; ℗⊜✳@🛜; Ⓜ Zócalo) The Gran Hotel flaunts the French art nouveau style of the pre-revolution era. Crowned by a stained-glass canopy crafted by Tiffany's in 1908, the atrium is a fin de siècle fantasy of curved balconies, wrought-iron elevators and chirping birds in giant cages. Rooms do not disappoint in comparison. Breakfast and brunch (M$210) are served on a terrace overlooking the Zócalo.

Breakfast deals and tour packages are available on the website. The hotel features in the James Bond film *Spectre*.

Hampton Inn & Suites
HOTEL $$$

(Map p74; ☑55-8000-5000; www.hampton mexicocity.com; Calle 5 de Febrero 24; r/ste incl breakfast from US$120/140; ⊜✳@🛜; ☐ Isabel La Católica) This well-maintained historic gem underwent an elaborate makeover to preserve its facade and Talavera-tiled walls. Well-appointed rooms with contemporary furnishings surround a six-story atrium with a stained-glass ceiling. A good seafood restaurant shares the property.

Hotel Catedral
BUSINESS HOTEL $$$

(Map p74; ☑55-5518-5232; www.hotelcatedral. com; Donceles 95; r incl breakfast M$1695; ℗⊜@🛜; Ⓜ Zócalo) This comfortable lodging clearly benefits from its prime location in the heart of Centro Histórico. Well-maintained rooms have flat-screens, desks, dark-wood furnishings and firm mattresses. For cityscape views, order a drink on the rooftop terrace.

Hotel Historico Central
HOTEL $$$

(Map p74; ☑55-5130-5138; www.central hoteles.com; Bolívar 28; d incl breakfast M$3960;

℗⊜✳🛜; Ⓜ Allende) Occupying a restored 18th-century building in the historic center, this colonial-style hotel gives you plenty of bang for your buck. All of the well-appointed rooms come with complimentary breakfast as well as free sandwiches and coffee at the 24-hour onsite cafe. Nearby sister property Zocalo Central offers more affordable digs but without the free grub.

🛏 Alameda Central & Around

Hotel Marlowe
HOTEL $$

(Map p74; ☑55-5521-9540; www.hotel marlowe.com.mx; Independencia 17; d/tw/ste M$1320/1425/1520; ℗⊜@🛜; Ⓜ San Juan de Letrán) Marlowe stands across from Chinatown's pagoda gate. The lobby says modern, but the thin-walled, low-ceilinged rooms have brown-and-beige retro charm with marble bathrooms. Grab a suite for a larger, brighter room with small balcony. Fitness fans will appreciate the gym with a view.

Chaya
BOUTIQUE HOTEL $$$

(Map p86; ☑55-5512-9074; www.chayabnb. com; Dr Mora 9, 3rd fl; d/ste incl breakfast from US$145/215; ⊜🛜; Ⓜ Hidalgo) Like a secret at the edge of Alameda Central, diminutive Chaya nestles on the top floor of an exquisite art deco building. Rooms exude utilitarian chicness, making slabs of gray, wood and cream look good. Plush beds and terrific Mexican breakfasts add to the feeling of escape within the city. Being so central brings occasional weekend noise from the park and bar below.

🛏 Plaza de la República & Around

Hostel Suites DF
HOSTEL $

(Map p86; ☑55-5535-8117; www.hostel suitesdf.com; Terán 38; dm/d/tr incl breakfast M$280/740/960; ⊜@🛜; ☐ Plaza de la República) Near the Monumento a la Revolución, this small HI-affiliated hostel offers pleasant common areas and a great central location that leaves you within walking distance of downtown. Dorm beds lack privacy curtains but have individual power points, and bathrooms are spacious and clean. The sociable terrace can stay noisy until midnight.

Casa de los Amigos
GUESTHOUSE $

(Map p86; ☑55-7095-7413; www.casadelos amigos.org; Mariscal 132; dm/s/d without bathroom M$170/330/440; ⊜@🛜; Ⓜ Revolución) ∅ The Quaker-run Casa is a guesthouse popular with NGO workers, activists and researchers, but it welcomes walk-in travelers too (minimum two nights). Vegetarian breakfast (M$30) is available and on Tuesdays and Thursdays guests can take free yoga or Spanish classes. You're not allowed to smoke or drink alcohol in the house, and 10pm to 7am are quiet hours.

See the website for volunteer work options.

Plaza Revolución Hotel
HOTEL $$

(Map p86; ☑55-5234-1910; www.hotelplaza revolucion.com; Terán 35; d/ste M$970/1100; P🐾❄@🛜; 🚇Plaza de la República) On a quiet street four blocks east of Plaza de la República and Monumento a la Revolución, this glossy establishment is a stylish option in an area where cut-rate hotels are the norm. Modern rooms with wooden floors are done up in neutral colors and kept impeccably clean.

Palace Hotel
HOTEL $$

(Hotel Palacio; Map p86; ☑55-5566-2400; Ramírez 7; s/d/tw M$725/800/965; P🐾@🛜; 🚇Plaza de la República) Run by gregarious Asturians, the Palace has large, neat rooms, some with broad balconies giving terrific views down palm-lined Ramírez to the domed Monumento a la Revolución. Request a street-facing room if you want brighter digs. Cash-paying guests get 12% to 20% discounts. Reservations booked directly only; no website and they don't use booking sites.

El Patio 77
B&B $$$

(☑55-5592-8452; www.elpatio77.com; Garcia Icazbalceta 77, Colonia San Rafael; d/ste incl breakfast from US$98/159; 🐾@🛜; Ⓜ San Cosme) 🍃 Stay in a 19th-century mansion with eight tastefully appointed rooms, each decked out with crafts from a different Mexican state. Like that Huichol bead art or Oaxacan black ceramics in your room? Take them home with you – guests can purchase basically anything in the house that's not bolted down. A daily-changing breakfast is served in the ecofriendly B&B's pleasant patio.

🛏 Zona Rosa & Reforma

Foreign businesspeople and tourists check in at the upscale hotels along or near Paseo de la Reforma in this international commerce and nightlife area. Less-expensive establishments dot the quieter streets of Colonia Cuauhtémoc, north of Paseo de la Reforma, and Juárez, east of Avenida Insurgentes Norte.

★ Capsule Hostel
HOSTEL $

(Map p128; ☑55-5207-7903; www.capsulehostel. com.mx; Hamburgo 41; dm/d without bathroom M$235/550; 🐾❄🛜; 🚇Hamburgo) This poshtel is less Japanese capsule hotel and more boutique hospital ward (with a similar level of cleanliness). Curtains wrap around the large dorm beds for privacy. Modern furnishings and surprisingly quiet rooms (request one away from the street) provide an excellent non-party, budget (finally) option near the embassies and action of Zona Rosa. No children allowed.

★ Casa González
GUESTHOUSE $$

(Map p128; ☑55-5514-3302; https://hotel casagonzalez.com; Río Sena 69; d/tw/ste M$1150/1950/1600; P🐾❄@🛜; 🚇Reforma) A family-run operation for nearly a century, the Casa is a perennial hit with travelers seeking peace and quiet. Set around several flower-filled patios and semiprivate terraces, it's extraordinarily tranquil. Original portraits and landscapes decorate some rooms, apparently done by a guest in lieu of payment.

Embassies, Reforma's buzzing boulevard and the *metrobús* to Centro Histórico are nearby, but an onsite restaurant makes it easy to stay in.

Hotel María Cristina
HOTEL $$

(Map p128; ☑55-5703-1212; www.hotelmaria cristina.com.mx; Río Lerma 31; d/ste from M$1200/1670; P🐾❄@🛜; 🚇Reforma) Dating from the 1930s, this facsimile of an Andalucian estate makes an appealing retreat, particularly for the adjacent bar with patio seating. Though lacking the lobby's colonial-era splendor, rooms are generally bright and comfortable. It's in a quiet area near the Reforma 222 shopping plaza.

MC Suites
BUSINESS HOTEL $$

(Map p128; ☑55-5566-6711; http://hotel-suites-mc.negocio.site; General Prim 106, Juárez; suites M$1265-2350; P🛜) The clean suites in this lofty building function like small, self-contained studios with minibar, basic kitchenette facilities, flat-screen TVs and very comfortable beds. Ceilings are low but the location near Reforma bars and cafes gives easy access to Zona Rosa and Alameda Central.

Hotel Geneve
HOTEL $$$

(Map p128; ☑55-5080-0800; www.hotelgeneve. com.mx; Londres 130; d/ste incl breakfast from M$4590/7140; P🐾❄@🛜; Ⓜ Insurgentes)

This Zona Rosa institution strives to maintain a belle epoque ambience dripping in gold despite the globalized mishmash around it. The lobby exudes class, with dark-wood paneling, oil canvases and high bookshelves. Rooms in the hotel's older rear section get a more pronounced colonial treatment, especially the 'vintage suites.'

🛏 Condesa

★Gael
HOSTEL $

(Map p120; ☑55-5919-1437; www.facebook. com/gaelcondesa; Nuevo León 179; dm incl breakfast M$265-340; 🛜; Ⓜ Chilpancingo) In fancy Condesa, budget digs of this quality are hard to come by. Helpful English-speaking staff are quick to point out the coworking space and sociable rooftop terrace. The small neat dorms have individual privacy curtains and provide a tranquil rest, though bathrooms could be cleaner. It's in a safe, pretty area near the metro and ample eating options.

Hostel Home
HOSTEL $

(Map p120; ☑55-5511-1683; www.hostelhome. com.mx; Tabasco 303; dm incl breakfast M$350; 🛜@🛜; 🚇 Durango) Housed in a fine old *porfiriato*-era building and managed by easygoing, English-speaking staff who celebrate diversity, this 20-bed hostel is on the narrow, tree-lined Calle Tabasco, a gateway to the Roma neighborhood. There's a kitchen and a nearby supermarket, a simple vegetarian *fonda* (family restaurant) and the bars of lively Fuente de Cibeles.

Stayinn Barefoot Hostel
HOSTEL $

(Map p120; ☑55-6286-3000; www.facebook. com/stayinnbarefoot; Juan Escutia 125; dm/d incl breakfast from M$420/870; 🛜; Ⓜ Chapultepec) On the edge of Condesa, this artfully designed hostel is a sociable option in a neighborhood lacking in budget accommodations. The cheerful lobby is done up in colorful mismatched tile floors and vintage furniture, while upstairs guests have use of a rooftop terrace. The Barefoot's welcoming mezcal bar seals the deal, but light sleepers might be kept awake till 2am on weekends.

★Izta 54
BOUTIQUE HOTEL $$

(Map p120; ☑55-7588-5240; www.izta54. com; Iztaccíhuatl 54; tw M$1045, studio M$2100-2950; 🛜; 🚇 Campeche) This converted art deco apartment in the heart of fashionable Condesa fulfills many fantasies of a charmed CDMX life. Wake up in a plush bed in a bright room with Scandinavian-style furnishings and stroll over to the cafes of adjacent Parque México. Or if in a studio, make coffee in the cute kitchens with minibar. Twin rooms have deluxe bunk beds.

★Red Tree House
B&B $$$

(Map p120; ☑55-5584-3829; www.theredtree house.com; Culiacán 6; s/d/ste incl breakfast from US$115/150/175; 🛜🛜; 🚇 Campeche) Condesa's first B&B has all the comforts of home, if your home happens to be decorated with exquisite taste in a splendid part of town. Each of the 17 bedrooms and suites is uniquely furnished, and the roomy penthouse has a private patio. Downstairs, guests have the run of a cozy living room and lovely rear garden. The Red Tree also has five pleasant rooms in a house located a half-block away on Citlaltépetl.

★Condesa Haus
BOUTIQUE HOTEL $$$

(Map p120; ☑81-1769-2769; https://condesahaus. com; Cuernavaca 142; d M$1920, apt M$2300; 🛜🛜; 🚇 Patriotismo) Owner and host extraordinaire Fernando took an old art deco home and turned it into one of the most stylish boutique hotels in Mexico City. Each room has a different theme and decor, but doesn't feel kitschy. Be sure to check out the original tiles and stained-glass window in the Puebla room.

★La Casona
BOUTIQUE HOTEL $$$

(Map p120; ☑55-5286-3001; www.hotellacasona. com.mx; Durango 280; r incl breakfast M$1675; 🛜✳🛜; 🚇 Sevilla) This stately mansion has been restored to its early-20th-century splendor to become one of the capital's most distinctive boutique hotels. The 29 rooms have comfy beds, high ceilings and are uniquely appointed with stylish wallpaper, ornate furniture and decorative musical instruments and artworks to bring out European charm. The relaxing area has some attractive restaurants, with both Condesa and Chapultepec a 10- to 15-minute stroll away.

Villa Condesa
BOUTIQUE HOTEL $$$

(Map p120; ☑55-5211-4892; www.villacondesa. com.mx; Colima 428; r incl breakfast from M$4230; 🛜🛜; 🚇 Chapultepec) You can say *adiós* to hectic Mexico City from the moment you set foot in the Villa's leafy lobby. The 14 rooms in this striking historic building combine classic touches (each has a piece of antique furniture) with the modern trappings of a first-rate hotel. Reservations required; children under 12 not allowed. Guests have free use of bicycles.

🛏 Roma

Hotel Milán
HOTEL $$

(Map p120; ☎55-5584-0222; www.hotelmilan.com.mx; Álvaro Obregón 94; s/d M$820/860; P🅿❄◎@☏; 🚇Álvaro Obregón) Sitting on the main corridor of gentrified-bohemian Roma, the Milán goes for minimalist decor and contemporary art in its lobby. Well maintained, small rooms come with quality bedding and feature bright bathrooms. One of the best-value modern options in the area. There's an onsite restaurant and breakfast is an extra M$70 per person.

Hotel Stanza
BUSINESS HOTEL $$$

(Map p120; ☎55-5208-0052; www.stanzahotel.com; Álvaro Obregón 13; d/tw/ste from M$1790/1940/2240; P🅿❄◎@☏; 🚇Jardín Pushkin) At the east end of the area's main road, Álvaro Obregón, the Stanza has its own restaurant and gym and makes a cushy base on the edge of Roma's cool-kid restaurant and bar scene.

🛏 Polanco

Hábita Hotel
BOUTIQUE HOTEL $$$

(Map p92; ☎55-5282-3100; www.hotelhabita.com; Av Presidente Masaryk 201; d incl breakfast from US$210; P🅿❄◎☏🏊; 🚇Polanco) Architect Enrique Norten turned a functional apartment building into a smart boutique hotel. Decor in the 36 rooms is boldly minimalist and the most economical digs measure 20 sq meters (call them cozy or just plain small). The rooftop bar, La Terraza (p132), is a hot nightspot.

Flowsuites Polanco
APARTMENT $$$

(Map p92; ☎55-4123-7506; www.flowsuites.com; Av Castelar 34; ste incl breakfast from US$250; ❄@☏; 🚇Auditorio) An affordable option by Polanco standards, the large comfy suites resemble deluxe apartments, giving you plenty of bang for your buck with minimalist designer furniture, quality plush bedding and a full kitchen. The well-maintained Flowsuites has no common areas, but breakfast is served to your door. Chapultepec park's main sights are within walking distance.

🛏 Xochimilco

La Llorona Cihuacoatl Campground
CAMPGROUND $

(☎55-5489-7773, cell 55-5591 4775; www.facebook.com/parqueecoturisticomichmani; Embar-

cadero Cuemanco, off Anillo Periférico Sur; campsites per person incl tent M$150, cabin M$650; P) 🍃 In Xochimilco, the ecotourism center Michmani arranges stays at La Llorona Cihuacoatl campground, which sits on a peaceful off-grid *chinampa*. The center rents out tents, but you'll have to bring a sleeping bag, or you can stay in a tiny rustic cabin with two beds. Also available are barbecue grills and temascals (steam baths; M$250).

To get here, go to metro General Anaya and exit the station on the east side of Calzada de Tlalpan, then walk 50m north to catch a 'Tláhuac Paradero' pesero. Get off at the Embarcadero Cuemanco entrance and walk about 1km to Michmani, just beyond the *embarcadero*. From there a boat will take you to La Llorona.

🛏 Coyoacán & Ciudad Universitaria

Hostal Cuija Coyoacán
HOSTEL $

(Map p103; ☎55-5659-9310; www.hostalcuijacoyoacan.com; Berlín 268; dm/d incl breakfast M$280/950; ❄@☏; 🚇Coyoacán) This lizard themed (for the roaming critters in the garden) HI hostel offers a clean and affordable base to check out Coyoacán's nearby sights. The house has pleasant common areas, but don't expect the smallish dorms and private rooms to wow you.

El Cenote Azul
HOSTEL $

(☎55-5554-8730; Alfonso Pruneda 24, Colonia Copilco el Alto; dm M$250; ❄☏; 🚇Copilco) This laid-back hostel near the UNAM campus has six neatly kept four- or two-bed rooms sharing three Talavera-tiled bathrooms. The downstairs bar of the same name is a popular hangout for university students, though was closed for remodeling when we visited. It's tucked away off Privada Ezequiel Ordoñes. Monthly deals are available.

★ Chalet del Carmen
GUESTHOUSE $$

(Map p103; ☎55-5554-9572; www.chaletdelcarmen.com; Guerrero 94; s/d/ste from M$899/999/1999; ❄☏; 🚇Coyoacán) 🍃 Run by a friendly Coyoacán native and his Swiss wife, this ecofriendly house strikes a warm blend of Mexican and European aesthetics. On offer are five rooms and two suites with antique furnishings and brilliant natural lighting. Guests have use of a kitchen and bicycles. Reservations a must; discounts for long-term stays.

Hostal Frida   GUESTHOUSE **$$**
(Map p103; ⌨ 55-5659-7005; www.hostalfridabyb. com; Mina 54; d/tr M$650/870; ☺☎; ⓜCoyoacán) Don't let the *hostal* tag fool you: this family-run place has decked out rooms more along the lines of a guesthouse. Each of the six wooden-floored doubles occupies its own level in adjacent structures, and three come with kitchens. Wi-fi is fast. Monthly rates available.

⌨ Airport

Hotel Aeropuerto   HOTEL **$$**
(⌨ 55-5785-5318; www.hotelaeropuerto.com. mx; Blvd Puerto Aéreo 388; d/tw M$1300/1500; ⓟ☺✱☎; ⓜTerminal Aérea) Although there are several upscale hotels linked to the terminals, this affordable hotel across the street serves just fine for weary travelers with budget-priced food and drinks in the bar-restaurant. The only nonchain in the zone, it has helpful reception staff and TV-equipped, neutral modern rooms, some overlooking the airport runway through soundproof windows.

Turn left outside the domestic terminal, and beyond the metro take a left onto Blvd Puerto Aéreo and cross via the pedestrian bridge.

✗ Eating

The capital offers eateries for all tastes and budgets, from soulful taco stalls to gourmet restaurants.

The trendiest cafes, ample vegan options and hottest restaurants for contemporary cuisine show up in **Roma**, centered on Álvaro Obregón and from there along Orizaba, which is bookended by two plazas loaded with restaurants. Picturesque **Colima** caters to fine dining.

Condesa is dressed up, though sometimes more show than substance. Dozens of informal bistros – many with sidewalk tables – crowd Condesa's restaurant zone (at the convergence of Michoacán, Vicente Suárez and Tamaulipas); casual eats ring Parque México, and the pleasant Fuente de Cibeles (corner of Durango and Medellín).

Polanco features five-star restaurants but inspiring budget eats are rare.

Though places on the immediate perimeter of the **Alameda** cater to tourists, head down Luis Moya or along Ayuntamiento, south of the Alameda, for rustic *torta* (sandwich) or taco stands. **Centro Histórico** is a tourist trap, but Calle de Motolinía off Madero has plenty of casual, local options.

Head to **Zona Rosa and Reforma** for good Korean barbecue or Japanese ramen. Great new restaurants and cafes are cropping up in the area known as Reforma. This comprises the **Colonia Cuauhtémoc**, north of Paseo de la Reforma, fast becoming known as 'Little Tokyo' for upmarket Japanese restaurants and bars.

✗ Centro Histórico

★Los Cocuyos   TACOS **$**
(Map p74; Bolívar 54; tacos M$18-25; ☺24hr; ⓜSan Juan de Letrán) *Suadero* (beef) tacos abound in the capital, but this always-open stand reigns supreme. Follow your nose to the bubbling vat of meats and go for the artery-choking *campechano* (mixed-beef-and-sausage taco). For the more adventurous eater, there are *ojo* (eye) or their speciality *lengua* (tongue) tacos; for vegetarians, there are *nopales* (cactus paddles). Be prepared to queue.

Café El Popular   CAFE **$**
(Map p74; ⌨ 55-5518-6081; Av 5 de Mayo 52; breakfasts M$80-109, mains M$98-146; ☺24hr; ⌨; ⓜAllende) So popular was this tiny round-the-clock, old-school diner that another more amply proportioned branch was opened next door. Fresh pastries, *café con leche* (coffee with milk) and good combination breakfasts are the main attractions to the booths here.

El Flaco   TACOS **$**
(Map p74; Calle 5 de Febrero 15-19; tacos M$9; ☺8am-8pm; ⌨; ⓜZócalo) The menu at this hole-in-the-wall hasn't changed since the family opened its shutters more than 50 years ago; it's one of the best spots to try *tacos de canasta* (tacos steamed inside a basket) with flavours like egg and potato or *chicharrón* (fried pork). Grab some napkins – things can get messy.

★Hostería de Santo Domingo   MEXICAN **$$**
(Map p74; ⌨ 55-5526-5276; http://hosteria santodomingo.mx; Belisario Domínguez 72; chile en nogada M$220, mains M$90-220; ☺9am-9pm Mon-Sat, to 8pm Sun; ☎; ⓟRepública de Chile) Whipping up classic Mexican fare since 1860, Mexico City's oldest restaurant has a festive atmosphere, enhanced by live piano music. The menu offers numerous dishes, but everyone comes here for the *chile en nogada* (an enormous *poblano* chili pepper stuffed with ground meat, dried fruit and

AROUND MEXICO ON A PLATE

Pasillo de Humo (Map p120; ☑55-5211-7263; www.facebook.com/pasillodehumo; 2nd fl, Av Nuevo León 107, Colonia Condesa; snacks M$120-180, mains M$174-288; ☉9am-10pm Mon-Wed, to 11pm Thu-Sat, to 7pm Sun; ☑; ☐Campeche) If you can't make it to culinary-capital Oaxaca, here's your chance to delve into authentic traditional cuisine from the region. You might try the *sopa oaxaqueña* (a delectable bean soup), *molotes istmeños* (plantain balls in *mole* sauce) or *tlayudas* (large tortillas filled with cheese, beans and aromatic herbs). The lovely dining area gets plenty of natural light.

Coox Hanal (Map p74; ☑55-5709-3613; www.cooxhanal.com; 2nd fl, Isabel La Católica 83, Centro Histórico; mains M$70-150; ☉10:30am-6:30pm; ℗☎; ⓜIsabel La Católica) Started in 1953 by boxer Raúl Salazar, this unpretentious establishment prepares Yucatecan fare just as it's done in don Raúl's hometown of Mérida. The *sopa de lima* (lime soup with chicken), *papadzules* (tacos stuffed with chopped hard-boiled egg and topped with pumpkin-seed sauce) and *cochinita pibil* (slow-cooked pork) are top-notch. Tables are set with the obligatory four-alarm habanero salsa.

Los Tolucos (☑55-5440-3318; Hernández y Dávalos 40, cnr Bolívar, Colonia Algarín; pozoles M$93-102, tacos M$29; ☉10am-9pm; ℗; ⓜLázaro Cárdenas) A popular local favorite for some of the best *pozole* (hominy and pork stew) in Mexico City. The Guerrero-style green *pozole* here has been drawing people from far and wide for more than four decades. A partial photo-menu with tacos and *carnitas* (braised pork) helps gets things started. It's three blocks east of metro Lázaro Cárdenas.

La Polar (☑55-5546-5066; www.facebook.com/restaurantelapolar; Prieto 129, Colonia San Rafael; birria M$146; ☉8am-1am; ℗; ⓜNormal) Run by a family from Ocotlán, Jalisco, this boisterous beer hall has essentially one item on the menu: *birria* (spiced goat stew). La Polar's version of this Guadalajara favorite is considered the best in town. Spirits are raised further by noisy mariachis and *norteña* combos who work the half-dozen salons here.

Tamales Chiapanecos María Geraldine (Map p103; ☑55-5608-8993; Plaza Hidalgo, Coyoacán; tamales M$35; ☉4-11pm Fri, 11am-10pm Sat & Sun; ⓜCoyoacán) Look for these incredible *tamales* by Chiapas native doña María Geraldine. Wrapped in banana leaves, stuffed with ingredients such as olives, prunes and almonds, and laced with sublime salsas, they're a meal in themselves. Her silver pots are at the passageway next to the arched wing of San Juan Bautista church, under the huge 'TAROT' sign.

Xel-Ha (Map p120; ☑55-5553-5968; Parral 78, Condesa; mains M$150-250; ☉1pm-midnight Mon-Sat, to 7pm Sun) Get a taste of the Yucatan without having to hop on another flight. Be sure to try the *cochinita pibil* tacos and *sopa de lima*.

bathed in a creamy walnut sauce). Beware: rumor has it the building is haunted.

The breakfast buffet (M$190) is worth getting up for.

★**El Cardenal**   MEXICAN **$$**
(Map p74; ☑55-5521-3080; www.restaurante elcardenal.com; Palma 23; breakfast M$104-150, lunch & dinner M$90-250; ☉8am-6:30pm Mon-Sat, from 8:30am Sun; ℗☎; ⓜZócalo) Possibly the finest place in town for a traditional meal, El Cardenal occupies three floors of a Parisian-style mansion and has a pianist playing sweetly in the background. Mexican breakfast is a must, like zucchini flower and cottage cheese croquettes, pastries and a pitcher of frothy, semisweet chocolate. For lunch the house specialty is the *pecho de ternera* (oven-roasted veal breast).

Another branch, **El Cardenal San Ángel** (Map p100; ☑55-5550-0293; Av de la Paz 32; breakfast M$104-150, lunch & dinner M$90-250; ☉8am-8pm Mon-Sat, 8:30am-6:30pm Sun; ℗☎; ☐La Bombilla), is in the south.

Los Vegetarianos   VEGETARIAN **$$**
(Map p74; ☑55-5521-6880; www.facebook.com/ losvegetarianosdemadero; Av Madero 56; menú del día M$95-145; ☉8am-8pm; ☑; ⓜZócalo) Despite its austere entrance, this is a lively upstairs restaurant where a pianist plinks out old favorites. The standard meat-free menu includes a range of variations on Mexican standards, such as *chile en nogada* filled with soy meat, and there are vegan options as well.

Al Andalus
MIDDLE EASTERN **$$**

(Map p74; ☑55-5522-2528; m_andalus171@ yahoo.com.mx; Mesones 171; mains M$140-220; ⊙9am-6pm; Ⓜ Pino Suárez) In a superb colonial-era mansion in the Merced textile district, Al Andalus caters to the capital's substantial Lebanese community with old standbys such as shawarma, falafel, baba ganoush, vine leaves, baklava and thick coffee.

Azul Histórico
MEXICAN **$$$**

(Map p74; ☑55-5510-1316; www.azul.rest; Isabel La Católica 30; mains M$178-410; ⊙9am-11pm; Ⓟ🛜; Ⓜ Zócalo) Chef Ricardo Muñoz reinvents traditional Mexican recipes such as *pescado tikin xic* (a grouper dish from the Yucatán with plantain and tortilla strips). This branch is in a beautiful complex of converted buildings and diners eat in an inner-courtyard among trees and romantic lighting, enclosed by stone archways. Rare for the *centro*, the Azul attracts upmarket visitors.

Los Girasoles
MEXICAN **$$$**

(Map p74; ☑55-5510-3281; www.facebook. com/LosGirasolesMexico; Xicoténcatl 1, cnr Tacuba; mains M$175-239; ⊙8-10pm Sun-Thu, to 11pm Fri & Sat; Ⓟ🛜; Ⓜ Allende) This fine restaurant overlooking the grand Plaza Tolsá boasts an encyclopedic range of Mexican fare, from pre-Hispanic ant larvae and grasshoppers to contemporary dishes such as red snapper encrusted with *huauzontle* flowers.

La Casa de las Sirenas
MEXICAN **$$$**

(Map p74; ☑55-5704-3345; www.lacasadelas sirenas.rest; República de Guatemala 32; mains M$240-310; ⊙11am-11pm Mon-Sat, to 7pm Sun; 🛜; Ⓜ Zócalo) Housed in a 17th-century relic, Sirenas has a top-floor terrace that looks toward the Zócalo via the Plaza del Templo Mayor. It's an ideal perch to enjoy regional dishes prepared with contemporary flair, such as chicken bathed in pumpkin-seed *mole,* and to linger with a mezcal margarita.

Casino Español
SPANISH **$$$**

(Map p74; ☑55-5521-8894; www.cassatt. mx; Isabel La Católica 29; 4-course lunch M$165, mains M$158-368; ⊙1-6pm Mon-Fri, restaurant also 8am-noon daily; 🛜; Ⓜ Zócalo) This old Spanish social center, housed in a fabulous *porfiriato*-era building, has a popular *mesón* (cantina-style eatery) downstairs, where the courses keep coming, and an elegant restaurant upstairs, which features classic Spanish fare such as *paella valenciana* (paella Valencia-style).

Café de Tacuba
MEXICAN **$$$**

(Map p74; ☑55-5521-2048; www.cafede tacuba.com.mx; Tacuba 28; mains M$177-326, 4-course lunch M$295; ⊙8am-11:30pm; 🛜; Ⓜ Allende) Before the band there was the restaurant. Way before. A fantasy of colored tiles, brass lamps and oil paintings, this Mexican icon has served *antojitos* (snacks such as tacos and *sopes* – corn tortillas layered with beans, cheese and other ingredients) since 1912. Lively *estudiantinas* (student musical groups) entertain the dinner crowd Wednesday through Sunday.

✖ Alameda Central & Around

★ El Huequito
TACOS **$**

(Map p74; ☑55-5518-3313; www.elhuequito. com.mx; Ayuntamiento 21; tacos al pastor M$19; ⊙8am-10pm; 🚇 Plaza San Juan) These old pros have been churning out delectable *tacos al pastor* (marinated pork roasted on a spit) since 1959, thus the higher than average asking price. Several downtown Huequito branches offer the sit-down experience, but for some reason the tacos are better here at the original hole-in-the-wall location.

Taquería Tlaquepaque
MEXICAN **$**

(Map p74; ☑55-5512-5583; Av Independencia 4; mains from M$70; ⊙8am-3am Sun-Thu, to 4am Fri & Sat; Ⓜ Bellas Artes) For a taste of Guadalajara in Mexico City, get yourself a seat at this traditional Mexican-style diner. The menu is long, but it's full of classics like *birria*, slow-roasted goat meat, and *chamorro*, slow-roasted pork leg. Every meal is served with tortillas, onions and cilantro.

Vegamo
VEGAN **$**

(Map p86; ☑55-7158-6934; www.vegamomx. com; Revillagigedo 47; mains M$90-110; ⊙9am-8pm Mon-Fri, to 9pm Sat, 10am-8pm Sun; 🛜✎; Ⓜ Juárez) The vegan dishes at this tiny cafe are a giant saviour if you want delectable, fresh Mexican meals like *pipian* eggplant in a creamy (almond) pepita sauce, burgers, or a satisfying *pozole* hominy-mushroom soup with chilies. Soy chai/turmeric/Mexican coffee lattes are excellent, and smoothies include coconut water with cardamom. Say yes to raw brownies and exotic-fruit waffles.

Mi Fonda
SPANISH **$**

(Map p74; ☑55-5521-0002; https://cocina -mi-fonda.negocio.site; López 101; paella M$100; ⊙11am-5:30pm Tue-Sun; 🚇 Plaza San Juan)

Working-class *chilangos* line up for their share of *paella valenciana,* made fresh daily and patiently ladled out by women in white bonnets. Jesús from Cantabria oversees the proceedings in the cute pastel diner.

★**Sin Nombre** MEXICAN $$
(Map p86; ☑55-5510-2697; Luis Moya 31; mains M$175-200; ⊙2-11:30pm Tue-Sat) Too good to keep hidden, the 'No Name' restaurant, located next to *mezcalería* Bósfaro, prepares handcrafted Mexican, slow-food dishes such as *conejo encacahuatado* (biodynamic rabbit in peanut salsa with sweet potato) and *pulpo en morita* (grilled squid with fruity smoked chilies) in earthenware cookware. Select ingredients are sourced from across Mexico and the industrial-chic atmosphere is just as charming. Spread the word.

Reservations highly recommended.

✕ Plaza de la República & Around

★**Terraza Cha Cha Chá** MEXICAN $$
(Map p86; ☑55-5705-2272; www.grupopalmares.com.mx; Av de la República 157; mains M$145-220; ⊙1:30pm-1:30am Mon-Sat, to 7pm Sun; ⊛☑; 🚇Plaza de la República) Just as festive as it sounds, a margarita and tuna *tostada* (large crispy tortilla) on the terrace overlooking the Monumento a la Revolución is a real *fiesta* starter. Groups and families love the big ballroom and varied menu – grilled meat and fish, oysters, *aguachile* (lime-cured shrimp), and tacos of beef tongue, duck, soft-shell crab or zucchini flower. Reserve to nab a terrace spot.

✕ Zona Rosa & Reforma

★**Tamales Madre** MEXICAN $
(Map p128; ☑55-5705-3491; www.tamalesmadre.com; Liverpool 44a, Colonia Juárez; tamales M$52-62; ⊙8am-5pm Tue-Sat, from 9am Sun; ⊛☑; 🚇Hamburgo) This is *tamales* heaven, especially for vegetarians. Cyclists blaring 'Tamales!' from speakers on CDMX's streets sell lard-based tamales that are stingy on the fillings. Stylish Tamales Madre artfully plates up packets of *mole* with chicken or vegan plantain, *hoja santa* (Mexican pepperleaf), or vegetarian pecan cream. All steamed in a corn husk or plantain leaf and without *manteca* (lard).

Yug Vegetariano VEGETARIAN $
(Map p128; ☑55-5333-3296; www.lovegetariano.com; Varsovia 3; buffet lunch M$115-135, mains M$65-85; ⊙7:30am-9pm Mon-Thu, to 8pm Fri, 8:30am-8pm Sat & Sun; ⊛☑; 🚇Sevilla) The mostly Mexican menu is taste-bud heaven for vegetarians and vast enough for most carnivorous folk to find something they fancy. Choose from specialties such as squash-flower crepes, or gorge on the buffet lunch (1pm to 5pm daily) upstairs, with all-you-can-eat simple mains, salads, soup and sugarless drinks. Yug's old-world decor attracts an unpretentious local crowd.

La Abuela STREET FOOD $
(Map p128; Río Amazonas, cnr Río Lerma; tacos M$10; ⊙6am-1pm; ☑; 🚇Reforma) There's certainly no shortage of *tacos de canasta* in Mexico City, but La Abuela (grandma) has been doing it for three decades – and it shows. Corn tortillas come filled with delectable ingredients such as refried beans, mashed potato and *cochinita pibil,* and they're dispensed by a kind man known as 'El Abuelo' (grandpa).

★**Café NiN** FRENCH $$
(Map p128; ☑55-9155-4805; www.cafenin.com.mx; Havre 73, Colonia Zona Rosa; snacks M$10-37, mains M$105-285; ⊙7am-9pm Mon-Sat, 7:30am-6pm Sun; ⊛☑; 🚇Insurgentes) This golden cafe-restaurant looks plucked from belle-epoque Paris with glorious patisserie and bakery treats as part of the Rosetta Panadería empire. The bar is great for coffee, sandwiches or solo egg brunches. A newer food menu brings European fusion to pork belly with plantains and cilantro or green-curry grouper fish. Save room for the grapefruit panna cotta.

WanWan Sakaba JAPANESE $$
(Map p128; ☑55-5514-4324; www.facebook.com/wanwansakaba; Londres 209; set lunch M$120-190, mains M$95-290; ⊙1-11pm Mon-Fri, noon-10pm Sat; ✳☑; 🚇Insurgentes) An authentic Japanese *izakaya* (pub-eatery) that's casual enough to tuck into ramen at the bar (or tables upstairs). Set lunches include perfectly simple grilled salmon, while the udon noodles and sake (rice wine) are Tokyo-good.

De Mar a Mar SEAFOOD $$$
(Map p128; ☑55-5207-5730; www.demaramar.mx; Niza 13, Zona Rosa; mains M$190-310; ⊙1-10pm Mon & Tue, to 11pm Wed-Sat, to 7pm Sun; ☑; 🚇Hamburgo) One of Zona Rosa's best restaurants, the menu here was designed by chef

Eduardo García, a rising star on the Mexico City culinary scene. All dishes, especially the ceviche and *tostadas* (baked or fried tortillas), stand out for their fresh ingredients. Dessert such as meringue with red berries is a slice of heaven

Don Asado
STEAK $$$

(Map p128; ☑ 55-5533-9000; www.donasado. mx; Río Lerma 210; mains M$149-235; ⊙ 1-11pm Tue-Sat, to 8pm Sun & Mon; ☎; Ⓜ Sevilla) One of the best and most reasonably priced steakhouses in town. Uruguayan-owned Don Asado rocks a large wood-burning grill to cook juicy cuts such as its popular *vacio con piel* (tender flank steak with a crispy outer layer of fat) or *bife de chorizo* (New York strip steak). Vegetarian options include handmade pasta and *empanadas* (turnovers).

✖ Condesa

★ Taquería Orinoco
TACOS $

(Map p120; www.taqueriaorinoco.com; Insurgentes 253; tacos M$19-35; ⊙ 1pm-4am Sun-Thu, to 5am Fri & Sat; Ⓜ Metrobus Álvaro Obregón) For a taste of the north, head to this excellent Monterrey-style taco restaurant. It's buzzing with hip locals after a night out but a queue forms by even 10pm. The *chicharrón* is the specialty here and different to the usual Mexico City offering.

The creamy *costra* (toasted-cheese) quesadilla is also special. Unusually, you order and pay at the entrance, but once seated you are free to add more onto a new bill.

El Faraón
TACOS $

(Map p120; ☑ 55-5514-2214; www.elfaraon.mx; Av Oaxaca 92-93; tacos M$17-55; ⊙ 1pm-5am; Ⓜ Sevilla) Thanks to its long hours and proximity to the clubs around the lively Fuente de Cibeles, this spacious taco restaurant is busiest around 3am, but the tacos are tasty all day long. An extensive menu includes everything from exquisite rib eye and *tacos al pastor* to mushroom quesadillas.

Degú
CAFE $

(Map p120; ☑ 55-6731-5294; www.degu.mx; Huichapan 25; mains M$80-115; ⊙ 8am-5pm Mon, to 7pm Tue-Fri, to 4pm Sat & Sun; ☎ ☑; Ⓜ Sonora) Around picturesquely overgrown Plaza Popocatéptl, this diminutive cafe creates splendid brunches like giant cassava-tortilla quesadillas overflowing with avocado, spinach and Oaxacan cheese; generous plates of exotic fruit on waffles;

nachos-like *chilaquiles* with steak (yes, for breakfast); and grilled fish, chicken, pork or cheese plates at lunch.

El Pescadito
SEAFOOD $

(Map p120; ☑ 55-2267-0641; https://elpescadito. mx; Atlixco 38; tacos M$38; ⊙ 11am-6pm Mon-Fri, from 10am Sat & Sun; Ⓜ Campeche) This bright-yellow taco joint is unmissable for the queue waiting for a (folding) seat. Nearly all nine fish/shrimp fillings are battered, Sonora style, for maximum crispy, juicy flavor. Just add your own toppings and sauces from a bar.

Pescadito's signature taco, '*que-sotote*' – a chili stuffed with shrimp and cheese – is worth holding out for.

El Moro
CHURROS $

(Map p120; http://elmoro.mx; Michoacán 27; 4 churros M$20; ⊙ 8am-11pm Mon-Sat, from 9am Sun; Ⓜ Campeche) Moro's blue-and-white tiles and Parque Mexico views make for a lovely, re-energizing stop. Doughnut-like sweet *churros* come rolled in cinnamon or *azúcar* (sugar) to complement the hot chocolate, ranging from gentle Mexicano style to heart-thumpingly syrupy, Español style.

El Farolito
TACOS $

(El Farolito; Map p120; ☑ 55-5273-0142; http:// taqueriaselfarolito.com.mx; Altata 19; tacos M$11-18; ⊙ 1pm-2am Mon-Thu, to 2am Fri & Sat, to midnight Sun; Ⓜ Patriotismo) This chain claims to have pioneered *tacos al carbón* (tacos cooked on charcoal). Whether it's true or not, it churns out some seriously delicious grilled meat. The *carnitas* are finished off on the grill, making them mouthwateringly good.

★ Lardo
FUSION $$

(Map p120; www.lardo.mx; Melgar 6, cnr Mazatlán; M$110-360; ⊙ 7am-10:45pm Mon-Sat, 8am-5pm Sun; ☑) It always seems sunny in this convivial stylish bistro, which takes Mexican flavors and matches them with European freshness. Part of the Rosetta patisserie family, Lardo's exquisite zucchini-and-spearmint pizzettas show baking prowess, and dishes such as red snapper with pepita sauce or *adobo* (red pepper) baby chicken are expertly balanced.

Green Corner
BISTRO $$

(Map p120; ☑ 55-6723-0318; www.thegreen corner.org; Av Mazatlán 81; mains M$95-155, set lunch M$135-165; ⊙ 7:30am-10pm; ☎ ☑) Healthy lunch along the plant-filled avenue outside this restaurant–organic grocery

Roma & Condesa

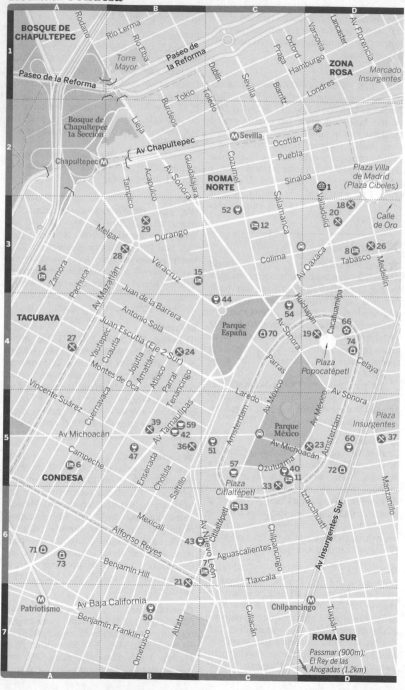

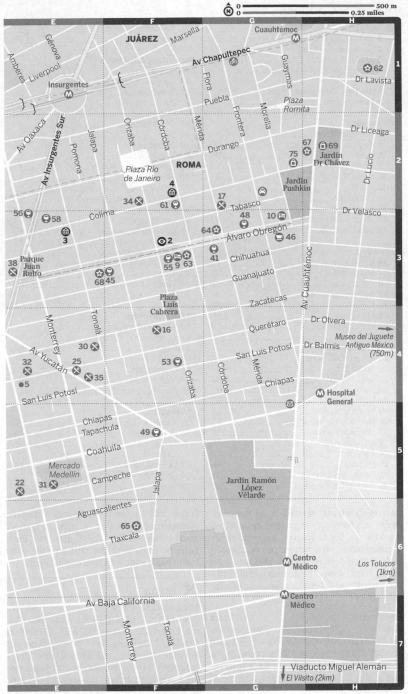

Roma & Condesa

store is stylish and relaxed. A set menu includes a choice of sugar-free *agua* (fruit drink) or tea, vegan soup or salad and either a macrobiotic, vegetarian or meat-based main before dessert. There's also acai fruit bowls, falafel wraps, pesto pasta, grilled turkey breast and interesting breakfasts with light options.

Merotoro MEXICAN **$$$**
(Map p120; ☑ 55-5564-7799; www.merotoro. mx; Amsterdam 204; mains M$230-405; ⊗1-11pm Mon-Sat, 1:30-6pm Sun; ☑; ☐ Campeche) For a taste of the Mexican coast, make a reservation at this Baja-style restaurant. The menu

is split into four sections: light fish starters, second courses of rice or pasta, a heavier meat course and, to finish, desserts. Each pairs perfectly with the next and the wine menu has a wide selection of Baja drops.

✖ Roma

Panadería Rosetta BAKERY **$**
(Map p120; ☑ 55-5207-2976; www.rosetta.com. mx; Colima 179; pastries M$20-50; ⊗7am-9pm Mon-Sat, 7:30am-7pm Sun; ☎☑; ☐ Durango) Sublime Mexican and French *pan dulce* (pastries), proper croissants and baguettes are made fresh daily at this tiny bakery, with

a bench for coffee, sandwiches and breakfasts. It's a tight squeeze so if queues form, try the lovely Café NiN (p118) branch in Zona Rosa.

It's owned by chef Elena Reygadas, sister of award-winning Mexican filmmaker Carlos Reygadas.

Por Siempre Vegana Taquería VEGAN $

(Map p120; 55-3923-7976; www.facebook. com/porsiempreveganataqueria; cnr Manzanillo & Chiapas; tacos M$10-20; 1pm-midnight Mon-Sat; ; Sonora) Vegans can join in the street-food action with soy and gluten taco versions of *al pastor, loganiza* (sausage) and chorizo. The late-night experience is complete with self-serve tubs of toppings – potato, *nopales*, beans and salsas.

There are also dairy-free cakes and Oaxacan ice cream at this street stall. Another branch with seating and the same hours is around the corner at Coahuila 169.

Mercado Medellín MARKET $

(Map p120; Campeche 101, Roma Sur; dishes M$35-85; 8:30am-6pm;) Self-caterers can stop into this colorful market for quality cuts of meat, fresh produce and nuts amongst the piñatas. It's also a popular spot for lunch: grab a stool at one of the vendors or *fondas* and enjoy *tamales, pozole* and tacos washed down with *horchata* (rice drink).

★**Expendio de Maíz** MEXICAN $$

(Map p120; 55-2498-9964; www.expendio demaiz.com; Av Yucatán 84; meals from M$200; 9:30am-6pm; ; Sonora) An unmissable, unique experience. No menu, no official name (except the 'corn dealer' description), just a relaxed, communal table with food straight from the *comal* (hot plate) to wow you. Bilingual staff explain each dish, such as the crunchy smoky-pork *carnitas* and Oaxacan cheese on house-made tortillas. Mostly organic, seasonal produce is used. When you've had enough, tell them to stop.

Expect to pay M$200 for four courses of generous snacks with a drink like kombucha or mezcal. Cash only.

★**El Hidalguense** MEXICAN $$

(Map p120; 55-5564-0538; Campeche 155; mains M$90-250; 7am-6pm Fri-Mon; ; Campeche) Slow-cooked over aged oak wood in an underground pit, the Hidalgo-style *barbacoa* at this family-run eatery is off-the-charts delicious. Get things started with a rich consommé or *queso asado* (grilled cheese with herbs), then move on to the tacos. Top it

off on a warm and fuzzy note by sampling the flavored *pulques*. Cash only.

★**Páramo** TACOS $$

(Map p120; 55-5941-5125; www.facebook. com/ParamoRoma; Av Yucatán 84; tacos M$40-70, mains M$140-360; 7pm-2am; ; Sonora) Named after Mexican novel *Pedro Páramo* about a ghost town, this jam-packed, sprawling restaurant–bar feels more like a house party. Tacos like the *huasca* wild boar in a beer reduction, or the seared tuna in honey set a high bar. There's also shrimp, meatballs, *longaniza* and vegetarian hibiscus flowers or stuffed chilies, all of which can be taken as mains.

Reservations recommended any night, otherwise wait an hour in the bar with a drink from the long menu – the refreshing *pepino* (cucumber) mezcal cocktail and their gins and tonic are excellent.

Broka Bistrot FUSION $$

(Map p120; 55-4437-4285; www.brokabistrot. com; Zacatecas 126; set lunch M$165, mains M$155-255; 2pm-midnight Mon-Sat, 11-5pm Sun; ; Álvaro Obregón) Set in a stylish hidden patio, Broka serves delectable Euro-Mexican fusion dishes such as a fish-and-*nopal* stack with blue-corn tortillas. The weekday lunch menu is hip and so photogenic that it's tweeted daily; check the website.

Buenavida MEXICAN $$

(Map p120; 55-5511-8293; Tabasco 101, Roma Norte; menú del dia M$115; 10am-10pm Mon-Sat, 1-8pm Sun; ; Cuauhtémoc) For a dressed-up *fonda* experience, head to this little cafe in Roma Norte. Opt for the *menú del día* (set menu), which usually includes a soup appetizer, a main of meat or a vegetarian option, rice and tortillas, and either coffee or sweetened juice.

Mercado Roma MARKET $$

(Map p120; 55-5564-1396; http://mercado roma.com; Querétaro 225; snacks M$20-150; 9am-8pm Sun-Wed, to 1am Thu-Sat; ; Sonora) Weekends at this gourmet food hall resemble a red-carpet event of well-to-do families and the best dressed (it has featured in top fashion mags). It is indeed an impressive, if cramped, space to meet, eat and drink. The nibbles are top-notch, representing a best-of from around town – Wagyu beef tacos, Mexican cheese, tapas, burrito-sushi, Vietnamese rolls and fine burgers.

Fonda Fina
MEXICAN $$

(Map p120; ✆55-5208-3925; www.fondafina.
com.mx; Medellín 79; appetizers M$75-120, mains
M$130-260; ☺1-11pm Mon-Wed, to midnight Thu-
Sat, to 7pm Sun; 🐾🍴; 🚇Álvaro Obregón) The
fonda concept of ordering a three-course
meal off a set menu does not apply here;
instead you select a main with your choice
of sauce and side dish. Appetizer and main
dish faves include *peneques rellenos de que-
so* (ricotta-filled tortillas with pumpkin-seed
mole) and *fideo seco con chilaquiles* (spicy
tortilla wedges on a bed of pasta).

Los Loosers
VEGAN $$

(Map p120; ✆55-4455-4875; www.facebook.
com/LosLoosers; Sinaloa 236, Colonia Roma; mains
M$150-220; ☺1-9pm Tue-Fri, noon-9pm Sat, noon-
6pm Sun; 🐾🍴; 🚇Chapultepec) Vegan food
done right. Reporter-turned-chef Mariana
Blanco cooks up something a little different
each day for a menu inspired by Mexican
and Asian cuisine, such as ramen *chilaquiles* (ramen noodles in spicy chili sauce).

Queues often form for the small space,
but free delivery service is available to your
hotel via Facebook. Cash only.

★ Máximo Bistrot
EUROPEAN $$$

(Map p120; ✆55-5264-4291; www.maximobistrot.
com.mx; Tonalá 133; mains M$350-900; ☺1-5pm &
7-11pm Tue-Sat, 1-4pm Sun; 🚇Álvaro Obregón) If
there's one place that best represents Mexico
City's exciting new culinary scene, it's Máxi-
mo Bistrot. The constantly changing menu,
which draws on European and some Mexi-
can recipes, features fresh, seasonal ingredi-
ents in dishes such as crab-stuffed courgette
flowers, while simple ingredients like white
string beans dusted in Parmesan take on
new life. Reservations a must.

Owner and chef Eduardo García honed
his cooking skills at Pujol (p124) under the
tutelage of famed chef Enrique Olvera.

★ Contramar
SEAFOOD $$$

(Map p120; ✆55-5514-9217; www.contramar.
com.mx; Durango 200; appetizers M$143-297,
mains M$263-583; ☺noon-6:30pm Sun-Thu, to
8pm Fri & Sat; 🅿🐾; 🚇Durango) Seafood is the
star attraction at this stylish dining hall with
a seaside ambience and impeccable service.
The specialty is tuna fillet Contramar-style
– split, swabbed with red chili and parsley
sauces and grilled to perfection. The creamy
tuna *tostada* topped with avocado slices is a
must-try appetizer – ask for a half serve to fit
it all in. Reservations recommended.

✘ Polanco

El Rey del Suadero
TACOS $

(Map p92; ✆55-5545-0560; Av Horacio 206;
tacos M$15-23; ☺9am-2am; 🚇Polanco) A one-
stop chomp to try two of Mexico City's
most iconic tacos: *suadero* and *al pastor*.
Suadero tacos can be combined with *lon-
ganiza* by ordering a *campechano*. One of
the more affordable options in the upscale
Polanco neighborhood, El Rey has received
a thumbs up from renowned Pujol chef Enrique Olvera.

★ Pujol
MEXICAN $$$

(Map p92; ✆55-5545-4111; www.pujol.com.
mx; Tennyson 133; menú degustación M$1840;
☺1:30-10:45pm Mon-Sat; 🅿; 🚇Polanco) Ar-
guably Mexico's best gourmet restaurant,
Pujol offers a contemporary take on classic
Mexican dishes in a stylish and modern,
Mexican-designed setting. Famed chef En-
rique Olvera regularly reinvents the menu,
which is presented as a *menú degustación*,
a multiple-course tasting extravaganza.
Tasty morsels include a charred aubergine
tamal, *infladita langosta* (a corn puff
filled with lobster), and brown-sugar roast-
ed pineapple with cilantro.

Tasting menus come as a choice of either
corn or seafood focused. It might take up to
several weeks to get a table here, so reserve
well ahead. Seats at the taco bar are easier to
book at short notice and come as 10 courses
of Asian-inspired bites with drinks, all de-
cided by the chef and your host.

★ Quintonil
MEXICAN $$$

(Map p92; ✆55-5280-1660; www.quintonil.com;
Newton 55; mains M$330-595, menú degustac-
ión M$2490; ☺1-4pm & 6:30-10pm Mon-Sat; 🐾;
🚇Polanco) This contemporary innovator con-
sistently makes the Top 50 Restaurants in
the World list for creatively showcasing traditional Mexican dishes. Chef Jorge Vallejo
gives local, organic ingredients starring roles,
which dazzle when Wagyu beef meets an
opulent *pulque*-and-*chipotle* reduction and
elevate crab *tostadas* to a smoky revelation.

It pays off, shining a spotlight on Mexico's culinary ascendancy. Book many weeks
ahead.

Dulce Patria
MEXICAN $$$

(Map p92; ✆55-3300-3999; https://marthaor-
tiz.mx; Anatole France 100; mains M$295-395;
☺1:30-11:30pm Mon-Sat, to 5:30pm Sun; 🅿🐾;
🚇Polanco) This restaurant owned by cook-

book author Martha Ortiz certainly lives up to her high standards, in spite of some unfortunate ruffled tablecloths and red velvet headrests. Reinvented traditional Mexican dishes such as *mole* enchiladas stuffed with plantain are deftly plated and delicious.

✗ San Ángel

Barbacoa de Santiago
MEXICAN $

(Map p100; ☑ 55-2365-8796; Plaza San Jacinto 23; tacos & flautas M$30; ☺ 9am-10pm Mon-Fri, to 11pm Sat & Sun; ☐ La Bombilla) A quick and affordable *taquería* off the plaza, this place is known for its *barbacoa* and *flautas ahogadas* (fried rolled tacos dipped in a *chile pasilla*-and-*pulque* sauce). You'll also find them at a minibranch in Mercado Roma.

★ Santana del Mar
SEAFOOD $$

(Map p100; ☑ 55-5550-7923; www.facebook. com/santanadelmarmx; Av de la Paz 39; tacos & ceviche M$18, mains M$98-182; ☺ 1-11:30pm Sun-Wed, 1pm-2am Thu-Sat; ☑ ; ☐ La Bombilla) The best-value seafood restaurant in CDMX *appears* pricey with a designer, nautical-themed dining hall roomy enough for groups to linger. For the price, it's hard to believe how good the *carnitas de atún* taco is, showing off slightly charred tuna and garlic sauce. The *jícama* swaps the tortilla for Mexican turnip around shrimp and mango for a refreshing taco.

Shareable mains include whole fried fish or zingy *torre de mariscos* (shrimp, octopus and avocado). Other goodies include ceviche and similar *aguachile* (lime-cured shrimp), spicy tuna *tostadas* (round corn chips), crab salad, vegetarian options and extremely cheap beer and cocktails (all M$18!). Non-Mexican dishes – ramen, pizzas, sushi – miss the mark.

El Péndulo Cafebrería
CAFE $$

(Map p100; ☑ 55-3640-4540; https://pendulo. com; Av Revolución 1500; mains M$95-190; ☺ 8am-11pm Sun-Wed, to midnight Thu & Fri, 9am-1am Sat; ⬢ ☎ ☑) Worth coming for the modern architecture alone, this library-sized cafe–bar–bookstore is built around a palm tree ascending over multiple well-stocked levels of books (many in English) and gifts. The ambience encourages spending hours over a coffee, burger, breakfast, Mexican or pasta dish (with plenty of interesting vegetarian options), or cocktail. The fruity *axiote* Yucatán-style fish with salsa is refreshing.

San Ángel Inn
MEXICAN $$$

(Map p100; ☑ 55-5616-1402; www.sanangelinn. com; Diego Rivera 50; breakfast M$90-160, lunch & dinner mains M$190-465; ☺ 7am-1am Mon-Fri, 8am-1am Sat, 8am-10pm Sun; ☑ ☎ ☎ ; ☐ Altavista) Classic Mexican meals are served in the garden and various elegant dining rooms of this historic estate opposite the Museo Casa Estudio Diego Rivera y Frida Kahlo. Try the *pollo con mole almendrado* (chicken with a spiced, almond sauce). On Saturday and Sunday mornings, the inn provides activities for kids in the rear garden, meaning it's margarita time for parents.

Vegetarians have slim pickings.

Taberna del León
MEXICAN $$$

(Map p100; ☑ 55-5616-2110; www.tabernadelleon. rest; Altamirano 46; mains M$240-495; ☺ 1:30-11:30pm Mon-Wed, to 12:30am Thu-Sat, to 6pm Sun; ☑ ☎ ; ☐ Dr Gálvez) Mónica Patiño is a modern, female star chef stirring up traditional cuisine in innovative ways. Seafood is the specialty here, with the likes of *róbalo a los tres chiles* (sea bass in three-pepper chili sauce) and corn blini with Norwegian salmon.

✗ Coyoacán & Ciudad Universitaria

Super Tacos Chupacabras
TACOS $

(Map p103; ☑ 618-163-6247; cnr Avs Río Churubusco & México; tacos M$15; ☺ 24hr; Ⓜ Coyoacán) Named after Mexico's mythical 'goat sucker' (a vampire-like creature), this famous *taquería* with seating under a freeway overpass slings wonderful beef and sausage tacos. The specialty is the *chupa,* a mixed-meat taco that contains 127 secret ingredients, or so they say. Avail yourself of the grilled onions, *nopales,* whole beans and other tasty toppings.

Mercado de Antojitos
MARKET $

(Map p103; Higuera 6; pozoles M$75, snacks from M$30; ☺ 9am-11pm; Ⓜ Coyoacán) Near Coyoacán's main plaza, this busy spot has all kinds of snacks, including deep-fried quesadillas, *pozoles* and *esquites* (boiled corn kernels served with a dollop of mayo). Look for the 'Pozole Estilo Michoacán' stall.

Picnic Helados
ICE CREAM $

(Map p103; ☑ 55-5510-9209; https://picnic-helados.negocio.site; Malintzin 205-2, Coyoacán; ice cream M$45-65; ☺ 11am-8pm Tue-Sun; ☑) A cone and a stroll is half the fun of Coyoacán. Picnic's organic *helados* (ice creams) and sorbets are the best around and miles ahead of the neon icy numbers on Coyoacán's plazas. Try creamy *mamey* (local fruit with a canteloupe–sweet potato flavour), dairy-free *guanábana* (soursop) or coffee with cardamom, depending on the season.

La Casa del Pan Papalotl

VEGETARIAN $$

(Map p103; ☑ 55-3095-1767; www.casadelpan. com; Av México 25; breakfasts M$125-165, mains M$90-150; ⊙ 8am-10pm; ☑; Ⓜ Coyoacán) This hugely popular vegetarian restaurant draws a loyal breakfast crowd thanks to its organic egg dishes, *chilaquiles* and fresh-made *pan* (bread). For lunch the lasagna with squash flowers, mushrooms and *poblano* chili is a big hit.

★ Los Danzantes

MEXICAN $$$

(Map p103; ☑ 55-6585-2477; www.losdanzantes. com; Jardín Centenario 12; mains M$155-370; ⊙ 12:30-11pm Mon-Thu, 9am-midnight Fri & Sat, 9am-11pm Sun; ☎☑⚄; Ⓜ Coyoacán) Los Danzantes puts a contemporary spin on traditional Mexican cuisine with dishes such as *huitlacoche* (trufflelike corn fungus) raviolis in *chile poblano* sauce, organic chicken in black *mole*, and *hoja santa* (Mexican pepperleaf) stuffed with cheese and *chipotle*. You'll also find top-shelf mezcal from its own famous distillery.

A different vegetarian option is featured each Monday.

During the 'Temporada de los Bichos' from early May to early June, dare to sample dishes featuring *escamoles* (ant larvae), *gusanos* (agave worms), *chicatanas* (flying ants) and other bugs.

Corazón de Maguey

MEXICAN $$$

(Map p103; ☑ 55-5659-3165; www.corazon demaguey.com; Jardín Centenario 9A; mains M$175-330; ⊙ 12:30pm-1am Mon, 9am-1am Tue-Thu, 9am-2am Fri & Sat, 9am-midnight Sun; ☎; Ⓜ Coyoacán) Adorned with old glass jugs used for transporting booze, this attractive restaurant does traditional Mexican fare that's typically prepared in mezcal-producing regions, such as stuffed *chile ancho* peppers from Queretaro, Oaxacan *tlayudas* and beef tongue in red *mole,* hailing from Puebla. It's also a prime spot to sample some of Mexico's finest mezcals.

Azul y Oro

MEXICAN $$$

(☑ 55-5424-1426; www.azul.rest; Centro Cultural Universitario, Av Insurgentes Sur 3000; mains M$135-350; ⊙ 10am-6pm Mon & Tue, to 8pm Wed-Sat, 9am-7pm Sun; Ⓟ☎; Ⓠ Centro Cultural Universitario) Chef Ricardo Muñoz searches Mexico high and low for traditional recipes and reinvents them to perfection. Fruits of his labor include *buñuelos rellenos de pato* (fried snacks filled with shredded duck and topped with *mole negro*) and *pescado tikin xic* (an elaborate grouper dish with plantain and tortilla strips). Azul y Oro is 8km southwest of Coyoacán. There's another branch downtown (p117).

✖ Tlalpan

La Voragine

ITALIAN $$

(☑ 55-2976-0313; Madero 107; mains M$90-140, pizzas M$135-245; ⊙ 1pm-2am Tue-Sat, to midnight Sun; ☎☑; Ⓠ Fuentes Brotantes) Run by a fun-loving couple from New York and CDMX, this muraled pizzeria-bar prepares savory pizzas, exquisite manicotti and *fungi trifolati* (flambéed mushrooms in white-wine sauce). Or just drop in for a Mexican microbrew and enjoy the sunny patio upstairs, or the occasional live music on Thursdays and Sundays. It's a half-block north of Tlalpan's main square.

✖ Colonia del Valle & Around

El Vilsito

MEXICAN $

(☑ 55-5682-7213; www.facebook.com/vilsitodia mante; Av Universidad, cnr Péten; tacos al pastor M$14; ⊙ 8pm-3am Mon-Thu, to 5am Fri & Sat, 4pm-midnight Sun; Ⓜ Eugenia) Auto-mechanic shop by day, taco diner by night. No worries, though: the experts slicing down those excellent *al pastor* (spit-cooked pork) tacos aren't the same ones rotating tyres. If you like *gringas* (wheat tortillas, pork and cheese), these old pros have been in the biz for 30 years. Just don't expect to find a seat at this post-party favourite.

El Rey de las Ahogadas

MEXICAN $

(☑ 55-5523-4989; Av Coyoacán 360, Colonia del Valle; flautas M$20-22, other snacks $27-55; ⊙ 11am-midnight Mon-Thu, to 1am Fri & Sat, to 11pm Sun; Ⓜ Poliforum) Deep-fried rolled tacos, aka *flautas,* are filled with your choice of refried beans, cheese, shredded beef, chicken, potato or marinated pork. They're topped with crumbled cheese, diced onion and served in a bowl of zesty *salsa verde. Flautas* are something of a fast-food staple throughout the city, but few can match the crunchy, spicy goodness of El Rey (The King).

Fonda Margarita MEXICAN $

(☑55-5559-6358; www.facebook.com/fonda
margarita; Adolfo Prieto 1354, Colonia Tlacoquemécatl del Valle; mains M$43-61; ⊙5:30am-noon
Tue-Sun; 🛜; 🚇Parque Hundido) Possibly the
capital's premier hangover-recovery spot,
this humble eatery under a tin roof whips
up batches of comfort food such as *longan-
iza en salsa verde* (sausage in green salsa)
and *frijoles con huevo* (beans with egg). The
fonda is beside Plaza Tlacoquemécatl, six
blocks east of Avenida Insurgentes.

It's years since the late Anthony Bourdain
visited, yet the queue remains – but it moves
fast.

🍸 Drinking & Nightlife

Cafes, bars and cantinas are all key social
venues on the capital's landscape. The traditional watering holes are, of course, cantinas – no-nonsense places with simple tables,
long polished bars and old-school waiters.
Alongside these, rustic *pulque* and mezcal
have returned as hip drinks.

🍸 Centro Histórico

Hostería La Bota BAR
(Map p74; ☑55-5709-9016; www.facebook.
com/labotacultubar; San Jerónimo 40; ⊙1pm-mid-
night Sun-Wed, to 2am Thu, to 3am Fri & Sat; 🛜;
Ⓜ Isabel La Católica) 🍷 *Cerveza,* mezcal
cocktails, tapas and deliciously oily pizza
are served amid a profusion of warped bullfighting bric-a-brac and recycled objects. A
portion of your bar tab sponsors local art
projects.

Cantina Tío Pepe BAR
(Map p74; ☑55-5521-9136; Independencia 26;
⊙noon-11pm Mon-Sat; Ⓜ San Juan de Letrán) A
must-visit on the downtown cantina crawl
circuit, Tío Pepe is one of the city's oldest
and most traditional watering holes. Over a
storied history that spans nearly 14 decades,
the saloon has poured *cerveza* and tequila
shots to influential Mexican politicians and
famous artists. It's said that author William
Burroughs wrote about this 'cheap cantina'
in *Junky.*

★ Bar La Ópera BAR
(Map p74; ☑55-5512-8959; www.barlaopera.
com; Av 5 de Mayo 10; ⊙1pm-midnight Mon-Sat,
to 6pm Sun; Ⓜ Allende) With booths of dark
walnut and an ornate copper-colored ceiling (said to have been punctured by Pancho
Villa's bullet), this late-19th-century water-

ing hole remains a bastion of tradition.
They serve some befittingly fine Mexican
meals too.

La Faena BAR
(Map p74; ☑55-5510-4417; Venustiano Carranza 49B; ⊙11am-11pm Mon-Thu, 10am-11:30pm
Fri-Sun; 🚇República del Salvador) This forgotten relic of a bar doubles as a bullfighting
museum, with matadors in sequined outfits
glaring intently from dusty cases, and bucolic canvases of grazing bulls. A new generation of younger, quietly cool drinkers have
rediscovered La Faena, helped by low beer
prices.

Farmacia Internacional CAFE
(Map p86; ☑55-5086-6220; Bucareli 128; coffee
M$35-45, breakfast M$45-90; ⊙8:30am-8pm Mon-
Fri, 9am-5pm Sat, 10am-4pm Sun; Ⓜ Balderas) A
perfect brunch spot to fuel up before a day
of exploring the Centro Histórico neighborhood. Head here for strong espresso-style
coffees with soy and macadamia milk options, housemade granola with yogurt, or
scrambled eggs and bacon on freshly baked
biscuits. They also have nice sandwiches, salads, and a selection of Mexican craft beers
available for lunch.

Bar Mancera BAR
(Map p74; ☑55-5521-9755; Venustiano Carranza
49; ⊙2-11pm Mon-Thu, to 2:30am Fri-Sun; 🚇Repú-
blica del Salvador) More than a century old, this
atmospheric gentlemen's salon is now open
to all but seems preserved in amber, with
ornate carved paneling and well-used dom-
ino tables. Regulars come for the good stuff:
mezcal and tequila as well as classics such as
gin and tonic, and Campari and orange.

Downtown Mexico BAR
(Map p74; ☑55-5282-2199; www.downtown
mexico.com; Isabel La Católica 30; ⊙10am-11pm
Sun-Thu, to 2am Fri & Sat; 🛜; Ⓜ Zócalo) The
rooftop lounge bar at boutique hotel Downtown Mexico has become a popular spot to
chill over drinks. It's also been known to
host the occasional pool party with open
bar and DJ sets.

🍸 Zona Rosa & Reforma

★ Xaman Bar COCKTAIL BAR
(Map p128; ☑55-4793-2614; https://xaman.bar;
Copenhague 6; ⊙6pm-2am; 🚇La Palma) This is
an underground bar, literally. Pass the hidden
entrance into the moody interior, and Xaman
resembles the laboratory of a cocktail cult.

Zona Rosa & Reforma

MEXICO CITY DRINKING & NIGHTLIFE

Zona Rosa & Reforma

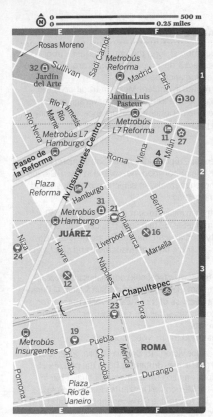

mole tamales (tamales in a spiced cacao sauce) or chalupas of mini-tortillas with chapulines for a savoury option. Pick up beautiful packaged chocolates as gifts...even if just for yourself.

🍷 Condesa

★Baltra   COCKTAIL BAR

(Map p120; ☑55-5264-1279; www.baltra.bar; Iztaccíhuatl 36D; ☺6pm-midnight Mon-Wed, 6pm-2am Thu-Sat, 6-11pm Sun; 🛜; ☒Campeche) This bar in affluent Condesa is dark enough to make everybody look lovely in a warm glow, with an excellent cocktail in hand. Knowledgeable, English-speaking staff can help work out what flavors you want, but a fine place to start is the 'Pacífica,' blending mezcal, cucumber and the right touch of habanero chili.

Baltra is the latest creation of lauded bar Licorería Limantour (p131) in Roma.

★Felina   COCKTAIL BAR

(Map p120; ☑55-5277-1917; Ometusco 87; ☺6pm-2am Tue-Sat; 🛜; Ⓜ Chilpancingo) Long-standing Felina has come of age. Quiet confidence is felt in its low-level music, and in cocktails that don't rely on sweetness but leverage real ingredients, such as fresh juniper berries in the gin.

Psychedelic wallpaper and vintage chairs give a nod to a 'funky' past, but times have changed, and the lounging crowd is well-dressed, but oh so casual.

Condesa df   BAR

(Map p120; ☑55-5241-2600; www.condesadf.com; Veracruz 102; ☺2-11pm Sun-Wed, noon-midnight Thu-Sat; 🛜; Ⓜ Chapultepec) The bar of the fashionable Condesa df hotel has become a popular stop on the Condesa circuit. Up on the roof, guests lounge on big-wheel wicker sofas and enjoy views of verdant Parque España across the way. There's suitably fashionable sushi for snacks.

Blend Station   COFFEE

(Map p120; http://blendstation.com.mx; Av Tamaulipas 60; coffee M$35-80; ☺8am-11pm Mon-Sat, 9am-10pm Sun; 🛜) A great spot for a morning coffee or an afternoon pick-me-up. Blend Station has one of the largest selections of Mexican coffee beans in the city, with serious attention given to small organic farmers in rural communities around the country. It's a favorite of caffeinated laptop warriors.

Herbs like sage daub smooth mezcal served in coconut shells, while smoke, capers and anise materialize from marble vessels. Designer spaces and drink names like 'astral travel' conjure a mystic-chic vibe. Wizardry aside, the cocktails are enchanting.

Sandwiches and other nibbles are available. Look for the doorbell to get in.

★La Rifa Chocolatería   CAFE

(Map p128; ☑55-9155-7684; Dinamarca 47, cnr Londres; drinks M$35-55; ☺8am-9pm Mon-Fri, 9am-9:30pm Sat, 9am-4pm Sun; 🛜; ☒Hamburgo) Pre-Hispanic cacao traditions are treated with artisanal respect at this pleasant outdoor plaza. The fermented hot chocolate has a deep, textured flavour. Choose water-based drinks for an authentic (as it was here thousands of years ago) yet creamy taste; you can ask for half-sweet or a touch of chilli.

The chocolate, mango and fig fruit salad and tarts are out of this world too. Or try

DON'T MISS

THE MEZCAL & PULQUE RENAISSANCE

In recent years the agave-based Mexican liquor mezcal, long thought of as just a poor rustic relative to tequila, has finally won the respect it deserves. Many bars around Mexico City now serve mezcal to a new breed of discerning aficionados.

A humbler kind of drinking establishment rooted in ancient Mexican tradition is the *pulquería*, which serves *pulque* (a pre-Hispanic, fermented alcoholic beverage made from the *maguey*). These places have also been experiencing a resurgence, with young *chilangos* rediscovering the joys of sharing a pitcher of the milky quaff.

Mezcalerías

Bósforo (Map p86; Luis Moya 31, cnr Independencia; ⊗6pm-midnight Tue-Sat; Ⓜ Juárez) Blink and you might walk right past the coolest neighborhood *mezcalería* in town. Behind the Bósforo's nondescript curtain await top-notch mezcals, an eclectic mix of music and surprisingly good bar grub in a dark and casual setting.

El Palenquito (Map p120; ☑55-5207-8617; http://en.milagrito.com; Av Álvaro Obregón 39, Roma Norte; ⊗6pm-midnight Mon-Wed, 6pm-2am Thu-Sat, 5-11pm Sun) This dark and dingy dive bar is one of the best spots in Mexico City for Oaxacan mezcal. Do as the locals do and sip yours alongside an ice-cold Victoria beer and a bowl of guacamole and *chicharrón* (fried pork fat).

Mano Santa Mezcal (Map p120; ☑55-3662-6088; www.facebook.com/manosantamezcal; Av Insurgentes Sur 219; mezcal M$85-160; ⊗4pm-2am Tue-Sat, to midnight Sun & Mon; Ⓡ Durango) Often compared to having a drink at home because of the cheap, quality mezcal (or because you live in a designer-school laboratory), this small bar quickly overflows with droves of the young and fashionable on weekends.

There's tacos, *tortas* and other Mexican bar food to line your stomach.

Alipús (☑55-6363-4375; www.alipus.com; Guadalupe Victoria 15, Colonia Tlalpan; ⊗12:30-11pm Sun-Wed, to midnight Thu & Fri, 10am-1am Sat; 🛜; Ⓡ Fuentes Brotantes) From the makers of the popular Oaxaca-based mezcal brands Alipús and Los Danzantes, this quaint bar in Tlalpan stocks some of the finest mezcal in all of Mexico (ie Danzantes Pechuga Roja). The regional *antojitos* (snacks) such as *tlayudas* (pizza-like Oaxacan topped tortilla) and Tlalpan-created soup *caldo tlalpeño* are wonderful as well.

La Clandestina (Map p120; www.milagrito.com; Álvaro Obregón 298, Colonia Roma; mezcal M$70-90; ⊗6pm-midnight Mon-Sat; Ⓡ Álvaro Obregón) Fashioned after a rural mom-and-pop shop, the Clandestina provides a detailed menu describing the distillation process of the mezcals, dispensed from jugs on high shelves.

In true clandestine fashion, the sign outside is tiny and for those in the know.

Pulquerías

Pulquería Los Insurgentes (Map p120; www.facebook.com/pulqueriainsurgentes; Av Insurgentes Sur 226; ⊗2pm-1:30am Sun-Wed, from 1pm Thu-Sat; Ⓡ Durango) A testament to the city's *pulque* revival, this three-story *porfiriato*-era house may not please the purists, but unlike a traditional *pulquería*, here you get live bands, DJ sets and other alcoholic drinks not called *pulque*.

Las Duelistas (Map p74; ☑55-1394-0958; www.facebook.com/pulquerialasduelistas; Aranda 28; ⊗10am-9pm Mon-Sat; Ⓡ Plaza San Juan) Now graffitied with pre-Hispanic psychedelia, this classic *pulquería* has been rediscovered by young artists and musicians. Despite this, the *pulque* (in a variety of flavors) is still dispensed straight from the barrel.

Pulquería La Botijona (Av Morelos 109, Xochimilco; ⊗10am-10pm; Ⓡ Xochimilco) Possibly the cleanest *pulque* dispenser in town, this institutional green hall near the Xochimilco train station is a friendly, family-run establishment with big plastic pails of the traditional quaff lining the shelves.

Flora Lounge　　　　　　　　BAR
(Map p120; Michoacán 54, cnr Av Nuevo León; ⊙9am-midnight Mon-Wed, to 1am Thu & Sat, to 2am Fri; 🛜; 🚇 Campeche) Condesa is overflowing with bars, but gay-friendly Flora Lounge strikes the right balance between good, fairly priced cocktails and drinks, and a casual-cute bistro atmosphere.

Flora serves an excellent range of Mexican and international food.

Pastelería Maque　　　　　　CAFE
(Map p120; ☑55-5212-1440; www.facebook. com/PasteleriasMaque; Av Ozuluama 4; ⊙8am-10pm Mon-Sat, to 9pm Sun; 🛜; 🚇 Campeche) Condesa sophisticates gather for coffee in the mornings and Irish coffee in the evenings at this Parisian-style cafe-bakery near Parque México. Waiters bring around trays of freshly baked croissants and *conchas* (round pastries sprinkled with sugar).

El Centenario　　　　　　　BAR
(Map p120; ☑55-5553-5451; Vicente Suárez 42; ⊙noon-midnight Mon & Tue, to 2am Wed-Sat; 🛜; 🚇 Campeche) Laden with bullfighting memorabilia, this dark cantina with unrenovated tiles and brick arches is an enclave of tradition amid the modish restaurant and bar zone. Not a place to dress up for, but great to start the night with fair prices on beer, mezcal, tequila and rum.

Tomás　　　　　　　　　TEAHOUSE
(Map p120; ☑55-4444-3918; http://tomas.mx; Av Tamaulipas 66; tea M$50-80; ⊙8am-10pm Mon-Fri, 9am-10pm Sat & Sun; 🛜) This artisanal teahouse has walls lined with teas from around the world. Order one to enjoy with a cake or cookie, or buy a jar to take back home with you.

🍴 Roma

★Licorería Limantour　　COCKTAIL BAR
(Map p120; ☑55-5264-4122; https://limantour.tv; Av Álvaro Obregón 106, Roma Norte; cocktails M$150-300; ⊙6pm-midnight Mon & Tue, to 1am Wed, to 2am Thu-Sat, to 11pm Sun; 🛜) This romantically lit cocktail bar regularly ranks as one of the top 50 bars in the world and the best bar in Latin America. The service and cocktails certainly live up to the hype, and thanks to the headlines this is also one of the busiest spots in Mexico City. Arrive early to get a table.

★Departamento　　　　　　CLUB
(Map p120; ☑55-2855-9154; www.departa mento.tv; 1st fl, Av Álvaro Obregón 154; club cov-er Wed M$100, Thu-Sat M$150; ⊙bar 6pm-2am Tue-Sat, upstairs club 9pm-3am Tue-Sat; 🚇 Álvaro Obregón) This upstairs club-performance space is like being invited to Roma's coolest friend-of-a-friend's apartment for an intimate live performance or dance in their living room. Quality cocktails and beers help the mix of visitors and cool locals mingle. Check the website for the calendar of Mexican and international musicians and DJs, who have included Sotomayor and the Rapture.

The street-level bar 'Departamento PB' is a stylish place to drink and pose.

★La Chicha　　　　　　　BAR
(Map p120; ☑55-5574-6625; Orizaba 171; ⊙noon-midnight Mon-Wed, to 2am Thu-Sat, 9am-11pm Sun; 🛜; 🚇 Hospital General) Mix one part Mexican vintage decor, one shot of rock vibe and throw in mezcal, beer and snacks (including veg options) and you have a bar full to its low-lit brim. Part of a growing row of bars that are too cool for the swankiness of Álvaro Obregón – with posing staff to match.

At lunch the *menú del día* (from M$130) usually includes interesting dishes such as falafel burgers and kale soup.

Falling Piano Brewing Co.　　MICROBREWERY
(Map p120; ☑55-7705-6145; Coahuila 99; ⊙4-11pm Mon & Tue, to midnight Wed, 2pm-2am Thu & Fri, noon-2am Sat, to 10pm Sun) A great addition to CDMX's craft-beer scene, this Roma Sur bar is one of few that make beer onsite. You'll pass the barrels as you walk through the entrance and upstairs to the spacious bar. Strong IPAs, fruity pale ales and rich porters all are reasonably priced for the area.

There's also Jenga to keep you entertained.

Bar Félix　　　　　　COCKTAIL BAR
(Map p120; ☑55-5264-0318; Álvaro Obregón 64, Roma Norte; ⊙6pm-2am Tue-Sat; 🛜; Ⓜ Niños Heroes) This trendy cocktail bar oozes chicness. Rooms are dimly lit; the tables are small; and the menu uses the word 'artisanal' in several instances. Cocktails are some of the best in Roma, and there's also a selection of mezcal and craft beer.

Traspatio　　　　　　BEER GARDEN
(Map p120; www.facebook.com/traspatiomx; cnr Córdoba & Colima; ⊙1:30pm-midnight Tue & Wed, to 2am Thu-Sat, 10am-10pm Sun; 🛜; 🚇 Durango) For the urban backyard-barbecue experience, this open-air beer garden is a fine choice.

It's a great little hideaway for chatting over a *cerveza*, mezcal, wine or gin and munching on a *choripán* (grilled sausage in a roll), tuna steak, vegan meatballs or portobello-mushroom burger.

Traspatio welcomes kids, just avoid the smoking area.

Patrick Miller CLUB
(Map p128; ☑ 55-5511-5406; www.facebook.com/PatrickMillerMX; Mérida 17; M$30; ⊙ 9pm-3am Fri; M Insurgentes) People-watching doesn't get any better than at this throbbing retro club, founded by Mexico City DJ Patrick Miller. With a clientele ranging from black-clad '80s throwbacks to cross-dressers and office workers gone wild, the Friday fun begins when dance circles open and regulars pull off moves that would make John Travolta proud. Beer is cheap, if you can make it through the crowds.

Dosis CAFE
(Map p120; ☑ 55-6840-6941; http://dosiscafe.com; Av Álvaro Obregón 24B, Roma Norte; ⊙ 9am-9pm Mon-Fri, from 10am Sat, from 11am Sun; ☎) Hip Roma locals flock to this chic cafe day and night; you can sit for hours at an outdoor table using the strong wi-fi and sipping an espresso, a cold brew with soy milk or a bottled craft beer. There's a small selection of salads and an incredibly indulgent dessert cabinet. We highly recommend the blondies.

Cantina Covadonga BAR
(Map p128; ☑ 55-5533-2701; www.banquetescovadonga.com.mx; Puebla 121; ⊙ 1pm-2am Mon-Sat, to 7pm Sun; M Insurgentes) Echoing with the sounds of clacking dominoes, this brightly lit old Asturian social hall is a traditionally male enclave, though hipsters of both sexes have increasingly moved in on this hallowed ground.

Spanish and Mexican dishes go down well with tequila, mezcal or wine; and the lack of music makes Covadonga good for chats without shouting.

La Bodeguita del Medio BAR
(Map p120; ☑ 55-5553-0246; www.labodeguitadelmedio.com.mx; Cozumel 37; ⊙ 1:30pm-2am Mon-Sat, to 12:30am Sun; M Sevilla) The walls are tagged with verses and messages at this animated re-creation of a famous Havana joint. A mojito (a Cuban drink of rum, lime juice and mint leaves) and the excellent *son cubano* combos that perform here often spark spontaneous dancing.

Jardín Chapultepec BEER GARDEN
(Map p128; www.facebook.com/jardinchapultepec.mx; Av Chapultepec 398, Colonia Roma; ⊙ 1-10pm Tue-Thu, 1-11pm Fri, 11am-11pm Sat, 11am-10pm Sun; ☎ ☎; M Insurgentes) This buzzy beer garden pours hoppy Mexican craft brew, and grills a mighty fine burger. You may find yourself sharing a picnic bench in the perpetually packed garden, but that just makes for a more convivial experience when knocking 'em back. As its name suggests, it's about a 15-minute walk from the east entrance of Bosque de Chapultepec.

 Polanco

Fiebre de Malta BEER HALL
(Map p92; ☑ 55-5531-6826; www.fiebredemalta.com; Av Presidente Masaryk 48; ⊙ noon-midnight Mon-Thu, to 2am Fri & Sat, to 10pm Sun; ☎; M Polanco) A pioneer of Mexico City's craft-beer boom, Fiebre de Malta has more than 30 brews on tap, with suds ranging from hoppy IPAs to German-style Hefeweizens. The menu describes the characteristics of each beer, including their origin and flavor details.

The large beer hall also does pub grub if you get the munchies.

La Terraza COCKTAIL BAR
(Área; Map p92; ☑ 55-5282-3100; www.hotelhabita.com; Av Presidente Masaryk 201; ⊙ 7pm-2am; ☎; M Polanco) Atop the designer Hábita Hotel, this open-air roof lounge does a brisk trade in exotic martinis, with sweeping city views as a backdrop and videos projected on the wall of a nearby building.

 San Ángel

La Camelia BAR
(Map p100; ☑ 55-5615-5643; Madero 3; ⊙ noon-8pm Sun-Thu, to 2am Fri & Sat; 🚃 La Bombilla) This restaurant-cantina has been drawing Mexican celebrities to San Ángel since 1931, evidenced by the stars' photos on the walls. On Friday and Saturday karaoke nights, it's your time to shine. Liquid courage comes in the form of tequila or *cerveza mexicana*. When we visited, the drinks outshone the food.

 Coyoacán

⭐ **Cantina La Coyoacana** BAR
(Map p103; http://lacoyoacana.com; Higuera 14; ⊙ 1pm-midnight Sun-Wed, to 1:45am Thu-Sat;

LGBTIQ+ MEXICO CITY

Since Mexico City approved a same-sex marriage law (with two-thirds of Mexican states following suit), the capital has been seen as a bastion of tolerance in an otherwise conservative country. During the annual Pride event, the city's mayor, Claudia Sheinbaum, tweeted a photo of government buildings resplendent in rainbow flags, declaring CDMX 'pluricultural.'

The longtime heart of gay life is Zona Rosa – in particular Calle Amberes – yet many night owls prefer the grungier downtown scene along República de Cuba. **GayCities** (http://mexicocity.gaycities.com) has useful information on gay-friendly hotels, bars and clubs. The Marcha del Orgullo Gay (Gay Pride) takes place one Saturday each June and sashays along Paseo de la Reforma from El Ángel to the Zócalo.

The **Clínica Condesa** (📞55-5515-8311; http://condesacdmx.mx; Gral Benjamín Hill 24; ⏱7am-5pm Mon-Fri; 🚇De La Salle) is a flagship health center specializing in sexual health, especially (but not only) LGBTIQ+ issues, with rapid HIV and STI tests, treatment and prevention, such as PEP medication, at no charge and without appointment, even for foreigners.

Look out for irregularly hosted alternative-queer parties **Traición** (www.instagram.com/traiciondf) and **BonBon Condesa** (Map p120; Av Nuevo León 163; cover from M$250; ⏱11pm-5am Thu monthly; 🚇Chilpancingo).

La Purísima (Map p74; www.facebook.com/Lapuri.oficial; República de Cuba 17, Colonia Centro; ⏱6pm-3am Thu-Sat; 🚇Bellas Artes) La Purísima is essentially two clubs in one: join the young, sweaty throng downstairs with dance hits, or head upstairs for mezcal, *pulque* and ironically bad/hip music. Drinks are cheap, but hold on tight as it gets crowded. Come early to avoid very long queues.

Marrakech Salón (Map p74; República de Cuba 18; cover charge after 9pm M$50; ⏱6pm-2:30am Wed-Sat; 🚇Allende) Typical sights and sounds at this gay bar include bare-chested bartenders serving cheap drinks, bar-top drag shows and festive music ranging from '80s pop to hip-shaking *cumbias* and current diva hits in English. It gets very crowded and sweaty, but no one seems deterred.

Tom's Leather Bar (Map p120; 📞55-5564-0728; www.toms-mexico.com; Av Insurgentes Sur 357; cover incl beer M$150-200; ⏱9pm-3am Tue-Sun; 🐾; 🚇Campeche) For those who dare to get medieval, Tom's provides the props, with heraldic shields and candelabras highlighting a decidedly decadent decor and a notorious dark room that must be crossed to reach the bathroom. Bears, cubs and daddies wear the crown here, though less so on busy Tuesdays.

Rico Club (Map p128; www.facebook.com/ricoclubcdmx; Niza 45; ⏱7pm-3am Wed-Sat, 5pm-2am Sun; 🚇Insurgentes) Three levels of house and retro might sound like your average Zona Rosa gay club, but it's the roof garden, cool student crowd and local drag stars that lure queues that can stretch around the block on weekends. It's grungy fun but hey, actor Ezra Miller has been spotted here twice.

Nicho Bears & Bar (Map p128; www.bearmex.com; Londres 182; ⏱8:30pm-2am Thu-Sat; 🚇Insurgentes) Popular with the 30-something crowd, this small Zona Rosa bear den has a slightly more mature air than many of the bars lining the raucous gay strip on nearby Amberes.

🐾; 🚇Coyoacán) Enter through the swinging saloon-style doors and head straight to the open-air patio, where wailing mariachis do their thing in this traditional drinking establishment – the most famous of Coyoacán.

There's also an ample menu of snacks and mains (M$145 to M$250).

Café Negro CAFE
(Map p103; www.cafenegrocoyoacan.com; Jardín del Centenario 16; coffee M$33-49, snacks M$65-75; ⏱8am-11pm; 🐾; 🚇Coyoacán) The best coffee for miles around with industrial-chic lamps to get some wi-fi-heavy work done. *Nopal* ciabatta, fig salad, vegetarian pasta and Mexican pastries are some of the snack offerings.

La Bipo BAR
(Map p103; ☑55-5484-8230; https://labipo.
com.mx; Malintzin 155; ☉noon-midnight Sun-Tue,
to 2am Wed-Sat; ☎; Ⓜ Coyoacán) This mock
cantina plays up the kitschier elements of
Mexican popular culture, with wall panels
fashioned from plastic crates and sliced tin
buckets as light shades. The menu of Mexican snacks is hit and miss, but good-value
drinks draw young punters. DJs spin assorted tunes upstairs from Wednesday to
Saturday.

Café El Jarocho CAFE
(Map p103; ☑55-5658-5029; www.facebook.
com/cafeljarocho; Cuauhtémoc 134; ☉6:30am-
1am Sun-Thu, to 2am Fri & Sat; Ⓜ Coyoacán) This
immensely popular, iconic joint churns out
coffee from Veracruz for long lines of bean
lovers – the *café de olla,* with a touch of cinnamon and other spices is a hit. As there's
no seating inside, people have their drink
standing in the street or sitting on curbside
benches.

A **branch** (Map p103; ☑55-5659-9107;
www.facebook.com/cafeljarocho; Av México 25C;
☉6am-11pm; Ⓜ Coyoacán) with seats is several
blocks northwest of Jardín Centenario.

Tlalpan

La Jalisciense BAR
(☑55-5573-5586; Plaza de la Constitución 6;
☉noon-11:30pm Mon-Sat; 🚍 Fuentes Brotantes)
This building opened its doors in 1870, making La Jalisciense arguably the oldest cantina in Mexico City – now that's a good reason
to pop in and wet your whistle with one of
their many tequilas while perusing the old
framed photos. The small *tortas* and Spanish dishes are also worthy.

Colonia del Valle

Passmar CAFE
(☑55-5669-1994; http://cafepassmar.com; Adolfo Prieto s/n, Local 237, cnr Av Coyoacán; ☉7am-
7:30pm; ☎; 🚍 Amores) You'll be hard-pressed
to find a place that takes a cup of joe more
seriously than Passmar, whose baristas have
won national awards. Unfancy-looking Passmar is in Mercado Lázaro Cárdenas, a block
and a half southwest of metrobús Amores.

☆ Entertainment

Cinema

Mexico City is a banquet for movie-goers,
with everything from open-air screenings,

film festivals and art-house cinema to block-
busters, many from the strong Mexican
film-production industry. Ticket prices are
around M$75, with many places offering
discounts on Wednesday. Most movies are
available in original languages with Spanish
subtitles (look for 'SUB' rather than 'ESP',
which is dubbed), except for children's fare.
Check individual cinema websites under
'cartelera' for screening times.

★ Cineteca Nacional CINEMA
(Map p103; ☑55-4155-1200; www.cineteca
nacional.net; Av México–Coyoacán 389, Colonia
Xoco; ☎; Ⓜ Coyoacán) Mexican and foreign
indie movies are shown daily on 10 screens
at the architecturally interesting Cineteca
in Coyoacán in the south. In November
the large complex hosts the Muestra Internacional de Cine, an international film
festival. From October to March you can
catch free open-air screenings at dusk in
the grass-covered rear garden.

The onsite **Galería de la Cineteca Nacional** is dedicated to Mexican cinema with
exhibitions related to international film.

Cine Tonalá CINEMA
(Map p120; www.cinetonala.com; Tonalá 261;
films M$65; ☎; 🚍 Campeche) A small, cool
multipurpose venue in Roma Sur for independent cinema, plays, stand-up comedy
and concerts.

Cinemex Casa de Arte CINEMA
(Cinemex Reforma; Map p128; ☑55-5257-6969;
www.cinemex.com; Río Guadalquivir 104; tickets
adult/child M$87/64; Ⓜ Insurgentes) Both art-
house and blockbuster flicks near El Ángel
and Reforma.

Filmoteca de la UNAM CINEMA
(☑55-5704-6338; www.filmoteca.unam.mx; Av
Insurgentes Sur 3000; films free-M$50; 🚍 Centro
Cultural Universitario) Two cinemas at the Centro Cultural Universitario of UNAM in the
south screen art and indie films from a collection of more than 43,000 titles, mostly in
Spanish. Many sessions have free admission;
check *'programación'* on the website.

Dance, Classical Music & Theater

Orchestral music, opera, ballet, contemporary dance and theater are all abundantly
represented in the capital's numerous theaters. Museums, too, serve as performance
venues (often for free), including the Museo
de la Secretaría de Hacienda y Crédito Público (p81) and the Museo de la Ciudad de

México (p84). The national arts council (www.mexicoescultura.com) provides a run-down of events on its website.

If your Spanish is up to it, you might like to sample Mexico City's lively theater scene. *Mejor Teatro* (www.mejorteatro.com) covers the major venues.

Palacio de Bellas Artes
PERFORMING ARTS

(Map p74; www.inba.gob.mx; Av Hidalgo 1; ☺ box office 11am-7pm; Ⓜ Bellas Artes) The Orquesta Sinfónica Nacional and prestigious opera companies perform in Bellas Artes' ornate theater, while chamber groups appear in the recital halls. The venue is most famous, though, for the **Ballet Folklórico de México** (Map p74; www.balletfolklorico demexico.com.mx; tickets from M$365; ☺ performances 8:30pm Wed, 9:30am & 9pm Sun), a two-hour festive blur of costumes, music and dance from all over Mexico. Tickets are usually available on the day of the show or from Ticketmaster.

Free guided tours of the theater are available in Spanish on Tuesdays and Fridays at 1pm and 1.30pm. Reserve by phone (☏ 55-8647-6500).

Salón Los Ángeles
DANCING

(☏ 55-5597-5181; www.salonlosangeles.mx; Lerdo 206, Colonia Guerrero; M$50; ☺ 5-11pm Tue & Sun; Ⓜ Tlatelolco) Fans of dance-hall music should not miss the outstanding orchestras or the graceful dancers who fill the vast floor of this atmospheric ballroom from 1937. The live music, consisting of salsa and *cumbia* (dance music originating in Colombia) on Sunday and swing and *danzón* on Tuesday, draws a mostly older crowd. It's located in the rough Colonia Guerrero, so take an authorized taxi or Uber.

Two-hour dance classes are offered on Monday at 6pm and Tuesday at 4pm.

Centro Nacional de las Artes
PERFORMING ARTS

(CENART; ☏ 55-4155-0000; www.cenart.gob.mx; Av Río Churubusco 79, Colonia Country Club; ☎; Ⓜ General Anaya) This sprawling cultural institute near Coyoacán has many free events across the artistic spectrum, including contemporary dance, theater, art shows and classical concerts. To get here, exit metro General Anaya (Línea 2) on the east side of Calzada de Tlalpan, then walk north to the corner and turn right.

Teatro de la Ciudad
CONCERT VENUE

(Esperanza Iris; Map p74; ☏ 55-5130-5740, ext 2006; http://teatros.cultura.cdmx.gob.mx; Donceles 36; ☺ box office 11am-2:30pm & 4-7pm Tue-Sun; Ⓜ Allende) Built in 1918 and modeled after Milan's La Scala opera house, this lavishly restored 1300-seat hall gets some of the more interesting touring acts in music, dance and theater.

Live Music

Mexico City's eclectic music offerings rock. On any given night, you can hear traditional Mexican, Cuban, jazz, electronica, garage, punk and so on. Music sounds off everywhere: in concert halls, bars, museums – even on public transportation. Free gigs often take place at the Zócalo and Monumento a la Revolución, while the thriving mariachi scene at Plaza Garibaldi gets going by about 8pm and stays busy until 3am. Both *Tiempo Libre* (www.tiempolibredigital.com.mx) and Ticketmaster (www.ticketmaster.com.mx) include show listings.

The grungy street market Tianguis Cultural del Chopo (p140) has a stage at its north end every Saturday afternoon for young and hungry metal and punk bands.

★ Salón Tenampa
LIVE MUSIC

(Map p74; ☏ 55-5526-6176; https://salontenampa.com; Plaza Garibaldi 12; ☺ 1pm-1am Sun-Thu, to 2am Fri & Sat; ☎; Ⓜ Garibaldi) Graced with murals of the giants of Mexican song and enlivened by its own songsters – and an extensive tequila, mezcal and food menu – Tenampa is a festive cantina on the north side of Plaza Garibaldi. If serenading at other tables is not enough, request a song (M$50 to M$100)

TICKETS

Ticketmaster sells tickets for all the major venues online (www.ticketmaster.com.mx), or visit one of its branches:

Liverpool Centro (Map p74; Venustiano Carranza 92; ☺ 11am-7pm; Ⓜ Zócalo)

Liverpool Polanco (Map p92; Mariano Escobedo 425; ☺ 11am-8pm; Ⓜ Polanco)

Mixup Centro (Map p74; Av Madero 51; ☺ 10am-9pm Mon-Sat, 11am-8pm Sun; Ⓜ Zócalo)

Mixup Zona Rosa (Map p128; Génova 76; ☺ 11am-8pm; Ⓜ Insurgentes)

from the mariachi, originating from across the country. A visit here is obligatory.

The Mexican food menu includes plenty of shareable snacks, meat grills and vegetarian enchiladas.

Casa Franca
JAZZ
(Map p120; ☑ 55-5533-8754; www.facebook.com/lacasamerida109; Mérida 109; ◷5pm-1am Tue & Wed, to 2am Thu-Sat; 🛜; 🚇Jardín Pushkin) **FREE** This upstairs bar is a labyrinth with more moods than a house party. The live jazz plays out in an intimate living room, while the corner balcony overlooking Álvaro Obregón captures that twinkle of Saturday night. The other (extremely) dark corners are made for lounging, sipping great cocktails and hand holding. Reservations recommended.

Centro Cultural de España
LIVE MUSIC
(Map p74; ☑ 55-5521-1925; www.ccemx.org; República de Guatemala 18; ◷10pm-2am Wed-Sat; Ⓜ Zócalo) Cool young things pack the terrace of this place each weekend for its excellent DJ and live-music sessions. Located directly behind the cathedral, the rebuilt colonial-era structure is usually quaking by midnight.

Parker & Lenox
LIVE MUSIC
(Map p128; ☑ 55-7893-3140; www.facebook.com/parkerandlenox; Milán 14; ◷1pm-1am Tue, to 2am Wed-Sat; 🛜; 🚇Reforma) Named after legendary saxophonist Charlie Parker and famed Harlem jazz club Lenox Lounge, Parker & Lenox is part American-style diner (specializing in hamburgers, M$140 to M$180), part backroom bar (cocktails M$140 to M$200) and concert venue featuring live jazz, blues, funk and swing bands. Groups take the stage around 10:30pm; reserve ahead for a table.

Cafebrería El Péndulo
LIVE MUSIC
(Foro del Tejedor; Map p120; ☑ 55-7470-34; www.forodeltejedor.com; Álvaro Obregón 86; events M$150-300; 🛜; 🚇Álvaro Obregón) Leading Mexican and Latin American artists of varying musical genres (especially acoustic guitar, tango and jazz) play at this cafe-bookstore's intimate rooftop venue in Roma. The adjoining open-air bar provides a nice atmosphere for hanging out after the show.

Multiforo Alicia
CONCERT VENUE
(Map p120; ☑ 55-5511-2100; http://twitter.com/multiforoalicio; Av Cuauhtémoc 91A; 🚇Jardín Pushkin) Behind the graffiti-scrawled facade is Mexico City's premier indie-rock club. A suitably dark, seatless space, the Alicia stages mostly up-and-coming punk, surf and ska bands, who hawk their music at the store downstairs. See their social media pages for show times.

Zinco Jazz Club
JAZZ
(Map p74; ☑ 55-5512-3369; www.zincojazz.com; Motolinía 20; events M$150-300; ◷9pm-midnight Wed-Fri, to 2am Sat; 🛜; Ⓜ Allende) A vital component in the rebirth of the *centro,* Zinco is a subterranean supper club featuring local jazz and funk outfits, as well as touring artists and tribute acts to Sinatra and Winehouse. The intimate basement room fills up fast when big-name acts take the stage.

LUCHA LIBRE

One of Mexico City's two wrestling venues, the 17,000-seat **Arena México** (Lucha Libre; CMLL; Map p120; ☑ 55-5588-0266; https://cmll.com; Dr Lavista 197, Colonia Doctores; tickets M$40-210; ◷7:30pm Tue, 8:30pm Fri, 5pm Sun; 🚇Cuauhtémoc) is taken over by a circus atmosphere each week, with flamboyant *luchadores* (wrestlers) such as Místico and Sam Adonis going at each other in tag teams or one-on-one. There are three or four bouts, building up to the headline match. Intermissions feature folkloric dancers. Tickets are nearly always available at the door.

Ignore claims by touts outside arenas that the match is sold out. The cheap seats may be higher up behind a wire fence, but this is where the most raucous locals sit, making it the most atmospheric spot for heckling the wrestlers. If you want to be close enough to smell the action from the pricier seats near the front, book in advance for Fridays (pick up tickets from window 1). Reasonably priced beers and other beverages can be bought and taken to your seat, or have your usher bring you drinks and snacks for a tip. No entrance with food or water. From this sketchy Doctores neighborhood, it's best to walk west in the direction of Roma rather than east.

Also check out the smaller, intimate **Arena Coliseo** (Map p74; ☑ 55-5526-1687; República de Perú 77; tickets M$40-210; ◷7:30pm Sat; 🚇República de Chile).

Pan y Circo
LIVE MUSIC

(Map p120; ☎ 55-2301-9522; www.facebook. com/panycircomxdf; Álavaro Obregón 160, Colonia Roma; ⊘ 6pm-midnight Mon-Wed, to 2am Thu-Sat; ☎; ▣ Álavaro Obregón) In trendy Roma, this three-story bar makes a nice place to unwind over mezcal or cocktails, especially during the week when the crowd thins out. On the 2nd floor you can catch live music on Thursday to Saturday nights in an interior patio, while upstairs you'll find a smoker-friendly *terraza* bar. See the Facebook page for weekly events.

El Bataclán
CABARET

(Map p120; ☎ 55-5511-7390; www.labodega. rest/eventos; Popocatépetl 25; ⊘ 9pm-midnight Tue & Wed, to 2am Thu-Sat; ▣ Álvaro Obregón) A theater within a fine restaurant (La Bodega), this classic cabaret venue showcases some of Mexico's more offbeat performers. Afterwards, catch top-notch Cuban *son combos* over a rum-based mojito.

El Hijo del Cuervo
LIVE MUSIC

(Map p103; ☎ 55-5658-7824; www.elhijodelcuervo. com.mx; Jardín Centenario 17; ⊘ 3pm-midnight Mon, 1pm-12:30am Tue-Sat, noon-midnight Sun; Ⓜ Coyoacán) A Coyoacán institution, this stone-walled bar around the central plaza stages jazz and rock groups on Tuesday, Wednesday and Thursday nights.

Check the website for other events in Spanish.

Cabaret

La Perla
CABARET

(Map p74; ☎ 55-3916-2699; www.facebook. com/cabaret.laperla; República de Cuba 44; M$150; ⊘ 8pm-2:30am, showtimes 11pm & 1am Fri & Sat; ▣ República de Chile) Once a red-light venue, this cabaret has been reborn in the age of irony as a cradle of kitsch, with hilarious drag shows featuring traditional Mexican songstresses. Between shows the dance floor opens. Tickets go fast; reservations are possible by direct online messenger or turn up by 9pm for a table, cash only.

Teatro Bar El Vicio
CABARET

(Map p103; ☎ 55-5659-1139; www.elvicio.com. mx; Madrid 13, Colonia del Carmen; tickets M$300-400; ⊘ 9:30pm-2am Thu-Sun, box office 2-8pm Tue-Sat; Ⓜ Coyoacán) With liberal doses of politically and sexually irreverent comedy and a genre-bending musical program, all in Spanish, this alternative cabaret is appropriately located in Frida Kahlo's old stomping ground.

Sports

The capital stages *fútbol* matches in the national Primera División almost every weekend of the year. Mexico City has three teams: América, nicknamed Las Águilas (the Eagles); Las Pumas of UNAM; and Cruz Azul. There are two seasons: January to June and July to December, each ending in eight-team play-offs and a two-leg final to decide the champion. The biggest match of all is El Clásico, between América and Guadalajara, which fills the **Estadio Azteca** (☎ 55-5487-3100; www.estadioazteca.com. mx; Calz de Tlalpan 3665; ▣ Estadio Azteca) with 100,000 flag-waving fans. Get tickets in advance for this one.

Tickets to *fútbol* matches (M$90 to M$650 for regular-season games) are usually available at the gate, or from Ticketmaster (p135). There are several stadiums that host games, including **Estadio Azul** (☎ 55-5563-9535; http://cruzazulfc.com.mx; Indiana 255, Colonia Nápoles; ▣ Ciudad de los Deportes) for Cruz Azul matches and Estadio Olímpico (p101) to see UNAM's Pumas play.

Mexico City has one *béisbol* (baseball) team in the Liga Mexicana de Béisbol, the Diablos Rojos. During the regular season (from April to July) it plays every other week at **Foro Sol** (http://diablos.com.mx; cnr Avs Río Churubusco & Viaducto Río de la Piedad, Colonia Granjas México; Ⓜ Ciudad Deportiva). From the metro, it's a five-minute walk to the ballpark. See the website for game times.

Most of the daily newspapers have a generous sports section where you can find out who is playing with which ball where. True enthusiasts should look for **La Afición** (www.laaficion.com), a daily devoted to sports.

Frontón México
SPECTATOR SPORT

(Jai Alai; Map p86; https://frontonmexico.com. mx/jai-alai; Plaza de la República 17, Colonia Tabacalera; tickets M$220; ⊘ ticket office 10am-6pm Mon-Wed, 10am-9pm Thu-Sun; Ⓜ Revolución) The lovely art deco building Frontón México hosts professional jai alai matches, one of the world's fastest ball sports, resembling squash. If you've never seen jai alai played live, you're in for a real treat. The season normally runs from March through June, but check the website for schedules. Frontón México doubles as a casino and expo hall.

🛍 Shopping

Shopping can be a real joy in Mexico City, with *artesanías* vendors, quirky shops and street markets all competing for your pesos. Most of the main museum gift stores stock unique, higher-quality designer *artesanías*. *Lucha libre* wrestling masks are sold outside arenas and at the main *artesanía* markets.

🛍 Centro Histórico & Around

★ Centro de Artesanías
La Ciudadela   ARTS & CRAFTS
(Map p86; 🗗 55-5510-1828; http://laciudadela. com.mx; cnr Balderas & Dondé; ⊙10am-7pm Mon-Sat, to 6pm Sun; Ⓜ Balderas) A favorite destination for good, and also mass-produced, handicrafts from all over Mexico. Worth seeking out are Oaxaca *alebrijes*, hand-painted Talavera tiles from Puebla, guitars from Paracho and Huichol beadwork. Stock up on sun hats for Teotihuacán and wrestling masks. Prices are generally fair, even before you bargain.

Take a break at the *fonda* at its centre. Outside are stalls selling books and vintage vinyl records.

★ Mercado San Juan   MARKET
(Map p86; www.mercadosanjuan.galeon.com; Pugibet 21; ⊙8am-5pm Mon-Sat, to 4pm Sun; 🚇 Plaza San Juan) Small market specializing in top-price gourmet food items such as *huitlacoche*, insects, *mole* pastes, crocodile, ostrich, deer and rare fruit. Local chefs and foodies come here to score ingredients not available elsewhere in the city. Eat the produce fresh at stalls with juices, paella and ceviche.

★ Plaza Downtown Mexico   MALL
(Map p74; http://theshops.mx; Isabel La Católica 30; ⊙11am-8pm Mon-Sat, to 6pm Sun; Ⓜ Zócalo) Shops surrounding the central courtyard of a beautifully restored, 18th-century colonial-era building sell upmarket crafts, ceramics, chocolate and clothes. For a shopping break, there are sleek restaurants to match.

★ Barrio Alameda   GIFTS & SOUVENIRS
(Map p86; 🗗 55-5512-3810; www.barrioalameda. com; Dr Mora 9; ⊙8am-11pm Sun-Wed, to 1am Thu, to 2am Fri & Sat; 🛜; Ⓜ Hidalgo) Enter this converted art deco building at the edge of the Alameda for inspired shopping, where plants drip from sleek railings and soft lamps. Three levels of boutiques showcase locally designed clothing, jewelry, furniture and gifts, plus stores dedicated to vinyl, photography and sports collectibles. Rest for good pizza, coffee and mezcal on the ground level or the rooftop restaurant with park views.

Mercado de la Merced   MARKET
(cnr Anillo de Circunvalación & General Anaya; ⊙6am-7pm Mon-Sat, to 4pm Sun; Ⓜ Merced) This gigantic market, Mexico City's largest, occupies four whole blocks dedicated to the buying and selling of daily needs, with photogenic displays of spices, chilies and every fresh Mexican foodstuff imaginable, from ant larvae to candied fruit. An atmospheric eating area serves all varieties of fresh tacos, moles and *tlacoyos* (pork- or cheese-filled oval tortillas).

On December 24, 2019, a fire burnt down 630 stalls and it will take some years to repair. Affected storeholders continue to sell from street stands and it is still a worthwhile cultural and sensory experience, even if you buy nothing.

Mumedi   GIFTS & SOUVENIRS
(Mexican Design Museum; Map p74; 🗗 55-5510-8609; www.mumedi.mx; Av Madero 74; ⊙8am-10pm, museum 10am-8pm Mon-Fri, 9am-9pm Sat & Sun; 🛜; Ⓜ Zócalo) This design-museum gift shop sells interesting pop-culture knick-knacks, handbags and jewelry crafted mostly by local artisans. Take a shopping break at the cute **cafe**.

Galería Eugenio   ARTS & CRAFTS
(Map p74; 🗗 55-4131-2870; Allende 84; ⊙11am-4pm Mon-Sat; Ⓜ Garibaldi) Galería Eugenio sells more than 4000 traditional, mostly wooden and clay masks from artisans across the country. Prices start from M$800. It's in the Lagunilla market area.

La Europea   ALCOHOL
(Map p74; 🗗 55-5512-6005; www.laeuropea. com.mx; Ayuntamiento 21; ⊙9am-8pm Mon-Sat, 11am-4pm Sun; 🚇 Plaza San Juan) Get reasonably priced tequila, mezcal and wine at this well-stocked liquor store with a better range than most. There are stores all over CDMX.

Dulcería de Celaya   FOOD
(Map p74; 🗗 55-5521-1787; www.dulceriadecelaya. com; Av 5 de Mayo 39; ⊙10:30am-7:30pm; Ⓜ Allende) This candy store has been operating since 1874 and it's worth a look for the ornate building alone. Candied fruits and coconut-stuffed lemons are some of the sweets on sale.

Mercado de Sonora MARKET
(http://mercadosonora.com.mx; cnr Fray Servando & Rosales, Colonia Merced Balbuena; ⊙9am-7pm Mon-Sat, to 5pm Sun; Ⓜ Merced) This place has all the ingredients for Mexican witchcraft. Aisles are crammed with stalls hawking potions, amulets, voodoo dolls and other esoterica. This is also the place for a *limpia* (spiritual cleansing), a ritual involving clouds of incense and a herbal brushing. Sadly some vendors at the market trade illegally in endangered animals. It's two blocks south of metro Merced.

Tianguis Dominical de Antiguedades la Lagunilla ANTIQUES
(González Bocanegra 66, cnr Paseo de la Reforma; ⊙8am-6pm Sun; Ⓜ Garibaldi) At this collector's flea market you can hunt for antiques, old souvenirs and bric-a-brac. Books and magazines are alongside the Lagunilla building.

🔒 Zona Rosa & Reforma

⭐**Fonart** ARTS & CRAFTS
(Map p128; ☑55-5546-7163; www.gob.mx/fonart; Paseo de la Reforma 116; ⊙10am-7pm Mon-Fri, to 4pm Sat & Sun; Ⓠ Reforma) This government-run crafts store sells quality wares from around Mexico, such as Olinalá-produced lacquered boxes and black pottery from Oaxaca. Prices are fixed.

Another branch is at **Mixcoac** (Patriotismo 691; ⊙10am-6pm Mon-Fri, to 7pm Sat; Ⓜ Mixcoac).

Fusión DESIGN
(Map p128; ☑55-5511-6328; http://casafusion. com.mx; Londres 37; ⊙noon-8pm Tue-Sat, 11am-7pm Sun; Ⓠ Hamburgo) From a converted house, a dozen boutique stores produce giftware, clothing and furniture, most with a Mexican spin. Each Friday to Sunday there's an ever-changing courtyard market showcasing products and food from a particular region, such as Michoacán. A cafe serves gourmet snacks such as grasshopper (or simply aubergine) pizza.

Antigüedades Plaza del Ángel ANTIQUES
(Map p128; www.antiguedadesplazadelangel. mx; Londres 161, btwn Amberes & Av Florencia; ⊙market 9am-4pm Sat & Sun, stores 10:30am-7pm daily; Ⓜ Insurgentes) Weekend flea market within a mall of high-end antique shops selling silver jewelry, paintings, ornaments and furniture in Zona Rosa.

🔒 Condesa & Roma

⭐**Vértigo** ARTS & CRAFTS
(Map p120; ☑55-5207-3590; www.vertigogaleria. com; Colima 23; ⊙10am-6pm Mon & Tue, noon-8pm Wed-Fri, 10am-5pm Sat; Ⓠ Jardín Pushkin) The store at this playfully stylish art gallery sells silk screens, graphic T-shirts and etchings made by popular Argentine illustrator Jorge Alderete and other artists from Mexico and abroad. The gallery has great appeal to fans of graphic novels and *Juxtapoz* magazine.

In addition to 'low brow' art shows, Vértigo stages acoustic music performances every so often.

Libreria Rosario Castellanos BOOKS
(Map p120; ☑55-5276-7110; www.fondodecultura economica.com; Av Tamaulipas 202, cnr Benjamín Hill; ⊙9am-11pm; 🕿; Ⓜ Patriotismo) Inside the impressive art deco Centro Cultural Bella Época is one of the largest bookstores in Latin America. It is easy, and permitted, to sit for hours perusing on the couches and in the cafe at its center. There are also CDs, DVDs and designer gifts. Check out their Facebook page for literary events.

La Naval ALCOHOL
(Map p120; ☑55-5584-3500; www.lanaval.com. mx; Av Insurgentes Sur 373; ⊙9am-9pm Mon-Sat, 11am-7pm Sun; Ⓠ Campeche) Name your poison: this gourmet store stocks a tantalizing selection of mezcals and tequilas, as well as Cuban cigars and hard-to-find imported gourmet food.

Under the Volcano Books BOOKS
(Map p120; www.underthevolcanobooks.com; Celaya 25; ⊙11am-6pm Mon-Sat; Ⓠ Sonora) Buys and sells used English-language titles. An excellent selection and very good prices. Cash only.

Casasola Fotografía GIFTS & SOUVENIRS
(Map p120; ☑55-5521-7883; www.casasolafoto. com; Nuevo Léon 22; ⊙10am-7pm Mon-Fri, to 3pm Sat; Ⓠ Sonora) Odds are you've probably seen this studio's world-famous, revolution-era sepia photos. Items on sale include framed pictures, calendars, T-shirts and postcards.

El Hijo del Santo GIFTS & SOUVENIRS
(Map p120; ☑55-5512-2186; www.elhijodelsanto. com.mx; Av Tamaulipas 219; ⊙10am-9pm Mon-Sat, 1-4pm Sun; Ⓜ Patriotismo) Owned by wrestler El Hijo del Santo – Mexico's most famous, iconic *lucha libre* star who rose to fame in

the 1980s – this small specialty store sells (you guessed it) all things Santo. Among the offerings are kitschy portraits, hip handbags and the ever-popular silver Santo mask.

🛍 Polanco

Antara
MALL

(Map p92; www.antara.com.mx; Av Ejército Nacional 843B; ⏰11am-11pm; Ⓜ Polanco) This cluster of upmarket and chain stores is half open-air and although there is little you won't find elsewhere in the world, it's a designer destination in itself in the fashionable Polanco area. There are travel and adventure goods at stores here and across the road.

Pasaje Polanco
SHOPPING CENTER

(Map p92; ☑55-5280-7976; Oscar Wilde 29, cnr Av Presidente Masaryk; ⏰9am-10pm; Ⓜ Polanco) A classy complex flanked by sophisticated boutiques, specialty stores and a large crafts shop selling handbags, wrestling masks and Day of the Dead folk art.

🛍 San Ángel

★Bazaar Sábado
ARTS & CRAFTS

(Map p100; ☑55-5616-0082; www.bazaar sabado.com; Plaza San Jacinto 11; ⏰10am-7pm Sat; 🚌La Bombilla) The Saturday bazaar showcases some of Mexico's best handcrafted jewelry, woodwork, ceramics and textiles including silver from Taxco and psychedelic Huichol beadwork from Zacatecas. Artists and artisans also display their work in Plaza San Jacinto itself and in adjacent Plaza Tenanitla.

A new website brings plenty of their products for sale online.

Jardín del Arte San Ángel
ART

(Map p100; www.jardindelarte.mx; Plaza San Jacinto; ⏰10am-4pm Sat; 🚌La Bombilla) Local artists set up on the west side of Plaza San Jacinto in San Ángel to sell their paintings while vendors hawk art supplies. There is another location northeast of here in **Plaza del Carmen** (Map p100; www.jardindelarte.mx; ⏰10am-4pm Sat; 🚌La Bombilla) and another in **Colonia San Rafael** (Map p128; btwn Sullivan & Villalongín, Colonia San Rafael; ⏰10am-6pm Sun; 🚌Reforma).

🛍 Other Neighborhoods

Tianguis Cultural del Chopo
MUSIC

(Calle Aldama s/n; ⏰10am-4pm Sat; Ⓜ Buenavista) A gathering place for the city's various youth subcultures – especially goth, metal, indie and punk – with most of the outdoor vendor stalls selling new and vintage clothes and CDs or offering tattooing, piercings and hair coloring. At the north end of the market is a concert stage for young-and-hungry bands with an often high audience.

The main entrance to the market is one block east of metro and metrobús Buenavista. Watch your belongings and expect to hear whispers for drug offers at this notorious market.

Mercado de Jamaica
MARKET

(https://mercadodejamaica.com; cnr Guillermo Prieto & Congreso de la Unión, Colonia Jamaica; ⏰24hr; Ⓜ Jamaica) Huge, colorful flower market, featuring both baroque floral arrangements, exotic blooms and plants. It's filled with marigolds, costumes and *papel picado* (decorative tissue-paper banners) in the weeks leading up to the Day of the Dead. There's colourful fruit and veg, and an eating area too. It's one block south of metro Jamaica.

ℹ Information

EMERGENCIES

Police & Fire ☑911

INTERNET ACCESS

Free wi-fi is available in nearly all accommodations and cafes. Since 2019 all major tourist-popular parks, plazas, shopping strips and airport terminals have official CDMX free access on networks with names starting with 'Gratis_CDMX…,' which require nothing more than ticking a checkbox and clicking '*Acceder*.' Internet services are everywhere; rates range from M$10 to M$30 per hour.

MEDICAL SERVICES

For recommendations for a doctor, dentist or hospital, call your embassy or Sectur (p142), the tourism ministry. A list of area hospitals and English-speaking physicians (with their credentials) is on the US Embassy website. A private doctor's consultation generally costs between M$500 and M$1200. Call Cruz Roja (Red Cross) on 911 for emergency medical attention. For non-urgent, simple checkups or routine prescriptions, most pharmacies (such as Farmacias Similares or Farmacias del Ahorro) have an attached office with doctors (rarely speaking English), who charge M$50 (or sometimes nothing) for consultations, though quality can be hit and miss.

The pharmacies in Sanborns department stores are among the most reliable.

Farmacia París (☑ 55-5709-5000; www.
farmaciaparis.com; República del Salvador 97,
cnr Calle 5 de Febrero; ⊘ 8am-11pm Mon-Sat,
9am-9pm Sun; 🚇 Isabel La Católica) Ornate,
well-stocked, late-opening pharmacy on a corner three blocks south of the Zócalo in Centro
Histórico.

Farmacia San Pablo (☑ 55-5354-9000; www.
farmaciasanpablo.com.mx; Chihuahua 232, cnr
Av Insurgentes Sur; ⊘ 24hr; 🚇 Álvaro Obregón)
Delivery service around the clock from Roma.

Hospital Ángeles Clínica Londres (☑ 55-
5229-8400, emergency 55-5229-8445;
https://hospitalesangeles.com/clinicalondres;
Durango 50, Colonia Roma; Ⓜ Cuauhtémoc)
Top notch private hospital and medical clinic.

Hospital Centro Médico ABC (American
British Cowdray Hospital; ☑ 55-5230-8000,
emergency 55-5230-8161; https://centromedi-
coabc.com; Sur 136 No 116, Colonia Las Américas; Ⓜ Observatorio) English-speaking staff
provide quality care.

MONEY

Most banks and *casas de cambio* (exchange
offices) change cash, but some handle only
euros and US or Canadian dollars. Rates vary,
so check a few places. Mexico City is one of
the few cities in the world where the exchange
offices at the airport actually offer competitive
rates. Exchange offices in town include **CCSole**
(☑ 55-5514-2823; www.ccsole.com.mx; Niza 11,
Zona Rosa; ⊘ 9am-6pm Mon-Fri; 🚇 Hamburgo)
and **Centro de Cambios y Divisas** (☑ 55-5705-
5656; www.ccd.com.mx; Paseo de la Reforma
87F; ⊘ 8am-9pm Mon-Fri, to 6pm Sat, 10am-
5pm Sun; 🚇 Reforma). Traveler's checks are
nearly impossible to exchange anymore because
of their history with scams.

The greatest concentration of ATMs, banks
and *casas de cambio* is on Paseo de la Reforma
between the Monumento a Cristóbal Colón
and El Ángel; and on Madero, the pedestrian
shopping street running to the Zócalo in Centro
Histórico.

POST

The Mexican postal service (www.correos-
demexico.gob.mx) website lists branches
throughout the city. For important items, it is
recommended to use a more reliable, private
courier service, which is not likely to lose items.

Palacio Postal (p81) The stamp windows,
marked 'estampillas,' at the city's main post
office stay open beyond normal hours. Even if
you don't need stamps, check out the sumptuous interior.

Post Office Cuauhtémoc Branch (Map
p128; ☑ 55-5207-7666; Río Tiber 87; ⊘ 8am-
7pm Mon-Fri, to 2pm Sat; Ⓜ Insurgentes) Near
El Ángel.

Post Office Roma Norte Branch (Map p120;
Coahuila 5; ⊘ 8am-6:30pm Mon-Fri, 9am-
2:30pm Sat; Ⓜ Hospital General) A small post
office branch, the only one that services the
Roma area.

SAFE TRAVEL

Most of the narco-related violence that makes
the news abroad happens in the northern and
Pacific states, far from Mexico City. While crime
rates remain significant in the capital, first-
time visitors are often surprised at how safe it
feels, and a few precautions greatly reduce any
dangers.

➔ Don't hail taxis off the street.

➔ Keep valuables out of sight and within a
zipped pocket or bag.

➔ Stick to main streets at night.

Assault

Although not as prevalent as in the 1990s, taxi
assaults still occur. Many victims have hailed
a cab on the street and been robbed by armed
accomplices of the driver, or the drivers themselves. Taxis parked in front of nightclubs or
restaurants should be avoided unless authorized
by the management. Rather than hailing cabs,
find a *sitio* (taxi stand) or request a radio taxi
or Uber – never accept food, drink or sweets
from the driver. In bars, drink spiking rarely but
sometimes occurs, so it's worth staying alert, as
in any large city.

Earthquakes

The danger posed by an earthquake is low, but
they do occur. On September 19, 2017, a major
earthquake rocked Mexico City, destroying
and damaging buildings and displacing hundreds of people. While there were hundreds
of deaths, it was far less devastating than the
1985 earthquake. It reflects, in part, the great
improvements that have been made to the
city's buildings and their ability to resist seismic
activity.

The *alerta sísmica* (public earthquake siren)
can give seconds of warning for you to evacuate
a building, and is now also connected to the
official government app 911 CDMX.

Although it is difficult to predict an earthquake, information on earthquake-prone areas
can be found on websites such as Smart Trav-
eller (www.smartraveller.gov.au) and the US
Department of State (http://travel.state.gov).

Theft

Robberies happen most often in areas frequented by foreigners, including Plaza Garibaldi, Zona
Rosa and Condesa late on weekend nights. Be
on your guard at the airport and bus stations.
Crowded metro cars and buses are favorite
haunts of pickpockets, many of whom work in
family-like groups, so keep a close eye on your

wallet and avoid carrying ATM cards or large amounts of cash. The exits of metro stations Zócalo and Bellas Artes are particularly popular for robbery by shoving. In case of robbery, don't resist – hand over your valuables rather than risk injury or death.

TOILETS

Use of the bathroom is free at some Sanborns department stores, but otherwise costs M$5. Most market buildings and holes-in-the-wall near metro stations have public toilets; just look for the 'WC' signs. Hygiene standards vary at these facilities and use of the facilities costs about M$5. Toilet paper is dispensed by an attendant on request.

TOURIST INFORMATION

Sectur (Map p92; ☑ 55-3002-6300, US 800-482-9832; www.gob.mx/sectur; Av Presidente Masaryk 172, Bosques de Chapultepec; ☉ 9am-7pm Mon-Fri; Ⓜ Polanco) The national tourism ministry hands out brochures on the entire country, though you're better off at the tourism kiosks for up-to-date information about the capital.

Mexico City Tourism Secretariat (☑ 800-008-90-90; https://turismo.cdmx.gob.mx) Has tourist-information kiosks in key areas, including the airport and bus stations. Staff usually speak English and have a map and practical guide. Most kiosks open 9am to 6pm daily.

TRAVEL AGENCIES

A number of hostels and hotels have onsite *agencia de viajes* or can recommend one nearby.

Mundo Joven Airport (☑ 55-2599-0155; www.mundojoven.com; Sala E1, international arrivals, Terminal 1; ☉ 9am-8pm Mon-Fri, 10am-5pm Sat; Ⓜ Terminal Aérea) Specializes in travel for students and teachers, with reasonable airfares from Mexico City. Issues ISIC, ITIC, IYTC and HI cards. Additional branches in **Polanco** (☑ 55-5250-7191; Av Homero 342, cnr Eugenio Sue; ☉10am-7pm Mon-Fri, to 2pm Sat; Ⓜ Polanco) and **Zócalo** (Map p74; ☑ 55-5518-1755; República de Guatemala 4; ☉ 9am-7pm Mon-Fri, 10am-2pm Sat; Ⓜ Zócalo).

USEFUL WEBSITES

CDMX Travel (www.cdmxtravel.com/en) The city's official travel site in English has a run-down on neighborhoods, experiences, tours and events.

Lonely Planet (www.lonelyplanet.com/mexico-city) Destination information, hotel bookings, traveler forum and more.

México es Cultura (www.mexicoescultura. com) A government-run promotion of what's on in the city (and the whole country).

Secretaría de Cultura del Distrito Federal (www.cartelera.cdmx.gob.mx) Lists festivals, museums and cultural events.

Sistema de Información Cultural (www.sic. gob.mx) Directory-like listings of festivals, museums and goings-on in the city.

VISAS

Instituto Nacional de Migración (National Migration Institute; Map p92; ☑ 800-00-46264; www.gob.mx/inm; Av Ejército Nacional 862; ☉ 9am-1pm Mon-Fri) You'll need to come to this immigration office in Polanco if you want to extend your tourist permit, replace a lost one, or deal with other nonstandard immigration procedures. Catch the 'Ejército' bus (M$7.50) from metro Sevilla; it terminates two blocks east of the office.

ⓘ Getting There & Away

AIR

Aeropuerto Internacional Benito Juárez (☑ 55-2482-2424; www.aicm.com.mx; Terminal 1, Capitán Carlos León s/n, Colonia Peñón de los Baños; ☎; Ⓜ Terminal Aérea) is Mexico City's only passenger airport, and Latin America's largest, with an annual capacity of about 32 million passengers. The airport has two terminals: terminal 1 (the main terminal) and terminal 2 (located 3km from the main terminal). Carriers operating out of terminal 2 include Aeromar, Aeroméxico, Copa Airlines, Delta and Lan. All other airlines depart from terminal 1. Construction of a second airport, far northeast of CDMX in Santa Lucía, began in October 2019, with a plan to open in March 2022 as Aeropuerto Internacional General Felipe Ángeles. Follow its progress at www. gob.mx/aisl.

Red buses (M$16, paid on board) run between the two terminals, making stops at *puerta* (door) 7 in terminal 1 and *puerta* 3 in terminal 2. From Terminal 2, the red bus makes a stop at metro Hangares (M$6). The terminals also are connected by an *aerotrén,* a free monorail service for ticketed passengers only, between *puerta* 6 in terminal 1 and *puerta* 4 in terminal 2.

Both terminals have *casas de cambio* and peso-dispensing ATMs. Car-rental agencies and luggage lockers are in *sala* (hall) A and *sala* E2 of terminal 1. Uber cars can pick you up from either terminal without charging additional fees. Select the door in the app.

More than 20 airlines provide international service to Mexico City. You can fly direct from more than 30 cities in the US and Canada, half a dozen each in Europe, South America and Central America/Caribbean, and from Tokyo. Seven different airlines connect the capital to about 50 cities within Mexico.

BUS

Mexico City has four long-distance bus terminals serving the four compass points: Terminal Norte (north), Terminal Oriente (called TAPO; east), Terminal Poniente (Observatorio; west) and Terminal Sur (Taxqueña; south). All terminals have baggage-check services or lockers, as well as tourist-information kiosks, newsstands, card phones, internet, ATMs and snack stalls.

There are also buses to nearby cities from the airport.

For trips of up to five hours, it usually suffices to go to the bus station, buy your ticket and go. For longer trips, many buses leave in the evening and tickets may sell out earlier, so buy beforehand.

For the main bus companies, it is now possible to purchase advance tickets directly from their websites with international debit and credit cards, then show the electronic ticket on your phone at the bus gate. You can also buy tickets at ubiquitous Oxxo convenience stores throughout the city and **Miescape** (☑ 55-5784-4652; www.miescape.mx), a booking agency for more than a dozen bus lines out of all four stations (a 10% surcharge is added to the cost of the ticket up to a maximum of M$50). Miescape also offers purchase by phone with Visa or MasterCard; and even queries by WhatsApp. Miescape branches are at **Buenavista** (Ticketbus; Map p86; ☑ 55-5566-1573; www.miescape.mx; Buenavista 13C, cnr Orozco y Berra; ⊙ 9am-2:30pm & 3:30-7pm Mon-Fri, to noon Sat; M Revolución) and at Terminal Oriente and Terminal Sur.

Lines

Check the individual bus websites for schedules and to buy electronic tickets online. Foreign debit and credit cards can be used.

ADO Group (☑ 55-5784-4652; www.ado.com.mx) One of the largest and most reliable companies with services all across the country. Includes ADO Platino (deluxe), ADO GL (executive), OCC (1st class), ADO (1st class) and AU (2nd class).

Autobuses Teotihuacán (☑ 55-5587-0501; www.autobusesteotihuacan.com.mx) Second-class services to the Teotihuacán ruins every 30 minutes. Ensure that your bus is marked 'ruinas' and not going to the nearby town of San Juan Teotihuacán.

Autovías (☑ 800-622-22-22; www.autovias.com.mx) Specializes in 1st-class services to Mexico state and Michoacán.

Estrella Blanca Group (☑ 55-5729-0807, 800-507-55-00; www.estrellablanca.com.mx) One of the largest and most reliable network of bus companies with services all across the country. Operates Futura (www.futura.com.mx), Costa Line and Elite (1st class).

Estrella de Oro (☑ 800-900-01-05, 55-5549-8520; www.estrelladeoro.com.mx) Specializes in services to Cuernavaca and cities in Guerrero state, such as Taxco and Acapulco. Executive and 1st class.

Estrella Roja (☑ 55-5130-1800, 800-712-22-84; www.estrellaroja.com.mx) Specializes in direct 1st-class services between Puebla and Mexico City's airport and TAPO.

ETN (☑ 55-5089-9200, 800-800-03-86; www.etn.com.mx) Arguably the most luxurious network of buses with services all over the country. Includes ETN (deluxe) and Turistar (executive and deluxe).

Ómnibus de México (☑ 55-5141-4300, 800-765-66-36; www.odm.com.mx) The most popular routes from Mexico City include Monterrey and San Luis Potosí, and even for the US to Houston and Dallas. Includes 1st class.

Primera Plus (☑ 800-375-75-87; www.primeraplus.com.mx) An extensive network of destinations, particularly for Jalisco, Michoacán, Guanajuato and Querétaro. Deluxe and 1st class.

Pullman de Morelos (☑ 800-022-80-00, 55-5445-0100; www.pullman.mx) Specializes in services to Cuernavaca. Executive, deluxe and 1st class.

Terminals

Terminal de Autobuses del Norte (☑ 55-5587-1552; Eje Central Lázaro Cárdenas 4907, Colonia Magdalena de las Salinas; M Autobuses del Norte) The largest of the four bus terminals. Serves points north, including cities on the US border, plus some points west (Guadalajara, Puerto Vallarta), east (Puebla) and south (Acapulco, Oaxaca). Deluxe and 1st-class counters are mostly in the southern half of the terminal. Luggage-storage services are at the far south end and in the central passageway. Buses to Teotihuacán depart from here. Connects with metro Autobuses del Norte on Línea 5 (yellow).

Terminal de Autobuses de Pasajeros de Oriente (TAPO; ☑ 55-5522-9381; Calz Zaragoza 200, Colonia Diez de Mayo; M San Lázaro) For eastern and southeastern destinations, including Puebla, Veracruz, Yucatán, Oaxaca and Chiapas. Known commonly as TAPO. Bus-line counters are arranged around a rotunda with a food court, internet terminals and ATMs. There's a left-luggage service in 'Túnel 1.' Connects with metro San Lázaro on Línea 1 (pink) and Línea B (dark green).

Terminal de Autobuses del Poniente (Observatorio; ☑ 55-5271-0149; Av Sur 122, Colonia Real del Monte; M Observatorio) The point for buses heading to Michoacán, Valle de Bravo, Toluca and shuttle services running to nearby Toluca. In addition, ETN offers service to Guadalajara. Commonly referred to by the adjacent metro name Observatorio, which is as the western end of Línea 1 (pink).

Terminal de Autobuses del Sur (Taqueña; 55-5689-9745; Av Tasqueña 1320, Colonia Campestre Churubusco; Ⓜ Tasqueña) Serves Tepoztlán, Cuernavaca, Taxco, Acapulco and other southern destinations, as well as Oaxaca, Huatulco and Ixtapa-Zihuatanejo. Estrella de Oro (Acapulco, Taxco) and Pullman de Morelos (Cuernavaca) counters are on the right side of the terminal, while OCC, Estrella Roja (Tepoztlán), ETN and Futura are on the left. In *sala* 3 you'll find luggage-storage service and ATMs. Commonly referred to by the adjacent metro name Tasqueña, which is at the southern end of Línea 2 (blue), with transfers to *tren ligero* for Xochimilco.

BUSES FROM MEXICO CITY

DESTINATION	TERMINAL IN MEXICO CITY	BUS LINES	FARE (M$)	TIME (HR)	FREQUENCY (PER DAY)
Acapulco	Sur	Costa Line, Estrella de Oro	605-720	5	hourly
	Oriente (TAPO)	ADO	675-720	5¾	7
Bahías de Huatulco	Sur	AltaMar, OCC, Turistar	1315-1585	14½-15½	3
	Norte	AltaMar	1350	16¾	1 (5:30pm)
Campeche	Oriente (TAPO)	ADO, ADO GL	1350-1495	17½-19½	3
	Norte	ADO	1350	18½	1 (2:30pm)
Cancún	Oriente (TAPO)	ADO, ADO GL	1666-1856	25-26	3
Chetumal	Oriente (TAPO)	ADO	1506	21½	1 (5:15pm)
Chihuahua	Norte	Estrella Blanca, Ómnibus de México	1560-1933	18-19¾	7
Cuernavaca	Sur	Estrella Blanca, Estrella de Oro, ETN, Pullman de Morelos	100-150	1½	frequent
Guadalajara	Norte	ETN, Futura Select, Ómnibus de México, Primera Plus	853-865	6½-7	frequent
	Poniente	ETN	1040	7½	4
Guanajuato	Norte	ETN, Primera Plus	680-835	4½-5½	14
Matamoros	Norte	ETN, Futura	1203-1475	12½-13½	3
Mazatlán	Norte	Elite, ETN, Pacífico	1055-1670	13-16	13
Mérida	Oriente (TAPO)	ADO, ADO GL	1488-1642	19½-20¼	6
Monterrey	Norte	ETN, Ómnibus de México	1130-1290	11-13	18
Morelia	Poniente	Autovías, ETN, Pegasso	350-635	4-4¼	frequent
Nuevo Laredo	Norte	ETN, Futura, Turistar	1335-1650	15-15½	8
Oaxaca	Oriente (TAPO)	ADO, ADO GL, ADO Platino	458-678	6½-7¼	frequent
	Sur	ADO GL, OCC	678-836	6½-7¼	5
Palenque	Oriente (TAPO)	ADO	1340	14	1 (6:20pm)
Papantla	Norte	ADO	438	4¼-5½	8
Pátzcuaro	Norte	Primera Plus	595	4¼-5	3
	Poniente	Autovías	610	5¼	9
Puebla	Airport	Estrella Roja	320	2	8
	Oriente (TAPO)	ADO, ADO GL, AU, Pullman de Morelos	200-320	2-2¼	frequent
Puerto Escondido	Sur	ETN, OCC, Turistar	1082-1555	12-17½	2

Aeropuerto Internacional Benito Juárez
(p142) Bus departures from Mexico City's airport include Cuernavaca, Pachuca, Puebla, Querétaro, Toluca, Córdoba, San Juan del Río, Orizaba and Celaya. Buses depart from platforms adjacent to *sala* E in terminal 1 and from *sala* D in terminal 2. Ticket counters in terminal 1 are on the upper level, off the food court. A pedestrian bridge off *sala* B leads to an

ADO bus terminal with service to Acapulco and Veracruz. Updated bus times, destinations and prices can be found on the airport website.

CAR & MOTORCYCLE
Rental

Rental-car companies have offices at the airport, bus stations and in the Zona Rosa area of the city. Rates generally start at about M$600 per

DESTINATION	TERMINAL IN MEXICO CITY	BUS LINES	FARE (M$)	TIME (HR)	FREQUENCY (PER DAY)
Puerto Vallarta	Norte	ETN, Futura, Primera Plus	1277-1565	12¼-13½	5
Querétaro	Norte	Estrella Blanca, ETN, Primera Plus	265-440	2¾-3	frequent
	Airport	Primera Plus	425	3	frequent
	Poniente	Primera Plus	335	3¾-4	15
San Cristóbal de las Casas	Oriente (TAPO)	ADO GL, OCC	1628	13¾-15	6
	Norte	ADO, OCC	1628	14½-16	5
San Luis Potosí	Norte	ETN, Primera Plus	647-745	4¾-5½	frequent
San Miguel de Allende	Norte	ETN, Primera Plus	520-635	3½-4½	hourly
Tapachula	Oriente (TAPO)	ADO GL, ADO Platino, OCC	1250-1450	18¼-19	6
Taxco	Sur	ADO, Costaline, Estrella de Oro, Pullman de Morelos	250-260	2¾	hourly
Teotihuacán	Norte	Autobuses Teotihuacán	52	1	hourly 7am-6pm
Tepoztlán	Sur	OCC	140	1¼	frequent
Tijuana	Norte	Elite, Pacífico	1789-2184	36½-46	13
Toluca	Airport	Caminante	200	1¾	5
	Poniente	ETN, Flecha Roja	67-90	1	frequent
Tuxtla Gutiérrez	Oriente (TAPO)	ADO, ADO GL, ADO Platino, OCC	1428-2140	12½-13½	10
Uruapan	Poniente	Autovías, ETN	745-905	5½-6¼	20
Veracruz	Oriente (TAPO)	ADO, ADO GL, ADO Platino, AU	568-992	5¾-7	frequent
	Norte	ADO, ADO GL	684-992	6	10
Villahermosa	Oriente (TAPO)	ADO, ADO GL, ADO Platino, AU	816-1234	11-14	19
Xalapa	Oriente (TAPO)	ADO, ADO GL, ADO Platino, AU	412-838	4½-5	frequent
Zacatecas	Norte	ETN, Ómnibus de México	1106-1330	8-9	14
Zihuatanejo	Sur	ADO, Costa Line	864-935	9-10	10
	Poniente	Autovías	919	9	4

day, but you can often do better by booking online. You can find a list of rental agencies online at the CDMX Tourism Secretariat (www.turismo.cdmx.gob.mx) website.

Roadside Assistance

If you leave the city, the **Ángeles Verdes** (Green Angels; ☑ 078, then press 2 for English; www.gob.mx/sectur/angelesverdes) can provide 24-hour highway assistance for tourists. Just phone and tell them your location.

Routes In & Out of the City

Whichever way you come into the city, once you're past the last *caseta* (toll booth) you enter a no-man's-land of poorly marked lanes and chaotic traffic. These *casetas* are also the points from which Hoy No Circula (p147) rules take effect.

To Puebla (east of CDMX) Take the Viaducto Alemán (Río de la Piedad) east. From Roma and Zona Rosa, this is most conveniently accessed off Avenida Cuauhtémoc (Eje 1 Poniente). Immediately after crossing over the Viaducto – by the Liverpool department store – turn left for the access ramp. From the Zócalo take Viaducto Tlalpan to get onto Viaducto Alemán then follow signs to Calzada Zaragoza. This leads to the highway to Puebla, or for Puebla airport head north along Blvd Puerto Aéreo.

To Oaxaca or Veracruz Also take the Viaducto Alemán to Calzada Zaragoza then follow the signs for Oaxaca until you join the Puebla highway.

To Querétaro (north of CDMX) Take Reforma from the Diana roundabout until you reach the Estela de Luz and turn right onto Calzada Gral Mariano Escobedo. Keep right and look for the signs to take the ramp to Querétaro. Pass through the toll at Tepotzotlán. Continue for 200km. Take the exit toward Centro from Carretera México–Querétaro.

To Pachuca, Hidalgo and northern Veracruz (north of CDMX) Take Avenida Insurgentes north (also the route to Teotihuacán), which feeds into the highway.

To Cuernavaca (south of CDMX) Turn right (south) at the Zócalo onto Pino Suárez, which becomes Calzada Tlalpan. About 20km south, signs indicate a left exit for the *cuota* (toll highway) to Cuernavaca.

To Toluca (west of CDMX) Heading out of the city, take Paseo de la Reforma, which feeds right into the *cuota*, passing the high-rises of Santa Fe, to Toluca.

ⓘ Getting Around

TO/FROM THE AIRPORT

The metro is a cheap option for getting to the airport, though hauling luggage amid rush-hour crowds while avoiding pickpockets can be a Herculean task. Authorized taxis and Uber provide a painless alternative that is far cheaper than most other countries, as does the *metrobús* if going to Centro Histórico.

Metro

The airport metro station is Terminal Aérea, on Línea 5 (yellow). It's 200m from terminal 1: leave by the exit at the end of *sala* A (domestic arrivals) and continue past the taxi stand to the station.

To the city center, follow signs for 'Dirección Politécnico.' At La Raza (seven stops away) change for Línea 3 (green) and follow signs for 'Dirección Universidad.' Metro Hidalgo, at the west end of the Alameda, is three stops south; it's also a transfer point for Línea 2 (blue) to the Zócalo.

To get to Zona Rosa from the airport, take Línea 5 to 'Pantitlán,' the end of the line. Change for Línea 1 (pink) and get off at metro Insurgentes.

There is no convenient metro link to terminal 2, but there is metrobús Línea 4, which connects to the TAPO bus terminal next to metro San Lázaro. Also, red buses at the entrance of terminal 2 go to metro Hangares (Línea 5).

Metrobús

Línea 4 of the metrobús has luggage racks and onboard security cameras, making it a more comfortable option than the metro.

Stops are at *puerta* 7 in terminal 1 and *puerta* 3 in terminal 2. The ride costs M$30, plus you'll need to purchase a smart card (valid for all metro and metrobús trips) for M$15 at machines inside the terminals. From terminal 1, it's about 45 minutes to reach the Zócalo.

The line runs five blocks north of the Zócalo, along República de Venezuela and Belisario Domínguez, then it heads west along Avenida Hidalgo past metro Hidalgo. To return to the airport, catch it along Ayuntamiento or República del Salvador. See www.aicm.com.mx/en for more information.

Taxi

Safe and reliable *taxis autorizados* (authorized taxis) are controlled by a fixed-price ticket system. Purchase taxi tickets from booths located in *sala* E1 (international arrivals) as you exit customs, and by the *sala* A (domestic arrivals) exit.

Fares are determined by zones. A ride to the Zócalo, Roma, Condesa or Zona Rosa and Reforma costs M$245. One ticket is valid for up to four passengers. 'Sitio 300' taxis are the best. If you have phone internet access (free wi-fi is available here), an Uber will cost about M$170 to the same destinations, and will allow you to select which *puerta* to be picked up from.

Porters may offer to take your ticket and luggage the few steps to the taxi, but hold on to the ticket and hand it to the driver. Drivers won't expect a tip for the ride, but will always welcome one.

TO/FROM THE BUS TERMINALS
The metro is the fastest and cheapest way to or from any bus terminal, but it's tricky to maneuver through crowded stations and cars. Taxis and app services (Uber and Didi) are easier options – all terminals have ticket booths for secure *taxis autorizados*, with fares set by zone. A 20% surcharge is applied from 11pm to 6am. An agent at the exit will assign you a cab.

Terminal Norte Metro Línea 5 (yellow) stops at Autobuses del Norte, just outside the terminal. To the city center, follow signs for 'Dirección Pantitlán,' then change at La Raza for Línea 3 (green) for 'Dirección Universidad.' (The La Raza connection is a six-minute hike through a 'Tunnel of Science.') The taxi kiosk is in the central passageway; a cab for up to four people to the Zócalo, Roma or Condesa costs about M$135.

Terminal Oriente (TAPO) This bus terminal is next door to metro San Lázaro. To the city center or Zona Rosa, take Línea 1 (pink) for 'Dirección Observatorio.' The authorized taxi booth is at the top (metro) end of the main passageway from the rotunda. The fare to the Zócalo is M$85; to Zona Rosa, Roma or Condesa it's M$110.

Terminal Poniente Metro Observatorio, the eastern terminus of Línea 1 (pink), is a couple of minutes' walk across a busy street. A taxi ticket to Roma costs M$110, Condesa M$85 and the Zócalo M$135.

Terminal Sur It's a two-minute walk from metro Tasqueña, the southern terminus of Línea 2, which stops at the Zócalo. For Zona Rosa, transfer at Pino Suárez and take Línea 1 to Insurgentes ('Dirección Observatorio'). Going to the terminal, take the 'Autobuses del Sur' exit, which leads upstairs to a footbridge. Descend the last staircase on the left then walk through a street market to reach the building. Authorized taxis from Terminal Sur cost M$140 to Centro Histórico, M$155 to Condesa and Roma, and M$170 to the airport. Ticket booths are in *sala* 3.

BICYCLE
Bicycles can be a viable way to get around town and are often preferable to overcrowded, recklessly driven buses. Although careless drivers and potholes can make Mexico City cycling an extreme sport, if you stay alert and keep off the major thoroughfares, it's manageable. The city government has encouraged bicycle use, with more bicycle-only lanes, and it's definitely catching on (see the boxed text on p107).

Bikes are loaned free from a kiosk on the west side of the Catedral Metropolitana. You'll also find booths at Plaza Villa de Madrid in Roma; at Fuente de Cibeles on Durango in Roma; at the intersection of Mazatlán and Michoacán in Condesa; and several along Paseo de la Reforma, near the Monumento a la Independencia and Auditorio Nacional. Leave a passport or driver's license for three hours of riding time. The kiosks operate from 10:30am to 6pm Monday to Saturday, and 9:30am to 4:30pm on Sunday.

Various app-based bike- and scooter-share services have come and gone in recent years, including Jump (provided by Uber) and Grin. They are the easiest option if you have phone internet access.

CAR & MOTORCYCLE
Touring Mexico City by car is strongly discouraged, unless you have a healthy reserve of patience. Even more than elsewhere in the country, traffic rules are seen as suggested behavior. Red lights may be run at will, no-turn signs are ignored and signals are seldom used. On occasion you may be hit with a questionable traffic fine. Nevertheless, you may want to rent a car here for travel outside the city.

---

❶ HOY NO CIRCULA (DON'T DRIVE TODAY) PROGRAM

To help combat pollution, Mexico City operates its 'Hoy No Circula' (www.hoy-no-circula.com.mx) program, banning many vehicles from being driven in the city between 5am and 10pm on one day each week. Additionally, vehicles nine years and older are prohibited from operating one Saturday a month. Exempted from restrictions are rental cars and vehicles with a *calcomanía de verificación* (emissions-verification sticker), obtained under the city's vehicle-pollution assessment system.

For vehicles without the sticker (including foreign-registered ones), the last digit of the license-plate number determines the day when they cannot circulate. See the official website for more information.

Day	Prohibited Last Digit
Monday	5, 6
Tuesday	7, 8
Wednesday	3, 4
Thursday	1, 2
Friday	9, 0

Parking

Avoid parking on the street whenever possible; most midrange and top-end hotels have guest garages. If you do park on the street, keep in mind that some neighborhoods, such as Cuauhtémoc, Roma and Polanco, have *parquímetros* (green parking meters usually located at the middle of the block). Feed them or your vehicle will be booted or wheel locked.

METRO

The metro system (www.metro.cdmx.gob.mx) offers the quickest way to get around Mexico City. Used by around 4.4 million passengers on an average weekday, it has 195 stations and more than 226km of track on 14 lines. Trains arrive every two to three minutes during rush hours. At M$5 a ride, it's one of the world's cheapest subways.

All lines operate from 5am to midnight weekdays, 6am to midnight Saturday and 7am to midnight Sunday and holidays. Platforms and cars can become alarmingly packed during rush hours (roughly 7:30am to 10am and 3pm to 8pm). At these times the forward cars are reserved for women and children, and men may not proceed beyond the pink 'Sólo Mujeres y Niños' gate. The metro is also chaotic during heavy rain.

With such crowded conditions, it's not surprising that pickpocketing occurs, so watch your belongings. Family-like groups have been known to 'accidentally' bump into victims.

The metro is easy to use. Lines are color-coded and each station is identified by a unique logo. Signs reading 'Dirección Pantitlán,' 'Dirección Universidad' and so on name the stations at the end of the lines. Check a map for the direction you want. Buy a rechargeable smart card for M$15 at any station and then add credit (the card also works for all metrobús lines). Additionally, the metro sells *boletos* (tickets) at the *taquilla* (ticket window). Feed the ticket into the turnstile and you're on your way. When changing trains, look for 'Correspondencia' (Transfer) signs. Maps of the vicinity around each station are posted near the exits.

PESERO, METROBÚS & TROLEBÚS

Mexico City's thousands of buses and peseros operate from around 5am till 10pm daily, depending on the route. Electric trolleybuses generally run until 11:30pm. Only a few routes run all night, notably those along Paseo de la Reforma. This means you'll get anywhere by bus and/or metro during the day, but will probably have to take a few taxis after hours.

Pesero

Peseros (also called microbúses or combis) are gray-and-green minibuses operated by private firms. They follow fixed routes, often starting or ending at metro stations, and will stop at virtually any street corner. Route information is randomly displayed on cards attached to the windshield. Fares are M$5 for trips of up to 5km, and M$5.50 for 5km to 12km. Add 20% to all fares between 11pm and 6am. Privately run green-and-yellow buses charge M$6 and M$7 for the same distances. A useful resource for route planning with the confusing number of peseros is the ViaDF (www.viadf.mx) website.

Useful routes include the following:

Metro Sevilla–Presidente Masaryk A purple bus ($7.50) between Colonia Roma and Polanco via Álvaro Obregón and Avenida Presidente Masaryk (stops at metro Niños Héroes, Avenida Insurgentes, metro Sevilla and Leibnitz).

Metro Tacubaya–Balderas–Escandón Between Centro Histórico and Condesa, westbound via Puebla, eastbound via Durango (stops at Plaza San Juan, metro Balderas, metro Insurgentes, Parque España and Avenida Michoacán).

Metrobús

The metrobús is a wheelchair-accessible long bus that stops at metro-style stations in the middle of the street, spaced at three- to four-block intervals. Access is by prepaid smart card, issued by machines for M$10 at the entrance to the platforms, and rides cost M$6. The rechargeable cards, which can also be used for the metro, are placed on a sensor device for entry. During crowded peak hours, the metrobús is a favorite for pickpockets. The front of the bus is for women and children only, marked out with pink seating. Most metrobús lines run from 5am to midnight. The most useful lines:

Línea 1 Plies a dedicated lane along Avenida Insurgentes from metro Indios Verdes in northern CDMX down to the southern end of Tlalpan.

Línea 4 Runs from metro Buenavista and cuts through Centro Histórico to metro San Lázaro. The line also has an *'aeropuerto'* bus that goes to and from the airport for M$30.

Línea 7 Covers most sights. A red double-decker that rides along Paseo de la Reforma from Plaza Garibaldi, passing key sights like Monumento a la Revolución, Zona Rosa and Reforma, El Ángel, Bosque de Chapultepec, Castillo de Chapultepec, Museo Tamayo and Museo de Antropología, terminating a stop after Auditorio Nacional. Closed on Sundays 6:30am to 2pm between Chapultepec and Auditorio (including Antropología), as the avenue becomes a bicycle-only zone for the Paseo Dominical.

Trolebús

Municipally operated *trolebuses* (trolleybuses) and full-sized cream-and-orange buses (labeled 'RTP') only pick up at bus stops. Fares are M$2 (M$4 for the express) regardless of distance traveled. The *trolebuses* should be replaced by a new fleet of comfortable black-and-blue vehicles by the time you read this and will only accept preloaded travel cards (as used on the metro and metrobús), no cash. Trolleybuses follow a number of the key *ejes* (priority roads) throughout the rest of the city. They generally run until 11:30pm. Route maps are on the trolleybus website (http://ste.cdmx.gob.mx). Useful routes include Autobuses del Sur and Autobuses del Norte, which travel along Eje Central Lázaro Cárdenas between the north and south bus terminals (stops at Plaza de las Tres Culturas, Plaza Garibaldi, Bellas Artes/Alameda and metro Hidalgo).

TAXI

Mexico City has several classes of taxi. Cheapest are the cruising pink-and-white street cabs, though they're not recommended due to the risk of assaults by the driver or accomplices. If you must hail off the street, check ¡or actual taxi license plates: numbers are preceded with the letters A or B. Check that the plate matches the number painted on the bodywork. Also look for the *carta de identificación* (called the *tarjetón*), a postcard-sized ID that should be displayed inside the cab, and ensure that the driver matches the photo. If the cab does not pass these tests, get another one.

In *libre* cabs (street cabs), fares are computed by *taxímetro* (meter), which should start at about M$9. The total cost of a 3km ride in moderate traffic – say, from the Zócalo to Zona Rosa and Reforma – should be M$30 to M$40. Between 11pm and 6am, add 20%.

Radio taxis, *taxis de sitio* or *taxis autorizados*, which come in many different colors, cost about two or three times as much as the others, but this extra cost adds an immeasurable degree of security. When you phone, the dispatcher will tell you the cab number and the type of car. If you have a smartphone or device with internet, you can order a safe cab via the popular apps Cabify, Didi or Uber. It is rare for scams to occur with these, but not unheard of. Do not accept a ride if has been cancelled in the app. Do not accept candy or drinks from any driver, as these can be drugged.

Reliable radio-taxi firms, available 24 hours, include the following:

Sitio de Taxis Parque México (Map p120; ☑ 55-5286-7129, 55-5286-7164; Michoacán s/n; ◷24hr)

Taxi Mex (Map p120; ☑ 55-9171-8888; www.taximex.com.mx; Colima 80; ◷24hr)

Taxis Radio Unión (Map p120; ☑ 55-5514-8074, 55-5514-7709; Frontera 100; ◷24hr)

AT A GLANCE

POPULATION
3 million

LANGUAGES
Spanish, Náhuatl

**BEST
ACTIVE VOLCANO**
Popocatépetl
(p180)

BEST PYRAMID
Pirámide del Sol
(p158)

BEST MOLE
El Mural de los
Poblanos (p170)

WHEN TO GO
May–Oct
Rainy season; after-
noon showers wash
the air clean and bring
wild mushrooms to
the forests.

Sep
The weeks before
Independence Day
are the time to
taste the seasonal
specialty *chiles en
nogada.*

Nov–Apr
Drier months; nomi-
nally cooler, making
for pleasant daytime
city exploration and
casual hikes.

Taxco (p203)
BELIKOVA OKSANA/SHUTTERSTOCK

Around Mexico City

The megalopolis of Mexico City is easy to escape from and can resemble the countryside in only 15 minutes' journey. The ancient ruins, *pueblos mágicos* (culturally rich 'magical villages') and stunning mountain landscape of the surrounding area should not be missed.

While many visitors to the region only take a day trip to the awe-inspiring archaeological complex at Teotihuacán, the area offers much more – from the captivating colonial cities of Taxco, Puebla and Cuernavaca to the eccentric small towns of Valle de Bravo, Malinalco and Tepoztlán. For those eager to taste some crisp, mountain air, there are *pueblitos* (small towns), volcanic giants, and the lesser-known ruins of Xochicalco and Cantona to visit.

Around Mexico City Highlights

1 Teotihuacán (p157) Being blown away by the spectacular pyramids.

2 Taxco (p203) Wandering the steep cobblestone streets linking the city's famed silver shops.

3 Malinalco (p215) Sashaying an easy path up to Aztec temples overlooking a newly trendy *pueblo*.

4 Tepoztlán (p189) Having a spiritual encounter at a mountaintop pyramid dedicated to the Aztec god of *pulque*.

5 Puebla (p163) Admiring the impressive Talavera-tiled historic churches.

6 Cuetzalan (p185) Enjoying a sunset drink at the tiny *zócalo* amid the dramatic scenery of the Sierra Madre Oriental.

7 Mineral del Chico (p162) Feeling mountain mists sweep over you.

8 La Malinche (p169) Climbing the slopes of a dormant volcano with panoramic views.

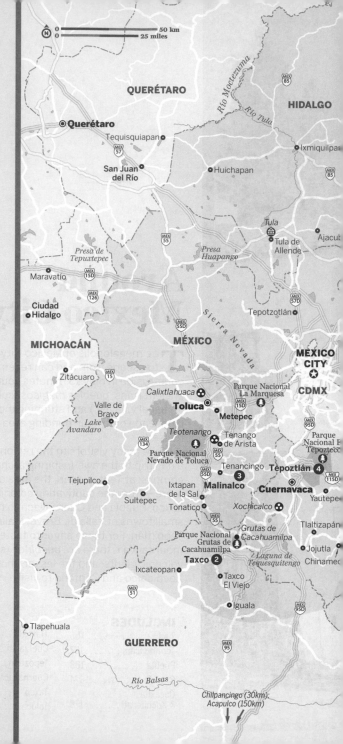

History

Long a cultural and economic crossroads, the region around present-day Mexico City has hosted a succession of important indigenous civilizations (notably the Teotihuacán, Toltec and Aztec). By the late-15th century, the Aztec had managed to dominate all but one of central Mexico's states. Many archaeological sites and museums preserve remnants of pre-Hispanic history – Puebla's Museo Amparo provides an excellent overview of the region's history and cultures.

Post-conquest, the Spanish transformed central Mexico, establishing ceramic industries at Puebla, mines at Taxco and Pachuca, and haciendas producing wheat, sugar and cattle throughout the region. The Catholic Church used the region as a base for its missionary activities and left a series of imposing cathedrals and fortified monasteries. Today, most towns retain a central plaza surrounded by colonial buildings.

ℹ Getting There & Away

The cities, towns and (to a lesser extent) villages around Mexico City enjoy excellent, often 1st-class bus links to both the capital and each other. Even the smallest backwaters have comfortable daily services to Mexico City and to the closest transportation hub. While airports also serve Puebla, Toluca, Cuernavaca and Pachuca, it's nearly always cheaper and easier to fly to Mexico City and travel onward from there – these destinations even have direct bus routes from the airport. For all but the most obscure sights, traveling by bus is the easiest and most affordable option. Highway robbery is rarely an issue for major destinations, but aim to travel in daylight hours to smaller towns.

NORTH OF MEXICO CITY

The biggest attraction north of Mexico City is the extraordinary complex at Teotihuacán, once the largest metropolis in the Americas and one of Mexico's most spectacular pre-Hispanic sights. Further north, the well-preserved stone statues at Tula also draw visitors.

Far less visited, but equally impressive, are Parque Nacional El Chico and the mining village of Mineral del Chico – the perfect escape from the big city, with stunning views, wide-open spaces and friendly locals.

Pachuca, the fast-growing capital of dynamic Hidalgo state, has brightly painted houses, an attractive colonial center and a Mexican twist on Cornish pasties. From Pachuca, well-paved routes snake east and north to the Gulf coast, through spectacular country such as the fringes of the Sierra Madre Oriental mountain range and the coastal plain.

Tepotzotlán

📓 55 / POP 45,900 / ELEV 2300M

This *pueblo mágico* is an easy day trip from Mexico City, but feels far from the chaotic streets of the capital, despite the fact that urban sprawl creeps closer to Tepotzotlán's colonial center every year. A small, pleasant *zócalo,* market and church make Tepotzotlán worth a quick stop.

⊙ Sights

★ **Museo Nacional del Virreinato** MUSEUM
(National Museum of the Viceregal Period; 📓 55-5876-0332; https://virreinato.inah.gob.mx; Plaza Virreinal; adult/student M$75/free; ⊙ 9am-4.45pm Tue-Sun) There's a very simple reason to visit this wonderful, expansive museum comprising the restored Jesuit **Iglesia de San Francisco Javier** and an adjacent **monastery.** Much of the folk art and fine art on display – silver chalices, pictures created from inlaid wood, porcelain, furniture and religious paintings and statues – comes from Mexico City cathedral's large collection, and the standard is very high.

Once a Jesuit college of indigenous languages, the complex dates from 1606. Additions were made over the following 150 years, creating a showcase for the developing architectural styles of Nueva España.

Don't miss the **Capilla Doméstica**, with a Churrigueresque main altarpiece that boasts more mirrors than a carnival fun house. The facade is a phantasmagoric array of carved saints, angels, plants and people, while the interior walls and the Camarín del Virgen adjacent to the altar are swathed with gilded ornamentation.

🎉 Festivals & Events

Pastorelas RELIGIOUS
(https://hosteriadelconvento.mx; La Hostería del Convento de Tepotzotlán, Plaza Virreinal 1; ⊙ Dec) Tepotzotlán's highly regarded *pastorelas* (nativity plays) are performed inside a former monastery in the weeks leading up to Christmas. Tickets, which include Christmas dinner and piñata smashing, can be purchased at La Hostería del Convento de Tepotzotlán after November 1 or via Ticketmaster.

🛏 Sleeping

Posada del Fraile HOTEL $
(🖉 55-5876-4110; Fraile 6, off Av Insurgentes; s/d/tr/q M$540/700/900/1100; 🅿🛜) Reflecting its name 'Friar's Inn', the rooms at this hotel are decked out in colorful Mexican blankets with painted stucco-like walls and decorative crosses, angels and mirrors. Some rooms are dark, so ask to see a few. The roof terrace and quiet location a few blocks east of the *zócalo* are perfect for meditation of all kinds.

Hotel Posada del Virrey HOTEL $
(🖉 55-5876-1864; Av Insurgentes 13; r with/without Jacuzzi M$720/480; 🅿🛜) A short walk from the *zócalo,* this retro-pastel, motel-style posada (inn) is popular with weekenders. Rooms can be a bit dark, but they're clean, quiet and have TVs.

🍴 Eating & Drinking

It's best to avoid the many almost indistinguishable, tourist-centric restaurants on the *zócalo,* where the food is mediocre and prices are high. A better option is to join the locals at the market behind the Palacio Municipal, where food stalls serve rich *pozole* (a thin stew of hominy, pork or chicken), *gorditas* (round masa cakes) and freshly squeezed juices all day long.

Mesón Vegetariano Atzin VEGETARIAN $
(🖉 55-4093-3321; Plaza Tepotzotlán, Local A; comida corrida M$70; 🕐noon-6pm; 🍴) The yoga-instructor owner-chef definitely sets the tranquil tone with her all-white outfits at this vegetarian restaurant in an inner courtyard. Set menus can include a simple salad, corn soup, sugar-free guava juice and natural yogurt with sunflower seeds. Tasty main dishes imitate meat favorites such as Veracruz-style 'fish' (from mushrooms) and gluten *milanesa* (Mexican schnitzel).

★La Hostería del Convento de Tepotzotlán MEXICAN $$
(🖉 55-5876-0243; https://hosteriadelconvento.mx; Plaza Virreinal 1; mains M$115-190; 🕐10am-5pm) Housed within the monastery's impressive bougainvillea-walled courtyard, La Hostería serves traditional brunch and lunch fare – *chiles tolucos* (Tepotzotlán specialty of *ancho* chilies stuffed with *chorizo* and cheese) and *cecina adobada* (Oaxacan-style chili-marinated pork) – to a well-dressed clientele.

El Rincón de la Catrina MEXICAN $$
(🖉 55-5876-6001; Mateos 15; menú del día M$110-155; 🕐10am-6pm Mon-Thu, to 9pm Fri & Sat, to 8pm Sun; 👶) Taking La Catrina (elegant female skeleton) as mascot and turning up the volume on Mexican colors, this restaurant has handy set-lunch meals such as *enchiladas de mole* (spiced sauce on chicken-filled tortillas) including rice and *café de olla* (spiced brewed coffee). The enclosed garden, occasional live music and festive vibe are great for groups and kids.

Los Molcajetes PUB
(Los Molca; 🖉 55-5876-8753; Pensador Mexicano s/n; 🕐6pm-late Tue-Sun) Weekends get busy here, with students and older couples head-nodding, and sometimes spontaneously dancing, to pop hits and Mexican classics. Start your night with a *'cucaracha'* (cockroach), a potent shot of tequila and Kahlua.

ℹ Getting There & Away

Tepoztlán (not to be confused with Tepoztlán, see p189, to the south of Mexico City) is on the Mexico City–Querétaro highway, about 40km from Mexico City.

From Mexico City's Terminal Poniente (Observatorio), **Primera Plus** (https://wl.primeraplus.com.mx) buses (M$115, 1½ hours, hourly) run conveniently to the center of Tepotzotlán. Return buses to Mexico City depart from the same terminal.

From Mexico City's Terminal Norte, 1st-class **Ovnibus** (http://ovnibus.com.mx) buses (M$101, 40 minutes, every 30 minutes) run direct to the Tepotzotlán bus terminal; **Autotransportes Valle del Mezquital** (AVM; http://ovnibus.com.mx) run 2nd-class buses (M$27, 40 minutes, every 20 minutes) to the terminal en route to Tula. **Pegasso** (www.pegasso.mx) buses (40 minutes, hourly) have a similar route. From the terminal, catch a combi (M$7.50) or secure taxi (M$35) to the *zócalo* (Plaza Virreinal).

Tula

🖉 773 / POP 27,295 / ELEV 2060M

A major city of the ancient, central Mexican culture widely known as Toltec, Tula is best known for its fearsome 4.5m-high stone warrior figures. Though less spectacular and far smaller than Teotihuacán, Tula is nonetheless fascinating and worth the effort of a day trip or overnight stay for those interested in ancient Mexican history.

The most attractive areas are the *zócalo* and Calle Quetzalcóatl, the pedestrianized street running north of the *zócalo* to a footbridge over the Tula river.

⊙ Sights

★ Zona Arqueológica de Tula
ARCHAEOLOGICAL SITE

(☑773-100-36-54; www.centrohidalgo.inah.gob.mx; Carretera Tula–Iturbe Km 2; adult/student M$70/free, Sun free, video camera use M$70; ⊙9am-5pm) Two kilometers north of Tula's center, ruins of the main ancient ceremonial site are perched on a hilltop. The highlight is standing atop a pyramid, virtually face-to-face with Toltec warrior statues, with views over rolling countryside (and the industrial sprawl nearby). Throughout the near-shadeless site, explanatory signs are in English, Spanish and Náhuatl. Near the main museum and the entrance to the site, you'll find souvenir markets on the weekends. Both of the onsite museums are free with site admission.

The main **site museum**, displaying ceramics, metalwork, jewelry and large sculptures, is near the entrance, at the north side of the *zona* from downtown on Calle Tollan. Outside the museum is a small, well-signed (in Spanish) cacti garden.

From the museum, the first large structure you'll reach is the **Juego de Pelota No 1** (Ball Court No 1). Archaeologists believe its walls were decorated with sculpted panels that were removed under Aztec rule.

Climb to the top of **Pirámide B**, also known as the Temple of Quetzalcóatl or Tlahuizcalpantecuhtli (the Morning Star), to see up close the impressive remains of three columnar roof supports – which once depicted feathered serpents with their heads on the ground and their tails in the air. The four basalt warrior telamones (male figures used as supporting columns; known as 'Los Atlantes') at the top, and the four pillars behind, supported the temple's roof. Wearing headdresses, breastplates shaped like butterflies and short skirts held in place by sun disks, the warriors hold spear throwers in their right hand and knives and incense bags in their left. The telamon on the left side is a replica of the original, now in Mexico City's Museo Nacional de Antropología (p91). The columns behind the telamones depict crocodile heads (which symbolize the Earth), warriors, symbols of warrior orders, weapons and Quetzalcóatl's head.

On the pyramid's north wall are some of the carvings that once surrounded the structure. These show the symbols of the warrior orders: jaguars, coyotes, eagles eating hearts, and what may be a human head in Quetzalcóatl's mouth.

Now roofless, the **Gran Vestíbulo** (Great Vestibule) extends along the front of the pyramid, facing the plaza. The stone bench carved with warriors originally ran the length of the hall, possibly to seat priests and nobles observing ceremonies in the plaza.

Near the north side of Pirámide B is the **Coatepantli** (Serpent Wall), which is 40m long, 2.25m high and carved with geometric patterns and a row of snakes devouring human skeletons. Traces remain of the original bright colors with which most of Tula's structures were painted.

Immediately west of Pirámide B, the **Palacio Quemado** (Burned Palace) is a series of halls and courtyards with more low benches and relief carvings, one depicting a procession of nobles. It was probably used for ceremonies or reunion meetings.

On the far side of the plaza is a path leading to the **Sala de Orientación Guadalupe Mastache**, a small museum named after one of the archaeologists who pioneered excavations here. It includes large items taken from the site, including the huge feet of caryatids (female figures used as supporting columns) and a visual representation of how the site might have looked in its prime.

Catedral de San José de Tula
CATHEDRAL

(☑773-732-00-33; cnr Zaragoza & Calle 5 de Mayo) **FREE** Tula's fortress-like cathedral, just off the *zócalo*, was part of the 16th-century monastery of San José. Inside, its vault ribs are decorated in gold.

🛏 Sleeping

Hotel Real Catedral
HOTEL $

(☑773-732-36-32; www.realhoteles.com/hotel-real-catedral; Av Zaragoza 106; d M$530-725, incl breakfast M$623-848; P❄🅿🛜) A street back from the plaza, the Real Catedral has some luxurious perks (a small gym, in-room coffee makers, hair dryers and safes) for the price. Many of the inside rooms lack natural light, but the suites offer balconies and street views. There's a restaurant, and a great selection of B&W photos of Tula in the lobby.

Hotel Casablanca
BUSINESS HOTEL $

(☑773-732-11-86; www.casablancatula.com; Pasaje Hidalgo 11; d/tr M$675/935; P🛜) This comfortable, practical business hotel is right in the heart of Tula, at the end of a narrow pedestrian passageway (look for the 'Milano' sign). Casablanca offers 36 rooms, all with cable TV, private bathroom and good wi-fi. Parking access is around the back, via Avenida Zaragoza.

Hotel Cuellar
BUSINESS HOTEL **$$**

(☑773-732-29-20; Calle 5 de Mayo 23; s/d/tr incl breakfast M$760/820/1400; P🐕❄) You may be in Tula for the pyramids, but here you can add a dip in the pool to your city escape. The palm trees, ample parking, low ceilings, frilly bedding and clashing pastel decor might make you swear you're at an LA motel and not near the *zócalo*. Comfortable clean beds make up for it.

Best Western Tula
BUSINESS HOTEL **$$**

(☑773-732-45-75; www.bestwesterntula.com; Av Zaragoza s/n; r from M$1100; P✳🐕) Small and friendly enough not to feel like an anonymous chain hotel, this Best Western has 18 cozy rooms and gives other midrange hotels in Tula a run for their money.

✗ Eating

Restaurant Casablanca
MEXICAN **$**

(☑773-732-22-74; www.casablancatula.com; Hidalgo 114; mains M$65-189, breakfasts M$149; ☺7am-9pm Mon-Fri, 7.30am-9pm Sat, 7.30am-6pm Sun; 🐕) While admittedly rather sterile – even Sanborns-esque – Casablanca has a full menu of Mexican standards, a good buffet (1pm to 6pm) and wi-fi. Just off the *zócalo*, it's one of the few sit-down options downtown, making it popular with businesspeople and travelers alike.

Mana
VEGETARIAN **$**

(☑773-100-31-33; Pasaje Hidalgo 13; menú del día/buffet M$50/70; ☺8am-5pm Sun-Fri; 🐕) This simple vegetarian restaurant serves a generous *menú del día* that includes wholewheat bread, vegetable soup and a pitcher of oat milk. There's also a selection of veggie burgers, *taquitos*, quesadillas, soups and salads. Everything's fresh, hearty and homemade.

❶ Getting There & Away

Tula's **bus terminal** (Central De Autobuses Tula; Xicoténcatl 14) is three blocks downhill from the cathedral. First-class **Ovnibus** (http://ovnibus. com.mx) buses travel to/from Mexico City's Terminal Norte (M$150, 1½ hours, every 30 minutes) and direct to/from Pachuca (M$140, 1½ hours, every 40 minutes). **Primera Plus** (https://wl.primeraplus.com.mx) has services to Querétaro (M$267, 2¼ hours, five daily). Companies often list the full name 'Tula de Allende'.

❶ Getting Around

If you arrive in Tula by bus, the easiest way to get around is on foot. To reach the *zócalo* (known locally as 'El Jardín') from the station, turn right on Xicoténcatl then immediately left on Rojo del Río and walk two blocks to Hidalgo. Take a right on Hidalgo, which dead-ends at Plaza de la Constitución and Jardín de Tula, Tula's main square.

To reach the Zona Arqueológica, continue right for 200m along Calle Zaragoza until the bridge over the river and catch a *taxi colectivo* (M$8.50, 10 minutes) to the Oxxo store outside the *zona*. Return taxis also depart from here. The site's secondary, south entrance is locked and defunct.

Unfortunately, the town's bus station lacks an *empaque* (baggage check), which is problematic for day trippers traveling with luggage.

Teotihuacán
☑594 / ELEV 2300M

This complex of awesome pyramids, set amid what was once Mesoamerica's greatest city, is the region's most visited destination. The sprawling site is comparable to the ruins of the Yucatán and Chiapas for significance and anyone lucky enough to come here will be inspired by the astonishing technological might of the Teotihuacán (teh-oh-tee-wah-*kahn*) civilization.

Set 50km northeast of Mexico City, in a mountain-ringed offshoot of the Valle de México, **Teotihuacán** (☑594-956-02-76; www.teotihuacan.inah.gob.mx; admission/parking M$75/45; ☺9am-5pm; P; 🚌 bound for Los Pirámides from Mexico City's Terminal Norte) is known for its two massive pyramids, the Pirámide del Sol (Pyramid of the Sun) and the Pirámide de la Luna (Pyramid of the Moon), which dominate the remains of the metropolis.

Though ancient Teotihuacán covered more than 20 sq km, most of what can be seen today lies along nearly 2km of the Calzada de los Muertos.

History

Teotihuacán was Mexico's biggest ancient city and the capital of what was probably Mexico's largest pre-Hispanic empire. It was a major hub of migration for people from the south, with multiethnic groups segregated into neighborhoods. Studies involving DNA tests in 2015 theorize that it was these cultural and class tensions that led to Teotihuacán's downfall.

The city's grid plan was plotted in the early part of the 1st century CE, and the Pirámide del Sol was completed – over an earlier cave shrine – by 150 CE. The rest of the city was developed between about 250 and 600 CE. Social, environmental and economic factors hastened its decline and eventual collapse in the 8th century.

The city was divided into quarters by two great avenues that met near La Ciudadela (the Citadel). One of them, running roughly north–south, is the famous Calzada de los Muertos (Avenue of the Dead), so called because the later Aztec believed the great buildings lining it were vast tombs, built by giants for Teotihuacán's first rulers. The major structures are typified by a *talud-tablero* style, in which the rising portions of stepped, pyramid-like buildings consist of both *talud* (sloping) and *tablero* (upright) sections. They were often covered in lime and colorfully painted. Most of the city was made up of residential compounds, some of which contained elegant frescoes.

Centuries after its fall, Teotihuacán remained a pilgrimage site for Aztec royalty, who believed that all of the gods had sacrificed themselves here to start the sun moving at the beginning of the 'fifth world,' inhabited by the Aztec themselves. It remains an important pilgrimage site: thousands of New Age devotees flock here each year to celebrate the vernal equinox (between March 19 and March 21) and to soak up the mystical energies believed to converge here.

◎ Sights

★ Pirámide del Sol ARCHAEOLOGICAL SITE
(Pyramid of the Sun) The world's third-largest pyramid – surpassed in size only by Egypt's Cheops (which is also a tomb, unlike the temples here) and the pyramid of Cholula – overshadows the east side of the Calzada de los Muertos. When Teotihuacán was at its height, the pyramid's plaster was painted bright red, which must have been a radiant sight at sunset. Clamber (carefully by rope) up the pyramid's 248 uneven steps – yes, we counted – for an inspiring overview of the ancient city.

The Aztec belief that the structure was dedicated to the sun god was validated in 1971, when archaeologists uncovered a 100m-long underground tunnel leading from the pyramid's west flank to a cave directly beneath its center, where they found religious artifacts. It's thought that the sun was worshipped here before the pyramid was built and that the city's ancient inhabitants traced the origins of life to this grotto.

The pyramid's base is 222m long on each side, and it's now just over 70m high. The pyramid was cobbled together around 100 CE, from three million tonnes of stone, without the use of metal tools, pack animals or the wheel.

No big backpacks are permitted up the Pirámide del Sol, and children must be accompanied by adults.

★ Pirámide de la Luna ARCHAEOLOGICAL SITE
(Pyramid of the Moon) The Pyramid of the Moon, at the north end of the Calzada de los Muertos, is smaller than the Pirámide del Sol, but more gracefully proportioned. Completed around 300 CE, its summit is nearly the same height as the Pirámide del Sol because it's built on higher ground, and is worth climbing for a perspective on the dominance of the larger pyramid, not to mention the best photos of the whole Teotihuacán complex.

The **Plaza de la Luna**, just in front of the pyramid, is a handsome arrangement of 12 temple platforms. Some experts attribute astronomical symbolism to the total number of 13 (made up of the 12 platforms plus the pyramid), a key number in the day-counting system of the Mesoamerican ritual calendar. The altar in the plaza's center is thought to have been the site of religious dancing.

Calzada de los Muertos ARCHAEOLOGICAL SITE
(Avenue of the Dead) Centuries ago, the Calzada de los Muertos must have seemed absolutely incomparable to its inhabitants, who were able to see its buildings at their best. Today it is the main path that connects most of the sights at Teotihuacán. Gate 1 brings you to the avenue in front of La Ciudadela. For 2km heading north, the avenue is flanked by former palaces of Teotihuacán's elite and other major structures, such as the Pirámide del Sol. The Pirámide de la Luna looms large at the north end. Look for the **puma mural** between the two pyramids.

★ Templo de Quetzalcóatl RUINS
(Temple of the Feathered Serpent) Teotihuacán's third-largest pyramid is the most ornate. The four surviving steps of the facade (there were originally seven) are adorned with striking carvings. In the *tablero* panels, the feathered serpent deity alternates with a two-fanged creature identified as the fire serpent, bearer of the sun on its daily journey across the sky. Imagine their eye sockets laid with glistening obsidian glass and the pyramid painted blue, as it once was. On the *talud* panels are side views of the plumed serpent.

Teotihuacán

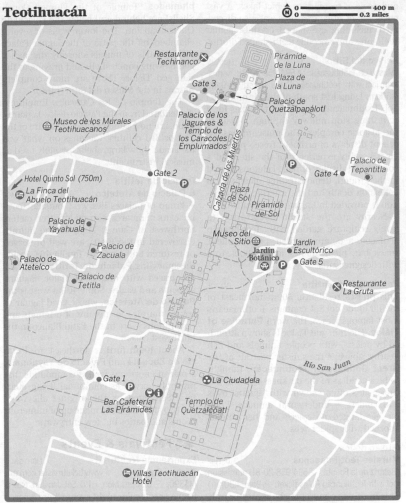

0 — 400 m
0 — 0.2 miles

Restaurante Techinanco

Pirámide de la Luna

Plaza de la Luna

Gate 3

Palacio de Quetzalpapálotl

Museo de los Murales Teotihuacanos

Palacio de los Jaguares & Templo de los Caracoles Emplumados

Calzada de los Muertos

Palacio de Tepantitla

Hotel Quinto Sol (750m)

Gate 2

Gate 4

La Finca del Abuelo Teotihuacán

Plaza de Sol

Pirámide del Sol

Palacio de Yayahuala

Palacio de Zacuala

Museo del Sitio

Jardín Escultórico

Jardín Botánico

Gate 5

Palacio de Atetelco

Palacio de Tetitla

Restaurante La Gruta

Río San Juan

Gate 1

La Ciudadela

Bar-Cafetería Las Pirámides

Templo de Quetzalcóatl

Villas Teotihuacán Hotel

The fearsome plumed serpent is a precursor to the later Aztec god Quetzalcóatl. Some experts think the temple carvings depict war, while others interpret them as showing the creation of time.

La Ciudadela
RUINS

(Citadel) This expansive square complex is believed to have been the residence of the city's supreme ruler, and its rooms may have been the city's administrative center. Four wide walls topped by 15 pyramids enclose a huge open space, with a major pyramid, the Templo de Quetzalcóatl (p158), built around 250 CE, to the east. The pyramids represented mountains during rituals where the plaza, representing the world of the living, was deliberately flooded.

Skeletal remains of 137 human victims have been found under and around this temple. DNA tests reveal they were brought from diverse parts of Mesoamerica to be sacrificed. Teotihuacán was a multiethnic city formed into different neighborhoods.

In 2003, heavy rains sculpted a sinkhole beneath La Ciudadela to reveal a tunnel 17m underground, installed with an impressive miniature landscape representing the underworld. The tunnel was decorated with fool's gold to represent the starry night sky and pools of mercury to depict lakes. A vast collection of ritual treasures was also discovered, including eye-shaped crystals, jaguar sculptures and crocodile teeth-shaped diorite.

Museo del Sitio   MUSEUM

(Museo de Teotihuacán; ☑ 594-958-20-81; admission incl with Teotihuacán Ruins ticket; ⊘ 9am-4:30pm) Lying just south of the Pirámide del Sol, Teotihuacán's site museum makes for a refreshing stop midway through a visit to the historic complex. The museum has excellent displays of artifacts, fresco panels, a virtual-reality experience of the site, and a confronting display of real skeletons buried in the ground, demonstrating ancient local beliefs on death and the afterlife. Information is provided in English and Spanish.

Nearby are the **Jardín Escultórico** (a lovely sculpture garden with Teotihuacán artifacts), a botanic garden, public toilets, snack bar, picnic tables and a bookstore with designer gifts.

Palacio de Tepantitla   PALACE

This priest's residence, 500m northeast of the Pirámide del Sol, contains Teotihuacán's most famous fresco, the worn **Paradise of Tláloc**. The rain god Tláloc is shown attended by priests, with people, animals and fish nearby. Above is the sinister portrait of the **Great Goddess of Teotihuacán**, thought to be a goddess of the darkness and war because she's often shown with jaguars, owls and spiders – underworld animals. Look for her fanged nosepiece and her shields adorned with spiderwebs.

Museo de los
Murales Teotihuacanos   MUSEUM

(Beatriz de la Fuente; ☑ 594-958-20-81; admission incl with Teotihuacán Ruins ticket; ⊘ 9am-4:30pm) This impressive museum showcases murals from Teotihuacán, as well as reconstructions of murals you'll see at the ruins. It's behind and to the left of the Pirámide de la Luna.

Palacio de Quetzalpapálotl   PALACE

(Palace of the Quetzal Butterfly) Off the Plaza de la Luna's southwest corner is the Palace of the Quetzal Butterfly, thought to be the home of a high priest. The remains of bears, armadillos and other exotic animals were discovered here, showing that the area was used by the elite for cooking and rituals – not the kind of animals an average person would have eaten.

The **Palacio de los Jaguares** (Jaguar Palace) and **Templo de los Caracoles Em-**

plumados (Temple of the Plumed Conch Shells) are behind and below the Palacio de Quetzalpapálotl. The lower walls of several chambers off the patio of the Jaguar Palace display parts of murals showing the jaguar god blowing conch shells and praying to the rain god Tláloc. There are more complete murals in the Museo del Sitio (p160).

The Templo de los Caracoles Emplumados, entered from the Palacio de los Jaguares' patio, is a now-subterranean structure of the 2nd or 3rd century. Carvings on what was its facade show large shells, possibly used as musical instruments.

Palacio de Tetitla
& Palacio de Atetelco   PALACE

A group of palaces lies west, outside Teotihuacán's main area, several hundred meters northwest of Gate 1. Many of the murals, discovered in the 1940s, are well preserved or restored and perfectly intelligible. Inside the sprawling **Palacio de Tetitla**, 120 walls are graced with murals of Tláloc, jaguars, serpents and eagles. Some 400m west is the **Palacio de Atetelco**, whose vivid jaguar or coyote murals – a mixture of originals and restorations – are in the Patio Blanco in the northwest corner.

About 100m further northeast are **Palacio de Zacuala** and **Palacio de Yayahuala**, a pair of enormous walled compounds that probably served as communal living quarters. Separated by the original alleyways, the two structures are made up of numerous rooms and patios but few entryways.

🎊 Festivals & Events

Experiencia Nocturna   LIGHT SHOW

(Night Experience; www.ticketmaster.com.mx; M$390; ⊘ 6:30pm Mon, Fri & Sat Jan-Jun, Nov & Dec) A spectacular night event where colored lights and video are projected onto the Pyramids of the Sun and Moon at Teotihuacán to a soundtrack. The 45-minute show may be slightly cheesy but it does give an impressive glimpse at the pyramids in their original red splendor. The 'Night Experience' is staged erratically, so check the website regularly, months in advance, as tickets sell out quickly.

🛏 Sleeping & Eating

Most people visit Teotihuacán as a day trip from Mexico City. If you want to start early at the site before the crowds arrive and don't want to take a dawn tour, the town of San Juan Teotihuacán, 2km from the archaeological zone, has a few good overnight options, though there is little life around.

Eating near the ruins is usually pricey and disappointing. You're much better off bringing a picnic, though there are a couple of enjoyable restaurants worth seeking out.

★ La Finca del Abuelo Teotihuacán   HOTEL $
(☑ 594-933-22-64; https://hotel-la-finca-del-abuelo-teotihuacan.negocio.site; cnr Juárez & 20 de Noviembre; d/tr/q M$735/920/1295; ⓅⓈ) The large manicured lawn with trickling fountains at this *finca* is an unexpected oasis a 10-minute walk to the eastern entrance to the pyramids, gate 2. It's not a true *finca* (farmhouse), but the spotless, tiled rooms with comfy beds set around upper-level balconies feel like a grandfather's country estate. There's even an old pool table in the onsite restaurant.

Hotel Quinto Sol   HOTEL $$
(☑ 594-956-18-81; www.facebook.com/hotelquintosolteotihuacan; Av Hidalgo 26, San Juan Teotihuacán; d/tr M$1200/1485; Ⓟ@Ⓢ☀) There's a reason most tourist groups stay at the Quinto Sol when visiting the ruins at Teotihuacán. With its fine facilities – including a decent-size pool, large, well-appointed fan-cooled rooms, good restaurant, in-room security boxes and room service – this is one of the best-equipped hotels in town.

Villas Teotihuacán Hotel   HOTEL $$$
(☑ 594-956-02-44; www.villasteo.com; Periférico Sur s/n, Zona Arqueológica; d from M$1850; Ⓟ✳@Ⓢ☀) Just south of the Zona Arqueológica, this elegant hotel has a small gym, a heated outdoor pool, a lit tennis court, a playground and a spa with temascal (pre-Hispanic steam bath). There's also a refined Mexican restaurant. Wi-fi is only accessible in the lobby.

Restaurante Techinanco   MEXICAN $$
(☑ 594-958-23-06; Zona Arqueológica ring road; mains M$100-140; ⊘10am-5.30pm; ⓓ) A short walk from gate 3, behind the Pirámide de la Luna, this cosy restaurant serves excellent home cooking at comparatively reasonable prices. The small menu takes in local favorites from enchiladas to homemade *moles* (chili sauce dishes) and vegan options. Cash only.

Ask about the curative massages or call in advance for a temascal.

★ Restaurante La Gruta   MEXICAN $$$
(☑ 594-956-01-27; www.lagruta.mx; Zona Arqueológica ring road; menú del día M$220, mains M$220-420; ⊘11am-7pm) Set in a vast, cool cave a short distance from gate 5, this tourist-centric restaurant is unapologetically gimmicky but definitely unique and kitsch fun. The Mexican and pre-Hispanic food, while pricey, is surprisingly decent. Go for the better-value *menú del día*. There's a 40-minute folkloric dance show on Saturdays at 3:30pm and Sundays at 1:30pm, 3:30pm and 5:30pm – reservations recommended.

ℹ Information

Information Booth (☑ 594-956-02-76; reservations 594-958-20-81; www.teotihuacan.inah.gob.mx; ⊘7am-6pm) Near the southwest entrance (gate 1) of Teotihuacán.

ℹ Getting There & Away

During daylight hours, **Autobuses México–San Juan Teotihuacán** (https://autobusesteotihuacan.com.mx) runs buses from Mexico City's Terminal Norte to the ruins (M$52, one hour) every hour from 7am to 6pm. When entering Terminal Norte, turn left to gate 8 for tickets, though ask which gate your bus departs from. Make sure your bus is headed for 'Los Pirámides,' not the nearby town of San Juan Teotihuacán (unless you are heading to accommodations in San Juan). Armed robberies still occasionally occur on these buses; for current warnings, search the **US State Department** (www.travel.state.gov) website for 'Teotihuacán.'

At the ruins, buses arrive and depart from near gate 1, also making stops at gates 2 and 3 via the ring road around the site. Your ticket allows you to re-enter through any of the five entrances on the same day. The site museum is just inside the main east entrance (gate 5).

Return buses are more frequent after 1pm. The last bus back to Mexico City leaves at 6pm; some terminate at Indios Verdes metro station, but most continue to Terminal Norte.

Alternatively, tours to the ruins are plentiful, are better value for solo travelers than renting a guide alone, and depart conveniently from Mexico City's Zócalo metro station or accommodations. Capital Bus (p108) and Turibús (p108) run daily minivan tours including a bilingual guide and entrance fee, with or without a visit to the Basílica de Guadalupe. Reservations are required.

ℹ Getting Around

To reach the pyramids from San Juan Teotihuacán, take a taxi (M$60) or any combi (M$14) labeled 'San Martín' departing from Avenida Hidalgo, beside the central plaza. Combis returning to San Juan stop on the main road outside gates 1, 2 and 3.

Mineral del Chico

📞 771 / POP 480

The charming old mining village of Mineral del Chico is among Mexico's newest *pueblos mágicos* and outshines the much larger Pachuca, the capital of Hidalgo state, at ground level. You can take an easy and very lovely day trip or weekend retreat from Pachuca to this 'little' town or the nearly 30-sq-km **Parque Nacional El Chico** (📞771-718-72-06; www.parqueelchico.gob.mx; per night cabins/campsites M$400/150; 🅿), which was established as a reserve in 1898.

The views are wonderful, the air is fresh and the mountains have some great hiking among spectacular rock formations and beautiful waterfalls. Most Mexicans who visit on the weekend hardly leave El Chico's cute main street (virtually the whole town) – not surprising when the locals are this friendly, proving their motto *'pueblo chico, gente grande'* (small town, great people).

👁 Sights

Peña del Cuervo Mirador   VIEWPOINT

FREE There are lovely wide-angled views of the green mountains in Parque Nacional El Chico from the Peña del Cuervo lookout, located on a peak at 2770m. People have visited this natural viewing point since the 1920s. The large stone figures in the distance are called Las Monjas (The Nuns) for their shape. Further away are more religiously named rocks, Los Frailes (The Friars).

From Mineral del Chico, *colectivos* marked 'Carboneras' (M$10) will drop you at the trailhead to the *mirador* (lookout). From there, it's about a 25-minute walk up a neglected cobbled staircase with a railing. Be careful after rain as there are plenty of loose stones. If you know what you're doing or have a guide, it's possible to walk back to town in about two hours.

🛏 Sleeping & Eating

Vagabundo de Media Noche   LODGE $

(📞771-157-59-55; Morelos s/n; d/ste M$700/1045; 🅿🛜) Like much in this budget, the hodge-podge of old linen screams outdated, but the beds are restful and clean and the spectacular views across the mountain are what you're probably really here for.

Hotel El Paraíso   LODGE $$

(📞771-715-56-54; www.hotelesecoturisticos.com.mx; Carretera Pachuca s/n; r M$1500; 🅿🛜) Nestled inside large, well-maintained grounds at the base of the mountain, with a fast-flowing stream running nearby, El Paraíso certainly has a location worthy of its name. The large, modern rooms lack individuality or charm, but they're very comfortable. A full-board option is available. Rates are reduced Sunday to Thursday.

La Trucha Grilla   SEAFOOD $$

(📞771-100-91-32; www.latruchagrilla.com.mx; El Calvario 3; mains M$120-250, breakfasts M$130; ⏱noon-9pm; 🍴) Fresh, locally grown vegetables, herbs and wild mushrooms are proudly on display and cooked up on the spot when you order at 'the Grilled Trout' restaurant. Naturally, the star is whole, fried or grilled fish, with fat shrimp skewers with optional salsas vying for attention too. Even salads are showy, with star fruit and dill zesting things up. Save room for lime-topped flan.

DON'T MISS

REAL DEL MONTE

This gorgeous mountain town is a tangle of houses, restaurants and *pastes* (pasties) shops scattered across a pine-tree-carpeted hillside. The air is thin here, so don't be surprised if you find yourself with a mild case of altitude sickness, but it's also clean, crisp and can get cold and windy suddenly (bring a sweater, if not a coat).

Two kilometers past the Hwy 105 turnoff for Parque Nacional El Chico, Real del Monte (officially known as Mineral del Monte) was the scene of a miners' strike in 1776, commemorated as the first strike in the Americas. Most of the town was settled in the 19th century after a British company commandeered the mines, and today Cornish-style cottages still line many of the steep, cobbled streets.

From central Pachuca, *colectivos* (M$11.50, 15 minutes, every 10 to 30 minutes) depart from Raza, near the corner of Carranza, opposite the Mercado Benito Juárez. Get off at the last stop, in the center of town, from where the last return bus to Pachuca departs at 10pm Monday to Saturday, or 9pm Sundays.

Set breakfasts include *chilaquiles* (fried tortillas with salsa and eggs or chicken) enchiladas and omelettes with coffee and house-made marmalade and bread.

ℹ Getting There & Away

From central Pachuca on Raza near the corner of Carranza, opposite the Mercado Benito Juárez, *colectivos* climb the winding roads up to Mineral del Chico (M$15, 40 minutes) every 20 minutes from 8am to 6pm. The last service back to Pachuca is at 7pm.

There's no direct transit service from Real del Monte, but those wanting to avoid a trip back to Pachuca to transfer *colectivos* can hire a taxi for about M$150.

Pachuca's **bus station** (☎ 771-713-34-47; Gómez) is 4km from downtown Pachuca. There's an ADO 1st-class bus service to/from Mexico City's TAPO terminal (M$109, two hours, hourly) and Terminal Norte (M$109, 1½ hours, every 15 minutes), as well as Poza Rica (M$296, 3 to 4½ hours, two daily) and Puebla CAPU (M$266, two hours, every one to two hours). Futura Estrella Blanca travels to Mexico City's two airport terminals (M$265, 2¼ hours, hourly, 3am to 8pm). Some routes have free wi-fi. Buses also go frequently to/from Tula and Querétaro.

Three scenic roads (Hwys 85, 105 and 130/132D) climb into the forested, often foggy, Sierra Madre Oriental.

EAST OF MEXICO CITY

The views get seriously dramatic as you head east from the capital, with the landscape peppered with the snowcapped, volcanic peaks of Popocatépetl, Iztaccíhuatl, La Malinche and Pico de Orizaba – the country's highest summit. The rugged Cordillera Neovolcánica offers anything from invigorating alpine strolls to demanding technical climbs. Unpredictable Popocatépetl, however, remains off-limits due to volcanic activity.

The gorgeous colonial city of Puebla – Mexico's fifth-largest city – is the dominant regional center, a local transportation hub and a big tourist draw with its churches dripping in tilework, plus rich culinary traditions, intriguing history and excellent museums. The surrounding state of Puebla is predominantly rural and home to approximately 500,000 indigenous people. Their rich handicraft culture ranges from pottery and carved onyx to embroidered textiles.

Attractive Cholula is now connected to Puebla by a convenient tourist train, making it easier than ever to drop by its youthful bars and chic restaurants.

Puebla

☑ 222 / POP 1.58 MILLION / ELEV 2160M

Once a bastion of conservatism, Catholicism and tradition, Puebla has come out of its colonial-era shell. The city retains a fantastically well-preserved center, a stunning cathedral and a wealth of beautiful churches, while younger *poblanos* (people from Puebla) are embracing the city's increasingly thriving art and nightlife scenes.

Puebla is well worth a visit, with 70 churches in the historic center alone, more than 1000 colonial-era buildings adorned with the Talavera-ware (painted ceramic tiles) for which the city is famous, and a long culinary history that can be explored at any restaurant or food stall. At its fringe, a museum dedicated to the baroque flaunts cutting-edge architecture that can compete with the world's showiest. For a city of its size, Puebla is far more relaxed and less gridlocked than you might expect.

History

Founded by Spanish settlers in 1531 as Ciudad de los Ángeles, with the aim of surpassing the nearby pre-Hispanic religious center of Cholula, the city became known as Puebla de los Ángeles (La Angelópolis) eight years later and quickly grew into an important Catholic center. Fine pottery had long been crafted from local clay, and after the colonists introduced new materials and techniques, Puebla pottery evolved as both an art and an industry. By the late-18th century, the city had emerged as a major producer of glass and textiles. With 50,000 residents by 1811, Puebla remained Mexico's second-biggest city until Guadalajara overtook it in the late-19th century.

In 1862 General Ignacio de Zaragoza fortified the Cerro de Guadalupe against the French invaders and on May 5 that year his 2000 men defeated a frontal attack by 6000, many of whom were handicapped by diarrhea. This rare Mexican military success is the reason for annual (and increasingly corporate-sponsored and drunken) celebrations in the US, where the holiday is far more significant than in Mexico and hundreds of streets are named Cinco de Mayo. Few seem to remember that the following year the reinforced French took Puebla and occupied the city until 1867.

Puebla

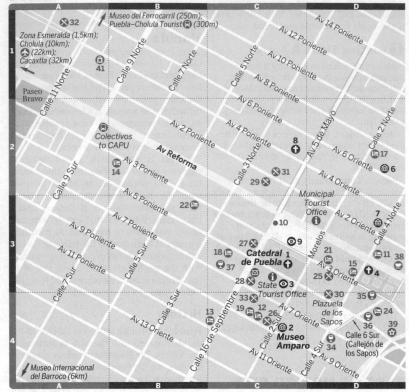

◉ Sights

Puebla's *centro histórico* (historic centre) is home to most of the attractions of interest, with the large, leafy *zócalo* and Mexico's tallest cathedral at its heart.

Most museums close on Mondays and have free admission on Tuesdays, but Museo Amparo is open and free on Sundays and Mondays, and Museo Internacional del Barroco is free on Wednesdays. The Zona Arqueológica in nearby Cholula is free on Sundays.

★ Catedral de Puebla
CATHEDRAL

(cnr Avs 3 Oriente & 16 de Septiembre; ◷ 9am-1pm & 4-8pm) **FREE** Puebla's impressive cathedral, which appeared on Mexico's M$500 bill until 2019, occupies the entire block south of the *zócalo*. Its architecture is a blend of severe Herreresque-Renaissance and early baroque styles. Construction began in 1550, but most of it took place under Bishop Juan de Palafox in the 1640s. At 69m, the towers are Mexico's tallest. The dazzling interior, the frescoes and the elaborately decorated side chapels are awe-inspiring; most have bilingual signs explaining their history and significance.

★ Museo Amparo
MUSEUM

(☏ 222-229-38-50; www.museoamparo.com; Calle 2 Sur 708; adult/student/child under 12yr M$35/25/free, Sun & Mon free; ◷ 10am-6pm Wed-Mon, to 9pm Sat; ♿) This superb private museum, housed in two linked 16th- and 17th-century colonial buildings, is loaded with pre-Hispanic artifacts, yet the interior design is contemporary and stylish. Displayed with explanatory information sheets in English and Spanish, the collection is staggering. Notice the thematic continuity in Mexican design – the same motifs appear again and again on dozens of pieces. An example: the pre-Hispanic cult skeleton heads are eerily similar to the candy skulls sold during Día de Muertos.

The wonderful cafe terrace hosts free live music from 8pm to 9pm every Friday. There

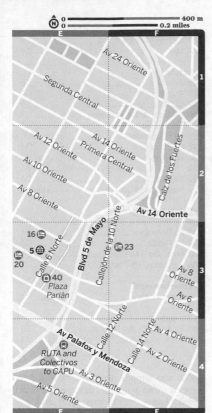

Inside, eight permanent and three temporary exhibition halls are joined by wavy staircases and curved walls in a nod to the baroque's obsession with water as a motif. This culminates in a central spiraling fountain and water views. In the upstairs education area, you can glimpse baroque art being restored. English explanations, modern audiovisual exhibitions, the breadth and variety covered and the architecture itself make this museum a star attraction and welcome addition to Puebla.

To get here from CAPU, take bus Perimetral 2, 14 La Loma, or 14 'A'. From the historic center, take bus 29 Verde Atlixcáyotl-CIS-Finanzas, 29 Verde Zavaleta, or 45 Prepa 2 de Octubre–Parque Ecológico; or a taxi (25 minutes) for about M$120. ADO and Ebus run direct buses to the nearby (2km) Paseo Destino terminal from Mexico City.

Zócalo
PLAZA

Puebla's central plaza was originally a marketplace where bullfights, theater and hangings occurred, before assuming its current arboretum-like appearance in 1854. The surrounding arcades date from the 16th century. The plaza fills with an entertaining mix of clowns, balloon hawkers, food vendors and people using the free wi-fi on weekend evenings.

Museo Casa del Alfeñique
MUSEUM

(☑ 222-232-04-58; Av 4 Oriente 416; adult/student M$40/20, Tue free; ☉10am-6pm Tue-Sun) This renovated colonial house is an outstanding example of the over-the-top 18th-century decorative style *alfeñique,* characterized by elaborate stucco ornamentation and named after a candy made from sugar and egg whites (evolving into modern-day Pueblan marzipan). The 1st floor details the Spanish conquest, including indigenous accounts in the form of drawings and murals. The 2nd floor houses a large collection of historic and religious paintings, local furniture and household paraphernalia. Labeling is in Spanish only.

Biblioteca Palafoxiana
LIBRARY

(☑ 222-232-34-83; http://palafoxiana.com/biblio teca; Av 5 Oriente 5; adult/student M$40/20, Tue free; ☉10am-6pm Tue-Sun) Situated above the Casa de la Cultura and founded in 1646, Biblioteca Palafoxiana was the first public library in the Americas. For this, Palafoxiana has been listed on the Unesco Memory of the World register. The handsome library

are often free art workshops for children on Saturday and Sunday. Free guided tours in Spanish are held daily at 4.30pm, as well as 6.30pm Saturdays and noon Sundays.

★ Museo Internacional del Barroco
MUSEUM

(http://mib.puebla.gob.mx; Atlixcáyotl 2501, Reserva Territorial Atlixcáyotl; adult/child M$80/40, Wed free, guided tour M$200; ☉10am-7pm Tue-Sun) This monumental white, architecturally spectacular museum is dedicated to the showy baroque movement – art, fashion, music and literature. The museum, designed by Japanese architect Itō Toyo, emerges from behind a lake, 7km southwest of Puebla's *zócalo,* evoking the drama of the 17th and 18th century. Reserve a whole afternoon to appreciate the art and the building. Expect rare violins, action-packed paintings by Rubens, performances by actors in period costumes, stained glass, gold crowns and ornate everything to convey the exuberance of baroque.

Puebla

houses thousands of rare books on its gorgeous shelves – carved cedar and white pine – including one of the earliest New World dictionaries and the 1493 *Nuremberg Chronicle,* with more than 2000 engravings.

Casa de la Cultura
NOTABLE BUILDING
(☎222-232-12-27; Av 5 Oriente 5; ◉8am-8pm Mon-Fri, 9am-1pm Sat, 10am-6pm Sun) **FREE** Occupying the entire block facing the south side of the cathedral, the former bishop's palace is a classic 17th-century brick-and-tile edifice that now houses government offices, the Casa de la Cultura and the State Tourist Office. Inside are art galleries, a bookstore and cinema, and a congenial cafe out back in the courtyard. Upstairs is the 1646 Biblioteca Palafoxiana.

Iglesia de la Compañía
CHURCH
(cnr Av Palafox y Mendoza & Calle 4 Sur; ◉entry 7am-2pm & 4-8pm, Mass 7pm) **FREE** This Jesuit church with a 1767 Churrigueresque facade is also called Espíritu Santo. Beneath the altar is a tomb said to be that of a 17th-century South Asian princess who was sold into slavery in Mexico and later freed.

She was supposedly responsible for the colorful *china poblana* costume – a shawl, frilled blouse, embroidered skirt and gold and silver adornments. This costume became a kind of 'peasant chic' in the 19th century. But *china* (*chee*-nah) also meant 'maidservant,' and the style may have evolved from Spanish peasant costumes.

Museo del Ferrocarril
MUSEUM
(☎222-774-01-06; http://museoferrocarriles mexicanos.gob.mx; Calle 11 Norte 1005; adult/child M$16/free, Sun free; ◉9am-5pm Tue-Sun; ⏵) This excellent railway museum with activities for kids is housed in Puebla's former train station and the spacious grounds surrounding it. There are ancient steam-powered monsters through to relatively recent passenger carriages, many of which you can enter. One carriage contains an excellent collection of photos of various derailments and other disasters that occurred during the 1920s and '30s.

Museo San Pedro de Arte
MUSEUM
(☎222-246-66-18; Calle 4 Norte 203; adult/student M$40/20, Tue free; ◉10am-6pm Tue-Sun) Opened in 1999 as Museo Poblano de Arte

Virreinal, this top-notch museum is now named after the 16th-century Hospital de San Pedro in which it is housed. Galleries display excellent contemporary art and there's a fascinating permanent exhibit on the hospital's history.

Templo de Santo Domingo   CHURCH
(cnr Avs 5 de Mayo & 4 Poniente; ⊙7.30am-2pm & 4-8pm) FREE This fine Dominican church features a stunning Capilla del Rosario (Rosary Chapel), south of the main altar, which is the main reason to come here. Built between 1650 and 1690, it's heavy on gilded plaster and carved stone, with angels and cherubs seemingly materializing from behind every gold leaf. See if you can spot the heavenly orchestra.

Outside the entrance, in the Zona de Monumentos, you'll often find sculpture exhibitions.

Museo de la Revolución   MUSEUM
(Casa de los Hermanos Serdán; ☑222-242-10-76; Av 6 Oriente 206; adult/student M$40/20, Tue free; ⊙10am-6pm Tue-Sun) This pockmarked 19th-century house was the scene of the first battle of the 1910 Revolution. The renovated house retains its bullet holes and some revolutionary memorabilia, including a room dedicated to female insurgents.

Betrayed only two days before a planned uprising against the dictatorship of Porfirio Díaz, the Serdán family (Aquiles, Máximo, Carmen and Natalia) and 17 others fought 500 soldiers until only Aquiles, their leader, and Carmen were left alive. Aquiles, hidden under the floorboards, might have survived if the damp hadn't provoked a cough that gave him away. Both were subsequently killed.

⚲ Tours

Turibus   BUS
(☑222-231-52-17; www.turibus.com.mx; tours adult/child Cholula M$160/90, Puebla centro M$80/45; ⊙tours Cholula 11am Mon-Fri, 11am & 1pm Sat, 1pm Sun; Centro every 40min 9am-9pm) Operated by ADO bus lines, this four-hour tour gives an overview of the nearby town of Cholula, including the pyramid (admission is a separate cost). There is also a red double-decker, hop-on/ hop-off bus route around Puebla's *centro histórico* (not including Museo Internacional del Barroco). Tours start from the west side of the *zócalo*; buy tickets on board.

🎊 Festivals & Events

Feria de Puebla   MUSIC
(⊙Apr-May) Starting in late April and ending in late May, this fair honors the state's achievements with cultural and music events.

Cinco de Mayo   PARADE
(⊙May 5) The city's May 5 celebrations mark the day in 1862 when the Mexican army defeated the French. There is a huge parade and celebrations over the following fortnight. Cinco de Mayo celebrations are generally a much bigger deal in the US than in Mexico, except for those in Puebla, which continue to grow in size.

Festival del Mole Poblano   FOOD & DRINK
(⊙Jun) In early June the city celebrates its most famous contribution to the culinary arts: *mole poblano,* a thick sauce of chilies, fruits, nuts, spices and chocolate.

Festival del Chile en Nogada   FOOD & DRINK
(⊙Aug) Leaving no culinary stone unturned, the city's savvy restaurateurs promote the country's 'patriotic recipe,' *chiles en nogada* – green chilies stuffed with *picadillo* (a mix of ground meat and fruit) and topped with a luscious walnut-cream sauce.

Día de Muertos   CULTURAL
(⊙Oct) Puebla has jumped on the bandwagon, with a fortnight-long citywide cultural program starting in late October devoted to the Day of the Dead and including nighttime museum visits and viewings of *ofrendas* (altars).

🛏 Sleeping

Puebla's hotel scene is competitive, with a huge range at all budgets and high standards in many boutique three- and four-star hotels. The Municipal Tourist Office (p173) on the *zócalo* provides flyers for budget hotels with prices. It's worth searching online for last-minute rates.

Many hotels can be spotted by illuminated 'H' signs over their entrance. Most of the colonial-era buildings have two types of room – interior (lacking windows) and exterior (exposed to a noisy street).

Hotel Elena Único   HOTEL $
(☑222-242-46-89; http://elenahotelunico.com; Calle 2 Norte 608; d incl breakfast from M$635; 🖲) The stuff of romance, with double-ceilinged rooms, plush four-poster beds and ornate wallpaper, even if it is a modern refurbishment of an old building. Road-facing rooms

have wooden shutters to block the light, though not the morning traffic noise; rooftop rooms are quiet and have their own private mini-terraces, for the same price.

Hotel El Descanso HOTEL $

(222-196-65-21; http://hoteleldescansopuebla.com; Av 6 Oriente 413, Barrio del Artista; d/tw M$700/850;) New in 2019 though decorated like a stylish ranch with stone arches ringing tranquil courtyards, Descanso is indeed 'restful' with its simple metal beds. Only the passageway-facing windows and lack of a lift might not be for everyone. The surrounding area is among the museums, bars and restaurants of the 'artist area' and an easy stroll to the *zócalo*.

Hotel Teresita HOTEL $

(Hotel Teresa; 222-232-70-72; www.hotelteresita.com.mx; Av 3 Poniente 309; s/d/q M$320/515/615;) Among the multiple dreary posadas near the *zócalo*, Hotel Teresita sparkles with modern rooms boasting private bathrooms. The trade-off is tiny space, ancient TVs and internal-facing windows (with footfall noise), but crisp white sheets, comfy beds and thorough cleanliness make Teresita a bargain.

Hostel Gente de Más HOSTEL $

(222-232-31-36; www.facebook.com/hostelgentedemas; Av 3 Poniente 713; dm/d/q M$180/450/600;) This fresh hostel has 'poshtel' aspirations with arty, rustic touches to the former house. Bathrooms are tiny and noise travels easily along the long halls, but the mostly windowless rooms are clean and comfortable. Bonuses include a roof terrace, interesting murals and games nights.

Hostal Casona Poblana HOSTEL $

(222-246-03-83; http://casonapoblana.com; Calle 16 de Septiembre 905; dm/d/tr/q incl breakfast M$175/560/700/820;) The tiled, sparse rooms at this bright hostel have an openness to them, being built around a covered courtyard that is sociable without being party central. This setup means noise and cold travel easily, though wi-fi not so much. There is also a roof garden and small kitchen. Look for the large 'Hostal' banner out front.

★**Hotel Colonial** HOTEL $$

(222-246-46-12, 800-013-00-00; www.colonial.com.mx; Calle 4 Sur 105; s/d/tr M$800/900/1000;) Once part of a 17th-century Jesuit monastery and existing as a hotel in various forms since the mid-19th century, the Colonial exudes heritage from its many gorgeously furnished rooms (half with colonial decor, half modern). There's a good restaurant and a fantastic 1890 gilt elevator. An unbeatable vibe and location despite occasional live-music and street noise.

Hotel Puebla de Antaño BOUTIQUE HOTEL $$

(222-246-24-03; www.hotelpuebladeantano.com; Av 3 Oriente 206; ste incl breakfast M$1340-1680;) This boutique hotel has marble washbasins, crown molding, in-room fireplaces and Jacuzzis, and vintage photographs on the walls. The ground floor is home to one of Puebla's more refined French-influenced restaurants, **Casa de los Espejos**, while the rooftop **Las Chismes de Puebla** bar is almost painfully chic (think summertime in the Hamptons).

Check the website for hefty discounts.

Hotel Isabel DESIGN HOTEL $$

(222-144-45-38; http://isabelhotelunico.com; Av 5 Poniente 125; d/tw from M$780/950;) Designer touches at good prices isn't too much to ask for, surely. Just soft hidden lighting, neutral tones, dark marble bathroom tiling, cotton sheets and some of the comfiest beds around – Isabel has it all. Some rooms even have Jacuzzi bathtubs.

Light sleepers, avoid staying at the front on the ground level, which is near a karaoke restaurant.

Hotel Nube HOTEL $$

(222-290-23-70; www.hotelnubepuebla.com; Av 4 Oriente 407; d/tr from M$1130/1500;) Floating near the *zócalo* but without the noise, the almost-designer Hotel Nube offers fresh rooms with clean beds, modern bathrooms and a roof garden with a view. A mini-gym, pet-friendly policy and helpful staff are pluses, though no English is spoken.

Room discounts available Sunday to Thursday.

Mesón Sacristía de la Compañía BOUTIQUE HOTEL $$

(222-232-45-13; http://mesones-sacristia.com; Calle 6 Sur 304; ste incl breakfast M$1200-1600;) With eight rooms set around a bright, kitschy, pink courtyard, this small inn feels like the home of an eccentric grandmother. The junior suites are actually just standard rooms, while the two master suites are bigger and more worthy of the title. The downstairs restaurant, which serves aromatic US-style breakfasts and refined *poblano* cuisine, gets rave reviews from guests.

LA MALINCHE VOLCANO

The long, sweeping slopes of this dormant 4460m **volcano**, named after Cortés' now much-maligned indigenous interpreter and concubine, dominate the skyline northeast of Puebla, and are visible on a clear day. La Malinche, Mexico's fifth-tallest peak, is snow-capped only a few weeks each year, typically in May. Hiking here is most popular with families on weekends.

Centro Vacacional IMSS Malintzi (☑ 800-623-23-23; http://centrosvacacionales. imss.gob.mx; campsites M$75, cabins up to 6 people M$1000, up to 9 people with kitchen M$1570; ℗), operated by the Mexican Social Security Institute, has 50 cabins, including rustic and 'luxury' options, at a frosty 3333m, and is the starting point of most hikes. The family-oriented resort has woodsy grounds and fine views of the peak. The remodeled cabins are basic, but include TV, fireplace, hot water and kitchen with refrigerator. It gets crowded from Friday to Sunday, but is quiet midweek. Prices are about M$100 higher on weekends and holidays. Those not staying can park here for M$40. An onsite restaurant operates from 9am to 9pm.

Beyond the vacation center, the road becomes impassable by car. It's about 1km by footpath to a ridge, from where it's an arduous five-hour round-trip hike to the top. Hikers should take precautions against altitude sickness.

The main route to the volcano is Hwy 136; turn southwest at the 'Centro Vacacional Malintzi' sign. Before you reach the center, you must register at the entrance of Parque Nacional La Malintzi. Some colectivos to the entrance leave at 8:20am from the town of Apizaco (M$30, 40 minutes) from the corner of Avenidas Hidalgo and Serdán outside Elektra, returning at 1pm, 3pm (Friday to Sunday) and 5pm. From CAPU in Puebla, ATAH buses (M$60) run to Apizaco.

Hotel Mesón de San Sebastián BOUTIQUE HOTEL **$$**
(☑ 222-242-65-23; www.mesonsansebastian.com; Av 9 Oriente 6; d/tw incl breakfast M$900/1700; ❧) This elegant boutique hotel has a colorful courtyard, accommodating staff who speak English, and a reputation for being family-friendly. Each of the 17 rooms is individually decorated and named after a saint. All rooms have TV, phone, safe, minibar and antique furnishings. Discounts are offered during quiet periods.

★**La Purificadora** BOUTIQUE HOTEL **$$$**
(☑ 222-309-19-20; www.lapurificadora.com; Callejón de la 10 Norte 802; d/ste from M$4610/7300; ℗❧☒) From the trendy hotel company that runs Mexico City's chic Condesa df, Purificadora's stunning design has sharp, dramatic angles and a magnificent infinity pool on the roof. As its sister hotel did in the capital, La Purificadora has fast become the hip hangout of the *poblano* elite. Prices vary widely and fall Sunday through Thursday, with frequent last-minute specials on the hotel website.

El Sueño Hotel & Spa BOUTIQUE HOTEL **$$$**
(☑ 222-232-64-23, 222-232-64-89; www.elsuenohotel.com; Av 9 Oriente 12; d/ste incl breakfast from M$1855/2588; ℗✳❧) An oasis of minimalist chic amid the colonial bustle of Puebla's old town, Sueño's 20 rooms are sleek, sumptuous, high-ceilinged and thematically decorated. Each is inspired by a different female Mexican artist. There's a hot tub and sauna, plasma TVs in the rooms and a martini bar and decorative pool around the lobby. Rooms are discounted Sunday to Thursday.

Casona de la China Poblana LUXURY HOTEL **$$$**
(☑ 222-242-03-61; https://casonadelachinapoblana .mx; cnr Calle 4 Norte & Av Palafox y Mendoza; d M$2800, ste M$3100-4000; ℗❧) This elegant boutique hotel is stunning and knows it. Shamelessly dubbing itself Puebla's 'most exclusive hotel,' China Poblana has massive, gorgeous suites decorated in a mixture of styles that all conjure the golden age of cinema, a lovely courtyard and La Cocina de la China Poblana restaurant.

Reserve on the website for a 20% discount and complimentary breakfast.

✖ Eating

Puebla's culinary heritage, of which *poblanos* are rightly proud, can be explored in a range of eateries throughout the city, from humble street-side food stalls to elegant colonial-style restaurants. However, given the city's renown as a culinary center, it's surprising how few truly excellent high-end restaurants there are.

★ La Zanahoria

VEGETARIAN $

(☑ 222-232-48-13; Av 5 Oriente 206; mains M$69-93, set meals M$90, daily buffet adult M$104-142, child M$63-85; ☺ 7.30am-7:30pm Mon-Sat, to 6.30pm Sun; ☺☎☑📶) This blessing for vegetarians is an excellent place for lunch, just moments from the *zócalo*. The draw is the popular daily buffet from 1pm to 6pm in the spacious interior colonial courtyard. It features more than 20 dishes, salads and desserts, such as soy-meat lasagna, *chilaquiles* and Middle Eastern tabbouleh, and includes a drink and coffee.

The extensive à la carte menu includes everything from soy or oat *hamburguesas* (popular at a mere M$29) to *nopales rellenos* (stuffed cactus paddles) and breakfasts. In the front of the restaurant is the express-service area (including a juice bar and a health-food snack shop).

★ Las Ranas

TACOS $

(☑ 222-242-47-34; Av 2 Poniente 102; tacos & tortas M$11-30; ☺ noon-9:30pm Mon-Sat, 2pm-9pm Sun) This local institution is *the* place to try one of Puebla's great dishes: the *taco árabe*. Unbelievably moist *al pastor* pork is marinated and spit-grilled then rolled in fresh, slightly charred Middle Eastern–style flatbread. This restaurant and the annex across the street, El Patio de las Ranas (Av 2 Poniente 205), are perpetually full but worth the wait for the unforgettable tacos.

An English menu and ample seating make things easy. Legend has it that Mexico's *taco árabe* and *al pastor* came into being in Puebla, as a fusion food of the kebab and shawarma of Middle Eastern residents.

Comal

MEXICAN $

(☑ 222-688-48-88; http://comal.com.mx; Av 16 de Septiembre 311B; mains M$79-139, snacks from M$22; ☺ 8am-midnight; ☎☑📶) Comal is your old dependable in Puebla. Come for flavorful, good-value *poblano* dishes like chicken *mole*, *cemitas* (a style of sandwich/burger unique to Puebla), *nopal* (cactus) soup, and tacos with cheese-stuffed chilies or *arrachera* (steak). Groups and families can breathe in the roomy, clean and cafe-like space. Trusty Comal opens early for breakfasts, and late for mezcal, wine, margaritas and snacks.

Mercado de Sabores Poblanos

MARKET $

(Av 4 Poniente, btwn Calles 11 & 13 Norte; snacks from M$10, menú del día from M$65; ☺ 7am-7pm; 📶) The 6570-sq-meter Mercado de Sabores Poblanos is a budget-friendly complement to Puebla's food scene with everything from snacks to full meals. A sparkling food court with space for families serves local specialties such as *cemitas* (a style of sandwich/burger unique to Puebla), *pipián verde* (chicken with green pumpkin-seed sauce) and *tacos árabes* (pita-bread pork taco) from 130-odd vendors.

It's quite a hike from the *zócalo* and best combined with other nearby sights or on your way back from Cholula.

★ El Mural de los Poblanos

MEXICAN $$

(☑ 222-225-06-50; www.elmuraldelospoblanos. com; Av 16 de Septiembre 506; mains M$175-350; ☺ 8am-midnight; ❋☎) Set back from the street in a gorgeous, plant-filled colonial courtyard, El Mural de los Poblanos serves excellent, traditional *poblano* dishes in an elegant setting. The house specialty is five kinds of *mole*. Other favorites include the

---

PUEBLA'S SEASONAL TREATS

Justly famous for its incredible cuisine, Puebla also offers an array of seasonal, local delicacies that adventurous eaters should not miss.

Escamoles (March to June) Ant larvae; looks like rice and is usually sautéed in butter.

Gusanos de maguey (April to May) Worms that inhabit the *maguey* plant, typically fried in a drunken chili and *pulque* (a low-alcohol brew made from the *maguey* plant) sauce.

Huitlacoche (June to October) Inky-black corn fungus with an enchanting, earthy flavor. Sometimes spelt *cuitlacoche*.

Chiles en nogada (July to September) Green chilies stuffed with *picadillo* (a mix of ground meat and dried fruit), covered with a creamy walnut sauce and sprinkled with red pomegranate seeds.

Chapulines (October to November) Grasshoppers purged of digestive matter then dried, smoked or fried in lime and chili powder.

smoky goat's-cheese-stuffed *chile relleno* and the trilogy of *cemitas*. Cocktails and other drinks are also excellent, and the service exceptional. At different times of the year you can try local insect dishes such as *escamoles* (ant larvae).

Reservations are a good idea on busy Friday and Saturday nights and holidays; it's open 365 days a year.

★ Nelhua
MEXICAN **$$**

(☑222-290-48-13; https://nelhua.mx; Av 7 Oriente 5; snacks M$70-90, mains M$180-310; ☺1-10pm Tue-Thu, 9am-10pm Fri & Sat, 9am-6pm Sun; 🛜) Talk about hitting all the right notes. The contemporary Mexican dishes at Nelhua highlight the complex flavors of *mole* – from smoked *poblano* on turkey to *pepián* on fish – not to mention the delightful edible flowers, sprouts and berries. Other wins are the industrial-chic lamps, bare walls and angular chairs, plus servers showing passion for their food.

Pop by the cafe level, where snacks such as quesadillas with *chapulines* (grasshoppers) and breakfast sandwiches are excellent. Upstairs is a bar mixing creative cocktails (how about avocado or amaranth?), if you never want to leave.

Augurio
MEXICAN **$$**

(☑222-290-23-78; www.augurio.mx; Av 9 Oriente 16; mains M$180-290; ☺8am-11pm Mon-Sat, to 6pm Sun; P🐾) Chef Ángel Vázquez has brought international flavors to Puebla in other ventures, but with Augurio he creates gourmet experiences in an intimate space out of local dishes such as the starter of *camarones en costra de chicharrón* (shrimp crumbed in pork crackling) and 10 kinds of *mole* mains, including trout in a red pepita *mole* with buttery *escamoles*.

There is a kids' play area.

Restaurante Sacristía
MEXICAN **$$**

(☑222-242-45-13; http://mesones-sacristia.com; Calle 6 Sur 304; mains M$145-195; ☺1-11pm Tue-Sat, 9am-6pm Sun) Set in the delightful colonial patio of the Mesón Sacristía de la Compañía (p168) hotel, this is an elegant place for a meal of authentic *mole* and creative twists on rich *poblano* cuisine, or a cocktail or coffee in the intimate **Confesionario** bar. Live piano and violin soloists (and flower petals by request) lend a romantic ambience most nights from around 9pm.

If you like what you taste, inquire about the small-group **cooking classes**.

Amalfi
PIZZA **$$**

(☑222-403-77-97; Av 3 Oriente 207B; pizzas M$150-190; ☺1-9:45pm Sun-Thu, to 11pm Fri & Sat; 🛜🐾) It's easy to see why this excellent wood-oven pizzeria – with dim lighting, terra-cotta walls and beamed ceilings – is a popular date spot. In addition to a wide selection of fine, thin-crust pizzas, there's decent wine and Italian classics such as caprese salads and pasta. Because the dining room is small, a reservation doesn't hurt.

La Purificadora
INTERNATIONAL **$$$**

(☑222-309-19-20; www.lapurificadora.com; Callejón de la 10 Norte 802, Paseo San Francisco, Barrio El Alto; mains M$170-410; ☺7am-11pm Sun-Thu, to midnight Fri & Sat; P🛜) The restaurant at La Purificadora (p169), one of Puebla's chicest boutique hotels, is set in a spare, loft-like space with unfinished walls and long, narrow wood-plank tables. The menu tends more toward the indulgent and elaborate, with dishes such as shrimp in hibiscus and passionfruit sauce or chicken *mole* with peanut polenta. There is also a good drinks list.

The only vegetarian choices are mushroom and matcha tacos or starters.

🍷 Drinking & Nightlife

During the day students pack the sidewalk tables along the pedestrian-only block of Avenida 3 Oriente, near the university. At night, mariachis lurk around Callejón de los Sapos – Calle 6 Sur between Avenidas 3 and 7 Oriente – but they're being crowded out by the bars on nearby Plazuela de los Sapos. These rowdy watering holes are packed on weekend nights, when many of them become live-music venues.

★ La Pasita
BAR

(☑222-232-44-22; Av 5 Oriente 602; shots from M$25; ☺1-5:30pm Wed-Mon) This tiny bar among the antique stores of La Plazuela de Los Sapos has been serving liqueur shots for over century. Try sweet and strong *la pasita* (raisin), *rompope* (eggnog), *almendra* (almond) or the romantically named 'artist's blood' of quince and apricot. The eclectic kitsch decor and old-world experience is worth the trip alone. Cash only.

Mezcalería Miel de Agave
COCKTAIL BAR

(☑222-688-46-46; Av 7 Poniente 110; ☺5-11pm Sun-Thu, to 1am Fri & Sat) A wall brimming with mezcal bottles could make you light-headed with choice, but the bartender-owner can guide you through the different varieties at this tiny bar. Sniff before you drink shots *a besos* (sipping with 'kisses') or in margaritas. Also try *pulque* and the *yolixpa*, a pre-Hispanic liqueur made with dozens of herbs from Sierra Norte, Puebla.

La Berenjena
CRAFT BEER

(🖉 222-688-47-54; www.laberenjenapizza.com; Av 3 Oriente 407; ⊘2-11pm Mon & Wed-Sat, to 7pm Sun; 🛜) Excellent artisanal pizzas are the specialty promoted at 'The Aubergine,' but the bar's long list of Mexican craft beers and mezcals are just as special. There is also wine, cocktails (mezcal mojito, anyone?) and fancy snacks to share such as honey-roasted goat's cheese and baba ghanoush (aubergine dip).

All Day Café & Bar
BAR

(🖉 222-242-44-55; www.facebook.com/allday cafeybar; Av 7 Oriente; snacks M$60; ⊘8.30am-10pm Mon-Thu, to 12:30am Fri & Sat, to 8pm Sun) This colorful cafe-bar, a student hangout just off Plazuela de los Sapos, is housed in a bright courtyard and turns into a club in the evenings. It serves a range of sandwiches, sushi, pastries, coffees and cocktails all day long, just as the name suggests.

Zaranda Café Palafox
CAFE

(🖉 222-242-09-88; http://zaranda.mx; Av Palafox y Mendoza 412; coffee M$18-32; ⊘8.30am-9pm; 🛜) Oh yes, Puebla now has excellent specialty coffee made by skilled baristas. Charming patio tables ringed by stone archways fit for a date? Yes, that too. Nab the indoor couches to relax with a croissant, bagel or chai and some travel reading.

☆ Entertainment

★ Celia's Cafe
LIVE MUSIC

(🖉 222-242-36-63; www.facebook.com/Celias CafePuebla; Av 5 Oriente 608; ⊘9am-10pm Wed-Fri, to 11:30pm Sat, 10am-6pm Sun) Live music adds old-world romance to the *poblano* decor at this sprawling bar-restaurant. Enjoy your meal with musicians playing *trova* (troubadour-type folk music; 8pm to 10pm Thursday), piano (8pm to 10pm Friday, breakfast and lunch Saturday and Sunday) or *bohemia* (love songs; 7pm to 9pm Saturday).

Every *mole poblano*, coffee and tequila shot is served up in (purchasable) Talavera-ware that is crafted in Celia's own studio. There's also a popular Friday breakfast buffet.

🛍 Shopping

The Zona Esmeralda, 2km west of the *zócalo*, is a stretch of Avenida Juárez with chichi boutiques, upscale restaurants and trendy nightclubs.

For quirky **antique stores**, head to Callejón de los Sapos, around the corner of Avenida 5 Oriente and Calle 6 Sur. Most shops open from 10am to 7pm. On Saturdays and Sundays, there is a lively outdoor antiques market here and at the Plazuela de los Sapos from 10am to 5pm.

A number of shops along Avenida 6 Oriente, to the east of Avenida 5 de Mayo, sell traditional handmade Puebla **sweets** such as *camotes* (candied sweet-potato sticks) and *jamoncillos* (bars of pumpkin-seed paste).

Puebla has plenty of shops selling the colorful, hand-painted ceramics known as **Talavera**. There are several good stores on Plazuela de los Sapos and the streets around it. Designs reveal Asian, Spanish-Arabic and Mexican indigenous influences. Bigger pieces are expensive, delicate and difficult to transport.

★ Talavera Uriarte
CERAMICS

(🖉 222-232-15-98; www.uriartetalavera.com.mx; Av 4 Poniente 911; ⊘10am-7pm Mon-Fri, to 6pm Sat, to 5pm Sun) Unlike most of Puebla's Talavera shops, Uriarte still makes its pottery onsite. The showroom displays a gorgeous selection of high-quality, intricately painted pieces. Founded in 1824, the company is now owned by a Canadian expat. Factory tours are offered 10am to 1pm Monday through Friday.

El Parián Crafts Market
ARTS & CRAFTS

(Plaza Parián; ⊘10am-7pm) Browse local Talavera, onyx and trees of life, as well as the kind of leather, jewelry and textiles that you'll find in other cities.

ℹ Information

ATMs are plentiful throughout the city, especially on Avenida Reforma near the *zócalo*, where banks have exchange facilities. Expect long queues on Friday afternoons.

Nearly all accommodations and cafes have free wi-fi access. There is patchy access in the *zócalo*. There are also several places to get online along Calle 2 Sur; most charge M$5 to M$10 per hour.

CAPU Tourist Kiosk (CAPU; ⊘10am-6pm Thu-Mon) English-speaking staff with pamphlets and transportation information within the bus terminal.

Hospital UPAEP (☎222-229-81-34, ext 6035; www.christusmuguerza.com.mx/hospital-upaep; Av 5 Poniente 715) Well equipped for emergencies with short wait times; only basic English is spoken.

Main Post Office (☎222-232-64-48; Av 16 de Septiembre s/n, cnr Av 5 Oriente; ⊗8am-6pm Mon-Fri, 10am-3pm Sat)

Municipal Tourist Office (☎222-309-43-00; www.turismopuebla.gob.mx; Portal Hidalgo 14; ⊗9:30am-8pm) English- and French-speaking staff; free maps, use of internet-connected PCs and excellent information about what's on. Through the archways on the *zócalo's* north.

State Tourist Office (Oficina de Turismo del Estado; ☎222-246-24-90; Av 5 Oriente 3; ⊗9am-8pm Mon-Sat, to 2pm Sun) Information for destinations outside Puebla. It's located in the Casa de Cultura building, facing the cathedral yard.

❶ Getting There & Away

AIR

Aeropuerto Hermanos Serdán (PBC; ☎227-102-50-80; www.aeropuertos.net/aeropuerto-internacional-de-puebla; Km 91.5), 22km northwest of Puebla off Hwy 190, has Aeroméxico, Volaris, VivaAerobús and Aeromar flights to/from Guadalajara, Tijuana, Monterrey, Cancún, Hermosillo and Chiapas most days. There is one daily international flight to/from Houston with United, and one to/from Dallas with American Airlines.

Service can be patchy and the airport closes whenever there is volcanic ash in the air. The Toluca airport (p212) is likely a better option.

BUS

Puebla's **Central de Autobuses de Puebla** (CAPU; ☎222-249-72-11; www.capu.com.mx; Blvd Norte 4222) – more commonly referred to as CAPU, including as a destination – is 4km north of the *zócalo* and 1.5km off the autopista.

From Mexico City and towns to the west, most buses to/from Puebla use the capital's TAPO station, though some travel to Terminal Norte, or Terminal Sur in Tasqueña. The trip takes about two hours.

Both **ADO** (www.ado.com.mx) and **Estrella Roja** (www.estrellaroja.com.mx) travel frequently between the two cities, operating both 1st-class and wi-fi-enabled deluxe buses.

From CAPU, there are buses at least once a day to almost everywhere to the south and east. The bus station website has a useful list of most of the destinations and bus companies.

Frequent 'Cholula' *colectivos* (M$7.50, 40 minutes) leave from Avenida 6 Poniente, near the corner with Calle 13 Norte.

For direct buses to the Museo Internacional del Barroco from Mexico City, take a direct ADO bus to the nearby (2km) Paseo Destino station from both Mexico City airport terminals (M$318, 15 daily), TAPO (M$244, three to six daily) or Terminal Sur (M$254, twice daily Friday and Saturday only); ADO also has services to/from Oaxaca City (M$900, 5¼ hours, twice daily) or Veracruz City (M$646-676, 4½ hours, three daily). **Ebus** (https://ebus.mx) also runs convenient Paseo Destino services (M$320-370, 2½ hours, one to five daily) aimed at executives to/from popular Mexico City business hubs (Santa Fe, World Trade Center, Antara in Polanco, El Ángel).

CAR & MOTORCYCLE

Puebla is 123km east of Mexico City by Hwy 150D. Traveling east of Puebla, 150D continues to Orizaba (negotiating a cloudy, winding 22km descent from the 2385m-high Cumbres de Maltrata en route), Córdoba and Veracruz.

TRAIN

The comfortable **Puebla–Cholula Tourist Train** (Tren Turístico Puebla–Cholula; www.trenturistico pueblacholula.com; Calle 11 Norte, cnr Av 18 Poniente; one way adult/child under 5yr M$30/free; ⊗departs Puebla 7am, 8:30am, 4:50pm Mon-Fri, every 45 mins 7am-5.30pm Sat & Sun) connects central Puebla with the pyramid in Cholula on a 17.4km, 40-minute route. The Puebla station is northwest of the *zócalo*.

❶ Getting Around

Most hotels and places of interest are within walking distance of Puebla's *zócalo*.

BUSES FROM PUEBLA

DESTINATION	FARE (M$)	TIME (HR)	FREQUENCY (PER DAY)
Cuetzalan	210	3½	14
Mexico City (TAPO, Terminal Sur, Terminal Norte or airports)	200-320	2-2½	75
Oaxaca City	565-665	4½-5	14
Veracruz City	438-564	4-5½	26

Within the CAPU bus station, buy a ticket at a kiosk for an authorized taxi to the city center (about M$81).

Alternatively, take a large **RUTA** (http://rutapuebla.mx) bus (similar to Mexico City's Metrobús) from the station just to the left upon exiting CAPU. RUTA Line 3 (5am to 11pm) was added in August 2018, connecting the *paradero* (outdoor bus station) at CAPU to the *paraderos* three blocks southeast of the *zócalo* (nearest *paradero*: Clínica 2) on comfortable buses with enough space for luggage (outside peak hours). Rides cost M$7.50 via a prepaid card (M$12.50) which you tap to enter the *paradero*. If you don't have a card, you can usually pay the fare directly to the guard, who will tap you in.

Combis are confusing but also possible. From CAPU, follow the signs for 'Autobuses Urbanos' and catch combi 51 (M$6) to the corner of Avenida 4 and Bulevar 5 de Mayo, three blocks east of the *zócalo*. The ride takes 15 to 20 minutes.

From the city center to the bus station, the most direct CAPU buses are branded with 'Boulevard CU' on the side, running along **Blvd 5 de Mayo** or **Calle 9 Sur**. All city buses and *colectivos* cost M$6.

Call **RadioTaxis Puebla** (☎222-222-22-22; http://radiotaxispuebla.com), or use Uber, for a secure taxi service within the city – a good idea if you're traveling alone or going out at night.

Cholula

☑222 / POP 120,000 / ELEV 2170M

Cholula's transformation from a colorful satellite town of Puebla into a proper boutique city-break stepped up a notch with the introduction of a tourist train. For now Cholula remains far different from Puebla in its history and relaxed daytime ambience. Owing to its large student population, the town has a surprisingly vibrant nightlife and an increasing range of chic restaurants and accommodations options within a short walk of the huge *zócalo*.

Cholula is also home to the widest pyramid ever built (yes, wider than any in Egypt) – the Pirámide Tepanapa. Despite this claim to fame, the town's ruins are largely ignored because, unlike those of Teotihuacán or Tula, the shrubbery-covered pyramid has been so badly neglected over the centuries that it's virtually unrecognizable as a human-made structure.

History

Between around 1 and 600 CE, Cholula grew into an important religious center, while powerful Teotihuacán flourished 100km to

the northwest. Around 600 CE, Cholula fell to the Olmec-Xicallanc, who built nearby Cacaxtla. Sometime between 900 and 1300 CE the Toltec and/or Chichimec took over and it later fell under Aztec dominance. There was also artistic influence from the Mixtec to the south.

By 1519 Cholula's population had reached 100,000 and the Pirámide Tepanapa was already overgrown. Cortés, having befriended the neighboring Tlaxcalans, traveled here at the request of the Aztec ruler Moctezuma, but it was a trap and Aztec warriors had set an ambush. The Tlaxcalans tipped off Cortés about the plot and the Spanish struck first. Within a day they killed 6000 Cholulans before the city was looted by the Tlaxcalans. Cortés vowed to build a church here for every day of the year, or one on top of every pagan temple, depending on which legend you prefer. Today there are 39 churches – far from 365 but still plenty for a small city.

The Spanish developed nearby Puebla to overshadow the old pagan center and Cholula never regained its importance, especially after a severe plague in the 1540s decimated its indigenous population.

⊙ Sights

★ **Zona Arqueológica**   ARCHAEOLOGICAL SITE
(☎222-247-90-81; Calz San Andres; M$70, Sun free; ⊙9am-6pm) Located two blocks to the southeast of Cholula's central plaza, the **Pirámide Tepanapa** looks more like a hill than a pyramid and has a domed church on top so it's tough to miss. The town's big drawcard is no letdown, with kilometers of tunnels veining the inside of the structure. The Zona Arqueológica comprises the excavated areas around the pyramid and the tunnels underneath.

The church grounds on the peak are worth the trip alone for panoramic views across Cholula to the volcanoes and Puebla.

Enter via the tunnel on the north side, which takes you on a spooky route through the center of the pyramid. Several pyramids were built on top of each other during various reconstructions, and more than 8km of tunnels have been dug beneath the pyramid by archaeologists to penetrate each stage, with 800m accessible to visitors. You can see earlier layers of the building, though not much else, from the access tunnel, which is a few hundred meters long.

The access tunnel emerges on the east side of the pyramid, from where you can

Cholula

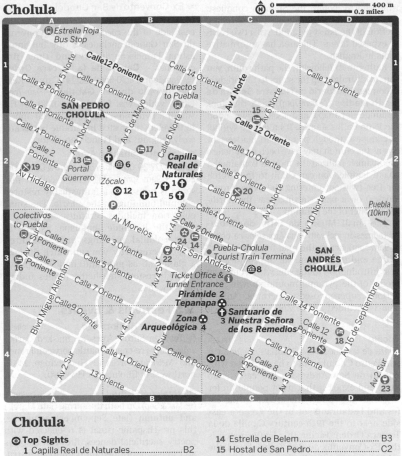

N 0 ——————— 400 m
0 ——————— 0.2 miles

Cholula

◎ Top Sights
1 Capilla Real de Naturales	B2
2 Pirámide Tepanapa	C3
3 Santuario de Nuestra Señora de los Remedios	C4
4 Zona Arqueológica	C4

◎ Sights
5 Capilla de la Tercera Orden	B2
6 Casa del Caballero Águila	B2
7 Ex-Convento de San Gabriel	B2
8 Museo de Sitio de Cholula	C3
9 Parroquia de San Pedro	B2
10 Patio de los Altares	C4
11 Templo de San Gabriel	B2
12 Zócalo	B2

🛏 Sleeping
13 Casa Calli	A2

14 Estrella de Belem	B3
15 Hostal de San Pedro	C2
16 Hotel La Quinta Luna	A3
17 Hotel Real de Naturales	B2
18 Piki Hotel y Hostal	D4

⊗ Eating
19 La Casa de Frida	A2
20 La Norberta	C2
21 Recaudo	D4

◎ Drinking & Nightlife
22 Bar Reforma	B3
23 Container City	D4

✪ Entertainment
24 Jazzatlán	B3

follow a path around to the **Patio de los Altares** on the south side. Ringed by platforms and unique diagonal stairways, this plaza was the main approach to the pyr-

amid. Three large stone slabs on its east, north and west sides are carved in the Veracruz interlocking scroll design. At its south end is an Aztec-style altar in a pit, dating from shortly before the Spanish conquest. On the mound's west side is a reconstructed section of the latest pyramid, with two earlier exposed layers. The area has informative signs in English.

Rather than following the path south, you can head straight up the stairs to the brightly decorated **Santuario de Nuestra Señora de los Remedios** (◎8am-7pm) **FREE** that tops Pirámide Tepanapa and looks down upon the Patio de los Altares. It's a classic symbol of conquest, though possibly an inadvertent one as the church may have been built before the Spanish realized the mound contained a pagan temple. You can climb to the church for free (without entering the Zona Arqueológica) on a path starting near the northwest corner of the pyramid.

The small **Museo de Sitio de Cholula** (admission incl with Zona Arqueológica ticket; ◎9am-5pm), across the road from the **ticket office** and down some steps, provides the best introduction to the site, with a cutaway model of the pyramid mound showing the various superimposed structures. Admission is included in the Zona Arqueológica ticket.

Zócalo　　　　　　　　　　　　PLAZA
(Plaza de la Concordia) Cholula's *zócalo* (in San Pedro Cholula, not to be confused with Zócalo de San Andrés to the east) is so huge and exposed that most people prefer to congregate under the arches in the cafes and restaurants, or in the greener east side near to the 19th-century Capilla de la Tercera Orden. Facing this leafier patch is the Ex-Convento de San Gabriel and the Arabic-style Capilla Real. In the center is the Templo de San Gabriel.

➡ ★**Capilla Real de Naturales**
(◎9:30am-1pm & 4-6pm Mon & Wed-Sat, 9am-3pm & 5-7pm Sun, closed Tue) **FREE** The Arabic-style Capilla Real has 49 domes and dates from 1540. The mosque-inspired design makes the yellow church unique to Mexico and creates a beautiful interior pattern of dome arches. It forms part of the Ex-Convento de San Gabriel. The church opens for extended hours (9am to 8pm) on the 25th of each month.

➡ **Parroquia de San Pedro**
(Av 5 de Mayo 401; ◎7am-7pm) **FREE** This distinctively yellow baroque church has the tallest tower in Cholula and has become an often-photographed icon of the city, at least at ground level. It was built in 1640 and the dome was reconstructed in 1782.

➡ **Ex-Convento de San Gabriel**
(Plaza de la Concordia; ◎9am-7pm) Facing the east side of the *zócalo*he, the Ex-Convento de San Gabriel includes a tiny but interesting Franciscan library and three fine churches – **Capilla de la Tercera Orden** (◎9am-1pm & 4:30-6pm) **FREE**, Capilla Real, and **Templo de San Gabriel** (◎9am-7pm) **FREE**, which was founded in 1530 on the site of a pyramid – all of which will appeal to travelers interested in antique books and early religious and Franciscan history.

➡ **Casa del Caballero Águila**
(☑222-777-29-00; cnr Av 5 de Mayo & Calle 4 Oriente; ◎9am-3pm) **FREE** This excellent museum is housed in a fantastically restored colonial building on the *zócalo*. The small collection includes ceramics and jewelry from the Pirámide Tepanapa, as well as later colonial paintings and sculptures. Most interestingly, you can watch through a glass wall as museum employees painstakingly restore smashed ceramics and repair jewelry.

✦ Festivals & Events

Carnaval de Huejotzingo　　　HISTORICAL
(◎Feb) On Shrove Tuesday, masked Carnaval dancers re-enact a battle between French and Mexican forces in Huejotzingo, 14km northwest of Cholula, off Hwy 190.

Quetzalcóatl Ritual　　　　　　CULTURAL
(◎Mar & Sep) On both the spring (late March) and autumn (late September) equinoxes, this pre-Hispanic ritual is re-enacted with poetry, sacrificial dances, firework displays and music performed on traditional instruments at the pyramid in Cholula.

Festival de la Virgen de los Remedios　　　　　　　　DANCE
(◎Sep) Perhaps the most important Cholulan holiday of the year, this festival is celebrated the week of September 1. There are traditional dances daily atop the Pirámide Tepanapa. It forms part of Cholula's regional *feria* held in the first few weeks of September.

🛏 Sleeping

With an increasing range of good-value hotels, a few boutique favorites and even new hostels, Cholula makes an attractive alternative to staying in Puebla for those who prefer a laid-back pace. Stay near the pyramid, in the area known as San Pedro Cholula, for the churches, museums and *zócalo*.

★**Hotel Real**
de Naturales BUSINESS HOTEL $
(☎222-247-60-70; www.hotelrealdenaturales.com; Calle 6 Oriente 7; d/tw/tr/ste M$650/750/850/1100; P🅿🛜❄) This 45-room hotel was built in the colonial style to blend into the surrounding architectural landscape and it succeeds with its shady courtyards, tiled baths, tasteful B&W photography and elegant archways. Beds are firm (like most at this budget in Mexico), but its central location and many considered details make it an excellent bargain.

Piki Hotel y Hostal HOSTAL $
(☎222-882-67-18; www.facebook.com/hotelpiki; Calle 14 Poniente 101A; dm M$385, ste M$1075-1685; 🛜) Is Piki a hostel or hotel? The chic metal dorm beds are a dream to sleep in and look more suited to a boutique hotel. The cheapest 'suites' are more akin to small, though comfortable, private rooms with colorful murals. Either way, it's a good option near the pyramid if you don't mind some noise to 1am from the bar next door.

Casa Calli BOUTIQUE HOTEL $
(☎222-261-56-07; www.hotelcasacalli.com; Portal Guerrero 11; d/tw/tr/ste M$750/850/1100/1200; P🅿🛜❄) Right on the *zócalo,* this hotel contains 40 stylishly minimalist rooms, an attractive pool and an Italian restaurant-bar in the lobby. Rooms are discounted slightly in quiet periods (Sunday to Thursday) and there are weekend spa packages available.

Hostal de San Pedro HOSTEL $
(☎222-178-04-95; www.facebook.com/HostalDe SanPedro; Av 6 Norte 1203; dm/d/tw incl breakfast M$270/580/930; P☺@🛜) This hostel is a quick stroll from the *zócalo* and has clean, comfy beds in a quiet location. There is no TV and no alcohol is allowed, but upstairs rooms are built around a sunny terrace where you could easily pass an afternoon alone. If you end up staying even longer, there are long-term deals with laundry use.

★**Estrella de Belem** LUXURY HOTEL $$$
(☎222-261-19-25; www.estrelladebelem.com. mx; Calle 2 Oriente 410; r incl breakfast M$2187-2958; P❄🛜❄) This majestic hotel has just six rooms, each with gorgeous, thoughtful touches such as radiant-heat floors, noise-blocking windows, bathtubs and LCD TVs. The master suites are especially luxurious, with fireplaces and Jacuzzis. Common areas include a lovely, grassy courtyard and a small, rooftop swimming pool that has views over the town. No children under 12.

Hotel La Quinta Luna LUXURY HOTEL $$$
(☎222-247-89-15; www.laquintaluna.com; Av 3 Sur 702; r incl breakfast M$1550-1900, ste M$2235-4230; P🅿🛜) This rarefied hotel is popular with a wealthy weekender crowd. The seven stylish rooms occupy a thick-walled 17th-century mansion set around a charming garden and boast a gorgeous mix of colonial antiques, plush bedding, flat-screen TVs and contemporary art. Meetings with the featured *poblano* artists are happily arranged.

There's a great library and the excellent **restaurant** is open to nonguests with a reservation.

✕ **Eating**

★**La Norberta** MEXICAN $
(☎222-247-28-49; www.facebook.com/LaNorberta; Av 6 Norte 602; mains M$70-90; ⊙9am-11pm Mon-Wed, to 1am Thu-Sat, to 9pm Sun; 🛜🍴) A cantina is a traditional Mexican bar with food, but Norberta forgoes saloon doors to welcome in families and young, discerning diners to eat *mole enchiladas* (chicken-filled tortillas in a spiced sauce), *aguachile* (lime-cured prawns), soups, salads and tacos at the kitsch-chic Formica tables in the courtyard. Naturally there's mezcal, *pulque* and a wide selection of beer, for tradition.

Live music is sometimes gently performed on weekend evenings.

Recaudo VEGETARIAN $
(www.facebook.com/recaudo; Calle 12 Poniente 105; mains M$75-85; ⊙8.30am-6pm Tue-Fri, 9am-6pm Sat, 9am-5pm Sun; 🍴) Healthy-eating delights in dishes made from organic, locally sourced ingredients. The seasonal vegetarian menu includes elaborate salads (mango, fig and amaranth), goat's cheese *tostadas* (crispy tortillas), *chilaquiles* (avocado, corn chips and salsa), bean burgers and pesto pasta alongside house-made bread. The terra cotta-roofed courtyard recalls a relaxing farmhouse and attracts vegetarians and omnivores alike.

La Casa de Frida MEXICAN $$
(☎222-178-23-03; Av Hidalgo 109; mains M$79-295, weekend buffet adult/child M$129/79; ⊙9:30am-6pm Mon-Thu, to 7pm Fri-Sun; 🛜🍴🍴) This cavernous gem gives a nod to Frida Kahlo's home in Mexico City. Mexican handicrafts (plus the artist-owner's murals) are splashed throughout the courtyard, where Mexican musicians croon on one side and excellent flame-grilled steaks sizzle on the other. Service is excellent, there is a kids' playroom and the *pipián verde* is exceptionally complex.

A weekend buffet (9am to 2pm) is a popular way to have a taste of all of the classic Mexican dishes on offer.

Drinking & Nightlife

Container City
BAR

(📞222-888-61-72; www.containercity.com.mx; cnr Calle 12 Oriente & Av 2 Sur; ⊙11am-2am Tue-Sat) This ramshackle collection of trendy(ish) bars, restaurants, clubs and shops buzzes at night. Set in revamped and stacked former shipping containers in eastern Cholula, it's the hangout of choice for the city's flashiest students and few fashionistas.

Bar Reforma
BAR

(📞222-247-01-49; cnr Avs 4 Sur & Morelos; ⊙6pm-midnight Mon-Sat, noon-4.30pm Sun) Attached to Hotel Reforma, Cholula's oldest drinking spot is a classic corner abode with swinging doors and plastic flowers, and specializes in iceless margaritas, mezcal and freshly prepared sangrias. After 9pm it's popular with the university pre-clubbing crowd.

★ Jazzatlán
LIVE MUSIC

(📞222-838-75-69; www.facebook.com/jazzatlan clubdejazz; Calle 2 Oriente 406; cover charge Wed-Sat M$100, Sun & Tue free; ⊙2pm-1am Tue-Sat, to 9pm Sun; 🛜) One of Mexico's jazz hot spots has diverse local and international musicians (playing live from 9.30pm Tuesdays to Saturdays; at 4pm, 6pm and 8pm Sundays) that include tribute acts to Dylan and Aretha, Latin-infused trios and Sunday swing afternoons. Check the website for the events calendar.

Good cocktails, craft beer and bistro meals are on offer. A rarity for Mexico, there is a happy hour from 6pm to 8pm Tuesdays to Fridays, and Wednesdays and Thursdays are half-priced gin or mezcal nights.

ℹ️ Getting There & Away

The much-needed, comfortable **Puebla–Cholula Tourist Train** (Tren Turístico Puebla–Cholula; www.trenturisticopueblacholula.com; cnr Avs Morelos & 6 Norte; one way adult/child under 5yr M$30/free; ⊙departs Cholula 7:45am, 12:20pm & 5:40pm Mon-Fri, every 45 minutes 7.45am-10am & 3:15-6.15pm Sat, Sun & holidays) began operation in 2017. It connects central Puebla with the pyramid in Cholula on a 17.4km, 40-minute route. A taxi for two people at M$150 may be an appealing option instead of the morning weekday train.

To travel to Puebla with locals on much windier routes, take a frequent **colectivo** (M$7.50, every 20 minutes) from the corner of Calle 5 Poniente and Av 3 Sur, or a larger **directo** (M$8, every 30 minutes) on Calle 12 Oriente near the corner with Calle 6 Norte. Buses and colectivos stop two or three blocks north of the zócalo and return from the same road. The trip takes 20 to 40 minutes, depending on how direct they go.

From Mexico City's TAPO bus station, **Estrella Roja** (https://estrellaroja.com.mx) runs four direct buses a day to **Cholula** (Calle 12 Poniente 522) for M$180. Return buses to Mexico City depart from the same stop on Calle 12 Poniente in Cholula, but check as some buses go to/from a stop further north at Plaza San Diego, a 10-minute taxi ride north of the pyramid.

Cacaxtla & Xochitécatl

The sister sites of Cacaxtla and Xochitécatl, about 20km southwest of Tlaxcala and 32km northwest of Puebla, are among Mexico's most intriguing ruins.

Cacaxtla (ca-*casht*-la) is one of Mexico's most impressive ancient ruins with its many high-quality, vividly painted depictions of daily life. Rather than being relegated to a museum collection, these works – including frescoes of a nearly life-size jaguar and eagle warriors engaged in battle – are on display within the site itself, though unfortunately they continue to fade. Discovered in 1975, the ruins are located atop a scrubby hill with wide views of the surrounding countryside.

The much older ruins at Xochitécatl (so-chi-*teh*-catl), 2km away and accessible from Cacaxtla on foot, include an exceptionally wide pyramid as well as a circular one. A German archaeologist led the first systematic exploration of the site in 1969, but it wasn't until 1994 that it was opened to the public.

◉ Sights

Cacaxtla
ARCHAEOLOGICAL SITE

(📞246-416-00-00; Circuito Perimetral s/n, San Miguel del Milagro; incl Xochitécatl & museums M$70; ⊙9am-5:30pm; 🅿) The large murals at Cacaxtla are intriguingly on display among the ruins rather than in a museum. They evoke a real sense of history where it happened and are worth seeing before they – unfortunately – continue to fade into history. The main attraction is a natural platform, 200m long and 25m high, called the **Gran Basamento** (Great Base), now sheltered under an expansive metal roof. Here stood Cacaxtla's main civic and religious buildings and the residences of its ruling priestly classes.

Starting at the parking lot opposite the site entrance, it's a 200m walk to the ticket office, museum and restaurant. From the ticket office it's another 600m downhill to the top of the entry stairs to the Gran Basamento in the **Plaza Norte**.

From here the path winds clockwise around the ruins until you reach the murals, many of which clearly show Maya influence among the symbols from the Mexican highlands. This combination of styles in a mural is unique to Cacaxtla.

Before reaching the first mural you'll come to a small patio, of which the main feature is an **altar** fronted by a small square pit, in which numerous human remains were discovered. Just beyond the altar you'll find the **Templo de Venus**, which contains two anthropomorphic sculptures – a man and a woman – in blue, wearing jaguar-skin skirts. The temple's name is attributed to the appearance of numerous half-stars around the female figure that are associated with Earth's sister planet, Venus.

On the opposite side of the path, away from the Plaza Norte, the **Templo Rojo** contains four murals, only one of which is visible. Its vivid imagery is dominated by a row of corn and cacao crops whose husks contain human heads.

Facing the north side of Plaza Norte is the long **Mural de la Batalla** (Battle Mural), dating from before 700 CE. It shows two warrior groups, one wearing jaguar skins and the other bird feathers, engaged in ferocious battle. The Olmec-Xicallanc (the jaguar warriors with round shields) are clearly repelling invading Huastecs (the bird warriors with jade ornaments and deformed skulls).

Beyond the Mural de la Batalla, turn left and climb the steps to see the second major **mural group**, behind a fence to your right. The two main murals (c 750 CE) show a figure in a jaguar costume and a black-painted figure in a bird costume (believed to be the Olmeca-Xicallanca priest-governor) standing atop a plumed serpent.

Cacaxtla is about 20km southwest of Tlaxcala and 32km northwest of Puebla.

Xochitécatl   ARCHAEOLOGICAL SITE
(🖉246-416-00-00; Circuito Perimetral s/n, San Miguel del Milagro; incl Cacaxtla & museums M$70; ⊙9am-5:30pm; P) About 2km from Cacaxtla, the much older ruins at Xochitécatl include a wide pyramid dedicated to a fertility god, and a circular pyramid. Because of its outline

and the materials used, archaeologists believe the circular **Pirámide de la Espiral** was built between 1000 and 800 BCE. Its form and hilltop location suggest it may have been used as an astronomical observation post, or as a temple to Ehécatl, the wind god. From here the path passes three other pyramids.

The **Basamento de los Volcanes**, which is all that remains of the first pyramid, is the base of the Pirámide de los Volcanes and it's made of materials from two periods. Cut square stones were placed over the original stones, visible in some areas, and then stuccoed over. In an interesting twist, the colored stones used to build Tlaxcala's municipal palace appear to have come from this site.

The **Pirámide de la Serpiente** gets its name from a large piece of carved stone with a snake head at one end. Its most impressive feature is the huge pot found at its center, carved from a single boulder, which was hauled from another region. Researchers surmise it was used to hold water.

Experts speculate that rituals honoring the fertility god were held at the **Pirámide de las Flores**, due to the discovery of several sculptures and the remains of 30 sacrificed infants. Near the pyramid's base – Latin America's fourth-widest – is a pool carved from a massive rock, where the infants were believed to have been washed before being killed.

❶ Getting There & Away

Considering how close the archaeological zone is to Mexico City, Tlaxcala and Puebla – it's roughly smack in the middle of the three cities – getting to and from Cacaxtla and Xochitécatl on public transit is inconvenient and time-consuming.

Cacaxtla is 1.5km uphill from a back road between San Martín Texmelucan (near Hwy 150D) and Hwy 119, the secondary road between Tlaxcala and Puebla. To reach the site from Tlaxcala, catch a 'San Miguel del Milagro' *colectivo* (M$9, 40 minutes) from the corner of Escalona and Sánchez Piedras (outside the market three blocks north of the *zócalo*), which will drop you off about 500m from Cacaxtla.

From Puebla, Flecha Azul buses go direct from the CAPU terminal to the town of Nativitas, about 3km east of Cacaxtla. From there, catch a 'Zona Arqueológica' *colectivo* to the site.

Between Cacaxtla and Xochitécatl, taxis (M$60) are available on weekends, or walk the 2km (about 25 minutes).

Tour operators run day trips on weekends from central Tlaxcala and charge about M$500 per person (minimum two people).

Popocatépetl & Iztaccíhuatl

Mexico's second- and third-highest peaks, volcanoes Popocatépetl (po-po-ka-*teh*-petl; 5452m) and Iztaccíhuatl (is-tak-*see*-watl; 5220m), form the eastern rim of the Valle de México, about 40km west of Puebla and 70km southeast of Mexico City. While the craterless Iztaccíhuatl is dormant, Popocatépetl (Náhuatl for 'Smoking Mountain'; also called Don Goyo and Popo) is very active and its summit has been off-limits since 1996.

The good news is that the fetching Iztaccíhuatl (White Woman), 20km north of Popo from summit to summit, remains open to climbers. From this vantage point there are panoramic views of the plateau, glaciers and across to Popo.

🏃 Activities

Hiking & Climbing

Izta's highest peak is **El Pecho** (5220m). All routes require a night on the mountain and there's a hut between the staging point at La Joya, the main southern trailhead, and Las Rodillas, one of Itza's lesser peaks, that can be used during an ascent of El Pecho. On average, it takes at least five hours to reach the hut from La Joya, then another six hours from the hut to El Pecho, and six hours back to the base.

Before making the ascent, climbers must register and pay the park entrance fee for an entry bracelet at the Parque Nacional Iztaccíhuatl-Popocatépetl **office** (📞597-978-38-29; www.conanp.gob.mx/conanp/dominios/iztapopo; Plaza de la Constitución 9B, Amecameca; per person per day M$30.50; ⊙7am-9pm), located on the southeast side of Amecameca's *zócalo*. The park website offers excellent maps, as well as a handy downloadable climbing guide and the registration form in English (to know what to expect).

About 24km up from Amecameca, there are lower-altitude trails through pine forests and grassy meadows near Paso de Cortés, the trailhead that leads to breathtaking glimpses of nearby peaks. La Joya is another 4km from Paso de Cortés.

Basic shelter with electricity is available at the **Refugio de Altzomoni** (Altzomoni Lodge; dm per person M$30.50), roughly halfway between Paso de Cortés and La Joya. You must reserve in advance at the park office and bring bedding, warm clothes and drinking water.

Climate & Conditions

It can be windy and well below freezing any time of year on Izta's upper slopes, and it's nearly always below freezing near the summit at night. Ice and snow are fixtures here; the average snow line is 4200m. The ideal months for ascents are November to February, when there is hard snowpack for crampons. The rainy season (April to October) brings with it the threat of whiteouts, thunderstorms and avalanches.

Guides

Izta should be attempted *only* by experienced climbers. Because of hidden crevices on the ice-covered upper slopes, a guide is advisable. In addition to the following guide, the park office has recommendations for groups.

Mario Andrade (📞cell 55-18262146; mount ainup@hotmail.com; hikes per person Nevado de Toluca/Iztaccíhuatl US$200/350) is a recommended authorized, English-speaking guide, based in Mexico City. The cost per person is reduced for groups, and includes round-trip transportation from Mexico City, lodging, mountain meals and rope usage.

❶ Getting There & Away

A guide is the most recommended option for climbing Iztaccíhuatl, with transportation included from Mexico City or Puebla. Otherwise, *colectivos* departing from Amecameca's *zócalo* for Paso de Cortés cost M$80. From the national park office (p180), taxis will take groups to La Joya (40 minutes) for a negotiable M$300.

Tlaxcala

📞246 / POP 13,000 / ELEV 2250M

The capital of Mexico's smallest state is unhurried and confident, with a compact colonial downtown defined by grand government buildings, imposing churches and a handsome central plaza. Despite its small stature, Tlaxcala is neither timid nor parochial. With a large student population, good restaurants and bars and a handful of excellent museums, the city has a surprisingly vibrant cultural life. Because there's no single attraction that puts Tlaxcala on tourist itineraries, it remains largely undiscovered, despite its location less than two hours' drive from Mexico City.

Two large central plazas converge at the corner of Avenidas Independencia and Muñoz Camargo. The northern one, which is surrounded by colonial buildings, is the *zócalo* called Plaza de la Constitución. The southern square is Plaza Xicohténcatl.

Tlaxcala

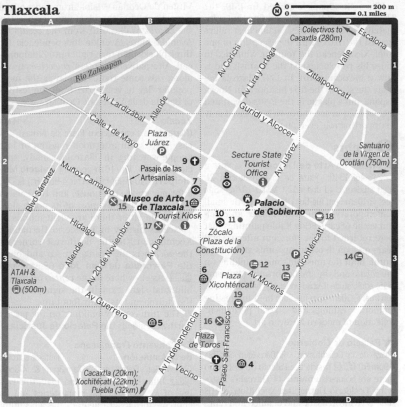

Tlaxcala

◎ Top Sights
1 Museo de Arte de Tlaxcala	B2
2 Palacio de Gobierno	C2

◎ Sights
3 Capilla Abierta	C4
4 Ex-Convento Franciscano de la Asunción	C4
5 Museo de Arte de Tlaxcala	B4
6 Museo de la Memoria Tlaxcala	C3
Museo Regional de Tlaxcala	(see 4)
7 Palacio de Justicia	B2
8 Palacio Municipal	C2
9 Parroquia de San José	B2
10 Zócalo	C3

⊕ Activities, Courses & Tours
11 Tranvía El Tlaxcalteca	C3

🛏 Sleeping
12 Hostería de Xicohténcatl	C3
13 Hotel Minatzín	C3
14 Posada La Casona de Cortés	D3

⊗ Eating
15 Desayunos Lupita	B2
16 Fonda del Convento	C4
17 Jaque's	B3

⊜ Drinking & Nightlife
18 11:11 Cafe Boutique	D3
19 Pulquería Tía Yola	C3

History

In the last centuries before the Spanish conquest, numerous small *señoríos* (warrior kingdoms) arose in and around Tlaxcala. Some of them formed a loose federation that remained independent of the Aztec empire as it spread from the Valle de México in the 15th century. The most important kingdom seems to have been Tizatlán, now in ruins on the northeast edge of Tlaxcala.

When the Spanish arrived in 1519, the Tlaxcalan fought fiercely at first but ultimately became Cortés' staunchest allies against the Aztec (with the exception of one chief, Xicohténcatl the Younger, who tried to rouse his people against the Spanish and is now a Mexican hero). In 1527 Tlaxcala became the seat of the first bishopric in Nueva España, but a plague in the 1540s devastated the population and the town has played only a supporting role ever since.

◉ Sights

★ Museo de Arte de Tlaxcala   MUSEUM

(☑246-462-15-10; Plaza de la Constitución 21; adult/student/child under 12yr M$20/10/free, Sun free; ◷10am-6pm Tue-Sun) This fantastic small contemporary-art museum houses an excellent cache of early Frida Kahlo paintings that were returned to the museum after several years on loan to other museums around the world. Both the museum's main building on the *zócalo* and the smaller **branch** (Av Guerrero 15; adult/student/child under 12yr M$20/10/free, Sun free; ◷10am-6pm Tue-Sun) hold interesting temporary exhibits and a good permanent collection of modern Mexican art.

★ Palacio de Gobierno   PALACE

(Plaza de la Constitución; ◷10am-6pm Sat-Thu, 4-9pm Fri) FREE Inside the Palacio de Gobierno there are color-rich murals of Tlaxcala's history by Desiderio Hernández Xochitiotzin. His style is vividly realistic and detailed and reminiscent of modern graphic novels. The 500 sq meters of painting in this governmental palace was the last of the large-scale murals of the muralist movement in the country and a delight to fans of an illustration style. English- and Spanish-speaking guides are available for tours of about an hour for M$200.

★ Santuario de la Virgen de Ocotlán   CHURCH

(☑246-462-10-73; Hidalgo 1, Ocotlán; ◷8am-7pm) FREE One of Mexico's most spectacular churches is an important pilgrimage site for those who believe the Virgin appeared here in 1541 – her image stands on the main altar in memory of the apparition. The classic Churrigueresque facade features white-stucco 'wedding cake' decorations contrasting with plain red tiles. During the 18th century, indigenous artist Francisco Miguel spent 25 years decorating the altarpieces and the chapel beside the main altar.

The effigy is the central figure in Tlaxcala's most famous festival, the Bajada de la Virgen de Ocotlán. Visible from most of the town, the hilltop church is 1km northeast of the *zócalo*. Walk north from the *zócalo* on Avenida Juárez/Avenida Independencia for three blocks then turn right onto Zitlalpopócatl. Alternatively, 'Ocotlán' *colectivos* travel along this same route. Sunday is the most popular day to visit apart from the festival of Bajada de la Virgen de Ocotlán.

Zócalo   PLAZA

(Plaza de la Constitución; Plaza de Armas) It's easy to pass an afternoon reading or just people-watching in Tlaxcala's shady, spacious *zócalo*. The 16th-century **Palacio Municipal** (◷10am-6pm Sat-Thu, 4-9pm Fri) FREE, a former grain storehouse, and the Palacio de Gobierno occupy most of its north side. Inside the latter there are vivid murals of Tlaxcala's history by Desiderio Hernández Xochitiotzin. Off the northwest corner of the *zócalo* is the orange-stucco and blue-tile **Parroquia de San José** (◷6am-9pm) FREE. As elsewhere in the *centro histórico*, bilingual signs explain the significance of the church and its many fountains.

The 16th-century building on the plaza's northwest side is the **Palacio de Justicia**.

Ex-Convento Franciscano de la Asunción   HISTORIC BUILDING

(Paseo San Francisco; ◷7am-3pm & 4-8pm) FREE Built between 1537 and 1540, this was one of Mexico's earliest monasteries and its church – the city's cathedral – has a beautiful Moorish-style wooden ceiling. It's up a shaded path from the southeast corner of Plaza Xicohténcatl.

Just below the monastery, beside the 19th-century Plaza de Toros (bullring), is a **capilla abierta** (◷24hr) FREE (open chapel) with three unique Moorish-style arches. One of the entrances to the grounds is locked, but you can get close (though not enter) the *capilla* from other gates.

Museo Regional de Tlaxcala (☑246-462-02-62; Paseo San Francisco; ◷10am-6pm) FREE, housed within the monastery building, has a large collection of religious paintings and sculptures and some pre-Hispanic artifacts from nearby archaeological sites.

Museo de la Memoria Tlaxcala   MUSEUM

(☑246-466-07-92; Av Independencia 3; adult/student M$20/free, Sun free; ◷10am-5pm) This modern history museum looks at folklore through a multimedia lens and has well-presented exhibits on indigenous government, agriculture and contemporary festivals. Explanations are in Spanish only.

🎓 Courses

Estela Silva's Mexican
Home Cooking School COOKING
(☑246-468-09-78; www.mexicanhomecooking.com) Learn to cook *poblano* cuisine with Señora Estela Silva and her sous-chef husband, Jon Jarvis, in the couple's Talavera-tiled kitchen in Tlacochcalco, 9km southeast of Tlaxcala. The English-Spanish bilingual course includes all meals plus lodging in private rooms with fireplaces (transportation to/from the school can be arranged). An all-inclusive, five-day/four-night, three-class course is US$1450.

🧭 Tours

Tranvía El Tlaxcalteca BUS
(☑246-458-53-24; Plaza de la Constitución, Portal Hidalgo 6; adult/child Mon-Fri M$100/90, Sat & Sun M$75/65; ☺departs hourly noon-6pm) This motorized streetcar visits 33 downtown sights with a Spanish-speaking guide on board in a 45-minute tour on Saturday and Sunday. During the week the tour extends to 1.5 hours to include visiting and walking around the Santuario de La Virgen de Ocotlán. No reservations necessary. Departs from the east side of the *zócalo*.

✨ Festivals & Events

Bajada de la Virgen de Ocotlán RELIGIOUS
(☺May) On the third Monday in May, the figure of the Virgen de Ocotlán is carried from its hilltop perch at the Santuario de La Virgen de Ocotlán to neighboring churches, attracting equal numbers of onlookers and believers. Throughout the month, processions along flower-decorated streets commemorating the miracle attract pilgrims from around the country.

Gran Feria de Tlaxcala CULTURAL
(☺Oct-Nov) People come from around the state for three weeks between late October and mid-November, when *charrería* (horsemanship) and other rodeo-inspired pageantry take center stage. Also known as Tlaxcala's Fiesta de Todos los Santos, the festival includes Día de Muertos activities.

🛏 Sleeping

Hotel Minatzín BOUTIQUE HOTEL $
(☑246-462-04-40; Xicohténcatl 6; d/tw from M$650/1100; 🅿❄🤙) This converted colonial

house has stone tiling, it's light, bright and airy and makes a fine match with Tlaxcala's nearby *zócalo*. All five spacious rooms have 3D TVs and feel more indulgent, and the beds much plusher, than the price suggests.

Hostería de Xicohténcatl GUESTHOUSE $
(☑246-466-33-22; www.hosteriadexicohtencatl.com; Av Morelos 10; s/d/tr/ste M$480/530/670/1425; 🅿🤙) Half of the 16 rooms at this straightforward budget *hostería* are large, multiroom suites with kitchens, making it a bargain for families, groups or those in town for an extended stay. The *hostería* is clean, if a bit sterile, and the location – right on Plaza Xicohténcatl – is excellent. Avoid rooms with balconies if you are noise-sensitive.

★Posada La Casona
de Cortés BOUTIQUE HOTEL $$
(☑246-462-20-42; http://lacasonadecortes.com.mx; Av Lardizábal 6; d/tw/tr from M$895/975/1500; 🅿🤙) Set around a lush courtyard with fruit trees and a fountain, this affordable boutique hotel seems almost too good to be true. The rooms, which have firm beds, tiled floors and high-pressure showers, are decorated with Mexican *artesanías*. The bar has a working 1950s jukebox and a roof deck with views of church steeples and volcanic peaks. Ask for a discount (up to 15%) during quiet periods.

🍴 Eating & Drinking

For a small city, Tlaxcala has an impressive number – and diversity – of good restaurants. The east side of the *zócalo* is overrun by underwhelming sidewalk cafes, but there are better options on the south side and on nearby Plaza Xicohténcatl. Tlaxcala's Mercado Emilio Sánchez Piedras is one of the most pleasant markets around. To get there from Parroquia de San José, walk along Avenida Lira y Ortega until the corner with Escalona.

Fonda del Convento MEXICAN $
(☑246-462-07-65; Paseo San Francisco 1; mains M$70-160; ☺8am-8pm Mon-Sat, to 6pm Sun) This unassuming home-style restaurant has been a local favorite for four decades. The menu focuses on traditional Tlaxcalteca cuisine, including *gusanos* (*maguey* worms), *escamoles*, *mole poblano*, rabbit in *pulque* and a family-recipe *pipián*.

Jaque's MEXICAN $
(☑246-466-09-53; Muñoz Camargo 2; menú del día M$80, mains M$45-100; ☺8am-6:30pm; 🤙) Jaque's is just a few steps from the *zócalo*,

but the Mexican fare is much better here than elsewhere in the area. Plus you still have the white tablecloths and bay windows peering down on the street. The *pechuga a la diabla* (chicken schnitzel stuffed with panela cheese in a spicy tomato sauce) is as devilishly good as the name suggests.

Desayunos Lupita   MEXICAN $
(☑ 246-462-64-53; Muñoz Camargo 14; set breakfasts M$55-95, mains $58-115; ☺ 8:30am-4pm Mon-Fri, to 1:30pm Sat & Sun) This ultrapopular breakfast and lunch spot serves quintessential *tlaxcalteca* food, like *huaraches* (an oblong, fried corn base with a variety of toppings), *tamales, atoles* (sweet, corn-based hot drinks) and quesadillas filled with everything from *huitlacoche* to squash flower. It's glorified street food, perfect for those with a taste for central Mexican specialties but squeamish about eating from carts and stalls.

Set breakfasts include your choice of main dish, fresh-squeezed juice, fruit salad and *café de olla*.

Pulquería Tía Yola   BAR
(☑ 246-462-73-09; Plaza Xicohténcatl 7; ☺ 11am-9pm Tue-Thu, to midnight Fri & Sat, 10am-8pm Sun) Sip one of a dozen-or-so flavors of house-made *pulque* in a colorful courtyard decorated with Día de Muertos figurines and mosaics of Aztec gods. The sidewalk tables along the plaza are a prime location for weekend people-watching. There is an extensive menu of good Mexican food too.

11:11 Cafe Boutique   CAFE
(☑ 246-144-01-81; Av Lardizábal 16; ☺ 9am-10pm Mon-Sat; 🐦) You would hardly know that this stylish cafe is down this quiet street, which makes it a popular spot for young couples and the local cool kids to hide away, sipping on frappés and good coffee with a matcha cake on the side.

ℹ Information

Several banks on Avenida Juárez, near the tourist office, exchange dollars and have ATMs. There is also an ATM inside the bus terminal.

Farmacia Cristo Rey (Av Lardizábal 15; ☺ 24hr) Around-the-clock pharmacy.

Hospital General (☑ 246-462-00-30; Corregidora s/n; ☺ emergencies 24hr, non-emergencies 8am-8pm Mon-Fri) Emergency services.

Secture State Tourist Office (☑ 246-465-09-60; cnr Avs Juárez & Lardizábal; ☺ 8am-5pm Mon-Fri, to 6pm Sat & Sun) The English-speaking staff are eager to sing Tlaxcala's praises and equip travelers with colorful bird's-eye-view maps and a handful of brochures. These are also found at the handy **tourist kiosk** (Plaza de la Constitución; ☺ 10am-5pm) on the west side of the *zócalo*.

ℹ Getting There & Away

Tlaxcala's **bus terminal** (cnr Castelar & Calle 1 Bis) sits on a hill 1km west of the central plaza. **ATAH** (☑ 246-466-00-87; http://atah.mx) runs (barely) 1st-class buses to Mexico City's TAPO terminal (M$150, two hours, every 30 minutes). Frequent 2nd-class Verde buses go to Puebla (M$29).

For Cacaxtla take a *colectivo* (M$9, 40 minutes) marked 'San Miguel del Milagro' from the corner of Escalona and Sánchez Piedras.

ℹ Getting Around

Most *colectivos* (M$6.50) passing the bus terminal head into town, although it takes just 10 minutes to walk. Exit the terminal, turn right down the hill until you hit Avenida Guerrero then turn right past the towering steps of Escalinata de Héroes. To reach the terminal from the center, catch a blue-and-white *colectivo* on the east side of Bulevar Sánchez. Taxis between the station and downtown cost M$35.

Huamantla

☑ 247 / POP 60,450 / ELEV 2500M

The most alluring – and famous – reason to visit colorful Huamantla is for the *tapetes,* where the streets are carpeted in colored sawdust and bright blooms, most spectacularly during the feria La Noche Que Nadie Duerme in August. At other times there are workshops to make your own *tapete*.

With La Malinche providing a perfect backdrop for the charming *zócalo,* this is a pleasant base camp for exploring the surrounding countryside, once you get past its sprawling suburbs. Most escapees from Puebla will just stay in town and enjoy the eye-popping paint job atop Huamantla's church, **Parroquia de San Luis Obispo**.

⊙ Sights

★**Museo Nacional del Títere**   MUSEUM
(☑ 247-472-10-33; Parque Juárez 15; adult/student & senior/child M$20/10/5, Sun free; ☺ 10am-5pm Tue-Sat, to 1pm Sun; 🔁) The national puppet museum displays dolls and marionettes from all around the world in a fantastic renovated building on the *zócalo*. It's a fun stop for the young and young at heart.

✨ Festivals & Events

Feria Huamantla FERIA
(⊙Aug) For two weeks in August, this festival features parades, cyclists and music, culminating in the spectacular La Noche Que Nadie Duerme ('The Night That Nobody Sleeps') on 14 August, when locals blanket 8km of the town's streets with elaborate carpets of flowers and colored sawdust. Festivities, crowds and candlelit processions continue to the wee hours; at 7am the carpets are swept clean.

The following weekend is Huamantlada, a running of the bulls similar to that in Pamplona – but more dangerous since the uncastrated males charge from two directions. The night before, human-sized puppets, musicians and bull-themed floats parade through the center of town in La Noche de los Burladeros.

🛏 Sleeping & Eating

Hotel Centenario HOTEL $
(📋247-472-05-87; http://hotelcentenariodehuamantla.com.mx; Juárez Norte 209; s/d/ste incl breakfast from M$440/480/680; 🅿 @ 🛜) Just a short walk from the *zócalo*, Hotel Centenario has 31 salmon-pink, clean and spacious rooms with black-out curtains, crisp white sheets and modernized bathrooms. The staff are helpful and there's an attached restaurant with good set-menu lunches (M$65, Monday to Saturday).

★Hacienda Soltepec HISTORIC HOTEL $$
(📋247-472-14-66; www.haciendasoltepec.com; Carretera Huamantla–Puebla Km 3; s/d/tw/ste from M$1100/1500/1500/1850; 🅿 🛜 🏊) A 4.5km drive south of town, this gorgeous renovated hacienda is a former movie set (María Félix stayed here for months while filming one of her classics) with views of La Malinche, horse stables, tennis courts and a fantastic restaurant. Bright rooms have high ceilings and polished floorboards. Its own *pulque* brewery is open for visits on Saturday and Sunday.

Xuni MEXICAN $$
(📋247-472-02-48; https://xuni.negocio.site; Reforma Sur 105A; mains M$100-220, Sunday brunch buffet M$155; ⊙7.30am-10pm; 🛜 🅿) Near Huamantla's sights, Xuni is set around a colorful courtyard and serves Mexican dishes such as *tacos gobernador* (shrimp-and-avocado tacos) and *cochinita pibil* (slow-roasted pork), pastas, and *menú del día* (week-day set lunch) as well as a popular Sunday brunch buffet.

The restaurant is inside Hotel Malinalli.

❶ Getting There & Away

Surianos (www.autobusesoro.com.mx) has services to/from Puebla CAPU (M$39, two hours) every 15 to 30 minutes. From Tlaxcala's main station, **ATAH** (www.atah.mx; M$38, frequent) and **ADO** (www.ado.com.mx; M$47, 12:50am, 6am, 3.45pm) buses to Huamantla take 1½ hours. Buses don't always stop at a station, so be sure to tell the driver you're going to Huamantla *centro* to avoid missing the town entirely. There are no direct services from Cuetzalan; you must first head to Puebla.

Supra operates a direct service between Mexico City's TAPO station (M$175, three hours, hourly) and Huamantla.

Cuetzalan

📋233 / POP 6000 / ELEV 980M

The gorgeous drive to Cuetzalan is one of the most exhilarating trips in the region and an adventure in itself. Beyond the Zaragoza turnoff, the road becomes dramatic, snaking up hills and around hairpin bends and offering breathtaking views. At the end of it all is the remote, humid town of Cuetzalan (Place of the Quetzals). Built on a precipitous slope, this striking town is famed for its vibrant festivals, weekend *voladores* (fliers) performances, and Sunday *tianguis* (street market) that attracts scores of indigenous people in traditional dress. On the clearest days you can see all the way from the hilltops to the Gulf coast, 70km away as the quetzal flies.

⊙ Sights

Start at the *zócalo*, Cuetzalan's central plaza with a *kiosko* (rotunda). Three structures rise above the skyline: the plaza's freestanding **clock tower**, the Gothic spire of the **Parroquia de San Francisco** to the northeast and, to the west, the tower of the French Gothic **Santuario de Guadalupe**, with its highly unusual decorative rows of *jarritos* (clay vases) and design based on the sanctuary in Lourdes.

Casa de la Cultura de Cuetzalan MUSEUM
(Museo Etnográfico Calmahuistic; 📋233-331-00-15; Av Miguel Alvarado 18; ⊙9am-6pm) FREE This small museum alongside the tourist office exhibits traditional daily dress of the region, arts and crafts, and some archaeological

OFF THE BEATEN TRACK

YOHUALICHÁN RUINS

Yohualichán ([☎]222-235-14-78; M$45; ⊙9am-5pm), a ceremonial pre-Hispanic site inhabited by the Totonaca, has niche 'pyramids' similar to El Tajín's (Veracruz) that are in varying states of ruin. The site is impressive and well worth a visit, not least for the great views from this side of the valley. It lies about 8km northeast of Cuetzalan, the last 2km along a steep cobblestone road. To get here, take a *colectivo* (M$6, 30 minutes) on Alvarado with the sign 'Yohualichán', or ask at the tourist office (p188).

The entrance is adjacent to Yohualichán's church and town plaza.

pieces from nearby Yohualichán. Fans of the *voladores* will appreciate the explanation of the history of this and other dances and ceremonial performances.

Jardín Botánico Xoxoctic   GARDENS
([☎]233-331-00-27; www.facebook.com/jbxoxoctic; San Antonio Rayón Km 2.8; M$50; ⊙9am-6pm Mon-Fri, to 5pm Sat, to 4pm Sun) A small but delightful botanical garden in a mountain forest with fine views 4km northeast of central Cuetzalan. Admission includes a Spanish-speaking guide who can explain the various local plants such as giant ferns, tropical cherries and endangered species, plus exotic orchids in the hothouse and butterflies in the butterfly house. It's an enjoyable stop on the way to Yohualichán.

Take a *colectivo* (M$6, 15 minutes, frequent) with the sign 'Yohualichán' or 'San Antonio Rayón' from outside Hotel Posada Molina at 68 Alvarado, four blocks northwest of the *zócalo*. The same *colectivos* continue 15 minutes to Yohualichán. A taxi from the *zócalo* or Yohualichán is about M$50.

**Cascada Las Brisas
& Cascada del Salto**   WATERFALL
(Río Tecolutla; M$10) About 5km southeast of town, there's a pair of lovely waterfalls. The shallow natural swimming pools beneath the falls are cold but enticing – bring your bathing kit, and footwear for the sharp underwater rocks. Rickshaw mototaxis will deposit you at the trailhead and await your return. From here it's an easy 15-minute walk to the waterfalls.

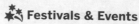

★★ Festivals & Events

Feria del Café y del Huipil   CULTURAL
(Plaza Celestino Gasca s/n; ⊙Oct) For several lively days around October 4, Cuetzalan celebrates both its patron saint, St Francis of Assisi, and the start of the coffee harvest with the Festival of Coffee and Huipiles. It features hearty drinking, traditional quetzal dancing and airborne *voladores*, the Totonac ritual in which men, suspended by their ankles, whirl around a tall pole.

🛏 Sleeping

Posada Quinto Palermo   HOTEL $
([☎]233-331-04-52; Calle 2 de Abril 2; s/d M$350/650; [🖥]) This basic hotel has the best location in town and a roof deck overlooking the palm trees and steeples of Cuetzalan's gorgeous *zócalo*. The 15 rooms have almost comically bad color schemes and tacky art. Ask for a room facing the front of the hotel, which has windows onto the plaza. Rates are greatly reduced in low season.

Parking (M$50) at a nearby lot can be arranged at check-in.

Hotel Taselotzin   LODGE $
([☎]233-331-04-80; www.taselotzin.mex. tl; Yoloxóchitl, Barrio Zacatipan; dm/s/d/tr M$180/420/700/930, cabins for up to 7 people M$1580; [P][🖥]) 🍴 Just 800m south of town, this lodge is run by an association of 100 welcoming Nahua craftswomen who campaign for fair trade. The 10-room lodgings have hard mattresses and patchy wi-fi but are clean and simply decorated with embroidery designs. Traditional massages are offered and a restaurant serves local dishes.

Follow the right-hand fork past the turnoff to the Puebla road; watch for an inconspicuous sign on the right-hand side, about 300m downhill.

Tosepan Kali   LODGE $
([☎]233-331-09-25; www.tosepankali.com; Carretera Cuetzalan Km 1.5, San Miguel Tzinacapan; dm/r/cabins per person incl breakfast M$290/406/522; [P][🖥][♨]) 🍴 High on a hill between Cuetzalan and the nearby town of San Miguel Tzinacapan to the north, Tosepan Kali ('our house' in Náhuatl) resembles a tree house nestled in foliage. With clean rooms constructed largely of bamboo and stone and a large pool with valley views, this beautiful, if run-down, ecohotel is the work of a local indigenous cooperative who collect rainwater.

The *cabañas* (cabins) are split-level and spacious. There are also *cuevañas*, cave-like bamboo cabins, a 50-minute drive away.

Hotel Posada Cuetzalan
HOTEL $$

(📞233-331-01-54; www.posadacuetzalan.com; Zaragoza 12; s/d/tr/q M$655/913/1085/1220; P🏊) This handsome hotel, 100m uphill from the *zócalo* and a short walk from the bus station, has three large courtyards full of chirping birds, a swimming pool, a good restaurant featuring local fruit liqueurs and 36 simple rooms with tropical colors, tiled floors, lots of lightly stained wood, and cable TV. The common-area-only wifi barely reaches the front rooms near the office.

Hotel La Casa de la Piedra
BOUTIQUE HOTEL $$

(📞233-331-00-30; www.lacasadepiedra.com; Carlos García 11; d/tw/ste from M$960/1580/1680; P🛜🏊) All 16 rooms in this renovated yet rustic former coffee-processing warehouse have picture windows and refinished wooden floors. Upstairs, the two-level suites accommodate up to four people and offer expansive views of the valley. Downstairs rooms have tiled bathrooms, rough stone walls and one or two beds.

🍴 Eating & Drinking

Restaurants are unfussy and family-friendly with no upmarket options. There are food stands at Mercado de Artesanías Matachiuj. Regional specialties, sold at many roadside stands, include fruit wines and smoked meats. Look for *xoco atol* (fermented rice drink), *yolixpa* (herbal liqueur with an anise flavor) and *dulce de tejocote* (yellow hawthorn fruit in anise syrup). Try the regional *café de la sierra* while you can, as climate change has decimated crops in recent decades.

Restaurante Yoloxóchitl
MEXICAN $

(📞233-331-03-35; Calle 2 de Abril 1; mains M$50-70, meals M$65-80; ⊗8am-9pm; 📶) Beautifully decorated with plants, antiques and ancient jukeboxes, Yoloxóchitl has views over the cathedral and a selection of salads, *antojitos* (tortilla-based snacks) and complete meals that include a filling regional Cuetzalan plate of *cecina* (beef) served with *tlacoyos* (stuffed tortilla), beans and wild mushrooms pickled in *chipotle* (smoked chili). Live music is common at lunch and dinner.

There are plenty of breakfast options, though no set menu.

La Terraza
SEAFOOD $

(📞233-331-04-16; Hidalgo 33; breakfasts M$65-75, mains M$65-162; ⊗8am-8pm) This family-run restaurant west of the *zócalo*, decorated with photos of the town's annual festivities, is extremely popular with locals for its large selection (and servings) of breakfasts, *mariscos* (seafood), quesadillas, *platillos de la región* and crawfish (in season). Handmade tortillas and clay tableware add rustic charm.

Bar El Calate
BAR

(📞233-112-50-36; Morelos 9B; ⊗noon-10pm Sun-Wed, to midnight Thu & Fri, to 2am Sat) On the west side of the *zócalo*, this is *the* place to sip homemade hooch. There are 36 flavors, including liquors infused with coffee, limes, berries – you name it. Try the all-curing *yolixpa*.

☆ Entertainment

★ Los Voladores
PERFORMING ARTS

(Parroquía de San Francisco de Asís, Plaza Celestino Gasca s/n; by donation; ⊗from 4pm Sat, from noon Sun) In the *danza de los voladores* (dance of the 'flyers'), airborne performers whirl around a 30m pole, suspended by their ankles while playing flutes. On weekends *voladores* twirl outside the church at the *zócalo*, several times a day for tourists (and tips). It's a remarkable, don't-miss performance. Unfortunately, hours are not fixed and sometimes dances don't happen, so check ahead with the tourist office.

This Mesoamerican ritual was recognized as Intangible Cultural Heritage by Unesco in 2009. It is estimated to have originated some time in the pre-Classic period (1000 BCE to 250 CE) in Veracruz. Four dancers represent the cardinal points and a fifth represents the sun. They spin 13 times, a number derived from 52 (the number of years in a pre-Hispanic century) divided by four ropes, to represent the dawn of a new sun.

Performances are canceled during heavy rain or wind.

Lienzo Charro El Potrillo
DANCE

(📞233-331-02-54; www.elrincon.mx; García 44; dinner & show per person M$240; ⊗9pm-midnight Sat) Vibrant Saturday dinner shows at this ranch move from pre-Hispanic times to the modern day through different folkloric dances, costumes and musical instruments. Included in the price is a hearty *molcajete* (grilled pork, *chorizo*, *nopal*, avocado and salsas) with an *agua fresca* (chilled fruit drink). The farm-like space is a good place

OFF THE BEATEN TRACK

CANTONA

Given its isolation from any town of significance, the vast and incredibly well-preserved Mesoamerican city of **Cantona** (☎ 276-596-53-07; Tepeyahualco; admission M$60, recording video M$45; ⊘ 9am-5pm, last entry 4pm) is virtually unknown to travelers. With 24 ball courts discovered, this is now believed to have been the biggest single urban center in Mesoamerica, stretching over 12 sq km in an ethereal lava-bed landscape dotted with cacti and yucca and offering incredible views of Pico de Orizaba to the south.

The site was inhabited from 600 to 1000 CE and is of interest for two main reasons. Unlike most other Mesoamerican cities, no mortar was used to build it, meaning all the stones are simply held in place by their weight. It's also unique in its design sophistication – all parts of the city are linked by an extensive network of raised roads connecting some 3000 residences. There are several small pyramids and an elaborate acropolis at the city's center. With good information panels in English and an access road, Cantona is being promoted as a tourist attraction, though there is only one place to eat outside the site and just one onsite store (selling mostly souvenirs) – so come prepared with food, water and sun protection, and be ready to walk a two-hour tour of the sprawling site. The **Museo de Sitio de Cantona** (☎ 276-596-53-07; ⊘ 9am-5pm) **FREE** is worth a visit, especially if you can read Spanish.

From Oriental, which is the nearest decent-sized town, combis leave when full from the corner of Carretera Federal Puebla–Teziutlan and 8 Poniente for Tepeyahualco near Cantona (M$30, 45 minutes). Tell the driver you want to go to the ruins and they can possibly make a side trip directly there, or you'll need to take a taxi *colectivo* (M$10) for the 10 minutes from Tepeyahualco.

Otherwise, taxis to the site from Oriental are M$150 or more for a round trip. If you have your own transportation, visiting Cantona makes for a good side trip en route to Cuetzalan.

to see local *voladores* flying around a pole. Reservations required.

The restaurant-ranch-hotel is a walkable four blocks north of the *zócalo*.

🛍 Shopping

Mercado de Artesanías Matachiuj   ARTS & CRAFTS
(Hidalgo 917; ⊘ 9am-7pm Wed-Mon) This small fair-trade market a few blocks west of the *zócalo* has a range of quality weavings and other crafts that come with the benefit of meeting the producer, as many wares are made onsite by local artisans. Food stalls and tourist guides can also be found here.

❶ Information

Tour guides (some speaking basic English) hang around the Mercado de Artesanías Matachiuj. The **tourist office** (Casa de la Cultura de Cuetzalan; ☎ 233-331-05-27; Av Miguel Alvarado 18; ⊘ 9am-5pm Mon-Fri, to 9pm Sat & Sun), two blocks west of the *zócalo*, has much-needed town maps and accommodations information, but no English is spoken. Next door there's a Santander **ATM**.

❶ Getting There & Away

Vía buses run between Puebla and Cuetzalan (M$210, 3½ hours, hourly), leaving Puebla CAPU from 6:45am to 8pm, returning 5am to 6pm.

It pays to check road conditions and buy your return bus tickets in advance during the rainy season. AU runs at least five buses a day, from 9am to 10pm, from Mexico City's TAPO bus station (M$394 to M$465, 5¾ to 6¼ hours), returning from Cuetzalan between 4:30am and 2:30pm. Additional services are offered by ADO Friday to Sunday.

❶ Getting Around

On the town's steep streets, three-wheeled moto-taxis (from M$25 or about M$100 an hour) offer rides with a thrill. Covered pickup trucks provide transportation to nearby *pueblitos* (M$8).

SOUTH OF MEXICO CITY

A host of great destinations sits south of the Mexican capital, including mystical Tepoztlán, breathtaking silver-mining cliff-hugging town of Taxco and the superb complex of caves at Grutas de Cacahuamilpa. Cuernavaca, 'the city of eternal spring,' is a longtime popular escape from Mexico City and a home-away-from-home for many North Americans and *chilangos* (Mexico City inhabitants) who own second houses here.

The state of Morelos, which encompasses Cuernavaca and Tepoztlán, is one of Mexico's smallest and most densely populated. Unfortunately, it suffered major damage in the earthquake of September 19, 2017, and some sights are temporarily closed for restoration work. Valleys at different elevations have a variety of microclimates, and many fruits, grains and vegetables have been cultivated here since pre-Hispanic times. You can visit palaces and haciendas in the region, along with 16th-century churches and monasteries. Those interested in the peasant revolutionary leader Emiliano Zapata should head to Cuautla, the first city that the Morelos hero conquered, and 6km further south to Anenecuilco, where he was born.

Tepoztlán

♩ 739 / POP 14,130 / ELEV 1700M

A weekend trip from the capital to Tepoztlán rarely disappoints. This beautifully situated small town with a well-preserved historic center surrounded by soaring jagged cliffs is just 80km south of Mexico City. As the birthplace of Quetzalcóatl, the omnipotent serpent god of the Aztec over 1200 years ago (according to Mesoamerican legend), Tepoztlán is a major Náhuatl center and a mecca for New Agers who believe the area has a creative energy.

This *pueblo mágico* boasts a great crafts market and a host of charming restaurants and hotels. It also retains indigenous traditions, with some elders still speaking Náhuatl and younger generations learning it in school, which makes it a rarity among the towns ringing the Mexican capital.

◎ Sights

Everything in Tepoztlán is easily accessible on foot, except the impressive cliff-top Pirámide de Tepozteco, a 2.5km strenuous hike away.

★ Pirámide de Tepozteco   ARCHAEOLOGICAL SITE
(☑ 777-314-40-48; Av del Tepozteco; M$55, Sun free; ☉ 9am-5.30pm) Tepoztlán's main sight is this 10m-high pyramid perched atop a sheer cliff at the end of a very steep paved path that begins at the end of Avenida del Tepozteco. Built in honor of Tepoztécatl, the Aztec god of harvest, fertility and *pulque,* the pyramid is more impressive for its location than actual size. At the top, depending on haze levels, the serenity and the panorama of the valley make the hike worthwhile.

Spotting the plentiful coati (raccoon-like animal) here is also a bonus for some, though they can be aggressive in pawing at you for food; trousers are recommended if this might bother you.

Tepotzteco is some 400m above the town. Be warned that the path is tough, so head off early to beat the heat and wear decent shoes. The 2.5km walk is not recommended to anyone not physically fit. A store at the peak sells refreshments, but you should bring water with you anyway. Video-camera use costs M$47. The hike itself is free, but to get close to the pyramid (and the view) you must pay the admission fee.

To get here walk north along the main road Avenida del Tepozteco, which is on the west side of the *zócalo.* After seven long blocks, the road becomes a steep, tree-covered path, marking the entrance to the path.

Ex-Convento Domínico de la Natividad   CHRISTIAN SITE
This monastery, situated east of the *zócalo,* and the attached church were built by Dominican priests between 1560 and 1588. The plateresque church facade has Dominican seals interspersed with indigenous symbols, floral designs and various figures, including the sun, moon and stars, animals, angels and the Virgin Mary. Upstairs, various cells house a bookstore, galleries and a regional history museum.

The monastery's arched west entryway is adorned with an elaborate seed mural of pre-Hispanic history and symbolism. Every year during the first week of September, local artists sow a new mural from 60 varieties of seeds.

At the time of writing the monastery remained closed for repairs, years after an earthquake, with only the south entrance on the ramp open for access to the grounds. Glimpsing Mass held in the surrounding outdoor grounds is interesting in itself. Check ahead to see if the monastery has reopened.

✨ Festivals & Events

Tepoztlán is a hyper-festive place, with many Christian feasts superimposed on pagan celebrations. With eight *barrios* and an equal number of patron saints, there always seems to be some excuse for fireworks.

Carnaval   DANCE
(☉ late Feb/early Mar) During the five days preceding Ash Wednesday (46 days before Easter Sunday), Carnaval features the

colorful dances of the Huehuenches and Chinelos, with feather headdresses and beautifully embroidered costumes, around central Tepoztlán.

Fiesta del Templo
RELIGIOUS

(Fiesta Tepozteco; ⊘ Sep 7) On September 7, an all-night celebration goes off on Tepozteco hill near the pyramid, with copious consumption of *pulque* in honor of Tepoztécatl. The following day is the Fiesta del Templo, a Catholic celebration featuring theater performances in Náhuatl. The pyramid is lit up with gaudy lights both evenings and access is closed off by 9pm, so arrive early.

The holiday was first intended to coincide with – and perhaps supplant – the pagan festival, but the *pulque* drinkers get a jump on it by starting the night before, congesting the main road Avenida del Tepozteco.

🛏 Sleeping

Tepoztlán has a range of good accommodations options, but in this small town it can sometimes be hard to find a room during festivals and on weekends. If you can't find a room, keep your eyes peeled for private homes marked with *hospedaje económico* or *posada* signs offering rooms for M$350 to M$700, especially along Las Industrias and Calle 22 de Febrero, just west of the *zócalo*. Loud fireworks continue late into the night during festivals.

Hospedaje Gema
GUESTHOUSE $

(🖉 739-395-17-33; www.facebook.com/hospedajegema; Rodríguez 6; d M$750-920, q M$1580; 🅿🛜) Tepoztlán attracts visitors seeking spiritual discovery, and what better place than this quiet home turned accommodations with a temascal in the wild garden or a massage in the spa room (both from M$400). Tiled rooms are simple with soft beds covered in mosquito nets, and the *abuela* (grandma) cooks hearty Mexican dishes. Children can't be accommodated.

Natural Mystic Hostal
HOSTEL $

(🖉 739-395-29-73; http://hostalnaturalmystictepoztlan.mex.tl; Av Zaragoza 29; dm M$325-360; 🛜) The most centrally located of Tepoztlán's few hostels promotes tranquility, attracting spirituality-seeking backpackers rather than party animals to its basic foam beds. The roof terrace is popular for hanging out in a hammock pondering nature's wonders in the cliffs.

★ Posada Nican Mo Calli
HOTEL $$

(🖉 739-395-31-52; www.hotelnican.com; Netzahualcóyotl 4A; d M$1400, ste M$1500-2600; 🅿🛜🏊) With brightly painted public areas, a heated pool, stylish rooms (some with balconies and great mountain views) and plenty of animals hanging around, Nican Mo Calli is just right for a romantic weekend away and one of the best options in town. Rates are discounted Sunday to Thursday.

Posada del Valle
RESORT $$

(🖉 739-395-05-21; www.posadadelvalle.com.mx; Camino a Mextitla 5; r from M$1480, spa packages M$4220-5220; 🅿🏊) Located east of town, this hotel-spa has quiet, romantic rooms and a good Argentine restaurant. Spa packages include accommodations for one or two nights, breakfast, massages and a visit to the temascal. It's 2km down Avenida Revolución 1910 – just follow the signs for the final 100m to the hotel. Children under 16 not allowed.

★ Posada del Tepozteco
LUXURY HOTEL $$$

(🖉 739-395-00-10; www.posadadeltepozteco.com; Paraíso 3; d/ste/q incl breakfast M$2730/4260/5620; 🅿@🛜🏊) This refined hotel was built as a hillside mansion in the 1930s. The 20 rooms are airy and individually decorated, with most boasting magnificent views over town, and share a wonderful garden and pool. The guest book contains famous names, including Angelina Jolie, who stayed in Room 5 when she dropped by. Rates are discounted up to 40% during the week.

🍴 Eating

This small town is hopping on weekends, when cafes and bars fill up with enthusiastic visitors. Unfortunately for those visiting midweek, many of the best spots are only open Friday to Sunday. Tepoztlán's growing expat population sustains plenty of vegetarian and fine-dining options with prices that match Mexico City.

El Tlecuil
VEGAN $

(www.facebook.com/eltlecuiltepoztlan; Mercado Municipal de Tepoztlán s/n; snacks M$40, meals M$120; ⊘9am-6pm; 🍴) The chaotic market hides a stall with mostly vegan pre-Hispanic food. Mainly this means *tortita* (croquette) taste bombs wrapped up as tacos or with rice and *mole*. Flavor highlights include *siete semillas* (mixed sunflower, pepita and other seeds) and an inventive apple hash. Croquettes are premade so ask for them to be cooked very hot.

Tepoztlán

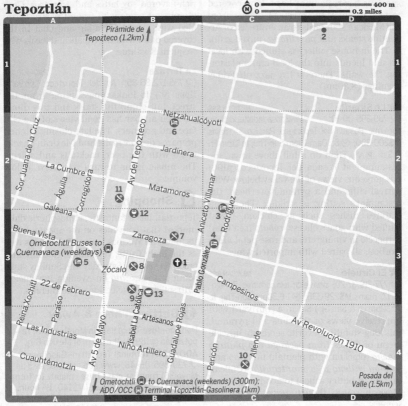

Tepoztlán

◎ Sights
1	Ex-Convento Domínico de la Natividad	B3

✛ Activities, Courses & Tours
2	La Villa Bonita	D1

⊟ Sleeping
3	Hospedaje Gema	C2
4	Natural Mystic Hostal	C3
5	Posada del Tepozteco	A3
6	Posada Nican Mo Calli	B2

⊗ Eating
7	El Ciruelo	B3
8	El Tlecuil	B3
9	La Luna Mextli	B3
	La Sibarita	(see 5)
10	La Veladora	C4
11	Los Colorines	B2

⊙ Drinking & Nightlife
12	La Terraza	B3
13	Rustique	B3

★ **Los Colorines**   MEXICAN **$$**
(☏ 739-395-01-98; www.facebook.com/loscolorines
oficial; Av del Tepozteco 13; mains M$96-192; ⊙ 9am-
9pm; 🖉 🍴) Inside the pink exterior of this
buzzing restaurant, the hearty traditional
Mexican fare bubbles away in *cazuelas* (clay
pots) – try the regional *chiles rellenos* or *hu-
auzontle* (broccoli-like flower buds). More

than the food, eating here is a joy for the
piñatas, terrace views, spaciousness and the
sense of being at a fiesta at grandma's colorful
ranch. Cash only.

La Luna Mextli   INTERNATIONAL **$$**
(☏ 739-395-20-67;   www.facebook.com/laluna
mextli; Av Revolución 1910 No 16; mains M$90-220;
⊙ noon-9pm Mon-Fri, 9am-10pm Sat & Sun) This

spacious bar-restaurant has a long covered terrace to enjoy the excellent dishes, from the Mexican standards to an entire list of Argentine steaks and *parrillada* (mixed grill).

The in-house gallery is stuffed with local art and blends into the local crafts plastering the walls. There is live jazz on Friday evenings (8.30pm).

★ La Sibarita   MEXICAN $$$

(☑739-395-00-10; www.posadadeltepozteco. com.mx; Posada del Tepozteco, Paraíso 3; mains M$200-300; ☺8:30am-10pm Sun-Thu, to 11pm Fri & Sat; P☎) High on a hill above town, the restaurant at Posada del Tepozteco (p190) has gorgeous views of the valley below. With surreal cliffs and a pyramid overhead, the restaurant's setting is striking. The menu features dishes such as chicken breast stuffed with goat's cheese, *róbalo* (sea bass) carpaccio in vinaigrette and rose-petal *nieve* (sorbet), all paired with imported wines.

★ El Ciruelo   MEXICAN $$$

(☑777-219-37-20; www.elciruelo.com.mx; Zaragoza 17; mains M$229-336; ☺1-6:30pm Sun-Thu, to 10:30pm Fri & Sat; ☎) Set in a courtyard with impressive views of the cliffs and pyramid, this long-standing favorite serves an upscale menu of dishes from *pechuga con plátano macho* (chicken with plantain in *mole*) and *salmón chileno a la mantequilla* (Chilean salmon in butter sauce) to good salads and Mexican soups, though prices match the scenery.

There's a wide selection of fine Mexican, Argentine, Chilean and Spanish wines, though only two offerings by the glass. On Saturday and Sunday there are play areas for kids.

La Veladora   FUSION $$$

(☑739-395-05-22; www.laveladora.mx; Niño Artillero 20, cnr Allende; mains M$220-380; ☺8am-10pm; ☎☎) A splendid grassy garden makes a wonderful evening out of the already artful meals at this boutique-hotel restaurant in the quiet backstreets of Tepoztlán. Good fish and pasta is outshined by a pre-Hispanic fusion of *amaranto* risotto, and tacos of *escamoles*, duck or soft-shell crab. There are elaborate salads and vegetarian options, and varied cocktails and wines.

🍷 Drinking & Nightlife

Rustique   CAFE

(☑777-135-39-86; Isabel La Católica 1; ☺7.30am-8pm; ☎) You can tell that this bakery-cafe roasts its own coffee beans onsite by its rich-flavored soy lattes and espressos. Grab a croissant or *concha* (round pastry sprinkled with sugar) for a sip and chat in the covered patio with the expats and locals who frequent Rustique.

La Terraza   ROOFTOP BAR

(☑735-172-85-85; Av del Tepozteco; ☺9am-11pm; ☎) It looks unassuming from the street, but climb the stairs and this dimly lit, open-air bar has good views of the cliff face and greenery. The late-closing kitchen prepares decent grills and Mexican snacks to go with the beer, cocktails and spirits. The music leans toward *ranchera* at low volume.

🔒 Shopping

Tepoztlán has a fantastic, atmospheric daily **market** that convenes on the *zócalo*. It's at its fullest on Wednesday and Sunday. As well as the daily fruits, vegetables, clothing and crafts on sale, on Saturday and Sunday stalls south of the *zócalo* on Avenida Revolución 1910 sell a wide selection of handicrafts.

ℹ️ Getting There & Away

Don't confuse Tepoztlán (in Morelos) with Tepotzotlán (p189) to the north of Mexico City.

ADO/OCC (Terminal Tepoztlán–Gasolinera; ☑739-395-06-46; www.ado.com.mx; Av 5 de Mayo 35) runs 1st-class buses mainly to/from Mexico City's Terminal Sur (M$140, 1¼ hours, every 20 to 40 minutes, 6am to 9.30pm), but also to Terminal Norte (M$146, 2¼ hours, two daily), and direct to/from Mexico City's airport (M$200, 1½ hours, three daily). ADO/OCC buses in Tepotzlán arrive at the ADO terminal 'Terminal Tepoztlán–Gasolinera' beside a gas station, from where a white micro (M$8, five minutes, frequent) can take you the 1.5km to the *zócalo*, or you can walk following the main road.

Ometochtli (☑739-395-07-44; www. ometochtli.com) runs 2nd-class direct buses to Cuernavaca's local-bus station (p203), four blocks northeast of the *zócalo* in Cuernavaca (M$28, 45 minutes, every 20 minutes 5am to 9pm). From Monday to Friday buses leave from opposite the Auditorio (with its mosaic mural of *chinelos*); buy tickets from sellers at the blue-and-white umbrella before boarding. On Saturday and Sunday, buses depart from the Ometochtli station five blocks south of the *zócalo* – walk the main street away from the pyramid. Do not take indirect buses, only the safer buses that say '*directo*' on their front. A secure taxi to Cuernavaca is about M$230.

Cuautla

📞 735 / POP 171,130 / ELEV 1300M

Cuautla (*kwout*-la) has none of Tepoztlán's scenic beauty, or the architectural merit of Cuernavaca, but it does have sulfur springs that have attracted people for centuries, as well as serious revolutionary credentials.

Cuautla was a base for one of Mexico's first leaders in the independence struggle, José María Morelos y Pavón, until he was forced to leave when the royalist army besieged the town in 1812. A century later it became a center of support for Emiliano Zapata's revolutionary army. However, if Mexican history and *balnearios* (bathing places) aren't your thing, there's not much for you here – modern Cuautla is perfectly pleasant, but there's little else to see and do.

⊙ Sights

The two main plazas are Plaza Fuerte de Galeana, better known as the Alameda (a favorite haunt of mariachis-for-hire at weekends), and the *zócalo*.

Ex-Convento de San Diego HISTORIC BUILDING
(Batalla 19 de Febrero s/n) In 1911 presidential candidate Francisco Madero embraced Emiliano Zapata at Cuautla's old train station in the sprawling monastery grounds of Ex-Convento de San Diego. Steam enthusiasts will want to come on Saturday, when Mexico's only steam-powered train fires up for short rides from 4pm to 9pm at the attached **Museo Vivencial Ferrocarril 279**. The Ex-Convento is now home to Cuautla's **tourist office** (📞735-352-52-21; Batalla 19 de Febrero s/n; ⊙8am-6pm Mon-Fri, to 8pm Sat, 9am-7pm Sun). The building was restored after earthquake damage in 2017 yet retains its charmingly dilapidated facade.

Museo Histórico del Oriente MUSEUM
(📞735-352-83-31; Callejón del Castigo 3; M$40, Sun free; ⊙9am-5.30pm Tue-Sun) The former residence of José María Morelos houses the Museo Histórico del Oriente. Each room here covers a different historical period with displays of pre-Hispanic pottery, good maps and early photos of Cuautla and Zapata. The Mexican War of Independence rebel leader's remains lie beneath the imposing Zapata monument in the middle of Plazuela Revolución del Sur.

🛏 Sleeping & Eating

Hotel Defensa del Agua HOTEL $
(📞735-352-16-79; Defensa del Agua 34; d/tw/tr/q M$350/450/530/610; 🅿🛜🐾) This old, clean hotel is set out in motel style with a small pool and spacious rooms with TV, phone and fan. There's no restaurant but a handy Italian Coffee Company branch in the building for breakfast. Avoid rooms with windows facing the noisy street.

Hotel & Spa Villasor RESORT $
(📞735-303-55-03; Av Progreso; s/d M$540/700; 🅿❄🛜🐾) Out of town and located opposite the Agua Hedionda baths, this modern place has a large pool and simple, clean and cheery rooms equipped with cable TV. With its own spa treatments, Villasor is the best option for relaxation.

Villasor is less convenient for those without transportation unless you plan on not leaving the area. Take an 'Agua Hedionda' combi (M$7.5) from Plazuela Revolución del Sur or Calle Niño Artillero in central Cuautla, stopping right outside Villasor.

DON'T MISS

CUAUTLA'S BALNEARIOS

Cuautla's best-known *balneario* (thermal bath) is the riverside **Agua Hedionda** (Stinky Water; 📞735-352-00-44; www.balneariosenmorelos.com.mx; end of Av Progreso, cnr Emiliano Zapata; adult/child Mon-Fri M$50/30, Sat & Sun M$75/40, before 9am Mon-Fri M$25; ⊙7am-5:30pm Mon-Fri, to 6pm Sat & Sun; 👜). Waterfalls replenish two lake-sized pools with sulfur-scented tepid water. There's a two-for-one deal on Thursdays. Take an 'Agua Hedionda' combi (M$7.50) from Plazuela Revolución del Sur.

Other *balnearios* worth visiting include **El Almeal** (Hernández; adult/child M$80/50; ⊙9am-6pm) and the nicer **Los Limones** (Gabriel Teppa 14; adult M$70-85, child M$55; ⊙8:30am-6pm; 👜). Both are served by the same spring (no sulfur) and have extensive shaded picnic grounds. Prices are reduced Monday to Friday. Children under three go free.

Check the website of **Balnearios Morelos** (www.balneariosenmorelos.com.mx) for a full list of thermal baths in the area.

¡VIVA ZAPATA!

A peasant leader from Morelos state, Emiliano Zapata (1879–1919) was among the most radical of Mexico's revolutionaries, fighting for the return of hacienda land to the peasants with the cry '*¡Tierra y libertad!*' (Land and freedom!). The Zapatista movement was at odds with both the conservative supporters of the old regime and their liberal opponents. In November 1911 Zapata disseminated his Plan de Ayala, calling for restoration of all land to the peasants. After winning numerous battles against government troops in central Mexico (some in association with Pancho Villa), he was ambushed and killed in 1919.

Ruta de Zapata

In **Anenecuilco**, 6km south of Cuautla, what's left of the adobe cottage where Zapata was born (on August 8, 1879) is now the **Museo de la Lucha para la Tierra** (Museo y Casa de Emiliano Zapata; ☑ 735-308-89-01; Ayuntamiento 33, cnr Av Zapata; M$35, Sun free; ⊙9am-5pm Tue-Sun), with a rousing mural of Zapata's life story.

About 20km south is the **Ex-Hacienda de San Juan Chinameca** (☑735-170-00-83; Cárdenas s/n; M$30, Sun free; ⊙9am-5pm Tue-Sun), in the town of the same name, where in 1919 Zapata was lured into a fatal trap by Colonel Jesús Guajardo, following the orders of President Venustiano Carranza, who was eager to dispose of the rebel leader and consolidate the post-revolutionary government. Pretending to defect to the revolutionary forces, Guajardo set up a meeting with Zapata, who arrived at Chinameca accompanied by a guerrilla escort. Guajardo's men gunned down the general before he crossed the abandoned hacienda's threshold.

The hacienda has a small museum with a meager collection of photos and newspaper reproductions. Following earthquake damage in 2017, the museum reopened with a makeover in late 2019, showing off an improved temporary exhibition of Zapata's life. Otherwise there's a statue of Zapata astride a rearing horse at the entrance, where you can still see the bullet holes where the revolutionary died and where old men gather to celebrate their fallen hero.

From Chinameca head 20km northwest to **Tlaltizapán**, the site of the excellent **Ex-Cuartel General de Zapata** (Museo de la Revolución del Sur; ☑734-341-51-26; Guerrero 2, Tlaltizapán; M$30; ⊙10am-6pm Tue-Sun) **FREE**, the main barracks of the revolutionary forces. Here you can see Zapata's rifle (the trigger retains his fingerprints), the bed where he slept and the outfit he was wearing at the time of his death (riddled with bullet holes and stained with blood). At the time of writing, all but the patio of the museum remained closed for earthquake repairs, but should be reopened by the time you read this; call ahead to confirm.

Though it's possible to do this route via *colectivo* (yellow 'Chinameca' combis traveling to Anenecuilco and Chinameca leave from the corner of Garduño and Matamoros in Cuautla every 10 minutes), it can be an all-day ordeal. The Morelos state tourist office (p202) in Cuernavaca arranges tours of the route.

Restaurant Vegetariano El Sol　VEGETARIAN $

(☑735-353-39-91; Av Insurgentes 126C; mains M$50-80, menú del día M$85; ⊙9am-6pm Mon-Sat; 🖋) Whether you want a meat-free quinoa-topped *tostada*, pizza, soy burger, set lunch, avocado 'prawn' cocktail or simply good-value healthy snack, El Sol is an unfussy place to pop in for something simple.

Las Golondrinas　MEXICAN $$

(☑735-354-13-50; www.facebook.com/restaurante. lasgolondrinas; Catalán 19A; mains M$85-190; ⊙8am-8pm) Set in a 17th-century building filled with plants and koi ponds, Las Golondrinas offers an attractive atmosphere and excellent service. House specialties include a range of *molcajetes*. Light breakfasts include egg-white omelettes.

ⓘ Getting There & Away

OCC (☑800-702-80-00; www.ado.com.mx; Calle 2 de Mayo 97) has 1st-class regular buses (M$158, 2¼, every 15 to 30 minutes) and express services (M$188, 1¾ hours, hourly 1pm to 7pm) from Mexico City's Terminal Sur, and Tepoztlán (M$30, 50 minutes, every 15 to 40 minutes).

Cuernavaca

⏚ 777 / POP 364,020 / ELEV 1480M

The 'city of eternal spring' is an easygoing weekend escape from Mexico City for its strollable town center, touches of fine dining, artworks by Diego Rivera and Frida Kahlo, and as a launchpad for the well-maintained ruins of nearby Xochicalco.

There's always been a formidable glamour surrounding Cuernavaca (kwehr-nah-*vah*-kah), the capital of Morelos state. With its vast, gated haciendas and sprawling estates, it has traditionally attracted high-society visitors year-round for its warmth, clean air and attractive architecture. Today this tradition continues, even though urban sprawl has put a decisive end to the clean air and you're more likely to see students of Spanish or Mexico City's wealthy visiting their holiday homes than meet international royalty or great artists in the street.

History

The first settlers to the valleys of modern Morelos are believed to have arrived in 1500 BCE. In the centuries between 200 CE and 900 CE they organized a highly productive agricultural society and developed Xochicalco and other large constructions throughout the region. Later, the dominant Mexica (Aztec) called them Tlahuica, which means 'people who work the land.' In 1379 a Mexica warlord conquered the settlement of Cuauhnáhuac, subdued the Tlahuica and exacted an annual tribute that included 16,000 pieces of *amate* (bark paper) and 20,000 bushels of corn. The tributes payable by the subject states were set out in a register the Spanish later called the Códice Mendocino, in which Cuauhnáhuac was represented by a three-branch tree. This symbol now graces Cuernavaca's coat of arms.

The Mexica lord's successor married the daughter of the Cuauhnáhuac leader, and from this marriage was born Moctezuma I Ilhuicamina, the 15th-century Aztec king, who was a predecessor to Moctezuma II Xocoyotzin, encountered by Cortés. Under the Aztec, the Tlahuica traded extensively and prospered. Their city was a learning and religious center, and archaeological remains suggest they had a considerable knowledge of astronomy.

When the Spanish arrived the Tlahuica were fiercely loyal to the Aztec. In April 1521 they were finally overcome and Cortés torched the city. Soon Cuauhnáhuac became known as Cuernavaca, a more Spanish-friendly version of its original appellation.

In 1529 Cortés received his belated reward from the Spanish crown when he was named Marqués del Valle de Oaxaca, with an estate that covered 22 towns, including Cuernavaca, and included the labor of 23,000 indigenous Mexicans. After Cortés introduced sugarcane and new farming methods, Cuernavaca became a Spanish agricultural center, as it had been for the Aztec. Cortés' descendants dominated the area for nearly 300 years.

With its salubrious climate, rural surroundings and colonial elite, Cuernavaca became a refuge for the rich and powerful in the 1700s and 1800s, including José de la Borda, the 18th-century Taxco silver magnate. Borda's lavish home was later a retreat for Emperor Maximilian and Empress Carlota. Cuernavaca has also attracted many artists and achieved literary fame as the setting for Malcolm Lowry's 1947 novel *Under the Volcano*.

⊙ Sights

★ **Museo Robert Brady**   MUSEUM

(⏚ 777-318-85-54; www.museorobertbrady.com; Netzahualcóyotl 4; adult/student M$50/30; ⊘ 10am-6pm Tue-Sun) Let's face it, who wouldn't want to be independently wealthy and spend their life traveling around the world collecting art for their lavish Mexican mansion? If that option isn't open to you, visit this museum – easily one of Cuernavaca's best – and live vicariously. The one-time home of American artist and collector Robert Brady (1928–86), the museum, which is housed in the Casa de la Torre, is a wonderful place to spend time appreciating the exquisite taste of one person.

Originally part of the monastery within the Recinto de la Catedral, the house is a stunning testament to a man who knew what he liked. Brady lived in Cuernavaca for 24 years after a spell in Venice, and has become a modern-day gay icon. His collections range from Papua New Guinea and India to Haiti and South America, and include personal photos with his pals.

Every room, including the two gorgeous bathrooms and kitchen, is bedecked in paintings, carvings, textiles, antiques and folk art from all corners of the Earth. Among the treasures are works by well-known Mexican artists, including Tamayo, Covarrubias

Cuernavaca

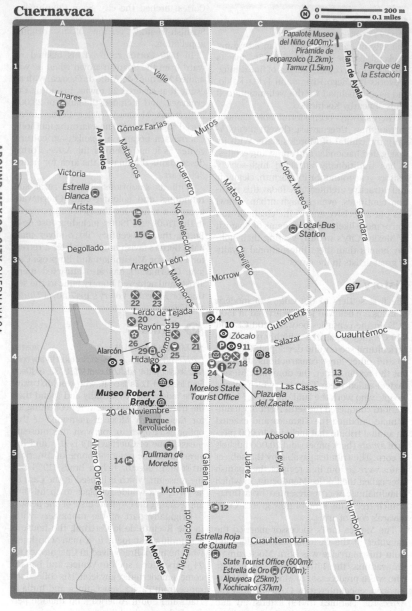

0 — 200 m
0 — 0.1 miles

Papalote Museo del Niño (400m);
Pirámide de Teopanzolco (1.2km);
Tamuz (1.5km)

Parque de la Estación

Plan de Ayala

Valle

Linares 17

Gómez Farías

Av Morelos

Matamoros

Guerrero

Muros

Mateos

López Mateos

Gandara

Victoria

Estrella Blanca
Arista

Degollado

16

15

Aragón y León

No Reelección

Matamoros

Clavijero

Morrow

Local-Bus Station

7

Gutenberg

Cuauhtémoc

22 23

Lerdo de Tejada
20
Rayón 19
26
Alarcón 29 25
3 Hidalgo

Comonfort

4
10
Zócalo
9 11
27 18
24
5
i
8
28

Salazar

Las Casas

13

2
6

Museo Robert
Brady 1

Morelos State
Tourist Office

Plazuela
del Zacate

20 de Noviembre
Parque
Revolución

Alvaro Obregón

14 Pullman de
Morelos

Galeana

Juárez

Leyva

Abasolo

Humboldt

Motolinía

Netzahualcóyotl

12

Av Morelos

Estrella Roja
de Cuautla

Cuauhtemotzin

State Tourist Office (600m);
Estrella de Oro (700m);
Alpuyeca (25km);
Xochicalco (37km)

and friends Rivera and Kahlo, as well as Brady's own paintings (check out his spot-on portrait of his buddy Peggy Guggenheim). There is a bedroom dedicated to his friend Josephine Baker, the French-American actor and black civil-rights activist. The gardens are lovely too, with a very tempting (but off-limits) swimming pool in one of them and a little **cafe** in the other.

Classic and contemporary films are shown in the museum's courtyard every Wednesday at 4pm and 6pm for a M$30 donation. Movies are in their original language with Spanish subtitles.

Cuernavaca

Guided tours are available by appointment for groups of up to 20 people for M$300.

Catedral de Cuernavaca CHURCH
(www.catedraldecuernavaca.org; Hidalgo 17; ☉7:30am-8pm) **FREE** Cuernavaca's cathedral, **Templo de la Asunción de María** is plain and solid with an unembellished facade. It stands in a large high-walled *recinto* (compound), built in a grand, fortress-like style in an effort to impress, intimidate and defend against the local people. Franciscans started work on what was one of Mexico's earliest Christian missions in 1526, using indigenous labor and stones from the rubble of Cuauhnáhuac. The compound entrance is on Hidalgo.

As you enter the cathedral compound there are two smaller churches. On the right is the pink **Templo de la Tercera Orden de San Francisco**. Its exterior was carved in 18th-century baroque style by indigenous artisans and its interior has ornate, gilded decorations. On the left is the yellow 19th-century **Capilla del Carmen**, where believers seek cures for illness.

Walking straight ahead upon entering the compound entrance is the cathedral side door (currently the main entryway), which shows a mixture of indigenous and European features – the skull and crossbones above it is a symbol of the Franciscan order. Inside are frescoes rediscovered early in the 20th century. Cuernavaca was a center for Franciscan missionary activities in Asia and the frescoes – said to show the persecution of Christian missionaries in Japan – were supposedly painted in the 17th century by a Japanese convert to Christianity.

In the left section of the cathedral is **Museo de Arte Sacro** (☎777-312-12-90; adult/student M$30/15; ☉10am-2pm & 4-6pm Tue-Fri, 10am-5pm Sat & Sun), a small museum (opened in 2018) displaying 92 pieces of religious paintings, ornaments and sculptures from the 16th to 20th centuries.

To the right of the cathedral lies an open chapel, the **Capilla Abierta de San José**, the compound's first structure (inaccessible at the time of writing, due to earthquake damage in 2017).

MMAPO MUSEUM
(Museo Morelense de Arte Popular; ☎777-318-62-00; http://mmapo.morelos.gob.mx; Hidalgo 239; ☉10am-5.30pm Tue-Sun) **FREE** This bright and inviting museum showcases handicrafts from Morelos, including life-size *chinelos* (costumed dancers with upturned chins from Morelos). Most of the pieces are displayed out in the open, not behind glass, so you can get close and admire the handiwork. The attached **store** sells quality pieces that you won't see in your average crafts market.

Museo Juan Soriano
MUSEUM

(MMAC; Museo Morelense de Arte Contemporáneo; ☑777-608-33-50; Dr Guillermo Gandara; ⊗museum 10am-6pm Wed-Mon, garden 8am-6.30pm daily, library 10am-6pm Mon & Wed-Sat) **FREE** Opened in 2018, this contemporary art museum is comprised of off-white cubes squatting a few blocks west of the *zócalo*. Temporary exhibits have included the grotesque sculptures of Javier Marín and the *cosmovisión* (worldview) of Ángela Gurría. The permanent collection displays the 1200 paintings, drawings and costume designs of modern Mexican artist Juan Soriano (1920–2006). A highlight are Soriano's sculptures in the shady garden, which flows around the lofty architecture, making a tranquil alternative to the Plaza de Armas, main square.

There is also an elegant library for research (no borrowing) specializing in books and magazines on modern and contemporary art.

Artwork explanatory text is in Spanish only. Admission is free, despite the price listed on the website; if this changes, Sundays will remain free, along with the garden and library.

Jardín Juárez
GARDENS

(Guerrero) **FREE** Adjoining the northwest corner of the Plaza de Armas is the Jardín Juárez, where the central gazebo (designed by tower specialist Gustave Eiffel) houses juice and sandwich stands. Live-band concerts on Thursday and Sunday evenings start at 6pm. Roving vendors sell balloons, ice cream and corn on the cob under the trees, which fill up with legions of cacophonous grackles at dusk.

Even more entertaining are the guitar trios who warm up their voices and instruments before heading to the cafes across the street to serenade willing patrons. You can request a ballad or two for around M$80.

Palacio de Cortés
HISTORIC BUILDING

(☑777-312-81-71; Leyva 100; M$55, Sun free; ⊗8am-6pm Tue-Sun) Cortés' imposing medieval-style fortress stands opposite the southeast end of the Plaza de Armas. This two-story stone palace was built in 1535 on the base of the city pyramid that Cortés destroyed after taking Cuauhnáhuac. The base is still visible from various points on the ground floor. An earthquake in 2017 damaged the building, and at the time of writing the Palacio remains closed for years-long repairs. Only a tiny exhibition remains open, with relics from pre-Hispanic cultures.

Papalote Museo del Niño
MUSEUM

(https://cuernavaca.papalote.org.mx; Av Vicente Guerrero 205; adult/child under 15yr M$50/60, group of 4 M$185; ⊗9am-6pm Mon-Fri, from 10am Sat & Sun; P♿) Built as part of a land deal with the city, this excellent children's museum has an odd location in a shopping center beside a Costco, about 4km north of downtown, but for travelers with children it's well worth seeking out. Geared toward education, technology and play, the museum includes a large Lego exhibit, musical elements and lots of bright colors. There's an IMAX theater in the same complex and discounts for families and groups.

It's 500m south of the Pullman de Morelos bus terminal 'Casino de la Selva', which has departures to Mexico City Terminal Sur.

Jardín Borda
GARDENS

(☑777-318-82-50; Av Morelos 271; adult/child M$30/15, Sun free; ⊗10am-5:30pm Tue-Sun) This extravagant property, inspired by Versailles (though with mere parklike results), features gardens formally laid out in a series of terraces with paths, steps and fountains. Duck into the house to get an idea of how Mexico's 19th-century aristocracy lived. In typical colonial style, the buildings are arranged around courtyards. In one wing, the **Museo de Sitio** has exhibits on daily life during the empire period and original documents with the signatures of Morelos, Juárez and Maximilian.

The property was designed in 1783 for Manuel de la Borda as an addition to the stately residence built by his father, José de la Borda. From 1866 Emperor Maximilian and Empress Carlota entertained their courtiers here and used the house as a summer residence.

Several romantic paintings in the **Sala Manuel M Ponce**, a recital hall near the entrance of the house, show scenes of the garden in Maximilian's time. One of the most famous paintings depicts Maximilian in the garden with La India Bonita, the 'pretty Indian' who later became his lover. Originally there was a botanical collection to show off, with hundreds of varieties of ornamental plants and fruit trees. Because of a water shortage, the baroque-style fountains now operate only on weekends.

Plaza de Armas
PLAZA

(Zócalo; Gutenberg) Cuernavaca's *zócalo*, Plaza de Armas, is flanked on the east by the Palacio de Cortés and giant 'Cuernavaca' letters,

XOCHICALCO

Atop a desolate plateau with views for miles around, **Xochicalco** (☎737-374-30-92; https://inah.gob.mx/zonas/13-zona-arqueologica-de-xochicalco; admission incl museum M$75, video permit M$45; ⊙9am-6pm, last entry 5pm) is an impressive and relatively easy day trip from Cuernavaca that shouldn't be missed. It's large enough to make the 38km journey worthwhile, but not so well known as to be overrun by tourists.

A Unesco World Heritage site and one of central Mexico's most important archaeological sites, Xochicalco (so-chee-*cal*-co) is Náhuatl for 'place of the house of flowers.' The collection of white stone ruins, many still to be excavated, covers approximately 10 sq km. They represent the various cultures – Tlahuic, Toltec, Olmec, Zapotec, Mixtec and Aztec – for which Xochicalco was a commercial, cultural and religious center. When Teotihuacán began to weaken around 650 to 700 CE, Xochicalco began to rise in importance, achieving its peak between 650 and 900 CE, with far-reaching cultural and commercial relations. Around 650 CE, Zapotec, Maya and Gulf coast spiritual leaders convened here to correlate their respective calendars. Xochicalco remained an important center until around 1200, when its excessive growth precipitated a demise similar to that of Teotihuacán.

The site's most famous monument is the **Pirámide de Quetzalcóatl**. Archaeologists have surmised from its well-preserved bas-reliefs that astronomer-priests met here at the beginning and end of each 52-year cycle of the pre-Hispanic calendar. Signage here is in English and Spanish, but information at the excellent, ecologically sensitive **museum**, situated 200m from the ruins, is in Spanish only.

A cave known as **El Observatorio** served as the 'observatory' for scientists studying the stars. From April 29 to August 13, El Observatorio is illuminated by natural sunlight. From December through May, the site offers an occasional **light show** (☎reservations 737-374-30-90; xochicalco.mor@inah.gob.mx; M$15; ⊙Dec-May) on Friday and Saturday nights. It's quite a spectacle, but call ahead because the shows haven't run in recent years.

From Cuernavaca's local-bus station (p203) outside Mercado Adolfo López Mateos, *colectivos* (M$20, 90 minutes, every 30 minutes) with 'Xochi' or 'Cuentepec' on their windshield depart for the site entrance. On arrival, you'll need to walk to the museum to buy tickets. The last return *colectivo* leaves around 6pm. Alternatively, take a taxi (M$35, five minutes) from the site to the nearby town of Alpuyeca for frequent *colectivos* back to Cuernavaca. Larger Pullman de Morelos buses (M$49, every 30 minutes) also run between their terminal a few blocks southeast of the *zócalo* in Cuernavaca and Alpuyeca, but only on Saturday and Sunday.

on the west by the **Palacio de Gobierno** (Plaza de Armas) and on the northeast and south by restaurants and roving bands of mariachis. It's the only main plaza in Mexico without a church, chapel, convent or cathedral overlooking it.

🎓 Courses

Cuernavaca is a well-established center for studying Spanish at all levels and has dozens of language schools. As such, standards are high, teaching is usually very thorough and prices competitive (generally US$200 to US$310 per week, plus registration- and study-material fees and housing). The best schools offer small-group or individual instruction at all levels with four to five hours per day of intensive instruction, plus a couple of hours' conversation practice. Classes begin each Monday and most schools recommend a minimum enrollment of four weeks.

With so many teaching styles and options, prospective students should research carefully. Visit www.languageinternational.com for some options.

✨ Festivals & Events

Carnaval　　　　　　　　　STREET CARNIVAL
(⊙Feb/Mar) Over the five days leading up to Ash Wednesday, Cuernavaca's colorful Carnaval celebrations feature parades, art exhibits and street performances by Tepoztlán's *chinelo* dancers.

Similar celebrations take place across Morelos.

Miquixtli CULTURAL
(Festividad Indígena y Popular de Día de Muertos; www.miquixtli.morelos.gob.mx; ⊙31 Oct–4 Nov) Cuernavaca's annual Day of the Dead festival started in 2018 with a series of free events – a crafts market, art exhibitions, *ofrendas* by indigenous groups of Morelos, traditional dance and music, theater and a *desfile* (parade) of people in costume, including as Catrinas. Most events take part in central Cuernavaca between Jardín Borda and the *zócalo*.

🛌 Sleeping

Some of the best boutique hotels in the country are here, aimed squarely at weekend escapees from the capital. Budget hotels tend to be spartan and not reservable online, while midrange hotels are few. The town fills up with visitors on weekends and holidays, when hotel prices rise significantly and places get booked out. Light sleepers should avoid anywhere within earshot of Plazuela del Zacate on (always rowdy) weekends.

Hotel Roma HOTEL $
(☑777-318-87-78; Matamoros 17; d M$575; 🛜🖥) The pick of the budget options – not difficult in Cuernavaca – for its clean beds with thick mattresses and crisp white bedding (rather than grandma's old animal-print blankets). It's on a hectic, central street but the small austere rooms are semi-enclosed in courtyard-like spaces, making them feel more private. There's even a tiny garden pool.

Hotel Antigua Posada HOTEL $$
(☑777-608-47-46; www.hotelantiguaposadamx .com; Galeana 69; d/tw/ste incl breakfast M$1260/1260/1560; 🅿🛜🖥) This exclusive hideaway is a short walk from the center of town and boasts just 11 rooms behind its unpromising exterior. But once inside you'll find a lovely courtyard, pool and great service. Rooms are gorgeous, complete with wooden beams and rustic touches.

Hotel Laam BUSINESS HOTEL $$
(☑777-314-44-11; Av Morelos 239; d/tw M$1050/1545; 🅿🛜🖥) With a motel feel and comfortable, if sterile, rooms (some with huge terraces), this slick hotel is good value. Set back from the road, giving it distance from street noise, Hotel Laam comes with a heated swimming pool and well-tended grounds.

Hotel Bajo El Volcán HOTEL $$
(☑777-312-48-73; www.hotelbajoelvolcan.com. mx; Humboldt 19; d/tw/tr/ste incl breakfast M$1100/1100/1500/1730; 🅿🛜🖥) There's a certain 1980s vacation-apartment vibe to this hotel with spacious tiled rooms (albeit sporting dated floral decor) set around a clean pool. Its leafy location two blocks east of the noisy *zócalo* is convenient yet tranquil (mariachi-free!). Or stay in your fan-cooled room with flatscreen TV and eat at the on-site restaurant.

★Hotel Hacienda de Cortés HISTORIC HOTEL $$$
(☑800-220-76-97, 777-315-88-44; www.hotel haciendadecortes.com.mx; Plaza Kennedy 90; d from M$2995; 🅿🛜🖥) Built in the 16th century by Martín Cortés (successor to Hernán Cortés as Marqués del Valle de Oaxaca), this former sugar mill was renovated in 1980 and boasts 23 rooms of various levels of luxury, each with its own private garden and terrace. There's also a swimming pool built around old stone columns, a gym and an excellent restaurant.

It's approximately 5km southeast of the center of town. Book months ahead for weekends. Good online promotions available via the website.

Las Mañanitas LUXURY HOTEL $$$
(☑777-362-00-00; www.lasmananitas.com.mx; Linares 107; ste incl breakfast M$3505-6005; 🅿❄🛜🖥) If you're really out to impress someone, book a room at this stunning place. It's a destination hotel – you may not want to leave the whole weekend – so the fact that it's not in the center of town isn't too important. The large rooms are beautifully understated, many with terraces overlooking the gardens, which are full of peacocks and boast a heated pool. Rates are cheaper midweek.

La Casa Azul BOUTIQUE HOTEL $$$
(☑777-314-21-41; www.hotelcasaazul.com.mx; Arista 17; r M$2915-3335; 🅿❄🛜🖥) This 24-room boutique hotel is a short walk from the town center and has lots of charm. Originally part of the Guadalupe Convent, the hotel has soothing fountains, two pools, a gym, and a great selection of local arts and crafts throughout, including in the spotless blue-and-white bathrooms. Suite-like rooms have air conditioning, safes and sofas.

🍴 Eating

Cuernavaca is a great food town with a few excellent high-end restaurants and plenty of good cafes. There are, however, surprisingly few enticing midrange options.

★ **La Maga Café** MEXICAN $
(www.facebook.com/lamagacafe; Morrow 9; buffet M$109; ⊘noon-9pm Mon-Sat; 🛜🍴) The colorful buffet (till 5pm) at La Maga features multitudes of glazed pots filled with salads, pastas, fruit, vegetables, and daily specials such as glistening *pollo en adobo* (chicken marinated in chili) and *tortas de elote* (cheesy corn croquettes). There are great vegetarian options, desserts, included coffee and a community vibe, sometimes with live music. Arrive early to nab a window seat.

Emiliano's MEXICAN $
(Rayón 5; menú del día M$45-75, mains M$35-85; ⊘8am-7pm) Quiz any local on their favorite place to eat and you'll be directed to the thatched roof of homey Emiliano's. Complex *mole* and other Mexican sure things, such as stuffed chilies, are only enhanced by tortillas you can watch being handmade. Add breakfast and you'll be here all day.

Iguana Greens MEXICAN $
(📱777-245-07-50; Rayón 190; menú del día M$45, mains M$40-90; ⊘8am-6:30pm) With authentic Mexican dishes this good and cheap, it would easy for Iguana to be another anonymous *fonda* (inn) and still draw crowds, but the friendly staff take pride in creating a festive space – with brightly colored chairs and tables and messages of appreciation scrawled on the walls.

La Cueva MEXICAN $
(📱777-255-79-59; Galeana 7; breakfasts from M$35, mains M$40-90; ⊘8am-10pm) This sloped bar, which opens onto the bustling crowds on Galeana, serves up superb *pozole* and other delicious snacks and dishes such as stewed *conejo* (rabbit), plus excellent breakfasts. This is a great place to eat with the locals at local prices.

★ **La India Bonita** MEXICAN $$
(📱777-312-50-21; www.laindiabonita.com.mx; Morrow 15B; mains M$160-240; ⊘8am-10pm Sun-Thu, to 11pm Fri & Sat) Set in a lush courtyard, Cuernavaca's oldest restaurant also has some of its best traditional Mexican food – from *brocheta al mezcal* (skewered meats marinated in mezcal) to *chile en nogada* – with the occasional enticing twist. La India Bonita also operates a tasty bakery-cafe next door.

★ **Restaurante**
Hacienda de Cortés INTERNATIONAL $$$
(📱777-315-88-44, 800-220-76-97; www.hotel haciendadecortes.com.mx; Plaza Kennedy 90; mains M$135-415; ⊘7am-11pm; 🅿⊕❄🛜🍴) Situated within Hotel Hacienda de Cortés, a 15-minute drive southeast of central Cuernavaca, this elegant but unpretentious hotel restaurant serves an excellent selection of salads and delicious international dishes, including a fantastic vegetarian lasagna, tuna in almond sauce with risotto, and well-prepared Angus steaks. The dining room is spectacular, with massive vines climbing the walls and wrought-iron chandeliers overhead.

Restaurant Las Mañanitas FRENCH $$$
(📱777-362-00-00; www.lasmananitas.com.mx; Linares 107; breakfasts M$120-285, mains M$290-430; ⊘8am-10:30pm; 🛜🍴) The restaurant and bar of Cuernavaca's most famous hotel, Las Mañanitas, is a luxurious splurge that's open to all. The expansive menu has a heavy French accent, with dishes such as entrecôte Bourguignon and sumptuous desserts. Traditional dishes include *maguey* grubs. Reserve a table inside the mansion or on the terrace, where you can watch wildlife wander among modern garden sculptures.

Casa Hidalgo MEXICAN $$$
(📱777-312-27-49; www.casahidalgo.com; Jardín de los Héroes 6; menú del día M$230, mains M$159-295; ⊘8am-11pm, to midnight Fri & Sat; 🛜🍴♿) Directly opposite the Palacio de Cortés, with a great terrace and upstairs balcony, this popular restaurant attracts a well-heeled crowd of local socialites. The menu is eclectic – try cold mango-agave soup with jicama, or *tlaxcalteca* chicken breast stuffed with cheese and *poblano* pepper with three salsas. There are breakfast and lunch set menus, vegetarian choices and a kids' menu.

🍷 Drinking & Nightlife

Cuernavaca's nightlife is kept buzzing by a student population, especially at rowdy bars and clubs at Plazuela del Zacate and the adjacent alley Las Casas (home of pumping house and techno clubs with that tell-tale accordion of Mexican *norteño*). All stay open until the last patron leaves, which is usually sunrise on weekends. For something more sophisticated, the best options are the restaurants opposite the cathedral or Mercado Comonfort.

Mercado Comonfort BEER GARDEN
(www.facebook.com/mercadocomonfort; Comonfort 4; ⊘2pm-midnight Mon-Thu, to 1am Fri & Sat, to 10pm Sun) A great drinking option away

from rowdy La Plazuela, this 'market' is a secluded courtyard with pubs and small terraced bars from where cool locals can be seen drinking cocktails or lattes and sometimes dancing. Beer and wine snacks include pizza, tapas, vegetarian meals, and Yucatecan and Oaxacan dishes. Some bars stay open well after midnight on weekends.

House Cafe + Lounge LOUNGE
(✆777-318-77-77; www.lascasasbb.com; Las Casas 110; ⏰8am-11pm Sun-Wed, to 12:30am Thu-Sat; 🛜) Housed inside a boutique hotel, the House has excellent food and cocktails, but the real reason that the beautiful people are drawn here is to be seen lounging around the pool by night in a more tranquil environment than the clubs on the same street.

☆ Entertainment

Hanging around the central plazas is a popular activity, especially on Sunday evenings, when open-air concerts are often staged. There are often recitals at Jardín Borda (p198) on Thursday nights, too. Live music is played at La Maga Café (p201) on some weekend evenings.

If your *español* is up to it, sample Cuernavaca's theater scene.

Los Arcos DANCE
(✆777-312-15-10; Jardín de los Héroes 4; minimum spend M$80; ⏰salsa 9-11pm Fri & Sun, live music Sat) Come here to dance salsa, not on a stage but around the tables of families having dinner on the terrace, with crowds of appreciative onlookers. The live band's carnival beats can be heard from the other side of the plaza and have a magnetic effect on your swiveling hips.

Cine Teatro Morelos CINEMA
(✆777-318-10-50; www.cinemorelos.com; Av Morelos 188; tickets from M$45; 🎦) Morelos' state theater hosts quality film festivals with subtitled movies in their original language, plays and dance performances. There's a full schedule posted out front and a bookstore and cafe inside.

🛍 Shopping

There are some good-quality *guayaberas* (men's appliquéd shirts), *huipiles* (long, sleeveless tunics) and upmarket souvenirs in the two plazas opposite the cathedral and along the same street. The MMAPO (p197) gift store has high-quality arts and crafts.

Mercado de Artesanías y Plata ARTS & CRAFTS
(Handicrafts & Silver Market; Juárez, cnr Hidalgo; ⏰8am-9pm) This relaxed market has handicrafts such as coconut lamps and hand-painted ceramics, found all over Mexico, as well as a plethora of handmade *chinelo* dolls with upturned beards, and souvenirs. It's a shady place to browse and prices are reasonable. To find the market, look for the huge statue of Morelos, the revolutionary himself, at the entrance.

Weekend Book and Crafts Market ARTS & CRAFTS
(Comonfort & Ruiz de Alarcón, cnr Hidalgo; ⏰10am-5pm Sat & Sun) The two streets opposite the cathedral entrance become pedestrianized (up to Calle Rayón) for two small markets to greet weekend visitors. On Ruiz de Alarcón you can find handicrafts such as decorated notepads and jewelry, while Comonfort sells new and used books and music.

ℹ Information

There's internet access at the Futura and Estrella Blanca bus station and internet cafes everywhere.

Cruz Roja (Red Cross; ✆777-322-26-10; https://cruzrojamorelos.org; Río Pánuco, cnr Leñeros; ⏰24hr) The Red Cross has professional medical consultations for M$100 (M$150 after 10pm), open to all. Some doctors speak some English, but it's pot luck. It's a 20-minute drive east of central Cuernavaca.

Main Post Office (Plaza de Armas; ⏰8am-5pm Mon-Fri, 10am-2pm Sat) At the south end of the *zócalo*.

State Tourist Office (✆800-987-82-24, 777-314-38-81; www.morelosturistico.com; Av Morelos Sur 187; ⏰9am-6pm) This excellent tourist office has a wealth of brochures, maps and information. It also has a **city center branch** (✆777-314-39-20; Hidalgo 5; ⏰9am-6pm) that can help book hotels.

There's an information booth in the cathedral, at the north end of the *zócalo* (9am to 6pm daily) and other kiosks around town, including at most bus stations. Ask for maps.

EMERGENCY NUMBERS
All emergencies ✆911
Tourist Police ✆ 800-903-92-00

ℹ Getting There & Away

Hwy 95D (the Mexico City–Acapulco toll road) skirts the city's east side. If you're driving from the north, take the Cuernavaca exit and cross to Hwy 95 (where you'll see a statue of Zapata on horseback). Hwy 95 becomes Bulevar Zapata then Avenida Morelos as you descend south into town. From Avenida Matamoros (still traveling south) the Avenida Morelos is one way, northbound only. To reach the center, veer left down Matamoros.

BUS

Cuernavaca's main-line bus companies operate separate long-distance terminals.

Estrella Blanca (Terminal de Autobuses Cuernavaca; ☑ 800-507-55-00; www. estrellablanca.com.mx; Av Morelos 503, btwn Arista & Victoria) Often referred to as Cuernavaca's main bus station. Futura, Costa Line, Elite, and executive ETN Turistar services leave from here. Departures include Toluca, Taxco, Tepotztlán, and Mexico City Terminal Sur and Terminal Norte.

Pullman de Morelos (PDM; ☑ 800-022-80-00; www.pullman.mx; cnr Abasolo & Netzahualcóyotl) The most conveniently located station, a few blocks southwest of the zócalo. Frequent, comfortable buses to Mexico City's airport and Terminal Sur.

Estrella de Oro (EDO; ☑ 777-312-30-55; www. estrelladeoro.com.mx; Av Morelos Sur 812) Departures to Taxco and Mexico City Terminal Sur; also OCC to Cuautla and Pluss to Acapulco. The bus station is 1.7km south of the zócalo in central Cuernavaca.

Estrella Roja de Cuautla (TER; ☑ 777-318-59-34; www.facebook.com/TransportesEstrellaRojaDeCuautla; cnr Galeana & Cuauhtemotzin) Tiny terminal with frequent services to Cuautla. Not the same company as Estrella Roja.

The **local-bus station** (López Mateos) outside Mercado Adolfo López Mateos has 2nd-class direct Ometochtli buses to Tepoztlán (five blocks southwest of its zócalo).

CAR & MOTORCYCLE

Cuernavaca is 89km south of Mexico City, a 90-minute drive on Hwy 95 or a one-hour trip on Hwy 95D. Both roads continue south to Acapulco – Hwy 95 detours through Taxco, while Hwy 95D is more direct and much faster.

ⓘ Getting Around

You can walk to most places of interest in central Cuernavaca. Local buses (M$6.50) advertise their destinations on their windshields. Many local buses, and those to nearby towns, leave from the local-bus station at the southern corner of the city's labyrinthine market, Mercado Adolfo López Mateos. There have been reports of robberies on local buses in Cuernavaca, so exercise caution if you must use them. Taxis to most places in town cost the base fare of M$35.

The bus depots are in walking distance of the zócalo, except the Estrella de Oro bus terminal, 1km south (downhill) of the center, which is reachable on Ruta 17 or 20 down Galeana. In the other direction, catch any bus heading up Avenida Morelos. Ruta 17 and 20 head up Avenida Morelos and stop within one block of the Pullman de Morelos terminal at Casino de la Selva.

The **Cuernabús** (☑ 777-135-04-68; http://cuernabus.mx; Hidalgo, cnr Juárez; per person M$100; ⊙ departs zócalo 11am, 1pm, 3pm & 5pm Fri-Sun) is a double-decker tourist bus taking in 22km of sights, starting at the zócalo and including parks and sights such as Jardín Borda, the Catedral de Cuernavaca and, most usefully, the Pirámide de Teopanzolco (if open again after repairs). It only has a Spanish-speaking guide.

Taxco

☑ 762 / POP 52,855 / ELEV 1800M

The first sight of Taxco's white buildings scattered across the steep valley as you approach it is enough to take your breath away. Surrounded by dramatic mountains and cliffs, its perfectly preserved colonial architecture and the twin belfries of its baroque masterpiece, Templo de Santa Prisca, make for one of the most beguiling views anywhere in the central highlands.

Taxco (tahs-ko), 160km southwest of Mexico City, has ridden the waves of boom and bust associated with wealthy silver deposits

BUSES FROM CUERNAVACA

DESTINATION	FARE (M$)	TIME (HR)	FREQUENCY (DAILY)
Acapulco	500	4	9
Cuautla	71	1-1½	28
Mexico City	100-150	1½	40
Mexico City Airport	250	2	24
Taxco	123	1½	14
Tepotztlán	160	3-4	4
Tepoztlán	28	¾	28

Taxco

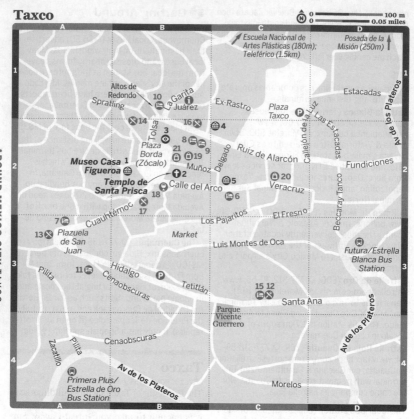

Taxco

⊚ Top Sights
1 Museo Casa Figueroa	B2
2 Templo de Santa Prisca	B2

⊚ Sights
3 Casa Borda	B2
4 Museo de Arte Virreinal	C2
5 Museo Guillermo Spratling	C2

⨭ Sleeping
6 Hostel Casa Taxco	C2
7 Hotel Casa Grande	A3
8 Hotel Emilia	B2
9 Hotel Los Arcos	B2
10 Hotel Mi Casita	B1
11 Hotel Santa Prisca	A3
12 Pueblo Lindo	C3

⊗ Eating
13 Hostería Bar El Adobe	A3
14 La Hacienda de Taxco	B2
La Sushería	(see 8)
15 Rosa Amaranto	C3
16 Sotavento	B2
17 Taxco de Mil Sabores	B2

⊜ Drinking & Nightlife
18 Bar Berta	B2

⊕ Shopping
19 EBA Elena Ballesteros	B2
20 Nuestro México Artesanías	C2
21 Patio de las Artesanías	B2

discovered here in the 16th century and then repeatedly until the early 20th century. With its silver now almost depleted, Taxco thrives on tourism. As such, it's a rare example of preservation-centric development in Mexico. Unlike many colonial-era towns, Taxco has not been engulfed by industrial suburbs, and new buildings must conform to the old in scale, style and materials. This preserves Taxco as a striking small city and one of the best weekend trips from the capital.

History

Taxco was called Tlachco (Ball-Playing Place) by the Aztec, who dominated the region from 1440 until the Spanish arrived. The colonial city was founded by Rodrigo de Castañeda in 1529, with a mandate from Hernán Cortés. Among the town's first Spanish residents were three miners, Juan de Cabra, Juan Salcedo and Diego de Nava, and the carpenter Pedro Muriel. In 1531 they established the first Spanish mine in North America.

The Spaniards came searching for tin, which they found in small quantities, but by 1534 they had discovered tremendous lodes of silver. That year the Hacienda El Chorrillo was built, complete with water wheel, smelter and aqueduct – the remains of the latter form the old arches (Los Arcos) over Hwy 95 at the north end of town.

The prospectors quickly depleted the first silver veins and fled Taxco. Further quantities of ore were not discovered until 1743. Don José de la Borda, who had arrived in 1716 from France at the age of 16 to work with his miner brother, accidentally unearthed one of the region's richest veins. According to the legend, Borda was riding near where the Templo de Santa Prisca now stands when his horse stumbled, dislodged a stone and exposed the precious metal.

Borda went on to introduce new techniques of draining and repairing mines, and he reportedly treated his indigenous workers better than most colonial mine owners. The Templo de Santa Prisca was the devout Borda's gift to Taxco. His success attracted more prospectors, and new silver veins were found and played out. With most of the silver gone, Taxco became a quiet town with a dwindling population and economy.

In 1929 a US architect and professor named William (Guillermo) Spratling arrived and, at the suggestion of the then US ambassador Dwight Morrow, set up a silver workshop as a way to rejuvenate the town. (Another version has it that Spratling was writing a book and resorted to the silver business because his publisher went bust. A third has it that Spratling had a notion to create jewelry that synthesized pre-Hispanic motifs with art deco modernism.) The workshop evolved into a factory, and Spratling's apprentices began establishing their own shops. Today Taxco is home to hundreds of silver shops, many producing for export.

◉ Sights & Activities

★ **Templo de Santa Prisca**   CHURCH
(Plaza Borda 1) **FREE** The icon of Taxco, Santa Prisca is one of Mexico's most beautiful and striking pieces of baroque architecture. Its standout feature (best viewed side-on) is the contrast between its belfries, with their elaborate Churrigueresque facade, and the far more simple, constrained and elegant nave. The rose-colored stone used on the facade is extraordinarily beautiful in sunlight – look for the oval bas-relief depiction of Christ's baptism above the doorway. Inside, the intricately sculpted, gold-covered altarpieces are equally fine Churrigueresque specimens.

Santa Prisca was a labor of love for town hero José de la Borda. The local Catholic hierarchy allowed the silver magnate to donate this church to Taxco on the condition that he mortgage his mansion and other assets to guarantee its completion. The project nearly bankrupted him, but the risk produced an extraordinary legacy. It was designed by Spanish architects Juan Caballero and Diego Durán, and was constructed between 1751 and 1758.

★ **Museo Casa Figueroa**   MUSEUM
(Casa de las Lágrimas; ☏ 762-622-00-03; https://sites.google.com/site/casafigueroataxco; Guadalupe 2; adult/student M$30/20; ⊙ 10am-6pm Wed-Mon) A splendid, envy-inducing home-turned-museum, with an interesting collection of vintage art and craftwork from across Mexico, comes to life alongside creepy features. Admission includes a guided tour in Spanish or basic English, retelling the building's construction in 1767 for the Count of Cadena (friend of Borda) by Tlahuic people who suffered mistreatment, lending the nickname 'House of Tears.' Eerie highlights are secret hiding spots for jewels, a panic room, and crawl spaces that once led to Santa Prisca.

Other oddities include statues of Jesus made with real human hair; beds where Morelos himself apparently slept when he took over the house as his army barracks; and photos of previous famous visitors including Elvis, Bette Davis and Richard Nixon. The kitchen is decked out in colorful pottery and leads into a secluded courtyard with a replica of the Aztec sun stone.

Museo Guillermo Spratling
MUSEUM

(☑762-622-16-60; www.inah.gob.mx/red-de-museos/301-museo-william-spratling; Delgado 1, cnr Celso Muñoz; adult/student M$55/free, Sun free; ⊙9am-5pm Tue-Sat, to 3pm Sun) This well laid-out three-story history and archaeology museum is off an alley behind Templo de Santa Prisca. It contains a small collection of pre-Hispanic jewelry, art, pottery and sculpture from US silversmith William Spratling's private collection. The phallic cult pieces are a particular eye-opener. The basement displays examples of Spratling's designs using pre-Hispanic motifs. The top floor hosts occasional temporary exhibits.

Museo de Arte Virreinal
MUSEUM

(☑762-627-42-58; Ruiz de Alarcón 12; adult/child M$20/15; ⊙10am-6pm Tue-Sun) This charming, rather ragtag religious-art museum is housed in a wonderful old house. It hosts a small but well-displayed collection of art, labeled in English and Spanish. The most interesting exhibit describes restoration work on Santa Prisca, during which some fabulous material (including tapestries, woodwork altarpieces and rich decorative fabrics) was discovered in the basement of the house. There is also an interesting display on the Manila Galleons, which pioneered trade between the Americas and the Far East.

Casa Borda
NOTABLE BUILDING

(☑762-622-66-17; Centro Cultural Taxco, Plaza Borda; ⊙10am-6pm Tue-Sun) FREE Built by José de la Borda in 1759, the Casa Borda serves as a cultural center hosting experimental theater and exhibiting contemporary sculpture, painting and photography by Guerrero artists. The building, however, is the main attraction. Due to the unevenness of the terrain, the rear window looks out on a precipitous four-story drop, even though the entrance is on the ground floor on the zócalo.

Teleférico
CABLE CAR

(www.montetaxco.mx; Los Plateros 3; one-way/round trip adult M$65/95, child M$45/65; ⊙7:45am-7pm Sun-Thu, to 10pm Fri & Sat) From the north end of Taxco, a Swiss-made gondola ascends 173m to the Hotel Monte Taxco resort, affording fantastic views of Taxco and the surrounding mountains from the hotel pool – ask at reception for directions.

Combis marked 'Arcos/Zócalo' (M$8) stop downhill from the cable-car entrance. Walk uphill from the south side of Los Arcos and turn right through the Escuela Nacional de Artes Plásticas gate.

The Hotel Monte Taxco bar-restaurant, El Taxqueño, has great views and is surprisingly more economical than the balcony restaurants around Taxco's zócalo.

★☆ Festivals & Events

Be sure to reserve your hotel in advance if your visit coincides with one of Taxco's annual festivals. Check exact dates of movable feasts with the tourist office (p209).

Fiestas de Santa Prisca & San Sebastián
RELIGIOUS

(⊙Jan) Taxco's patron saints are honored on January 18 (Santa Prisca) and January 20 (San Sebastián), when locals parade by the Templo de Santa Prisca for an annual blessing, with their pets and farm animals in tow.

Día del Jumil
FOOD & DRINK

(⊙Nov) The Monday after the Día de Muertos (Day of the Dead; November 2), locals celebrate the jumil – the edible beetle said to represent the giving of life and energy to Taxco residents for another year. Many families camp on the Cerro de Huixteco (above town) over the preceding weekend, and townsfolk climb the hill to collect jumiles and share food and camaraderie.

Feria de la Plata
FERIA

(⊙Nov/Dec) The weeklong national silver fair convenes in late November or early December. Craft competitions are held and some of Mexico's best silverwork is on display. Other festivities include rodeos, concerts, dances and burro (donkey) races.

Las Posadas
CULTURAL

(⊙Dec) From December 16 to 24, nightly candlelit processions fill Taxco's streets with door-to-door singing. Children are dressed up to resemble biblical characters. At the end of each night, they attack piñatas.

🛏 Sleeping

Taxco has a wealth of hotels, from large four- and five-star resorts to charming family-run posadas. During holiday weekends, when the hordes arrive from Mexico City, it's a good idea to reserve ahead.

Earplugs are also a good idea. Owing to the innumerable Volkswagen taxis that serve as transportation in this, the steepest of hill towns, street noise is a problem nearly everywhere. The bells of Santa Prisca also chime hourly from morning till midnight.

WORTH A TRIP

CACAHUAMILPA CAVERNS

One of central Mexico's most stunning natural sights, the **Cacahuamilpa Caverns** (Grutas de Cacahuamilpa; 721-104-01-55; www.facebook.com/lasgrutasdecacahuamilpaoficial; adult/child incl guide M$80/70; 10am-5pm; P) are a must-see for anyone visiting Taxco or Cuernavaca. The scale of the caves is hard to imagine, with vast chambers up to 82m high leading 2km beneath the mountainside, inside which are mind-blowing stalactites and stalagmites.

Unfortunately, individual access to the (perfectly safe) pathway through the caves is not allowed. Instead, visitors are allocated free guides who lead large group tours (departures each hour on the hour), with constant stops to point out shapes (Santa Claus, a kneeling child, a gorilla) in the rock. At the end of the hour-long tour, you can wander back to the entrance – with the lights now off – at your own pace. Most guides do not speak English.

From the cave exit it's possible to follow a steep path for 15 minutes to the fast-flowing Río Dos Bocas. There are spectacular views year-round and tranquil pools for swimming during the dry season. Bring bug spray.

Weekends are often very crowded, with long lines and large group tours, making mid-week a more pleasant time for a visit. There are restaurants, snacks and souvenir stores near the entrance. Between the entrance and the caves, it's possible to take a short zip-line (M$70) across the treetops, or you can just walk the 150m around.

To reach the caves, take an Estrella Roja 'Grutas' bus from the Futura bus terminal in Taxco (M$43, 40 minutes, every 40 minutes to 6.30pm) or taxi (M$180). Buses deposit you at the *crucero* (crossroads) to Cuernavaca. From there, walk 350m downhill to the park's visitor center. Return buses leave from the same crossroads (every 40 minutes, last bus 8:30pm). Pullman de Morelos has direct services to the caves from Cuernavaca (M$70, two hours, every two hours to 7:43pm; last return bus 6pm) and Mexico City Terminal Sur (M$225, 8.29am and 9.29am, Saturday and Sunday only).

Hostel Casa Taxco   HOSTEL $

(762-622-70-37; www.facebook.com/hostelcasa taxco; Veracruz 5; dm/d/tw M$300/600/600;) Taxco is getting with the times, starting with this beautiful converted house with its artisanal tiles and furnishings and the calm vibe of a colonial home. There's also an open-plan kitchen and a roof terrace with cathedral views (and hourly bells), though staff could provide more local knowledge. Rooms are two-bed dorms except for one twin and one double with private bathroom.

Hotel Casa Grande   HOTEL $

(762-622-09-69; www.facebook.com/hotel casagrandedetaxco; Plazuela de San Juan 7; d/tw/tr/q M$515/590/690/790, tw without bathroom M$420;) Its excellent location and hypnotic terrace views over the *plazuela* make Casa Grande an attractive budget option, but bring your earplugs as the music from attached restaurant-bar La Concha Nostra plays until 1am Thursday to Sunday. Rooms are small, fanless and rough around the edges but have fresh cotton sheets.

Hotel Emilia   HOTEL $

(762-622-13-96; www.hotelemilia.com.mx; Ruiz de Alarcón 7; d & tw M$760;) All rooms are spotlessly clean and have beautiful tiled bathrooms. Owned by a family of famous silver workers, this intimate hotel has colonial charm and includes free use of the pools at nearby Hotel Agua Escondida. Sadly, it's in a location noisy for traffic – ask for a room at the back, but don't miss the views from the rooftop terrace.

Hotel Santa Prisca   HOTEL $

(762-622-00-80; www.facebook.com/santa prisca.hotel; Cenaobscuras 1; d/tr M$635/715;) The 31-room Santa Prisca has traditional Mexican decor and a welcoming courtyard garden. It has a great location too, right in the thick of things. Rooms are small-ish, but most have breezy private balconies. All have two beds, and newer, sunnier rooms cost a bit more. The parking lot is reached through a tunnel at the hotel's uphill end.

★ Hotel Los Arcos   HISTORIC HOTEL $$

(762-622-18-36; www.hotellosarcosdetaxco.com; Ruiz de Alarcón 4; d/tr from M$1254/1490;) With plenty of plant-filled terraces, courtyards, rooftop space and chic cushioned areas to lounge about, this beautiful old hotel could be a destination in itself. Rooms are large and rustic with comfortable beds and touches of Mexican decoration, and the location near the *zócalo* is convenient, though street-facing rooms have some traffic noise.

★ Hotel Mi Casita
INN $$

(☑762-627-17-77; www.hotelmicasita.com; Altos de Redondo 1; r incl breakfast from M$1490; ❁@❂❃) This elegant colonial home run by a family of jewelry designers boasts 12 beautifully and individually decorated rooms just moments from the *zócalo,* with wraparound balconies giving views over the cathedral. The comfortable rooms feature original hand-painted bathroom tiles, three with Talavera bathtubs, some with private terraces and all with fans.

★ Pueblo Lindo
SPA HOTEL $$

(☑762-622-34-81; www.pueblolindo.com.mx; Hidalgo 30; ste incl breakfast M$1090-1940; ❂❃❄❅❆) This luxurious hotel manages to balance style and substance, embracing a modern Mexican-inspired aesthetic with bright colors and wooden furnishings. The knockout views over Taxco are the highlight here, enjoyed from the rooftop pool, some of the rooms (all suites) and the cafe-bar. Rooms are restfully dark and quiet. Other treats are the wonderful Mexican restaurant, spa treatments, mini-gym and excellent service.

Posada de la Misión
LUXURY HOTEL $$

(☑762-622-00-63, 800-008-29-20; http://posadamision.com; Cerro de la Misión 32; d/tr/q incl breakfast M$1525/2265/2620; ❂❃❄) On a steep hill overlooking town, the rambling grounds of La Misión are a luxurious escape from Taxco's bustle. Rooms are large, bright and airy, and many have balconies with breathtaking views. There's also a gorgeous pool and Jacuzzi under a mosaic of Cuauhtémoc, and an excellent restaurant.

It's a steep, winding 1km walk to the *zócalo* from the hotel. Primera Plus buses from Mexico City stop here briefly on the way to their terminal.

✕ Eating & Drinking

The *jumil* (similar to a stink beetle) is a delicacy in Taxco, notably during the Día del Jumil (p206) festivity – look for them in a *cucurucho* (paper cone) in the market. They are traditionally eaten live in a tortilla, but are more commonly seen crushed into a sauce.

For street food, try the excellent barbecued pork tacos in Plazuela de San Juan at night. The reasonably priced hotel restaurant at the top of the *teleférico* has impressive views.

Taxco de Mil Sabores
MEXICAN $

(Cuauhtémoc 4D; breakfasts $45, menú del día $65-85; ❂8am-8pm) As you traipse through a jewelry store to this hidden spacious restaurant, the last thing you might expect are 180-degree views of the town from its balcony. Budget Mexican lunch and dinner classics stick to hearty basics, such as *mole verde* (chicken stew in a pepita sauce), *chile relleno* (cheese-stuffed chili), and include a simple soup and rice.

Look for the stack of nine arches and enter from the rightmost arch.

La Sushería
JAPANESE $

(☑762-622-13-96; www.facebook.com/lasusheria taxco; Ruiz de Alarcón 7; sushi M$75-115; ❂3-10pm Sun-Fri, to 11pm Sat; ❃❄) This sushi restaurant in the lobby of Hotel Emilia (p207) reflects modern Taxco with its designer furniture but casual vibe. The sushi is fresh and finished nicely with the green-tea ice cream – heaven in a cocktail glass. If you're here on a date or a business lunch, the slick booths will impress.

There are popular two-for-one specials on Wednesday and Sunday evenings.

★ Rosa Amaranto
MEXICAN $$

(www.facebook.com/RosaAmarantoTaxco; Hidalgo 30; mains M$99-219; ❂8am-10.30pm Sun-Fri, to 11pm Sat; ❃) The roof terrace of Pueblo Lindo (p208) hotel is one of the most spectacular spots for panoramic views of Taxco over a lunch of *enchiladas de jamaica* (chicken-or cheese-stuffed tortillas bathed in hibiscus sauce) or dinner of baked fish in spicy mango and cucumber relish, steak or pasta. You could also simply come for margaritas or chocolate mousse by moonlight.

★ Sotavento
MEXICAN $$

(☑762-627-12-17; Ruiz de Alarcón 4; mains M$80-168; ❂8am-10.30pm Thu-Tue) It's easy to be wooed by the cobblestone arches in the warm lighting of Sotavento's leafy, tranquil courtyard. Classic Mexican dishes such as enchiladas and chicken *mole* are some of the best in town, and there are cocktails and some surprisingly good European options too. The Sunday breakfast buffet (M$130) is wonderful.

La Hacienda de Taxco
MEXICAN $$

(☑762-622-11-66; www.aguaescondida.com; Plaza Borda 4; mains M$90-180; ❂7:30am-10pm Sun-

Thu, to 11pm Fri & Sat; 🍴🖥) Offering an extensive menu of traditional Mexican dishes (including house-made jam in the morning and a 20-ingredient, house-made *mole* in the afternoon), La Hacienda also has considerate menu options, like the egg-white-only breakfasts, vegetarian dishes and smaller portions for kids. The wooden furniture and attempt at decorative plating add photogenic touches. Rooftop and window-side tables have good views.

Hostería Bar El Adobe MEXICAN $$
(☎762-622-14-16; www.eladoberestaurante.info; Plazuela de San Juan 13; mains M$80-230; ⊙8am-11pm Mon-Thu, to 11.30pm Sat, to 10pm Sun) This place doesn't have the *zócalo* views, but the interior is charmingly decorated with B&W photos of everyone from Pancho Villa to Elvis, and the cute balcony tables are more private. Good, simple dishes include pan-fried chicken or fish in salsa with rice and veg. There's *pozole* (M$65) on Thursday, live *trova* music on Saturday night and a buffet (M$125) on Sunday.

Bar Berta BAR
(☎762-107-55-90; www.facebook.com/barbertataxco; Cuauhtémoc; ⊙noon-10pm Wed-Mon) A clientele of local roughs knock back stiff drinks in this kitsch-chic bar, which displays memorabilia harking back to when it opened in 1930. Upstairs, there's a tiny terrace for people-watching over the *zócalo*. Try a Berta (tequila, honey, lime and mineral water), the house specialty.

🛍 Shopping

EBA Elena Ballesteros JEWELRY
(☎762-622-37-67; www.ebaplata.com; Muñoz 4; ⊙9:30am-7pm Mon-Sat, 10am-6pm Sun) EBA Elena Ballesteros produces creative, well-crafted silver designs in Taxco.

Nuestro México Artesanías ARTS & CRAFTS
(☎762-622-09-76; Veracruz 8; ⊙10am-6pm) Treasure hunters will love rummaging in this storehouse of handicrafts from across Mexico. Most of the favorite souvenirs are here – coconut masks, papier-mâché devils, flying cherubs, fish wind chimes and, yes, silver. The prices are marked and close to what you pay on the street outside.

Patio de las Artesanías JEWELRY
(Plaza Borda; ⊙9am-6pm Tue-Sun) If you are looking for silver, there are several fine shops to wander through in the Patio de las Artesanías building.

ℹ Information

Several banks around the main plazas and bus stations have ATMs.

Hospital General Adolfo Prieto (☎762-622-93-00; Chorrillo 20; ⊙24hr)

Tourist Office (Secretaría de Turismo Municipal; ☎762-622-13-79; Juárez 6, cnr Plazuela del Exconvento; ⊙9am-8pm) Next to the post office, it offers maps and good information. Note that the tourism kiosk on the main plaza mostly exists to hand out brochures and push tours.

ℹ Getting There & Away

The shared **Futura/Estrella Blanca terminal** (Av de los Plateros) is the main bus station (the streets opposite head up to the *zócalo*), from where Costaline and buses to the Cacahuamilpa Caverns also depart; left-luggage storage (M$5 to M$15 per hour) is offered. The **Primera Plus/Estrella de Oro (EDO) terminal** (Av de los Plateros) is 750m away at the south end of town along the main road, where taxis offer rides for M$27 to the main plazas. The Futura bus to Mexico City runs mostly on the hour.

For more frequent bus services to the coast, take a shared taxi (M$30) from in front of the bus station to the nearby town of Iguala, about 30 minutes away.

Buses serve Acapulco (M$302, 4½ hours, five daily) from the EDO terminal; Cuernavaca from EDO (M$108, 1¼ hours, 8.05am daily, also 5.30pm Saturdays) and Futura (on Costaline buses; M$123, 1½ hours, 14 daily); and Mexico City's Terminal Sur from EDO (M$250, 2¾ hours, four to seven daily) and Futura (M$260, mostly hourly).

ℹ Getting Around

While one of the joys of Taxco is getting lost while aimlessly wandering the pretty streets, it's actually a very easy place to find your way around. The twin belfries of Santa Prisca make the best landmark, situated as they are on the *zócalo*, or Plaza Borda.

Nearly all of the town's streets are one way; the only major two-way street is the main road, Avenida de los Plateros. This is where both bus stations are located and is the road for entering and leaving the town. The basic *colectivo* route is a counterclockwise loop going north on Avenida de los Plateros and south through the center of town.

Apart from walking, combis and taxis are the best way to navigate Taxco's steep and narrow cobbled streets.

Combis (white Volkswagen minibuses; M$8) are frequent and operate from 7am to 8pm. 'Zócalo' combis depart from Plaza Borda, travel down Cuauhtémoc to Plazuela de San Juan then head down the hill on Hidalgo. They turn right at Morelos, left at Avenida de los Plateros and go north, passing the Futura bus station, until La Garita, where they turn left and return to the *zócalo*. 'Arcos/Zócalo' combis follow the same route except that they continue past La Garita to Los Arcos, where they do a U-turn and head back to La Garita. Combis marked 'PM' (for Pedro Martín) go to the south end of town from Plaza Borda, past the Estrella de Oro bus station. Taxis cost M$27 to M$37 for trips around town.

WEST OF MEXICO CITY

This area contains two wonderful colonial small towns. Malinalco has some fascinating pre-Hispanic ruins perched above it and is slowly transforming from a sleepy remote village to a cosmopolitan getaway. Its chic sibling Valle de Bravo is located on the shores of a large, artificial reservoir, a dramatic two-hour drive west of Toluca.

Toluca is immediately west of Mexico City but it's mostly a large industrial, transportation-hub city. While pleasant, it has little to recommend it to travelers and most bypass it en route to the towns or the countryside surrounding Toluca itself – a landscape of scenic pine forests, rivers and a huge extinct volcano, Nevado de Toluca.

Toluca

📞722 / POP 562,995 / ELEV 2660M

Toluca is an enjoyable place to spend a day exploring attractive plazas, lively shopping arcades, art galleries, museums and a spectacular botanical garden with stained-glass panels that is worth a quick visit alone.

Like many colonial Mexican cities, Toluca's development has created a ring of urban sprawl around what remains a very picturesque old town. The traffic problems alone can be enough to dampen the city's appeal, but as a major hub for buses and planes, those who linger here will find Toluca a pleasant, if bustling, small city.

◉ Sights

The 19th-century **Portal Madero**, running 250m along Avenida Hidalgo, is lively, as is the commercial arcade along the pedestrian street to the east ringed by *arcos* (archways), which attracts mariachis after 9pm and where most of the city's action happens. A block north, the large, open expanse of **Plaza de los Mártires** is surrounded by fine old government buildings; the 19th-century **cathedral** and the 18th-century **Templo de la Santa Veracruz** are on its south side. On Plaza Garibay's north side is the 18th-century **Templo del Carmen**. All museums are closed on Mondays and have free admission on Wednesdays and Sundays.

★**Cosmovitral Jardín Botánico**   GARDENS
(Cosmic Stained-Glass Window Botanical Garden; 📞722-214-67-85; Juárez s/n, cnr Lerdo de Tejada; adult/child M$10/5; ⊙10am-6pm Tue-Sat, to 3pm Sun) At the northeast end of Plaza Garibay, the stunning and unique Cosmovitral Jardín Botánico was built in 1909 as a market. The building now houses 3500 sq meters of lovely gardens, lit through 48 stained-glass panels designed by the Tolucan artist Leopoldo Flores with the help of 60 artisans. The 500,000 pieces of glass come in 28 different colors from seven countries, including Japan, Belgium and Italy.

Depicted in the stained glass is the evolution of humans across history and our relationship to the stars, reflected in the 'cosmo' aspect of the name. Also shown are the dualities at work in our universe – creation and destruction, life and death, day and night.

The eastern section shows a man and a woman in relation to the Andromeda nebula; at the center, the creation of the universe is brought to life in coloured glass.

Museo de Culturas Populares   MUSEUM
(Museum of Popular Culture; 📞722-274-54-58; Bulevar Reyes Heroles 302; adult/child M$10/5, Wed & Sun free; ⊙10am-6pm Tue-Sat, to 3pm Sun) This museum has a wonderfully varied collection of Mexico's traditional arts and crafts, with some astounding 'trees of life' from Metepec, whimsical Day of the Dead figures and a fine display of *charro* (cowboy) gear. There are also mosaics, traditional rugs, a loft and a **gift shop**.

**Museo de Arte Moderno
del Estado de México**   MUSEUM
(Museum of Modern Art; 📞722-274-12-66; Bulevar Reyes Heroles 302; adult/student M$10/5, Wed & Sun free; ⊙9am-6pm Tue-Sat, to 3pm Sun) Tracing the development of Mexican art from the late-19th-century Academia de San Carlos to the Nueva Plástica, the Museo de Arte Moderno includes paintings by Tamayo, Orozco and many others. There's an impressive spherical mural of people fighting against slavery, which makes up part of the building itself, as well as exhibits of challenging pieces of contemporary art.

Museo de Antropología y História MUSEUM

(Museum of Anthropology & History; ☑722-274-12-00; Blvd Reyes Heroles 302; adult/student M$10/5, Wed & Sun free; ⊙9am-6pm Tue-Sat, to 3pm Sun) This standout museum presents exhibits the state's history from prehistoric times to the 20th century, with a good collection of pre-Hispanic artifacts. It also traces pre-Hispanic cultural influences up to the modern day in tools, clothing, textiles and religion. Most labeling is in Spanish only.

Museo Luis Nishizawa MUSEUM

(☑722-215-74-65; www.facebook.com/Museo TallerLuisNishizawa; Bravo Norte 305; adult/student M$10/5, Wed & Sun free; ⊙10am-6pm Tue-Sat, to 3pm Sun) This musuem exhibits the work of modern Mexican-Japanese muralist and landscape artist Luis Nishizawa (1918–2014). Nishizawa was born in the state of Mexico and trained in both Mexican and Japanese artistic styles, which is reflected in murals constructed from ceramics. He is known for his mixed-media sculptures and intensely colorful ink paintings of nature and people. His works are held in collections across the world, including MOMAK in Kyoto.

Museo de Bellas Artes de Toluca MUSEUM

(Museum of Fine Art; ☑722-215-53-29; Degollado 102; adult/student M$10/5, Wed & Sun free; ⊙10am-6pm Tue-Sat, to 3pm Sun) The ex-convent buildings adjacent to Templo del Carmen, on the north side of Plaza Garibay, house Toluca's Museo de Bellas Artes, with paintings from the colonial period to the early 20th century.

⚲ Tours

Tranvía TRAM

(☑722-330-50-52; www.turismotolucalabella.com; Independencia, cnr Bravo; adult/child M$65/50; ⊙departs hourly 11am-5pm Fri-Sun) This motorized trolley visits two dozen sites in the city in an hour with a Spanish-only guide. From mid-October to early November there are also Tranvía del Terror night tours (adult/child M$100/80, 6:30pm and 8pm Friday to Sunday, 1½ hours, every 1½ hours), visiting 12 sites accompanied by a guide and actors recounting spooky *leyendas* (legends) associated with each building.

🛏 Sleeping

Hotel Maya HOTEL $

(☑722-214-48-00; Hidalgo 413; r with/without bathroom M$400/300; 🕿) The extremely central location of this one-grandma-run posada makes a handy, if very no-frills, base for a quick visit of Toluca's sights. Wi-fi is patchy but rooms are clean. If street noise bothers you, choose a darker interior room.

Hotel Don Simón BUSINESS HOTEL $$

(☑722-213-26-96; www.hoteldonsimon.com; Matamoros 202; d/tr M$1200/1400; 🅿@🕿) The rooms at Don Simón are immaculately clean and bright, if a little heavy on the brown furnishings of yesteryear, which continue into the attached restaurant. It's a balanced all-rounder in central Toluca – the staff are friendly, the street is quiet and it's just a short walk to Cosmovitral.

Fiesta Inn Toluca Centro BUSINESS HOTEL $$

(☑722-167-89-00; www.fiestainn.com; Allende Sur 124; r/ste M$1430/1975; 🅿@🕿) The modern, sleek, 85-room Fiesta Inn has airy, comfortable rooms, a small gym and a cafe-bar-restaurant in the lobby. There's another branch near the airport.

🍴 Eating

Toluqueños take snacking and sweets very seriously and you can join them in the arcades around Plaza Fray Andrés de Castro. Other stalls sell candied fruit and *jamoncillos*, and *mostachones* (sweets made of burned milk). Most eateries in the center are open from around 8am to 9pm.

★La Gloria Chocolatería y Pan 1876 CAFE $

(Quintana Roo; snacks M$30-55, mains M$65-120; ⊙9am-11:30pm) You'll probably be the only foreigner at this wonderful, friendly, family-run cafe. It serves a tempting menu of local cuisine, from *tacos al pastor* to delicious *sermones* (sandwiches) stuffed with oven-baked pork or shredded chicken bathed in *mole poblano*.

La Vaquita Negra del Portal SANDWICHES $

(☑722-167-13-77; http://lavaquitanegra.com. mx; Portal Reforma 124B; sandwiches M$24-41; ⊙8:30am-8pm) On the northwest corner of the arcades, smoked hams and huge green-and-red sausages hanging over the deli counter signal first-rate *tortas*. Try a messy *toluqueña* (red pork *chorizo*, white cheese, cream, tomato and *salsa verde*), and don't forget to garnish your heaped sandwich with spicy pickled peppers and onions, as they have done here since 1943.

Bistró Mecha BISTRO $$

(https://bistro-mecha-centro-historico.negocio. site; Aldama 102; mains M$90-190; ☺8.30am-11pm Mon-Thu, to 1am Fri & Sat, to 8pm Sun; 📶🏃) A meal or a wine in the courtyard of Mecha makes for a pleasant escape from shopping frenzy of central Toluca. European bistro-style dishes feature, including vegetarian lasagna, *involtini* (rolled pizza), pork escalope in blackberry salsa, and seafood and meat grills. There are also excellent salad choices.

★**Petra Fonda** FUSION $$$

(📞722-174-50-80; www.facebook.com/PetraFonda; Matamoros 213; mains M$180-380, breakfasts M$90-150; ☺8am-11pm Mon-Sat, to 6pm Sun) Gourmet delights have arrived for Toluca's foodies. Creative, exquisite dishes include *mole de coco* (chicken rolled around garlic shrimp in a coconut sauce), and grilled tuna with a *mora* (smoked) chili mayonnaise and side of *chapulines*. The multiple dining spaces are fit for a gallery and worth looking sharp for.

Chandeliers and vintage gilded mirrors mix with designer chairs and airy high ceilings. Daring breakfasts like beef red-curry crepes and zucchini-flower omelettes are also available. Petra is reason enough to make a stop in central Toluca.

🛍 Shopping

★**Casart** ARTS & CRAFTS

(Casa de Artesanía; 📞722-217-51-08; Aldama 102; ☺9am-7pm Mon-Fri, to 5pm Sat) This downtown location of Casart – the state organization promoting local crafts – is fantastic both for its beautiful home, set around a courtyard, and its wonderful selection of quality arts and crafts. Prices are fixed and therefore higher than you might be able to get haggling in markets for an inferior product (for the best prices, go directly to the source).

ℹ Information

There are banks with ATMs near Portal Madero.

City Tourist Office (Oficina de Información Turística; 📞ext 104 722-384-19-00; Edificio B, Local 6, Planta Baja, Plaza Fray Andrés de Castro; ☺9am-7pm Mon-Fri, from 10am Sat & Sun) English-speaking staff provide free city maps and can help book accommodations.

State Tourist Office (📞722-212-59-98; Urawa 100, cnr Paseo Tollocan; ☺9am-6pm Mon-Fri) Inconveniently located 2km southeast of the center, but with English-speaking staff and good maps.

Tourist Information Kiosk (www.turismo tolucalabella.com; Palacio Municipal; ☺9am-6pm Mon-Fri, 10am-7pm Sat & Sun) Helpful kiosk with free city map.

ℹ Getting There & Away

AIR

The modern, efficient and low-stress **Aeropuerto Internacional de Toluca** (TOL; 📞722-279-28-00; www.aeropuertodetoluca.com.mx; Blvd Miguel Alemán Valdez) is an excellent alternative to Mexico City's massive and intimidating airport – though in recent years some airlines have abandoned Toluca in favor of the capital. Conveniently located off Hwy 15, about 10km from downtown, the airport is adjacent to the industrial zone and a group of business-friendly chain hotels.

Toluca is the hub for budget airline **Interjet** (www.interjet.com.mx), which offers flights to Los Angeles, Houston, Vancouver, Toronto, Havana (Cuba), and all over Mexico. **VivaAerobús** (www.vivaaerobus.com) has flights to Cancún and Monterrey.

Europcar, Dollar and Alamo all have rental-car offices at the airport.

BUS

There are frequent Caminante shuttle buses from Toluca's airport to Mexico City's Observatorio bus terminal (M$202) daily to about 7pm or 8pm; and to the capital's airport (M$200, five daily). Both take an hour or two, depending

BUSES FROM TOLUCA

DESTINATION	FARE (M$)	TIME (HR)	FREQUENCY (PER DAY)
Cuernavaca	71-290	2	24
Mexico City (Poniente)	67-90	1	55
Morelia	294-468	3½-4	16
Taxco	144	3	7
Valle de Bravo	80	2¼	10
Zihuatanejo	887	8	1

on traffic. Interjet has shuttles to Cuernavaca (M$255). An authorized taxi from the airport to downtown Toluca costs about M$35 and takes 20 to 30 minutes.

Toluca's **bus station** (Terminal Toluca; www.terminaltoluca.com.mx; Berriozábal 101) is 2km southeast of the center. Ticket offices for many destinations are on the platforms or at the gate entrances, and it's fair to say it can be a confusing place. Look for monitors at gate entrances that reveal which gates sell which destination. Suggestions include **Autovías** (http://autovias.com.mx) for Morelia, San Miguel de Allende or Zihuatanejo; **Flecha Roja** (https://flecharoja.com.mx) for Cuernavaca, Mexico City (Poniente or Terminal Norte) or Taxco; **ETN** (https://etn.com.mx) for luxury services to Mexico City (Terminal Sur) or Cuernavaca; and **Zina-bus** (http://autobuseszinacantepec.com.mx) for Morelia or Valle de Bravo.

ℹ Getting Around

The main road from Mexico City becomes Paseo Tollocan on Toluca's eastern edge, before bearing southwest and becoming a ring road around the city center's southern edge. Toluca's bus station and the huge Mercado Juárez are 2km southeast of the center, off Paseo Tollocan.

Large 'Centro' buses depart from outside Toluca's bus station to the town center (M$10, 20 minutes) along Lerdo de Tejada and by Plaza de los Mártires. From Juárez in the center, 'Terminal' buses go to the bus station. Taxis from the bus station to the city center cost around M$45.

Nevado de Toluca

Among the highest peaks in the region, the long-extinct volcano Nevado de Toluca (also known as Xinantécatl) is Mexico's fourth-tallest peak. Nevado has two summits on the crater rim, each worth hiking for magnificent views across two snow-fringed crater lakes – Sol and Luna. The lower summit, Pico del Águila (4620m), is closer to the parking area and is the more common day hike. The main or highest summit is called Pico del Fraile (4704m) and requires an additional three to four hours of hiking.

In 2013 the Mexican government redesignated the national park as a *zona protegida* (protected area), thus legalising and legitimising the unregulated mining activity that had been going on there. Most people still continue to call it a national park.

English-speaking Mario Andrade (p180) leads one-day private climbs up Nevado de Toluca and Iztaccíhuatl (near Puebla).

Just beyond the Parque de los Venados gate, **Posada Familiar** (☑722-214-37-86; campsite/dm M$85/150, closed Sat & Sun), the only accommodations in the park, offers basic lodging at a heavily used refuge with shared hot showers, a kitchen (without utensils) and a common area with a fireplace. Bring extra blankets. It is best to reserve two weeks ahead. On Saturdays and Sundays the park police stay here, making it unavailable.

ℹ Getting There & Away

The best way to get to Nevado de Toluca is with a private guide or tour.

From Toluca from Monday to Friday, taxis will take you to the trailhead for upwards of M$350, or there and back (including time for a look around) for a negotiable M$750. Be sure to hire a newer taxi (the road up is very rough and dusty) from an official taxi stand with the driver's photo displayed inside the vehicle. Most international car-rental companies also have offices in Toluca.

From the park entrance a road winds 3.5km up to the **main gate** (Carretera Temascaltpec Km 18, San Antonio Acahualco; per vehicle/camioneta M$20/40; ☉10am-5pm, last entry 3pm). From there it's a 17km drive along an unsurfaced road up to the crater. On Saturdays, Sundays and holidays, taxis can't drive up to the trailhead; instead take a *camioneta* (M$50 per person, one way) from the main gate to the trailhead and back.

Dress warmly – it gets extremely cold up top.

Valle de Bravo

☑726 / POP 33,445 / ELEV 1800M

With one of the loveliest colonial centers in central Mexico, the *pueblo mágico* of Valle de Bravo is an utter charmer and a wonderful spot for an escape from Mexico City. The setting here is reminiscent of the northern Italian lakes, with thickly wooded, mist-clad hills and red terracotta roofing used throughout the town. Valle, as it's known, is famous for being the weekend retreat of choice for the capital's well-connected upper classes.

There are stunning views at the shore of Lago Avándaro – an artificial lake, the result of the construction of a hydroelectric station – but the beguiling and largely intact colonial center is arguably the real draw here. Boating on the lake is very popular as well, as are hiking and camping in the hills around the town. Valle is set up well for visitors while still feeling lived in.

🏃 Activities

Boating on the pleasant lake is the main activity here and you will be approached by plenty of operators anywhere near the water. *Lanchas* (small boats) with a captain run about M$400/700 for 30 minutes/one hour. Many include visits to a waterfall. Make sure the boat includes *chalecos salvavidas* (life jackets) – child-sized, if required.

Hiking opportunities to butterfly farms, haciendas, waterfalls and even a Buddhist temple are possible through tour operators or self-guided (the most popular trail is 'La Pena' for lofty lake views); ask at the tourist information stand on the *zócalo*.

Paragliding and parasailing are also popular.

✴️ Festivals & Events

Festival de las Almas CULTURAL
(☉ Oct/Nov) In late October or early November, the weeklong Festival de las Almas, an international arts and culture extravaganza, brings in music and dance troupes from all over Europe and Latin America. Events are held in central Valle, including the *zócalo*.

🛏 Sleeping

For a small town, this popular weekend escape from Mexico City has a good selection of budget posadas and midrange hotels. The most affordable, shabby options are within two blocks of the bus station. Camping and sleeping in huts is also possible; the tourist information stand on the *zócalo* has information.

★ Hotel San José HOTEL $
(☎726-262-09-72; Callejón San José 103; d/tw/tr M$600/700/1350; 🛜) This converted ranch-style hotel is just a block from the *zócalo*, but hidden down an alley away from the noise, with a small terrace garden where you can admire the view of the hills. Large, basic rooms have extremely comfortable beds, and light-filled tiny bathrooms with luxury trimmings – heavy shower curtains and plush bath rugs. Most have kitchenettes. A steal at this budget.

★ Hotel San Sebastian BOUTIQUE HOTEL $$
(☎726-688-50-15; hotel_sansebastian@outlook.es; San Sebastian 101, cnr Callejón Machinhuepa; d/tr/penthouse M$1600/1700/4200; ✳️🛜) Some of the best lake and terra cotta–tile views are from the balcony of the small rooms at this fresh hotel. Bathrooms are modern and spotless and beds are very comfortable, making for a top romantic getaway, even for solo travelers. There is also room service from the adjacent restaurant. A penthouse sleeps six and has a kitchen and terrace.

Hotel Casanueva BOUTIQUE HOTEL $$
(☎726-262-17-66; Villagrán 100; d/tw/ste M$1000/1300/1700; 🛜) Set on the west side of the *zócalo*, the Casanueva has individually designed rooms decorated with tasteful arts and crafts, though they have thin walls. One of the most stylish options downtown, the hotel's suite, which sleeps four, is especially lovely. Some rooms have private balconies over the square.

El Santuario RESORT $$$
(☎726-262-91-00; www.elsantuario.com; Carretera Colorines, San Gaspar; ste from M$6025; ℗✳️🛜🏊) Twenty minutes northwest of town, this gorgeous hillside hotel has an infinity pool, fountains, an in-house spa and rooms with magnificent lake views and personal mini-pools. There's also a golf course, horse stables and a marina with sailboat rentals.

🍴 Eating & Drinking

There are scores of restaurants and cafes along the wharf and around the *zócalo*, many of which only open Friday through Sunday. If there ever was a time to try *esquites* (lime and chili-flavored corn in a cup) from street stalls, this is it. Villagrán, on the west side of the *zócalo*, has very clean food stands. The *trucha* on most menus is farmed in the mountains, not from the lake.

El Punto BISTRO $
(☎726-262-18-79; www.elpuntovalle.com; Santa María 137; mains M$85-120; ☉ 8am-6pm; 🛜🍽) Dishes at sleek Punto are so stylish they are hardly recognisable. The enchiladas include stuffed tortillas but they go easy on the *mole* and artfully present ripe produce. Most ingredients are organic and locally sourced, and Puntos bake its own bread and desserts. There are also wonderful breakfasts, lattes (coffee, matcha or turmeric), Mexican craft beer and set lunches Monday to Thursday.

La Michoacana MEXICAN $$
(☎726-262-16-25; Calle de la Cruz 100; mains M$150-260; ☉ 8am-11pm; 🛜) A large restaurant with colorful indoor spaces and a great terrace with excellent wide-angled views of the town and lake. Mexican favorites include chicken *mole, salmón en salsa de*

almendra and lots of snacks and drinks to take it slowly. Waiters are eager to practice their English.

Soleado
FUSION **$$**

(☎726-262-58-31; Pagaza 314; mains M$105-265; ⊘1-9pm Tue-Thu, 1-10pm Fri, 10am-10pm Sat, 10am-8pm Sun; 🖥🖉🕪) Soleado calls itself *cocina del mundo* and indeed there is a dish and a dessert from many a 'kitchen of the world' on offer. Admittedly, most dishes, from Indian curry to Italian veg lasagna, have a (tasty) Mexican twist. The low-lit restaurant with lofty views is a great place for groups, with dishes to please all tastes.

There are breakfasts with organic eggs, and a menu for kids.

Restaurante Paraíso
SEAFOOD **$$**

(☎726-262-47-31; Fray Gregorio Jiménez de la Cuenca s/n; mains M$160-210, menú del día M$150; ⊘8am-10pm Tue-Sun) Restaurante Paraíso has fantastic lake views and a sprawling menu of seafood specialties, plus excellent and imaginatively prepared local trout. Come early and watch the sunset from the rooftop patio. A set lunch with fish options is good value.

LocaL
CAFE

(☎726-262-51-74; Calle 5 de Mayo 107; ⊘9am-6:30pm; 🖥) LocaL tries to be a bit of everything – cafe, co-working space with free printing deals, a library with design and architecture books, roof terrace with nursery, and a small bakery with vegan items – but its most solid triumph is being the hippest place in Valle de Bravo.

ℹ Information

There's a tourist-info kiosk on the wharf and essential services, including ATMs and internet cafes, are found around the main plaza, a 10-minute walk uphill from the waterfront.

ℹ Getting There & Away

Considering the hordes of tourists who descend on Valle each weekend, transportation options are relatively few. Most visitors are affluent Mexicans, who come by car.

Zina-bus (www.autobuseszinacantepec.com.mx) runs 1st-class *directo* buses from early morning to late afternoon between Mexico City's Terminal Poniente and Valle de Bravo's small bus terminal on Calle 16 de Septiembre (M$245, 2¼ hours, every one to two hours). For a scenic ride ask for the southern, 'Los Saucos' route, which travels along Hwy 134 and through a national park. If driving, that's the route to take as well.

There is no direct bus between Malinalco and Valle de Bravo. You have to travel via Toluca (M$80, 2¼ hours, frequent) on a 2nd-class bus or via Mexico City.

Malinalco
📞714 / POP 8045 / ELEV 1740M

Set in a valley of dramatic cliffs and ancient ruins, this *pueblo mágico* continues its awakening as the next Tepoztlán or Valle de Bravo. Weekends see crowds, but still far fewer than those that descend more easily accessible weekend escapes. The drive to Malinalco is one of the most enjoyable to be had in the area, with dramatic scenery lining the road south of Toluca.

There is a clutch of boutique 'hippie' stores, a handful of international restaurants and a surprising number of boutique hotels with pools. The town is far from fully developed, though, and midweek you'll often have the quiet backstreets all to yourself.

The village itself has a charming colonial core comprising a well-preserved convent, a lively *zócalo* with a rotunda, and a small plaza with obligatory giant 'Malinalco' letters. Weekends add food and craft stalls.

⊙ Sights

Aztec Temples
ARCHAEOLOGICAL SITE

(Zona Arqueológica Cuauhtinchan; ☎722-215-85-69; Av Progreso s/n; M$60; ⊘9am-5pm Tue-Sun, last entry 4pm) An invigorating 358-step hike up the mountainside above Malinalco takes you to one of the country's few reasonably well-preserved temples (even surviving recent earthquakes), from where there are stunning views of the valley and beyond. The small, fascinating site includes the mural *El paraíso de los guerreros* that once covered an entire wall and depicts fallen warriors becoming deities and living in paradise. From the *zócalo* follow signs to the *zona arqueológica*, taking you up the hillside on a well-maintained, signed footpath.

The Aztec conquered the region in 1476 and were busy building a ritual center here when they were conquered by the Spanish. **El Cuauhcalli** (Temple of the Eagle and Jaguar Knight, where sons of Aztec nobles were initiated into warrior orders) survived because it was hewn from the mountainside itself. The entrance is carved in the form of a fanged serpent.

Temple IV, located on the far side of the site, continues to baffle archaeologists.

As the room is positioned to allow the first rays of sunlight to hit it at dawn, there has been speculation that this place was part of a Mexican sun cult, a solar calendar or a meeting place for nobles – or some combination of these.

To dodge the crowds, avoid Sundays when entry is free for Mexican residents with ID.

Situated 50m before the site entrance, the **Museo Universitario Dr Luis Mario Schneider** (M$15) explores the region's history and archaeology in a beautiful, modern museum space.

Museo Vivo
ANIMAL SANCTUARY

(Los Bichos; ☑714-147-22-42; www.museovivo.org; Pensamiento s/n, cnr Violetas & Rosa Blanca; admission incl guide M$50; ◷10am-4.30pm Thu-Sun; ♠) This interactive collection of live and mounted insects and other creepy crawlies is a giggly delight. You can join a continual circuit tour where you can cradle a tarantula, shoulder a snake, eat a meal worm and sniff at Mexican plants. Kids and adults are encouraged to rethink attitudes to nature – in Spanish, though interactive elements are universal.

From the *zócalo,* take Morelos south for nine blocks. From the *criadero* (trout farm), head to the main road Miguel Negrete, then two blocks west.

Augustinian Convent
CHURCH

(Convento Agustino de Malinalco; Morelos s/n, cnr Hidalgo; ◷9am-6pm) A well-restored 16th-century convent, fronted by a tranquil tree-lined yard, faces the *zócalo.* Impressive frescoes fashioned from flower- and herb-based paint adorn its cloister.

At the time of research, the main buildings still suffered the damage from the 2017 earthquake and were clad in wooden supports. Entry is not possible and services are held outside on makeshift seating, which is in itself interesting to see.

☞ Tours

Tour Gastronómico Prehispánico
FOOD & DRINK

(☑cell 55-55091411; www.facebook.com/Gastronomia.Prehispanica; tours per person M$1200, minimum 5 people) This pre-Hispanic food tour includes a visit to the market, a cooking class using traditional utensils and methods, and a three-course meal. The guide is an expert in the anthropology and cuisine of the region and speaks English. Tours can be run any day but the market is liveliest on Wednesdays, Saturdays and Sundays.

🛌 Sleeping

This small town has an inordinate number of hotels, many boutique with pools, but reservations remain essential. Because Malinalco is geared toward weekend visitors, you'll have no trouble finding a room Sunday to Thursday night (often with a negotiable discount), though some nicer hotels aren't open for walk-ins midweek. Budget options near the *zócalo* suffer from weekend bar music into the wee hours.

⭐El Asoleadero
HOTEL $

(☑714-147-01-84; Aldama, cnr Comercio; s/d M$600/700, r with kitchen M$800; ▣ 🗢 ☒) Just uphill from Malinalco's main drag, El Asoleadero offers spacious, modern and airy rooms with stunning views of the *pueblito* and surrounding cliffs. You can enjoy the million-peso vista from the courtyard's small pool with a cold beer from the lobby. Discounts of M$100 Sunday to Thursday; reserve at least a week ahead for Saturdays.

⭐Casa Navacoyan
BOUTIQUE HOTEL $$$

(☑714-147-04-11; www.casanavacoyan.mx; Prolongación Calle Pirul 62; s/d/ste incl breakfast from M$2600/2835/3400; ▣ 🗢 ☒) This beautiful hotel on the outskirts of town has just six rooms, each decorated with an upscale, home-style aesthetic, like staying at your wealthy aunt's house in the country. The immaculately groomed yard is the real attraction, with palm trees, a gorgeous heated pool and views of Malinalco's famed hills and cliffs.

Casa Limón
BOUTIQUE HOTEL $$$

(☑714-147-02-56; www.casalimon.com; Río Lerma 103; r/ste incl breakfast from M$2700/3100; ▣ 🗢 ☒) Surrounded by a stark high-desert landscape, this ultra-trendy hotel with bright fan-cooled rooms, a slate pool and intriguing artworks has a seductive indoor-outdoor bar and tree house–like restaurant. Pricey mains (M$300) are classic international, from coq au vin to almond trout, and the wine list is superb. To get here, from east of the *zócalo,* take Morelos seven blocks south.

🍴 Eating & Drinking

Perhaps surprisingly for such a small town, Malinalco has a few very good restaurants. Unfortunately for those visiting midweek, though, most of the better options (on Avenida Hidalgo and around the *zócalo*) are only open Thursday through Sunday. There is a small but well-stocked supermarket on the northeast corner of the *zócalo*.

Most bars are dotted on Vincente Guerrero and around the *zócalo* and only open Friday to Sunday. Look for new Malinalco mezcales; in 2018, mezcal producers in 12 municipalities around Malinalco gained official denomination of origin to use the 'mezcal' name.

Casa Vieja
MEXICAN $

(☎714-147-0756; www.facebook.com/Casavieja malinalco; Av Hidalgo; menú del día M$50-75; ⊙9am-6pm; ☑🖶) The ample, semi-outdoors seating, murals and colorful wooden tables give this converted 'Old House' courtyard vibes. It's an inviting casual restaurant for families and groups for good-value set menus including *huevos rancheros* (eggs sunny side up on tortillas, bathed in salsa) for breakfast and enchiladas (tortillas stuffed with chicken) for lunch.

Truchas Los Comales
MEXICAN $$

(Camino a Las Truchas; trout meals M$95-135; ⊙10am-6pm) Pick fresh *trucha* from the tank at this family restaurant, or fish it yourself at the nearby *criadero* for cooking here. Then have your fish grilled multiple ways – try it wrapped in banana leaves with *nopal* and *epazote* (pre-Hispanic medicinal herb). Take a taxi (M$50) for the *criaderos* from between the two plazas in central Malinalco.

Similar small *trucha* restaurants line the street but the open space at Comales allows stretching out your full belly. It's about a 30-minute walk from the *zócalo*.

La Casa de Valentina
BISTRO $$

(☎cell 55-40755459; Av Hidalgo 213; mains M$105-200; ⊙1-11pm Fri, 9am-11pm Sat, 8am-8pm Sun; ⊙🕸☑) Popular weekend bistro-restaurant near the *zócalo* with spaces to suit every mood, from courtyard to cosy nook or stylish space for live classical music. Burgers, focaccia, al dente pasta, salads, milk-free cocoa drinks and homemade ice cream dominate the long, bilingual picture menu.

Casa Diablitos
BAR

(☎722-585-68-63; Vicente Guerrero 8; ⊙11am-11pm Fri, 11am-1am Sat, 10am-8pm Sun) A shot of Malinalco mezcal with quesadillas filled with *chapulines* (grasshoppers) in this cave-like bar is part of the local weekend experience. Give in to your *diablito* (little devil) with the *cata* (taste-test flight) of mezcales that include *chicatana* (flying-ant) infusions.

❶ Getting There & Away

Flecha Roja (☎800-224-84-52; https://flecharoja.com.mx) runs two direct buses daily from Mexico City's Terminal Poniente to the centre of Malinalco (M$114, 2½ hours, 4:20pm and 6:20pm), with an additional service Saturdays and Sundays (8:45am). Return buses depart from the same drop-off point (outside the Santander bank on Avenida Hidalgo) daily in the wee hours (4:40am, also 3:30am Mondays) with an additional service Saturdays and Sundays (5pm). Otherwise, take a taxi *colectivo* (M$15, 25 minutes) from Casa de Cultura at the *zócalo* to hectic Chalma for more frequent Flecha Roja buses to Mexico City's Terminal Poniente (M$125, 2½ hours, every 20 to 30 minutes). Note that Flecha Roja buses do not have toilets on board.

Though the distances are short, traveling from Malinalco to Cuernavaca can take hours. It is, however, possible to hire a taxi (M$175, about one hour) and travel between the two towns via the incredibly scenic route through Puente Caporal–Palpan–Miacatlán to the town of Alpuyeca, near the Xochicalco ruins. From there it's easy to flag one of the frequent buses traveling along Hwy 95, and continue either north (to Cuernavaca and Mexico City) or south (to Taxco and the coast).

AROUND MEXICO CITY MALINALCO

AT A GLANCE

POPULATION
8.1 million

CAPITAL
Xalapa

BEST COFFEE EXPERIENCE
Museo del Café Córdoba (p246)

BEST FESTIVAL
Día de la Candelaria (p260)

BEST RAFTING TRIP
Expediciones México Verde (p244)

WHEN TO GO
Feb & Mar
Veracruz Carnaval kicks off the biggest party on Mexico's eastern coast.

Jul
Nonstop processions and masked dances in Xico in honor of the town's patron saint.

Nov–Feb
Peak tourist season for non-Mexicans with less rain and balmy temperatures.

El Tajín (p254)
INSPIRED BY MAPS/SHUTTERSTOCK

Veracruz

Taking up much of Mexico's Gulf coastline, the long and diverse state of Veracruz is where the Spanish conquest of the Aztec began. It was also the cradle of the Veracruz Mesoamerican culture at El Tajín and is home to Mexico's highest peak, Pico de Orizaba.

It's routinely overlooked by travelers, and while it's true that the beaches are better in the Yucatán and the colonial towns more impressive in the highlands, Veracruz has both, without the crowds. There's also World Heritage site Tlacotalpan, the inspiring Reserva de la Biosfera Los Tuxtlas and some seductively pretty, historic *pueblos mágicos*, including Orizaba, Papantla, Coatepec and Xico.

Its biggest attraction, though, is its quietness, with unique discoveries just waiting to be made.

History

The Olmec, Mesoamerica's earliest known civilization, built their first great center around 1200 BCE at San Lorenzo in southern Veracruz state. In 900 BCE the city was violently destroyed, but Olmec culture lingered for several centuries at Tres Zapotes. Between 250 and 900 CE, the Gulf coast developed another distinctive culture, known as the Classic Veracruz civilization. Its most important center was El Tajín, which was at its peak between 600 and 900 CE. In the post-Classic period the Totonac established themselves in the region south of Tuxpan. North of Tuxpan, the Huastec civilization flourished from 800 to 1200 CE. During this time, the warlike Toltec also moved into the Gulf coast area. In the mid-15th century, the Aztec took over most of the Totonac and Huastec areas, exacting tributes of goods and sacrificial victims, and subduing revolts.

When Hernán Cortés arrived in April 1519, he made Zempoala's Totonac his first allies against the Aztec by vowing to protect them against reprisals. Cortés set up his first settlement, Villa Rica de la Vera Cruz (Rich Town of the True Cross), and by 1523 all the Gulf coast was in Spanish hands. Slavery, newly introduced diseases and the ravages of war severely reduced indigenous populations.

Veracruz harbor became an essential trade and communications link with Spain and was vital for anyone trying to rule Mexico, but the climate, tropical diseases and pirate threats inhibited the growth of Spanish settlements.

Under dictator Porfirio Díaz, Mexico's first railway linked Veracruz to Mexico City in 1872, stimulating industrial development. In 1901, oil was discovered in the Tampico area, and by the 1920s the region was producing a quarter of the world's oil. In the 1980s, the Gulf coast still held well over half of Mexico's reserves and refining capacity. Today, the region is not as large a player as it used to be, but is still a significant contributor to Mexico's oil economy.

VERACRUZ CITY

🎵 229 / POP 428,323

Veracruz, like all great port cities, is an unholy mélange of grime, romance and melted-down cultures. Having celebrated its 500th birthday in 2019, this is Mexico's oldest European-founded settlement. However, usurped by subsequent inland cities, it's neither the nation's most historic spot nor its most visually striking. Countless sackings by the French, Spanish and North Americans have ravaged the prettiest buildings, leaving a motley patchwork of working docks and questionable hybrid architecture, punctuated by the odd stray colonial masterpiece.

But Veracruz' beauty is in its grit rather than its grandiosity. A carefree spirit reigns in the *zócalo* (main square) most evenings, where the primary preoccupation is the *danzón* (traditional couples dance). There are places to dive and snorkel off the coast and some passably OK beaches south of the city center.

History

Hernán Cortés arrived at the site of today's Veracruz on Good Friday, April 21, 1519, and began his siege of Mexico. By 1521 he had crushed the Aztec empire.

Veracruz provided Mexico's main gateway to the outside world for 400 years. Invaders and pirates, incoming and outgoing rulers, settlers, silver and slaves – all came and went, making Veracruz a linchpin in Mexico's history. In 1569, English sailor Francis Drake survived a massive Spanish sea attack here. In 1683, vicious Frenchman Laurent de Gaff and his 600 men held Veracruz' 5000 inhabitants captive, killing escapees, looting, drinking and raping. Soon after, they left much richer.

Under bombardment from a French fleet in the Pastry War, General Antonio López de Santa Anna was forced to flee Veracruz in 1838, wearing nothing but his underwear. But the general managed to respond heroically, expelling the invaders. When Winfield Scott's army attacked Veracruz during the Mexican–American War, more than 1000 Mexicans died before the city surrendered.

In 1861, Benito Juárez announced that Mexico couldn't pay its debts to Spain, France and Britain. The British and Spanish planned only to take over Veracruz' customhouse, but retreated on seeing that Frenchman Napoleon III sought to conquer Mexico. After Napoleon III's five-year intervention ended, Veracruz experienced revitalization. Mexico's first railway was built between Veracruz and Mexico City in 1872, and foreign investment poured into the city.

US troops occupied Veracruz in 1914, halting a delivery of German arms to dictator

Veracruz Highlights

1 **Orizaba** (p248)
Strolling by the river and enjoying the architecture, museums and mountainous landscape of this magical town.

2 **Museo de Antropología** (p233) Deciphering a triumvirate of Mesoamerican cultures in Xalapa's architecturally magnificent museum.

3 **El Tajín** (p254) Imagining past glories at these extensive ruins.

4 **Coatepec** (p240) Sipping gourmet coffee in this cloud forest–encased highland town.

5 **Jalcomulco** (p243) Riding the white water of one of Mexico's best rivers for rafting.

6 **Veracruz's Zócalo** (p222) Swaying along to the *danzón* concerts in the city's most happening square.

7 **Papantla** (p253) Watching grown men fly at a one-of-a-kind *voladores* (fliers) ceremony.

8 **Tlacotalpan** (p259) Marveling at the many colors of this sleepy colonial town, perhaps Mexico's least-known World Heritage site.

Veracruz

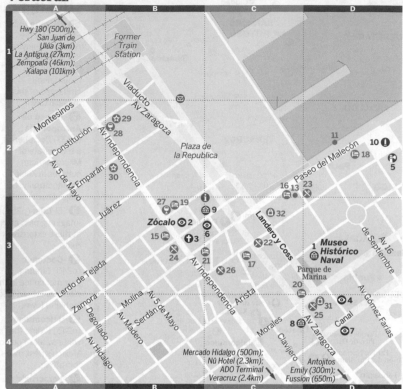

Victoriano Huerta. Later in the Revolution, Veracruz was briefly the capital of the reformist Constitutionalist faction led by Venustiano Carranza.

Today, Veracruz is an important deep-water port, handling exports, manufacturing and petrochemical industries. Tourism, particularly from the domestic sector, is another large income earner.

◉ Sights

★ Zócalo   PLAZA
Any exploration of Veracruz has to begin with its *zócalo* (also called the Plaza de Armas and Plaza Lerdo), the city's unofficial outdoor 'stage' where inspired organized events overlap with the day-to-day improvisation of Mexican life. The handsome public space is framed by *portales* (arcades), the 17th-century **Palacio Municipal** (Zamora s/n) and an 18th-century **cathedral** (http://diocesis deveracruz.mx; Mario Molina 173; ◐8am-7pm).

The level of activity accelerates throughout the day until the evening, when the *zócalo* becomes thick with souvenir sellers, musical entertainers, merrymakers and bystanders.

★ Museo Histórico Naval   MUSEUM
(☏229-931-40-78; Arista 418; adult/student/child under 6yr M$45/30/free; ◐10am-5pm Tue-Sun) Occupying a former naval academy, this high-tech museum offers a titanic lesson in Mexico's maritime heritage, with plenty of interactive displays and an attractive layout. Displays cover pre-Hispanic navigation and Columbus' arrival in the New World to trade with Asia, the growth of Veracruz and the role of the present-day navy. There are also exhibits focusing on the US attacks on Veracruz in 1847 and 1914, a ship simulator and plenty of armaments through the ages.

The in-house cafe offers a place for a quiet rest. Most of the displays are in Spanish only.

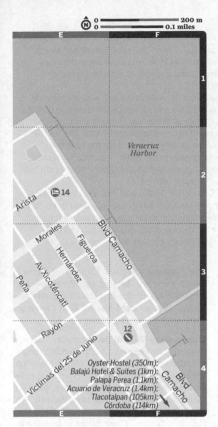

Veracruz

◎ Top Sights
1 Museo Histórico Naval D3
2 Zócalo B3

◎ Sights
3 Catedral de la Virgen de la
    Asunción B3
4 Centro Cultural La Atarazana D4
5 Faro Carranza D2
6 Fototeca C3
7 Instituto Veracruzano de Cultura D4
8 Museo de la Ciudad de Veracruz C4
9 Palacio Municipal C3
10 Statue of Venustiano Carranza D2

◎ Activities, Courses & Tours
11 ASDIC D2
12 Scubaver F4
13 Tours Amphibian C2

◎ Sleeping
14 Fiesta Inn E2
15 Gran Hotel Diligencias B3
16 Hawaii Hotel C2
17 Hotel Amparo C3
18 Hotel Emporio D2
19 Hotel Imperial B3
20 Mesón del Mar C3
21 Mucara Hotel C3

◎ Eating
22 Cochinito de Oro C3
23 Gran Café de la Parroquia D2
24 Gran Café del Portal B3
    Los Canarios .... (see 18)
25 Tacos David D4
26 Toks C3

◎ Drinking & Nightlife
    Bar El Estribo .... (see 15)
27 Bar Prendes B3
28 Miraloco B2

◎ Entertainment
29 Las Barricas B2
30 Teatro Principal Francisco Javier
    Clavijero B2

◎ Shopping
31 Mar Adentro D4
32 Plaza de las Artesanías C3

San Juan de Ulúa   FORTRESS
(☑229-938-51-51; www.sanjuandeulua.inah.gob.mx;
adult/student & child M$48/free; ◎9am-4:30pm
Tue-Sun) The city's colonial fortress is almost
hidden amid the container ships and cranes
across the harbor. The central part of the
fortress was a prison, and a notoriously in-
humane one, during the Porfirio Díaz regime.
Today, San Juan de Ulúa is an empty ruin
of passageways, battlements, bridges and
stairways undergoing lengthy renovations.
To get here, take a taxi (M$55) or a *lancha*
(boat taxi; M$40) from the *malecón* (beach
promenade).

The fort was originally built on an island
that's since been connected to the mainland
by a causeway. The earliest fortifications
date from 1565, and a young Francis Drake
got his comeuppance here in a violent battle
in 1569. During the colonial period, the fort
and island became the main entry point for
Spanish newcomers to Mexico.

**Centro Cultural
La Atarazana**   CULTURAL CENTER
(☑229-932-89-21; www.facebook.com/Centro
culturalatarazanas; Montero s/n; ◎10am-6pm
Tue-Fri & Sun, 10am-2pm & 3-6pm Sat) FREE This
colonial-era warehouse has been beautifully converted into an exhibition space and
sports a striking mural by Melchor Perado.
Worthwhile temporary exhibitions, such as

DANZÓN DAYS

The highlight of Veracruz is heading to the *zócalo* (p222) on Friday and Saturday evenings to find the plaza full of romantic *jarochos* (inhabitants of Veracruz) indulging in the city's favorite pastime, the *danzón*. An elegant tropical dance, it melds aspects of the French contradance with the rhythms of African slaves.

As with most Latin American dances, *danzón* has its roots in Cuba. It was purportedly 'invented' in 1879 by popular band leader Miguel Failde, who showcased his catchy dance composition *Las alturas de Simpson* in the port city of Matanzas. Elegant and purely instrumental in its early days, the *danzón* required dancers to circulate in couples rather than groups, a move that scandalized polite white society of the era. By the time the dance arrived in Mexico, brought by Cuban immigrants in the 1890s, it had become more complex, expanding on its peculiar syncopated rhythm, and adding other instruments such as the conga to form an *orquesta típica* (popular orchestra).

Though the *danzón* faded in popularity in Cuba in the 1940s and '50s with the arrival of the mambo and the cha-cha, in Mexico it continued to flourish. Indeed, since the 1990s the *danzón* has undergone a huge revival in Veracruz, particularly among mature citizens. The bastion of the dance is the *zócalo*, where bands play many evenings (always on Fridays and Saturdays) and couples in matching outfits go through their moves.

ceramic art and installations by contemporary artists, are held regularly.

Instituto Veracruzano de Cultura
CULTURAL CENTER

(IVEC; ☎229-931-69-62; www.ivec.gob.mx; Francisco Canal 1517; ⊙9am-8pm Mon-Fri, until 6pm Sat & Sun) FREE A converted church and cloister house some excellent temporary exhibitions as well as works by local contemporary artists.

Acuario de Veracruz
AQUARIUM

(☎229-931-10-20; www.acuariodeveracruz.com; Blvd Camacho s/n; adult/child M$140/85, shark feeding M$445/245; ⊙10am-7pm Mon-Thu, to 7:30pm Fri-Sun) Allegedly the best of its kind in Latin America, this aquarium does a good job of showcasing the denizens of the Gulf of Mexico, as well as fishy oddities such as arapaima and albino shark catfish. Situated 2km south of the center, on the waterfront, its centerpiece is a large doughnut-shaped tank filled with tiger, reef and nurse sharks, barracuda, and eagle rays that glide around visitors.

Visitor participation in shark feedings is possible.

The aquarium also features a tank full of sad manatees. Aquarium authorities claim they are aiding manatee conservation and research, but animal-welfare groups around the world claim that such exhibits are cruel.

Museo Agustín Lara
MUSEUM

(☎229-937-02-09; Ruíz Cortines s/n, Boca del Río; ⊙10am-5pm Tue-Sun) FREE A monument to one of Veracruz' most famous musical icons, this museum displays a range of Agustín Lara's personal belongings, furniture and memorabilia in the musician's old city residence. It is situated just off Blvd Camacho, 4km south of the city center.

Museo de la Ciudad de Veracruz
MUSEUM

(Veracruz City Museum; ☎229-931-63-55; http://amiweb.com.mx; Av Zaragoza 397; ⊙10am-5pm Tue-Sun) FREE Housed in a charming colonial-era building, this museum recounts Veracruz's history from the pre-Hispanic era. Standout exhibits include some Totonac and Huastec figures. There is some labeling in English, and plenty about Veracruz at different stages in its history, which gives a feel for the essence of this proud and lively city.

Faro Carranza
LIGHTHOUSE

(Xicoténcatl) Facing the waterfront on the *malecón*, this early-20th-century building holds a lighthouse and navy offices guarded by a large **statue of Venustiano Carranza** (Map p222; Paseo del Malecón). It was here that the 1917 Mexican Constitution was drafted. Every Monday at 8am members of the Mexican navy go through an elaborate flag-raising parade in front of the building.

Fototeca
ARTS CENTER

(☎229-932-87-67; Portal de Miranda 9; ⊙10am-6pm Tue-Sun) FREE On the southeast side of the *zócalo*, this small arts center has rotating photographic and video exhibitions. It's spread over three floors of a restored colonial building, though usually only the ground floor is open.

🏃 Activities

You wouldn't expect high-visibility diving right near such an oil-rigged city, but Veracruz has some pretty good options (including at least one accessible wreck) on the reefs near the offshore islands. Visibility is best in May. Contact either **Scubaver** (☑229-932-39-94; www.scubaver.net; Francisco Hernández y Hernández 563; 2 dives M$900) or **Mundo Submarino** (☑229-980-63-74; www.mundo submarino.com.mx; Blvd Camacho 3549; beginner dives from M$1000) both of which offer PADI courses and a range of diving excursions.

Tours Amphibian   ADVENTURE
(☑229-931-09-97; www.amphibianveracruz.com; Paseo Insurgentes Veracruzanos 432; tours from M$900; ◎9am-5pm) Amphibian conducts themed city tours of Veracruz, as well as rafting and rappeling expeditions to Jalcomulco, tours of the coffee region that include Xico and Xalapa, and historical tours of the Zempoala and Quiahuiztlán ruins.

Aventura Extrema   ADVENTURE
(☑229-147-6029; www.aventuraextrema.com.mx; Avenida Salvador Díaz Mirón; ◎11am-6pm Mon-Fri) Offers rappeling, horseback riding, rafting and hiking around Veracruz, mostly in the Jalcomulco area.

ASDIC   CRUISE
(☑229-935-94-17; www.asdic.com.mx; adult/child from M$100/55; ◎9am-6pm) Boats from the *malecón* offer 35-minute cruises of the harbor. The company also runs trips out to the nearby islands for snorkelling ($180).

🎊 Festivals & Events

★ Carnaval de Veracruz   CARNIVAL
(http://carnavaldeveracruz.com.mx; ◎Feb or Mar) Veracruz throws one of Mexico's greatest fiestas with this nine-day party before Ash Wednesday. Flamboyant parades wind through the city daily, beginning with one devoted to the 'burning of bad humor' and ending with the 'funeral of Juan Carnaval.' There are also fireworks, dances, concerts, handicrafts, folklore shows and more.

🛏 Sleeping

At busy times (mid-July to mid-September, Carnaval, Semana Santa, Christmas and New Year) prices may increase by as much as 40%. There are historic hotels around the *zócalo* and some inexpensive places are dotted around the city center and further south. Boca de Río and around is full of business and resort hotels.

Oyster Hostel   HOSTEL $
(☑229-348-83-94; www.oysterhostelveracruz. bookdreams.co; Xicotencatl 1076; dm/d/q incl breakfast M$150/350/500; ❇⤬) Bright, clean and well run, this is the best backpackers in town, though it can be low on atmosphere. The breakfast spread is unusually good for this price bracket, and it's close to the waterfront and within walking distance of many of the town's sights.

Hotel Amparo   HOTEL $
(☑229-932-27-38; www.hotelamparo.com.mx; Serdán 482; s/d/tr M$250/400/500; 🅿❇⤬)

VERACRUZ BEACHES & LAGOONS

Inseparable from the *jarocho* (Veracruz) identity is the beach. You'll find reasonably pleasant stretches of beach all the way down through Boca del Río. As a rule of thumb, the further from the oil rigs the better, but locals can be seen enjoying them all.

Alternatively, you may be able to find *lanchas* (motorboats; M$110 Monday to Thursday and M$150 Friday to Sunday) by the aquarium that will take you to **Cancuncito**, a sandbar off the coast that is sometimes completely submerged: you can paddle and snorkel here. Another part of the *lancha* beat is around the **Isla de Sacrificios**, an island once used for Totonac human sacrifice and later as a leper colony. It's now part of a protected nature and marine reserve called **Parque Marino Nacional Sistema Arrecifal Veracruzano**, so boats don't land here.

Some 11km from the center, the gritty, off-shoot town of **Boca del Río** has a smattering of brightly colored seafood restaurants overlooking the mouth of the river on Blvd Camacho; one of the best is Villa Rica Mocambo (p228). *Lanchas* offering boat tours to mangrove forests leave from here. Over the bridge, the coastal road continues about 8km further down the coast from Boca del Río to **Mandinga**, known for its seafood (especially *langostinos bicolores* – two-colored shrimp), where you can hire a boat (from the *zona de restaurantes*) to take you around mangrove lagoons rich with wildlife.

This mosaic-tile-fronted, family-run hotel represents the best value for your peso in the historic center, if not the city. Yes, the rooms are snug bordering on cozy and are fan-cooled rather than air-conditioned, but they're clean, have en suites and are steps away from most of Veracruz's attractions.

Hawaii Hotel
HOTEL $

(☎229-989-88-88; Paseo del Malecón 458; s/d/tr M$600/700/900; P♨❀🛜🌊) Who knows why it's called the Hawaii Hotel? The 30-room hotel looks more like the prow of a boat, with marble-and-white decor inside. However, it's the best value on the *malecón*, and some of the spacious, sunlight-filled rooms have marvelous views. Extras such as hairdryers and fridges make for a comfortable stay.

Nû Hotel
HOTEL $

(☎229-937-09-17; www.nuhotel.com.mx; Av Lafragua 1066; s/d M$550/650; P♨❀🛜🌊) The Nû has pitched itself amid the scruffy next-to-bus-station hovels and declared war. It's no contest really, especially at these prices. Savor the clean, minimalist-chic rooms; young, casual staff; and modern downstairs cafe. The only real drawback is the location, 3km south of the *zócalo*, which isn't really handy for anything – except the buses, of course.

★ Mesón del Mar
BOUTIQUE HOTEL $$

(☎229-932-50-43; Morales 543; r/ste from M$950/1295; ❀🛜) One of Veracruz' most atmospheric midrange options, this colonial charmer boasts friendly staff and well-cared-for rooms with tall ceilings (many have mezzanines with extra sleeping spaces), beautifully tiled bathrooms, ceiling fans and wooden furniture. Rooms facing busy Avenida Zaragoza can be noisy, however.

Mucara Hotel
HOTEL $$

(☎229-358-52-64; www.hotelmucara.com.mx; Mario Molina 168; s/d from M$600/800; ❀🛜) New in 2019, this centrally located hotel in a revamped old building offers a touch more style in its decor than similar midrange options. Plus there are spacious balconies attached to most rooms

Balajú Hotel & Suites
HOTEL $$

(☎229-201-08-08; www.balaju.com; Blvd Camacho 1371; r incl breakfast from M$950; P❀🛜🌊) The room design follows the tried-and-tested tiled floor/neutral color scheme formula, but on the upside, this smart, pleasant hotel overlooks the sea (pick a corner room for best views), the staff are efficient and friendly, and it's handy for either the aquarium or the city center. Note, the pool is tiny.

Hotel Imperial
HISTORIC HOTEL $$

(☎229-276-19060; Miguel Lerdo de Tejada 153A; r/ste from M$900/1350; ♨❀🛜🌊) Claiming to be the oldest hotel in the Americas, the Imperial has been in business since 1794. Its suites and public areas are suitably ornate (check out the 1904 stained-glass elevator!) and will certainly please colonial-history buffs, and you can't beat the location. The standard rooms, however, are as bland as unseasoned porridge.

Gran Hotel Diligencias
LUXURY HOTEL $$

(☎229-923-02-80, 800-505-55-95; www.granhoteldiligencias.com.mx; Av Independencia 1115; r/ste from M$1200/2000; P♨❀🛜🌊) The fanciest option on the *zócalo* has a smart lobby full of fresh flowers and buzzes with livery-clad bellhops. Upstairs, big rooms deliver solid, old-fashioned elegance and perks such as cable TV and coffee makers. They also have a spa but the outdoor pool is pretty small.

You'll find more atmosphere downstairs in the adjoining **Bar El Estribo** (⊙9am-late; 🛜) and **Villa Rica** seafood restaurant.

Fiesta Inn
BUSINESS HOTEL $$

(☎229-923-15-00; www.fiestainn.com; Figueroa 68; r from M$1342; P♨❀🛜🌊) A block away from the *malecón* and overlooking the sea, this chain hotel is all spacious rooms and blond-wood furniture. A decent onsite restaurant, small pool, gym, helpful bilingual staff and proximity to the city's attractions, plus a quiet location, add to its charm.

★ Hotel Emporio
LUXURY HOTEL $$$

(☎229-989-33-00; www.hotelesemporio.com; Paseo del Malecón 244; r from M$1751; P♨❀🛜🌊) The Emporio is shot through with arty touches, and the rooms are spacious, with beautifully appointed bathrooms. Each comes with a large balcony, and it's worth splurging on a sea view. It also has three pools, a gym, a cocktail bar and a dynamite location on the most picturesque stretch of the *malecón*.

Out-of-season deals can see prices drop 40% on the listed rack rates. It's restaurant **Los Canarios** (http://loscanarios.com.mx/emporio-veracruz; mains M$115-305; ⊙1-11pm; 🛜) is also highly rated.

🍴 Eating

Seafood features heavily on the menus of most restaurants, from the strip of *palap-*

DON'T MISS

VERACRUZ' LECHERO

No visit to Veracruz is complete without dropping into the **Gran Café de la Parroquia** (www.laparroquia.com; Gómez Farías 34; mains M$70-200; ☉6am-midnight), a fixture of the city's coffee-drinking and dining scene since 1808. It's not so much about the immense but un-showy interior. Rather it's all about the overall atmosphere with patrons chatting, mariachis strumming their guitars and – crucially – the white-jacketed waiters serving the establishment's famous *lechero*.

It goes like this: a waiter or customer taps their spoon on their coffee glass, an old Parroquia tradition, to attract attention. Another waiter arrives carrying two huge brass kettles, one filled with coffee and the other with hot milk. An espresso measure is poured in the bottom of a glass while a stream of hot milk poured from on high tops up the glass with scientific precision.

The Parroquia (which is a great breakfast and light-meal joint, too, with eggs prepared at least a dozen different ways) has inspired several imitators around town. We also particularly like the equally venerable **Gran Café del Portal** (☎229-931-27-59; Av Independencia 1187; mains M$70-200; ☉7am-midnight; ☎) near the *zócalo*. And there's a great, newer branch of the **Parroquia** (cnr Av George Washington & Blvd Manuel Ávila Camacho; mains M$70-200; ☉6am-midnight) overlooking the beach in the south of the city.

as (thatched-roof shelters) on the *malecón* just south of the aquarium to seafood restaurants in Boca del Río. Fusion and international places are scattered throughout the city, and some of the best cheap eats, including street food, are found in the historical center.

Tacos David STREET FOOD $
(Morales 536; tacos M$10; ☉9am-5pm Mon-Sat) Late morning and lunchtime, locals congregate at simple tables around this beloved taco spot that specializes in one thing: *cochinita pibil* (slow-cooked pork) tacos served in a fragrant, mildly spicy broth. Four tacos is a good-sized portion and there are extra chilies if you want to spice it up.

Antojitos Emily MEXICAN $
(☎229-955-09-36; Zapata 436; mains from M$10; ☉9am-2:30pm) Its generally low-key appearance belies the fact that this little neighborhood eatery does some of the best *gordas* (filled pastry), *pellizcadas con chicharrón* (cornflour 'nests' topped with pork crackling), *antojitos con chorizo* (fried tortillas with tomato salsa, chorizo and cheese) and other snacks.

Mercado Hidalgo STREET FOOD $
(Av Hidalgo; mains M$30-100; ☉7am-8pm Mon-Sat, until 5pm Sun) Join *jarochos* at this atmospheric covered market where you can find nooks that serve cheap, delectable local favorites. **Tampico Mariscos** is a good bet for the monster seafood cocktail *vuelve a la vida* ('come back to life' – a hangover

remedy), while **Los Michoacanos** serves all manner of meaty tacos, as does **Taquería Rosita**.

Cochinito de Oro MEXICAN $
(☎229-932-36-77; Zaragoza 190; mains M$50-100; ☉7am-6pm) A couple of blocks away from the *zócalo*, you can actually escape the hawkers and incredible price inflation. The food is simple, plentiful and tasty, and includes all manner of *antojitos* (snacks), including those involving *cochinita pibil*. The set menu is M$60.

Palapa Perea SEAFOOD $$
(☎229-200-98-94; http://palapaperea.com; Av 16 de Septiembre; mains M$69-185; ☉9am-8pm) This rustic place, with models of sharks dangling from a straw roof, deserves its reputation for serving some of the best seafood in Veracruz. Its location, a few blocks back from the seafront, means that it's mostly locals who come here. The rice and seafood stew, *arroz a la tumbada*, will fill you up nicely.

Bistro Marti FRENCH $$
(☎229-213-95-73; www.facebook.com/bistromarti veracruz; Calle Magallanes 213; mains M$120-230; ☉5pm-midnight Mon-Sat, until 10pm Sun; ☎) This highly regarded French restaurant, with just a hint of Italian, serves a seasonally changing menu that can be loaded with treats, such as delicately presented scallops or mussels in white wine sauce. The setting manages to be romantic, modern and cozy all at once.

Toks

MEXICAN $$

(☑229-931-04-67; www.toks.com.mx; Serdán 566; mains M$138-190; ⊘7am-11pm; ☎) It's a chain restaurant but Toks stands out for being based in a huge decommissioned church dating back to 1645 and for its crowd-pleasing menu that delivers a wide range of options from breakfast through dinner. You can also buy some products such as *mole*, chocolate and jam developed with indigenous communities from around Mexico.

★Dos

MEXICAN $$$

(☑229-935-47-84; http://dosboca.mx; Navegantes 96, Fraccionamiento Virginia; mains M$290-395, set menu $785; ⊘1:30-10:30pm Tue-Sat, until 7pm Sun) At the best restaurant in the city, the six-course tasting menu is the way to go, each small dish is supremely satisfying and brings a new taste angle to simple things such as a taco or enchilada. Chef Erik Guerrero sources the produce for his inspired contemporary Mexican cuisine from across the state.

★Fussion

MEXICAN $$$

(☑229-932-6164; www.restaurantefussion.com.mx; 1º de Mayo 632; mains M$175-320; ⊘1-10pm Mon-Thu, until midnight Fri & Sat, until 8pm Sun) With dishes such as tuna tataki in *mole*, octopus risotto and delicious shrimp tacos, Fussion delivers a more contemporary take on Mexican cuisine. The atmosphere in the light-blue painted house is charming with arty, homely decorations and fine service.

★Mariscos Villa Rica Mocambo

SEAFOOD $$$

(☑229-922-55-87; www.villa-rica.com; Calz Mocambo 527, Boca del Río; mains M$120-325; ⊘11am-10pm Sun-Wed, to midnight Thu-Sat; ☎) This restaurant in particular is reason enough to make the pilgrimage to Boca del Río. Fish is the all-encompassing ingredient, from *camarones enchipotlados* (smoky *chipotle* shrimp) to stuffed sea bass, and the beachside service is attentive. It's one of the best seafood operations in Veracruz.

There's a couple more branches in Veracruz, including one at Gran Hotel Diligencias (p226) on the *zócalo*.

🍷 Drinking & Nightlife

The *portales* cafes on the *zócalo* are drinking strongholds. But head south some distance on the *malecón* and you'll find the majority of the city's fast-paced and ever-changing nightlife along Blvd Camancho.

★Impetus

COFFEE

(☑229-284-61-80; www.impetus.mx; Fernando de Magallanes 661, Fraccionamiento Reforma; ⊘8am-10pm Mon-Fri, 2-8pm Sat, noon-8pm Sun; ☎) The baristas have won awards at this creative, third-wave coffeehouse that's a fab alternative to Veracruz's most traditional caffeine haunts. Its cold-brew coffee served in a cut glass with a giant ice cube made of frozen coffee is an inspired way to cool down on a sultry day. The salads and snack dishes are excellent, too.

Miraloco

BAR

(Independencia 816A; ⊘1:30pm-10pm) The food is OK at this cantina (opened in 2019), but we prefer it as place to have a drink and relax in retro-shabby chic surroundings. Occasionally on weekends they have live music.

Bar Prendes

BAR

(☑229-922-21-13; Lerdo de Tejada 1056; ⊘noon-1am) For a front-row seat for whatever's happening in the *zócalo* on any given night, look no further than Prendes; it occupies a prize slice of real estate under the *portales*. The food served here comes courtesy of the Mariscos Villa Rica group.

☆ Entertainment

Of course, there are always marimbas and mariachis on the *zócalo*. And the coastline boulevard is known as *la barra más grande del mundo* (the biggest bar in the world), *barra* referring both to the sandbar and the drinks bar. There is also a bona fide theater and some live-music venues.

Las Barricas

LIVE MUSIC

(☑229-931-18-86; www.facebook.com/Lasbarricas bar; Constitución 72; cover Sat & for live music M$50; ⊘1pm-4am Tue-Sat) This popular live-music venue and club plays a variety of music: salsa, pop, rock etc. Come late and expect it to be packed in with the raucous, jovial crowd, especially on weekends.

Teatro Principal Francisco Javier Clavijero

THEATER

(☑229-200-22-47; Emparán 166; ⊘hours vary) This theater has a long history and has had many incarnations. It moved here in 1819 and adopted its current architectural style (French neoclassical with some tremendous mosaics in the entrance lobby) in 1902. Plays, musicals and classical concerts are performed here.

🔒 Shopping

Avenida Independencia is the city's main shopping thoroughfare. Souvenirs, including bottles of vanilla and good-quality coffee, can be procured at the **Plaza de las Artesanías** (Insurgentes Veracruzanos s/n; ☺9am-10pm) and the market that lines the *malecón*. Jewelry – especially silver – is also economical and sometimes engraved with interesting indigenous motifs.

Mar Adentro   BOOKS
(☑229-375-11-90;   https://libreriamaradentro
.negocio.site; E Morales 524; ☺10am-10pm Mon-Sat;
☎) Top-quality bookshop with a small English section and many other titles, including antiquarian books, over two floors. Worth visiting for the lovely 18th-century building alone, which includes a cafe with seats in a peaceful courtyard.

🛈 Information

Most banks change US dollars, and some change euros as well. ATMs are generally widely available throughout the city. There's a cluster of banks with ATMs a block north of the *zócalo*, including both **Banco Santander** and **HSBC** on the corner of Avenidas Independencia and Juárez (both open 24 hours).

Hospital Beneficencia Española de Veracruz
(☑229-262-23-00; https://heveracruz.mx; Av 16 de Sepiembre 955; ☺24hr) Best hospital in the city, with general medical services.
Hospital Regional (☑229-932-11-71; Av 20 de Noviembre 1074; ☺24hr) General hospital.
Post Office (Marina Mercante 210; ☺9am-4pm Mon-Fri, to 1pm Sat) A five-minute walk north of the *zócalo*.
Tourist Office (☑229-200-20-00; http://veracruz.mx; Palacio Municipal, Lerdo; ☺8am-4pm Mon-Fri) Has helpful staff and plenty of maps and brochures.

🛈 Getting There & Away

AIR

Veracruz International Airport (VER; ☑229-934-90-08; www.asur.com.mx; Carr Veracruz–Xalapa Km 13.5) is 18km southwest of the center, near Hwy 140. There are flights to Cancún, Guadalajara and Monterrey with VivaAerobus (www.vivaaerobus.com), to Cuidad del Carmen, Tampico and Mérida with TAR Aerolíneas (https://tarmexico.com), Villahermosa with Aeromar (www.aeromar.com.mx), and frequent flights to Mexico City with Aeroméxico (www.aeromexico.com), Aeromar, Interjet (www.interjet.com.mx) and a number of international airlines. Volaris (www.volaris.com) and Interjet also fly to Guadalajara. Direct flights to/from Houston are offered by United (www.united.com).

BUSES FROM VERACRUZ CITY

Daily 1st-class ADO departures from Veracruz include the following:

DESTINATION	FARE (M$)	TIME (HR)	FREQUENCY (PER DAY)
Campeche	964-1248	12½-13	2 (6:45pm & 7pm)
Cancún	1278-1482	20	2 (1:15pm & 3:45pm)
Catemaco	240	4	7
Chetumal	1409	17¼	1 (4:45pm)
Córdoba	173-191	1½	frequent
Mérida	1118-1286	15½	2 (1:05pm & 3:15pm)
Mexico City	538-940	5½-7¼	frequent
Oaxaca	595-775	8	4
Orizaba	190-219	2½	frequent
Papantla	345	3¾	4
Puebla	438-598	3¾-5¼	frequent
San Andrés Tuxtla	227	3¼	frequent
San Cristóbal de las Casas	1131-1338	9	2 (3:55pm & 10:55pm)
Santiago Tuxtla	223	2¾	10
Tuxpan	455-512	5½-6	frequent
Villahermosa	710	6½-8¾	frequent
Xalapa	140-184	2	frequent

BUS

Veracruz is a major hub, with good services up and down the coast and inland along the Córdoba–Puebla–Mexico City corridor. Buses to and from Mexico City can be heavily booked at holiday times.

The **bus station** (☑ 229-937-57-44; Av Díaz Mirón btwn Tuero Molina & Orizaba) is located 3km south of the *zócalo* and has ATMs. The 1st-class/deluxe area is in the part of the station closest to Calle Orizaba. For more frequent, slightly cheaper and slower 2nd-class services, enter on the other side from Avenida Lafragua. There's a 24-hour luggage room there.

CAR & MOTORCYCLE

Local and international car-rental agencies, such as Hertz (www.hertz.com) and Dollar (www.dollar.com) have desks at Veracruz airport. There are also some other agencies scattered around town. Rates start at M$400 per day.

❶ Getting Around

There's no bus service connecting the airport with Veracruz; official taxis cost M$250 to the *zócalo*: buy a ticket from a booth in the arrivals hall. Going the other way you *may* be able to find a taxi to take you for M$200 but be prepared to bargain.

To get downtown from the 1st-class bus station, take a bus marked 'Díaz Mirón y Madero' (M$9). It will head to Parque Zamora then up Avenida Madero. For the *zócalo*, get off on the corner of Avenida Madero and Lerdo de Tejada and turn right. Returning to the bus stations, pick up the same bus going south on Avenida 5 de Mayo. Booths in the 1st- and 2nd-class stations sell taxi tickets to the center (*zócalo* area; M$45 to M$50). In some hotels, such as the Gran Hotel Diligencias (p226), you can get a summary sheet of official taxi-ride costs, which is helpful for guarding against tourist price inflation.

Buses marked 'Mocambo-Boca del Río' (M$10 to Boca del Río) leave regularly from the corner of Avenida Zaragoza and Arista, near the *zócalo;* they go via Parque Zamora and Blvd Camacho to Playa Mocambo (20 minutes) and on to Boca del Río (30 minutes). AU buses also go there from the 2nd-class station.

CENTRAL VERACRUZ

From Veracruz, curvy Hwy 180 follows the coast past dark-sand beaches to the busy transportation hub of Cardel, where Hwy 140 branches west to Xalapa, the state capital, surrounded by coffee-growing highland villages and home to one of Mexico's best museums. Two of Mexico's white-water-rafting hubs, Tlapacoyan and Jalcomulco, lie north and south of Xalapa, respectively.

Just south of Veracruz, Hwy 150D heads southwest to Córdoba and Orizaba, on the edge of the Sierra Madre. Orizaba is a particularly appealing town, with Mexico's highest mountain looming beyond it.

Between Nautla and Veracruz, the coast is remarkably wild and unexplored, despite its weighty historical significance. The sleepy village of La Antigua (home to the atmospheric ruins of Casa de Cortés) and the impressive archaeological sites Cempoala and Quiahuiztlán are all worth a visit, and can easily be combined into a day trip from Veracruz.

La Antigua

☑ 296 / POP 988

The village of Veracruz's second incarnation (1525–99) and the second-oldest Spanish settlement in Mexico, La Antigua reveals little of its past identity with its languid grid of sleepy, cobbled streets and moss-covered ruins. It's a pleasant, soporific backwater these days, worth a detour for its historical significance and good seafood.

A Spanish settlement was established here in 1525, and it's rumored that this is where conquistador Cortés moored his boats to a **ceiba tree**. The tree – gnarly and gigantic – is still standing, not far from the pedestrian bridge spanning the Río Antigua.

La Anitgua's main site is **Casa de Cortés** (Venustiano Carranza; by donation; ⊙8:30am-4:30pm). All that's keeping up much of the ruined walls of this 16th-century stone building is a lattice of tree roots. Whether or not Cortés stayed here is unclear, but for certain it was used as a customs house. It's an atmospheric spot to explore – also check out the adjacent alley of **street art** including an image of La Malinche, Cortés' interpreter and concubine.

The compact whitewashed **La Ermita del Rosario** (cnr Av Independencia & Elodia Rosales) is believed to be the oldest church in Mexico. Parts of it date back to 1525, but the chapel was expanded to its present size in 1695. Look for the original glazed tiles studding the surrounding walls.

Lanchas will motor you along the pleasant Río Antigua for around M$100 per person, depending on how many people want to go.

On the waterfront, closest to a pedestrian suspension bridge, **Las Delicias Marinas** (☑296-971-60-38; www.lasdeliciasmarinas.com; mains M$130-255; ☺10:30am-7:30pm) is a long-established restaurant that specializes in fresh and saltwater fish and seafood. The charcoal-grilled seafood mix and the *camarones enchipotlados* (shrimp in chipotle sauce) are both excellent, as is the hearty *arroz a la tambada en pulpa*, a soupy stew of seafood and rice that's a Veracruz specialty. On Saturday and Sunday around 3pm there is a music and dance show.

Colectivo (shared) taxis charge M$10 or so from the village to the highway 1km away, where buses to Veracruz and Cardel pass every 15 minutes or so. Flag down the driver just north of the toll booth or just walk for 20 minutes from the highway.

Villa Rica

☑296

Standing in this tiny, dusty fishing village 69km north of Veracruz, it's hard to believe you're gazing at the site of the first European-founded settlement north of Panama in mainland America. These days the historic settlement hardly merits a label on most maps and there's little to show for Cortés' connection to the place.

Founded as Villa Rica de la Vera Cruz in 1519, the Spanish settlement here lasted only until 1524, when it was moved to present-day La Antigua. There's a small and attractive curved beach, and you can trace it around past some dunes and across an isthmus to the Cerro de la Cantera, a rocky outcrop famed for its plunging *quebraditas* (ravines). Weekends are most lively with visiting Veracruz residents.

◉ Sights

★**Quiahuiztlán**   ARCHAEOLOGICAL SITE
(http://sic.gob.mx; off Hwy 180; M$45; ☺8:30am-4pm) Perched like a mini–Machu Picchu on a plateau beneath a horn-shaped mountain, Quiahuiztlán is a pre-Hispanic Totonac town and necropolis. Enjoying a commanding view of the Gulf coast, the site has two pyramids, more than 70 tombs and some carved monuments.

Buses plying Hwy 180 drop you at the Quiahuiztlán turnoff, from where the site is reachable via a pleasant 3km walk up a winding paved road.

The inhabitants of Quiahuiztlán (Place of the Rains) were the only pre-Hispanic civilization to bury their dead in tombs resembling miniature temples. Counting 30,000 inhabitants at the time of Cortés' arrival in 1519, its history before that is sketchy, although there was certainly a settlement here by 800 CE.

A short trail leads up from the main plateau that overlooks the ocean to a higher site with four tombs. The adventurous can continue up from here along an unmarked trail towards the summit for unparalleled views of the coast and the greenery-clad valley, with buzzards circling overhead. Otherwise, follow the steps down from the main site to the remains of the ball court where Totonac teams played for the 'honor' to be sacrificed.

In spite of its lofty location, the settlement was subjugated first by the Toltec between 800 and 900 CE, and then by the Aztec around 1200. You can contemplate this amid nature and in solitude, as you're likely to have the place entirely to yourself.

⚡ Activities

★**EcoGuías La Mancha**   OUTDOORS
(☑296-100-11-63; www.ecoturismolamancha.com; La Mancha–Actopan, Carretera Federal Cardel–Nautla Km 31; kayak tours/horseback riding M$175/400) ✈ All hail this progressive local association for developing a grassroots environmental-education center. The facilities, 1km from the beach, offer interpretive walks, bird-watching excursions, horseback riding and kayak tours where you can see mangroves and wildlife. Follow the 'El Mangal' signs from the La Mancha eastbound turnoff on Hwy 180 for 1km. Bring insect repellent.

Accommodations are rustic (campsites with own tent M$80; nine-person thatched cabins with shared bathrooms per person/entire M$175/1575), but it's a great off-the-beaten-path choice that supports the local community. There's also a **cafe** here open 8am to 6pm.

🛏 Sleeping & Eating

Villas Arcon   HOTEL $$
(☑296-964-91-72; www.villasarcon.com; s/d M$700/950; P❄❄🛜🏊) At the northern entrance to Villa Rica, this bright orange, low-rise resort hotel sits amid immaculate grounds in the shade of trees and bamboo thickets. Spartan, clean rooms surround two pools, and it's a short walk through the village to the beach. The onsite restaurant

DON'T MISS

CEMPOALA

As Hernán Cortés approached the Totonac settlement of **Cempoala** (Morelos Oriente s/n; M$55; ⊙9am-6pm) in 1520, one of his scouts reported that the buildings were made of silver – but it was only white paint shining in the sun. Cempoala's chief, Xicomacatl – a corpulent fellow nicknamed *el cacique gordo* (the fat chief) by the Spanish – struck an alliance with Cortés for protection against the Aztec. But the chief's hospitality didn't stop the Spanish from smashing statues of his gods and lecturing his people on the virtues of Christianity. It was at Cempoala in 1520 that Cortés defeated the expedition sent by Cuba's Spanish governor to arrest him. A smallpox epidemic in 1575–77 decimated Cempoala and most of the survivors moved to Xalapa.

The archaeological remains of this Totonac town of around 30,000 people date to around 1200 CE and sit on the outskirts of modern-day **Zempoala**, reachable by frequent buses from Cardel (M$20). The temples and buildings at this quiet, grassy site have undergone extensive renovation works, and most are studded with smooth, rounded riverbed stones, though many were originally plastered and painted. Cempoala once had defensive walls, and underground water and drainage pipes, and human sacrifices were held in its temples.

As there is no labeling at the site itself, have a look inside the adjoining small **museum** first. Apart from interesting clay figurines, polychrome plates, obsidian flints and pottery used in ceremonies, there are photos and descriptions (in Spanish) of every major building on the site. Also, check out the clay figure of Xipe Totec – a deity in whose honor slaves and prisoners were sacrificed and skinned, with the skin then placed on ill people to cure them of their ailments.

Guides are available at the site to show you around but none have particularly fluent English; if that's what you need it's best to arrange a bilingual guide in Veracruz.

By the entrance, the **Templo del Muerte** (Temple of the Dead) once featured a tomb containing Mixtecachihuatl, the goddess of dead women. The **Templo Mayor** (Main Temple), uncovered in 1972, is an 11m-high pyramid with a wide staircase ascending to the remains of a shrine. When they first encountered Zempoala, Cortés and his men lodged in the **Templo de Las Chimeneas**, whose battlement-like teeth *(almenas)* were thought to be chimneys – hence the name. The circle of stones in the middle of the site is the **Círculo de los Guerreros**, where lone captured soldiers were made to fight against groups of local warriors. Few won.

There are two main structures on the west side. One is known as the **Templo del Sol** and has two stairways climbing its front in typical Toltec-Aztec style. The sun god was called Tonatiuh and sacrifices were offered to him here on the **Piedra de Sacrificios**. Xicomacatl sat facing the macabre spectacle on the appropriately large altar. To its north, the second structure is the **Templo de la Luna**, with a structure similar to Aztec temples to the wind god, Ehécatl. East of Las Chimeneas is **Las Caritas** (Little Faces), named for niches that once held several small pottery skulls, now displayed at the museum.

Another large temple to the wind god, known as the **Templo Dios del Aire**, is in the town itself – go back south on the site entrance road, cross the main road in town and then go around the corner to the right. The ancient temple, with its characteristic circular shape, is beside an intersection.

---

serves fish and seafood dishes, including excellent *camarones enchipotlados*.

Restaurant Miriam SEAFOOD **$**
(☏296-105-26-40; mains M$50-140; ⊙8am-6pm) Friendly Miriam and her extended family serve up delicious seafood dishes to order, in what is essentially an extension of their living room. Be warned, when she offers you her *picantísimo* (spiciest) dish, she's not kidding!

It's only a few steps from the beach where you'll find several other simple places for refreshments.

ⓘ Getting There & Away

Villa Rica is about 1km east of the main Hwy 180. Ask any bus driver on the Cardel–Nautla run to stop at the entrance road to the Quiahuiztlán ruins. From here it's an easy walk to the village.

Xalapa

📄 228 / POP 424,755 / ELEV 1417M

Familiar to the world primarily due to the super-hot green chili that was named after it, Xalapa (also spelled Jalapa, but always pronounced ha-*la*-pa) is actually about as different to the fiery jalapeño as can be. Unlike sweaty coastal Veracruz city, Xalapa's highland location makes it temperate and often quite cloudy. Thanks to its alternative vibe and large student population, the city is lively at night and has a thriving cultural scene.

Xalapa has an alluring center, full of well-kept parks, bustling pedestrian streets and colonial architecture. Don't miss the superb anthropological museum with its gargantuan pre-Hispanic relics, but also enjoy the city's galleries, funky bars, many bookstores and a superb array of quality coffee joints, making this one of Mexico's most enjoyable state capitals.

History

Founded by the Totonac in the early 1200s, Xalapa was part of the Aztec empire when Hernán Cortés and his men passed through in 1519. Because of its appealing climate and location, Spain strategically placed a monastery here to proselytize the indigenous population. By the 17th century it had evolved into a commercial axis and meeting hub. In 1824 it was made the state capital of Veracruz and today is a thriving commercial center for coffee, tobacco and flowers.

⊙ Sights

★ Museo de Antropología   MUSEUM
(📄 228-815-09-20; www.uv.mx/max; Av Xalapa s/n; adult/student M$55/30, audioguide M$55; ⊙ 9am-5pm Tue-Sun) Attached to spacious gardens, 4km northwest of the center, this remarkable museum contains Mexico's second-finest archaeological collection. The focus is on the main pre-Hispanic civilizations from the Gulf coast, principally the Olmec, the Totonac, the Huastec and Classic Veracruz, and the beautifully displayed artifacts are presented in chronological order in a series of interconnecting galleries that descend the side of a lush hill.

The exhibits' scale and breadth rival the museum's intricate layout. Standout exhibits include the world's largest collection of giant Olmec heads, a reconstruction of the

Las Higueras temple, jade masks, and the museum's most celebrated piece: the jade Olmec sculpture, *El señor de Las Limas*, from southern Veracruz. There are also dramatic stone representations of the main pre-Hispanic deities, namely Quetzalóatl (aka the Feathered Serpent), god of creation and knowledge; Tláloc, the bespectacled god of rain and fertility; Tlazoltéotl (aka the Eater of Filth), the patron deity of adulterers and goddess of carnal desire; and Xipe Totec, deity of life-death-rebirth, celebrated with the sacrifice of a slave and the priest wearing the flayed skin of the corpse. There is also an array of fine work associated with the pre-Hispanic ball game.

It has a small **cafe** on the upper floor and an excellent **bookstore**, while the walk back up the hill through the beautifully kept garden is a delight.

All information panels are in Spanish, but there is an excellent iPhone/audioguide in English (bring ID to leave as collateral).

If taking public transportation, hop on a 'Camacho-Tesorería' **bus** (Av Camacho; M$10) from Enríquez near Parque Juárez. To return, take a bus marked 'Centro.' A taxi costs M$35.

Parque Juárez   PLAZA
Xalapa's central main square doubles as a terrace, with its south side overlooking the valley below and, in clear weather, the snow-capped cone of Pico de Orizaba beckoning in the distance. Greener and better kept than most other plazas in Mexico, you'll find monkey puzzle trees and manicured hedges among the shoe-shiners, snack stalls, balloon sellers and wandering minstrels.

On its lower levels look for the gallery **El Ágora de la Ciudad** (📄 228-818-57-30; www.facebook.com/AgoraXalapa; Parque Juárez; ⊙ 9am-7pm Tue-Fri, 10am-9pm Sat & Sun) FREE, which also screens art-house movies; the giant mosaic sculpture of the plumed serpent **Quetzalcóatl** that doubles as a kids' climbing frame and slide; and the 1931 sculptures of the **Virtues**: strength, justice, prudence and temperance.

Palacio de Gobierno   NOTABLE BUILDING
(Map p234; Parque Juárez) Veracruz' state government occupies a palatial neoclassical building. On its north and east facades, under the arcades, are superb murals depicting historical events and people. Pop inside to see the murals above the stairways of both entrances painted by Mario Orozco Rivera (1930–98).

VERACRUZ XALAPA

Xalapa

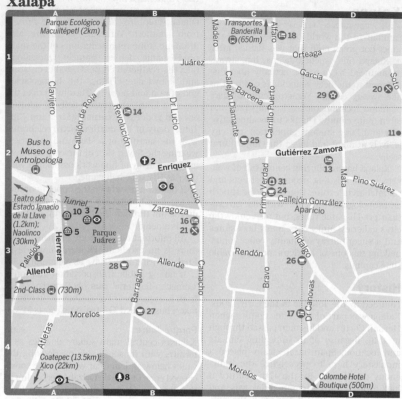

Catedral Metropolitana CATHEDRAL
(☑228-817-36-40; www.arquidiocesisdexalapa.
com; cnr Enríquez & Revolución; ☺8am-6pm) A
mélange of neo-Gothic and baroque, Xalapa's cathedral lacks a second tower but
still impresses with its scale and grandiosity.
The architecture makes full use of the steep
hillside location to inspire awe as you enter,
forcing you to raise your head to see the altar and giant crucifix centerpiece.

The church contains the remains of St
Rafael Guízar y Valencia, beatified by Pope
John Paul II in 1995.

Galería de Arte Contemporáneo GALLERY
(☑228-817-03-86; http://gacxalapa.blogspot.com;
Xalapeños Ilustres 135; ☺10am-9pm Tue-Sun) FREE
Xalapa has several contemporary art galleries
and this one, in a renovated colonial building
1km east of the center, shows an interesting
range of temporary exhibitions by local artists. Also here is a small movie theater that
screens art-house films for free.

Parque Paseo de los Lagos PARK
(Zona Universitaria) 🏊 *Xalapeños* escape
the monstrous traffic just south of Parque
Juárez in this serendipitous park, which has
3km of delightful lakeside paths, most commonly used for jogging (and making out).

At its northern, **Casa de Lago** (☑228-817-
28-83; www.uv.mx/cluv; Paseo de los Lagos s/n;
☺11am-3pm Sat & Sun) FREE is the cultural
center of Universidad Veracruzana – there are
often free concerts and events in the evenings
as well as exhibitions at the weekend.

Pinacoteca Diego Rivera GALLERY
(☑228-818-18-19; www.facebook.com/Pinacoteca
DiegoRivera.IVEC; Herrera 5; ☺10am-7pm Tue-Sat)
FREE This small gallery houses a modest
collection of Rivera's works, and also exhibits
paintings by other Mexican artists.

Parque Ecológico Macuiltépetl PARK
(☑228-132-89-04; http://macuiltepetl.org; off
García Barna; museum adult/child M$18/9, observa-
tion platform M$4; ☺5am-7pm) Atop a hill north

Xalapa

of the city, this 40-hectare park is actually the heavily wooded cap of an extinct volcano. Spiraling to the top, the park's paths are a treasure for the city's robust fraternity of joggers, and provide expansive views of Xalapa and the surrounding area.

The park includes a small **botanical museum** and an **observation platform** both open 10am to 6pm.

Museo Casa de Xalapa   MUSEUM
(☎228-841-98-02; Herrera 7; ⊙10am-7pm Tue-Sun) FREE For a quick exposé of Xalapan history, head to this museum in an old colonial house close to Parque Juárez. Exhibits (in Spanish) run the gamut from prehistory to the growth and urbanization of Xalapa, the city's culture and commerce, and a replica *xalapeño* kitchen.

Parroquia de San José   CHURCH
(Alcalde y García 4) Xalapa's oldest church was founded back in 1535, with the current building completed in 1770. Architecturally, it displays an unusual blend of baroque and Mudejar styles, including some horseshoe arches. Your best chance of finding it open is to head here during services on Sunday.

🏃 Activities & Courses

Local tour operators offer cultural trips to the outlying *pueblos mágicos* (magical villages) of Xico, Coatepec and Naolinco, as well as archaeological sites, and also provide easygoing, sports-oriented outdoor excursions such as hiking, rafting and rappeling.

WORTH A TRIP

DAY TRIPS FROM XALAPA

Twelve kilometres southeast of Xalapa just off the Veracruz highway is **Museo Ex-Hacienda El Lencero** (☎228-820-02-70; off Carretera Xalapa-Veracruz Km 10; adult/child M$40/30; ☺10am-5pm Tue-Sun). Almost as old as New Spain itself, this former posada was initiated in 1525 by Juan Lencero, a soldier loyal to Hernán Cortés, and served as a resting place for travelers toiling between a newly Europeanized Mexico City and the coast. Now a museum, it incorporates a superbly restored house furnished with antiques, a chapel and some delightful gardens with a small lake and a 500-year-old fig tree. Catch one of the regular 'Miradores' buses (M$10) from Xalapa's Plaza Cristal shopping center; the museum is a 10-minute walk from the highway.

Also with a history stretching over 500 years is the pretty *pueblo mágico* of **Naolinco** (http://naolinco.emunicipios.gob.mx/; Hwy 65), 33km drive north of the Xalapa. Its *artesanos* (craftspeople) are renowned for their leatherwork and for making colorful masks used during various celebrations. This is also one of the more atmospheric places to see the Día de los Muertos celebrations in Veracruz. Take a bus (M$30, 1¼ hours) from **Transportes Banderilla** (☎228-818-64-46; Pípila 65).

Robert Straub   BIRD-WATCHING
(☎228-818-18-94; http://wildsidenaturetours.com/leaders/robert-straub) Local bird-watching guide Robert Straub, a member of COAX (a conservation-minded bird-watching club), offers tours in the area or can hook up birders with experienced local guides if he is busy. Straub authored a bird-watching guide to Veracruz, *Guía de sitios* – proceeds go to Pronatura, a conservation nonprofit.

Aventura en Veracruz   CULTURAL
(☎228-979-26-16; www.facebook.com/aventuraver) English-speaking and experienced guide Armando Lobato can arrange tours of Xalapa and surroundings, from cultural jaunts to Naolinco to coffee tours of Coatepec's *fincas* (coffee farms) and rafting excursions to Jalcomulco.

Veraventuras   ADVENTURE SPORTS
(☎228-818-97-79; www.veraventuras.com; Degollado 83; ☺9am-7pm) Offers rafting excursions, camping trips and many other activities, including trips to the El Carrizal hot springs, 49km southeast of Xalapa.

**Escuela para
Estudiantes Extranjeros**   LANGUAGE
(School for Foreign Students; ☎228-817-86-87; www.uv.mx/eee; Gutiérrez Zamora 25; 7-week courses from M$2900, plus registration fee US$300) The Universidad Veracruzana offers short-term, accredited programs on the Spanish and Náhuatl languages and on Mexican culture and history. Most students choose to stay in one of the homestay programs organized by the university.

🛏 Sleeping

Xalapa is blessed with some charming places to stay, such as several centrally located hotels inside centuries-old colonial mansions. There's also a bona fide hostel. Prices are reasonable.

★**Posada del Cafeto**   HISTORIC HOTEL **$**
(☎228-817-00-23; www.pradodelrio.com; Dr Canovas 8; s/d/ste M$590/690/890; ❄🐾🛜) This appealing posada offers Xalapa's best combination of value and traditional Mexican character. It's centrally located, but on a quiet side street. The dual inner patios with their finely sculpted stairways, arches and plenty of greenery create a 'secret garden' feel. Rooms are spacious, individually decorated and very comfortable. Breakfast is served in a cute onsite cafe.

★**Posada La Mariquinta**   GUESTHOUSE **$**
(☎228-818-11-58; www.posadalamariquinta.com; Alfaro 12; s/d/ste M$580/735/1400; 🐾🛜) Set in an 18th-century colonial residence, this guesthouse is built like a fortress. Inside, tranquility reigns. The airy, individually decorated rooms are arranged around a lush flower-filled garden. Service is friendly and art, antiques and general curiosities can be found in the fabulous library-cum-reception room.

Mesón del Alférez Xalapa   HISTORIC HOTEL **$**
(☎228-818-01-13; www.pradodelrio.com; Camacho 2; r/ste M$790/990; ❄🛜) This classy, 19th-century colonial mansion is a partial retreat from the roaring traffic outside (the rooms don't quite block out the noise). It

offers beautiful split-level rooms (beds upstairs, living room below), heavy wooden beams, flower-filled greenery and the best breakfast in town (guests get 10% off the bill) in its refined La Candela restaurant.

Majova Inn
BUSINESS HOTEL $

(☑228-818-18-66; www.hotelmajovainn.com; Zamora 80; s/d/tr from M$500/600/700; P✳🖙) A study in creams and browns, with welcome splashes of color, Majova is slick and modern if a little antiseptic. Tiled rooms are as neat as a pin, all with cable TV and contemporary bathrooms. The hotel is comfortable, clean, central and comes with its own parking – a boon for motorists.

Hostal de la Niebla
HOSTEL $

(☑228-817-21-74; www.facebook.com/hostal.dela niebla; Zamora 24; dm/r with shared bathroom incl breakfast M$160/380; P🖙) This modern hostel is no half-baked nod to the backpacker market. Rather, it's a spotless, well-organized place featuring airy rooms with decks and terraces. There's access to lockers and a kitchen. Accommodations are in either six-bed dorms or large private rooms.

Hotel Limón
HOTEL $

(☑228-817-22-04; Revolución 8; s/d M$230/290; 🖙) The term 'musty jewel' could have been invented with this 1894-vintage hotel in mind. The 'musty' part refers to the dark rooms on the ground floor, with high ceilings and fans but no windows. The 'jewel' is the patterned-tiled courtyard. An economical option for the unfussy, it's also very central.

Colombe Hotel Boutique
BOUTIQUE HOTEL $$

(☑228-817-57-30; www.colombehotel.com; Calle Vista Hermosa 16; s/d incl breakfast from M$1026/1152; P✳🖙🖙) A short way out of the city center, this small hotel has 13 rooms that all differ from one another and range from the Río, which is a bit like sleeping inside a technicolor rainbow, to the mellow tones of the Aqua room and the local-flavored Suite México. A stylish restaurant and cocktail bar and helpful staff are among the perks.

✖ Eating

Stylish cafes and restaurants abound in Xalapa, many offering interesting regional menus and vegetarian choices. Many are centrally located, but a few fine dining options require a taxi ride. One local specialty worth trying is *chiles rellenos* (stuffed chili).

Verde Raiz
VEGAN $

(☑228-200-16-31; www.facebook.com/verderaiz xalapa; Leño 28; mains M$50-90; ⊙9:30am-6pm Mon-Sat; 🖙🖉) 🍃 Raw food and tofu tacos have arrived in Xalapa and have become hugely popular with the resident student population. Get here early to grab one of the three tiny tables and tuck into a bowl of muesli, some *chilaquiles* (fried tortilla strips with salsa and fresh cheese) or one of its celebrated smoothies or juices.

Postodoro
ITALIAN $

(☑228-841-20-00; www.postodoro.com; Primo Verdad 11; mains M$39-112; ⊙9-12:30am Sun-Thu, until 1:30pm Fri & Sat; 🖙) With its cheery yellow walls, appealing courtyard dining space lit with fairy lights and comfy leather booths, this place has won itself many local fans. The pasta dishes and thin crust pizzas are nicely executed, portions are ample, and inexpensive sangria and wine flow generously.

Siwapan
MEXICAN $

(☑228-409-70-93; Soto 17; mains M$25-140; ⊙8am-5pm Wed-Mon; 🖙) With its low prices, leafy murals and tasty slow-cooked food it's no wonder this laid-back place is a hit with Xalapa's student population. Try out the *memelas*, which are essentially a larger version of a taco and come with a variety of toppings.

★El Brou
MEDITERRANEAN $$

(☑228-165-49-94; www.facebook.com/elbrou restaurante; Soto 13; mains M$98-258; ⊙9am-5:30pm; 🖙🖉) Housed in a delightful high-ceilinged colonial lounge, El Brou gets it right on all counts. The varied menu offers a delicious and arty take on Mediterranean, Lebanese and Mexican cuisine, and the modern touches to its traditional decor give it a chic look and feel. Settle in for a memorable meal of tuna tartare, tabbouleh and Greek-style moussaka.

★La Candela
BREAKFAST $$

(☑228-818-01-13; www.pradodelrio.com; Camacho 2; mains M$85-170; ⊙7:30am-4:30pm Mon-Sat, from 8am Sun; 🖙) This brightly decorated place attracts a crowd of loyal regulars who come for the inventive Mexican cuisine and great steaks at lunchtime, but it's the breakfasts, which are accepted by nearly all *xalapeños* as being the best in town, that really please hungry tummies.

It's downstairs from Mesón del Alférez Xalapa,

VERACRUZ XALAPA

El Itacate
MEXICAN $$

(☑228-690-87-08; www.facebook.com/elitacate fonda; Soto 4; mains M$75-180; ☺7am-5pm; 👪) Big colorful murals of beloved Mexican celebrities, including María Félix, Augustín Lara and Pedro Infante, cover the walls of this eminently popular spot. Ladies make tortillas from scratch at the door where some of the recommended dishes of the day are displayed. It's also family-friendly with a kids' menu and a playroom upstairs.

Vinissimo
INTERNATIONAL $$$

(☑228-812-91-13; Av Araucarias 501; mains M$130-280; ☺2pm-midnight Mon-Sat; 📶) Elegant, but certainly not pretentious, Vinissimo offers imaginative dishes made from fresh market produce. The often-changing menu takes its risottos and pastas from Italy, and seafood flavors from the wild coastline of Spanish Galicia. It has a comprehensive wine and cocktail list and service is attentive. It's a 10-minute cab ride east of the center.

🍷 Drinking & Nightlife

Xalapa has numerous cafes serving excellent highland coffee harvested from surrounding estates. Being a university town, it also has a vivacious nightlife. The loudest buzz can be found in Callejón González Aparicio, between Primo Verdad and Mata, an alley stacked with late-night bars and clubs with little to choose between them.

★Flor Catorce
CAFE

(www.facebook.com/florcatorcemx; Morelos 1; 228-812-08-27; ☺8am-11pm Mon-Sat) Flor Catorce is one of Xalapa's top social hubs. It combines an artisan coffeehouse, with the intimate live-music venue **Cauz**, which also doubles as a fine **bookshop**. Surrounded by the quirky surreal art of Gerardo Vargas (his prints are for sale), you can sip excellent local coffee, Mexican craft beers and 10 types of mezcal.

Caferencial
COFFEE

(☑228-153-50-73; Hidalgo 10; ☺10am-2pm & 4-8pm; 📶) We love the stripped-back simplicity of this third-wave coffee bar serving brews with tasting notes and five types of preparation method. The tiled floors are gorgeous and there's a small **art gallery**.

Reformanda
COFFEE

(☑228 818 96-83; www.reformandabarracafe.com; Allende 23; ☺8am-10pm Mon-Fri, 9am-1pm Sat; 📶) They roast their own coffee beans at this slick, multilevel cafe. It has a great roof terrace providing views of the town while you sip your espresso or savour one of their many other specialty caffeinated brews.

Café Cali
CAFE

(☑228-818-13-39; www.cafecali.com.mx; Callejón Diamante 23A; ☺9am-10pm Mon-Sat, 10am-7pm Sun) The enticing smell of roasting coffee beans wafts down the alleyway and seems to envelop the entire block surrounding Café Cali. The interior of the cafe is classic bohemia, and the range of coffees is pure caffeine-drenched bliss.

Angelo Casa de Té
CAFE

(☑228-841-08-39; Primo Verdad 21A; tea from M$15; ☺8am-9pm Mon-Sat) A pleasant change of scene in coffee-centric Xalapa. The shelves at this cute little place are lined with tins of different kinds of tea, the walls are adorned with pictures of tea-pickers and fields the world over, and it has good chocolate and homemade cookies to tuck into.

☆ Entertainment

Xalapa has a lively cultural life, with entertainment and events running the gamut from poetry slams to theater. For full details of what's on, consult https://ayuntamiento.xalapa.gob.mx/web/tucartelera.

Centro Recreativo Xalapeño
ARTS CENTER

(☑228-195-82-24; www.facebook.com/xalapare creativa; Xalapeños Ilustres 31; ☺8am-8pm) This cultural center in an attractive 19th-century colonial building packs in plenty of offerings, including jam sessions, dance classes, art expos, and art-house movie screenings; check out the Facebook page for upcoming events.

Tierra Luna
PERFORMING ARTS

(☑228-812-13-01; http://tierraluna.com.mx; Rayón 18; ☺9am-10pm Mon-Sat; 📶) A sanctuary for arty types, the historic high-ceilinged Tierra Luna provides a changing roster of poetry readings, theater performances and music gigs. It also serves tasty cafe fare, including a breakfast menu and a range of alcoholic drinks. It has a small **bookstore**, too.

Teatro del Estado Ignacio de la Llave
THEATER

(☑228-818-43-52; www.facebook.com/teatrode lestado.ivec; Ignacio de la Llave 2; ☺from 8pm) The impressive state theater hosts both the **Orquesta Sinfónica de Xalapa** and the **Ballet Folklórico** of the Universidad Veracruzana. It is situated 1.5km northwest of Parque Juárez, up Avenida Ávila Camacho.

🔒 Shopping

An epicenter of Xalapa's alternative culture is Callejón Diamante, an alley lined with boutiques and street vendors selling cheap jewelry, incense and paraphernalia. Bookstores line Xalapeños Ilustres.

Café Colón　　　　　　　　　　COFFEE
(☑ 228-817-60-97; Primo Verdad 15; ☺ 9am-8pm Mon-Sat, 10am-1pm Sun) 🍴 Old-school coffee roasters will grind Coatepec's best in front of your eyes in this aromatic store. It sells for around M$180 per kilogram.

Mercado Alcalde y García　　　MARKET
(Justo Sierra; ☺ 6am-8pm) This attractive old market building houses a handful of stalls selling the region's famous flowers alongside the usual fruit and veg and other household items. The cooked food stalls here are also a good place for a cheap meal and there are some cool bars beneath the main hall.

ℹ️ Information

There are banks with 24-hour ATMs along Enríquez and Gutiérrez Zamora.
Centro de Especialidades Médicas (☑ 228-814-45-00; www.cemev.gob.mx; Ruíz Cortines 2903; ☺ 24hr) Medical care around the clock.
Post Office (cnr Gutiérrez Zamora & Leño; ☺ 9am-5pm Mon-Fri, to 2pm Sat)
Tourism Xalapa (☑ 229-820-37-14; http://visitaxalapa.com; Palacios 9; ☺ 9am-8pm) Main tourist office: there are also several booths around town including one at the bus station.

ℹ️ Getting There & Away

Xalapa is a transportation hub with excellent connections throughout the state and beyond.

BUS
Xalapa's modern and well-organized bus station, the **Central de Autobuses de Xalapa** (CAXA; ☑ 228-842-25-00; Av 20 de Noviembre 271), is 2km east of the center. **Second-class buses** (1º de Mayo, Mercado Los Sauces) for Xico and Coatepec regularly leave from the southern side of Mercado Los Sauces, about 1km west of the center.

Buses to Jalcomulco leave from the **Azteca bus station** (☑ 228-818-74-56; Carranza 66), 2km north of the center.

CAR & MOTORCYCLE
Xalapa is notorious for its traffic-choked streets, and driving here is a challenge; just negotiating the sprawling suburbs to find the center can be difficult as signage is poor.

Hwy 140 to Puebla is narrow and winding until Perote; the Xalapa–Veracruz highway is very fast and smooth. Going to the northern Gulf coast, it's quickest to go to Cardel, then north on Hwy 180.

There are numerous parking lots in the center (around M$17 per hour).

ℹ️ Getting Around

For buses from CAXA to the center, follow signs to the taxi stand, then continue downhill to the main Avenida 20 de Noviembre. The bus stop is to your right. Any bus marked 'Centro' will pass within a block or two of Parque Juárez (M$10).

For a taxi to the center, you have to buy a ticket in the bus station (M$45).

To return to the bus station, take the 'Camacho-CAXA-SEC' bus from Avenida Ávila Camacho or Hidalgo. Taxi rides across Xalapa cost M$30 to M$40, depending on the distance.

BUSES FROM XALAPA

Daily ADO and AU services from CAXA.
　Destinations also served include Acayucan, Campeche, Cancún, Catemaco and Mérida.

DESTINATION	COST (M$)	TIME (HR)	FREQUENCY (PER DAY)
Cardel	98-116	1	frequent
Córdoba	278	3	18
Mexico City (TAPO)	390-534	4¼-4¾	frequent
Orizaba	300	4	18
Papantla	367	4-4½	16
Puebla	276-355	2½-3	frequent
Veracruz	140-252	2	frequent
Villahermosa	849-1244	8¼-9	6

Coatepec

📞 228 / POP 86.696 / ELEV 1200M

Waking up and smelling the coffee has rarely been this epiphanic. Cradled in the Sierra Madre foothills, Coatepec's coffee production has long been its raison d'être, a fact that will become instantly clear as soon as you step off the bus and inhale. The settlement dates from 1701 and coffee has been grown in the surrounding cloud forests for almost as long. The crop has brought wealth to the town; Coatepec – which lies a mere 15km south of Xalapa – is adorned with rich, gaudily painted colonial buildings. One of Mexico's *pueblos mágicos*, it makes a laid-back alternative to nearby Xalapa.

🔾 Sights & Activities

★ Museo El Café-tal Apan   MUSEUM

(📞 228-816-61-85; www.elcafe-tal.com; Carretera Coatepec–Las Trancas Km 4, El Grande; M$40; ⊘ 9am-5pm) 🅿 If you want to learn about the history of coffee in the region, visit this excellent museum, which displays antique coffee-making tools alongside modern machinery. There are hands-on demonstrations showing how coffee is grown, washed, sorted and roasted, and also coffee tastings. Purchase your coffee beans, coffee and *chipotle* salsa and other caffeinated goodies here. It's a bit out of town; a taxi will cost around M$45.

Basílica Menor de
Nuestra Señora de Guadalupe   CHURCH

(cnr Aldama & Hidalgo) This salmon-pink neo-Gothic beauty of a church was completed in 1853. If you think the exterior is pretty jazzy, wait until you go inside where the wall paintings by Coatepecan master Gregorio Sosa are off the scale.

Cascada Bola de Oro   WATERFALL

(Camino a Chopantla s/n) FREE For a pleasant nature walk aim for this waterfall about 5km north of central Coatepec. Follow Calle 5 de Mayo north to a bridge, continue north on Calle Prieto and then turn left into Calle Altamirano. After passing the last shop, hang a right, cross a bridge and turn left onto a path. The tourist office dispenses useful maps.

Museo de la Orquídea   GARDENS

(📞 228-304-08-53; www.facebook.com/Museo delaOrquidea; Aldama 20; M$40; ⊘ 10am-5pm Tue-Sun) A 40-year labor of love by the late botanist Dr Contreras Juárez, this orchid garden features 5584 species of orchids from around the world, including 1274 of Mexico's indigenous species, some of which are so minuscule that they can only be properly appreciated with a magnifying glass. A guided tour shows off some of the beauties.

Cerro de las Culebras   VIEWPOINT

(off Independencia; ⊘ 24hr) Cerro de las Culebras (Snake Hill; Coatepec in the Náhuatl language) is easily accessible from the town center. The walk takes you up cobbled steps to a lookout tower with a white statue of Christ on top. From here there are magnificent city and mountain views (it's best to go in the morning).

Parque Miguel Hidalgo   PLAZA

At the center of Coatepec's lush green main square stands a *glorieta* (bandstand), which doubles as a cafe. Set back from the road on the eastern side is the unashamedly baroque **Parroquia de San Jerónimo**, named after the city's patron saint.

✫✫ Festivals & Events

Fiesta de San Jerónimo   CULTURAL

(⊘ late Sept) Held at various venues across town, this week-long festival includes music, dance and art exhibitions all in celebration of the local patron saint, San Jerónimo.

🛏 Sleeping

Ashram Coatepec   HOSTEL $

(📞 228-816-10-55; www.ashramdecoatepec.org; Mina 100; dm or campsite M$120; 🅿 ⊖) On the outskirts of town, this ashram has yoga, meditation and walking trails through its lush grounds. The dorms are basic and all food served here is vegetarian.

Hotel Boutique Casabella   BOUTIQUE HOTEL $$

(📞 228-186-09-64; www.hotelcasabellacoatepec. com.mx; Calle 16 de Septiembre 33; r from M$980; 🅿 🛜) With its split-level rooms clustered around two greenery-filled courtyards, this historic hotel has plenty of charming features: a bona fide well in the central courtyard, heavy wooden beams and antique coffee presses scattered about. This blends seamlessly with contemporary creature comforts: good beds, cable TV and rain showers.

Hotel Mesón del
Alférez Coatepec   BOUTIQUE HOTEL $$

(📞 228-816-67-44; www.pradodelrio.com; Jiménez del Campillo 47; d/ste incl breakfast M$930/1190; 🅿 ⊖ ❄ 🛜) Behind the mustard-yellow walls of this historical town house lies a courtyard with a fountain and a jungle of flowers, surrounded by a horseshoe of split-level rooms filled with heavy timber furnishings, polished floors, wood beam ceilings and colonial accents. It's a gorgeous place to stay and has helpful staff.

Casa Real del Café HISTORIC HOTEL $$
(☑ 228-816-63-17; www.casarealdelcafe.com; Gutiérrez Zamora 58; r incl breakfast from M$960; P ❀ 🛜) This colonial-style hotel is owned by local coffee farmers whose aromatic products fortuitously find their way into the onsite **Antiguo Beneficio** cafe. It has a variety of appealing rooms including some split-level ones; we found the showers lacked pressure, though. There's a communal courtyard to relax in and a small spa for treatments on the top floor.

★**Posada Coatepec** HISTORIC HOTEL $$$
(☑ 228-816-05-44; www.posadacoatepec. mx; Hidalgo 9; d/ste incl breakfast M$1307/2000; P ❀ 🛜 🏊) Coatepec's hallmark hotel oozes character. The resplendent colonial-era building has an atmospheric central courtyard overflowing with plants and features a gurgling fountain. It boasts a pool, exhibits from local artists, tranquil gardens, an antique coach and even a stuffed lion! Rooms are spacious and individually decorated, with beautifully tiled bathrooms.

✖ Eating

Chéjere MEXICAN $
(☑ 228-202-66-05; www.facebook.com/Chejerecafe; Jiménez del Campillo 37; mains M$35-125; ☉ 9am-10pm) There's a good-value daily set lunch (M$60) served at this characterful, colorfully decorated spot. It's also decent for snacks and light meals such as tacos and sandwiches.

★**Casa Bonilla** MEXICAN $$
(☑ 228-816-00-09; www.facebook.com/casa.bonilla; cnr Juárez & Cuauhtémoc; mains M$100-385; ☉ 8am-8pm; 🛜) Claiming to be the 'most famous corner in Coatepec,' Casa Bonilla has been in business since 1939 and certainly knows what it's doing when it comes to food and drink. It's best known for its seafood dishes but it also serves a variety of craft beers (including its own brews on tap) and a whopping 350 different mezcals.

The attached **shop** sells coffee, craft beer, mezcal and other souvenirs.

Finca Andrade MEXICAN $$
(☑ 228-816-48-87; Lerdo 5; mains M$99-205; ☉ 7:30am-9pm; 🛜) This large, colorful restaurant is renowned for its smoky, flavorful *chilpochole de camarón* (chili-laden shrimp soup), as well as chicken with the restaurant's secret *mole* recipe and a variety of tasty *antojitos* – both are delicious.

🍷 Drinking

★**El Café de Avelino** CAFE
(☑ 228-180-95-77; www.facebook.com/elcafede avelino; Rebolledo 21; ☉ 2-9pm) Some of the best coffee in Coatepec comes from a cafe with two tables and four chairs (five if you count the owner's). Owner Avelino Hernández – known locally as the *Poeta del café* (coffee poet) – brews minor miracles from his Coatepec, Cosailton, Xico and Teocelo brands.

M Cafe COFFEE
(☑ 228-838-91-41; http://mcafe.mx; Constitución 6; ☉ 8am-10pm; 🛜) Although this coffee-roasting and -brewing operation has more contemporary design to its drinking areas than other Coatepec cafes, the shop front is designed like an old-time pharmacy. They sell pastries to go with the drinks and have a **gift shop** selling coffee souvenirs, too.

Casú CAFE
(La Casa del Café; ☑ 228-202-04-41; www.facebook. com/cafecasucoatepec; Calle 5 de Mayo 11; ☉ 9am-9pm; 🛜) A charming cafe run by a friendly team of coffee roasters who serve up their delicious wares (think fantastic coffee and mouthwatering cakes) in a lovely back garden space a short distance from the main square.

🛍 Shopping

Coatepec is *the* place to stock up on gourmet coffee, which is sold in many cafes and shops. A couple of good central spots to browse for souvenirs are **Plazuela El Zaguán** (Lerdo 3; ☉ 9am-8pm) and **Plaza Los Azulejos** (www.facebook.com/coatepecplaza losazulejos; De Aldama 4; ☉ 9:30am-9pm).

Enriqueta COFFEE
(☑ 228-816-86-59; www.facebook.com/enriqueta mx; Rebolledo 11; ☉ 9am-8pm) At one of the better coffee shops in town, the heady brew can be purchased as beans or ground – fine, extra fine and coarse. For 500g you'll pay around M$90. They also sell teas, coffee-flavoured sweets and other edible treats.

ℹ Information

Tourist Office (☑ 228-203-90-58; http:// somoscoatepec.com; cnr Rebolledo & Arteaga, Palacio Municipal s/n; ☉ 8am-6pm Mon-Fri, 11am-7pm Sat & Sun) A helpful office in the Palacio Municipal on Parque Hidalgo.

❶ Getting There & Away

Second-class buses (M$10) connect with Xalapa's Mercado Los Sauces terminal, or a taxi is M$120. Buses for Xico (M$10) leave from along Juárez. The ADO **bus station** (📞228-816-96-19; Trinidad Plaza, Río Sordo s/n; ☺9-12:30am Mon-Fri, until 9pm Sat) serves only Mexico City direct (M$535, five hours, 12:30am) but you can book tickets here for destinations out of Xalapa.

Xico

📞228 / POP 18,652 / ELEV 1297M

Quiet and hilly Xico is a small, beguiling town that's one of Mexico's government-sanctioned *pueblos mágicos*. Just 8km from Coatepec, Xico attracts devotees of *mole* and handicrafts rather than coffee. It has several quirky museums, cobbled streets and varied colonial architecture – all making it a popular weekend retreat. Exuberant masked and costumed dances are a vital part of Xico's many fiestas, and within Mexico the town is best known for its annual Fiesta de Santa Magdalena, held each July and famous for a running of the bulls à la Pamplona in Spain.

◉ Sights

★**Cascada de Texolo** WATERFALL

(off Camino a la Cascada; ☺24hr) FREE From Xico, it's a pleasant, signposted 3km walk (or short drive along a potholed road) to the spectacular, plunging, 80m Cascada de Texolo. From the viewpoint, cross the bridge. A five-minute walk leads to the **Cascada de la Monja**, featured in the film *Romancing the Stone* (1984); said 'stone' was hidden behind it. The main trail continues up to a viewpoint restaurant; take the steep Sendero de Ocelot path (M$10) down for an up-close look at Cascada de Texolo.

Though some locals swim in the Cascada de la Monja, à la Kathleen Turner and Michael Douglas, the current is strong, so you take your safety into your own hands.

Museo del Danzante Xiqueño MUSEUM

(📞228-129-66-97; Av Hidalgo 76; M$10; ☺10am-6pm Tue-Fri) FREE This excellent, colorful museum is devoted to the centuries-old history of Xico's costumed dances that take pride of place during the town's celebrations dedicated to its patron saint. The mask-carving tradition is also explained, as is the role of each masked character – the bull, the clown, the *negro separado* – in each dance. All signs are in Spanish.

Café Pepe PLANTATION

(📞228-855-09-70; Miguel Hidalgo 2; tours M$60; ☺10am-7pm) 🖉 This small plantation, which produces almost-organic, shade-grown coffee, offers tours (call ahead) and sells delicious coffee and liquors.

Casa Museo Totomoxtle MUSEUM

(cnr Aldama & Juárez; donation M$10; ☺8am-9pm) FREE Basically a room in a house, come here to view the Xico craft of making intricate and detailed figures from *hojas de maíz* (corn leaves): the dolls in various settings – coffee plantation, dance celebration – are charming. Only in Xico! Opening hours can be flexible.

Museo del Vestido de Santa María Magdalena MUSEUM

(Parroquia de Santa María Magdalena, Av Hidalgo s/n; M$5; ☺4-7pm Tue-Fri, 11am-6pm Sat & Sun) Go through Xico's main church to the courtyard behind to find this esoteric, niche display of St María Magdalena's past festival dresses – hundreds of them! – dating from 1910.

✸ Festivals & Events

★**Fiesta de Santa Magdalena** RELIGIOUS

(Parroquia de Santa María Magdalena, Av Hidalgo; ☺Jul 15-24) The mother of all festivals involving exuberant costumed dances, processions and more. The Magdalena statue in the Parroquia de Santa María Magdalena is clothed in a different elaborate dress each day for 30 days around the fiesta. A running of the bulls takes place through the streets on July 22.

Gigantic floral arches are raised, and streets are artistically decorated with carpets of colored sawdust in preparation for the saint's procession.

🛏 Sleeping

Hotel Coyopolan HOTEL $

(📞228-813-12-66; Venustiano Carranza Sur s/n; s/d incl breakfast from M$450/585; 🅿☺🖃) It's all about bright colors and lively Mexican design at this OK place down beside the river, south of the town center. There's the pleasant **La Molienda** restaurant and the staff can help arrange hiking, canyoning and rappeling in the surrounding mountains and canyons. Some rooms are windowless but open out onto balconies.

Posada los Naranjos HOTEL $

(📞228-153-54-54; Av Hidalgo 193; r from M$400; 🅿🖃) Right in the center of town, this no-frills place is a will-do-for-a-night budget option.

Rooms have high ceilings and, though clean, are windowless and sometimes musty. It's a short amble down Xico's main street from the church and there's a coffee roasters out the front.

The dawn chorus of the church bells is either a boon or a bane, depending on your outlook.

⭐ **Las Magdalenas**   BOUTIQUE HOTEL **$$**
(☑228-813-03-14; https://lasmagdalenas.com; Hidalgo 123; r incl breakfast from M$1390; P 🛜) This gorgeous colonial house has been impressively transformed into a delightful boutique hotel. It boasts a courtyard garden full of flowers, common areas with gilded mirrors and beautiful floor tiles, and split-level rooms that are surprisingly light and modern for such an old-world setting.

✖️ Eating

Los Portales Texolo   MEXICAN **$$**
(☑228-129-81-43; Av Hidalgo 107; mains M$110-155; ⏰8am-8pm Tue-Sun) Facing onto a small square that is popular with ecstatic birds at sunset, this friendly local place serves delicious *xiqueño* specialties such as *chiles en nogada* (stuffed green chilies) and *mole*. Dine outside under the building's arches to take in Xico's colonial splendor.

⭐ **Restaurante Mesón Xiqueño**   MEXICAN **$$**
(☑228-813-07-81; Av Hidalgo 148; mains M$95-170; ⏰9am-9pm) Near the corner with Calle Carranza is Xico's best-known restaurant. Dine inside the lovely courtyard and sample the famous local *mole*, served in a number of different ways, as well as stuffed jalapeño, soup with the fragrant *xonequi* herb and more.

La Casona de Don Gonzalo   MEXICAN **$$**
(☑228-129-80-47; cnr Morelos & Pavón; mains M$75-120; ⏰8am-9pm) Facing onto Xico's main square, with a few outdoor tables should the weather be fine, this atmospheric place serves the usual range of meats doused in the local *mole* as well as seafood cooked in a variety of ways. Meals come with a complimentary tot of local herbal liquor.

🛍️ Shopping

La Casa de Lili   FOOD
(Av Hidalgo 148; ⏰10am-7pm) Step back in time at this tiny, picturesque grocery store, where you can pick up Xico's trademark *mole* as well as organic coffee.

Casa Doria   ARTS & CRAFTS
(☑228-140-19-08; Av Hidalgo 195; ⏰11am-7pm) Check out all of the local handicrafts at Casa Doria, including the distinctive, painted wooden masks worn by dancers during the town's many festivals.

ℹ️ Information

Tourist office (☑228-813-16-18; Av Hidalgo 76; ⏰9am-6pm) Inside the Casa de la Cultura.

ℹ️ Getting There & Away

From the **bus terminal** (☑228-813-03-91; Nava s/n), frequent buses run to Xalapa's Los Sauces terminal (M$20) and to Coatepec (M$10).

Jalcomulco

☑279 / POP 4690 / ELEV 423M

Sitting in a lush valley, 30km southeast of Xalapa, tiny Jalcomulco hugs the Río Antigua (this stretch known as the Río Pescados) and is surrounded by jungle-covered hills. The area is rich with caves and luscious swimming spots, but it's most famous for its rapids – some of Mexico's best – which accommodate white-water enthusiasts from beginners through to the more advanced. On weekends the place comes to life with numerous adventurers descending on it, but the rest of the time Jalcomulco remains a soporific village amid mango plantations and sugarcane fields.

🏃 Activities

Numerous operators, including some of the best places to stay, offer day and multiday rafting packages; these typically include other adventure activities, such as rappeling, horseback riding, mountain biking, canyoning, trekking, paint-balling (called 'gotcha' in these parts) and sweating it out in a temascal (herbal steam room). Book ahead as often there are minimum numbers needed for each activity.

⭐ **Jalco Expediciones**   RAFTING
(☑279-832-36-87; www.facebook.com/jalco expedicionestumejoraventura; Calle 20 de Noviembre 17; day package M$780) Very professional rafting company with excellent equipment and English-speaking staff. A bonus is the wood-fired pizza from its associated restaurant waiting for customers upon return. Day packages and multiday adventures available.

★**Expediciones**
México Verde ADVENTURE SPORTS
(☑800-362-88-00, 279-832-37-30; www.mexico
verde.com; Carretera Tuzamapan–Jalcomulco Km
4; rafting trip M$890, kayaking M$1195) Based in
jungly grounds 4km north of town, México
Verde is one of the longest-standing adventure activity operators in Jalcomulco. The
list of white-knuckle, wet-and-wild adrenaline activities offered by this professional
establishment will get the heart of even the
most reckless racing.

Day-long and accommodations packages
including all meals are the way to go; if you
overnight it's in a choice of spacious, luxury safari tents with either shared or private
bathrooms. They also have a restaurant,
pool, spa and temascal.

Armonía Rafting OUTDOORS
(☑279-832-35-80; www.armoniarafting.com;
Zaragoza 56; rafting day trip M$520) One of
Jalcomulco's top rafting operators offering a wide variety of packages that include
accommodations (camping/hostel/hotel
M$2390/2590/2790 per person), two rafting
outings, rappeling, zip-lining, meals, transportation, guide and a steaming session in a
temascal. Day activities also available.

🛏️ **Sleeping & Eating**

Posada del Río HOTEL $
(☑279-832-35-27; cnr Zaragoza & Madero; r
M$680; ❄🛜🏊) This centrally located hotel
has just 14 compact rooms clustered around
a courtyard filled with greenery and a tiny
pool. There's a rustic mansion vibe to the
place, the onsite restaurant prepares delicious local dishes (mains M$80 to M$155),
and the service is helpful and friendly.

Aldea Ecoturismo TENTED CAMP $$
(☑279-832-37-51; www.aldeajalcomulco.com.mx;
Carretera Tuzamapan–Jalcomulco Km 3; tent per
person M$500, s/d bungalow from M$647/1200; 🛜)
Around 3km out of town, this leafy property
allows you to live out your jungle fantasies by
camping, sleeping in a tree-house or adobe
cabins. Rafting and other adrenaline-packed
activities are on the menu, and you can steam
your aching muscles afterward in a traditional temascal or go meditate beside the camp's
stupa, one of only two in Mexico.

★**Picocanoa Rodaventa** RESORT $$$
(☑279-822-35-96; www.picocanoarodavento.
com; Constitución s/n; 3-/4-person bungalow
M$1638/1810, safari tent M$2155; ❄🛜🏊) Just

south of the river, adorable, snug thatch-roofed bamboo bungalows (with extra loft
beds) and luxurious, spacious safari tents
surround a pool and a *palapa*-style restaurant that sit amid lush grounds. The decor
inside the lodgings is vibrant, with bold
splashes of color, and there's a luxury spa
and traditional temascal to chill out in.

The resort specializes in multiday packages
that include rafting, rappeling, white-water
kayaking, canyoning, zip-lining and more.

★**Restaurante Nachita** SEAFOOD $$
(☑228-832-35-19; Madero 4; mains M$99-360;
⊙8am-9pm; 🛜) Sit on the deck overlooking
the river and order one of the restaurant's
specialties: *manuelitos* (locally caught
crawfish) in salsa verde or chipotle sauce,
a hearty *torta be mariscos* (seafood pie) or
seafood *cazuela* (casserole) washed down
with generous-sized glasses of *agua de jamaica* (hibiscus iced tea). Popular with
groups as it's a big place.

ℹ️ **Getting There & Away**

Buses to Xalapa's Azteca terminal (M$40, 1½
hours, six daily) and to Coatepec (M$30, 45
minutes, hourly) leave from the main square.
Adventure tour operators from Veracruz city and
elsewhere offer transfers to Jalcomulco as part
of their rafting packages.

Tlapacoyan
☑225 / POP 58,084
At the mouth of the Río Filobobos (known
as Río Bobos and famous for its rapids),
head 60km inland from Nautla on Hwy 129
and you'll hit Tlapacoyan, where a handful
of rafting companies are based, and where
the waterfall Cascada de Encanto provides a
gorgeous swimming spot. Tlapacoyan itself
is a fairly unexciting agricultural town, surrounded by banana plantations and citrus
fruit groves, but it's worth an overnight stopover, if only to visit the two archaeological
sites nearby, Caujilote and Vega de la Peña,
collectively referred to as Filobobos and
both very much off the beaten track.

◉ **Sights**

★**El Cuajilote** ARCHAEOLOGICAL SITE
(M$55; ⊙9am-5pm) Only discovered in the
early 1990s, this beautiful site dates back to
600–900 CE and was once home to peoples
unknown. It consists of temples, platforms
and shrines, partially reclaimed from the

jungle, around a long, rectangular plaza, and is worth visiting for the beauty of the surroundings alone; you are likely to have the serene place to yourself.

Follow the 'Filobobos' signs south from Tlapacoyan along a paved road; the last 1km is unpaved and very bumpy. Rancho Grande–bound taxis can drop you at the 1km turnoff.

As you enter the site, the first two buildings on your right are a ball court. Directly opposite is the excavated **Templo Mayor**, an impressive multitiered pyramid. Along the two sides of the plaza you can make out the shapes of other platforms and temples beneath the lush vegetation. A brook separates the Templo Mayor from the remains of shrines in the middle of the plaza. The archaeological project is ongoing and the origins of El Cuajilote's residents are yet to be determined. Over 1500 phallic fertility figures were found at **Shrine A4**, suggesting the influence of a Huastec fertility cult, whereas the earliest buildings at the site (possibly dating back to 1000 BCE) seem to be Olmec in appearance and stone sculptures found here appear to be similar to Totonac in style.

Archaeologists believe that it is also possible that the two sites that make up Filobobos were, in fact, settled by a hitherto-unknown Mesoamerican civilization.

Vega de la Peña   ARCHAEOLOGICAL SITE
(M$55; ⊗9am-5pm) Reachable only on foot and covering 8 sq km, the remains of this pre-Hispanic settlement have been only partially excavated. It shows Olmec, Huastec, Totonac and Toltec influences and its history spans more than 1500 years, from 100 BCE to 1500 CE, though its heyday seems to have been between 1200 and 1500. It's 2.5km away from the El Cuajilote site, where you can get directions.

It's not as visually impressive as its sister site; there's a small ball court and some residential buildings, but the underlying idea is mindblowing. It is possible that the yet-to-be-excavated ruins are considerably more extensive than currently believed, and that the complex civilization that flourished here played a considerably more prominent role in terms of Mesoamerican trade and influence than previously believed.

🏃 Activities

★ Aventurec   RAFTING
(☑225-315-43-00; www.aventurec.com; off Hwy 129, El Encanto; day rafting packages from M$600,

overnight packages including accommodations, meals and rafting adult/child from M$1300/1000) Quite apart from running wet-and-wild rafting and kayaking trips on Río Filobobos, Aventurec is a gorgeous place to stay. Choose between camping, staying in dorms or in private cabins, all surrounded by lush greenery. Delicious buffet meals are included and there's a great swimming pool.

And you don't have to go rafting: the zip-lining and hiking offered here also come highly recommended. If you plan to camp you'll need to bring your own tent.

🛏 Sleeping & Eating

Hotel Posada Oliver   HISTORIC HOTEL **$**
(☑225-315-42-12; Av Cuauhtémoc 400; r M$450; ❄️🛜) The pick of Tlapacoyan's hotels (not that it's much of a horse race), Posada Oliver is just off the main square, with stone arches and a greenery-filled courtyard adding much-needed character. Rooms are simple but comfortable, with cable TV and air-con.

Las Acamallas   MEXICAN **$$**
(☑225-315-02-91; Héroes de Tlapacoyan s/n; mains M$65-215; ⊗8am-10pm) Just off the main square, two-tiered Las Acamallas is a sure bet for breakfast, enchiladas and chicken cooked a dozen ways.

ℹ Getting There & Away

From the **bus terminal** (Zaragoza s/n) there are ADO services to Mexico City (M$844, 8½ hours, 10pm), Puebla (M$654, 6¼ hours, 10pm) and Xalapa (M$185, 2½ hours, 10 daily). For connecting services to Veracruz or Papantla, you need to take a 2nd-class bus to Martínez de la Torre, 22km east, and change there.

Córdoba

☑271 / POP 142,500 / ELEV 817M

Not to be confused with its famous namesakes in Spain and Argentina, Córdoba has an illustrious history and a justifiable sense of civic pride; the contract that sealed Mexico's independence was signed here in 1821. The city itself was originally founded in 1618 as a staging post between Mexico City and the coast, with the purpose of protecting the Spanish crown's interests from the local slave rebellion, led by Gaspar Yanga, which was strong in the area.

Córdoba is far less lovely than nearby Orizaba; however, a quick visit here is worth considering for the sights around its buzzing main plaza, Parque de 21 de Mayo.

◎ Sights

Córdoba's key attractions ring its main plaza, Parque de 21 de Mayo, which is a sight in itself. It's a 24-hour live 'show:' theater-goers in high heels dodge hungry pigeons and grandpas moonlight as marimba players. Watching over it all is an impressive baroque cathedral, one of the state's most resplendent.

★ Museo del Café Córdoba   MUSEUM

(Av 3 112; M$50; ⊙ 9:30am-5pm Tue-Sun) The ground floor of the city's cultural center have been transformed into this well-designed museum on Córdoba's prime product: coffee. Most explanation panels have English translations and entry includes an excellent tasting session in the museum's **cafe** where you'll learn plenty more about the drink. A good gift shop also provides a chance to purchase local specialty beans and other souvenirs.

Catedral de la
Inmaculada Concepción   CATHEDRAL

(Calle 1; ⊙ hours vary) Dating from 1688, the pale-blue baroque cathedral has an elaborate facade flanked by twin bell towers. The ornate interior has gold-leaf detailing and marble floors. The chapel features candlelit statues with altars, such as a gruesome Jesus on the cross and an eerily despairing Virgen de la Soledad. The mixture of glitz and gore is a visual metaphor for a disturbing historical dichotomy: the richness of the conquistadors and the misery that the indigenous people endured.

Portal de Zevallos   HISTORIC BUILDING

(Av 1 101) On the northeast side of Parque de 21 de Mayo, this 1687 building is the former home of the *condes* (counts) of Zevallos. Plaques in the courtyard record that Juan O'Donojú and Agustín de Iturbide met here on August 24, 1821, and agreed on the terms for Mexico's independence. They also concurred that a Mexican, not a European, should be head of state.

The building is now full of restaurants and cafes as well as an excellent new boutique hotel.

Palacio Municipal   ARCHITECTURE

(Calle 1 102) Cordoba's neoclassical municipal palace, built in 1905, is worth a quick look for its stairway covered by a historical mural created in 2010 by Jaime Sanches Nava. The local artist's work can also be seen in the Museo del Café Córdoba and some of the cafes on the ground floor of the Portal de Zevallos.

Museo de Córdoba   MUSEUM

(☑ 271-712-09-67; Calle 3 316; M$10; ⊙ 9am-5pm Mon-Fri) FREE This museum has a modest collection of artifacts including a fine Aztec ballcourt marker, some Olmec figurines, and a replica of the statue of *El señor de Las Limas* that resides in Xalapa's Museo de Antropología (p233). You'll find it just off the main square, opposite the Coffee Museum.

★✦ Festivals & Events

Good Friday   RELIGIOUS

On the evening of Good Friday, Córdoba marks Jesus's crucifixion with a silent procession, in which thousands of residents walk through the streets behind an altar of the Virgin. Everyone holds a lit candle, no one utters a word and the church bells are strangely quiet.

🛏 Sleeping

A warning about hotels near Córdoba's Parque de 21 de Mayo: when we say the music goes on all night in and around the central square, we do mean *all* night. If you stay here, bring heavy duty earplugs to ensure a sound night's sleep.

Hotel Los Reyes   HOTEL $

(☑ 271-712-25-38; www.losreyeshotel.com; cnr Calle 3 & Av 2; s/d M$280/450; ❀ 🛜) Just half a block from the main square, this cheapie distinguishes itself with friendly service and its attention to detail, with good beds and quality bed linens (embroidered with the hotel name) in the fan-cooled rooms. Half the rooms face indoors; of the outdoor-facing ones, rooms 203 to 206 are the best, as they face the marginally quieter Calle 3.

Casa Bonita   HOSTEL $

(☑ 271-717-80-99; http://casabonitahotel.mystrik ingly.com; Av 5 1601; dm/d/trp M$150/380/400; ❀❄🛜) Something approaching a backpackers hostel, the brightly decorated Casa Bonita has one large six-bed dorm and several private rooms, a few of which have their own bathrooms. There's no kitchen though and barely a communal area. It's a good 10-minute walk northwest of the city center.

★ Casa Zevallos   BOUTIQUE HOTEL $$

(☑ 271-157-81-33; www.casazevallos.com; Av 1 101, 2nd flr; r incl breakfast from M$1500; 🅿❀❄🛜) It's not every day that you get to sleep in such an historic property as the Portal de Zevallos. Even better is that the five rooms here are truly boutique, each creatively mixing the antique aspects of the building with quirky contemporary style – think copper baths, tiled ceilings and wild wallpaper and art.

You'll find the hotel on the building's 2nd floor, with the rooms ranged around the back away from the noisy plaza.

Hotel Mansur   HOTEL **$$**
(☑271-712-60-00; www.hoteleshm.com; Av 1 No 301; r/ste from M$950/1053; P⊖❀🛜) Claiming five stories of prime viewing space above Córdoba's main plaza, the venerable Mansur, with its vast balconies equipped with thick wooden chairs, makes you feel as if you're part of the 'show' going on below. It's a solid, business-style hotel that has traded in its old-world glamour for modern conveniences.

Some rooms have private terraces, but with that comes the square's noise; request a room at the back of the hotel if you desire relative peace and quiet.

✕ Eating & Drinking

Córdoba has a lively eating and cafe scene with plenty of choice. Numerous options line the ground-floor arches of Portal de Zocallos.

El Patio de la Abuela   MEXICAN **$**
(☑271-712-06-06; Calle 1 No 208; mains M$35-120; ⊗8am-midnight; 🛜) This friendly, informal eatery serves a variety of tacos, *picaditas* (thick tortillas with different toppings) and *tamales*, as well as hearty *pozole* (spiced hominy and pork stew), *mondongo* (cow tripe soup – a hangover cure!) and gut-busting helpings of grilled meats. Just like *abuela* used to make.

★El Balcón del Zevallos   MEXICAN **$$$**
(☑271-714-66-99; Av 1 No 101; mains M$130-560; ⊗2pm-1am; 🛜) The upper floor of the historic Portal de Zevallos claims the prize for Córdoba's most-famous restaurant. It has a wonderful setting – a balcony overlooking the plaza – an extensive wine list (including some

decent Mexican reds) and quality meat and seafood dishes cooked *a la parrilla* (on the barbecue) at your table. Service is excellent.

Calufe Café   CAFE
(☑217-717-75-46; Calle 3 No 212; ⊗10am-11pm; 🛜) If only all cafes could be like this. Calufe occupies the interior of an agreeably peeling colonial mansion with eclectic nooks arranged around a dimly lit, plant-filled courtyard. Guitar and vocal duos provide a melancholy musical backdrop in the evenings. Calufe sells its own blend of coffee, along with melt-in-the-mouth coffee cake and other diet-busting snacks.

❶ Information

Banks around the Plaza de Armas have 24-hour ATMs.

Hospital Covadonga (☑271-714-55-20; www.corporativodehospitales.com.mx; Av 7 No 1610; ⊗24hr) Urgent medical care at all hours.

Tourist Office (☑271-712-43-44; Centro Cultural Municipal, cnr Av 3 & Calle 3; ⊗9am-5pm Mon, until 7pm Tue-Sun) Helpful staff offer maps and information.

❶ Getting There & Away

BUS

Córdoba's **bus station** (☑271-712-22-57; Blvd Augin Millan), which has deluxe, 1st-class and 2nd-class services, is 2.5km southeast of the plaza. To get to the town center from the station, take a local bus marked 'Centro' or buy a taxi ticket (M$40). To Orizaba, it's more convenient to take a local bus from the corner of Avenida 11 and Calle 3 than to go out to the Córdoba bus station.

CAR & MOTORCYCLE

Córdoba and Orizaba are linked by toll Hwy 150D, the route that most buses take, and by the much slower Hwy 150. A scenic back road goes through the hills from Fortín de las Flores, via Huatusco, to Xalapa.

VERACRUZ CÓRDOBA

BUSES FROM CÓRDOBA

Deluxe and 1st-class buses from Córdoba include the following:

DESTINATION	FARE (M$)	TIME (HR)	FREQUENCY (PER DAY)
Mexico City (TAPO)	424-568	5-5½	frequent
Oaxaca	601	5¼-7	4
Orizaba	47	¾	frequent
Puebla	264-315	2½-3½	frequent
Veracruz	173-191	1¾	frequent
Xalapa	278	3	11

Orizaba

📱 272 / POP 124,000 / ELEV 1242M

Veracruz' most appealing town rewards the visitor with a pleasant old colonial center, some lovely parks and a gorgeous riverside walk. It's also within easy reach of Mexico's highest mountain, the magnificent Pico de Orizaba (5636m). The most striking sight in Orizaba itself is Gustave Eiffel's art nouveau Palacio de Hierro (Iron Palace). There's also an excellent art museum, home to Mexico's second-largest Diego Rivera collection. Add to that a varied dining scene and numerous coffee shops, and you may find yourself lingering here longer than expected.

◎ Sights

★ Teleférico de Orizaba   CABLE CAR

(Sur 4 btwn Avs Poniente 3 & Poniente 5; M$50; ◷9am-5pm Mon-Fri, to 7pm Sat, Sun & holidays) For a fab excursion, ride this cable car that glides smoothly from its riverside site across from the Palacio Municipal up to the top of the Cerro del Borrego hill (1240m). From here there are incredible views over the city and easy access to hiking routes. It takes just five minutes to travel nearly 1km and climb some 320m.

At Cerro del Borrego, you'll find signed walking trails and an 'eco-park,' which has a cafe, picnic areas, a small military museum, playgrounds, and a tower you can climb to gain a view of snow-capped Pico de Orizaba (should the weather be clear). There's also a zip-line (M$100, Tuesday to Sunday) and between 2pm and 5pm on Saturday and Sunday, costumed locals re-create a military battle that took place here in the late-19th century.

★ Palacio de Hierro   MUSEUM

(📱272-728-91-36; Norte 1; ◷9am-7pm) FREE Alexandre Gustave Eiffel's 'Iron Palace' is Orizaba's fanciful art nouveau landmark. The palace's interior has been converted into several small museums (none of them particularly inspiring), including the Museo de la Cerveza, tracking Orizaba's beer industry; the Museo de Fútbol (soccer); the Museo Interactivo, with a small planetarium and some science exhibits, including a bed of nails you can lie on; and the Museo de las Raíces de Orizaba, displaying archaeological artifacts.

The master of metallurgy who gave his name to the Eiffel Tower and engineered the Statue of Liberty's framework, designed this pavilion, which was built in Paris. Oriz-

aba's mayor, eager to acquire an impressive European-style Palacio Municipal, bought it in 1892. Piece by piece it was shipped out, then reassembled in Orizaba.

Poliforum Mier y Pesado   MUSEUM

(📱272-688-52-27; Av Oriente 6 No 1653; ◷gardens 7am-10pm, museums 10am-7pm; 🚻) FREE Dating from 1944, this palatial-style building set in manicured grounds about 2km east of central Orizaba was once an asylum. It now houses several excellent exhibitions, the best being the ones devoted to traditional costumes from around Mexico and to the children's song composer Francisco Gabilondo Soler (1907–90) who was born in Orizaba.

Kids will be charmed by the Soler exhibition, with its many cartoon-character-filled displays. Also in the building are several popular cafes and restaurants.

Museo de Arte del Estado   MUSEUM

(State Art Museum; 📱272-724-32-00; cnr Av Oriente 4 & Sur 25; M$16; ◷10am-7pm Tue-Sun) The State Art Museum is housed in a gorgeously restored colonial building attached to the side of the elaborate La Concordia church dating from 1679. The museum is divided into rooms that include Mexico's second-most-important permanent Diego Rivera collection, with 33 of his original works. Guides give complimentary tours in Spanish. The museum is about 2km east of Parque Castillo.

Parque Alameda Gabilondo Soler   PARK

(Av Poniente 2 & Sur 10; ◷6am-10pm; 🚻) This leafy park doesn't lack activity. Aside from the obligatory statues of dead heroes, you'll find an outdoor gym, a bandstand, food carts, shoe-shiners and a playground for kids. Practically the whole city rolls in at weekends after Sunday Mass.

From 10am to 6pm Friday to Sunday and on holidays, you can also clamber between the trees on the Canopy aerial park (M$150).

Parque Castillo   PLAZA

(Av Colón Oriente; ◷24hr) Smaller than your average Mexican city plaza, Parque Castillo is watched over by the 17th-century **Catedral de San Miguel Arcángel** and the neoclassical **Teatro Ignacio de la Llave**, an 1875 theater that continues to hosts a variety of concerts and other performances.

🏃 Activities

★ Paseo del Río   WALKING

(Orizaba's clean eponymous river is bordered by walking paths decorated with

Orizaba

Orizaba

many colorful murals and abstract sculpture toward its southern end, beyond the cable car. There are 13 bridges along the way, including a suspension bridge and the arched Puente La Borda, dating from 1776. A good starting point is Avenida Poniente 8, about 600m northwest of the Palacio de Hierro.

From Avenida Poniente 8 heading north you'll pass a collection of animal enclosures beside the walkway, containing monkeys, parrots, lizards, crocodiles, llamas and even a tiger. All of the animals were born in captivity and cannot be released into the wild.

★ Turismo Aventura   OUTDOORS
(☑ cell 272-725-14-91; www.turismoaventuraorizaba. com; Av Poniente 9 No 27) This long-established adventure-tour operator runs guided climbs to the summit of Pico de Orizaba with an English-speaking guide. Check its website for details as they have a variety of packages, including day-long sightseeing trips and other outdoor activities in the area.

Alberto Gochicoa   OUTDOORS
(☑ cell 272-703-29-51; www.facebook.com/alberto. gochicoa) A recommended guide who can help organize various outdoor activities in nearby hills, mountains and canyons, including climbs partway up Pico de Orizaba. Highlights of the area include the gorgeous Cañón de la Carbonera near Nogales and the Cascada de Popócatl near Tequila.

⌓ Sleeping

Orizaba has something to suit all budgets, from higher-end options on the Avenida Oriente 6 traffic strip and near Parque Alameda, to lower-end choices in or near the center.

Hotel del Río   HOTEL $
(Map p249; ☑ 272-726-66-25; http://hoteldelrio .tripod.com; Av Poniente 8 No 315; s/d from M$475/590; P ❈ ☏) A pleasant place and a good-value price make this a surefire winner. It has an attractive location right by the Río

PICO DE ORIZABA

At a cloud-scraping and breathless 5636m, snowcapped Pico de Orizaba is Mexico's tallest mountain and the third tallest in North America after USA's Mt Denali and Canada's Mt Logan. It dominates the horizon for miles around, although to get a view of it from Orizaba itself you'll need to take the cable car up to Cerro del Borrego and keep your fingers crossed for clear weather.

Called Citlaltépetl (Star Mountain) in the Náhuatl language, the views from the summit of this massive dormant volcano take in the mountains of Popocatépetl, Iztaccíhuatl and La Malinche to the west and the Gulf of Mexico to the east.

For a closer look, Turismo Aventura (p249) offers a variety of day-trip packages that can get you closer to the mountain, including, weather permitting, up to 4520m near Fausto González Gomar hostel, the highest point you can go by a car.

Attaining the summit is a serious undertaking suitable only for experienced, well-equipped mountain climbers prepared for extreme cold and possible altitude sickness. Traversing ice fields in the last section of the ascent is particularly demanding. Acclimatization over several days before you attempt the climb is necessary.

All but the most experienced climbers will need a guide. Local operators apart from Turismo Aventura include **Servimont** (☑ 245-451-50-19, cell 222-6275406; www.servimont.com.mx; Ortega 1A), based in the small town of Tlachichuca (2600m) in Puebla, which is a common starting point for expeditions, along with Orizaba and the old colonial town of Coscomatepec (1535m), 37km north of Orizaba.

The recommended climbing season is October to March, with the most popular time being December and January. Book your expedition well in advance and allow four to seven days to acclimatize, summit and return. Do not attempt to rush up this mountain because altitude sickness, which at these heights can be deadly, is a very real concern. If you experience any kind of symptoms, descend immediately.

Orizaba, simple modern rooms with tacky 'art' in an old building, and a congenial owner.

Hotel Plaza Palacio HOTEL **$**
(☑ 272-725-99-33; https://hotel-plaza-palacio.negocio.site; Av Poniente 2 No 2-Bis; r from M$400; 🛜) You can't get more central than this place; the windows look directly onto the Palacio de Hierro. It's nothing special architecturally, and the rooms are clean but not particularly characterful. But you do get cable TV and a fan, as well as the town right on your doorstep.

Orizaba Inn HOTEL **$**
(☑ 272-725-06-26; www.hotelorizabainn.com.mx; Av Oriente 2 No 117; r/ste from M$649/1049; 😊 🕸 🛜) The interior of this hotel offers bright, white-washed rooms, with turquoise accents, and thoroughly modern bathrooms and mod cons. Some rooms come with balconies; have a look at a few if you can. Friendly staff and a decent breakfast up this hotel's game.

★**Gamma Orizaba**
Grand Hotel de France HOTEL **$$**
(www.gammahoteles.com; Av Oriente 6 No 186; r from $1240; 🅿 🕸 🛜 🌊) In 2019 the Gamma hotel group breathed fresh, contemporary life into this old central property set around a large internal courtyard. Rooms are large and stylish and there's a major plus with the expansive rooftop including a bar, decent-sized pool and wonderful city views.

★**Hotel Tres79** BOUTIQUE HOTEL **$$**
(☑ 272-725-23-79; http://tres79hotelboutique.com; Av Colón Poniente 379; r/ste incl breakfast from M$1470/2229; 🅿 😊 🕸 🛜) Each of the 14 rooms at this truly stylish hotel is individually themed around a Mexican writer, musician or artist (we particularly like the Agustín Lara room), with bold furnishings and great attention to creature comforts (hypoallergenic bedding, rain showers). There's big courtyard with a tiled fountain, and the restaurant is excellent.

Hotel Misión Orizaba BOUTIQUE HOTEL **$$$**
(☑ 272-106-92-94; www.hotelesmision.com.mx; Av Oriente 6 No 64; r/ste from M$1670/1970; 🅿 🕸 🛜 🌊) The comfortable but somewhat-plain rooms here, set around a courtyard and a tiny swimming pool, are enlivened by fresh flowers, writing desks and coffee machines. Plus the staff are very helpful.

✖ Eating & Drinking

Orizaba's dining scene is excellent and incorporates fusion, steak and seafood restaurants, as well as atmospheric cafes. Head to the plaza for noteworthy Orizaban snacks including *garnachas* (open tortillas with chicken, onion and tomato salsa) or scour Avenida Oriente 4 in search of the best tacos.

Taco T STREET FOOD $
(☑272-106-10-49; Av Oriente 4 No 1247; tacos from M$4-39; ⊗1pm-midnight) Join the locals in the bustling dining hall of the most popular *taquería* of the many strung along Avenida Oriente 4, and watch the cooks expertly slice off sizzling hunks of meat from the rotating skewers. Or get your tacos to go and enjoy them in the leafy plaza across the street.

★ Gran Café de Orizaba CAFE $
(☑272-728-83-49; www.grancafedeorizaba.com; cnr Av Poniente 2 & Madero, Palacio de Hierro; snacks M$40-80; ⊗9am-10:30pm; 🛜) It's not every day that you can you sit back and enjoy a coffee and cake on the balcony of a regal cafe that's part of an iron palace designed by Gustave Eiffel. The delightful decor, smart staff and selection of sandwiches, crepes and cake make this an obvious place to break up your exploration of Orizaba.

La Antigua Casa Marrón FUSION $$
(☑272-724-01-39; www.facebook.com/marron cocinagaleria; Sur 7 No 64; mains M$38-275; ⊗1-10pm Mon & Wed-Fri, until 11pm Sat, until 8pm Sun; 🛜🅿🐾) Occupying a gorgeous courtyard space, this arty and cool fusion restaurant has an easy, informal and convivial atmosphere. Some of the best items on the menu are Italian-Mexican fusion, such as wonderful, spicy *lasagna de mi suegra* (my mother-in-law's lasagna). They do decent thick-crust pizza, too, and several vegan dishes.

★ Trogon MEXICAN $$
(☑272-173-01-41; Poniente 2; mains M$130-450; ⊗8am-midnight) Sample traditional ingredients such as *chapulines* (deep fried grasshoppers) and *escamoles* (ant larvae) at this excellent modern Mexican restaurant in the city center. Trogon occupies the courtyard inside, while on the exterior of the corner complex is **La Casona**, a pleasant spot for breakfast, light lunch, coffee and dessert.

Casa Lara CAFE
(☑272-229-06-90; www.facebook.com/casalara rooftop; De Sur 4; ⊗2-11pm) Don't miss having a drink and taking in the city and surrounding mountain views from this cute rooftop cafe-bar, named after the famous Mexican songwriter Agustín Lara (1897–1970) – there's a bronze statue of him sitting on a bench in the tiny square outside the building entrance.

El Interior COFFEE
(☑272-726-45-31; cnr Av Oriente 4 & Sur 9; ⊗9am-8:30pm; 🛜) Books, coffee and art – a small handily located literary cafe connected to a book store.

🛍 Shopping

Mercado de Artesanías ARTS & CRAFTS
(www.facebook.com/MercadodeartesaniasOrizaba; Norte 3 btwn Avs Poniente 2 & 4; ⊗11am-8pm) Handmade woolly ponchos and sweaters, funky T-shirt designs, wood carvings and wooden kitchen utensils, and all manner of assorted gifts are represented at this large craft market in the heart of town.

ℹ Information

Banks with ATMs are on Avenida Oriente 2, a block south of the plaza.
Hospital Covadonga (☑272-725-50-19; www.corporativodehospitales.com.mx; Sur 5 No 398; ⊗24hr)

VERACRUZ ORIZABA

BUSES FROM ORIZABA

Daily 1st-class buses include the following:

DESTINATION	FARE (M$)	TIME (HR)	FREQUENCY (PER DAY)
Córdoba	47	¾	frequent
Mexico City (TAPO)	399-546	4½	frequent
Mexico City (Terminal Norte)	399-483	4½-5½	9
Oaxaca	416-564	4½-6	4
Puebla	248-292	2½	frequent
Veracruz	190-219	2-3	frequent
Xalapa	300	3¼-4	11

Orizaba Pueblo Mágico It's well worth downloading this app, a comprehensive guide to the town's attractions.

Tourist Office (☑ 272-728-91-36; www.orizaba. travel; Palacio de Hierro, Norte 1; ⊙ 9am-7pm) Has enthusiastic staff and plenty of brochures.

ℹ Getting There & Away

BUS

Local buses to and from Córdoba (cnr Av Oriente 9 & Norte 14) stop four blocks north and six blocks east of the town center, while the **AU 2nd-class bus station** (☑ 272-725-19-79; www. ado.com.mx; Poniente 8 No 425), a short walk northwest of the center, also has plenty of buses to Córdoba (M$25).

The modern 1st-class **bus station** (☑ 222-107-22-55; www.ado.com.mx; cnr Av Oriente 6 & Sur 13) handles ADO, ADO GL and deluxe UNO services.

CAR & MOTORCYCLE

Toll Hwy 150D, which bypasses central Orizaba, goes east to Córdoba and west, via a spectacular ascent, to Puebla (160km). Toll-free Hwy 150 runs east to Córdoba and Veracruz (150km) and southwest to Tehuacán, 65km away over the hair-raising Cumbres de Acultzingo.

NORTHERN VERACRUZ

The northern half of Veracruz state, between the coast and southern fringes of the Sierra Madre Oriental, mainly consists of lush rolling pastureland. Laguna de Tamiahua is the region's largest wetland, while the Gulf's Costa Esmeralda has some fine isolated (though sometimes polluted) beaches, which are popular with local holidaymakers. The major attraction is El Tajín archaeological site; it's reachable from the historic *pueblo mágico* of Papantla and is refreshingly untouristed compared to some of Mexico's more renowned archaeological sites. On the coast, less than an hour from Papantla, Tecolutla is a quintessential Mexican resort with decent beaches and some very good seafood, while two hours north, Tuxpan is a possible stopover if you're heading north to Tampico and beyond.

Papantla

☑ 784 / POP 51,716 / ELEV 180M

Spread across a succession of verdant hills, the solidly indigenous *pueblo mágico* of Papantla has a history, look and feel that stares firmly back in time to a pre-Hispanic or,

more precisely, Totonac period of grandeur. Predating the Spanish conquest, the town was founded around 1230 CE. A launching pad for people visiting the nearby ruins of El Tajín, Papantla has carved its own niche in recent years, stressing its indigenous heritage and promoting its central position in the world's best vanilla-growing region. You'll see Totonacs wearing traditional clothing here – the men in loose white shirts and baggy white trousers, and the women in embroidered blouses. Meanwhile *voladores* 'fly' and local artisans peddle handicrafts in the attractive main square that seems in permanent fiesta mode.

⊙ Sights

Catedral de Nuestra
Señora de la Asunción   CATHEDRAL
(16 de Septiembre 216; ⊙ 8am-7pm) Overlooking the *zócalo* from its high platform, this cathedral is notable for its large cedar doors and quartet of indoor canvases by a Jalisco artist. Begun in 1570 by the Franciscans, it was added to in stages over the subsequent centuries; the bell tower wasn't completed until 1875.

Outside stands a 30m-high *voladores* pole. Mesmerizing, ritual performances normally take place every two hours between 9am and 5:30pm Friday to Sunday; in high season (January, February and main holidays) the performances are daily.

Parque Israel C Téllez   PLAZA
(zócalo) The bustling heart of Papantla, there always seems to be something going on in or around this *zócalo* terraced into the hillside – head here on Friday evenings to watch or take part in the *danzón* when a live band serenades dancers. Facing the square is a symbolic 50m-long bas-relief mural, designed by Papantla artist Teodoro Cano in 1979 and depicting Totonac and Veracruz history.

A serpent stretches along the mural, bizarrely linking a pre-Hispanic stone carver, El Tajín's Pirámide de los Nichos, and an oil rig.

Museo de la Ciudad Teodoro Cano   MUSEUM
(☑ 228-156-71-83; Curti 101; M$10; ⊙ 10am-6pm Tue-Sun) ✐ This small and immensely satisfying museum displays the fine paintings of celebrated local artist Teodoro Cano (b 1932). His monochromatic and super colorful images pulse with life and are drawn almost exclusively from Totonac culture. The Totonac theme extends to the museum's other artifacts, including photos and traditional clothing displays.

DANCE OF THE FLYERS: PAPANTLA'S VOLADORES

Papantla's Totonac *voladores* (fliers) have been flinging themselves off 30m-high wooden poles (with zero safety equipment) for centuries. Indeed, so old is the 'dance of the flyers' that no one is quite sure how or when it started. In 2009, Unesco recognized the ritual ceremony as Intangible Cultural Heritage.

The rite begins with four men in elaborate ceremonial clothing climbing to the top of the pole where they each attach themselves to a rope. They sit on the edges of a small frame at the top and rotate the frame to twist the ropes around the pole. A fifth man then climbs to top and dances on the platform above them while playing a *chirimía*, a small drum with a flute attached. When he stops playing, the others fall backward. Arms outstretched, they revolve gracefully around the pole and descend to the ground, hanging upside down, as their ropes unwind.

One interpretation of the ceremony is that it's a fertility rite and the fliers make invocations to the four corners of the universe. It's also noted that each flier circles the pole 13 times, giving a total of 52 revolutions. The number 52 is not only the number of weeks in the modern year but also was an important number in pre-Hispanic Mexico, which had two calendars: one corresponding to the 365-day solar year, the other to a ritual year of 260 days. The calendars coincided every 52 solar years.

Voladores ceremonies are best observed at El Tajín, outside Papantla's cathedral, and occasionally at Cempoala (p232).

Volador Monument   MONUMENT

(Callejón Centenario s/n) There are fine views from the hill atop which towers this 1988 statue by Teodoro Cano portraying a *volador* musician playing his pipe and preparing for the four fliers to launch. To reach the monument, take Calle Centenario heading uphill from the southwest corner of the cathedral yard, before turning left into steep Callejón Centenario.

👉 Tours

Gaudencio Simbrón González   WALKING
(📱784-126-41-90; per day M$450) Guide Gaudencio Simbrón is more commonly known as *el de la ropa típica* (the guy who wears traditional clothes) because he sports Totonac costume. He can guide you through El Tajín, Papantla and its environs. He's based at Centro Cultural Ecoturistico Nuestras Raíces a couple of kilometres away from El Tajín.

✨ Festivals & Events

Feria de Corpus Christi   CULTURAL
(www.facebook.com/CorpusChristiPapantla; ⊘Jun) This is the big annual event in Papantla. As well as the bullfights, parades and *charreadas* (Mexican rodeos) that are usual in Mexico, Papantla celebrates its Totonac cultural heritage with spectacular indigenous dances. The main procession is on June 15 when *voladores* fly in elaborate ceremonies several times a day.

Festival de Vainilla   FOOD & DRINK
(⊘Dec) A major celebration in Papantla, the Vanilla Festival features indigenous dancers, gastronomic delights sold in street stalls, and all manner of vanilla products.

🛏 Sleeping

Papantla has an uninspiring selection of budget and midrange places to stay. However, prices are low and rooms are generally clean.

★Hotel Tajín   HOTEL $
(📱784-842-01-21; http://hoteltajin.mx; Núñez 104; s/d/tr M$690/770/940, ste from M$1200; 🅿❄🛜🏊) The retro Tajín is an intrinsic part of the Papantla experience with a prime edge-of-*zócalo* location and a stone-arch-fringed pool and onsite restaurant. It's not a fancy hotel by any means, but the whole place oozes character. Rooms do vary though – best to request one on the upper floors, which get more natural light.

Hotel Provincia Express   HOTEL $
(📱784-842-16-45; http://hotelprovinciaexpress. com; Enríquez 103; s/d M$500/750; ❄🛜) This welcoming hotel offers spacious, bright and pleasant rooms looking out across the main square – great for catching the town's atmosphere, but not so brilliant if you're after a quiet place to rest.

Hotel Hostal del Moncayo   GUESTHOUSE $
(📱784-842-04-98; http://hotelpapantla.web cindario.com; Zaragoza 108; s/d from M$500/780;

P ✳ 🛜) Looking like an eccentric castle, this family-run place is in a quieter part of town, less than 10 minutes' walk from the center. It has some pleasant, airy rooms upstairs, but avoid the darker, musty ones downstairs. There's limited parking on site.

🍴 Eating

The *zócalo* is surrounded by a good selection of local restaurants, cafes and busy street food stalls. Mercado Juárez, off the southwest corner of the plaza opposite the cathedral, has stalls on its upper floor that sell cheap, fresh regional food.

Café Catedral   BAKERY, CAFE $
(📞 784-842-53-17; cnr Núñez y Domínguez & Curato; cakes from M$30; ⊘ 9:30am-10pm) There are far fancier cafes in town but this unpretentious place is the best one (ask any local) and it doubles as a bakery. Grab a cake, muffin or *pan dulce* (sweet bread) from one of the display cases and sit down to enjoy a great cup of coffee.

★ Nakú Restaurante Papanteco MEXICAN $$
(📞 784-842-31-12; https://m.facebook.com/Naku Corazon; Colegio Militar s/n; mains M$70-179; ⊘ 8am-8pm; 🛜) This touristy restaurant, a couple of kilometers northeast of town, has traditionally dressed waitstaff serving supposedly authentic Totonac cuisine. The garden setting is nice, the food very tasty and the bread is baked in a big mud-clay oven.

On weekends during the afternoon there are traditional dance performances here. A taxi here from Papantla is M$25.

Al Son de Chapala   MEXICAN $$
(📞 784-842-22-67; Reforma 100; mains M$75-160; ⊘ 8am-10pm; 🛜) Perched like a theater box above the *zócalo* action, this colorfully decorated, popular cafe serves hearty portions of tasty Mexican food covering all the bases from tacos to prawns in a delicious smoky-chipotle sauce.

Plaza Pardo   MEXICAN $$
(📞 784-842-00-59; www.facebook.com/Restaurante PlazaPardo; Enríquez 105, 1st fl; mains M$85-170; ⊘ 7:30am-11:30pm; 🛜) There's no place better to absorb the atmosphere of Papantla than the Plaza Pardo's delightful balcony overlooking the *zócalo*. While the interior is perfectly pleasant, it's a big step down in romance and views. The menu offers a large range of *antojitos,* fish and meats, all cooked in pleasant but unmemorable ways.

Restaurante la Parroquia   INTERNATIONAL $$
(📞 784-842-01-21; http://hoteltajin.mx/restau rantes; Núñez y Domínguez 104, Hotel Tajín; mains M$75-140; ⊘ 8am-10pm; ✳ 🛜) With its exposed stone arches, this hotel bar-restaurant has plenty of atmosphere (particularly on the poolside terrace) and an extensive international menu that runs the gamut from *antojitos* and enchiladas to burgers. It also serves cocktails made with locally produced vanilla extract.

★ Ágora Alta Cocina   FUSION $$$
(📞 784-842-75-64; www.facebook.com/agorapa pantla; Libertad 301, 3rd fl; mains M$295-1250; ✳ 🛜) An unexpected surprise in a quiet residential part of town, Ágora Alta Cocina is indeed high – both in terms of location and the sky-high aspirations. The food? Nicely executed fusion, from smoked salmon with pear, goat's cheese and asparagus to delicate, herb-filled Asian-style shrimp and noodle soup and seared steak. Attentive young service and good desserts, too.

🛍 Shopping

Here in Mexico's leading vanilla-growing center, you'll find quality vanilla extract, vanilla pods and *figuras* (pods woven into the shapes of flowers, insects or crucifixes). Also good buys are traditional embroidered Totonac clothing and handmade baskets.

ℹ Information

Tourist office (Reforma 100; ⊘ 8am-5pm Mon-Fri) A kiosk inside the Ayuntamiento building, off the *zócalo*.

ℹ Getting There & Away

A few long-distance buses leave from Papantla's **Terminal ADO** (📞 784-101-35-01; cnr Juárez & Venustiano Carranza), a short, steep walk from the center. Taxis from the ADO to the center are M$20. Local buses leave from **Terminal Transportes Papantla** (cnr Av 20 de Noviembre & Olivo), just off the plaza by the Pemex station, for the coastal towns to the south and to Martínez de la Torre for connections to Tlapacoyan.

El Tajín

This wonderfully evocative and relatively under-visited **ancient city** (off Hwy 127; M$75; ⊘ 9am-5pm) is one of the best-preserved and most important pre-Hispanic cities in Mesoamerica, El Tajín's pyramids and temples burst off a plain surrounded by low, verdant hills 7km west of Papantla. These extensive ruins are the most impressive reminder of Classic Veracruz civilization. Come as late in the day as possible in order to catch the reddening sky, bubbling clouds and reflective calm of the site shortly before closing.

Among El Tajín's special features are rows of square niches on the sides of buildings, numerous ball courts, and sculptures depicting human sacrifice connected with the ball game. Archaeologist José García Payón believed that El Tajín's niches and stone mosaics symbolized day and night, light and dark, and life and death in a universe of dualities.

History

It was originally thought that El Tajín (the name is Totonac for 'thunder,' 'lightning' or 'hurricane') was settled in three phases between 100 BCE and 1200 CE, but the most recent research suggests that it reached its zenith as a city and ceremonial center between 800 and 900. Around 1200 the site was abandoned, possibly after a fire and attacks by Chichimec. Quickly engulfed by the jungle, it lay unknown until it was 'rediscovered' accidentally by an officious Spaniard looking for illegal tobacco plantations in 1785.

⊙ Sights

The site stretches across 10 sq km. To see everything, you'll walk a few kilometers over a couple of hours. There's little shade and it can get blazingly hot, so come early or late. Most buildings and carvings have some labeling in English and Spanish, but a guide would greatly aid your understanding.

★ Pirámide de los Nichos
ARCHAEOLOGICAL SITE

El Tajín's most emblematic structure, the beautifully proportioned Pyramid of the Niches, is just off the Plaza Menor. The six lower levels, each surrounded by rows of small square niches, climb to 18m. Archaeologists believe that there were originally 365 niches, suggesting that the building may have been used as a kind of calendar. In its heyday, it was painted red with black niches.

Museo El Tajín
MUSEUM

(⊙9am-5pm) Do drop in to the onsite museum at the entrance to El Tajín (included in your ticket price) to see an excellent model of the site. It also displays a collection of statuary, pottery, delicate bas reliefs and part of a burial site from the ruins.

El Tajín

Ⓝ 0 —— 200 m
0 —— 0.1 miles

Plaza de las Columnas
Edificio B
Edificio A
Edificio D
Plaza El Tajín Chico
Gran Greca
Edificio C
Pirámide de los Nichos
Edificio I
Juego de Pelota de las Pinturas
Juego de Pelota Norte
Estructura 3
Plaza De Dios Tajin
Templo de las Alamenas
Juego de Pelota de Venus
Juego de Pelota Sur
Plaza del Arroyo
Juego de Pelota de las Serientes
Museo El Tajín, Visitor Center, ♿, Parking Lot (180m)

VERACRUZ EL TAJÍN

Juego de Pelota de las Pinturas
ARCHAEOLOGICAL SITE

The Juego de Pelota de las Pinturas (Ball Court of the Paintings), to one side of the Pirámide de los Nichos, is so called as it has two very impressively preserved red-and-blue geometric friezes on its north-facing side.

El Tajín Chico
ARCHAEOLOGICAL SITE

El Tajín Chico was the government area of the ancient city and would have been home to the ruling classes. Many of the buildings have geometric stone mosaic patterns known as 'Greco' (Greek). The raised level here gives an excellent view of the lower site.

The path north toward Plaza El Tajín Chico passes the **Juego de Pelota Norte** (Northern Ball Court), which is smaller and older than the southern court and has fainter carvings on its sides.

Edificio I, probably once a palace, has some terrific carvings and beautifully preserved, blue, yellow and red paintwork. **Edificio C**, on the east side, with three levels and a staircase facing the plaza, was initially painted blue and sports some unusual whorled decorations. **Edificio A**, on the plaza's north side, has an arch construction known as a corbeled arch, with two sides jutting closer to each other until they are joined at the top by a single slab, which is typical of Maya architecture. Its presence here is yet another oddity in the jigsaw puzzle of pre-Hispanic cultures.

Northwest of Plaza El Tajín Chico is the unreconstructed **Plaza de las Columnas** (Plaza of the Columns), one of the site's most important structures. It originally housed a large open patio and adjoining buildings stretching over the hillside. Some wonderful reassembled carved columns are displayed in the museum.

Juego de Pelota Sur   ARCHAEOLOGICAL SITE
(Southern Ball Court) Some 17 ball courts have been found at El Tajín. The Juego de Pelota Sur dates from about 1150 and is the most famous of the courts, owing to the six relief carvings on its walls that depict various aspects of the ball-game ritual.

The panel on the northeast corner is the easiest to make out: in the center, three ball-players perform a ritual post-game sacrifice with one player ready to plunge a knife into the chest of another, whose arms are held by the third player. Death gods and a presiding figure look on. The other panels depict various scenes of ceremonial drinking of *pulque* (a milky, low-alcohol brew made from the *maguey* plant).

Plaza Menor   PLAZA
Beyond the Plaza del Arroyo in the south of the site, flanked by pyramids on four sides, is the Plaza Menor (Lesser Plaza), part of El Tajín's main ceremonial center and possible marketplace, with a low platform in the middle. All of the structures around this plaza were probably topped by small temples, with some decorated with red or blue paint, traces of which remain.

⁜ Festivals & Events

★ **Voladores Performances**   CULTURAL
(⊙noon-5pm) A 30m-high *voladores* pole stands outside the entrance to the ruins next to the mass of souvenir stalls. Totonacs perform the *voladores* rite several times per day. Before they start, a performer in Totonac regalia requests donations (around M$20 per person should suffice) from the audience.

ⓘ Information

The **visitor center** (off Hwy 127; ⊙9am-5pm) has a left-luggage room and information desk. Those seeking more information should look for the book *Tajín: Mystery and Beauty*, by Leonardo Zaleta, sometimes available in several languages in the souvenir shops.

ⓘ Getting There & Away

From Papantla, buses (M$20) marked 'Pirámides Tajín' leave every 20 minutes or so from Calle 16 de Septiembre, directly behind Hotel Tajín. The site is 300m from the highway – buses drop you off near the market, before the entrance to Tajín. Taxis to/from Papantla cost M$70.

Tecolutla

📞766 / POP 24,258

This relaxed seaside town, with a reasonable strip of sand and a slew of seafood restaurants and inexpensive hotels, passes for one of Veracruz' more pleasant beachfronts. Cancún this most definitely isn't. Instead, the place is as dead as a doornail midweek, though on weekends, in high summer and during Semana Santa it's a different story. There are banks and ATMs on the plaza. For more information see https://tecolutlaveracruz.mx.

🕺 Activities

★ **Vida Milenaria**   VOLUNTEERING
(📞766-846-04-67; www.vidamilenaria.org.mx; Niños Héroes 1; donation required; ⊙7am-9am Jun-Nov)
🌿 This small turtle conservation place (at the beach end of Niños Héroes) is run by Fernando Manzano Cervantes, known locally as 'Papá Tortuga.' In addition to educating the public, he has been effectively protecting and releasing green and Kemp's ridley turtles here for over 35 years. Visitors gather in droves to watch baby-turtle releases most mornings in season.

If you stop by, think about buying a souvenir because this is a privately funded show. Volunteers are especially needed here in April and May, when patrolling the beaches (35km worth) and collecting the turtle eggs is imperative (when possible the eggs are left in their original nest site but at others time they're reburied in a safer area). Most of the patrolling is done at night between 10pm and 6am. Camping and the use of kitchen and bathroom facilities is free to volunteers.

The highest number of turtles is released in June, but in late October you can join hundreds of locals in celebrating the release of the baby turtles in the Festival de Las Tortugas.

Boat & Fishing Trips   BOATING
(📞766-115-10-95; off Ribera del Río; boat from M$500) Walk toward the Río Tecolutla on Emilio Carranza and you'll hit the *embarcadero* (pier), where boats wait to take you

fishing or on trips through dense mangrove forests rich with wildlife, including pelicans and alligators. For more information contact friendly, English-speaking guide Arutoro.

🛏 Sleeping & Eating

There's no shortage of accommodations in this tourist-reliant town, with plenty of cheap hotels near the plaza and nicer ones toward the ocean. Rates plummet midweek and during quiet periods.

On the beach, all the *palapa* places sell cold beer, while vendors hawk seafood cocktails. In the evenings, vendors around the main square do a brisk business.

★ Punta Bocana HOTEL **$$**
(☑766-846-01-12; http://puntabocanaspa.com.mx; Centenario s/n; r/ste from M$900/1100; P🌐🛜🏊) Heads above the competition, Punta Bocana is a serene resort offering spacious, comfortable rooms decorated in soothing pastel tones with hammocks on their private balconies. Note the cheapest rooms don't have sea views but the property is set in verdant, flower-filled grounds adjacent to the beach.

Aqua Inn Hotel HOTEL **$$**
(☑766-846-03-58; www.tecolutla.com.mx/aquainn; cnr Aldama & Av Obregón; r from M$800; P🌐🛜🏊) This modern place in the middle of town and a short walk from the water has clean, functional rooms, all with cable TV. It has a small rooftop pool and the attached **Porteño Café** (cnr Aldama & Av Obregón; ⊙8am-10pm) which is good for breakfast, coffee and snacks. Rates start at M$1200 in peak times.

★ El Camarón Desvelado SEAFOOD **$$**
(☑766-846-02-35; Aldama 13; mains M$80-280; ⊙8am-9pm) The Sleepless Shrimp is the standout seafood restaurant in town, briskly serving platters of *arroz a la tumbada*, garlic shrimp, octopus in its own ink and fish stuffed with seafood, among other ocean goodies. Also check out the taxidermy marine specimens decorating one wall!

ℹ Getting There & Away

Tecolutla is 41km east of Papantla. There are regular 2nd-class Transportes Papantla buses between Tecolutla and Papantla (M$60) but you'll likely have to transfer through Gutiérrez Zamora, from where you can also catch shared taxi to the seaside (M$15).

OFF THE BEATEN TRACK

COSTA ESMERALDA

The 'Emerald Coast' is a 25km or so long stretch of beachfront running between Tecolutla and Nautla. Large and small resort hotels are strung along it at regular intervals. One of the best is minimalist design **Hotel Azúcar** (☑232-321-06-78; www.hotelazucar.com; Carretera Federal Nautla–Poza Rica Km 83.5; r incl breakfast from US$171; P🌐🛜🏊), which offers 20 chic villas with hammocks and private terraces, gorgeous whitewashed public areas topped in thatch, a sumptuous pool, an impressive spa and a decent restaurant.

From the 1st-class ADO **bus station** (cnr Abasolo & Ahumada) a few blocks from the main plaza, there are services to some major cities including Mexico City's Terminal Norte (M$467, 5¼ hours, six daily), as well as services to Papantla (M$83, one hour, seven daily).

Tuxpan
☑783 / POP 78,523

Of all the major towns in the north of the state, the one you may want to stop over in is Tuxpan (sometimes spelled Túxpam). This steamy fishing town and minor oil port, 300km north of Veracruz and 190km south of Tampico, is no great beauty, but is well set up for overnighting travelers. Arrange a diving trip, treat yourself to excellent seafood, take a trip across the broad Río Tuxpan to visit a little museum devoted to Cuban-Mexican friendship, or join vacationing Mexicans on Playa Norte, the beach 14km northeast of the center.

◉ Sights

Museo de la Amistad México-Cuba MUSEUM
(Mexican-Cuban Friendship Museum; ☑783-834-05-97; Obregón 1; ⊙9am-5pm) FREE This modernist house is now a small museum commemorating the colonial histories of Mexico and Cuba and their significance to Fidel Castro's ill-fated uprising of 1956. Murals and photos of Castro and Che Guevara abound and there's a tiny model of the revolutionary yacht, *Granma*. To get here, take a *lancha* (M$5) across the river from the quay near the ADO bus station.

On November 25, 1956, the errant lawyer-turned-revolutionary, Fidel Castro, set sail from the Río Tuxpan with 82 poorly equipped soldiers, including Che Guevara and Castro's brother Raúl, to start an uprising in Cuba. The sailing was made possible thanks to an encounter in Mexico City between Castro and Antonio del Conde Pontones (aka 'El Cuate'). On meeting Castro for the first time, Pontones, a legal arms dealer, was immediately taken by the Cuban's strong personality and agreed to help him obtain guns and a boat. To smooth the process, he bought a house on the south side of the Río Tuxpan, where he moored the boat and allowed Fidel to meet in secret. Today that house is the Museo de la Amistad México-Cuba.

Activities

The diving and snorkeling around **Isla Lobos** around 2¾ hours by boat from Tuxpan, is highly recommended. The slinky sandbar island can also be reached from Tamiahua, 42km north, where you can also take boats tours or go kayaking in the third-largest coastal lagoon in Mexico. Contact either **Escuela De Buceo Tuxpan** (☑783-117-78-60; www.buceotuxpan.com.mx; Carretera a la Barra Norte; diving from M$2160; ⊙9am-6pm) or **Puerto Lobos Dive Camp** (☑768-857-94-21, 555-606-36-02; http://puertolobos.net; Mangles 25, Tamiahua; diving from M$2160) to arrange such activities.

🛏️ Sleeping & Eating

Hotel Reforma HOTEL **$$**
(☑783-834-02-10; http://hotel-reforma.com.mx; Av Juárez 25; s/d M$900/1000; P🏳️🏳️) The grand exterior of the Reforma leads into a smart atrium lobby with a small fountain and some 98 comfortable if rather functional rooms. They include flat-screen TVs

and relentless brown carpeting. There's a smart **restaurant** downstairs.

★ Taquería Los Nuevos 4 Vientos STREET FOOD **$**
(☑783-134-48-76; Morelos s/n; tacos from M$10; ⊙9:30am-midnight) One of four *taquerías* in a row, this one wins our praise for its extensive collection of fresh salsas, which complement the nine types of meat (*asado,* tripe, *pastor* etc) that are deftly fried and scooped into tacos. Perpetually packed with locals at mealtimes, it clearly gets their vote, too.

Restaurante Mora SEAFOOD **$$**
(☑783-837-09-93; www.facebook.com/Restaurante. Mora; Ribera del Pescador s/n; mains M$100-160; ⊙noon-9pm) The first of a long row of simple seafood restaurants along the Laguna de Tampamachoco, Mora serves up stuffed crabs, *camarones enchipotlados*, oysters on the half shell, and the fresh catch of the day, which is grilled, fried, stuffed with shrimp or *a la diabla* (hot!).

ℹ️ Information

Tourist Booth (☑783-110-28-11; http://tuxpan.com.mx; Juárez 25, Palacio Municipal; ⊙9am-7pm Mon-Fri, 10am-2pm Sat) Staff at this booth have vast reserves of enthusiasm: you'll go away overloaded with maps and brochures.

ℹ️ Getting There & Away

Most 1st-class buses leaving Tuxpan are *de paso* (passing through). Booking a seat in advance might be a good idea. There are several bus terminals, but the 1st-class ADO **bus station** (☑783-834-01-02; cnr Rodríguez & Av Juárez) is the most convenient from the center.

There is a M$5 ferry service across the river at various points between Guerrero and Parque Reforma.

BUSES FROM TUXPAN

First-class departures from the ADO station include the following:

DESTINATION	FARE (M$)	TIME (HR)	FREQUENCY (PER DAY)
Mexico City (Terminal Norte)	430-486	4-5½	12
Papantla	110	2	13
Tampico	308	3¼	frequent
Veracruz	455-512	5½-6½	18
Villahermosa	1114	12¾-13½	6
Xalapa	465	5¾-6½	10

SOUTHERN VERACRUZ

Southeast Veracruz is arguably the most beautiful part of the state, and yet tourism is still on a very modest scale. Here you'll find languorous wetlands, volcano-dappled rainforest, breathtaking lakes, some beautiful beaches along the little-visited Costa de Oro, and the superb Reserva de la Biosfera Los Tuxtlas, a well-run ecological reserve that will appeal to anyone wanting to get off the beaten track. The wilder, volcanic portion of the reserve is accessed via San Andrés Tuxtla, whereas the Laguna Catemaco portion is renowned for bird-watching and is closer to the eponymous town. The Olmec civilization flourished here over 2000 years ago; learn something about their ancient culture at the archaeological site Tres Zapotes. And there's Tlacotalpan, an enchanting Unesco World Heritage site notable for its colonial-era architecture. If you're heading south into Tabasco, the unpretty commercial center of Acayucan is a passable stopover.

Tlacotalpan

📞 288 / POP 8,850

Once an important river port, this Unesco World Heritage town has changed little since the 1820s. The color palette is extraordinary here; the lucid sunsets over the adjacent Río Papaloapan add subtle oranges and yellows to the rainbow of single-story colonial houses, bringing to mind a more soporific Havana.

In September 2010, Tlacotalpan was hit by devastating floods, which inundated 500 historic buildings and prompted the evacuation of 8500 people. The recovery has been remarkable, with only a high watermark drawn onto a wall on Calle Alegre to show how disastrous the flooding was.

Its smattering of ho-hum museums aside, this is the kind of town where the greatest pleasure is found in wandering the technicolor streets and taking in the atmosphere. Tlacotalpan has two appealing plazas, Parque Hidalgo and Plaza Zaragoza, directly adjacent to each other. Be sure to take a stroll by the riverside and down Cházaro.

⊙ Sights

Villin Montalio GALLERY
(📞 288-884-25-16; Av 5 de Mayo 53; ⊙9am-6pm Mon-Sat) Tlacotalpan is well known for its locally made cedar furniture, including rocking chairs. Drop by this workshop in business since 1944 to see it being made,

and to see some of the handsome finished products on display, including in the family's personal rooms.

Capilla de la Candelaria CHURCH
(Parque Hidalgo) The pale-salmon-painted Capilla de la Candelaria dates from 1779. Its mid vault is made of Veracruz coral stone and the interior is elaborately painted.

Parroquía San Cristóbal CHURCH
(Plaza Zaragoza; ⊙8am-6pm) This neoclassical church, begun in 1812, is gorgeously painted in blue and white and is the star of Plaza Zaragoza.

Museo Salvador Ferrando MUSEUM
(Alegre 6; M$20; ⊙11am-7pm) Named after a Tlacotalpan artist, this is the best of Tlacotalpan's handful of mini-museums based within a charming old colonial mansion. Its exhibits are eclectic, ranging from vintage Singer sewing machines, old muskets and paintings of local notables.

Teatro Netzahualcóyotl THEATER
(Av Carranza; M$10; ⊙8am-3pm Mon-Fri) Step into the gorgeous French-style Teatro Netzahualcóyotl, built in 1891, and the caretaker will turn on the auditorium and stage lights so you can take in its full splendor. It occasionally hosts events.

Casa Cultural de Agustín Lara MUSEUM
(📞288-884-22-55; Cházaro 2; M$20; ⊙10am-6pm Mon-Sat) This museum features old photos of Tlacotalpan, and those of *tlacotalpeño* Agustín Lara (1897-1970) – a legendary musician, composer and Casanova – as well as a Frankenstein-lookalike mannequin of the man seated by a piano. Its appeal is perhaps greater to Mexicans than it is to foreign tourists.

🏃 Activities

Bici Cletando CYCLING
(📞229-2156-83-46; Cházaro; per hour M$50; ⊙9am-6pm) Wonderfully flat, Tlacotalpan is a perfect spot for bike riding. You can arrange bike hire through Bici Cletando, which rents out bikes from a gift shop on the corner of Plaza Zaragoza.

Boat Rides BOATING
(1hr M$350) If you walk the *malecón* near the restaurants, you're bound to run into a *lanchero* (boatman) offering to whisk you down the scenic river for an hour-long boat ride to see a nearby lagoon. It's not the Amazon, but it's a lovely way to spend a late afternoon.

✨ Festivals & Events

Día de la Candelaria RELIGIOUS
(☉ Jan & Feb) In late January and early February, Tlacotalpan's huge Candelaria festival features bull-running in the streets. An image of the Virgin is also floated down the river, followed by a flotilla of small boats.

🛏 Sleeping

There's a smattering of mostly midrange guesthouses inside beautiful colonial buildings. Prices triple or quadruple during the Candelaria holiday, during which reservations, which should be made weeks ahead of time, are essential.

★Hotel Doña Juana GUESTHOUSE $
(☑288-884-34-80; http://hoteldonajuana.com; Juan Enríquez 32; r M$650-750; ❄🤶) This modern multilayered building has small, well-kept rooms. The ample use of terracotta colors and statement art make it stand out from many similarly priced places, as do the helpful, smiling staff. Avoid the single dark room with a partial view of the inner courtyard.

Hostal El Patio GUESTHOUSE $
(☑288-884-31-97; www.hostalelpatio.com.mx; Alvarado 52; r M$550-650; ⓟ@🤶) This friendly guesthouse combines a warm color scheme with spacious, well-appointed rooms (with rain showers) and a leafy courtyard. There's a resident miniature schnauzer to love too.

Hotel Posada Doña Lala HISTORIC HOTEL $
(☑288-884-25-80; http://hoteldonalala.com.mx; Av Carranza 11; r/ste M$700/1000; ⓟ⊖❄🤶🏊) Doña Lala is a handsome colonial-style hotel with spacious, elegant rooms with high ceilings. For great views try to get a room overlooking the riverside square; half the rooms are dark and face the inner courtyard. It has an excellent restaurant downstairs and even a pool to enjoy.

Hotel Casa del Río HOTEL $$
(☑288-884-29-47; www.casadelrio.com.mx; Cházaro 39; r/ste M$850/1100; ⊖❄🤶) Creating modern, stylish, minimalist rooms in a colonial mansion is definitely a challenge, but the Hotel Casa del Río does a good job of it with its nine spacious offerings. Its best feature is definitely the terrace overlooking the river.

🍴 Eating & Drinking

The riverside is lined with fish restaurants that operate from lunchtime to sunset each day, serving up the catch of the day. See which one looks busiest and join the locals. There are several dining options on and around Plaza Zaragoza as well – but make sure you slather up with mosquito repellent in the evenings.

Restaurant Doña Lala MEXICAN $$
(Av Carranza 11; mains M$60-325; ☉7am-7pm; 🤶) The smartest eating option in town, this place inside the eponymous hotel has a friendly staff and is patronized by a crowd of local eccentrics who vie for the best seats on its terrace. The wide-ranging selection of Mexican dishes won't disappoint and the locally caught seafood (especially the prawns) is very good.

Rokala MEXICAN $$
(☑288-884-22-92; Plaza Zaragoza; mains M$80-220; ☉5:30pm-midnight; 🤶) With its unbeatable position under the colonial arches on the Plaza Zaragoza, this friendly place with alfresco dining buzzes all year-round. Mains range from fresh fish and prawns plucked straight from the river to meat grills and typical *antojitos*. For atmosphere alone it's a clear winner, but the food itself is only average.

El K-Fecito CAFE
(www.facebook.com/elkfe; Plaza Zaragoza; ☉5pm-2am) At the junction of the two main plazas, serving great coffee, cakes and various simple snacks, El K-Fecito is a good spot to relax and take in the passing parade each evening.

ℹ Information

Tourist Office (☑288-884-33-05; www.tlacotalpan-turismo.gob.mx; Plaza Zaragoza, Ayuntamiento; ☉9am-3pm Mon-Fri) Right on Plaza Zaragoza, with helpful maps and other information.

ℹ Getting There & Away

Hwy 175 runs from Tlacotalpan up the Papaloapan valley to Tuxtepec, then twists and turns over the mountains to Oaxaca (320km). The riverside ADO **station** (☑288-884-21-25; Cházaro 37) is situated outside the Mercado Municipal, three blocks east of the center – services include Mexico City (TAPO; M$844, 8½ hours, 10pm), Puebla (M$654, 6¼ hours, 10pm), San Andrés Tuxtla (M$126, two hours, three daily) and Xalapa (M$337, three hours, 6:30am).

TRV buses connect to Veracruz ($113, 2 hours).

Santiago Tuxtla

☑ 294 / POP 15,500 / ELEV 300M

Santiago Tuxtla centers on a lovely, verdant main plaza – one of the state's prettiest and all atweet with Mexican grackles – and is surrounded by the rolling green foothills of the volcanic Sierra de los Tuxtlas. It's far more laid-back and considerably more charming than its built-up neighbor San Andrés, with its plaza strewn with women arm-in-arm, couples lip-to-lip and shoes getting vigorously shined. Its museum and its giant Olmec head alone make it worth a quick visit.

◉ Sights

Olmec Head   MONUMENT
(Plaza Olmeca) Dominating the main plaza, this stone monolith is known as the 'Cobata Head,' after the estate where it was found. Thought to be a very late Olmec production, it's the biggest known Olmec head, 3.4m in height and weighing in at 40 tonnes, and is unique in that its eyes are closed.

Museo Tuxteco   MUSEUM
(☑294-947-10-76; www.inah.gob.mx; Plaza Olmeca; M$55; ⊙9am-5pm Tue-Sun) This small museum on Santiago Tuxtla's main plaza focuses on the pre-Hispanic peoples that inhabited this region from 1600 BCE to around 1200 CE, with a particular emphasis on the Olmec, Mexico's first-known major civilization. Artifacts include a Totonac effigy of a woman who died in childbirth, ceramic plates used in human-sacrifice ceremonies on the Isla de Sacrificios, Olmec stone carvings (including a colossal head), a monkey-faced *hacha* (ax) with obsidian eyes, and a Tres Zapotes altar replica.

🛏 Sleeping & Eating

★Mesón de Santiago   HOTEL $
(☑294-947-16-70; Calle 5 de Mayo 8; d M$760; P❄🖥🐾) With a well-preserved colonial exterior and enormous, creeper-covered trees in the peaceful courtyard, this fantastic place right on the main plaza is unexpected in such a quiet and little-visited place. Rooms are tastefully decorated, with deeply burnished wood furniture, beautifully tiled bathrooms and domed staircases.

There's also a small pool.

La Joya   MEXICAN $
(☑294-947-01-77; cnr Juárez & Comonfort; mains M$45-90; ⊙7am-11pm) The plastic tablecloths, alfresco-only chairs and rustic open-to-view kitchen scream 'Moctezuma's revenge,' but fear not: La Joya delivers where it matters –

VERACRUZ SANTIAGO TUXTLA

Los Tuxtlas

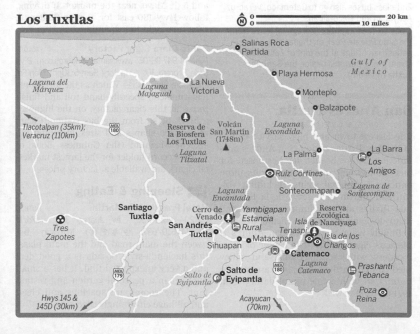

BUSES FROM SANTIAGO TUXTLA

First-class bus services include the following:

DESTINATION	FARE (M$)	TIME (HR)	FREQUENCY (PER DAY)
Córdoba	353-402	4	4
Mexico City (TAPO)	721-847	9-10½	5
Puebla	510-682	6½-7¾	4
San Andrés Tuxtla	47-65	⅓	frequent
Tlacotalpan	108	1½	3
Veracruz	223	2½-3	10
Villahermosa	501	6½	1 (9pm)
Xalapa	365	4¾	3

good, tasty Mexican food. It's on a corner of the main plaza, to one side of the Olmec head.

❶ Getting There & Away

Most buses arrive and depart from the **bus station** near the junction of Morelos and the highway. ADO buses **stop** (☑ 294-947-04-38; cnr Hwy 180 & Guerrero) on the highway. To get to the center, continue down Morelos, then turn right into Ayuntamiento, which leads to the main plaza, a few blocks away.

All local and regional buses and *taxis colectivos* to San Andrés Tuxtla are frequent and stop at the junction of Morales and Hwy 180. A private taxi between the towns is M$80. Frequent 2nd-class buses also go to Catemaco, Veracruz, Acayucan and Tlacotalpan.

Taxis to Tres Zapotes (Zaragoza) leave from the Sitio Puente Real, on the far side of the pedestrian bridge at the foot of Zaragoza (the street going downhill beside the Santiago Tuxtla museum).

San Andrés Tuxtla

☑ 294 / POP 61,800 / ELEV 360M

The largest town and busy service center of the Las Tuxtlas region, San Andrés puts function before beauty. It's best used for bus connections and link-ups to its more enticing peripheral sights, including Volcán San Martín in Reserva de la Biosfera Los Tuxtlas and the impressive waterfall Salto de Eyipantla. Cigar aficionados will definitely want to visit, as San Andrés is Mexico's cigar capital. The center of town is orderly, with a soaring orange-and-yellow tiled church on the main plaza and a *casa municipal* with a fine mural dating from 1971 on its stairwell.

◉ Sights

★ **Salto de Eyipantla** WATERFALL
(Salto de Eyipantla; M$20; ◷ 8am-6pm) Twelve kilometers southeast of San Andrés, in the eponymous village, a 250-step staircase leads down to the absolutely spectacular Salto de Eyipantla, a 50m-high, 40m-wide waterfall. Scenes from the movie *Apocalypto* were filmed here. To avoid the steps (and a soaking at the base) there's a *mirador* (lookout) at the top of the falls, which is free.

Frequent TLT buses (M$15) and taxis (shared/whole M$30/100) run from San Andrés, leaving from the corner of Cabada and 5 de Mayo, near the market. If driving, follow Hwy 180 east for 4km to Sihuapan, then turn right to Eyipantla.

Santa Clara Cigar Factory FACTORY
(☑ 294-947-99-06; www.santaclarapuros.com; Blvd 5 de Febrero 10; ◷ factory 9am-5:30pm Mon-Fri, shop 9am-8pm) **FREE** Watch as the *torcedores* (cigarmakers) speedily hand roll and finish *puros* at this cigar factory, on the highway, a block or so from the bus station. Cigars of assorted shapes and sizes, including the 48.3cm Magnum (the Guinness Book of World Record holder for the largest marketed cigar), are available at factory prices.

🛏 Sleeping & Eating

Hotel Posada San Martín HOTEL $
(☑ 294-942-10-36; Av Juárez 304; s/d/tr M$524/610/697; 🅿🕸📶🌊) Midway between the main road and the main plaza, this hacienda-style posada is a good deal and a very unexpected find. It has a small pool set in a peaceful garden and restaurant. The rooms are spacious and clean and all have charmingly tiled sinks.

Winni's CAFE $

(☑294-942-01-10; 20 de Noviembre s/n; mains M$60-180; ⊙7am-midnight; ☎) Join the rest of San Andrés on the corner of the main plaza and sip an espresso while munching on a plate of eggs (cooked a dozen ways), some *chilaquiles* or other mains. For lunch there's a good two-course special including a drink and cookie for dessert for M$68.

★ **Mr Taco Segovia** STREET FOOD $

(www.facebook.com/Mr.TacoSegovia; cnr Madero & Allende; tacos M$9; ⊙7.30pm-2am) Satisfying late-night munchies since 1996, this taco stand is a study in nose-to-tail eating, Mexico-style. Watch the guys fry up the tortillas and top them with *suadero* (cut of beef from between the belly and the leg), *tripita* (tripe), *seso* (brain) and more, and add some spice with homemade salsa.

ⓘ Information

Tourist Office (☑294-947-93-00 ex 613; Independencia; ⊙9am-3pm Mon-Fri) Head downhill from the central square and look for the building with a mural on the left. The small tourist office on the 1st floor here can provide up-to-date info on the Reserva de la Biosfera Los Tuxtlas and other local sights.

ⓘ Getting There & Away

San Andrés is the transportation center for Los Tuxtlas, with fairly good bus services in every direction. First-class buses with ADO and 2nd-class with AU depart from their respective **stations** (☑294-942-08-71; cnr Juárez & Blvd 5 de Febrero) just off the Santiago Tuxtla–Catemaco highway, and about a 10-minute walk from the center. Frequent **taxis colectivos** (5 de Mayo s/n) to Catemaco and Santiago leave from the market – they're the fastest way of getting to local destinations but cost a fraction more than the rickety 2nd-class TLT buses that also leave from a block north of the market and skirt the north side of town on Blvd 5 de Febrero (Hwy 180).

Catemaco

☑294 / POP 27,615 / ELEV 340M

The tourist town of Catemaco sits pretty on the shore of the 16km-long Laguna Catemaco (actually a lake) ringed by verdantly cloaked and softly shaped volcanic hills. With a long tradition of witchcraft – shamans who will exorcise your nasty spirits – a gorgeous lakeside setting, proximity to some great bird-watching, swimming holes and pristine, isolated beaches, Catemaco is an ideal base for exploring Los Tuxtlas and surrounds.

DON'T MISS

TRES ZAPOTES

One of Veracruz's most important archaeological sites, the late-Olmec settlement of Tres Zapotes, lies around 21km west of Santiago Tuxtla. The site was an Olmec settlement for over 2000 years, from around 1200 BCE to 1000 CE, and was probably first inhabited while the great Olmec center of La Venta (Tabasco) still flourished. After the destruction of La Venta (about 400 BCE), the city carried on in what archaeologists call an 'epi-Olmec' phase – the period during which the Olmec culture dwindled, as other civilizations (notably Izapa and Maya) came to the fore.

Tres Zapotes is now just a series of mounds in cornfields, but the eponymous archaeological **museum** (☑294-947-01-96; www.inah.gob.mx; Estela Núñez, Tres Zapotes; M$45; ⊙9am-5pm Tue-Sun) showcases important finds from the site. The biggest piece, Stela A, depicts three human figures in the mouth of a jaguar. Other pieces include a sculpture of what may have been a captive with hands tied behind his back, and the upturned face of a woman carved into a throne or altar. The Olmec preceded Mexico's other major civilizations, and are notable for sculpting giant human heads, a 1.5m example of which, dating from 100 BCE, takes pride of place in the museum. The museum attendant is happy to answer questions in Spanish or give a tour (tipping is appreciated).

From Santiago Tuxtla, take a 2nd-class bus (M$35) or taxi (M$50/200 *colectivo/ private*). If driving, the road to Tres Zapotes goes southwest from Santiago Tuxtla; a 'Zona Arqueológica' sign points the way from Hwy 180. Eight kilometers down this road, you fork right onto a paved stretch for the last 13km to Tres Zapotes. It comes out at a T-junction, from where you go left then left again to reach the museum.

Catemaco

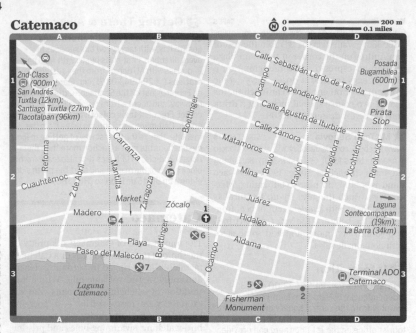

Catemaco

⊙ Sights & Activities

Basílica del Carmen   CHURCH
(Aldama 8) Resplendent in blue and white on Catemaco's *zócalo*, this church was named a basilica (ie a church with special ceremonial rights) in 1961, due primarily to its position as a pilgrimage site for the Virgen del Carmen. It's said she appeared to a fisherman in a cave by Laguna Catemaco in 1664, in conjunction with a volcanic eruption. A couple of statues of the virgin, whose feast day is July 16, reside in the church.

The intricately decorated interior and splendid stained glass of the church belie its modernity; the current building only

dates from 1953, though it looks at least a century older.

**★ Reserva Ecológica
de Nanciyaga**   OUTDOORS
(☎294-943-01-99; www.nanciyaga.com; Carretera Catemaco–Coyame; ⊙ day visits 9am-6pm) 🌿 On the northeast shore of the Laguna Catemaco, 8km from Catemaco, this well run ecological reserve preserves a small tract of dense rainforest. Here you can take part in a variety of activities including guided nature walks (from M$80), kayaking (M$60), mud baths (M$250) or sweating in a temascal (M$250). Arrive by *pirata* (pickup truck; M$12), taxi (M$80) or by boat (M$80 per person; hire in Catemaco).

There's a very pleasant lakeside **restaurant** (mains M$110-175) and it's possible to stay overnight in solar-powered **cabins** (packages incl meals & activities M$1100-1900). You have to walk to the bathrooms, so it's a mix of rustic and high-quality. It's not for everyone, but it provides an incredible experience for those who want to be very close to nature while being reasonably comfortable.

Laguna Catemaco Cruises   BOATING
🚤 Numerous *lancheros* along the *malecón* offer similar boat trips around the lake, charging either per person (around M$150) or

around M$900 for the whole boat for around an hour. Outings typically include stops on several islands to check out the wildlife.

You can visit several islands on the lake; on the largest, **Isla Tenaspi**, Olmec sculptures have been discovered. **Isla de los Changos** (Monkey Island) shelters red-cheeked monkeys, originally from Thailand, introduced by the Universidad Veracruzana in 1974. **Isla Agaltepec** is home to endangered (and very vocal) howler monkeys. East of town are a few modest gray-sand beaches where you can take a dip in cloudy water if you don't mind Morelet's crocodiles who live in the lake (and haven't attacked a human to date).

🛏 Sleeping & Eating

The lake provides the specialties here: *tegogolo* (a snail, reputed to be an aphrodisiac, eaten with chili, tomato, onion and lime) sold by street vendors, and *chipalchole* (shrimp or crab-claw soup). Many similar-standard restaurants serving fresh fish line the *malecón*.

★ **Posada Bugambilea**   GUESTHOUSE $
(✆ 294-943-18-25; www.posadabugambilia.com; 20 de Octobre 5; r M$350-750; 🅿 ❄ 🛜) On the edge of town and drowning in bougainvillea blossoms, with two cats and a small dog playing on the patio, this immaculate guesthouse is run by Chepina, the loveliest proprietor in town, who'll shower you with advice and attention. Rooms are spacious and airy and benefit from the quiet you won't find in the town center.

From the upstairs terrace there's a view of the lake.

Hotel Los Arcos   HOTEL $
(✆ 294-943-00-03; Madero 7; r/q incl breakfast from M$450/600; 🅿 ❄ 🛜 🏊) Centrally located, Los Arcos is a friendly, well-run place with neatly decorated, small rooms with their own semi-private outdoor space and seating area. There's even a (very) small pool. Sound carries, though, so you may feel as if you're in bed with your neighbors.

Hotel Acuario   HOTEL $
(✆ 294-943-04-18; cnr Boettinger & Carranza; s/d/tr from M$450/550/700; 🅿 ❄ 🛜) This friendly budget option has 25 clean rooms just off the *zócalo*. It's well kept, though plain. Some rooms have balconies and views – try for one of these, as those at the back lack natural light. Cable TV is a bonus.

La Casa de Los Tesoros   CAFE $
(✆ 294-943-29-10; Aldama 4; mains M$50-120; ⊙ 10am-10pm Mon-Thu, 9am-10pm Fri-Sun; 🛜) This hippie-styled place is part cafe-restaurant, part used bookstore (spot some vintage Lonely Planet guides here), part gallery and part arty gift shop, selling locally produced handicrafts. It's renowned among locals for its breakfasts (build-your-own omelettes) in particular, but there are also burgers, sandwiches, brownies, herbal teas and more.

La Ola   SEAFOOD $$
(✆ 294-943-00-10; Paseo del Malecón s/n; mains M$80-185; ⊙ 8am-8pm; 🛜) There's a nice view from this large waterfront restaurant on the *malecón*, serving all the seafood you could want, including reasonable *pargo* (red snapper), barbecued shrimp and more.

THE WITCHING HOUR

On the first Friday in March each year, hundreds of *brujos* (shamans), witches and healers from all over Mexico descend on Catemaco to perform a mass cleansing ceremony on Cerro Mono Blanco, a little way north of the town. The event is designed to rid them of the previous year's negative energies, though in recent years the whole occasion has become more commercial than supernatural. Floods of Mexicans also head into town at this time to grab a shamanic consultation or *limpia* (cleansing), and eat, drink and be merry in a bizarre mix of otherworldly fervor and hedonistic indulgence.

Witchcraft traditions in this part of Veracruz go back centuries, mixing ancient indigenous beliefs, Spanish medieval traditions and voodoo practices from West Africa. Many of these *brujos* multitask as medicine men or women (using both traditional herbs and modern pharmaceuticals) and shrinks, or black magicians who cast evil spells on enemies of their clients. Catemaco is known for its brotherhood of 13 prominent *brujos* (Los Hermanos), who are seen as the high priests of their profession. If you want to arrange a consultation, it's best to take advice from locals to find out what services are provided during the rituals and how much you're likely to be paying, and also to avoid scammers.

BUSES FROM CATEMACO

ADO's 1st-class bus services include the following:

DESTINATION	FARE (M$)	TIME (HR)	FREQUENCY (PER DAY)
Mexico City	394-871	10-11½	6
Puebla	305-700	7¾-9	4
San Andrés Tuxtla	10-47	½	frequent
Santiago Tuxtla	65-73	1	16
Veracruz	112-240	3½-4½	14
Xalapa	213-229	5½-6¼	4

Il Fiorentino   ITALIAN $$
(📞294-943-27-97; Paseo del Malecón 11; mains M$65-220; ⊙7-11pm Tue-Fri, from 3pm Sat, from 1pm Sun; 🕸) Smarter than your average Italian-abroad restaurant, Il Fiorentino serves handmade pasta, Piedmontese wine, cappuccinos and great cake.

ℹ Information

http://catemaco.info A useful website on regional attractions.

ℹ Getting There & Away

ADO and AU buses operate from a lakeside **bus terminal** (cnr Paseo del Malecón & Revolución). Local **2nd-class TLT buses** (Hwy 180) run from a bus station 700m west of the plaza by the highway junction and are a bit cheaper and more frequent than the 1st-class buses. *Colectivo* taxis arrive and depart from **El Cerrito** (Carranza s/n), a small hill about 400m to the west of the plaza on Carranza.

To arrive at communities surrounding the lake and toward the coast, take inexpensive *piratas*. They leave from a **stop** (cnr Lerdo de Tejada & Revolucíon) five blocks north of the bus station.

Reserva de la Biosfera Los Tuxtlas

The various nature reserves around San Andrés Tuxtla and Catemaco were conglomerated in 2006 into this biosphere reserve under Unesco protection. This unique volcanic region, rising 1680m above the coastal plains of southern Veracruz, lies 160km east of the Cordillera Neovolcánica, making it something of an ecological anomaly. Its complex vegetation is considered the northernmost limit of rainforest in the Americas.

The nature reserve spans the Laguna Catemaco and its surrounds, and its heart is the **Volcán San Martín** (1748m) at the foot of which sits **Ruíz Cortines** (📞cell 294-100-50-35; Ejido Ruíz Cortines) 📞. An hour north of San Andrés Tuxtla, this little village has installed very rustic cabañas (M$450) and offers horseback riding, hikes to caves and guided ascents of the volcano, for which you'll need to be fit. A taxi from San Andrés Tuxtla costs M$120, while a *pirata* costs M$30.

Laguna Encantada (off Valencia), the 'Enchanted Lagoon' occupies a small volcanic crater 3.5km northeast of San Andrés Tuxtla in jungle-like terrain. A dirt road goes there, but no buses do. It's not advisable to walk by the lake alone as muggings have occurred in the past; check with the guides at the nearby Yambigapan homestay for updates. There are also good views of the lake and surrounding countryside from atop the 650m hill within the nearby **Cerro de Venado** (off Valencia; M$10; ⊙8am-6pm) 📞 nature reserve.

Despite its many charms, the region receives few international visitors and has little tourism infrastructure. This all makes it a wonderful area to explore for those with a love of nature and the off the beaten track. Get the latest update on Ruíz Cortines at the San Andrés tourist office (p263), and take a guide with you, as locals are wary of strangers: **Braulio Malaga** (📞294-100-43-26; Ruíz Cortines) is a recommended guide.

🛏 Sleeping & Eating

Yambigapan Estancia Rural   CAMPGROUND $
(📞294-115-76-34; www.facebook.com/Restaurant Yambigapan; Camino a Arroyo Seco Km 3.5; camping per person M$35, s/d M$350/450; 🅿) 📞 Three kilometers or so from San Andrés Tuxtla, this family-run rural homestay has two very rustic *cabañas* with spectacular views. Not to be missed are the cooking classes from the *doña* of the house, Amelia, who will teach you traditional Mexican cooking and its history (in Spanish) in her kitchen for M$250. Taxi (around M$45) is the easiest way to arrive.

There's a great **restaurant** (☑294-115-76-34; www.facebook.com/RestaurantYambigapan; mains M$70-100; ☺9am-5pm Sat & Sun; ☎) on the premises, open on weekends only; swimming in the nearby river, Arroyo Seco; and guided hikes. An all-day summit of Volcán San Martín can also be arranged. If you're counting your pesos, ask a *pirata* (about M$10) going to Ruíz Cortines to leave you at the turnoff and follow the signs for Yambigapan that eventually lead you up a long dirt driveway.

❶ Getting There & Away

From San Andrés Tuxtla, there are *piratas* and *colectivo* taxis to Ruíz Cortines; these pass by Laguna Encantada. From Catemaco, *piratas* and *colectivo* taxis ply the lakeshore road along the Laguna Catemaco.

Costa de Oro

☑294

From Catemaco, a mostly paved, 92km-long road runs toward the coast, passing through what's dubbed 'the Switzerland of Mexico' (presumably because of the green hills and cows) before it reaches the lagoon-side town of **Sontecomapan**, from where you can take boat trips through the mangroves. Further north along the coast, the idyllic fishing villages **La Barra** and **Montepío** are renowned for their seafood, and several beautiful, pristine beaches, including those at the appropriately named villages of **Playa Hermosa** and **Costo de Oro**, before turning inland again and rejoining Hwy 180, some 22km north of Santiago Tuxtla. Take a day or two to slowly explore some of the least-visited and most beautiful parts of the Veracruz coast.

◉ Sights & Activities

Playa Escondida   BEACH
This is probably the single best beach in the whole state, but it's not an easy one to access. Turn off the main road onto a dirt road just before Balzapote village. Follow this potholed road for 10 minutes to a moldering relic of a hotel. From there, find the path leading to a long set of crumbling stairs going to fittingly named Playa Escondida (Hidden Beach).

During the work week in the low season, you'll probably have the gorgeous blond sands and turquoise waters to yourself.

Laguna de Sontecomapan   BOATING
In the town of Sontecomapan, 15km north of Catemaco, there are some lagoonside eateries where you can hire a boat (for up to six people)

for an hour-long jaunt through the beautiful mangroves (M$450) or for a trip to La Barra (M$650 for the whole boat or M$100 per person). From Catemaco you can catch a taxi (M$80) or *pirata* (M$20) to Sontecomapan.

Pozo de los Enanos   SWIMMING
(Sontecomapan) The idyllic Pozo de los Enanos (Well of the Dwarfs) swimming hole, where local youths launch, Tarzanlike, from ropes into the water, is a five-minute walk from the boat landing in Sontecomapan.

🛏 Sleeping & Eating

★**Rancho Los Amigos**   ECOLODGE $
(☑294-100-78-87; www.losamigos.com.mx; Sontecomapan; incl breakfast dm M$270, cabañas 2 people M$580-900, 6 people M$1200-1700; ☎) 🌿 This peaceful, nature-surrounded retreat close to where the Laguna Sontecomapan enters the ocean is a blissful escape. The fantastic *cabañas* tucked into the verdant hillside have lovely balconies with spectacular views of the bay. There are nature trails to a beautiful lookout, and a good restaurant serving fresh seafood. The boat ride from Sontecomapan is about 20 minutes.

Kayaking in the mangroves, yoga and relaxing in a temascal (M$400 for up to six people) are among the get-away-from-it-all attractions.

★**La Barra**   SEAFOOD $
(mains M$70-120; ☺10am-9pm) Wiggle your toes in the sand and dig into fish so fresh it may have jumped onto your plate straight from the ocean. Whether grilled, or cooked *al mojo de ajo* (with garlic), and served with homemade salsa, fried plantain, rice and an ice-cold beer, it's as close as it gets to perfection.

The fare at the various *palapas* is comparable in quality, but we particularly like the *palapa* at the very end of the road because of the estuary views.

❶ Getting There & Away

Piratas run reasonably frequently from Catemaco to Montepío (M$40) via Sontecomapan (M$15). For La Barra, if you don't have your own wheels, it's best to take a boat from Sontecomapan (M$650 for the whole boat or M$100 per person). *Piratas* beyond Montepío are infrequent, so to drive the whole Costa de Oro it's best to have your own car.

The road is mostly paved, but somewhat potholed, with one really slow stretch of giant cobblestones near the turnoff for Playa Escondida and Balzapote.

AT A GLANCE

⭐

POPULATION
5.1 million

CAPITALS
Mérida (Yucatán),
Chetumal (Quintana
Roo), Campeche
(Campeche)

BEST MAYA RUINS
Uxmal (p333)

BEST MUSEUM
Gran Museo del
Mundo Maya
(p320)

**BEST BEACH
FOR SWIMMING**
Playa Norte (p282)

📅

WHEN TO GO
Dec–Apr
Mérida Fest is held in
January; the weather
is much cooler
during this time.

Jul & Aug
Hot and humid
throughout the
peninsula. Hurricane
season begins and
hotel rates rise.

Sep–Nov
Weather is cooler
September to Novem-
ber. Great hotel deals.
Crowds thin out.

Cenote (limestone sinkhole)
TATYANA BAKUL/SHUTTERSTOCK

Yucatán Peninsula

Only one Mexican destination can dazzle you with ancient Maya ruins, azure Caribbean and Gulf of Mexico waters, and colonial cities all in one fell swoop – the Yucatán Peninsula.

The peninsula comprises parts of Belize and Guatemala, as well as three separate Mexican states: Yucatán, Quintana Roo and Campeche. Quintana Roo boasts tourism mega-destinations Cancún, Tulum and Playa del Carmen. But head just a couple of hours west for Mérida, Yucatán state, whose colonial architecture and contemporary restaurants are a satisfying change of pace, not to mention the many cenotes (limestone sinkholes) nearby. Finally, neighboring Campeche state is home to mind-blowing Maya ruins galore.

Gulf of Mexico

Progreso

Sisal

Reserva de
la Biosfera 🕭
Ría Celestún

Dzibilchaltún

Kinchil

Mérida 1

Celestún

Umár

MEX
281

MEX
261

Maxcanú

Bécal

Santa
Cruz

Calkiní

Uxmal

Hecelchakán

Kabah

Tenabo

MEX
180

Bolonchén
de Rejón

Campeche 9

San Antonio
Cayal

Hopelchén

Edzná 🕭

Pich

Dzibalchén

Champotón

Bahía de
Campeche

MEX
180

CAMPECHE

Sabancuy

MEX
261

Isla del
Carmen

Puerto
Real

Ciudad del
Carmen

Laguna
de Términos

Escárcega

MEX
186

Balamkú

Frontera

MEX
180

Zacatal

Conhuas

Chicanná

TABASCO

MEX
180

MEX
186

Candelaria

Calakmul 4

Jonuta

Reserva de
la Biosfera 🕭
Calakmul

Ciudad
Pemex

Catazajá

Emiliano
Zapata

Parque Nacional El Mirador-
Dos Lagunas-Río Azul 🕭

MEX
186

CHIAPAS

GUATEMALA

Río Candelaria

Yucatán Peninsula Highlights

1 Mérida (p320)
Wandering a stunning colonial
capital, feasting on local treats.

2 Parque Dos Ojos
(p306) Diving in this
extraordinary cave system.

3 Isla Holbox (p286)
Snorkeling with 15-ton whale
sharks or spotting rare birds.

4 Calakmul (p363)
Exploring some of the Maya's

largest pyramids, with
awesome jungle views.

5 Chichén Itzá (p342)
Staring at the massive El
Castillo pyramid and learning
about Maya culture.

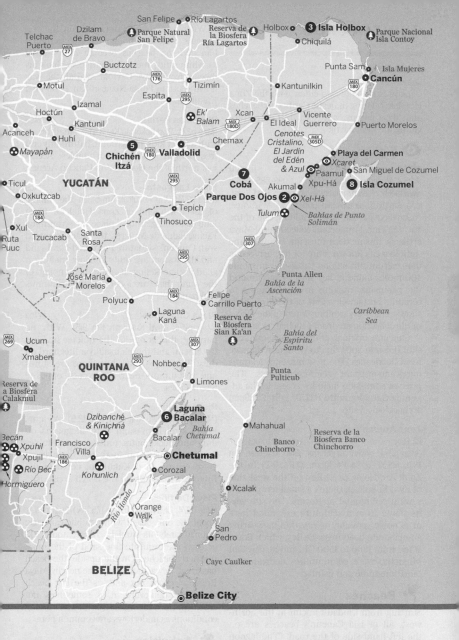

6 Laguna Bacalar (p314)
Plunging into deep Cenote
Azul to delight at the lake of
seven colors.

7 Cobá (p308) Marveling
as the jungle awakens with

birdcalls and light filters
through the canopy.

8 Isla Cozumel (p295)
Diving in coral reefs at one of
the world's best underwater
destinations.

9 Campeche (p354)
Enjoying the colonial beauty of
a town overflowing with pastel-
colored houses.

QUINTANA ROO

Cancún
📞 998 / POP 743,600

Cancún is a tale of two cities, with the Zona Hotelera offering majestic Caribbean beaches and Maya culture, and Cancún Centro providing the local flavor.

⊙ Sights

★ **Museo Maya de Cancún**   MUSEUM
(Maya Museum; Map p274; 📞 998-885-38-43; www.facebook.com/museomayacancun; Blvd Kukulcán Km 16.5; adult/child under 13yr M$75/free; ⊘ 9am-6pm Tue-Sun; 🚌 R-1) Holding one of the Yucatán's most important collections of Maya artifacts, this modern museum is a welcome sight in a city known more for its party scene than cultural attractions. On display are some 400 pieces found at key sites in and around the peninsula, ranging from sculptures to ceramics and jewelry. One of the three halls shows temporary exhibits. Many of the pieces in the collection are from Chichén Itzá.

Cancún's original anthropology museum shut down in 2004 due to structural damage from hurricanes. The new museum features hurricane-resistant reinforced glass. The price of admission includes access to the adjoining **San Miguelito** (M$70; ⊘ 9am-5:30pm) archaeological site.

**Zona Arqueológica
El Rey**   ARCHAEOLOGICAL SITE
(Map p274; www.inah.gob.mx; Blvd Kukulcán Km 18.5; M$55; ⊘ 8am-4:30pm; 🚌 R-1, R-2) In the Zona Arqueológica El Rey, on the west side of Blvd Kukulcán, there's a small temple and several ceremonial platforms. The site gets its name from a sculpture excavated here of a noble, possibly a *rey* (king), wearing an elaborate headdress. El Rey, which flourished from 1200 to 1500 CE, and nearby San Miguelito were communities dedicated to maritime trade and fishing.

🏖 Beaches

Starting from Ciudad Cancún in the northwest, all of Isla Cancún's beaches are on the left-hand side of the road. (The lagoon is on the right; don't swim there – it has crocodiles!) The first beaches are Playas Las Perlas, Juventud, Linda, Langosta, Tortugas and Caracol. With the exception of Playa Caracol, these are Cancún's most swimmable beaches.

When you round Punta Cancún the water gets rougher (though it's still swimmable) and the beaches become more scenic as white sands meet the turquoise-blue Caribbean, from Playa Gaviota Azul all the way down south to Punta Nizuc at Km 24 on Blvd Kukulcán.

Playa Las Perlas   BEACH
(Map p274; Blvd Kukulcán Km 2.5) A small beach with a great kids' playground, bathrooms and free *palapa* (thatched-roof) tables. Access just north of the Holiday Inn Cancun Arenas.

Playa Langosta   BEACH
(Map p274; Blvd Kukulcán Km 5) In the middle of the north end of Zona Hotelera, Playa Langosta is a gem of a place for swimming. Facing Bahía de Mujeres, the beach is coated with Cancún's signature powdered-coral sand and the waters are quite shallow, making it good for snorkeling. If you've had enough of the water there are lots of beach restaurants and bars.

Playa Chac-Mool   BEACH
(Map p274; Blvd Kukulcán Km 9.5) With no parking, this is one of the quieter beaches in Cancún and there's usually a lifeguard on duty. There's no food, but there are stores and restaurants near the access, opposite Señor Frogs.

Playa Marlin   BEACH
(Map p274; Blvd Kukulcán Km 12.5) A long, lovely stretch of sand with lifeguards on duty and deck chairs, umbrellas and tables for rent. There's no food, but there is an Oxxo out on Blvd Kukulcán, north of the Kukulcán Plaza where the beach access is.

Playa Delfines   BEACH
(Map p274; Blvd Kukulcán Km 17.5; 🅿) Delfines is about the only beach with a public car park; unfortunately, its sand is coarser and darker than the exquisite fine sand of the more northerly beaches. On the upside, the beach has great views, there are some nearby Maya Ruins to check out and, as the last beach along the boulevard, it is sometimes not crowded. Heed the signs regarding swimming conditions as undertows are common here.

🏃 Activities

★ **Museo Subacuático de Arte**   SNORKELING
(MUSA; Map p274; www.musamexico.org; snorkeling tour US$47, 1-tank dive US$90-115) 🤿 Built to divert divers away from deteriorating coral reefs, this unique aquatic museum

PARQUE NACIONAL ISLA CONTOY

Spectacular **Isla Contoy** (☑998-234-99-05; contoy@conanp.gob.mx) is a bird-lover's delight: an uninhabited national park and sanctuary that is an easy day trip from Cancún or Isla Mujeres. About 800m at its widest point and more than 8.5km long, it has dense foliage that provides ideal shelter for more than 170 bird species, including brown pelicans, olive cormorants, turkey birds, brown boobies and frigates, and is also a good place to see red flamingos, snowy egrets and white herons.

Whale sharks are often sighted north of Contoy between June and September. In an effort to preserve the park's pristine natural areas, only 200 visitors are allowed access each day. Bring binoculars, mosquito repellent and sunblock. Guided tours to Isla Contoy give you several hours of free time to explore the island's interpretive trails, climb a 27m-high observation tower and get in a little snorkeling.

For more information on the island, **Amigos de Isla Contoy** (Map p274; ☑998-884-74-83; www.islacontoy.org; Local E-1, 2nd fl, Plaza Bonita Mall; ⊕9am-5pm Mon-Fri) has detailed information on the island's ecology. Tour operators based out of Cancún run trips to Contoy.

---

features hundreds of life-size sculptures in the waters of Cancún and Isla Mujeres. Only snorkeling is allowed at the 4m-deep artificial reef at Cancún's Punta Nizuc gallery, while the deeper Isla Mujeres' gallery is ideal for first-time divers. Organize outings through dive shops; Scuba Cancún is recommended.

The underwater museum is a creation of British-born sculptor Jason deCaires Taylor.

Scuba Cancún   DIVING
(Map p274; ☑998-849-52-25; www.scubacancun.com.mx; Blvd Kukulcán Km 5.2; 1-/2-tank dive US$62/77; ⊕7am-8pm, from 8am Sun) A PADI-certified and family-owned dive operation with many years of experience, Scuba Cancún was the city's first dive shop. It offers a variety of snorkeling and diving expeditions (including cenote and night dives). It also runs snorkeling and diving trips to the underwater sculpture museum, aka MUSA, as well as outings to see whale sharks.

☞ Tours

Captain Hook   BOATING
(Map p274; ☑998-849-44-51; www.capitanhook.com; Blvd Kukulcán Km 5, Marina Capitán Hook; adult US$89-109, child 2-12yr US$40-53; ⊕tour 7-10:30pm; ⊕) There's nothing like a swashbuckling adventure with sword fights and cannon battles to get kids' imaginations running wild. This 3½-hour tour aboard a Spanish galleon replica includes dinner service, and it costs a pretty doubloon if you opt for the steak and lobster option. On the other hand, kids cost only US$5 if they eat strictly from the buffet bar.

Asterix   TOURS
(☑998-886-42-70; www.contoytours.com; Vialidad s/n, V&V Marina; adult/child 5-12yr including dock fees US$113/93; ⊕tours 9am-5:30pm Tue-Sun) Boats to Isla Contoy depart from the V&V Marina (aka La Amada), just north of the Punta Sam car-ferry terminal. The tours include guide, breakfast, lunch at Isla Mujeres, open bar and snorkeling gear. Hotel pickup costs an additional US$10 per person.

⊨ Sleeping

The city has a variety of accommodations ranging from budget to mind- and budget-blowing. Almost all hotels offer discounts during 'low' season, but many have up to five different rate periods: Christmas and New Year are always at a premium, with high rates sometimes running from December through to US spring break in March and then again in July and August (when locals have their summer vacation). Many places have great online promotions available.

Grand Royal Lagoon   HOTEL $$
(Map p274; ☑800-552-46-66, 998-883-27-49; reservar.grlagoon@hotmail.com; Quetzal 8A; r M$1500; ⓟ⊕❄☎☀; ⊡R-1, R-2) Though pleasantly breezy and relatively affordable for the Zona Hotelera, rooms at the old-school Grand Royal are looking a bit worn and tired these days. Most have two double beds, while some have kings, lagoon views and balcony. The property has a small pool, and wi-fi reaches common areas only. It's 100m off Blvd Kukulcán Km 7.5.

Cancún

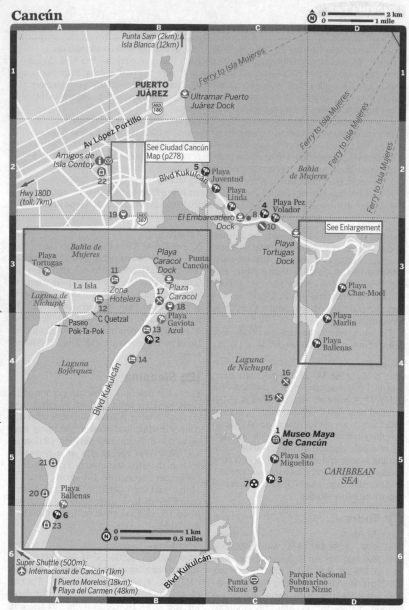

Puerto Juárez

Punta Sam (2km);
Isla Blanca (12km)

PUERTO
JUÁREZ

Ferry to Isla Mujeres

Ultramar Puerto
Juárez Dock

Av López Portillo

Amigos de
Isla Contoy

22

Hwy 180D
(toll; 7km)

See Ciudad Cancún
Map (p278)

Blvd Kukulcán

5   Playa
     Juventud

Playa
Linda

Bahía
de Mujeres

Ferry to Isla Mujeres

19

Playa Pez
4   Volador

8

El Embarcadero
Dock

10

See Enlargement

Playa
Tortugas
Dock

Playa
Tortugas

Bahía de
Mujeres

11

La Isla

Zona
Hotelera

Playa
Caracol
Dock

Punta
Cancún

Playa
Chac-Mool

Laguna de
Nichupté

12

Paseo
Pok-Ta-Pok

C Quetzal

17   Plaza
      Caracol

18

13   Playa
      Gaviota
2   Azul

Playa
Marlin

Playa
Ballenas

14

Laguna
Bojórquez

Blvd Kukulcán

Laguna
de Nichupté

16

15

1   Museo Maya
    de Cancún

21

20   Playa
      Ballenas

6

23

Super Shuttle (500m);
Internacional de Cancún (1km)

Puerto Morelos (18km);
Playa del Carmen (48km)

Playa San
Miguelito

7   3

CARIBBEAN
SEA

Blvd Kukulcán

Punta
Nizuc

9

Parque Nacional
Submarino
Punta Nizuc

Hotel Antillano   HOTEL $$

(Map p278; 998-884-11-32, 998-884-15-32;
www.hotelantillano.com.mx; Claveles 1; d M$1226;
P✹❂☎✉; R-1) Just off Avenida Tulum is
this very pleasant and quiet place with a relaxing lobby, nice pool, good central air-con
and cable TV, and a bar in the lobby. Rooms

on the *avenida* catch more street noise.
Rates drop considerably during low season.

Hotel Plaza Caribe   HOTEL $$

(Map p278; 998-884-13-77; www.hotelplaza
caribe.com; Pino 19; r from M$1270; P✹❂
☎✉; R-1, R-2) Directly across from the

Cancún

◎ Top Sights
1 Museo Maya de Cancún.........................C5

◎ Sights
2 Playa Chac-Mool....................................B4
3 Playa Delfines.......................................C5
4 Playa Langosta......................................C2
5 Playa Las Perlas....................................B2
6 Playa Marlin..A6
7 Zona Arqueológica El Rey.....................C5

◎ Activities, Courses & Tours
8 Captain Hook...C3
9 Museo Subacuático de Arte C6
10 Scuba Cancún......................................C3

◎ Sleeping
11 Beachscape Kin Ha Villas & Suites.......B3
12 Grand Royal Lagoon.............................A3

13 Hostel Natura..B4
14 Le Blanc..B4

◎ Eating
15 Crab House..C4
16 Harry's Steakhouse & Raw Bar.............C4
17 Taco Factory..B3

◎ Drinking & Nightlife
18 City..B3
19 Marakame Café......................................B2

◎ Shopping
20 La Europea...A5
21 La Isla Shopping Village.........................A5
22 Mercado 28..A2
23 Plaza Kukulcán.......................................A6

bus terminal, this hotel offers comfortable rooms, a pool, restaurant and gardens with peacocks roaming about. Request one of the remodeled rooms, which sport newer furnishings than those in the older wing.

Hotel Colonial Cancún — HOTEL $$
(Map p278; ☏ 998-884-15-35; www.hotelcolonial cancun.com; Tulipanes 22; d M$1150; ❄❋⛛⬚; ☐R-1, R-2) Rooms are anything but colonial, but they're pleasant enough and they overlook a leafy central courtyard with a gurgling fountain. The hotel has a small pool area.

Hotel Bonampak — HOTEL $$
(Map p278; ☏ 998-884-02-80; www.hotelbonam pak.com; Av Bonampak 225; d incl breakfast M$1200; ⓟ❄❋@⛛⬚; ☐R-1, R-2) Good value by Cancún standards, rooms at this business-style hotel have comfy mattresses, dark-wood furnishings and flat-screen TVs. Ask for one overlooking the sunny pool area.

Ciudad Cancún

'Budget' is a relative term; prices in Cancún are higher for what you get than almost anywhere else in Mexico. There are many cheap lodging options within several blocks of the bus terminal, northwest on Avenida Uxmal. The area around Parque de las Palapas has several hostels and budget digs as well.

Midrange in Cancún is a two-tiered category; the Cancún Centro area is much cheaper than the Zona Hotelera and only a short bus ride away from the Zona's beaches.

★ Hostel Ka'beh — HOSTEL $
(Map p278; ☏ 998-892-79-02; www.facebook. com/hostelkabeh; Alcatraces 45; dm/r/tr incl

breakfast from M$230/750/1200; ❄❋@⛛; ☐R-1) A friendly central option just off the buzzing Parque de las Palapas, this small hostel has a lived-in feel that goes hand in hand with the relaxed vibe. Expect many social activities at night, most organized around food and drink. Trips depart to the beach at noon and to the Zona Hotelera after dinner.

At the time of research plans for a pool were underway, as well as expansion to provide sleepers with some quieter quarters away from the 'Fiesta Party House.' And what other hostel offers over 30 craft beers from its fridge?

Mezcal Hostel — HOSTEL $
(Map p278; ☏ 998-217-53-15; www.nomads experience.com/mezcal.php; Mero 12; dm/r US$16/70; ❄❋⛛⬚; ☐R-1) Mezcal Hostel occupies a beautiful two-story house and some adjoining properties in a quiet residential area off Avenida Náder. Smoke can be thick in the common areas, but the dorms are smoke-free. There's a pool, large bar and restaurant, lots of activities, and even a tattoo parlor. What's next, a wedding chapel?

Cancún International Suites — HOTEL $$
(Map p278; ☏ 998-884-17-71; www.cancuninter nationalsuites.com; Gladiolas 11, cnr Alcatraces; r/ ste M$1480/1860; ❄❋⛛; ☐R-1) Colonial-style rooms and suites in this remodeled hotel are comfortable and quiet and the location is great – right off Parque de las Palapas and conveniently close to downtown's restaurant and bar zone.

YUCATÁN PENINSULA CANCÚN

Soberanis Hotel
HOTEL **$$**

(Map p278; ✆998-884-45-64; www.soberanis.mx; Av Cobá 5 s/n; d M$1300; ❄@❂; ☐R-1) Location, location, location. The Soberanis sits right on a busy intersection where you can catch buses to practically anywhere in town, including Zona Hotelera, and there's a supermarket right next door. Rooms have comfortable, clean beds with wood furnishings. No elevator means the lotsa-luggage crowd may want to look elsewhere.

Náder Hotel & Suites
HOTEL **$$**

(Map p278; ✆998-884-15-84; www.suitesnadercancun.com; Av Náder 5; d/ste incl breakfast M$1450/1950; ❄❉❂; ☐R-1) The Náder caters to business travelers, but it's also a hit with families thanks to its ample rooms and suites with large common areas and kitchens. Even the 'standard' setup here gets you digs with some serious elbow room, with a work desk and chair, track lighting, and a comfy chaise to nap on.

Hotel El Rey del Caribe
HOTEL **$$$**

(Map p278; ✆998-884-20-28; www.elreydelcaribe.com; Av Uxmal 24; r incl breakfast from US$90; ❄❉❂✖; ☐R-1) 🍃 El Rey is a true ecohotel – it recycles, employs solar collectors and cisterns, uses gray water on the gardens, and has some rooms with composting toilets. It also has a swimming pool and Jacuzzi in a jungly courtyard that's home to a small family of *tlacuaches* (opossums). Each room has a fully equipped kitchenette, comfortable beds and a fridge. Offers good online deals.

🛏 Zona Hotelera

With few exceptions, most hotels lining Blvd Kukulcán are of the top-end variety. Many offer all-inclusive packages, often at reasonable rates if you're willing to forgo eating elsewhere. Often the best room rates are available through hotel-and-airfare packages, so shop around.

Hostel Natura
HOSTEL **$$**

(Map p274; ✆998-883-08-87; www.facebook.com/hostelcancunnatura; Blvd Kukulcán Km 9.5; dm US$30, r with/without bathroom US$100/75; ❄❉❂; ☐R-1, R-2) Above a health-food restaurant of the same name, this fun, vibrant Zona Hotelera hostel offers private rooms with lagoon views and somewhat cramped dorms, offset by the airy rooftop terrace and a nice common kitchen area. The party zone is just a stumble away, and the staff are helpful and friendly.

★Le Blanc
RESORT **$$$**

(Map p274; ✆998-881-47-48, USA 800-986-5632; www.leblancsparesort.com; Blvd Kukulcán Km 10; d/ste all-inclusive from US$793/868; P❄❉❂✖; ☐R-1, R-2) You can't miss the glaring white exterior of the aptly named Le Blanc, arguably Cancún's most sophisticated resort. This adults-only retreat comes with all the amenities you'd expect in this category: gorgeous infinity pool, cold welcome drink on check-in, scented hand towels – the works. There's even butler service should life in Cancún become too complicated. Discounts for multiple-night stays.

Guests get free valet parking as well.

Beachscape Kin Ha Villas & Suites
RESORT **$$$**

(Map p274; ✆998-891-54-00; www.beachscape.com.mx; Blvd Kukulcán Km 8.5; d/ste incl breakfast from M$5210/6060; P❄❉@❂✖; ☐R-1) A good family spot, Beachscape offers a babysitting service, a play area for kids and a swimmable beach with calm waters. You'll never need to leave the hotel's grounds (though we think you should), as there are bars, markets, travel agencies and more on the premises. All rooms feature a balcony and two double beds or one king-sized bed.

🍴 Eating

Where you go to eat often is based on where you are staying: the hotel zone or downtown. Each place has a range of options, though meals are (not surprisingly) pricier in the hotel zone. That said, even a fancy meal here is often a fraction of the cost of a night out in New York or Tokyo, and cheap eats are tasty and filling.

Los Huaraches de Alcatraces
CAFETERIA **$**

(Map p278; ✆998-884-39-18; Alcatraces 31; mains M$30-60, menú del día M$135; ❂9am-5:30pm Tue-Sun; ✖) A casual cafeteria-style place that's packed with locals and sometimes even has live music to boot. Grab a tray, point at a few items that look tasty, and prepare to chow cheaply. In addition to dozens of entrees, they also have excellent *aguas* (fruit drinks) and desserts.

Taco Factory
MEXICAN **$**

(Map p274; ✆998-883-07-50; www.facebook.com/taco.factory.cancun; Blvd Kukulcán Km 9; tacos M$36-48; ❂11am-7am; ☐R-1) This casual open-air restaurant boasts the best authentic Mexican tacos in the Cancún Hotel Zone, and its convenient location in the central alley right by the nightclub strip makes it perfect for late-night cravings.

La Parrilla
MEXICAN **$$**

(Map p278; ✆998-287-81-18; www.laparrilla.com.mx; Av Yaxchilán 51; mains M$140-830; ☉noon-1am Sun-Thu, to 2am Fri & Sat) Colorful decoration, a large outdoor bull, and the sounds of a mariachi band invite you in to La Parrilla. Open since 1975, it fills with locals and tourists alike thanks to its tasty *tacos al pastor* (spit-roasted pork tacos) and extensive menu of authentic Mexican cuisine. Mariachis play from 7:30pm to 11:30pm.

La Fonda del Zancudo
INTERNATIONAL **$$**

(Map p278; ✆998-884-17-41; www.facebook.com/lafondadelzancudo; Av Uxmal 23; mains M$155-295; ☉6pm-midnight Mon-Sat; 🛜; 🚌R-1) Softly lit, with strings of lights, lanterns and moonlight, this alluring little restaurant sits within an enchanting walled patio on downtown Cancún's central Avenida Uxmal. The main menu boasts artisanal creations made primarily with local organic ingredients, and the daily specials wall always has tempting culinary surprises and inventive cocktails to try.

★ Peter's Restaurante
INTERNATIONAL **$$$**

(Map p278; ✆998-251-93-10; www.facebook.com/peterscancun; Av Bonampak 71, btwn Sierra & Róbalo; dinner M$210-655; ☉6-10pm Tue-Sat) Peter's Restaurante has a homey charm and some of the best cooking in the city. Dutch chef Peter Houben has blended European, Mexican and international cuisine, with beautifully prepared dishes like the mushroom-ravioli appetizer and fresh salmon fillet in lemon sauce with a spicy hint of *chile de arbol* (tree chili). Try the poached pear for dessert.

Irori
JAPANESE **$$$**

(Map p278; ✆998-892-30-72; www.iroricancun.com; Av Tulum 226; mains M$150-300; ☉1-10:30pm Mon-Sat, to 9:30pm Sun; 🛜🅿; 🚌R-27, R-1, R-2) Enjoy this Japanese-run restaurant serving sushi and many other Japanese favorites in an intimate setting. There's even a kids' menu and playroom for those with little sushi-scoffers in tow. You'll find the entrance on Calle Viento. It may close early on slow nights. From Zona Hotelera use R-1 or R-2 buses and get off at Avenida Tulum.

Harry's Steakhouse & Raw Bar
STEAK **$$$**

(Map p274; ✆998-840-65-50; www.harrys.com.mx; Blvd Kukulcán Km 14.2; mains M$380-1290, steak up to M$3900; ☉1pm-1am; 🚌R-1, R-2) Stunning, renowned Harry's serves house-aged steaks, plus superfresh fish and a famous cotton-candy treat. The architecture's impressive too, with outdoor waterfalls, plenty of decking over the lagoon and two **bars** – one indoors and one out. Service is impeccable. Try the **jungle-theme lounge** or the new exclusive **roof nightclub**, and don't miss peeking at the tequila and mezcal display. Yum!

Crab House
SEAFOOD **$$$**

(Map p274; ✆998-193-03-50; www.crabhousecancun.com; Blvd Kukulcán Km 14.7; dishes M$485-2950; ☉noon-11:30pm; 🅿🛜; 🚌R-1, R-2) Offering a lovely view of the lagoon that complements the seafood, the long menu here includes many shrimp and fish-fillet dishes. Stone crab is the specialty, which (along with lobster) is priced by the kilo. Both are served from crystal-clear tanks. The establishment prides itself on having no holidays, not even for hurricanes.

🍷 Drinking & Nightlife

Many clubs and restaurants are open for drinks for much of the day. Cancún's hotel zone doesn't offer much in the way of a gay and lesbian scene but downtown has a few nightspots.

Grand Mambocafé
CLUB

(Map p278; ✆998-884-45-37; www.facebook.com/grandmambocafecancunoficial; 2nd fl, Plaza Hong Kong, cnr Avs Xcaret & Tankah; cover M$60-180; ☉9:30pm-3am Wed-Sat; 🚌R-2) The large floor at this happening club is the perfect place to practice those Latin dance steps you've been working on. Live groups play Cuban salsa and other tropical styles.

Nomads Hostel & Bar
COCKTAIL BAR

(Map p278; ✆998-898-31-92; www.nomadsexperience.com; cnr Av Náder & Mero; ☉7-11:30pm Tue-Sun; 🚌R-1) Showing off with an artsy vibe where geometric tiles meet concrete and brick, Nomads draws in Cancún's young 'in crowd' with creative cocktails and innovative Mexican cuisine. The indoor area allows friends to sit down to a late dinner (mains M$90 to M$170), while the back area under the stars is standing-room only. A pool table adds to the vibe.

City
CLUB

(Map p274; ✆998-883-33-33; www.thecitycancun.com; Blvd Kukulcán Km 9; open bar US$65; ☉10:30pm-4am Fri; 🚌R-1) The largest nightclub in Latin America still manages to fill up every Friday night. Frequently hosting

Ciudad Cancún

N

0 ____ 400 m
0 ____ 0.2 miles

Hwy 180 (1km);
Puerto Juárez (4km)

Hwy 180
(850m)

18

Flamboyan

Av Tulum

Av Uxmal

Roble

Palmera

Flamboyan

Chaca

Av Náder

Naranja

Cereza

Laurel

Bus Stop to
Zona Hotelera

Punta Allen

Av Yaxchilán

Nicchehabi

7

Pino

Colectivos to Puerto
Juárez & Punta Sam

Laurel

ADO Bus
Terminal

Playa Express
Buses

6

Av Uxmal

12

Punta Cotoco

13

Margaritas

Rosas

Av
Sunyaxchén

Jazmines

Margaritas

Azucenas

17

Ayuntamiento
Benito
Juárez

8

Mercado 28
(200m)

Jazmines

Av Yaxchilán

Gladiolas

Parque de las
Palapas

Tulipanes

Av Tulum

Av Bonampak

Gladiolas

1

5

Tulipanes

Orquideas

2

14

Claveles

3

9

Av Náder

Orquideas

Claveles

Alcatraces

Crisantemos

Alcatraces

Av Cobá

10

City Tourism
Office

15

Sierra

16

Av Xcaret

Av Cobá

Av Cobá

Jaleb

Brisa

Nube

Lluvia

Tejón

Lluvia

Nube

Pecari

Av Tulum

Agua

Cielo

Av Bonampak

Pecari

Agua

Cielo

Viento

Tierra

Viento

Tierra

11

4

Mar

Fuego

Park

Fuego

Av Sayil

Ciudad Cancún

🛏 Sleeping
1 Cancún International Suites	B3
2 Hostel Ka'beh	B4
3 Hotel Antillano	C4
4 Hotel Bonampak	D7
5 Hotel Colonial Cancún	C3
6 Hotel El Rey del Caribe	D2
7 Hotel Plaza Caribe	B2
8 Mezcal Hostel	D3
9 Náder Hotel & Suites	C4
10 Soberanis Hotel	C4

🍴 Eating
11 Irori	C7
12 La Fonda del Zancudo	D2
13 La Parrilla	B2
14 Los Huaraches de Alcatraces	B4
15 Peter's Restaurante	D5

🍷 Drinking & Nightlife
16 Grand Mambocafé	A5
17 Nomads Hostel & Bar	C3

🛍 Shopping
18 Mercado 23	B1

world-famous DJs and musicians, this massive place offers wild nightlife, whether you're dancing on top of the central stage or watching it all from the stadium-style side levels. Due to the large crowds and 'party hearty' atmosphere, it can feel overwhelming at times.

Marakame Café BAR
(Map p274; ☎ 998-887-10-10; www.marakamecafe.com; Av Xpujil, Circuito Copán 19; ⊙ 8am-1am Mon-Fri, 9am-2am Sat, to midnight Sun; 🛜; 🚌 R-27) An excellent open-air breakfast and lunch spot by day, and a popular bar with live music by night. The bartenders, or mixologists if you will, prepare martinis and mango margaritas, and they do mimosas for Saturday and Sunday brunch (adult/child M$288/128). It's a short taxi ride from downtown.

🛍 Shopping

Shopaholics will enjoy downtown's colorful markets and the Zona Hotelera's modern open-air malls. Locals head to either **Mercado 28** (Map p274; ☎ 998-892-43-03; www.facebook.com/mercado28cancunmexico; cnr Avs Xel-Há & Sunyaxchén; ⊙ 8am-7pm) or **Mercado 23** (Map p278; www.facebook.com/mercado23cancun; Jabín 9; ⊙ 8am-7pm; 🚌 R-1) for clothes, shoes, inexpensive food stalls and so on. Of the two, Mercado 23 is less frequented by tourists. If you're looking for a place without corny T-shirts, this is the place to go.

La Europea DRINKS
(Map p274; www.laeuropea.com.mx; Blvd Kukulcán Km 12.5; ⊙ 10am-9pm Mon-Sat, 11am-7pm Sun; 🚌 R-1) A gourmet liquor store with reasonable prices, knowledgeable staff and the best booze selection in town, including top-shelf tequilas and mezcals.

Plaza Kukulcán MALL
(Map p274; ☎ 998-193-01-60; www.kukulcanplaza.mx; Blvd Kukulcán Km 13; ⊙ 10am-10pm; 🛜; 🚌 R-1) The largest of the indoor malls is Plaza Kukulcán. Of note here are the temporary art exhibits, the many stores selling silverwork, and La Ruta de las Indias, a shop featuring wooden models of Spanish galleons and replicas of conquistadors' weaponry and body armor.

ℹ Information

EMERGENCY
These emergency numbers may not work as quickly as getting to the nearest hospital.

Cruz Roja (Red Cross)	☎ 911, 065, 998-884-16-16
Fire	☎ 911, 998-884-12-02
Police	☎ 911, 066
Tourist Police	☎ 911, 066, 998-885-22-77

IMMIGRATION
The **immigration office** (Immigration Office; ☎ 998-881-35-60; www.gob.mx/inm; cnr Av Náder 1 & Uxmal; ⊙ 9am-1pm Tue-Fri) can replace lost tourist cards for M$558, but you can also have this done at the airport on your departure if you're leaving by plane.

MEDICAL SERVICES
Hospital Playa Med (☎ 998-140-52-58; www.hospitalplayamed.com; Av Náder 13, cnr Av Uxmal; ⊙ 24hr; 🚌 R-1) Modern facility.

MONEY
There are numerous banks with ATMs throughout the Zona Hotelera and downtown on Avenida Tulum. Cancún's airport also has ATMs and money exchange.

POST
There is no post office in the Zona Hotelera, but some hotels' reception desks sell stamps and will mail letters.

The **Main Post Office** (Map p274; cnr Avs Xel-Há & Sunyaxchén; ⊙ 8am-4pm Mon-Fri, 9am-12:30pm Sat) is downtown at the edge of Mercado 28. You can also post mail in the red postal boxes sprinkled around town, but you're best off handing them to the clerk in person. The red boxes are increasingly misused as trash bins.

TOURIST INFORMATION

City Tourism Office (Map p278; ☑ 998-887-33-79; cnr Avs Cobá & Náder; ⊙ 9am-4pm Mon-Fri) A small city tourist office with supplies of printed material and knowledgeable staff.

❶ Getting There & Away

AIR

Aeropuerto Internacional de Cancún (Cancún International Airport; ☑ 998-848-72-00; www. asur.com.mx; Hwy 307 Km 22) is the busiest airport in southeast Mexico. It has all the services you would expect from a major international airport: ATMs, money exchange and car-rental agencies. It's served by many direct international flights and by connecting flights from Mexico City. Low-cost Mexican carriers VivaAerobus, Interjet and Volaris have services from Mexico City.

There are flights to Cancún from Guatemala City and Flores (Guatemala), Havana (Cuba), Panama City and São Paulo (Brazil). Some Havana–Cancún flights continue to Mérida.

For a full list of the carriers with flights to Cancún, see the airport website. Mexican carriers include the following.

Aeroméxico (☑ 998-884-21-54; www.aeromexico.com; Plaza Hollywood, Local 32; ⊙ 9am-6:30pm Mon-Fri, to 6pm Sat; ☒ R-1) Direct flights from Mexico City and New York. Office just west of Avenida Bonampak.

Interjet (☑ 998-892-02-78; www.interjet.com; Av Xcaret 35, Plaza Hollywood; ⊙ 9am-7pm Mon-Fri, to 6pm Sat, 10am-3pm Sun) Flies direct to Miami and Havana.

Magnicharters (☑ 998-884-06-00, 800-201-14-04; www.magnicharters.com.mx; Av Náder 94, cnr Av Cobá; ⊙ 9am-8pm Mon-Fri, to 2pm Sat, 10am-3pm Sun; ☒ R-1) To Mexico City.

VivaAerobus (☑ 818-215-01-50; www.vivaaerobus.com; Hwy 307 Km 22, Cancún International Airport) Nonstop to Mexico City.

Volaris (www.volaris.com; Hwy 307 Km 22, Cancún International Airport) Service to Mexico City and other parts of Mexico.

BOAT

There are several ferry departure points for Isla Mujeres from Cancún. From the Zona Hotelera, you can depart from **El Embarcadero** (Map p274; Blvd Kukulcán Km 4), **Playa Caracol** (Map p274; Blvd Kukulcán Km 9.5; parking per day M$100) or **Playa Tortugas** (Map p274; Blvd Kukulcán Km 6.5). From Cancún Centro, there are two passenger ferry terminals in Puerto Juárez: **Ultramar** (Map p274; ☑ 998-293-90-92; www.ultramarferry.com; Juárez adult/child one-way M$160/130, Hotelera adult/child one-way US$15/10) and a less popular dock about 500m north shared by Marinsa (www.

marinsaturismo.com) and Naveganto (www.naveganto.mx), though at the time of research only Ultramar was running regularly. From Puerto Juárez, one-way fares cost M$140 to M$160, while leaving from the Zona Hotelera runs about M$270.

If you want to take a vehicle across you'll need to head to Punta Sam's **Marítima Isla Mujeres** (☑ Isla Mujeres 998-307-10-19, Punta Sam 998-201-93-76; www.maritimaislamujeres.com; Av Rueda Medina s/n), 8km north of Cancún Centro (basic one-way/return auto fare M$295/590, including driver), but it's much easier to rent a golf cart or scooter on the island.

For Isla Contoy, boats (p273) depart from the V&V Marina, just north of the Punta Sam car-ferry terminal.

BUS

Cancún's modern **bus terminal** (Map p278; www.ado.com.mx) occupies the wedge formed where Avenidas Uxmal and Tulum meet. It's a relatively safe area, but be aware of your bags and make sure to establish the fare before getting into a taxi.

Across Pino from the bus terminal, a few doors from Avenida Tulum, is the ticket office and mini-terminal of **Playa Express** (Map p278; Pino s/n, cnr Av Tulum), which runs air-conditioned buses down the coast to Playa del Carmen every 10 minutes until early evening, stopping at major towns and points of interest. ADO covers the same ground and beyond with its 1st-class and 2nd-class lines. To reach Isla Holbox up north, take a bus to Chiquilá.

ADO sets the 1st-class standard. Mayab provides good 'intermediate class' (tending to make more stops than 1st class) to many points.

CAR & MOTORCYCLE

Cars can be rented at Cancún airport, where you'll find multiple kiosks and offices in and around the terminals. **Avant** (☑ 998-883-94-34; www.avantrentacar.com; Hwy 307 Km 15.2; US$40 per day, minimum 3 days; ⊙ 9am-5pm), an upstart, will pick you up at the airport and offers no-dickering: the price you've reserved for includes full insurance already, often at a fraction of the cost of the bigger rental agencies.

In the city, there are several rental offices just south of **La Isla Shopping Village** (Map p274; ☑ 998-883-50-25; www.facebook.com/laislacancun; Blvd Kukulcán Km 12.5; ⊙ 10am-10pm; ☒; ☒ R-1). Be aware that Hwy 180D, the *cuota* (toll road) running much of the way between Cancún and Mérida, costs M$504. An economy-size rental car with basic liability insurance starts at about M$700 per day.

Alamo (☑ 998-886-01-01; www.alamo.com.mx; Hwy 307 Km 22, Cancún International Airport; ⊙ 24hr)

Avis (📞 998-883-14-36; www.avis.com.mx; Blvd Kukulcán Km 12.5, La Isla Shopping Village; ⊙7am-10pm)

Hertz (📞 999-911-80-40; www.hertz.com; Hwy 307 Km 22, Cancún International Airport; ⊙24hr)

National (📞 998-881-87-60, toll free 800 737 3722; www.nationalcar.com; Hwy 307 Km 22, Cancún International Airport; ⊙7am-11pm)

🛈 Getting Around

TO/FROM THE AIRPORT

Frequent ADO buses go to Cancún Centro (M$88) between 8:15am and 12:30am. They depart from outside the terminals. Once in town, the buses travel up Avenida Tulum to the bus terminal on the corner of Avenida Uxmal. Going to the airport from Cancún Centro, the same ADO airport buses leave regularly from the bus station. ADO also offers bus services out of the airport to Playa del Carmen, Tulum and Mérida.

Airport shuttle vans **Super Shuttle** (📞 998-193-17-42; www.supershuttle.com; Hwy 307 Km 22, Cancún International Airport) and Yellow Transfer run to and from Cancún Centro and the Zona Hotelera for about US$10 per person for shared rides and US$60 for nonstop service.

Regular taxis run from the airport into town or to the Zona Hotelera and cost up to M$650 (up to four people). Expect to pay about M$370 for a city cab when returning to the airport.

BUS

To reach the Zona Hotelera from Cancún Centro, catch any **bus** (Map p278; Av Tulum) with 'R-1', 'Hoteles' or 'Zona Hotelera' displayed on the windshield as it travels along Avenida Tulum toward Avenida Cobá then eastward on Avenida Cobá. South of Avenida Cobá, along Avenida Tulum, you can also catch the 'R-27' to the Zona Hotelera. The fare is M$12.

To reach Puerto Juárez and the Isla Mujeres ferries, you can either take a northbound 'Punta Sam' or 'Puerto Juárez' **colectivo** (Map p278) from a bus stop on Avenida Tulum (across from the ADO terminal), or you can wait on Avenida Tulum for an R-1 'Puerto Juárez' bus.

TAXI

Cancún's taxis do not have meters. Fares are set, starting as low as M$35, but you should always agree on a price before getting in; otherwise you could end up paying for a 'misunderstanding.' From Cancún Centro to Punta Cancún it's usually M$100 to M$130, to Puerto Juárez M$50 to M$70. Trips within the Zona Hotelera or downtown zones cost around M$40 to M$50. Hourly and daily rates should be about M$250 and M$2000, respectively.

BUSES FROM CANCÚN

DESTINATION	COST (M$)	TIME	FREQUENCY (PER DAY)
Bacalar	312-467	5-5½hr	frequent
Cancún International Airport	88	½hr	frequent
Chetumal	487	5½-6hr	frequent
Chichén Itzá	334	3-4hr	hourly
Chiquilá	270	3-3½hr	4
Felipe Carrillo Puerto	246	3½-3¾hr	frequent
Mahahual	218-497	5½-5¾hr	2 (6:45am & 4:45pm)
Mérida	460-754	4-5hr	frequent
Mexico City (Norte)	1588	27¼hr	1 (6:30pm)
Mexico City (TAPO)	1588-1770	25-26½hr	5
Palenque	832-1288	13-13¼hr	4
Playa del Carmen	42-88	1½hr	frequent ADO & Playa Express
Puerto Morelos	28-37	½-¾hr	frequent ADO & Playa Express
Ticul	296	8hr	frequent
Tizimín	166	6hr	2-5 until 6:50pm
Tulum	73-181	2¼-2¾hr	frequent
Valladolid	191-252	2-2¼hr	frequent
Villahermosa	1036-1258	12¾-14¾hr	frequent

Isla Mujeres

998 / POP 19,500

Isla Mujeres generally has a quieter and more relaxing vibe than what you'll find across the bay in Cancún, and there's just enough here to keep you entertained: scuba diving and snorkeling, visiting a turtle farm or simply swimming and lazing around on the island's gorgeous north shore.

Sure, there are quite a few ticky-tacky tourist shops, but folks still get around by golf cart and the crushed-coral beaches are undeniably lovely. As for the calm turquoise water of Isla Mujeres, well, you really just have to see it for yourself.

Come sunset, there are plenty of dining options, and the nightlife scene moves at a carefree pace.

Some people plan their vacation around Cancún and pencil in Isla Mujeres as a side trip, but the island is truly a destination in its own right, and a surprisingly affordable one at that.

Sights

Isla Mujeres Turtle Farm
FARM

(Isla Mujeres Tortugranja; www.facebook.com/tortugranja.mx; Carretera Sac Bajo Km 5; M$30; ⊙9am-5pm;) Although they're endangered, sea turtles are still killed throughout Latin America for their eggs and meat. In the 1980s, efforts by a local fisherman led to the founding of this *tortugranja* (turtle farm), 5km south of town, which safeguards breeding grounds and protects eggs. It's a small spot, with a number of sizes of turtles and a few different species. The farm is easily reached from town by taxi (M$75 to M$100) or golf cart.

The farm provides refuge for loggerhead, hawksbill and green turtles ranging in weight from 150g to more than 300kg. It also has a small but interesting aquarium, displays on marine life and a pen that holds large nurse sharks and manta rays. Tours are conducted in Spanish.

Punta Sur
VIEWPOINT, GARDENS

(ruins M$30) At the island's southernmost point you'll find a lighthouse, a sculpture garden and the worn remains of a temple dedicated to Ixchel, Maya goddess of the moon and fertility. Various hurricanes have pummeled the ruins over time and there's now little to see other than the sculpture garden, the sea and Cancún in the distance. Taxis from town cost M$105.

Beaches

⭐ Playa Garrafón
BEACH

Head to this beach for excellent snorkeling. It's 6.5km from the tourist center. A cab costs M$100.

Playa Norte
BEACH

(Map p284) Once you reach Playa Norte, the island's main beach, you won't want to leave. Its warm, shallow waters are the color of blue raspberry syrup and the beach is crushed coral. Unlike most of the island's east coast, Playa Norte is safe for swimming and the water is only chest deep, even far from shore.

Playa Secreto
BEACH

(Map p284;) The lagoon separating a large hotel complex from the rest of the island has a shallow swimming spot that's ideal for kids. Despite the depth (or lack of it), a number of pretty fish circle around the swimmers looking for handouts.

Activities

Within a short boat ride of the island there's a handful of lovely dives, such as **La Bandera**, **Arrecife Manchones** and **Ultrafreeze** (El Frío), where you'll see the intact hull of a 60m-long cargo ship, thought to have been deliberately sunk in 30m of water. Expect to see sea turtles, rays and barracuda, along with a wide array of hard and soft corals.

There's good shore-snorkeling near **Playa Garrafón** and at **Yunque Reef**. As always, watch for boat traffic when you head out snorkeling.

Snorkeling with whale sharks is another popular activity. The peak season runs from July through August, when there can be up to a dozen boats circling one whale shark. Most dive shops offer whale-shark excursions; ask about their ethical practices before committing. See the boxed text on p287 for more on this question.

⭐ Hotel Garrafón de Castilla
SNORKELING

(Carretera Punta Sur Km 6; admission M$100, snorkel-gear rental M$50; ⊙8am-5pm) Avoid the overpriced Playa Garrafón Reef Park and instead visit Hotel Garrafón de Castilla's beach club for a day of snorkeling in translucent waters. A taxi from town costs M$105.

Aqua Adventures Eco Divers
DIVING

(Map p284; 998-188-41-50, cell 998-3228109; www.diveislamujeres.com; Juárez 13; 2-tank dives incl equipment from US$120, whale-shark tour US$125; ☻9am-7pm Mon-Sat, 10am-6pm Sun) Great option for snorkeling with whale sharks and goes to 15 sites for reef dives. Find them across from Javi's Cantina.

Mundaca Divers
DIVING

(Map p284; ☑cell 998-1212228; www.facebook.com/mundaca.divers; Madero 10; 2-tank dives for certified divers US$90-120, snorkeling US$47, bay fishing US$450; ☻8am-8pm) Does everything from shark-cave dives and fishing expeditions to snorkeling trips to a unique underwater sculpture museum known as MUSA (p272).

🛏 Sleeping

Apartments Trinchan
APARTMENT $

(Map p284; ☑cell 998-1666967; atrinchan@prodigy.net.mx; Carlos Lazo 46; r/apt M$800/900; ❈⏣) This is one of the best budget deals in town – and the beach is right around the corner. Opt for one of the large apartments with full kitchen, but avoid No 8, which catches noise from a nearby hostel's late-night beach parties. Unlike nearly every other hotel, you can smoke inside the rooms. (So this may be a bad choice for nonsmokers!)

Hotel Francis Arlene
HOTEL $$

(Map p284; ☑998-877-08-61; www.francisarlene.com; Av Guerrero 7; r with fan/air-con from M$1200/1500; ❈❋⏣) This place offers comfortable, good-sized rooms with fridge. Most have a king-sized bed or two doubles, and many have balcony and partial sea views. The lounging-frog sculptures are cute. Good low-season rates, August to September.

Hotel Rocamar
HOTEL $$$

(Map p284; ☑998-877-01-01; www.rocamar-hotel.com; cnr Calle Bravo & Av Guerrero; r US$113-143, casas US$286; ℗⏣❋⏣⏣) Modern rooms (the glass-walled bathrooms in some do have curtains) feature private balcony with sea views. The view from the pool ain't too shabby either. *Casas* are available with a full kitchen. Prices drop considerably in low season. Wi-fi extends through the lobby area only.

🍴 Eating

Aluxes Coffee Shop
CAFE $$

(Map p284; www.aluxesisla.com; Matamoros 11; breakfast M$80-100, lunch & dinner M$95-290; ☻8am-10pm Wed-Mon; ⏣) Aluxes serves bagels, baguettes and mighty fine banana

Isla Mujeres

Punta Norte

See Isla Mujeres Town Map (p284)

Punta Sam (6km)

Ferry to Puerto Juárez (10km)

Ferries to Cancún's Zona Hotelera (13km)

Car Ferries to Punta Sam

CARIBBEAN SEA

Av Rueda Medina

Laguna Makax

Mango Café

Bahía de Mujeres

Carretera Sac Bajo

Av Rueda Medina

Salina Grande

Isla Mujeres Turtle Farm

Playa Pescador

Carretera Punta Sur

Playa Lancheros

Playa Indios

Hotel Garrafón de Castilla

Playa Garrafón

Punta Sur

bread, and it's one of the friendliest joints in town.

Mango Café
BREAKFAST $$

(www.facebook.com/mangocafeisla; Payo Obispo 101, Colonia Meterológico; mains M$105-170; ☻7am-3pm; ⏣) See the south side of town and drop by Mango Café for some self-serve coffee and a hearty Caribbean-inspired breakfast. The hot items here are coconut French toast and eggs Benedict in a curry hollandaise sauce. It's a short bike or cab ride away, about 3km south of the ferry terminal. Cash only. No pets.

Isla Mujeres Town

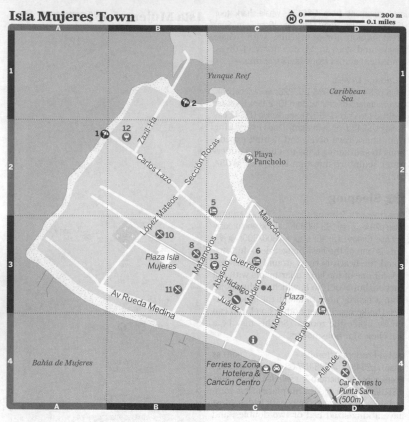

Isla Mujeres Town

◎ Sights
1 Playa Norte A2
2 Playa Secreto B1

✚ Activities, Courses & Tours
3 Aqua Adventures Eco Divers C3
4 Mundaca Divers C3

🛏 Sleeping
5 Apartments Trinchan C2
6 Hotel Francis Arlene C3

7 Hotel Rocamar D3

🍴 Eating
8 Aluxes Coffee Shop B3
9 La Lomita D4
10 Lola Valentina B3
11 Olivia B3

🍸 Drinking & Nightlife
12 Buho's B2
13 El Patio C3

La Lomita   MEXICAN $$
(Map p284; ☑ cell 998-2903866; www.facebook.
com/restaurantlalomita; Juárez Sur 25; mains
M$120-205; ⊙9am-10pm) 'Little Hill' serves
good, cheap Mexican food in a small, colorful
setting. Seafood and chicken dishes predomi-
nate. Try the fantastic bean and avocado soup,
or the ceviche (seafood marinated in citrus,
garlic and seasonings). There's also a little al-
fresco dining section with umbrellas.

Lola Valentina   FUSION $$$
(Map p284; ☑ 998-105-85-83; www.facebook.com/
lolavalentinaislamujeres; Hidalgo s/n; mains M$245-
540; ⊙8am-midnight; 🔊🖉) Overlooking the
quieter north side of the restaurant strip, Lola
does popular Mexican fusion with dishes like
coconut shrimp, plus several gluten-free and
vegan items, and the decidedly nonvegan,
non-GF Latin Surf 'n' Turf. It has swings at the
bar (fun!) and a tasty cocktail menu.

Olivia MEDITERRANEAN $$$
(Map p284; ☑998-877-17-65; www.olivia-isla
-mujeres.com; Matamoros s/n; mains M$150-380;
⊗5-9:45pm Mon-Sat; 🔊) This lovely Israeli-run
restaurant makes everything from scratch,
from Moroccan-style fish on couscous to
chicken shawarmas wrapped in pita bread.
Ask for a candlelit table out back in the gar-
den, and save room for the house-made cher-
ry ice cream. Usually closes September to
mid-October. Reservations recommended.

Drinking & Nightlife

Buho's BAR
(Map p284; ☑998-877-03-01; Carlos Lazo 1, Playa
Norte; ⊗10:30am-11pm; 🔊) The quintessential
swinger experience. Literally: it has swings
at the bar. You can also take morning and
afternoon yoga classes here. Any closer to
the beach and you'd be in the water.

El Patio BAR
(Map p284; www.facebook.com/elpatioislamujeres;
Hidalgo 17; ⊗4:30pm-midnight; 🔊) The self-pro-
claimed 'house of music' has an open-air pa-
tio and rooftop terrace where you can catch
mediocre rock cover bands and relatively
subdued acoustic sets amid a near-100%
gringo crowd. Happy hour is from 5pm to
7pm, with discount drinks and food.

ⓘ Information

MONEY
Several banks are directly across from the ferry
dock. Most exchange currency and all have ATMs.
HSBC (☑998-877-00-05; Av Rueda Medina 3,
btwn Bravo & Av Morelos; ⊗9am-5pm Mon-Fri)

MEDICAL SERVICES
Hospital Comunitario Isla Mujeres (Bo-
quinete s/n, cnr Picuda, Colonia La Gloria;
⊗24hr) About 5km south of the town center;
doctors available 24/7.

Hyperbaric Chamber (☑cell 998-1349310,
cell 998-8458147; Guerrero s/n, cnr Morelos;
⊗9am-4pm, on call 24hr) Just north of the
main square. It's often closed but there's 24-
hour telephone assistance.

TOURIST INFORMATION
Tourist Information Office (Map p284; Av
Rueda Medina 130, btwn Madero & Morelos;
⊗9am-4pm Mon-Fri) Offers a number of bro-
chures. Some staff members speak English.

ⓘ Getting There & Away

There are several points of embarkation from
Cancún to reach Isla Mujeres. Most people cross

on Ultramar passenger ferries. The R-1 'Puerto
Juárez' city bus in Cancún serves all Zona Ho-
telera departure points and Puerto Juárez, in
Ciudad Cancún. If you arrive by car, daily parking
fees in and around the terminals cost between
M$100 and M$180, but can be as low as M$50 if
you go further from the terminal.

Ultramar fares for ferries departing from the
Zona Hotelera are in US dollars. If you're on a tight
budget, it's much cheaper to leave from Puerto
Juárez. Ultramar ferries (www.ultramarferry.
com) depart from the following docks.

➡ **El Embarcadero** (Blvd Kukulcán Km 4) Nine
daily departures; one-way US$15.

➡ **Playa Caracol** (Blvd Kukulcán Km 9.5) Six
daily departures; one-way US$15.

➡ **Playa Tortugas** (Blvd Kukulcán Km 6.5)
Twelve daily departures; one-way US$15.

➡ **Puerto Juárez** (4km north of Ciudad Cancún)
Depart every 30 minutes; one-way M$160.

At the time of research, neither of the alternate
passenger ferries Marinsa (www.marinsaturismo.
com) and Naveganto (www.naveganto) were
operating to or from Isla Mujeres.

Punta Sam, 8km north of Cancún Centro, is
the only ferry that transports vehicles and bikes.
From Punta Sam, drivers are included in prices
for the following one-way fares: cars (M$295),
motorcycles (M$90) and bicycles (M$20); addi-
tional passengers pay M$46. Get there an hour
before if you're transporting a vehicle. See www.
maritimaislamujeres.com for departure times.
To reach Punta Sam, take a taxi or northbound
'Punta Sam' colectivo along Avenida Tulum. Car
ferries for **Punta Sam** (☑998-293-90-92; www.
ultramarferry.com; Av Rueda Medina s/n; one-way
fare incl passenger M$295; ⊗6:30am-9:30pm)
and **passenger ferries to Cancún** (Map p284;
Av Rueda Medina s/n) leave from different docks.

ⓘ Getting Around

BICYCLE
Cycling is a great way to get around on the island's
narrow streets and to explore outlying areas.

Rentadora Fiesta (☑cell 998-7349862; Av
Rueda Medina s/n, btwn Morelos & Bravo; bike
per hour/day M$50/150, scooter/golf cart per
day M$400/750; ⊗9am-5pm) Rents mountain
bikes and beach cruisers.

MOTORCYCLE & GOLF CART
Inspect all scooters carefully before renting.
Costs vary, and are sometimes jacked up in high
season, but generally start at about M$400 per
day (9am to 5pm).

Many people find golf carts a good way to get
around the island, and caravans of them can be
seen tooling down the roads. The average cost is
M$800 per day (9am to 5pm).

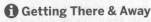

YUCATÁN PENINSULA ISLA MUJERES

Gomar (☑998-877-16-86; cnr Av Rueda Medina & Calle Bravo; scooter/golf cart per day M$400/800; ⊙9am-9pm) Offers reasonable golf-cart and scooter rentals.

Mega Ciro's (☑cell 998-5785266; www.facebook.com/cirosgolfcartrentals; Av Guerrero 11; golf cart per day US$60; ⊙9am-5pm) Well-maintained golf carts.

TAXI

Taxi rates are set by the municipal government and posted at the **taxi base** (Map p284; ☑998-877-18-38; Av Rueda Medina s/n; M$50-115; ⊙24hr) just south of the passenger-ferry dock.

Isla Holbox

☑984 / POP 1600

Isla Holbox (hol-bosh) has sandy streets, colorful Caribbean buildings, lazing, sundrunk dogs, and sand so fine its texture is nearly clay. The greenish waters are a unique color from the mixing of ocean currents, and on land there's a mixing too: of locals and tourists, the latter hoping to escape the hubbub of Cancún.

While there are no throbbing nightclubs here, and while its beaches are beautiful, it's not exactly peaceful (what with the throngs of people and constant buzzing of noisy gasoline-powered golf carts). It's also the one place in nearly all Mexico you'll find a 'tourists-go-home' attitude from (some) locals.

It's a fantastic spot for wildlife. Lying within the **Yum Balam** reserve, Holbox is home to more than 150 bird species, including roseate spoonbills, pelicans, herons, ibis and flamingos. In summer, whale sharks congregate nearby.

◉ Sights

For most people, the island is synonymous with powdery sand, but there are some lovely lagoons, low forest and lots of wildlife. Some of the best 'sights' are underwater: whale sharks and sea turtles.

★Punta Mosquito   BEACH

On the eastern side of the island, Punta Mosquito is about 2.5km east of the downtown area. It has a large sandbar and is a good place to spot flamingos. It's not named 'Mosquito' for nothing: bring repellent!

⟜ Tours

★VIP Holbox Experience   TOURS

(☑984-875-21-07; www.vipholbox.com; Av Damero s/n; whale-shark tours per person US$150,

night kayak tours US$55; ⊙9am-1pm & 5-9pm) VIP Holbox Experience goes the extra mile to ensure that guests understand they are part of a delicate ecosystem – for the whale-shark tours, they offer biodegradable sunscreen, no plastic bottles and follow strict guidelines to make sure these incredible animals are properly protected. Tours include delicious ceviche and a stop for snorkeling.

It also offers English-language guides and a variety of other tours, including bird-watching and a nighttime kayaking outing to observe a fascinating bioluminescent phenomenon that occurs in Holbox's waters from April to November.

🛏 Sleeping

Not surprisingly, *cabañas* (cabins) and bungalows are everywhere along the beach. Some of the most upscale places can be found east of town, out along the island's northern shore in the Zona Hotelera. Most budget and midrange accommodations are clustered within several blocks of the plaza.

Hostel Tribu   HOSTEL $

(☑984-875-25-07; www.tribuhostel.com; Av Pedro Joaquín Coldwell s/n; dm/d/ste M$380/1050/1600; ⊜❋⍥) With so many activities available here (from salsa lessons to yoga and kayaking), it doesn't take long to settle in with the tribe. Slightly more expensive dorms come with air-con, as does the private suite, and all rooms are clean and cheerful. Tribu also has a bar that hosts weekly jam sessions. From the plaza, it's one block north and two blocks west.

Also worthy of note are the double **bars** (open to nonguests too) and the common areas. Oversize lockers make it easy to secure your stuff.

★Casa Takywara   HOTEL $$$

(☑984-875-22-55; www.casatakywara.com; Av Pedro Joaquín Coldwell s/n; ste/bungalow incl breakfast from M$4100/5400; ⊜❋⍥) Out on the quiet western end of town, this beautiful waterfront hotel stands out for its striking architecture and stylishly decorated rooms with kitchenette and sea-view balcony. It's built next to a patch of protected wetland where you'll hear the song of chirping cicadas. Rates drop considerably during the low season. It's 1km west of Tiburón Ballena. Wi-fi in the reception area only.

SWIM WITH THE WHALE SHARKS?

Between mid-May and mid-September, massive whale sharks congregate around Isla Holbox to feed on plankton. They are the largest fish in the world, weighing up to 15 tons and extending as long as 15m from gaping mouth to arching tail. Locals call them 'dominoes' because of their speckled skin.

The best time to track these gentle giants is in July and August, but that also happens to be the busy Mexican vacation season, when you can get up to two-dozen boats rotating around a single whale shark.

The World Wildlife Fund has been working with the local community since 2003 to develop responsible practices for visiting the whale sharks, trying to balance the economic boon of these tours with the environmental imperatives of protecting a threatened species.

If you choose to go swimming with the whale shark, only three swimmers (including your guide) are allowed in the water at a time. You are not allowed to touch the fish, and are required to wear either a life jacket or wetsuit to ensure you do not dive below the shark.

Hotel Casa Bárbara   HOTEL $$$
(📞984-875-23-02; www.hotelcasabarbara.mx; Tiburón Ballena s/n; d from M$3000; 🅿️❄️🛜🏊) A very comfortable hotel with a swimming pool surrounded by a verdant garden. Rooms are decked out with rustic furnishings and cushy beds, and most have porches overlooking the garden. It's halfway between the ferry dock and the beach.

Hotel La Palapa   HOTEL $$$
(📞984-875-21-21; www.hotellapalapa.com; Morelos 231; r from US$195; 🅿️❄️🛜) La Palapa offers cozy beachfront rooms, some with balconies overlooking the sea, and a cloistered beach area complete with an outdoor bar that serves scrumptious international food. The ocean view from the rooftop terrace is simply awesome. It's 100m east of Tiburón Ballena, along the beach.

🍴 Eating & Drinking

Dinners in Holbox, with a few exceptions, are surprisingly average, especially in the seafood department (a travesty, given it's an island!). Avoid overpriced lobster options, especially at the spots edging the plaza. Breakfasts, on the other hand, are great, with lots of inexpensive, tasty options in a wide range of cuisines.

★ Le Jardin   FRENCH $
(📞cell 984-1158197; www.facebook.com/lejardin panaderia; Lisa 30; bread M$25-35, coffee M$24-45; 🕐8:30am-12:30pm Wed-Sun; 🛜♿) Very tasty French pastries and morning breakfast selections make this a welcome spot if you're craving something other than Mexican morning food. Coffee is delicious as well, and the airy *palapa*, surrounded by plumeria and butterflies, makes for a comfortable spot to sit and chat with fellow diners. Kids will love the large toy selection to play with as adults dine.

Arte Sano   CAFE $
(Aguilar s/n, btwn Tiburón Ballena & Palomino; breakfast mains M$110-160, lunch mains M$90-190; 🕐9am-9pm Wed-Mon; 🛜) A small, intimate, *palapa* cafe with bright colored tablecloths and even cheerier service. A mix of veggie and meat options, with good green juice smoothies and other treats. A giant *alebrije* (colorful wooden animal figure) sits outside the door.

Las Panchas   SEAFOOD $$
(📞cell 984-1208354; Esmedregal s/n; snacks M$14-39, mains M$160-280; 🕐8-11am & 1-7pm) Ask just about anyone in town where to go for Holbox seafood and they'll probably point to Las Panchas, where you can get delicious Mexican and Caribbean seafood favorites like spicy *diabla*-style octopus, refreshing ceviches, seafood soup and fish tacos, plus some excellent Yucatecan snacks. Be prepared to wait for a table, especially on weekends in high season. Cash only.

Roots   PIZZA $$
(📞cell 984-2415953; www.facebook.com/pizza rootswood; Porfirio Díaz s/n, btwn Palomino & Carito; pizzas M$100-250, lobster pizza M$600; 🕐noon-11:30pm) Like most pizzerias in town, the hot item here is the seasonal lobster pizza and Roots' version ranks among the best of them. All of the wood-fired, thin-crust pies come with a zesty Morita salsa on the side. The open-air restaurant also carries a fantastic selection of Mexican-only liquor, beers and mezcal (150 different ones!).

★ El Chapulím
MEXICAN $$$

(✐cell 984-1376069; elchapulim@gmail.com; Tiburón Ballena s/n; mains from M$350-550; ◷6-9pm Mon-Sat) El Chapulím has no menu and the kitchen closes when the food runs out – usually before 9pm – so come aware of the quirks involved. Food is excellent, and chef Erik comes to your table personally. This may be the only place in Holbox where you can depend on lobster to be worth the pretty price tag. Cash only.

Hot Corner
BAR

(✐cell 984-8752293; www.facebook.com/the hotcornerholbox; Av Pedro Joaquín Coldwell s/n; ◷noon-2am) Truly living up to its name, this corner gastro-bar is Holbox's go-to spot for live music, dancing, spirited boozing and late-night munchies. Much to the neighbors' chagrin, the nightly fiesta often spills onto the sand street.

☆ Entertainment

Tribu Bar
LIVE MUSIC

(☑984-875-25-07; www.tribuhostel.com/bar; Av Pedro Joaquín Coldwell s/n; ◷7pm-2am Tue-Sun) Drop by the *palapa* bar at Hostel Tribu (p286) for live music, weekly salsa classes and Tuesday pub quizzes.

ℹ Information

Holbox has one **bank** (Tiburón Ballena s/n, btwn Cortéz & Kuka; ◷8:30am-6:30pm Mon-Sat, ATM 24hr). There's an ATM on the plaza above the police station, but it often runs out of money so bring lots of cash.

ℹ Getting There & Around

Ferries (Chiquilá dock; one-way M$150; ◷6am-9:30pm) run to Holbox from the port town of Chiquilá. It takes about 25 minutes to reach the island. Smaller, faster and wetter *lanchas* (motorboats) can make the crossing after dark for M$1200.

Buses to Cancún (M$200 to M$270, 3½ hours), Mérida (M$305 to M$436, five hours) and other destinations leave from the small Chiquilá ADO station a block south of the plaza. One departure to Cancún airport (M$355) leaves per day. Alternatively, you have the option of taking shared or private shuttle vans to/from Cancún airport with **Transfer Holbox** (☑cell 984-8752104; Av Damero, cnr Carito; M$350 per person; ◷9am-9pm) or Holbox Shuttle (www.holboxshuttle.com). *Colectivos* cost M$200 to Cancún Centro and M$350 to the airport.

Private air charters with **Flights Holbox** (✐cell 984-1368852; www.flights-holbox.com; Av Pedro Joaquín Coldwell s/n, Holbox Airport) are surprisingly economical if you have a small group. Per plane (up to five passengers), a Cancún flight costs US$545. They also run to Playa del Carmen (US$650), Cozumel (US$719), Mérida (US$1320) and other destinations.

If you're driving, your vehicle will be safe in Chiquilá parking lots for M$50 to M$100 per 24 hours. You won't be allowed to bring a tourist car to the island.

The good news is that you really won't need a car. Holbox's sand streets are narrow and deeply rutted, and golf carts have become ubiquitous, buzzing noisily up and down like giant bumblebees. You can rent them easily enough, but consider using your walking shoes instead. Golf-cart taxis cost M$30 to M$50 in town and M$100 out to Punta Coco.

Rent golf carts at **Rentadora El Brother** (☑984-875-20-18; Tiburón Ballena s/n; cart per hour/day M$250/1200; ◷9am-8pm).

Puerto Morelos
☑998 / POP 37,500

Halfway between Cancún and Playa del Carmen, Puerto Morelos retains its quiet, small-town feel despite the encroaching building boom north and south of town. While it offers enough restaurants and bars to keep you entertained by night, it's really the shallow Caribbean waters that draw visitors here. Brilliantly contrasted stripes of bright green and dark blue separate the shore from the barrier reef – a tantalizing sight for divers and snorkelers – while inland a series of excellent cenotes beckon the adventurous. There's a nice market just south of the plaza with a good selection of crafts and handmade hammocks that are of a much higher quality than those you'll find in Cancún or Playa.

◉ Sights

Crococun Zoo
ZOO

(☑998-850-37-19; www.crococunzoo.com; Hwy 307 Km 31; adult/child 6-12yr US$32/22; ◷9am-5pm) About 23km south of the Cancún airport, this former crocodile farm now calls itself a conservationist zoo that protects some of the area's endangered species and rescue animals. The price of admission includes a guided tour in which visitors are allowed to interact with some of the animals, such as white-tailed deer, boa constrictors, macaws, crocs and spider monkeys. Bring mosquito repellent.

Jardín Botánico
Dr Alfredo Barrera Marín
GARDENS

(Jardín Botánico Yaax Che; ☑ 998-206-92-33; www.facebook.com/jbpuertomorelos; Hwy 307 Km 320; adult/child 3-10yr M$120/50; ☺8am-4pm; ⛳) One of the largest botanical gardens in Mexico, this 65-hectare reserve has about 2km of trails and sections dedicated to epiphytes (orchids and bromeliads), palms, ferns, succulents (cacti and their relatives) and plants used in traditional Maya medicine. The garden also holds a large animal population, including the only coastal troops of spider monkeys left in the region.

🏃 Activities

The barrier reef that runs along most of the coast of Quintana Roo is only 600m offshore here, providing both divers and snorkelers with views of sea turtles, sharks, stingrays, moray eels, lobsters and loads of colorful tropical fish. Several sunken ships make great wreck diving, and the dive centers offer cenote trips as well.

Aquanauts
DIVING

(☑ 998-206-93-65; www.aquanautsdiveadventures.com; El Cid Marina; 1-/2-tank reef dive US$85/113, 2-tank cenote dive US$210, snorkeling US$35, lion-fish hunting M$140; ☺8am-4pm Mon-Sat) Runs many interesting tours, including drift diving, cenote and shipwreck dives, and lionfish fishing. Though there is an office in town, the actual dives leave from the El Cid Marina, 3km south of town.

🛏 Sleeping & Eating

Casitas Kinsol
GUESTHOUSE $$

(☑ 998-206-91-52; www.casitas-kinsol.com; Av Zetina Gazca 18; d with air-con/fan US$61/39; ☺✷🏧) Great for people who want to see what life's like on the other side of town (yes, there are signs of life west of the highway!), Kinsol offers fan-cooled *palapa*-style huts with beautiful design details such as Talavera tile sinks and handcrafted furnishings. It's a peaceful spot where even the dogs and cats get along. It's 3km west of town.

A resident tortoise wanders around in the verdant garden. Bike rentals available.

★ Posada El Moro
HOTEL $$$

(☑ 998-871-01-59; www.hotelelmoro.mx; Av Rojo Gómez s/n; r/ste incl breakfast from M$1900/2500; ℙ☺✷🏧🏊) A pretty property, with cheery geraniums in the halls and courtyard. Some rooms have kitchenette, most have couches that fold out into futons, and there's a small pool in a tropical garden. Prices drop substantially in low season or if you book via their website (not the booking sites). It's northwest of the plaza.

Casa Caribe
B&B $$$

(☑ 998-251-80-60; www.casacaribepuertomorelos.com; Av Rojo Gomez 768; r incl breakfast US$185; ☺✷🏧) Rooms with terra-cotta floors at this tastefully decorated B&B afford sweeping beach views from large balconies with hammocks, and all get fantastic sea breezes. Breakfast is served on a hacienda-style terrace overlooking a walled garden area.

There's a three-night minimum stay.

El Nicho
BREAKFAST $$

(☑ cell 998-2010992; www.elnicho.com.mx; cnr Avs Tulum & Rojo Gómez; breakfast M$79-140; ☺7:30am-2pm; 🏧) Puerto Morelos' most popular breakfast spot, El Nicho serves organic egg dishes, eggs Benedict, *chilaquiles* (fried tortilla strips in salsa) with chicken and organic coffee from Chiapas. Vegetarians will find many good options here. Cash only.

★ Al Chimichurri
STEAK $$$

(☑ 998-252-46-66; www.facebook.com/alchimichurri; Av Rojo Gómez s/n; mains M$182-495; ☺5-11pm Tue-Sun) You definitely can't go wrong with the fresh pasta and wood-fired pizza here, but this Uruguayan grill is best known for its steaks. The star cuts are a *Flintstones*-size rib eye, tender flank steak and filet mignon in homemade beef gravy. It's just south of the plaza.

John Gray's Kitchen
INTERNATIONAL $$$

(☑ 998-871-06-65; www.facebook.com/johngrayskitchen; Av Niños Héroes 6; breakfast M$60-100, dinner M$270-450; ☺8am-10pm Mon-Sat Nov-Apr, from 3pm May-Oct) One block west and two blocks north of the plaza, this 'kitchen' turns out some truly fabulous food. The chef's specialty, though not listed on the regularly changing menu, is the duck in chipotle, tequila and honey sauce. It opens for breakfast too.

🛍 Shopping

★ Artisans Market
ARTS & CRAFTS

(Av Rojo Gómez s/n; ☺9am-8pm) The hammocks sold here differ from what you'll find elsewhere because they're created right here in Puerto Morelos by a local family that's been making them for decades. (Ask for Mauricio or Martin!) You can also buy dream catchers, *alebrijes* (from San Martín Tilcajete), handbags, masks, jewelry and more.

ℹ Getting There & Away

Playa Express vans and ADO buses to Puerto Morelos drop you on the highway, where you can walk the 2km into town or take a taxi (M$30) waiting at the turnoff. ADO and Playa Express have frequent departures to Cancún (M$28 to M$37) and Playa del Carmen (M$28 to M$37). You can purchase ADO tickets at a **bus station** (www.ado.com.mx; Hwy 307, cnr Morelos) next to the highway turnoff.

From Cancún airport (p280), buses depart frequently to Puerto Morelos for M$127. They usually run from 7am to 8:30pm.

Cabs parked at the town plaza will take you back to the highway. Some drivers will tell you the fare is per person or overcharge in some other manner; strive for M$30 for as many people as you can stuff in. *Colectivos* to/from town to the highway cost M$8. A taxi to the airport runs M$450.

Playa del Carmen

📋 984 / POP 210,000

Playa del Carmen, now one of Quintana Roo's largest cities, ranks right up there with Tulum as one of the Riviera's trendiest spots. Sitting coolly on the lee side of Cozumel, the town's beaches are jammed with superfit sun worshipers. The waters aren't as clear as those of Cancún or Cozumel, and the sand isn't quite as powder-perfect as they are further north, but still Playa grows and grows.

The town is ideally located: close to Cancún's international airport, but far enough south to allow easy access to Cozumel, Tulum, Cobá and other destinations. The reefs here are excellent and offer diving and snorkeling close by. Look for rays, moray eels, sea turtles and a huge variety of corals. The lavender sea fans make for very picturesque vistas.

With cruise-ship passengers visiting from Cozumel, Playa can feel crowded along the first several blocks of the tourist center.

◉ Sights

Playa del Carmen is primarily known for its beaches and outdoor party life, but there are a few sights worth checking out on rainy days.

Aquarium   AQUARIUM

(El Acuario de Playa; 📋 984-879-44-62, 998-287-53-13; www.elacuariodeplaya.com; 2nd fl, Calle 14 Norte 148, Plaza Calle Corazón; M$270; ⊗11am-10pm) An impressive three-story aquarium with 200 marine species and 45 exhibits. One of the few options in Playa for non-beach days. Last entry is at 9pm.

🏖 Beaches

Avid beachgoers won't be disappointed here. Playa's lovely white-sand beaches are much more accessible than Cancún's: just head down to the ocean, stretch out and enjoy. Numerous restaurants front the beach in the tourist zone and many hotels in the area offer an array of water-sport activities.

If crowds aren't your thing, go north of Calle 38, where a few scrawny palms serve for shade. Here the beach extends for uncrowded kilometers, making for good camping, but you need to be extra careful with your belongings, as thefts are a possibility.

Some women go topless in Playa (though it's not common in most of Mexico, and is generally frowned upon by locals – except the young, of course). **Mamita's Beach**, north of Calle 28, is considered the best place to let loose and it's LGBTIQ+ friendly to boot.

About 3km south of the ferry terminal, past a group of all-inclusives, a refreshingly quiet stretch of beach sees relatively few visitors.

🏃 Activities

In addition to great ocean diving, many outfits offer cenote dives. Prices are similar at most shops: two-tank dives (US$100), cenote dives (US$160), snorkeling (US$30), whale-shark tours (US$190) and open-water certification (US$450).

French, English and Spanish are spoken at **Phocea Mexico** (📋984-873-12-10; www.phocea-mexico.com; Calle 10 Norte s/n; 2-tank dive incl gear US$95, cenote dives incl gear US$150; ⊗7:15am-9pm; 🚗). The shop does dives with bull sharks (US$90) for advanced divers, usually from November to March.

≋ Courses & Tours

International House
Riviera Maya   LANGUAGE

(📋984-803-33-88; www.ihrivieramaya.com; Calle 14 Norte 141; per week US$230) Offers 20 hours of Spanish classes per week. You can stay in residence-hall rooms (US$26, no meals), even if you're not taking classes, but the best way to learn the language is to take advantage of the school's homestays (including breakfast, US$33 to US$39) with Mexican host families.

Río Secreto   ADVENTURE

(📋984-242-00-74; www.riosecreto.com; Carretera 307 Km 283.5; adult/child 4-12yr from US$79/40; ⊗tours 9am-1pm) Hike and swim through a 1km-long underground cavern 5km south of

RIVIERA THEME PARKS

Always a big hit with children, there are several theme parks between Cancún and Tulum, many with fantastic scenery – truly some of the most beautiful lagoons, cenotes and natural areas on the coast. Sure, some will find these places cheesy, but the kids couldn't care less. Some parks are pricey but their websites often offer presale online discounts.

It's worth mentioning that some parks offer an optional swim-with-dolphins activity, and though it may seem like a lovely idea, animal welfare groups suggest interaction with dolphins and other sea mammals held in captivity creates stress for these creatures.

Here are some of the most popular parks.

Aktun Chen (☑cell 984-8064962, toll free 800-099-07-58; www.aktun-chen.com; Hwy 307 Km 107; full tour incl lunch adult/child 6-10yr US$128/102; ☻9:30am-5:30pm; 🐾) This small park 40km south of Playa del Carmen features a 585m-long cave, a 12m-deep cenote, 10 zip-lines and a small zoo.

Xplor (☑984-206-00-38, 998-883-31-43; www.xplor.travel; Hwy 307 Km 282; adult/child 5-11yr US$130/65; ☻9am-5pm & 5:30-11pm Mon-Sat; 🐾) This large park 6km south of Playa del Carmen operates circuits that take you zip-lining, rafting, driving amphibious jeeps, swimming in an underground river and hiking through caverns. Xplor has nighttime activities as well.

Xel-Há (☑984-206-00-38, 998-883-3034; www.xelha.com; Hwy 307 Km 240; adult/child 5-11yr from US$100/50; ☻8:30am-6pm; 🐾) Billing itself as a natural outdoor aquarium, it's built around an inlet 13km north of Tulum. There are lots of water-based activities on offer, including a river tour and snorkeling.

Xcaret (☑984-206-00-38; www.xcaret.com; Hwy 307 Km 282; adult/child 5-12yr from US$110/55; ☻8:30am-1pm; 🐾) One of the originals in the area, with loads of nature-based activities and stuff for grown-ups like a Mexican wine cellar and day spa. It's 6km south of Playa del Carmen. Hosts a pretty Day of the Dead festival in November.

Selvática (☑998-881-3033; www.selvatica.com.mx; Ruta de los Cenotes Km 19; adult/child 8-15yr US$199/99; ☻tours 9am, 10:30am, noon & 1:30pm; 🐾) Inland from Puerto Morelos, this adventure outfit only runs prearranged tours. Come for adrenaline-pumping zip-lining, swimming in a cenote and more. Check the website for age restrictions for each tour.

Playa del Carmen. Some aspects are hyped, but there is a lot that is just plain awesome.

🛏 Sleeping

Hostel 3B　　　　　　　　　　HOSTEL $
(☑984-803-29-01; www.hostel3b.com; Av 10 Sur s/n, cnr Calle 1 Sur; dm/r incl breakfast from M$180/690; ❄✳🛜🏊) Known for its popular rooftop pool parties on Friday and Sunday, the electronic-music fiestas last until about 2am, something to consider if you value shut-eye. Conveniently close to the beach, bus and ferry terminals, 3B features clean, air-conditioned mixed dorms and colorful private rooms. Avoid booking rooftop rooms.

★**Hotel Playa del Karma**　BOUTIQUE HOTEL $$
(☑984-803-02-72; hplayadelkarma@gmail.com; 15 Av Norte, btwn Calles 12 & 14; d M$1380; ❄✳🛜🏊) The closest you're going to get to the jungle in this town; rooms here face a lush courtyard with a small – no, make that tiny – pool. All rooms have air-con and TV, sitting area

and a sweet little porch with a hammock. The hotel arranges tours to nearby ruins and diving sites.

Petit Lafitte　　　　　　　　RESORT $$$
(☑984-877-40-00; www.petitlafitte.com; Carretera Cancún–Chetumal Km 292; d/bungalow incl breakfast & dinner from US$370/515; 🅿❄✳🛜🏊) Occupying quiet Playa Xcalacoco, 6km north of Playa del Carmen, Petit Lafitte is an excellent and safe family vacation spot. Stay in a room or a 'bungalow' (essentially a wood cabin with tasteful rustic furnishings, some of which sleep up to five guests). Kids stay entertained with the large pool, small animal shelter, games room, paddleboards and other water activities.

See website for directions.

🍴 Eating

Playa has a great range of dining choices, from cheap eats (away from the tourist center) to fancy date spots, to great regional

Playa del Carmen

0 — 200 m
0 — 0.1 miles

Calle 16 Norte Bis

Chez Céline (600m);
La Bodeguita del Medio (650m);
La Cueva del Chango (1km)

Calle 14 Norte Bis

Calle 14 Norte

2

1

Calle 12 Norte Bis

5

ADO
Terminal
Alterna

Calle 12 Norte

Calle 10 Norte Bis

7

6

Calle 10 Norte

3

20 Av Norte

15 Av Norte

10 Av Norte

Quinta Av (5 Av) Norte

1 Av Norte

1 Av Norte Bis

Parque 28
de Julio

15 Av Norte

Playa

Calle 8 Norte

Calle 6 Norte Bis

Calle 6 Norte

10

9

8

Calle 4 Norte

CARIBBEAN
SEA

20 Av Norte

15 Av Norte

10 Av Norte

Quinta Av (5 Av) Norte

Calle 2 Norte

Playa
Express

Parque
Leona
Vicario

ADO
Terminal
Turística

Plaza
Mayor

Av Juárez

4

Hwy 307 (450m);
Cozumel (10km)

Winjet

Ultramar

Cozumel Ferry
Ticket Booths

Calle 1 Sur

20 Av Norte

10 Av Norte

Quinta Av (5 Av) Norte

Calle 1 Sur

Cozumel
(19km)

Lara & Luca (400m)

YUCATÁN PENINSULA PLAYA DEL CARMEN

Playa del Carmen

and international food. Or hit the markets for some home-style regional cooking.

★ **Lara & Luca**　　　　　　　　　CAFE
(☏984-176-33-05; www.larayluca.com; Av Aviación s/n; breakfast mains M$106-146; ⊙7:30am-10pm Mon-Sat, to 2pm Sun; ⓅⓏ) 'Okay, but first, coffee' is the motto here, and they sure do coffee well. They do everything well, actually: from tasty fruit-and-yogurt bowls to green juice and smoothies to eggs Benedict with pork confit and bacon that will have you wondering if you can take it on the plane. Well worth the trip out of the town center.

Kaxapa Factory　　　　　SOUTH AMERICAN $
(☏984-803-50-23; www.kaxapa-factory.com; Calle 10 Norte s/n; mains M$75-165; ⊙8am-9pm Tue-Sun; ⓇⓏ) The specialty at this Venezuelan restaurant on the park is *arepas* (delicious corn flatbread stuffed with your choice of shredded beef, chicken or beans and plantains). There are many vegetarian and gluten-free options here and the refreshing freshly made juices go nicely with just about everything on the menu.

★ **Chez Céline**　　　　　　　　BREAKFAST $
(☏984-803-34-80; www.chezceline.com.mx; cnr 5 Av Norte & Calle 34 Norte; breakfast M$34-118, lunch M$90-265; ⊙7:30am-11pm; ❄ⓇⓏ) Good, healthy breakfasts (some vegan!) and a range of yummy baked goods are what keeps this French-run bakery-cafe busy. Sa-

vory croissants with smoked salmon or ham, cheese, and béchamel.

★ **La Cueva del Chango**　　　　MEXICAN $$
(☏984-147-02-71; www.lacuevadelchango.com; Calle 38 Norte s/n, btwn Av 5 Norte & beach; breakfast M$62-138, lunch & dinner M$196-238; ⊙8am-10:30pm Mon-Sat, to 2pm Sun; Ⓡ) The 'Monkey's Cave,' known for its fresh and natural ingredients, has seating in a jungly *palapa* setting or a verdant garden out back. Service is friendly, but the kitchen can be slow. The food is delicious; try the *sopa de coco con camarones* (coconut milk with shrimp). Yum!

La Famiglia　　　　　　　　　ITALIAN $$$
(☏984-803-53-50; www.lafamiglia.mx; 10 Av Norte s/n, cnr Calle 10 Norte; mains M$140-550; ⊙noon-11pm; ⓇⓏ) Pay a visit to the family and enjoy superb wood-fired pizza and handmade pasta, ravioli and gnocchi. Playa is a magnet for Italian restaurants, but this definitely ranks among the best of them. Dairy-free, gluten-free and vegan options are all available.

🍸 Drinking & Nightlife

Playa is quite the party. You'll find everything from mellow, tranced-out lounge bars to thumping beachfront discos here. The fun generally starts on Quinta Avenida then heads down toward the beach on Calle 12.

Tiny Tiki Hut　　　　　　　COCKTAIL BAR
(☏984-149-09-07; www.facebook.com/tinytikihut; Av 20, btwn Calles 4 Norte & 6 Norte; ⊙4-11pm Mon-Sat) If you're tired of Mexico and need some Hawaii in your night, head to Tiny Tiki Hut, with tasty original cocktails, old Tiki faves like mai tais, and (loud record scratching sound here)...ramen noodles all on the menu. Oddly, it all fits perfectly and you can actually have a conversation here, unlike most other Playa bars.

La Bodeguita del Medio　　　　DANCING
(☏984-803-39-50; www.labodeguitadelmedio.com.mx; 5 Av Norte s/n, cnr Calle 34 Norte; ⊙6pm-1am; Ⓡ) The writing is literally on the walls (and on the lampshades, and pretty much everywhere) at this Cuban restaurant-bar. After a few mojitos you'll be dancing the night away to live *cubana* music. Get here at 7pm on Tuesday and Thursday for free salsa lessons.

Playa 69
GAY

(www.facebook.com/sesentaynueveplaya; off 5 Av Norte, btwn Calles 4 & 6 Norte; cover after 10pm from M$60; ⊘9pm-4am Wed-Sun) This popular gay dance club proudly features foreign strippers from such far-flung places as Australia and Brazil, and it stages weekend drag-queen shows. It may also open Tuesdays at key vacation times. Find it at the end of the narrow alley.

☆ Entertainment

★ **Fusion**
LIVE MUSIC

(☑cell 984-1478420; www.facebook.com/fusion beachbarcuisine; Calle 6 Norte s/n; ⊘8am-2am) This beachside bar and grill stages live music, along with a fun belly-dancing and fire-dancing show. The fire-dancing comes later in the evening (around 11:30pm). From 6pm on it's a cool spot to have a beer or cocktail and listen to rock, reggae and Latin sounds.

ⓘ Information

Everything Playa del Carmen (www.everything playadelcarmen.com) is a good online source of information about restaurants, day trips, public transportation services and more.

ⓘ Getting There & Away

BOAT

Passenger ferries depart frequently to Cozumel from Calle 1 Sur, where you'll find two companies with **ticket booths** (Av 1 Sur s/n, cnr Calle 1 Sur). Prices are subject to change. The **Calica-Punta Venado terminal** (Terminal Marítima Punta Venado; Hwy 307 Km 282), 8km south of Playa, operates car ferries to Cozumel.

Winjet (☑984-872-15-88; www.winjet.mx; Av 1 Sur s/n; one-way adult/child 6-11yr M$170/110; ⊘8am-10pm) Online promotions can bring fares down by about 20% for all travelers.

Transcaribe (☑987-872-76-71; www.trans caribe.net; Hwy 307 Km 282, Calica–Punta Venado; one-way M$500) Daily car ferries to Cozumel. One-way fare includes passengers.

Ultramar (☑998-881-58-90, 998-293-90-92; www.ultramarferry.com/en; Av 1 Sur s/n; one-way adult/child 6-11yr M$220/140; ⊘7am-11pm) The most spiffy of the ferries, and claims to be the least prone to causing seasickness. Offers a 1st-class option with a lounge, more room, priority boarding and leather seats. Also operates car ferries from the Calica–Punta Venado terminal.

BUS

Playa has two bus terminals; each sells tickets and provides information for at least some of the other's departures. You can save money by buying a 2nd-class bus ticket, but remember that it's often stop-and-go along the way.

The **ADO Terminal Alterna** (www.ado.com. mx; 20 Av Norte s/n, cnr Calle 12; ⊘24hr) is where most long-distance bus lines arrive and depart. Buses heading to destinations within the state of Quintana Roo leave from the **ADO Terminal Turística** (Terminal del Centro; www.ado. com.mx; 5 Av Norte s/n, cnr Av Juárez; ⊘24hr).

Playa Express (Calle 2 Norte s/n) shuttle buses are a much quicker way to get around the Riviera Maya between Playa del Carmen and Cancún. It has frequent service to Puerto Morelos (M$28, 40 minutes) and downtown Cancún (M$42, 1¼ hours).

COLECTIVO

Colectivos (Calle 2 Norte s/n, cnr 20 Av; ⊘5am-11:30pm) are a great option for cheap travel southward to Tulum (M$45) and north

BUSES FROM PLAYA DEL CARMEN

DESTINATION	FARE (M$)	TIME (HR)	FREQUENCY (PER DAY)
Cancún	79	1-1¼	frequent
Cancún International Airport	206	1	frequent
Chetumal	398	4½-5½	frequent
Chichén Itzá	194	3-4	3 (7:30am, 8am & 9:30am)
Cobá	164	2	frequent
Laguna Bacalar	376	4-4½	frequent
Mahahual	414	4-4½	2 (8:05am & 5:55pm)
Mérida	503-756	4¼-5¾	frequent
Palenque	986-1178	11½-12	7
San Cristóbal de las Casas	726-1216	20-21	6
Tulum	89	1	frequent
Valladolid	252	2½-3½	frequent

to Cancún (M$42). They depart as soon as they fill (about every 15 minutes) and will stop anywhere along the highway between Playa and Tulum. Luggage space is somewhat limited, but colectivos are great for day trips. There are also daily departures to Isla Holbox (M$250) between 8:30am and 6:30pm. Local trips around Playa cost M$15.

Isla Cozumel

☑ 987 / POP 86,400

Fascinating for its dual personality, Cozumel offers an odd mix – quietly authentic neighborhoods existing alongside tourist-friendly playgrounds. Leaving the tourist area behind, you'll find garages that still have shrines to the Virgin and a spirited Caribbean energy in the air. And, of course, there are epic experiences to be had, such as diving at some of the best reefs in the world.

While diving and snorkeling are the main draws, the town square is a pleasant place to spend the afternoon, and it's highly gratifying to explore the less-visited parts of the island on a rented scooter or in a convertible car. The coastal road leads to small Maya ruins, a marine park and cliffside bars, passing captivating scenery along the unforgettable windswept shore. And while the nightlife has nothing on Playa del Carmen's or Cancún's, there's plenty to do after the sun goes down.

⊙ Sights

El Cedral   ARCHAEOLOGICAL SITE
(Map p297; per person M$38; ⊙24hr) This Maya ruin, a fertility temple, is the oldest on the island. It's the size of a small house and has no ornamentation. El Cedral is thought to have been an important ceremonial site; the small church standing next to the tiny ruin today is evidence that the site still has religious significance for locals.

The town of El Cedral is 3km west of Carretera Costera Sur. The turnoff is near Km 17, across from the Alberto's Restaurant sign. Look for the white-and-red arch.

🏖 Beaches

Access to many of Cozumel's best stretches of beach has become limited. Resorts and residential developments with gated roads create the most difficulties. Pay-for-use beach clubs occupy some other prime spots, but you can park and walk through or around them and enjoy adjacent parts of the beach without obligation. Sitting under club umbrellas or otherwise using the facilities requires you to fork out some money, either a straight fee or a *consumo mínimo* (minimum consumption of food and drink), which can add up in some places. However, charging is not always strictly applied, especially when business is slow.

Playa Palancar   BEACH
(Map p297; ☑cell 987-1185154; www.buceopalancar.com.mx; Carretera Costera Sur Km 19.5; dives 1/2-tank incl equipment US$65/90; ⊙9am-5pm) About 17km south of San Miguel, Palancar is a great beach to visit during the week when the crowds thin out. It has a beach club renting snorkel gear (US$10) and there's a **restaurant**. Nearby, Arrecife Palancar (Palancar Reef) has some excellent diving (it's known as Palancar Gardens) and fine snorkeling (Palancar Shallows, US$35).

A dive shop here runs snorkeling and diving trips to nearby sites.

🏊 Activities

Cozumel and its surrounding reefs are among the world's most popular diving spots.

The sites have fantastic year-round visibility (commonly 30m or more) and a jaw-droppingly impressive variety of marine life that includes spotted eagle rays, moray eels, groupers, barracudas, turtles, sharks, brain coral and some huge sponges.

The island can have strong currents (sometimes around 3 knots), making drift dives the standard, especially along the many walls. Even when diving from the beach you should evaluate conditions and plan your route carefully, selecting an exit point down-current beforehand, then staying alert for shifts in currents. Always keep an eye out (and your ears open) for boat traffic as well.

There are scores of dive operators on Cozumel. All limit the size of their groups to six or eight divers, and the good ones take pains to match up divers of similar skill levels. Some offer snorkeling and deep-sea fishing trips as well as diving instruction.

Prices are usually quoted in US dollars. In general expect to pay anywhere between US$100 and US$115 for a two-tank dive (equipment included) or an introductory 'resort' course. PADI open-water certification costs US$440.

Multiple-dive packages and discounts for groups or those paying in cash can bring rates down significantly.

If you encounter a decompression emergency, head immediately to the hyperbaric chamber at **Cozumel International Hospital** (☑ 987-872-14-30; www.hospitalcozumel.com; Calle 5 Sur 21B, btwn Avs Melgar & 5 Sur; ⊙ 24hr).

If diving is your primary goal, you may want to time your trip for September or October, when weather conditions are ideal. Severe weather can affect turbidity and prevent the boats from leaving, among other hassles.

Deep Blue (Map p298; ☑ 987-872-56-53; www.deepbluecozumel.com; Salas 200; 2-tank dives incl equipment US$112, snorkeling incl gear US$65; ⊙ 7am-9pm) is a PADI and National Association of Underwater Instructors (NAUI) operation with knowledgeable staff, state-of-the-art gear and fast boats that give you a chance to get more dives out of a day. A snorkeling outing visits three sites.

🛏 Sleeping

Amigo's Hostel　　　　　　　　HOSTEL $
(Map p298; ☑ 987-872-38-68, cell 987-1199664; www.cozumelhostel.com; Calle 7 Sur 571, btwn Avs 25 Sur & 30 Sur; dm/d US$15/54; ⊛❄@🗜⊛) Unlike some cramped budget digs, here you get a large garden with labeled trees, an inviting pool and a good lounge area stocked with reading material. Some guests say it's too far removed from the tourist center; others like it that way. Snorkel-gear rentals available (M$100). Air-con May to October only, from 10pm to 8am.

Recent additions include a permanent grill for guests to use, and reinforced roofing.

Sun Suites Cozumel　　　　　　HOTEL $$
(Map p298; ☑ 987-872-29-28; www.facebook.com/sunsuitesczm; Av 10 Norte 19; d incl breakfast M$1150; ⊛❄🗜⊛) Spacious, tile-floored rooms are spick-and-span, with large fridge, air-con, coffee maker and flat-screen TV. Guests have breakfast on a shady courtyard and there's an inviting grassy pool area at the back, with lounge chairs.

★ **Hotel B Cozumel**　　BOUTIQUE HOTEL $$$
(Map p297; ☑ 987-872-03-00; www.hotelbcozumel.com; Carretera San Juan Km 2.5; d/ste incl breakfast US$193/287; ⊛❄🗜⊛) This trendy hotel on the north shore may not have that sand beach you're after, but just wait till you get a look at the crystalline saltwater pool and oceanfront hot tub. Rooms are fitted with handmade furnishings, there's live jazz on Thursdays and free bikes are available.

Rates quoted are for jungle-view rooms; ocean views cost extra.

It's about 3km north of the ferry terminal.

Casa Mexicana　　　　　　　　HOTEL $$$
(Map p298; ☑ 987-872-90-90; www.casamexicanacozumel.com; Av Melgar 457; d incl breakfast US$193-205; P⊛❄❅@🗜⊛) The breezy open-air lobby with swimming pool and ocean view is pretty awesome here. Rooms are standard issue for the most part, but all in all Casa Mexicana offers good value given its prime location and free breakfast buffet. The 'deluxe city view' with balcony is the best deal.

Hotel Flamingo　　BOUTIQUE HOTEL $$$
(Map p298; ☑ 987-872-12-64, USA 800-806-1601; www.hotelflamingo.com; Calle 6 Norte 81; d/casa incl breakfast M$2333/5950; ⊛❄🗜) The colorful Hotel Flamingo is a nicely decorated place offering spacious rooms loaded with amenities. There's a large penthouse apartment (the *casa*), too. Common areas include a leafy courtyard and a popular **bar** (Map p298; ⊙ 7am-10pm; 🗜). The hotel can arrange various activities, including diving.

🍴 Eating & Drinking

Taquería El Sitio　　　　　　　TACOS $
(Map p298; Calle 2 Norte 124; tacos & tortas M$16-40; ⊙ 8am-2pm) For something quick, cheap and tasty, head over to El Sitio for breaded shrimp and fish tacos or a *huevo con chaya torta* (egg and tree-spinach sandwich). The folding chairs and concrete floor are nothing fancy, but the food is good.

Camarón Dorado　　　　　　　SEAFOOD $
(Map p297; ☑ 987-872-72-87, cell 987-1181281; www.facebook.com/camaron.dorado; cnr Av Juárez & Calle 105 Sur; tortas M$29-58, tacos M$18-34; ⊙ 7am-1:30pm Tue-Sun; 🗜) If you're headed to the windward side of the island or just want to see a different aspect of Cozumel, drop by the Camarón Dorado for a bite, assuming you're early enough. Be warned: the *camarón empanizado* (breaded shrimp) *tortas* and tacos are highly addictive. It's 2.5km southeast of the passenger-ferry terminal.

Jeanie's　　　　　　　　　　MEXICAN $$
(Map p298; ☑ 987-878-46-47; www.jeaniescozumel.com; Av Melgar 790; breakfasts M$90-115, mains M$100-280; ⊙ 7am-10pm; 🗜) The views of the water are great from the outdoor patio here. Jeanie's serves waffles, hash browns, eggs, sandwiches and other tidbits including vegetarian fajitas. Frozen coffees beat the midday Lovely happy hour between 5pm and 7pm.

Isla Cozumel

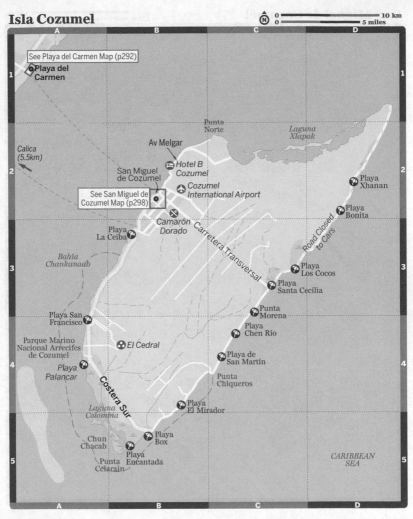

★**Kinta** BISTRO **$$$**
(Map p298; ☑987-869-05-44; www.kinta
restaurante.com; Av 5 Norte 148; mains M$280-
380; ⊘5-11pm; ☎) Putting a gourmet twist
on Mexican classics, this chic bistro is one
of the best restaurants on the island. The
Midnight Pork Ribs are a tried-and-true
favorite, while the wood-fired oven turns
out spectacular oven-baked fish. For des-
sert treat yourself to a *budín de la abue-
lita,* aka 'granny's pudding.' It currently
has a delicious six-course tasting menu for
M$700.

Guido's Restaurant ITALIAN **$$$**
(Map p298; ☑987-869-25-89; www.guidos
cozumel.com; Av Melgar 23; mains M$250-495,
pizzas M$230-280; ⊘11am-11pm Mon-Sat, from
3pm Sun; ☎) Drawing on recipes handed
down from her father, Guido, chef Yvonne
Villiger has created a menu ranging from
wood-fired pizzas and homemade pastas to
prosciutto-wrapped scallops. To accompany the meal, order a pitcher of sangria, the
house specialty. The cocktail menu is equally
impressive; there is even house-made tonic
syrup for your G&Ts.

San Miguel de Cozumel

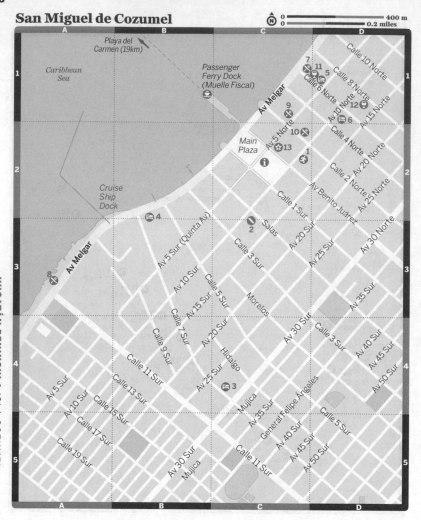

La Cocay COCKTAIL BAR
(Map p298; ☎987-872-55-33; www.lacocay.com;
Calle 8 Norte 208; mains M$160-480; ⊗5:30-
11:30pm; 🛜) This restaurant's food is underwhelming and the service slow; but it's good
for a romantic, candlelit après-meal tipple, or
for coffee and dessert. The full bar can fix just
about any cocktail you're craving, a refreshing change from the out-of-a-can margaritas
often served elsewhere.

⭐ Entertainment

Woody's Bar & Grill LIVE MUSIC
(Map p298; www.cozumelradio.wixsite.
com/woodys; Av Juárez s/n, btwn Avs 5 & 10;

⊗9am-midnight Mon-Fri, to 1am Sat & Sun; 🛜)
Though the cocktails here barely pass mus-
ter, there are some pretty decent live acts –
not only covers, but some nice original stuff
too. The beers are icy and this is a fun spot
to people-watch, chat with new friends, or
just listen.

ℹ️ Information

Tourist Information Office (Map p298;
☎987-869-02-12; www.cozumel.travel; Av
5 Sur s/n, Plaza del Sol, 2nd fl; ⊗8am-3pm
Mon-Fri) You can pick up maps and travel
brochures here.

San Miguel de Cozumel

Getting There & Away

AIR

Cozumel's small **airport** (Map p297; 987-872-20-81; www.asur.com.mx; Blvd Aeropuerto Cozumel s/n) is some 3km northeast of the ferry terminal, and is signed along Avenida Melgar. There are direct services from the US with United, Delta and American airlines; flights from Europe are generally routed via the US or Mexico City. Cozumel is also served by Mexican airlines Interjet, Volaris and MAYAir.

Interjet (800-011-23-45, USA 866-285-9525; www.interjet.com; Cozumel International Airport) Direct flights to Mexico City.

MAYAir (987-872-36-09; www.mayair.com.mx; Cozumel International Airport) Flights to Cancún with onward service to Mérida.

Volaris (55-1102-8000; www.volaris.com; Cozumel International Airport) Nonstops to Guadalajara and Monterrey.

BOAT

Passenger ferries operated by Ultramar (p294) and Winjet (p294) run frequently to Cozumel from Playa del Carmen from 7am to 11pm (one-way M$160), leaving from and arriving at the **Passenger Ferry Dock** (Map p298).

To transport a vehicle to Cozumel, go to the Calica–Punta Venado car-ferry terminal (officially known as the Terminal Marítima Punta Venado; p294), about 8km south of Playa del Carmen. There are four daily departures (three on Sundays). See the ferries' websites for schedules. You'll need to line up at least one hour before departure, two hours before in high season. Fares cost M$500, including passengers, or more depending on the size of the vehicle.

Getting Around

TO/FROM THE AIRPORT

Frequent, shared shuttle vans run from the airport into town (M$85), to hotels on the island's north end (M$140) and to the south side (M$140 to M$200). To return to the airport in a taxi, expect to pay about M$110.

BICYCLE & SCOOTER

Touring the island solo by scooter is a blast, provided you have experience with scooters and with driving in Mexico. Two people on a bike is asking for trouble, though, as the machines' suspension will be barely adequate for one. Riders are injured in crashes on a regular basis, so always wear a helmet and stay alert. Collision insurance is not usually available for scooters: you break, you pay. Be sure to carefully inspect the scooter for damage before driving off or you may get hit with a repair bill.

To rent, you must have a valid driver's license and leave a credit-card slip or put down a cash deposit. There is a helmet law, and it is enforced. Rentadora Isis (p302) is a worthwhile rental place; **Best Bikes Cozumel** (Map p298; cell 987-8788602; www.bestbikescozumel.com; Av 10 Norte 14; per hour M$30-50, per day M$150-250; 9am-6pm Apr–mid-Oct, 8am 8pm mid Oct Mar) rents good bicycles.

CAR

A car is the best way to get to the island's furthest reaches, and there are plenty of places where you can rent one. All rental contracts should automatically include *daños a terceros* (liability insurance). Check that taxes are included in the quoted price: often they are not. Collision insurance is usually about M$380 extra, with a 10% vehicle value deductible for the cheapest vehicles.

Rates start at around M$880 all-inclusive, though you'll pay more during late December and January. There are plenty of agencies around the main plaza, but prices are about 50% lower from the dock to the fringes of the tourist zone, where you can sometimes find a jalopy or clunker for M$600 or so.

Before renting, check with your hotel to see if it has an agreement with any agencies, as you can often get discounts. Some agencies will deduct tire damage (repair or replacement) from your deposit, even if tires are old and worn. And always check your car's brakes before driving off.

If you rent, observe the law on vehicle occupancy. Usually only five people are allowed in a vehicle. If you carry more, the police will fine you. You'll need to return your vehicle with the same amount of gas it had when you signed it

YUCATÁN PENINSULA ISLA COZUMEL

MATTEO COLOMBO / GETTY IMAGES ©

CHRISONTOUR84 / SHUTTERSTOCK ©

1. Cenote, Valladolid (p349)

It's possible to visit, and swim in, many of the stunning cenotes (natural sinkholes) within easy distance of this charming city.

2. Becán (p365), Campeche

One of the largest and most elaborate Maya sites, surrounded by lush forest.

3. Laguna Bacalar (p314)

Strikingly beautiful Laguna Bacalar is a 60km-long lagoon – the largest on the Yucatán Peninsula – and a great place to relax and unwind.

4. Mérida (p320)

Stunning Mérida – the cultural capital of the Yucatán Peninsula – is full of narrow cobbled streets and plazas studded by beautifully maintained ornate colonial-era buildings.

TATI NOVA PHOTO MÉXICO / SHUTTERSTOCK ©

out or pay a premium. There's a **gas station** (cnr Avs Juárez & 30 Sur) five blocks east of the main square, and several near the town center.

Rentadora Isis (☑ 984-879-31-11, 987-872-33-67; www.rentadoraisis.com.mx; Av 5 Norte 181; per day scooters from US$25, cars US$35-60; ☺ 8am-6:30pm) is a fairly no-nonsense, family-run place with cars ranging from great shape to total clunkers; this branch rents convertible VW Beetles, Golfs and scooters, with little seasonal variation in prices.

TAXI

As in some other towns on the Yucatán Peninsula, the taxi syndicate on Cozumel wields a good bit of power. Fares are around M$50 (in town), M$100 (to the Zona Hotelera) and M$1500 for a five-hour day trip around the island. Fares are posted just outside the ferry terminal.

Tulum

☑ 984 / POP 32,700

Tulum's spectacular coastline – with all its confectioner-sugar sands, cobalt water and balmy breezes – makes it one of the top beaches in Mexico. Where else can you get all that *and* a dramatically situated Maya ruin? There's also excellent cave and cavern diving, fun cenotes and a variety of lodgings and restaurants to fit every budget.

Some may be put off by the fact that the town center, where the really cheap eats and sleeps are found, sits right on the highway, making the main drag feel more like a truck stop than a tropical paradise. But rest assured that if Tulum Pueblo isn't to your liking, you can always head to the coast and find that tranquil, beachside bungalow, though it's gonna cost you.

Exploring Tulum's surrounding areas pays big rewards: there's the massive Reserva de la Biosfera Sian Ka'an, secluded fishing village Punta Allen and the ruins of Cobá.

History

Most archaeologists believe that Tulum was occupied during the late post-Classic period (1200–1521 CE) and that it was an important port town during its heyday. The Maya sailed up and down this coast, maintaining trading routes all the way down into Belize. When Juan de Grijalva sailed past in 1518, he was amazed by the sight of the walled city, its buildings painted a gleaming red, blue and yellow and a ceremonial fire flaming atop its seaside watchtower.

The ramparts that surround three sides of Tulum (the fourth side being the sea) leave little question as to its strategic function as a fortress. Several meters thick and 3m to 5m high, the walls protected the city during a period of considerable strife between Maya city-states. Not all of Tulum was situated within the walls. The vast majority of the city's residents lived outside them; the civic-ceremonial buildings and palaces likely housed Tulum's ruling class.

The city was abandoned about 75 years after the Spanish conquest. It was one of the last of the ancient cities to be abandoned; most others had been given back to nature long before the arrival of the Spanish. But Maya pilgrims continued to visit over the years, and indigenous refugees from the War of the Castes took shelter here from time to time.

'Tulum' is Maya for 'wall,' though its residents called it Zama (Dawn). The name Tulum was apparently applied by explorers during the early-20th century.

Once a small fishing town, present-day Tulum is growing fast: since 2006 the population has more than doubled and city limits continue to expand. The Zona Hotelera, once quiet and peaceful, is now full of glitz and glamour, with people there to be seen (and take selfies). Development has even run deep into the coastline of the Sian Ka'an Biosphere Reserve, as property owners sell and people put up mansions. For a trip back in time to a Tulum of 'yesterdecade,' pick up a copy of *Sunsets of Tulum*, a literary novel set in a Tulum circa 2007.

◉ Sights

★**Tulum Ruins**   ARCHAEOLOGICAL SITE
(www.inah.gob.mx; Hwy 307 Km 230; M$75, early/late M$255, parking M$180, tours from M$700; ☺ 6:30am-8am, 8am-5pm, 5:30-7pm; ℗) The ruins of Tulum preside over a rugged coastline, a strip of brilliant beach and green-and-turquoise waters that'll leave you floored. It's true the extents and structures are of a modest scale and the late-post-Classic design is inferior to those of earlier, more grandiose projects – but, wow! Those Maya occupants must have felt pretty smug each sunrise!

You can see (at a premium price) the sunrise yourself on a sunrise tour. Late-risers may prefer the sunset tour, though the sun sets over the jungle, not the sea. Tulum is a prime destination for large tour groups. To best enjoy the ruins without feeling like part of the herd, you should visit them early in the morning, another benefit of the sunrise tour. A train (M$55) takes you to the ticket booth from the entrance, or just hoof the 500m. You'll find cheaper parking (M$50 to M$100) just east of the main parking lot, along the old entrance road. There's a less-used southern foot entrance from the beach road.

Exploring the Ruins

Visitors are required to follow a prescribed route around the ruins. From the ticket booth, head north along nearly half the length of Tulum's enormous wall, which measures approximately 380m south to north and 170m along its sides. Once inside, head east toward **Casa del Cenote**, named for the small pool at the base of the structure. Incredibly, the muddy pool (sometimes with visible minnows) connects underground to the vast cenote system beneath the Yucatán.

Passing the **Templo del Dios del Viento** (Temple of the Wind God), you'll come to a lovely stretch of beach, sometimes roped off, and beyond it, the impressive **Estructura 25**, which contains a beautiful stucco frieze of the Descending God (alternatively the Diving God), which appears elsewhere in Tulum and in nearby ruins such as Cobá. Interpretations of the significance vary, some suggesting it's a stylized bee sipping nectar.

Most impressive is **El Castillo** – the Castle – as it was dubbed by the Spanish: a massive structure impressively perched at the top of the cliff overlooking the Caribbean. It has figures both of the Descending God and the Plumed Serpent (echoing Chichén Itzá). Nearby is the **Templo del Dios Descendente**, named for the relief figure above the door.

Wooden steps lead down to a lovely (though often packed) beach, where you can take a dip if you (like many) are wearing your swimsuit. You won't be the only one enjoying the sunshine: some of the ruin's largest iguanas will be basking next to you or in the rocky cliffs.

Last in the route is **Templo de las Pinturas**, constructed in several stages around 1400 to 1450 CE. Its decoration is among the most elaborate in Tulum and once included relief masks and colorful murals, which have mostly been lost due to the proximity with the harsh sea air. In places it has been restored.

In addition to the iguanas and tourists, other wildlife you'll spot if you're lucky are frigate birds (look for the distinctive V-shaped tail), pelicans, jays, and the occasional agouti (a shy, cat-sized rodent with antelope-like legs).

Tulum Ruins 🛞

🏃 Activities & Tours

Zacil-Há SWIMMING
(📱cell 984-2037621; www.facebook.com/cenotezacilha; Hwy 109 Km 8; M$100, snorkel gear M$30, zip-line M$10; ⊙10am-5:30pm) At this cenote you can combine swimming, snorkeling and zip-lining. It's 8km west of Avenida Tulum on the road to Cobá. There's even a bar, and if you fancy staying overnight, grab a *cabaña* for two/eight people for M$1000/1200.

Xibalba Dive Center DIVING
(📱984-8712953; www.xibalbadivecenter.com; Andromeda Oriente 7, btwn Libra Sur & Geminis Sur; 1-/2-cavern dive incl gear US$100/160) One of the best dive shops in Tulum, Xibalba is known for its safety-first approach to diving. The center specializes in cave and cavern diving, visiting sites such as Dos Ojos and the spooky **Cenote Angelita** (Hwy 307 Km 213; cenote dives M$300, snorkeling M$200; ⊙7am-5pm). Xibalba doubles as a hotel (rooms from US$100) and offers attractive packages combining lodging, diving trips and courses.

Uyo Ochel Maya TOURS
(📱WhatsApp only 983-1248001; Muyil; adult/child M$900/600, parking M$50; ⊙8am-4pm) Tour Chunyaxche and Muyil lagoons and swim in a centuries-old Maya canal. It's a lovely way

Tulum

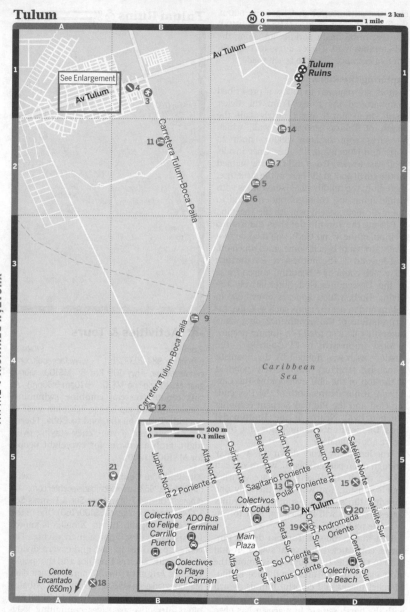

to see the second-largest lagoon in Quintana Roo, and the mangroves harbor orchids, saprophytes and numerous birds. To reach the lagoon shore by car, turn down a dirt road about 250m south of the Muyil archaeological site.

🛏 Sleeping

The biggest decision, aside from budget, is whether to stay in the town center or out along the beach. Both have their advantages: most of the daytime action happens at the

Tulum

beach or ruins, while at night people tend to hang at restaurants and bars in town.

You'll find better deals in town, where hostels and midrange options abound.

⭐ **Mayan Monkey** HOSTEL $
(☎984-122-13-01; www.mayanmonkey.com; Carretera Tulum–Boca Paila s/n; dm/r M$250/1400; P❄❋@🛜🏊) If you want your hostel to be more an all-inclusive place, with spotless beds, private rooms that rival upscale hotels, a swing bar, giant patio/breakfast area and neon-lit swimming pool, then look no further than the Mayan Monkey. It has RFID wristbands that act as keys, three stories of sleeping options and a variety of activities.

As luxurious as it is, despite the snaz, it's a bit lacking in warmth, and guests here are more likely to be on their phones than making friends. Still, it remains a great option for people looking for boutique on the cheap.

🛏 Tulum Pueblo

Weary Traveler HOSTEL $
(☎cell 984-2112608; www.wearytravelerhostel. rocks; Polar Poniente, Tulum Pueblo, btwn Orión Norte & Beta Norte; dm/r M$400/1000; ❄❋🛜) Once the only hostel in a tiny, out-of-the-way spot called Tulum, the Weary Traveler is now one of many options for the budget traveler in the town center. The hostel offers a free breakfast, which can include custom-made omelettes, or guests can make their own meals at the communal kitchen. The common areas are a great way to meet people.

Hotel Kin-Ha HOTEL $$
(☎984-871-23-21; www.hotelkinha.com; Orión Sur s/n, btwn Sol Oriente & Venus Oriente; d incl breakfast US$246-276; P❄❋❈🛜) A small Italian- and Mexican-owned hotel with pleasant rooms surrounding a small courtyard with hammocks. The location is ideal – the bus stop for *colectivos* going to the beach is right around the corner. At last visit, Kin-Ha was still renovating rooms and planning to install a rooftop hot tub and bar.

⭐ **L'Hotelito** HOTEL $$$
(☎984-160-02-29; www.hotelitotulum.com; Av Tulum, btwn Beta & Orión; d incl breakfast US$100-150; ❄❋@🛜) Brick and wood boardwalks pass through a jungle-like side patio to generous, breezy rooms at this characterful, Italian-run hotel. The attached restaurant does good breakfasts, too. Two rooms upstairs come with wide balconies, but they also catch more street noise from the main strip down below. Towels are twisted into the shape of rabbits or swans. Check online for discounts.

🛏 Zona Hotelera

Cenote Encantado CAMPGROUND $
(☎WhatsApp only 55-30282253; www.cenoteencantado.com; Carretera Tulum–Boca Paila Km 10.5; tents per person/treehouses/campsites M$500/120./350; ❄) A rare budget option near the beach, this new-agey spot gets its name from a cenote right in the campground's backyard. Guests stay in large tents with beds, rugs and nightstands; there's a yoga and meditation room too. It's not on the beach, but you can walk there. Rates go up in December and January.

Though the area is set to get electricity, water, and (yep!) fiber-optic internet, the venerable 'Juicycle' blender-bike isn't going to the trash heap just yet. They've put some rocks in the cenote, and you can swim, kayak or snorkel here surrounded by nature, including iguanas, birds, and land crabs. It's 6.5km south of the T-junction, near the Reserva de la Biosfera Sian Ka'an entrance.

Zazil-Kin
CABAÑAS **$$**

(📞 984-124-00-82; www.zzk.mx; Carretera Tulum–Boca Paila Km 0.47; cabañas M$2068, without bathroom M$1509, r from M$3121; 🅿️😊❄️📶) About a 10-minute walk from the ruins, this beachside place resembles a little Smurf village with its painted *cabañas*. Bare-bones cabins (basically just a bed with mosquito net) have electricity available from 7pm to 8am, while more expensive air-conditioned rooms run on 24-hour electricity. Apparently, cleanliness is not a virtue here. Bring insect repellent!

There are swings and a jungle gym for kiddos.

Cabañas Playa Condesa
CABIN **$$**

(📞cell 984-2341413; Carretera Tulum–Boca Paila Km 3, Zona Hotelera; d M$2000; 📶) About 1km north of the T-junction, this group of no-frills, thatched *cabañas* and basic rooms is one of the cheaper options on the beach, though the service sometimes comes up short. All accommodations have private bathroom and you get mosquito nets (believe us, you'll need them). The coast is rocky here, but there's a sandy beach 100m away.

Reservations by telephone only.

Diamante K
CABAÑAS **$$$**

(📞cell 984-8762115; www.diamantek.com; Carretera Tulum–Boca Paila Km 2.5; cabin US$250, ste US$700-800; 🅿️😊📶) Diamante K is one of those spots that really can't be any closer to the beach. Its nine cabins have a shared bathroom and thus remain relatively affordable; all rooms are lovely, with hammocks, incredible ocean views, palm trees, and almost Tolkienesque accents and decor.

El Paraíso
HOTEL **$$$**

(📞cell 984-1137089; www.elparaisohoteltulum.com; Carretera Tulum–Boca Paila Km 1.5; r incl breakfast from US$309; 🅿️😊❄️📶) Eleven rooms in a one-story hotel-style block, each with two good beds, private hot-water bathroom, fine cross-ventilation and 24-hour electricity. The restaurant is very presentable, and the level beach, with its palm trees, *palapa* parasols, swing-chaired bar and soft white sand, is among the nicest you'll find on the Riviera Maya. Bikes are free for guests.

★La Posada del Sol
BOUTIQUE HOTEL **$$$**

(📞cell 984-1348874; www.laposadadelsol.com; Carretera Tulum–Boca Paila Km 3.5; r incl breakfast US$300; 😊📶) 🚲 Using recycled objects found on the property after a hurricane, Posada del Sol stands out for its natural design details and creative architecture. All 11 rooms have air-con, but the pricier ones on the beach side of the road usually catch a nice ocean breeze. The solar- and wind-powered hotel has a sweet beach and a great crafts store too.

Rooms do not have TVs. The hotel works with local turtle-nesting organizations, too. It's just before the much larger Marina del Sol hotel.

Posada Margherita
HOTEL **$$$**

(📞WhatsApp only 984-8018493; www.posada margherita.com; Carretera Tulum–Boca Paila Km 4.5; d US$200-300; 😊📶) This is a beautiful spot

---

DON'T MISS

PARQUE DOS OJOS

About 1km south of amusement park Xel-Há (p291) is the turnoff to the enormous **Dos Ojos** (📞cell 984-1600906; www.parquedosojos.com; Hwy 307 Km 124; dives M$3000-5000, snorkeling M$400; 🕐8am-5pm) cave system. Operating as a sustainable tourism project by the local Maya community, Dos Ojos offers guided snorkeling tours of some amazing underwater caverns, where you float past illuminated stalactites and stalagmites in an eerie wonderland. For diving, you must go with a dive shop.

With an extent of about 83km and some 30 cenotes, it's one of the largest underwater cave systems in the world. One of the most popular sites for experienced divers is the Pit, a 110m-deep cenote in which you can see ancient human and animal remains. If you are not a certified diver, you can pay the price of admission and go swimming or snorkeling. Dive rates run about M$3000 to M$5000 depending on the number of tanks and the type of cave.

right in the center of the Hotel Zone, with the beach just steps away. The restaurant below makes incredible food using local, fresh, organic ingredients. All rooms have good bug screening, 24-hour lights and a terrace or balcony, some with hammocks. Cash only.

✗ Eating

Tulum is ritzy and glitzy and ever-more shallow, but one good reason to come here is the food. The town has everything from cheap tourist food to high-end cuisine, all of it tasty, with lots of Italian and international options if you need a break from Yucatecan. Be aware that many of the restaurants in the Zona Hotelera cannot accept credit cards because they're off the grid. Most hotel restaurants welcome nonguests.

La Eufemia   TACOS $
(Carretera Tulum–Boca Paila Km 7.5; tacos M$25-65; P) Odd for a casual beachside taco joint, there's valet parking at La Eufemia, where you can gorge on great cheap food (think 'In your *face*, pricey Zona Hotelera!') and hang out with a mostly younger, tattooed, and often smoking-doobage kind of crowd. Chairs are painted with portraits of rock greats like Freddy Mercury or Jim Morrison. The beach is just steps away, if you fancy a swim.

La Gloria de Don Pepe   TAPAS $$
(cell 984-1524471; www.facebook.com/lagloria dedonpepe; Orión Sur, cnr Andromeda Oriente; tapas M$60-210; 2-11pm Tue-Sun) With its 'A meal without wine is called breakfast' sign, this spot tickles the taste buds with delicious tapas plates and fine seafood paella. And wine – did we mention there's wine? A perfect place to come to talk to a friend for a couple of hours without being drowned out by noise. Alfresco seating is also possible.

Acqua e Farina da Mario   ITALIAN $$
(984-100-91-52; Satelite Norte s/n; mains M$120-200; 1-4pm & 7:30-10:30pm) A taste of real Italy on the streets of central Tulum. This cafe is cramped (luckily there are some alfresco tables) but somehow Mario makes it well worth the wait: get perfectly cooked al dente pasta, ravioli, or fish and seafood specials that will make you think you're in Roma. Wines are excellent, and you can even order a Negroni (rare in Mexico) if you're feeling the Old World vibe.

★ Hartwood   FUSION $$$
(www.hartwoodtulum.com; Carretera Tulum–Boca Paila Km 7.5; mains M$365-550; 5:30-10pm

WORTH A TRIP

GRAN CENOTE

About 4km west of Tulum, **Gran Cenote** (Hwy 109 s/n; adult/child under 120cm M$180/90, snorkeling gear M$80, diving M$200; 8:10am-4:45pm) is a worthwhile stop on the highway out to the Cobá ruins, especially if it's a hot day. You can snorkel among small fish and see underwater formations in the caverns if you bring your own scuba gear. A cab from Tulum costs M$100 one-way (but check first to avoid surprises).

Wed-Sun) Assuming you can get in (it accepts walk-ins and online reservations made one month in advance), this sweet 'n' simple nouvelle-cuisine restaurant down on the beach road will definitely impress. Ingredients are fresh and local; flavors and techniques are international. The chalkboard menu changes daily, and the solar-powered open kitchen and wood-burning oven serve to accentuate the delicious dishes.

El Asadero   STEAK $$$
(984-157-89-98; www.facebook.com/elasadero. tulummexico; Av Satélite Norte 23; mains M$160-550; 4-11pm Mon-Sat;) Somewhat pricey but worth it, this spot has grilled *arrachera* served with sides of potato, *nopal* (cactus paddle) and sausage, which pairs nicely with the Mexican craft beers on offer. Pescatarians and vegetarians won't be disappointed with the grilled tuna and loaded potatoes.

Posada Margherita   ITALIAN $$$
(WhatsApp only 984-8018493; www.posada margherita.com; Carretera Tulum–Boca Paila Km 4.5; mains M$345-570; 7:30am-10pm) This hotel's beachside restaurant is candlelit at night, making it a beautiful, romantic place to dine. The fantastic food, including pasta, is made fresh daily and consists mostly of organic ingredients. The wines and house mezcal are excellent. It's 3km south of the T-junction. Cash only.

Parking can be a nightmare.

♟ Drinking & Nightlife

Clandestino   BAR
(Carretera Tulum–Boca Paila Km 6.5; 1pm-2am) There are several bars here and a bunch of tables, all clustered around a cenote (yes!) that's actually swimmable, so if you get bored with your drink or want to cool off (or

BUSES FROM TULUM

DESTINATION	COST (M$)	TIME (HR)	FREQUENCY (PER DAY)
Belize City (Belize)	831	6	1 (1:50am)
Cancún	181-250	2-2½	frequent
Cancún International Airport	266	2	5
Chetumal	240-359	3¼-4	frequent
Chichén Itzá	252	2½-2¾	2 (9am & 2:45pm)
Chiquilá (for Isla Holbox)	365	3½	1 (8:10am)
Cobá	50	1	10:11am
Felipe Carrillo Puerto	69-75	1¼	4 (consider taking a frequent *colectivo*)
Laguna Bacalar	220-270	3	frequent
Mahahual	327	3-3½	1 (7:10pm)
Mérida	264-392	4-4½	frequent
Playa del Carmen	44-89	1	frequent
Valladolid	103-148	1½-1¾	frequent

show off!) then just dive right in. Nobody will mind, and the water is as clear as glass. Drinks are excellent, with a number of original cocktails and the usual beach faves.

★ **Batey**   BAR
(📱cell 984-7454571; www.facebook.com/batey tulum; Centauro Sur 7, btwn Av Tulum & Andrómeda Oriente; ⊙12pm-2am Mon-Sat, 4:30pm-1am Sun) Mojitos sweetened with freshly pressed cane sugar are the main attraction at this popular Cuban bar, with fun music acts in the rear garden. Most nights the crowd spills into the street, while inside cane is pressed on top of an iconic, painted VW bug.

❶ Getting There & Away

The 24-hour **ADO bus terminal** (📞984-871-21-22; www.ado.com.mx; Av Tulum, btwn Alfa Norte & Júpiter Norte; ⊙24hr) is simple but adequate, with some chairs for waiting, but not much else.

Colectivos leave from Avenida Tulum for **Playa del Carmen** (Av Tulum s/n, cnr Júpiter Sur; M$45; ⊙45min). **Colectivos to Felipe Carrillo Puerto** (Av Tulum s/n, cnr Júpiter Norte; M$70; ⊙1hr) depart from a block south of the bus terminal. Colectivos to Cobá (p310) depart every two hours or so from 9am to 6pm.

❶ Getting Around

Colectivos (cnr Venus Oriente & Centauro Sur; M$20-40; ⊙7am-midnight) to the beach run frequently from 7am to midnight. The shared vans turn right at the beach-road T-junction and go as far south as the Sian Ka'an Biosphere Reserve entrance, before turning around.

To reach the ruins, any Playa del Carmen–bound colectivo will drop you on the highway at

the ruins (M$20), where it's about a 1km walk to the site's main entrance.

Bicycles and scooters can be a good way to go back and forth between the town and beach. Many hotels and hostels have free bikes for guests. **I Bike Tulum** (📞984-802-55-18; www.ibiketulum.com; Av Cobá Sur, btwn Sol Oriente & Gama Oriente; per day bicycle M$150-250, scooter M$670; ⊙8:30am-5:30pm Mon-Sat) has a good selection of bike and scooter rentals.

Taxi fares are fixed, from either of the two taxi stands in Tulum Pueblo: **one** (Av Tulum, cnr Júpiter Norte) in front of the bus terminal, the **other** (Av Tulum, cnr Centauro Norte) four blocks north. They charge M$100 to the ruins and M$150 to M$200 from town to the Zona Hotelera, depending on how far south you need to go.

Cobá

📞984 / POP 1300

Cobá's ruins are a treat and exploring them is a big part of the reason for coming here: the state's tallest pyramid, a beautiful ball court and a variety of other structures make for a fun few hours. The village is quiet and cute, with a croc-filled lagoon, a series of cenotes, and a growing number of hotels and restaurants...but people mostly come for the ruins. In droves. By the busload. In fact, that's its biggest problem: arrive after 11am and you'll be one of literally hundreds of other people coming in from Cancún, Playa and Tulum. So come at 8am. You'll thank the stars you did.

From a sustainable-tourism perspective, it's great to stay the night in small communities like Cobá, but don't plan on staying up late.

History

Cobá was settled earlier than Chichén Itzá or Tulum, and construction reached its peak between 800 and 1000 CE. Archaeologists believe that this city once covered 70 sq km and was home to some 40,000 Maya.

Cobá's architecture is a mystery; its towering pyramids and stelae resemble the architecture of Tikal, which is several hundred kilometers away, rather than the much nearer sites of Chichén Itzá and the northern Yucatán Peninsula.

Archaeologists say they now know that between 200 and 600 CE, when Cobá had control over a vast territory of the peninsula, alliances with Tikal were made through military and marriage arrangements in order to facilitate trade between the Guatemalan and Yucatecan Maya. Stelae appear to depict female rulers from Tikal holding ceremonial bars and flaunting their power by standing on captives. These Tikal royal females, when married to Cobá's royalty, may have brought architects and artisans with them.

Archaeologists are still baffled by the extensive network of *sacbeob* (ceremonial limestone avenues or paths between great Maya cities) in this region, with Cobá as the hub. The longest runs nearly 100km west from the base of Cobá's great Nohoch Mul pyramid to the Maya settlement of Yaxuna. In all, some 40 *sacbeob* passed through Cobá, parts of the huge astronomical 'time machine' that was evident in every Maya city.

The first excavation at Cobá was led by Austrian archaeologist Teobert Maler in 1891. There was little subsequent investigation until 1926, when the Carnegie Institute financed the first of two expeditions led by Sir J Eric S Thompson and Harry Pollock. After their 1930 expedition, not much happened until 1973, when the Mexican government began to finance excavation. Archaeologists now estimate that Cobá contains more than 6500 structures, of which just a few have been excavated and restored, though work is ongoing.

◉ Sights

★ **Cobá Ruins**   ARCHAEOLOGICAL SITE
(www.inah.gob.mx; M$75, sunset entry M$255, guides M$800-850, parking M$50; ⊘8am-4pm & 4:30-7pm; ℗) Cobá's ruins include the tallest pyramid in Quintana Roo (the second tallest in all the Yucatán) and the thick jungle setting makes you feel like you're in an Indiana Jones flick. Many of the ruins are yet to be excavated; for now they are mysterious piles

of root- and vine-covered rubble. Walk along ancient *sacbeob*, climb up ancient mounds and ascend Nohoch Mul for a spectacular view of the surrounding jungle.

If walking to the various sites is too taxing, you can rent a bike (M$80) or hire a peditaxi (M$125 to M$180).

➡ **Juego de Pelota**

An impressive ball court, one of several in the ruins. Don't miss the relief of a jaguar and the skull-like carving in the center of the court.

➡ **Templo 10**

Here you can see an exquisitely carved stela (730 CE) depicting a ruler standing imperiously over two captives.

➡ **Grupo Cobá**

The most prominent structure in the Grupo Cobá is **La Iglesia** (the Church). It's an enormous pyramid; if you were allowed to climb it, you could see the surrounding lakes (which look lovely on a clear day) and the Nohoch Mul pyramid. To reach it walk just under 100m along the main path from the entrance and turn right.

Take the time to explore Grupo Cobá; it has a couple of corbeled-vault passages you can walk through. Near its northern edge, on the way back to the main path and the bicycle concession, is a very well-restored juego de pelota.

➡ **Grupo Macanxoc**

(Cobá Ruins) Grupo Macanxoc is notable for its numerous restored stelae, some of which are believed to depict reliefs of royal women from Tikal. Though many are worn down by the elements, a number are still in good condition and are worth a detour.

➡ **Grupo de las Pinturas**

The temple at Grupo de las Pinturas (Paintings Group) bears traces of glyphs and frescoes above its door and remnants of richly colored plaster inside. You approach the temple from the southeast. Leave by the trail at the northwest (opposite the temple steps) to see two stelae. The first of these is 20m along, beneath a *palapa*. Here a regal figure stands over two others, one of them kneeling with his hands bound behind him.

Sacrificial captives lie beneath the feet of a ruler at the base. You'll need to use your imagination, as this and most of the other stelae here are quite worn. Continue along the path past another badly weathered stela and a small temple to rejoin a path leading to the next group of structures.

➡ **Grupo Nohoch Mul**

Nohoch Mul (Big Mound) is also known as the Great Pyramid (which certainly sounds a lot better than Big Mound). It reaches a n impressive height of 42m, making it the second-tallest Maya structure on the Yucatán Peninsula (Calakmul's Estructura II, at 45m, is the tallest). Climbing the old steps can be scary for some. Two diving gods are carved over the doorway of the temple at the top (built in the post-Classic period, 1100–1450 CE), similar to sculptures at Tulum.

The view from up top is over many square kilometers of flat scrubby forest, with glimpses of lake.

➡ **Xaibé**

This is a tidy, semicircular stepped building, almost fully restored. Its name means 'the Crossroads,' as it marks the juncture of four separate *sacbeob*.

⚡ Activities

Cenotes Choo-Ha,
Tamcach-Ha & Multún-Ha   SWIMMING

(📞cell 985-1040472; per cenote M$100; ⊗8am-6pm) About 6km south of the town of Cobá, on the road to Chanchen I, you'll find a series of three locally administered cenotes: Choo-Ha, Tamcach-Ha and Multún-Ha. These cavern-like cenotes are nice spots to cool off with a swim, or a snorkel if you bring your own gear. Children under 10 enter free.

🛏 Sleeping & Eating

Hacienda Cobá   HOTEL $$$

(📞cell 998-2270168; www.haciendacoba.com; Av Principal; d incl breakfast US$80; 🅿⊗❄🛜🏊) Lovely if simple hacienda-style rooms with rustic furniture sit in a pleasant jungle setting with lots of chirping birdies and the occasional spider-monkey sighting. It's about 200m south of the Hwy 109 turnoff to Cobá and 2.7km from the ruins, so you'll either need a car or be willing to walk or cab it into town.

Chile Picante   MEXICAN $$

(📞cell 984-1443006; www.facebook.com/restaurantechilepicante; Av Principal s/n; mains M$75-220; ⊗7:30am-11pm; 🛜) Located at Hotel Maya, Chile Picante does everything from vegetarian omelettes with *chaya* and fresh fruit plates to *panuchos* (handmade fried tortillas with beans and toppings).

Restaurant La Pirámide   MEXICAN $$

(📞984-173-74-70; Av Principal s/n; mains M$80-180, buffet M$180; ⊗8am-5pm; 🛜) At the end of the town's main drag, by the lake, this restaurant is pretty touristy but does decent Yucatecan fare like *cochinita* or *pollo pibil* (*achiote*-flavored slow-cooked pork or chicken), or you can opt for the lunch buffet between noon and 3pm. The open-air setup allows for nice lagoon views.

ℹ Getting There & Away

Most buses serving Cobá swing down to the ruins to drop off passengers at a small **bus stop**; but you can also get off **in town** (Av Principal s/n).

Buses run eight times daily between Tulum and Cobá (M$52 to M$95, one hour) and there are about five daily departures to Playa del Carmen (M$98 to M$160, two hours). Buses also go eight times daily to Valladolid (M$51, one hour), where you'll find frequent **bus services** (📞985-856-34-48; www.ado.com.mx; cnr Calles 39 & 46; ⊗24hr) to Chichén Itzá and Mérida (M$177).

Day-trippers from Tulum can reach Cobá by taking **colectivos** (M$70) that depart every two hours or so from Calle Osiris Norte and Avenida Tulum.

The arrow-straight road from Cobá to Chemax is in good shape. If you're driving to Valladolid or Chichén Itzá, this is the way to go.

Cobá-based taxis charge M$450 to Tulum and M$650 to Valladolid. You can visit all three nearby cenotes by taxi for M$450.

Punta Allen

📞984 / POP 470

The tiny town of Javier Rojo Gómez is more commonly called by the name of the point 2km south, Punta Allen. The village, which is truly the end of the road, exudes a laidback ambience reminiscent of the Belizean cays. There's also a healthy reef 400m from shore that offers snorkelers and divers wonderful sights. To get here you have to enter the incredible Sian Ka'an Biosphere Reserve, a vast tract of mangrove swamp, lagoon, beaches and jungle that supports a variety of endemic species, including the elusive jaguar.

The village is known primarily for its catch-and-release bonefishing; tarpon and snook are very popular sportfish as well. Cooperatives in town offer fishing trips, dolphin-watching outings and snorkeling expeditions.

Hurricane Gilbert nearly destroyed the town in 1988, and there was some damage and a lot of wind-scrubbed palms after Hurricane Dean in 2007. But Punta Allen is still standing.

◉ Sights

Reserva de la Biosfera Sian Ka'an   NATURE RESERVE

(Sian Ka'an Biosphere Reserve; M$36; ⊙ sunrise-sunset) Sian Ka'an (Where the Sky is Born) is home to a small population of spider and howler monkeys, American crocodiles, Central American tapirs, four turtle species, giant land crabs, more than 330 bird species (including roseate spoonbills and some flamingos), manatees and some 400 fish species, plus a wide array of plant life.

There's an entrance gate to the reserve about 10km south of Tulum. At the gate, there's a short nature trail taking you to a rather nondescript cenote (Ben Ha). The trail's short, so go ahead and take a second to have a look.

About 8km south of the reserve entrance is a modest visitor area, a pull-off where you'll find a watchtower that provides tremendous bird's-eye views of the lagoon.

The road can be a real muffler-buster between gradings, especially when holes are filled with water from recent rains, making it difficult to gauge their depth. The southern half, south of the bridge beyond Boca Paila, is the worst stretch – some spots require experienced off-road handling or you'll sink into the mud. It is doable even in a non-4WD vehicle, but bring along a shovel and boards just in case – you can always stuff palm fronds under the wheels to gain traction – and plan on returning that rental with a lot more play in the steering wheel.

There are no hiking trails through the heart of the reserve; it's best explored with a professional guide. If you'd like to see more of Sian Ka'an, Maya-run **Community Tours Sian Ka'an** (www.siankaantours.com.mx) runs various expeditions into the sprawling biosphere reserve.

For remote coastal camping, this is where intrepid adventuring really takes off. Bring a tent, a couple of hammocks, lots of water, mosquito nets and food supplies. Around 30km from the entrance gate is an excellent camping spot with the lagoon on one side and glorious blue ocean on the other.

Lagoon tours around the lagoon in *lanchas* (boats) cost M$2700 for up to six people for a 2½-hour tour.

🛏 Sleeping & Eating

★ Serenidad Shardon   GUESTHOUSE $$$

(☑ Mexico 984-146-15-87, USA 616-827-0204, WhatsApp only 984-1074155; www.shardon.com; Punta Allen Rd; cabañas M$3400, house M$11,500, camping US$25) Serenidad (serenity) couldn't be a more fitting description for this white-sand oceanfront property on the southern end of town. On offer are a large beach house that sleeps eight, a romantic honeymoon *cabaña* for two and a larger *cabaña* with a balcony, kitchen and lovely interior design details. There are also affordable camping options available.

Muelle Viejo   SEAFOOD $$

(Punta Allen; mains M$95-170; ⊙ 12:30-9pm Tue-Sun; ℗) Service here can be as slow as the frigates circling overhead, but it's hard not to use this as a chance to relax and enjoy. Overlooking a dock where fishers bring in the daily catch, this colorful beach house serves fresh seafood ceviche, decent fried-fish dishes and lobster when it's in season.

❶ Getting There & Away

The best way to reach Punta Allen is by driving a rental car or scooter, but prepare to drive very slowly and expect more than a few transmission-grinding bumps. The ride can take three to four hours or as little as two, depending on the condition of the road. Keep a sharp eye out while driving for the numerous sunbathing iguanas, snakes and other wildlife.

You can also get there by *colectivo*, which costs about M$200 to/from Tulum center and departs several times per day.

Mahahual

☑ 983 / POP 920

Mahahual changed forever when the cruise-ship dock was completed, and it grows larger every year. Despite the (literally) boatloads of tourists, there's a lovely, relaxed, Caribbean vibe that you won't find further north, and once the passengers have returned to their ships, a quiet calm settles over the town. Mahahual is the only spot in the Costa Maya that's large enough to support a diversity of sleeping and eating options, while still being right on the beach.

New restaurants and bars are cropping up on the north side of town, a residential area

YUCATÁN PENINSULA MAHAHUAL

known as Casitas that's home to both locals and foreigners. Or go south toward Xcalak and you'll have no problem finding your own private beach with sugar-white sand.

There's great diving and snorkeling in Mahahual, and just enough nightlife along the beachfront *malecón* to keep you entertained.

◉ Sights & Activities

★ Chacchoben RUINS
(M$60; ⊘8am-5pm) Chacchoben means 'Place of Red Corn' in Maya and like so many ruins, its origin and use remain a mystery. It has several impressive structures, including two pyramid-shaped temples. It is a popular stop today because it is the only major ruin within a few hours' reach of Mahahual, where cruise ships dock, so the vast majority of visitors come from there for a day trip among the ruins. Do not confuse it with the eponymous town nearby.

Come at peak time and you'll find the place crowded with bus tours. If there aren't any ships in port, you may have this good-sized ruin all to yourself. The site consists of three major structures, none of which you are allowed to climb, but which you can walk entirely around. The largest sits on a raised base and if you're lucky there'll be spider monkeys aplenty hanging out in the trees. There are also a host of other animals and birds to see. A taxi from Mahahual costs M$2500; *colectivos* to the Hwy 307 intersection runs M$15, then about M$60 to reach Mahahual.

★ Banco Chinchorro DIVE SITE
Divers won't want to miss the reefs and underwater fantasy worlds of the Banco Chinchorro, the largest coral atoll in the northern hemisphere and known for its shipwreck sites, coral walls and canyons. Some 45km long and up to 14km wide, Chinchorro's western edge lies about 30km off the coast, and dozens of ships have fallen victim to its barely submerged ring of coral.

The atoll and its surrounding waters were made a biosphere reserve (Reserva de la Biosfera Banco Chinchorro) to protect them from depredation. But the reserve lacks the personnel and equipment needed to patrol such a large area, and many abuses go undetected. Consequently, Amigos del Mar (☑cell 984-1516758; www.amigosdelmar. net; Malecón s/n, cnr Coronado; 1-/2-tank dive incl equipment US$90/150, snorkeling US$100;

⊘9am-6pm) is one of only several dive shops authorized to run scuba trips to Chinchorro.

Most dives here go to an average of 18m as there are no decompression chambers for miles. And with a ban on wreck dives lifted, there are plenty of shipwreck sites worth exploring. Along the way you'll also spot coral walls and canyons, rays, turtles, giant sponges, grouper, tangs, eels, nurse sharks, and occasionally, tiger and hammerhead sharks.

There's good snorkeling as well, including *40 Cannons*, a wooden ship in 5m to 6m of water.

Mahahual Dive Center DIVING
(☑983-102-09-92; www.mahahualdive.com; Malecón Km 1, cnr Atún; 1-/2-tank dives incl equipment US$69/99, snorkeling US$25; ⊘9am-5pm Mon-Sat, to 4pm Sun) Right on the *malecón* (waterfront promenade), Mahahual Dive Center does scuba trips to nearby sites, snorkeling outings and day trips.

Doctor Dive DIVING
(☑983-834-56-19; www.doctordive.com; cnr Malecón & Coronado; 2-tank dive US$100, snorkeling incl equipment US$25; ⊘8am-9pm) In addition to scuba and snorkeling excursions, the Doctor can offer training courses at many different levels, including open-water PADI certification (US$420).

Victor Rosales BIRD-WATCHING
(☑WhatsApp only 983-1362827) Victor Rosales is a Mahahual-based tour guide who can arrange a variety of tours throughout the area, including bird-watching and even jaguar-tracking in the Sian Ka'an or nearby areas. He is a certified ethnobotanist and knows a wealth of info about birds.

🛏 Sleeping & Eating

★ Posada Pachamama HOTEL $$
(☑983-834-57-62; www.posadapachamama.net; Huachinango s/n, btwn Coronado & Martillo; d/q M$1500/2500; ▣☻✳🛜🐾) Rooms at the Pachamama (which means Mother Earth in Quechua, the language of the Inca) range from small interior singles and doubles with partial ocean views to more ample digs that sleep four. The staff are very knowledgeable about local activities and the accommodations are fairly priced by Mahahual standards. The beach is a 10m stumble away.

Hostal Jardín Mahahual HOSTEL $$
(☑983-834-57-22; www.mahahualjardin.com; Sardina s/n, btwn Rubia & Sierra; dm/r M$250/695;

😊🕸📶) This is a surprisingly stylish little hostel with seven private rooms and a six-bed mixed dorm. Rooms are spotless and the dorm is the best in town by far. It's set back two blocks from the beach, near Calle Rubia.

Quinto Sole   BOUTIQUE HOTEL $$$

(📱983-834-59-42; www.quintosole.mx; Carretera Mahahual–Xcalak Km 0.35; r/ste M$1800/2500; 🅿😊🕸📶) One of the fancier hotels in town, the rooms here have cushy beds and private balcony. It's on a quiet beach north of the boardwalk and 350m south of the lighthouse at the town's entrance. There's also a restaurant. Rates are for jungle views; ocean views cost more.

Panadería La Tartaleta   BAKERY $

(Sierra s/n, btwn Huachinango & Malecón; coffee M$35-55, bread M$15-35; ⊙7am-10pm) Hopping in the mornings, the tiny Tartaleta has decent expressos, pastries and freshly baked bread. Expect a queue. It's in the pedestrian section of Sierra just before it intersects with the *malecón*.

★Nohoch Kay   SEAFOOD $$

(Big Fish; 📱983-834-59-81; miplayanohochkay@outlook.com; cnr Malecón & Cazón; mains M$150-240; ⊙12:30-8:30pm; 📶) Nohoch Kay, aka the Big Fish, definitely lives up to its name. Don't miss this beachfront Mexican-owned restaurant, where they prepare succulent whole fish in a garlic and white-wine sauce, and seafood paella for two (M$395), which includes mussels, clams, shrimp, calamari and octopus.

❶ Getting There & Away

Mahahual is 125km south of Felipe Carrillo Puerto, and 105km northeast of Laguna Bacalar.

There's no official bus terminal in Mahahual. Los Hijos del Maíz restaurant sells tickets for a twice-daily northbound bus, which departs Mahahual at 10:30am and 5:30pm for Felipe Carrillo Puerto (M$183, 1¾ hours), Tulum (M$327, three hours), Playa del Carmen (M$414, four hours) and Cancún (M$497, 5½ hours). A Xcalak-bound Caribe bus (M$52, 40 minutes) stops here as well, usually around 8:10am and 6:40pm. Hourly westbound buses to Limones (M$60, one hour), Laguna Bacalar (M$90, 1½ hours) and Chetumal (M$100 to M$244, 2½ to three hours) leave from 6:30am to 6:30pm.

Shuttle vans leave hourly from 5:20am to 8:20pm to Chetumal (M$100, 2½ hours), Laguna Bacalar (M$60, two hours) and Limones (M$60, one hour), where you can catch frequent northbound buses. The terminal is on the corner of Calles Sardina and Cherna, on the soccer field's north end.

There's a Pemex gas station in Mahahual if you need to fill your tank. The Xcalak turnoff is about 100m west of the gas station.

Xcalak

📱983 / POP 375

The rickety wooden houses, beached fishing launches and lazy gliding pelicans make this tiny town plopped in the middle of nowhere a perfect escape. And by virtue of its remoteness and the Banco Chinchorro, Xcalak may yet escape the development boom.

Come here to walk along dusty streets and sip frozen drinks while frigate birds soar above translucent green lagoons. Explore a mangrove swamp by kayak, scuba-dive at Banco Chinchorro or do some excellent fly-fishing. Xcalak has a few nice restaurants and an easygoing mix of foreigners and locals.

The mangrove swamps stretching inland from the coastal road hide some large lagoons and form tunnels that invite kayakers to explore. They, and the drier forest, teem with wildlife; in addition to the usual herons, egrets and other waterfowl, you can see agoutis, jabirus (storks), iguanas, javelinas (peccaries), parakeets, kingfishers, crocodiles and more.

🏃 Activities

XTC Dive Center   DIVING

(📱WhatsApp 984-2401557; www.xtcdivecenter.com; Coast Rd Km 0.3; 2-tank Chinchorro dives US$275, snorkeling trips US$50-75; ⊙dive shop 8am-6pm) XTC is the one-stop spot for all your travel needs. It offers dive and snorkel trips to the wondrous barrier reef offshore and to Banco Chinchorro. It also rents out diving equipment, provides PADI open-water certification (US$600), and operates fishing and bird-watching tours (US$75). Kayaks, free for guests, can be rented for a half/full day for US$40/60.

Additionally, XTC rents nice **rooms** (US$115-130) and a larger **apartment** (US$250), and has a good **restaurant-bar**. It's 300m north of town.

🛏 Sleeping & Eating

Accommodations here are simple: even the nicer ones. Most places don't accept credit cards without prior arrangement and are best contacted through their websites, via email or WhatsApp.

Food in Xcalak tends to be tourist-grade seafood or Mexican, though some of it is quite good.

Casa Paraíso HOTEL $$$
(📞 Canada 416-277-6774, WhatsApp 983-1587008; www.casaparaisoresort.com; Coast Rd Km 2.5; r incl breakfast US$140; 🛜) Bright, cheery yellow Casa Paraíso has four guest rooms with large, hammock-equipped balconies facing the sea. Each room has a king-sized bed and a kitchen with fridge, and the bathrooms try to outdo one another with their beautiful Talavera tilework. Includes free use of kayaks, snorkel gear and bicycles.

Costa de Cocos INTERNATIONAL $$
(📞 WhatsApp 983-1167744; www.costadecocos.com; Coast Rd Km 5.2; breakfast US$3-5, lunch & dinner US$9-26; ⊘ 7am-9pm; 🅿🛜) This fishing lodge's restaurant-bar is one of the better options in town for eating and drinking. It serves both American- and Mexican-style breakfasts and does fish tacos for the lunch and dinner crowd. The bar produces its own craft whiskey and has pale ale on tap.

Toby's SEAFOOD $$
(📞 cell 983-1075426; tobyxcalak@hotmail.com; town center; mains M$85-350; ⊘ 11:30am-8pm Mon-Sat but varies) On the main drag in town, the friendly chitchat and well-prepared fish and seafood dishes make this a popular expat spot. Try the coconut shrimp or lionfish and you'll know why. Toby's also rents **camping sites** (M$100) across the street.

❶ Getting There & Away

Buses to Chetumal (M$130) and Mahahual (M$50, where you can grab northbound buses) leave at 4:50am and 1:50pm; they stop on the coast road behind the lighthouse and pass through Mahahual before heading west. From Chetumal, buses leave at 5:40am and 4:10pm.

Cabs from Limones, on Hwy 307, cost M$1000 (including to the northern hotels).

From the Hwy 307 turnoff, drive south about 52km and then turn right at the signs pointing to Xcalak (another 60km). Keep an eye out for the diverse wildlife that frequents the forest and mangrove; a lot of it runs out onto the road. Large land crabs, snakes and tortoises are common. The cat-sized Yucatecan fox is another resident.

At last visit, the bumpy coastal road from Xcalak to Mahahual was closed, so you'll have to take the paved inland road instead: a much faster option but far less scenic.

Laguna Bacalar
📅 983 / POP 39,000

Laguna Bacalar, the peninsula's largest lagoon, comes as a surprise in this region of scrubby jungle. More than 60km long with a bottom of sparkling white sand, this crystal-clear lake offers opportunities for camping, swimming, kayaking and simply lazing around, amid a color palette of blues, greens and shimmering whites that seems more out of Photoshop than anything real life could hold.

Some would say this area is the 'new' Tulum. Small and sleepy, yet with enough tourism to have things to do and places to eat, the lakeside town of Bacalar lies east of the highway, 115km south of Felipe Carrillo Puerto. It's noted mostly for its old Spanish fortress and popular *balnearios* (bathing places). There's not much else going on, but that's why people like it. Around the town plaza, you'll find ATMs, a money-exchange office, a small grocery store, a taxi stand and a tourist information office.

◉ Sights & Activities

Fort FORTRESS
(📞 museum cell 983-8361065; cnr Av 3 & Calle 22; adult/child 9-17yr M$100/25; ⊘ museum 9am-7pm Tue-Sun) The fortress above the lagoon was built in 1733 to protect Spanish colonists from pirate attacks and rebellions by local indigenous people. It also served as an important outpost for the Spanish in the War of the Castes. In 1859 it was seized by Maya rebels, who held the fort until Quintana Roo was conquered by Mexican troops in 1901.

Today, with formidable cannons still on its ramparts, the fortress remains an imposing sight. It houses a museum exhibiting colonial armaments and uniforms from the 17th and 18th centuries.

Balneario SWIMMING
(📞 983-835-55-05; Av Costera s/n, cnr Calle 14; ⊘ 9am-5pm) **FREE** This beautiful public swimming spot lies several blocks south of the fort, along Avenida Costera. Though admission is free, parking costs M$10.

Cenote Azul SWIMMING
(Hwy 307 Km 34; adult/child under 11yr M$25/free; ⊘ 10am-6pm) Just shy of the south end of the *costera* (coastal highway) and about 3km south of Bacalar's town center is this cenote, a 90m-deep natural pool with an onsite bar and restaurant. It's 200m east of Hwy 307, so

many buses can drop you nearby. Taxis to the cenote from the main square cost M$50.

🛏 Sleeping

Yak Lake House HOSTEL $
(☑983-834-31-75; www.yakbacalar.com; Av Costera s/n, btwn Calles 24 & 26; dm/r M$450/2000; P⊜❄🐾) If lounging around all day in your bikini is your idea of fun, then Yak House won't disappoint. It's steps away from Laguna Bacalar and there are ample chairs, docks and decks on which to soak up the sun. Free breakfast, friendly staff, clean rooms and comfy mixed dorms make this a sweet spot to park yourself for several days.

Amigo's Hotelito Bacalar HOTEL $$
(www.amigoshotelito.com; Av Costera s/n; d US$85; P⊜❄🐾) Right on the lake and about 500m south of the fort, this ideally located property has five spacious guest rooms with king-size beds, hammocks, satellite TV, terraces and a *palapa* common area with a lake view.

Hotel Laguna Bacalar HOTEL $$
(☑983-834-22-05; www.hotellagunabacalar.com; Av Costera 479; d with fan/air-con M$1360/1500, bungalow from M$3000; P⊜❄🐾🏊) This breezy, old-school place boasts a swimming pool, restaurant and fairly basic rooms with spotty wi-fi and excellent views of the lagoon, which you can explore by kayak or boat tours. It's 2km south of town and 150m east of Hwy 307, so if you're traveling by bus you can ask the driver to stop at the turnoff.

★ Rancho Encantado CABAÑAS $$$
(☑998-884-20-71, cell 983-1004141; www.encantado.com; Hwy 307 Km 24; d/ste incl breakfast from M$2872/4099; P⊜❄🐾🏊) Laguna Bacalar is absolutely beautiful in its own right, so imagine staying at one of the most striking locations along the shore. A typical day on the *rancho* (ranch) goes something like this: wake up in comfy cabin or room; have breakfast with lagoon view; kayak or swim in calm, translucent waters; and unwind in a Jacuzzi. Wi-fi in reception only.

The ranch is 3km north of Bacalar.

🍴 Eating

Christian's Tacos TACOS $
(☑cell 983-1149094; www.facebook.com/taqueria christiansbacalar; Calle 18 s/n, btwn Avs 7 & 9; tacos M$14-30, nachos M$70-125; ⊙6pm-1am) If Christian's were in Mexico City – the *al pastor* capital – it would compete with the best of

them. The popular, yet artery-choking, *pastor* nachos are topped with slices of pork, beans and cheese. The new **bar** means you can wash down your food with your favorite alcoholic libations as well.

Mango y Chile VEGAN $$
(☑983-688-20-00; www.facebook.com/mangoy chile; Av 3 s/n, btwn Calles 22 & 24; mains M$100-150; ⊙1-9pm Wed-Mon; P⊜🐾) Bacalar's first and only all-vegan dining option, Mango y Chile has a beautiful, large deck overlooking the fort and the lagoon, and friendly service. Vegans will rejoice that there's a spot here to dine worry-free. The burgers are tasty, though the food is on the salty side.

★ Nixtamal GRILL $$$
(☑cell 983-1347651; www.facebook.com/nixtamal cocinaafuegoyceniza; López Mateos 525, cnr Calle 12; mains M$130-300; ⊙5-11pm Wed-Mon; 🐾) The *slooow*-food experience here pushes your patience to the limit, but grill-master Rodrigo Estrada makes it well worth the wait. Exquisite dishes such as marinated rib eye and whole grilled lobster are cooked over a wood-and-charcoal grill and finished in a wood-fired oven (no gas or electrical appliances are used). The candle-lit open-air restaurant stages live music on weekends.

La Playita SEAFOOD $$$
(☑983-834-30-68; www.laplayitabacalar.com; Av Costera s/n, cnr Calle 26; mains M$160-300; ⊙9am-11:45pm; 🐾) A sign outside reads, 'Eat, drink and swim' – and that about sums it up. Fish and seafood dishes are tasty, albeit on the smallish side, but the mezcal and fine swimming certainly make up for that. An enormous rubber tree, which provides shade in the gravel garden section, was nearly uprooted in 2007 when Hurricane Dean pummeled the coast.

☆ Entertainment

Galeón Pirata Espacio Cultural LIVE MUSIC
(☑cell 983-1577558; www.facebook.com/galeon piratabacalar; Av Costera s/n, btwn Calles 30 & 32; ⊙varies depending on events, to 2am Fri & Sat) This indie cultural center hosts live music, art exhibits, movie screenings and plays, while doubling as a restaurant-bar. Hours can be erratic, but when it's happening, it's a fun time. Galeón hosts an annual indie-art festival in March.

ℹ Getting There & Away

Buses don't enter town, but taxis and some *colectivos* will drop you at the town square. Buses arrive at Bacalar's ADO station. From there it's about a 10-block walk southeast to the main square, or you can grab a local taxi for M$20.

If you're driving from the north and want to reach the town and fort, take the first Bacalar exit and continue several blocks before turning left (east) down the hill. From Chetumal, head west to catch Hwy 307 north; after 25km on the highway you'll reach the signed right turn for Cenote Azul and Avenida Costera, aka Avenida 1.

Chetumal

📞 983 / POP 224,000

The capital of Quintana Roo, Chetumal is a relatively quiet city going about its daily paces. The bayside esplanade hosts carnivals and events, and the modern Maya museum is impressive (though a bit short on artifacts). Excellent Maya ruins, amazing jungle and the border to neighboring Belize are all close by. Though sightings are rare (there are no tours), manatees can sometimes be seen in the rather muddy bay or nearby mangrove shores. The lagoon should not be used for swimming, as there is a risk of crocodiles, despite the locals' joke that there's only one (named Harry) and he's tame. It may be their way of getting rid of pesky tourists, so swim in your hotel pool to be safe.

History

Before the Spanish conquest, Chetumal was a Maya port used for shipping gold, feathers, cacao and copper to the northern Yucatán Peninsula. After the conquest, it wasn't until the late-19th century when the Mexican government took full control of the city to put a stop to the arms and lumber trade carried on by descendants of the Maya who fought in the War of the Castes. The government declared May 5, 1898 as the city's 'founding' date. The town was initially dubbed Payo Obispo, and later renamed Chetumal, in 1936. In 1955, Hurricane Janet virtually obliterated it, and 2007's Hurricane Dean did a bit of damage to the town's infrastructure too.

◉ Sights

★ **Laguna Milagros**   LAGOON

(off Hwy 186, in Huay-Pix; 🚌 Nicolás Bravo) Paddle out on a kayak or simply have a swim in the azure waters of Laguna Milagros, about 23km west of Chetumal, in the town of Huay-Pix.

Waterfront seafood restaurant El Abuelo (☎ cell 983-1171536; www.facebook.com/restaurante labuelohuaypix; Av Laguna Milagros; mains M$140-210; ⏰ 10am-7:30pm; 🅿 🛜; 🚌 Nicolás Bravo colectivo) rents kayaks (M$100 per hour) and serves tasty fresh fish.

Museo de la Cultura Maya   MUSEUM

(☎ 983-833-38-68; www.facebook.com/museo delaculturamaya; Av de los Héroes 68, cnr Av Gandhi; adult/child under 8yr M$105.61/free; ⏰ 9am-7pm Tue-Sun) The Museo de la Cultura Maya is the city's claim to cultural fame – a bold showpiece that's beautifully conceived and executed, though regrettably short on artifacts. It's organized into three levels, mirroring Maya cosmology. The main floor represents this world, the upper floor the heavens and the lower floor Xibalbá, the underworld. The various exhibits cover all the Mayab (lands of the Maya). Though original pieces are in short supply, there are replicas of stelae and a burial chamber from Honduras' Copán.

The museum's courtyard, which you can enter for free, has salons for temporary exhibitions of modern artists. In the middle of the courtyard is a *na* (thatched hut) with implements of daily Maya life on display: gourds and grinding stones.

Museo de la Ciudad   MUSEUM

(Local History Museum; www.icaqroo.com; Av Héroes de Chapultepec 66, cnr Av de los Héroes; M$105.61; ⏰ 9am-7pm Tue-Fri, to 5pm Sat & Sun) The Museo de la Ciudad is small but neatly done, displaying historic photos, pre-Hispanic and military artifacts, and old-time household items (even some vintage telephones, linotypes and cameras). Explanatory text is in Spanish.

🛏 Sleeping & Eating

Hotel Xcalak   HOTEL $

(☎ 983-129-17-08; www.facebook.com/xcalak hotelboutique; Av Gandhi 181, cnr Av 16 de Septiembre; r M$500; ❄ ✴ 🛜) A clean and reliable budget option, though the wi-fi is spotty at best. It's near the city's best museum (Museo de la Cultura Maya) and transportation to Laguna Bacalar, and there's a decent restaurant downstairs, La Pantoja (☎ 983-832-39-57; mains M$80-110, set menu M$75; ⏰ 8am-6pm Mon-Sat; 🛜), serving affordable eats.

Hotel Los Cocos   HOTEL $$

(☎ 983-835-04-30; www.hotelloscocos.com.mx; Av de los Héroes 134, cnr Héroes de Chapultepec; d/ste with air-con from M$912/1140; 🅿 ⊝ ✴ @ 🛜 ⚊) With a great location, Hotel Los

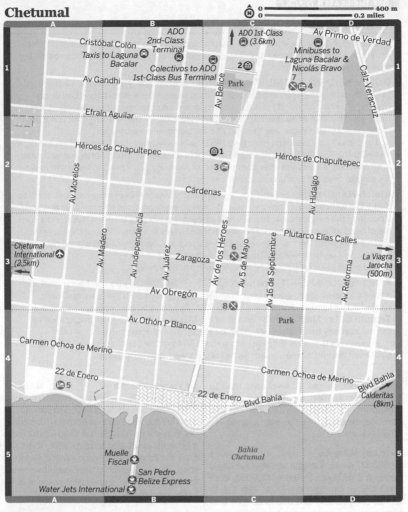

Chetumal

Chetumal

◎ Sights

🛏 Sleeping

🍴 Eating

Cocos has a mirrored lobby that gets your inner disco-dancer rising. There's also a swimming pool, Jacuzzi and restaurant. All rooms have small fridges and some have a balcony. It runs 'promotions' year-round, so it's likely you'll pay less than the official rates listed here – check the website for details.

Noor Hotel　　　　　　　　　HOTEL **$$**
(☑ 983-835-13-00; www.hotelnoor.mx; cnr Blvd Bahía & Av Morelos; r M$1500-1800; 🅿 ⊕ ❄ 🛜 🏊) Right on the bay, the Noor will appeal to those looking to get away from the bustling center. Bay-view rooms, though pricier, are

CORREDOR ARQUEOLÓGICO

The Corredor Arqueológico comprises archaeological sites that include Dzibanché, Kinich-Ná and Kohunlich, three intriguing and seldom-visited Maya ruins that can be visited on a day trip from Chetumal.

Dzibanché (☑ 983-837-24-11; off Hwy 186; M$60; ⊗ 8am-5pm; ℗) Though it's a chore to get to, this site is definitely worth a visit for its secluded, semi-wild nature. Dzibanché (meaning 'writing on wood') was a major city extending over more than 40 sq km and there are a number of excavated palaces and pyramids, though the site itself is not completely unearthed. On the way there you'll pass beautiful countryside.

The turnoff for Dzibanché from Hwy 186 is about 44km west of Chetumal, on the right just after the Zona Arqueológico sign. From there it's another 24km north and east along a narrow road. About 2km after the tiny town of Morocoy you'll need to turn right again. It's easy to miss the sign unless you're looking for it.

Kinich-Ná (off Hwy 186; ⊗ 8am-5pm; ℗) Part of Dzibanché (ticket price includes entry to both), but well removed from the main site, Kinich-Ná consists of one building. But what a building: the megalithic **Acrópolis** held at least five temples on three levels and a couple of dead VIPs with offerings. The site's name derives from the frieze of the Maya sun god once found at the top of the structure. It's an easy 2km drive along a good narrow road leading north from near Dzibanché's visitors center.

The ticket price for Dzibanché includes entry to Kinich-Ná.

Kohunlich (☑ 983-837-24-11; off Hwy 186; M$75; ⊗ 8am-5pm; ℗) This archaeological site sits on a jungle-backed grassy area. The ruins, dating from both the late pre-Classic (100–200 CE) and the early Classic (300–600 CE) periods, are famous for the great **Templo de los Mascarones** (Temple of the Masks), a pyramid-like structure with a central stairway flanked by huge, 3m-high stucco masks of the sun god.

Kohunlich's turnoff is 3km west along Hwy 186 from the Dzibanché turnoff, and the site lies at the end of a 9km road. It's a straight shot from the highway.

your best bet, as ground-level ones tend to have poor ventilation. There's a pool, and the restaurant prepares international cuisine. The boardwalk across the way is good for afternoon strolls.

Café Los Milagros CAFE $
(☑ 983-832-44-33; Zaragoza s/n, btwn Avs de los Héroes & 5 de Mayo; breakfast M$90-160, lunch M$32-105; ⊗ 7am-3pm Mon-Fri, to 2pm Sat, to 1pm Sun; ⊛) Simple and laid-back spot that serves great espresso and food. A favorite with Chetumal's student and intellectual set, it's a good spot to chat with locals or while away the time with a game of dominoes.

Sergio's Pizzas PIZZA $$
(☑ 983-832-29-91; www.sergiospizzas.com.mx; Av Obregón 182, cnr Av 5 de Mayo; mains M$85-320; ⊗ 7am-11pm; ⊛⊛) Walk in here and you'll feel like you're in a Hollywood mafia movie: the service and decor are old-school, with stiff, formal waiters in starched shirts who never seem to smile. But the food's good, and it has a nice range of Mexican and Italian dishes, plus steaks and seafood.

La Viagra Jarocha MEXICAN $$
(☑ 983-144-39-05; www.laviagrajarocha.com; Blvd Bahía 98A; mains M$150-300; ⊗ 8am-8pm Mon, to 10pm Tue-Sun; ⊛) Fun and festive, with a goofy dolphin statue outside, La Viagra Jarocha is a hit with locals and tourists alike, most notably for its namesake '*sopa viagra*' (seafood soup). The breezes keep the mosquitoes away, too, and when you're done eating, you're close to the local nightclub scene.

❶ Information

There are numerous banks and ATMs around town, including an ATM inside the 1st-class bus terminal.

CI Banco (☑ 983-832-38-83; www.cibanco. com; Av Obregón 232; ⊗ 8:30am-5pm Mon-Fri, 9am-2pm Sat) For ATM, bank services and money exchange.

❶ Getting There & Away

AIR

Chetumal's small **airport** (☑ ext 3302 983-832-96-39; Av Revolución 660, Colonia Industrial) is roughly 2km northwest of downtown.

There are flights to Mexico City with **Interjet** (☎ 983-833-31-47; www.interjet.com; ⊙ 8am-7pm Mon-Sat, from 7am Sun) and **Volaris** (☎ 55-1102-8000; www.volaris.com); both have offices at the airport.

The airport is best reached by taxi (M$120).

BOAT

Belize-bound ferries depart from the **muelle fiscal** (Dock; Blvd Bahía). Remember that in addition to the ferry fee you'll pay an exit fee of M$558 on departure, unless you can provide proof that you already paid the fee when you purchased your airline ticket, which is often the case. Immigration will need to see an itemized receipt detailing payment of the fee.

San Pedro Belize Express (☎ 983-832-16-48; www.belizewatertaxi.com; Av Blvd Bahía s/n, Muelle Fiscal; one-way M$950-1050; ⊙ 8:30am-4pm) Boat transportation to Belize City, Caye Caulker and San Pedro.

Water Jets International (☎ 983-833-32-01; www.sanpedrowatertaxi.com; Blvd Bahía s/n, Muelle Fiscal; one-way M$1100-1200; ⊙ 9am-3:30pm) Water taxis to San Pedro and Caye Caulker, in Belize.

BUS

Long-distance buses arrive at and depart from the ADO 1st-class terminal.

ADO 1st-Class Terminal (☎ 983-832-51-10; www.ado.com.mx; Av Insurgentes s/n, cnr Av Palermo) Services to Cancún, Campeche,

Mérida, Valladolid, Mahahual and other destinations, including points in Belize. Most 2nd-class buses also stop at the 1st-class terminal.

ADO 2nd-Class Terminal (www.ado.com.mx; Av Belice s/n, cnr Colón) Buses to Mahahual, Xcalak, Laguna Bacalar and Tulum.

Minibus Terminal (cnr Avs Primo de Verdad & Hidalgo) Minibuses serve Laguna Bacalar (M$42) from 7:30am to 1:30pm; however, you'll find more frequent departures to Bacalar at the taxi *colectivo* base on Avenida Independencia.

TAXI & CAR

City cabs charge about M$25 to M$40 for short trips, but always ask the price before getting in.

Taxis (Av Independencia s/n, btwn Av Gandhi & Efraín Aguilar; per person M$45) on Avenida Independencia charge M$45 per person for Laguna Bacalar. Night trips have an additional surcharge.

Gibson's Tours & Transfers (☎ cell in Belize 501-6002605; www.facebook.com/gibsons storageandparking; Santa Elena-Corozal border; transportation for up to 4 people from US$100) can bring up to four people across to Corozal for US$100.

❶ Getting Around

Most places in Chetumal's tourist zone are within walking distance. To reach the main bus terminal from the center, catch a 'Lagunitas' **colectivo** (Gandhi s/n, btwn Avs Juárez & Belice) from the corner of Avenidas Belice and

BUSES FROM CHETUMAL

Unless noted otherwise, the following buses depart from the ADO 1st-class terminal.

DESTINATION	FARE (M$)	TIME (HR)	FREQUENCY (PER DAY)
Bacalar	45	¾	frequent
Belize City (Belize)	390	4-4½	1 (4:40am)
Campeche	570	6	1 (noon)
Cancún	406-486	5½-6½	frequent
Corozal (Belize)	195	1	1 (4:40am)
Escárcega	361	4	10
Felipe Carrillo Puerto	100	2¼-3	frequent
Mahahual	120	2-2½	1 (10:30am, 2nd-class terminal)
Mérida	473	5½-6	frequent
Orange Walk (Belize)	300	2¼	1 (4:40am)
Palenque	680-808	7	3
Tulum	323-359	3¼-4	12
Valladolid	250	5½	3 (2nd-class terminal)
Veracruz	1409	17¾	1 (6:30pm)
Villahermosa	767	8½-9	5
Xcalak	130	3-3½	2 (5:40am and 4:10pm, 2nd-class terminal)
Xpujil	195	1¾	7

Gandhi, just around the corner from the 2nd-class bus station.

You'll find 'Calderitas' *colectivos* lined up across the street from the 2nd-class bus station.

YUCATÁN STATE & THE MAYA HEARTLAND

Sitting regally on the northern tip of the peninsula, Yucatán state sees less mass tourism than its flashy and mass-market neighbor, Quintana Roo. It is sophisticated and savvy, and the perfect spot for travelers more interested in cultural exploration than beach life. While there are a few good beaches in Celestún and Progreso, most people come to this area to explore the ancient Maya sites peppered throughout the region, like the Ruta Puuc, which will take you to four or five ruins in just a day.

Visitors also come to experience the past and present in the cloistered corners of colonial cities, to experience *henequén* haciendas (vast estates that produced agave-plant fibers, used to make rope) lost to time or restored by caring hands to old glory, and to discover the energy, spirit and subtle contrasts of this diverse corner of southeastern Mexico.

For planning, a useful website is www.yucatan.travel.

Mérida

☑ 999 / POP 893,000

Since the Spanish conquest, Mérida has been the cultural capital of the entire Yucatán Peninsula. A delightful blend of provincial and cosmopolitan, it is a town steeped in colonial history, with narrow streets, broad central plazas and the region's best museums, including a fantastic collection of Maya archaeological finds. Expect excellent cuisine, some wonderful accommodations options, thriving markets and events happening just about every night. It's also a perfect place from which to kick off your adventure into the rest of Yucatán state, with dozens of sites within easy striking distance.

Long popular with European travelers looking to go beyond the hubbub of Quintana Roo's resort towns, Mérida attracts many tourists, but is too big to feel like a tourist trap. And as the capital of Yucatán state, Mérida is also the cultural crossroads of the region.

History

Francisco de Montejo (the Younger) founded a Spanish colony at Campeche, about 160km to the southwest, in 1540. From this base he took advantage of political dissension among the Maya, conquering T'ho (now Mérida) in 1542. By decade's end Yucatán was mostly under Spanish colonial rule.

When Montejo's conquistadors entered T'ho, they found a major Maya settlement of lime-mortared stone that reminded them of the Roman architecture in Mérida, Spain. They promptly renamed the city and proceeded to build it into the regional capital, dismantling the Maya structures and using the materials to construct a cathedral and other stately buildings. Mérida took its colonial orders directly from Spain, not from Mexico City, and Yucatán has had a distinct cultural and political identity ever since.

During the War of the Castes only Mérida and Campeche were able to hold out against the rebel forces. On the brink of surrender, the ruling class in Mérida was saved by reinforcements sent from central Mexico in exchange for Mérida's agreement to take orders from Mexico City.

Mérida today is the peninsula's center of commerce, a bustling city that has been growing rapidly ever since *maquiladoras* (low-paying, for-export factories) started cropping up in the 1980s and '90s, and as the tourism industry picked up during those decades as well. The growth has drawn migrant workers from all around Mexico. and there's a large Lebanese community in town.

☉ Sights

★**Gran Museo del Mundo Maya**   MUSEUM
(☑ 999-341-04-30; www.granmuseodelmundo maya.com.mx; Calle 60 Norte 299E; adult/child under 13yr M$150/25; ☺ 9am-5pm Wed-Mon; ℗) A world-class museum celebrating Maya culture, the Gran Museo houses a permanent collection of more than 1100 remarkably well-preserved artifacts, including a reclining chac-mool sculpture from Chichén Itzá and a cool underworld figure unearthed at Ek' Balam (check out his punk-rock skull belt and reptile headdress). If you're planning on visiting the area's ruins, drop by here first for some context and an up-close look at some of the fascinating pieces found at the sites.

Inaugurated in 2012, the contemporary building was designed in the form of a ceiba, a sacred tree believed by the Maya to connect the living with the underworld and the heavens above. On a wall outside, the museum offers a free **light-and-sound show** at night.

You'll find it about 12km north of downtown on the road to Progreso. Public transportation running along Calle 60 will leave you at the museum's entrance.

★ **Palacio Cantón**   MUSEUM
(Regional Anthropology Museum; ☎999-923-05-57; Paseo de Montejo 485; adult/child under 13yr M$60/free; ⊙8am-5pm Tue-Sun) This massive mansion was built between 1909 and 1911, though its owner, General Francisco Cantón Rosado (1833–1917), lived here for only six years before his death. The Palacio's splendor and pretension make it a fitting symbol of the grand aspirations of Mérida's elite during the last years of the Porfiriato – the period from 1876 to 1911 when Porfirio Díaz held despotic sway over Mexico.

It hosts temporary exhibitions and the entry fee may depend on what's on.

Casa de Montejo   MUSEUM
(Museo Casa Montejo; ☎999-253-67-39; www.fomentoculturalbanamex.org; Calle 63 No 506, Palacio de Montejo; ⊙10am-7pm Tue-Sat, to 2pm Sun) FREE Casa de Montejo is on the south side of Plaza Grande and dates from 1540. It originally housed soldiers, but was soon converted into a mansion that served members of the Montejo family until the 1800s. Today it houses a bank and museum with a permanent exhibition of renovated Victorian, neo-rococo and neo-renaissance furnishings of the historic building.

Outside, take a close look at the facade, where triumphant conquistadors with halberds stand on the heads of generic barbarians (though they're not Maya, the association is inescapable). Typical of the symbolism in colonial statuary, the vanquished are rendered much smaller than the victors; works on various churches throughout the region feature big priests towering over or in front of small indigenous people. Also gazing across the plaza from the facade are busts of Montejo the Elder, his wife and his daughter.

Parque Santa Lucía   PARK
(cnr Calles 60 & 55) The pretty little Parque Santa Lucía has arcades on the north and west sides; this was where travelers would get on or off the stagecoaches that linked towns and villages with the provincial capital. Today it's a popular restaurant area and venue for **Serenatas Yucatecas** (Yucatecan Serenades), a free weekly concert on Thursday at 9pm.

BIKE-FRIENDLY MÉRIDA
....
In an effort to make the city more bike-friendly, Mérida closes down stretches of Paseo de Montejo and Calle 60 to traffic on Sunday morning. For night tours, the bicycle collective **Ciclo Turixes** (www.facebook.com/colectivociclo turixes) gathers at Parque Santa Ana most Wednesdays at around 8:30pm.

Museo Fernando García Ponce-Macay   MUSEUM
(Museo de Arte Contemporáneo; ☎999-928-32-36; www.macay.org; Pasaje de la Revolución s/n, btwn Calles 58 & 60; ⊙10am-5:15pm Wed-Mon) FREE Housed in the former archbishop's palace, the attractive museum's impressive collection holds permanent exhibitions of three of Yucatán's most famous painters of the Realist and Ruptura periods (Fernando Castro Pacheco, Fernando García Ponce and Gabriel Ramírez Aznar), as well as rotating exhibitions of contemporary art from Mexico and abroad.

Paseo de Montejo   ARCHITECTURE
Paseo de Montejo, which runs parallel to Calles 56 and 58, was an attempt by Mérida's 19th-century city planners to create a wide boulevard similar to the Paseo de la Reforma in Mexico City or the Champs-Élysées in Paris. Though more modest than its predecessors, the Paseo de Montejo is still a beautiful green swath of relatively open space in an urban conglomeration of stone and concrete, and there are some wonderful buildings built along it.

Plaza Grande   PLAZA
One of the nicest plazas in Mexico, huge laurel trees shade the park's benches and wide sidewalks. It was the religious and social center of ancient T'ho; under the Spanish it was the Plaza de Armas, the parade ground, laid out by Francisco de Montejo (the Younger).

A ceremony is held daily marking the raising and lowering of the Mexican flag, there's a crafts market on Sunday, and dance or live music nearly every night.

Catedral de San Ildefonso   CATHEDRAL
(Calle 60 s/n; ⊙6am-noon & 4:30-8pm) On the site of a former Maya temple is Mérida's hulking, severe cathedral, begun in 1561 and completed in 1598. Some of the stone from the Maya temple was used in its construction. The massive crucifix behind the altar

Mérida

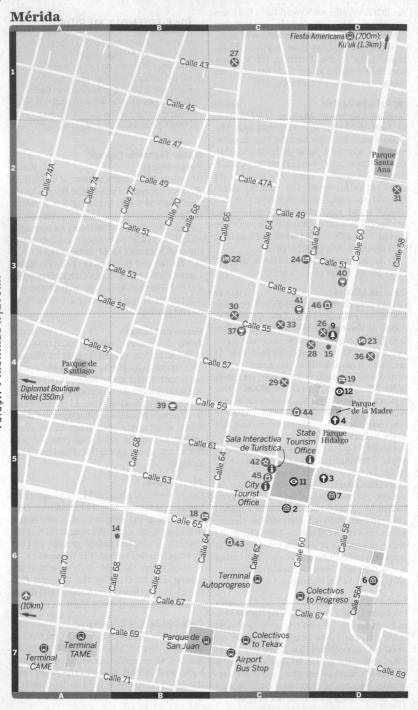

Fiesta Americana (700m);
Ku'uk (1.3km)

Calle 43

27

Calle 45

Calle 47

Parque
Santa
Ana

Calle 74A

Calle 74

Calle 72

Calle 49

Calle 70

Calle 68

Calle 47A

Calle 47A

31

Calle 51

Calle 66

Calle 64

Calle 49

Calle 62

Calle 60

Calle 58

Calle 53

22

24

Calle 51

40

Calle 55

Calle 53

41

46

30

33

26

9

37

Calle 55

28

15

23

36

Calle 57

Calle 57

29

19

Parque de
Santiago

12

Diplomat Boutique
Hotel (350m)

39

Calle 59

44

Parque
de la Madre

4

Calle 68

Calle 61

State
Tourism
Office

Parque
Hidalgo

Calle 64

Sala Interactiva
de Turística

Calle 63

42

45

City
Tourist
Office

11

3

7

2

18

Calle 65

14

43

Calle 64

Calle 70

Calle 68

Calle 66

Calle 62

Calle 60

Calle 58

Terminal
Autoprogreso

Calle 56A

Calle 67

6

Colectivos
to Progreso

(10km)

Calle 67

Calle 69

Calle 69

Terminal TAME

Parque de
San Juan

Colectivos
to Tekax

Terminal
CAME

Airport
Bus Stop

Calle 71

Calle 69

is **Cristo de la Unidad** (Christ of Unity), a symbol of reconciliation between those of Spanish and Maya heritage.

To the right over the south door is a painting of Tutul Xiu, *cacique* (indigenous chief) of the town of Maní paying his respects to his ally Francisco de Montejo at T'ho. (De Montejo and Xiu jointly defeated the Cocome people; Xiu converted to Christianity, and his descendants still live in Mérida.)

In the small chapel to the left of the altar is Mérida's most famous religious artifact, a statue called **Cristo de las Ampollas** (Christ of the Blisters). Local legend says the statue was carved from a tree that was hit by lightning and burned for an entire night without charring. It is also said to be the only object to have survived the fiery destruction of the church in the town of Ichmul (though it was blackened and blistered from the heat). The statue was moved to the Mérida cathedral in 1645.

Other than these items, the cathedral's interior is largely plain, its rich decoration having been stripped away by angry peasants at the height of anticlerical fervor during the Mexican Revolution.

Museo de Arte Popular de Yucatán
MUSEUM

(Yucatán Museum of Popular Art; Calle 50A No 487; ☉10am-5pm Tue-Sat, to 3pm Sun) **FREE** In a building constructed in 1906, the Museo de Arte Popular de Yucatán has a small rotating exhibition downstairs that features popular art from around Mexico. The permanent exhibition upstairs gives you an idea of how locals embroider *huipiles* (long, woven, white sleeveless tunics with intricate, colorful embroidery) and it explains traditional techniques used to make ceramics. Watch out for jaguars drinking toilet water!

Museo de la Ciudad
MUSEUM

(City Museum; ☎999-924-42-64; Calle 56 No 529A, btwn Calles 65 & 65A; ☉9am-6pm Tue-Fri, to 2pm Sat & Sun) **FREE** The Museo de la Ciudad is housed in the old post office and offers a great reprieve from the hustle, honks and exhaust of this market neighborhood. There are exhibits tracing the city's history back to preconquest days up through the belle-epoque period, when *henequén* (sisal) brought riches to the region, and into the 20th century.

Iglesia de Jesús
CHURCH

(Iglesia de la Tercera Orden; Calle 60 s/n) The 17th-century Iglesia de Jesús was built by Jesuits in 1618. It's the sole surviving edifice

Mérida

from a complex of buildings that once filled the entire city block. The church was built from the stones of a destroyed Maya temple that had occupied the site. On the west wall facing Parque Hidalgo, look closely and you can see two stones still bearing Maya carvings.

Teatro Peón Contreras   THEATER
(☏ 923-13-34-35; www.sinfonicadeyucatan.com. mx; cnr Calles 60 & 57; tickets from M$150; ⊙9am-9pm) The enormous Teatro Peón Contreras was built between 1900 and 1908, during Mérida's *henequén* heyday. It boasts a main staircase of Carrara marble, a dome with faded frescoes by Italian artists, and various paintings and murals throughout the building. The **Yucatán Symphony Orchestra** performs here Friday at 9pm and Sunday at noon (in season). See the website for more information.

➢ Courses & Tours

Los Dos   COOKING
(☏ 999-191-26-20; www.los-dos.com; Calle 68 No 517; 1-day courses & tours from US$125) Formerly run by the late US-educated chef David Sterling, this cooking school continues to offer courses with a focus on flavors of the Yucatán under the direction of chef Mario Canul, who worked with David for many years. It offers a one-day *cocina económica* class for US$125 per person and a Taste of Yucatán Class for US$200 per person.

Instituto Benjamín Franklin   LANGUAGE
(☏ 999-928-00-97; www.benjaminfranklin.com.mx; Calle 57 No 474A; 1hr class US$18) This nonprofit teaches intensive Spanish-language courses.

★**Turitransmérida**   TOURS
(☏ 999-924-11-99; http://turitransmerida.com. mx; Calle 55, btwn Calles 60 & 62; ⊙8am-7pm Mon-Fri, to 1pm Sat, to 11am Sun) Turitransmérida does good day-long group tours to sites around Mérida, including Celestún (M$950 per person), Chichén Itzá (M$750), Uxmal and Kabah (M$700), and Izamal (M$700). Also does a day trip around the Ruta Puuc (M$850). You can arrange in advance for guides who speak your language. Four-person minimum.

Nómadas Travel TOURS
(☑ 999-924-52-23; www.nomadastravel.com; Calle 62 No 433) Nómadas arranges a variety of tours, such as day trips including transportation and guide to Reserva de la Biosfera Ría Celestún (M$1100) and outings to Chichén Itzá (M$750) and Uxmal, Yaxkopoil and a cenote (M$750). The hostel also provides informative DIY sheets with written instructions detailing costs and transportation tips for more than a dozen destinations in the region.

✦ Festivals & Events

Mérida Fest CULTURAL
(www.merida.gob.mx; ☉ Jan) This cultural event held throughout most of January celebrates the founding of the city with art exhibits, concerts, theater and book presentations at various venues.

Festival de las Aves Toh FESTIVAL
(Toh Bird Festival; www.festivalavesyucatan. com; ☉ Feb-Nov) Toh holds various events throughout the year, culminating with a 'bird-a-thon' (bird-counting competition) in late November.

Otoño Cultural CULTURAL
(www.culturayucatan.com; ☉ Sep & Oct) Typically held in September and October, this three-week autumn fest stages more than 100 music, dance, visual-art and theater events.

Paseo de Ánimas STREET CARNIVAL
(Festival of Souls; ☉ around Oct 31) Hundreds of locals flaunt their skeleton-style and parade through the altar-lined streets for Day of the Dead celebrations. Musical renditions, artist performances and local food carts add to the festivities.

⌂ Sleeping

★**Nómadas Hostel** HOSTEL $
(☑ 999-924-52-23; www.nomadashostel.mx; Calle 62 No 433; dm from M$215, d M$640, without bathroom M$500, incl breakfast; P ❋ ☞ ☲) One of Mérida's best hostels, Nómadas has mixed and women's dorms as well as private rooms with bathroom. Guests have use of a fully equipped kitchen, as well as spotless showers, toilets and hand-laundry facilities. It even has free salsa, yoga, *trova* (troubadour-type folk music) and cooking classes, and an amazing pool out back that is always buzzing with a young party-friendly crowd.

The owner, Señor Raul, was one of the first 'contemporary' hosteliers in Mexico, and he knows his stuff. See the website for various tours to nearby ruins.

Hostel Le Juj HOSTEL $
(☑ 999-285-43-23, 999-285-41-61; Calle 59 No 596; dm/d incl breakfast M$150/450; ❊ ❋ ☞) Named after a small type of local black iguana, Le Juj (pronounced *khookh*) is just west of downtown Mérida and has a spacious and stylishly minimalist lobby leading to private rooms and dorms upstairs (each of which has its own bathroom) and a small kitchen, plunge pool and social area downstairs. The whole place exudes an atmospheric *meridano* charm.

There is currently wi-fi downstairs only.

Casona Hostel Boutique HOSTEL $
(☑ 999-268-98-19; www.hostelmerida65.wixsite. com/casonahostal; Calle 65 No 523A, btwn Calle 64 & 66; dm M$200, r M$700-800; ☞ ☲) This charming addition to Mérida's hostel scene has an enviable location in a converted colonial building just a couple of blocks from Plaza Grande. There are six rooms, of which two are privates and four dorms (one is female only). There's a lovely large courtyard with a well in the middle, a pool and small gym to boot.

Hotel La Piazzetta HOTEL $
(☑ 999-923-39-09; www.hotellapiazzettamerida. com; Calle 50A No 493, btwn Calles 57 & 59; d incl breakfast from M$750; ❊ ❋ ☞) Off a quiet side street overlooking **Parque de la Mejorada**, this friendly little hotel has lovely views of the park or the pleasant patio area. Each of the well-appointed rooms is decked out with a contemporary feel: stressed wooden tables, hanging baskets with towels and the like. Bike loans are available. An airy, pleasant onsite cafe forms the lobby.

★**Luz en Yucatán** HOTEL $$
(☑ 999-924-00-35; www.luzenyucatan.com; Calle 55 No 499; r US$58-100; P ❊ ❋ ☞ ☲) Luz en Yucatán has a perfect downtown location, 15 individually decorated rooms, fabulous common areas and a wonderful pool-patio area out back that combine to make it one of Mérida's very best accommodations. Knowledgeable and enthusiastic owners Tom and Donard and their helpful, English-speaking staff assist with every need and can arrange tours and activities.

A free tasting bar lets you sip tequila, triple sec or anise liqueur any time, while a new coffee shop was being built when we visited.

Casa Ana B&B   B&B $$

(☑999-181-66-55, 999-924-00-05; www.casa ana.com; Calle 52 No 469; r incl breakfast US$50; ⊜❋❂≋) Casa Ana is a casual but intimate escape and one of the best deals in town. It has a small pool and a cozy overgrown garden. The four rooms are spotless and have Mexican hammocks and mosquito screens. The Cuban owner Ana is on site, which adds a personal, friendly touch.

Hotel Julamis   BOUTIQUE HOTEL $$

(☑999-924-18-18, cell 998-1885508; www.hotel julamis.com; Calle 53 No 475B; r incl breakfast US$75-110; ❋❂) The highlight of this B&B is its breakfast, prepared by the gourmet-chef owner, Alex. The rooms are very pleasant (each features unique design details, such as colorful murals and original tiled floors), if a tad tired. But the 6pm tequila tastings and sociable happy hour make for a pleasant stay. All rooms come with fridges stocked daily with free beverages.

★**Casa Lecanda**   BOUTIQUE HOTEL $$$

(☑999-928-01-12; www.casalecanda.com; Calle 47 No 471, btwn Calles 54 & 56; d/ste incl breakfast from US$290/393; ❋❂≋) Behind its beautiful but unassuming facade, Casa Lecanda is a cut above Mérida's other boutique options thanks to attention to detail in both the design and the guest service. A 19th-century mansion stuffed with antiques and restored to stunning effect, it only has seven rooms, each decorated with a nod to traditional styles while including plentiful amenities and luxurious bathrooms.

The courtyard surrounds a small pool, which looked like it needed a bit of a refresh on our last visit, but there's a lovely shady area for hammocks and lush gardens. Continental breakfasts are served in the colonial-style dining room and an array of tequilas and Mexican wines can be sampled at the bar.

★**Diplomat Boutique Hotel**   B&B $$$

(☑999-117-29-72; www.thediplomatmerida.com; Calle 78 No 493A, btwn Calles 59 & 59A; r US$175-325; ⊜❋❂≋) A beautiful, intimate oasis, just southwest of the historic center in a neighborhood of Santiago, the Diplomat oozes style and charm. The four rooms err on minimalist, with touches of flair such as greenery and tasteful ornamentation. The hospitable Canadian hosts provide a gourmet breakfast spread served on the terrace, treats by the pool, and fabulous ideas for cuisine and exploration.

While high-season rates may be pushing the budget (and often require a minimum three-night stay), low-season rates provide better value. As if things couldn't get better, a complimentary tequila bar and welcome cocktails await.

Rosas y Xocolate   BOUTIQUE HOTEL $$$

(☑999-924-29-92; www.rosasandxocolate.com; Paseo de Montejo 480; r/ste from US$327/505; ℗❋❂≋) Built from the remains of two mansions and reusing much of the original materials, this medium-sized hotel is rosy indeed, though much of its interior is painted in restrained and muted tones. It goes all out with custom-made furniture, Nespresso machines, Bose sound systems and open-air baths in each room. An air-conditioned gym, full day spa and gourmet restaurant are also onsite.

Los Arcos Bed & Breakfast   B&B $$$

(☑999-928-02-14; www.losarcosmerida.com; Calle 66 No 448B; d incl breakfast US$85-95; ℗⊜❋❂≋) Certainly not for minimalists – there's art on every wall and knickknacks filling every space – Los Arcos is a lovely, gay-friendly ('everyone-friendly') B&B with two guestrooms at the end of a drop-dead-gorgeous garden and pool area. Rooms have an eclectic assortment of art and antiques, plus excellent beds and bathrooms. No pets or minors.

Hotel Casa del Balam   HOTEL $$$

(☑999-924-88-44; www.casadelbalam.com; Calle 60 No 488, btwn Calles 55 & 57; d/ste M$1800/3000; ℗⊜❋@❂≋) This place is centrally located, has an attractive pool and large, quiet colonial-style rooms with shiny tiles and extra-firm beds with wrought-iron bedheads. It often offers hefty discounts during quiet times, which make it solid value.

✗ Eating

Mérida is a culinary treat, with all kinds of cuisines for all kinds of budgets. You can dine on cheap but mind-blowingly delicious street food or try modern Mexican and international fusion at a range of world-class establishments. Don't miss **Mérida en Domingo**, an all-day food and crafts market in the Plaza Grande every Sunday. It's a great place to try a wide variety of regional dishes at bargain prices.

★**Pola**   ICE CREAM $

(☑999-330-34-41; www.polagelato.com; Calle 55 s/n, btwn Calles 62 & 64; ice cream from M$30;

noon-10pm Mon-Sat, from 11am Sun) You'd head to this place even if were you in the Arctic, it's that good. Get your tongue around full-cream, 100% natural gelati with some of the quirkiest flavours in ice-cream land. Flan de la Cubanita (Cuban-style vanilla custard) is quite addictive, while other flavors include cardamom, blue cheese and apple, and avocado.

Wayan'e
TACOS $

(999-291-94-22; cnr Calles 59 & 46; tacos M$14-20, tortas M$22-50; 7am-2:30pm Mon-Sat) Popular for its *castakan* (crispy pork belly), Wayan'e (meaning 'here it is' in Maya) is one of Mérida's premier breakfast spots. Vegetarians will find options here, such as the *huevo con xkatic* (egg with chili) taco and fresh juices. But if you eat meat, it's all about the greasy goodness of the *castakan torta* (crispy pork-belly sandwich).

Taquería de la Union
TACOS $

(999-389-60-77; www.facebook.com/taqueria delaunionmid; Calle 55 No 488; tacos M$15-22; 8am-midnight Mon-Sat, to 5pm Sun;) The sharp minds behind this superb *taquería* combine the flavors and variety found on taco carts all over town, but in a pristine, air-conditioned environment with comfortable seating and table service to boot. A good option for anyone not too keen on trying street food, but interested in sampling authentic local fillings: don't miss the *cochinita pibil.*

★ SOCO Mérida
BAKERY $$

(999-458-06-55; Calle 51 No 492C; mains M$90-160; 7am-3pm Tue-Sun;) This smart, friendly bakery and breakfast joint has an open kitchen, a stylish bar counter for single diners and a great jazz-and-blues soundtrack. You'll find some of the best eggs Benedict in Mexico here, served on a crispy croissant. The coffee and pastries are also superb.

Bistro Cultural
FRENCH $$

(Calle 66 No 377C, btwn Calles 41 & 43; mains breakfast M$60-80, lunch M$95-125; 8:30am-5:30pm Mon-Sat, to 4:30pm Sun;) While the cuisine is French, the influence is Yucatecan, and locally grown, organic products are used where possible. The small menu varies but includes a local twist on a croque monsieur, and there is a daily special on top of the normal menu, all served in a pleasant courtyard garden. Delectable French pastries (M$15 to M$20) are also on sale.

Sukra Bar de Café
CAFE $$

(999-923-44-53; www.facebook.com/sukracafe; Paseo de Montejo 496, btwn Calles 43 & 45; mains M$70-135; 9am-6pm Mon-Sat, to 2pm Sun;) This easygoing spot, at the beginning of Paseo de Montejo, is framed by pretty plants and features an eclectic mix of tables and chairs, more reminiscent of a great aunt's house than a cafe overlooking the poshest street in town. The excellent salads and sandwiches are equally as down to earth. Dig in and watch the world go by.

Manjar Blanco
MEXICAN $$

(999-923-00-03; www.facebook.com/elmanjar blanco; Calle 47, btwn Calles 58 & 60; mains M$75-155; 8am-6pm;) This modernised colonial building with contemporary local art on the walls puts a gourmet twist on regional favorites and makes a good downtown lunch spot between museums. The *tortillitas tropicales* (fried plantains topped with smoked pork) are delicious, while the house specialty, *queso relleno* (a stuffed ball of cheese filled with ground meat and spices) is also superb.

Lo Que Hay
VEGAN $$

(999-924-54-72; www.hotelmediomundo.com; Calle 55 No 533; 3-course menu M$200; 7-10pm Tue-Sat;) Even nonvegans usually give an enthusiastic thumbs up to this dinner-only restaurant, where three-course themed vegan meals are served in a serene courtyard. The dishes range from Mexican and Lebanese cuisine to raw vegan. Lo Que Hay is in the Hotel Medio Mundo and it welcomes nonguests.

★ Oliva Enoteca
ITALIAN $$$

(999-923-30-81; www.olivamerida.com; cnr Calles 47 & 54; mains M$190-600; 1-5pm & 7pm-midnight Mon-Sat;) This contemporary restaurant with black-and-white tiled floors, Edison light bulbs, designer chairs and an open kitchen is a magnet for the local smart set who descend en masse for excellent and creative Italian cuisine. Those craving something other than a margarita will love the cocktail selection, as well as the wines. Desserts are to die for.

★ Ku'uk
INTERNATIONAL $$$

(999-944-33-77; www.kuukrestaurant.com; Av Rómulo Rozo 488, cnr Calle 27; mains M$290-550, tasting menu M$1600, with wine pairing M$2500; 1:30-11pm Tue-Sat, to 5pm Sun) The stunning historic home, at the end of Paseo Montejo, sets the scene for what's to come: a high-end, gourmet meal that will end up setting a very high benchmark for Mexican cuisine. You can dine in a number of elegant,

YUCATÁN PENINSULA MÉRIDA

BACK ROADS SOUTH OF MÉRIDA

Hacienda Yaxcopoil (📞999-900-11-93; www.yaxcopoil.com; Hwy 261 Km 186; adult/child under 12yr M$100/free; ⏰8am-6pm Mon-Sat, 9am-3pm Sun; 🅿🚻) If you visit one hacienda, make it this one. This vast estate grew and processed henequén (agave plant fibers, used to make rope); many of its numerous French Renaissance–style buildings have undergone picturesque restorations. The interior of the main building is superb. You can enter the sheds with the giant rasping machines that turned the leaves into fiber. The caretaker used to work cutting henequén and has stories to share (should you speak Spanish; tip suggested).

Hacienda San Pedro Ochil (📞999-924-74-65; www.facebook.com/haciendasanpedroochil yucatan; Hwy 261 Mérida–Muna Km 175; M$40; ⏰10am-6pm; 🅿🚻) There's no lodging (or old house) here, but it provides an interesting look at how henequén was grown and processed. From the parking lot, follow the tracks once used by small wheeled carts to haul materials to and from the processing plant. You'll pass hemp and filigree workshops, and a small museum with changing exhibitions. The casa de maquinas (machine shed) and smokestack still stand.

Grutas de Calcehtok (Grutas de X'Pukil; 📞cell 999-2627292; off Hwy 184; tours M$100-300; ⏰8am-5pm; 🅿🚻) The Calcehtok caves are said to comprise the longest dry-cave system on the Yucatán Peninsula. More than 4km have been explored so far, and two of the caves' 25 vaults exceed 100m in diameter (one has a 30m-high 'cupola'). The caves hold abundant and impressive natural formations; however, if you're claustrophobic, have a fear of dark spaces or don't like getting dirty, this definitely isn't for you.

Oxkintok (www.inah.gob.mx; M$60, guides M$600; ⏰8am-5pm; 🅿) Archaeologists have been excited about the ruins of Oxkintok for several years. Inscriptions found at the site contain some of the oldest-known dates in the Yucatán, and indicate the city was inhabited from the pre-Classic to the post-Classic period (300 BCE to 1500 CE), reaching its greatest importance between 475 and 860 CE.

Cenote X-Batún & Dzonbakal (📞999-132-80-26; San Antonio Mulix; M$80; ⏰9am-5:45pm) A cooperative from the tiny village of San Antonio Mulix runs this lovely swimming spot consisting of two cenotes, 800m apart. Pay at the Centro Comunitario, then drive 2km along a dirt road. At the end of the road turn right to X-Batún or left to Dzonbakal. X-Batún enjoys far more sunlight and is the more attractive of the two, though Dzonbakal is perhaps the more atmospheric, with its cenote essentially a giant cave you can swim in.

if slightly bare, rooms. The cuisine gives a nod to Yucatecan cuisine with contemporary preparation and flavor twists.

⭐ **Apoala**　　　　　　　　　　　MEXICAN $$$
(📞999-923-19-79; www.apoala.mx; Calle 60 No 471, Parque Santa Lucía; mains M$140-480; ⏰1pm-midnight Mon-Sat, 2-10pm Sun; 🛜) With influences from Oaxaca, which like the Yucatán is known for its extraordinary regional cuisine, Apoala reinvents popular dishes such as *enmoladas* (stuffed tortillas in a rich *mole* sauce) and *tlayudas* (a large tortilla with sliced beef, black beans and Oaxaca cheese). It's in a lovely spot on Parque Santa Lucía and also boasts some of Mérida's best cocktails.

Nectar　　　　　　　　　　　YUCATECAN $$$
(📞999-938-08-38; www.nectarmerida.mx; Av García Lavín 32; mains M$192-605; ⏰1:30pm-midnight Tue-

Sat, 2-6pm Sun) Inventive and delicious takes on traditional Yucatecan cuisine, a setting that would win design awards and superfriendly staff make for a winning combination at this north Mérida destination restaurant (take a taxi). The pork-belly tacos, *cebollas negras* (blackened onions), venison tartare and any of the fish mains are all superb and well worth the price and distance.

La Chaya Maya　　　　　　　　MEXICAN $$$
(📞999-928-22-95; www.lachayamaya.com; Calle 55 No 510; mains M$100-340; ⏰7:30am-11pm; 🛜) Popular with locals and tourists alike, this restaurant's main outlet can be found in charming downtown premises that are always busy. Consider La Chaya your introduction to classic Yucatecan fare (and it's a good one): dishes include *relleno negro* (black turkey stew) and *cochinita pibil*.

South of Mérida

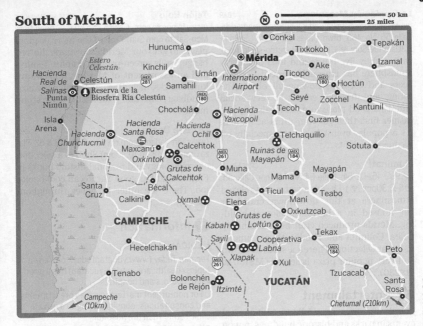

The **original location** (☑999-928-47-80; cnr Calles 62 & 57; mains M$100-340; ☺7am-11pm; 🛜) can be found just off Parque Santa Lucia.

Eureka
ITALIAN $$$

(☑999-926-26-94; www.facebook.com/eureka cucinaitaliana; Av Rotary Internacional 117, cnr Calle 52; mains M$150-350; ☺1:30-10:30pm; P🛜🐾) A stylish, intimate Italian spot outside the center. The signature dish of chef Fabrizio Di Stazio is the *riccioli eureka,* freshly made pasta in white ragu sauce with mushrooms and an aromatic hint of truffle. It's east of Paseo Montejo and an easy taxi ride. Try some homemade *limoncello* (lemon liqueur) after the meal.

🍷 Drinking & Nightlife

★Pipiripau Bar
COCKTAIL BAR

(Calle 62 No 461; ☺5pm–2am Sun-Thu, from 1pm Fri & Sat) This historic cantina is easily one of Mérida's most charming and atmospheric spots. Its gorgeous bar is original and there are several grand rooms for knocking back the excellent mezcal cocktails, as well as a garden where there is sometimes live music. This is a real hotspot on the weekend, when it's often packed with locals and visitors alike.

★Manifesto
COFFEE

(www.manifesto.mx; Calle 59 No 538, btwn Calles 66 and 68; ☺8am-9pm Mon-Sat; 🛜) This place, run by a trio from Calabria, Italy, offers an ambitious 'manifesto' indeed: a revolution in coffee brought about by fusing Italian preparation methods with the very best beans Mexico has to offer. It's a compelling combination, and the sleek premises is the kind of place where you'll want to order your coffee to drink in.

They roast their beans here, too, and you can buy packets with beans originating from all over Southern Mexico.

Mercado 60
COCKTAIL BAR

(www.mercado60.com; Calle 60, btwn Calles 51 & 53; ☺6pm-late) For a fun night of booze and cheap(ish) international eats, head to this atmospheric, lively and diverse culinary market, where the margaritas will have you dancing alongside locals to live salsa music. This modern concept is a cocktail bar meets beer hall, with different businesses serving up different concoctions.

The cuisine – ranging from Mexican gourmet tacos to ramen noodles – is also served from small kiosks. Dishes, while tasty, could be better but they do the 'soaking-up' trick...

La Fundación Mezcalería BAR

(www.facebook.com/lafundacionmezcaleriamerida; Calle 56 No 465, btwn Calles 53 & 55; ⏲8pm-2:30am Tue-Sun; 🛜) This loud, retro-styled bar with nightly live music and tons of Mérida atmosphere has reasonably priced mezcals, beers and cocktails flowing all night. The young and friendly crowd is very social and it's a good place to meet locals. Pay the cashier first, then get your drink at the bar. It's a popular cyclist hangout, especially on Wednesday nights.

Illuminati CRAFT BEER

(📞999-461-02-64; Calle 64 No 461, cnr Calle 55; ⏲5-11:30pm; 🛜) There's a warm and relaxed atmosphere at this downtown craft-beer bar housed in a barnlike colonial building. Mérida-produced craft beers including Ceiba, Colimita and Thodes Ale are among its great selection. There's a student crowd and very popular pizza is served (M$100 to M$230).

☆ Entertainment

Mérida organizes many folkloric and musical events in parks and historic buildings, put on by local performers of considerable skill. Admission is mostly free. The tourist publication *Yucatán Today* has a good summary of weekly events.

Centro Cultural Olimpo CONCERT VENUE

(📞999-924-00-00 ext 80130; www.merida.gob. mx/capitalcultural; cnr Calles 62 & 61) This cultural center on Plaza Grande always has something going on: films, concerts, art installations and other events, many of which are free.

🛍 Shopping

Guayaberas Jack CLOTHING

(Calle 59 No 507A; ⏲10am-8pm Mon-Sat) The *guayabera* (embroidered dress shirt) is the classic Mérida shirt, but in buying the wrong one you run the risk of looking like a waiter. Drop into this famous shop to avoid getting asked for the bill.

Cielo Hamacas ARTS & CRAFTS

(📞999-924-04-40; www.hamacasmerida.com.mx; Calle 65 No 510, btwn Calles 62 & 64; ⏲9am-7pm Mon-Fri, to 1pm Sat) Has a large catalog with all kinds of sizes, shapes and colors of locally produced hammocks, Maya hanging chairs and all accessories for creating that perfect hang-out space. It can ship purchases worldwide.

Tejón Rojo GIFTS & SOUVENIRS

(www.tejonrojo.com; Calle 53 No 503; ⏲noon-9pm Mon-Sat, to 6pm Sun) One of the more original places to get your Mérida souvenirs, the 'red badger' sells screen-printed graphic T-shirts and an assortment of Mexican pop-culture knickknacks, including coffee mugs, jewelry, handbags, caps and – inevitably – wrestling masks.

Librería Dante BOOKS

(www.libreriadante.com.mx; cnr Calles 61 & 62, Plaza Grande; ⏲8am-10:30pm) Shelves a selection of archaeology and regional-history books in English and has good Yucatecan cookbooks, too. There are other branches throughout the city.

ⓘ Information

MEDICAL SERVICES

Yucatán Today (www.yucatantoday.com/en/topics/healthcare-merida-yucatan) has a good list of doctors and hospitals.

For non-urgent matters, such as prescriptions and consultations, consider going to a private clinic rather than the hospital.

Clínica de Mérida (📞999-942-18-00; www.clinicademerida.mx; Av Itzáes 242, cnr Calle 25; ⏲24hr; 🚌R-49) Good private clinic with laboratory and 24-hour emergency service.

Hospital O'Horán (📞999-930-33-20; cnr Avs de los Itzáes & Jacinto Canek; ⏲24hr) A centrally located public hospital for emergencies.

MONEY

Banks and ATMs are scattered throughout the city. There is a cluster of both along Calle 65 between Calles 60 and 62, one block south of Plaza Grande. *Casas de cambio* (money-exchange offices) have faster service and longer opening hours than banks, but often have poorer rates.

POST

Post Office (📞999-928-54-04; Calle 53 No 469, btwn Calles 52 & 54; ⏲8am-7pm Mon-Fri, to 3pm Sat) Central post office.

TOURIST INFORMATION

You'll find tourist information booths at the airport. Tourist offices downtown have basic brochures and information and maps.

City Tourist Office (📞ext 80119 999-942-00-00; www.merida.gob.mx/turismo; Calle 62, Plaza Grande; ⏲8am-8pm) Right on the main plaza, it is staffed with helpful English speakers. Here you can hook up free walking tours of the city, which depart daily at 9:30am.

State Tourist Office (📞999-930-31-01; www.yucatan.travel; Calle 61 s/n, Plaza Grande; ⏲8am-8pm) In the entrance to the Palacio de

DZIBILCHALTÚN

Lying about 17km due north of central Mérida, **Dzibilchaltún** (Place of Inscribed Flat Stones; M$152, parking M$20; ⊗ site 8am-5pm, museum 9am-5pm Tue-Sun, cenote 9am-3:30pm; **P**) was the longest continuously used Maya administrative and ceremonial city, serving from around 1500 BCE until the European conquest in the 1540s. At the height of its greatness, Dzibilchaltún covered 15 sq km. Some 8400 structures were mapped by archaeologists in the 1960s and only few of these have been excavated. Aside from the ruins, the site offers a lovely, swimmable cenote and a Maya museum.

Enter the site along a nature trail that terminates at the modern, air-conditioned **Museo del Pueblo Maya**, featuring artifacts from throughout the Maya regions of Mexico, including some superb colonial-era religious carvings and other pieces. Exhibits explaining both ancient and modern Maya daily life are labeled in Spanish and English. Beyond the museum, a path leads to the **central plaza**, where you'll find an **open chapel** that dates from early Spanish times (1590–1600).

In some ways the site might feel a little unimpressive if you've already seen larger places, but twice a year humble Dzibilchaltún truly shines, in some ways even more than Chichén Itzá; at sunrise on the equinoxes (approximately March 20 and September 22), the sun aligns directly with the main door of the **Templo de las Siete Muñecas** (Temple of the Seven Dolls), which got its name from seven grotesque dolls discovered here during excavations. As the sun rises, the temple doors glow, then 'light up' as the sun passes behind. It also casts a cool square beam on the crumbled wall behind. Many who have seen both feel the sunrise here is more spectacular than Chichén Itzá's famous snake, and is well worth getting up at the crack of dawn to witness.

Within the site, the **Cenote Xlacah** is more than 40m deep and a fine spot for a swim after exploring the ruins. In 1958 a National Geographic Society diving expedition recovered more than 30,000 Maya artifacts, many of ritual significance, from the cenote. The most interesting of these are now on display in the site's museum. South of the cenote is **Estructura 44** – at 130m it's one of the longest Maya structures in existence. Note that for some reason you're not allowed to bring backpacks into the ruins, so plan accordingly.

Chablekal-bound *colectivos* depart frequently from Calle 58 (between Calles 57 and 59) in Mérida. They'll drop you about 300m from the site's entrance.

Gobierno. There's usually an English speaker on hand.

Sala Interactiva (Calle 62, btwn Calles 61 and 63, Palacio Municipal; ⊗ 9am-8pm) On the plaza, with fancy touch screens and multimedia info displays.

🛈 Getting There & Away

AIR

Aeropuerto Internacional de Mérida (Mérida International Airport; ☑ 999-940-60-90; www.asur.com.mx; Hwy 180 Km 4.5; 🚌 R-79) is a 10km, 20-minute ride southwest of Plaza Grande off Hwy 180 (Av de los Itzáes). It has car-rental desks, several ATMs, currency-exchange services and an information desk to assist you to find transportation into town.

Most international travelers to Mérida will need to make connections through Mexico City. Nonstop international services are provided by Aeroméxico and United Airlines.

Low-cost airlines Interjet, VivaAerobus and Volaris serve Mexico City. Mayair operates pro-peller planes to Cancún and Cozumel. All of the airlines have offices at the airport.

Aeroméxico (☑ 800-021-40-00; www.aeromexico.com) Flies direct from Miami.

Interjet (☑ 800-011-23-45, US 866-285-9525; www.interjet.com) Serves Mexico City, where you can catch connecting flights to New York, Miami and Houston.

Mayair (☑ 800-962-92-47; www.mayair.com.mx) Runs propeller planes to Cancún that continue on to Cozumel.

VivaAerobus (☑ 818-215-01-50, US 888-935-9848; www.vivaaerobus.com) Service to Mexico City and Monterrey.

Volaris (☑ Mexico City 55-1102-8000, US 866-988-3527; www.volaris.com) Direct to Mexico City and Monterrey.

BUS

Mérida is the bus transportation hub of the Yucatán Peninsula. Take care with your bags on night buses and those serving popular tourist destinations (especially 2nd-class buses): there have been reports of theft on some routes.

There are a number of bus terminals, and some lines operate from (and stop at) more than one terminal. Tickets for departure from one terminal can often be bought at another, and destinations overlap greatly among bus lines. Check out www.ado.com.mx for ticket info on some of the lines.

Terminal CAME (Terminal de Primera Clase; ☑ 999-924-08-30 ext 2406; Calle 70 s/n, btwn Calles 69 & 71; ⊙ 24hr; 🕾) Mérida's main bus terminal has (mostly 1st-class) buses – including ADO, OCC and ADO GL – to points around the Yucatán Peninsula and faraway places such as Mexico City.

Fiesta Americana Bus Terminal (☑ 999-924-83-91; cnr Calle 60 & Av Colón; 🚌 R-2) A small 1st-class terminal on the west side of the Fiesta Americana hotel complex servicing guests of the luxury hotels on Avenida Colón, north of downtown. ADO buses run between here and Cancún, Playa del Carmen, Villahermosa and Ciudad del Carmen.

Noreste Bus Terminal (Autobuses del Noreste y Autobuses Luz; ☑ 999-924-63-55; cnr Calles 50 & 67) Noreste and Luz bus lines use this terminal. Destinations served from here include many small towns in the northeast part of the peninsula, including Tizimín and Río Lagartos; Cancún and points along the way; and small towns south and west of Mérida, such as Celestún, Ticul, Ruinas de Mayapán and Oxkutzcab. Some Oriente buses depart from Terminal TAME and stop here.

Parque de San Juan (Calle 69, btwn Calles 62 & 64) From all around the square and church, *colectivos* (vans and minibuses) depart for Muna (M$30), Oxkutzcab (M$55), Tekax (M$75), Ticul (M$45) and other points, between about 5am and 10pm daily.

Terminal Autoprogreso (Progreso Bus Terminal; ☑ 999-928-39-65; www.autoprogreso.com; Calle 62 No 524; ⊙ 5am-10pm) There's a separate terminal with buses leaving for the northern beach town of Progreso.

Terminal TAME (Terminal de Segunda Clase; ☑ 999-924-08-30; Calle 69, btwn Calles 68 & 70; ⊙ 24hr) This terminal is just around the corner from Terminal CAME. ADO, Mayab, Oriente, Sur, TRT and ATS run mostly 2nd-class buses to points in the state and around the peninsula, including Ticul, Valladolid and Tizimín.

Colectivo to Tekax (Calle 62, btwn Calles 67 & 69)

Colectivo to Progreso (Calle 60)

CAR & MOTORCYCLE

The most flexible way to tour the many archaeological sites around Mérida is to travel with a rental

BUSES FROM MÉRIDA

DESTINATION	FARE (M$)	TIME (HR)	FREQUENCY (PER DAY) & TERMINAL
Campeche	264-341	2½-3	hourly (6am-11:45pm)
Cancún	476-496	4½-6½	hourly; Terminal CAME, Terminal TAME
Celestún	60	2½	frequent; Noreste, Terminal TAME
Chetumal	339-446	5½-6	3-4; Terminal TAME
Chichén Itzá	99-180	1½-2	frequent; Terminal CAME, Noreste, Terminal TAME
Escárcega	306-430	4-4½	3 (8:30am, 2:15pm, 9pm); Terminal TAME
Felipe Carrillo Puerto	234	6	frequent; Terminal TAME
Izamal	31	1½	frequent; Noreste
Mayapán	37	1½	hourly; Noreste
Mexico City	999-1900	20	7; Terminal CAME, Terminal TAME
Palenque	662-729	7½-10	4; Terminal CAME, Terminal TAME
Playa del Carmen	304-498	4-6	frequent; Terminal CAME, Terminal TAME
Progreso	21	1	frequent; Terminal Autoprogreso
Río Lagartos/San Felipe	170-250	3½	3 (5:30am, 9am, 4pm); Noreste
Ruta Puuc (round-trip; 30min at each site)	99	8-8½	weekly (8am Sunday); Terminal TAME
Ticul	57	1¾	frequent; Terminal TAME
Tizimín	125-190	4-5	frequent; Noreste
Tulum	205-356	4-4½	5; Terminal CAME, Terminal TAME
Uxmal	76	1½	5; Terminal TAME
Valladolid	125-240	2½-3	frequent; Terminal CAME, Terminal TAME

car. Assume you will pay M$1000 to M$2500 per day (tax and insurance included) for short-term rental of an economy-size vehicle. Getting around Mérida's sprawling tangle of one-way streets is normally better on foot or by bus, though driving is perfectly possible in the city as well.

Several agencies have branches at the airport and on Calle 60, between Calles 55 and 57. You'll get the best deal by booking online.

Easy Way (📲 999-930-95-00; www.easyway rentacar.com; Calle 60 No 484, btwn Calles 55 & 57; car rental incl basic insurance from US$50 per day; ⊘7am-11pm)

National (📲 999-923-24-93; www.national-car.com; Calle 60 No 486F, btwn Calles 55 & 57; economy car incl basic insurance from M$2500; ⊘8am-1pm & 4-8pm)

❶ Getting Around

TO/FROM THE AIRPORT

The taxi companies **Transporte Terrestre** (📲 999-946-15-29; www.transporteterrestre demerida.com; per car M$250) and **ADO** (📲 999-454-18-01; www.taxiadoaeropuerto. mx/en; M$250) provide speedy service between the airport and downtown, charging M$200 (same price for hotel pickup). A street taxi from downtown to the airport should cost M$120. If you want to get this same price *from* the airport, you'll need to walk out to the main road and flag down a city cab.

A city bus labeled 'Aviación 79' (M$8) travels between the main road of the airport entrance. The bus does not enter the airport, but instead **stops outside** (cnr Calles 62 & 69) and connects downtown every 15 to 30 minutes until 9pm, with occasional service until 11pm. The best place to catch the same bus to the airport is at Parque San Juan, from the corner of Calles 62 and 69.

BICYCLE

See the boxed text on p321.

BUS

City buses are cheap at M$8, but routes can be confusing. Some start in suburban neighborhoods, skirt downtown and terminate in another distant suburban neighborhood. **Transpublico. com** (https://merida.transpublico.com) provides detailed maps of all the routes.

To travel between Plaza Grande and the upscale neighborhoods to the north along Paseo de Montejo, catch the R-2 'Hyatt' or 'Tecnológico' lines along Calle 60. To return to downtown, catch any bus heading south on Paseo de Montejo displaying the same signs and/or 'Centro.' A bus heads to/from the airport, too.

TAXI

More and more taxis in town are using meters these days. If you get one with no meter, be sure to agree on a price before getting in. M$30 to M$50 is fair for getting around downtown and to the bus terminals. Taxi stands can be found at most of the barrio parks (dispatch fees may cost extra).

Radio Taxímetro del Volante (📲 999-928-30-35) For 24-hour radio taxi service.

Uxmal

Uxmal (pronounced oosh-mahl) is an impressive set of **ruins** (M$75; ⊘8am-5pm), easily ranking among the top (and unfortunately most crowded) Maya archaeological sites. It is a large site with some fascinating structures in good condition and bearing a riot of ornamentation. Adding to its appeal is Uxmal's setting near the hilly Puuc region, which lent its name to the architectural patterns in this area. *Puuc* means 'hills,' and these, rising to about 100m, are the first relief from the flatness of the northern and western portions of the peninsula.

For an additional cost, Uxmal projects a nightly **light-and-sound show**.

For an entirely different experience, outside the ruins, the **Choco-Story museum** (📲 999-289-99-14; www.choco-storymexico.com; Hwy 261 Km 78, near Hotel Hacienda Uxmal; adult/child 6-12yr M$140/90; ⊘9am-7:30pm) takes a look at the history of chocolate.

◉ Sights

Casa del Adivino   ARCHAEOLOGICAL SITE
(Pirámide del Adivino) As you approach Uxmal, the Casa del Adivino comes into view. This 35m-high temple (the name translates as 'Magician's House') was built in an unusual oval shape. What you see is a restored version of the temple's fifth incarnation, consisting of round stones held rudely together with lots of cement. Four earlier temples were completely covered in the final rebuilding by the Maya, except for the high doorway on the west side, which remains from the fourth temple.

Decorated in elaborate Chenes style (a style that originated further south), the doorway proper forms the mouth of a gigantic Chaac mask.

Cuadrángulo de las Monjas   ARCHAEOLOGICAL SITE
The 74-room, sprawling Nuns' Quadrangle is directly west of the Casa del Adivino. Archaeologists guess variously that it was a military academy, royal school or palace complex. The long-nosed face of Chaac appears everywhere on the facades of the four separate temples that form the quadrangle.

The northern temple, the grandest of the four, was built first, followed by the southern, then the eastern and finally the western.

Several decorative elements on the exuberant facades show signs of Mexican, perhaps Totonac, influence. The feathered-serpent (Quetzalcóatl, or in Maya, Kukulcán) motif along the top of the west temple's facade is one of these. Note also the stylized depictions of the *na* over some of the doorways in the northern and southern buildings.

Passing through the corbeled arch in the middle of the south building of the quadrangle and continuing down the slope takes you through the **Juego de Pelota** (Ball Court). From here you can turn left and head up the steep slope and stairs to the large terrace. If you have time, you could instead turn right to explore the western **Grupo del Cementerio** (which, though largely unrestored, holds some interesting square blocks carved with skulls in the center of its plaza), then head for the stairs and terrace.

Casa de las Tortugas ARCHAEOLOGICAL SITE

The House of the Turtles, which you'll find on top of a hillside overlooking the Juego de Pelota, takes its name from the turtles carved on the cornice. The Maya associated turtles with the rain god, Chaac. According to Maya myth, when the people suffered from drought, so did the turtles, and both prayed to Chaac to send rain.

The frieze of short columns, or 'rolled mats,' that runs around the temple below the turtles is characteristic of the Puuc style.

On the west side of the building a vault has collapsed, affording a good view of the corbeled arch that supported it.

Palacio del Gobernador ARCHAEOLOGICAL SITE

The Governor's Palace, with its magnificent facade nearly 100m long, is arguably the most impressive structure at Uxmal. The buildings have walls filled with rubble, faced with cement and then covered in a thin veneer of limestone squares; the lower part of the facade is plain, the upper part festooned with stylized Chaac faces and geometric designs, often lattice-like or fretted.

Other elements of Puuc style are decorated cornices, rows of half-columns (as in the Casa de las Tortugas) and round columns in doorways (as in the palace at Sayil).

Researchers recently discovered some 150 species of medicinal plants growing on the east side of the palace. Due to the high concentration of plants growing there it's believed they were cultivated by the Maya to treat stomach infections, snake bites and many other ailments.

Gran Pirámide ARCHAEOLOGICAL SITE

The 30m-high, nine-tiered pyramid has been restored only on its northern side. Archaeologists theorize that the quadrangle at its summit was largely destroyed in order to construct another pyramid above it. That work, for reasons unknown, was never completed. At the top are some stucco carvings of Chaac, birds and flowers.

El Palomar ARCHAEOLOGICAL SITE

West of the Gran Pirámide sits a structure whose roofcomb is latticed with a pattern reminiscent of the Moorish pigeon houses built into walls in Spain and northern Africa – hence the building's name, which means the Dovecote or Pigeon House. Honeycombed triangular 'belfries' sit on top of a building that was once part of a quadrangle.

🛏 Sleeping

There is no town at Uxmal, only several resort-style hotels aimed at tour groups, and no budget options. A good range of midrange lodgings can be found in Santa Elena, 16km southeast, or in Ticul, 30km east, though most people press on to either Mérida or Campeche.

Hotel Hacienda Uxmal HISTORIC HOTEL $$$

(☑800-719-54-65, US 877-240-5864; www.mayaland.com/hacienda-uxmal; Hwy 261 Km 78; r incl breakfast from US$118; 🅿❄🛜🏊) This attractive Mayaland Resort is 500m from the ruins. It housed the archaeologists who explored and restored Uxmal. Wide, tiled floors, lots of wrought iron, high ceilings, great bathrooms and a beautiful swimming pool make for a pleasant stay. There are even rocking chairs to help you kick back after a hard day of exploring.

Lodge at Uxmal LUXURY HOTEL $$$

(☑997-976-20-31, USA 877-240-5864; www.mayaland.com/the-lodge-at-uxmal; Hwy 261 Km 78; r incl breakfast from US$208; 🅿❄🛜🏊) Rooms could be nicer for the price, but you can't beat the easy access to the ruins, and the pool certainly adds value. Some of the more expensive rooms have Jacuzzis. We don't suppose Stephens and Catherwood enjoyed

Uxmal

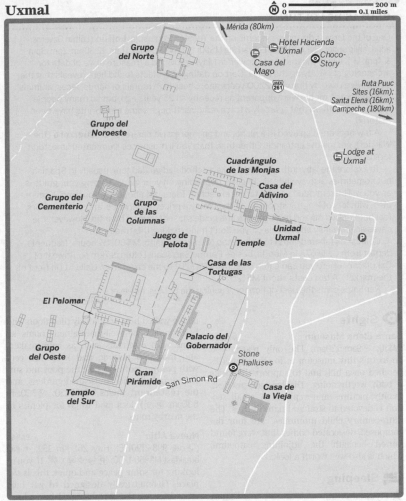

such luxury when they passed through the area in the late 1830s. Private guides to the ruins are available for M$800.

Getting There & Away

Uxmal is 80km from Mérida. Departures (M$76, 1½ hours, four daily) on the Sur bus line leave from Mérida's Terminal TAME (p332). But going back to Mérida, passing buses may be full. If you get stuck, a taxi to nearby Santa Elena costs M$150 to M$200.

Tours offered by Nómadas Hostel (p325) in Mérida are always a good option, or rent a car and also visit other ruins in the area. Alternately, take a *colectivo* for about M$30.

Santa Elena

997 / POP 3500

Originally called Nohcacab, the town today known as Santa Elena was virtually razed in 1847 in the War of the Castes. '*Ele*-na' means burnt houses in Maya. The Mexican government changed the name to Santa Elena in a bold PR stunt.

If you're up for a little DIY adventure, head 4km outside town to the **Mulchic pyramid**; locals can tell you how to get there. Santa Elena also makes a great base to explore the nearby ruins of Uxmal, Kabah and those along the Ruta Puuc.

GRUTAS DE LOLTÚN

One of the largest dry-cave systems on the Yucatán Peninsula, **Loltún** (Loltún Caverns; adult/child under 13yr M$140/free, parking M$50; ☺ tours 9:30am, 11am, 12:30pm, 2pm, 3pm & 4pm; [♿]), which means 'stone flower' in Maya, provided a treasure trove of data for archaeologists studying the Maya. Carbon dating of artifacts found here reveals that the caves were used by humans 2200 years ago. Chest-high murals of hands, faces, animals and geometric motifs were apparent as recently as 25 years ago, but so many people have touched them that scarcely a trace remains, though some handprints have been restored.

A few pots are displayed in a niche, and an impressive bas-relief, **El Guerrero** (the Warrior), guards the entrance. Other than that, you'll mostly see illuminated limestone formations.

To explore the labyrinth, you must take a scheduled guided tour, usually in Spanish but sometimes also available in English, depending on your guide. Tipping your guide is, as you will be reminded several times, expected. Tours last about one hour and 20 minutes, with lots of lengthy stops. It's undoubtedly a pricey experience, and some visitors feel both ripped off and frustrated by the guide's laser focus on their tip. However, the caves are certainly spectacular, if you don't mind making this trade-off.

Colectivos (shared vans) to Oxkutzcab (osh-kootz-kahb; M$60, 1½ hours, frequent) depart from Calle 67A in Mérida, beside Parque San Juan. Loltún is 7km southwest of Oxkutzcab, where you can catch *colectivos* (M$20) to the caves from Calle 51 (in front of the market). A taxi costs about M$120.

Renting a car is the best option for reaching the Grutas, however.

◉ Sights

Santa Elena Museum   MUSEUM
(M$10; ☺ 9am-5:30pm) The only reason you go to this tiny museum is for the view (it's perched on a hill) and to support the locals – both worth doing. Displays are modest, mainly pictures and replicas. A small section is devoted to sisal and natural dyes. The '18th-century child mummies,' are four decomposed, desiccated bodies that were found buried beneath the adjoining cathedral, which is also well worth a look.

⌇ Sleeping

★ Flycatcher Inn   B&B $$
(☎ 997-978-53-50; www.flycatcherinn.com; off Hwy 261; r incl breakfast US$70-117; ☺ mid-Oct–Aug; [P ❋ ☲]) Flycatcher Inn features seven squeaky-clean rooms, all with great porches, high-quality hammocks, excellent screenage and spacious bathrooms. It is surrounded by a pleasant garden, and a number of bird and animal species can be seen here, including the flycatchers that gave their name to the place. A lovely pool and high-quality breakfasts make it a great overnight stop.

Pickled Onion   B&B $$
(☎ 997-111-79-22; www.thepickledonionyucatan.com; Hwy 261; d incl breakfast US$55-70; [P ⊖ ☲ ⊠]) The charming Pickled Onion offers modern adobe-walled huts with lovely tiled floors and bathrooms. The well-maintained rooms all come with essentials such as coffeemakers and mosquito netting, and keep you cool with *palapa* roofs. We love the pool and surrounding lush and landscaped gardens, and the **restaurant** (mains M$100-130; ☺ 7:30am-8:30pm; [P ☲]) does food to go for picnics in the nearby ruins.

Nueva Altia   B&B $$
(☎ cell 998-2190176; Hwy 261 Km 159; r incl breakfast M$950-1200; [P ⊖ ☲ ⊠]) ✎ If you're looking for some peace and quiet, this is *the* place. Geometrically designed to get nice cross breezes, the spiral-shaped bungalows were inspired by ancient Maya architecture. And, as with many locales, unearthed Maya ruins are tucked away on the pretty, wooded grounds. Each room has two double beds and its own hammock. Wi-fi is in the lobby only.

❶ Getting There & Away

It's handy to have your own wheels here, especially if you're using it as a base to visit the ruins of Uxmal, plus to explore the Ruta Puuc. Second-class Sur Mayab buses run between Mérida and Campeche stopping in Uxmal and Santa Elena (plus Oxcutzcab, five daily, around M$75).

Kabah

Kabah (Hwy 261; M$60, guides M$500; ☺8am-5pm) is one of the few Maya settlements in the area that has retained its original name (meaning 'the powerful hand'). Second only to Uxmal in the Puuc Region, this is a hugely impressive sight, spread out on both sides of the main road, though at present only one side of the complex is open to the public. The site was occupied in the 3rd century BCE, but most of the structures standing today date from 7th–11th centuries.

Upon entering the site, head to the right and climb the stairs of **El Palacio de los Mascarones** (Palace of the Masks). Standing in front of it is the **Altar de los Glifos**, whose immediate area is littered with many stones carved with glyphs. The palace's facade is an amazing sight, covered in nearly 300 masks of Chaac, the rain god or sky serpent. Most of their huge noses are broken off; the best intact beaks are at the building's south end.

These curled-up noses may have given the palace its modern Maya name, **Codz Poop** (Rolled Mat; it's pronounced like 'codes pope'). When you've had your fill of noses, head north and around to the back of the Poop to check out the two restored **atlantes** (male figures used as supporting columns). These are especially interesting, as they're some of the very few 3D human figures you'll see at the main Maya sites. One is headless and the other wears a jaguar mask atop his head.

Descend the steps near the *atlantes* and turn left, passing the small **Pirámide de los Mascarones**, to reach the plaza containing **El Palacio**. The palace's broad facade has several doorways, two of which have a column in the center. These columned doorways and the groups of decorative *columnillas* (little columns) on the upper part of the facade are characteristic of the Puuc architectural style.

The souvenir ticket office sells snacks and cold drinks. For good lodging, stay in Santa Elena (p335), about 8km north of Kabah.

Kabah is 104km from Mérida. It's easiest to reach the site by car, or from Mérida you can take a Sur bus (five daily). Turi-transmérida (p324) and Nómadas Hostel (p325) both run tours here.

Ruta Puuc

The Ruta Puuc (Puuc Route) meanders through rolling hills dotted with seldom-visited Maya ruins sitting in dense forests. A road branches off to the east (5km south of Kabah) and winds past the ruins of Sayil, Xlapak and Labná, eventually leading to the Grutas de Loltún. The sites offer some marvelous architectural detail and a deeper acquaintance with the Puuc Maya civilization.

◎ Sights

★ Labná   ARCHAEOLOGICAL SITE
(M$55; ☺8am-5pm; Ⓟ) This is *the* Ruta Puuc site not to miss. Archaeologists believe that, at one point in the 9th century, some 3000 Maya lived at Labná. To support such numbers in these arid hills, water was collected in *chultunes* (cisterns); there were some 60 *chultunes* in and around the city, and several are still visible. El Palacio, the first building you encounter, is one of the longest in the Puuc region, and much of its decorative carving is in good shape.

On the west corner of the main structure's facade, straight in from the big tree near the center of the complex, is a serpent's head with a human face peering out from between its jaws, the symbol of the planet Venus. Toward the hill from this is an impressive Chaac mask, and nearby is the lower half of a human figure (possibly a ball-player) in loincloth and leggings.

The lower level has several more well-preserved Chaac masks, and the upper level contains a large *chultún* that still holds water. The view of the site and the hills beyond from there is impressive.

Labná is best known for **El Arco**, a magnificent arch once part of a building that separated two quadrangular courtyards. It now appears to be a gate joining two small plazas. The corbeled structure, 3m wide and 6m high, is well preserved, and the reliefs decorating its upper facade are exuberantly Puuc in style.

Flanking the west side of the arch are carved *na* with multi-tiered roofs. Also on these walls, the remains of the building that adjoined the arch, are lattice patterns atop a serpentine design. Archaeologists believe a high roofcomb once sat over the fine arch and its flanking rooms.

Standing on the opposite side of the arch and separated from it by the *sacbé* is a pyramid known as **El Mirador**, topped by a temple. The pyramid itself is largely stone rubble. The temple, with its 5m-high roofcomb, is well positioned to be a lookout, hence its name.

Labná is 14km east of the Ruta Puuc junction with Hwy 261.

Sayil
ARCHAEOLOGICAL SITE

(M$55; ◷ 8am-5pm) Sayil is best known for **El Palacio**, the huge three-tiered building that has an 85m-long facade. The distinctive columns of Puuc architecture are used often here, either as supports for the lintels, as decoration between doorways or as a frieze above them, alternating with stylized Chaac masks and 'descending gods.'

Xlapak
ARCHAEOLOGICAL SITE

(◷ 8am-5pm) **FREE** The ornate *palacio* at Xlapak (shla-pak), also spelled Xlapac, is quite a bit smaller than those at nearby Kabah and Sayil, measuring only about 20m in length. It's decorated with the inevitable Chaac masks, columns and colonnettes and fretted geometric latticework of the Puuc style. The building is interesting and on a bit of a lean.

❶ Getting There & Away

Turitransmérida (p324) offers Ruta Puuc tours, as do some of the hostels and accommodations.

On Sundays only, an ATS bus leaves Mérida's Terminal TAME (p332) at 8am and visits Uxmal, Kabah and all three Ruta Puuc sites, giving you time to see each and costing just M$99. It returns between 3pm and 4pm, so it's a whirlwind trip, but the easiest and best-value way to visit all five sites without your own transportation.

Ruinas de Mayapán

Though far less impressive than many Maya sites, Mayapán (M$45; ◷ 8am-4:30pm) is historically significant – it was one of the last major dynasties in the region and established itself as the center of Maya civilization from 1200 to 1440. The site's main attractions are clustered in a compact core, and visitors usually have the place to themselves. It is also one of few sites where you can ascend to the top of the pyramid.

The city of Mayapán was large, with a population estimated to be around 12,000; it covered 4 sq km, all surrounded by a great defensive wall. More than 3500 buildings, 20 cenotes and traces of the city wall were mapped by archaeologists working in the 1950s and in 1962. The late-post-Classic artisanship is inferior to that of the great age of Maya art.

Among the structures that have been restored is the **Castillo de Kukulcán**, a climbable pyramid with fresco fragments around its base and, at its rear side, friezes depicting decapitated warriors. The reddish color is still faintly visible. The **Templo Redondo** (Round Temple) is vaguely reminiscent of El Caracol at Chichén Itzá.

Don't confuse the ruins of Mayapán with the Maya village of the same name, which is about 40km southeast of the ruins, past the town of Teabo.

The Ruinas de Mayapán are just off Hwy 184, a few kilometers southwest of the town of Telchaquillo and some 50km southeast of Mérida. Although some 2nd-class buses run to Telchaquillo (M$50, 1½ hours, hourly), consider renting a car to get here.

Celestún

📞 988 / POP 6800

West of Mérida, Celestún is a sleepy sunscorched fishing village that moves at a turtle's pace. While it's not a historic or particularly attractive town, it does have some nice beaches, and the wonderful Reserva de la Biosfera Ría Celestún, a wildlife sanctuary abounding in waterfowl, where large colonies of flamingos are the star attraction.

It makes a good beach-and-bird day trip from Mérida, and you can even spend a night or two here if you fancy a break from Maya sights. Fishing boats dot the appealing white-sand beach that stretches north for kilometers, and afternoon breezes cool the town on most days.

◎ Sights

★ Reserva de la Biosfera Ría Celestún
WILDLIFE RESERVE

The 591-sq-km Reserva de la Biosfera Ría Celestún is home to a huge variety of animals and birdlife, including a large flamingo colony. You can see flamingos (via boat tours) year-round in Celestún, but they're usually out in full force from November to mid-March.

Hacienda Real de Salinas
HISTORIC BUILDING

FREE This abandoned hacienda, a few kilometers southeast of town, once produced dyewood and salt, and served as a summer home for a Campeche family. It's 5km in from the mouth of the estuary. Out in the *ría* (estuary) you can see a cairn marking an *ojo de agua dulce* (freshwater spring) that once supplied the hacienda.

The buildings are decaying in a most scenic way; you can still see shells in the wall mixed into the building material, as well as pieces of French roof tiles that served as ballast in ships on the journey from Europe. Many intact tiles with the brickworks' name and location (Marseille) are still visible in what's left of the roofs.

The hacienda makes a good bicycle excursion from town. Coming south on Calle 4, go left at the Y junction (a dirt road that flanks Puerto Abrigo), then turn right to reach El Lastre (the Ballast), a peninsula between the estuary and its western arm. Flamingos, white pelicans and other birds are sometimes seen here. If the water is high enough, it's possible to ask your flamingo-tour captain to try stopping here on the way back from the birds. You'll find bike rentals on the town square.

Tours

Flamingo tours in the Reserva de la Biosfera Ría Celestún are Celestún's main draw. Normally the best months for viewing the flamingos are from around end November to mid-March.

Trips from the beach last 2½ hours and begin with a ride along the coast for several kilometers, during which you can expect to see egrets, herons, cormorants, sandpipers and many other bird species. The boat then turns into the mouth of the *ría*.

Continuing up the *ría* takes you under the highway bridge where other boat tours begin and beyond which lie the flamingos. Depending on the tide, hour, season and climate conditions, you may see hundreds or thousands of the colorful birds. Don't encourage your captain to approach them too closely; a startled flock taking wing can result in injuries and deaths (for the birds). In addition to taking you to the flamingos, the captain will wend through a 200m mangrove tunnel and visit freshwater springs welling into the saltwater of the estuary, where you can take a refreshing dip.

Tours from the bridge run 1½ hours, between 8am and 5pm daily.

Hiring a boat on the beach can be frustrating at times. Operators tend to try to collect as many people as possible, which sometimes means a lot of waiting around. Prices are often quoted based on six passengers, but if fewer people show up, the quoted price rises. You can avoid this problem by coming up with a group of six on your own.

Expect to pay around M$1500 for a boat of up to six people plus the M$69 per person entry to the biosphere reserve.

With either the bridge or beach option, your captain may or may not speak English.

★**Manglares de Dzinitún** ECOTOUR
(999-645-43-10; www.facebook.com/manglar celestun; 90min tour canoe/kayak for up to 3 people from M$1000) About 1km inland past the bridge (follow the signs to 'Paseos: canoas y kayak') you'll find an operator offering ecotours in a double kayak (where you do the work) or canoe (the guide paddles). These run through a mangrove tunnel and good birding spots, made better by the lack of engine noise and knowledgeable guides; a couple have basic English.

To get here from the beach, turn right on the street after the second transmission tower. It's about 300m ahead. Prices depend a lot on the group configuration, so call and ask. For a large group, it may be M$500 per person for a kayak tour. Flamingo tours are M$1500 for two kayakers.

Sleeping & Eating

Most of Celestún's hotels are on Calle 12, within a short walk of one another, though many are in poor condition. Most of the better options are along the seafront just north of town.

Eco Hotel Flamingo Playa HOTEL $$
(988-916-21-33; drivan2011@hotmail.com; Calle 12 No 67C; r from M$850; P❄️✳️🛜🏊) One of the better budget hotels in town, this rather shabby family-run hotel has direct beach access and its own pool. Weathered sinks and showers could use some maintenance, and the rooms are humid, but the place is clean. It's 800m north of Calle 11.

★**Playa 55**
Beach Escape BOUTIQUE HOTEL $$$
(988-916-20-00; www.playa55beachescape. com; Calle 12 No 55K; r from US$143; ✳️🛜🏊) Injecting Celestún with some much-needed style and elegance, this eight-room boutique hotel offers smart and tasteful accommodations without any pretense. There's a great pool, direct access to a perfect stretch of normally empty beach and you're just a short walk into town. Rooms are white, pared down, and all have balcony or outdoor space and bright furnishing accents.

Casa de Celeste Vida GUESTHOUSE $$$
(☑988-916-25-36; www.hotelcelestevida.com; Calle 12 No 49E; r/apt from US$95/130; P ⊕ 🐕 🛜 🐾) This friendly Canadian-owned place offers two comfortably decked-out rooms with kitchenette (think toaster and coffeemaker) and an apartment that sleeps four – all with water views and the gorgeous, empty beach at your doorstep. Kayak and bike use are free for guests. The hosts are happy to arrange flamingo tours and a nighttime crocodile excursion. It's 1.5km north of the town center.

A large communal kitchen means you can cook your own meals, or you can use the barbecue. Breakfast baskets cost an extra US$10 for two people. It's open all year. Paddleboard rental is US$10 per hour.

La Playita SEAFOOD $$
(☑988-916-20-52; Calle 12 No 99; mains M$100-160; ☺10am-7pm; 🐕) Of all the sandy-floored, plastic-table-and-chairs beachfront joints here, this one gets the thumbs-up from the locals. Fresh seafood and ceviche are its main draws, as is access to the sea and cold beers.

La Palapa SEAFOOD $$
(☑998-916-20-63; restaurant-lapalapa@hotmail .com; Calle 12 No 105; mains M$125-235; ☺11:30am-6pm; 🐕) A cut above the other seaside joints, La Palapa has an expansive dining area looking down to the sea, as well as a number of tables right on the beach. The go-to dish is the coconut-coated shrimp served in a coconut shell. The perfect spot if you want to swim while waiting for your meal.

❶ Information

There are no banks in town. You'll find an ATM inside Super Willy's, located on the plaza. The best bet is to bring cash in case the ATMs run out of money (which occurs frequently).

❶ Getting There & Away

Calle 11 is the road into town (it comes due west from Mérida), ending at Calle 12, the road paralleling the beach.

Frequent buses head for Celestún (M$60, 2½ hours) from Mérida's Noreste bus terminal. The route terminates at Celestún's plaza, a block inland from Calle 12.

There are also *colectivos* on the plaza that will take you to downtown Mérida for around M$45.

Progreso

☑969 / POP 39,000

If Mérida's heat has you dying for a quick beach fix, or if you want to see the longest pier (6.5km) in Mexico, head to Progreso (aka Puerto Progreso). The *malecón* can get packed with diners, drinkers and over-sunned tourists, as can the beach (even though it's loooong). Nevertheless, Progreso maintains a relaxed beach-town vibe. As with other Gulf beaches, the water is murky, even on calm days. Winds can hit full force in the afternoon and evenings, especially from December to March when *los nortes* (northern winds) kick up.

Meridanos come in droves on weekends, especially during July and August when it can be difficult to find a room with a view and, sadly, you'll see more litter on the beach. Once or twice a week the streets flood with cruise-ship tourists, but the place can feel empty on off nights, which makes a refreshing change.

🏃 Activities

El Corchito SWIMMING
(☑999-158-51-55; Hwy 27 s/n, cnr Calle 46; adult/child under 12yr M$90/35; ☺9am-4pm) Take a refreshing dip in one of three freshwater swimming holes surrounded by mangroves at nature reserve El Corchito. Motorboats take visitors across a canal to the reserve. El Corchito is home to iguanas, boa constrictors, small crocs, raccoons and a band of coatis. The racoons and coatis are skilled food thieves, something to consider if you bring lunch.

El Corchito sees a lot of visitors, especially on weekends, so get there early for a more peaceful swim.

'Tecnológico' buses (M$6.50) departing from a bus station at Calles 82 and 29 in Progreso will leave you a block and a half from El Corchito.

🛏 Sleeping & Eating

Hotel Yaxactún HOTEL $$
(☑969-103-93-26; www.hotelyrestauranteyaxac tun.com; Calle 66 No 129, btwn Calles 25 & 27; r M$750; ⊕ ❄ 🛜 🏊) The brown-and-cream Yaxactún is one of the better hotels in town. Street-facing rooms get good natural light and have balconies. The hotel also has a small onsite restaurant specializing in Yucatecan food, and there's a swimming

pool with a kiddie corral. It's three blocks from the beach.

There's little greenery and lots of concrete.

El Naranjo
YUCATECAN $

(Calle 27 s/n, btwn Calles 78 & 80; tacos/tortas M$10/20; ☺6am-noon) One of the best options in the market for *cochito* (slow-cooked pork) tacos and tortas – and it's squeaky clean.

Milk Bar
CAFE $$

(Malecón s/n, btwn 72 & 74; mains M$88-155; ☺8am-11pm; 🕸) The 'cow in a rowboat' indicates you've arrived at this laid-back Texan-run spot. Despite the name, it doesn't specialize in milk-based drinks, but is definitely the place to go for hefty sandwiches, burgers and salads. It's a popular hangout for expats who enjoy the eclectic decor and large servings. It's also a great breakfast and brunch spot.

Crabster
SEAFOOD $$$

(🕿969-103-65-22; www.facebook.com/crabster mx; mains M$205-390; ☺8am-8pm; 🕸) At the current posh spot on the strip, with its blond-wood chairs, pink velvet trim and designer lighting, you could be in an international hotel, not smack on the beachfront. But this spot pulls in the moneyed visitor for, you guessed it, seafood dishes. Service is a nice combo of friendly-professional.

❶ Getting There & Away

Progreso is 33km north of Mérida along a fast four-lane highway that's basically a continuation of the Paseo de Montejo.

To get to Progreso from Mérida, go to the Progreso bus terminal (p332) or catch a *colectivo* one block east of the terminal on Calle 60. These are not ADO buses, so if you're continuing onward beyond Mérida you'll need to have different tickets.

Traveling to Mérida, frequent buses (M$21) depart from Progreso's **bus terminal** (Calle 29 No 151, btwn Calles 80 & 82).

Izamal

🕿988 / POP 16,000

In ancient times Izamal was a center for the worship of the supreme Maya god, Itzamná, and the sun god, Kinich-Kakmó. A dozen temple pyramids were devoted to these or other gods. No doubt these bold expressions of Maya religiosity are why the Spanish colonists chose Izamal as the site for an enormous and impressive Franciscan monastery,

which still stands at the heart of this town, about 70km east of Mérida.

The Izamal of today is a quiet and provincial place, nicknamed La Ciudad Amarilla (the Yellow City) for the traditional bright yellow colonial-era buildings that line its town center like a budding daisy. It's easily explored on foot, though some visitors prefer to hire a horse-drawn carriage for a tour. It's an obvious lunch stop between Mérida and Valladolid.

◉ Sights

Centro Cultural y Artesanal
MUSEUM

(Calle 31 No 201; M$25; ☺9am-8pm) 🖉 Just across the square from the monastery, this cultural center and museum showcases popular art from around Mexico. Explanatory cards in English give an excellent summary. Its excellent shop sells fair-trade-certified crafts made by artisans from about 40 indigenous communities. Any purchase you make is a direct source of income for rural indigenous families.

Kinich-Kakmó
ARCHAEOLOGICAL SITE

(Calle 27 s/n, btwn Calles 26B & 28; ☺8am-5pm) **FREE** Though not worth detouring wildly for, if you're here already, three of the town's original 12 Maya pyramids have been partially restored. The largest (and the third largest in Yucatán) is the 34m-high Kinich-Kakmó, three blocks north of the monastery. Legend has it that a deity in the form of a blazing macaw would swoop down from the heavens to collect offerings left here.

★Convento de San Antonio de Padua
MONASTERY

(Calle 31 s/n; museum M$10; ☺5:30am-8pm, museum from 9am) When the Spaniards conquered Izamal, they destroyed the major Maya temple, the Ppapp-Hol-Chac pyramid, and in 1533 began to build from its stones one of the first monasteries in the western hemisphere. Work on Convento de San Antonio de Padua was finished in 1561. Under the monastery's arcades, look for building stones with an unmistakable mazelike design; these were clearly taken from the earlier Maya temple.

🛏 Sleeping & Eating

Your best bet is Yucatecan fare. Several *loncherías* (simple restaurants) occupy spaces in the market on the monastery's southwest side, but there are a few spots that cater more to tourists.

Hotel Casa Colonial   HOTEL $
([📞]988-954-02-72; hotelcasacolonializamal@ hotmail.com; Calle 31 No 331, cnr Calle 36; s/d M$500/600; [P][❄][🛜][🏊]) A clean and spacious option compared to some of the other more rundown and cramped budget hotels in town. All rooms are even decked out with dining table, microwave and minifridge.

⭐**Hacienda Hotel Santo Domingo**   HOTEL $$
([📞]988-967-61-36; www.izamalhotel.com; Calle 18, btwn Calles 33B & 35; r/ste from M$1650/2375; [P][🍽][🛜][🏊]) Set on a 13-hectare property with lush gardens, walking trails, a pool and *palapa* restaurant, this serene, upscale and well-run spot (the owner is always on site) will win over nature lovers and those who enjoy a touch of style. All rooms are attractive, some with natural stone sinks and indoor-outdoor showers. A great reason to stay in Izamal overnight.

⭐**Kinich**   MEXICAN $$
([📞]988-954-04-89; www.facebook.com/kinich izamal; Calle 27 No 299, btwn Calles 28 & 30; mains M$150-250; [🕐]11am-7pm; [🛜]) Kinich showcases fresh, handmade Yucatecan cuisine at its finest. The *papadzules kinich* – rolled tortillas stuffed with diced egg and topped with pumpkin-seed sauce and smoky sausage (M$124) – is a delightful starter that's a house specialty. Kinich is also famous for its *dzic de venado,* a shredded venison dish (M$244) and its excellent empanadas.

The setting is a massive *palapa* and the servers are dressed in traditional *huipiles.*

❶ Getting There & Around

Frequent buses run out of Izamal's **Oriente bus terminal** ([📞]988-954-01-07; Calle 32 s/n, cnr Calle 31A; [🕐]4:30am-8pm) and the nearby **Terminal de Autobuses Centro** ([📞]988-967-66-15; www.autobusescentro.com; Calle 33 No 302, cnr Calle 30; [🕐]5am-9pm).

Chichén Itzá

[📞]985 / POP 5500 (PISTÉ)

The most-famous and best-restored of the Yucatán Maya sites, **Chichén Itzá** (www. chichenitza.inah.gob.mx; off Hwy 180, Pisté; adult/ child under 13yr M$481/75, guided tours M$1200; [🕐]8am-5pm, last entry 4pm; [P]), while tremendously crowded, will still impress even the most jaded visitor. Indeed, its inclusion in the New Seven Wonders of the World in 2007 came as no surprise at all: it's a stunning ruin with spectacular, iconic structures and historical importance. The granddaddy of Maya sites in Mexico, Chichén Itzá (meaning 'mouth of the well of the Itzáes' in Mayan) is visible even from faraway Ek' Balam.

Many mysteries of the Maya astronomical calendar are made clear when one understands the design of the 'time temples' here. However, since a fatal accident in 2006, climbing on the structures is not allowed, making Chichén feel significantly tamer than many less-regulated Mesoamerican sites elsewhere in Mexico.

The heat, humidity and crowds in Chichén Itzá can be fierce, as can competition between the craft sellers who line the paths. To avoid this, explore the site either early in the morning or late in the afternoon, though note that the 5pm closing is a hard exit: all visitors must be through the gates well beforehand, and many areas of the site are out-of-bounds from 4:30pm onward.

History

Most archaeologists agree that the first major settlement at Chichén Itzá, during the late Classic period, was pure Maya. In about the 9th century CE, the city was largely abandoned for reasons unknown.

It was resettled around the late-10th century, and shortly thereafter it is believed to have been invaded by the Toltec, who had migrated from their central highlands capital of Tula, north of Mexico City. The bellicose Toltec culture was fused with

BUSES FROM IZAMAL

DESTINATION	FARE (M$)	TIME (HR)	FREQUENCY (PER DAY) & TERMINAL
Cancún	188-214	5	3 (6:10am, 2:26pm, 4:35pm), Oriente; approx every 2hr Centro
Mérida	33-42	1½	frequent, Centro; hourly, Oriente
Tizimín	95	2½	2 (7:25am, 6:10pm), Oriente
Valladolid	69	2	frequent, Centro

that of the Maya, incorporating the cult of Quetzalcóatl (Kukulcán, in Maya). You will see images of both Chaac, the Maya rain god, and Quetzalcóatl, the plumed serpent, throughout the city.

The substantial fusion of highland central Mexican and Puuc architectural styles makes Chichén unique among the Yucatán Peninsula's ruins. The fabulous El Castillo and the **Plataforma de Venus** are outstanding architectural works built during the height of Toltec cultural input.

The sanguinary Toltec contributed more than their architectural skills to the Maya: they elevated human sacrifice to a near obsession, and there are numerous carvings of the bloody ritual in Chichén demonstrating this.

After a Maya leader moved his political capital to Mayapán while keeping Chichén as his religious capital, Chichén Itzá fell into decline. Why it was subsequently abandoned in the 14th century is a mystery, but the once-great city remained the site of Maya pilgrimages for many years.

◎ Sights

El Castillo
ARCHAEOLOGICAL SITE

Upon entering Chichén Itzá, El Castillo (aka the Pyramid of Kukulcán) rises before you in all its grandeur. The first temple here was pre-Toltec, built around 800 CE, but the present 25m-high structure, built over the old one, has the plumed serpent sculpted along the stairways and Toltec warriors represented in the doorway carvings at the top of the temple. You won't see the carvings, however, as ascending the pyramid was prohibited after a fatal accident here in 2006.

The structure is actually a massive Maya calendar formed in stone. Each of El Castillo's nine levels is divided in two by a staircase, making 18 separate terraces that commemorate the 18 20-day months of the Maya Vague Year. The four stairways have 91 steps each; add the top platform and the total is 365, the number of days in the year. On each facade of the pyramid are 52 flat panels, which are reminders of the 52 years in the Maya calendar round.

At the vernal and autumnal equinoxes (around March 20 and September 22), the morning and afternoon sun produces a light-and-shadow illusion of the serpent ascending or descending the side of El Castillo's staircase. The site is mobbed on these dates, however, making it difficult to see, and after

❶ NAVIGATING CHICHÉN ITZÁ

To fully take in the details of the site and avoid the crowds, you can hire a guide, which will allow you to enter the grounds between 5am and 8am. The tour costs M$1500 per person, including transport and entry to the site, and can be arranged through **Kukulkan Rising Tours** (☑985-106-47-57; pitzz4525@hotmail.com).

If a guide's not in your budget, just walking around offers a fascinating insight into one of the greatest cities of pre-Hispanic civilization.

the spectacle, parts of the site are sometimes closed to the public. The illusion is almost as good in the week preceding and following each equinox (and draws much smaller crowds), and is re-created nightly (except Mondays) in the light-and-sound show (p344) year-round. If you're in the area around the equinox and you have your own car, it's easy to wake up early for the fiery sunrise of Dzibilchaltún (p331), a site north of Mérida, and then make it to Chichén Itzá by midafternoon, catching both spectacles on the same day.

The older pyramid inside El Castillo has a red jaguar throne with inlaid eyes and spots of jade; also lying behind the screen is a chac-mool (Maya sacrificial stone sculpture). The entrance to **El Túnel**, the passage up to the throne, is at the base of El Castillo's north side. You can't go in, though.

Researchers in 2015 learned that the pyramid most likely sits atop a 20m-deep cenote, which puts the structure at greater risk of collapsing.

Gran Juego de Pelota
ARCHAEOLOGICAL SITE

The great ball court, the largest and most impressive in Mexico, is only one of the city's eight courts, indicative of the importance the games held here. The court, to the left of the visitors center, is flanked by temples at either end and is bounded by towering parallel walls with stone rings cemented up high. Along the walls of the ball court are stone reliefs, including scenes of decapitations of players.

There is evidence that the ball game may have changed over the years. Some carvings show players with padding on their elbows and knees, and it is thought that they played

SOUND & LIGHT SHOW

A 45-minute **sound-and-light show** (www.nochesdekukulkan.com; M$510 Tue-Sat, M$255 Sun) begins each evening at 8pm in summer and 7pm in winter. You must preorder your tickets online.

a soccer-like game with a hard rubber ball, with the use of hands forbidden. Other carvings show players wielding bats; it appears that if a player hit the ball through one of the stone hoops, his team was declared the winner. It may be that during the Toltec period, the losing captain, and perhaps his teammates as well, were sacrificed.

The court exhibits some interesting acoustics: a conversation at one end can be heard 135m away at the other, and a clap produces multiple loud echoes.

Templo del Barbado　　ARCHAEOLOGICAL SITE
The structure at the ball court's north end, called the Temple of the Bearded Man after a carving inside it, has finely sculpted pillars and reliefs of flowers, birds and trees.

Plataforma de los Cráneos　　ARCHAEOLOGICAL SITE
The Platform of Skulls (Tzompantli in Náhuatl) is between the **Templo de los Jaguares y Escudos** and El Castillo (p343). You can't mistake it, because the T-shaped platform is festooned with carved skulls and eagles tearing open the chests of men to eat their hearts. In ancient days this platform was used to display the heads of sacrificial victims.

Plataforma de las Águilas y los Jaguares　　ARCHAEOLOGICAL SITE
Adjacent to the Platform of Skulls, the carvings on the Platform of the Eagles and Jaguars depict those animals gruesomely grabbing human hearts in their claws. It is thought that this platform was part of a temple dedicated to the military legions responsible for capturing sacrificial victims.

Cenote Sagrado　　ARCHAEOLOGICAL SITE
From the Plataforma de Venus (p343), a 250m rough stone *sacbé* runs north to the huge sunken well that gave this city its name. The Sacred Cenote is some 60m in diameter and 35m deep. The walls between the summit and the water's surface are ensnared in tangled vines and other vegetation, and sadly it's hard to see much of the water, but spare a thought for the children and adults sacrificed to the gods here over the centuries.

There are ruins of a small steam bath next to the cenote.

Grupo de las Mil Columnas　　ARCHAEOLOGICAL SITE
This group east of El Castillo (p343) pyramid takes its name – which means 'Group of One Thousand Columns' – from the forest of pillars stretching south and east. The star attraction here is the **Templo de los Guerreros** (Temple of the Warriors), adorned with stucco and stone-carved animal deities. At the top of its steps is a classic reclining chac-mool figure, sadly not visible from behind the ropes.

Many of the columns in front of the temple are carved with figures of warriors. Archaeologists working in 1926 discovered a structure known as the Temple of the Chac-Mool lying beneath the Temple of the Warriors.

You can walk through the columns on its south side to reach the **Columnata Noreste**, notable for the 'big-nosed god' masks on its facade. Some have been reassembled on the ground around the statue. Just to the south are the remains of the **Baño de Vapor** (Steam Bath or Sweat House) with an underground oven and drains for the water. The sweat houses (there are two onsite) were regularly used for ritual purification.

El Osario　　ARCHAEOLOGICAL SITE
The Ossuary, otherwise known as the Bonehouse or the Tumba del Gran Sacerdote (High Priest's Grave), is a ruined pyramid to the southwest of El Castillo. As with most of the buildings in this southern section, the architecture is more Puuc than Toltec. It's notable for the beautiful serpent heads at the base of its staircases.

A square shaft at the top of the structure leads down into a cave that was used as a burial chamber; seven tombs with human remains were discovered inside.

El Caracol　　ARCHAEOLOGICAL SITE
Called El Caracol (the Snail) by the Spaniards for its interior spiral staircase, this observatory, to the south of the El Osario, is one of the most fascinating and important of all Chichén Itzá's buildings. Its circular design resembles some central highlands structures, although, surprisingly, not those of Toltec Tula.

Chichén Itzá

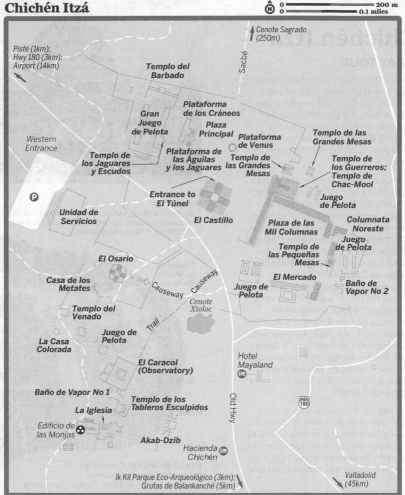

Chichén Itzá

0 ————— 200 m
0 ————— 0.1 miles

Cenote Sagrado
(250m)

Pisté (1km);
Hwy 180 (3km);
Airport (14km)

Templo del
Barbado

Sacbé

Plataforma
de los Cráneos

Gran
Juego
de Pelota

Plaza
Principal

Plataforma
de Venus

Western
Entrance

Templo de
los Jaguares
y Escudos

Plataforma de
las Águilas
y los Jaguares

Templo de
las Grandes
Mesas

Templo de las
Grandes Mesas

Templo de
los Guerreros;
Templo de
Chac-Mool

Entrance to
El Túnel

Unidad de
Servicios

El Castillo

Plaza de las
Mil Columnas

Juego
de Pelota

Columnata
Noreste

Juego
de Pelota

El Osario

Casa de los
Metates

Causeway

Causeway

Cenote
Xtoloc

Templo de
las Pequeñas
Mesas

El Mercado

Juego de
Pelota

Baño de
Vapor No 2

Templo del
Venado

Trail

Juego de
Pelota

La Casa
Colorada

Hotel
Mayaland

El Caracol
(Observatory)

Old Hwy

MEX
180

Baño de Vapor No 1

Templo de los
Tableros Esculpidos

La Iglesia

Edificio de
las Monjas

Akab-Dzib

Hacienda
Chichén

Ik Kil Parque Eco-Arqueológico (3km);
Grutas de Balankanché (5km)

Valladolid
(45km)

YUCATÁN PENINSULA CHICHÉN ITZÁ

In a fusion of architectural styles and religious imagery, there are Maya Chaac rain-god masks over four external doors facing the cardinal points. The windows in the observatory's dome are aligned with the appearance of certain stars at specific dates. From the dome the priests may have decreed the times for rituals, celebrations, corn-planting and harvests.

Edificio de las Monjas   ARCHAEOLOGICAL SITE
Thought by archaeologists to have been a palace for Maya royalty, the so-called Edificio de las Monjas (Nunnery), with its myriad rooms, resembled a European convent to the con-

quistadors, hence their name for the building. The building's dimensions are imposing: its base is 60m long, 30m wide and 20m high.

The construction is Maya rather than Toltec, although a Toltec sacrificial stone stands in front. A smaller adjoining building to the east, known as **La Iglesia** (the Church), is covered almost entirely with carvings.

🏃 Activities

Tsukán Santuario de Vida   HEALTH & FITNESS
(☎ 999-648-0109; www.tsukan.com.mx; Carretera Piste–Yokdzonot; adult/child M$225/125; ☺ 9am-5pm) The centerpiece of this spa

Chichén Itzá

A DAY TOUR

It doesn't take long to realize why the Maya site of Chichén Itzá is one of Mexico's most popular tourist draws. Approaching the grounds from the main entrance, the striking castle pyramid **1** **El Castillo** jumps right out at you – and the wow factor never lets up.

It's easy to tackle Chichén Itzá in one day. Within a stone's throw of the castle, you'll find the Maya world's largest **2** **ball court** alongside eerie carvings of skulls and heart-devouring eagles at the Temple of Jaguars and the Platform of Skulls. On the other (eastern) side are the highly adorned **3** **Group of a Thousand Columns** and the **4** **Temple of Warriors**. A short walk north of the castle leads to the gaping **5** **Sacred Cenote**, an important pilgrimage site. On the other side of El Castillo, you'll find giant stone serpents watching over the High Priest's Grave, aka El Osario. Further south, marvel at the spiral-domed **6** **Observatory**, the imposing Nunnery and Akab-Dzib, one of the oldest ruins.

Roaming the 47-hectare site, it's fun to consider that at its height Chichén Itzá was home to an estimated 90,000 inhabitants and spanned approximately 30 sq km. So essentially you're looking at just a small part of a once-great city.

TOP TIPS

➤ Arrive at 8am and you'll have a good three hours or so before the tour-bus madness begins. Early birds escape the merchants, too.

➤ Remember that Chichén Itzá is the name of the site; the actual town where it's located is called Pisté.

El Caracol
Observatory
Today they'd probably just use a website, but back in the day priests would announce the latest rituals and celebrations from the dome of the circular observatory.

Edificio de las Monjas (Nunnery)

6

Akab-Dzib

Entrance

Grupo de las Mil Columnas
Group of a Thousand Columns
Not unlike a hall of fame exhibit, the pillars surrounding the temple reveal carvings of gods, dignitaries and celebrated warriors.

El Castillo
The Castle
Even this mighty pyramid can't bear the stress of a million visitors ascending its stairs each year. No climbing allowed, but the ground-level view doesn't disappoint.

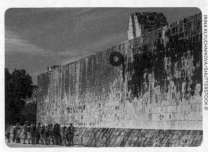

IRINA KLYUCHNIKOVA/SHUTTERSTOCK ©

Gran Juego de Pelota
Great Ball Court
How is it possible to hear someone talk from one end of this long, open-air court to the other? To this day, the acoustics remain a mystery.

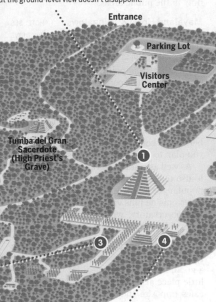

Entrance

Parking Lot

Visitors Center

Tumba del Gran Sacerdote (High Priest's Grave)

Templo de los Jaguares (Temple of Jaguars)

1

2

3

4

5

Plataforma de los Cráneos (Platform of Skulls)

Cenote Sagrado
Sacred Cenote
Diving expeditions have turned up hundreds of valuable artifacts dredged from the cenote (limestone sinkhole), not to mention human bones of sacrificial victims who were forced to jump into the eternal underworld.

Templo de los Guerreros
Temple of Warriors
The Maya associated warriors with eagles and jaguars, as depicted in the temple's friezes. The revered jaguar, in particular, was a symbol of strength and agility.

MATYAS REHAK/SHUTTERSTOCK ©

complex is its absolute knockout cenote, which is easily one of the most attractive in Yucatán and certainly the fanciest. For the relatively enormous entry fee, you can spend all day here, swimming (only in life jackets, annoyingly), sunbathing, eating and drinking. It's just off the main road, 8km west of Pisté.

🛏 Sleeping & Eating

Most of Chichén Itzá's lodgings, restaurants and services are arranged along 1km of highway in the town of Pisté to the western (Mérida) side of the ruins. It's about 1.5km from the ruins' main (west) entrance to the nearest hotel in Pisté, and 2.5km from the ruins to Pisté's town plaza.

Don't hesitate to haggle for a bed in low season (May through June and August to early December). Sadly, quality of both food and lodgings is poor here, though perfectly fine for an overnight stop.

The highway (Calle 15) through Pisté is lined with dozens of simple places to eat, large and small. The cheapest are clustered in a roadside market, known as Los Portales, on the west end of town.

Pirámide Inn   HOTEL $

(☑ 985-851-01-15; www.piramideinn.com; Calle 15 No 30; campsite M$100, r with/without air-con M$600/400; 🅿 ❄ ✳ 🛜 🏊 🐾) While in fairly desperate need of some TLC, this is one of the few budget options in town and is also relatively close to the ruins. Campers can pitch a tent in the large gardens, which feature an unexcavated Maya site themselves. The spacious rooms have adequate bathrooms and two double beds. Pets are welcome and vibe is super-relaxed.

Hotel Chichén Itzá   HOTEL $$

(☑ 998-887-24-95, toll free from Mexico 800-719-54-65, toll free from USA 877-240-5864; www.mayaland.com; Calle 15 No 45; r from M$1320; 🅿 ❄ ✳ 🛜 🏊) This hotel has 42 pleasant rooms with tiled floors and old-style brick-tiled ceilings. Rooms in the upper range face the pool and the landscaped grounds, and all have firm beds and good bathrooms. Parents may bring two kids under 12 years old for free. The hotel is part of the Mayaland chain, with its private entrance to the archaeological site.

★ Hacienda Chichén   RESORT $$$

(☑ 999-920-84-07, USA 877-631-0045; www.haciendachichen.com; Zona Hotelera Km 120;

d from US$198; 🅿 ❄ ✳ 🛜 🏊) About 300m from the entrance to Chichén Itzá, this resort sits on the well-manicured grounds of a 16th-century hacienda with an elegant main house and towering ceiba trees. The archaeologists who excavated Chichén Itzá during the 1920s lived here in bungalows, which have been refurbished and augmented with new ones. Monthly activities on offer include Maya cooking classes and bird-watching.

One additional plus is that the spot has a private entrance to the ruins, meaning you get to skip the lines. The restaurant's prices are eye-opening (be warned), and the wi-fi is only in the public areas.

Mayaland Hotel & Bungalows   HOTEL $$$

(☑ 998-887-24-95, US 877-240-5864; www.mayaland.com; Zona Hotelera Km 120; d/bungalow from M$2100/3100; 🅿 ❄ ✳ 🛜 🏊) Getting long in the tooth at this point, and somewhat officious rather than personal, the Mayaland is less than 100m from Chichén Itzá and has a 'private' entrance. The rooms are good, however, and the expansive public areas attractive, though there's actually very limited benefit in being so close to the site, unless you plan to visit multiple times.

As well as restaurants and all the services, it also offers cultural programs, including a popular 'Be Maya' activity where you cook Maya cuisine plus visit the resort's own replica 'observatory,' while learning about the roles of Maya people.

Cocina Económica Fabiola   MEXICAN $

(Calle 15 s/n; mains M$45-75; ⊙ 7am-11pm) For a good, honest, cheap meal hit this humble little place at the end of the strip of simple cafes opposite the church. Since the mid-'90s it's been churning out *sopa de lima* (lime soup; M$45) and *pollo yucateco* (Yucatecan chicken; M$75). There are half a dozen similar places nearby.

Las Mestizas   MEXICAN $$

(☑ 985-851-0069; Calle 15 s/n; mains M$70-115; ⊙ 9am-10pm; ✳ 🛜) One of the town's better restaurants, Las Mestizas serves up decent Yucatecan fare. There's indoor and outdoor seating – depending on the time of day, an outdoor table may mean you'll be getting tour-bus fumes (and lines of people) to go along with that *poc chuk* (pork marinated in orange juice and garlic and grilled; M$115).

BUSES FROM CHICHÉN ITZÁ

DESTINATION	FARE (M$)	TIME (HR)	FREQUENCY (PER DAY)
Cancún	172-335	3-4½	hourly 8:30am-9:30pm
Cobá	85	2	12:30am, 7:30am, 1pm, 5pm, 7pm
Mérida	99-178	1¾-2¾	hourly
Playa del Carmen	174-367	3½-4	12:30am, 7:30am, 1pm, 5pm, 7pm
Tulum	123-252	2½-3	12:30am, 7:30am, 8:25am, 1pm, 4:30pm, 5pm, 7pm
Valladolid	34-106	1	hourly

ⓘ Getting There & Away

Oriente has ticket offices near the east and west sides of Pisté, and 2nd-class buses passing through town stop almost anywhere along the way.

Most 1st-class buses arrive and depart from the ruins only. These also head to Mérida and Valladolid, as well as to coastal locations in Quintana Roo: Playa del Carmen, Tulum and Cancún. If you plan to see the ruins and then head directly to another city by 1st-class bus, to secure your seat, buy your bus ticket at the visitors center gift shop before going into the ruins.

Colectivos to Valladolid (M$35, 40 minutes) enter the car park.

ⓘ Getting Around

Buses to Pisté generally stop at the **bus station** (📞985-851-00-52; ⊗10am-6pm); you can make the hot walk to and from the ruins in 20 to 30 minutes. First-class buses stop at the ruins; for others, check with the driver.

There is a taxi stand near the west end of town; the prices are around M$50 to the ruins, M$80 to Cenote Ik Kil and M$150 to Grutas de Balankanché.

Valladolid

📞985 / POP 52,000

Once known as the Sultana of the East, Yucatán's third-largest city is famed for its quiet streets and sun-splashed pastel walls. It's worth staying here for a few days or longer, as the provincial town makes a great hub for visits to Río Lagartos, Chichén Itzá, Ek' Balam and a number of nearby cenotes. The city resides at that magic point where there's plenty to do, yet it still feels small, manageable and affordable.

History

Valladolid has seen its fair share of turmoil and revolt. The city was first founded in 1543 near the Chouac-Ha lagoon some 50km from the coast, but it was too hot and there were way too many mosquitoes for Francisco de Montejo, nephew of Montejo the Elder, and his merry band of conquerors. So they upped and moved the city to the Maya ceremonial center of Zací (sah-*see*), where they faced heavy resistance from the local Maya. Eventually the Elder's son – Montejo the Younger – took the town. The Spanish conquerors, in typical fashion, ripped down the town and laid out a new city following the classic colonial plan.

During much of the colonial era, Valladolid's physical isolation from Mérida kept it relatively autonomous from royal rule, and the Maya of the area suffered brutal exploitation, which continued after Mexican independence. Barred from entering many areas of the city, the Maya made Valladolid one of their first points of attack following the 1847 outbreak of the War of the Castes in Tepich. After a two-month siege, the city's occupiers were finally overcome. Many fled to the safety of Mérida; the rest were slaughtered.

Today Valladolid is a prosperous seat of agricultural commerce, augmented by some light industry and a growing tourist trade.

⊙ Sights

★**Casa de los Venados** MUSEUM
(📞985-856-22-89; www.casadelosvenados.com; Calle 40 No 204, btwn Calles 41 & 43; M$100; ⊗tours 10am or by appointment) Featuring over 3000 pieces of museum-quality Mexican folk art, this private collection is interesting in that objects are presented in an actual private house, in the context that they were originally designed for, instead of being displayed in glass cases. The tour (in English or Spanish) touches on the origins of some of the more important pieces and the story of the award-winning restored colonial mansion that houses them.

Valladolid

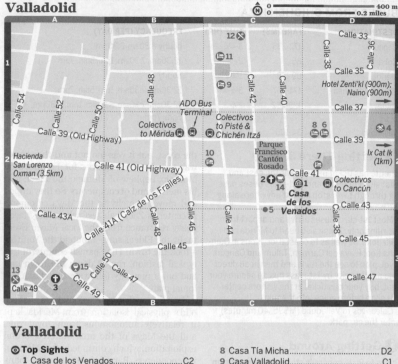

Valladolid

While there are tours every day at 10am, for which you don't need a reservation, there are also tours on the hour each hour until 1pm when demand is high. Note that though the fee is officially called a 'donation,' the guides make it abundantly clear that those on the tour should pay M$100, and that a tip is appreciated as well. It's actually a small price to pay for entry to a truly impressive collection, but the term 'donation' is misleading.

Iglesia de San Servacio   CATHEDRAL
(San Gervasio; Parque Francisco Cantón Rosado) The original edifice of Valladolid's main

church was built in 1545, but was demolished and rebuilt in the early 1700s following a violent atrocity the town wished to forget. Following Valladolid's role in the War of the Castes against Spain (1847–1901), the church was given a north-facing entrance (all the others in Yucatán are east-facing), a form of punishment handed down to the local upstarts for challenging royal authority.

🏃 Activities & Tours

★**Hacienda San Lorenzo Oxman**   SWIMMING
(off Calle 54; cenote M$80, cenote & pool M$100; ⊙8am-6pm) Once a *henequén* plantation

and a refuge for War of the Castes insurgents in the mid-19th century, today the hacienda's main draw is a gorgeous cenote that's usually less crowded than other sinkholes in the area, especially if you visit Monday through Thursday. If you buy the entry to both, you have a M$50 credit to use at the cafe.

A taxi to the hacienda from Valladolid costs around M$100.

Cenote X'Kekén y Samulá SWIMMING
(Cenote Dzitnup & Samulá; 1/2 cenotes M$80/125; ⏰8:30am-6:30pm) One of two cenotes at Dzitnup (also known as X'Kekén Jungle Park), X'Kekén is popular with tour groups. A massive limestone formation with stalactites hangs from its ceiling. The pool is artificially lit and very swimmable. Here you can also take a dip in cenote Samulá, a lovely cavern pool with *álamo* roots stretching down many meters. You can also rent horses (M$225 per 30 minutes), ATVs (M$275 per 30 minutes) or bikes (M$100 per hour).

Pedaling a rented bicycle to the cenotes takes about 20 minutes. By bike from Valladolid's center take Calle 41A (Calzada de los Frailes), a street lined with colonial architecture. Go one block past the **Templo de San Bernardino** (Convento de Sisal; cnr Calles 49 & 51; M$30 Mon-Sat, Sun free; ⏰9am-7pm) along Calle 54A, then make a right on Calle 49, which becomes Avenida de los Frailes and hits the old highway. Follow the *ciclopista* (bike path) paralleling the road to Mérida for about 3km, then turn left at the sign for Dzitnup and continue for just under 2km.

Shared *colectivos* also depart for Dzitnup.

Cenote Zací SWIMMING
(☎985-856-08-18; Calle 36 s/n, btwn Calles 37 & 39; adult/child 3-11yr M$30/15; ⏰10am-5pm) One of few cenotes in Valladolid itself, Cenote Zací is a handy place to cool off. While it's a gorgeous spot, don't expect crystalline waters. You might see catfish or, overhead, a colony of bats. If you spend over M$100 at the pleasant **restaurant** under a large *palapa* (mains M$50 to M$150) here, your entry is free.

MexiGo Tours TOURS
(☎985-856-07-77; www.mexigotours.com; Calle 43 No 204C, btwn Calles 40 & 42; ⏰9am-1pm & 3-7pm Mon-Sat) MexiGo Tours has a good reputation for its trips that cover a range of cultural and nature activities in one day.

You might be swimming in a cenote in one hour and sampling tequila the next. Not to mention visits to ruins and action further afield, such as boat tours to see flamingos at Río Lagartos. It can also arrange airport pickup in Mérida or Cancún.

Also offers bike hire per hour/day from M$25/150.

🛏 Sleeping

⭐**Hostel Candelaria** HOSTEL $
(☎985-856-22-67; www.hostelvalladolidyucatan. com; Calle 35 No 201F; dm/d/tr/q incl breakfast from M$200/630/860/1120; ❄✳🐾🛜) A friendly place on a quiet little square, this hostel can get a little cramped when full, but its charming decor, good kitchen, gorgeous elongated garden complete with hammocks, female-only dorm and plenty of hangout space make it one of the best hostels in town. It also rents out bikes for M$20 per hour.

⭐**Hostal Mamachá** HOSTEL $
(☎985-856-36-59; Calle 41 No 209A, btwn Calle 44 & 46; dm without/with air-con M$200/230; 🛜) This small but unusually stylish hostel has just three dormitories sleeping between seven and 11 people, each with its own spacious bathroom featuring stone basins and good showers. The bunks are made from high-quality wood, there's a large garden at the back and plenty of space for socializing. Our only gripe is the very basic kitchen.

Casa Valladolid BOUTIQUE HOTEL $$
(☎985-856-55-15, 985-121-01-44; Calle 44 No 176, btwn Calles 35 & 37; r incl breakfast from M$1200; ❄✳🛜✖) This spot promises big things on entry – the reception is located in a lovely colonial building with stunning floor tiles. The rooms are in a new section, set around a small pool and patio. Rooms are pleasant, if a little plain. The smaller rooms are less appealing (several don't have external windows); those with terraces and balconies are the nicest.

Casa San Roque B&B $$$
(☎985-856-26-42; www.casasanroquevalladolid. com; Calle 41 No 193B; r M$1190-1725; 🅿❄✳ 🛜✖) With just seven colonial rooms on offer you'll get more privacy and personalized attention here than at some of the larger hotels on the main plaza. The full breakfast (M$100 per person) and a pool with dual fountains in the rear garden are the clinchers.

Hotel Zenti'k
BOUTIQUE HOTEL $$$

(☎985-104-91-71; www.zentikhotel.com; Calle 30 No 192C, btwn Calles 27 & 29; cabañas incl breakfast from M$1500; P❄✦🛜🖥🏊) This hippyish boutique hotel some way from the town center offers a choice of 10 spacious and imaginatively designed *cabañas* within intimate surrounds. A gorgeous pool, a spa and an usual underground swimming cave are the real highlights, as is its fabulous restaurant and the fact that the owner rescues local stray animals and finds them homes.

You'll need your own transportation to get here as it's just beyond walkable from the center for some, especially at night. Prices are significantly lower outside high season and that's when you get real value for money. Several walls are covered in impressive murals by contemporary artists.

Casa Tía Micha
BOUTIQUE HOTEL $$$

(☎985-856-04-99; www.casatiamicha.com; Calle 39 No 197; r incl breakfast from M$1450; P❄✦🛜🖥) The corridor and rear garden are beautifully lit at night in this family-run boutique hotel just off the plaza. Some of the tastefully adorned colonial-style rooms have king-sized beds, and the upstairs suite comes with a Jacuzzi. If the Tía is booked, on the same block you'll find sister property **Casa Marlene** (Calle 39 No 193; r incl breakfast M$1800-2150; P❄✦🛜🖥), whose pool guests here can use.

Eating

★ Yerbabuena del Sisal
MEXICAN $

(☎985-856-14-06; www.yerbabuenadelsisal.com; Calle 54A No 217; mains M$80-120; ☉8am-5pm Tue-Sun; 🛜🖥) 🌿 Wonderfully healthy dishes are served in this gorgeous open-sided space with a peaceful garden right on Parque Sisal. Tortilla chips and three delectable salsas come to the table while you look over the menu, which offers all-vegetarian and largely organic dishes, such as the delightful *tacos maculum* (with handmade corn tortillas, beans, cheese and aromatic Mexican pepper leaf).

La Palapita de los Tamales
MEXICAN $

(☎998-106-34-72; Calle 42 s/n, cnr Calle 33; tamales from M$45; ☉8-10pm Mon-Sat; 🖥) The menu changes daily here, but you'll always find a welcome *tamal* to snack on. Sweetcorn and pork was on the menu recently, as was excellent *pozole* (a pork-and-hominy soup). There's casual indoor or patio seating, and takeout is popular. Great juices, breakfasts and vegan options, too.

★ Ix Cat Ik
MAYA $$

(☎985-104-16-05; www.ixcatik.mx; Calle 39, btwn Calles 20 & 22; mains M$165-265; ☉noon-10pm; 🛜🖥) Take a cab to reach this superb place, your best opportunity to eat Maya cooking in Valladolid. Its knowledgeable English-speaking staff will help you decide between the numerous choices, including dishes cooked in the *píibil*, a Maya woodfired oven built into the soil, which you can see in the garden. Try the *sopa de lima* and the *empanada de chaya*.

Naino
INTERNATIONAL $$

(☎985-104-90-71; www.facebook.com/zentikproject; Calle 30 No 192, btwn Calles 27 & 29; mains M$80-180; ☉7am-10:30pm; P🛜) Located on the outskirts of town, on the premises of the resort Zenti'k, this pleasant open-air restaurant is an option for breakfast, lunch or dinner. The food is creative with some extremely creative takes on local cooking fused with international flavors. If you're craving something a bit different then this is the spot.

🍷 Drinking & Nightlife

Taberna de los Frailes
COCKTAIL BAR

(☎985-856-06-89; www.tabernadelosfrailes.com; Calle 49 s/n, cnr Calle 41A; ☉10am-10pm; 🛜) This pretty and rather romantic spot with a verdant garden is a top spot to get a tasty cocktail at a place where you can actually have a quiet conversation. There's an excellent selection of mezcals and tequilas.

Los Portales
CAFE

(☎985-856-09-99; Calle 41 No 202B; ☉7am-11pm) Don't expect award-winning mixology at Los Portales, but as its name suggests, it's all about location: hard to beat the alfresco experience on the plaza if you're looking to relax, sip something and marvel at beautiful Valladolid.

ℹ Getting There & Away

BUS
Valladolid's main bus terminal is the convenient ADO bus terminal (p310), which has both 1st- and 2nd-class services.

Buses to Chichén Itzá/Piste normally stop at the ruins during opening hours, though double check with the driver.

COLECTIVO
Colectivos depart as soon as their seats are filled (or you can elect to pay the full fare). Most operate from 7am or 8am to about 7pm, but some leave as early as 3am or as late as 10pm.

BUSES FROM VALLADOLID

DESTINATION	FARE (M$)	TIME (HR)	FREQUENCY (PER DAY)
Cancún	252	2½-3½	frequent
Chichén Itzá/Pisté	35-118	¾	frequent
Chiquilá (for Isla Holbox)	201	4	9:50am
Cobá	51	1	6 daily
Izamal	80	2½	12:50pm
Mérida	240-250	2-3½	frequent
Playa del Carmen	252	3-4	frequent
Tizimín	31	1	frequent
Tulum	100-148	1-2	frequent

Direct services run to **Mérida** (Calle 39, near the ADO bus terminal; M$200; ⊘2hr) and **Cancún** (Calle 41, cnr Calle 38, 1 block east of the plaza; M$200; ⊘2hr); confirm they're nonstop. *Colectivos* for **Pisté & Chichén Itzá** (Calle 39; M$35; ⊘1hr) leave north of the ADO bus terminal. For **Ek' Balam** (Calle 44, btwn Calles 35 & 37; M$50) take a 'Santa Rita' *colectivo*.

ⓘ Getting Around

The old highway passes through the town center, though most signs urge motorists toward the toll road north of town. To follow the old highway eastbound, take Calle 41; westbound, take Calle 39.

Bicycles are a great way to see the town and get out to the cenotes. You can rent them at Hostel La Candelaria (p351) or MexiGo Tours (p351) for around M$20 to M$25 per hour.

It's possible to get to many of the cenotes by public transportation. *Colectivos* depart from different points around the center; ask the locals. Note that these tend to leave in the mornings only.

Ek' Balam

The tiny village of Ek' Balam is worth a visit to see what a traditional Maya village looks like. There's not a lot here, except a handful of artisan stands (mainly selling hammocks) along the main plaza, which also serves as the town's soccer field, and a decent accommodations option.

⊙ Sights

Ek' Balam   ARCHAEOLOGICAL SITE
(adult/child 4-12yr M$431/75; guide M$600; ⊘8am-4pm) The fascinating ruined city of Ek' Balam reached its peak in the 8th century CE, before being suddenly abandoned.

Vegetation still covers much of the archaeological site, but it's well organized and has a lovely, lush setting. Interesting features include a pyramid-like structure near the entrance, as well as a fine arch and a ball court. Most impressive, though, is the gargantuan **Acrópolis**, whose well-restored base is 160m long and holds a 'gallery' – actually a series of separate chambers.

Built atop the base of the Acrópolis is Ek' Balam's massive **main pyramid**, reaching a height of 32m and sporting a gaping jaguar mouth. Below the mouth are stucco skulls, while above and to the right sits an amazingly expressive figure. On the right side stand unusual winged human figures (some call them Maya angels, although a much more likely explanation is that they are shamans or medicine people).

The turnoff for the archaeological site is 17km north of Valladolid, and the ruins are another 6km east from the turnoff.

⎘ Sleeping

⭐**Genesis Eco-Oasis**   GUESTHOUSE $$
(☑cell 985-1010277; www.genesisretreat.com; Ek' Balam pueblo; r US$45-79; ⊝⊚⚇) ⦚ This retreat offers B&B intimacy in a quiet, laid-back ecofriendly setting. Mostly it's environmentally friendly: gray water is used for landscaping, the rooms' architecture (pitched, thatched roofs) encourages passive cooling and there's a dehydrating toilet or two. There's a swimming pool and it offers delicious veggie meals made from scratch.

ⓘ Getting There & Away

Colectivos (M$50) to Ek' Balam depart Valladolid from Calle 44, between Calles 35 and 37.

YUCATÁN PENINSULA EK' BALAM

Río Lagartos

📞 986 / POP 3000

On the windy northern shore of the peninsula, sleepy Río Lagartos (Alligator River) is a fishing village that also boasts the densest concentration of flamingos in Mexico, supposedly two or three flamingos per resident, if one believes the provided math. Lying within the Reserva de la Biosfera Ría Lagartos, this mangrove-lined estuary shelters bird species including snowy egrets, red egrets, tiger herons and snowy white ibis, as well as the crocodiles that gave the town its name. It's a beautiful area. At the right time of year you can see numerous species of birds without even getting out of your vehicle.

🧭 Tours

⭐ **Río Lagartos Adventures**   BOATING
(📱986-100-83-90; www.riolagartosadventures.com; Calle 19 No 134; per boat 4hr from M$3425, 2hr flamingo tour per boat M$2000) This outfit run by local expert Diego Núñez Martinez does various water and land expeditions, including flamingo- and crocodile-watching, fly-fishing and excursions designed for photography. Diego is a licensed, fluent-English-speaking guide with formal training as a naturalist. He's well up to date on the area's fauna and flora, which includes some 400 bird species.

He organizes the tours out of **Ría Maya Restaurante** (www.riolagartosadventures.com; Calle 19 No 134, cnr Calle 14; mains M$120-300; ⊗9am-8:30pm) and trains local guides.

🛏 Sleeping & Eating

**Restaurant y
Posada Macumba**   GUESTHOUSE $
(📱986-862-00-92; ⊗s/d M$750/950; ❄🖥) The waterfront Macumba has six smallish and very comfortable rooms, decked out in Caribbean design, and it is in a nice location, right on the waterfront. It is also the site of a skippable restaurant on the 1st floor.

El Perico Marinero   HOTEL $$
(📱986-862-00-58; www.elpericomarinero.com; Calle 9, near Calle 19; d incl breakfast M$650-950; 🅿❄🖥🐕) This cozy hotel offers 14 pleasant rooms, some with estuary vistas and handmade wood furnishings, and all with excellent beds. The pool isn't enormous, but is adequate for cooling off. Breakfasts are simple, but coffee is brewed, not instant.

ⓘ Getting There & Away

Several Noreste buses run daily between Río Lagartos and Tizimín (M$47, 1¼ hours), Mérida (M$250, three to four hours) and San Felipe (M$20, 20 minutes). Noreste serves Valladolid and Cancún, but you'll need to transfer in Tizimín. If you are traveling to Valladolid, be sure to catch the 4pm bus from Río Lagartos; the 5pm doesn't make the connection in Tizimín.

The bus terminal is on Calle 19, between Calles 8 and 10.

CAMPECHE STATE

Tucked into the southwestern corner of the Yucatán Peninsula, Campeche state is home to low-key villages, vast stretches of tangled jungle, bird-dotted mangroves and lagoons, and some of the region's most imposing Maya ruins – many of which you might have all to yourself. The walled capital city of Campeche is the quiet-but-gorgeous colonial town at the center of it all, providing a great jumping-off point for your adventures into this offbeat hinterland.

Campeche is the least visited of the Yucatán's states, laced through with lonely back roads, friendly people, quiet coastlines and a provincial, lost-land charm. It makes a welcome break from the tourist hordes that descend on the peninsula's more popular destinations; here you'll find peace, surprising attractions and very genuine local experiences.

Campeche

📞 981 / POP 250,000

Campeche is a historical fairyland, its walled city a tight enclave of restored pastel buildings, narrow cobblestone streets, fortified ramparts and well-preserved mansions. Added to Unesco's list of World Heritage sites in 1999, the state capital may lack the buzz and smarts of nearby Mérida, but wandering its near perfectly preserved colonial streets is a wonderful experience. Leave the inner walls and you'll find a genuine Mexican provincial capital complete with a frenetic market, peaceful *malecón* and old fishing docks.

Besides the walls and numerous mansions built by wealthy Spanish families during Campeche's heyday in the 18th and 19th centuries, seven of the *baluartes* (bastions or bulwarks) have also survived. Two preserved colonial forts guard the city's outskirts, one of them housing the Museo Arqueológico de Campeche, an archaeological museum with many world-class pieces.

History

Once a Maya trading village called Ah Kim Pech (Lord Sun Sheep-Tick), Campeche was first briefly approached by the Spaniards in 1517. Resistance by the Maya prevented the Spaniards from fully conquering the region for nearly a quarter-century. Colonial Campeche was founded in 1531, but later abandoned due to Maya hostility. By 1540, however, the conquistadors had gained sufficient control, under the leadership of Francisco de Montejo (the Younger), to found a permanent settlement. They named the settlement Villa de San Francisco de Campeche.

The settlement soon flourished as the major port of the Yucatán Peninsula, but this made it subject to pirate attacks. After a particularly appalling attack in 1663 (p359) left the city in ruins, the king of Spain ordered construction of Campeche's famous bastions, putting an end to the periodic carnage.

Today the city's economy is largely driven by tourism.

◉ Sights

★ Museo Arqueológico de Campeche & Fuerte de San Miguel   MUSEUM, FORT
(Campeche Archaeological Museum; Av Escénica s/n; M$55; ⊘8:30am-5pm Tue-Sun; ℗) Campeche's largest colonial fort, facing the Gulf of Mexico some 4km southwest of the city center, is home to the most important of Maya museums, which has recently undergone a full renovation with an expanded collection, including many finds never before displayed publicly.

Plaza Principal   PLAZA
Shaded by carob trees and ringed by tiled benches and broad footpaths radiating from a belle-epoque kiosk, Campeche's appealingly modest central square started life in 1531 as a military camp. Over the years it became the focus of the town's civic, political and religious activities and remains the core of public life. *Campechanos* come here to chat, smooch, have their shoes shined or cool off with an ice cream after the heat of the day.

Malecón   WATERFRONT
A popular path for joggers, cyclists, strolling friends and cooing sweethearts, the *malecón,* Campeche's 7km-long waterfront promenade, makes for a breezy sunrise ramble or sunset bike ride.

Mansión Carvajal   HISTORIC BUILDING
(Calle 10, btwn Calles 51 & 53; ⊘8am-2:45pm Mon-Fri) FREE Once the mansion of wealthy landowner Fernando Carvajal, this beautiful building now houses state offices. Visitors are welcome to take a peek inside, however. Black-and-white tiled floors, Doric columns, elaborate archways and a dramatic marble-and-ironwork staircase are highlights. Note the historical plaque.

Museo del Archivo General de Estado   MUSEUM
(☑981-816-09-39; Calle 12 No 159; ⊘8am-3pm Mon-Fri) FREE At this small museum, learn how Campeche came to be. It's free and air-conditioned, and you get to check out old documents and maps, and watch a video (in Spanish or English) that recounts the history of the state.

Catedral de Nuestra Señora de la Purísima Concepción   CATHEDRAL
(Calle 55; ⊘7am-9pm) FREE Dominating Plaza Principal's east side is the two-towered cathedral. The limestone structure has stood on this spot for more than three centuries and it still fills beyond capacity most Sundays for mass. Statues of Sts Peter and Paul occupy niches in the baroque facade; the sober, single-nave interior is lined with colonial-era paintings. And at night, the gauzy lights on the illuminated church and other central landmarks create a magical atmosphere.

Centro Cultural Casa Número 6   CULTURAL CENTER
(Calle 57 No 6; M$20; ⊘8am-9pm Mon-Fri, from 9am Sat & Sun) During the prerevolutionary era, when this mansion was occupied by an upper-class *campechano* family, Número 6 was a prestigious plaza address. Wandering the premises, you'll get an idea of how the city's high society lived back then. The front sitting room is furnished with Cuban-style pieces of the period. Inside are exhibition spaces, a tourist information desk and a gift shop.

Ex-Templo de San José & Bazar Artesanal   HISTORIC BUILDING
(former San José Church; cnr Calles 10 & 63; ⊘10am-8pm) Faced with blue-and-yellow

Campeche

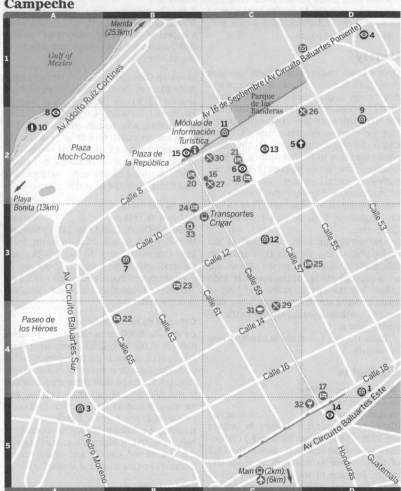

tiles, the Ex-Templo de San José is a wonder; note the lighthouse, complete with weather vane, atop the right spire. Built in the early-18th century by Jesuits, who ran it as an institute of higher learning until they were booted out of Spanish domains in 1767.

Museo de la Arquitectura Maya MUSEUM
(Calle 8; M$45; ☺8:30am-5:30pm Tue-Sun) The Baluarte de Nuestra Señora de la Soledad, designed to protect the Puerta del Mar, contains the fascinating Museo de la Arquitectura Maya. It provides an excellent overview of the sites around Campeche

state and the key architectural styles associated with them. Currently, four halls display stelae taken from various sites, accompanied by graphic representations of their carved inscriptions with brief commentaries in flawless English.

Monument to the City Gates MONUMENT
Next to the Plaza Moch-Couoh is this modern monument to the city's four famous gates (land, sea, San Román and Guadalupe); these entrances were in the city walls that surrounded the city. The first two are still standing.

Baluartes

After a particularly blistering pirate assault in 1663, the remaining inhabitants of Campeche set about erecting protective walls around their city. Built largely by indigenous labor with limestone extracted from nearby caves, the barrier took more than 50 years to complete. Stretching more than 2.5km around the urban core and rising to a height of 8m, the hexagonal wall was linked by eight bulwarks. The seven that remain display a treasure trove of historical paraphernalia and artifacts of varying degrees of interest. You can climb atop the bulwarks and stroll sections of the wall for sweeping views of the port.

Two main entrances connected the walled compound with the outside world. The **Puerta del Mar** (Sea Gate; cnr Calles 8 & 59) provided access from the sea, opening on to a wharf where small craft delivered goods from ships anchored further out. (The shallow waters were later reclaimed so the gate is now several blocks from the waterfront.) The **Puerta de Tierra** (Land Gate; Calle 18; ◎9am-6pm), on the opposite side, was opened in 1732 as the principal ingress from the suburbs.

Baluarte de San Francisco & Baluarte de San Juan HISTORIC BUILDING

(Calle 18; M$25; ⊙ 8am-9pm Mon-Wed, to 6pm Thu & Fri, from 9am Sat & Sun) FREE Once the primary defensive bastion for the adjacent Puerta de la Tierra, the Baluarte de San Francisco houses a pirate exhibition in both English and Spanish. You also enter here to walk along the Baluarte de San Juan, the smallest of the seven bulwarks. Here you can see the bell that was rung to alert the population in times of danger – different bells around the city had different sounds and meanings.

Baluarte de San Pedro HISTORIC BUILDING

(cnr Avs Circuito Baluartes Este & Circuito Baluartes Norte; M$15; ⊙ 8am-3pm) FREE Directly behind Iglesia de San Juan de Dios, the Baluarte de San Pedro served a post-piracy defensive function when it repelled a punitive raid from Mérida in 1824. Carved in stone above the entry is the symbol of San Pedro: two keys to heaven and the papal tiara. Inside you'll find a few small rooms with exhibitions on pirate history.

Baluarte de Santiago & Jardín Botánico
Xmuch Haltún GARDENS, HISTORIC BUILDING

(cnr Calles 8 & 49; M$15; ⊙ 8am-9pm Mon-Fri, from 9am Sat & Sun) Completed in 1704 – the last of the bulwarks to be built – the Baluarte de Santiago houses the Jardín Botánico Xmuch Haltún, a botanical garden with numerous endemic and some introduced plants. It's not a huge place, but provides a green and peaceful respite when the sun gets particularly brutal.

Baluarte de Santa Rosa HISTORIC BUILDING

(cnr Calle 14 & Av Circuito Baluartes Sur; ⊙ 8am-8pm) FREE The Baluarte de Santa Rosa has a gallery that houses temporary exhibitions.

Tours

Kankabi' Ok TOUR

(✆ 981-811-27-92; www.kankabiok.com.mx; Calle 59 No 3; ⊙ 9am-1pm & 5-9pm Mon-Sat) This reliable outfit offers a huge number of tours from four-hour guided walks around Campeche to day trips to archaeological sites such as Edzná, Chenes, Calakmul and the Ruta Puuc. It also rents out bikes (per hour M$30) and does ecotourism and beach trips. Prices vary depending on your group size and itinerary, so it's best to get in touch to discuss.

Sleeping

Hostal Viatger HOSTEL $

(✆ 981-811-45-00; Calle 51 No 28, btwn Calles 12 & 14; dm/d/tr incl breakfast M$245/500/550; P ⊖ ※ ⊚) This hostel enjoys a good location in the historic center (but away from the crowds) and has a friendly atmosphere. Dorms are nothing fancy, but women can enjoy their own space and there's the option of private doubles and triples, some with TVs and air-con. There's a kitchen and an outdoor social area out the back in the yard.

Hotel Campeche HOTEL $

(✆ 981-816-51-83; Calle 57, btwn Calles 8 & 10; s/d with fan M$285/345, with air-con M$380/450; ※ ⊚) Not much in the way of frills here, but the location by the plaza and big rooms in this classically crumbling building make this about the best budget hotel in town. Of the 40 rooms, seven have little balconies looking out over the plaza, which are a steal at this price.

Hostal Casa Balché HOSTEL $

(✆ 981-811-00-87; Calle 57 No 6; dm/d/tr/ste M$260/850/1000/1000; ※ ⊚) With its unbeatable location on the Plaza Principal, this breezy, bright and friendly hostel offers a combination of dorms and private rooms, all with their own dedicated bathroom outside each room. It's a stylish set up, with lots of social spaces, including a roof terrace remodeled in 2019. The kitchen is very basic, though.

★ Hotel López HOTEL $$

(✆ 981-816-33-44; Calle 12 No 189; r/ste M$750/850; ⊖ ※ ⊚ ⊛) This business hotel is by far one of Campeche's best midrange options. Modern, comfortably appointed rooms open on to curvy art-deco-styled balconies around oval courtyards and pleasant greenery. There's also a lovely pool out back. Prices are considerably lower outside high season, though the standard rooms are on the small side and it's worth paying a little extra for more space.

Hotel Misión Campeche HOTEL $$

(✆ 981-816-45-88; www.hotelesmision.com.mx; Calle 10 No 252; r from M$1220; P ※ ⊚) Part of a national chain of midrange hotels, this excellently located and atmospheric place has a traditional courtyard and 42 large, clean rooms spread along arcade corridors. The downside is that the rooms can vary widely in size and brightness, so check some out first.

Hotel Francis Drake HOTEL $$
(☑ 981-811-56-26; www.hotelfrancisdrake.com; Calle 12 No 207; incl breakfast s/d M$935/1030, ste from M$1300; ❀❅☎) A somewhat baroque lobby leads to 25 cool, but now rather faded looking rooms with a sprinkling of tasteful decoration. Bathrooms and balconies are tiny, but the rooms are huge (other hotels would call them suites) with king-sized beds and separate sitting areas. Wi-fi is in the lobby only.

★**Hacienda Puerta Campeche** BOUTIQUE HOTEL $$$
(☑ 981-816-75-08; www.luxurycollection.com; Calle 59 No 71; r from US$240; ❅☎❆) This beautiful Marriott-run hotel has 15 suites with high ceilings and separate lounges. Perfectly manicured gardens and grassy lawns offer peace, while the creatively designed pool cuts through the property and has nearby hammocks fit for a Maya king. There's an on-site spa, restaurant and bar in case you really don't want to leave the premises, and service is charming.

It also runs a restored luxury hacienda 26km outside the city, on the way to the Edzná ruins.

Hotel Socaire BOUTIQUE HOTEL $$$
(☑ 981-811-21-30; www.hotelsocaire.com; Calle 57 No 19, btwn Calles 12a & 14a; r/ste from M$1550/1990; ☎❆) A charmingly converted colonial building leads through to a variety of spacious rooms in the rear. The walls have curios and antiques in the nooks and crannies, and the lovely pool is a perfect way to cool down in the heat of the day. It's in a great central location and is excellent value.

Hotel Boutique Casa Don Gustavo BOUTIQUE HOTEL $$$
(☑ 981-816-80-90; www.casadongustavo.com; Calle 59 No 4; r/ste from M$3300/4000; ℗❅☎❆) The 10 rooms here are decorated with antique furniture and have huge modern bathrooms, while the public areas look more like a museum than anything else. There's a small pool with hammocks and colorful tiled hallways line an outdoor courtyard. Its location on the main pedestrian street can make some rooms a little noisy, however.

✗ Eating

You can try some good local dishes in Campeche, especially seafood and the likes of *cochinita pibil*. Overall the city doesn't have a particularly interesting foodie scene, but a few places offer an escape from the bland offerings of many restaurants in the historic center.

Luan Restaurante y Café CAFE $
(☑ 981-811-52-05; Calle 59 No 35, btwn Calles 12a & 14a; M$75-115; ❂8am-10pm Mon-Fri, to 1pm Sat-Sun; ☎) This breezy and cool place in an old colonial building overlooking the prettiest section of pedestrian Calle 59 serves Mexican breakfast and brunch dishes, from eggs (any way you want them) to pancakes and freshly made sandwiches. Reasonable coffee and excellent smoothies make it a great place for a welcome break from the heat.

★**La María Cocina Peninsula** MEXICAN $$
(☑ 981-816-36-18; Calle 8 No 173; mains M$130-245; ❂2-9pm Wed-Mon; ☎✐) Despite not looking

---

MARAUDING PIRATES OF CAMPECHE

Where there's wealth, there are pirates – this was truer in the 1500s than it is today. And Campeche, which was a thriving timber, chicle (gum) and logwood (a natural source of dye) port in the mid-16th century, was the wealthiest place around.

Pirates (or 'privateers,' as some preferred to be called) terrorized Campeche for two centuries. Time and time again the port was invaded, ships sacked, citizens robbed and buildings burned – typical pirate stuff. The buccaneers' hall of shame included the infamous John Hawkins, Francis Drake, Henry Morgan and the notorious 'Peg-Leg' himself. In their most gruesome assault, in early 1663, the various pirate hordes set aside rivalries to converge as a single flotilla upon the city, massacring Campeche's citizens.

This tragedy finally spurred the Spanish monarchy to take preventive action, but it was another five years before work on the 3.5m-thick ramparts began. By 1686 a 2.5km hexagon incorporating eight strategically placed bastions surrounded the city. A segment of the ramparts extended out to sea so that ships literally sailed into a fortress to gain access to the city. With Campeche nearly impregnable, pirates turned to other ports and ships at sea. In 1717 the brilliant naval strategist Felipe de Aranda began a campaign against the buccaneers, and eventually made this area of the Gulf safe from piracy.

much different from other Mexicana-heavy old-town restaurants replete with sombreros, national flags and Yucatecan art, one look at the menu here will confirm you've entered a different culinary universe. Some of the dishes might sound downright odd (shrimp *aguachile* with seasonal fruit sorbet, anyone?), but this is Campeche's most innovative dining spot right now.

La Parrilla Colonial
MEXICAN $$

(☑ 981-127-11-62; Calle 59, btwn Calles 8 & 10; mains M$100-200; ◷1pm-1am Mon-Wed, to 2am Thu-Sat; 🛜) Despite its relentlessly clichéd decor that takes in as many national tropes as possible, this is actually one of the best of the restaurants spread out along Calle 59. There's a full and interesting menu of Yucatecan specialties and good service from a fleet of efficient staff in national dress.

Marganzo
MEXICAN $$$

(☑ 981-811-38-98; Calle 8 No 267; mains M$180-350; ◷7am-10:45pm; 🛜) Marganzo is a popular with tourists and locals alike for good reason – the food is great, the portions large and the complimentary appetizers numerous. An extensive menu offers everything from international fare to regional treats such as *cochinita pibil* and a famous seafood platter. Wandering musicians provide entertainment.

La Pigua
SEAFOOD $$$

(☑ 981-811-33-65; www.lapigua.com.mx; Miguel Alemán 179A; mains M$200-380; ◷1-6pm) Campeche's most upscale restaurant can be found just outside the old city walls and is an elegant space with white linen tablecloths. Service is attentive and the specialties include *camarones al coco* (coconut shrimp), fish fillet in cilantro sauce and grilled squid with ground almonds and paprika. Reservations advised.

Drinking & Nightlife

Chocol-Ha
CAFE

(☑ 981-811-78-93; Calle 59 No 30; drinks M$25-55, snacks M$35-80; ◷8am-10:30pm Mon-Sat; 🛜) For chocolate cravings, head to this cute little cafe with a patio in front and grassy yard in back. Try bittersweet hot chocolate with green tea or chili, and a chocolate frappé. Sweet treats such as cake, crepes and even tamales (yep, all chocolate!) will give you a sugary high, while nonchocolate dishes are also available.

Salón Rincón Colonial
BAR

(☑ 981-816-83-76; Calle 59 No 60; ◷10am-9pm) With ceiling fans high over an airy hall and a solid wood bar amply stocked with rum, this Cuban-style drinking establishment appropriately served as a location for *Original Sin,* a 2001 movie with Antonio Banderas and Angelina Jolie that was set in Havana. The *botanas* (appetizers) are exceptionally fine and go down well with a local beer.

🛍 Shopping

Casa de Artesanías Tukulná
ARTS & CRAFTS

(☑ 981-127-17-68; Calle 10 No 333; ◷9am-9pm) A central collection of shops selling a lovely, high-quality range of textiles, clothing, hats, hammocks, wood chairs, sweets and so on – all made in Campeche state.

ℹ Information

Campeche has numerous banks with ATMs.

Call ☑ 911 in an emergency.

Central Post Office (cnr Av 16 de Septiembre & Calle 53; ◷8:30am-4pm Mon-Fri, 8-11:30am Sat)

Hospital General De Especialidades (☑ 981-127-39-80; Las Flores)

Hospital Dr Manuel Campos (☑ 981-811-17-09; Av Circuito Baluartes Norte, btwn Calles 14 & 16)

HSBC Bank (Calle 10, btwn Calles 53 & 55; ◷9am-5pm Mon-Fri, to 3pm Sat) Open Saturday.

Módulo de Información Turística del Municipio de Campeche (☑ 981-811-39-89; www.campeche.travel; Puerta del Mar, Calle 8; ◷8am-9pm Mon-Fri, from 9am Sat & Sun) Basic information on Campeche city.

ℹ Getting There & Away

AIR

Campeche's small-but-modern airport is 6km southeast of the center; it has car-rental offices and a tiny snack bar. Aeroméxico and Interjet provides services to Mexico City.

BUS

Campeche's **main bus terminal** (☑ 981-811-99-10; Av Patricio Trueba 237), usually called the ADO or 1st-class terminal, is about 2.5km south of Plaza Principal via Av Central. Buses provide 1st-class and deluxe service to Mérida, Cancún, Chetumal (via Xpujil), Palenque, Veracruz and Mexico City, along with 2nd-class services to Sabancuy (M$148, two hours), Hecelchakán (M$50, one hour) and Candelaria (M$218, four hours).

BUSES FROM CAMPECHE

DESTINATION	FARE (M$)	TIME (HR)	FREQUENCY (PER DAY)
Cancún	755	7	2
Chetumal	570	6½	1
Ciudad del Carmen	240-270	3	hourly
Mérida	264	2½	hourly
Mérida (via Uxmal)	120-180	4½	5 from 2nd-class terminal
Mexico City	1200-2100	18	3
Palenque	497	5	4
San Cristóbal de las Casas	709	15	2
Villahermosa	380-609	6	frequent
Xpujil	240-414	4½	2pm

The **2nd-class terminal** (Terminal Sur; ☑ 981-816-34-45; Av Gobernadores 479), often referred to as the 'old ADO' station' or 'Autobuses del Sur,' is 700m east of the Mercado Principal. Second-class destinations include Hopelchén (M$74, 1½ hours), Xpujil (M$245, four hours), Uxmal (M$141, one hour) and Bécal (M$63, 1¾ hours).

Transportes Crígar (☑ 981-145-61-62; Calle 10 No 329; ⊘ 8am-10pm) is a handy spot to buy ADO (1st-class) bus tickets. Or try other travel agencies around town.

To get to the main bus terminal, catch any 'Las Flores,' 'Solidaridad' or 'Casa de Justicia' microbus by the post office. To the 2nd-class terminal, catch a 'Terminal Sur' bus from the same point.

A taxi to either bus station from the walled city costs M$40 to M$50.

ℹ Getting Around

Taxis from the airport to the center cost M$160 (shared taxis M$70 per person); buy tickets at the taxi booth inside the terminal. Going to the airport, some street taxis (ie those not called from your hotel, which are more expensive) charge M$150; penny-pinchers can try taking the hourly bus to Chiná (a village outside Campeche; around M$15) from the market, and getting off at the airport entrance, then walking 500m to the airport doors.

Within Campeche city, taxis charge M$30 to M$60; prices are 10% more after 10pm, and 20% more from midnight to 5am.

Most local buses (around M$7) have a stop at or near the Mercado Principal.

Consider pedaling along the *malecón;* get bike rentals at Kankabi' Ok (p358).

Drivers should note that even-numbered streets in the *centro histórico* take priority, but go slowly until you get the hang of the cross streets.

Northern Campeche

Northern Campeche offers a fascinating blend of experiences. An enticing mix of colonial and Maya elements, blended with centuries-old tradition and lush nature, it's worth spending time here. Wander through the alluring complex of Edzná (one of the region's finest sets of ruins) or marvel over the unique features of architecture at the Chenes sites. Most of these places are doable as separate day trips from Campeche.

Chenes Sites

Northeastern Campeche state is dotted with more than 30 sites in the distinct Chenes style, recognizable by the monster motifs around doorways in the center of long, low buildings of three sections, and temples atop pyramidal bases. Most of the year you'll have these sites to yourself. The three small sites of El Tabasqueño, Hochob and Dzibilnocac make for an interesting day trip from Campeche if you have your own vehicle, though even if you don't, you can take a tour from Campeche with Kankabi' Ok Tours (p358).

◉ Sights

Dzibilnocac ARCHAEOLOGICAL SITE
(⊘ 8am-5pm) **FREE** Though it only has one significant structure, Dzibilnocac possesses an eerie grandeur that merits a visit. Unlike the many hilltop sites chosen for Chenes structures, Dzibilnocac ('big painted turtle' is one translation) is on a flat plain, like a large open park. As Stephens and Catherwood observed in 1842, the many scattered hillocks in the zone, still unexcavated today, attest to the presence of a large city.

YUCATÁN PENINSULA NORTHERN CAMPECHE

The single, clearly discernible structure is **A1**, a palatial complex upon a 76m platform with a trio of raised temples atop rounded pyramidal bases. The best preserved of the three, on the east end, has fantastically elaborate monster-mask reliefs on each of its four sides and the typically piled-up Chaac masks on three of the four corners.

Dzibilnocac is located beside the village of Iturbide (also called Vicente Guerrero), 20km northeast of Dzibalchén. From Campeche's 2nd-class bus terminal there are several buses daily to Iturbide via Hopelchén (M$110, three hours). There's no place to stay here so you'll need to make it back to Hopelchén by nightfall.

Hochob   ARCHAEOLOGICAL SITE

(M$45; ⊘8am-5pm) About 60km south of Hopelchén, Hochob, 'the place where corn is harvested,' is among the most beautiful and terrifying of the Chenes-style sites. The **Palacio Principal** (Estructura 2, though signposted as 'Estructura 1') is on the north side of the main plaza, faced with an elaborate doorway representing Itzamná, creator of the ancient Maya, as a rattlesnake with open jaws.

Facing it across the plaza, **Estructura 5** has two raised temples on either end of a long series of rooms; the better-preserved eastern temple retains part of its perforated roofcomb.

To reach Hochob, go 5km south from El Tabasqueño, then turn right just before the Pemex station at Dzilbalchén. Now go 7.5km to the Chencoh sign, turn left, then after 400m go left again; then drive another 3.5km.

El Tabasqueño   ARCHAEOLOGICAL SITE

(⊘8am-5pm) FREE Supposedly named after a local landowner from Tabasco, El Tabasqueño boasts a **temple-palace** (Estructura 1) with a striking monster-mouth doorway, flanked by stacks of eight Chaac masks with hooked snouts. Estructura 2 is a solid **free-standing tower**, an oddity in Maya architecture.

To reach El Tabasqueño, go 30km south from Hopelchén. Just beyond the village of Pakchén, there's an easy-to-miss sign at a turnoff on the right; follow this rock-and-gravel road 2km to the site.

ℹ Getting There & Away

If you don't have your own wheels, head off on a day trip from Campeche with Kankabi' Ok Tours (p358). There is no easy public transportation to these or other Chenes sites.

Edzná

If you only have the time or inclination to visit one archaeological site in northern Campeche, **Edzná** (M$60, guide M$500; ⊘8am-5pm) should be your top pick. It's located about 60km southeast of Campeche.

Edzná's massive complexes, that once covered more than 17 sq km, were built by a highly stratified society that flourished from about 600 BC to the 15th century CE. During that period the people of Edzná built more than 20 complexes in a melange of architectural styles, installing an ingenious network of water-collection and irrigation systems. (Though it's a long way from such Puuc Hills sites as Uxmal and Kabah, some of the architecture here has elements of the Puuc style.)

Edzná means 'House of the Itzáes,' a reference to a predominant governing clan of Chontal Maya origin. Most of the visible carvings date from 550 to 810 CE. The causes leading to Edzná's decline and gradual abandonment remain a mystery; the site remained unknown until its rediscovery by *campesinos* in 1906.

Edzná's rulers recorded significant events on stone stelae. Around 30 stelae have been discovered adorning the site's principal temples; a handful are on display underneath a *palapa* just beyond the ticket office.

A path from the *palapa* leads about 400m through vegetation; follow the 'Gran Acrópolis' sign. Soon, to your left, you'll come upon the **Plataforma de los Cuchillos** (Platform of the Knives), a residential complex highlighted by Puuc architectural features. The name is derived from an offering of silica knives that was found within.

Crossing a *sacbé* (stone-lined, grass walkway), you arrive at the main attraction, the **Plaza Principal**. Measuring 160m long and 100m wide, the Plaza Principal is surrounded by temples. On your right is the Nohochná (Big House), a massive, elongated structure topped by four long halls likely used for administrative tasks, such as the collection of tributes and the dispensation of justice.

Across the plaza is the **Gran Acrópolis**, a raised platform holding several structures, including Edzná's major temple, the 31m-high Edificio de los Cinco Pisos (Five-Story Building). The current structure is the last of four remodels and was done primarily in the Puuc style. It rises five levels from its base to the roofcomb and contains many vaulted rooms. Note the well-preserved glyphs along the base of the central staircase.

South of Plaza Principal is the **Templo de los Mascarones** (Temple of the Masks), with a pair of reddish stucco masks underneath a protective *palapa*. Personifying the gods of the rising and setting sun, these extraordinarily well-preserved faces display dental modification, crossed eyes and huge earrings, features associated with the Maya aristocracy.

🛈 Getting There & Away

Combis (around M$40; ⏱1hr) leave when full from Calle Chihuahua near Campeche's Mercado Principal. Most drop you 200m from the site entrance unless the driver is feeling generous. The last *combi* back is midafternoon (some say 2pm, others 3pm, others 5pm...you get the idea), so ask the driver to make sure. Weekdays you'll likely find a last return as late as 6pm; weekends it may be 3pm.

A taxi from Campeche with a one-hour wait at the ruins costs M$500. Kankabi' Ok (p358) in Campeche provides guided tours of Edzná (including transportation) for around M$900 per person.

Southeastern Campeche

The southern peninsular region from Escárcega to Xpujil, which borders modern-day Guatemala, was the earliest-established, longest-inhabited and most-densely populated region in the Maya world. Here you'll find the most-elaborate Maya archaeological sites on the Yucatán Peninsula.

Among the region's archaeological sites, the Río Bec architectural style dominates. To see all elements in one place you'll need to arrange a visit to the **Río Bec ruin** (ATV/pickup M$900/1000, guide M$700, park entry M$55; ⏱8am-5pm) 🆓, but more-accessible ruins contain some of these distinct characteristics. It is actually a hybrid of styles fusing elements from the Chenes region to the north and Petén to the south (in Guatemala). The most significant is the spectacular Calakmul set amid the ecologically diverse, and very lush, **Reserva de la Biosfera Calakmul** (⏱6am-5pm), however each site contains unique structures, carvings or discoveries that will fascinate ruin explorers.

Calakmul

A magnificent experience, **Calakmul** (combined admission M$198; ⏱8am-5pm) is made even better by its history as a leading city from around 250 CE. 'Discovered' in 1931 by American botanist Cyrus Lundell, and located deep in the jungle miles from modern civilization, the site bears comparison in size and historical significance to Tikal in Guatemala, its chief rival for hegemony over the southern lowlands during the Classic Maya era. It boasts the largest and tallest known pyramid in Mexico's Yucatán, and was once home to over 50,000 people.

But visiting Calakmul is not just a historical experience, it's also an ecological one. Lying at the heart of the vast, untrammeled Reserva de la Biosfera Calakmul (which covers close to 15% of the state's total territory), the ruins are surrounded by rainforest and a seemingly endless canopy of vegetation.

👁 Sights

A central chunk of the 72-sq-km expanse of Calakmul has been restored, but most of the city's approximately 6000 structures lie covered in jungle. In 2004, amazingly well-preserved painted murals were discovered at the Chiik Naab acropolis of Estructura 1. They depicted something never before seen in Maya murals – the typical daily activities of ordinary Maya (as opposed to the usual political, ceremonial or religious themes). Unfortunately, the murals and frieze are not open to the public, but their reproductions can be seen at Calakmul's modern **Museo de Naturaleza y Arqueología** (⏱8am-3pm) 🆓, at Km 20 on the 60km side road to Calakmul.

Note that the outer gates close for entry at 2:30pm, as you'll need over an hour's driving time to reach the site itself. Also note that there is no water or food on sale within the reserve, so be sure to bring plenty of supplies.

Gran Plaza   ARCHAEOLOGICAL SITE
The Gran Plaza, with its ancient buildings and many stelae, is a good place to begin your Calakmul explorations. You'll find Estructura II at the south side of the plaza; a path on the left (east) side of Estructura II leads past Estructura III; and walking south from Estructura III you come to Estructura I.

➡ **Estructura I**
Estructura I is Calakmul's second great pyramid (surpassed by Estructura II). American botanist Cyrus Lundell named the site

Calakmul

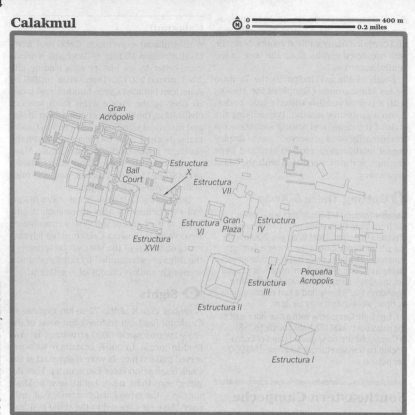

Calakmul, Maya for 'two adjacent mounds,' in reference to the pair of then-unexcavated pyramids that dominated the site. The steep climb pays off handsomely with top-of-the-world views.

⇒ **Estructura II**

Climbing the enormous Estructura II, at the south side of the Gran Plaza, is a must. Each of this pyramid's sides is 140m long, giving it a footprint of just under 2 hectares – making it by some estimates the largest and tallest known Maya structure. After a good climb you'll come to what appears to be the top of the building, but go around to the left to reach the real apex.

From here, 45m above the forest floor, you'll have magnificent views of Estructura I to the southeast and Estructura VII to the north – as well as jungle canopy as far as you can see. Facing southwest, you'll be looking toward the Maya city El Mirador, in neighboring Guatemala.

⇒ **Estructura III**

The palatial Estructura III consists of a dozen rooms atop a raised platform. Archaeologists found a tomb inside the 5th-century structure that contained the body of a male ruler of Calakmul surrounded by offerings of jade, ceramics and shell beads. He was wearing not one but three jade-mosaic masks – one each on his face, chest and belt.

Gran Acrópolis

The Gran Acrópolis is a labyrinthine residential zone with a ceremonial sector containing a ball court. (From the northern perimeter of this zone, you can head east and follow the path back to the entrance.)

⇒ Tours

From Campeche, Kankabi' Ok (p358) runs tours to Calakmul.

From Xpujil, **Ka'an Expeditions** (983-158-26-69, 983-871-60-00; www.kaanexpeditions.com; Av Calakmul s/n; per person US$75; ⓢnoon-

8pm Tue-Sun) runs a convenient tour; or a good English-speaking outfit is **Calakmul Adventures** (☑ 983-184-13-13; www.calakmul adventures.com; around M$1350).

Just west of Xpujil, **Río Bec Dreams** (☑ 983-126-35-26; www.riobecdreams.com; Hwy 186 Km 142, Becán; cabañas M$1300-2175; P 🐕 🛜) arranges tours with English-speaking guides, but these are only available to its guests.

If you want to arrange something on the hop, certified guides wait at the turnoff from Hwy 186 (at the entrance to the 20km of lands owned by the local community of Conhuas). They charge around M$800 for a multihour visit, but you need your own transportation. Most speak Spanish only. For those who speak English add at least another M$400 to the fee. Most importantly, do not try to get a guide at the site entrance, an hour's drive deep into the rainforest; you can normally only pick up guides on the turnoff to Calakmul on Hwy 186.

If you want a real DIY experience, you can hire a taxi from Escárgeca or Xpujil (around M$1500 with a three-hour wait). You don't need a guide at Calakmul, but a good one will infinitely improve your experience as the site is enormous and rather confusing.

🛏️ Sleeping

Campamento Yaax' Che   CAMPGROUND $
(Servidores Turísticos Calakmul; ☑ 983-101-19-21, 983-134-88-18; own/fixed tent M$100/320) This is the closest campground to the Calakmul site, and the nearest thing to a camping experience in the jungle. It's several kilometers after the turnoff from Hwy 186 on the road to Calakmul and another 700m in on a rough road. It's a relaxed, wilderness-style campground with sites for BYO tents. Or you can opt for ready-pitched tents.

It can be muddy when wet. There are environmentally friendly dry toilets and 'natural' showers plus a communal *palapa*. Meals can be arranged at the onsite restaurant. Head honchos Fernando and Leticia offer tours, too, including a three-hour jungle tour (around M$950 per person; five to six people) and a tour of archaeological sites (from M$1200; eight-person minimum).

ℹ️ Getting There & Away

Calakmul is 60km south of Hwy 186 at the end of a dirt road (the turnoff is 56km west of Xpujil). There are no buses after the turnoff, but a taxi from Xpujil can take you for M$1500 and wait

while you tour the ruins. Taxis wait at the turnoff and can bring one to four people the 60km and back for M$1200 per person, including a wait at the ruin. Shuttles can take up to 14 people for M$2400.

Chicanná & Becán

Chicanná and Becán are two interesting sites that are easily accessible from Hwy 186, located 10km and 8km respectively west of Xpujil. They represent fascinating examples of Chenes and Río Bec styles.

👁️ Sights

Chicanná   ARCHAEOLOGICAL SITE
(M$55; ⊙ 8am-5pm) Aptly named 'House of the Snake's Jaws,' this Maya site is best known for one remarkably well-preserved doorway with a hideous fanged visage. Located 10km west of Xpujil and 400m south of Hwy 186, Chicanná is a mixture of Chenes and Río Bec architectural styles buried in the jungle. The city attained its peak during the late Classic period, from 550 to 700 CE, as a sort of elite suburb of Becán.

Beyond the admission pavilion, follow the rock paths through the jungle to **Estructura XX**, which boasts two monster-mouth doorways, one above the other. The top structure is impressively flanked by rounded stacks of crook-nosed Chaac masks.

A five-minute walk along the jungle path brings you to **Estructura XI**, with what remains of some of the earliest buildings. Continue along the main path about 120m northeast to reach the **main plaza**. Standing on the east side is Chicanná's famous **Estructura II**, with its gigantic Chenes-style monster-mouth doorway, believed to depict the jaws of the god Itzamná – lord of the heavens and creator of all things. Note the painted glyphs to the right of the mask. A path leading from the right corner of Estructura II takes you to **Estructura VI**, which has a well-preserved roofcomb and some beautiful profile masks on its facade. Circle around the back, noting the faded red-painted blocks of the west wing, then turn right to hike back to the main entrance.

Chicanna is 10km west of Xpujil and 2km west of Becán.

★ Becán   ARCHAEOLOGICAL SITE
(M$60; ⊙ 8am-5pm) The Maya word for 'canyon' or 'moat' is *becán*, and indeed a 2km moat snakes its way around this must-visit Maya site. Seven causeways provide access

across the moat to the 12-hectare site, within which are the remains of three separate architectural complexes. A strategic crossroads between the Petenes civilization to the south and Chenes to the north, Becán displays architectural elements of both, with the resulting composite known as the Río Bec style.

The elaborate defenses surrounding the site allude to the militaristic nature of the city, which, from around 600 to 1000 CE, was a regional capital encompassing Xpujil and Chicanná.

Enter the complex via the western causeway, skirting Plaza del Este on your left. Proceed through a 66m-long arched passageway and you will emerge on to the **Plaza Central**, ringed by three monumental structures. The formidable 32m **Estructura IX**, on the plaza's north side, is Becán's tallest building – though the sign says not to climb it, a rope is provided and there's a steady stream of visitor traffic ascending and descending. **Estructura VIII** is the huge temple on your right, with a pair of towers flanking a colonnaded facade at the top. It's a great vantage point for the area; with binoculars, you can sometimes make out Xpujil's ruins to the east. Across the plaza from VIII is **Estructura X**, with fragments of an Earth Monster mask still visible around the central doorway. You can climb Estructura X, but it's tricky to descend it on the other side, so if you're facing Estructura X, walk to your right around it, which will take you on to the west plaza, with a ritual **ball court**. Walk through the ball court and go left to check out the encased stucco mask on display.

Follow around the right side of the mask to another massive edifice, **Estructura I**, which takes up one side of the eastern plaza. Its splendid south wall is flanked by a pair of amazing Río Bec towers rising 15m. Ascend the structure on the right side and follow the terrace alongside a series of vaulted rooms back to the other end, where a passage leads you into the **Plaza del Este**. The most significant structure here is **Estructura IV**, on the opposite side of the plaza; experts surmise it was a residence for Becán's aristocrats. A stairway leads to an upstairs courtyard ringed by seven rooms with cross motifs on either side of the doorways. Finally, go around Estructura IV to complete the circle.

Becán is located 8km west of Xpujil, 500m north of the highway.

Eating

Río Bec Dreams Restaurant INTERNATIONAL
(☑ 983-126-35-26; www.riobecdreams.com; Hwy 186 Km 142; mains M$120-300; ⊙ 7:30am-9pm) This wonderful open-air restaurant, set amid tropical plants, has the best homemade food in the area. The wide variety of main dishes includes roasted pork loin, Mediterranean pasta, Indian curry and chili con carne. Ingredients are high quality and fresh.

❶ Getting There & Away

Your own transportation is required to get to these sites. Alternatively, a taxi from Xpujil costs around M$500 with a one-hour wait at each.

Xpujil

☑ 983 / POP 4000
Although unremarkable, the small town of Xpujil (shpu-*heel*) has expanded over the last few years, largely due to its proximity to the area's many ruins. As such, it's a useful base, and as there's nothing else around for miles, you're pretty much bound to spend the night here between Campeche and Quintana Roo. It has a few hotels, some unexceptional cafes, several ATMs (one at supermarket Willy's), an exchange house (Elektra Dinero on Calle Chicanná near Xnantún) and a bus terminal. Most services are along the seven-block main drag, Avenida Calakmul (aka Hwy 186) and one street heading inland. There are three gas stations in the area.

◉ Sights

Xpuhil ARCHAEOLOGICAL SITE
(M$60; ⊙ 8am-5pm) The ruins of Xpuhil are a striking example of the Río Bec style. The three towers (rather than the usual two) of Estructura I rise above a dozen vaulted rooms. The 53m central tower is the best preserved. Its banded tiers and impractically steep stairways leading up to a temple that displays traces of a zoomorphic mask, give you a good idea of what the other two towers must have looked like in Xpuhil's 8th-century heyday.

Go around back to see a fierce jaguar mask embedded in the wall below the temple. The ruins are located on the western edge of Xpujil town; it's about a 1km walk from the entrance to the ruins, which are in a pretty setting.

HORMIGUERO

The buildings of **Hormiguero** (⊘8am-5pm) `FREE` date as far back as 50 CE; the city (whose modern name is Spanish for 'anthill') flourished during the late-Classic period. Until recent times, the site was not easy to reach; and even today the road, although mostly sealed, is largely overgrown and riddled with potholes. Hormiguero has two impressive and unique buildings in an impressive, lush setting that are worth the trek. Best of all, you will almost certainly have the site to yourself.

As you enter you'll see the 50m-long **Estructura II**. The facade's chief feature is a very menacing Chenes-style monster-mouth doorway, jaws open wide, set back between a pair of Classic Río Bec tiered towers. Around the back is intact Maya stonework and the remains of several columns. Follow the arrows 60m north to reach **Estructura V**, with a much smaller but equally ornate open-jawed temple atop a pyramidal base. Climb the right side for a closer look at the incredibly detailed stonework, especially along the corner columns that flank the doorway.

This site is reached by heading 14km south from Xpujil's stoplight, then turning right and going 8km west on a sealed road (the final 2km are on a rough, dirt road).

🛏 Sleeping & Eating

Xpujil's sleeping options are all along the main highway, which can be noisy. Around the bus terminal at the east end of town you'll find cheap hotels; the nicer hotels are at the west end of town.

Aside from the hotel restaurants, various greasy spoons are clustered around the bus station and roadside *taquerías* (taco stands) toward the Xpuhil ruins. There's a small supermarket next to the bus station.

Hotel Maya Balam   HOTEL $
(☑ 983-871-62-90; Calle Xpujil s/n, btwn Avs Calakmul & Silvituc; d/tr M$540/760; P ⊖ ❋ 🛜) The best of a fairly basic lot in town, this quiet place has decent, clean rooms, an outdoor restaurant and friendly service. There's not much outlook (back rooms face on to the car park), but it's fine for a night or two if you're exploring the area. It's a short stroll from the center of town.

Sazón Veracruzano   MEXICAN $$
(☑ 983-871-62-99; Av Calakmul 92; mains M$130-170; ⊘7am-11pm Mon-Sat; 🛜) Even though this casual place has a bright-orange exterior and even-more-vibrant plastic tablecloths, it's as smart as you'll get in Xpujil. It offers a big menu of Mexican dishes (with a focus on Veracruz, where the owners are from), such as *fajita la arrachera* (beef strips) and fried fish fillet, all served on an elevated roadside terrace.

❶ Getting There & Away

The **bus terminal** (☑ 983-871-65-11; ⊘24hr) is just east of the Xpujil stoplight next to Hotel Victoria. Services head to/from Campeche (M$245 to M$414, 4½ hours, six daily; via Champotón) and Chetumal (M$120 to M$198, two hours, six to eight daily).

There are also *colectivos* to Chetumal (M$120 per person, 1½ hours) and Escárcega (M$130, two hours). You'll find these near the traffic circle opposite the bus terminal.

AT A GLANCE

POPULATION
7.9 million

CAPITALS
Tuxtla Gutiérrez
(Chiapas), Villaher-
mosa (Tabasco)

**BEST COFFEE
EXPERIENCE**
Cafeología (p391)

BEST WATERFALL
Agua Azul (p408)

BEST CEVICHE
La Cevichería
Tabasco (p432)

WHEN TO GO
Jan
Fiesta Grande de
Enero in Chiapa de
Corzo, and San Juan
Chamula's change of
cargo-holders.

Jun–Nov
Nesting season for
sea turtles along the
Pacific coast; heat
and heavy rains in
Tabasco.

Nov–Apr
The driest months in
both states, but eve-
nings in San Cristóbal
are chilly November
to February.

San Juan Chamula (p395)
JEREMY WOODHOUSE/GETTY IMAGES

Chiapas & Tabasco

Chilly pine-covered highlands, sultry rainforest jungles and pretty colonial cities exist side by side in Chiapas, Mexico's southernmost state – a region awash with the legacy of Spanish rule and remnants of ancient Maya civilization. Palenque and Yaxchilán are evocative vestiges of powerful Maya kingdoms, and the presence of modern Maya is a constant reminder of the region's rich history. Colonial towns San Cristóbal de las Casas and Chiapa de Corzo give way to fertile plots of coffee and cacao around Tapachula and sandbar beaches in the Soconusco, while Lagos de Montebello offers unmissable outdoors adventures.

To the north, the state of Tabasco has more water than land, and harbors Maya ruins and an expansive biosphere reserve.

Chiapas & Tabasco Highlights

1 Palenque Ruins (p399) Scaling the jungly hills and soaring Maya temples.

2 San Cristóbal de las Casas (p379) Strolling the high-altitude cobblestone streets.

3 Reserva de la Biosfera La Encrucijada (p424) Experiencing the remote communities via their mangrove-lined waterways.

4 Lagos de Montebello (p420) Flitting between the sapphire and emerald lakes.

5 Yaxchilán (p414) Wandering amid the roar of howler monkeys at the riverside Maya ruins.

6 Villahermosa (p431) Admiring the giant Olmec heads on display in Parque-Museo La Venta.

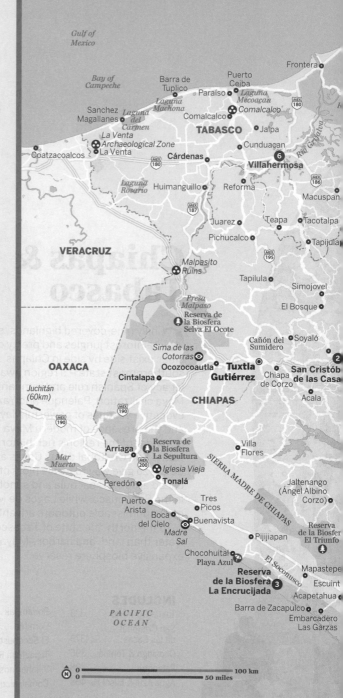

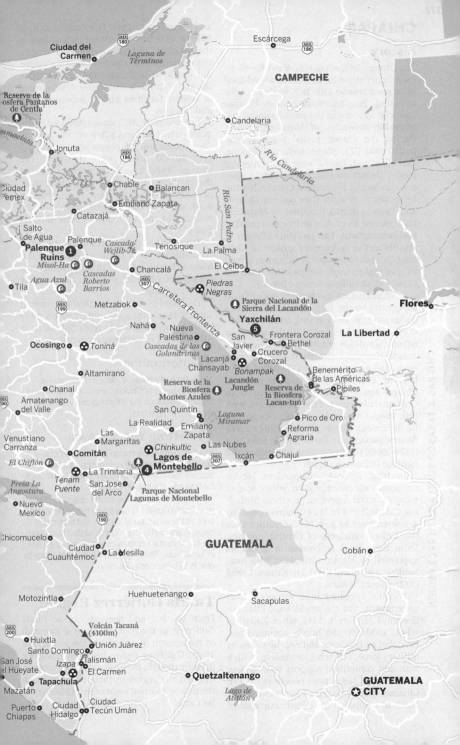

CHIPAS

History

The Olmec civilization, renowned for its extraordinary stone carvings, established itself in Tabasco around 1500 BCE while later, the low-lying, jungle-covered eastern Chiapas gave rise to some of the most splendid and powerful city-states of Maya civilization. During the Classic period (approximately 250–900 CE), places such as Palenque, Yaxchilán and Toniná were the centers of power, though dozens of lesser Maya powers – including Bonampak, Comalcalco and Chinkultic – prospered in eastern Chiapas and Tabasco during this time, as Maya culture reached its peak of artistic and intellectual achievement. The ancestors of many of the distinctive indigenous groups of highland Chiapas today appear to have migrated to that region from the lowlands after the Classic Maya collapse around 900 CE.

Central Chiapas was brought under Spanish control by the 1528 expedition of Diego de Mazariegos, and outlying areas were subdued in the 1530s and '40s, though Spain never gained full control of the Lacandón Jungle. New diseases arrived with the Spaniards, and an epidemic in 1544 killed about half of Chiapas' indigenous population. Chiapas was ineffectively administered from Guatemala for most of the colonial era, with little check on the colonists' excesses against its indigenous people, though some church figures, particularly Bartolomé de Las Casas (1474–1566), the first bishop of Chiapas, did fight for indigenous rights.

In 1822, a newly independent Mexico unsuccessfully attempted to annex Spain's former Central American provinces (including Chiapas), but in 1824 Chiapas opted (by a referendum) to join Mexico rather than the United Provinces of Central America. From then on, a succession of governors appointed by Mexico City, along with local landowners, maintained an almost feudal control over the state.

Periodic uprisings bore witness to bad government, but the world took little notice until January 1, 1994, when Zapatista rebels suddenly and briefly occupied San Cristóbal de las Casas and nearby towns by military force. The rebel movement, with a firm and committed support base among disenchanted indigenous people in eastern Chiapas, quickly retreated to remote jungle bases to campaign for democratic change

and indigenous rights. The Zapatistas have failed to win any significant concessions at the national level, although increased government funding steered toward Chiapas did result in noticeable improvements in the state's infrastructure, the development of tourist facilities and a growing urban middle class.

In September 2017, a magnitude 8.2 earthquake struck around 87km off the coast of Chiapas. Around 98 people were killed and over 40,000 homes were damaged. The damage could have been much worse, but the earthquake occurred far underground. At time of research some reconstruction work was still taking place, mainly on the churches in and around San Cristóbal de las Casas.

Tabasco, meanwhile, continues to suffer economically as a result of the privatization of the oil industry in 2014, which saw the closure of many jobs with the formerly state-run Pemex.

The border regions, particularly around Tapachula, are busy with migrants en route to USA, including many from Sub-Saharan Africa, living in rudimentary conditions.

ℹ Information

At the time of research, dengue fever was reported in parts of Chiapas, including Tuxtla and around. Check on the situation and wear insect repellant at all times.

ℹ Getting There & Away

Bus links within the region and to other states are very good; for regional routes, minibuses, combis and *colectivo* taxis are speedier (though far less spacious) alternatives.

There aren't lots of car-rental options in Chiapas. Tuxtla Gutiérrez has a number of agencies both at the airport and in town, but otherwise options are pretty thin. San Cristóbal has a couple of car rental companies, and there are a few in Tapachula. The only other convenient place to rent is Villahermosa, Tabasco.

Tuxtla Gutiérrez Region

From the hot and heaving city of Tuxtla Gutiérrez to the cool splash of a waterfall or the screech of a parrot in the jungle, the Tuxtla Gutiérrez region has a lot going for it. Sadly though, most visitors hurry straight through the region in their haste to reach the nearby colonial town of San Cristóbal de las Casas.

Tuxtla Gutiérrez

[📞] 961 / POP 550,000 / ELEV 530M

In Chiapas, Tuxtla Gutiérrez is as close to a big city as you're going to get. A busy modern metropolis and transportation hub, the state capital doesn't overwhelm with style, though it makes up for it with lots of amenities and nightlife. Most travelers pass through either the shiny modern airport or the bus station on the way to somewhere else, but it's a comfortable, worthwhile and welcoming place to spend a day.

A few blocks west of the Jardín de la Marimba, Avenida Central becomes Bulevar Belisario Domínguez; many of the Tuxtla's best hotels and restaurants are strung along this road, as well as the city's big-box megastores.

◉ Sights

★ Jardín de la Marimba
PLAZA

To take your evening *paseo* (stroll) with the locals, stop by this leafy plaza, just eight blocks west of Plaza Cívica. The whole city seems to turn out here for the free nightly marimba concerts (6pm to 9pm), especially at weekends, and couples of all ages dance around the central bandstand.

Museo de la Marimba
MUSEUM

([📞] 961-600-01-74; 9a Calle Poniente Norte; M$30, Sun free; ⊙10am-9pm) On the Jardín de la Marimba, this small museum showcases 120 years of this ubiquitous instrument, with both antique and modern models on display and a photo exhibition of the most revered marimba performers.

★ Jardín Botánico Dr Faustino Miranda
GARDENS

(M$10; ⊙9am-3:45pm Tue-Sun) The lush oasis of the Jardín Botánico Dr Faustino Miranda is a gorgeous place to visit, as well as being a nice respite from the city heat. The collection is entirely endemic to Chiapas and features everything from palms and fig varieties to cacti and medicinal plants. Various *puentes colgantes* (suspended bridges or 'tree top' walks) provide a lovely means of truly immersing yourself in the jungle. Take a Ruta 3 or 20 *colectivo* from 6a Avenida Norte Poniente.

★ Zoológico Miguel Álvarez del Toro
ZOO

(Zoomat; [📞] 961-639-28-56; www.zoomat.chiapas.gob.mx; Calz Cerro Hueco s/n; adult/child M$25/15; ⊙8:30am-4:30pm Tue-Sun) Chiapas, with its huge range of natural environments, has the highest concentration of animal species in North America, including several varieties of big cat, 1200 butterfly species and more than 600 birds. About 180 of these species, many of them in danger of extinction, are found in spacious, forested and generally natural-looking enclosures at Tuxtla's excellent zoo. Beasts you'll see here include ocelots, jaguars, pumas, tapirs, red macaws, toucans, snakes, spider monkeys and three species of crocodile.

Most interpretive materials are in both English and Spanish. To get to the zoo, take a Ruta 60 'Zoológico' colectivo (M$7, 30 minutes) from the corner of 1a Calle Oriente Sur and 7a Avenida Sur Oriente. A taxi from the center costs around M$60.

Museo del Café
MUSEUM

([📞] 961-611-14-78; https://es-la.facebook.com/museodelcafedechiapas; 2a Calle Oriente Norte 236; M$25; ⊙9am-5pm Mon-Sat) This small museum, housed inside an attractive colonial building, contains exhibits on the cultivation and processing of everyone's favorite bean. It's hardly high-tech and descriptions are in Spanish only, but English-speaking guides are available. The rooms are pleasantly air-conditioned and at the end of the tour visitors receive a cup of brew to savor in the building's pretty courtyard.

Even if you're not visiting the museum, you can drop by for a coffee at the small **cafe**, or drop in for a free cultural event on Thursday and Friday evenings.

Museo Regional de Chiapas
MUSEUM

(Calz de los Hombres Ilustres; M$60; ⊙9am-6pm Tue-Sun) The Museo Regional de Chiapas, an imposing modern building constructed in 1982, was under much-needed renovation at the time of research (it's a fabulous design but had been left to deteriorate). It is worth checking out when it reopens in 2020. It has a sampling of lesser archaeological pieces from Chiapas' many sites, and a history section, running from the Spanish conquest to the Mexican Revolution, all in Spanish only.

🖝 Tours

Transporte Panorámico Cañón del Sumidero
TOURS

([📞] cell 961-1663740) If there are enough people, this company has three available tours: viewing the canyon from above at five *miradores* (lookouts; M$200, 2½ hours), a *lancha* (motorboat) trip with

Tuxtla Gutiérrez

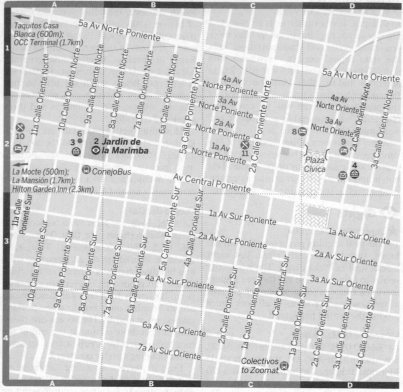

return transportation (M$350, 4½ hours) and an all-day *miradores*-and-*lancha* trip (M$450, morning departure only). Call a day beforehand to confirm departure; Señor Escobar doesn't speak English.

Private regional tours also available.

🛏 Sleeping

Reasonable budget hotels cluster in the downtown area, while most midrange and luxury hotels – primarily big international chains – are strung out along Avenida Central Poniente and Bulevar Belisario Domínguez west of the center. The larger hotels offer sizable online and weekend discounts.

★ **Hostal Tres Central** HOSTEL $
(📞 961-611-36-74; www.facebook.com/TresCentral; Calle Central Norte 393; dm M$174, r with/without bathroom M$646/446; ➹✳@🛜) Tuxtla's one and only hostel is actually one of the best in Mexico. A stylish Ikea-esque affair with comfortable beds in either four-person

dorms or spacious private rooms (those with shared bathroom have a shower and sink in the room). The rooftop terrace views of the surrounding hills can't be beat. No kitchen facilities, though there is an onsite cafe-bar.

Hotel Casablanca HOTEL $
(📞 961-611-03-05; 2a Av Norte Oriente 251; s with fan from M$270, d with fan/air-con M$395/465; ➹✳🛜) Practice your jungle explorer moves as you wade through the foliage-filled courtyard of this super helpful and friendly little hotel absolutely square in the middle of town. The rooms might be dated, but they're kept polished and clean and there are little desks to work at and big mirrors to admire yourself in.

Holiday Inn Express BUSINESS HOTEL $$
(📞 800-907-458; www.ihg.com; Av Central Poniente 1254; r from M$1500; 🅿➹✳🛜) Even if you're not a fan of chain hotels, this one is well worth a look. It has a prime position just two blocks from the Jardín de la Marimba, slick and friendly service, soothing color combinations,

◎ **Top Sights**
1 Jardín Botánico Dr Faustino Miranda..................F1
2 Jardín de la Marimba..........................A2

◎ **Sights**
3 Museo de la Marimba..........................A2
4 Museo del Café.................................D2
5 Museo Regional de Chiapas..............F1

⦿ **Activities, Courses & Tours**
6 Transporte Panorámico Cañón del Sumidero....................................A2

▣ **Sleeping**
7 Holiday Inn Express...........................A2
8 Hostal Tres Central...........................D2
9 Hotel Casablanca..............................D2

✕ **Eating**
10 Florentina Pizzas.............................A2
11 La Macarena..................................C2

ℹ **Information**
Municipal Tourism Office............(see 3)

joyable cafes cluster in the center around the Jardín de la Marimba.

★**Taquitos Casa Blanca**　　TACOS $
(cnr 16 Poniente & 3a Norte 428; tacos/pozol M$10/13; ⏱ 7:30am-3:30pm) One of a number of earthy, budget eateries around this neighbourhood, Taquitos Casa Blanca has made a name for itself for serving no-frills, filling, cheap and delicious tacos, as well as rich cocoa *pozol* (a drink comprising fermented corn and chocolate; something of an acquired taste!). No trip to Tuxtla is really complete without eating here once. Busy with local workers at lunchtime.

★**Florentina Pizzas**　　PIZZA $$
(☎ 961-613-91-91; www.facebook.com/florentina. pizzas; 12a Calle Poniente Norte 174A; pizzas from M$110; ⏱ 5-11:30pm Sun, Tue & Wed, to 1am Thu-Sat; 🛜) Thin-crust, wood-fired pizza, washed down with craft beer in Tuxtla? Yep – this is the most frequently recommended pizzeria in town, for good reason. The atmosphere's cool and fun, the colors are bright, prices are reasonable and there's occasional live music. (Oh, and there are good salads and margaritas, too).

La Macarena　　SPANISH $$
(2a Av Norte Poniente 369; tapas M$70-150; ⏱ 1:30-10pm) This reliable Spanish option has a fun flamenco-filled vibe, plus it serves

well-equipped rooms, lightning-fast internet and an impressive breakfast spread. Prices outside high season are significantly cheaper.

All up it will be hard for any other hotel in town to match the Holiday Inn Express for price and quality.

Hilton Garden Inn　　HOTEL $$
(☎ 961-617-18-00; www.tuxtlagutierrez.hgi.com; cnr Bulevars Belisario Domínguez & Los Castillos; r/ste from M$1050/1350; 🅿 ⊕ ❄ @ 🛜 ≋) The luxurious 167-room Hilton sits in a commercial area 2.5km west of the Jardín de la Marimba. Gadget-lovers will appreciate the MP3 player/alarm clock, adjustable pillow-top mattresses and internet-ready TVs, and style fans will groove on the rain-forest showerheads and Herman Miller chairs.

✕ Eating & Drinking

Many upscale and international chain options are west of the center, along Bulevar Belisario Domínguez, and a number of en-some genuine tapas dishes and wines from the (colonial) mother country. This means there's also sangria and paella dishes. It's a good choice if you're after an alternative to Mexican flavors.

La Mansión
MEXICAN $$$

(☑961-617-77-33; www.lamansion.com.mx; Sur Poniente 105; mains M$130-300; ☺1-11pm Mon-Sat, to 6pm Sun; 🅿✳) Mixing classic white-tablecloth elegance with blue-and-red disco lighting, this upmarket restaurant, which is inside the Marriott Hotel, serves creative, sassy modern Mexican cuisine. Think tacos in a rainbow of colors and red meats beautifully prepared, and served with lightly barbecued vegetables.

La Mocte
MEXICAN

(☑961-279-76-95; www.facebook.com/LaMOCTE; Circ Tapachula 263, entre 14a y 15a Poniente; mains M$80-250; ☺1pm-1:30am; 🍴) This fun and smart(ish) cantina is all things to all people. Expect lots of action (think downing of shots) or enjoy watching the groups in action: everyone from ladies' night attendees to families to business folk gulping down a meal on the way home. Music, cocktails and massive meals are all part of the melody and mix.

ℹ Information

There's an **ATM** at the departure level of the airport.

Banorte (Av Central Oriente, btwn 2a Calle Oriente Sur & 3a Calle Oriente Sur; ☺9am-5pm Mon-Fri, to 2pm Sat) Changes dollars.

Municipal Tourism Office (9a Calle Poniente Norte; ☺10am-2pm & 4-8pm) More of a module than an office. Limited information but staff are pleasant and may be able to answer queries. It's located inside the Museo de la Marimba.

Post Office (2a Calle Oriente Norte 227; ☺8am-4:30pm Mon-Fri, 10am-noon Sat) In the Palacio Federal.

Secretaría de Turismo (☑961-617-05-50, 800-280-35-00; www.turismochiapas.gob.mx; Edificio Torre, Level 5, Bulevar Andrés Serra Rojas 1090; ☺8am-4pm Mon-Fri) The main state tourism office has a toll-free phone number for Chiapas information; English speakers rarely available.

ℹ Getting There & Away

AIR

Tuxtla's small and gleaming **Aeropuerto Ángel Albino Corzo** (☑961-153-60-99; www.chiapas aero.com; Sarabia s/n) is 35km southeast of downtown and 18km south of Chiapa de Corzo. Aeroméxico (www.aeromexico.com), Interjet (www.interjet.com) and Volaris (www.volaris. com) have nonstop services to Mexico City. VivaAerobus (www.vivaaerobus.com) has services to Cancún, Guadalajara and Monterrey.

BUS, COLECTIVO & COMBI

Free wi-fi and a huge supermarket are bonuses of the modern **OCC terminal** (☑961-125-15-80, ext 2433; 5a Av Norte Poniente 318). It's about 2.5km northwest of the Jardín de la Marimba and houses all the 1st-class and deluxe buses and the 2nd-class Rápidos del Sur line. More 2nd-class buses and combis depart from the **Terminal de Transporte Tuxtla** (☑961-600-1212; cnr 9a Av Sur Oriente & 13a Calle Oriente Sur), with frequent departures for destinations including San Cristóbal, Ocosingo and Ocozocoautla.

For Chiapa de Corzo (M$15, 45 minutes), combis leave every few minutes between 5am and 10:30pm from **1a Avenida Sur Oriente**.

BUSES FROM TUXTLA GUTIÉRREZ

DESTINATION	FARE (M$)	TIME (HR)	FREQUENCY (PER DAY)
Cancún	1278-1458	17-20	5
Comitán	132	3	frequent
Mérida	1058-1734	13-14	5
Mexico City (TAPO & Norte)	950-1392	11½-12	11
Oaxaca	855-711	10	4
Palenque	310	6-6½	frequent
Puerto Escondido	769	11-12	2
San Cristóbal de las Casas	77-91	1¼	frequent
Tapachula	449-576	4½-6	frequent
Tonalá	180-209	2-2½	frequent
Villahermosa	300-471	4-5	12

To San Cristóbal

For San Cristóbal de las Casas (around M$50, one hour), minibuses and combis are faster and more frequent (every 10 minutes) than the bus.

Corazón de María (☑961-600-12-12) Combis depart from Parque 5 de Mayo near Avenida Central Oriente; services 4am to 9pm.

Ómnibus de Chiapas (☑961-128-94-07; 15A Oriente Sur & 4a Sur, Lerma Centro) Comfortable minibuses (called 'sprinters'); departures 5am to 10pm.

CAR & MOTORCYCLE

In addition to companies at the airport, in-town rental agencies include **Alamo** (☑967-602-16-00; www.alamo.com; 5a Av Norte Poniente 2260; ☺7am-10pm), near the OCC bus station, and **Europcar** (☑961-121-49-22; www.europcar.com; Bulevar Belisario Domínguez 2075; ☺8am-6pm Mon-Fri, to 4pm Sat & Sun).

❶ Getting Around

TO/FROM THE AIRPORT

From the airport, prepay taxis (one to three passengers) meet all flights and go to central Tuxtla (M$350, 40 minutes), Chiapa de Corzo (M$362, 30 minutes) and San Cristóbal (M$800, 1¼ hour). ADO (www.ado.mx) runs frequent buses directly from the terminal to San Cristóbal (M$200, 1½ hours) roughly every one or two hours between 8am and 11pm, although there is a three-hour pause in the service between 3pm and 6:30pm.

BUS

A biodiesel bus service called **ConejoBus** (☺5am-11pm) plies Bulevar Belisario Domínguez–Avenida Central; you'll need a prepaid card (M$7 from the Palacio de Gobierno on the Parque Central) to ride. For other areas, consult www.tuxmapa.com.mx for local combi routes. Taxi rides within the city cost M$45 to M$70.

West of Tuxtla Gutiérrez

◎ Sights

Sima de las Cotorras   CENOTE
(Abyss of the Parrots; www.simaecoturismo.com; adult M$20; ☺5:30am-7pm) The Sima de las Cotorras is a dramatic 160m-wide sinkhole that punches 140m down into the earth into a crater thick with rainforest. At sunrise, a green cloud of screeching parrots spirals out for the day, trickling back before dusk. With binoculars you can see a series of red pre-Hispanic rock paintings that decorate one side of the cliff face, and you can also hike or rappel (M$700) down into the hole.

For serious bird-watchers this is an essential stop.

Lodging (☑cell 968-117-80-81; www.simaecoturismo.com; campsites M$150, d/q M$500/750, 6-person cabañas M$1500; P ☺) is available (the spacious six-person, two-room *cabañas* – cabins – are well worth the extra cost), and there is a good restaurant serving scrumptious *tamales* (fried, stuffed corn *masa*) and handmade tortillas.

From the last stop in Ozocoautla (Coita), located on Hwy 190 right at the signed turnoff for the Sima, take a taxi (around M$320, 50 minutes). Three daily Piedra Parada *colectivos* (M$14) also leave from this stop, but let you off 4km before the Sima. Driving from Tuxtla, it's reasonably well signed all the way. Go all the way through Ozocoautla, turning right at the minibus terminal (there's a blue turnoff sign here, but it's not visible coming from this direction), go 3.5km north, then 12km on a good dirt road.

El Aguacero   WATERFALL
(www.cascadaelaguacero.com; M$35; ☺7am-5pm) Plunging into the sheer Río La Venta canyon, El Aguacero is a gorgeous series of frothy stairsteps that tumble and spray. You'll descend over 700 steps to access the water. In drier months (usually December through May), you can stroll along sandy riverbed beaches to the waterfall. When the water's high, it's a half-hour hike along a shady jungle trail.

From December through May, you can also explore an underground river running through the 200m-long **El Encanto cave** (M$25). An hour-long tour (M$200) includes all equipment (helmet, headlamp etc).

Camping (campsites per person M$100, 4-person cabins M$800) and hammock space (with showers) is available, and a simple restaurant.

From Ozocoautla (Coita), *colectivos* to El Gavilán/Las Cruces (M$12) can drop you off at the highway turnoff, and it's a 3km walk down to the entrance. Drivers should look for the turnoff sign about 15km west of Ozocoautla.

Chiapa de Corzo
☑961 / POP 45,000 / ELEV 450M

Set 12km east of Tuxtla Gutiérrez on the way to San Cristóbal, Chiapa de Corzo is a small and attractive colonial town with an easygoing, provincial air. Sitting on the north

CHIAPAS & TABASCO CHIAPA DE CORZO

bank of the broad Río Grijalva, it's the main starting point for trips into the Cañón del Sumidero.

Chiapa de Corzo has been occupied almost continuously since about 1200 BCE. Before the Spaniards arrived, the warlike Chiapa tribe had their capital, Nandalumí, a couple of kilometers downstream, on the opposite bank of the Grijalva. When Diego de Mazariegos invaded the area in 1528, the Chiapa hurled themselves by the hundreds to their death in the canyon rather than surrender.

Mazariegos founded a settlement called Chiapa de Los Indios here, but quickly shifted his base to San Cristóbal de las Casas, where he found the climate and indigenous inhabitants more manageable.

◎ Sights

The *embarcadero* (jetty) for Cañón del Sumidero boat trips is two blocks south of the plaza down Calle 5 de Febrero. Look for the road lined with vendors.

Cañón del Sumidero   CANYON

The Sumidero Canyon is a spectacular fissure in the earth. In 1981, the Chicoasén hydroelectric dam was completed at its northern end, damming the Río Grijalva, which flows through the canyon, and creating a 25km-long reservoir. Traveling between Tuxtla and Chiapa de Corzo, the road crosses the Grijalva just south of the canyon mouth.

The most impressive way to see the canyon is from a **lancha** (return trip M$250; ◎8am-4pm) that speeds between the canyon's towering rock walls. It's about a two-hour return trip, starting at either Chiapa de Corzo or the Embarcadero Cahuaré, 5km north of Chiapa along the road to Tuxtla. You'll rarely have to wait more than half an hour for a boat to fill up. Bring a drink, something to shield you from the sun and, if there's any chance of bad weather, some warm clothing or a waterproof jacket.

It's about 35km from Chiapa de Corzo to the dam. Soon after you pass under Hwy 190, the canyon walls tower an amazing 800m above you. Along the way you'll see a variety of birds – herons, cormorants, vultures and kingfishers – plus probably a crocodile or two. The boat operators will point out a few odd formations of rock and vegetation, including one cliff face covered in thick hanging moss, resembling a giant Christmas tree. Disappointingly, the *lanchas* sometimes have to plow through float-

ing plastic garbage when wet-season rains wash in trash from Tuxtla Gutiérrez.

Plaza   PLAZA

Impressive arcades frame three sides of the plaza, and a beefy tree called **La Pochota** buckles the sidewalk with its centuries-old roots. Venerated by the indigenous people who founded the town, it's the oldest ceiba tree along the Río Grijalva. But the focal point of the plaza is **La Pila** (also called the Fuente Colonial), a handsome brick fountain completed in 1562 in Mudejar-Gothic style. It's said to resemble the Spanish crown.

Templo de Santo Domingo de Guzmán   CHURCH

(Mexicanidad Chiapaneca 10; ◎8am-5pm) The large Templo de Santo Domingo de Guzmán, one block south of the main plaza, was built in the late 16th century by the Dominican order. Its adjoining (former) convent is now the **Centro Cultural** (☑997-616-00-55; www.facebook.com/CentroculturalExconvento; ◎10am-5pm Tue-Sun) **FREE**, home to an exposition of the wood and lino prints of talented Chiapa-born Franco Lázaro Gómez (1922–49), as well as the **Museo de la Laca**, which is dedicated to the local craft specialty: lacquered gourds. The museum holds pieces dating back to 1606.

At the time of research, all the buildings were closed due to damage sustained in the 2017 earthquake.

⁂ Festivals & Events

Fiesta Grande de Enero   CULTURAL

(◎Jan) Held for a week in mid-January, this is one of Mexico's liveliest and most extraordinary festivals, including nightly dances involving cross-dressing young men, known as Las Chuntás. Women don the highly colorful, beautifully embroidered *chiapaneco* dress, and blond-wigged, mask-toting *Parachicos* (impersonating conquistadors) parade on a number of days. A canoe battle and fireworks extravaganza follow on the final evening.

🛏 Sleeping & Eating

Less hectic than Tuxtla and much less touristy than San Cristóbal, Chiapa de Corzo makes for a fine place to stay (though standards are not quite as high as Tuxtla). It's also very close to Tuxtla airport so is handy for transit passengers.

Restaurants on the *embarcadero* have near-identical, generally overpriced menus.

The river views are nice, though battling marimba players tend to amp up the noise level. The market (southeast of the plaza) is your best bet for an inexpensive meal. *Tascalate* (a sweet concoction of ground cacao, pine nuts, toasted corn, cinnamon and annatto) is sold by vendors (in small plastic bags), and many shops sell the drink powder.

Posada Rocío   HOTEL $

(☑ 961-223-75-54; Zaragoza 347; s/d/tr from M$250/300/350; 🛜) Just off the main plaza, this humble little faded orange guesthouse ticks all the budget-hotel boxes with its decent-sized clean rooms, friendly management and a good location.

Hotel La Ceiba   HOTEL $$

(☑ 961-616-03-89; www.laceibahotel.com; Av Domingo Ruíz 300; r M$745; P ⊜ ❄ 🛜 ⊠) By far the most upscale place in town (though the rooms are quite simple), La Ceiba has a full-service spa and restaurant, an inviting pool, a lush garden and 80 well-kept air-conditioned rooms in an arched and domed colonial-flavored building. It's two blocks west of the main plaza. Ask for the remodeled rooms; prices halve outside high season.

Los Sabores de San Jacinto   MEXICAN $

(☑ 961-218-46-88; Calle 5 de Febrero 144; mains M$80-130; ⊙ 1-11:30pm Wed-Mon) This no-frills place, with a handful of tables inside the orange dining room and a couple more outside on the terrace overlooking the street, serves hearty, simple but very tasty south Mexican staples. The service is fast and it's one of the few places open in the evenings.

D'Avellino   ITALIAN $$

(☑ 961-153-07-33; www.davellino.com.mx; Calz Grajales 1103; mains M$110-270, pizza M$150-300; ⊙ 1pm-1am Mon-Sat, to midnight Sun) A cute Italian restaurant with a rustic old-world dining room and patio seating, D'Avellino serves fresh pastas and good pizza in a warm and convivial atmosphere. It's 1.5km northwest of the plaza (a 15-minute stroll), along the main Tuxtla-bound road.

Restaurant Jardines de Chiapa   MEXICAN $$

(☑ 961-616-01-98; www.restaurantesjardines.com. mx; Madero 395; mains M$95-180; ⊙ 8:30am-6:30pm) Not too far from the main plaza, this large place is set around a garden patio with atmospheric brick arches. The long menu includes the tasty house special *cochinito al horno* (oven-baked pork). Be warned that it can

get a bit hectic at lunchtime with tour groups pouring in for the buffet lunch (M$289). Alternatively, stick with the huge à la carte menu.

❶ Information

There's a small tourist kiosk on the northern side of the plaza. It doesn't have much in the way of materials, but staff are delightful.

❶ Getting There & Away

Combis from Tuxtla Gutiérrez (M$15, 45 minutes) leave frequently from 1a Avenida Sur Oriente (between Calles 5a and 7a Oriente Sur) between 5am and 10:30pm. They arrive (and return to Tuxtla) from the north side of the main plaza.

There's no direct transportation between San Cristóbal and the center of Chiapa de Corzo. From San Cristóbal, catch a Tuxtla-bound combi and ask to be let off at the Chiapa de Corzo stop on the highway (M$55, 30 minutes). From there, cross the highway and flag down a combi (M$8) to the plaza. From Chiapa de Corzo to San Cristóbal, catch a combi from the plaza back to the highway and then flag down a combi heading to San Cristóbal. You'll rarely wait more than a few minutes for a connecting combi in either direction.

San Cristóbal Region

All tourist roads in Chiapas lead, sooner or later, to the pastel-painted, cobbled streets of the gorgeous mountain city of San Cristóbal de las Casas. Although the city is rich in cultural attractions, for many visitors it's the bright highland light, humming street life and the chance to mingle with the local indigenous people – a people who are descended from the ancient Maya and maintain some unique customs, traditional dress and beliefs – that is the greatest draw.

Markets and festivals often give the most interesting insight into indigenous life, and beyond the valley bowl in which San Cristóbal nestles, lots of village markets and festivals take place. Full of life and the hues of a hundred different colors, the weekly markets at the villages are today nearly always held on Sunday. Proceedings start as early as dawn, and wind down by lunchtime.

San Cristóbal de las Casas

☑ 967 / POP 185,000 / ELEV 1940M

Set in a gorgeous highland valley surrounded by pine forest, the colonial city of San Cristóbal (sahn cris-*toh*-bal) has been a popular travelers' destination for decades.

CHIAPAS & TABASCO SAN CRISTÓBAL DE LAS CASAS

INDIGENOUS PEOPLES OF CHIAPAS

Of the 4.8 million people of Chiapas, approximately a quarter are indigenous, with language being the key ethnic identifier. Each of the eight principal groups has its own language, beliefs and customs, a cultural variety that makes Chiapas one of the most fascinating states in Mexico.

Travelers to the area around San Cristóbal are most likely to encounter the Tsotzil and the Tzeltal. Their traditional religious life is nominally Catholic, but integrates pre-Hispanic elements. Most people live in the mountains outside the villages, which are primarily market and ceremonial centers.

Tsotzil and Tzeltal clothing is among the most varied, colorful and elaborately worked in Mexico. It not only identifies wearers' villages but also continues ancient Maya traditions. Many of the seemingly abstract designs on these costumes are in fact stylized snakes, frogs, butterflies, birds, saints and other beings. Some motifs have religious-magical functions: scorpions, for example, can be a symbolic request for rain, since they are believed to attract lightning.

The Lacandón people dwelled deep in the Lacandón Jungle and largely avoided contact with the outside world until the 1950s. They now number fewer than 1000 and mostly live in three main settlements in that same region (Lacanjá Chansayab, Metzabok and Nahá), with low-key tourism being one of their major means of support. Lacandón people are readily recognizable in their white tunics and long black hair cut in a fringe. Most have now abandoned their traditional animist religion in favor of Presbyterian or evangelical forms of Christianity.

Traditionally treated as second-class citizens, indigenous groups mostly live on the least productive land in the state, with the least amount of government services or infrastructure. Many indigenous communities rely on subsistence farming and have no running water or electricity, and it was frustration over lack of political power and their historical mistreatment that fueled the Zapatista rebellion, putting a spotlight on the region's distinct inequities.

Today, long-standing indigenous ways of life are challenged both by evangelical Christianity – opposed to many traditional animist-Catholic practices and the abuse of alcohol, including in religious rituals – and by the Zapatista movement, which rejects traditional leadership hierarchies and is raising the rights and profile of women. Many highland indigenous people have emigrated to the Lacandón Jungle to clear new land, or to Mexican and US cities in search of work.

Despite all obstacles, indigenous identities and self-respect survive. Indigenous people may be suspicious of outsiders, and may resent interference in their religious observances or other aspects of their life, but if treated with due respect they are likely to respond in kind.

It's a pleasure to explore San Cristóbal's cobbled streets and markets, soaking up the unique ambience and the wonderfully clear highland light. It's very much on the tourist map, and offers all the services, from good accommodations and restaurants, to tour and transport services.

Surrounded by dozens of traditional Tsotzil and Tzeltal villages, San Cristóbal is at the heart of one of the most deeply rooted indigenous areas in Mexico. A great base for local and regional exploration, it's a place where ancient customs coexist with modern luxuries.

The city shook violently during the September 2017 Chiapas earthquake; the cathedral and other buildings were damaged and, at the time of research, remained closed for renovation.

History

Diego de Mazariegos founded San Cristóbal as the Spanish regional base in 1528. Its Spanish citizens made fortunes from wheat, while the indigenous people lost their lands and suffered diseases, taxes and forced labor. The church afforded some small protection against colonist excesses. Dominican monks reached Chiapas in 1545, and made San Cristóbal their main base. The town is now named after one of them, Bartolomé de Las Casas, who was appointed bishop of Chiapas and became the most prominent Spanish defender of indigenous people in colonial times. In modern times Bishop Samuel Ruiz, who passed away in 2011, followed in Las Casas' footsteps, defending the oppressed indigenous people and earning the hostility of the Chiapas establishment.

San Cristóbal was the state capital of Chiapas from 1824 to 1892, but remained relatively isolated until the 1970s, when tourism began to influence its economy.

Recent decades have seen an influx of indigenous villagers into the 'Cinturón de Miseria' (Belt of Misery), a series of impoverished, violence-ridden, makeshift colonies around San Cristóbal's *periférico* (ring road). Many of these people are here because they have been expelled from San Juan Chamula and other communities as a result of internal politico-religious conflicts. Most of the craft sellers around Santo Domingo church and the underage hawkers around town come from the Cinturón de Miseria.

San Cristóbal was catapulted into the international limelight on January 1, 1994, when the Zapatista rebels selected it as one of four places from which to launch their revolution, seizing and sacking government offices in the town before being driven out within a few days by the Mexican army. The city remains a hot spot for sympathizers (and some opponents) of the Zapatista rebels, and a central location for organizations working with Chiapas' indigenous people. Political and social tensions remain, but San Cristóbal continues to attract travelers, real-estate investment and a growing middle class.

◎ Sights

San Cristóbal is very walkable, with straight streets rambling up and down several gentle hills. Heading east from Plaza 31 de Marzo, Real de Guadalupe has a long pedestrian-only section with a concentration of places to eat and drink. The other principal pedestrian mall, the Andador Turístico, runs up Hidalgo and Avenida 20 de Noviembre.

★ **Na Bolom**   HISTORIC BUILDING
(☑967-678-14-18; www.nabolom.org; Guerrero 33; M$60, incl tour M$70; ⊙9am-7pm) An atmospheric museum-research center, Na Bolom for many years was the home of Swiss anthropologist and photographer Gertrude Duby-Blom (Trudy Blom; 1901–93) and her Danish archaeologist husband Frans Blom (1893–1963). Na Bolom means 'Jaguar

House' in the Tsotzil language (as well as being a play on its former owners' name). It's full of photographs, archaeological and anthropological relics, and books.

The house tour provides a revealing insight into the lives of the Bloms and the Chiapas of half a century and more ago – though the picture presented of the Lacandones does dwell more on their past than their present. The Bloms bought the 19th-century house in 1950, and while Frans explored and surveyed ancient Maya sites all over Chiapas (including Palenque, Toniná and Chinkultic), Trudy studied, photographed and fought to protect the scattered Lacandón people of eastern Chiapas and their jungle environment.

Since Trudy's death, Na Bolom has continued the thrust of the Bloms' work, with the house operating as a museum and research center for the study and support of Chiapas' indigenous cultures and natural environment. The library of more than 9000 books and documents here is a major resource on the Maya.

Na Bolom also offers guest rooms (p388) and meals made with organic vegetables grown in its garden.

★ **Templo & Ex-Convento de Santo Domingo de Guzmán**   CHURCH
(Av 20 de Noviembre; ⊙6:30am-1:45pm & 4-8pm Mon-Sat, 7am-9pm Sun) **FREE** Located just north of the center of town, the imposing 16th-century Templo de Santo Domingo is San Cristóbal's most beautiful church, especially when its facade catches the late-afternoon sun. This baroque frontage, with outstanding filigree stucco work, was added in the 17th century and includes the double-headed Hapsburg eagle, then the symbol of the Spanish monarchy.

The interior is lavishly gilded, especially the ornate pulpit. At the time of research, the church was being repaired from earthquake damage; you can enter from the side but the golden interior is covered in plastic sheeting. On the church's western side, the attached former monastery contains a regional museum and the excellent Centro de Textiles del Mundo Maya (p385). Around Santo Domingo and the neighboring **Templo de la Caridad**, built in 1712, Chamulan women and bohemian types from around Mexico conduct a colorful daily crafts market. The weavers' showroom of Sna Jolobil (p392) is now in a separate light-filled building on the northwest section of the grounds.

San Cristóbal de las Casas

Museo de la Medicina Maya (400m)

Combis to San Juan Chamula

Río Amarillo

Honduras

Colombia

Real de Mexicanos

Brasil

Av 16 de Septiembre

Escuadrón 201

Av 5 de Mayo

Venezuela

Argentina

Canada

Museo de Sergio Arturo Castro Martínez 1

Av 12 de Octubre

Río Amarillo

Guadalupe Victoria

Calle 5 de Febrero

Calle 1 de Marzo

Av 5 de Mayo

Calle 28 de Agosto

27

34

55

17

36

21

9

28

Puente Tiboli

Combis to Zinacantán

Caminero

Robledo

Díaz Ordaz

Bermudas

Tonalá

Diagonal Arriaga

Chiapa de Corzo

Colón

Yajalón

Tercera Calle

Segunda Calle

Primera Calle

Dugelay

Calz Lázaro Cárdenas

Utrilla

61

5

26

3

Templo & Ex-Convento de Santo Domingo de Guzmán

11

20

14

Plaza

38

48

Dr. Navarro

Calz Roberta

Calz Franz Blom

Comitán

Tapachula

Cintalapa

Ejército Nacional

Colón

Paniagua

MA Flores

Real de Guadalupe

Belisario Domínguez

Utrilla

Av 20 de Noviembre

Na Bolóm 2

Isabel La Católica

Real de Guadalupe

Huixtla

Guerrero

25

32

62

59

6

N

0   400 m
0   0.2 miles

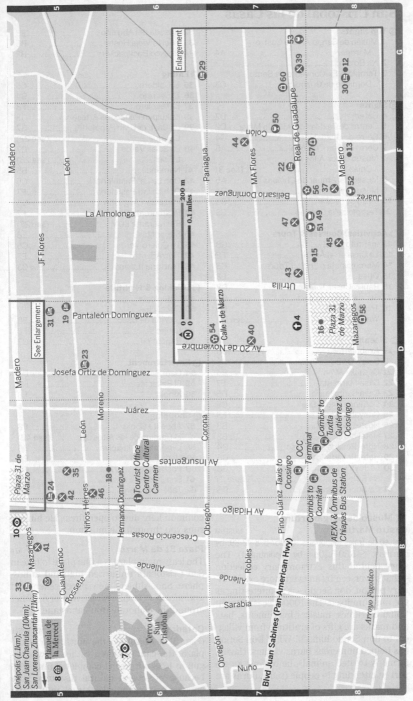

San Cristóbal de las Casas

★ **Museo de Sergio Arturo
Castro Martínez** MUSEUM
(Museo de Trajes Regionales; ☎967-678-42-89; by
donation; ⊙5:30-6:30pm by appointment) The
story behind this extraordinary collection
– that's overseen by an even more extraordinary person, don Sergio – is as interesting as
the museum itself. The 1000 pieces of traditional costumes, musical instruments, hats
and masks are gifts of gratitude from villagers to don Sergio himself. Why? Don Sergio
has helped numerous burns victims. Having
formerly treated animals, he became an expert in attending to people (sadly, burns are

common here due to open fires). He himself
runs you through the museum.

Plaza 31 de Marzo PLAZA
The leafy main plaza is a fine place to take in
San Cristóbal's unhurried highland atmosphere. Shoe-shiners, newspaper sellers and
ambulantes (mobile street vendors) gather
around the elaborate iron bandstand.

Catedral CATHEDRAL
(Plaza 31 de Marzo) On the north side of the
plaza, the candy-colored cathedral was begun in 1528 but wasn't completed until 1815
because of several natural disasters. Sure
enough, new earthquakes struck in 1816 and

also 1847, causing considerable damage, but it was restored again from 1920 to 1922. The gold-leaf interior has lots of incense smoke and candlelight as well as five gilded altar-pieces featuring 18th-century paintings by Miguel Cabrera.

The cathedral was closed at time of research due to damage sustained from the 2017 earthquake.

Museo de los Altos de Chiapas MUSEUM

(📞967-678-16-09; Calz Lázaro Cárdenas s/n; M$60; ⏱9am-5:45pm Tue-Sun) One of two world-class museums inside the Ex-Convento de Santo Domingo (on the western side of the Templo de Santo Domingo), this exhibits several impressive archaeological relics – including stelae from Chinkultic – as well as exhibits on the Spanish conquest and evangelization of the region. Admission is bundled with Centro de Textiles del Mundo Maya.

Museo de la Medicina Maya MUSEUM

(Ciudadela Salomón González Blanco 10; M$30; ⏱9am-5pm Mon-Fri, to 6pm Sat & Sun) This space pays homage to the various techniques and practices of indigenous traditional medicine of the Tsotzil and Tzeltal peoples in Chiapas. The exhibit style is à la 1950s (that is, dated), but for those interested in natural healing and culture, it's very interesting.

Museo del Ámbar de Chiapas MUSEUM

(📞967-674-58-99; www.museodelambardechiapas. org.mx; Plazuela de la Merced; M$25; ⏱10am-2pm & 4-8pm Tue-Sun) Chiapas amber – fossilized pine resin that's around 30 million years old – is known for its clarity and diverse colors. Most is mined around Simojovel, north of San Cristóbal. This small museum explains all things amber (with information sheets in English, French, German, Japanese and Italian).

Note that a number of nearby jewelry shops have appropriated the museum's name, but this is the only place around that's housed in an ex-convent – you can't miss it.

Centro de Textiles del Mundo Maya MUSEUM

(📞967-631-30-94; www.centrotextilesmayas. org; Calz Lázaro Cárdenas; M$60; ⏱9am-2pm & 4-6pm) Upstairs inside the Ex-Convento de Santo Domingo, this excellent museum showcases over 500 examples of handwoven textiles from throughout Mexico and Central America. There's more than meets the eye here; be sure to open the drawers that showcase most of the collection! Two perma-nent exhibition rooms display *huipiles* and videos show how materials and clothes are created, with some explanations in English. Admission is bundled with the Museo de los Altos de Chiapas (note the pre-Hispanic textiles here).

Museo del Cacao MUSEUM

(📞967-631-79-95; www.kakaw.org; 1ro de Marzo 16; M$30; ⏱11am-8pm Mon-Sat, to 6pm Sun) This chocolate museum runs along an open upstairs balcony of a cafe. Learn about the history of chocolate and how it was used by the Maya. Also on display are modern chocolate drinking vessels and utensils; exhibits cover the process of creating the delicious substance. Includes a small tasting. The chocolateria-cum-cafe is open later.

🎓 Courses

Several good language schools offer instruction in Spanish, with flexibility to meet most level and schedule requirements. Weekly rates normally include three hours' tuition five days a week, but many variations (classes only, hourly instruction, homestays etc) are available.

La Casa en el Árbol LANGUAGE

(📞967-674-52-72; www.facebook.com/lacasaen elarbol.mexico; Madero 29; individual classes 1/10/20hr M$150/1400/2600, homestay & meals per week M$1800; ⏱8:30am-8:30pm) The 'Tree House' is an enthusiastic, socially committed school that teaches various languages including Tzeltal and Tsotzil. It offers lots of out-of-school activities and is also a base for volunteer programs. Mexican cooking classes are also available (four to five hours; M$650).

Instituto Jovel LANGUAGE

(📞967-678-40-69; www.institutojovel.com; Madero 45; individual/group classes per week from US$215/140, homestay per week from US$140) Instituto Jovel is professional and friendly, and has a top-class reputation among students. Most tuition is one-to-one, and it has a beautiful location. Classes in indigenous cultures of Chiapas (US$110 per week), Mexican cooking (US$26 to US$34 per class), history (US$110 per week) and salsa dancing (US$6 per class) are offered too.

👉 Tours

Agencies in San Cristóbal (open approximately 8am to 9pm) offer a variety of tours, often with guides who speak English,

French or Italian, though many offer transportation only. Typical day trips run to Chiapa de Corzo and Cañón del Sumidero (from M$350, six to seven hours), Lagos de Montebello and El Chiflón waterfalls (M$300, nine to 10 hours) and Palenque, Agua Azul and Misol-Ha (M$450, 14 hours). All prices are per person (usually with a minimum of four people).

★ **Walking Tour**   WALKING
(☑ What'sApp 951-135-09-06; by donation) Fun and informative walking tours in English and Spanish depart daily at 10am and 5pm from the wooden cross in Plaza de la Paz. These cover interesting snippets about the town, plus give great recommendations for local nosh and drinks, music and shopping. Tours can last for several hours but you're welcome to peel off. You choose the amount you pay.

★ **SendaSur**   ECOTOUR
(☑ 967-678-39-09; www.sendasur.com.mx; 5 de Febrero 29) 🖉 A highly professional, partner-based ecotourism network based in San Cristóbal de las Casas, but operating throughout Chiapas, SendaSur can help with independent travel and reservations in the Lacandón and El Ocote jungle regions for trips from two days to two weeks. Will organize itineraries in advance. English not spoken.

Raúl & Cesar Tours   CULTURAL
(☑ 967-678-91-41; www.alexyraultours.wordpress. com; per person M$250) Enjoyable and informative minibus tours in English, French or Spanish. Raúl and/or a colleague wait at the wooden cross in front of San Cristóbal's cathedral from 8:45am to 9:30am daily, going to San Juan Chamula and Zinacantán (minimum of two people). Trips to Tenejapa, San Andrés Larraínzar or Amatenango del Valle can also be arranged for a minimum of four people.

Jaguar Adventours   CYCLING
(☑ 967-631-50-62; www.adventours.mx; Barrio de Diego; bicycle rental per hr/day M$50/250; ⊙9am-8pm) Does bicycle tours to Chamula (M$700), plus longer expeditions. Also rents out quality mountain bikes with helmet and lock.

Otisa   TOURS
(Jalapeño Tours; ☑ 967-678-19-33; www.otisatravel. com; Real de Guadalupe 3C) In the main pedestrian drag, the company's activity arm, Jalapeño Tours, offers the standard tours.

Marcosapata o En Bici Tours   CYCLING
(☑ 967-141-72-16; www.marcosapata1.wordpress. com) Offers tailored hiking tours (M$250) and excellent bike tours visiting San Lorenzo Zinacantán, San Juan Chamula, Rancho Nuevo or the Cañón del Sumidero. Tours cost between M$600 and M$900 (for example, a five to seven hour trip to three villages costs M$800). English and French spoken. Ask for Marco Antonio Morales at the clothing store at Utrilla 18, above which he is based.

Trotamundos   TOURS
(☑ 967-116-03-07; www.facebook.com/trotamundos agencia; Av Insurgentes 17) Regional transportation, airport transfers and trips to Laguna Miramar (minimum four people; M$4500).

🎊 Festivals & Events

Semana Santa   RELIGIOUS
The Crucifixion is acted out on Good Friday in the Barrio de Mexicanos, northwest of town.

Feria de la Primavera y de la Paz   CULTURAL
(Spring & Peace Fair) Easter Sunday is the start of this week-long town fair, with parades, musical events and bullfights.

Festival Internacional Cervantino Barroco   CULTURAL
(www.conecultachiapas.gob.mx; ⊙ late Oct) FREE
This free week-long cultural program keeps things hopping with world-class music, dance and theater.

🛏 Sleeping

San Cristóbal has a wealth of budget accommodations, but also a number of appealing and atmospheric midrange hotels, often set in colonial or 19th-century mansions, along with an ever-growing number of top-end luxury choices. The high seasons here are during Semana Santa and the following week, and the months of July and August, plus the Día de Muertos and Christmas–New Year holidays. Most prices dip at least 20% (and up to 50%) outside high season.

🛏 Real de Guadalupe Area

Casa Margarita   HOTEL $$
(☑ 967-678-72-66; www.hotelcasamargarita.mx; Real de Guadalupe 34; s/d/tr from M$855/1073/1275; 🅿😊🛜) This popular and well-run travelers' haunt offers impeccably clean, though rather dark, rooms with reading lights and a good city-center location. A lovely plant-filled garden adds to the appeal.

🛌 West of Plaza 31 de Marzo

★ Puerta Vieja Hostel
HOSTEL $

(☎ 967-631-43-35; www.puertaviejahostel.com; Mazariegos 23; dm incl breakfast M$180, r with/without bathroom M$450/550; ⊜ 🛜) Spacious, modern, traveler-savvy; this hostel is in a high-ceilinged colonial building with a large garden strung with hammocks, kitchen, temascal (pre-Hispanic steam bath) and sheltered interior courtyard. Its dorms (one for women only) are a good size, and the rooftop ones have fab views. Six private rooms have one queen and a bunk bed. There's occasional karaoke in the garden.

Hostal Akumal
HOSTEL $

(☎ cell 967-1161120; www.hostalakumal.com; Av 16 de Septiembre 33; dm/d incl breakfast M$170/500; 🛜) Friendly, live-in owners and a big cooked breakfast that changes daily are winning points at this tiny, but centrally located house-come-hostel. There's a roaring fireplace in the lounge for chilly nights, a small courtyard, and the rooms and dorms are adequate, if nothing exciting.

Dominga Bed & Desk
HOSTEL $

(☎ 967-135-80-94; www.hostaldominga.com; Andador Miguel Hidalgo 1; dm/d incl breakfast M$180/300; 🛜) The jury is still out about this new spot, a millenials' dream design, with an off-the-radar funk factor and industrial chic design. There's an open kitchen area, a boardroom table with retro office chairs, and bright, airy living spaces. The dorms have bunks with great storage, though a couple seem airless, as the windows don't open.

But hey, given Dominga's other spaces (these rival the offices of a famous US search engine company), and the fact that breakfast is included, this ultra-modern space could be a winner.

Hotel Posada El Paraíso
HOTEL $$

(☎ 967-678-00-85; www.hotelposadaparaiso.com.mx; 5 de Febrero 19; s/d/tr M$1150/1450/1750; ⊜🛜) Combining colonial style with the feel of a boutique-hotel, El Paraíso has a bright-blue wood-pillared patio, a jungly garden sitting area and loads of bohemian character. The high-ceilinged rooms are not huge, but all have natural light, and several are bi-level with an extra bed upstairs. The in-house restaurant, L'Eden, is excellent.

★ Casa del Alma
BOUTIQUE HOTEL $$$

(☎ 967-674-90-90; www.casadelalma.mx; Av 16 de Sepiembre 24; ste incl breakfast from M$3658;

DON'T MISS

TWO VIEWPOINTS
••••••••••••••••••••••••••••••••••
Want to take in the best views in town? Well, you'll have to work for them, because at this altitude the stairs up these hills can be punishing. The **Cerro de San Cristóbal** (off Hermanos Domínguez) and **Cerro de Guadalupe** (off Real de Guadalupe) lord over the town from the west and east, respectively, and churches crown both lookouts. The Iglesia de Guadalupe becomes a hot spot for religious devotees around the **Día de la Virgen de Guadalupe**.

These areas are not considered safe at night.

🅿⊜🛜) This very central, boutique hotel has it all. The rooms, which offer a fine mix of colonial charm and modern comforts, are notable for the floor-to-ceiling artworks and creative bedheads. Each comprises the material specific to a neighborhood, such as wood or metal. Beautiful bathrooms and views over terracotta tiled roofs from the private terraces and balconies.

The communal areas are just as impressive with a stylish reception area and a restaurant, El Secreto (p391), with a modern art ceiling and lots of leafy plants. Service is top-notch and there's a spa and secure underground parking – a huge plus in the city center.

Hotel b̈o
BOUTIQUE HOTEL $$$

(☎ 967-678-15-15; www.hotelbo.mx; Av 5 de Mayo 38; r from M$6000; 🅿⊜@🛜) It's all about the snob value at Hotel b̈o, a boutique hotel that seems to be more Miami Beach than San Cristóbal; it definitely breaks the traditional colonial-architecture barrier. Think supermodern, trendy lines and unique, artsy touches. The large rooms and suites are elegant and feature glass-tile bathrooms with ceiling showers, while the flowery gardens host fine water features.

The excellent Restaurante LUM (p389) is on the premises.

🛌 South of Plaza 31 de Marzo

Parador Margarita
HOTEL $$

(☎ 967-116-01-64; www.hotelparadormargarita.mx; JF Flores 39; s/d/tr incl breakfast M$1310/1593/2053; 🅿🛜) A three-story hotel with moderately sized rooms sporting one king- or two queen-sized beds; some include details like fireplaces, stained-glass windows and bathroom skylights. Other pluses include in-room heaters and a pleasant back patio overlooking a large lawn.

Azabache
HOTEL $$

(☑cell 967-1040670; www.casaazabache.com; Francisco León 46; d M$762-1090; ☎) One of the town's newer budget-cum-midrange options located about a 10-minute walk from the plaza. The owner, a carpenter, has outfitted the compact rooms in a minimalistic, industrial chic way. You can forgive any small glitches given the fair price that you pay. A small **cafe** is attached that serves good breakfasts. Staff are super helpful.

★ La Joya Hotel
BOUTIQUE HOTEL $$$

(☑967-631-48-32; www.lajoyahotelsancristobal. com; Madero 43A; r incl breakfast US$170-220; P❄🐾☎) This extraordinary boutique hotel is a visual feast in which every corner contains something interesting and beautiful. The five rooms have been ripped from a design magazine and have exquisite cabinetry, enormous bathrooms and antiques curated from the owners' world travels. Fireplace sitting areas and heaters grace each room, and rooftop terraces beckon with hill views.

But that's just the beginning of the equation. Delightful owners (Ann and John), wonderful staff, plus attentive service equals one of the very best boutique hotels you've ever stayed in. There are also snacks and late arrival or early departure treats. Needless to say, booking ahead is essential. Minimum two-night stay.

Casa Santa Lucía
BOUTIQUE HOTEL $$$

(☑967-631-55-45; www.hotelcasasantalucia.mx; Av Josefa Ortíz de Domínguez 13; r M$1600-2000, ste M$2500-3000; P❄☎) This discreet boutique hotel has been touched by the hand of an artist. Moroccan lamps hang from polished wood beams, geraniums add a touch of pink, leopards and Day of the Dead skulls grin from shady corners, and ethnic textiles and antique carved furnishings fill the bedrooms. Guests enjoy the warm welcome, free laundry service and delicious breakfasts.

Other thoughtful touches are the complimentary cookies.

🛏 North of Plaza 31 de Marzo

Rossco Backpackers
HOSTEL $

(☑967-674-05-25; www.backpackershostel.com.mx; Real de Mexicanos 16; dm from M$139, d with/without bathroom M$550/400; P❄@☎) Rossco Backpackers is a friendly, sociable and well-run hostel with good dorm rooms (one for women only), a guest kitchen, a movie-watching loft and a grassy garden. Private upstairs rooms have nice skylights. A free night's stay if you arrive by bicycle or motorcycle!

Posada del Abuelito
HOSTEL $

(☑967-678-17-41; www.posadadelabuelito.com; Tapachula 18; dm M$160, r with/without bathroom M$380/320; ☎) Featuring a good mix of private rooms and dorms (including one mixed and one female-only) set around a sweet little hammock-lined patio, this quiet, central hostel, the longest running in the city, has all the expected conveniences plus a rustic old-timey feel. All up, it's more a relax and chill hostel than a party hostel.

Phone reservations are not accepted, but you can book online.

Hotel Posada Jovel
HOTEL $$

(☑967-678-17-34; www.hoteljovel.com; Paniagua 28; r from M$1000; P❄☎) The colonial-style Jovel offers one of the better deals in town. The rooms are filled with the light, color and character of Mexico and they surround a pretty garden with fountains and tropical flowers where you can have breakfast.

Na Bolom
HOTEL $$

(☑967-678-14-18; www.nabolom.org; Guerrero 33; r incl breakfast from M$1100; P❄☎) This famous museum/research institute, about 1km from Plaza 31 de Marzo, has 16 character-filled guest rooms with gorgeous textiles and furniture (all but two have log fires). Meals are served in the house's stately dining room. Room rates include a house tour. Proceeds go towards running the NGO programs promoting the environment, heritage and culture.

Guayaba Inn
HOTEL $$$

(☑967-674-76-99; www.guayabainn.com; Comitán 55; r incl breakfast from M$2000; ☎) With something of an old country farmhouse feel to it, this gorgeous, rustic and quirky place is one of the best-looking hotels in town. The artist owners' attention to detail shines through in everything from the tranquil garden spaces to the light, spacious and divinely decorated rooms. All rooms have fireplaces, big separate tubs and minibars, and there's a sauna/massage suite.

Bela's B&B
B&B $$$

(☑967-121-55-78, 967-678-92-92; www.belasbandb. com; Dr Navarro 2; s/d incl breakfast US$100, without bathroom US$40/55; P❄☎🐾) A dreamy oasis in the center of town, this tranquil American-run B&B will seduce you with its lush garden, electric under-blankets and towel heaters. The five comfortable rooms are trimmed in traditional local fabrics and some have lovely mountain views. There's a virtual Noah's Ark of dogs, so if you're not a doggy fan look elsewhere.

A larger apartment sleeps four (M$150). There's a three-night minimum stay for all.

✖ Eating

The region's foodie jackpot, San Cristóbal has more tantalizing food options than any other place in the state. Vegetarians are almost embarrassingly spoiled for choice. A great **food court** is in Plaza San Agustín. *¡Provecho!*

✖ Real de Guadalupe Area

Self-caterers can stock up at the centrally located **Super Más** (Madero s/n; ⊗8am-10pm) market, and there are a number of fruit and vegetable shops on Dugelay where the pedestrianized section of Real de Guadalupe ends.

TierrAdentro   MEXICAN $
(☑967-674-67-66; Real de Guadalupe 24; set menu M$75-210; ⊗8am-11pm; 🛜🅿) A popular gathering point for political progressives and coffee-swigging, laptop-toting locals (not that they're mutually exclusive), this large indoor-courtyard restaurant, cafe and pizzeria is a comfortable place to while away the hours. It's run by Zapatista supporters, who hold frequent cultural events and conferences on local issues.

La Casa del Pan Papalotl   VEGETARIAN $
(☑967-678-72-15; www.casadelpan.com; Real de Guadalupe 55; mains M$50-180; ⊗8am-10pm Mon-Sat, 9am-4pm Sun; 🛜🅿) 🍽 This attractive and relaxed restaurant-bakery is *the* place in San Cristóbal for vegetarian, vegan and bio dishes and there's an emphasis on using local ingredients. It offers great breakfasts and a daily three-course fixed-price menu, light lunches and some of the best *empanadas* (turnovers) around (great for lunch to go or self caterers).

La Lupe   MEXICAN $$
(☑967-678-12-22; Real de Guadalupe 23; mains M$70-170, breakfast from M$75; ⊗7am-11:30pm) This very popular cafe has farmhouse decorations splayed across the walls and good, authentic Mexican country fare served

in clay pots or on wooden boards. It's renowned for its filling breakfasts of *huevos mexicanos* and tasty fruit juices.

✖ West of Plaza 31 de Marzo

Namandí   CRÊPES $
(☑967-678-80-54; Mazariegos 16C; crepes M$71-99; ⊗8am-11pm Mon-Sat, 8:30am-10:30pm Sun; 🛜🅿) Nattily attired staff serve baguettes, pastas and good coffee at this large cafe and restaurant, but the fresh-off-the-griddle crepes are the main draw. Try a savory *crepa azteca* with chicken, corn and peppers drizzled with *salsa poblana*. Kids love the glassed-in modern play space, and frazzled parents can take advantage of free childcare while they're onsite (paid babysitting also available).

L'Eden   MEXICAN, INTERNATIONAL $$
(☑967-678-00-85; Hotel Posada El Paraíso, 5 de Febrero 19; mains M$90-210; ⊗7am-10pm; 🅿) This smart, colorful restaurant has a tempting and reliable European and Mexican menu that includes an authentic *fondú suiza* (Swiss fondue), *sopa azteca* (tortilla, chili, onion and herb broth topped with shredded chicken, cheese, lime, avocado and coriander) and succulent meat dishes, all served around a cozy fireplace or out in the leafy courtyard. There's a good-sized wine list too.

★**Restaurante LUM**   MEXICAN $$$
(☑967-678-15-16; www.hotelbo.mx/restaurante-san-cristobal-de-las-casas; Hotel b̄o, Av 5 de Mayo 38; mains M$200-350; ⊗7am-11pm) This swanky indoor-outdoor restaurant in San Cristóbal's first designer hotel serves up exciting blends of Chiapas, Veracruz and Yucatán cuisine fused with tastes and ideas from around the culinary planet. Custom-made lamps, reflecting pools and walls of geometrically stacked firewood create a funky contemporary ambience. We're still in raptures of delight over the shrimp with almond sauce.

✖ South of Plaza 31 de Marzo

★**Ooh La La! Pastelería**   PASTRIES $
(https://sancristobalenlascasas.com/pasteleria-oh-lala; San Augustín Plaza; snacks from M$20; ⊗8:30am-11pm) Bite into these authentic, fresh French pastries and you might have to recalibrate your location; a whiff of Paris comes with a sugary hit. There's *pain au raisin*, custard-filled cakes and much more.

THE ZAPATISTAS

On January 1, 1994, the day the North American Free Trade Agreement (Nafta) was implemented, a previously unknown leftist guerrilla army emerged from the forests to occupy San Cristóbal de las Casas and other towns in Chiapas. The Ejército Zapatista de Liberación Nacional (EZLN; Zapatista National Liberation Army) linked antiglobalization rhetoric with Mexican revolutionary slogans, declaring that they aimed to both overturn the oligarchy's centuries-old hold on land, resources and power, and improve the wretched living standards of Mexico's indigenous people.

The Mexican army evicted the Zapatistas within days, and the rebels retreated to the fringes of the Lacandón Jungle to wage a propaganda war, mainly fought via the internet. The Zapatistas' balaclava-clad, pipe-puffing Subcomandante Marcos (a former university professor named Rafael Guillén) rapidly became a cult figure. High-profile conventions against neoliberalism were held, international supporters flocked to Zapatista headquarters at La Realidad, and Zapatista-aligned peasants took over hundreds of farms and ranches in Chiapas.

A set of accords on indigenous rights and autonomy was negotiated between the Zapatistas and the Mexican government but never ratified, and tension and killings escalated in Chiapas through the 1990s. According to Amnesty International, the paramilitary groups responsible for a massacre in Acteal in 1997 were armed by the authorities. By 1999, an estimated 21,000 villagers had fled their homes after a campaign of intimidation.

After a high-profile Zapatista media campaign, La Otra Campaña (The Other Campaign), during Mexico's 2006 presidential election, the EZLN has mostly remained dormant, with only the occasional conference and mobilization, its political influence slight outside its own enclaves. The movement still maintains five regional 'Juntas de Buen Gobierno' (Committees of Good Government) and many autonomous communities, though some former supporters have grown disillusioned and many have left the movement.

In 2016, in a break with tradition, the Zapatistas elected to put forward a candidate for the 2018 presidential elections, that ended 20 years of the Zapatista's rejection of Mexican politics. In 2019, the EZLN announced it had expanded into 11 new regions (four of which are autonomous, the others 'organizing regions'); President López Obrador did not disapprove, but stressed there be no violence.

Further background is available in *The Zapatista Reader,* an anthology of writers from Octavio Paz and Gabriel García Márquez to Marcos himself, and Bill Weinberg's *Homage to Chiapas: The New Indigenous Struggles in Mexico.*

Snag a seat at this cafe branch or grab a few things for a picnic from its take-out location on **Real de Guadalupe** (https://sancristobalen lascasas.com/pasteleria-oh-lala; Real de Guadalupe 2; ⊕8:30am-10pm).

El Tacoleto MEXICAN $
(☑967-678-64-86; Belisario Domínguez 1; mains M$50-150; ⊕1-11pm) The name and taste on everyone's lips, it seems. Great quality tacos – with all the toppings you can ever desire – in a fun, casual eatery. Check it out on Facebook.

Te Quiero Verde VEGETARIAN $
(Niños Héroes 4; mains from M$80; ⊕9am-10pm; 🛜🍴) 🍃 If you've ever doubted that a vegan burger can be truly tasty, you need to head here. The soups and salads are OK too, but the burgers and homemade fries steal the show.

El Caldero MEXICAN $
(☑967-116-01-21; Av Insurgentes 5; soups from M$90; ⊕7am-10pm; 🍴) Perfect for a cold day, simple, friendly little El Caldero specializes in delicious Mexican soups – *pozole* (shredded pork in broth), *mondongo* (tripe) and *caldo* (broth). Although calling them mere 'soups' does them an injustice: these are more massive portions of thick, hearty stews than watery soups and they come with a spread of avocados, tortillas and salsas.

Restaurante Belil MEXICAN $$
(☑967-115-2022; https://es-la.facebook.com/ RestaurantBelil; MA Flores 20; mains M$130-230; ⊕8am-9:30pm) Run by a passionate owner who promotes not only indigenous artworks and textiles (without taking a monetary cut), but also delightful tastes of Chiapas. The likes of *chipilín* salsa with *chile relleno* (stuffed chile) and a local

bread soup. Brightly colored wooden decor, fresh flowers, and an open modern ambience add to the appeal.

★ **El Secreto** INTERNATIONAL $$
(☏967-674-91-21; Av 16 de Septiembre 24; mains M$185-240; ⊗7am-11pm) Possibly San Cristóbal's best choice for fine dining and one of the best-value places this side of the equator. High end gourmet cuisine in a color palette and presentation that would make Frida Kahlo blush. Get your senses around everything from mushroom ceviche to suckling pig tacos to Zinancantan bass.

Good Mexican breakfasts, too (M$120 to M$130). Two words: don't miss.

Plaza San Augustín INTERNATIONAL $$
(cnr Andador Miguel Hidalgo & Cuauhtémoc; ⊗9am-11pm) This wonderful food court, housed in a refurbished two-storey colonial building, is chock-a-block with food options for all budgets and tastes, from Thai to Italian. Standards for all are high and reliable; the joy is in the choosing according to your mood and taste buds. Once you've had your fill, you can browse the several Mexican-themed home-decor stores, too.

✕ North of Plaza 31 de Marzo

Kukulpan Panadería Artesanal BAKERY $
(☏967-631-59-99; www.facebook.com/Kukulpan; Dr Navarro 10; cakes from M$20, lunch mains M$55-80; ⊗8am-10:30pm) This artisanal bakery and vegetarian hotspot has a few seats on a tiny plaza. Bites here are perfect for a quick lunch (or take out) and include organic breads, perfect for the tasty sandwiches. Delicious pastries, too.

La Salsa Verde TACOS $
(☏967-678-72-80; Av 20 de Noviembre 7; 5 tacos M$60-90; ⊗8am-midnight; ☏) Meat sizzles on the open-air grill and TVs blare at this taco institution (more than 30 years in business), with tables of families and club-goers packed into its two large, noisy dining rooms.

Trattoria Italiana ITALIAN $$
(☏967-678-58-95; Dr Navarro 10; mains M$128-200; ⊗2-10pm Mon-Sat, to 6pm Sun, closed Tue) Set inside a pastel-colored colonial building and with some tables outside under the trees, this Italian-run local delivers in Tuscan style, right down to the checked tablecloths. Fresh pasta is the specialty. Try the ravioli, handmade fresh every day. And you can expect fillings of sea bass with eggplant,

cheeses with walnut and arugula, or rabbit with rosemary and olive.

The sauces are divine – don't miss the mango, chipotle and gorgonzola if it's around.

🍸 Drinking & Nightlife

The aroma of roasted highland-grown coffee beans wafts through the streets of San Cristóbal, and a strong dose is never far away. Fabulous bars dot the town, too.

★ **Cafeología** CAFE
(Casa Cafeologo; ☏967-678-77-38; www.cafeologia.org; Real de Guadalupe 13; ⊗8:30am-10pm; ☏) Coffee hounds, we've sniffed out the bean scene and this is the best place in town. Here's the checklist: single origin/single-farmer production (tick). Smooth flavours (tick again). Fair trade. Brewed in house. Baristas (triple tick). International methods (you name it, they'll do it).

While we're at it, the place is lovely, too – modern and sleek with great wi-fi. Plus, if you really want to smell, taste, brew and or prepare your own, do one of the 'coffee experience' courses (M$350 to M750 per person).

★ **Cocoliche** COCKTAIL BAR
(☏967-631-46-21; Colón 3; mains M$60-210; ⊗1pm-midnight; ☏) By day Cocoliche is a bohemian restaurant with lots of Asian dishes, but in the evening its vintage lanterns and wall of funky posters set the scene for drinking boozy or virgin cocktails with friends. Jostle for a spot near the fireplace on chilly evenings, and check out the nightly jazz, funk and swing music.

Panóptico BAR
(☏967-631-73-56; Real de Guadalupe 63A; ⊗3pm-2am) A small bar with more of a local clientele than many city-center places, it has a good range of artisan beers and the barman knows how to mix a mean mojito and other cocktails with flair.

La Viña de Bacco WINE BAR
(☏967-119-19-85; Real de Guadalupe 7; ⊗1:30pm-midnight) At San Cristóbal's first wine bar, chatty patrons spill out onto the pedestrian street. It's a convivial place, pouring a large selection of global options, starting at a reasonable M$25 per glass. A free tapa comes with every glass of wine.

Latino's CLUB
(☏967-678-99-27; Madero 23; Fri & Sat M$50; ⊗8pm-3am Mon-Sat) A bright restaurant and

dance spot where the city's *salseros* (salsa musicians or dancers) gather to groove. Latin DJs spin from 8pm every night, and a salsa/merengue/*cumbia/bachata* band plays at 11pm Wednesday through Saturday.

☆ Entertainment

Most live-music venues are free, and clubs generally enforce the no-smoking law.

San Cristóbal is a fine place to immerse yourself in Mexican and Latin American cinema, political documentaries and art-house movies. West of the center, the **Cinépolis** (www.cinepolis.com; Paniagua 50; tickets M$60) multiplex plays first-run flicks.

★ Café Bar Revolución   LIVE MUSIC
(☑ 967-678-66-64; www.facebook.com/elrevomx; Calle 1 de Marzo 11; ⊘1pm-3am) There's always something fun at Revolución, with two live bands nightly and an eclectic line up of salsa, rock, blues, jazz and reggae. Dance downstairs or order a mojito or caipirinha and chat in the quieter upstairs *tapanco* (attic).

El Paliacate   ARTS CENTER
(☑ 967-125-37-39; www.facebook.com/elpaliacate; Av 5 de Mayo 20; ⊘4pm-2am Tue-Sat) An alternative cultural space with a small restaurant and a bar serving wine, beer and artisan mezcal, El Paliacate's main stage hosts music events including rock en Tsotzil, *son jarocho* (folk music from Veracruz) and experimental bands, plus the occasional documentary film or theater presentation. There's bike parking inside and chill-out rooms upstairs.

Kinoki   CINEMA
(☑ 967-678-50-46; www.forokinoki.blogspot.com; Belisario Domínguez 5A; tickets M$30; ⊘12:30pm-midnight; 🛜) With a beautiful upstairs space and terrace, this art gallery and tea salon screens films and holds events. Private cinema rooms available with over 3500 movies on hand.

🔒 Shopping

Real de Guadalupe and the Andador Turístico have some upscale craft shops, but the busy daily crafts market around the Santo Domingo and La Caridad churches is also a good place to check out. In addition to textiles, another Chiapas specialty is amber, sold in numerous jewelry shops. When buying amber, beware of plastic imitations: the real thing is never cold and never heavy, and when rubbed should produce static electricity and a resiny smell.

Poshería   DRINKS
(Real de Guadalupe 46A; ⊘10am-11pm Sun-Wed, 10am-1am Thu-Sat) Pick up a bottle of artisanal *pox* (pronounced 'posh'; alcohol made from sugarcane) infused with honey, chocolate or fruits like *nanche* (a sweet, yellow fruit). Definitely not what the common folk are drinking, since bottles sell for M$50 to M$250 and the alcohol content averages only about 14%.

Sna Jolobil   ARTS & CRAFTS
(☑ 967-678-26-46; www.facebook.com/SnaJolobil; Calz Lázaro Cárdenas s/n; ⊘9am-2pm & 4-7pm Mon-Sat) Next to the Templo de Santo Domingo, Sna Jolobil – Tsotzil for 'Weaver's House' – exhibits and sells some of the very best *huipiles*, blouses, skirts, rugs and other woven items, with prices ranging from a few dollars for small items to thousands for the best *huipiles* (the fruit of many months' work).

A cooperative of 800 weavers from the Chiapas highlands, it was founded in the 1970s to foster the important indigenous art of backstrap-loom weaving, and has revived many half-forgotten techniques and designs.

Abuelita Books   BOOKS
(Colón 2; ⊘12:30-8:30pm Wed-Mon; 🛜) A great place for a leisurely browse over hot coffee or a steamy tea and simple snacks; come here to replenish your reading material from an excellent selection of new and used books in English (other languages also available). Free English movies on Thursday nights.

★ Taller Leñateros   ARTS & CRAFTS
(☑ 967-678-51-74; www.tallerlenateros.com; Paniagua 54; ⊘9am-5pm Mon-Fri, to 2pm Sat) 🖉 A society of Maya artists, the 'Woodlanders' Workshop' crafts exquisite handmade books, posters and fine-art prints from recycled paper infused with local plants, using images inspired by traditional folk art. It's an open workshop, so you can watch the art in progress.

Lágrimas de la Selva   JEWELRY
(Plaza 31 de Marzo; ⊘10am-9pm Mon-Sat, noon-9pm Sun) A lovely jewelry store where you can watch jewelers work with amber.

El Camino de los Altos   ARTS & CRAFTS
(☑ 967-631-69-44; www.facebook.com/elcaminodelosaltosAC; Miguel Hidalgo 6; ⊘noon-10pm Wed-Mon) Creators of exquisite furnishings and textiles, El Camino de los Altos is a collaboration of French textile designers and 130 Maya weavers.

Nemi Zapata ARTS & CRAFTS
(www.nemizapata.com; MA Flores 57; ⊙9am-2pm & 3:30-7pm Mon-Sat) 🖉 A fair-trade store that sells products made by Zapatista communities: weavings, embroidery, coffee and honey, as well as EZLN cards, posters and books.

❶ Information

Most banks require your passport if you want to change cash, though money is only changed Monday through Friday. There are also handy **ATMs** at the OCC bus station and on the southern side of the Plaza 31 de Marzo.

Banamex (Av Insurgentes, btwn Niños Héroes & Cuauhtémoc; ⊙9am-4pm Mon-Fri) Has an ATM; exchanges dollars.

Dr Patrick Rueda Trujillo (☑ cell 967-102-01-06) Reliable and speaks English; makes house calls.

Hospital de la Mujer (☑ 967-678-07-70; Av Insurgentes 24; ⊙24hr) General hospital with emergency facilities.

Main Post Office (Allende 3; ⊙8am-5pm Mon-Fri, 10am-2pm Sat)

Tourist Office Centro Cultural Carmen (Av Hidalgo 15; ⊙9am-8pm) Tiny office outside the cultural center with a few fliers on local events

❶ Getting There & Away

A fast toll autopista (M$57 for cars) zips to San Cristóbal from Chiapa de Corzo. Follow the highways signs that say 'cuota' (toll).

At the time of research, because of security concerns and the inconvenience of ongoing blockades, the prolific 4am tour company departures to Palenque (via Misol-Ha and Agua Azul

waterfalls) were heading in convoy to Palenque via Ocosingo. However, large buses (eg ADO) were not traveling the same route; most were instead taking the much more circular and longer route via Villahermosa. If you do travel to Palenque via Ocosingo, it's best to travel during daylight, as highway holdups and assaults – though by no means common – have occurred. When taking a bus along this route, stow your valuables in the checked luggage compartment.

AIR
San Cristóbal's airport has no regular passenger flights; the main airport serving town is at Tuxtla Gutiérrez. Frequent direct ADO minibuses (M$242) run to the Tuxtla airport from San Cristóbal's main bus terminal; book airport-bound tickets in advance, and consult www.ado.com.mx for schedules to/from 'Ángel Albino Corzo Aeropuerto.'

A number of tour agencies run shuttles to Tuxtla airport for around M$200 to M$400 per person (shared transport) or M$800 for a private trip.

Taxis from the airport will cost at least M$650.

BUS & COLECTIVO
The Pan-American Hwy (Hwy 190, Bulevar Juan Sabines, 'El Bulevar') runs through the southern part of town, and nearly all transportation terminals are on it or nearby. From the OCC bus terminal, it's six blocks north up Insurgentes to the central square, Plaza 31 de Marzo.

The main 1st-class **OCC terminal** (cnr Pan-American Hwy & Av Insurgentes) is used by ADO 1st-class and deluxe buses. Tickets can also be purchased at **Ticket bus** (☑ 967-678-85-03; Real de Guadalupe 16; ⊙7am-10:30pm) in the center of town. **AEXA buses and Ómnibus de**

CHIAPAS & TABASCO SAN CRISTÓBAL DE LAS CASAS

BUSES FROM SAN CRISTÓBAL DE LAS CASAS

DESTINATION	COST (M$)	TIME (HR)	FREQUENCY (PER DAY)
Campeche	717	14	2 ADO
Cancún	1278	23	3 ADO
Ciudad Cuauhtémoc (Guatemalan border)	181	4	3
Comitán	93	2	frequent ADO & *colectivos*
Mérida	1074	17	2
Mexico City (TAPO & Norte)	1577	15	frequent
Oaxaca	784	12	4
Palenque	351	9	7
Puerto Escondido	855	13	3
Tuxtla Gutiérrez	77	1¼	frequent
Tuxtla Gutiérrez airport (Ángel Albino Corzo)	242	1½	12
Villahermosa	544	6½-7	5

Chiapas minibuses share a terminal across the street from the OCC terminal.

All *colectivo* vans (combis) and taxis have depots on the Pan-American Hwy a block or so from the OCC terminal. They generally run from 5am until 9pm and leave when full, including to **Comitán** and **Tuxtla Gutiérrez and Ocosingo**. Combis to **Zinacantán** and **San Juan Chamula** (Honduras) leave from further north. *Colectivo* taxis to Tuxtla, Comitán and **Ocosingo** are available 24 hours; if you don't want to wait for one to fill, you must pay for the empty seats. (Check on the security status of traveling to Ocosingo; at the time of research there were occasional blockades.)

For Tuxtla Gutiérrez, comfortable Ómnibus de Chiapas 'sprinter' minibuses (M$55) are the best bet; they leave every 10 minutes.

For Guatemala, most agencies offer a daily van service to Quetzaltenango (M$450, eight hours), Panajachel (M$450, 10 hours) and Antigua (M$600, 12 hours). Otherwise, go to Ciudad Cuauhtémoc and pick up onward transportation from the Guatemala side.

CAR & MOTORCYCLE

One of San Cristóbal's few car-rental companies, **Óptima** (☑ 967-674-54-09; optimacar1@hotmail .com; Mazariegos 39; ⊗ 9am-7pm Mon-Fri, 9am-2pm & 4-7pm Sat, 9am-1pm Sun) rents out cars with manual transmission. Rates vary wildly depending on the season and demand. Sizable discounts are given for payment in cash. Drivers must be 25 or older and have a credit card.

❶ Getting Around

Combis (M$8) go up Crescencio Rosas from the Pan-American Hwy to the town center. Taxis cost M$35 to M$40 within town and slightly more at night.

Croozy Scooters (☑ cell 967-6832223; Belisario Domínguez 7; bicycles/scooters/motorcycles per day M$220/500/800; ⊗10am-7pm) rents well-maintained Italika CS 125cc scooters and 150cc and 200cc motorcycles. The price includes locks and helmets; passport and M$500 deposit required.

Around San Cristóbal de las Casas

San Juan Chamula

📞 967 / POP 3300 / ELEV 2200M

The Chamulans are a fiercely independent Tsotzil group, and you will feel it. Their main village, San Juan Chamula, 10km northwest of San Cristóbal, is the center for some unique religious practices. It's an interesting place to visit, but do be aware of local sensibilities, as locals guard their privacy.

Chamulan men wear loose homespun tunics of white wool (sometimes, in cool weather, thicker black wool), but *cargo*-holders – those with important religious and ceremonial duties – wear a sleeveless black tunic and a white scarf on the head. Chamulan women wear fairly plain white or blue blouses and/or shawls and woolen skirts.

Sunday is the weekly market; people from the hills stream into the village to shop, trade and visit the main church. A corresponding number of tourist buses also stream in, so you might prefer to come another day (though due to local superstitions, there are fewer worshippers on Wednesdays).

◉ Sights

★ Templo de San Juan   CHURCH

(M$25) Standing beside the main plaza, Chamula's main church is a ghostly white, with a vividly painted arch of green and blue. Inside the darkened sanctuary, hundreds of flickering candles, clouds of copal incense, and worshippers kneeling with their faces to the pine-needle-carpeted floor make a powerful impression. Chamulans revere San Juan Bautista (St John the Baptist) above Christ. NOTE: It is strictly forbidden to take photos in the church. Please do not abuse the privilege of entering.

Chanting *curanderos* (literally 'curers'; medicine men or women) may be treating their patients' bodies with eggs or bones, and worshippers often drink soft drinks (burps are believed to expel evil spirits) or copious amounts of *pox*. Images of saints are surrounded with mirrors and dressed in holy garments.

You must obtain tickets (M$25) at the ticket office beside the plaza before entering.

Nearby, around the shell of an older church, is the village **graveyard**. Though it's no longer practiced, traditionally black crosses were for people who died old, white for the young, and blue for others.

WORTH A TRIP

GRUTAS DE RANCHO NUEVO

The entrance to **Grutas de Rancho Nuevo** (M$40, parking M$30; ⊗ 8am-6pm) is situated in pine woods 9km southeast of San Cristóbal, a five-minute walk south of the Pan-American Hwy. The first 350m or so of the cave is lit and open for viewing, with a concrete walkway threading through a dazzling chasm of stalagmites and stalactites. Beyond that you have the option of continuing (extra M$30) in total darkness with just a flashlight, helmet and jacket (provided) for company for another few hundred meters.

Horseback riding is available from the parking area, where you'll also find *comedores* (food stalls).

To get here, take a Teopisca-bound combi (M$25) from the Pan-American Hwy, about 150m southeast of the OCC bus station in San Cristóbal, and ask for 'Las Grutas.'

✦ Festivals & Events

Carnaval   CARNIVAL

(⊗ Feb/Mar) During Carnaval, groups of minstrels stroll the roads in tall, pointed hats with long, colored tassels, strumming guitars and chanting. Much *pox* is drunk. Festivities also mark the five 'lost' days of the ancient Long Count calendar, which divided time into 20-day periods (18 of these make 360 days, leaving five to complete a year).

❶ Getting There & Away

From San Cristóbal, combis to San Juan Chamula (M$18) leave from spots on Calles Honduras and Utrilla frequently. It's best to come with a guide.

San Lorenzo Zinacantán

📞 967 / POP 3900 / ELEV 2558M

The orderly village of San Lorenzo Zinacantán, about 11km northwest of San Cristóbal, is the main village of the Zinacantán municipality (population 36,000). Zinacantán people, like Chamulans, are Tsotzil. The men wear distinctive pink tunics embroidered with flower motifs and may sport flat, round, ribboned palm hats. Women wear pink or purple shawls over richly embroidered blouses.

AMATENANGO DEL VALLE

The women of this Tzeltal village by the Pan-American Hwy, 37km southeast of San Cristóbal, are renowned potters. Pottery here is still fired by a pre-Hispanic method, building a wood fire around the pieces rather than putting them in a kiln. Amatenango children find a ready tourist market with *animalitos* – little pottery animal figures that are inexpensive but fragile. If you visit the village, expect to be surrounded within minutes by young vendors. From San Cristóbal, take a Comitán-bound bus or combi.

The welcoming people of Zinacantán are great flower growers. Their church (reopened in 2019 after repair to damage caused by the 2017 earthquake) is a glorious sight when decorated in flowers. Entrance to the village costs M$15.

The huge central **Iglesia de San Lorenzo** was rebuilt following a fire in 1975. Today there are often masses of flowers on the altar. Photography is banned in the church and churchyard.

ⓘ Getting There & Away

For Zinacantán, combis (M$20) and *colectivo* taxis (M$20) go at least hourly, from a yard off Robledo in San Cristóbal de las Casas. Transportation runs from before daybreak to around dusk.

Ocosingo & Toniná

📞 919 / POP 42,000 / ELEV 900M

A respite from both the steamy lowland jungle and the chilly highlands, the bustling regional market town of Ocosingo sits in a gorgeous and broad temperate valley midway between San Cristóbal and Palenque. The impressive Maya ruins of Toniná are just a few kilometers away.

At the time of research, the town of Ocosingo was perfectly safe to visit (the plaza is a lovely spot to watch the world go by). Unfortunately, however, there have been some security issues on roads in and out of the city, relating to ongoing blockades. These are more of an inconvenience than a danger and locals here suffer for the lack of visitors.

Some tours still pass through Ocosingo on the way to/from Palenque, but if traveling on your own, check the latest before venturing here as the protests can, and do, flare up now and again.

⊙ Sights

★ **Toniná**   ARCHAEOLOGICAL SITE
(📞919-108-22-39; M$60; ⊙8am-5pm Tue-Sun) The towering ceremonial core of Toniná, overlooking a pastoral valley 14km east of Ocosingo, is one of the most spectacular archaeological sites in Chiapas. This was the city that temporarily brought mighty Palenque to its knees. However, despite the ruins here being veritable poems in stone, and the sheer importance of the site, few people bother to visit – which is all the better for those who do.

The year 688 CE saw the inauguration of the Snake Skull–Jaguar Claw dynasty, with ambitious new rulers bent on controlling the region. Palenque was their rival state, and when Toniná captured the Palenque ruler K'an Joy Chitam II in 711, it's likely that he had his head lopped off here.

Toniná became known as the Place of the Celestial Captives, because its chambers held the captured rulers of Palenque and other Maya cities, who were destined to be ransomed for large sums or decapitated. A recurring image in Toniná sculpture is of captives before decapitation, thrown to the ground with their hands tied.

To enter the site, follow the road from the entrance and **site museum** (⊙Tue-Sun) **FREE**, which details Toniná's history (in Spanish) and contains most of the best artifacts. The road turns into a footpath, crosses a stream and climbs to the broad, flat **Gran Plaza**. At the south end of the Gran Plaza is the **Templo de la Guerra Cósmica** (Temple of Cosmic War), with five altars in front of it. Off one side of the plaza is a **ball court**, inaugurated around 780 CE under the rule of the female regent Smoking Mirror. A decapitation altar stands cheerfully beside it. In 2011 archaeologists discovered two life-size stone sculptures of captive warriors inscribed as being from Copán (in Honduras), confirming that Maya kingdom's wartime alliance with Palenque.

To the north rises the ceremonial core of Toniná, a hillside terraced into a number of platforms, rising 80m above the Gran Plaza. At the right-hand end of the steps, rising from the first to the second platform, is the entry to a **ritual labyrinth of passages**.

Higher up on the right-hand side is the **Palacio de las Grecas y de la Guerra** (Palace of the Grecas and War). The *grecas* are a band of geometrical decoration forming a zigzag x-shape, possibly representing Quetzalcóatl. To its right is a rambling series of chambers, passages and stairways, believed to have been Toniná's **administrative headquarters**.

Higher again is Toniná's most remarkable sculpture, the **Mural de las Cuatro Eras** (Mural of the Four Eras). Created between 790 and 840 CE, this stucco relief of four panels – the first, from the left end, has been lost – represents the four suns, or four eras of human history. The people of Toniná believed themselves to be living in the fourth sun – that of winter, the direction north, mirrors and the end of human life. At the center of each panel is the upside-down head of a decapitated prisoner. Blood spurting from the prisoner's neck forms a ring of feathers and, at the same time, a sun. In one panel, a dancing skeleton holds a decapitated head. To the left of the head is a lord of the underworld, resembling an enormous rodent.

Up the next set of steps is the seventh level, with remains of four temples. Behind the second temple from the left, more steps descend into the very narrow **Tumba de Treinta Metros** (Thirty-Meter Tomb), an impossibly slim passageway that's definitely not for the claustrophobic!

Above here is the **acropolis**, the abode of Toniná's rulers and site of its eight most important temples – four on each of the two levels. The right-hand temple on the lower level, the **Templo del Monstruo de la Tierra** (Temple of the Earth Monster), has Toniná's best-preserved roof-comb, built around 713 CE.

On the topmost level, the tallest temple, the **Templo del Espejo Humeante** (Temple of the Smoking Mirror), was built by Zots-Choj, who took the throne in 842 CE. In that era of the fourth sun and the direction north, Zots-Choj had to raise this, Toniná's northernmost temple, highest of all, which necessitated a large, artificial northeast extension of the hill.

Guides wait at the entrance; some speak English. They charge around M$300 to M$400 for up to four people.

Combis to Toniná (M$15) leave from a roofed depot next to Ocosingo's Tianguis Campesino every 30 minutes. The last one returns around 5:30pm. A taxi costs between M$150 and M$180. There are currently no security issues surrounding a visit here.

🛏 Sleeping & Eating

Hotel Central   HOTEL $
(📞 919-673-00-24; Av Central 5; s/d M$350/400; P😊❄️🛜) With great plaza views from the 1st-floor terrace, the colorful Hotel Central has smallish rooms with cable TV and fan. Ask for one of the upstairs rooms; corner room 12 is especially bright and breezy.

Casa Lobe   INTERNATIONAL $$
(📞 919-688-03-26; www.casalobe.mx; Calle 2a Poniente Norte; mains M$120-160; ⏰8am-10pm) With two trained chefs as the owners, you're in safe hands at this new place, a stylish spot that's housed within the small courtyard of a restored home. It specializes

---

ⓘ ROAD TRAVEL TO OCOSINGO

The valleys known as Las Cañadas de Ocosingo, between Ocosingo and the Reserva de la Biosfera Montes Azules to the southeast, form one of the strongest bastions of support for the Zapatistas, and Ocosingo saw the bloodiest fighting during the 1994 uprising, with about 50 rebels killed here by the Mexican army. The occasional skirmish continues to flare up to this day.

Many other 'copycat' communities, too, disgruntled by the lack of services, have taken to expressing their frustrations through ongoing and intermittent road blockades. It means drivers must pay small payments to individuals 'representing' the *ejidos* (communal landholding communities). Visitors do not often understand how these demands should be dealt with, which has had serious repercussions in the past.

At the time of research, large company buses were not running to Ocosingo for possible inconveniences and trouble, taking the longer route via Villahermosa to areas like Palenque. It is still possible, however, to get to the town by *colectivo* (but even these might travel by a much-longer route.) Tour buses to/from Palenque were running via this route, leaving at 4am daily. It's imperative that you check with authorities and tour companies before traveling to and from Ocosingo. The town itself is safe and is a pleasant place to visit.

in international cuisine with regional influences and all the pastas are home made. We'd go as far to say that it might have put Ocosingo back on the map.

Our favorite dish is the *pasta cremosa de camarones y chipilín*, noodles served with shrimp and the local herb in a creamy sauce.

🛍 Shopping

Tianguis Campesino   MARKET
(Peasants' Market; cnr Av 2 Sur Oriente & Calle 5 Sur Oriente; ⊙6am-5pm) The Tianguis Campesino is for the area's small-scale food producers to sell their goods direct. It's a colorful sight, with most of the traders in traditional dress.

❶ Getting There & Away

Ocosingo's OCC bus terminal is on Hwy 199, 600m west of the plaza; at the time of research, large buses were not running due to the inconvenience of intermittent blockades, but combis are still running. The main *colectivo* terminal is across the street from OCC. There are frequent departures to Palenque (M$80, four hours) and San Cristóbal de las Casas (M$70, 2½ hours). *Colectivos* sometimes take very roundabout routes to avoid roadblocks or known trouble areas.

A walled lot behind the market is the terminus for trucks to Nahá (M$65, three hours, 7:30am and 1pm) and Laguna Miramar. For Nahá, shared taxis cost M$125 per person (three hours).

Palenque

📞 916 / POP 43,000 / ELEV 80M

Swathed in morning jungle mists and echoing to a dawn chorus of howler monkeys and parrots, the mighty Maya temples of Palenque are deservedly one of the top destinations of Chiapas and one of the best examples of Maya architecture in all of Mexico. By contrast, modern Palenque town, a few kilometers to the east, is a sweaty, humdrum place without much appeal except as a jumping-off point for the ruins and tours to the Lacandón jungle. Many prefer to base themselves at one of the forest hideouts along the road between the town and the ruins, including the grungy travelers' hangout of El Panchán.

History

The name Palenque (Palisade) is Spanish and has no relation to the city's ancient name, which may have been Lakamha (Big Water). Palenque was first occupied around 100 BCE, and flourished from around 630 to around 740 CE. The city rose to prominence under the ruler Pakal, who reigned from 615 to 683 CE. Archaeologists have determined that Pakal is represented by hieroglyphics of sun and shield, and he is also referred to as Escudo Solar (Sun Shield). He lived to the then-incredible age of 80.

During Pakal's reign, many plazas and buildings, including the superlative Templo de las Inscripciones (Pakal's own mausoleum), were constructed in Palenque. The structures were characterized by mansard roofs and very fine stucco bas-reliefs.

Pakal's son Kan B'alam II (r 684–702), who is represented in hieroglyphics by the jaguar and the serpent (and is also called Jaguar Serpent II), continued Palenque's expansion and artistic development. He presided over the construction of the Grupo de las Cruces temples, placing sizable narrative stone stelae within each.

During Kan B'alam II's reign, Palenque extended its zone of control to the Río Usumacinta, but was challenged by the rival Maya city of Toniná, 65km south. Kan B'alam's brother and successor, K'an Joy Chitam II (Precious Peccary), was captured by forces from Toniná in 711 CE, and probably executed there. Palenque enjoyed a resurgence between 722 and 736, however, under Ahkal Mo' Nahb' III (Turtle Macaw Lake), who added many substantial buildings.

After 900 CE, Palenque was largely abandoned. In an area that receives the heaviest rainfall in Mexico, the ruins were soon overgrown, and the city remained unknown to the Western world until 1746, when Maya hunters revealed the existence of a jungle palace to a Spanish priest named Antonio de Solís. Later explorers claimed Palenque was capital of an Atlantis-like civilization. The eccentric Count de Waldeck, who in his 60s lived atop one of the pyramids for two years (1831–33), even published a book with fanciful neoclassical drawings that made the city resemble a great Mediterranean civilization.

It was not until 1837, when John L Stephens, an amateur archaeology enthusiast from New York, reached Palenque with artist Frederick Catherwood, that the site was insightfully investigated. Another century passed before Alberto Ruz Lhuillier, the tireless Mexican archaeologist, uncovered Pakal's hidden crypt in 1952. Today it continues to yield fascinating and beautiful secrets – most recently, a succession of sculptures and frescoes in the Acrópolis del Sur area, which have vastly expanded our knowledge of Palenque's history.

◉ Sights

Hwy 199 meets Palenque's main street, Avenida Juárez, at the **Glorieta de la Cabeza Maya** (Map p402; Maya Head Statue), a roundabout with a large statue of a Maya chieftain's head, at the west end of the town. The main ADO bus station is here, and Juárez heads 1km east from this intersection to the central square, **El Parque** (Map p402).

A few hundred meters south of the Maya head, the paved road to the Palenque ruins, 7.5km away, diverges west off Hwy 199. This road passes the site museum after about 6.5km, then winds on about 1km further uphill to the **main entrance** (Map p401; Upper Entrance) to the ruins.

Museo de Sitio   MUSEUM
(Map p401; Carretera Palenque–Ruinas Km 6.5; with ruins ticket free; ⊙9am-4:30pm Tue-Sun) Palenque's site museum is well worth a wander, displaying finds from the site and interpreting, in English and Spanish, Palenque's history. Highlights include a the copy of the lid of Pakal's sarcophagus (depicting his rebirth as the maize god, encircled by serpents, mythical monsters and glyphs recounting his reign) and finds from Templo XXI.

El Panchán   AREA
(Carretera Palenque–Ruinas Km 4.5) Just off the road to the ruins, El Panchán is a legendary travelers' hangout set in a patch of dense rainforest. It's the epicenter of Palenque's alternative (and slightly grungy) scene and home to a bohemian bunch of Mexican and foreign residents and wanderers.

Once ranchland, the area has been reforested by the remarkable Morales family, some of whom are among the leading archaeological experts on Palenque. Today El Panchán has several (mostly rustic) places to stay, a couple of restaurants, a set of sinuous streams rippling their way through every part of the property, nightly entertainment (and regular drumming practice), a meditation temple, a temascal and a constant stream of quirky visitors from all over the world.

Palenque Ruins   ARCHAEOLOGICAL SITE
(Map p401; M$75, plus M$35 national park entry fee; ⊙8am-5pm, last entry 4:30pm) Ancient Palenque stands at the precise point where the first hills rise out of the Gulf coast plain, and the dense jungle covering these hills forms an evocative backdrop to Palenque's exquisite Maya architecture. Hundreds of ruined buildings are spread over 15 sq km, but only a fairly compact central area has been excavated. Everything you see here was built without metal tools, pack animals or the wheel.

As you explore the ruins, try to picture the gray stone edifices as they would have been at the peak of Palenque's power: painted blood red with elaborate blue and yellow stucco details. The forest around these temples is still home to howler monkeys, toucans and ocelots. The ruins and surrounding forests form a national park, the Parque Nacional Palenque, for which you must pay a separate admission fee at Km 4.5 on the road to the ruins.

Palenque sees more than 1000 visitors on an average day, and visitation spikes in the summer-holiday season. Opening time is a good time to visit, when it's cooler and not too crowded, and morning mist may still be wrapping the temples in a picturesque haze. Refreshments, hats and souvenirs are available outside the main entrance. For better or worse, vendors line many of the paths through the ruins.

Official site guides are available by the entrance and **ticket office**. Two Maya guide associations offer informative two-hour tours for up to seven people, which cost M$1300 in Spanish or US$95 in English, French, German or Italian. French, German and Italian speakers may have to wait a bit longer as there are fewer guides available.

Most visitors take a combi or taxi to the ruins' main (upper) entrance, see the major structures and then walk downhill to the museum, visiting minor ruins along the way.

Combis to the ruins (M$25 each way) run about every 10 minutes during daylight hours. In town, look for 'Ruinas' combis anywhere on Juárez west of Allende. They will also pick you up or drop you off anywhere along the town–ruins road.

Be aware that the mushrooms sold by locals along the road to the ruins from about May to November are the hallucinogenic variety.

➡ **Templo de las Inscripciones Group**
As you walk in from the entrance the vegetation suddenly peels away to reveal many of Palenque's most-magnificent buildings in one sublime vista. A line of temples rises in front

of the jungle on your right, culminating in the Templo de las Inscripciones about 100m ahead; El Palacio, with its trademark tower, stands to the left of the Templo de las Inscripciones; and the Grupo de las Cruces rises in the distance beneath a thick jungle backdrop.

The first temple on your right is Templo XII, called the **Templo de la Calavera** (Temple of the Skull) for the relief sculpture of a rabbit or deer skull at the foot of one of its pillars. The second temple, **Templo XI**, has little interest. Third is **Templo XIII**, containing a tomb of a female dignitary, whose remains were found colored red (as a result of treatment with cinnabar) when unearthed in 1994. You can look into the **Tumba de la Reina Roja** (Tomb of the Red Queen) and see her sarcophagus. With the skeleton were found a malachite mask and about 1000 pieces of jade. Based on DNA tests and resemblances to Pakal's tomb next door, the theory is that the 'queen' buried here was his wife Tz'ak-b'u Ajaw. The **tomb of Alberto Ruz Lhuillier**, who discovered Pakal's tomb in 1952, lies under the trees in front of Templo XIII.

The **Templo de las Inscripciones** (Temple of the Inscriptions), perhaps the most-celebrated burial monument in the Americas, is the tallest and most stately of Palenque's buildings. Constructed on eight levels, the Templo de las Inscripciones has a central front staircase rising 25m to a series of small rooms. The tall roofcomb that once crowned it is long gone, but between the front doorways are stucco panels with reliefs of noble figures. On the interior rear wall are three panels with the long Maya inscription, recounting the history of Palenque and this building, for which Mexican archaeologist Alberto Ruz Lhuillier named the temple. From the top, interior stairs lead down into the **tomb of Pakal** (now closed to visitors indefinitely, to avoid further damage to its murals from the humidity inevitably exuded by visitors). Pakal's jewel-bedecked skeleton and jade-mosaic death mask were removed from the tomb to Mexico City, and the tomb was re-created in the Museo Nacional de Antropología. The priceless death mask was stolen in an elaborate heist in 1985 (though recovered a few years afterward), but the carved stone sarcophagus lid remains in the closed tomb – you can see a replica in the site museum.

➡ El Palacio

Diagonally opposite the Templo de las Inscripciones is El Palacio (the Palace), a large structure divided into four main courtyards, with a maze of corridors and rooms. Built and modified piecemeal over 400 years from the 5th century on, it was probably the residence of Palenque's rulers.

Its **tower**, built in the 8th century by Ahkal Mo' Nahb' III and restored in 1955, has remnants of fine stucco reliefs on the walls, but you're not allowed to climb up inside it. Archaeologists believe the tower was constructed so that Maya royalty and priests could observe the sun falling directly into the Templo de las Inscripciones during the winter solstice.

The northeastern courtyard, the **Patio de los Cautivos** (Patio of the Captives), contains a collection of relief sculptures that seem disproportionately large for their setting; the theory is that they represent conquered rulers and were brought from elsewhere.

In the southern part of the complex, the extensive subterranean bathrooms included six toilets and a couple of steam baths.

In April 2018, a stucco mask thought to represent Pakal, along with ceramic figurines and pots, carved bones and other ancient artifacts, were discovered in El Palacio's House E.

➡ Grupo de las Cruces

Pakal's son, Kan B'alam II, was a prolific builder, and soon after the death of his father started designing the temples of the Grupo de las Cruces (Group of the Crosses). All three main pyramid-shaped structures surround a plaza southeast of the Templo de las Inscripciones. They were all dedicated in 692 CE as a spiritual focal point for Palenque's triad of patron deities.

The **Templo del Sol** (Temple of the Sun), on the west side of the plaza, has the best-preserved roofcomb at Palenque. Carvings inside, commemorating Kan B'alam's birth in 635 CE and accession in 684, show him facing his father. Some view this beautiful building as sure proof that Palenque's ancient architects were inspired by the local hallucinogenic mushrooms. Make up your own mind!

Steep steps climb to the **Templo de la Cruz** (Temple of the Cross), the largest and most elegantly proportioned in this group. The stone tablet in the central sanctuary shows the lord of the underworld smoking tobacco on the right and Kan B'alam in full royal attire on the left. Behind is a reproduction of a panel depicting Kan B'alam's accession.

Palenque Ruins

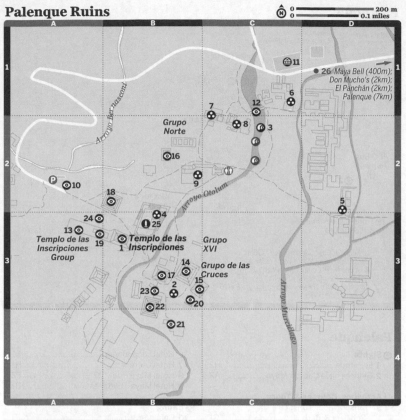

N 0 ——————— 200 m
0 ——————— 0.1 miles

● 26 Maya Bell (400m);
Don Mucho's (2km);
El Panchán (2km);
Palenque (7km)

Grupo Norte

Arroyo Bernasconi

Arroyo Otolum

Grupo XVI

Templo de las Inscripciones Group

Templo de las Inscripciones

Grupo de las Cruces

Arroyo Murciélago

Palenque Ruins

On the **Templo de la Cruz Foliada** (Temple of the Foliated Cross), the corbel arches are fully exposed, revealing how Palenque's architects designed these buildings. A well-preserved inscribed tablet shows a king (probably Pakal) with a sun shield emblazoned on his chest, corn growing from his shoulder blades, and the sacred quetzal bird on his head.

Palenque

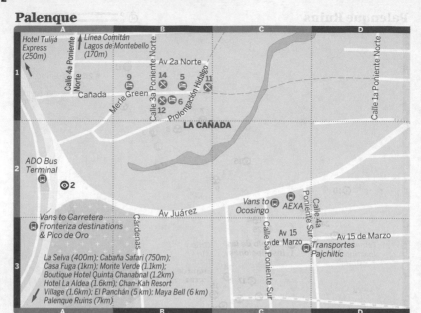

Palenque

Sights

The 'cross' carvings in some buildings here symbolize the ceiba tree, which in Maya belief held up the universe.

➤ **Acrópolis Sur**

In the jungle south of Grupo de las Cruces is the Southern Acropolis, where archaeologists have made some terrific finds in recent excavations. You may find part of the area roped off. The **Acrópolis Sur** appears to have been constructed as an extension of the Grupo de las Cruces, with both groups set around what was probably a single long open space.

Templo XVII, between the Cruces group and Acrópolis Sur, contains a reproduction carved panel depicting Kan B'alam standing with a spear, and a bound captive kneeling before him (the original is in the site museum).

In 1999, in **Templo XIX**, archaeologists made the most important Palenque find for decades: an 8th-century limestone platform with stunning carvings of seated figures and lengthy hieroglyphic texts that detail Palenque's origins. A reproduction has been placed inside Templo XIX. The central figure on the long south side of the platform is the ruler Ahkal Mo' Nahb' III, who was responsible for several of the buildings of the Acrópolis Sur, just as the Grupo de las Cruces was created by Kan B'alam II. Also on view is a wonderful reproduction of a tall stucco relief of U Pakal, the son of Ahkal Mo' Nahb'.

Also discovered in 1999, **Templo XX** contains a red-frescoed tomb built in 540 that is currently Palenque's most active dig. Archaeologists began restoration work inside

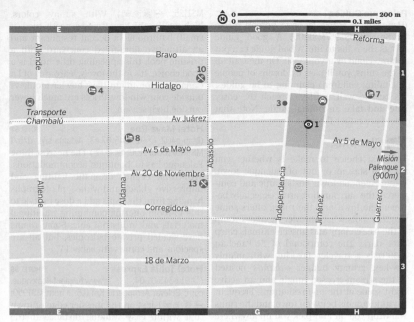

the tomb in 2012, and now believe that it might be the final resting place of K'uk B'alam I, an ancestor of Pakal.

In 2002, archaeologists found in **Templo XXI** a throne with very fine carvings depicting Ahkal Mo' Nahb', his ancestor the great Pakal, and his son U Pakal.

➧ **Grupo Norte**

North of El Palacio is a **Juego de Pelota** (Ball Court) and the handsome buildings of the Northern Group. Crazy Count de Waldeck lived in the so-called **Templo del Conde** (Temple of the Count), constructed in 647 CE.

➧ **Palenque Northeastern Groups**

East of the Grupo Norte, the main path crosses Arroyo Otolum. Some 70m beyond the stream, a right fork will take you to **Grupo C**, a set of jungle-covered buildings and plazas thought to have been lived in from about 750 to 800 CE.

If you stay on the main path, you'll descend some steep steps to a group of low, elongated buildings, probably occupied residentially from around 770 to 850 CE. The path goes alongside the Arroyo Otolum, which here tumbles down a series of small falls forming natural bathing pools known as the **Baño de la Reina** (Queen's Bath). Unfortunately, you can't bathe here anymore.

The path then continues to another residential quarter, the **Grupo de los Murciélagos** (Bat Group), and then crosses the **Puente de los Murciélagos**, a footbridge across Arroyo Otolum.

Across the bridge and a bit further downstream, a path goes west to **Grupo I** and **Grupo II**, a short walk uphill. These ruins, only partly uncovered, are in a beautiful jungle setting. The main path continues downriver to the road, where the museum is a short distance along to the right.

☞ Tours

★ **Transportador Turística Scherrer & Barb** TOURS
(Map p402; ☎ cell 916-1032153; fermerida_69@hotmail.com; Hotel Wayak, Central Poniente 2) Scherrer & Barb offers the most eclectic tours in town, including the remote Lacandón communities of Metzabok and Nahá (two days M$6300), Guatemala's Piedras Negras archaeological site (M$7740), and cool day trips off the Carretera Fronteriza like the Cascada de las Golondrinas, Cascadas Roberto Barrios, Cascada Welib-Já and various bird-watching and kayaking destinations. All with a minimum of four people. Owner Fernando Mérida speaks English and Italian.

Palenque Guides
TOURS

(Map p401; 1½ hr tour for up to 7 people in English/Spanish US$95/M$1300) A good guide brings the ruins to life. A bad guide can put a damp cloud over your visit. On the trail up to the ruins, you'll pass by dozens of people (including children) claiming to be guides. It's best to wait until you reach the entry gate and take an official guide. Note that prices are rather flexible!

🛏 Sleeping

The first choice to make is whether you want to stay in or out of Palenque town. While Palenque town hosts traffic and commerce, the surrounding area, especially between the town and the ruins, offers some magical spots where howler monkeys romp in the tree canopy and unseen animals chirp after dark. The compound of El Panchán (p399) is a traveler favorite, with mainly low-key, grungy budget *cabañas* nestled in the stream-crossed jungle and an active night scene at the one restaurant. Frequent daytime combis between town and the ruins will drop you off and pick you up anywhere along this road.

Except for the leafy La Cañada area in the west, Palenque town is not particularly attractive, but if you stay here you'll have plenty of restaurants and services nearby.

🛏 In Town

Hostal San Miguel
HOTEL $

(Map p402; ☎916-345-01-52; www.hotelsanmiguelpalenque.mx; Hidalgo 43; d from M$400; ❈🛜) This formal hostel is in the process of being revamped into a decent budget hotel. It has good natural light and views from the upper floors and it's clean and quiet and revamped rooms have flat screen TV. Rooms with air-con cost an extra M$100 on the price listed.

Hotel Lacandonia
HOTEL $

(Map p402; ☎916-345-00-57; Allende 77; s/d/tr M$600/700/800; P❈🛜) A modernish hotel with airy rooms, all with wrought-iron beds, reading lights and cable TV. Most rooms face into a courtyard which serves as a motel-style car park. The upstairs rooms facing the street have cute balconies and the best light. Decent **restaurant** attached.

★ Hotel Chablis Palenque
HOTEL $$

(Map p402; ☎916-345-08-70, 916-142-03-77; www.hotelchablis.com; Merle Green 7; r from

M$1125; ❄❈🛜🖥) With sunny colors, high-quality, thick mattresses, neatly tiled (if small) bathrooms, a decent restaurant and an attractive flora-filled courtyard with a pristine pool, this appealing little hotel is a good choice. It's in the lovely, leafy area of La Cañada so you might have howler monkeys outside your window. Prices are much lower outside high season.

Hotel Maya Rue
HOTEL $$

(Map p402; ☎916-345-07-43; Aldama s/n; d/tr/f M$900/1000/1100; ❈@🛜) The nearest thing Palenque has to 'boutique' accommodations. Tree-trunk beams, dramatic lighting and impressive black-and-white photographs hanging from the walls add a dose of style to this 13-room offering combining traditional materials and industrial chic. Some rooms have shaded private balconies, but all are spacious and come with cable TV.

Hotel Tulijá Express
HOTEL $$

(☎916-345-01-04; www.tulijahotelpalenque.com; Bulevar Aeropuerto Km 0.5; r from M$1950; ❄❈🛜🖥) Just on the messier edge of town (but within easy walking distance to the center), this is an excellent-value midrange hotel. It's the town's 'grand dame' with a good onsite restaurant, and a great pool area. It's not bursting with character, but is a solid midrange choice nonetheless. Prices can drop significantly to that listed.

Hotel Lacroix
HOTEL $$

(Map p402; Hidalgo 10; s/d/tr/f M$750/830/920/1000; P❄❈🛜🖥) This well-tended, family-friendly 16-room hotel on a pedestrian strip near El Parque sports white rooms – the upper ones with small balconies – and attention-grabbing wall murals of the ruins. The grounds hint at better days (the restaurant is no longer open), but the pool is still working, and the service is super friendly. Great value.

Hotel Maya Tulipanes
HOTEL $$$

(Map p402; ☎916-345-02-01; www.mayatulipanes.com.mx; Cañada 6, La Cañada; d from M$1700; ❄❈🛜🖥) Entered through a muraled foyer, this spot has plain, comfortable, air-conditioned rooms with wrought-iron double beds and minimalist decor. It's designed around a pretty garden with a small pool and a restaurant.

Misión Palenque
HOTEL $$$

(☎916-345-02-41; www.hotelmisionpalenque.com; Periférico Oriente s/n; r from M$2000; P❈🛜🖥)

Set on lush, sprawling grounds just to the east of the center, this 207-room behemoth (part of a Mexican chain) has all the trimmings you'd expect: comfy rooms with lime-green splashes of color, pleasant gardens and pool area, a good on-site restaurant and attentive staff. Prices fluctuate according to season and supply and demand.

🛏 Outside Town

Cabaña Safari   CABAÑAS $
(☑916-345-00-26; Carretera Palenque–Ruinas Km 1; r M$1200, campsites with gear M$150; P❋🛜🏊) Fourteen enjoyable, jungly *palapa*-roofed *cabañas* with air-con and private porches. Rocks, tree branches and wall murals give personality to the spacious (including some two-level) rooms. There's a plunge pool, temascal and full restaurant (open 7am to 10pm).

It's better value in low season when the price almost halves.

★ Hotel La Aldea   HOTEL $$
(☑916-345-16-93; www.hotellaaldea.net; Carretera Palenque–Ruinas Km 2.8; r M$1500; P❋🛜🏊) The four-star Aldea has 35 large, beautiful and bright *palapa*-roofed rooms set amid lovely grounds. Each room has an outside terrace with hammock and easy chair. It's a simple, stylish place, with a peaceful hilltop restaurant and a wonderful pool area with two places for dipping! There are no TVs, making it an ideal place to get away from it all.

Maya Bell   HOTEL $$
(☑916-341-69-77; www.mayabell.mx; Carretera Palenque–Ruinas Km 6; cabañas without bathroom M$350, r with fan/air-con M$950/1200; P❋🛜🏊) At first glance, this spot looks very inviting, especially the attractive jungle setting and the sprawling jungleside pool (frequented by vocal howler monkeys). On closer inspection, however, the rooms, while comfortable, are looking a tad tired around the edges for what you pay, and some reception staff can be a bit unfriendly.

But, it's in a lovely spot and it's the closest accommodations to the ruins (it's just 400m from Palenque's site museum). Note: being inside the national park means you have to pay the park entry fee if you arrive between 7am and 8pm.

Hotel Casa Lakyum   HOTEL $$
(☑916-780-34-52; www.casalakyum.com.mx/en/home; Km 3.5, Palenque; d from M$1200; P🛜🏊) This understated spot should be shouting

its existence from the jungle tops. Or they're leaving that to the howler monkeys (and the macaws) that do just that in the surrounding jungle. Simple, but spacious, rooms with lovely views, outside hammocks and a pool for cooling off. Great family rooms, too. It's within walking distance of El Panchán (for dinner).

★ Boutique Hotel
Quinta Chanabnal   BOUTIQUE HOTEL $$$
(☑916-345-53-20; www.quintachanabnal.com; Carretera Palenque–Ruinas Km 2.2; r US$177-413; P❋🛜🏊) The Maya-inspired architecture and impeccable style and service at this decadent boutique hotel will leave you swooning. Enter through heavy wood doors (carved by local artisans) into spacious stone-floor suites that contain majestically draped four-poster beds, outlandish Mexican art and cavernous bathrooms. Water features on the premises include a creek, a small lagoon and a natural rock, multi-tiered swimming pool.

Massages, a temascal and a fine restaurant are available. The Italian owner, Rafael, is a Maya expert and also speaks German, French, English and Spanish.

Piedra de Agua   BOUTIQUE HOTEL $$$
(☑916-345-08-42; www.palenque.piedradeagua.com; Carretera Palenque–Ruinas Km 2.5; r from US$100; P☕🛜🏊) Elegant and romantic off-white-and-wood minimalism marks this fab designer *cabaña* compound that pampers guests with oodles of natural bath products, plush robes, private terrace tubs with bubble bath and hammocks outside every room. Massages are available, though the lap pool and Jacuzzi are the most popular amenities. A perfect place to indulge after a sweaty day at the ruins.

Chan-Kah Resort Village   RESORT $$$
(☑916-345-11-34; www.chan-kah.com.mx; Carretera Palenque–Ruinas Km 3; r/ste incl breakfast M$2450/4650; P☕❋@🛜🏊) This large, quality resort on the road to the ruins is an ideal choice for families. It has arty, well-spaced wood-and-stone cottages, some of which have four beds, and all come with generous bathrooms, ceiling fans, terrace and air-con. Kids and swimmers will also love the Chan-Kah's stupendous multilayer 70m stone-lined swimming pool in lush jungle gardens.

🍴 Eating

Palenque is definitely not the gastronomic capital of Mexico. There's a decent variety of restaurants, though some are laughably overpriced. La Cañada is the most pleasant spot for eating.

★ **Café Jade**   INTERNATIONAL $

(📞916-688-00-15; Prolongación Hidalgo 1; breakfast M$67-132, mains M$87-130; ⏱7am-11pm; 📶🍴) This very cool bamboo construction has indoor and outdoor seating and is one of the most popular places in town. Has fabulous staff, and serves good breakfasts, some Chiapan specialties and international traveler classics such as burgers. There is a reasonable number of vegetarian options and really good fresh juices too. Fast wi-fi to boot.

Don Mucho's   INTERNATIONAL $

(📞916-112-83-38; Carretera Palenque-Ruinas Km 4.5, El Panchán; mains M$70-185; ⏱7am-1am Tue-Thu, to 2am Fri, to 3am Sat, to midnight Sun & Mon) In El Panchán, popular Don Mucho's provides great-value meals in a jungly setting, with a candlelit ambience at night. Busy waiters bring pasta, fish, meat, plenty of *antojitos* (typical Mexican snacks), and pizzas (cooked in a purpose-built Italian-designed wood-fired oven).

★ **Monte Verde**   ITALIAN $$

(mains M$120-290; ⏱2-10:30pm Sun-Tue, Thu & Fri, to 11pm Sat) There's a real Mediterranean vibe to this Italian restaurant tucked away in the forest (do a bit of bird- and monkey-watching while waiting for your lunch!), and though most people go for the delicious thin-crust pizzas, the meat and pasta dishes are worthy of your time. Try the seafood tagliatelle piled high with giant prawns and you'll leave happy.

Frequent live music in the evenings.

El Huachinango Feliz   SEAFOOD $$

(📞916-129-82-31; Hidalgo s/n; mains M$130-200; ⏱8am-11pm) A popular, atmospheric restaurant in the leafy La Cañada neighborhood. It has an attractive front patio with plastic chairs and umbrellas, and there's also an upstairs covered terrace. Seafood is the specialty here: order seafood soup, seafood cocktails, grilled fish that's beautifully crunchy on the outside and soft on the inside, or shrimp served 10 different ways. The service can be slow but the food is worth the wait.

Restaurant Las Tinajas   MEXICAN $$

(📞916-345-49-70; cnr Av 20 de Noviembre & Calle Abasolo; mains M$95-150; ⏱7am-10:30pm) It doesn't take long to figure out why this place is always busy. It slings enormous portions of excellent home-style food – enough to keep you fueled up for hours. *Pollo a la veracruzana* (chicken in a tomato, olive and onion sauce) and *camarones al guajillo* (shrimp with a not-too-hot type of chili) are both delicious, as is the house salsa.

La Selva   MEXICAN $$

(📞916-345-17-42; Av 7a Poniente Sur s/n; mains M$85-220; ⏱11:30am-10:30pm) A small, neat and slightly upscale (for Palenque anyway) restaurant serving up well-prepared steaks, seafood, salads and *antojitos* under an enormous *palapa* roof, with jungle-themed murals at the back. Known for its *empanadas de camarón*.

Restaurant Maya Cañada   MEXICAN $$

(📞916-345-02-16; Merle Green s/n; breakfast M$110-165, mains M$130-230; ⏱7am-midnight; 📶) This relatively upmarket and professionally run restaurant in the shady La Cañada area serves fine steaks, regional specialties and terrific seafood kebabs, all of which are beautifully presented. It has a cool upstairs terrace.

★ **Restaurante Bajlum**   MEXICAN $$$

(📞916-107-85-18; mains M$270-370; ⏱2-10pm) Creative and stunningly presented Maya gastronomy fills the menu at this upmarket but inviting restaurant. The house specials include the delicious rabbit with 'jungle herbs' and duck with orange. Much of the produce is locally sourced and whatever you order, the owner is sure to come over and explain the story behind each dish. Impressive cocktail list.

It's a little tucked away down a side lane on the left shortly before the ruins. Cash only.

🍸 Drinking & Nightlife

Palenque doesn't have much of a nightlife scene. In the evenings, you'll often spot more travelers waiting for a night bus than out on the town. Along the ruins road you can listen to live music in a few places, while bars in the town center tend toward the unsavory.

Casa Fuga   BAR

(📞916-119-43-47; drinks from M$25; ⏱5-11pm Tue-Sun) There's an air of secrecy about this smart, concrete-heavy place nestled away in a jungle garden, but that's how Casa Fuga seems to like it (*fuga* means 'escape'). It offers a mix of drinks, from hot chocolates to hard liquors, all served in style in a locale that's more suited to Mexico City than here, several kilometers from Mayan ruins.

Café de Yara CAFE $$
(Hidalgo 66; breakfast M$75-145, mains M$95-170; 7am-11pm; ❄ 📶) A sunny start to the day, this slightly dated, deep-orange-colored corner cafe has huge and tasty breakfasts. Next door, a hole-in-the-wall dishes out an excellent range of organic Chiapan coffee – just what you need before or after a visit to the ruins.

ℹ️ Information

Whichever direction you come from, it's safer to travel in Palenque in daylight hours as blockades (and in the past, armed holdups) along roads leading to Palenque are not unheard of. At the time of research, larger buses were not travelling between Ocosingo to Palenque (taking an alternative, and much longer but safer, route), though the tour companies were, by keeping daily check on the status of any flare-ups. In the past, there have also been reports of thefts on the night bus from Mérida. When taking buses along these routes, consider stowing valuables in the checked luggage compartment.

Both of the following banks change dollars and euros (bring a copy of your passport).
Banco Azteca (Av Juárez, btwn Allende & Aldama; 9am-9pm)
Bancomer (Av Juárez 96; 8:30am-4pm Mon-Fri) Also has an ATM.
Médica Palenque (Clínica Palenque; 916-407-15-01; Velasco Suárez 33; 9am-1pm & 2-6pm) Sometimes English-speaking doctors.
Post Office (Independencia s/n; 8am-5pm Mon-Fri, 10am-2pm Sat)
Tourist Information Office (cnr Av Juárez & Calle Abasolo; 9am-9pm Mon-Sat, to 1pm Sun) The state tourism office's help center is thin on the ground for hefty materials, though it has regional and transportation information, and sometimes maps. However, more accurate information is normally available from hotel staff.

ℹ️ Getting There & Away

AIR

A small airport is serviced by irregular and expensive flights. Interjet has twice-weekly service to/from Mexico City. Otherwise, the closest major airport is Villahermosa; ADO runs a direct airport service (M$350) in comfortable minibuses.

BUS

In a spacious location behind the Maya head statue, **ADO** (www.ado.com.mx) has the main bus terminal, with deluxe and 1st-class services, an ATM and left-luggage facilities. In high season, it's a good idea to buy your outward bus ticket a day in advance. Note that due to security issues buses are not currently running direct to Ocosingo and most companies are routing buses through Villahermosa instead.

AEXA (www.autobusesaexa.com.mx; Av Juárez 159), with 1st-class buses, and Cardesa (2nd class) is about 300m east on Avenida Juárez.
Línea Comitán Lagos de Montebello (916-345-12-60; Velasco Suárez, btwn Calles 6a & 7a Poniente Norte), west of Palenque market, runs frequent vans to Benemérito de las Américas (M$150, 3:30am to 4.30pm), with a couple continuing around the Carretera Fronteriza to the Lagos de Montebello (around M$300, nine hours to Tziscao) and Comitán (M$375, eight hours).

COLECTIVOS

Vans to Ocosingo (M$80) wait on Calle 5a Poniente Sur and leave when full. The route is prone to security issues and vans do not always go on the most direct road. Be prepared for canceled services or very circuitous routing.

Most people do the Carretera Fronteriza (including Lacanjá Chansayab, Bonampak, Yaxchilán and Benemérito de las Américas) on a tour from Palenque or San Cristóbel. If you do decide to do it alone, it's doable, though expect to spend many hours in the crowded vans. Many

CHIAPAS & TABASCO PALENQUE

BUSES FROM PALENQUE

DESTINATION	COST (M$)	TIME (HR)	FREQUENCY (PER DAY) & COMPANY
Campeche	440	5-5½	5 ADO
Cancún	430-970	13¾-14¼	5 ADO
Mérida	628	8	4 ADO
San Cristóbal de las Casas	9		8 ADO, 4 AEXA
Tulum	866-1118	11½	5 ADO
Tuxtla Gutiérrez	280-320	7½	7 ADO, 4 AEXA
Villahermosa	150-240	2½	frequent ADO & AEXA
Villahermosa airport	400	2¼	5 ADO (Sprinter)

combis for destinations along the Carretera Fronteriza and for Pico de Oro leave from an outdoor *colectivo* **terminal** just south of the ADO bus station.

Vans operated by **Transportes Pajchiltic** (Av 15 de Marzo) run to Metzabok (M$120, three hours) and Nahá (M$120, four hours) whenever they're full (morning is best). Transportation back again often leaves in the middle of the night.

ⓘ Getting Around

Taxis charge around M$100 to El Panchán, Maya Bell, and the ruins. Combis (M$25) run by **Transporte Chambalú** (☑ 916-345-28-49; Hidalgo) from the center ply the ruins road until dark. **Radio Taxis Santo Domingo** (☑ 916-345-01-26) and **Taxistas Maya Pakal** (☑ 916-341-11-50) have on-call services. There's a **taxi stand** on El Parque.

Agua Azul & Misol-Ha

These spectacular water attractions – the thundering cascades of Agua Azul and the 35m jungle waterfall of Misol-Ha – are both short detours off the Ocosingo–Palenque road. During the rainy season they lose part of their beauty as the water gets murky, though the power of the waterfalls is magnified.

Both are usually visited on an organized day tour from Palenque or as part of a tour between San Cristóbal and Palenque.

◉ Sights

Agua Azul   WATERFALL
(M$50) Agua Azul is a breathtaking sight, with its powerful and dazzling white waterfalls thundering into turquoise (outside rainy season) pools surrounded by verdant jungle. On holidays and weekends the place is packed; at other times you'll have few companions. The temptation to swim is great, but take extreme care, as people do drown here. The current is deceptively fast, the power of the falls obvious, and there are many submerged hazards like rocks and dead trees.

If you're in decent shape, keep walking upstream – the crowds thin out the further up you go.

The turnoff for Agua Azul is halfway between Ocosingo and Palenque, some 60km from each. A paved road leads 4.5km down to Agua Azul from Hwy 199. A well-made stone and concrete path with steps runs 700m up beside the falls from the parking area, which is packed with food and souvenir stalls. Basic lodging is also available.

Unfortunately, theft isn't uncommon, so don't bring valuables, keep an eye on your belongings and stick to the main paved trail.

Misol-Ha   WATERFALL
(M$40; ⊙ 6am-7pm) Just 20km south of Palenque, Misol-Ha cascades approximately 35m into a wonderful wide pool surrounded by lush tropical vegetation. It's a sublime place for a dip when the fall is not excessively pumped up by wet-season rains. A path behind the main fall leads into a cave, which allows you to experience the power of the water close up. Misol-Ha is 1.5km off Hwy 199 and the turnoff is signposted, and two separate *ejidos* charge admission (around M$30).

The downside is that the path can get crowded, thanks to the early-morning tours from San Cristóbal.

🛏 Sleeping

Centro Turístico Ejidal
Cascada de Misol-Ha   CABIN $
(☑ 967-164-21-49; www.misol-ha.com; cabin M$290; ⊙ restaurant 7am-7pm; 🅿 🐾 📶) Atmospheric wooden cabins among the trees near the waterfall, with fans, hot-water bathrooms and mosquito netting, plus a good open-air restaurant (mains M$80 to M$160). Nighttime swims are dreamy.

ⓘ Getting There & Away

Most Palenque (and San Cristóbal) travel agencies offer daily Misol-Ha and Agua Azul trips. Trips cost around M$350 (M$400 from San Cristóbal) including admission fees, and last six or seven hours, spending 30 to 60 minutes at Misol-Ha and two to three hours at Agua Azul. If coming from San Cristóbal, you can stay in Palenque at the end. From Palenque, companies may charge you to head to San Cristóbal afterward (around M$150). *Colectivos* (around M$50) run from Palenque to the turnoff for Misol-Ha from where it's a 20- to 30-minute walk to the falls.

Bonampak, Yaxchilán & the Carretera Fronteriza

Close to the Guatemala border, the ancient Maya cities of Bonampak and Yaxchilán might not be the largest Maya ruins, but one thing's for sure: they're certainly among the most wildly romantic. Fringed by the Lacandón Jungle, the area is characterized by bright tropical birds flitting between crumbling monuments and monkeys hooting from the trees. Bonampak, famous for its frescoes, is 152km by road from Palenque;

the bigger and more important Yaxchilán, with a peerless jungle setting beside the broad and swift Río Usumacinta, is 173km by road, then about 22km by boat.

Access to Bonampak and Yaxchilán is via the Carretera Fronteriza, which also gives handy access to a number of excellent ecotourism projects, dreamy waterfalls, Lacandón villages and lesser-known archaeological ruins.

☞ Tours

Organized tours can be helpful in this region if you have limited time and aren't driving. These operate out of both San Cristóbal and Palenque. Always check package inclusions and exclusions, so you can plan your meals and park fees. The only problem is that the day trips are ridiculously long (often around 16 hours, with many hours in a vehicle). Following are the standard tours (including entry fees and some meals) per person offered by Palenque travel agencies:

Bonampak and Yaxchilán Day trips (M$800 to M$2000) Usually include two meals and transportation in air-conditioned vans – a good deal since independent transportation to both is time-consuming and tours include the Bonampak transportation fee; two-day trips (M$3000 to M$4000) include an overnight stay at Lacanjá Chansayab.

Transportation to Flores, Guatemala Transportation (around M$1000, 10 to 11 hours) is by van to Frontera Corozal, river launch up the Usumacinta to Bethel in Guatemala, and public bus on to Flores. It's just as easy to organize it all yourself and go entirely by public transportation.

Flores via Bonampak and Yaxchilán Two days (around M$2700) with an overnight in Lacanjá Chansayab.

If you want to arrange your own itinerary that allows for more flexibility, in Palenque, Transportador Turística Scherrer & Barb (p403) organizes more off-the-beaten-path trips to the region, including the Lacandón

---

THE LACANDÓN JUNGLE

Chiapas contains swaths of wild green landscape that have nourished its inhabitants for centuries. But this rich trove of natural resources also makes it a contentious prize in the struggle for its water, lumber, and oil and gas reserves.

The Selva Lacandona (Lacandón Jungle), in eastern Chiapas, occupies just 0.25% of Mexico. Yet it contains more than 4300 plant species (about 17% of the Mexican total), 450 butterfly species (42% of the national total), at least 340 bird species (32% of the total), and 163 mammal species (30% of the Mexican total). Among these are such emblematic creatures as the jaguar, red macaw, white turtle, tapir and harpy eagle.

This great fund of natural resources and genetic diversity is the southwest end of the Selva Maya, a 30,000-sq-km corridor of tropical rainforest stretching from Chiapas across northern Guatemala into Belize and the southern Yucatán. But the Lacandón Jungle is shrinking fast, under pressure from ranchers, loggers, oil prospectors, and farmers desperate for land. From around 15,000 sq km in the 1950s, an estimated 3000 to 4500 sq km of jungle remains today and it continues to shrink at a rate of about 5% per year. Waves of land-hungry settlers deforested the northern third of the Lacandón Jungle by about 1960. Also badly deforested are the far eastern Marqués de Comillas area (settled since the 1970s) and Las Cañadas, between Ocosingo and Montes Azules. Most of what's left is in the Reserva de la Biosfera Montes Azules and the neighboring Reserva de la Biosfera Lacan-tun.

The Mexican government deeded a large section of the land to a small number of Lacandón families in the 1970s, creating tensions with other indigenous communities whose claims were put aside. Land within the region remains incredibly contested. Lacandón people and their advocates consider themselves to be an environmentally sensitive indigenous group, defending their property against invasive settlers. Other communities within the reserve, who provide some of the Zapatista rebels' strongest support, view it as an obfuscated land grab and pretext for eviction under the guise of environmental protection. Zapatista supporters also argue that the settlers are using the forests in unsustainable ways, and claim that the government seeks to exploit the forests for bio-prospecting (and patenting) traditional plants.

REFORMA AGRARIA

The small village of Reforma Agraria is the home of an impressive community program to protect the endangered *guacamaya* (scarlet macaw). This huge and spectacular member of the parrot family, which is so colorful it looks like a flying rainbow, once ranged as far north as Veracruz, but sadly its only Mexican home today is far-eastern Chiapas. Numbers at Reforma Agraria have increased since 1991, when the 14.5-sq-km macaw reserve was founded. Guides here can take you in search of the birds, but remember that they can move in and out of the reserve in seasonal pursuit of food; the best months for observing them are December to June, when they are nesting. Ask to see the chick aviary onsite at Las Guacamayas, and about the possibility of accompanying staff when they monitor nests (outside of the breeding season there's not a great deal to see.)

Las Guacamayas (☑ in Guatemala 502-5157-96-10; www.lasguacamayas.org.mx; Ejido Reforma Agraria; dm M$330, cabaña M$805-2065, ste M$2375; P ⊛ ⊜) is a beautiful and welcoming ecolodge on the bank of the broad Río Lacantún, one of the Usumacinta's major tributaries, with the Reserva de la Biosfera Montes Azules on the opposite bank. Large, superbly comfortable thatch-roofed *cabañas* – with mosquito screens, verandas and bathrooms with hot showers – are spread around the extensive grounds, linked by wooden walkways.

Dorms are shared two-bed rooms with common bathrooms. Wake up to a chorus of howler monkeys and take a stroll through the beautiful gardens before breakfast on the restaurant veranda.

The road to Reforma Agraria turns west off the Carretera Fronteriza 8km south of Benemérito.

villages of Nahá and Metzabok and waterfalls in the area. San Cristóbal–based SendaSur (p386) organizes fabulous itineraries and can help with reservations for independent travelers. The company focuses on community lodges and projects and can provide drivers.

ℹ Information

SAFE TRAVEL

Drug and human trafficking are facts of life in this border region, and the Carretera Fronteriza more or less encircles the main area of Zapatista rebel activity and support. Expect a few military checkpoints along the road and from this area to Palenque and Comitán. For your own security, it's best to be off the Carretera Fronteriza before dusk. Little, if any, public transportation ever runs after dark. Aim to get to all border crossings with Guatemala early in the day.

In the rainy months of September and October, rivers are usually too swollen for safe swimming.

Don't forget insect repellent; dengue fever has been reported here over the last couple of years.

ℹ Getting There & Away

The Carretera Fronteriza (Hwy 307) is a good paved road running parallel to the Mexico–Guatemala border, all the way from Palenque to the Lagos de Montebello. From Palenque, Autotransporte Chamoán runs vans run to Frontera

Corozal (around M$145, 2½ to three hours, every 40 minutes from 4am to 5pm), leaving from the outdoor *colectivo* terminal near the Maya head statue and south of the bus station. Use them for visits to Bonampak and Lacanjá Chansayab, because upon request they'll stop at the junction closest to the ruins, known as Crucero Bonampak (M$95, two hours), instead of the San Javier stop on the highway.

Línea Comitán Lagos de Montebello, west of Palenque market, runs frequent vans to Benemérito de las Américas (M$150, 3:30am to 4.30pm), with a couple continuing around the Carretera Fronteriza to the Lagos de Montebello (around M$300, nine hours to Tziscao) and Comitán (M$375, eight hours).

Both companies stop at San Javier (around M$90, two hours), the turnoff for Lacanjá Chansayab and Bonampak, 140km from Palenque, and at Crucero Corozal (around M$100, 2½ hours), the intersection for Frontera Corozal. For Cascada Welib-Já and Nueva Palestina, take any Carretera Fronteriza–bound combi from Palenque.

Gas stations along the Carretera Fronteriza are limited. From Palenque to Comitán (via the Chajul cutoff road) you'll find them in Chancalá and Benemérito only, but plenty of entrepreneurial locals sell reasonably priced gasoline from large plastic containers. Look for homemade '*Se vende gasolina*' signs. If you're driving yourself make sure you are safely off the roads before dark.

Palenque to Bonampak

★ Cascada de las Golondrinas WATERFALL

(Nueva Palestina; M$35, campsite M$100; ⊘ restaurant 9am-4pm; Ⓟ) A lovely water feature tucked 10km off the highway, where two rivers cascade dramatically from a high point of 35m and you can swim in clear blue water during the dry season. A wooden boardwalk crosses the outflow, and at dusk hundreds of swallows duck in to bed down in a cave beneath the falls, streaming out at dawn.

You can camp here in lovely shady spots with basic facilities. From Palenque take a combi to the turnoff for Nueva Palestina (M$80, two hours), where taxis charge M$150 one way to the falls. Arrange a return pickup. Drivers should go 9km toward Nueva Palestina to the signed turnoff; the falls are another 1km in.

A fun alternative to get here is to walk from Lacanjá via the pretty jungle walkway called Sendero Ya Toch Kusam (p413) just outside the Sok Nak cabañas.

★ Cascada Welib-Já WATERFALL

(M$30; ⊘ 8am-7pm; Ⓟ) Thirty kilometers from Palenque, these 25m-high curtains of water aren't the most-dramatic water features in the area, but the turquoise river pools make excellent swimming spots and there are few people. It's in a gorgeous setting on the edge of a jungle swathe and you can hear howler monkeys as you swim. There's a fun cross-river zip-line (M$100) and a simple restaurant. From Palenque, take a combi to the well-signed highway entrance (M$25, 30 minutes); it's a 700m walk in.

The well-organized community members are keen to help with directions and activities. Life jackets are available for rent and in high season there's a life guard.

Cascadas Roberto Barrios WATERFALL

(M$30; ⊘ 8am-5pm; Ⓟ) This attractive set of cascading rapids and waterfalls is the latest attraction of the tour agencies, thanks to its easy access from the road (other falls around are more appealing, though more of an effort to get to). While the waterfalls are lovely, the paths are rudimentary and muddy and care for them is a bit ad hoc. As with all the other falls, waters swell in rainy season and lose their color; don't swim during this time.

Roberto Barrios is 38km southeast of Palenque.

Bonampak

It's setting in dense jungle kept Bonampak, one of the outstanding archaeological sites of Chiapas, hidden from the outside world until 1946. The site is most renowned for its vivid frescoes, which really bring the Maya world to life. Getting here is a bit of a hassle but the reward is well worthwhile. The ruins are spread over 2.4 sq km, but all the main ruins stand around the rectangular Gran Plaza.

The Bonampak site abuts the Reserva de la Biosfera Montes Azules, and is rich in wildlife. Keep your eyes peeled for monkeys and macaws.

⊙ Sights

The most impressive surviving monuments at the ruins (☑ 961-612-83-60; community entry M$30, ruins M$70; ⊘ 8am-5pm) were built under Chan Muwan II, a nephew of Yaxchilán's Itzamnaaj B'alam II, who acceded to Bonampak's throne in 776 CE. The 6m-high Stele 1 in the Gran Plaza depicts Chan Muwan II holding a ceremonial staff at the height of his reign. He also features in Stele 2 and Stele 3 on the Acrópolis, which rises from the south end of the plaza.

However, it's the vivid frescoes inside the modest-looking Templo de las Pinturas (Edificio 1) that have given Bonampak its fame – and its name, which means 'Painted Walls' in Yucatecan Maya. Some archaeologists theorize that the murals depict a battle between Bonampak and the city of Sak T'zi', which is believed to be Plan de Ayutla.

Diagrams outside the temple help interpret the murals, which are the finest known from pre-Hispanic America, but which have

Bonampak Ⓝ 0 ——— 50 m

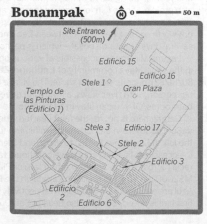

weathered badly since their discovery. (Early visitors even chucked kerosene over the walls in an attempt to bring out the colors!)

Sala 1, on the left as you face the temple, shows the consecration of Chan Muwan II's infant son, who is seen held in arms toward the top of the right end of the room's south wall (facing you as you enter). Witnessing the ceremony are 14 jade-toting noblemen. The central **Sala 2** shows tumultuous battle scenes on its east and south walls and vault, while on the north wall Chan Muwan II, in jaguar-skin battle dress, presides over the torture (by fingernail removal) and sacrifice of prisoners. A severed head lies below him, beside the foot of a sprawling captive. Recently restored and now blazing with vivid color, **Sala 3** shows a celebratory dance on the Acrópolis steps by lords wearing huge headdresses, and on its east wall three white-robed women puncture their tongues in a ritual bloodletting.

The sacrifices, the bloodletting and the dance may all have been part of the ceremonies surrounding celebrating winning a war (some say it was for the new heir.) If the latter is correct, the infant prince probably never got to rule Bonampak; the place was abandoned before the murals were finished, as Classic Maya civilization evaporated. Don't forget to look up at the intricately carved lintels when entering **Edificios 1** and **6**.

❶ Getting There & Away

Bonampak is 12km from San Javier, the turnoff town on the Carretera Fronteriza. If you get dropped off at San Javier instead of Crucero Bonampak (8km further in), taxis from San Javier charge around M$40.

Get ready to open your wallet: the community charges M$30 per person to enter the town of Lacanjá, and private vehicles are prohibited beyond the Crucero Bonampak, where van drivers charge an exorbitant M$250 (one person) or M$300 (two or three persons) round trip per van to the ruins and back. Note: despite what drivers may tell you, the ruins operate by official government time.

Lacanjá Chansayab

POP 380 / ELEV 340M

Lacanjá Chansayab, the largest Lacandón Maya village, is 6km from San Javier on the Carretera Fronteriza, and 12km from Bonampak. Its family compounds are scattered around a wide area, many of them with

---

OFF THE BEATEN TRACK

LAGUNA MIRAMAR

Ringed by rainforest, pristine Laguna Miramar, 140km southeast of Ocosingo in the **Reserva de la Biosfera Montes Azules** (Montes Azules Biosphere Reserve), is one of Mexico's most remote and exquisite lakes. Frequently echoing with the roars of howler monkeys, the 16-sq-km lake is bathtub-warm and virtually unpolluted. Rock ledges extending from three small islands make blissful wading spots, and petroglyphs and a turtle cave are reachable by canoe. The area is rich in wildlife. As you swim, you might find yourself being ogled by spider monkeys, tapirs, macaws and toucans; butterflies are also prolific. Locals fish for *mojarra* (perch), and will assure you that the lake's few crocodiles are not dangerous. Take note though: getting to the lake can be a real mission. It's not worth coming unless it's between December and April (drier season) and you have several days at your disposal – which is part of its appeal: it sees few visitors.

Laguna Miramar is accessible at various points, but the easiest ecotourism project in the small Maya community of **Emiliano Zapata** (☎ community phone 200-124-88-80/81/82), near its western shore. The village has a handful of simple *cabañas* (M$150 per person) with river views, all with one queen and one twin-bed room, a fan and shared bathrooms. Or you can stay in a family house for M$600.

Getting here is not for the faint hearted. The easiest way is on a three day trip with SendaSur (p386) from San Cristóbal (minimum four people, M$4500). Alternatively, ask the folk at Las Nubes (p416) to drive (and then walk you). There's a short cut from here to access points. Hard-core travelers should take a combi from Comitán to La Democracia (across the bridge from Amatitlán) or Plan de Río Azul and hire a *lancha* (around M$2000 per boat) to Emiliano Zapata on the Río Jataté. La Democracia and Plan de Río Azul are a rough 16km and 20km respectively from the Carretera Fronteriza highway; the first half is paved. Combis also head to San Quintín, another access point, from Comitán.

creeks or even the Río Lacanjá flowing past their grassy grounds. Tourism is now an important income earner, and many families run *campamentos* with simple rooms, camping and hammock space. As you approach the village, you'll cross the Río Lacanjá on a bridge, from where it's about 700m to a central intersection where roads go left (south), right (north) and straight (west).

🏃 Activities

Sendero Ya Toch Kusam   HIKING
(M$75) The Sendero Ya Toch Kusam is a 2.5km self-guided walking trail that starts at Sok Nak accommodation (buy tickets from reception). You can access Cascadas de Ya Toch Kusam from here.

🛏 Sleeping & Eating

★ Campamento Río Lacanjá   CABAÑAS $$
(www.ecochiapas.com/lacanja;   r with/without bathroom M$1100/750; P) This fabulous setup might lack material luxury, but it's rich in jungle atmosphere. Comfortable, semi-open-air, wood-framed cabins with mosquito nets stand close to the tree-shrouded Río Lacanjá and let in the sights and sounds of the forest and river. A separate group of larger rooms have two solid wooden double beds, tiled floors, fans and hot-water bathrooms.

As well as guided walks, rafting trips on the Río Lacanjá – which has waterfalls up to 2.5m high but no rapids – are offered for a minimum of four people. Set dinners cost M$100 and breakfast is M$85.

Campamento Topche   CABAÑAS $$
(www.sendasur.com.mx; r from M$600; P 🐾 🛜) About 550m west of the central intersection, this *campamento* is run by a local family and has several options that are spread around a messy garden: wood-cabin rooms with shared bathroom; comfortable rooms with terra-cotta–tiled floors and a vaulted roof; and detached, spacious, and more upmarket jungly *cabañas* next to the river. All have hot water and mosquito nets.

Sak Nok   CABAÑAS $$$
(📱916-165-07-41; Lacanjá Chansayab; from M$1600; P 🛜) The most upmarket of the options in Lacanjá Chansayab, with massive *cabañas* featuring solid wooden bed frames. The generous room sizes are good for families and groups. The *palapa* roofs and grass give it the feeling of a resort, though that might be a stretch.

Restaurant Chankin   MEXICAN $
(meals M$90; ⊙7:30am-9pm) This calm and quiet garden restaurant has fragrant walls of flowers that attract swarms of hyperactive hummingbirds, while the food, which is hearty country fare, attracts travelers who are a lot less hyperactive. You can munch away while looking over gentle cascades in the near distance. Offers decent cabin-style accommodations, too (from M$500 per double).

ℹ Getting There & Away

Combis for Lacanjá Chansayab (M$150) and other destinations along the Carretera Fronteriza leave Palenque from an outdoor *colectivo* terminal just south of the ADO bus station. If you're traveling from Yaxchilán, combis charge around M$50 between Crucero Corozal and San Javier.

The community collects M$30 per person at the town entrance.

Frontera Corozal

POP 5200 / ELEV 200M

This riverside frontier town is the stepping-stone to the beautiful ruins of Yaxchilán, and is on the main route between Chiapas and Guatemala's Petén region. Inhabited mainly by Chol Maya, who settled here in the 1970s, Frontera Corozal is 16km by paved road from Crucero Corozal junction on the Carretera Fronteriza. The broad Río Usumacinta, flowing swiftly between jungle-covered banks, forms the Mexico–Guatemala border here.

Long, fast, outboard-powered *lanchas* come and go from the river *embarcadero*. Almost everything you'll need is on the paved street leading back from the river here, including the **immigration office** (⊙8am-6pm), 400m from the *embarcadero*, where you should hand in/obtain a tourist permit if you're leaving for/arriving from Guatemala.

If it's open, the one-roomed **Museo de la Cuenca del Usumacinta** (Museum of the Usumacinta Basin; M$26; ⊙9am-5pm), opposite the immigration office, has some information in Spanish on the area's postconquest history. Pride of place goes to two fine and intricately carved stelae retrieved from the nearby site of Dos Caobas.

🛏 Sleeping & Eating

Nueva Alianza   CABAÑAS $$
(📱in Guatemala 502-463-824-47; www.hotel nuevaalianza.org;   r with/without bathroom M$950/300; P 🛜) Friendly Nueva Alianza,

among trees 150m along a side road from the museum, has a plain but cheerful budget section with wooden walls that don't reach the ceiling (think noise among friends!). Its stand-alone rooms with bathrooms are better, though, with wooden furniture and fans. A pleasant onsite restaurant (mains from M$110) has the only internet access in town.

Escudo Jaguar CABAÑAS $$
(🏠in Guatemala 502-5353-56-37; www.escudo jaguar.com; campsites per person M$120, d from M$640; 🅿🏊) Often used by tour groups, the pretty, community-run Escudo Jaguar overlooks the river 300m from the main *embarcadero*. Its solidly built thatched *cabañas* are spotless, and have fans and mosquito netting. The best are very spacious and have hot showers and terraces strung with hammocks. The smart-looking restaurant serves straightforward, but well-prepared Mexican dishes (mains from M$110, breakfasts from M$80).

Restaurante Imperio Maya MEXICAN $
(mains M$80-130; ⊙7:30am-3pm) Attached to the museum, this spacious *palapa* restaurant has a lengthy menu of Mexican standards and caters to Yaxchilán-bound tourists.

❶ Getting There & Away

If you can't get a bus or combi direct to Frontera Corozal, get one to Crucero Corozal, 16km southeast of San Javier on the Carretera Fronteriza, where *colectivo* taxis (M$50 per person) run to Frontera Corozal. The *ejido* hits up visitors entering or leaving Frontera Corozal for a M$30 per person toll; keep your ticket for exiting unless you're continuing on to Guatemala.

Autotransporte Chamoán vans run hourly from Frontera Corozal *embarcadero* to Palenque (around M$145, 2½ to three hours), with the last departure at 4pm or when full.

Lancha organizations have desks in a thatched building near the *embarcadero*, and all charge about the same prices for service to **Bethel, Guatemala** (boat 1-4 people M$1400, 5-7 people M$1700, 8-10 people M$2200), which is 40 minutes upstream. From Bethel, hourly buses depart to Flores (4½ hours) from 8am to 4pm. Make sure that the driver stops at the Bethel immigration office.

Yaxchilán

Jungle-shrouded Yaxchilán (yas-chee-*lan*) has a terrific setting above a horseshoe loop in the Río Usumacinta. The control this location gave it over river commerce, and a series of successful alliances and conquests, made Yaxchilán one of the most important Classic Maya cities in the Usumacinta region. Archaeologically, Yaxchilán is famed for its ornamented facades and roofcombs, and its impressive stone lintels carved with conquest and ceremonial scenes. A flashlight is helpful for exploring parts of the site.

Saraguates (howler monkeys) inhabit the tall trees here, and are an evocative highlight. You'll almost certainly hear their visceral roars, and you stand a good chance of seeing some. Spider monkeys, and occasionally red macaws, can also be spotted here at times.

History

Yaxchilán peaked in power and splendor between 681 and 800 CE under the rulers Itzamnaaj B'alam II (Shield Jaguar II, 681–742), Pájaro Jaguar IV (Bird Jaguar IV, 752–68) and Itzamnaaj B'alam III (Shield Jaguar III, 769–800). The city was abandoned around 810 CE. Inscriptions here tell more about its 'Jaguar' dynasty than is known of almost any other Maya ruling clan. The shield-and-jaguar symbol appears on many Yaxchilán buildings and stelae; Pájaro Jaguar IV's hieroglyph is a small jungle cat with feathers on its back and a bird superimposed on its head.

Most of the main monuments have information boards in three languages, including English.

◉ Sights

As you walk toward the **ruins** (M$70; ⊙8am-5pm, last entry 4pm), a signed path to the right leads up to the **Pequeña Acrópolis**, a group of ruins on a small hilltop – you can visit this later. Staying on the main path, you soon reach the mazelike passages of **El Laberinto (Edificio 19)**, built between 742 and 752 CE, during the interregnum between Itzamnaaj B'alam II and Pájaro Jaguar IV. Dozens of bats shelter under the structure's roof today. From this complicated two-level building, you emerge at the northwest end of the extensive **Gran Plaza**.

Though it's difficult to imagine anyone here ever wanting to be any hotter than they already were, **Edificio 17** was apparently a sweat house. About halfway along the plaza, **Stele 1**, flanked by weathered sculptures of a crocodile and a jaguar, shows Pájaro Jaguar IV in a ceremony that took place in 761 CE. **Edificio 20**, from the time of Itzamnaaj B'alam III, was the last significant structure built at Yaxchilán; its lintels are now in Mex-

Yaxchilán

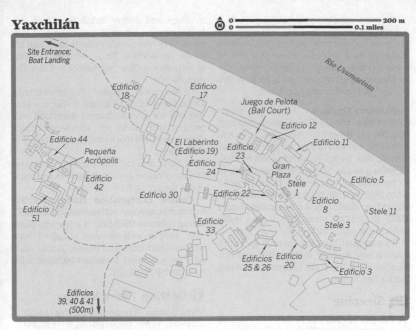

ico City. **Stele 11**, at the northeast corner of the Gran Plaza, was originally found in front of Edificio 40. The bigger of the two figures visible on it is Pájaro Jaguar IV.

An imposing stairway climbs from Stele 1 to **Edificio 33**, the best-preserved temple at Yaxchilán, with about half of its roofcomb intact. The final step in front of the building is carved with ball-game scenes, and splendid relief carvings embellish the undersides of the lintels. Inside is a statue of Pájaro Jaguar IV, minus his head, which he lost to treasure-seeking 19th-century timber cutters.

From the clearing behind Edificio 33, a path leads into the trees. About 20m along this, fork left uphill; go left at another fork after about 80m, and after some 10 minutes, mostly going uphill, you'll reach three buildings on a hilltop: **Edificio 39**, **Edificio 40** and **Edificio 41**.

ⓘ Getting There & Away

Lanchas take 40 minutes running downstream from Frontera Corozal (p414), and one hour to return. The three boat companies are in a thatched building near the Frontera Corozal *embarcadero*, all charging about the same price for trips. The return journey with 2½ hours at the ruins costs M$1400 for one to four people, M$1700 for five to seven people, and M$2200 for eight to 10 people. *Lanchas* normally leave frequently until around 2pm; try to arrive early to hook up with other travelers or a tour group to share costs.

Las Nubes

Near the community of Las Nubes, milky-blue river waters spill over smooth granite boulders and crash and tumble over a series of impressive waterfalls surrounded by tropical forest. The river is a deliciously laid-back spot in which to while away a couple of days swimming, walking or, for the more active, throwing caution to the wind by going zip-lining, rappelling or trying other adrenaline sports.

⊙ Sights & Activities

Río Santo Domingo   RIVER

The Río Santo Domingo is a beautiful, turquoise mess of cascades and rapids accessed from the community lodging at Las Nubes and Ecoturismo Xbulanjá. Some of the river pools are great swimming spots; it's M$25 per person to swim here if you're not staying the night. A swinging bridge straddles a fierce section of water-carved canyon, making an excellent vantage point from which to swoon over the grandest waterfalls. You can walk to *miradores*, head out in a kayak, and spelunk and rappel from February through June.

There are some enjoyable walking opportunities along the riverbank and into the forest. The most popular short walk is the 15-minute amble up to a *mirador* where you will be rewarded with blue-green jungle views. The bird-watching all around here is great. Activities are paid for through Las Nubes.

Ecoturismo Xbulanjá   RAFTING
(☑ What'sApp 664-113-37-16; www.xbulanja.com; Jerusalen Las Margaritas) From Embarcadero Jerusalén, just east of the Las Nubes highway turnoff, this Tzeltal cooperative offers Class III rafting to Las Nubes for M$1800 (two to six passengers, three hours). It has pleasant cabin lodging with mosquito nets (M$800 to M$900 per double) and a restaurant (mains M$75 to M$130; open high season only). Rafting trip prices include the drive back.

It's a modest but very friendly spot with a lovely setting right on the river and is a cheaper than the local alternative, Causas Verdes Las Nubes.

🛏 Sleeping

★**Causas Verdes Las Nubes**   LODGE $$
(☑ in Guatemala 502-4972-02-04; www.lasnubes chiapas.com; cabañas from M$1250; 🅿 🛜) Beautifully situated close to the main falls, this nicely landscaped, professionally run, and very peaceful complex has 15 well-built *cabañas* with hot water and pleasant porches. The waterside restaurant serves meals (mains M$120 to M$170), but no alcohol, though you can bring your own. Lodging rates drop hugely in low season. We love cabin number 9, right by the cascades.

You can walk, swim (in calm conditions; be aware the river swells in rainy season), kayak and simply relax. It's one of the nicest options around.

🛈 Getting There & Away

Las Nubes is 12km off the Carretera Fronteriza, 55km from Tziscao. From Comitán there are three daily combis (M$100, 3½ to four hours) with Transportes Tzovol (p420) between 7:30am and 4:30pm.

Metzabok & Nahá

Situated in the Lacandón Jungle between Ocosingo and the Carretera Fronteriza town of Chancalá, the small and isolated Lacandón villages of Metzabok and Nahá straddle a network of underground rivers in a protected biodiversity zone that's home to wildlife including jaguars, tapirs, howler monkeys and ocelots. Inhabitants here still follow many Lacandón traditions and customs. Very few people make it here, and it's worth considering for a wonderful cultural immersion. You pay M$35 to enter the community.

In Metzabok, villagers offer *lancha* trips along forest-ringed Laguna Tzibana, where you can see a moss-framed limestone wall painted with vivid red prehistoric pictograms, and hike to a lookout point above the tree canopy.

In Nahá, you can hire a guide to travel on foot or by canoe to various lagoons and learn about the area's flora and fauna.

Centro Ecoturístico Nahá (www.naha ecoturismo.com; cabin incl breakfast M$1350-2080, without bathroom M$72-820) is a friendly place with simple well-screened thatched huts with mosquito nets and bags of *Tarzan* character or startlingly luxurious *cabañas* with hot-water bathrooms.

🛈 Getting There & Away

From Palenque, Transportes Pajchiltic (p408) vans leave for Metzabok (M$120, three hours) and Nahá (M$120, four hours) whenever they're full (morning is best). Transportation back again often leaves in the middle of the night. Note that service to Metzabok is unreliable in both directions; it will stop at the junction (6km away) if the driver decides there aren't enough passengers to bother with the detour. From Ocosingo, trucks to Nahá (M$65, three hours) leave from a walled lot behind the market whenever there are enough passengers. Shared taxis cost M$125 per person (three hours).

Comitán Region

With a heady mixture of natural world wonders, towns laced with pretty colonial architecture and impressive ancient sites, the Comitán region has a lot going for it. It's therefore a little odd then that the region isn't more heavily touristed. But, for those in the know, this is one of the most enticing parts of Chiapas to explore. The regional capital is Comitán, a likeable small town of attractive buildings and lots of local color.

Comitán

☑ 963 / POP 98,000 / ELEV 1560M
With a pretty plaza of modern sculpture pieces, an eye-catching church and mature, carefully manicured flat-topped trees

Comitán

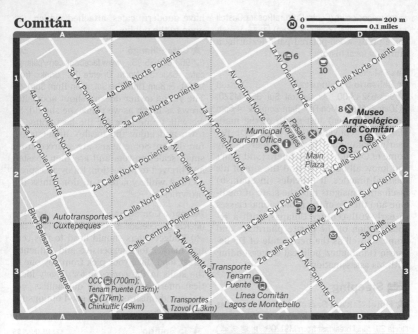

N 0 —————————— 200 m
0 —————————— 0.1 miles

Comitán

where birds flock and chirp in the evening, the colonial-flavoured town of Comitán has a very pleasant, artsy atmosphere. Set on a high plain 90km southeast of San Cristóbal de las Casas, Comitán has a gentle climate and a couple of reasonable places to stay and eat. There's a few interesting museums but not a great deal to do in the town itself. However, less than an hour away in the verdant countryside, there are several fabulous natural and archaeological attractions.

⊙ Sights

★Museo Arqueológico de Comitán
MUSEUM

(📞963-632-57-60; 1a Calle Sur Oriente; ⊙9am-6pm Tue-Sun) **FREE** Although this excellent museum is very small it's crammed with treasures from the area's many archaeological sites (Spanish signage only). It's arranged in chronological order and is a great way to learn about Maya culture and history. Despite all the beautiful artistic items from across the ages, the highlights for most people are the misshapen pre-Hispanic skulls on display – deliberately 'beautified' by squeezing infants' heads between boards. Going to the dentist will never seem quite so bad again...

Iglesia de Santo Domingo
CHURCH

(⊙7am-2pm & 4-8pm) On the plaza, pretty apricot-yellow Iglesia de Santo Domingo dates back to the 16th and 17th centuries, and sports unusual and handsome blind arcading on its tower. Its former monastic buildings next door are now the **Centro Cultural Rosario Castellanos** (📞963-632-06-24;

www.facebook.com/CentroCulturalRosarioCastellanos; 1a Av Oriente; ⊗8am-8:30pm) **FREE**, which has a pretty wood-pillared patio featuring a mural on local history.

Casa Museo Dr Belisario Domínguez
MUSEUM

(☏963-632-13-00; Av Central Sur 35; M$20; ⊗10am-6:45pm Mon-Fri, 9am-2pm & 4-6pm Sat, 10am-2pm Sun) Just south of the main plaza, the renovated Casa Museo Dr Belisario Domínguez is the former family home of Comitán's biggest hero (and won't you know all about it) and the site of his medical practice. It provides (in Spanish) fascinating insights into the state of medicine and the life of the professional classes in early-20th-century Chiapas, with a reconstruction of the onsite pharmacy and home, as well as the heroic tale of Dr Belisario Domínguez' political career, ending with his assassination.

🛏 Sleeping

★ Hotel Nak'am Secreto
HOTEL **$$**

(☏963-636-73-85; www.nakan.mx; 1a Av Oriente Norte 29; r incl breakfast from M$1209; 🅿❄🛜🚐) With sharp, modern and spacious rooms, some charming common areas and fabulously detailed service, this is Comitán's best-value hotel. The super central location, big leafy plants in terra-cotta pots and views from the rooftop garden seal the deal.

The only downer (for some) might be that you can't open the massive windows, but there's a rarity here (for Comitan) – a desk!

★ Hotel Casa Delina
BOUTIQUE HOTEL **$$$**

(☏963-101-47-93; www.hotelcasadelina.com; 1a Calle Sur Poniente 6; r M$1300; 🅿🛜🛜) When a team of contemporary Mexican and international artists were let loose in this stunningly restored 250-year-old mansion, they created something truly memorable. Think outlandish light fittings hanging from original wood-pillared arches, walls festooned in pouting lips and leaping horses, and a gorgeous, leafy tropical garden surrounded by eight industrial-chic rooms. This is truly something special.

An onsite cafe serves excellent organic Chiapan coffees.

🍴 Eating & Drinking

A handful of good restaurants, both Mexican and international, are within, or close to, the center. Most of the boutique hotels have modern cafes attached which are open to the public.

★ Café Pillangó
CAFE

(☏963-632-35-95; www.facebook.com/pillangocafe; Calle 2a Norte Oriente 12; drinks from M$20; ⊗8am-11pm Tue-Sat, noon-11pm Sun) 🍃 The young owner doesn't shout about her brews as much as we think she should. So we will. Come here for the best coffee in town and enjoy the locale's understated, fun design. Some beans are sourced from small scale growers and are then roasted and brewed to perfection. Enjoy an espresso (and while you're at it, don't miss the brownies.)

Mercado Comedors
MEXICAN **$**

(Mercado; quesadillas M$20-30; ⊗8am-5pm; 🍴) Budget eaters should head to this central market for inexpensive and authentic street food. Take your pick from any one of the stalls in the *comedor* for largely identical offerings. The filling quesadillas, *nopales* and mushrooms are good options for vegetarians.

★ Ta Bonitio
MEXICAN **$$**

(☏963-632-80-87; www.facebook.com/tabonitio.mx; Av Central Norte 5; mains M$130-300; ⊗8am-11pm) Ever had an octopus-tentacle burger? Highly imaginative and quirky modern Chiapas dishes are served up at this easygoing place that, as much as possible, uses only local produce. As well as unexpected main courses and great mezcal, it's also well regarded for its large and varied breakfast spreads.

500 Noches
SPANISH **$$**

(☏963-101-38-11; Main Plaza, Calle Central; mains M$120-230; ⊗4pm-2am; 🛜) Soaring ceilings and romantic nooks populate this cavernous restaurant-bar specializing in tapas and 80-plus wines, as well as craft beers. The big draw is the live *trova* folk music (Thursday to Saturday at 8pm), so it's worth coming by for drinks or dessert. Great hot chocolate and churro bar, too.

ℹ Information

BBVA Bancomer (cnr 1a Av Oriente Sur & 1a Calle Sur Oriente; ⊗8:30am-4pm Mon-Fri) Changes euros and dollars Monday through Friday; has an ATM.

Municipal Tourism Office (www.visitcomitan. com; Av Central Norte; ⊗8am-8pm)

Post Office (Av Central Sur 45; ⊗8:30am-4:30pm Mon-Fri, to noon Sat)

SIGHTS AROUND COMITÁN

Chinkultic Ruins

With a dearth of other tourists, the **Chinkultic Ruins** (⊙8am-5pm) is one of those magical archaeological sites where the sense of wild atmosphere is as enthralling as the stories written into the stones. Chinkultic was a minor Maya power during the late Classic period and, like Tenam Puente, may have survived into post-Classic times. Of 200 mounds scattered over a wide area of dramatically situated ruins, only a few have been cleared, but it's easy to let your imagination color in the rest.

The ruins are in two groups. From the entrance, first take the path to the left, which curves around to the right below one of Chinkultic's biggest structures, **E23**, which is covered in vegetation. The path reaches a grassy plaza with several weathered **stelae**, some carved with human figures, and a ball court on the right.

Return to the entrance, from which another path heads to the **Plaza Hundida (Sunken Plaza)**, crosses a stream, then climbs steeply up to the **Acrópolis**, a partly restored temple atop a rocky escarpment, with remarkable views over the surrounding lakes and forests and down into a cenote 50m below – into which the Maya used to toss offerings of pottery, beads, bones and obsidian knives.

Chinkultic is about 48km from Comitán, on the road to the Lagos de Montebello. Combis for the lakes can drop you at the intersection (M$50 from Comitán); the site is 2km north via a paved access road.

El Chiflón

The mighty **El Chiflón** (📞963-126-81-65; Cascadas de Chiflón M$50; Velo de Novia M$30; ⊙9am-5:30pm) waterfalls tumble 120m off the edge of an escarpment 20km southwest of Comitán. In a region with a surfeit of impressive waterfalls, these ones really are something special. In the dry season, from roughly February through July, the falls form a foamy line and the blue river water is safe enough to swim in. But during the rainy season, rapid currents turn the river a muddy brown, the falls gush with abandon and swimming is a life-threatening proposition.

There are two community-run enterprises, each on alternate sides of the river. For the first, **Cascadas de Chiflón**, you can walk the 1km approach road (or take a mototaxi for M$10) that heads up from Hwy 226 to the parking area. From here, a well-made path leads 1.3km up alongside the forest-lined river (which has nice swimming spots) to a series of increasingly dramatic and picturesque waterfalls. Reaching the main Velo de Novia (Bridal Veil) falls, prepare to be drenched by flying spray. You can also fly across the river on several zip-lines that are at various points along the route (from M$150). A small **interpretive center** provides information (in Spanish) on the river and wildlife in the area.

The second community enterprise, **Velo de Novia**, has lower entrance fees and it also offers zip-lining.

From Comitán, Autotransportes Cuxtepeques (p420), runs hourly vans and buses to the El Chiflón turnoff on Hwy 226 (M$35, 45 minutes) from around 6am to 7pm. For Cascadas de Chiflón, mototaxis wait at the entrance to ferry passengers up the road. Drivers should take the Tzimol turnoff from the Pan-American Hwy, 5km south of central Comitán.

Tenam Puente Maya Ruins

These sprawling Maya **ruins** (M$45; ⊙8am-5pm) feature three ball courts, a 20m tiered pyramid and other structures rising from a wooded hillside. Tenam Puente was one of a set of Classic Maya settlements in this region that seem to have survived in the post-Classic period, possibly to as late as 1200 CE. Although the main structures have been fully restored, the lesser ones remain half buried in the undergrowth, which, combined with the lack of visitors, gives the site a reflective, dreamy atmosphere.

A 5km-long paved road leads west to the site from Hwy 190, 9km south of Comitán. **Transporte Ejidal Tenam Puente** (3a Av Poniente Sur 8) runs combis (M$25) every 45 minutes from 7am to 7pm. The last combi from the ruins returns at 4pm. A taxi costs about M$300 return (with an hour at the ruins).

BUSES FROM COMITÁN

DESTINATION	FARE (M$)	TIME (HR)	FREQUENCY (PER DAY)
Ciudad Cuauhtémoc	140	1¾	4
Palenque	420	10½	1
San Cristóbal de las Casas	60	2	frequent
Tapachula via Motozintla	353	7½	6
Tuxtla Gutiérrez	130	3½	frequent

ⓘ Getting There & Away

The Pan-American Hwy (Hwy 190), named Blvd Belisario Domínguez here but usually just called 'El Bulevar,' passes through the west of town.

Comitán's **OCC bus terminal** (☑ 963-632-09-80; Blvd Belisario Domínguez Sur 43) is on the Pan-American Hwy. Among many others here are buses to Mexico City, Villahermosa, Playa del Carmen and Cancún. Across the road from the OCC terminal, 'centro' combis (M$7) run to the main plaza; a taxi is around M$35.

Numerous *colectivos* have terminals on Hwy 190 between 1a and 2a Calles Sur Poniente, about 500m north of the OCC terminal; they depart when full. For San Cristóbal, vans (M$55) and *colectivo* taxis (M$60) are available until 9pm. Vans for Ciudad Cuauhtémoc (M$47, until 8pm), which usually say 'Comalapa,' and Tuxtla Gutiérrez (M$95, until 6pm) are also available.

Línea Comitán Lagos de Montebello (☑ 963-632-08-75; www.facebook.com/montebello2019; 2a Av Poniente Sur 23) runs vans to the Lagos de Montebello and along the Carretera Fronteriza, with departures to Laguna Bosque Azul (M$75, one hour) and Tziscao (M$50, 1¼ hours) every 15 minutes from 3am to 6pm; to Reforma Agraria (M$200, 4½ hours) hourly until 2pm; and to Palenque (M$350, nine hours) hourly from 2:30am to 10am. Schedules don't use daylight saving time.

Transportes Tzovol (☑ 963-632-77-39; cnr 4a Av Poniente Sur 1039 & 13a Calle Sur Poniente) runs vans to Reforma Agraria (M$195, nine hours) four times daily from 2:30am to 3pm, as well as to Plan de Río Azul (M$120, 3½ hours), the connection for boats to Laguna Miramar, three times a day between 3:30am and 1pm. It also runs to Las Nubes (M$90, four hours) three times daily between 7:30am and 4pm and to Lagos de Montebello (M$55, one hour) every 15 minutes. It doesn't use daylight saving time.

Autotransportes Cuxtepeques (Blvd Belisario Domínguez Sur, btwn 1a & 2a Calles Norte Poniente) runs hourly vans and buses to the El Chiflón waterfall turnoff on Hwy 226 (M$35, 45 minutes) from 4am to 8pm.

GETTING TO GUATEMALA

Frequent *colectivos* (M$50) and intermittent buses (M$65) run between Ciudad Cuautémoc and Comitán (1½ hours). From Ciudad Cuautémoc, two daily ADO buses run to San Cristóbal de las Casas (M$181, four hours) and beyond, but it's usually quicker to get to Comitán and pick up onward transportation there. Other (infrequent) destinations include Palenque, Cancún and Tapachula.

Mexican immigration (Ciudad Cuauhtémoc; ◷ 8am-10pm) is across the street from the OCC terminal; *colectivos* generally assume that travelers need to be dropped off there. The Guatemalan border post is 4km south at La Mesilla, and 'Línea' combis (M$8) and taxis (around M$20 *colectivo*, M$50 private) ferry people between the two sides. There are banks and money changers on both sides of the border, which closes to car traffic from 9pm to 6am.

From La Mesilla, mototaxis can drop you at the 2nd-class bus depot. Second-class buses leave very frequently from 6am to 6pm for Huehuetenango (two hours) and Quetzaltenango (four hours), where you can find onward connections to Guatemala City. About 1km inside the border, 1st-class Línea Dorada (www.lineadorada.com.gt) has direct daily departures to Guatemala City (eight hours).

There's a **Guatemalan consulate** (☑ 963-110-68-16; www.minex.gob.gt; 1a Calle Sur Poniente 35, Int 3 4th fl, Comitán; ◷ 9am-1pm & 2-5pm Mon-Fri) in town that issues tourist visas.

Lagos de Montebello

The temperate pine and oak forest along the Guatemalan border east of Chinkultic is dotted with more than 50 small lakes of varied hues, known as the Lagos (or Lagunas) de Montebello. The area is very picturesque, peaceful and, after the steamy heat of the nearby jungles, beautifully cool and refreshing. Most people just come on a day trip from Comitán, or en route from eastern Chiapas, but the lakes make an ideal place at which to spend a couple of peaceful days wandering.

◉ Sights

Lagunas de Colores   LAKES
From the park ticket booth, the northward road leads to the Lagunas de Colores, five lakes with vivid hues that range from turquoise to deep green: **Laguna Agua Tinta**, **Laguna Esmeralda**, **Laguna Encantada**, **Laguna Ensueño** and, the biggest, **Laguna Bosque Azul**, on the left where the paved road ends.

Laguna Pojoj & Laguna Tziscao   LAKES
Laguna Tziscao, on the Guatemalan border, comes into view 1km near the Pojoj junction. The turnoff to the Chuj-speaking village of **Tziscao**, a pretty and spread-out place stretching down to the lakeside, is a little further on. The local *ejido* charges a M$25 entrance fee to access the lake areas along the Tziscao road; pay once and keep your receipt for the other lakes.

Near to Tziscao, a track leads 1km north to cobalt-blue **Laguna Pojoj**, which has an island in the middle that you can visit on simple rafts.

☞ Tours

In the Laguna Ensueño (and sometimes Bosque Azul) parking lot, local boys offer multilake horseback excursions that include **Dos Cenotes** (M$200, two to three hours), a pair of sinkholes in the forest, or to the **Laguna de Montebello** (about one hour away). There are also tours to see orchids, including a small flower museum which in reality is just boards with information in Spanish.

From Laguna de Montebello, more boys offer horseback rides to Dos Cenotes.

🍴 Sleeping & Eating

Villa Tziscao   CABAÑAS $$
(☏ Guatemala 502-5780-27-75; www.ecotziscao.com; campsites per person M$100, d M$750, cabaña M$750-1314; ℙ☺🛜) By the lake in Tziscao village (2km from the highway turnoff), this medium-sized lakeside complex is run by an *ejido*. Extensive, grassy grounds (shame about the tree stumps) include a sandy beach with terrific views across the lake to the foothills of the Cuchumatanes in Guatemala. Comfortable rooms in the main hotel building have decent beds and bathroom tiling, plus flat-screen TVs.

More rustic wooden *cabañas* are also available. All accommodations have a private bathroom with hot water, and campers can use the kitchen. The hotel also has a restaurant (breakfast M$50 to M$80, mains from M$100).

You can arrange to rent two-person kayaks (M$100 per person per hour).

Comedores   MEXICAN $
(dishes from M$45; ⊙7am-3pm) Beside the Laguna Bosque Azul parking lot are several basic *comedores* that serve drinks and simple plates of *carne asada* (roasted meat) or quesadillas; food options exist at most other lakes as well.

Restaurante Paraiso   MEXICAN $$
(www.cabaniasparaisotziscao.com/servicio-de-restaurante; Tziscao; mains M$80-M$180; ℙ) This sunny and airy spot serves up the standard Mexican favorites, from quesadillas to *milanesa de pollo* (chicken schnitzel), but it's the nicest option around these parts. It's located on the edge of the Lago

CHIAPAS & TABASCO COMITÁN REGION

Lagos de Montebello

DON'T MISS

PARADOR-MUSEO SANTA MARÍA

You'll feel like aristocracy staying in this beautiful **hotel-museum** (📞963-596-34-17; www. paradorsantamaria.com.mx; Carretera La Trinitaria–Lagos de Montebello Km 22; r from M$2420; 🅿️🕑🛜🐕), 1.5km off the road from Comitán to Lagos de Montebello. The restored 19th-century hacienda is decorated throughout with period furniture and art; some of the eight rooms have tiled bathtubs and fireplaces, and all have rough stone floors, grand wooden beds and look out over expansive grassy lawns to the countryside beyond.

There's little to do here but relax, though it's close enough to ruins and waterfalls and it's perfect if you want some luxury after visiting the jungle.

The small chapel is a **religious art museum** (M$25; 🕑9am-5pm) with an interesting array of colonial-era work from Europe and the Philippines as well as Mexico and Guatemala. **Restaurant Los Geranios** (mains M$235-380; 🕑8am-9pm) serves Chiapan and international dishes prepared with organic ingredients (including coffee) grown onsite.

Look for the 22km marker from La Trinitaria on the Montebello road.

Tzsicao and near Lago Internacional (the Guatemalan border), it has large windows to view the watery world beyond.

ℹ️ Getting There & Away

The paved road to Montebello is east off Hwy 190 just north of La Trinitaria, 16km south of Comitán. If coming from Comitán, it passes Chinkultic after 32km, and enters the Parque Nacional Lagunas de Montebello 5km beyond. A further 800m along is a ticket booth, where you must pay a M$34 park admission fee. (If you're coming from the east you must buy a ticket to a community, plus a ticket to the park which will cover you for the various lakes). Here the road forks: north to the Lagunas de Colores (2km to 3km) and east to the village of Tziscao (9km), beyond which it becomes the Carretera Fronteriza, continuing east to Ixcán and ultimately circling back up to Palenque.

Public transportation from Comitán is a snap, making it an easy day trip, but getting around is a little fiddly. Vans go to the end of the road at Laguna Bosque Azul and to Tziscao, and will drop you at the turnoffs for Museo Parador Santa María, Chinkultic and the other lakes, but you'll need to walk. The last vehicles back to Comitán leave Tziscao and Laguna Bosque Azul in the early evening.

From San Cristóbal, a number of agencies offer tours that take in the lakes, throw in a visit to El Chiflón and get you back by dinnertime.

El Soconusco & Beaches

Chiapas' fertile coastal plain, 15km to 35km wide, is called El Soconusco, and is named for the Aztecs' most distant 15th-century province, called Xoconochco. It's hot and humid year-round, with serious rainfall from mid-May to mid-October. The lushly

vegetated Sierra Madre de Chiapas, rising steeply from the plain, provides an excellent environment for coffee, bananas and other crops. Olive ridley and green sea turtles and the occasional leatherback nest along the coastline from June through November, and turtle preservation projects exist in Puerto Arista, Boca del Cielo, La Encrucijada and Chocohuital/Costa Azul.

The endless beach and ocean here is more wild and wooly than the tropical cliché and you should take care where you go in – the surf is often rough, and riptides (known as *canales*) can quickly sweep you out a long way. Bring bug repellent for overnights, as sandflies can be fierce from May through October.

Tonalá

📞966 / POP 35,000

This sweaty, bustling town on Hwy 200 is the jumping-off point for the beaches in the northern part of El Soconusco. The town has no attractions as such but the wonderful Zona Arqueológica de Iglesia Vieja is nearby. Assuming you don't arrive too late in the day, there's little reason to spend the night here.

There are good travel connections to larger inland towns and you'll need to get cash if you're heading for nearby beaches such as Puerto Arista, as there are no ATMs there.

👁️ Sights

⭐ **Zona Arqueológica de Iglesia Vieja** ARCHAEOLOGICAL SITE
(🕑8am-5pm) **FREE** Believed to be the regional capital of the Zoque during the Classic period, these ruins were inhabited between 250 and 400 CE. The site's most prominent

characteristics are its use of megalithic granite architecture, and its most impressive structure, the namesake 'Old Church,' is a 95m by 65m pyramid utilizing stone blocks weighing over a ton each. Instead of steps, the apex is reached via a ramp – look for the petroglyph cross at the south side of its base.

The other distinctive feature here is the presence of many carved anthropomorphic and zoomorphic monuments scattered throughout the site. The most well-known are the **Sapodrilo** (it appears to be a cross between a toad and a crocodile) and the **Altar de las Cuatras Caras** (Altar of the Four Faces).

Few people make the really quite minimal effort required to visit, which gives the ruins a haunting, deserted quality. From the signed turnoff at Km 10 on the Tonalá–Arriaga highway, it's about 9km (30 minutes) east off the main road; a high-clearance vehicle is required mid-May through November because the last 2km up can be washed out, but walking a section may still be required. There is no public transportation.

An exuberant authority on regional archaeological sites, the distinguished **Ricardo López Vassallo** (☑ cell 966-1008768, landline 966-663-01-05; rilova36@hotmail.com) lives in Tonalá and can organize transportation.

🛏 Sleeping & Eating

Hotel Galilea HOTEL **$**
(☑966-663-02-39; Hidalgo 138; r M$500; P❋🛜) Virtually on the central plaza, the mellow yellow Hotel Galilea has a convenient restaurant and boring medium-sized rooms around a parking area, with dark wooden furniture. It's a 'hey-passable-if-you-get-stuck-in-Tonalá' option.

Restaurant Nora MEXICAN **$$**
(www.facebook.com/nora.restaurante; Independencia 10; mains M$85-200; ⊘8am-5pm Mon-Fri, to 1pm Sat) There's always a fun family atmosphere and lots of checked tablecloths at the Restaurant Nora, one block east from the plaza (behind the Hotel Galilea), and one of the few good options to eat in town. The shrimp are something of a house specialty, but then they've had plenty of time to get them right – they've been in business since 1964.

ℹ️ Getting There & Away

From the central plaza, the **OCC bus terminal** (Hidalgo) is 600m west and the 2nd-class **Rápidos del Sur** (RS; Hidalgo, btwn Belisario

Domínguez & Iturbide) is 250m east. Both lines have frequent services to Tapachula (M$145 to M$318, three to four hours), Pijijiapan (M$145 to M$160, one hour) and Tuxtla Gutiérrez (M$108 to M$200, 2½ to three hours).

Colectivo taxis for Puerto Arista (M$25, 20 minutes), Boca del Cielo (M$38, 35 minutes) and the *embarcadero* for Madre Sal (M$70, 45 minutes) run from Matamoros between 20 de Marzo and Belisario Domínguez, four blocks east of the plaza and one block downhill. Puerto Arista combis (M$25) leave from Juárez between 20 de Marzo and 5 de Mayo, one block further downhill. Combis to Madre Sal (M$45) depart from near the market on 5 de Mayo between Juárez and Allende; a private taxi costs around M$300. *Colectivo* taxis for Pijijiapan (M$50) can be found on Hidalgo between 5 de Mayo and 20 de Mayo. Taxis and combis run until about 7pm.

Puerto Arista

🖉 994 / POP 900

The state's most-developed beach town is 18km southwest of Tonalá, though unless you visit during weekends, summer or holidays – when hotel prices rise and vacationing *chiapanecos* jam the place and its *palapa* seafood eateries along the beachfront – it's a small, ultra-sleepy fishing town. With a faded white lighthouse as its landmark, it's shabby and otherwise unremarkable, only okay for those after a 100% Mexican beach experience. If music, drinking and palm fronds aren't for you, look elsewhere. Note: be careful of rip tides; swimming here can be dangerous.

◉ Sights

Centro de Protección & Conservación de la Tortuga Marina en Chiapas ANIMAL SANCTUARY
(⊘10am-5pm) FREE During the nesting season, the state government collects thousands of newly laid olive ridley turtle eggs from 40km of beach, incubating them in protected beachside nests and releasing the hatchlings when they emerge seven weeks later. At this center located on the main road about 3km west of the lighthouse (mototaxis charge M$15), you can stop in to see the turtle nursery.

🛏 Sleeping

José's Camping Cabañas CABAÑAS **$**
(☑994-600-90-48; campsites per person M$70, RV sites M$250, dm M$130, s/d M$350/400, without bathroom M$250/275; P🚗) Run by a longtime Canadian expat, this laid-back fruit

tree–filled compound has simple, but very pleasant *cabañas,* some with bathrooms. All have mosquito netting, fans and screens, and shaded sitting areas. Breakfast is M$50 and José even makes organic coffee (M$20). Go 800m southeast from the lighthouse, then follow the signs (inland).

José knows a lot about the area. He also rents canoes (M$100) so that you can paddle through the gorgeous mangroves of Estero Prieto, accessed from the bottom of his garden.

Garden Beach Hotel HOTEL $$
(☑994-600-90-42; www.gardenbeach.mx; Bulevar Mariano Matamoros 800; r from M$1000; ⓟ❉🛜🏊) Across the street from the beach and 800m southeast of the lighthouse, and spread over two different grounds, this hotel has pastel-shaded, air-conditioned rooms that are past their best. All rooms have flat-screen TVs and there's no fly screens. The upper floors have great ocean views.

❶ Getting There & Away

At weekends and in holidays there's a near-constant stream of *colectivo* taxis bustling between Puerto Arista and Tonalá (M$25, 20 minutes). During the working week you'll likely have to wait a little longer for transportation.

Reserva de la Biosfera La Encrucijada

Stretching from the community of Chochuital (near Pijijlapan) to Barra San Simón (near Tapachula), this large biosphere reserve protects a 1448-sq-km strip of coastal lagoons, sandbars, wetlands, seasonally flooded tropical forest and the country's tallest mangroves (some above 30m). The ecosystem is a vital wintering and breeding ground for migratory birds, and harbors one of Mexico's biggest populations of jaguars, plus spider monkeys, turtles, crocodiles, caimans, boa constrictors, fishing eagles and lots of waterfowl. Despite the apparent quantity of wildlife, you'd have to be very dedicated and patient to see many of the flagship creatures. Bird-watching, however, is good at any time of year, but best during the November-to-March nesting season. The reserve can be visited via access points from Pijijiapan and Escuintla, and *lancha* rides take you through towering mangroves.

◉ Sights

Playa Azul BEACH
A laid-back coastal jewel, the beautiful black sandbar of Playa Azul is a thin strip of palm-fringed land between the ocean and the lagoon accessed from the Chocohuital *embarcadero,* 20km southwest of Pijijiapan. Camping is generally free, though restaurants ask that you eat your meals (seafood M$150 to M$230) there to do so. Outside of the busy high season, many places are closed. *Lanchas* (one way M$25) ferry passengers to the sandbar, and birding and mangrove trips can also be organized.

If you don't want to camp, head 300m north of the Chocohuital dock and pull up a pool chair at the **Refugio del Sol** (☑962-117-30-73, cell 962-625-27-80; www.refugiodelsol.mx; Ribera Costa Azul; r from US$80; ⓟ❉🛜🏊) hotel.

Red de Ecoturismo La Encrucijada COMMUNITIES
Accessed from the jetty community known as Embarcadero Las Garzas, the swamps and estuaries in Encrucijada reserve are home to local communities, including La Palma, El Ballenato, La Lupe, Barra Zacapulco and El Castaño. The backwaters here serve as their 'streets' and *lanchas* are the only public transport links. With some planning (around the rather-flexible boat schedule), you can hop between the communities via *lanchas.*

Under the banner Red de Ecoturismo La Encrucijada (see www.ecoturismolaencrucijada.com), together the communities run tourism activities, including basic accommodations.

Activities on offer include private *lancha* tours (M$1200 to M$2500, up to 10 passengers) to local beaches and to some superb bird-watching spots.

One of the easiest communities to access is **Barra de Zacapulco** – whose cooperative runs **Las Conchitas** (☑918-596-25-00; Zacapulco; r M$500; 🏊), 15 *cabañas* with fans, screened windows and cold-water bathrooms. You can usually camp or sling a hammock for free if you eat your meals at one of its simple *comedores* (seafood plates M$150).

It also has a sea-turtle breeding center and in season, you can watch the turtles being released.

MADRE SAL

Drift to sleep pondering the waves crashing onto the black-sand beach at **Madre Sal** (☑USA 966-100-7296, USA 966-666-6147; www.elmadresal.com; Manuel Ávila Camacho; campsites M$250, cabañas from M$700; ℗), an ecotourism project 25km south of Puerto Arista on the Pacific Coast. Named for a mangrove species, its **restaurant** (meals M$120 to M$150) and 18 thatched two-bed en suite **cabañas** sit astride a skinny bar of pristine land between a lagoon and the Pacific that's reached via *lancha* (M$25) through mangroves.

Crabs skitter along the sand when stars fill the night sky. In season, sea turtles come ashore to lay eggs, and the night watchman can wake you if you want to watch or help collect the eggs for the Boca del Cielo hatchery.

Though the water can be rough, the beach is spotless, and there's excellent bird-watching in the mangroves (there are 250 species of birds in the area), including 13 species of heron. Two- to three-hour *lancha* trips are available (per boat M$800, maximum 12 people), including one for bird- and crocodile-spotting (per boat M$1200).

From Tonalá, take a taxi (M$50 shared, M$500 private) or combi (M$40) to the *embarcadero* at Manuel Ávila Camacho; or from the village you can walk five minutes or ride on the back of a motorbike (M$10).

ⓘ Getting There & Away

For Playa Azul, combis for Chocohuital (M$25, 40 minutes, 5am to 6pm) leave hourly from 1a Av Norte Poniente 27 in Pijijiapan between 2a and 3a Poniente Norte; the last one returns at 8pm.

To get to Embarcadero Las Garzas, take a bus along Hwy 200 to Escuintla, then a *colectivo* taxi to Acapetahua (M$10, 10 minutes). If coming from Tapachula, shared taxis go direct to Acapetahua, bypassing the need to go to Escuintla first. From Acapetahua, take a shared truck 18km to Embarcadero Las Garzas (M$25, 40 minutes, every 30 minutes until 5pm). From Embarcadero Las Garzas, shared *lanchas* serve the communities including Barra de Zacapulco (M$120 return, 25 minutes one way). The last boat back from Barra de Zacapulco may be as early as 4pm, and the last truck from Embarcadero Las Garzas to Acapetahua goes at about 5pm.

Tapachula Region

Often treated as a mere stepping stone between northern Guatemala and better known attractions elsewhere in southern Mexico, it's nevertheless well worth devoting a few days to the Tapachula area. The region is known for producing some of the best coffee in Mexico and a few of the coffee farms offer tours and boutique accommodations. Highlights elsewhere in the area include the pretty village of Santo Domingo, reaching for the clouds by climbing one of the tallest volcanoes in Mexico

and exploring little known pre-Hispanic ruins. The regional capital, Tapachula, is a gritty town but makes for a convenient overnight stop.

Tapachula

📞 962 / POP 216,000 / ELEV 180M

Mexico's bustling southernmost city, the 'Pearl of the Soconusco,' doesn't quite live up to its nickname, though it does have an interesting combination of gritty border town feel, tropical tempo and commercial center (it does a lot of cross-border trade with Guatemala).

A hot, humid and busy place year-round, Tapachula's heart is the lively Parque Hidalgo, with vistas of the towering 4100m cone of Volcán Tacaná to the north on clear days. Most travelers simply pass through here on their way to or from Guatemala, but it is the gateway to a number of interesting nearby attractions.

At the time of research, thousands of asylum seekers from Central America and some African countries, had set up camp here.

⊙ Sights

Parque Hidalgo   PLAZA

Tapachula's heart is the large, very lively Parque Hidalgo, with vistas of the towering 4100m cone of Volcán Tacaná to the north on clear days. Anybody and everybody, it seems, from locals to visitors to Central American and African asylum seekers, seem to gather here.

Tapachula

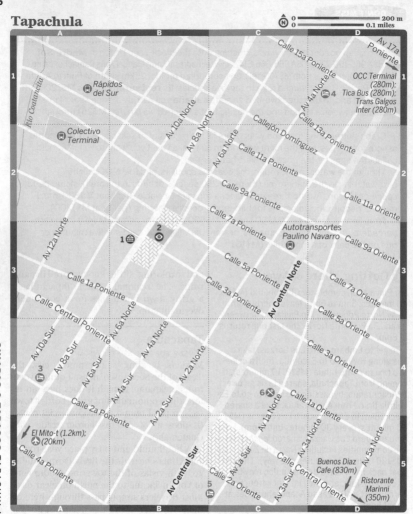

Museo de Tapachula MUSEUM
(Ex-Palacio Municipal, Plaza Central; ⊙10am-7pm Tue-Sat, to 6pm Sun) **FREE** Opened in August 2019, it's worth coming here, even if it's just to tour the lovely building, a former palace. The museum's intentions are good: to promote the history of the city, including the influence of the migrants who ventured here (there's a fascinating section on the Japanese and Chinese). However, it's light on exhibits and heavy on textual descriptions. If you can read Spanish, these provide an in-depth look at the growth of the city and surrounds.

☞ Tours

Tours Discover Chiapas TOUR
(☑cell 962-1336820) Run by a delightful and intelligent English- and French- speaking guide, Miguel Ángel, tours cover the surrounding region: the Coffee Route; the 'chocolate towns,' where chocolate is prepared by traditional means; boat trips through mangroves; and Santo Domingo and Union Juárez. Miguel provides excellent commentary. Tours start at around US$55 per person, minimum of two to four people, depending on the tour.

Tapachula

◎ Sights

🛌 Sleeping

✖ Eating

🛌 Sleeping

Hotel & Suites Mo Sak
HOTEL $

(☎962-626-67-87; Av 4a Norte 97; s/d from M$600/800; P🐕❄🛜) A popular choice, this modern and fair-priced hotel has big windows, bold artwork and minimalist furniture. Helpful, attentive staff and free morning coffee help round out the deal. King-bed rooms have kitchenettes.

★Casona Maya Mexicana
BOUTIQUE HOTEL $$

(☎962-626-66-05; www.casonamaya.com; Av 8a Sur 19; r from M$975; P🐕❄@🛜🏊) This vine-covered and quirkily charming boutique hotel pays homage to Mexican women in history. Guests can choose from 10 sumptuous (if slightly tired) rooms named for heroines such as human rights lawyer Digna Ochoa or Zapatista commander Ramona. Antiques, a small tropical garden-patio, and interesting art create a pleasant oasis from Tapachula's frenzy. There's a small pool, too.

In addition, there's a small bar and a restaurant with excellent homemade meals and great service, all of which makes this a fabulous place to stay.

Suites Ejecutivas Los Arcos
HOTEL $$

(☎962-625-31-31; www.suitesejecutivasarcos.com; Av 1a Sur 15; s/d from M$814/932; ❄🛜) This is one of those delightfully home-arty hotels for the midrange budget which Mexico so excels at. Paper butterflies and real plants enliven common areas and a tangle of art fills the walls. It has a great downtown location, rooms are generously sized and come equipped with kitchenette and balconies overlooking the lush gardens. The owner's personality matches the decor.

✗ Eating & Drinking

★Buenos Díaz Cafe
CAFE

(☎962-625-93-60; www.facebook.com/buenos diazcoffee; 7a Av Sur 53; from M$20; ⊘6am-10pm) Given that Tapachula is the gateway to the Coffee Route (Chiapas' coffee *fincas*), it's surprising how few contemporary cafes there are here. Thanks to Buenas Díaz, coffee snobs can enjoy a good brew. The interior has funky timber decor and the baristas (yes, it's a word here!) produce some fabulous coffees in line with third-wave coffee trends.

★La Jefa
MEXICAN $$

(☎962-118-17-20; Av 1a Norte Esquina; mains M$80-180; ⊘noon-6pm Mon-Sat) This classic Tapachula *parrillada* is a great night out with a group friends. Huge hunks of meat sizzle over the barbecue, cold beers are slapped down onto the tables, while TVs blare out. This is rustic Mexican eating at its finest. If you're here for drinking alone, each alcoholic drink comes with a small snack, such as a taco.

El Mito-t
MEXICAN $$

(☎962-620-02-80; 4a Av Sur 133; mains M$90-160; ⊘1pm-midnight Mon-Sat, to 7pm Sun) You get to be the chef at this fun place – well, kind of anyway. Known far and wide for its salsas, it piles a dozen or more different kinds onto your table when you sit down and then leave it to you to order the tacos and fillers. The shrimp and calamari are a hit with everyone.

★Ristorante Marinni
ITALIAN $$$

(☎962-625-39-97; www.facebook.com/Marinni Ristorante; Av 11a Sur 1; mains M$135-285; ⊘9am-11pm Mon-Sat) Held in high regard by locals, this Italian restaurant has a sophisticated and softly lit indoor dining room and an outdoor patio cloaked in dramatic greenery. Taste highlights include the wood-fired thin-crust pizza, the lasagna and the *medallón al balsámico* (beef medallions in red wine and balsamic vinegar). Has good breakfast deals, too.

ℹ Information

CI Banco (www.cibanco.com; 4a Av Sur; ⊘9am-5pm Mon-Fri, to 2pm Sat) Fast and efficient.

Ciudad Salud (☎962-642-44-01; Carretera Tapachula Puerto Madero s/n) Recommended public hospital

Hospital Metropolitano (☎962-626-65-80; Central Sur s/n, Los Naranjos) Private hospital.

ℹ Getting There & Away

AIR

Tapachula's modern **airport** (Airport code: TAP; ☎962-626-22-91; Carretera Tapachula–Puerto Madero Km 18.5; 🛜) is 20km southwest of the

BUSES FROM TAPACHULA

DESTINATION	FARE (M$)	TIME (HR)	FREQUENCY (PER DAY) & COMPANY
Comitán via Motozintla	353	7¼	5 ADO
Escuintla	75-136	1½-2	2 ADO, very frequent RS
Mexico City	800-1183	18-20	frequent ADO
Oaxaca	700	13	1 ADO
San Cristóbal de las Casas via Motozintla	250-447	9	7 ADO
Tonalá	210-351	3½-4½	very frequent ADO & RS
Tuxtla Gutiérrez	250-600	5½-6	very frequent ADO & RS

city. It's a drowsy place, with just three daily flights to/from Mexico City on **Aeroméxico** (☑ 962-626-39-21; www.aeromexico.com; Central Oriente 4) and Volaris (www.volaris.com).

BUS

Deluxe and 1st-class buses go from the **OCC terminal** (☑ 962-626-28-81; Calle 17a Oriente, btwn Avs 3a & 5a Norte), 1km northeast of Parque Hidalgo. The main 2nd-class services are by **Rápidos del Sur** (RS; ☑ 962-626-11-61; Calle 9a Poniente 62).

Other buses from the OCC station go to Palenque, Puerto Escondido and Villahermosa. There are also daily buses from here to Guatemala City (five to six hours), with tickets sold at the main counter: The main operator is **Tica Bus** (☑ 962-625-24-35; www.ticabus.com; Terminal OCC, Calle 17a Oriente, btwn Avs 3a & 5a Norte; ⊗ 6am-2pm Mon-Sat) which has a 7am departure.

Trans Galgos Inter (www.transgalgosintergt. com; Calle 13a Oriente 43) and Tica Bus run buses to San Salvador, El Salvador (from M$650, nine hours). Tica Bus continues all the way to Panama City, with several long overnight stops en route.

For destinations in western Guatemala, including Quetzaltenango, it's best to get a bus from the border.

COLECTIVO

A large **colectivo terminal** (Calle 5a Poniente) houses most of the regional taxi and combi companies. **Autotransportes Paulino Navarro** (☑ 962-626-11-52; Calle 7a Poniente 5) runs rather ancient combis to Ciudad Hidalgo (M$34, 50 minutes) every 10 minutes from 4:30am to 10pm.

❶ Getting Around

CAR & MOTORCYCLE

Tapachula's two rental agencies carry both automatic and manual-transmission cars. Prices for a small car start at around M$600 per day.

AVC Rente un Auto (☑ 962-626-23-16; www.avcrenteunauto.com; Av Tapachula 2A; ⊗ 7:30am-6pm Mon-Fri, 8:30am-6pm Sat, 9am-5pm Sun) In-town pickup service available.
Europcar (www.europcar.com; Airport; ⊗ 9am-11:30pm) Best rates online.

TAXI

Taxis within the central area (including the OCC terminal) cost M$40 to M$50.

Taxis charge around M$230 per person (up to four people) for a *colectivo* from the airport to the center.

North of Tapachula

The hills north of Tapachula are home to numerous coffee *fincas* (ranches), many of them set up by German immigrants more than a century ago and today offering tours, restaurants and overnight accommodations.

🛌 Sleeping

★ **Finca Argovia**   RESORT $$$
(☑ 962-621-12-23; www.argovia.com.mx; r M$2350, bungalow M$3445; ➌❀❅✾) This gorgeous boutique hotel on a working coffee farm high in the cool, misty hills north of Tapachula offers comfortable wood-paneled rooms. Here, you can while away hours in hammocks, count orchids in the jungle gardens, or go on informative coffee-farm tours. And then there's the pool and spa and a lovely restaurant. The highlight is the delightful owner Bruno Giesemann and staff.

Finca Argovia follows permacultural practices with a twist. Everything, from coffee plants to shampoo ginger flowers, have been planted in the jungle to adhere to natural principles. Rates are cheaper outside of high season.

To get here, taxis cost around M$400. Alternatively, regular *colectivos* marked 'Saragosa' depart from Mercado San Juan (M$27, 1¼ hours). Alight at Nueva Alemania (five minutes from the *finca*; they will collect you).

Finca Hamburgo   CABAÑAS **$$$**
(☏ 962-626-75-78; www.fincahamburgo.com; Carr a Nueva Alemania Km 54; d/ste M$2350/3570; P☺☎🖵) Founded by German settlers in 1888, this historic coffee farm, perched atop a hill, offers breathless views over lush, rugged countryside (best enjoyed, cup of coffee in hand, from an easy chair on your room terrace), bush-chic wooden cabins that are comfortable without being over the top, spa services, a gourmet restaurant (mains M$200 to M$250) and tours of the property and surrounds.

There are several options to get here. Finca Hamburgo can arrange pick up from Tapachula (from M$1200 return trip). Combis run twice daily from Mercado San Juan at 5:45am and 11am (three hours). An easier alternative is to take a combi to Finca Argovia and arrange in advance for Finca Hamburgo to pick you up in a jeep (M$150 round trip). It's very doable and has improved over the years but, given the steep road conditions, the 12km trip takes around 35 minutes. Rates are cheaper outside of high season.

Izapa

The small and peaceful pre-Hispanic ruins at **Izapa** (☺ 9am-5pm Wed-Sun) **FREE** contain three groups of ruins. The northern group (Grupo F) is on the left side of the road if you're arriving from Tapachula – watch for the low pyramid mounds; you'll also see a ball court and several carved stelae and altars. Grupo A has 10 very weathered stele-and-altar pairings around a field. Grupo B is a couple of grass-covered mounds and more stone sculptures, including three curious ball-on-pillar affairs.

Izapa flourished from approximately 200 BCE to 200 CE, and its carving style (mostly seen on tall slabs known as stelae, fronted by round altars) shows descendants of Olmec deities with their upper lips unnaturally lengthened. Some Maya monuments in Guatemala are similar, and Izapa is considered an important 'bridge' between the Olmec and the Maya. Izapa had 91 known stele-and-altar pairings.

Groups A and B are a little way from the northern group. To reach them go back 700m toward Tapachula and take a signposted road to the left. After 800m you'll reach a fork with signs to Izapa Grupo A and Izapa Grupo B, each about 250m further on and looked after by caretaker families that may request a small donation.

ℹ CROSSING THE BORDER

If you're not taking a direct bus to Guatemala from the OCC station, you can go to the border for connections. It's 20km from Tapachula to the international border at Talismán, opposite El Carmen in Guatemala. The border crossing between Ciudad Hidalgo, 37km from Tapachula, opposite Ciudad Tecún Umán in Guatemala, is busier and has more onward connections. Both border points have money-changing facilities and are open 24 hours – though you should get through by early afternoon for greater security and to guarantee onward transportation. Watch out for money changers passing counterfeit bills at both crossings.

Combis for Talismán (M$20, 30 minutes) leave from near the front of the OCC station, roughly every 10 minutes from 5am to 9pm. The majority of bus services from El Carmen, which include around 20 a day to Guatemala City (seven hours), go via Ciudad Tecún Umán, and then head along the Pacific slope route. For Quetzaltenango, you can take one of these and change at Coatepeque or Retalhuleu, but it's easier to get a *colectivo* taxi to Malacatán, on a more direct road to Quetzaltenango via San Marcos, and then look for onward transportation from there.

From Tapachula, regular combis head to Ciudad Hidalgo (M$34, 50 minutes). Across the border in Ciudad Tecún Umán, frequent buses leave until about 6pm for Guatemala City (five hours) by the Pacific slope route, through Retalhuleu and Escuintla. Buses to Quetzaltenango (three hours) depart hourly during the day.

For Lake Atitlán or Chichicastenango, you need to get to Quetzaltenango first.

Izapa is around 11km east of Tapachula on the Talismán road. To get there from Tapachula, take a combi (M$16) from the *colectivo* terminal or any Talismán-bound bus.

Santo Domingo, Unión Juárez & Volcán Tacaná

☑ 962

At 4100m, Volcán Tacaná's dormant cone towers over the countryside north of Tapachula. Even if you're not interested in climbing to its summit, two villages, Santo Domingo and Unión Juárez, on its gorgeously verdant lower slopes make an attractive day trip, their cooler climates offering welcome relief from the Tapachula steam bath. The scenic road up is winding but well paved.

◉ Sights

Santo Domingo   VILLAGE
Santo Domingo lies 34km northeast of Tapachula, amid coffee plantations. The village's gorgeous three-story wooden 1920s *casa grande* (big house), **Casa Braun**, has been restored. It belonged to the German immigrants who formerly owned the coffee plantation here, but it's now a community cooperative, **Centro Ecoturístico Santo Domingo** (M$5; ☺8am-8pm). There's a **restaurant** (mains M$70 to M$180), a small creaky-floored, dusty **coffee museum** (M$10), and a well-tended **tropical garden and pool** (M$10; free with a meal).

From the back entrance, be sure to wander up the hill for 50m to see a historic coffee-processing plant made of corrugated iron that is still in use. (Great photo opportunities.)

Keep an eye out for the fabulous small houses made of timber planks, built to German design.

Unión Juárez   VILLAGE
About 9km beyond Santo Domingo, passing some gorgeous waterfalls tucked in around tight turns, Unión Juárez (population 2600, elevation 1300m) is the starting point for ascents of Tacaná and other, less-demanding walks. Tapachula folk like to come up here on weekends and holidays to cool off and feast on *parrillada*, a cholesterol-challenging plate of grilled meat and a few vegetables.

🏃 Activities

The best months to climb Tacaná are late November to March. There are several routes up the mountain from Unión Juárez. These do not require any technical climbing, but you need to allow two or three days for either, preferably plus time to acclimatize. Be prepared for extreme cold at the top. The less-steep route is via Chiquihuites, 12km from Unión Juárez and reachable by vehicle. From there it's a three-hour walk to Papales, where you can sleep in huts for a small donation. The ascent from Papales to the summit takes about five hours. The other route is via Talquián (a one hour walk from Unión Juárez, or take a *colectivo*) and Trigales (two hours from Talquián). It takes about six hours to climb from Trigales to the summit. The two routes meet at the crater, and on both you have access to camping areas.

It's a good idea to get a guide for Tacaná in Unión Juárez or organize one to meet you. Casa Morayma can find guides (about M$1500 for one to two people) with a couple of days' notice.

🛌 Sleeping

Hotel Colonial Campestre   HOTEL $
(☑ 962-647-22-37; Unión Juárez; r from M$350; ℗ 🛜) Rambling and Escher-esque, this hotel has extremely basic rooms in need of a good pick-me-up. Room 26 has good views. It also has a restaurant (mains M$70 to M$120, *parrillada* for two M$250). Look for the arch a couple of blocks below the plaza.

★ Casa Morayma   HOTEL $
(☑ 962-122-25-84; www.facebook.com/casamorayma; Unión Juárez; d M$700; ☻) Offering by far the best night's sleep in Unión Juárez, this small, arty hotel on the town's entrance road stands out for its terra-cotta–red paintwork and vines creeping up the outside of the building. The botanical theme continues inside with a little water garden feature, bright flowery paintings and travel-inspired photo art.

Señora Morayma, a marathon runner (note the medals hanging upstairs) or other staff can organize Tacaná treks (around M$1500 per day for two people).

❶ Getting There & Away

From Tapachula, take a combi from the *colectivo* terminal to Cacahoatán (M$20, 30 minutes), 20km north. From where these terminate in Cacahoatán, other combis travel to Santo Domingo (M$14, 30 minutes) and Unión Juárez (M$21, 45 minutes).

TABASCO

They say that the state of Tabasco has more water than land, and looking at all the lagoons, rivers and wetlands on the map you can certainly see why, especially during the rainy season. It's always hot and sweaty here, but marginally less so when you catch a breeze along the Gulf of Mexico or venture into the southern hills. Travelers to Villahermosa and coastal Tabasco should note the region is subject to seasonal floods, though few travelers linger in Tabasco longer than it takes to see the outstanding Olmec stone sculpture in Villahermosa's Parque-Museo La Venta. Located north of Chiapas and abutting the Gulf of Mexico, Tabasco is the site of onshore and offshore oil extraction by Mexico's former state oil company (Pemex). With the privatization of the oil industry around 2014, thousands lost their jobs and the region has continued to suffer.

Villahermosa

📞 993 / POP 353,000

This sprawling, flat, hot and humid city, with more than a quarter of Tabasco's population, has never been the 'beautiful town' its name implies. And that's not likely to change. What it lacks in the looks department, though, it makes up for with its buzzy atmosphere and welcoming inhabitants. The city makes a good base for day trips to some of the state's more-alluring attractions. Most people use it as an arrival or departure point for Chiapas or other areas.

◉ Sights

The central area of this expansive city is known as the Zona Luz, and extends north–south from Parque Juárez to the Plaza de Armas, and east–west from the Río Grijalva to roughly Calle 5 de Mayo. The main bus stations are between 750m and 1km north of the center.

★ **Parque-Museo La Venta** MUSEUM
(www.iec.tabasco.gob.mx/content/parque-museo-de-la-venta; Av Ruíz Cortines; M$50; ⊙8am-4pm; P🚲) This fascinating outdoor park and museum was created in 1958, when petroleum exploration threatened the highly important ancient Olmec settlement of La Venta in western Tabasco. Archaeologists moved the site's most significant finds, including three colossal stone heads, to Villahermosa. There's also a zoo but the

DON'T MISS

MALPASITO RUINS

The Maya ceremonial site of **Malpasito** (M$50; ⊙7am-5pm) is 600m (signposted) uphill from the village of the same name. Apart from the beautiful setting, what's remarkable about this little-visited site, dating from 700 to 900 CE, are its petroglyphs. More than 100 petroglyphs showing birds, deer, monkeys, people, and temples with stairways are scattered around the Malpasito area, of which about 10 are at the archaeological site. Interpretive signs are in Spanish and English.

You need your own wheels to get here but if you do, the site is easily accessible between Tuxtla Gutiérrez and Villahermosa. It's located just over the border of Chiapas on the main highway 145D, 115km north of Tuxtla Gutiérrez (1¾ hours), or 140km (two hours) south of Villahermosa.

cages are shabby and depressing; this can be avoided when making your way to the sculpture trail.

There's an informative display in English and Spanish on Olmec archaeology as you pass through the sculpture trail, the start of which is marked by a giant ceiba (the sacred tree of the Olmec and Maya; this one is over 120 years old). All pieces are numbered in order. This 1km walk is lined with finds from La Venta. Among the most impressive, in the order you come to them, are **Stele 3 (number 4)**, which depicts a bearded man with a headdress; **Altar 5 (number 10)**, depicting a figure carrying a child; **Monumento 77 (number 11)**, 'El Gobernante,' a very sour-looking seated ruler; the monkey-faced **Monumento 56 (number 16)**; **Monumento 1 (number 24)**, the colossal head of a helmet-wearing warrior; and **Stele 1 (number 31)**, showing a young goddess (a rare Olmec representation of anything female). Animals that pose no danger (such as coatis, squirrels and black agoutis) roam freely around the park.

At 7pm, 8pm, 9pm and 10pm Tuesdays to Sundays, there's a **sound-and-light show** (M$116).

Plan two to three hours for your visit, and take mosquito repellent (the park is set in humid tropical woodland). Parque-Museo La Venta lies 2km northwest of the Zona

CHIAPAS & TABASCO VILLAHERMOSA

ⓘ AIRPORT BUS TO PALENQUE

The Villahermosa airport has a handy counter for ADO (www.ado.com.mx), with almost hourly minibuses departing daily to Palenque (M$350, 2¼ hours) between 5:20am and 9:20pm. Check the website for schedules to/from 'Aeropuerto Villahermosa.'

Luz, beside Avenida Ruíz Cortines, the main east–west highway crossing the city. It's a M$50 or so taxi ride.

★ Museo Regional de Antropología

MUSEUM

(www.iec.tabasco.gob.mx/content/museo-antro pologia; Periférico Carlos Pellicer; M$23; ⊙ 9am-5pm Tue-Sun; ℗) Villahermosa's excellent regional anthropology museum (even the shiny modern building it's housed in is impressive) holds some stunning exhibits on Olmec, Maya, Nahua and Zoque cultures in Tabasco – including Tortuguero #6, the infamous tablet *solely* responsible for the dire 'end of world' predictions forecast for December 21, 2012, which just goes to show that you can't believe everything you read! It's in the CICOM complex, a 15-minute walk from Zona Luz and just south of the Paseo Tabasco bridge.

Casa de los Azulejos

MUSEUM

(Av 27 de Febrero; M$33; ⊙ 9am-5pm Tue-Fri, to 6pm Sat & Sun) This lovely historic home, diagonally opposite the Palacio Gobierno, is more interesting for its Spanish tiles, than its museum contents (which tell the story of the region's history). Constructed between 1889 and 1915, each room is covered in a series of unique, and very stunning, Catalan tiles. There are 42 different patterns, with influences of Moorish, Gothic, baroque and Renaissance styles throughout. The building later housed the city's first pharmacy before it was turned into a museum.

🛏 Sleeping & Eating

As a former oil town, Villahermosa has scores of business-style midrange and top-end chain hotels, most of which offer heavily discounted online and weekend rates. Inviting budget options are scarce.

Hotel Olmeca Plaza

HOTEL $$

(☎ 993-358-01-02; www.hotelolmecaplaza.com; Madero 418; d from M$800; ℗ ⊛ ❋ @ �� ⛱) This downtown hotel has a flash lobby, an open-air pool and a well-equipped gym. But that's about it. Reception can be terse. The rooms are basic and dated, but comfortable, with ample desks and decent bathrooms. A plus is the onsite restaurant (open 7am to 11pm).

★ Sleep Inn

BUSINESS HOTEL $$

(www.choicehotels.com/mexico/villahermosa/sleep-inn-hotels; Av Jose Maria Pino Suárez 216; r incl breakfast from M$900; ⊛ ❋ �) One of several business-oriented spots in downtown Villahermosa, this brand new option (as at 2019) won't disappoint. Ultra-professional staff, a central locale and neat-as-a-pin rooms (if lacking in personality). Big-screen TVs and good wi-fi make it a fine choice if you're arriving in or departing from the city. Light sleepers should avoid rooms near the lifts (there are loud pings).

One Villahermosa Centro

BUSINESS HOTEL $$

(☎ 993-131-71-00; www.onehotels.com; Carranza 101; r incl breakfast from M$1204; ❋ �) A large, business-style hotel, this one wins points for attentive staff and a super-central location. Rooms are what you'd expect for the price – big and comfortable but lacking much sense of place. Even so, if it's a good night's kip you want, then you won't find a better option downtown.

★ La Cevichería Tabasco

SEAFOOD $$

(☎ 993-345-00-35;www.facebook.com/lacevicheria tabascov; Francisco José Hernández Mandujano 114; mains M$130-250; ⊙ 11am-6pm Tue-Fri, from 10am Sat & Sun; ❋) A stellar seafood place just over the river from downtown. With bright murals inside and out and a friendly neighborhood vibe, this busy, and slightly chaotic, place serves seafood dishes that are so arty you might prefer to just gaze in wonder at your meal rather than eat it. The tacos stuffed with marlin are especially impressive.

Coctelería Rock & Roll

SEAFOOD $$

(☎ 993-334-21-90; Reforma 307; mains M$160-220; ⊙ 10am-10pm) A maelstrom of heat, swirling fans and blaring TVs. Everyone's here for the large and delicious seafood cocktails (though it also has good ceviche and seafood stew) and cheap beer. It's on a pedestrian street across from the Miraflores Hotel, and has 60 years (and three generations of owners) under its belt. A Villahermosa institution if ever there was one.

La Dantesca ITALIAN $$
(📞993-351-51-62;www.facebook.com/LaDantesca;
Hidalgo 406, near Parque Los Pajaritos; mains
M$110-220, pizzas from M$170; ⏰1-10pm; 🏮) Lo-
cals enjoy this lively trattoria for its fantastic
brick-oven pizzas, house-made pastas and
scrumptious desserts. Most folks come for
the pizza, but the trio of lasagna, *lomo* (pork
loin) and ravioli is superb. Give the cook the
slightest hint of encouragement and he'll
start spinning pizza bases around like he's
mixing a cocktail (wow, and around a wood-
fired oven in 38 degree temperatures; we
salute him).

Mar & Co SEAFOOD $$$
(📞993-315-05-05; http://marcompany.com.mx;
Paseo Tabasco 1011; mains M$110-300; ⏰1-10pm
Mon-Wed, to midnight Thu-Sat, noon-7pm Sun) A
little out of the center, on the strip known as
Paseo Tabasco, but worth coming for its outstandingly good seafood. Culinary highlights
are the octopus and shellfish. Many locals
insist it's the best seafood joint in town. The
building itself, a dozen or so old shipping
containers piled like Lego atop each other, is
as memorable as the food.

ℹ Information

Most banks have **ATMs** and exchange dollars
or euros.
HSBC (cnr Juárez & Lerdo de Tejada; ⏰9am-
5pm Mon-Fri) Bank branch on a pedestrianized
street.
**Oficina de Convenciones y Visitantes de
Tabasco** (OCV; 📞993-310-97-00; www.
tabasco.gob.mx/turismo; Plaza Río, 1st Floor,
Av Paseo Usumacinta 1504; ⏰9am-3pm Mon-
Fri) This changes with the government (as for
the rest of Mexico), so expect varying service.

ℹ Getting There & Away

AIR
Villahermosa's **International Airport**
(Aeropuerto Carlos Rovirosa Pérez; 📞993-
356-01-57; www.asur.com.mx; Carretera Villa-
hermosa–Macuspana Km 13) is 13km east of
the center, off Hwy 186. Aeroméxico is the major
airline; there are daily nonstop flights to/from
Villahermosa.
Aeroméxico (www.aeromexico.com) Flights
daily to Mexico City; lots of international con-
nections via Mexico City.
Interjet (www.interjet.com.mx) To Mexico
City.
MAYAir (www.mayair.com.mx) To Mérida.
VivaAerobus (www.vivaaerobus.com) To
Cancún, Mérida, Mexico City, Monterrey and
Guadalajara.
Volaris (www.volaris.com) To Mexico City.

BUS & COLECTIVO
Deluxe and 1st-class buses depart from the **ADO
bus station** (📞993-312-84-22; Mina 297; 📶),
which has wi-fi and 24-hour left luggage and is
located 750m north of the Zona Luz.
Transportation to most destinations within
Tabasco leaves from here, or other terminals
within walking distance north of ADO, including the 2nd-class **Cardesa bus station** (cnr
Hermanos Bastar Zozaya & Castillo) and the
main 2nd-class bus station, the **Central de
Autobuses de Tabasco** (CAT; 📞993-312-29-77;
cnr Av Ruíz Cortines & Castillo) on the north side
of Avenida Ruíz Cortines (use the pedestrian
overpass).

BUSES FROM VILLAHERMOSA

DESTINATION	FARE (M$)	TIME (HR)	FREQUENCY (PER DAY) & COMPANY
Campeche	550-635	6½-9	frequent ADO
Cancún	625-1100	12½-14½	10 ADO
Comalcalco	110	2	frequent Cardesa, 1 ADO
Mérida	695-855	8-11½	frequent ADO
Mexico City (TAPO or Norte)	670-1235	12-13	frequent ADO
Oaxaca	400-1000	14	3 ADO
Palenque	140-240	2-2½	frequent ADO & Cardesa
San Cristóbal de las Casas	240-575	6½	5 ADO
Tenosique	130-150	3-4	frequent ADO & CAT
Tuxtla Gutiérrez	300-680	4½-6	frequent ADO
Veracruz	750-870	6½-8½	frequent ADO

❶ Getting Around

Comfortable ADO minibuses ferry passengers between the airport and the ADO bus terminal (M$212); they run hourly between 6am and 9pm. Taxis to the center cost around M$300. Alternatively, walk 500m past the airport parking lot for a *colectivo* (M$25) from the Dos Montes taxi stand. These terminate in the market on Carranza, about 1km north of the Zona Luz.

A system of *colectivo* taxis (M$25) provides the backbone of the center's public transit. Flag one down to ask if it's going your way, or join a queue at a stand outside a large store or transportation terminal, where proficient handlers ask for your destination and quickly assign you a shared taxi. There's no fee for the match-up, and no haggling necessary. Private taxis charge around M$30 within the center.

Comalcalco

📞 933 / POP 40,000

The small town of Comalcalco, around 55km northwest of Villahermosa, is a scrappy, low-rise place of little visual appeal. However, just on the outskirts of town is an enjoyably under-visited Maya site that is one of the big attractions of Tabasco. The town is also known for its cacao production and small chocolate factories, some of which are open to the public. Ancient monuments and divine chocolate: what better reason to make the easy day trip from Villahermosa does a person need?

◉ Sights

Small though Comalcalco might be, there are a couple of attractions in and around the town to make for an enjoyable day trip from Villahermosa, which is between one and two hours away.

★**Comalcalco**   ARCHAEOLOGICAL SITE
(www.inah.gob.mx/zonas/9-zona-arqueologica-de-comalcalco; M$60; ◷8am-4pm) Surrounded by jungle and little visited by tourists, the small but impressive Maya ruins of ancient Comalcalco are the most westerly known Maya ruins. Architecturally they're unique due to many of the buildings being constructed of bricks and/or mortar made from oyster shells. Comalcalco was at its peak between 600 and 1000 CE, when it was ruled by the Chontal. It remained an important center of commerce for several more centuries, trading in a wealth of pre-Hispanic luxury goods.

At the entrance to the complex is a small **museum** with a fine array of sculptures and engravings of human heads, deities, glyphs and animals, such as crocodiles and pelicans.

Beyond the museum, the first building you encounter is the great brick tiered pyramid, **Templo I**. At its base are the remains of large stucco sculptures, including the feet of a giant winged toad. Further temples line **Plaza Norte**, in front of Templo I. In the far (southeast) corner of the site rises the **Gran Acrópolis**, which has views from its summit over a canopy of palms to the Gulf of Mexico. The Acrópolis is fronted by **Templo V**, a burial pyramid that was once decorated on all sides with stucco sculptures of people, reptiles, birds and aquatic life. At Templo V's western foot is **Templo IX**, which has a tomb lined by nine stucco sculptures showing a Comalcalco lord with his priests and courtiers. Above Templo V is the crumbling profile of **El Palacio**, with its parallel 80m-long, corbel-arched galleries, probably once Comalcalco's royal residence. Information is in both Spanish and English.

If coming via public transport, there are several options. The easiest, but most expensive way is via taxi from the center of Comalcalco (around M$60). From Villahermosa, if you take Comalli or ADO buses to the center of Comalcalco, ask to be directed to the supermarket Chedraui. From here, take a combi (direction Paraíso) and ask to be let off at the ruins turn-off. From here it's a 20-minute walk along a pleasant house-lined street. Alternatively, from Villahermosa, ask the Comalli buses to drop you near the ruins turn off *if* they head that way; be aware that you are on a main highway.

Hacienda La Luz   PLANTATION
(📞933-337-11-22; www.haciendalaluz.mx; Bulevar Rovirosa 232; 1hr tour per person from M$100; ◷tours 9am, 11am, 1pm & 3pm) Hacienda La Luz, one of several local plantations making chocolate from home-grown cacao, offers informative guided tours (a basic tour is one hour, but longer and more detailed tours are available) round the gardens and cacao plantation (the house is still lived in). You will be shown the traditional methods of turning cacao beans into chocolate, and, yep, the bit you were waiting for, the tour concludes with a chocolate drink. For a tour in English, it's wise to reserve in advance.

The hacienda is just 300m from Comalcalco's central Parque Juárez: walk 250m west along Calle Bosada to its end at Bulevar Rovirosa, turn right and you'll see the hacienda's white gateposts across the road.

RESERVA DE LA BIOSFERA PANTANOS DE CENTLA

This 3030-sq-km **biosphere reserve** (M$36; ⊙ visitor center Thu-Sun, boat trips daily) protects a good part of the wetlands around the lower reaches of two of Mexico's biggest rivers, the Usumacinta and the Grijalva. These lakes, marshes, rivers, mangroves, savannas and forests are an irreplaceable sanctuary for countless creatures, including the West Indian manatee and Morelet's crocodile (both endangered), six kinds of tortoise, tapirs, ocelots, jaguars, howler monkeys, 60 fish species and 255 bird species.

The **Centro de Interpretación Uyotot-Ja** (☏ 913-106-83-90; www.casadelagua.org. mx; Carretera Frontera–Jonuta Km 12.5; admission M$40, reserve fee M$36, boat ride M$1000; ⊙ 9am-5pm Thu-Sun) visitor center, or 'Casa de Agua,' is 13km along the Jonuta road from Frontera, beside the broad, winding Río Grijalva. A 20m-high observation tower overlooks the awesome confluence of the Grijalva, the Usumacinta and a third large river, the San Pedrito – a spot known as Tres Brazos (Three Arms). Boat trips (two hours, up to seven people M$1000), offered by a changing schedule of local communities on rudimentary *lanchas*, are available into the mangroves, where you might see crocodiles, iguanas, birds and, with luck, howler monkeys. The boats are rudimentary at best, so it's better value with a group. Note: these operate daily (while the Centro de Interpretación Uyotot-Ja does not). March to May is the best birding season.

From Villahermosa, ADO and Cardesa buses service Frontera (near the site of conquistador Hernán Cortés' 1519 first battle against native Mexicans), from where *colectivos* run the 15-minute trip to the reserve (M$25). A taxi from Frontera costs around M$100.

🍴 Eating

There are a number of taco stands and other cheap eats in and around the Parque Benito Juárez García, which is a little to the west of the main road through town. There is also one exceptional place close to the archaeological site.

★**Cocina Chontal**   MEXICAN $
(☏ 933-158-56-96; www.facebook.com/nelly. cordovamorillo.5; Buenavista; mains M$150-180; ⊙ noon-5pm Wed-Sun) Run by the larger-than-life, traditionally dressed Nelly Córdova, this delightful open-air restaurant is located near the archaeological site (ask to cut through the site itself). It is a basic but fun spot and specializes in rekindling half-forgotten traditional Tabasco dishes, including some from

the Maya period. These include thick chocolate *moles*, turkey stew and bananas stuffed with beans and pork.

Everything is cooked on open wood fires and served in clay bowls. Oh, and roll up your sleeves because there's no cutlery, so you can ignore everything your mother ever said about eating with your fingers.

ⓘ Getting There & Away

There are frequent ADO buses (M$90, two hours) to and from Villahermosa. The best and more frequent option is to take the **Comalli** (Reforma Sur 503) vans that depart the Comalli Terminal – located in the town center (ask any local) – between 4:50am and 10:30pm daily when full (M$40; departures at least half hourly).

AT A GLANCE

POPULATION
4.1 million

CAPITAL
Oaxaca City

BEST MEZCAL BAR
Mezcaloteca
(p456)

BEST SURFING
Playa Zicatela
(p474)

**BEST
OAXACAN CUISINE**
Casa Oaxaca
(p455)

WHEN TO GO
Jan–Mar
Driest months; best
hiking conditions
in the Sierra Norte;
whale-watching.

Jul & Aug
The Guelaguetza
festival is held in
Oaxaca city and
outlying towns.

Late Oct & Nov
Día de Muertos in
and around Oaxaca
city; Fiestas de
Noviembre in Puerto
Escondido.

Hierve El Agua (p467)
BYELIKOVA_OKSANA/GETTY IMAGES

Oaxaca

The state of Oaxaca (wah-*hah*-kah) has a special magic felt by Mexicans and foreigners alike. A bastion of indigenous culture, it's home to the country's most vibrant crafts and art scene, some outstandingly colorful and extroverted festivities, a uniquely savory cuisine and diverse natural riches.

At the center of the state in every way stands beautiful, colonial Oaxaca city, an elegant and fascinating cultural hub. Nearby, in the forested Sierra Norte, community-tourism ventures enable visitors to hike, bike and ride horses amid dramatic green mountainscapes. To the south, across rugged, remote ranges, is Oaxaca's fabulous tropical coast, with great beaches, seas full of surf, dolphins and turtles, and a string of relaxed beach towns and villages.

Oaxaca Highlights

1 **Oaxaca City** (p440)
Soaking up culture, cuisine, architecture, crafts and mezcal in this festive, colonial city.

2 **San Agustinillo** (p490)
Chilling for longer than you

planned at this travelers' beach hangout, one of several laid-back villages on the coast.

3 **Puerto Escondido** (p474) Surfing at this low-key town's gorgeous beaches.

4 **Pueblos Mancomunados** (p471) Hiking otherworldly cloud forests between mountain villages.

5 **Monte Albán** (p461)
Exploring the majestic setting

Gulf of Mexico

Tlacotalpan

Santiago
Tuxtla

Catemaco

Laguna
Catemaco

Bahía de
Campeche

Laguna
El Carmen

osamaloapan

Río Papaloapan

MEX
175

Agua
Dulce

Coatzacoalcos

TABASCO

Loma
Bonita

Isla

MEX
145

Acayucan

MEX
145D

Minatitlán

MEX
180

MEX
180D

MEX
17

VERACRUZ

Río Coatzacoalcos

Las Choapas

Río Uxpanapa

MEX
145D

MEX
179

Zacatepec

Zempoaltépetl
(3400m)

MEX
147

Istmo de
Tehuantepec

Presa
Netzahualcóyotl

OAXACA

Río El Corte

Ayutla

Matías
Romero

MEX
185

Sierra Atravesada

CHIAPAS

MEX
190

Niltepec

MEX
190

MEX
190D

MEX
190

Jalapa del
Marqués

Presa
Juárez

Ixtepec

MEX
185D

La Ventosa

Guiengola

Juchitán

Tapanatepec

Arriaga

MEX
200

Tehuantepec

Laguna
Superior

Laguna
Inferior

Mar
Muerto

Tonalá

Salina
Cruz

San Mateo
del Mar

MEX
190

MEX
200

Concepción
Bamba

Golfo de Tehuantepec

Barra de
la Cruz

Bahías de
Huatulco

N

0   50 km
0   25 miles

and mysterious architecture of
a vista-rich archaeological site.

6 **Chacahua** (p484)
Riding across bird-filled
lagoons to a stunning beach at
this tranquil village.

7 **Bahías de Huatulco**
(p495) Enjoying beach life
with creature comforts.

8 **Playa Escobilla** (p485)
Seeing thousands of turtles
arriving ashore to nest.

9 **Valles Centrales** (p461)
Experiencing indigenous
village life at markets, fiestas
and artisan workshops.

History

Pre-Hispanic cultures in Oaxaca's Valles Centrales (Central Valleys) reached heights rivaling those of central Mexico. The hilltop city of Monte Albán became the center of the Zapotec culture, which conquered much of Oaxaca and peaked between 300 and 700 CE. From about 1200 the Zapotecs came under the growing dominance of Mixtecs from Oaxaca's northwest uplands. Mixtecs and Zapotecs alike were conquered by the Aztecs in the 15th and early 16th centuries.

The Spanish sent at least four expeditions before they felt safe enough to found the city of Oaxaca in 1529. The indigenous population declined quickly and disastrously, though rebellions continued into the 20th century.

Benito Juárez, the great reforming president of mid-19th-century Mexico, was a Zapotec from the Oaxaca mountains. Another Oaxacan, Porfirio Díaz, rose to control Mexico with an iron fist from 1877 to 1910, bringing the country into the industrial age but fostering corruption, repression and, eventually, the Revolution in 1910.

Today, while tourism thrives in and around Oaxaca city and on the coast, underdevelopment prevails in the backcountry. There is still a wide gulf between the state's rich, largely mestizo (people of mixed ancestry) elite and its poor, disempowered, heavily indigenous majority.

OAXACA CITY

951 / POP 264,250 / ELEV 1555M

A cultural colossus fit to rival anywhere in Latin America for history, gastronomy and colorful manifestations of indigenous culture, Oaxaca is a complex but intensely attractive city whose majestic churches and refined plazas have deservedly earned it a Unesco World Heritage badge. Lovers of culture come here to indulge in the Mexico of Zapotec and colonial legend. Flowing through handsome yet tranquil streets, life pulsates with an unadulterated regional flavor. See it in the color palette of historic boutique hotels, a meet-the-producer artisan store or an intentionally grungy *mezcalería* (plying locally manufactured alcoholic beverages). But what makes Oaxaca especially interesting are its undercurrents. While largely safe and attractive by Mexican standards, snippets of political protest in recent years have lent the city a grittier edge. It bubbles up in satirical street art, bohemian bars and been-around-forever street markets. Trust us: there's far more to this city than just pretty churches.

⦿ Sights

Oaxaca's sights start with its historic whole – listed as a Unesco World Heritage site since 1987. Downtown overflows with churches, art galleries, museums and attractive green spaces. If it's your first trip, you're best off targeting the highlights.

★ Museo de las Culturas de Oaxaca   MUSEUM

(951-516-29-91; Alcalá s/n; adult/child under 13yr M$75/free, guided tour per hour M$600; ⊙10am-6pm Tue-Sun) Got two hours? You'll need it for the Museum of Oaxacan Cultures, housed in the beautiful monastery buildings adjoining the Templo de Santo Domingo. This is one of Mexico's best regional museums. The rich displays take you right through the history and cultures of Oaxaca state up to the present day, emphasizing the continuity between pre-Hispanic and contemporary cultures in areas such as crafts, medicine and food.

A gorgeous stone cloister serves as antechamber to the museum proper. The greatest treasure is the Mixtec hoard from Tomb 7 at Monte Albán, in Room III (the first on the right upstairs). This dates from the 14th century, when Mixtecs reused an old Zapotec tomb at Monte Albán to bury one of their kings and his sacrificed servants, along with a stash of beautifully worked silver, turquoise, coral, jade, amber, pearls, finely carved bone, crystal goblets, a skull covered in turquoise and a lot of gold. The treasure was discovered in 1932 by Alfonso Caso.

Halls I to IV are devoted to the pre-Hispanic period, halls V to VIII to the colonial period, halls IX to XIII to Oaxaca in the independence era and after, and the final room (XIV) to Santo Domingo Monastery itself. At the end of the long corridor past hall IX, glass doors give a view into the beautifully ornate choir of the Templo de Santo Domingo.

Some of the museum's explanatory material is in English, but most is in Spanish. Also, there's a good book/souvenir shop and a fascinating onsite library with 30,000 titles in various languages, with some books dating to the 15th century.

★ Templo de Santo Domingo   CHURCH

(cnr Alcalá & Gurrión; ⊙7am-1pm & 4-8pm except during Mass) Gorgeous Santo Domingo is the

CONTEMPORARY ART IN OAXACA

Of Mexico's major art hubs, Mexico City may have the most and the fanciest galleries, and Monterrey the most impressive presentations – but only in Oaxaca will you find such a dense concentration of talent, innovation and galleries within a small, accessible area.

A delight in color and light, a dreamlike feeling and references to indigenous mythology have long been trademarks of Oaxacan art. Two artists laid the basis for today's flourishing scene: the great muralist Rufino Tamayo (1899–1991) and European-influenced Francisco Gutiérrez (1906–45). The next generation was led by three artists. The colorful art of Rodolfo Morales (1925–2001) from Ocotlán, with its childlike angel figures, has deep roots in local myths. Rodolfo Nieto (1936–85) populated his work with vivid fantasy animals and dream figures. Francisco Toledo (1940–2019), from Juchitán, worked in many media, often focusing on grotesque beasts. He was always an active figure in Oaxacan cultural life.

Workshops for young artists organized by Tamayo in the 1970s encouraged talents such as Abelardo López, Ariel Mendoza and Alejandro Santiago. Their work is highly varied, but indigenous roots and a dreamlike quality run through a lot of it. More or less contemporary is Sergio Hernández, whose limitless imagination melds the figurative with the abstract and fantastic. Artists who appeared around the turn of the 21st century, such as Demián Flores, Soid Pastrana and Guillermo Olguín, tend to reject representation and 'folklorism' in favor of postmodernism, video and symbol-loaded graphic compositions designed to make us ponder.

Top Museums & Galleries

Museo de Arte Contemporáneo de Oaxaca (p446) Changing exhibits of first-rate contemporary Mexican and international art in a beautifully revamped colonial house.

Museo de los Pintores Oaxaqueños (MUPO, Museum of Oaxacan Painters; ☑951-516-56-45; www.facebook.com/mupoax; Independencia 607; M\$23, Sun free; ☺9am-7pm) Exhibitions by artists from Oaxaca and elsewhere – often provocative contemporary work.

Arte de Oaxaca (☑951-514-09-10; www.artedeoaxaca.com.mx; Murguía 105; ☺11am-3pm & 5-8pm Mon-Sat) **FREE** A commercial gallery presenting a wide range of quality art, it includes a room devoted to Rodolfo Morales' work.

Centro Fotográfico Álvarez Bravo (☑951-516-98-00; www.cfmab.com.mx; Bravo 116; ☺9:30am-8pm Wed-Mon) **FREE** With a taste for provocative social commentary, this photo gallery displays weird and wonderful work by international photographers.

La Máquina (☑951-501-21-64; www.facebook.com/lamaquinataller; 5 de Mayo 413; ☺10am-7pm Mon-Fri) **FREE** Works on display in the showroom range from talented up-and-comers to established artists such as Demián Flores.

Instituto de Artes Gráficas de Oaxaca (IAGO, Oaxaca Graphic Arts Institute; ☑951-516-69-80; www.facebook.com/iagomx; Alcalá 507; ☺9:30am-8pm Wed-Mon, library closed Sun) **FREE** Offers changing exhibitions of graphic art plus a superb arts library open to all.

La Mano Mágica (☑951-516-42-75; www.lamanomagica.com.mx; Alcalá 203; ☺10:30am-3pm & 4-8pm Mon-Sat) **FREE** You'll find art by leading figures such as Tamayo, Morales and Hernández, plus a small but fine selection of handicrafts, at this commercial gallery founded by the master weaver Arnulfo Mendoza (1954–2014) from Teotitlán del Valle.

Espacio Zapata (p444) A bona-fide art collective peddling revolutionary art, often with a political bent.

most splendid of Oaxaca's churches, with a finely carved baroque facade and nearly every square centimeter inside decorated in 3D relief with intricate gilt designs swirling around a profusion of painted figures. Most elaborate of all is the 18th-century Capilla de la Virgen del Rosario (Rosary Chapel) on the south side. The whole church takes on a magically warm glow during candlelit evening Mass.

Santo Domingo was built mainly between 1570 and 1608 as part of the city's Dominican monastery, with the finest artisans from

Oaxaca City

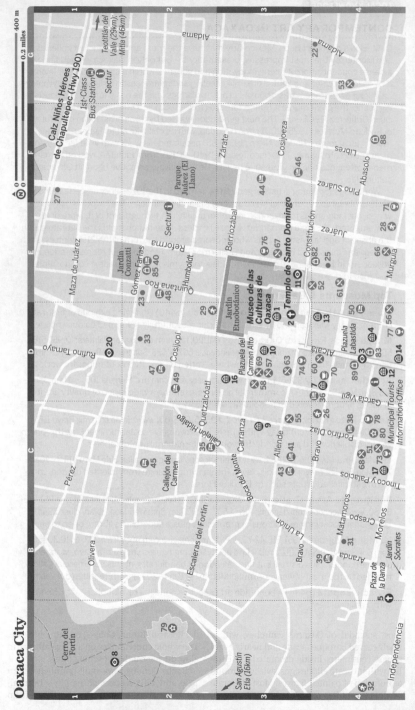

400 m
0.2 miles

Cerro del Fortín

San Agustín Etla (16km)

Teotitlán del Valle (29km); Mitla (46km)

Calz Niños Héroes de Chapultepec (Hwy 190)

1st-Class Bus Station

Sectur

Parque Juárez (El Llano)

Jardín Conzatti

Jardín Etnobotánico

Museo de las Culturas de Oaxaca

Templo de Santo Domingo

Plazuela del Carmen Alto

Plazuela Labastida

Municipal Tourist Information Office

Plaza de la Danza

Jardín Sócrates

Rufino Tamayo

Streets: Aldama, Zárate, Berriozábal, Reforma, Humboldt, Quintana Roo, Gómez Farías, Maza de Juárez, Pérez, Olivera, Escaleras del Fortín, Callejón del Carmen, Cosijopí, Callejón Hidalgo, Quetzalcóatl, Boca del Monte, Carranza, Allende, Bravo, Tinoco y Palacios, La Unión, Aranda, Matamoros, Crespo, Morelos, Independencia, Porfirio Díaz, García Vigil, Alcalá, Constitución, Juárez, Pino Suárez, Libres, Abasolo, Murguía, Cosijoeza, Zárate

Locations numbered: 1, 2, 3, 4, 5, 7, 8, 9, 10, 11, 12, 13, 14, 16, 17, 20, 22, 23, 25, 26, 27, 28, 29, 31, 32, 33, 35, 36, 38, 39, 40, 41, 43, 44, 45, 46, 47, 48, 49, 50, 51, 52, 53, 55, 56, 57, 58, 60, 61, 63, 66, 67, 68, 69, 70, 71, 73, 74, 76, 77, 78, 79, 80, 82, 83, 85, 88, 89

Santa María Atzompa (6km);
Atzompa Ruins (8km)

Tlayudas el
Negro (150m)

54

59

37

42

Murguia

Santos Degollado

González Ortega

Hidalgo

Libres

Morelos

Independencia

Reforma

Doblado

Xochitl

La Carbonera

34

87

Xicoténcatl

Ocampo

Guerrero

Colón

Rayón

Arteaga

La Noria

(6km);
Ocotlán (31km) Xochitl

84

18

81

30

5 de Mayo

Fiallo

Valdivieso

Municipal Tourist
Information Kiosk

Portal
Benito
Juárez

6

21

19

65

Armenta y López

Eclipse 70

Express
Service

Zaachila
Yoo

Líneas
Unidas

64

15

Alameda
de León

Portal de
Flores

Bustamante

86

Flores Magón

Cabrera

Autobuses
Halcón

Monte Albán
(6km)

62

75

20 de Noviembre

Zaragoza

Arista

JP García

24

JP García
Aldama

Mina

72

Huatulco
2000

Expressos
Colombo
Huatulco

Mier y Terán

Hidalgo

Trujano

Las Casas

Díaz Ordaz

Autobuses
Turísticos to
Monte Albán

Victoria

Terminal AU (250m);
2nd-class (350m);
Central de Abastos (450m)

Transportes
Villa del
Pacífico

Galeana

Periférico

Prolongación Victoria

Oaxaca City

Puebla and elsewhere helping in its construction. Like other big buildings in this earthquake-prone region, it has immensely thick stone walls.

Santo Domingo de Guzmán (1172–1221), the Spanish monk who founded the Dominican order, appears as the right-hand one of the two figures holding a church in the center of the facade, and his elaborate family tree adorns the ceiling immediately inside. The Dominicans observed strict vows of poverty, chastity and obedience, and in Mexico they protected the indigenous people from other colonists' excesses.

Andador Turístico
STREET

Historic, romantic, dignified and safe, Calle Alcalá (traffic-free since the 1980s) is what Oaxaca is all about. It runs north from the cathedral to Templo de Santo Domingo and is lined by typical colonial-era stone buildings that are now home to artisan shops, galleries, museums, cafes and bars. Always good for a stroll, it's particularly atmospheric at night.

Zócalo
PLAZA

Traffic-free, shaded by tall trees and surrounded by elegant *portales* (arcades), the Zócalo is the perfect place to start soaking up the Oaxaca atmosphere. It bustles with life by day and night, as marimba ensembles, brass bands and roving buskers float their melodies among the crowds, hawkers try to offload pretty carpets and hideous balloons, and lovers parade in slow rounds under the trees, while anyone and everyone sits, drinks and watches from the sidewalk cafes.

Espacio Zapata
GALLERY

(🖉 951-126-71-10; www.facebook.com/espacio zapata; Porfirio Díaz 509; ⏰10am-8pm Mon-Sat) **FREE** In a city of provocative graphic art, this workshop and gallery is a key agitator. Founded by the art collective Asaro (Asamblea de Artistas Revolucionarios de Oaxaca) in 2006, and never satisfied to put down its paintbrush for long, it broadcasts an ever-changing menu of events, discussions, workshops and expos. Even the mural on the facade is regularly repainted.

Stick your head in for a browse or a chat.

Museo Rufino Tamayo
MUSEUM

(Museo de Arte Prehispánico de México Rufino Tamayo; 🖉 951-516-76-17; www.facebook.com/museo tamayooaxaca; Morelos 503; M$90; ⏰10am-2pm

& 4-7pm Mon & Wed-Sat, 10am-3pm Sun) A top-class museum, even by Oaxaca's high standards, showing off a wondrous collection of pre-Hispanic art donated by the city's most famous artist, Rufino Tamayo (1899–1991). It traces artistic developments in preconquest times and includes some truly beautiful pieces laid out in color-coded backlit cases in a series of uncluttered rooms set around a lovely 17th-century patio.

The abundant figurines – some as old as 1250 BCE – are from sites all around Mexico and are displayed as art rather that archaeology.

Jardín Etnobotánico   GARDENS
(Ethnobotanical Garden; ☑951-516-53-25; www.jardinoaxaca.mx; cnr Constitución & Reforma; 2hr tours in English or French M$100, 1hr tours in Spanish M$50; ☺tours English 11am Tue, Thu & Sat, Spanish 10am, noon & 5pm Mon-Sat, French 5pm Tue) In former monastic grounds behind the Templo de Santo Domingo, this garden features plants from around Oaxaca state, including a staggering variety of cacti. Though it has been growing only since the 1990s, it's already a fascinating demonstration of Oaxaca's biodiversity. Due to acts of vandalism, visits are by guid-ed tour only; be there five minutes before they start.

Basilica de Nuestra Señora de la Soledad   BASILICA
(☑951-516-50-76; Independencia 107; admission by donation; ☺museum 9am-2pm & 3-7pm Tue-Sun) Oaxaca doesn't lack distinguished churches, but many locals rate the Soledad as their favorite. The original baroque facade dates from 1690; while the florid and gold-tinged interior, which emits an extra sparkle above the altar, is a product of the late 19th century. Among some of the finer touches are the eight sculpted angels each holding up a chandelier. Don't miss the small **museum** around the back crowded with stained glass, saintly paintings and depictions of the Virgin of Solitude.

Catedral de Nuestra Señora de La Asunción   CATHEDRAL
(☑951-516-44-01; Av de la Independencia 700; ☺7:30am-7:30pm) Oaxaca's cantera stone cathedral is suitably massive and old, but in a city as culturally rich as Oaxaca, it is arguably only the third most impressive church behind the Soledad and the Templo de Santo Domingo (p440). Construction

began in 1553 and finished (after several earthquakes) in the 18th century. It enjoys a grand placement just north of the Zócalo with its main facade, featuring typical if not lavish baroque carving, facing the Alameda.

Palacio de Gobierno NOTABLE BUILDING
(Trujano s/n, Plaza de la Constitución; ☺9am-5pm Mon-Fri) **FREE** A 19th-century wonder of marble and murals, the State Government Palace occupies the Zócalo's southern flank. The large, very detailed stairway mural (1980), by Arturo García Bustos, depicts famous Oaxacans and Oaxacan history, including Benito Juárez, his wife Margarita Maza, José María Morelos, Porfirio Díaz, Vicente Guerrero (being shot at Cuilapan) and the 17th-century nun and love poet Juana Inés de la Cruz.

Museo de Arte Contemporáneo de Oaxaca MUSEUM
(MACO; ☎951-514-22-28; www.museomaco.org; Alcalá 202; M$20; ☺10:30am-8pm Wed-Mon) Exhibitions of first-rate contemporary Mexican and international art in a beautifully revamped colonial house.

Museo de Sitio Casa de Juárez MUSEUM
(☎951-516-18-60; www.museocasajuarez.blogspot. com.es; García Vigil 609; M$55; ☺10am-7pm Tue-Sun) The simple house of bookbinder Antonio Salanueva, who supported the great 19th-century Mexican leader Benito Juárez during his youth, is now an interesting little museum. The binding workshop is preserved, along with Benito memorabilia and period artifacts.

Xochimilco Aqueduct LANDMARK
(Callejón Rufino Tamayo) Wander northwest of the historical core and you'll ultimately encounter this arched aqueduct rendered in typical green cantera stone that runs the length of Callejón Rufino Tamayo. Built between 1727 and 1751, it was designed to bring fresh drinking water from the hillsides of Cerro de San Felipe into downtown. It served its purpose until 1940, when it was replaced by a more modern if less architecturally elegant system.

Cerro del Fortín HILL
Oaxaca's sentinel hill with stairs, statues, a park and – of course – views makes a robust early-morning run or walk. It starts on Calle Crespo at the bottom of the Escaleras del Fortín, a wide stairway busy every morning with exercising locals. Duck under the

muraled underpass at the top and you'll be at the foot of the Auditorio Guelaguetza (p449), beside which stands a noble **statue of Benito Juárez** admiring a fine view of the city that helped shape him.

Further up, a road leads to a planetarium, a space observatory and, beyond that, a Christian cross. The upper reaches of the hill are best avoided at dusk and after dark.

Museo Textil de Oaxaca MUSEUM
(☎951-501-11-04; www.museotextildeoaxaca.org. mx; Hidalgo 917; ☺10am-8pm Mon-Sat, to 6pm Sun) **FREE** This textile museum promotes Oaxaca's traditional textile crafts through exhibitions, workshops, films, presentations and a library. Themed selections from its stock of around 10,500 Oaxacan and international textile pieces, many of them a century or more old, are always on view. There's a top-quality crafts shop here too.

One-hour guided visits are given at 5pm on Wednesday, in English and/or Spanish.

🏃 Activities

★Tierraventura OUTDOORS
(☎951-390-84-09; www.tierraventura.com; División Oriente 129; day trips per person M$1400-2000; ☺10am-2pm & 4-6pm Mon-Fri) 🖉 Tierraventura, set up by a Swiss-German couple in 1999, is the antidote to the rest of the tour-guide pack, offering trips to places few others think to tread. Local guides accompany travelers wherever possible.

Options include hiking in the Sierra Norte, trips to Santiago Apoala, and some truly off-the-beaten-track destinations such as Santiago Quiotepec in the dramatic La Cañada area (where you'll see a rarely visited Zapotec fort, Mexico's last military macaws and some amazing cardón cacti), or the northern village of Santo Domingo Cacalotepec, where lauded coffee and everything else is grown organically and you'll swim beneath waterfalls and hike through ancient high-altitude rainforest.

Expediciones Sierra Norte OUTDOORS
(☎951-514-82-71; www.sierranorte.org.mx; Bravo 210A; ☺9am-7:30pm Mon-Fri, to 2pm Sat) 🖉 Some of Oaxaca's most exhilarating outdoor experiences are to be had among the mountain villages of the Pueblos Mancomunados, where this community-run outfit maintains a network of good trails, comfortable *cabañas* (cabins), guide services, and horse and bike rentals. This city office has copious information (including a guide map; M$50),

some English-speaking staff, and can make reservations for all services.

Mundo Ceiba
CYCLING

(☑ cell 951-1920419; www.mundoceiba.org; Berriozábal 109; bike/tandem rentals per day M$100/200; ⊙ 8am-11pm) Oaxaca's bike hub inhabits a large garage with an onsite cafe and is instrumental in organizing the Paseos Nocturnos en Bicicleta, a free communal bike ride that heads out four evenings a week into the cobbled streets of downtown. Rental bikes and tandems for this or any other necessity are available.

Horseback Mexico
HORSEBACK RIDING

(Rancho Pitaya; ☑ cell 951-1997026; www.horsebackmexico.com; Murguía 403; rides per person from US$85; ⊙ 11am-6pm Sun-Fri) This experienced, enthusiastic Canadian–American-run outfit offers equestrian adventures for all levels from beginners up: two-hour rides on Arabian and Mexican Criollo horses in the countryside around their ranch at Rojas de Cuauhtémoc, 15km east of the city. Rates include round-trip transportation from Oaxaca.

Courses

Language Classes

Oaxaca has numerous good, professional language schools, all offering small-group instruction at varied levels and most emphasizing spoken language. At most schools you can start any Monday (at some you can start any day). Most also offer individual tuition if wanted, plus volunteer opportunities and optional activities like dance or cooking classes, trips and *intercambios* (meetings with locals for conversation). If you're looking for some social life with other students, the bigger schools are best. Enrollment/registration fees, textbooks and materials are extra costs at some schools.

Schools can arrange accommodations with families or in hotels, apartments or their own student houses. Homestays with a private room typically cost around US$20/25/28 a day with one/two/three meals.

★ Ollin Tlahtoalli
LANGUAGE

(☑ 951-514-55-62; www.ollinoaxaca.org.mx; Ocampo 710; 15/20hr per week from US$150/186) Not just a mere language school, Ollin can teach you far more than how to conjugate Spanish verbs. It also offers Mixtec and Zapotec language classes and content courses on the Mexican Revolution, Latin American economics, Mexican literature and

up-to-the-minute street art. Email or call in to discuss your individual needs. They're extremely flexible.

Instituto Cultural Oaxaca
LANGUAGE

(ICO; ☑ 951-515-34-04; www.icomexico.com; Juárez 909; 15/20/40hr per week US$155/175/195; ☻) A large, long-established school with a professional approach and ample gardens where some of the classes take place. The 40-hours-a-week main program includes eight hours of cultural workshops (dance, cooking, arts, crafts and more) and four hours' *intercambio*. You can study for any period from one week up.

Courses in medical and business Spanish, and for children and teachers, are also offered.

Becari Language School (Bravo)
LANGUAGE

(☑ 951-514-60-76; www.becari.com.mx; Bravo 210; 15/20/30hr per week US$150/200/300; ☻) The Bravo branch of the highly rated, medium-sized Becari Language School. Group sizes range from one to five, and optional extras include salsa, wood carving, weaving and cooking. It also offers special courses such as Zapotec language and Spanish for children. There's another branch at **Gómez Farías** (☑ 951-503-84-48; Gómez Farías 118; ☻).

Spanish Immersion School
LANGUAGE

(☑ cell 951-1964567; www.spanishschoolinmexico.com; Matamoros 502; 15/20/25hr per week US$225/300/375) This school employs the novel method of giving one-on-one classes in cafes, parks, libraries, homestays or on the move while visiting markets, museums and galleries. They're very flexible: you can study from three to eight hours daily, for as long as you like, or even just take a teacher for a day's excursion.

Cooking Classes

Oaxaca has its own memorable take on Mexican cuisine, based on its famous seven *mole* sauces (p454), ancient culinary traditions and unforgettable flavor combinations. Numerous cooks regularly impart their secrets to visitors – in classes that are (or can be) held in English, and include market visits to buy ingredients and a meal to enjoy the fruits of your work!

Casa de los Sabores
COOKING

(☑ 951-516-66-68; www.casadelossabores.com; La Olla, Reforma 402; per person US$85) Pilar Cabrera, owner of the excellent La Olla (p454), gives classes most Wednesday and Friday mornings. Participants prepare and eat one of 17 varied lunch menus. Make inquiries and reservations at La Olla; participants meet there at 9:30am and are delivered back at around 2:30pm after a market visit and the class and lunch at Pilar's house.

Alma de Mi Tierra COOKING

(🖉951-513-92-11; www.almademitierra.net; Aldama 205, Barrio Jalatlaco; per person US$75-95) Nora Valencia, from a family of celebrated Oaxacan cooks (her parents run La Casa de Mis Recuerdos, p452), conducts five-hour morning classes at her home in quaint Barrio Jalatlaco; 48 hours' notice is needed.

🖝 Tours

The abundance of heavyweight sights surrounding Oaxaca make it an ideal base for guided tours. Such trips can save transportation hassles, be a lot of fun and tell you more than you might otherwise learn. An affordable option for a small-group day trip can be booked directly through travel agency **Turismo El Convento** (🖉951-516-18-06; www.oaxacatours.mx; Quinta Real, Calle 5 de Mayo 300; tours M$450-990; ⊙8:30am-7pm Mon-Sat, 9am-2pm Sun), which offers excursions to outlying towns that cost anywhere between M$450 to M$990 per person. Admission fees and meals are usually extra.

Zapotrek HIKING, CYCLING

(🖉951-502-59-57, cell 951-2577712; www.zapotrek.com; Xólotl 110B; tours per person US$110-150; ⊙9am-2pm & 4-7pm Mon-Sat) 🖉 Zapotrek specializes in hiking, biking and driving trips amid indigenous Zapotec villages and

their often-spectacular countryside with the help of local guides and experts. The outings open windows on Zapotec culture and usually include meals in villagers' homes. It's run by English-fluent Eric Ramírez, a native of nearby Tlacolula.

Traditions Mexico CULTURAL

(🖉cell 951-2262742; www.traditionsmexico.com; day tours per person US$85-119; 🚺) These expertly guided trips yield insights into Oaxacan crafts, food, festivals and culture that few tours match, getting off the beaten track into artisans' workshops and locals' kitchens for hands-on encounters with indigenous Zapotec culture. Eight-hour day trips explore a different facet of Zapotec life each day.

Fundación En Vía CULTURAL

(🖉951-515-24-24; www.envia.org; Instituto Cultural Oaxaca, Juárez 909; tour per person M$850; ⊙tours 1pm Thu & 9am Sat) 🖉 Run out of the Instituto Cultural Oaxaca (p447), nonprofit organization En Vía provides financial aid to small groups of village women to help them develop small businesses. The program's funded by En Vía's unique six-hour tours, which take you into the women's houses for lunch and explanations of the local crafts and economy, providing a rare close-up look at village life.

Bicicletas Pedro Martínez CYCLING, HIKING

(🖉951-514-59-35, cell 951-1844506; www.bicicletaspedromartinez.com; Aldama 418; half-/full-day tours from M$1500/1800; ⊙9am-8pm Mon-Sat, 10am-3pm Sun) 🖉 This friendly team headed by Mexican Olympic cyclist Pedro Martínez offers mostly off-road rides (and some great day walks) amid some of Oaxaca state's best

---

DON'T MISS

NIGHTTIME BIKE RIDES

Oaxaca is a famously attractive city and its beauty can be fully appreciated at night when the city-center traffic subsides. Mundo Ceiba (p447), a bike-rental shop responsible for organizing regular communal bike rides designed to cut pollution and push alternative means of transportation, organizes the so-called **Paseos Nocturnos en Bicicleta**, which began in 2008 as a once-a-week jaunt around Oaxaca's cobbled core. The outing quickly became so popular with both locals and tourists that they now run four times a week on Wednesday, Friday, Saturday and Sunday. Cyclists meet at 9pm on Calle Alcalá outside the Templo de Santo Domingo (p440). The ride, which is leisurely and highly sociable, runs for 1½ hours and covers 8km. A customized tricycle pedals at the front playing galvanizing music and looking out for errant drivers. On special days and festivals, riders have been known to don fancy dress. There isn't a better way to see after-dark Oaxaca while communing with the locals.

Bikes for the ride can be rented beforehand at Mundo Ceiba, a couple of blocks from the starting point.

scenery. Van support cuts out the less interesting bits and hardest climbs. A popular option is the full-day La Culebra–Las Salinas ride, which includes stops for sampling mezcal and swimming in a river.

✥ Festivals & Events

★ Guelaguetza   DANCE
(⊘10am & 5pm, last 2 Mon of Jul) The Guelaguetza is a brilliant feast of Oaxacan folk dance staged on the first two Mondays after July 16 in the large, semi-open-air **Auditorio Guelaguetza** (Carretera Panamericano) on Cerro del Fortín. Magnificently costumed dancers from the seven regions of Oaxaca state perform a succession of dignified, lively or comical traditional dances, tossing offerings of produce to the crowd as they finish.

Excitement climaxes with the incredibly colorful pineapple dance by women of the Papaloapan region, and the stately Zapotec Danza de las Plumas (Feather Dance), which symbolically reenacts the Spanish conquest.

The auditorium holds around 11,000 people; tickets for the front sections of seating (A and B, together holding about 5000 people) for each show go on sale about two months ahead through the state tourism office, Sectur (p459), and at www.super boletos.com for M$850 to M$1175. The remaining 6000 or so seats (sections C and D) are free and first come, first served.

The event takes place at 10am and 5pm on each of the Mondays, lasting about three hours. The dates vary only when July 18, the anniversary of Benito Juárez' death, falls on a Monday. Guelaguetza then happens on July 25 and August 1.

The Guelaguetza period also sees many other colorful celebrations in Oaxaca, including concerts, exhibitions, a mezcal fair in Centro Cultural y de Convenciones and fantastically festive Saturday-afternoon parades along Calle Alcalá. Thousands of people flock into the city for the festivities (including visiting pickpockets, so stay alert).

Smaller Guelaguetzas are held in outlying towns and villages, such as Zaachila, Tlacolula, Atzompa, Mitla, Tlacochahuaya and San Agustín Etla, and even Tututepec down near the Oaxaca coast, usually on the same days, and can make a refreshing change from what might seem the overcommercialized hubbub of Oaxaca.

The Guelaguetza celebrations have their origins in a colonial-era fusion of indigenous festivities with Christian celebrations for the Virgen del Carmen. The current format dates to 1932.

Día de Muertos   TRADITIONAL
(⊘Oct 31-Nov 2) Oaxaca's Día de Muertos (Day of the Dead) celebrations are among Mexico's most vibrant, with concerts, exhibitions and other special goings-on starting days beforehand. Homes, cemeteries and some public buildings are decorated with fantastic *altares de muertos* (altars of the dead); streets and plazas are decked with *tapetes de arena* (colored sand patterns and sculptures); and *comparsas* (satirical fancy-dress groups) parade the streets.

Oaxaca FilmFest   FILM
(www.oaxacafilmfest.com; ⊘Oct) Growing bigger with each year, the Oaxaca FilmFest presents a weeklong program of independent films from Mexico and around the world in the first half of October. All showings are in their original language with subtitles in Spanish, English or both.

🛏 Sleeping

Oaxaca is a dreamland of beautiful non-franchise accommodations loaded with authentic local charm. There's a good stash of cheap but well-kept hostels in interesting old houses, some brilliant B&Bs, an extravagant array of boutique hotels and plenty of evocative historic nooks. 'Spoiled for choice' would be a huge understatement.

Most places raise rates around four main festivals: Semana Santa, Guelaguetza, Día de Muertos and Christmas to New Year's Eve.

★ Casa Ángel   HOSTEL $
(☑951-514-22-24; www.casaangelhostel.com; Tinoco y Palacios 610; dm M$260-500, d M$1000-1200, d without bathroom M$800, all incl breakfast; ✳ @ 🛜) Deservedly popular, this 'boutique' hostel is run by a friendly, helpful young team and kept scrupulously clean. Rooms are thoughtfully designed and the bright common areas include a good kitchen, a plasma screen with Netflix, and a great roof terrace with a barbecue every Sunday.

Some of the 'superior' dorms have their own little terraces, and the standard dorms (two of them women only) have good solid bunks with private reading lights. The newer 'deluxe' dorms are capsule-style, with curtained, comfy, wood-paneled bunks equipped with their own air-con, electrical plugs and USB chargers. There's plenty of local info on offer too.

Hostal de las Américas   HOSTEL $

(☑ 951-514-13-53; www.hostaldelasamericas.mx; Porfirio Díaz 300; dm/r incl breakfast M$220/600; ✱ 🛜) In a recently renovated city-center house, this hotel-standard hostel has seven separate-sex dorms, each with its own bathroom. Every bunk has its own reading light and electrical plug. There are three private rooms too, plus a roof terrace, filtered drinking water and a well-equipped kitchen. It's kept impeccably clean and adds up to a sound budget choice.

Azul Cielo   HOSTEL $

(☑ 951-205-35-64; www.azulcielohostel.com; Arteaga 608; dm M$170-180, d M$620, all incl breakfast; @🛜) This backpacker's favorite is a cross between a hostel and a B&B. A sunny garden that generates the comfy atmosphere of a private home lies at its heart. A semi-open lounge area sits at one end, along with three dorms and a modern kitchen. The eight brightly decorated private rooms at the other end have murals, fans and wooden furniture.

Free bikes (two hours a day) and cooked breakfasts add to the appeal.

Posada Don Mario   INN $

(☑ 951-514-20-12; www.facebook.com/posadadonmario; Cosijopí 219; d incl breakfast M$900, without bathroom M$700; 🛜) Cute, cheerful and friendly, this colorful courtyard inn has an intimate feel, with neat, brightly decorated rooms – the five up on the roof terrace being particularly appealing. There's free drinking water, and helpful services include bookings for cooking classes, tours and transportation to the coast.

La Villada Inn   INN $

(☑ 951-518-62-17; www.facebook.com/lavillada.hostel; Felipe Ángeles 204, Ejido Guadalupe Victoria; dm/s/d/q US$350/380/625/900; 🅿@🛜♨🛜) Though it's set on the city's far northern edge, La Villada is preferred by some people for its good facilities, helpful English-speaking staff, spacious, relatively tranquil premises and rural views. The mostly adobe-built rooms have good Mexican furniture, and there's a reasonably priced cafe, plus an excellent swimming pool, bar, yoga room, tour service and hammocks.

If you call ahead, or from the bus station, they'll send a taxi to pick you up for M$70. It's 5.5km north of the Zócalo.

★ La Betulia   B&B $$

(☑ 951-514-00-29; www.labetulia.com; Cabrera Carrasquedo 102; d/apt incl breakfast US$82/145; 🅿🛜) There's good service and then there's the Betulia, an eight-room B&B with a pretty walled patio where the owners sit and mingle with guests over breakfast as if they were old amigos. Nothing is too much trouble here, be it offering tips about the best local places for live music or satisfying special requests for breakfast (which changes daily).

The rooms are simple but highly contemporary, rendered with the kind of underlying artiness that Mexico – and, in particular, Oaxaca – seems to excel in. If available, the two-bedroom apartment upstairs is a steal.

Hotel La Casa de María   BOUTIQUE HOTEL $$

(☑ 951-514-43-13; www.lacasademaria.com.mx; Juárez 103; s M$750, d M$990-1245; ✱🛜) A subtle boutique hotel with an interior mix of virgin white splashed with sharp color accents and the odd Frida Kahlo–esque painting or drawing. Bonuses, aside from the surgically clean rooms, are a bright patio, roof deck, small attached restaurant (with room service available) and beyond-the-call-of-duty staff. This being Oaxaca, they also serve fabulous coffee.

Hotel Casa del Sótano   HOTEL $$

(☑ 951-516-24-94; www.hoteldelsotano.com.mx; Tinoco y Palacios 414; s/d M$1190/1290; 🛜) Set off by a small but beautiful plant-filled courtyard and topped by a sunset-viewing terrace, this bargain-for-what-you-get hotel is one of the city's best deals, with attractive, spotless rooms that are pleasantly old rather than 'olde.' Enjoy the sturdy beds, traditional furniture and punctuations of antique art. There's a fine cafe onsite.

Hotel Las Golondrinas   HOTEL $$

(☑ 951-514-20-95; www.lasgolondrinasoaxaca.com; Tinoco y Palacios 411; d/tr incl breakfast M$1270/1370; ✱🛜) A profusion of plants of all types fills the three patios that beautify this excellent-value small hotel, which is worth the price for the gardens alone. The rooms are a little more prosaic but immaculately clean, and fruity breakfasts served in one of the patios are well worth climbing out of your hammock for.

El Diablo y la Sandía   B&B $$

(☑ 951-514-40-95; www.eldiabloylasandia.com; Libres 205; s/d incl breakfast US$80/90; ⊖🛜) Is there any better place in the world to enjoy breakfast than Oaxaca? After a few days at the 'Devil and the Watermelon' B&B, you'll answer 'probably not.' There are six rooms painted lily white in these wonderful accommodations. All are punc-

LAPIZTOLA & THE RISE OF STREET ART

Following a path first blazed by Mexican muralists Diego Rivera and José Clemente Orozco in the 1930s and '40s, Oaxaca's modern street artists have captured a global audience in recent years with provocative exhibitions in places as diverse as Brazil, Sweden, the UK and Cuba.

The street-art renaissance can be traced back to a series of mass protests in 2006, when a teachers' strike in the state capital turned violent, resulting in over a dozen deaths. Against this backdrop of volatility and political turmoil, angry art collectives began to take shape using their graphic stencils as a form of political protest.

Sitting at the forefront of the movement, **Lapiztola** (www.lapiztola.tumblr.com) is an art collective, pioneered by creative luminaries Rosario Martínez and Roberto Vega, and whose name is a clever juxtaposition of the words *lápiz* (pencil) and *pistola* (pistol). Never shy to comment graphically on the 2006 protests and their aftermath, the artists have been quoted as describing their vivid if often ephemeral art as 'a shout on a wall.'

While philosophically anchored in the traditions of Mexican muralism, Lapiztola's work stylistically owes more to the satirical graffiti of artists such as Banksy in the UK and Blek le Rat in France. Working under the radar, they copy their stencils guerrilla-style onto walls and buildings around the city using politically tinged graffiti to highlight the injustices in contemporary Mexico, be it drug wars, environmental degradation, migrant issues or the trials of innocent youth. Some decry it as vandalism; others see it as part of a vast public gallery that has been instrumental in shaping ideas and pushing debate.

Like it or not, Oaxaca's street art continues to highlight the dichotomies that exist in the city today: an attractive Unesco World Heritage site on one hand, yet a place where divisive political issues fester beneath the surface on the other. Not surprisingly, Lapiztola is just the point of the pencil. Other important art collectives include **Asaro** (Asamblea de Artistas Revolucionarios de Oaxaca, p444) and **Yescka** (www.guerilla-art.mx), while plenty more small independent galleries plying prints, pop art and T-shirts lie scattered around the city.

tuated with very Mexican color accents and sprinkled with original Oaxacan *artesanías* (crafts).

Hotel Casa Conzatti
HOTEL $$

(☏951-513-85-00;   www.casaconzatti.com.mx; Gómez Farías 218; r M$1460-1780; ☒☎) An understated but good-value hotel (named after an Italian botanist) that is located opposite a quiet park about a 10-minute walk from the city-center action. Rooms are well equipped with coffee machines and regularly replenished toiletries. Onsite is a thoroughly decent restaurant where you can enjoy breakfast, lunch or dinner. A rooftop terrace adds extra sparkle.

Hotel Las Mariposas
HOTEL $$

(☏951-515-58-54;   www.lasmariposas.com.mx; Suárez 517; r M$850-950; ☎) ✿ The fan-cooled rooms and studios with kitchens at this solar-powered hotel surround two tranquil plant-filled patios with a book exchange and dining area where complimentary coffee and sweet bread are served in the morning. The tile-floor rooms are kept

impeccably clean and jazzed up a bit with local art and crafts.

Hotel Azucenas
HOTEL $$

(☏951-514-79-18; www.hotelazucenas.com; Aranda 203; s/d M$850/900; ☎) Painted in the warm colors of a Mexican sunset, the Azucenas is a small, friendly, well-run hotel in a beautifully restored century-old house. The 10 rooms have ample bathrooms and a continental buffet breakfast (M$60) is served on the panoramic roof terrace.

Casa Adobe
B&B $$

(☏951-517-72-68;   www.casaadobe-bandb.com; Independencia 801, Tlalixtac de Cabrera; s/d incl breakfast US$56/59, apt US$50-52; ☎) On a quiet lane in the village of Tlalixtac de Cabrera, 8km east of the city, this is a charming retreat full of lovely art and crafts, and a good base for visits to the city and exploring outlying areas. Breakfast is served in the verdant little patio, and there's a nice roof terrace and cozy sitting room.

The amiable owners will pick you up on arrival in Oaxaca and offer free rides to town in the mornings. They'll also tell you about good restaurants locally. Minimum stay is two nights for the three rooms, and three nights for the two apartments.

★ Casa de las Bugambilias
B&B $$$

(☎951-516-11-65, USA & Canada 866-829-6778; www.lasbugambilias.com; Reforma 402; s US$80-130, d US$90-135, all incl breakfast; ❋🛜) 🖉 The 10 rooms, all named after flowers, are works of art (equipped with beds embellished with wood-carved or hand-painted headboards); breakfast, with organic/fair-trade ingredients, will have you thinking that Mexico is the best place in the world to wake up; and it's all stitched together by above-and-beyond service at this fabulous B&B.

Some rooms have little balconies. We really like the 'Violeta' room. Gorgeous little decor details leave you in no doubt that you're in the cultural heart of Mexico.

La Casona de Tita
HERITAGE HOTEL $$$

(☎951-516-14-00; www.lacasonadetitaoaxaca.com; García Vigil 805; r incl breakfast M$4235-5500; ❋🛜) Would you like the room with the 18th-century wrought-iron headboard, or one with a precious 16th-century wardrobe, or perhaps the one with the beautiful Filipino chest brought to Mexico in a Chinese boat during the colonial era? The Tita is one of Oaxaca's most exquisite and exclusive digs, with six huge rooms decorated with a mix of antiques and modernity.

And if you grow attached to that fabulous modern painting hung up in your room, you can take it home with you when you leave – for a price.

Quinta Real Oaxaca
HISTORIC HOTEL $$$

(☎951-501-61-00; www.quintareal.com; 5 de Mayo 300; r from M$4500; ❋🛜) As far as historic colonial hotels go, the Quinta is a five star among the five stars. The place is literally dripping with attention-grabbing details, from the multiple green patios to the knightly Don Quixote–esque decor. Built in the 16th century as a convent, in 1970 the Quinta was the first religious building in Mexico to become a hotel.

The old chapel is a banquet hall, one of the five palatial courtyards contains a swimming pool and sturdy thick stone walls help to keep the place cool. The 91 rooms are sympathetically rendered in colonial styles, with high ceilings, though the ordinary (nonmaster) suites are modestly sized. If you start to feel claustrophobic, walk the colonial corridors with the ghosts of conquistadors past.

La Casa de Mis Recuerdos
B&B $$$

(☎951-513-90-78; www.lacasademisrecuerdos. com; Pino Suárez 508; d incl breakfast US$95-110, without bathroom US$70-80; ❋🛜) A marvelous decorative aesthetic prevails throughout this welcoming guesthouse, with old-style tiles, mirrors, masks and all sorts of other Mexican art and crafts adorning the rooms and halls. The best rooms overlook a fragrant central patio, and the Oaxacan breakfast (one of numerous highlights) is served in a beautiful dining room. There's a three-night minimum at some peak periods.

Family member Nora Valencia gives cooking classes at Alma de Mi Tierra (p448).

Casa Oaxaca
BOUTIQUE HOTEL $$$

(☎951-514-41-73; www.casaoaxaca.com.mx; García Vigil 407; r/ste incl breakfast from M$4235/5456; P🛜@🛜🛜) Huge rooms, luxury pool, arty food and contemporary-meets-colonial courtyard in a converted 18th-century colonial mansion. What more could you want? Fabulous service? They have that too, along with art exhibits, an excellent little patio restaurant, mezcal tastings and cooking classes with the chefs. No kids under 12.

Ollin Bed & Breakfast
B&B $$$

(☎951-514-91-26; www.oaxacabedandbreakfast. com; Quintana Roo 213; r incl breakfast US$95-130; ❋@🛜🛜) The Ollin has most of those wonderful Oaxacan calling cards: characterful rooms imbued with a tangible Mexican flavor, gourmet breakfasts, hands-on staff, and color and interest in every corner. Raising the yardstick even higher is the courtyard swimming pool, big roof terrace and lovely Oaxacan handicrafts sprinkled around. All that and they keep the room prices pretty reasonable.

✗ Eating

Surely one of the world's great food cities, Oaxaca is a gastronomic powerhouse full of fabulous creative restaurants, big-name chefs, cooking schools and curious local dishes (grasshoppers anyone?). You can eat grandly or cheaply any night of the week without complaint. The selection is dizzying.

★ Boulenc Pan Artesano
BAKERY, CAFE $

(☎951-351-36-48; www.boulenc.com; Porfirio Díaz 207; sandwiches M$54-110, pizzas M$60-135; ⏱8:30am-11pm Mon-Sat; 🛜) Oaxaca's best bakery comes with a trendy cafe next door where the most popular dish is – guess what? – avocado toast. Guys with beards or girls in Doc Martens serve you excellent coffee in terracotta mugs and cakes of your choice (peruse the bakery case first) in a patio with terrace seating upstairs.

Impossibly addictive are the almond croissants, sourdough pizzas and the *shak-shouka* (poached eggs in a tangy tomato sauce).

Lechoncito de Oro   STREET FOOD $

(cnr Libres & Murguía; tacos/tortas M$15/40; ☺8pm-5am Mon-Sat) You'll usually see a long row of cars double-parked on the street beside this popular late-night stall known for its *tacos de lechón con chicharrón* (tender pork tacos topped with crispy pork rinds and spicy green salsa). It's pure artery-choking joy.

Tlayudas El Negro   OAXACAN $

(✆951-227-10-29; www.facebook.com/tlayudas negrooax; Guerrero 1029; tlayudas M$59-129; ☺1pm-1am) Ask where to get the best *tlayudas* in town and locals will often point you in the direction of El Negro, where large grilled tortillas are filled with refried beans, cheese, lettuce and topped with optional beef, sausage or shrimp. El Negro has six locations but we like the atmospheric smoke-filled patio of the original Calle Guerrero joint.

Tamales de San Agustín Yatareni   STREET FOOD $

(cnr Armenta y López & Colón; tamales M$15-30; ☺2:30-7:30pm Tue-Sat) Find out why *oaxaqueños* queue up to buy these large *tamales* filled with ingredients such as squash blossom, chicken in salsa verde, *mole* and *chapulines* (grasshoppers). Takeout only.

Gourmand   EUROPEAN $

(✆951-516-44-35; www.facebook.com/gourmand delicatessen; Porfirio Díaz 410A; dishes M$55-110; ☺9am-1am Mon-Sat; ☎🖱) Like a cross between a deli and a tapas bar, Gourmand does baguettes and deli sandwiches with roast beef, hummus or turkey breast, *tablas* (boards) of cold meats and cheeses, homemade sausages with mustard, assorted burgers (including veggie) and good breakfast options including eggs Benedict.

Big bonus – you can order craft beers in from the adjoining nano-brewery, La Santísima Flor de Lúpulo (p456).

Jaguar Yuú   CAFE $

(✆951-526-36-18; www.facebook.com/cafejaguar yuu; Murguía 202; breakfasts & light dishes M$65-130; ☺8am-11pm Mon-Thu, to 2am Fri & Sat; ☎🖱) The best coffee in Oaxaca comes from the mountains overlooking the Pacific and is served in this quietly hip but unmistakably Mexican cafe that also does a fine line in smoothies, baguettes, crepes, waffles and other appetite satisfiers. Jaguar Yuú pronounced in Spanish sounds similar to 'How are you' in English.

Fonda Florecita   MARKET $

(✆951-513-53-64; Nicolás del Puerto, Mercado de la Merced; mains M$35-75; ☺7:30am-5pm Wed-Mon) A popular local haunt for more than 50 years, *this* is the classic Oaxaca market-food experience. There's no printed menu, so you might try the *salsa de queso* (cheese in a spicy tomato-based sauce) with a chocolate *atole* (a sweet-corn-based drink). Nothing fancy here, just good cheap grub served on long, shared tables.

Mercado 20 de Noviembre   MARKET $

(20 de Noviembre 512; dishes M$25-70; ☺7am-9pm) Looking for cheap street food? Look no further. Dozens of good, clean *comedores* (food stalls) fill this large market where wait staff will thrust menus to within an inch of your nose as you stroll past.

The biggest treat for carnivores is the smoky Pasillo de Carnes Asadas (Grilled Meat Passage) on the east side, where a dozen stands specialize in grilling *tasajo* (beef) or *cecina* enchilada (slices of chili-coated pork) over hot coals.

El Destilado   FUSION $$

(✆951-516-22-26; www.eldestilado.com; 5 de Mayo 409; mains M$150-300, tasting menu M$900; ☺5-11pm Tue-Sat; ☎) Belly up to the bar here and order a Mexican corn whiskey, a small-batch mezcal or one of the innovative cocktails. Or simply go for a local craft beer, which pairs nicely with the outstanding tempura fish tacos topped with roasted pineapple and tamarind salsa. You can also delve into a six-course tasting menu featuring creative Mexican and international dishes.

Destilado's rooftop terrace serves tacos and *tostadas* from Thursday to Sunday.

Zandunga   OAXACAN $$

(✆951-516-22-65; www.zandungasabor.com; García Vigil 512E; mains M$90-240; ☺1-11pm Mon-Sat, to 10pm Sun; ☎) The Isthmus of Tehuantepec has its own take on Oaxacan cuisine based on ingredients like tropical fruits and seafood, with many dishes cooked in banana leaves. Festive Zandunga brings those flavors to Oaxaca, and the *botana zandunga* (a sampler of dishes that easily serves two) is perfect for whiling away a couple of hours with some of its many mezcals.

La Popular   MEXICAN $$
(www.facebook.com/lapopularoaxaca; García Vigil 519; dishes M$75-200; ⊘9:30am-11:30pm Tue-Sat, from 2:30pm Sun & Mon; 🛜🍽️) Cheap, quick, boisterous and – as the name implies – popular, this little corner restaurant with a sideline as an art gallery does a variety of interesting *antojitos* (Mexican snacks) and other more substantial Oaxacan and Mexican dishes. Trendy it isn't, which could be something of a relief if you've been overdosing in Oaxaca's rash of hip new *mezcalerías* (mezcal bars).

The soft tacos are good. The mushrooms in garlic are even better. Arrive early. 'Tis busy.

La Olla   OAXACAN $$
(📋951-516-66-68; www.laolla.com.mx; Reforma 402; mains M$75-210, menú del día M$150; ⊘noon-10pm Mon-Sat; 🛜🍽️) La Olla (the cooking pot) is very much its own invention. It's not a trying-too-hard bohemian cafe, or a fancy fusion restaurant or a purveyor of nouveau cuisine. It's just, for want of a better word, good – very good, in fact. One day, they'll be serving international dishes; another day,

street food; another, whatever's on sale at the local market.

You can take stock of it all in the slick ground-floor restaurant, but far more attractive views await upstairs on the roof terrace where the guacamole, *moles* and tortillas seem to taste so much better.

La Biznaga   OAXACAN, FUSION $$
(📋951-516-18-00; García Vigil 512; mains M$110-260; ⊘10am-10pm Mon-Thu, to 11pm Fri & Sat, 1-10pm Sun; 🛜) Locals and visitors alike jam the large colonial courtyard for well-rendered nouveau-Oaxacan fusion dishes. The choices are chalked on blackboards: you might start with the *sopa del establo* (a creamy Roquefort and *chipotle* chili soup), follow up with turkey breast in a blackberry *mole negro*, and finish with the delectable chocolate mousse and guava.

Tastavins   MEDITERRANEAN $$
(📋951-514-37-76; www.facebook.com/tastavins oficial; Murguía 309; dishes M$50-165; ⊘1pm-midnight Mon-Sat; 🛜🍽️) The best Oaxaca tapas experience supported by some small Italy-worthy pasta, all served on typically Mexican ceramics, can be found in the pleasantly cramped confines of Tastavins (seven tables and three or four barstools,

---

HOLY *MOLE*

Oaxaca's multicolored *moles* ('moh-les'; nut-, chili- and spice-based sauces) are its culinary signature. To Mexicans, the meat these sauces are served over is secondary in importance to the *mole* itself. Oaxaca's most famous variety, *mole negro* (black *mole*), is a smoky, savory delight bearing a hint of chocolate. It's the most complex and labor-intensive to create, though its popularity ensures that it's easy to find. While in Oaxaca, seek out the other colors of the *mole* family.

Mole amarillo A savory *mole* using a base of tomatillo (a small, husked tomato-like fruit), spiced with cumin, cloves, cilantro and hierba santa (Mexican pepperleaf), and often served over beef. To the untutored eye, it's more red than *amarillo* (yellow).

Mole verde A lovely, delicate sauce thickened with corn dough and including tomatillos, pumpkin seeds, the herbs *epazote* and hierba santa, and different nuts such as walnuts and almonds. Often served with chicken.

Mole colorado A forceful *mole* based on *ancho, pasilla* and *cascabel* chilies, black pepper and cinnamon.

Mole coloradito (or mole rojo) This tangy, tomato-based blend might remind gringos of their neighborhood Mexican joint back home; it is exported in dumbed-down form as enchilada sauce.

Mancha manteles The brick-red 'tablecloth stainer' has a deep, woody flavor, often used to complement tropical fruit.

Chíchilo negro A rare *mole* whose defining ingredients include *chilhuacle negro, mulato* and *pasilla* chilies, avocado leaves (which give a touch of anise flavor), tomatoes and corn dough.

all usually taken by around 8pm). They also ply fine Latin-world wine that tastes infinitely better with a plate of cheese and cured meat.

Xuncu Choco OAXACAN $$
(☑951-351-48-08; www.facebook.com/xuncuchoco; Matamoros 302; mains M$80-150, menú del día M$70; ⊗8am-10pm Mon-Sat, 9am-5pm Sun; 🐀) What wonderful treats emerge from this small place specializing in cuisine from the Isthmus of Tehuantepec. Regional dishes include *pescadillas* (fish quesadillas) or *camarones nanixhe* (spicy sautéed shrimp). It also does a rich variety of breakfast omelettes, organic coffee and an affordable three-course *menú del día* (set menu) from 2pm to 6pm, Monday to Friday.

★Casa Oaxaca FUSION $$$
(☑951-516-85-31; www.casaoaxacaelrestaurante. com; Constitución 104A; mains M$400-600; ⊗1-11pm Mon-Sat, to 9pm Sun; 🐀) It's not easy living up to the mantle of Oaxaca's best restaurant, but this place consistently achieves. A glamorous rooftop terrace, theatrical tableside preparation, a posh cocktail scene, and an array of ravishing dishes – seared tuna, heirloom pepper stuffed with ceviche, duck in black *mole* sauce, and grilled octopus among them. Iron your shirt and make a reservation.

★Los Danzantes FUSION $$$
(☑951-501-11-84; www.losdanzantes.com; Alcalá 403; mains M$145-410; ⊗1-10:30pm Sun-Thu, to 11pm Fri & Sat) Excellent Mexican-fusion food in a spectacular architect-designed patio makes Los Danzantes one of Oaxaca's special dining spots. The hierba santa (Mexican pepperleaf) rolled around two cheeses are a great starter, and the goat's-cheese flan with figs, chocolate and honey is a perfect dessert. In between, try a fish fillet in *mole amarillo* (yellow *mole*) or a rib-eye steak.

Restaurante Catedral INTERNATIONAL $$$
(☑951-516-32-85; www.restaurantecatedral.com. mx; García Vigil 105; mains M$185-350; ⊗8am-11pm Wed-Mon; 🐀) Perhaps Oaxaca's most refined and romantic eating choice, with sharp but nonshowy service on a patio or in a variety of interior rooms. The specialty is roast pork, but there is the usual variety of *moles* and – highlight – the multifarious of meat-heavy *plato oaxaqueña*, a platter of the town's best food bites with cheese, *chorizo*, stuffed chilies and cured meat.

Pescatarians can attempt the *pulpo a las brasas* (grilled octopus), while vegetarians can dive figuratively into the mushroom mountain soup.

Pitiona OAXACAN $$$
(☑951-514-06-90; www.pitiona.com; Allende 114; mains M$190-345, tasting menu M$1200; ⊗1-11pm Mon-Sat, to 9:30pm Sun) Food as art. Oaxacan chef José Manuel Baños, who has worked at the renowned El Bulli in Spain, takes the ingredients and flavors of his homeland to new creative heights at Pitiona. The delicious *sopa de fideos* (noodle soup) comes with floating capsules of liquid cheese, and the *tacos de lechón* (pork tacos) are deftly prepared as well.

Some dishes are so artistically presented it's a shame to eat them – but the restaurant's atmosphere is refreshingly relaxed. The 10-course tasting menu is eternally popular.

Los Pacos OAXACAN $$$
(☑951-516-17-04; www.lospacosrestaurante.mx; Abasolo 121; mains M$70-265, mole tasting menu M$280; ⊗8am-10pm; 🐀) *Moles* are the prize here and, to make things easier, a tasting menu allows you to sample all seven of the revered sauces along with tortillas for dipping. The *mole negro* with chicken rules. It also offers *tasajo* (thinly sliced grilled beef) done 15 different ways. Grab a table on the rooftop terrace.

There's another Los Pacos – older, more local and more family-oriented – in the Colonia Reforma neighborhood in the northern suburbs.

Vieja Lira ITALIAN $$$
(☑951-516-86-76; www.viejalira.com; Reforma 502; mains M$140-435; ⊗1-11pm; 🐀) Every city needs an Italian restaurant and Oaxaca has several, though few are better than the authentic and casually refined Vieja Lira with its thin-crust pizzas, al-dente pastas and inviting interior flecked with memories of Florence. The extensive wine list makes a welcome time away from mezcal and margaritas.

🍸 Drinking & Nightlife

Mezcal is the (sometimes slurred) word on most people's lips when ordering a drink in Oaxaca. This once poor man's alternative to tequila is now officially trendy, as exemplified by the city's large and growing cache of divey-hip *mezcalerías*. Craft beer is also making inroads.

Alcalá, García Vigil and nearby streets are the main party zone on Friday and Saturday nights.

Cuish
MEZCALERÍA

(☑ 951-516-87-91; www.mezcalescuish.mx; Díaz Ordaz 712; ⊙ 10am-10pm Mon-Sat, 11am-7pm Sun) ✐ Cuish is an outlet for small organic producers making mezcal from wild agaves. Here you can book mezcal tastings or just pop in and try what's available. If you want to take some mezcal back home with you, Cuish sells three-bottle sets encased in beautifully designed boxes.

★ Mezcaloteca
BAR

(☑ 951-514-00-82; www.mezcaloteca.com; Reforma 506; ⊙ 5-9pm Mon-Thu, from 11am Fri & Sat) This swanky tasting room is by far the best place in the city to visit if you want to learn about mezcal. Not only can the staff here teach you about how mezcal is made, but you will get a crash course in how to taste it and what to look for in a quality product.

Call ahead to book a tasting session. Pay based on how many mezcals you want to taste, and come prepared to ask questions. Hosts will offer you a selection from the house brands based on your tastes. They work with small-batch producers to create a number of unique, blended, wild-crafted and aged mezcals that can't be found anywhere else.

Sabina Sabe
COCKTAIL BAR

(☑ 951-514-34-94; www.facebook.com/sabinasabe oaxaca; 5 de Mayo 209; ⊙ 1pm-midnight Sun, Mon, Wed & Thu, to 1:30am Fri & Sat) An upscale mezcal bar with well-prepared cocktails such as mezcal mixed with ginger beer, Mexican pepperleaf and cucumber. For a tasty snack, try the blue-corn raviolis filled with grasshoppers, cheese and topped with a squash-blossom sauce.

Candela
CLUB

(☑ 951-351-36-41; www.facebook.com/candelaoaxac; Murguía 413; cover M$50; ⊙ 10pm-2am Thu, 8pm-3am Fri & Sat) Candela's writhing Latin bands and beautiful colonial-house setting have kept it high on the Oaxaca nightlife lists for years. Get there soon after opening for a good table. Latin dance classes are held here too.

Txalaparta
CLUB

(☑ 951-514-43-05; Matamoros 206; ⊙ noon-3am Mon-Thu, to 4am Fri & Sat, 7pm-3am Sun) Take a vague Wild West theme, the cool menace of *Reservoir Dogs* and the appeal of *cumbia*

sounds (music originating from Colombia), and you've got a rough feel for Txalaparta. This quietish hookah bar has plenty of dark nooks to hide away in by day, but morphs into a jiving hive at night with spirited DJ sets.

It mostly draws a crowd of youngsters in their 20s to mid-30s, who pile in to dance to assorted rhythms from Latin to tropical, world music, trip hop, reggae and more.

La Santísima Flor de Lúpulo
BREWERY

(☑ 951-516-44-35; www.facebook.com/lasantisima flordelupulo; Allende 215; ⊙ 10am-1am Mon-Sat; ☎) Goodbye Corona, hello Lúpulo (meaning 'hop,' as in the plant). Oaxaca's cherished nano-brewery (that's a brewery even smaller than a microbrewery) offers a constantly rotating batch of made-onsite craft beers served in a space barely large enough to swing a small kitten. For full immersion, order the three-glass taster board with a burger from deli/bakery Gourmand (p453), next door.

In Situ
MEZCALERÍA

(☑ 951-514-18-11; www.insitumezcaleria.com; Morelos 511; ⊙ 3-11pm Mon-Sat; ☎) A don't-miss stop on any mezcal trail, In Situ stocks a vast variety of artisanal mezcals, many of them unusual, and the owner is an encyclopedia of the so-called oven-cooked agave.

Los Amantes
MEZCALERÍA

(☑ 951-501-06-87; www.losamantes.com; Allende 107; ⊙ 4pm-midnight) Squeeze into this standing-room-only bar stuffed to the rafters with peculiar knickknacks for a short, sharp intro to Mexico's smokiest spirit. Friendly bar staff will explain all about the three different artisanal mezcals that they give you to taste for around M$210.

Cafébre
CAFE

(☑ cell 951-2524899; www.cafebre.com; Bravo 108; ⊙ 7:30am-10pm; ☎) ✐ This pleasant cafe offers a small lunch menu to pair with a wide selection of single-origin coffee, prepared in a variety of ways, depending on batch and preference. If you want to be able to choose between an AeroPress, French press, Chemex, espresso or moka pot, this is your place.

Mayordomo
CAFE

(☑ 951-516-16-19; www.chocolatemayordomo.com. mx; Mina 219; ⊙ 7am-9pm) A synonym for chocolate in Oaxaco, Mayordomo has numerous branches, but the best is just south of the Mercado 20 de Noviembre (p453). Walk in through the sweet-smelling grinding room

MEZCAL

When Oaxacans tell you mezcal is a *bebida espirituosa* (spirit), they're not just saying it's a distilled liquor; they're hinting at an almost-spiritual reverence for the king of Oaxacan drinks. When you sip mezcal, you're imbibing the essence of an agave plant that has taken at least seven, and sometimes 70, years to reach maturity. Mezcal is a drink to be respected while being enjoyed, a drink that can put people into a kind of trance – *'Para todo mal, mezcal,'* they say. *'Para todo bien, también.'* ('For everything bad, mezcal; for everything good too.)

In the past decade or so, this once little-trumpeted liquor has become positively fashionable, not just in Mexico but also in the US and beyond. *Mezcalerías* (mezcal bars), from the trendy to the seriously connoisseurish, have proliferated in Oaxaca, Mexico City and elsewhere, and a mind-boggling diversity of mezcal varieties and brands has hit the market.

It's strong stuff (usually 40% to 50% alcohol content), and best sipped slowly and savored. A glass of reasonable mezcal in a bar is unlikely to cost less than M$40 and a top-shelf one might cost M$300.

Mezcal-type drinks are produced in many parts of Mexico, but only those that meet established criteria from certain specific areas can legally be marketed as 'mezcal.' Otherwise they are known as *destilados de agave*. Around 60% of mezcal (and most of the best) is produced in and around Oaxaca's Valles Centrales.

Mezcal can be made from around 20 different species of agave (or *maguey* – the words are synonymous). The majority comes from the widely cultivated *espadín*, which has a high sugar content and matures relatively quickly. Mezcals from *agaves silvestres* (wild, uncultivated agaves) are specially prized for their organic nature, unique tastes and usually small-scale production methods. Best known of these is the *tobalá*, which yields distinctive herbal notes.

The mature plant's *piña* (heart), with the leaves removed, is cooked for several days over a wood fire, typically in an oven in the ground. Thus sweetened, it is crushed to fibers that are fermented with water for up to three weeks. The resulting liquid is distilled twice to produce mezcal. It can be drunk *joven* (young), *reposado* (aged in oak for between two months and one year) or *añejo* (aged in oak for at least a year). A *pechuga* mezcal is one with flavors imparted by a chicken or turkey breast *(pechuga)* and/or fruits and spices placed in the distillation vessel.

You can observe the mezcal-making process and sample the product at dozens of mezcal factories and *palenques* (small-scale producers) in the Oaxaca area, especially around Mitla, and above all at the town of Santiago Matatlán, which produces about half of all Oaxaca's mezcal. About 9km southeast of Santiago Matatlán you'll find the turnoff to San Baltazar Guelavila, a worthwhile stop to try complex mezcals produced from wild agaves at **3 Mezquites de Don Goyo** (☑ cell 951-1897978; 5 de Mayo, San Baltazar Guelavila). Buses to Santiago Matatlán (M$40, 1¼ hours) depart from Oaxaca's 2nd-class terminal (p460).

If you really want to get down to grass roots and learn about the mezcal-making process firsthand and in detail, take a trip with **Mezcal Educational Tours** (☑ 951-132-82-03; www.mezcaleducationaltours.com; tour from US$44 per hour for 2 people, minimum 5hr) ✆. Another good tour outfit, **Experience Agave** (☑ 503-922-17-71; www.experienceagave.com; day tour per person US$200), runs customized day trips and multiday outings to the heart of mezcal country.

The taste variations of different mezcals are amazingly wide, and as a general rule you get what you pay for – but the only sure way to judge a mezcal is by how much you like it!

The infamous *gusano* (worm) is actually a moth caterpillar that feeds on the agave and is found mostly in bottles of cheaper mezcal. While no harm will come from swallowing the *gusano*, there is definitely no obligation! Mezcal is, however, often served with a little plate of orangey powder, *sal de gusano*, which is a mix of salt, chili and ground-up *gusanos*. Along with slices of orange, this nicely counterpoints the mezcal taste. *Salud!*

OAXACA OAXACA CITY

and make a beeline for the bar where you can order a cup of Oaxacan chocolate (hot or cold) and become mesmerized by the cooks making breakfast or lunch.

☆ Entertainment

Teatro Macedonio Alcalá THEATER
(🖂 951-516-83-12; www.facebook.com/teatro macedonioalcala; Independencia 900; ⊗ ticket office 10am-5pm Mon-Fri) The city's main theater is a riot of frescoes and gilded boxes built in Louis XV style in 1909 during a renaissance of Mexican theater known as *chico mexicano*. Performances here range from plays and ballet to classical and pop concerts. There's a ticket/info office next to the lobby.

La Nueva Babel LIVE MUSIC
(🖂 cell 951-5213494; Porfirio Díaz 224; ⊗ 8am-2am Mon-Sat) A mural of Bowie as Aladdin Sane juxtaposed with the Virgin of Guadalupe sets Babel's alternative tone, a kind of Mexican dive bar with regular live music from an eclectic cache of performers – it could be *son* (folk), blues, *trova* (troubadour-type folk), jazz or *cumbia*. The chairs are covered in old newspaper, should you get bored.

Guelaguetza Show DANCE
(🖂 951-501-61-00; Quinta Real Oaxaca, 5 de Mayo 300; with buffet dinner M$640; ⊗ 6:30-9:30pm Fri) If you're not in Oaxaca for the Guelaguetza dance festival itself (July), it's well worth attending one of the regular imitations. The highly colorful three-hour show in the beautiful hotel Quinta Real (p452) is the best of them.

🔒 Shopping

The state of Oaxaca has the richest, most inventive folk-art scene in Mexico, and the city is its chief marketplace. You'll find the highest-quality crafts mostly in stores and galleries, but prices are lower in the markets. Some artisans have grouped together to market their products directly in their own stores.

Oaxaca's crowded commercial area stretches over several blocks southwest of the Zócalo. Oaxacans flock here, and to the big Central de Abastos market, for all their everyday needs.

Voces de Copal ARTS & CRAFTS
(🖂 951-516-83-41; www.vocesdecopal.com; Alcalá 303; ⊗ 8am-10pm) A classy crafts shop with superb *alebrijes* from the workshop of Jacobo and María Ángeles in San Martín Tilcajete (p468). These brightly painted wooden figurines, primarily depicting animals and birds, are unique and highly sought-after crafts, but they'll cost you a pretty peso as some take months to make.

Texier CHOCOLATE
(🖂 951-514-21-35; www.texier.mx; Colón 518; ⊗ 8am-8pm Mon-Sat) Beware: the boxed chocolate bites sold here, known as 'Texoros,' are highly addictive. The gourmet Oaxacan treats come in 10 varieties, including hazelnut, cardamom and 'cacao crush.' French transplant David Texier has dedicated a better part of his life to chocolate-making and it shows.

Huizache ARTS & CRAFTS
(🖂 951-501-12-82; www.facebook.com/huizachearte vivodeoaxaca; Murguía 101; ⊗ 8am-9pm) A kind of greatest hits of Oaxacan crafts – including black pottery, rugs, clothes, shoes and *alebrijes* (painted wood carvings) – collected from around the state by a cooperative of artisans. A handy place to shop if you can't make it out to the village markets.

El Nahual ARTS & CRAFTS
(🖂 951-516-42-02; www.elnahualfolkart.blogspot. ca; Reforma 412A; ⊗ 11am-3pm & 5-8pm Mon-Fri, 10am-7pm Sat) Folk-art shop run by a Teotitlán del Valle weaving family, meaning it's stuffed with quality rugs, clothes and embroidery, as well as work from other affiliated artisans.

La Casa del Rebozo ARTS & CRAFTS
(www.lacasadelrebozo.com.mx; 5 de Mayo 114; ⊗ 9:30am-9pm Mon-Sat, 10am-6pm Sun) A cooperative of more than 80 artisans from around Oaxaca state, La Casa del Rebozo stocks quality pottery, textiles, *alebrijes*, tinware, bowls and baskets made from pine needles, and palm-leaf bags, baskets, mats and hats.

La Contra ALCOHOL
(🖂 951-515-23-35; www.facebook.com/lacontra oaxaca; Gómez Farías 212B; ⊗ 11am-9pm Mon-Fri, to 8pm Sat) Stocks a good selection of quality mezcal, wines from Baja California's Valle de Guadalupe and Mexican craft beer.

Mercado Juárez MARKET
(cnr Flores Magón & Las Casas; ⊗ 6am-9pm) This daily indoor market, a block south of the Zócalo, peddles a mix of flowers, hats, shoes, cheap clothes and jewelry, baskets,

leather belts and bags, fancy knives, mezcal, herbs (medicinal and culinary), spices, meat, cheese, ready-made *mole*, fruit, vegetables, grasshoppers and almost every other food an Oaxacan could need – a fascinating browse.

Unión de Palenqueros de Oaxaca   ALCOHOL
(☑951-513-04-85; Abasolo 510; ⊙9am-9pm)
This hole-in-the-wall place is the outlet for a group of small-scale mezcal producers from Santiago Matatlán. It has decent and very well priced *reposado, pechuga* and smoky *añejo* varieties.

Central de Abastos   MARKET
(Periférico; ⊙6am-8pm) The enormous main market, nearly 1km west of the Zócalo, is a hive of activity all week, with Saturday the biggest day. You can find almost anything here, and it's easy to get lost among the household goods, *artesanías* and overwhelming quantities of fruit, vegetables, sugarcane, maize and other produce grown from the coast to the mountaintops.

ℹ Information

INTERNET ACCESS
There are still a few internet cafes; most charge around M$10 per hour. There is free wi-fi in some public spaces, including Parque Juárez, and in nearly all hotels.

MONEY
There are plenty of ATMs around the center, and several banks and *casas de cambio* (exchange houses) that will change US dollars, euros and other major currencies.
Scotiabank (☑951-501-57-20; Av Independencia 801; ⊙8:30am-4pm Mon-Fri, 10am-3pm Sat) Exchanges foreign currency and has an ATM.

POST
Main Post Office (☑951-514-13-78; Antonio de León 2; ⊙8am-7pm Mon-Fri, to 3pm Sat)

TOURIST INFORMATION
Municipal Tourist Information Kiosk (García Vigil, Alameda de León; ⊙9am-6pm)
Municipal Tourist Information Office (☑951-514-14-61; www.facebook.com/visitaoaxacacd; Matamoros 102; ⊙9am-6pm)
Sectur (☑ext 1506 951-502-12-00; www.oaxaca.travel; Juárez 703; ⊙9am-7pm) The Oaxaca state tourism department's main information office. Also has desks at the **1st-class bus station** (5 de Mayo 900, Barrio Jalatlaco; ⊙9am-7pm).

ℹ Getting There & Away

AIR
Aeropuerto Internacional Xoxocotlán (☑951-511-50-88; www.asur.com.mx; Hwy 175 Km 7.5) Oaxaca city's airport is 6km south of the center, 500m west off Hwy 175, and is served by numerous airlines. Most international flights connect through Mexico City.

Airlines
Aeroméxico (☑951-516-10-66; www.aeromexico.com; Hidalgo 513; ⊙9am-6pm Mon-Fri, to 3pm Sat) To/from Mexico City at least five times daily.
Aerotucán (☑951-502-08-40; www.aerotucan.com; 5 de Mayo 1022, Hotel Oaxaca Inn Express; ⊙8am-2pm & 4-7pm Mon-Fri, 8:30am-5pm Sat) Thirteen-seat Cessnas make half-hour hops to Puerto Escondido (M$2728) and Bahías de Huatulco (M$2594), on the Oaxaca coast, both daily – spectacular flights, but these are sometimes canceled or rescheduled at short notice.
American Airlines (☑55-5209-1400; www.aa.com) Daily nonstop flights to Dallas, Texas.
Interjet (☑951-503-34-76; www.interjet.com.mx; Hwy 175 Km 7.5, Oaxaca Airport; ⊙7:30am-1:30pm & 5-7:30pm Sun-Fri, 7:30am-2pm Sat) Flies to Mexico City three times daily.
TAR Aerolíneas (☑55-2629-5272; www.tarmexico.com) Weekly direct flights to Guadalajara and Huatulco.
United (☑55-5283-5500; www.united.com) Flies to Houston, Texas, daily.
Vivaaerobus (☑81-8215-0150; www.vivaaerobus.com) Budget airline flying to/from Mexico City and Monterrey two or three times weekly.
Volaris (☑55-1102-8000; www.volaris.com) Low-cost Mexican airline with direct flights to Mexico City, Tijuana and Los Angeles.

BUS & VAN
For destinations on the Oaxaca coast, buses from the 1st-class bus station take a long and expensive route via Salina Cruz. Unless you're prone to travel sickness on winding mountain roads, it's cheaper and quicker to use one of the comfortable 12- to 18-seat van services that go directly to Puerto Escondido, Pochutla, Zipolite, Mazunte or Huatulco (prices from between M$200 and M$260). Some hostels can arrange for these services to pick you up for an extra charge of around M$50.
1st-class bus station (Terminal ADO; ☑951-502-05-60; www.ado.com.mx; 5 de Mayo 900, Barrio Jalatlaco) Two kilometers northeast of the Zócalo; used by ADO Platino and ADO GL (deluxe service), ADO and OCC (1st class). You can book online at **Mi Escape** (☑ext 2422 951-502-05-60; www.miescape.mx; 5 de Mayo 900; ⊙9am-2pm & 5-8pm Mon-Sat).

2nd-class bus station (Central de Autobuses de Segunda Clase; Juárez Maza) Mainly useful for some buses to villages around Oaxaca; it's 1km west of the Zócalo.

Terminal AU (☎ 951-514-90-03; Periférico 606) AU and Sur (2nd class) buses depart from this terminal.

Autobuses Halcón (☎ 951-516-01-83; Bustamante 606A) Buses to San Bartolo Coyotepec.

Eclipse 70 (☎ 951-516-10-68; Armenta y López 504) Vans to San José del Pacífico, Zipolite, San Agustinillo and Mazunte.

Express Service (☎ 951-516-40-59; Arista 116) Vans to Puerto Escondido.

Expressos Colombo Huatulco (☎ 951-514-38-54; www.expressoscolombohuatulco.com; Trujano 600) Vans to Bahías de Huatulco.

Huatulco 2000 (☎ 951-516-31-54; Hidalgo 208) Vans to Bahías de Huatulco and Pluma Hidalgo.

Líneas Unidas (☎ 951-187-55-11; Bustamante 601) Vans to Pochutla and Zipolite.

Transportes Villa del Pacífico (☎ cell 951-1605160; Galeana 322A) Vans to Puerto Escondido.

CAR & MOTORCYCLE

Hwy 135D branches off the Mexico City–Veracruz highway (150D) to make a spectacular traverse of Oaxaca's northern mountains to Oaxaca city. Automobile tolls from Mexico City to Oaxaca total M$482; the trip takes five to six hours.

The roads of Oaxaca state are mostly poorly maintained; among the several winding highways from Oaxaca to the coast, Hwy 175 has the best driving conditions. Away from Oaxaca city, traffic is light and the scenery is fantastic.

Walk-in car-rental prices in Oaxaca start at around M$800 a day with unlimited kilometers and liability coverage.

Europcar (☎ 951-143-83-40; www.europcar.com.mx; Oaxaca Airport; ⊙ 6am-10:30pm) At the airport.

Only Rent-A-Car (☎ 800-227-66-59; www.onlyrentacar.com; 5 de Mayo 215A; ⊙ 8am-8pm Mon-Sat, from 9am Sun)

ⓘ Getting Around

TO/FROM THE AIRPORT

The Transporte Terrestre shuttle service in the airport charges M$90 per person to get anywhere downtown in a shared van, or you can pay M$350 for one of their private vans. Enquire on board about reserving the same service for your return trip. Street taxis to the airport generally cost M$300.

BUS

City buses cost M$8. From the main road outside the 1st-class bus station, westbound 'Juárez' buses will take you down Juárez and Ocampo, three blocks east of the Zócalo; westbound 'Tinoco y Palacios' buses go down Tinoco y Palacios, two blocks west of the Zócalo. To return to the bus station, take an 'ADO' bus north up Pino Suárez or Crespo.

TAXI

Taxis anywhere within the central area, including the bus stations, cost M$50 to M$60.

BUSES & VANS FROM OAXACA CITY

DESTINATION	FARE (M$)	TIME (HR)	FREQUENCY (PER DAY)
Bahías de Huatulco	240-386	7-8	13 Expressos Colombo, 10 Huatulco 2000, 5 from 1st-class terminal
Mazunte	240	7	5 Eclipse 70
Mexico City (TAPO)	310-823	6¾-8½	hourly from 1st-class terminal & Terminal AU
Pochutla	200-514	6-10	30 Líneas Unidas, 4 from 1st-class terminal
Puebla	263-572	4½-6	hourly from 1st-class terminal
Puerto Escondido	235-528	7-11	12 Express Service, 20 Transportes Villa del Pacífico, 4 from 1st-class terminal
San Cristóbal de las Casas	402-487	10½-12	4 from 1st-class terminal
Tapachula	710	13	7:10pm from 1st-class terminal
Tehuantepec	180-287	4¾	16 from 1st-class terminal, 9 from Terminal AU
Veracruz	409-461	7½-8	6 from 1st-class terminal
Zipolite	210	6¾	5 Líneas Unidas, 5 Eclipse 70

VALLES CENTRALES

The historic yet sophisticated city of Oaxaca is ringed by a slightly more rustic collection of towns and villages that tout some of the state's biggest calling cards: ancient Mesoamerican ruins, indigenous crafts, industrious markets, riotous festivals and fields full of mezcal-producing agave plants. There are three main geographical arteries: the Valle de Tlacolula, stretching 50km east from the city; the Valle de Zimatlán, running about 100km south; and the Valle de Etla, reaching about 40km north. All are within easy day-trip distance of Oaxaca city. The people of these Valles Centrales (Central Valleys) are mostly indigenous Zapotec.

Monte Albán

The city from which the ancient Zapotecs once ruled Oaxaca's Valles Centrales, **Monte Albán** (☑ 951-516-70-77; Carretera a Monte Albán; adult/child under 13yr M$75/free; ⊘ 8am-5pm; ℗) towers 400m above the valley floor from a hilltop a few kilometers west of Oaxaca. This is one of Mexico's most culturally rich archaeological sites, with the remains of temples, palaces, tall stepped platforms, an observatory and a ball court all arranged in orderly fashion, with wonderful 360-degree views over the city, valleys and distant mountains.

Monte Albán traces its roots to 500 BCE and its 1300-year history is usually split into five archaeological phases. The city reached its apex between 300 and 700 CE, but was abandoned long before the Spanish arrived in the 1520s.

While busy compared to other Oaxaca archaeological sites, Monte Albán avoids the tour-bus circus of some of the better-known ruins around Mexico City and Cancún.

History

Monte Albán was first occupied around 500 BCE, probably by Zapotecs moving from the previous main settlement in the Valles Centrales, the less defensible San José El Mogote in the Valle de Etla. Monte Albán had early cultural connections with the Olmecs to the northeast.

The years up to about 200 BCE (known as phase Monte Albán I) saw the leveling of the hilltop, the building of temples and probably palaces, and the growth of a town of 10,000 or more people on the hillsides. Hieroglyphs

OAXACA MONTE ALBÁN

ⓘ COLECTIVOS: A BEGINNER'S GUIDE

Colectivos are shared taxis that run along fixed routes in the localities in and around Oaxaca. However, because you are sharing the ride with other people, the cost is a lot cheaper than a regular taxi (but slightly more expensive than a bus). In Oaxaca, *colectivos* are dark red and white and display their destination on a banner at the top of the windscreen. Many congregate at the north side of Oaxaca's 2nd-class bus station, but will stop unscheduled en route to pick up passengers if they have room (stick your arm out to flag one down). *Colectivos* carry four passengers and leave when full (some try to squeeze in five people). They are generally faster than buses – some would say a little too fast!

---

and dates in a dot-and-bar system carved during this era may mean that the elite of Monte Albán were the first people in Mexico to use a developed writing system and written calendar. Between 200 BCE and 300 CE (phase Monte Albán II) the city came to dominate more and more of the Oaxaca region.

The city was at its peak from about 300 to 700 CE (Monte Albán III), when the main and surrounding hills were terraced for dwellings, and the population reached about 35,000. This was the center of a highly organized, priest-dominated society, controlling the extensively irrigated Valles Centrales, which held at least 200 other settlements and ceremonial centers. Many buildings here were plastered and painted red. Nearly 170 underground tombs from this period have been found, some of them elaborate and decorated with frescoes, though none of these are regularly open to visitors today.

Between about 700 and 950 (Monte Albán IV) the place was abandoned and fell into ruin. Phase Monte Albán V (950–1521) saw minimal activity, although Mixtecs arriving from northwestern Oaxaca reused some old tombs here to bury their own dignitaries – notably Tumba 7, where they placed a famous treasure hoard, now seen in the Museo de las Culturas de Oaxaca (p440).

◉ Sights

Gran Plaza
PLAZA

About 300m long and 200m wide, the Gran Plaza is the heart of Monte Albán. Some of its structures were temples; others were elite residential quarters. Many of them are now cordoned off to prevent damage by visitors' feet.

Plataforma Norte
VIEWPOINT

The North Platform is almost as big as the Gran Plaza, and affords the best views. It was rebuilt several times over the centuries. The 12 column bases at the top of the stairs were part of a roofed hall. On top of the platform is a ceremonial complex created between 500 and 800 CE, which includes the **Patio Hundido** (Sunken Patio), with an altar at its center; **Edificios D, VG** and **E**, which were topped with adobe temples; and the **Templo de Dos Columnas**.

Edificio de los Danzantes
NOTABLE BUILDING

This structure combines an early (Monte Albán I) building, which contained famous carvings known as Danzantes (Dancers), with a later structure that was built over it. There are a few original Danzantes in a short passage that you can enter, and copies of others along the wall outside. Carved between 500 and 100 BCE, they depict naked men, thought to be sacrificed leaders of conquered neighboring towns.

The Danzantes generally have thick-lipped open mouths (sometimes down-turned in Olmec style) and closed eyes. Some have blood flowing where they have been disemboweled.

Plataforma Sur
VIEWPOINT

The 40m-high South Platform, with its wide staircase, is the tallest in Monte Albán and is great for a panorama of the plaza and the surrounding mountains. Unlike some Mexican ruins, you are allowed to climb to the top of the structure.

Monte Albán

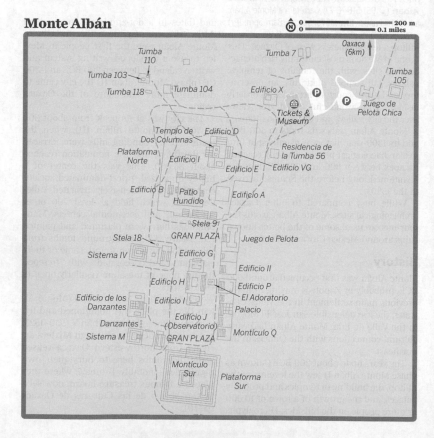

Juego de Pelota ARCHAEOLOGICAL SITE

The stone terraces of the deep Ball Court, constructed about 100 BCE, were probably part of the playing area, not seats for spectators. It's thought they were covered with a thick coating of lime, meaning the ball would roll down them.

Edificio J NOTABLE BUILDING

Arrowhead-shaped Building J, constructed about 100 BCE and riddled with tunnels and staircases (unfortunately you can't go inside), stands at an angle of 45 degrees to the other Gran Plaza structures and was an observatory. Astronomical observation enabled the ancients to track the seasons, calculate agricultural cycles and make prophesies. Figures and hieroglyphs carved on the building's walls record Monte Albán's military conquests.

Edificio P NOTABLE BUILDING

Building P was topped by a small pillared temple and was probably an observatory of some sort. The sun shines directly down into a small opening near the top at the solar zenith passages (when the sun passes directly overhead at noon on May 5 and August 8).

👉 Tours

Official guides offer their services outside the ticket office (around M$600 for a small group). Alternatively, numerous companies in central Oaxaca offer Monte Albán as a half-day trip from around M$450 including guide and transportation.

❶ Getting There & Away

It's easy to get to Monte Albán from Oaxaca either independently or as part of an organized trip. **Autobuses Turísticos** (☑951-516-61-75; Mina 501, Oaxaca; round-trip M$60) has bus departures hourly (half-hourly on Saturday and Sunday) from 8:30am to 3:30pm, starting back from the site between noon and 5pm. Buses stop two blocks west of Mercado 20 de Noviembre.

Valle de Tlacolula

Valle de Tlacolula, east of Oaxaca, has the Valles Centrales' most condensed booty of sights – it's home to two pre-Hispanic sites (Mitla and Yagul) and an even more ancient tree. Craft-wise, this is where you come for weaving (cloths and rugs abound) and artisan mezcal (there are numerous distilleries). The cherry on top is the glorious infinity pools and petrified waterfalls at Hierve El Agua.

Yagul Ruins ARCHAEOLOGICAL SITE

(Tlacolula; adult/child under 13yr M$75/free; ⊘8am-5pm; Ⓟ) If you want photos of Zapotec ruins without hordes of tourists milling around in the background, Yagul is your kind of place. The ruins (known as 'Pueblo Viejo' by locals) are finely sited on a cactus-covered hill, about 1.5km north of the Oaxaca–Mitla road, 34km from Oaxaca. Unless you have a vehicle, you'll have to walk the 1.5km.

Prehistoric Caves of Yagul & Mitla CAVE

(Guilá Naquitz) Approaching Yagul from the main road, you can make out a large white rock painting of a person/deity/tree/sun on a cliff face on the **Caballito Blanco** rock outcrop to your right. This is the most obvious feature of the Unesco World Heritage site, the Prehistoric Caves of Yagul and Mitla, which stretches about 6km east from here.

Caves here have yielded evidence of the earliest plant domestication in North America, about 10,000 years ago, and other valuable details about the transition from hunting and gathering to agriculture over a period of several thousand years.

The Unesco-protected caves are difficult to visit independently. Your best bet is to hook up with Tierraventura (p446) on a day tour to the important Guilá Naquitz cave (M$1500 per person). The trip includes a three-hour hike.

El Rey de Matatlán DISTILLERY

(☑951-516-23-46; www.mezcalelrey.com; Hwy 190 Km 26; ⊘9am-7pm) **FREE** A popular place to taste and buy artisan mezcal right next to the fields where they grow the agave. Granted, it's a hot spot on the tour-bus circuit (if you're on a tour you'll probably stop here), but the smoky-flavored mezcal is authentic and the terracotta-shaded hacienda with its bar, mill, traditional ovens and fermentation plant is more rustic than industrial. Free explanations of the mezcal-making process are given throughout the day. Afterward you can get tipsy tasting it.

❶ Getting There & Away

El Tule, Teotitlán del Valle, Tlacolula and Yagul are all close to the Oaxaca–Mitla road, Hwy 190. Buses to Mitla (M$24, 1¼ hours) leave about every hour from Oaxaca's 2nd-class bus station and will drop you anywhere along this road.

Alternatively, you can catch *taxis colectivos* (shared taxis) direct to El Tule (M$14, 15 minutes), Teotitlán (M$18, 30 minutes), Tlacolula (M$20, 40 minutes) or Mitla (M$25, one hour)

Valles Centrales & Pueblos Mancomunados

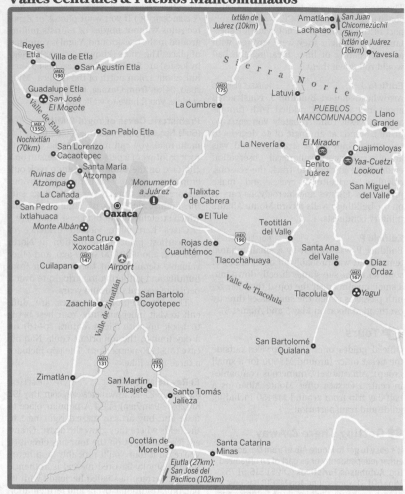

Ixtlán de Juárez (10km)

Amatlán
San Juan Chicomezúchil (5km); Ixtlán de Juárez (16km)
Lachatao
Yavesía

Reyes Etla
Villa de Etla
San Agustín Etla
MEX 190

Sierra Norte

Latuvi

MEX 175

La Cumbre

PUEBLOS MANCOMUNADOS
Llano Grande

Guadalupe Etla
San José El Mogote
Valle de Etla

Nochixtlán (70km)
MEX 135D

La Neveria
El Mirador
Cuajimoloyas

San Pablo Etla

San Lorenzo Cacaotepec
Santa María Atzompa
Benito Juárez
Yaa-Cuetzi Lookout

Ruinas de Atzompa
Monumento a Juárez
San Miguel del Valle

La Cañada
Tlalixtac de Cabrera

San Pedro Ixtlahuaca

Oaxaca
El Tule
Teotitlán del Valle

Monte Albán
MEX 190

Santa Cruz Xoxocatlán
Rojas de Cuauhtémoc
Santa Ana del Valle

MEX 147
Airport
Tlacochahuaya
Díaz Ordaz
MEX 167

Cuilapan
Valle de Tlacolula
Tlacolula
Yagul

Zaachila
San Bartolo Coyotepec
Valle de Zimatlán

San Bartolomé Quialana

MEX 131
MEX 175

Zimatlán
San Martín Tilcajete
Santo Tomás Jalieza

Ocotlán de Morelos
Santa Catarina Minas

Ejutla (27km); San José del Pacífico (102km)

from the corner of Hwy 190 and Derechos Humanos, 500m east of Oaxaca's 1st-class bus station, immediately past the baseball stadium.

El Tule

☎ 951 / POP 7640 / ELEV 1565M

El Tule, 10km east of Oaxaca along Hwy 190, draws crowds of visitors for one very good reason: El Árbol del Tule, a huge tree reckoned to be as old as the Monte Albán ruins. The tree anchors a pleasant little Mexican town complete with church, square and market that contrasts with the more urban scene of the big city nearby.

El Árbol del Tule   LANDMARK

(Tree of Tule; M$10; ⊙ 8am-8pm) Visitors flock to the village of El Tule to behold El Árbol del Tule, which is, by some counts, the fattest tree in the world. California's General Sherman sequoia is ahead in total volume, but at 14m in diameter, El Árbol del Tule certainly has the world's widest trunk. This vast *ahuehuete* (Montezuma cypress), 42m high, dwarfs the pretty 17th-century village church in whose churchyard it towers.

The tree is estimated to be over 2000 years old, which means it was already growing when the ancient city of Monte Albán was in its infancy. Much revered by

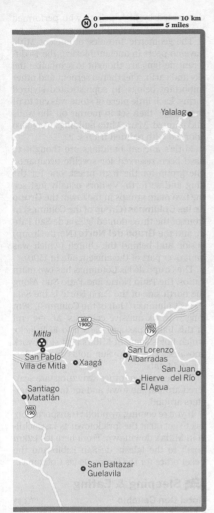

10 km
0
5 miles

Yalalag

Mitla

MEX 190D

MEX 179

San Pablo
Villa de Mitla   Xaagá
San Lorenzo
Albarradas
San Juan
Hierve del Río
El Agua

Santiago
Matatlán

MEX 190

San Baltazar
Guelavila

Oaxacans, the Árbol del Tule appears to be healthy, though there are potential threats to it from local urban growth and irrigated agriculture, which tap its water sources.

El Milenario OAXACAN $$
(☑ 951-502-59-57; www.facebook.com/restaurante elmilenario; Guerrero 4A; mains M$80-135; ⊙ 9am-8pm) This popular, family-run restaurant one block south of the Árbol del Tule (past the Mercado de Artesanías) is a great place to stop, serving classic Oaxacan dishes such as *moles* with chicken and *salsa de queso* in a cheerful atmosphere set off by the tortilla-maker stationed outside.

OAXACA VALLE DE TLACOLULA

Teotitlán del Valle

☑ 951 / POP 4360 / ELEV 1680M

A famous weaving village, located about 25km southeast of Oaxaca, Teotitlán has been renowned for its weaving wares since pre-Hispanic times: the village had to pay tributes of cloth to the Aztecs. Quality today is high, and traditional dyes made from natural sources like indigo, cochineal and moss have been revived (though some weavers still use much cheaper synthetic dyes). The variety of designs is enormous – from Zapotec gods and Mitla-style geometric patterns to imitations of paintings by Rivera and Picasso.

Many tour groups only get as far as the larger weaving showrooms on the road approaching the village, which tend to dominate the craft here by buying up weavers' products or employing weavers directly to weave for them. For more direct interaction, head on into the village itself, where blankets and rugs wave at you from workshops and a cultural center provides background on this ancient local tradition.

⊙ Sights

**Centro Cultural Comunitario
de Teotitlán del Valle** CULTURAL CENTER
(☑ 951-348-36-07; Av Hidalgo; by donation; ⊙ 11am-6pm Tue-Sun) A new cultural center with exhibits focused primarily on, you guessed it, all things weaving. Definitely worth a peek if you want to learn more about textiles and the town's interesting Zapotec customs.

Iglesia Preciosa Sangre de Cristo CHURCH
(Aldama 7; ⊙ 6am-6pm) From the plaza, steps rise to this handsome 17th-century church with a fine broad churchyard and colorful 18th-century frescoes inside. It was built atop a Zapotec ceremonial site, many of the carved stones of which can be seen in the church walls; look especially in the inner patio.

⮂ Courses

El Sabor Zapoteco COOKING
(☑ 951-524-46-58; www.cookingclasseselsabor zapoteco.blogspot.com; Av Juárez 30; per person US$75) Learn to prepare classic village dishes using traditional methods under the tutelage of Reyna Mendoza in her open-air kitchen in Teotitlán. Classes, which include round-trip transportation from Oaxaca city, are normally held Tuesday and Friday mornings (Teotitlán's main market days). The pickup point in Oaxaca is outside the Jardín Etnobotánico (p445).

✗ Eating

Tierra Antigua
OAXACAN $$

(☎951-166-61-60; www.facebook.com/tierraantigua; Av Juárez 175; mains M$125-250; ⊗9:30am-6:30pm; P) A talented husband-and-wife team run this inviting Zapotec restaurant and gallery where you can stop for traditional *mole negro* or *mole estofado* (stewed ribs in *mole*) and shop for colorful wool rugs and handbags made onsite. Offers classes in cooking (M$1500) and weaving (M$1400), too.

Tlacolula

POP 13,820 / ELEV 1600M

Tlacolula, 31km from Oaxaca, holds one of the Valles Centrales' biggest markets every Sunday, with the area around the church becoming a packed throng. Crafts, foods and plenty of everyday goods are on sale. It's a treat for lovers of market atmosphere – and market food.

Tlacolula's main church, **Santa María de la Asunción** (Av 2 de Abril 42; ⊗7am-8pm), is notable for its ornate baroque side chapel, known colloquially as the **Capilla de la Plata** (Silver Chapel), a dazzling riot of indigenous-influenced decoration comparable to the Capilla del Rosario in Oaxaca's Santo Domingo (p440). Among the ceiling ornamentation, spot the plaster martyrs holding their own severed heads and the playful angels clutching various musical instruments.

San Pablo Villa de Mitla

☎951 / POP 8170 / ELEV 1680M

The small town of San Pablo Villa de Mitla, 46km southeast of Oaxaca, is famous for the ruins of Ancient Mitla replete with unique stone 'mosaics' that stand today in the midst of a modern Zapotec settlement.

Mitla is also a hive of craft shops peddling embroidery and liquor stores selling potent locally made mezcal.

◉ Sights

Zona Arqueológica de Mitla
ARCHAEOLOGICAL SITE

(Mitla Archaeological Zone; Camino Nacional; M$75; ⊗8am-5pm; P) Second only to Monte Albán in their importance, though not as old, the ruins of ancient Mitla date from the final two or three centuries before the Spanish conquest in the 1520s, and comprise what was probably the most important Zapotec religious center at the time – a cult center

dominated by high priests who performed literally heart-wrenching human sacrifices.

The geometric 'mosaics' of ancient Mitla have no peers in ancient Mexico: the 14 different designs are thought to symbolize the sky and earth, a feathered serpent and other important beings, in sophisticated stylized forms. Each little piece of stone was cut to fit the design, then set in mortar on the walls and painted. Many Mitla buildings were also adorned with painted friezes.

Mitla's ancient buildings are thought to have been reserved for specific occupants: one group for the high priest, one for the king and so forth. Visitors usually just see the two main groups in the town: the **Grupo de las Columnas** (Group of the Columns) in front of the three-domed Iglesia de San Pablo, and the **Grupo del Norte** (North Group) beside and behind the church (which was built over part of the ancient site in 1590).

The Grupo de las Columnas has two main patios, the Patio Norte and Patio Sur. Along the north side of the Patio Norte is the Sala de las Columnas (Hall of the Columns), 38m long with six massive columns. At one end of this hall, a passage leads into El Palacio, which holds some of Mitla's best stonework 'mosaics.' The Patio Sur holds two underground tombs.

The remains of other structures are scattered around the town and for many kilometers around.

If you're coming by public transportation, ask to get off at the fork known as La Cuchilla in Mitla's downtown. From here it's 1.2km north to the Iglesia de San Pablo and the ticket office for the Grupo de las Columnas.

🛌 Sleeping & Eating

Hotel Don Cenobio
HOTEL $$

(☎951-568-03-30; www.hoteldoncenobio.com; Av Juárez 3; r M$987-1364; P🛜❄) Set on the central plaza, this is one of Mitla's best lodging options, with its 23 comfortable rooms sporting multicolored carved furnishings from Guadalajara. In and around the grassy central garden are a swimming pool, bar and the hotel's restaurant (open 8am to 5pm), serving Oaxacan fare.

Casa Regina
BOUTIQUE HOTEL $$$

(☎cell 951-1900521; www.hotelcasaregina.com; Camino a Xaagá; M$2600-3000; P🛜❄) Mitla's most luxurious hotel makes a quiet, comfy base for visiting Hierve El Agua and mezcal country. Cool adobe brick rooms with rustic-chic stylings surround an outdoor pool and open-air restaurant with views of the sierra. An onsite temascal (pre-Hispanic steam bath) allows you to sweat out the party toxins.

Restaurante Doña Chica OAXACAN $
(☑951-568-06-83; www.facebook.com/rest-donachica; Av Morelos 41; mains M$100-150; ☺10am-7pm; 🐾) If you're hungry after viewing the Mitla ruins, fret not. Bright Doña Chica serves delicious Oaxacan dishes like *moles,* enchiladas and *tasajo* from an open kitchen. Good soups, *antojitos,* salads and desserts round out the menu – and your stomach.

Hierve El Agua

ELEV 1800M
Hierve El Agua consists of a series of spectacularly sited mineral springs and rock formations 65km southeast of Oaxaca and 35km beyond Tlacolula. It's a popular outing for *oaxaqueños* on their days off and a good place to end a trip to the Valle de Tlacolula.

★Mineral Springs NATURAL POOL
(San Isidro Roaguía; M$25; ☺7:30am-7:30pm; 🅿) Natural springs have never looked this good. Set in truly ethereal surroundings amid low brush-covered mountains, Hierve El Agua (meaning 'the water boils,' but the water temperature is actually cool) is a set of bubbling mineral springs that run into natural infinity pools right on a cliff's edge with spectacular panoramas of the sierra. Water dribbling over the cliff edge for millennia has created unique white mineral formations that resemble huge frozen waterfalls. Arrive early to avoid the crowds.

There are two ghostly 'waterfalls' at the site. The **cascada chica** is the one nearer the visitor car park and supports four popular mineral pools (the one nearest to the lip of the cliff is human-made). From here you get perfect views of the more impressive **cascada grande**. To get to the second 'waterfall' follow the trail for 1km to its end, where you can enjoy a much quieter more natural spot (with few bathers).

The mineral-laden water is cool to cold, though usually swimmable. Altogether it's an utterly unique bathing experience and stunningly beautiful to boot. There are changing rooms just above the pools.

Unofficial roadblocks – the result of a local feud – sometimes spring up close to the springs and charge you an extra M$10 to enter.

❶ Getting There & Away

Hierve El Agua is on the itinerary of day tours from Oaxaca, and there's public transportation by the *camionetas* (pickup trucks) of Transportes Zapotecos del Valle Oriente (M$50 one way) from La Cuchilla in Mitla. They leave when they have enough passengers.

If you're driving, 'Hierve El Agua' signs approaching Mitla will lead you on to the new Hwy 190D toll road, which bypasses Mitla: you turn off (signposted to Hierve El Agua) after 19km then go another 7km (unpaved for the last 4km). Alternatively, drive through Mitla and follow the older Hwy 179, which more or less parallels the toll road; the signed turnoff to Hierve El Agua comes up 18km from Mitla.

Valle de Zimatlán

South from Oaxaca, Hwy 175 goes through San Bartolo Coyotepec, famed for its black pottery; Ocotlán, with one of the Valles Centrales' busiest weekly markets; and – much further on – San José del Pacífico, famed for its magic mushrooms, en route to Pochutla near the coast. The less busy Hwy 147 goes to Cuilapan just west of Oaxaca Airport.

Cuilapan

☑951 / POP 12,360 / ELEV 1560M
Cuilapan (Cuilápam), 9km southwest of Oaxaca, is one of the few Mixtec towns in the Valles Centrales. It's the site of a historic Dominican monastery, the Ex Convento Dominicano, most people's primary reason for visiting.

Ex Convento Dominicano MONASTERY
(cloister M$45; ☺9am-5:30pm; 🅿) Standing by the highway in dusty Cuilapan, the Ex Convento Dominicano (aka Santiago Apóstol) with its pale 'green' stone walls seems almost to grow out of the land. With half the building missing a roof, one's immediate conclusion is that it's just another ruin. On the contrary, the building was never actually finished. Work on the long low church in front of the monastery with its stately arches and detailed stone carving stopped in 1560 due to financial disputes.

Behind is the church that succeeded it, which contains the tomb of Juana Donají (daughter of Cosijoeza, the last Zapotec king of Zaachila) and is normally open only for Mass (noon and 5pm Saturday and Sunday). Adjoining the church is a two-story Renaissance-style cloister. A painting of Mexican independence hero Vicente Guerrero hangs in the small room where he was held in 1831 before being executed by soldiers supporting the rebel conservative Anastasio Bustamante. Outside, a monument marks the spot where he was shot.

Aside from its roofless church and Guerrero associations, the convent is notable for its Moorish architectural influences and faded murals that incorporate some unusual indigenous themes.

❶ Getting There & Away

Zaachila Yoo (Bustamante 601) runs buses from Oaxaca to Cuilapan (M$9, 45 minutes) about every 15 minutes.

San Bartolo Coyotepec

✍ 951 / POP 3980 / ELEV 1520M

Barro negro, the polished, surprisingly light, black pottery (candlesticks, jugs and vases, and decorative animal and bird figures) that you find in hundreds of forms around Oaxaca, comes from San Bartolo Coyotepec, 11km south of the city. For the original source, head to Alfarería Doña Rosa, a short walk east off the highway.

Alfarería Doña Rosa   HANDICRAFTS
(☑ 951-551-00-11; www.facebook.com/alfareriadonarosabarronegro; Juárez 24; ⊙ 9am-7pm; 🅿) It was doña Rosa Real Mateo (1900–80) who invented the method of burnishing *barro negro* with quartz stones for the distinctive shine. Her family *alfarería* (potters' workshop) is now the biggest in the village, and they demonstrate the process to visitors after 4pm. The pieces are hand-molded by an age-old technique that uses two saucers functioning as a rudimentary potter's wheel. They are fired in pit kilns and turn black from smoke and from the iron oxide in the clay.

The workshop doubles as a shop and is also something of a museum. It's well worth visiting, even if you have no intention of buying.

**Museo Estatal de
Arte Popular de Oaxaca**   MUSEUM
(☑ 951-551-00-36; www.facebook.com/artepopulardeoaxaca; Independencia; adult/child under 13yr M$20/free; ⊙ 10am-6pm Tue-Sun) San Bartolo's excellent, modern, folk-art museum, with its bright pink facade, is on the south side of the main village plaza. It's very nicely done and features a collection of fine *barro negro*, plus exhibits of quality folk art from around Oaxaca state.

❶ Getting There & Away

Autobuses Halcón (p460) runs buses from Oaxaca city to San Bartolo (M$10, 20 minutes) about every 10 minutes.

San Martín Tilcajete

✍ 951 / POP 1730 / ELEV 1540M

San Martín Tilcajete, 1km west of Hwy 175, 24km south of Oaxaca, is the source of many of the bright copal-wood *alebrijes* – those distinctive colorful wooden animal figures – seen in Oaxaca. Dozens of villagers carve them, and you can see and buy them in makers' houses, many of which have 'Alebrijes' or 'Artesanías de Madera' (Wooden Handicrafts) signs outside.

Azucena Zapoteca   OAXACAN $$
(☑ 951-524-92-27; www.facebook.com/azucenazapoteca; Hwy 175 Km 23.5; mains M$90-195; ⊙ 8am-6pm; 🅿 🛜) Good *alebrijes* and other crafts are displayed and sold at this popular lunch stop, which also serves good Oaxacan fare, beside Highway 175 opposite the Tilcajete turnoff. The menu features a *desayuno de Jacobo* (steak and onions with bacon, egg and beans), which is a breakfast dish named after the skilled local wood-carver, Jacobo Ángeles.

⭐ **Jacobo & María Ángeles**   ARTS & CRAFTS
(☑ 951-524-90-47; www.jacoboymariaangeles.com; Callejón del Olvido 9; ⊙ 8am-6pm) Jacobo and María Ángeles have been making particularly wonderful *alebrijes* for over 25 years and now run a workshop providing employment for 100 people. Visitors get a free tour and see the incredibly detailed *alebrijes* being made. It's very labor-intensive. An average-sized piece takes up to a month to make.

Many of the figures made here are based on the sacred animals of Zapotec mythology. The best pieces sell for many thousands of pesos, and some huge and very detailed ones can take up to four years to make. The workshop is about 2km from the highway. The couple's work can also be found in crafts-store Voces de Copal (p458) in central Oaxaca.

❶ Getting There & Away

Ocotlán-bound **buses** (Bustamante 622, Oaxaca) from Oaxaca will drop you at the turnoff to San Martín (M$20, 35 minutes). *Taxis colectivos* run from Ocotlán itself.

Ocotlán de Morelos

☑ 951 / POP 15,000 / ELEV 1500M

Ocotlán de Morelos is a town of fine art, esoteric pottery and a dense, industrious Friday market. The art is courtesy of homegrown artist Rodolfo Morales (1925–2001), who turned his international success to the area's benefit by setting up the Fundación Cultural Rodolfo Morales (www.fcrom.org.mx), which has done marvelous renovation work on local churches and promotes the area's arts, heritage, environment and social welfare.

The pottery was put on the international map by the Aguilar family, a quartet of talented sisters who pioneered a style of sculpture captured in unusually beautiful clay figurines reflecting religion, Frida Kahlo and Day of the Dead iconography.

Most visitors come to Ocotlín on Friday, when its big spirited covered market takes over the central plaza and its surroundings.

Ex-Convento de Santo Domingo MUSEUM
(Amador 1; M$15; ⊙9am-1pm & 3-6pm) This rehabilitated former convent, previously a dilapidated jail, is now a first-class art museum and includes a room dedicated to the work of local magic realist artist, Rodolfo Morales. Morales was responsible for driving much of the restoration of the building, which began in 1995. His ashes are interred here too.

After enjoying the art, it's also worth perusing the adjacent church framed by a lovely avenue of slender trees.

Guillermina Aguilar HANDICRAFTS
(☑ cell 951-1255441; Morelos 430; ⊙10am-6pm Mon-Sat, to 4pm Sun) Ocotlán's most renowned artisans are the four Aguilar sisters and their families, who create whimsical, colorful pottery figures of women with all sorts of unusual motifs. Their houses are together on the west side of the main road entering Ocotlán from the north, almost opposite the Hotel Real de Ocotlán.

Most renowned is Guillermina Aguilar, the eldest of the sisters, who turns out, among other things, miniature 3D re-creations of Frida Kahlo works. The artisan pottery work was initially inspired by Guillermina's mother and the skill has since been carried through the generations to her grandchildren.

Mercado Morelos MARKET
(Pueblos Unidos; ⊙7am-8pm) This covered market, on the south side of the central plaza, opens daily. Food, clothes, pottery, textiles, mezcal, chickens, art and cheap junk – it's difficult to work out what it doesn't sell. On Fridays, the stalls are integrated into Ocutlán's massive weekly market that spills over several city blocks.

❶ Getting There & Away

Automorsa (p468) runs buses (M$25) and vans (M$30) from Oaxaca to Ocotlán (45 minutes) about every 10 minutes from 6am to 9pm.

Zaachila

☑ 951 / POP 13,960

This part-Mixtec, part-Zapotec town 6km southeast of Cuilapan is an authentic place with a big, busy Thursday market known for its food stalls – expect a noisy mélange of squawking chickens, buzzing three-wheeler taxis and gossiping locals. It was a Zapotec capital from 1400 CE until the Spanish conquest. Behind the village church overlooking the main plaza, a sign indicates the entrance to Zaachila's Zona Arqueológica, a relatively unexplored site where tourism has yet to disturb the tranquility.

Zona Arqueológica ARCHAEOLOGICAL SITE
(Archaeological Zone; ☑ cell 951-1625065; Alarii 30; M$45; ⊙9am-6pm) Ancient Zaachila, rather like Mitla, was a post-Classic Zapotec city that took root after the demise of Monte Albán. It was later conquered by the Mixtec. The rough date of its establishment is sketchy, but it probably reached its apogee in the 1300s. The Zona Arqueológica consists of a small assortment of mounds where you can enter two small tombs used by the ancient Mixtecs.

❶ Getting There & Away

Zaachila Yoo (p468) runs buses between Oaxaca and Zaachila (M$9, 40 minutes) about every 15 minutes.

Valle de Etla

Etla (meaning land of beans) is a subvalley of the Valle de Oaxaca and stretches about 40km to the northeast of the state capital. It has some recently excavated ruins and an inspirational factory-turned-arts center.

Santa María Atzompa

☑ 951 / POP 21,800 / ELEV 1580M

Perched 3km above Santa María Atzompa (and 6km from central Oaxaca), the hilltop archaeological site of Atzompa on the Cerro de la Campaña is a fascinating complement to the larger, more famous, parent city of Monte Albán. Together with Santa María Atzompa village's museum and crafts market, it provides proof of the continuity of Atzompa's pottery-making expertise from pre-Hispanic times to the present day.

Atzompa Ruins ARCHAEOLOGICAL SITE
(☑951-516-70-77; Av Independencia, Cerro de la Campaña; ⊙8am-5pm; 🅿) FREE If you like your pre-Hispanic Mexican ruins suitably 'ruined' and crowd-free without compromising on authenticity or spectacular setting, opt for Atzompa. The site gets a tiny fraction of Monte Albán's visitors (it's not unusual to have the place to yourself), meaning your imagination can run wild conjuring up images of Zapotecs in feathery attire playing the Mesoamerican ball game.

Only thoroughly excavated in the early 21st century and not opened to the public until 2012 (when the access road was built), Atzompa was a residential satellite city of nearby Monte Albán. It was probably established around 650 CE and abandoned 300 years later.

Three ceremonial plazas, several ball courts (including the largest in the Oaxaca area) and the remains of two large residences have been exposed to view. A specially intriguing feature is the reconstructed pottery-firing oven on the north side – identical to ovens still used by potters in modern Atzompa. Excavation at the site is ongoing.

Museo Comunitario de Atzompa MUSEUM
(☑951-244-19-40; www.facebook.com/atzompa museo; Av Independencia; M$20; ⊙10am-5pm; 🅿) Two kilometers down the road from the ruins (p470) toward Santa María Atzompa, the neglected Community Museum exhibits some very fine pieces of pottery found at the archaeological site, including detailed effigies of nobility or deities and huge pots used for storing water, grain or seeds.

Mercado de Artesanías ARTS & CRAFTS
(Crafts Market; ☑951-558-92-32; Av Libertad 303; ⊙9am-9pm) The work of over 100 contemporary Atzompa potters is on sale in the Mercado de Artesanías: items range from animal figures and lampshades to pots, plates, cups and more – some bearing Atzompa's traditional green glaze, others in more colorful, innovative styles. Prices are reasonable but much of the best work goes to shops in Oaxaca and elsewhere.

🛈 Getting There & Away

Access to the ruins is by paved road, either 3km up from Santa María Atzompa village, or 2.5km up from La Cañada village on the road from Oaxaca to San Pedro Ixtlahuaca. From Monte Albán, vehicles can drive direct to La Cañada and the ruins without returning to Oaxaca. *Taxis colectivos* and buses to Santa María Atzompa leave from Trujano on the north side of Oaxaca's 2nd-class bus station and cost M$10 for the 20-minute journey. From Santa María Atzompa, hail a moto-taxi (M$15) to the ruins. Private cabs from Oaxaca charge about M$180 round trip to the site.

San Agustín Etla
☑951 / POP 3700 / ELEV 1760M
Pretty San Agustín sits on the Valle de Etla's eastern slopes, 18km northwest of Oaxaca. Its large, early-20th-century textile mill has been superbly restored as the Centro de las Artes de San Agustín, an arts center used for concerts, conferences and top-notch art or craft exhibitions.

**Centro de las Artes
de San Agustín** ARTS CENTER
(CaSa; ☑951-521-25-74; www.casa.oaxaca.gob.mx; Independencia s/n, Barrio Vistahermosa; ⊙9am-8pm) 🗲FREE San Agustín's spectacular arts center features two long, large halls. The lower hall is used as a gallery for often wonderful craft or art exhibitions; the upper one is a setting for concerts, conferences and other events. The center also hosts courses and workshops in a great variety of arts and crafts. Check the website for upcoming events and expos.

The sublime pools surrounding the building are part of a gravity-powered water system that cools the roof and also supplies a paper-making workshop down the hill. The design features – both arty and ecological – are the brainchild of Oaxaca artist Francisco Toledo, who helped turn the abandoned factory into an arts center in the early 2000s.

🛈 Getting There & Away

The turnoff for San Agustín is on the east side of Hwy 190, 13.5km from central Oaxaca, marked by a tiny 'San Sebastián Etla' sign beside the largish Instituto Euro-Americano. It's 4km up to the village. *Taxis colectivos* to San Agustín (M$16, 30 minutes), from Trujano on the north side of Oaxaca's 2nd-class bus station, will take you to CaSa.

San José del Pacífico

☑ 951 / POP 550 / ELEV 2562M

High in the misty mountains that close off the south end of the Valles Centrales, 135km from Oaxaca, San José del Pacífico is chiefly renowned for one thing – the hallucinogenic mushroom *Psilocybe mexicana*. Though their consumption is officially illegal, these *hongos mágicos* (magic mushrooms) help to make San José quite a popular travelers' stop en route between Oaxaca city and the coast. There's a significant community of alternative lifestylers here and in nearby villages. Mushrooms or no mushrooms, San José has a touch of magic anyway and is a beautiful place to break a journey. When the clouds clear, the views over pristine forested ranges and valleys are fabulous. There are good walks, a handful of surprisingly good places to stay, and several places where you can take a temascal steam bath.

🛏 Sleeping & Eating

There are several cafes and small restaurants along the main road in the village, plus a few shops selling food.

La Puesta del Sol CABAÑAS $

(☑ 951-190-82-56; www.sanjosedelpacifico.com; Hwy 175 Km 131; r M$400-500, cabañas M$600-800, all incl breakfast; P🛜🐕) Just below the highway 500m north of town, La Puesta del Sol is usually considered to be San José's posh digs. The cozy, clean *cabañas* have porches affording marvelous views and all except the cheapest have fireplaces.

Refugio Terraza de la Tierra CABAÑAS $$

(www.terrazadelatierra.com; Hwy 175 Km 128; r M$550-850, breakfast/dinner M$140/180; P🛜) 🌿 A beautiful mountain retreat, solar-powered Terraza de la Tierra has nine lovely rooms in adobe and wood *cabañas* around its large organic garden, on a 1.5-sq-km hillside property with over 20 waterfalls. Excellent vegetarian meals are served, and there are cute little glass meditation pyramids and a big-windowed yoga room. They offer yoga classes and guided bird-watching trips.

It's 300m off the highway, 3.5km north of town.

La Taberna de los Duendes ITALIAN $$$

(☑ cell 951-4776879; www.facebook.com/latabernadelosduendes; Hwy 175 Km 132; mains M$210-400; ☺1-9:30pm Mon-Sat, to 9pm Sun; 🌿) The Italian-owned 'elves tavern' serves generous

portions of pasta, pepper-rubbed steak and fried trout, plus there's affordable mezcal to sip on as you drift off to the dreamy sounds of Pink Floyd.

❶ Getting There & Away

San José sits on Hwy 175, the Oaxaca–Pochutla road, 33km south of Miahuatlán. All the frequent van services running between Oaxaca (M$110, three hours) and Pochutla (M$110, 2¾ hours), Zipolite (M$150, 3¼ hours) or Bahías de Huatulco (M$190, three hours) stop here.

SIERRA NORTE

The mountains separating the Valles Centrales from low-lying far-northern Oaxaca are called the Sierra Juárez, and the more southerly parts of this range, rising from the north side of the Valle de Tlacolula, are known as the Sierra Norte. These beautiful, forested highlands are home to several successful community ecotourism ventures providing a wonderful opportunity to get out on foot, mountain bike or horseback into pristine landscapes. Over 400 bird species, 350 butterfly species, all six species of Mexican wild cat and nearly 4000 plant varieties have been recorded in the Sierra Norte. Be prepared for cool temperatures: in the higher, southern villages it can snow in winter. The wettest season is from late May to September; there's little rain from January to April.

Pueblos Mancomunados

The Pueblos Mancomunados (Commonwealth of Villages) comprises eight remote villages (**Amatlán**, **Benito Juárez**, **Cuajimoloyas**, **La Nevería**, **Lachatao**, **Latuvi**, **Llano Grande** and **Yavesía**) protected under the umbrella of a unique and foresighted ecotourism project. Communally they offer great wilderness escapes and an up-close communion with Zapotec village life. More than 100km of high-country trails run between the villages and to local beauty spots and places of interest, and you can easily enjoy several days exploring them. Elevations in these hills range from 2200m to over 3200m, and the landscapes, with canyons, caves, waterfalls and panoramic lookouts, are spectacular.

For centuries these villages have pooled the natural resources of their 290-sq-km territory,

---

ℹ️ HOW TO VISIT THE PUEBLOS MANCOMUNADOS

Tourism in seven of the villages is administered by a locally run indigenous organization called Expediciones Sierra Norte (p446) that has a useful booking office in central Oaxaca. Although it is perfectly fine to turn up at any of the villages unannounced and organize your activities independently, booking through the agency makes things a lot easier and also ensures that your money goes directly back into the communities.

Expediciones Sierra Norte can arrange all types of trips into the mountains (including hiking, biking and horseback riding), as well as accommodations in appealing rustic cabins, local guide services and transportation to and from Oaxaca. Zip-lining is also available. Itineraries are extremely flexible and you can usually get things sorted at a day's notice (reserve earlier if you want an English-speaking guide). Hikers must pay a one-time access fee of M$60 for routes from 8km to 12km and M$100 for hikes 13km or longer.

One of the villages – Yavesía – doesn't fall under the Expediciones Sierra Norte umbrella and must be dealt with separately through **Lachatao Expediciones** (📞 951-159-71-94, cell 951-1810523; www.facebook.com/lachataoexpediciones) .

---

sharing profits from forestry and other enterprises. In recent years they have also turned to ecotourism to stave off economic difficulties. Currently 120 souls work in a tourist industry that attracts 17,000 annual visitors, and 90% of the money goes back into the communities.

🏃 Activities

Hiking

Over 100km of trails link the eight villages. You can spend one afternoon or up to four days wandering at will. If you're short on time, the 3½-hour walk between Benito Juárez and Cuajimoloyas on the **Needa-Naa-Lagashxi trail** includes a visit to **El Mirador**, a craning lookout tower perched high above the village; the **Piedra Larga**, a giant rock you can scramble up to for views of Pico Orizaba (Mexico's highest mountain peak) on a clear day; and a bouncy **suspension bridge** across a ravine.

Other good day walks include the **Ruta Loma de Cucharilla** from Cuajimoloyas to Latuvi (about six hours, nearly all downhill), and two ancient tracks leading on from Latuvi: the **Camino Real** to San Juan Chicomezúchil and Amatlán, and the beautiful **Latuvi–Lachatao canyon trail** passing through cloud forests festooned with bromeliads and hanging mosses (keep your eyes peeled for trogons on this route).

Using a basic map available from Expediciones Sierra Norte (p446), it is possible to hike on your own, but beware: signposting is sometimes lacking.

Cycling

Welcome to mountain-biking paradise. Cycling routes meander between all eight villages. Of note is the **Circuito Taurino Mecinas Ceballos**, a 30km circuit linking Benito Juárez, Latuvi and La Nevería. Another possibility is the **Ruta Ka-Yezzi-Daa-Vii**, a 28km (one-way) ride between Cuajimoloyas and Lachatao. Beware of rough and steep sections. Reasonable bike-handling skills are essential.

Bike rentals are available in Benito Juárez and Cuajimoloyas for M$240 for three hours (from M$420 with a guide).

Horseback Riding

Horseback riding is an adventurous and highly satisfying way of exploring the Sierra Norte. Costs are M$350/480 per three/four hours.

Zip-Lining

A spectacular 1km-long zip-line (M$240) starts on the slopes of 3200m-high Yaa-Cuetzi and carries you over the rooftops of the village of Cuajimoloyas at speeds reaching 65km/h.

There's another shorter zip-line circuit (three cables) in Benito Juárez costing M$200 per person.

ℹ️ Getting There & Away

Benito Juárez is the nearest of the villages from Oaxaca city, 60km away by road heading northeast.

Check with Expediciones Sierra Norte (p446) in Oaxaca for current public transportation details. For private transportation, Sierra Norte operates a shared van (making stops along the way) that goes to Benito Juárez, Cuajimoloyas, Latuvi or La Nevería for M$170 to M$230 (one way) and private vans to most villages for M$800 (one way) for two people. It can also transport groups of up to 14 people by van to any of the villages for M$4000 to M$4500 round trip: reserve at least one day before.

THE SOUTHERN VILLAGES

Faden runs buses from Oaxaca's 2nd-class station (p460) to Cuajimoloyas (M$80, two hours) and Llano Grande (M$90, 2½ hours) leaving daily at 7am, 9am, noon, 2pm, 4pm and 8pm. For Benito Juárez get off at the Benito Juárez turnoff ('desviación de Benito Juárez'), 3km before Cuajimoloyas, and walk 3.5km west to Benito Juárez. From Benito Juárez, La Nevería is an 8km walk west, and Latuvi 12km north.

AMATLÁN & LACHATAO

Your best options to reach these villages are either by car or arranging transportation with Expediciones Sierra Norte, which charges M$2200 round trip for two people.

WESTERN OAXACA

Western Oaxaca is dramatic and mountainous, with a fairly sparse population and some thick forests as well as overfarmed and deforested areas. Along with adjoining parts of Puebla and Guerrero states, it is known as the Mixteca, for its Mixtec indigenous inhabitants. The region offers a chance to get well off the beaten track, enjoy hiking or biking in remote areas and see some outstanding colonial architecture. Guided trips are available from Oaxaca with operators such as Tierraventura (p446) and Bicicletas Pedro Martínez (p448).

Santiago Apoala

POP 190 / ELEVATION 1980M

In the heart of Oaxaca's Mixtec region, this small, remote village is nestled in a green, Shangri-la–like valley flanked by cliffs. Though still little publicized, it is a lovely spot for hiking, biking and climbing. The village, which is small and rustic, practices a form of community tourism similar to that in the Pueblos Mancomunados.

In traditional Mixtec belief, this valley was the birthplace of humanity, and the scenery around Apoala is appropriately spectacular, with the 60m waterfall **Cascada Cola de Serpiente**, the 400m-deep **Cañón Morelos** and a number of caves, ancient rock carvings and paintings among the highlights.

The easy way to get here is with an agency from Oaxaca – Tierraventura (p446) does a good two-day tour – but it's cheaper to make your own way and arrange things directly

with the village's community-tourism unit, Ecoturismo Comunal Yutsa To'on (p473).

Ecoturismo Comunal
Yutsa To'on   CABAÑAS $

(WhatsApp only 951-2291813; r M$200, cabañas M$500-700, mains M$60-70; P) Santiago Apoala's cozy *cabañas* are run by the village's community-tourism unit. They have bathrooms with hot water, and a wonderfully tranquil riverside location. There are also two rooms available in town, where the tourism center has its office and restaurant, but you can't beat the sheer beauty of the cabins' surroundings.

Getting There & Away

Santiago Apoala is 40km north of the town of Nochixtlán, by a rough, unpaved road that takes about two hours to drive. Nochixtlán is served by 20 daily buses from Oaxaca's 1st-class bus station (M$73 to M$173, 1½ to two hours). Between Nochixtlán and Apoala, your best bet is taking a **taxi** (cnr 2 de Abril & Altamirano; one way M$300) (M$300). A half block north of 2 de Abril is the not so reliable *camioneta* bus, which normally leaves Nochixtlán at noon on Wednesday, Saturday and Sunday (M$60, two hours), and heads back to Nochixtlán the following day at 6am. Beware: the schedule is 'flexible.'

OAXACA COAST

Oaxaca's beautiful, little-developed Pacific coast is home to several varied, relaxed beach destinations, and a near-empty shoreline strung with long golden beaches and lagoons full of wildlife. Offshore are turtles (this is a major global sea-turtle nesting area), dolphins and whales, plus diving, snorkeling, sportfishing and some of North America's best surfing swells. In this tropical climate, the pace is never too hectic, the atmosphere is relaxed and the people are welcoming. Everywhere the scenery is spectacular and you're in direct touch with the elements wherever you go, from the half-hidden sandy beaches to the crashing surf to the river-threaded mountains rising just inland. No need to pack too many clothes!

The area spins on three main hubs: the restrained resort zone of Huatulco, the loose federation of beach villages south of Pochutla (including nude-friendly Zipolite, laid-back San Agustinillo and yoga-practicing Mazunte) and the carefree surf town of Puerto Escondido.

Puerto Escondido

🎵 954 / POP 42,000

Is this where surfers go when they die? Many places claim to be the world's best surfing beach, but Puerto Escondido's Playa Zicatela – 3.5km of golden sand and crashing waves – would make most wave-riders' top 10. Even if you have no desire to test your balance as a 20ft wave curls over your head, Mexico's 'hidden port' is a highly desirable place, a small mellow town where Mexicans, expats and world travelers intermingle.

While it's hardly undiscovered these days, PE remains pleasantly rough around the edges and, thanks to its spread-out nature, rarely feels urban. Plus there's more to do here than just ride white-knuckle on waves. Playa Carrizalillo – the superstar of Mexico's beaches – is a gorgeous place to hang out, swim and live vicariously as a surfer dude(ette), while nearby Rinconada has emerged as Puerto's culinary hot spot. For late-night mischief, Zicatela's casual beach bars host spirited dance parties.

👁 Sights

★ Playa Zicatela   BEACH

(Map p478; 🅿) Legendary 3.5km-long Zicatela is the best-known surfing spot in Mexico courtesy of the tempestuous surfing waves of the Mexican Pipeline. The heart of the action, including the Pipeline, is at Zicatela's northern end. Nonsurfers beware: the waters here have a lethal undertow and are not safe for the boardless, or beginner surfers either. Lifeguards rescue several careless people most months. Surfing aside, the beach is a beauty: wide, golden and gloriously laid-back – man!

The main beach area is backed by **Calle del Morro**, a kind of gringo-ville meets Mexican beach town where locals, along with visitors from colder climes, mix seamlessly.

The **Punta Zicatela** area at Zicatela's far southern end has mellower surf and a mellower vibe to go with it. With its unpaved roads overlooked by vegan cafes and yoga retreats, it's favored chiefly by backpackers and beginner surfers.

★ Playa Carrizalillo   BEACH

(Map p476) Small is beautiful at Carrizalillo, set in a sheltered cove west of the center that's reached by a stairway of 157 steps. It's popular for swimming and bodyboarding, and is *the* place for beginner surfers. Book a lesson and

you'll probably end up here making a splash or three 50m offshore. There's a mellow line of *palapa* beach bars when you finish.

Casa Wabi   ARTS CENTER

(www.casawabi.org; Hwy 200 Km 113; M$250; ⊘ guided visits 4pm Tue & Thu, 10am Sat) 🎋 Casa Wabi, a sprawling artists' residency that occupies a wonderfully airy building designed by famed Japanese architect Tadao Ando, runs tours three times a week at its sublime oceanfront property 27km west of Puerto Escondido. Founded by Mexican contemporary artist Bosco Sodi, the multidisciplinary arts center features an indoor gallery and several outdoor exhibits on the beach.

Tour proceeds for the nonprofit go to an outreach program in which resident artists impart workshops in 14 local communities. Casa Wabi is best reached by car.

Bahía Puerto Angelito   BEACH

(Map p476) The sheltered bay of Puerto Angelito has two smallish beaches with shallow, usually calm waters: the western **Playa Angelito** and the eastern **Playa Manzanillo**. Both have lots of seafood *comedores* and are very popular with Mexican families on weekends and holidays. Manzanillo has the more relaxed vibe. You can rent snorkel gear for around M$50 per hour.

Bahía Principal   BEACH

(Map p476) Puerto Escondido's central bay is long enough to accommodate restaurants at its west end, a fleet of fishing boats in its center (Playa Principal), and sun worshippers and bodyboarders at its east end (Playa Marinero), where the waters are a little cleaner. Pelicans wing in centimeters above the waves, boats bob on the swell and a few hawkers prowl up and down with a low-key sales pitch.

🏃 Activities

Diving & Snorkeling

Typical visibility is around 10m, rising to as much as 30m between May and August, when the seas are warmest. The reefs are of volcanic rock, with lots of marine life, including big schools of fish, spotted eagle rays, stingrays and turtles. Most dive sites are within a 15-minute boat ride. Puerto's dive outfits offer snorkeling and marine-life-spotting trips as well as dives for certified divers and a variety of courses.

Deep Blue Dive   DIVING, SNORKELING

(Map p478; 📱cell 954-1278306; www.deep bluedivemexico.com; Calle del Morro, Beach Hotel

Inés; 1-/2-tank dives US\$55/85, snorkeling tour US\$30; ⊙9am-2pm & 4:30-8pm Mon-Sat) This professional, European-run outfit with Professional Association of Diving Instructors (PADI) dive master guides does one-tank, two-tank and night dives for certified divers, one-morning Discover Scuba sessions and a range of PADI diving courses. A two-hour snorkeling outing visits three different beaches and includes gear.

Aventura Submarina   DIVING
(Map p476; ☑cell 954-5444862; bravoescondido@gmail.com; Av Pérez Gasga 609; snorkeling/2-tank dive M\$500/1600; ⊙9am-5pm Mon-Sat) PADI instructor Jorge Pérez Bravo has more than three decades' experience diving local waters, and offers two-tank dives, plus a range of diving courses and snorkeling trips.

Fishing

Local fishers will take two to four people fishing for marlin, sailfish, tuna or smaller inshore fish: a four-hour trip costs around US\$300 for up to four people. Contact **Omar's Sportfishing** (Map p476; ☑cell 954-5594406; www.omarsportfishing.com; Playa Angelito; whale- & dolphin-watching per person US\$25, half-/full-day fishing per boat US\$300/450). Catch-and-release is encouraged, but boat owners can also arrange for some of the catch to be cooked for you at one of the town's seafood restaurants.

Surfing

Puerto Escondido has surfable waves most days of the year. The Zicatela **Pipeline** is one of the world's heaviest and scariest beach breaks; it's normally best with the offshore winds in the morning and late afternoon, and at its biggest between about May and August. Even when the Pipeline is flat, the point break at Punta Zicatela works almost day in, day out. Playa Carrizalillo has good beginners' waves. Several professional surf contests are held annually at Zicatela: dates depend partly on swell forecasts, but there's always an event during the November fiestas. In 2015 the World Surf League's Big Wave Tour came to Zicatela for the first time.

Long- or shortboard rental is typically M\$200 to M\$500 per day; bodyboards are normally M\$100 to M\$150. You can buy secondhand boards for between M\$3000 and M\$5000 at several surf shops in Zicatela.

Numerous surf shops, schools and individuals at Zicatela, Punta Zicatela and Rinconada offer surfing lessons. Lessons normally last 1½ to two hours in the water,

LOCAL KNOWLEDGE

RESPONSIBLE WHALE-WATCHING

The federal government has created a new 280-sq-km whale-watching zone off the southern coast of Puerto Escondido that requires licensed tour-boat operators to abide by certain rules on excursions. Boats visiting the designated observation area must maintain a safe distance of at least 60m from the whales and passengers are prohibited from swimming with the cetaceans, a practice that's been known to cause stress for aquatic mammals. Whale-watching can be done from November to March but the best months of the year for spotting the gentle giants are January and February. You'll typically see humpback whales in the waters of Puerto Escondido and Mazunte, both of which now have protected zones. Omar's Sportfishing (p475) and Deep Blue Dive (p474) offer whale-watching trips.

with prices including board use and transportation to wherever the waves are most suitable (often Carrizalillo).

Puerto Surf   SURFING
(Map p478; ☑954-122-01-72, cell 954-1096406; www.puertosurf.com.mx; Nuevo León, Punta Zicatela; 1-/3-day classes M\$750/2100, board rental per day M\$250, r M\$600-900) Run by the amiable David Salinas, the youngest of six well-known Puerto surfer brothers, Puerto Surf offers good three-day surf courses that can be taken individually or with a group. One-day classes are also available, and they have a comfortable seven-room guesthouse in La Punta.

🎓 Courses

Experiencia   LANGUAGE
(Map p476; ☑954-582-18-18; www.spanishpuerto.com; Andador Revolución 21; Spanish-surfing package per week US\$283-410, with lodging from US\$523) Experiencia has a reputation for professionalism and a good atmosphere, and combines language learning with activities, excursions and volunteer projects (including turtles). Tuition is in small groups or one-to-one, and programs range from 10 to 40 hours per week, with all levels catered for. The Spanish-surfing package is popular (try conjugating subjunctive tense while trying to stand on a surfboard).

Puerto Escondido

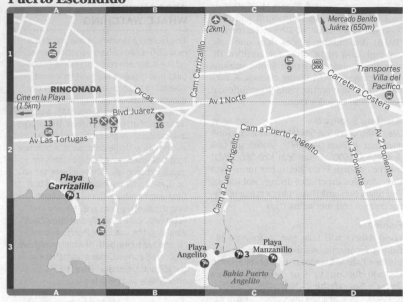

Puerto Escondido

Instituto de Lenguajes Puerto Escondido LANGUAGE
(Puerto School; Map p478; ☎ 954-582-20-55; www.puertoschool.com; Carretera Costera s/n, Zicatela; small-group/private classes per person per hour US$8/12) This small, student-centered school emphasizes both spoken and written Spanish and receives good reports for teaching quality. Excursions and activities, including surfing, salsa and art workshops, are available at extra cost. It's set in tropical gardens overlooking Zicatela beach, with wi-fi and student bungalows available onsite.

You can start any day, at any level, and study for as long as you like.

☞ Tours

★**Gina's Tours** CULTURAL, HISTORICAL
(Map p476; ☎ 954-582-02-76, cell 954-5595518; www.ginainpuertoescondido.wordpress.com; Av Pérez Gasga, Tourist Information Kiosk; market tour M$400, tours to Playa Escobilla/Tututepec M$900/1000, food & mezcal tour M$1200; ⊗ 10am-1:30pm & 4-6pm Mon-Fri, 10am-1:30pm Sat) Gina Machorro, Puerto's energetic and knowledgeable tourist information officer, leads a variety of personally guided tours including trips to Playa Escobilla (p485) to observe nesting turtles, and popular Saturday-morning visits to the Mercado Benito Juárez (p481) with

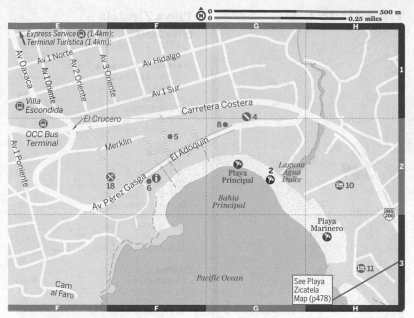

an introduction to local history, market food and religion (two hours). She also runs food and mezcal tours with transportation to and from your hotel.

Or consider a guided visit to **Tututepec** village, an ancient indigenous Mixtec capital west of Puerto Escondido, which has ruins, Mixtec *artesanías* and a good little archaeological museum. Tututepec trips include lunch and a 20-minute local dance and music performance.

★**Lalo Ecotours**   BIRD-WATCHING
(Map p478; ☎954-582-16-11, cell 954-5889164; www.lalo-ecotours.com; Calle del Morro; bird-watching/bioluminescense/turtle-release tours per person M$800/350/300; ☉office 9am-9pm) 🌱 Lalo's is run by an experienced local bird guide who lives right next to the Laguna de Manialtepec (p483). *Lancha* (motorboat) trips include pickups from Puerto Escondido. Lalo's also offers night tours to observe the lagoon's bioluminescense as well as trips to turtle-release beaches and coffee farms.

Campamento Tortuguero Palmarito   WILDLIFE
(☎cell 958-1044707; donation M$100; 🚸) 🌱 A few kilometers west of Puerto Escondido, the Palmarito sea-turtle camp collects tens

of thousands of newly laid turtle eggs each year, and reburies them in a fenced enclosure to protect them from human and animal predators. When the baby turtles hatch after about six weeks, visitors can help release them into the sea.

Lalo Ecotours (p477) and other agencies take groups from town to participate for around M$300 per person: look for 'Liberación de Tortugas' signs. The camp is down a track off Hwy 200 just after the Km 134 marker, 3km past the airport. Call ahead to ask when they will be releasing turtles and expect to pay a donation.

La Puesta del Sol   BIRD-WATCHING
(☎cell 954-5889055, cell 954-1328294; www.facebook.com/lapuestamanialtepec; Hwy 200 Km 124; bird-watching/bioluminescence tours M$1600/200, kayaks per hour M$100; ☉restaurant 8am-6pm, bioluminescence tour 8pm; 🚸) This pretty, family-run, lakeside restaurant, just off Hwy 200 about 2.5km from the eastern end of Laguna Manialtepec, is a good base if you're getting to Manialtepec under your own steam. It serves excellent food (breakfast dishes M$60 to M$100, lunch M$100 to M$200), and does two-hour bird-watching boat trips and evening bioluminescence tours of the lagoon.

OAXACA PUERTO ESCONDIDO

Playa Zicatela

0 _____ 100 m
0 _____ 0.05 miles

See Puerto Escondido Map (p476)

MEX 200

Playa Zicatela 1

PACIFIC OCEAN

Calle del Morro

Carretera Costera

Bajada Las Brisas

COLONIA SANTA MARÍA

Punta Zicatela (2km)

Jacarandas

Vista Hermosa

Punta Zicatela

Tamaulipas

Brisas

Justo Salvador Maldonado

Alejandro Cárdenas Peralta

PACIFIC OCEAN

Heroes Oaxaqueños

Playa Zicatela

◎ Top Sights
1 Playa Zicatela A2

◎ Activities, Courses & Tours
Deep Blue Dive ....(see 7)
2 Instituto de Lenguajes Puerto
Escondido................................ B2
3 Lalo Ecotours................................ A3
4 Puerto Surf.................................... A7
5 Viajes Dimar.................................. A3

◎ Sleeping
6 Aqua Luna B4
7 Beach Hotel Inés A3
8 Casamar B6
9 Frutas y Verduras......................... A7
10 Hostal One Love B5
11 Hotel Buena Vista A2
12 Hotel Casa de Dan......................... B4
Hotel Rockaway.......................(see 3)
13 Hotelito Swiss Oasis B2

◎ Eating
14 Alaburger....................................... A6
15 Dan's Café Deluxe B4
16 El Cafecito A3
17 El Coste A2
18 La Hostería Bananas A3
19 Lychee A7
One Love...................................(see 10)
20 Pepe's Tacos................................. B5

◎ Drinking & Nightlife
21 Casa Babylon................................ A2

◎ Entertainment
22 Mar & Wana A4

Viajes Dimar TOURS
(Map p476; ☏954-582-02-59; www.viajes
dimar.com; Av Pérez Gasga 905; tours per person
M$300-1000; ⊙6am-8pm Mon-Sat, to 5pm Sun)
Long-established and reliable Dimar offers a
good range of day and half-day trips to Manialtepec, Chacahua, waterfalls, hot springs
and other places of interest in the area, with
English-speaking guides.

There's also a **Zicatela branch** (Map
p478; ☏954-582-23-05; Calle del Morro s/n, Zicatela; ⊙9am-9pm Mon-Sat, to 5pm Sun).

✷ Festivals & Events

Fiestas de Noviembre CULTURAL, SPORTS
(⊙Nov) Puerto buzzes throughout November with many events and festivities, including the Festival Costeño de la Danza
(folk dance), sportfishing and surfing tournaments, motocross contests, and plenty
more.

🛏 Sleeping

Accommodations are scattered from the Rinconada and Bacocho areas in the west of town to the central Adoquín area and out to the southeast along Playa Zicatela.

During the Christmas to New Year and Easter vacations, prices can double or even more, but in the low season many rates drop dramatically. It's worth reserving ahead in the busy seasons.

★ Hotel Casa de Dan   HOTEL $
(Map p478; ☑954-582-27-60; www.hotelcasa dan.com; Jacarandas 14, Colonia Santa María; r M$500-1000; P❄🅟🛜🏊) Run by an expat Canadian, these magnificent accommodations just back from Zicatela beach are head and shoulders above much of the opposition. The 14 individualistic *cabañas* and apartments have all the usual bells and whistles (comfortable beds, large bathrooms and plenty of Mexican craft touches), but with a few notable extras, such as kitchens.

Here you can enjoy a proper lap pool, a veritable library of books, a deluxe affiliated cafe and the charming presence of Dan himself (and/or his excellent staff). And it all comes at a highly reasonable price. Book ahead; it's understandably popular.

Hostal One Love   HOTEL, HOSTEL $
(Map p478; ☑cell 954-1298582; www.hostal puertoescondido.com; Brisas de Zicatela; dm M$250, r M$700-950; 🛜) The big dilemma at One Love is whether to stay in the John Lennon room or the Jim Morrison suite or, if you're feeling a little more bluesy, the *habitación de* Janis Joplin. Classier than many of the hippie joints in La Punta, One Love is a high-walled, wonderfully private domain packed with lush ferns and music legends.

The circular rooms are decorated with art and photos of the peace-loving rock heroes they are named after and are exceedingly comfortable, especially the 'One Love' suite. Bonus: there's an excellent onsite restaurant (p481) that generously accepts nonguests.

Casa Losodeli   HOSTEL $
(Map p476; ☑954-582-42-21; www.losodeli.com; Prolongación 2a Norte; dm M$180-200, r M$750-850; P❄🅟🛜🏊) Popular, well-run Losodeli, located between the bus stations and Rinconada, provides most things a budget traveler needs: clean accommodations with a choice between bunk dorms and private rooms (some very spacious), friendly staff, a well-equipped, well-organized kitchen, a good pool in the central garden, free bikes, breakfast available (M$50), and bookings for many outings and activities.

Hotel Buena Vista   HOTEL $
(Map p478; ☑954-582-14-74; www.facebook. com/hotelbuenavistapuertoescondido; Calle del Morro s/n; r M$500-500, with air-con M$730-790; ❄🛜) The 11 no-frills rooms at this hillside Zicatela hotel are big and spotless, with two beds, mosquito screens, breezy balconies and some have kitchens. It's fine value, centrally located and the 'good view' is as advertised.

Frutas y Verduras   CABAÑAS, ROOMS $
(Map p478; ☑cell 954-1230473; www.facebook .com/frutasyverdurasmexico; Cárdenas s/n, Punta Zicatela; r M$600-1000, without bathroom M$500-800, apt M$2000-3000; ❄🛜🏊) 'Fruit & Veg' might sound like a strange name for a hotel, but this is the surfer-hippie enclave of La Punta where being weird is considered relatively normal. Gelling eloquently with the rustic jungly feel of the 'hood, this place sports tiny simple *cabañas* with mosquito nets, highly colorful screened rooms, and three apartments – some with private bathroom.

Surprise: there's a small pool, a new 'chillout' lounge upstairs, an inviting restaurant called Café Olé and free bicycles.

Casamar   SUITES $$
(Map p478; ☑954-582-25-93; www.casamar suites.com; Puebla 407, Brisas de Zicatela; r US$58-125; P❄🛜🏊) North American–owned Casamar is a luxurious, comfortable and health-conscious vacation retreat. The 17 spacious, air-conditioned rooms are instantly impressive and all have gorgeous kitchens and tasteful Mexican art and crafts decor, much of it locally made. At the center of things is a large, fern-draped garden with a sizable pool.

Hotel Rockaway   HOTEL $$
(Map p478; ☑954-582-06-68; www.hotelrock away.com; Calle del Morro; d/ste incl breakfast from M$1380/2370; P❄🛜🏊) This newish hotel is Zicatela's fledgling posh abode, advertising itself in slick white with purple accents. Rooms are as attractive as they are spotless, the beach is across the road and the hotel incorporates a wider complex that also includes a decent gym (guests get free access).

Hotel Villa Mozart y Macondo
BUNGALOW $$

(Map p476; ☑954-104-22-95; villamozarty macondo@hotmail.com; Av Las Tortugas 77, Rinconada; r M$850-1300; ☞) The work of art here is not courtesy of Wolfgang Amadeus, instead it's a verdant tropical garden (Jardín Macondo) filled with avant-garde Peruvian sculptures. Around the sides are the adults-only accommodations – four rooms with bright, artistic touches and all mod cons (some have king-sized beds and one features a kitchenette.

Three obvious bonuses: there's a pleasant onsite cafe, the owner is super-welcoming and Playa Carrizalillo (Puerto's best swimming beach) is a short walk away.

Hotel Suites La Hacienda
HOTEL $$

(Map p476; ☑954-582-02-79; www.facebook. com/hotelsuiteslahacienda; Av Atunes 15, Rinconada; r from M$1448; ❉❄) Colonial-style rooms, some with full kitchen and sitting area, overlook attractive courtyards with fountains and a large pool area edged by a tropical garden. Great restaurants, sidewalk cafes and Puerto's best beach are all within walking distance.

Hotelito Swiss Oasis
HOTEL $$

(Map p478; ☑954-582-14-96; www.swissoasis. com; Andador Gaviotas 1; r US$50-65; ☞❄) This small hotel provides a guest kitchen with free coffee, tea and purified water, and a pool in the pretty garden, in addition to eight fan-cooled rooms and one apartment with good beds, mosquito screens and attractive color schemes. The well-traveled Swiss owners speak four languages and are very helpful with local information. No under-15s.

Hotel Flor de María
HOTEL $$

(Map p476; ☑954-582-05-36; www.mexonline. com/flordemaria.htm; 1a Entrada a Playa Marinero; r US$50-65; ℗☞❄) A popular Canadian-owned hotel with 24 ample rooms sporting good large bathrooms, folksy Mexican decor and pretty wall and door paintings. A highlight is the expansive roof terrace with its fabulous views, bar and small pool. No under-12s.

Beach Hotel Inés
HOTEL $$

(Map p478; ☑954-582-07-92; www.hotel ines.com; Calle del Morro s/n; r M$1080-1350; ℗❉☞❄) German-run Inés has a wide variety of bright, cheerful *cabañas*, rooms, apartments and suites, around a shaded pool area with a restaurant serving good Euro/ Mexican food. Most accommodations have air-con available, and some come with kitch-en or Jacuzzi. You can arrange horseback riding, surf lessons, diving and other outings – and security is particularly good here.

Aqua Luna
HOTEL $$

(Map p478; ☑954-582-15-05; www.hotelaqua luna.com; Vista Hermosa s/n, Colonia Santa María; d M$500-600, with air-con M$900-1000, apt M$1200; ❉☞❄) In contrast to the beach shacks often beloved of surfers, Aqua Luna offers cool, contemporary black-and-white minimalism with a few nods to Mexican style (a poolside *palapa* and a panoramic deck with a hot tub). The brainchild of an Aussie surfer, it still attracts plenty of boarders thanks to excellent-value rooms, some with kitchen. All-day breakfasts and light dishes are served at the poolside bar.

★ Villas Carrizalillo
BOUTIQUE HOTEL $$$

(Map p476; ☑954-582-17-35; www.villas carrizalillo.com; Av Carrizalillo 125, Rinconada; apt US$185-240; ℗❉☞❄) There's no shortage of inspired accommodations perched on spectacular headlands on the Oaxacan coast, but the Carrizalillo stands out even on this dreamy littoral. It helps that it overlooks one of the area's most gorgeous beaches, has a plush restaurant (Espadin) on a covered terrace, and spacious, stylish, air-conditioned apartments with one to three bedrooms.

Nearly all the grandly decorated apartments have kitchen and private terrace, and about half afford panoramic coastal views. A path goes directly down to the beach. Discounts are offered for cash payments.

Hotel Escondido
CABAÑAS $$$

(☑954-582-22-24; www.hotelescondido.com; Hwy 200 Km 113; cabañas US$400-450; ℗☞❄) Escapists will love the quiet calm of this remote, adults-only beach getaway 27km west of Puerto Escondido. On offer are 16 minimalist-style thatched-roof *cabañas* with painted wood floors, plush beds, private patios sporting plunge pools, an excellent onsite Mexican-fusion restaurant and a long, serene beach that you'll pretty much have to yourself.

Hotel Santa Fe
HOTEL $$$

(Map p476; ☑954-582-47-00; www.hotelsanta fe.com.mx; Calle del Morro s/n; r from M$1950; ℗❉❄) Bringing some taste to the menu of hotel architecture, the Santa Fe is a neo-colonial-style beauty filled with greenery, birdsong, terracotta pots and a subtle folkloric theme. The 60 rooms with attractive terracotta-tile floors and wood furnishings are set around two pools shaded by palms, and the reputable restaurant (p482) overlooking Zicatela beach is pescatarian, serving strictly fish and vegetarian dishes.

✖ Eating

Virginia's Supercafe CAFE $
(Map p476; ✆cell 954-1003464; www.facebook. com/virginiassupercafe; Andador La Soledad 2; breakfast M$70-120; ۞7:30am-2pm Wed-Mon; ⬥) Hidden away off a quiet stairway, Virginia's cafe is pretty super, particularly if you're judging it by its coffee (among the best in the city and roasted onsite) and its waffles (chunky with inventive toppings). The ultimate breakfast stop.

Dan's Café Deluxe INTERNATIONAL $
(Map p478; ✆954-582-27-60; www.facebook. com/danscafedeluxe; Jacarandas 14, Colonia Santa María; breakfast M$49-75, light meals M$55-95; ۞7am-4pm; ⬥✐) Dan was one of the founders of local legend El Cafecito (p482) and this spot next to his eponymous hotel is great for hearty, surfer-pleasing breakfasts, juices and *licuados* (smoothies), and healthy lunch options like salads, wholewheat sandwiches and vegetable stir-fry. Dan's also does fish and shrimp tacos on weekends.

One Love EUROPEAN, MEXICAN $
(Map p478; ✆cell 954-1298582; www.hostal puertoescondido.com; Tamaulipas s/n, Brisas de Zicatela; mains M$75-170; ۞8am-9:30pm Tue-Sun; ⬥✐) Excellent Euro-Mexican dishes with fresh local ingredients are served in this restaurant run by a Mexican–French couple. You could start with the 'One Love taco' (a ceviche wrap with a dressing of mango and habanero chili) and follow up with 'Give Peace a Chance' (breaded catch of the day with tabbouleh and chili mayo), but there's plenty of choice, including vegetarian dishes.

Pepe's Tacos TACOS $
(Map p478; www.facebook.com/pepesfishtacos; cnr San Luis Potosí & Calfornia, Brisas de Zicatela; tacos M$60; ۞2-10pm Wed-Mon) Popular with surfers, this hidden sand-floor shack serves large coconut-encrusted shrimp and battered fish tacos topped with a colorful variety of chopped fruit and veggies. They're mighty tasty, we just wish the gringo-friendly salsas had a bit more heat. There's no sign outside so follow your nose.

El Sultán MIDDLE EASTERN $
(Map p476; ✆954-582-05-12; www.facebook. com/elsultanptoescondido; Blvd Juárez, Rinconada; dishes M$55-80; ۞9am-10pm Tue-Sat; ⬥✐) For a puff on a hookah pipe and a dose of falafel served with strong coffee, park yourself on one of the cushions at Sultán, an unlikely oasis of cheap Middle Eastern snack food on the posh Rinconada strip (they also do shawarma and hummus).

Mercado Benito Juárez MARKET $
(Calle 8a Norte, btwn Calles 3a & 4a Poniente; mains M$40-120; ۞7am-7pm) For local flavors and the true PE atmosphere, head to the main market in the upper part of town, where dozens of *comedores* serve fresh fish and shrimp, soups and *antojitos* at ridiculously cheap prices. Wander the flower, food and craft stalls and try out some of the unusual offerings at the line of juice stalls.

'Mercado' buses (M$8) run up Av Oaxaca.

Alaburger INTERNATIONAL $$
(Map p478; ✆cell 954-1816068; Cárdenas s/n, Punta Zicatela; mains M$100-250; ۞11am-11pm; ⬥) Talk about simple. Alaburger inhabits a beach garden where its congenial owners have constructed an open kitchen under a thatched roof. But, oh the food! Baked potatoes, pizzas, burgers, grilled fish and a vegan menu good enough to turn you into one. The best culinary alchemy often emerges from the most modest food shacks – like this one.

El Nene MEXICAN, FUSION $$
(Map p476; ✆cell 33-11754842; www.facebook. com/restaurantelnene; Blvd Juárez, Rinconada; mains M$90-265; ۞2:30-10:30pm Mon-Sat; ⬥) El Nene serves enormous tacos and Mexican- and international-style fish, shrimp and chicken mains. Fish of the day prepared Cajun-style is a good choice, and you could start with flavorsome mussels in white wine. The plant-fringed patio setting adds to one of Puerto's best eating experiences.

Lychee THAI $$
(Map p478; ✆cell 954-1345718; www.facebook. com/lycheemex; cnr Cárdenas & Héroes Oaxaqueñas, Punta Zicatela; mains M$140-190; ۞5-11:30pm; ✐) La Punta resembles in some ways a sybaritic Thai beach and Lychee doesn't have to try hard to meld in with superb Thai dishes – green curries, chicken satay, spicy coconut soup – and other Southeast Asian standards cooked up in the middle of a large, rectangular wooden bar, with

alfresco log tables and benches set on the earth around it.

Save room for the chocolate lava cake!

Pez Gallo SEAFOOD $$
(✆954-582-03-50; www.facebook.com/restaurante pezgallo; Club de Playa Villasol, Playa Bacocho; mains M$130-220; ⊗8am-7pm; 🕾🍴) Seafood dishes such as the catch of the day encrusted in coconut are popular at this beach club's oceanfront *palapa* restaurant, plus you get the added perks of free access to one of Puerto Escondido's most swimmable beaches and a large onsite pool (always a splash hit with the kids).

El Cafecito MEXICAN, INTERNATIONAL $$
(Map p478; ✆954-582-05-16; www.facebook.com/elcafecitopuertoescondido; Calle del Morro s/n; breakfast dishes M$59-122, mains M$78-279; ⊗6am-11pm; 🕾🍴) Cafecito has cornered the market in crossover gringo-Mexican fusion food with large surfer appetites in mind. Herein are some of the best breakfasts on the coast: endless egg concoctions, huge fruit dishes, pasta and bowls of rich Oaxacan chocolate. Icing on the cake is the onsite Carmen's bakery with a walk-up window offering coffee and baked goods.

There's another equally busy branch in Rinconada.

La Hostería Bananas ITALIAN, MEXICAN $$
(Map p478; ✆954-582-00-05; Calle del Morro s/n; mains M$145-210; ⊗8am-11:30pm; 🕾🍴) The Hostería is an Italian labor of love, from its gleaming kitchen (with computerized wood-fired pizza oven) to the Talavera-tiled bathrooms. A broad selection of dishes, including many veggie and homemade pasta options, is paired with a great drinks list, good breakfast deals and strong coffee. The seafood skewers are epic.

Hotel Santa Fe VEGETARIAN, SEAFOOD $$
(Map p476; ✆954-582-47-00; www.hotelsantafe.com.mx; Calle del Morro s/n; mains M$90-283; ⊗7:30am-10pm; 🕾🍴) The attractive Hotel Santa Fe's restaurant sits on a covered terrace looking along Zicatela beach and is a pescatarian affair (no meat – just fish and veg). Options include tofu dishes, vegetarian *antojitos* and a Mediterranean plate with hummus, tabbouleh, Greek salad and pita bread.

★**Almoraduz** MEXICAN $$$
(Map p476; ✆954-582-31-09; www.almoraduz.com.mx; Blvd Juárez 11-12, Rinconada; mains M$295-580, tasting menu M$800; ⊗1:30-10pm Mon-Sat,

from 6pm Sun; 🕾🍴) Almoraduz' husband-and-wife culinary alliance creates memorable flavor combinations in one of the Oaxaca's coast's few true gourmet restaurants. It's not at all pretentious. The open dining space in the rising Rinconada quarter is small, tasteful and distinguished. The menu changes frequently: their most popular offerings range from black seafood risotto or fish in green *mole* to chocolate lava cake.

For the 'full monty' opt for the seven-course tasting menu. The drinks selection, including artisan mezcals, craft beers and original fruit drinks, is top-notch too.

El Coste SEAFOOD $$$
(Map p478; ✆954-104-40-80; www.facebook.com/elcostepuertoescondido; Calle del Morro s/n; dishes M$145-350; ⊗1-11pm Thu-Tue; 🕾) Inhabiting a deluxe *palapa* on Zicatela beach, the highly successful El Coste is all about its grilled fish and seafood (take your pick from snapper, bass, prawns and octopus). For those favoring cured seafood, this is arguably the best place in town for ceviche.

🍷 Drinking & Nightlife

Casa Babylon BAR
(Map p478; ✆954-582-08-75; www.facebook.com/casababylonmexico; Calle del Morro s/n; ⊗9am-2am; 🕾) Psychedelic Babylon has a terrifying Mexican mask collection, a sprawling library of books to exchange and varied live music or a DJ Thursday to Saturday performing on a stage surrounded by winged angels and flying nymphs. Word on the street says the mojitos and mezcal margaritas are to die for.

☆ Entertainment

★**Mar & Wana** LIVE MUSIC
(Map p478; ✆954-127-11-95; www.facebook.com/marandwana; Calle del Morro; ⊗5pm-midnight Tue-Thu, to 1am Fri-Sun) Occupying part of a rocky iguana habitat, this sand-floor garden hosts live bands and DJs, while an onsite food court offers gourmet burgers, tacos and Asian fare. Grab a mezcal or cocktail and check out the cool (somewhat hidden) hangout spots up on the rocks.

Cine en la Playa CINEMA
(Cinema on the Beach; ✆954-582-03-50; www.facebook.com/hotelvillasol; Playa Bacocho; ⊗7-9pm Wed Nov-May) A varied program of movies, from recent feature films to art house, classics and documentaries, is shown on the sands of Playa Bacocho at Hotel Suites

WORTH A TRIP

LAGUNA DE MANIALTEPEC

The 6km-long Laguna de Manialtepec, beginning 14km west of Puerto Escondido along Hwy 200, is an essential spot for bird enthusiasts and a fascinating place for anyone interested in nature. Ibises, roseate spoonbills, parrots, pelicans, falcons, ospreys, herons, kingfishers and several types of hawk and iguana call Manialtepec home for at least part of the year. The best bird-watching months are December to March, and the best time of day is soon after dawn.

The lagoon is mainly surrounded by mangroves, but tropical flowers and palms accent the ocean side, and the channel at the west end winds through to a pristine sandbar beach.

Several operators run three-hour bird-watching trips in motorized *lanchas* (outboard boats), with English-speaking guides, binoculars and round-trip transportation from your accommodations in Puerto Escondido. Manialtepec is also a bioluminescent bay where phosphorescent plankton appear for a few nights several times a year. At these times nocturnal boat trips are offered, and you can swim or trail your hand in the water to activate the strange phosphorescent glow. July, August, November and December are often good months for this. Don't bother going when there's a full moon or after heavy rain.

From Puerto Escondido, take a *taxi colectivo* (shared taxi) bound for San José Manialtepec from Av 4 Poniente (M$20 to La Puesta del Sol, 15 minutes), running from about 6am to 8pm, or a Río Grande–bound minibus (M$25) from Av Hidalgo 5, leaving about every 30 minutes from 4am to 9pm.

Villasol's beach club. Films are generally in Spanish with English subtitles, or vice versa.

ⓘ Information

MONEY

Playa Zicatela has a couple of ATMs, but the ones in town work more reliably.

HSBC (☑ 954-582-18-25; Av 1 Norte, btwn Av 2 Poniente & Carretera Costera; ◎ 9am-5pm Mon-Fri, to 2pm Sat) Has a dependable ATM.

Santander (☑ 954-582-38-86; Carretera Costera; ◎ 9am-4pm Mon-Fri, 10am-2pm Sat) Bank with several reliable ATMs and a welcoming blast of air-con.

TOURIST INFORMATION

Tourist Information Kiosk (Map p476; ☑ cell 954-5595518; ginainpuerto@yahoo.com; Av Pérez Gasga; ◎ 10am-1:30pm & 4-6pm Mon-Fri, 10am-1:30pm Sat) Gina Machorro, the energetic, dedicated, multilingual information officer, knows everything that's happening in and around Puerto, happily answers your every question and conducts her own interesting tours (p476).

ⓘ Getting There & Away

AIR

Aeropuerto Internacional de Puerto Escondido (☑ cell 954-1493975; Hwy 200 Km 6.5) Three kilometers west of the center on Hwy 200. Flights to Mexico City and Oaxaca.

Aeromar (☑ 55-5133-1111; www.aeromar. mx; Airport) Up to three daily flights to/from Mexico City.

Aerotucán (☑ 954-582-34-61; www.aerotucan. com; Airport; ◎ 7am-3pm Mon-Sat, 10am-noon Sun) Flies 13-seat Cessnas daily to/from Oaxaca (M$2210). Flights are sometimes rescheduled at short notice.

Interjet (☑ cell 954-1079957; www.interjet. com; Airport; ◎ 8am-5pm Sun-Fri, to 2pm Sat) To/from Mexico City four to seven times weekly.

VivaAerobus (☑ 81-8215-0150; www.vivaaerobus.com; Airport) Budget airline flying daily to/from Mexico City. Flights bought in advance can cost less than M$800.

Volaris (☑ 55-1102-8000; www.volaris.com; Airport) Four weekly flights to/from Mexico City and twice weekly to Guadalajara.

BUS & VAN

OCC Bus Terminal (Map p476; ☑ 954-582-10-73; www.ado.com.mx; Carretera Costera 102) Used by OCC 1st-class and Sur and AU 2nd-class services.

Terminal Turística (Central Camionera; cnr Avs Oaxaca & 4 Poniente) Located in the upper part of town; used by AltaMar (1st class), Turistar (deluxe) and Villa Escondida's vans to Oaxaca.

Oaxaca

The most convenient way of traveling to Oaxaca is in the comfortable van services via Hwy 131 (seven hours) offered by at least two companies. OCC's 1st-class buses (M$280 to M$528, 11 hours, four daily) take a much longer route via Salina Cruz and Hwy 190.

BUSES FROM PUERTO ESCONDIDO

DESTINATION	FARE (M$)	TIME	FREQUENCY (PER DAY)
Acapulco	528	8-9hr	8 AltaMar
Bahías de Huatulco	85-191	2½hr	12 from OCC terminal, 5 from Terminal Turística
Mexico City (Terminal Sur)	1233-1550	12-13hr	3 AltaMar, 1 Turistar 7:45pm
Pochutla	88-124	1¼hr	12 from OCC terminal, 5 from Terminal Turística
Salina Cruz	341-365	5¼hr	11 from OCC terminal
San Cristóbal de las Casas	469-622	13hr	3 from OCC terminal

Express Service (☑ 954-582-24-68; Terminal Turística, cnr Avs Oaxaca & 4 Poniente) Vans to Oaxaca (M$235) hourly from 7am to 2pm, and at 10pm, 11pm and 11:30pm.

Transportes Villa del Pacífico (Map p476; ☑ 954-1325643; Av Hidalgo 5) Frequent vans to Oaxaca (M$220).

Villa Escondida (Map p476; ☑ 954-104-24-69; Av Hidalgo s/n) Vans to Oaxaca (M$250) hourly from 1am to 11pm. Has another office in Terminal Turística (p483). Vans call at both.

Other Destinations

For Mexico City, the AltaMar and Turistar services from the Terminal Turística go via the outskirts of Acapulco and are much quicker than OCC, which takes a longer route via Salina Cruz.

CAR & MOTORCYCLE

To/from Oaxaca city, the winding Hwy 131 via Sola de Vega will one day be superseded by a new highway linking Hwy 200 just east of Puerto Escondido with Hwy 175 south of Ejutla. This will reduce driving time from about seven hours to about four. The highly delayed project is slated for completion in 2022.

Between Puerto Escondido and Acapulco, figure on about seven hours for the 400km drive along Hwy 200, which is well enough surfaced but has a lot of speed bumps.

Los Tres Reyes (☑ 954-582-33-35; www.lostresreyescarrent.com; Carretera Costera 113, Colonia Santa María; ⊙ 7am-8pm) rents economy cars from M$800 per day. They have offices on the highway above Colonia Santa María and at the airport. Slightly cheaper is **Úcar** (☑ cell 954-1490304; www.u-car.mx; Calle del Morro; ⊙ 7am-7pm Mon-Sat, 8am-5pm Sun) with cars from M$770 per day and scooters from M$350.

❶ Getting Around

Shared ticket taxis from the airport will drop you in town for M$50 per person (M$70 to Punta Zicatela). You can usually find a whole cab for a similar price on the main road outside the airport. Taxi rides within town cost M$30 to M$40.

Taxis colectivos, local buses and *camionetas* marked 'Zicatela' or 'La Punta' (all M$8) run approximately every 20 minutes to Punta Zicatela from Mercado Benito Juárez up in the north of the town (near the Terminal Turística), from sunrise to about 8:30pm. They travel down Calle 3 Poniente then east along the Carretera Costera; for El Adoquín or Playa Zicatela you can hop off and walk down in two minutes.

Parque Nacional Lagunas de Chacahua

West of Manialtepec, Hwy 200 winds its way along a coast studded with lagoons, pristine beaches and prolific bird and plant life. Settlements in this region are home to many Afro-Mexicans, descendants of slaves who escaped from the Spanish.

The area around the coastal lagoons of Chacahua and La Pastoría forms the beautiful 149-sq-km Parque Nacional Lagunas de Chacahua, which attracts many migratory birds from Alaska and Canada in winter. Mangrove-fringed islands harbor roseate spoonbills, ibises, cormorants, wood storks, herons and egrets, as well as mahogany trees, crocodiles and turtles. El Corral, a tunnel-like waterway filled with countless birds in winter, connects the two lagoons. The boat trip along the lagoons is fabulous, and at its end Chacahua village sits upon a gorgeous beach curving at least 20km eastward, inviting you to stop for a meal or a night in rustic *cabañas.*

◉ Sights

Cocodrilario de Chacahua   WILDLIFE RESERVE
(Chacahua Crocodile Sanctuary; Chiapas; guided tour by donation; ⊙ 9am-6pm) 🅿 The Cocodrilario de Chacahua houses over 200 crocodiles, releasing some of them into the lagoons occasionally as part of a successful program to save the local wild croc population from extinction at the hands of poach-

ers. It's not specifically set up to receive visitors, but you're welcome to drop by.

Local *lanchas* (M$15 per person) will whiz you across the channel to the inland half of the village where the Cocodrilario is situated.

🛏 Sleeping & Eating

Many of the beach restaurants also have basic *cabañas* costing around M$250 to M$400 for two people.

Cabañas La Isla CABAÑAS $
(📱 cell 954-1305168; M$700-900; 🛜) Locals refer to La Isla as Chacahua's 'luxury' option, and while the four fan-cooled *cabañas* with handcrafted wood furnishings and sliding glass doors are certainly a step above the rest, the cabins are fairly basic. Balconies and decks strewn with hammocks are nice additions.

Restaurante Siete Mares CABAÑAS $
(📱 cell 954-1322263, cell 954-1140062; cabañas M$250) Siete Mares, at the beach's west end (nearest the river), has simple *cabañas*, each with two double beds, fans, mosquito nets, electric light and curtained-off showers in the corner. There's also a pleasant onsite restaurant.

ℹ Getting There & Away

The starting point for boat trips along the lagoons to Chacahua village is the small fishing village of Zapotalito, at the eastern end of Laguna La Pastoría, 63km from Puerto Escondido.

From Puerto Escondido, take a van bound for Pinotepa Nacional from Av Hidalgo 5 (departures about every 20 minutes, 4am to 9pm) and get out at the Zapotalito turnoff (M$50, 1¼ hours), 58km from Puerto (and 8km past the town of Río Grande). From the turnoff, taxis will shuttle you the 5km to Zapotalito for M$80 (M$20 by *colectivo*).

Competing boat cooperatives offer *lancha* services from Zapotalito to Chacahua village, charging approximately M$1500 round trip for up to 10 people, depending on your negotiating skills. When there is sufficient traffic, *colectivo* boats run hourly for M$150 per person one way. All prices go up about 40% at peak holiday times such as Christmas–New Year's and Semana Santa.

For drivers, a mostly unpaved road heads 27km south to Chacahua village from San José del Progreso on Hwy 200. It's passable for normal cars except when waterlogged, which it often is between May and November.

Pochutla

📱 958 / POP 13,700

Bustling, sweaty Pochutla is the market town and transportation hub for the central part of the Oaxaca coast, including the nearby beach spots of Puerto Ángel, Zipolite, San Agustinillo and Mazunte. There's no other reason to pause here.

Hwy 175 from Oaxaca runs through Pochutla as Av Cárdenas, the narrow main street, and meets the coastal Hwy 200 about 1.5km south of town. The bus and van terminals cluster toward the southern, downhill end of Cárdenas.

Hotel San Pedro (📞 958-584-11-23; www.hotel-sanpedro.com.mx; Av Cárdenas 1; s/d M$450/550; 🅿❄🛜), 300m south of the main bus station, does just fine for a night,

OAXACA POCHUTLA

LOCAL KNOWLEDGE

PLAYA ESCOBILLA

This 15km-long beach, beginning about 30km east of Puerto Escondido, is one of the world's major nesting grounds for the olive ridley turtle (*tortuga golfina* to Mexicans). Up to a million female olive ridleys a year arrive at Escobilla to lay their eggs, with numbers peaking at night for a period of about a week around the full moons from July to February – a spectacular phenomenon known as an *arribada* or *arribazón*. The olive ridley is one of the smaller sea turtles (around 70cm long), but still an impressive animal, especially when seen emerging from the surf at a rate of several thousand per hour, as happens during Escobilla's biggest *arribadas*.

To protect the turtles, there is no general public access to the beach; however, **Centro Ecoturístico Escobilla** (📱 WhatsApp 55-11336942; www.facebook.com/ecoturismo.escobilla; Hwy 200 Km 180.5, Escobilla; 👪) 🦎 releases turtles throughout most of the year around 7pm and you can participate for M$150 per person.

Some Puerto Escondido agencies run organized trips to Escobilla; a great option is Gina's Tours (p476).

BUSES FROM POCHUTLA

DESTINATION	FARE (M$)	TIME	FREQUENCY (PER DAY)
Bahías de Huatulco	30-74	1hr	TRP every 15min, Sur hourly, 9 OCC
Mexico City (Terminal Sur)	1089	13½hr	Turistar 8pm
Puerto Escondido	70-124	1¼hr	Sur hourly 7am-8pm, 10 OCC, 4 AltaMar
Salina Cruz	264-276	3¾hr	10 OCC & AU
San Cristóbal de las Casas	493-508	11-12hr	3 OCC
Tapachula	875	12hr	OCC 7pm

but realistically Pochutla is mainly a way station for the coastal villages nearby.

Finca de Vaqueros (☑ cell 958-1004858; Hwy 175 Km 4, El Colorado village; mains M$210-320; ⊙ 10am-10pm; ℗) is a ranch-style restaurant with long tables in a large, open-sided barn that is worth an expedition from anywhere on the coast for its superb grilled meats. It's 2km south of Pochutla on the Puerto Ángel road (M$60 by taxi). Order some *frijoles charros* (bean soup with bacon bits) and *queso fundido* (melted cheese) to start, followed by some tender *arrachera* (skirt steak).

❶ Information

Scotiabank ATM (Av Cárdenas 57; ⊙ 8:30am-4pm Mon-Fri) About 350m north of the bus station along the main street.

❶ Getting There & Away

OAXACA

Oaxaca is 245km away by the curvy Hwy 175 – six hours in the convenient and fairly comfortable air-conditioned van services for around M$200 offered by several companies. The same services will drop you in San José del Pacífico (M$110, three hours). Drivers will also usually stop when you need a bathroom break, or need to vomit, as a few people do on this route. OCC runs four daily 1st-class buses to Oaxaca (M$514, nine hours) from the Terminal de Autobuses San Pedro Pochutla, but they take a much longer and more expensive route via Salina Cruz.

Líneas Unidas (☑ 958-584-67-65; Av Cárdenas 94; one way to Oaxaca M$200) Across the street from the main bus terminal, with vans to Oaxaca every 30 to 60 minutes from 1am to midnight (M$200, six hours).

OTHER DESTINATIONS

Terminal de Autobuses San Pedro Pochutla (☑ 958-584-02-74; cnr Av Cárdenas & Constitución) The main bus station is toward the south end of Av Cárdenas. It's used by ADO, Turistar (deluxe), OCC and AltaMar (1st class),

and Sur and AU (2nd class) services. For distant destinations with limited service, such as San Cristóbal de las Casas and Mexico City, it's advisable to get tickets at least one day ahead.

Taxis to the Beach Villages (TRP; cnr Jamaica & Matamoros) Follow Calle Jamaica west off Av Cárdenas just north of the main bus station. After 150m you will reach a small chapel. To the left, a car park acts as a departure point for shared *taxis colectivos* to the beach villages of Zipolite, San Agustinillo and Mazunte. Prices run from M$20 to M$30. Slightly more expensive shared taxis parked in front of the bus station charge M$35 to the beach.

Transportes Rapidos de Pochutla (TRP; Av Cárdenas 85; to Huatulco M$30) Frequent air-conditioned vans to Huatulco; 5am to 8pm.

Puerto Ángel

☑ 958 / POP 2645

The scruffy entry point to this slice of nirvanic coast has the feel (and smell) of a Mexican fishing village. Boats rather than surfboards embellish the sheltered curve of beach known as Playa Panteón and the food is more tortilla than pizza and pasta. Most travelers don't stop here at all, preferring instead to press on to the beach bliss of San Agustinillo or Mazunte further west without looking back. But a night or two needn't be wasted, especially if you prefer the gritty to the pretty.

⊙ Sights & Activities

Playa La Boquilla BEACH
(℗) The coast east of Puerto Ángel is dotted with small hidden beaches, none of them very busy on weekdays. Playa La Boquilla, on a gentle bay about 7.5km from town by road, is the site of the Bahía de la Luna hotel and restaurant, and is good for snorkeling and swimming. It's fun to go by boat (M$600 one way): ask at Puerto Ángel pier or Playa Panteón.

You can also get here by a rough 3.5km unpaved road from a turnoff 4km out of Puerto Ángel on the Pochutla road. A taxi from Puerto Ángel costs around M$150, or from Pochutla about M$200. Some taxis won't tackle the road in the rainy season.

Azul Profundo   WATER SPORTS
(☑ cell 958-1060420; www.excursionesazulprofundo. com; Playa Panteón; snorkeling per person M$220, fishing boat per hour M$700, kayak rentals per hour M$50) Well-organized Azul Profundo specializes in boat trips (with snorkeling and wildlife-watching thrown in) and sportfishing for marlin, swordfish, sailfish, tuna or mahi-mahi. Its main base is at Hotel Cordelias overlooking Puerto Ángel, but you can also make bookings in the internet cafe (p490) in Zipolite from where they can arrange pickups.

Four-hour snorkeling boat trips take in four bays and go looking for turtles, dolphins and, with luck (from December to March), whales. All guides speak at least a little English.

Kayaks are available for paddling around in Puerto Ángel's sheltered bay for M$50 per hour.

🛏 Sleeping & Eating

Hotel Cordelias   HOTEL $$
(☑ 958-584-30-21; www.hotelcordelias.com; Playa Panteón; r M$800-1200; ❋ 🐾) Not many elect to stay in Puerto Ángel, but, if you do, head to this bright, white hotel run by the owners of boat-tour specialists Azul Profundo. Rooms are large (most with two double beds) and 10 overlook Puerto's merry beach and harbor. There's a fresh-fish restaurant downstairs and boat trips push off from the adjacent jetty. Just the package!

Bahía de la Luna   BUNGALOW $$$
(☑ 958-589-50-20; www.bahiadelaluna.com; Playa La Boquilla; r incl breakfast from M$2200; 🅿 🐾) This rustic-chic hideaway sits in splendid isolation at lovely Playa La Boquilla – a place for really escaping the world. The simple fan-cooled bungalows are scattered over a tree-covered hillside overlooking the beach. Some have kitchens, but there's also an informal Mexican/international-fusion beach restaurant (lunch from M$85 to M$150, two-course dinner from M$350), with excellent seafood and steaks and generous margaritas.

Snorkel gear, kayaks and a paddleboard are free for guests. Expect spotty wi-fi. A taxi from Puerto Ángel costs M$150 or you can hire a motorboat for M$600.

ℹ Information

Banco Azteca (☑ 958-584-34-79; Blvd Uribe; ⊙ 8am-8pm) Changes cash US dollars and euros.

ℹ Getting There & Away

A *taxi colectivo* costs M$10 to Zipolite and M$15 to Pochutla. A private cab to either is M$70 to M$100, depending on the hour. Private taxis to Mazunte run M$150.

Zipolite
📋 958 / POP 1060

There's a naked sunbather with dreadlocks meditating on the beach, a bobbing crowd of surfers bravely fighting aggressive waves, a couple of aging hippies looking (apart from their cell phones) like they've just arrived in a time machine from 1975 and a local artisan shop doing a roaring trade in Frida Kahlo bags. Welcome to Zipolite, a chilled-out strip of *palapas,* beach shacks and intentionally rustic boutique hotels that hasn't yet been discovered by big resort developers or people who play golf.

The largest of the three beach towns that decorate the coast west of Puerto Ángel, Zipolite is known for its surfing, clothing-optional beach and unashamed 'do nothing' vibe. Plenty of expats have discovered its tranquil charms and opened small businesses (most notably Italians), but the place still retains a touch of erstwhile bohemian magic. Long may it continue.

⊙ Sights & Activities

The essence and glory of Zipolite is that organized activity is minimal. This is a place for hanging out and doing just as little as you like.

Azul Profundo provides free transportation for its fishing, diving and snorkeling trips from Puerto Ángel: you can reserve at an internet shop (p490) on Privada Huaje.

You can partake in yoga classes (M$90) at La Loma Linda (p488) at 9am from Wednesday through Sunday.

★ Playa Zipolite   BEACH
Zipolite's beach is huge, running for a good 1.5km and dispatching massive waves. It's famous for its nudity; you'll see people randomly swimming, sunbathing or happily walking across the wet sand minus their clothes at any time of day, although it is more common in a couple of coves at the

OAXACA ZIPOLITE

western end of the beach and in the small bay called Playa del Amor at the east end, which is a favorite spot for gay men.

The eastern end of Zipolite (nearest Puerto Ángel) is called Colonia Playa del Amor, the middle part is Centro, and the western end, where most of the traveler scene is centered, is Colonia Roca Blanca, where you'll find what amounts to the main street, Av Roca Blanca (also called El Adoquín), a block back from the beach.

Surfing is better toward the west. For more seclusion and the best boutique hotels, retreat to the far western end of the beach behind several rocky knolls.

🛏 Sleeping

The majority of accommodations are in and around the Roca Blanca area at the west end of Zipolite and are literally steps from the beach. A smaller, plusher cluster sits at the top of a headland to the west.

Posada México   ROOMS $
(☏ 958-584-31-94; www.posadamexico.com; Av Roca Blanca s/n; r M$750-1350, without bathroom M$500-650; 🅿🛜) ⚡ This Italian-run beachfront joint is on a friendly, personal scale and has smallish but clean, colorful rooms with good beds, four-poster mosquito nets, clever water-saving showers and sandy little hammock areas. Best are the two larger, more expensive, beach-facing rooms. There's a fine **restaurant-bar** (mains M$55-180; ⊗8am-2pm Tue, to 11pm Thu-Mon; 🛜⚡) too.

Lo Cósmico   CABAÑAS $
(☏ cell 958-1002130; www.locosmico.com; west end Playa Zipolite; cabañas M$600-800, without bathroom M$400-500; ⊗restaurant 8am-4pm Tue-Sun; 🅿🛜) Lo Cósmico is old-school Zipolite, a throwback to the days when this place really was undiscovered, except by the odd cosmically minded hippie. Despite being destroyed and rebuilt after a 1997 hurricane, it has retained its 1970s essence: simple conical-roofed rustic *cabañas* made out of local materials, dotted around a tall rock outcrop.

The onsite open-air restaurant (dishes M$50 to M$80) serves excellent crepes, salads and breakfasts from an impeccably clean kitchen.

A Nice Place on the Beach   ROOMS $
(☏958-584-31-95; www.facebook.com/aniceplace onthebeach; Av Roca Blanca; d M$500-600, d/q without bathroom M$400/550; 🛜) Aptly named and aptly subtitled too (the second stanza reads: 'Where people come to do nothing'), Nice Place has eight basic rooms, split four upstairs with wooden walls and private bathrooms, and four downstairs with concrete walls and shared bathrooms. Step out of the door and your feet are on soft sand right beside the onsite bar and restaurant.

Casa Kalmar   HOTEL $$
(☏cell 958-5892675; www.casakalmar.com; Arco Iris 12; r/ste incl breakfast from M$1500/4000; 🅿❄🛜≋) The hilltop vantage point from Casa Kalmar's blue-tiled infinity pool and lovingly designed ocean-facing rooms imbues a sense of calm, as the hotel's name suggests. Guests chill out in an open-air lounge area where the attentive staff serves breakfast in the morning. A stairway just outside the property descends to the west side of Playa Zipolite.

Las Casitas   BUNGALOW $$
(☏958-100-34-55; www.las-casitas.net; cabins M$850-1400; 🅿🛜) Peaceful Las Casitas sits like a lighthouse on a lane behind the west end of Playa Zipolite. Six detached rooms done out with tasteful Mexican color schemes and cute decorative details are set in palm-thatch-and-wood bungalows scattered around a steep terraced garden. All have private bathroom, kitchen and spacious hangout area.

La Loma Linda   HOTEL $$
(☏958-584-31-98; www.lalomalinda.com; Principal; d US$50-75, without bathroom US$35-45; 🅿🛜) Stacked on a steep hillside away from the tourist center, this handsome yoga retreat is an aesthetic joy with six exceptionally well designed bungalows with private bathrooms and four individual rooms that share a bathroom encased in a hexagonal Mudéjar-style tower. The gardens and terraces are impeccable and there's a yoga studio offering classes Wednesday through Sunday (nonguests welcome).

Rooms have fridge, mozzie nets, hammocks and huge stone terrace with ocean or garden views. Book ahead as the German owners often host retreats.

Hotel Nude   HOTEL $$
(☏958-584-30-62; www.facebook.com/nude zipolite; Av Roca Blanca; r from M$1200, ste M$2000; 🅿❄🛜≋) Tapping into Zipolite's clothing-optional vibe, the Nude wears its nudist reputation fairly subtly (guests usually save their nudity for the beach). Attractive

two-story thatched bungalows are arranged around a kidney-shaped pool with a palm tree in the middle. Well-scrubbed interiors are simple and white, but all have large porches with hammocks. Bonuses include a spa, beachfront restaurant and eager-to-please service.

★ **Heven** APARTMENT $$$
(☎55-4164-9111, cell 958-1062018; www.heven residence.com; Arco Iris 1; ste M$1960-2460, apt M$2460-2970, all incl breakfast; 🖥🌊) Heven, at the risk of sounding trite, is pretty heavenly: a beautifully designed walled compound arranged around an infinity pool, lush gardens and winding stairways punctuated with balconies and a shapely tower that (intentionally) recalls the whitewashed glories of the Amalfi Coast. The rooms, which have lured musicians and writers in the past, are classy and charismatic.

Most have kitchen facilities, and all have fans and handsome handcrafted Mexican furniture.

El Alquimista BUNGALOW $$$
(☎958-587-89-61; www.elalquimistahotel.mx; Camino a Shambala s/n, west end Playa Zipolite; r M$2668-3779, cabañas M$2223-2445; P🖩🖥🌊) The Alquimista has rustic-boutique thatch-roofed *cabañas* just off the beach (all with king-sized beds and air-con) and big, bright rooms set back up the luxuriant hillside with ample terraces. The decor is all about hammocks, lazy terraces, trance music and twinkling oil lamps at night.

One of Zipolite's best restaurants (p490) is here too, plus there's a good pool and a spa, **Espacio Shanti** (☎cell 958-1115097; www. shantispazipolite.com; ⊙10am-7:30pm), which uses locally made organic materials.

✗ Eating & Drinking

Zipolite's beachfront restaurant-bars have perfect locations for drinks from sunset onward, and beach bonfires and the occasional fire-dancing provide the focus for informal partying when the surfers get home.

Orale! Cafe BREAKFAST $
(☎cell 958-1177129; off west end Av Roca Blanca; breakfast dishes M$50-85; ⊙8am-3pm Thu-Mon; 🖥) This shady tropical-garden cafe feels like a rough clearing in the jungle and its food tastes pretty good too, especially if you order their branded coffee or ask for a fruit plate (with yogurt and granola) that comes full of ambrosial bites that might conceiv-

ably have fallen off a nearby tree straight onto your plate.

It also serves eggs for breakfast and baguettes for lunch.

Postres del Sol CAFE $
(☎cell 958-1070249; www.facebook.com/postres delsol; Calle Principal; cakes M$20-40; ⊙9am-9pm Tue-Fri, from 10am Sat & Sun; 🖉) An apparition by the dusty roadside heading west out of Zipolite, this cafe with four alfresco tables, and usually as many dogs, lures people out of passing taxis with its strategically positioned display case full of rich cakes – chocolate and tropical cheesecake among them. They bake vegan cookies and the joe's pretty good too.

★ **La Providencia** MEXICAN, FUSION $$
(☎cell 958-1009234; www.laprovidenciazipolite. com; mains M$135-225; ⊙6:30-10:30pm Wed-Sun Nov-Apr, Jul & Aug; 🖥) Zipolite's outstanding dining option, on a road behind the beach's western end, combines exquisite flavors, artful presentation and relaxed ambience. You can sip a cocktail in the open-air lounge while you peruse the menu. It's a contemporary Mexican treat, from amaranth-encrusted eggplant to beef medallions with red-wine reduction or coconut-crusted prawns with mango sauce. Save room for the chocolate mousse!

Reservations advised for December through March.

Sal y Pimienta MEXICAN $$
(☎cell 958-1200353; Playa Zipolite; mains M$120-250; ⊙noon-10pm; P🖥) So close to the ocean you barely need to get off your surfboard, the 'Salt & Pepper' serves unsophisticated but delicious *comida* from plastic tables set out on the sand. Portions are huge and the *pescado entero a las brasas* (grilled whole fish) tastes oh-so-good with a cold beer.

Piedra de Fuego SEAFOOD $$
(☎cell 958-1139935; Mangle; mains M$90-120; ⊙2-10pm) If you came to Zipolite to eat Mexican rather than Italian food, this is your bag with generous servings of fresh fish fillet or shrimp, accompanied by rice, salad and potatoes. It's simple, superb and run by a local family. Good *aguas de frutas* (fruit cordials) too.

La Fenice PIZZA $$
(☎cell 958-1116964; www.facebook.com/cristiano bordogni; Av Roca Blanca; pizzas M$110-200; ⊙7-10:30pm Thu-Sun) While there are a number of pizza restaurants along the coast, including several in Zipolite, most of them with

much the same menu, La Fenice is the place to go for truly authentic Italian quality and flavor. Hours vary.

El Alquimista INTERNATIONAL **$$$**
(☑ cell 958-1362858; www.elalquimistahotel.mx; Camino a Shambala s/n, west end Playa Zipolite; mains M$140-265; ☻ 8am-11pm; [P][☎][⊿]) The Alchemist is delightfully sited alfresco in a quiet sandy cove, and atmospherically lit by oil lamps and candles at night, conjuring up an intentionally romantic air. The wide-ranging menu runs from fresh salads to good meat, seafood and pasta, and hard-to-pass-up desserts. In terms of setting, it's definitely Zipolite's most refined choice.

El Bicho BAR
(www.facebook.com/elbichomeetpoint; beach, south of Hotel Descalzo; ☻ 3pm-midnight) Take in a glorious sunset over cocktails while swaying back and forth on a swing at this *palapa* beach bar. Often hosts live music events on weekends.

☆ Entertainment

Cine Luciernaga
(Firefly Cinema) OUTDOOR CINEMA
(www.facebook.com/groups/fireflycineluciernaga zipolite; Mangle; FREE) A neat little makeshift cinema with indoor and outdoor seating areas and a small bar. It usually screens one or two evening shows. From December through March there's also live music.

🛍 Shopping

Tienda de Artesanías
Piña Palmera ARTS & CRAFTS
(☑ 958-688-55-88; www.pinapalmera.org; cnr Pelícano & Carretera, Colonia Roca Blanca; ☻ 9am-5pm Mon-Sat) 🎗 This little shop sells wooden toys, recycled paper products, coconut oil and other stuff made at the **Piña Palmera** (☑ 958-584-31-47; www.pinapalmera.org; Principal, Colonia Roca Blanca) 🎗 rehabilitation center and in the communities where Piña Palmera works.

ℹ Information

Ostensibly Zipolite is a place for peace and tranquility and most travelers enjoy a quiet, trouble-free stay here. However, some crimes against tourists have been reported in recent years, especially on the beach after dark. Enjoy the laid-back ambience, but don't drop your guard too low. Always lock your bedroom door and think twice before spending the night on a hammock alfresco on the sand.

A more natural danger is Zipolite's surf. It's fraught with riptides, changing currents and a strong undertow. Going in deeper than your knees can be risking your life. Local voluntary lifeguards rescue many, but people still drown here every year. The shore break is one only experienced surfers should attempt. Heed the warning flags: yellow means don't go in deeper than your knees; red means don't go in period.

INTERNET
Internet Cafe (☑ 958-584-34-37; Privada Huaje; internet per hour M$15; ☻ 9am-9pm) Also takes bookings for Azul Profundo (p487).

MONEY
There is an ATM inside Hotel Nude (p488) on Av Roca Blanca, but it's known to run out of cash. The nearest other ATMs are in Mazunte and Pochutla.

ℹ Getting There & Away
After dark, taxis are your only option for getting to Puerto Ángel, San Agustinillo or Mazunte. Expect to pay M$80 to M$100.

Líneas Unidas (☑ 958-119-66-66; Principal) and **Eclipse 70** (☑ 954-854-32-14; Principal) have comfortable vans that depart for San José del Pacífico (M$150, three hours) and Oaxaca (M$200, six hours), each with five daily departures.

San Agustinillo
☑ 958 / POP 290

True, it's a bit like comparing heaven with nirvana, but San Agustinillo might just possess the nicest slice of sand on this glorious coast. The village is smaller than Mazunte, its 'twin' to the west, with everything clinging to the main drag, Calle Principal. The waves are a little more manageable too, making this place perfect for bodyboarding and learning to surf. There's a local surf school should you need assistance.

🏃 Activities

Local fishers will take you on boat trips to observe turtles, dolphins, birds, manta rays and whales (best from November to March for these last two). The cost for three hours is normally M$300 per person (usually with a minimum of four) including a snorkeling stop. The fishers also offer sportfishing trips, usually M$1300 to M$1500 for three or four hours. Ask at your accommodations.

🐚 Courses

Tropical Surf SURFING
(☑ cell 958-1222398, cell 958-1302557; www.facebook.com/tropicalsurfsanagustinillo; on the beach;

class/board rentals per hour M$400/100; ☻9am-6pm) For surfing classes or board rentals, head to this beachfront *palapa* next to Casa Aamori (p492). Tropical emphasizes safety first and the friendly instructors know the area's best surf spots according to your skill level.

🛏 Sleeping

Most places to stay and eat are right on the beach. Rooms have either mosquito-screened windows or mosquito nets.

Recinto del Viento
GUESTHOUSE $

(🗹WhatsApp 958-1135236; recintodelviento@gmail.com; d M$650-750, without bathroom M$500; ℗) This budget option looks like some frozen relic from San Agustinillo's pre-tourist days and sits 100m up steps opposite Bambú with surf views from its hammock-slung terrace. The guest kitchen helps create a sociable atmosphere and there's a no-wi-fi policy to encourage guests to interact. The seven rooms are simple and small; three have their own bathroom.

Posada Paloma
INN $

(🗹cell 958-1282201; posadapalomasanagustinillo@gmail.com; Principal; r from M$600; 🛜) A decent budget option on the east end of town, the fan-cooled rooms at Posada Paloma overlook a small garden and open-air lobby with an onsite restaurant and bar. The larger, pricier rooms upstairs get good natural light and share a balcony with a partial ocean view.

Bambú
CABAÑAS $$

(www.bambuecocabanas.com.mx; Principal; cabañas M$1500-1900; ℗🛜) 🏄 The seven *cabañas* here, toward the beach's east end, are large, open to as much breeze as possible, and set under high *palapa* roofs that look faintly Indonesian. All are cleverly constructed, mainly from bamboo, with pretty tilework, fans, good mozzie nets, and quirky details like seashell shower heads and trees growing inside several rooms. The tree-house-like 'Pelicano' cabin rules.

The large guest kitchen area includes a barbecue grill and long communal table. Reserve online.

Paraíso del Pescador
HOTEL $$

(🗹cell 958-5895101; paraiso_forever5@hotmail.com; Principal; r M$700-1200; ℗❄🛜) Sunny rooms with adjoining kitchens (equipped with large fridges) and broad balconies characterize this orange-hued posada above a restaurant along San Agustinillo's main

drag. The rooms aren't flashy, but the view is, especially from room seven.

Rancho Cerro Largo
CABAÑAS $$

(www.ranchocerrolargo.wix.com/ranchocerrolargo; Playa Aragón; r M$1350-1600, cabañas M$1800-200, all incl breakfast & dinner; ℗🛜) 🏄 The Rancho has all the calling cards of a quintessential Oaxacan yoga resort: quiet clifftop location; comfortable but simple ocean-view *cabañas*, most constructed of mud and wattle (and some with open walls overlooking the crashing surf below); and top-notch mainly vegan and vegetarian meals taken communally with other guests. Online reservations only.

There probably isn't a better place to sit in the lotus position and feel at one with nature.

Access is by a signed driveway from the Zipolite–San Agustinillo road.

★ Casa Bagus
HOTEL $$$

(🗹cell 958-1098829; www.casabagus.com.mx; Playa San Agustinillo; r M$2450; ℗❄🛜) 🏄 Six tastefully designed oceanfront rooms and a breezy open-air restaurant overlook San Agustinillo's most beautiful – and most swimmable – stretch of beach. All accommodations come with private balcony and hammocks, furnishings crafted from wood and stone objects, local artwork and biodegradable bathroom products. Your energetic host Manu aims to please. Reserve well ahead.

Punta Placer
CABAÑAS $$$

(🗹cell 958-1076644; www.puntaplacer.com; Principal; r/apt M$1800/2500; ℗🛜) The eight beautiful circular rooms and one large apartment here have a fresh, open-air feel thanks to their breezy terraces and wood-slat windows. With welcome touches like good reading lights and stone-lined hot showers with excellent water pressure, they're a grade above most other San Agustinillo accommodations.

Hotel Casa La Ola
BOUTIQUE HOTEL $$$

(🗹cell 55-31036257; www.casalaola.mx; Principal; s/d/ste M$1800/2600/3100; ℗❄🛜❄) A plush bricks-and-mortar affair set above the main road at the village's western limits, rooms are classy and supermodern, using local wood and stone in an enviably creative way. Most are large and ocean-facing with fridge, wooden deck and relaxing deck chairs. Breakfast in the onsite cafe is an extra M$180.

Casa Aamori BOUTIQUE HOTEL $$$
(☎55-5436-2538; www.aamoriboutiquehotel.com;
Principal; r M$2380-3570; ✻🛜🏊) San Agus-
tinillo's classiest accommodations, lovingly
designed Casa Aamori stands toward the
east end of the beach. The 12 large, attrac-
tive rooms, on themes from Copacabana
to Goa to Africa, feature floor mosaics and
original crafts from around the world. Four
look straight out on to the ocean.

The pool-and-restaurant deck leads on to
a sandy area over the beach, with hanging
beds under the palms. The hotel is for adults
only and may require a multiple-night stay
during the busy season from December
through March.

✖ Eating

⭐**Restaurante La Mora** MEXICAN, ITALIAN $$
(☎cell 958-5846422; www.lamoraposada.com;
Principal; mains M$65-200, r M$850-950, apt
M$1800; ⊗8am-2pm & 6:30-10pm Wed-Mon;
🅿✻🛜) Tucked onto a sheltered slice of
beach, there's something of the old posada
about La Mora. You can park yourself in the
tavern-like interior or feel the salt spray on
the narrow terrace. The food – good Italian
and seafood dinners, breakfasts, massive
fruit plates and organic, fair-trade coffee –
will be equally memorable.

Upstairs are four cheerful rooms, and
above them is a bright, spacious apartment
that's good for families. All three floors have
terraces with close-up sea views.

El Navegante SEAFOOD $$
(☎cell 958-1180842; Principal; mains M$120-
300; ⊗6-10pm Tue-Sat; 🅿) A Catalan chef
whips up innovative fish and seafood dish-
es at this intimate sand-floor restaurant
perched above the main strip. Mains in-
clude lobster in *guajillo* chili sauce, snap-
per with grilled yams, several meat and
vegetarian options, and they have mezcal
and craft beer too.

La Ola SEAFOOD $$
(☎cell 958-1368942; Playa San Agustinillo; mains
M$80-245; ⊗10am-6pm; 🛜) A slightly more
refined *palapa* than is standard in these
parts, La Ola (the wave) is right on the
beach and delivers fine fish concoctions to
its wooden periwinkle tables with aplomb.
Honorable mentions should go to the tuna
tostadas (with raw marinated spicy tuna)
and the *taco de pulpo zarandeado* (grilled
octopus).

La Termita ITALIAN $$
(☎cell 958-5893046; www.posadalatermita.com;
Principal; pizzas M$135-220; ⊗8am-11pm Thu-Tue;
🛜🅿🏠) The service leaves much to be de-
sired but La Termita's wood-oven pizzas are
the best in town, and there are good salads
to go with them and carrot or chocolate cake
to follow!

ℹ Getting There & Away

San Agustinillo is linked to the other villages on
the coast by regular *colectivos* and *camionetas
pasajeras* (small trucks). Flag them down on the
main road. Vans (p490) to Oaxaca depart from
Zipolite.

Mazunte

📞958 / POP 870

Mazunte is a counterpart of Zipolite, a hud-
dle of thatch and abode buildings that hug
two elemental beaches – Playas Rinconcito
and Mermejita – on either side of a wave-
lashed headland called La Cometa. Well
known on the independent travelers' circuit,
it's a motley mélange of tattoo parlors, coffee
shops, Che Guevara T-shirts and people who
see their future in tarot cards. It's also very
beautiful and – courtesy of a recent *pueblo
mágico* (magical village) listing – the most
visited of the beach villages hereabouts.

Mazunte is known for its sea turtles: an
interesting research center just off the main
drag has an aquarium open to the public. It's
also a good place to learn Spanish, practice
yoga or simply do nothing.

⊙ Sights

⭐**Punta Cometa** VIEWPOINT
This rocky cape, jutting out from the west
end of Mazunte beach, is the southernmost
point in the state of Oaxaca and a fabulous
place to hike at sunset amid crashing waves
and dreamy Pacific vistas.

To walk to the cape, take the lane toward
Playa Mermejita off Calle Rinconcito, and go
left up the track immediately after the cem-
etery to reach the community nature reserve
entrance after 250m. Here you have two
choices. Take the path leading down to the
right (Sendero Corral de Piedra Poniente)
and you'll join a winding, sometimes rough
trail that ultimately gets you to the Punta
in 20 to 30 minutes (the last part crosses
a small beach). Take the central path and
you'll be led more directly through trees
and then across a grassy headland to the

Punta. Ideally you can combine both paths for a round trip that takes around one hour without stops.

Centro Mexicano de la Tortuga · AQUARIUM
(Sea Turtle Center; ☑ ext 19001 55-5449-7000; www.centromexicanodelatortuga.org; Av Paseo del Mazunte; M$36; ⊙ 10am-4:30pm Wed-Sat, to 2pm Sun; ⛢) ✔ With a wonderful and very appropriate setting overlooking the ocean, this two-part turtle center ushers visitors on a walk around a collection of outdoor tanks filled with all kinds of exotic breeds of turtle before diving (metaphorically) into an indoor aquarium where you can get very close to some very big reptiles. The research center contains specimens of all the world's eight marine-turtle species (seven of which frequent Mexico's coasts), plus some fresh-water and land varieties.

🎓 Courses

Instituto Iguana · LANGUAGE
(☑ 958-583-53-77; www.institutoiguana.com; Instituto Iguana s/n; classes 10/20hr per week M$2200/4200) ✔ In keeping with the Mazunte vibe, this language school is a relaxed, friendly place where you can start Spanish classes any day and study as intensively as you like. Run by a Mexican–German non-profit organization, which also gives free English classes to villagers, it has a lovely breezy hilltop site centered on a beautiful big *palapa* area.

One-on-one classes are available any time and the school can help arrange accommodations onsite or in family-run guesthouses nearby (from M$300 to M$400 per night). For courses for two people using the same teacher, you'll pay M$1800 each for 10 hours per week. The school is 400m inland off the main road, signposted beside the bridge in the middle of Mazunte.

🎉 Festivals & Events

Festival Internacional de Jazz · MUSIC
(www.facebook.com/festivalinternacionalde jazzdemazunte; ⊙ mid-Nov) This festival brings three days of top-quality international jazz and other music, plus workshops and exhibitions, to Mazunte around mid-November. All events are free!

🛏 Sleeping

Most of the accommodations are collected in two huddles – one around Playa Rinconcito at the end of the eponymous dirt street,

and the other over the 'hump' overlooking Playa Mermejita. The latter area has the pick of the bunch.

★ Hotel Arigalan · HOTEL $
(☑ cell 958-1086987; www.arigalan.com; Cerrada del Museo de la Tortuga; dm/cabañas/bungalows M$450/700/1200, ste M$1800-2000; ⓟ ❄ 🛜 🏊) The best of both worlds can be found high above the lofty headland between Mazunte and San Agustinillo where you get spectacular views of two beaches and rooms ranging from affordable dorms to comfy virgin-white suites with plunge pools, hammocks and an air of casual refinement. No under-18s accepted here. Breakfast available on request.

Posada del Arquitecto · CABAÑAS $
(☑ cell 958-1258852; www.posadadelarquitecto. com; Rinconcito; dm M$150, estrellas M$180-200, cabins M$550-2100; ⓟ 🛜) Arquitecto looks slightly grungy from beach level, but venture inside its rooms and the quality shines through. Its quirk is its *camas colgantes* (hanging beds) also known as *estrellas*. Some of them are set on the hillside *en plein air,* sheltered only by *palapas;* others are suspended from the ceiling on ropes inside cabins and encased in white mosquito nets.

You can rock yourself to sleep to the sound of crashing waves (Playa Rinconcito is inches away). There are cheaper dorm rooms on offer too.

Hospedaje El Rinconcito · HOTEL $
(☑ cell 984-1573056; Rinconcito; d M$700, with air-con M$900; ⓟ ❄ 🛜) Inhabits a terra-cotta-hued building on Calle Rinconcito and is fronted by a row of crafty shops, including La Baguette (p494) bakery. Rooms are gathered on the 2nd floor around a courtyard parking lot and are relatively simple with a few dashes of color. Most have two double beds. Some have air-conditioning.

Cabañas Amaia · B&B $$
(☑ cell 55-61620351; www.facebook.com/cabanas amaia; Camino a Mermejita; cabañas incl breakfast M$800-930; ⓟ 🛜) This well-run B&B near Punta Cometa has just four *cabañas,* each with its own private garden and terrace. Expect immaculate rooms adorned with Oaxacan crafts, delicious breakfast, spot-on service and plenty of peace and quiet.

El Copal · CABAÑAS $$
(☑ cell 55-41942167; www.elcopal.com.mx; Playa Mermejita; cabañas & teepees from M$1550; ⓟ 🛜) ✔ Hard-to-find Copal hugs a forested hill

behind Playa Mermejita with steps leading up to an arty **restaurant** (☑cell 55-41942167; www.elcopal.com.mx; Playa Mermejita; mains M$90-180; ⊙7:30am-10:30pm; 🛜), along with a pool that appears as infinite as the sea beyond. It's a leafy secluded spot with solar-powered *cabañas* of adobe, wood and palm-thatch, all containing a double bed on the ground floor and two or three singles above.

Recently added are some pretty basic tepees. The bathrooms are quaint open-air affairs with views.

★**Oceanomar** CABAÑAS $$$
(☑cell 958-5876232; www.oceanomar.com; Camino a Mermejita, Playa Mermejita; r M$1200, cabañas M$1800-2200; 🅿🛜🏊) On a lovely and cleverly landscaped hillside site with great views over Playa Mermejita, Italian-owned Oceanomar has a gorgeous pool and five spacious, well-built *cabañas* with nice craft details, hammock-slung terraces and good bathrooms. There's a great little onsite restaurant also called Oceanomar (mains M$120-200; ⊙8am-9pm; 🍴), serving meals for guests all day and open to nonguests in the evening.

There are also two smaller, more affordable rooms here.

Casa Pan de Miel HOTEL $$$
(☑cell 958-1004719; www.casapandemiel.com; Cerrada del Museo de la Tortuga; r US$150-350; 🅿❄🛜🏊) This is a place for real relaxation, equipped with a lovely infinity pool in front of an inviting large *palapa* dining/lounge area. The nine bright, elegant air-conditioned rooms are adorned with varied Mexican art, and all have sea views, kitchen or kitchenette, and terraces with hammocks. The excellent breakfasts (US$9 to US$15) include organic eggs and homemade jams, breads and yogurt.

It's up a steep track from the main road at the east end of Mazunte and enjoys wonderful views. Children under 12 are not accepted because of the clifftop position.

Celeste del Mar ROOMS $$$
(☑cell 958-1075296; www.celestedelmar.com; Playa Mermejita; r US$90-125; 🛜) 🌿 A few steps from Playa Mermejita, this small hotel offers eight carefully designed rooms in two-story *palapa*-roofed cottages with attractive contemporary decorative details. The four airy upstairs rooms feature loft areas with big double hammocks under their high roofs; no under-18s.

✖ **Eating & Drinking**

Maralto BAKERY $
(☑958-1730615; www.facebook.com/maralto cocinartesanal; Av Paseo del Mazunte; sandwiches M$60-85, pizzas M$90-150; ⊙8am-8pm Wed-Mon) Under-the-radar Maralto makes its own marmalades, freshly baked bread and pastries, bagels, pizzas, sandwiches and more. The Reuben, a corned-beef sandwich with Russian dressing and sauerkraut on rye, is deli done right. The small bakery also pours joe hailing from Pluma Hidalgo, Oaxaca's best coffee-producing region.

La Baguette BAKERY, CAFE $
(☑cell 958-1095599; Rinconcito; baked goods M$5-25; ⊙7am-9:30pm) On your way down Calle Rinconcito to the beach you'll surely have to stop for this little bakery well stocked with ready-made baguettes, muffins, pizza slices and coffee made in a stove-top pot.

★**Alessandro** ITALIAN $$
(☑cell 958-1736645; Rinconcito; mains M$95-200; ⊙6-10:30pm Wed-Mon; 🛜🍴) On Oaxaca's coast you're never far from an expat Italian chef who's generously imported his/her culinary know-how and opened a restaurant. Few are as good as Alessandro. His small but brilliant place has just eight tables in a corner of the Posada del Arquitecto (p493), but it has wonderful homemade pasta (eg in arugula-and-avocado pesto).

Also on offer is fresh fish (maybe served in *guajillo* chili and tomatillo sauce), filet minon (beef tenderloin in white wine and olive oil, with Parmesan) and desserts (don't miss the mousse of Oaxacan chocolate with orange-and-rum perfume). Good drinks include Argentine wine, Oaxacan mezcal and thirst-quenching *aguas de frutas*. Go early to avoid waiting.

La Cuisine MEDITERRANEAN, MEXICAN $$
(☑cell 958-1071836; La Barrita; mains M$130-230; ⊙7-11pm Tue-Sat; 🛜) An immediate success when it opened in 2015, La Cuisine has a menu that changes daily according to the market-fresh ingredients that the dedicated French cook acquires; dishes such as filet mignon and the catch of the day are posted each night on a chalkboard. There's live music on Thursdays.

La Mezcalería BAR
(La Barrita; ⊙7pm-midnight Fri & Sat) One of the few spots in Mazunte where you can get some dance grooves on. Live bands play

cumbia, salsa and reggae under an open-air *palapa* that serves up good times, cold beer and mediocre mezcal.

🛍 Shopping

Cosméticos Naturales
Mazunte   HEALTH & WELLNESS
(www.cosmeticosmazunte.com; Av Paseo del Mazunte; ⊙9am-4pm Mon-Sat, 10am-2pm Sun) ✍ This very successful small cooperative, toward the village's west end, makes and sells products such as shampoo, cosmetics, mosquito repellent, soap and herbal medicines, using natural sources like maize, coconut and essential oils. You'll find its toiletries in hotel bathrooms all over Oaxaca state. It also sells organic coffee and tahini, and you can have a look at the workshop while here.

ℹ Information

Banco Multiva ATM (Paseo del Mazunte) Just west of the church on the main drag. Sometimes runs out of money.

ℹ Getting There & Away

Eclipse 70 (p490) and Líneas Unidas (p490) operate comfortable vans with service to San José del Pacífico (M$150, three hours) and Oaxaca (M$240, six hours), each with five daily departures from Zipolite. Eclipse 70 vans coming from Oaxaca will drop you in Mazunte but you need to catch them in Zipolite for the return.

Local transportation to the nearby villages is provided by *colectivos* and *camionetas pasajeras*. Flag them down anywhere on the main street. There's a taxi base on the main drag, next to the bridge.

La Ventanilla

📞958 / POP 90
Some 2.5km along the road west from Mazunte, a sign points to the tiny beach village of La Ventanilla, 1.2km down a dirt road. La Ventanilla is home to a community-led eco-project protecting turtles, crocodiles and a long, wild beach and lagoon. You can take a boat trip on the lagoon to observe crocodiles and birds, and you can also ride horses along the beach. Somehow this tiny village manages to have two rival cooperatives offering these services: both have some English-speaking guides and do a fine job.

Lagarto Real   WILDLIFE
(✉WhatsApp 958-1425921; www.facebook.com/lagartoreal.ventanilla; Playa Ventanilla; 1½hr lagoon tours adult/child M$80/40; ⊙tours 8am-6pm) ✍ Lagarto Real, the members of which wear red shirts, has its office on the roadside at the turnoff and another in the village itself. It offers lagoon boat trips (without an island stop), early-morning bird-watching (M$150 per person per hour) and nocturnal turtle-nesting observation.

Servicios Ecoturísticos
La Ventanilla   WILDLIFE
(✉249-596-04-10; www.laventanilla.com.mx; Playa Ventanilla; 1½hr lagoon tours adult/child M$100/50; ⊙tours 8am-5pm) ✍ With its office and restaurant by the roadside as you enter the village, this cooperative (with white-shirt wearing members) runs 12-passenger boat trips on the mangrove-fringed lagoon to spot endangered river crocodiles (there are hundreds in the local protected area), waterbirds (most prolific from November to March), and a few deer, monkeys and coatis in enclosures on an island.

It also arranges three-hour horseback rides (M$750); reserve both the day before. From June to December there's the chance to release turtle hatchlings or join night patrols to see turtles laying eggs (M$100).

ℹ Getting There & Away

Camionetas and *taxis colectivos* on the Zipolite–Mazunte–Pochutla route pass the Ventanilla turnoff, leaving you with a 1.2km walk. A taxi from Mazunte should cost M$100. From Zipolite, bank on M$150.

Bahías de Huatulco

📞958 / POP 19,000
Huatulco is an interesting experiment in resort development. Until the mid-1980s, this thickly forested slice of Pacific coast hosted nothing more than a few hard-to-reach fishing villages. Then along came government-funded tourist agency Fonatur, with a mandate to develop the region's nine ruggedly handsome bays for tourism. But Cancún this isn't. Huatulco's development has followed a more ecological bent. Big hotels are spread out, low-rise and relatively low-key; tracts of virgin forest are protected in a national park; and the area's unobtrusive infrastructure doesn't really feel like a resort. Indeed, the main settlement, Crucecita (which houses the coast's original inhabitants), could pass as any authentic Mexican town with its church, park and street stalls.

The somewhat restrained approach means Huatulco appeals to a broad cross-section of travelers who come here to appreciate what has always been the region's raison d'être: world-class beaches nestled in sheltered coves backed by broccoli-colored forest.

👁 Sights

Huatulco's beaches are beautiful and sandy with clear turquoise waters. Some have coral offshore and excellent snorkeling. As in the rest of Mexico, all beaches are under federal control, and anyone can use them, even when hotels appear to treat them as private property.

The area is popularly described as having nine different bays protecting over a dozen named beaches.

★ Playa Salchi   BEACH
Halfway between the western edge of Parque Nacional Huatulco and Puerto Ángel awaits some of the most precious coastline in Oaxaca. The water can be somewhat rough on the main beach but there are several swimmable beaches nearby that you can easily walk to along jungly dirt roads.

Ask for directions at **Manta Raya Hotel** (📱cell 958-1113111; www.mantaraya-hotel.com; Playa Salchi; r incl breakfast M$2000-2750, ste M$3150), where you can stop for lunch or spend the night in spacious oceanfront rooms with private balcony. The Swiss owner Reto will gladly point you in the right direction. To get here, take Hwy 200 west to the Cuatunalco turnoff and follow the Manta Raya signs along a dirt road for about 7km.

Bahía San Agustín   BEACH
This long, sandy beach, 14km west of Santa Cruz Huatulco, is backed by a fishing village, and in contrast to Huatulco's other settlements, there's absolutely no resort-type development – just a line of rustic *comedores* stretching along the beach, serving seafood and fish dishes and simple *antojitos*. Usually the waters are calm, and there is coral with very good snorkeling around the rocks in the bay and at **Playa Riscalillo** around the corner to the east.

San Agustín is popular with Mexicans on weekends and vacations, but quiet at other times. Some restaurants rent out snorkel gear, and most of them can arrange boats to Riscalillo or Playa La India. **El Capi** (📱958-103-90-54, cell 958-1001164; elcapi.rest@gmail.com; Playa San Agustín; cabañas M$800-1000,

tents M$100; 🅿🛜), on the northeast end, sits on quiet sands and has an onsite restaurant, rustic *cabañas* and tents for rent.

A 13km dirt road heads south to San Agustín from a crossroads on Hwy 200, 1.7km west of the airport. Buses between Huatulco and Pochutla will drop you at the turnoff, where taxis wait to carry people to San Agustín (M$130, or M$30 per person by *colectivo*).

Hagia Sofia   FARM
(www.hagiasofia.mx; Apanguito; incl round-trip transportation & breakfast M$1000; 🅿🍴) 🌿 One of Huatulco's loveliest and most interesting day trips, this 'agro-ecotourism' operation includes a large organic fruit orchard and a gorgeous 500m riverside trail with 60 kinds of tropical flowering plants that attract colorful birds and butterflies. You can have a refreshing dip beneath a waterfall while you're there. It's 9km northwest of Santa María Huatulco and about 30km from La Crucecita (a 45-minute drive).

You can visit any day, but reserve the day before in person or by phoning the **office** (📞958-587-08-71, cell 958-5837943; Local 7, Mitla 402; ⊙9am-2pm & 4-7:30pm Mon-Fri, 11am-5pm Sat) in Santa Cruz Huatulco: tours are given in English or Spanish and most people stay about four hours.

Bahía Cacaluta   BEACH
Cacaluta is a 1km-long slice of paradise that's protected by an island, backed by dunes and usually deliciously deserted. The Mexican road-trip movie *Y Tú Mamá También* was famously filmed there. Swimming is possible, although there can be undertow. Snorkeling is best around the island. There are no services at the beach, so bring plenty of water. A paved road off Hwy 200 leads to a 2.5km trail to the beach.

Alternatively, you can reach the beach by motorboat (M$2000 per boat) departing from Santa Cruz harbor.

Bahía Conejos   BEACH
The oddly named 'rabbit bay,' 3km east of Tangolunda, has a long main beach divided by a small rocky outcrop into the western **Playa Arenas** and the eastern **Playa Punta Arenas**, both reachable by short walks from the paved road. The surf can be strong here. At the east end of the bay is the more sheltered **Playa Conejos**, site of the super-plush Secrets Huatulco Resort (p501), but still accessible to Joe Public.

Bahías de Huatulco

5 km
2.5 miles

Río Copalita

Parque
Eco-Arqueológico
Copalita

Playa La
Bocana

La Bocana

Playa
Conejos

Playa
Magueyito

Barra de la
Cruz (14km)

Copalita

Bahía Conejos

Playa
Arenas

Residencial
Conejos

PACIFIC
OCEAN

Tangolunda

Bahía
Tangolunda

Playa
Tangolunda

Playa
Arrocito

Huatulco
Expediciones

Playa
Chahué

Bahía
Chahué

Bahía de Santa Cruz

Parque
Ecológico
Rufino Tamayo

Chahué

Playa La Entrega

Las Palmas

Playa
Santa Cruz

La Crucecita

Santa Cruz Huatulco

Bahía El
Organo

Playa El
Organo

Bahía
Maguey

Playa
Maguey

Sendero
Zanate

Río Cacaluta

Sendero Sabanal

Bahía Cacaluta

Parque Nacional
Huatulco

Playa
Cacaluta

MEX
200

Parque Nacional
Huatulco

Playa La
India

Bahía
Chachacual

Playa
Chachacual

Río San Agustín

Santa María
Huatulco (9km);
Pluma Hidalgo (38km)

Airport

Playa Salchi (19km);
Pochutla (30km)

Playa
Riscalillo

Playa San
Agustín

Bahía San
Agustín

San Agustín

Bahía Maguey   BEACH
(Playa El Maguey; **P** **[icon]**) Three kilometers west of Santa Cruz and easily walkable along a roadside pavement, Maguey's fine 400m beach curves around a calm bay between forested headlands. A line of a dozen or more family-friendly *palapas* serves fresh fish and seafood dishes, along with rather nice piña coladas. There's good snorkeling around the rocks on the east side of the bay; **Escualo** (**[icon]** cell 958-5854240; snorkeling gear per hour M$100; ☺ 8am-6pm) rents out gear. Taxis waiting in the parking lot charge M$70 to Santa Cruz.

Bahía Chachacual   BEACH
Inaccessible by land, Chachacual has two beaches: the easterly **Playa La India** is one of Huatulco's most beautiful scimitars of sand and one of the area's best places for snorkeling. The eponymous **Playa Chachacual** is longer with strong sea currents. There are no facilities on either beach but you'll find the odd local selling coconuts. Catch a motorboat from Santa Cruz harbor.

Bahía El Órgano   BEACH
Just east of Bahía Maguey, this lush 250m beach has calm waters good for snorkeling, and no crowds because there's no vehicle access and no restaurants. You can come by boat (most do), or walk to the beach by a 1km path through the forest. The trail starts about 1.3km back toward Santa Cruz from the Maguey parking lot; the easy-to-miss entry is next to a nondescript bus stop and marked by signs telling people not to disturb wildlife.

It becomes a mini-river in the rainy season.

Parque Eco-Arqueológico
Copalita   ARCHAEOLOGICAL SITE
(**[icon]** 958-587-15-91; Blvd Copalita-Tangolunda; Mexican/non-Mexican M$60/80, parking M$10; ☺ 8am-4pm Tue-Sun; **P**) Granted, it's no Monte Albán, but this pre-Hispanic site 600m north of La Bocana village is your only true glimpse of history in made-in-the-1980s Huatulco. Excavations are ongoing, but, to date, a ball court and two fairly modest temples have been uncovered. Adding to the appeal is a small museum, a jungle path to a spectacular clifftop lookout (site of an ancient 'guiding stone' possibly also used for sacrifices) and some explanatory signs in Spanish and English.

The site was occupied by different groups between about 600 BCE and 750 CE, and again from 1000 to the 16th century. You can wander around on your own or hire a guide (M$480 for up to four people).

A taxi to Crucecita costs M$100.

Playa La Entrega   BEACH
(**P** **[icon]**) La Entrega lies toward the outer edge of Bahía de Santa Cruz, a five-minute motorboat trip or 2.5km walk/drive along a bendy road from Santa Cruz. This 300m beach, backed by a line of seafood *palapas*, can get busy, but it has decent (if sometimes crowded) snorkeling on a coral plate from which boats are cordoned off. Gear is available at **Renta de Snorkel Vicente** (**[icon]** cell 958-1065211; snorkeling gear M$100, kayak per hour M$250; ☺ 8am-5pm) on the beach's northern end.

'La Entrega' means 'The Delivery': in 1831 Mexican independence hero Vicente Guerrero was handed over here to his political enemies by a Genoese sea captain. Guerrero was then taken to Cuilapan near Oaxaca and shot.

La Bocana   BEACH
(**P**) About 1.5km east of Playa Conejos, just before the Parque Eco-Arqueológico Copalita, lies Hutatulco's most low-key beach. Less pretty than other spots, Bocana is the surfers' choice courtesy of a decent right-hand break near the mouth of the Río Copalita. There's a **surf school** (**[icon]** cell 958-1301832; www.facebook.com/bocanasurfschool; surf lesson US$75; ☺ hours vary) offering lessons and rentals onsite (look out for the VW camper-van mural).

Bahía Tangolunda   BEACH
Tangolunda, 5km east of Santa Cruz Huatulco, is the site of most of the major top-end hotel developments. The long, wide, spotlessly clean beach is accessible to the public at its west end just beyond the golf course. A rocky headland (climbable with care) splits the beach in two.

Corredor Turístico   STREET
One of Huatulco's more recent developments is a wide terraced walkway that leads from Crucecita to the Santa Cruz harbor. The path then carries on west paralleling the road all the way out to Playa Maguey.

Bahía Chahué   BEACH
(**P**) The beach here, 1km east of Santa Cruz Huatulco, is wide with soft sand, but offers little in the way of shade, plus the surf can be surprisingly strong. There's a marina at its east end. Locals use it as an impromptu soccer pitch.

Parroquia de Nuestra
Señora de Guadalupe
CHURCH

(Plaza Principal, La Crucecita; ⏰7am-9pm) Let it not be said that the age of great church building is dead. Crucecita's pale-orange colonial-style ecclesial dame dates from – ahem – 2000, but what it lacks in history it makes up for in neck-tilting beauty. A huge 20m-long painting of the Virgin of Guadalupe is etched on the ceiling. Complementing Mexico's patron saint are a couple of colorful side chapels filled with mosaics and other murals.

🏃 Activities

Huatulco Expediciones
RAFTING

(📞958-108-31-73, cell 958-1080570; www.huatulco expediciones.com; Hwy 200 Km 256, Puente Tangolunda, Comunidad La Jabalina; rafting trips per person M$500-900; 🖐) Runs rafting trips on the Río Copalita near Huatulco, from all-day outings on the Class III–IV Alemania section starting 800m above sea level (generally from July to December) to a gentler 2½-hour jaunt down the Copalita's final 5km to the ocean at La Bocana (available all year and suitable for children).

Diving & Snorkeling

You can rent snorkeling gear, including life jacket and fins, at Santa Cruz harbor for M$150 a day if you're taking a boat trip from there. Renters at one or two beaches have slightly lower rates. The best snorkeling sites include the coral plates at La Entrega, San Agustín and the inshore side of the island at Cacaluta. You can either hire a *lancha* from Santa Cruz to take you to snorkel sites or take a snorkeling tour with one of Huatulco's diving outfits.

The Huatulco coast has over 100 dive sites and 45 hectares of coral reefs. There are 150 species of fish and 10 types of coral, plus dolphins, turtles and (from about December to March) humpback whales. This is a good place to learn to dive, with warm waters, varied underwater scenery, and calm conditions almost year-round. Visibility averages 10m to 20m. There's a decompression chamber in the local navy hospital.

Hurricane Divers
DIVING, SNORKELING

(📞958-587-11-07; www.hurricanedivers.com; Mitla 402, Playa Santa Cruz; 2-tank/night dives US$110/85, Discover course US$170; ⏰9am-6pm Mon-Fri, to 4pm Sat) This very professional international crew is one of Mexico's few PADI 5-Star Dive Resorts. Options include two-tank dives and

night dives for certified divers (additional US$15 for buoyancy control device, regulator and wetsuit if needed), and half-day PADI Discover Scuba courses for beginners, which include two short dives.

Huatulco Dive Center
DIVING, SNORKELING

(📞958-583-42-95; www.huatulcodivecenter.com; Marina Chahué; 2-tank dive M$1800, snorkeling M$700, Discover course M$2000-2500; ⏰9am-1pm Mon-Sat) A highly efficient PADI dive shop at the Marina Chahué. They offer two-tank dives, Discover Scuba courses in the open water for first-timers and a range of PADI courses and snorkeling trips.

Diving excursions usually set out at 9pm. Most dive sites are within 20 minutes of boat launch.

Hiking & Mountain Biking

There are several trails within the Parque Nacional Huatulco, but travelers are strongly pushed into doing them as part of an organized excursion. Huatulco Salvaje (p499) is your best bet for interesting guided hikes and bike trips in this area.

👉 Tours

Practically every agency in town offers the 'Seven Bays Tour' that calls into seven of Huatulco's nine bays with stops for snorkeling and lunch. Prices for shared motorboats are a fairly generic M$350 and might include an additional M$40 in harbor and national-park fees.

There are also trips to local waterfalls, rafting on the Copalita River and several undemanding hiking and biking excursions. You'll see these and other trips well advertised in hotels and information kiosks throughout town.

⭐ Huatulco Salvaje
ADVENTURE

(📞cell 958-1193886, cell 958-5874028; www.face book.com/senderosyhumedales; Local 2, Plaza María Bonita, Dársena de Santa Cruz; snorkeling tours per boat M$2650, wildlife-watching per person M$650, bike rental per hour/day M$40/250; ⏰9am-2pm & 4:30-7:30pm Mon-Sat; 🖐) 🌿 Huatulco Salvaje is a group of certified tour guides from the local community, many of them from village families displaced when the Parque Nacional Huatulco was created in the 1990s. They know their stuff when it comes to nature tours hereabouts.

Pop into their office at Santa Cruz's harbor to organize seaborne activities including five-hour snorkeling boat outings, various walking

OAXACA BAHÍAS DE HUATULCO

PLUMA HIDALGO

The majestic coffee-producing region of Pluma Hidalgo often gets overlooked but it's well worth a day trip, or even an overnight stay if you're feeling the love. There's not much going on in this small village, population 600, but the sweeping views from misty mountains rising 1300m above the coast are spectacular, and the coffee produced in these parts ranks among Mexico's best; in fact, many of Oaxaca city's gourmet java shops purchase their beans from farms here. **Cafetería Origen Mágico** (☑ cell 958-5258057; www.facebook.com/origenmagico; Allende; ⊙ 8am-10pm), off the tiny town square, serves excellent joe on a hillside deck that exudes tranquility – just the place to get all hopped up on caffeine! For lodging, **Finca Don Gabriel** (☑ 958-589-83-38, cell 958-1080763; www.fincadongabriel.com; Colonia Palogrande; d M$800-1100; P ☒) makes a fine spot to decompress with its pleasant rustic cabins offering striking mountain views, a cliffside pool and tours focused on coffee production or bird-watching. Here you can also hike to a 70m waterfall, known as Arcoiris or Providencia (look for the 'cascadas' sign just south of town). To get to Pluma Hidalgo, Huatulco 2000 (p503) has frequent shared vans (M$90, 1¼ hours) departing near Plaza El Madero in downtown Crucecita.

trips, and whale-, dolphin- and turtle-watching (October to April, four hours, minimum five people).

They also rent bikes.

🛏 Sleeping

You'll find all budget and many midrange options in La Crucecita. Further midrange possibilities are in Chahué and Santa Cruz. The top-end resort hotels are at Tangolunda and beyond, and are typically all-inclusive.

Flight-and-lodging package deals are your best bet for a good-value vacation in a top-end Huatulco hotel.

Hotel Nonni   HOTEL **$**
(☑ 958-587-03-72; www.facebook.com/hotelnonni; Bugambilia 203, La Crucecita; r from M$600; ☒ 🛜) Nonni has managed to preserve a newish look in rooms with modern fittings, freshly tiled showers and an aura of underlying cleanliness. While modest in ambition, it's no ugly duckling and has some well-thought-out details, with plenty of power sockets, good lighting and large beds with mattresses comfortable enough to make getting up in the morning a chore.

Hotel María Mixteca   HOTEL **$**
(☑ 958-587-09-90; www.mariamixtecahuatulco.com; Guamuchil 206, La Crucecita; r M$650-750; ☒ 🛜) María Mixteca offers 14 prettily decorated yellow-and-white rooms on two upper floors around an open patio, with super-comfy beds, air-conditioning, all-you-need bathrooms and room safes. It's half a block east of the Plaza Principal and shares digs with El Sabor de Oaxaca (p502) restaurant.

Misión de los Arcos   HOTEL **$$**
(☑ 958-587-01-65; www.misiondelosarcos.com; Gardenia 902, La Crucecita; r M$750-800, ste M$1000; ☒ 🛜) Surprise! Huatulco's best-loved hotel isn't one of the big all-inclusives but these more humble yet fiercely traditional accommodations near Crucecita's Plaza Principal. While not particularly old, the Misión is nonetheless embellished by a touch of colonial style with interior greenery, bright air-conditioned rooms, very comfortable beds and homey touches, all of which normally costs much more in other places.

We just hope the nearby school band practice doesn't jolt you out of bed. There's walk-through access to the good onsite Terra-Cotta (p502) restaurant.

Hotel Posada Edén Costa   HOTEL **$$**
(☑ 958-587-24-80; www.edencosta.com; Zapoteco 26, Chahué; r/ste incl breakfast M$1000/1500; P ☒ 🛜) Mediterranean-style Edén Costa, 500m inland from Bahía Chahué, has attractive rooms with avian touches in the form of colorful bird murals. Most rooms have two double beds and overlook the small central pool. Suites have their own kitchens. The attached restaurant, **L'Échalote** (mains M$145-250; ⊙ 4-11pm Tue-Fri, from 2pm Sat & Sun), is a bonus.

Habitación Azul   GUESTHOUSE **$$**
(☑ cell 958-1224134; huxboy@me.com; Vialidad 4; M$800-1100; P ☒) A good midrange option, Habitación Azul is one of three color-themed rooms tucked away in the rear garden of this Mexican family's home. Guests have use of a shared kitchen, a pretty

pool area and private parking in this quiet residential area 1km east of downtown Crucecita. Your amiable host Federico is a good source of local info.

★ Las Palmas
VILLA **$$$**

(☑ cell 958-1091448; www.laspalmashuatulco. com; Camino a Playa La Entrega; casitas/villas US$236/898; P ❋ 🛜 ☲) On a lovely site looking down on little Playa Violín, along the road between Santa Cruz and Playa La Entrega, Las Palmas is a marvelous discovery for couples, families or larger groups who have a vehicle and want to self-cater. The three bright, spacious four-bedroom villas enjoy large sitting/eating areas opening on to their own infinity pools.

The five smaller but also attractive casitas (villas, for up to four people) share a kitchen, pool and large *palapa* dining area. The tilework and crafts are beautiful, kayaks and mountain bikes are provided free, and the whole place has an expansive but private feel.

Secrets Huatulco Resort & Spa
RESORT **$$$**

(☑ USA 866-467-3273; www.secretsresorts.com mx; Bahía de Conejos; d all-inclusive US$519-597; P ❋ @ 🛜 ☲) Opened in 2012 and still looking as plush as the day it was born, Secrets is a pretty ravishing offering. For starters, there's the location, perched above the golden ribbon of Playa Conejos between two spinach-colored headlands. Then there's the Vegas-sized super-rooms with Jacuzzi baths, Nespresso machines, dressing gowns, slippers and private pools, not to mention the more prosaic essentials.

Hotel Binniguenda
RESORT **$$$**

(☑ 958-583-26-00; www.binniguendahuatulco. com.mx; Blvd Santa Cruz 201, Santa Cruz Huatulco; s/d all-inclusive from M$3150/4200; ❋ @ 🛜 ☲) Not as monstrous in size as your average all-inclusive, the Binniguenda is a historical monument in Huatulco years. It was the resort's first hotel when it opened in 1987. With its refined ambience, small attractive pool and colonial-style architecture, it hasn't aged badly. Indeed, a 2012 renovation has meant it remains proudly plush.

While not on the beach, the hotel is close to Santa Cruz's sand and has a nice quiet feel. With only 77 rooms, it is just small enough to merit a more intimate personable level of service. Look for online deals.

Camino Real Zaashila
LUXURY HOTEL **$$$**

(☑ 958-583-03-00; www.caminoreal.com; Blvd Juárez 5, Tangolunda; r from M$3000; P ❋ 🛜 ☲)

The Zaashila is rendered in smooth white adobe on a lovingly manicured terraced slope above the ocean, giving it a palpable Greek islands feel. You'll probably feel a bit like Zeus or Aphrodite when you book into your large ocean-facing room with its luxuriant sheets, Jacuzzi bathtub and king-of-the-gods-sized bed.

The other draw – if you need one – is the food. Two particularly fine restaurants slot seamlessly into the Garden of Eden grounds, including Azul Profundo (p502).

✖ Eating

Many of the best eating options are in 'downtown' Crucecita. Several of the beaches – most notably Playas Santa Cruz, Entrega, Maquey and San Agustín – have lines of generically good *palapas*. Being an all-inclusive area, Tangolunda is more limited, although there are a couple of lunch places.

La Tosta
SEAFOOD **$**

(☑ 722-8440556; www.facebook.com/latosta huatulco; Blvd Juárez, Santa Cruz Huatulco; tostadas M$45-85, tacos M$55-90; ⊙ noon-/pm Tue-Sun) Artfully prepared *tostadas* come piled high with fresh tuna, octopus, shrimp and ceviche at this local fave. The seared tuna *tostada* (not on the menu) is a great option and the 'rokamarones' (shrimp tempura) come highly recommended. There was no sign outside at last visit; it's in front of Hotel Binniguenda.

Antojitos Los Gallos
MEXICAN **$**

(☑ 958-587-01-39; cnr Carrizal & Palma Real, La Crucecita; dishes M$45-70; ⊙ 2-10pm Wed-Sun; 🛜) The beauty of Crucecita is that it looks, feels and *is* Mexican despite its actual youth. Indeed, if you grab a cafeteria-style table in this very simple little diner, a fount of unadulterated Mexican home cooking – it tastes authentically Mexican too. Start with *caldo tlalpeño* (a chicken and vegetable soup) before launching into a *tlayuda* (a large tortilla), or maybe enchiladas.

El Grillo Marinero
SEAFOOD **$$**

(☑ 958-587-07-83; Carrizal 908, La Crucecita; mains M$135-190; ⊙ 1-8pm Wed-Mon) Huge portions of fish (try the mahi-mahi if it's available) served in a no-nonsense family-run restaurant that has most locals sighing with affection. Expect ice-cold beer in a bottle, *chipotle* sauce in a plastic container and super-fresh seafood served under a thatched roof. All in all, a classic.

Giordanas ITALIAN **$$**

(📞958-583-43-24; www.giordanas-delizie.com; Gardenia, La Crucecita; mains M$115-240; ⏰noon-10pm Tue-Sat; 📶🍴) The talented Italian chef here makes almost everything herself, including the pasta. Options include ravioli with a choice of five fillings and nine sauces, meat or vegetarian lasagna, and some pretty good antipasti, including carpaccios and Parma ham with melon. Plus there's a choice of Italian wine. Also a great selection of baguettes with Italian cheeses and salamis.

Terra-Cotta MEXICAN, INTERNATIONAL **$$**

(📞958-587-11-35; www.facebook.com/terracotta restaurante; Gardenia 902, La Crucecita; mains M$129-285; ⏰8am-11pm; 📶) One of Crucecita's classiest restaurants is affiliated with the equally classy Misión de los Arcos (p500) and inhabits a refined air-conditioned dining room and adjacent patio to resemble a pleasant summer's day in Paris. The menu is international with a Mexican bias, but here you get complimentary bread rather than default chips. Choose from shrimp, steaks, fish, pasta, baguettes and pizza.

El Sabor de Oaxaca OAXACAN **$$**

(📞958-587-00-60; Guamuchil 206, La Crucecita; mains M$125-195; ⏰7:30am-11pm; 📶) Sit amid the sound of roosting birds and whirring fans and let friendly servers bring you classic Oaxacan food. Lots of local specialties are on show here, including *tlayudas* and *moles*. You can go the 'full monty' (Oaxacan-style) if you order your *tlayuda* with *chapulines*.

Xipol CAFETERIA **$$**

(📞958-105-16-78; www.xipol.com.mx; Guanacastle 311, La Crucecita; breakfast & snacks M$55-250; ⏰7am-11:30pm; 📶) Bivouacked beneath bohemian La Crema, this open-air spot can claim to be equally arty (a mural by noted Zapotec graffiti artist Irving Cano beautifies one wall). It can deliver in the mezcal stakes and it also offers breakfast washed down with superb coffee. A couple of flat-screen TVs placate travelers missing their European soccer fix.

Azul Profundo SEAFOOD **$$$**

(📞958-583-03-00; Camino Real Zaashila, Blvd Juárez 5, Tangolunda; mains M$230-360, lobster M$1800; ⏰7-11pm Mon, Wed, Fri & Sat) Unusual for an all-inclusive, the Camino Real Zaashila (p501) allows nonguests into its best restaurant, a romantic candlelit affair aside the ocean, to experience rich but expensive seafood. If you've ever dreamed of lobster and champagne over a tangerine sunset, bust out your credit card.

 Drinking & Nightlife

Palapas (ie beach bars) are common and can usually rustle up large potent cocktails inches from the waves. All-inclusive resorts put on their own slightly canned entertainment (expect Elvis impersonators and cheesy cabaret). Downtown Crucecita has a modest bar scene embellished by mellow musicians and a bit of mezcal-fueled karaoke.

⭐**La Crema** BAR

(📞958-587-07-02; Gardenia 311, La Crucecita; ⏰7pm-2am; 📶) Part of the success of Huatulco is that it can cough up something as cool as La Crema, a dark-lit upstairs bar where a thrown-together mesh of old sofas and retro decor attracts anyone who's into live music, mezcal and good pizza. It's always an interesting atmosphere, especially when they stage bands (weekends mainly).

El Tonel BAR

(📞958-107-11-20; Carrizal 504, La Crucecita; ⏰9pm-5am Tue-Sun; 📶) Plunge into Crucecita's popular mezcal dive bar, which is actually rather large compared to your average *mezcalería*, with moody lighting, lurid graffiti and plenty of stools upon which to perch. Music of the salsa variety loosens the limbs on Friday and Saturday nights.

Casa Mayor CAFE

(📞958-587-18-81; www.facebook.com/cafe casamayor; Bugambilia 601, La Crucecita; ⏰8am-midnight Mon-Sat, from 4pm Sun; 📶) 🍴 Overlooking the Plaza Principal, Casa Mayor serves good organic coffee from Pluma Hidalgo, one of Oaxaca's best coffee-producing regions. Decent breakfast is served on the terrace and there's a smaller **branch** (cnr Gardenia & Guanacastle, La Crucecita; coffees M$15-40; ⏰7am-11pm) 🍴 on the far corner of the plaza that does the same excellent coffee and other drinks. There's often a live troubadour strumming plaintively in the evenings.

 Shopping

Paradise ARTS & CRAFTS

(📞958-587-02-68; www.facebook.com/paradise hux; Gardenia 803; ⏰9:30am-9:30pm) Crucecita doesn't lack shops, but if you're looking for something a bit quirkier than underpants and socks, this local craft outlet can oblige with black clay pottery, copal-wood *alebrijes* and some psychedelic clothes.

ℹ Getting There & Away

AIR

Possibly the world's handsomest airport, with white walls and a gabled thatched roof, **Bahías de Huatulco International Airport** (www.asur.com.mx; Hwy 200 Km 237) is 400m north of Hwy 200, 15km west of La Crucecita. From November to April (or parts of that period) there are weekly flights to/from several Canadian airports with **Air Canada** (☑ 888-247-2262; www.aircanada.com), **Air Transat** (☑ USA & Canada 877-872-6728; www.airtransat.ca), **Sunwing Airlines** (☑ USA & Canada 877-786-9464; www.flysunwing.com) and **WestJet** (☑ USA & Canada 888-937-8538; www.westjet.com; Huatulco Airport), and to/from Minneapolis with **Sun Country Airlines** (☑ USA 651-905-2737; www.suncountry.com).

Other airlines include the following.

Aeroméxico (☑ 958-581-91-26; www.aeromexico.com; Huatulco Airport; ⊗ 9:30am-6:30pm) Mexico City twice daily.

Aerotucán (☑ 958-581-90-85, cell 958-5876066; www.aerotucan.com; Huatulco Airport; ⊗ 8am-noon) Flies 13-seat Cessnas daily to/from Oaxaca (M$2510). Flights are sometimes canceled or rescheduled at short notice.

Interjet (☑ 958-581-91-16; www.interjet.com; Huatulco Airport; ⊗ 9am-5pm) Mexico City at least twice daily.

Magnicharters (☑ 55-5141-1351; www.magnicharters.com; Huatulco Airport) Mexico City daily except Tuesday.

TAR Aerolíneas (☑ 55-2629-5272; www.tarmexico.com; Huatulco Airport; ⊗ 9am-5pm) Oaxaca four times weekly, Querétaro twice weekly.

Volaris (☑ 55-1102-8000; www.volaris.com; Huatulco Airport) Mexico City twice weekly, plus flights to Chicago.

BUS, VAN & TAXI COLECTIVO

Some buses to Huatulco are marked 'Santa Cruz Huatulco,' but they still terminate in La Crucecita. Make sure your bus is not headed to Santa María Huatulco, which is some way inland.

Shared vans to Pochutla (M$30, one hour) leave frequently from the street corner beside Soriana supermarket on Blvd Chahué, 200m west of the ADO Bus Terminal in La Crucecita.

ADO Bus Terminal (www.ado.com.mx; Blvd Chahué, La Crucecita) Located 500m north of the Plaza Principal; used by ADO GL (deluxe), OCC (1st class) and Sur and AU (2nd class) buses.

Central Camionera (Carpinteros s/n, Sector V, La Crucecita) Located 1.2km northwest of central La Crucecita; used by Turistar (deluxe), AltaMar (1st class), Transportes Rápidos de Pochutla (TRP; 2nd class) and Istmeños (2nd class) buses.

Expressos Colombo (☑ 958-587-23-11; www.expressoscolombohuatulco.com; cnr Gardenia & Sabalí, La Crucecita; to Oaxaca M$260) Passenger vans to Oaxaca; the terminal is 400m north of the Plaza Principal.

Huatulco 2000 (☑ 958-587-29-10; Guamuchil, La Crucecita; to Oaxaca M$260) Passenger vans to Oaxaca and Pluma Hidalgo. Located 150m east of the Plaza Principal.

OAXACA BAHÍAS DE HUATULCO

OFF THE BEATEN TRACK

CONCEPCIÓN BAMBA

The coast west from Salina Cruz is spectacular, with long, sweeping sandy beaches, monster dunes and forested mountains rising just inland. It has surfers in raptures for its long-peeling, sand-bottom, right-hand point breaks and several beach and jetty breaks. Concepción Bamba, or La Bamba as it's known, 40km west of Salina Cruz, sits on a 6km beach with two point breaks in the middle. The surfing season is from about March to October, but swells don't come every day so check the forecasts.

There's a community turtle camp on the beach, where turtle eggs (laid between October and March) are collected and incubated in a protected enclosure, with hatchlings being released into the ocean after about six weeks. There's an excellent surf camp here, **Cocoleoco**, which offers lodging and meals, but it was shut down at last visit. If it remains closed you can always head 80km west to **Barra de la Cruz**, where you'll find great surf and plenty of accommodations, including **Posada Blanca** (☑ cell 958-1156677; www.facebook.com/posadablancarooms; cabañas M$800, without air-con M$350-500; ℗ ☜).

The signposted turnoff to Concepción Bamba is at Km 352 on Hwy 200: a 2.5km unpaved road leads to the village. Buses between Huatulco and Salina Cruz will drop you at the turnoff, where three-wheeler moto-taxis (M$15 per person) run to the village from about 7am to 6pm.

BUSES & VANS FROM BAHÍAS DE HUATULCO

DESTINATION	FARE (M$)	TIME (HR)	FREQUENCY (PER DAY) & LOCATION
Mexico City (Terminal Sur) via Puerto Escondido	1253-1510	14-15	AltaMar 3:45pm & 5:30pm, Turistar 5pm from Central Camionera
Mexico City (TAPO)	808-1275	15-16	3 from ADO terminal
Oaxaca via Salina Cruz	279-305	8	4 from ADO terminal
Oaxaca via San José del Pacífico	260	6½-7	13 Expressos Colombo, 10 Huatulco 2000
Pochutla	30-89	1	frequent from ADO terminal, TRP every 10min from Central Camionera
Puerto Escondido	81-205	2½	23 from ADO terminal
Salina Cruz	100-250	2¾	TRP & Istmeños every 30min from Central Camionera, 12 from ADO terminal
San Cristóbal de las Casas	405-464	10-10½	3 from ADO terminal
Tehuantepec	120-206	3-3½	TRP & Istmeños frequent from Central Camionera, 9 from ADO terminal

❶ Getting Around

TO/FROM THE AIRPORT

Shared *taxis autorizados* (authorized taxis) cost M$150 per person or M$450 for a whole cab from the airport to La Crucecita, Santa Cruz, Chahué or Tangolunda, but you can usually get private taxis for half this price, or less, by walking 300m down to Hwy 200, where drivers wait at the airport intersection. From the same intersection, you can also catch a bus to La Crucecita (M$14): they pass about every 15 minutes from 6am to 8pm.

To get back to the airport from La Crucecita taxis cost M$180.

BICYCLE

You can rent bikes for M$250 per day from Huatulco Salvaje (p499). Roads are light on traffic and regular *topes* (speed bumps) prevent speeding.

BOAT

Some of the western bays and most of the eastern ones are accessible by road, but a boat ride is more fun, if more expensive, than a taxi. *Lanchas* will whisk you out to most beaches from Santa Cruz harbor any time after 8am and return to collect you by dusk. Round-trip rates for up to 10 people: Playa La Entrega M$1000, Bahía Órgano M$1500, Bahía Maguey M$1500, Bahía Cacaluta M$2500, Playa La India M$3500 and Bahía San Agustín M$4000. For the bays lying west of Playa La Entrega, visitors may be asked to pay a M$36 national-park fee. Use of nonbiodegradable sunscreen and insect repellent is prohibited within the national park.

BUS & TAXI

Taxis are the main modus operandi around Huatulco's spread-out sights. They have set rates clearly displayed at every taxi rank. Sample rates from Crucecita are M$35 to Santa Cruz or the Central Camionera, M$60 to Tangolunda or Playa La Entrega and M$70 to Bahía Maguey.

Blue-and-white local buses run frequently during daylight. To Santa Cruz Huatulco they depart from Plaza El Madero on Guamuchil, two blocks east of the main plaza in La Crucecita. It costs M$7.

CAR & MOTORCYCLE

Car rental is available with rates fluctuating between M$600 to M$1100, depending on the time of year.

Europcar (☏ 958-100-40-97; www.europcar. com; Huatulco Airport; ⊗ 8am-6pm) Reasonable rates and good service.

Los Tres Reyes (☏ cell 958-1005443; www. lostresreyescarrent.com; Lote 20, Blvd Chahué Manzana 1, La Crucecita; ⊗ 8am-7pm) Efficient local firm with fair prices.

Zipping around on a scooter or motorcycle can be a fun way to get around Huatulco. **Aventura Mundo** (☏ 958-581-01-97; www.aventuramundo. net; Blvd Juárez; scooter/motorcycle rentals per day from M$450/900; ⊗ 9am-2pm Mon-Sat) in Tangolunda rents out good machines, with helmets and a map. There's generally no insurance available with scooter or motorcycle rentals.

WALKING

The whole area from La Bocana in the east to Playa Maguey in the west has a wide, relatively smooth pavement running alongside the road, making walking both safe and easy.

ISTHMUS OF TEHUANTEPEC

The southern half of the 200km-wide Isthmus of Tehuantepec (teh-wahn-teh-*pek*), Mexico's narrow waist, forms the flat, hot, humid eastern end of Oaxaca state. Indigenous Zapotec culture is strong here, with its own regional twists. In 1496 the isthmus Zapotecs repulsed the Aztecs from the fortress of Guiengola, near Tehuantepec, and the isthmus never became part of the Aztec empire. An independent spirit pervades the region to this day.

Few travelers take the time to linger here, but those who do encounter a lively, friendly populace whose open and confident women take leading roles in business and government. Many fiestas feature the *tirada de frutas,* in which women climb on roofs and throw fruit down onto the men below!

Of the three main towns, isthmus culture is stronger in Tehuantepec and Juchitán than in Salina Cruz, which is dominated by its oil refinery. All three towns can be uncomfortably hot in the day, but evening breezes are refreshing.

Tehuantepec

971 / POP 42,000

Tehuantepec, 245km from Oaxaca city, is a friendly but hot and sweaty town, and most travelers blow through here on their way to somewhere else. June and August are the main months for partying in the fiestas of Tehuantepec's 15 barrios (neighborhoods). Each barrio has its own colonial church, and many are prettily painted and floodlit after dark.

Sights

Ex Convento Rey Cosijopí HISTORIC BUILDING
(971-715-01-14; Callejón Rey Cosijopí; 8am-8pm Mon-Fri, 9am-2pm Sat) FREE This former Dominican monastery, built in the 16th century, houses Tehuantepec's **Casa de la Cultura**, where arts and crafts workshops and activities are held, though at last visit it remained closed for repairs due to structural damage from the 2017 earthquake. It bears traces of old frescoes, and some rooms hold modest exhibits of traditional dress, archaeological finds and historical photos. It's on a short lane off Guerrero, 400m northeast of the central plaza.

Sleeping & Eating

Hotel Calli HOTEL $$
(971-715-00-85; www.hotelcalli.com; Hwy 185 Km 790; d incl breakfast M$975; P图令图) Bland but comfortable, the Calli offers a quiet stay away from Tehuantepec's busy downtown and you get plenty of open space in a grassy garden surrounding a palm-fringed pool. For most people, it's an overnighter – nothing more – in which case it passes the test. It's beside Hwy 185, 1km east of the main bus station.

Hotel Donaji HOTEL $
(971-715-00-64; betty_hdonaji@hotmail.com; Ortiz de Domínguez 10; d M$470-570; 图令) A journeyman hotel that's serves to break a journey (which is Tehuantepec's main function). It's pretty central with a slightly dingy affiliated cafe, air-con units and smallish rooms.

Restaurante Scarú MEXICAN $$
(971-715-06-46; Callejón Leona Vicario 4; mains M$145-180; 8am-9pm; 令) Scarú occupies an 18th-century house with a scruffy patio

---

THE 2017 EARTHQUAKE

A major 8.2 magnitude earthquake (the strongest in Mexico in over a century) dealt a devastating blow to the Oaxaca coast in September 2017, particularly the area around the Isthmus de Tehuantepec. Juchitán was the city that fared the worst with many of its older structures in and around central Jardín Juárez collapsing completely or suffering major damage. The most public of images was the sight of the Palacio del Ayuntamiento, a graceful 19th-century town hall with 31 arches, partially caved in. Another casualty was the 16th-century Vicente Ferrer church around the corner, which lost one tower with the other one left hanging precariously over the adjacent Lidxi Guendabiaani like a loose piece of Lego. The school in front of the church, the Centro Escolar Juchitán, had to be demolished completely due to irrevocable structural damage.

The town of Tehuantepec, 28km southwest of Juchitán, suffered less severe damage, although roofs on some of the older colonial structures failed to withstand the tremors.

BUSES FROM TEHUANTEPEC

DESTINATION	FARE (M$)	TIME (HR)	FREQUENCY (PER DAY)
Bahías de Huatulco	205-238	3½	6
Mexico City (TAPO or Sur)	550-1423	12-13	10
Oaxaca	172-287	4¾-5¼	20
Pochutla	298	4¾	4
Puerto Escondido	361-382	6	5

made infinitely prettier by some striking typically Mexican murals. Sit beneath a fan, quaff a *limonada* and sample one of the varied dishes on offer. Seafood is the specialty and the prawns stuffed with *acelga* (chard) are a good choice.

To find it go 200m south from the east side of the plaza to the end of Juárez, then one block east.

ⓘ Information

There's an erratically staffed **Tourist Information Office** (☑ 971-713-76-53; Hwy 185; ☺ 8am-4pm Mon-Fri, 9am-2pm Sat) beside the highway, two blocks west from the central plaza.

ⓘ Getting There & Away

Tehuantepec's main bus station, known as **Terminal ADO** (☑ 971-715-01-08; www.ado.com.mx; Ixtaltepec 20), is by Hwy 185, 1.5km northeast of the central plaza. It's shared by deluxe, 1st-class and 2nd-class services of the ADO/OCC group. Second-class Istmeños buses to Juchitán (M$28, 30 minutes) and Salina Cruz (M$18, 30 minutes) stop on the highway outside La Terminal at least every half-hour during daylight.

Juchitán

☑ 971 / POP 74,800

Isthmus culture is strong in this friendly town, where about 30 different neighborhood *velas* (festivals) fill the calendar with music, dancing, drinking, eating and fun from April to September. Juchitán is also famed for its *muxes* – a third gender identifying openly gay, frequently cross-dressing people assigned male at birth, who hold their own *vela* in November.

In September 2017, an 8.2 magnitude earthquake hit Juchitán hard, the first in recorded history to strike in this region. The area's structures were not designed to withstand the quake, and so it destroyed many buildings and severely damaged others.

Homes around town are still in various states of reconstruction, with new structures abandoning the classic Juchitán style for safer designs. The downtown market, known for its excellent regional cuisine, has been rebuilt and was set to reopen at last visit.

⊙ Sights

Parque Benito Juárez   PLAZA
(El Zócalo) Parque Juárez is the city's always interesting central square. This is where the city's vendors moved after the market was destroyed in the 2017 earthquake. You can find locally made hammocks, traditional Tehuana clothing and jewelry, plus a wide selection of fruits and vegetables, meat and fish, and freshly baked bread.

The splendid 19th-century Palacio del Ayuntamiento, the governmental palace building, with its 31 arches runs down the square's east side. Unfortunately, it was badly damaged in the 2017 earthquake, when part of it caved in, and reconstruction continues.

⌚ Sleeping & Eating

The town has a reasonable stash of affordable if unspectacular places to stay, some of which were rebuilt after the 2017 earthquake. Juchitán's famed market on Calle 2 de Abril, beloved for its affordable home-style eats, was completely rebuilt behind a new red-brick facade.

Hotel Central   HOTEL $
(☑ 971-712-20-19; www.hotelcentral.com.mx; Av Efraín Gómez 30; s/d M$380/500; ❉ @ ☎) Renovated after the 2017 earthquake, the new-look Central offers freshly painted rooms with comfy beds, some with more natural light than others. It's conveniently located near the market, a must-stop to sample regional fare. The owners are friendly and they have a great website (www.turismo.hotelcentral.com.mx) that lists nearby day trips to seldom-visited beaches, freshwater springs and more.

BUSES FROM JUCHITÁN

DESTINATION	FARE (M$)	TIME (HR)	FREQUENCY (PER DAY)
Bahías de Huatulco	233-333	3½-4	10
Mexico City	725-1374	12-13½	20
Oaxaca	185-305	5-6	20
Pochutla	309-339	4½-5¼	6
San Cristóbal de las Casas	294-483	5¾-6¾	4
Tapachula	373-554	7-7½	3

Lidxi Guendaro MEXICAN $
(☑ 971-711-02-23; www.facebook.com/lidxiguendaro; Juárez 71; M$70-160; ☺ 4-10:30pm Mon-Sat) Traditional *istmeña* food like *garnachas*, *tlayudas*, *mole* and *pozole* (hominy soup) is served with a smile in this family's pretty plant-filled patio.

La Inter CAFETERIA $$
(☑ 971-711-42-08; www.lainterpuebla.com; 16 de Septiembre 25; mains M$43-185; ☺ 8am-10:30pm; ☜) Suspend your judgment on this light, bright eating option. Inter might be part of a three-cafe chain and look a bit plastic on first impression, but it's rich pickings in hot, steamy post-earthquake Juchitán, with polite, fleet-footed staff, a comprehensive, not unhealthy, menu and life-reaffirming air-conditioning.

Drinking & Nightlife

Restaurant Bar Jardín BAR
(☑ 971-711-20-51; www.facebook.com/barjardin85; Calle 5 de Mayo 21; ☺ 1pm-midnight Mon-Wed, to 1am Thu, to 2am Fri & Sat) After a hot day unwind with a cold beer or cocktail at the popular open-air Jardín, which also serves traditional *istmeña* dishes and stages live music.

ⓘ Getting There & Away

The main bus station, **Terminal ADO** (☑ 971-711-10-22; www.ado.com.mx; Prolongación 16 de Septiembre), is used by deluxe, 1st-class and 2nd-class services of ADO/OCC and is 100m south of Hwy 185 on the northern edge of town. Many buses depart inconveniently between 11pm and 7am.

Second-class Istmeños buses to Tehuantepec (M$28, 30 minutes) and Salina Cruz (M$44, one hour) leave at least every 30 minutes during daylight, from the next corner south of the main terminal.

ⓘ Getting Around

Moto-taxis between the bus station and the central Jardín Juárez cost M$15.

AT A GLANCE

POPULATION
2 million

LANGUAGES
Spanish, Huichol,
Purépecha, Cora

BEST BEACH
Playa Maruata
(p564)

**BEST
CRAFTS STORE**
Galería Colectika
(p553)

**BEST
LGBTIQ+ HOTEL**
Almar Resort
(p550)

WHEN TO GO
Feb
Perfect beach
weather; the Carnaval
reigns in Mazatlán.

Jun & Jul
Surf's up and prices
are down at Pacific
Mexico's prime surf-
ing destinations.

Nov & Dec
Puerto Vallarta
celebrates sport-
fishing and gourmet
food, and ushers in
the whale-watching
season in December.

Play Pichilinguillo (p563)
ARTUROGI/GETTY IMAGES ©

Central Pacific Coast

Giant aquamarine waves provide the backdrop and pulsating rhythm to any visit to Mexico's central Pacific coast, a land of stunning beaches and hot sunsets. You can indulge in all the tropical clichés here: eating sublime seafood under palm-frond roofs, drinking chilled coconut water in a hammock, or enjoying poolside cocktails at a ritzy resort. The nightlife in the cities is great and there's a beach for everyone, whether you prefer yours backed by high-rise hotels or tumbledown cabins.

There's even more going on in the ocean, where you can surf world-class breaks and spot humpback whales breaching on the horizon, mother turtles arriving to lay their eggs, pelicans flying in formation or pods of dolphins rising from the waves.

Central Pacific Coast Highlights

1 Mazatlán (p511) Hanging out in the beautifully restored downtown and enjoying superb cultural offerings.

2 Troncones (p565) Dreaming of making a life in this beach town before heading out for a day of surfing.

3 Puerto Vallarta (p539) Cherishing the diverse art of this coastal city and visiting remote beaches.

4 San Francisco (p533) Soaking up the mellow party vibe and hitting the waves in this tranquil village.

5 Zihuatanejo (p570) Savoring the thriving culinary scene, great beaches and atmospheric bars.

6 Playa Ventura (p595) Disconnecting from everything and chilling on the impossibly perfect beach.

7 Michoacán coast (p563) Exploring pristine surfing beaches and indigenous settlements.

8 Acapulco (p581) Watching daredevils dive off cliffs and looking down at the bay from a petroglyph site.

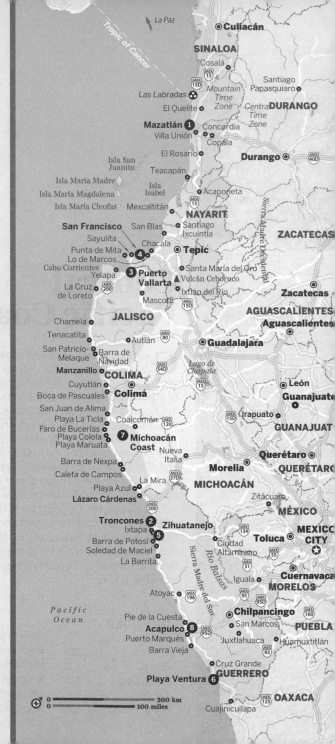

Mazatlán

📍 669 / POP 449,515

Thanks to 20km of sandy beaches, Mazatlán became one of Mexico's most alluring and inviting beach destinations in the mid-20th century, prior to which it had worn other hats: smuggler haven, thriving Pacific port. Though the city has gone through a slump since the 1980s, the cruise ships are now back and Mazatlán's sensitively restored 'tropical neoclassical' historic core has got its second wind, with creative restaurants and businesses popping up like mushrooms after the rain. The result is a coastal city with plenty of allure, its cosmopolitan heritage evident in its architecture, and German influence felt in the strains of local *banda* (big-band) music and in the cold, crisp taste of Pacífico beer.

To take the pulse of Mazatlán, go to the Zona Dorada (Golden Zone) for the beaches, then return to wander the characterful streets of the old town and to linger on the *malecón* (beach promenade) for the sunsets and the people-watching.

◉ Sights

◉ Old Mazatlán

★ Old Mazatlán AREA
(Map p517) Mazatlán's restored old town is a picturesque compendium of noble 19th-century buildings and pretty plazas. It's set back from Playa Olas Altas (p514), a small cove beach where the waterfront road – with its old-fashioned bars and hotels – strongly evokes the 1950s. Though overlooked by the ugly radio masts of Cerro de la Nevería, this old quarter is delightful, with student life and numerous art galleries, cafes, restaurants and bars.

★ Plaza Machado SQUARE
(Map p517; cnr Av Carnaval & Constitución; 🚌 Sábalo-Centro) Surrounded by splendid 19th-century buildings, this gorgeous tree-lined plaza comes alive in the evening, when market stalls pop up, couples stroll hand-in-hand and its numerous terrace restaurants are serenaded by musicians.

Teatro Ángela Peralta THEATER
(Map p517; 📞 669-982-44-46, ext 103; http://culturamazatlan.com/es/teatro-angela-peralta; Av Carnaval 47; self-guided visit M$20; ⊙10am-2pm & 4-6pm Mon-Fri, 10am-2pm Sat; 🚌 Sábalo-Centro)

Named after a 19th-century soprano and constructed between 1869 and 1874, this 1366-seat theater just off Plaza Machado was a thriving center of local cultural life for nearly a century. Revived from its decaying state by dedicated local citizens in the late 1980s, the three-level interior has been restored to its former splendor. All kinds of cultural events are again staged here, from temporary art exhibitions to the annual Festival Cultural Mazatlán (p516).

El Faro LIGHTHOUSE
(Map p512; Joel Montes Camarena; miradór M$10; ⊙park 5am-8pm, miradór 7:30am-7:30pm; 🚌 Playa Sur) At the Mazatlán peninsula's southern end, a prominent rocky outcrop is the base for this lighthouse, which is 135m above sea level. Join the locals either early in the morning or around sunset for a climb up here (it takes around 20 minutes) for a spectacular view of the city and coast. For M$10, you can wander out onto the see-through plexiglass Miradór de Cristal at the top.

Catedral de la Inmaculada Concepción CATHEDRAL
(Map p517; cnr Juárez & Calle 21 de Marzo; ⊙6:30am-1pm & 4-7:30pm; 🚌 Sábalo-Centro) FREE At the center of the old town is this striking 19th-century Romanesque and neo-Gothic mélange of a cathedral with yellow twin towers. The dramatic interior has gilt ceiling roses supporting chandeliers and blocks of stone in alternating colors. It's located on the greenery-filled **Plaza Principal**.

El Clavadista VIEWPOINT
(Map p517; Paseo Olas Altas) Although not as famous nor as spectacular as Acapulco's cliff divers, local *clavadistas* cast their bodies from a couple of platforms at the eponymous viewpoint into the treacherous ocean swells for your enjoyment. Tip accordingly. They usually perform around lunchtime and in the late afternoon, but they won't risk their necks until a crowd has assembled.

Museo Arqueológico de Mazatlán MUSEUM
(INAH; Map p517; 📞669-981-14-55; www.inah.gob.mx/es/red-de-museos/210-museo-arqueologico-de-mazatlan; Sixto Osuna 76; adult/child under 12yr M$45/free; ⊙9am-6pm Tue-Sun; 🚌 Sábalo-Centro) This absorbing museum focuses on pre-Hispanic Sinaloan civilizations. Among obsidian tools and ceramics, standout exhibits include beautiful Aztatlán pottery (900–1200 CE), a funereal urn, *malacates* (spindles), an intricate upper

Greater Mazatlán

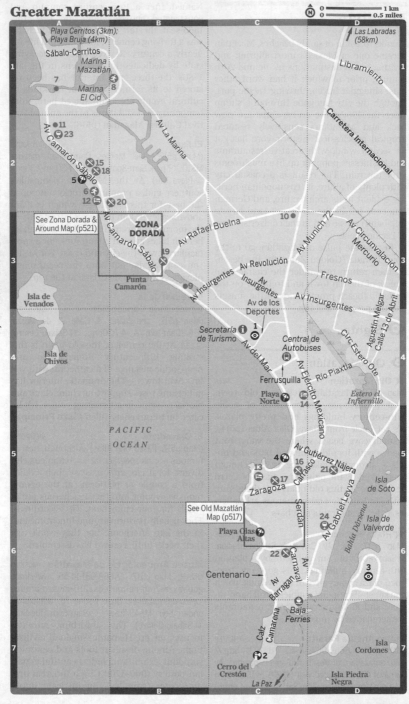

Playa Cerritos (3km);
Playa Bruja (4km)

Las Labradas
(58km)

Sábalo-Cerritos

Marina
Mazatlán

Marina
El Cid

Libramiento

Carretera Internacional

Av La Marina

Av Camarón Sábalo

See Zona Dorada &
Around Map (p521)

ZONA
DORADA

Av Camarón Sábalo

Punta
Camarón

Av Rafael Buelna

Av Munich 72

Av Circunvalación
Mercurio

Fresnos

Av Insurgentes

Av Revolución

Av
Insurgentes

Av de los
Deportes

Av Insurgentes

Agustín Melgar
Calle 13 de Abril

Circ Estero Ote

Secretaría
de Turismo

Central de
Autobuses

Ferrusquilla

Av del Mar

Av Ejército Mexicano

Río Piaxtla

Estero el
Infiernillo

Isla de
Venados

Isla de
Chivos

PACIFIC
OCEAN

Playa
Norte

Av Gutiérrez Nájera

Carrasco

Isla
de Soto

Zaragoza

Serdán

See Old Mazatlán
Map (p517)

Av Gabriel Leyva

Isla de
Valverde

Bahía Dársena

Playa Olas
Altas

Av
Carnaval

Centenario

Av
Barragán

Baja
Ferries

Isla
Cordones

Calz
Camarena

Cerro del
Crestón

La Paz

Isla Piedra
Negra

Greater Mazatlán

torso adornment made of 1922 pieces of shell and coral, and a statue of a hunchback, *Jorobado de la Nautical,* believed to be in possession of special powers. The mammoth skeleton in the entry hall harks back to the days when these beasts roamed Sinaloa.

Museo de Arte   MUSEUM
(Map p517; ☎669-985-35-02; www.facebook.com/museodeartedemazatlan; cnr Sixto Osuna & Carranza; ☺10am-6pm Tue-Fri, 11am-5pm Sat & Sun; ☒Sábalo-Centro) FREE This small museum in a sprawling colonial courtyard complex makes a convincing case for the vitality and innovation of contemporary Mexican art, with changing exhibitions of digital works, sculptures, prints and paintings.

Isla de la Piedra   ISLAND
(Map p512; return boat M$35; ☒Playa Sur) A popular half-day escape from the city, this peninsula (not an actual island) is just southeast of Old Mazatlán and boasts a beautiful, long sandy beach bordered by coconut groves. Surfers come for the waves, and its simple *palapa* (thatched-roof) restaurants draw Mexican families, particularly on weekends. Water taxis depart frequently (6am to 6pm) from the Playa Sur *embarcadero* (dock).

'Playa Sur' buses leave for the *embarcadero* from the corner of Serdán and Escobedo, two blocks southeast of Plaza Principal in Old Mazatlán.

◎ Zona Dorada

Resembling breaching whales, the three photogenic islands jutting from the sea off shore from the Zona Dorada offer secluded beaches and clear waters ideal for snorkeling, plus great multitudes of seals and marine birds. On the left is **Isla de Chivos** (Goat Island); **Isla de Pájaros** (Bird Island) is on the right. The most visited is the one in the middle, **Isla de Venados** (Deer Island). The islands are part of a wildlife refuge designated to help protect the local birds and marine fauna. Any boat operator can take you out there; day tours typically depart from Marina El Cid around 9:30am, returning at 4pm, with prices (around M$1300) including lunch, activities and drinks.

Onilikan   DISTILLERY
(Map p521; ☎669-668-23-70; www.onilikan.com; Av Playa Gaviotas 505; ☺9am-6pm Mon-Fri, to 2pm Sat; ℗; ☒Sábalo-Centro) FREE This tiny distillery is the only one of its kind, specializing in brewing up mango liquors, which can be sampled here in their pure form or as part of a cocktail. You can also try *aguardiente de agave* (tequila in all but name), plus fiery vodkas flavored with three types of chili. It's in the heart of the Zona Dorada, and you can just drop in for a friendly short explanation and free tasting.

Acuario Mazatlán   AQUARIUM
(Map p512; ☎669-981-78-15; http://acuariomazatlan.com; Av de los Deportes 111; adult/child 3-11yr M$115/85; ☺9:30am-5pm; ℗; ☒Sábalo-Centro) One of Mexico's largest aquariums has tanks with hundreds of species of freshwater, pelagic and reef fish, a display of skeletons, birds and frogs in the garden. The eerie jellyfish tanks are particularly mesmerizing.

However, its sea-lion shows and much-hyped shark-riding experience are a big concern to animal welfare groups, who say that activity of this sort is harmful to the creatures and should be avoided.

🏊 Beaches

With over 20km of beaches, it's easy to find a suitable stretch of sand. The following beaches are listed in geographical order, from south to north.

In Old Mazatlán, crescent-shaped **Playa Olas Altas** (Map p517; Paseo Olas Altas; Sábalo-Centro) is where tourism first flourished from the 1920s onwards; buffeted by heavy surf, it's better for bodyboarding than swimming.

Backed by a promenade popular with joggers and cyclists, the golden sands of **Playa Norte** (Map p512; Sábalo-Centro) begin just north of Old Mazatlán. The beach arcs toward **Punta Camarón**, a rocky point dominated by the conspicuous, castle-like **Fiesta Land** (Map p521; 669-989-16-00; www.fiesta land.mx; Av Camarón Sábalo s/n; 9pm-4am Thu-Sun; ; Sábalo-Centro) nightclub complex.

The most luxurious hotels face pretty **Playa Las Gaviotas** (Map p521; Sábalo-Centro) and **Playa Sábalo** (Map p512; Sábalo-Centro), the latter extending north of the Zona Dorada. Sheltered by picturesque islands, the waters here are generally calm and ideal for swimming and water sports.

Further north, past **Marina El Cid** and the ever-evolving **Marina Mazatlán**, are **Playa Bruja** (Cerritos-Juárez) – a once-serene beach that has seen a flood of high-rise development in recent years – and **Playa Cerritos** (Cerritos-Juárez). Both have a smattering of seafood restaurants and decent surf. To reach these northern beaches, catch a 'Cerritos–Juárez' bus along Avenida Camarón Sábalo in the Zona Dorada.

🏃 Activities

Mazatlán boasts some noteworthy surfing sites, including Playa Bruja (p514). There are several spots to rent boards and a handful of surf schools. Other water-sports equipment can be hired from the beaches of most large beachfront hotels.

Jah Surf School   SURFING
(cell 669-1494699; http://jahsurfschool.com; class US$50, board rental per hour/day US$10/25;) Friendly, reader-recommended instructor who is happy to take on whole families. Also rents out boards and equipment.

Aqua Sports Center   WATER SPORTS
(Map p512; 669-913-04-51; www.aquasports center.com; Hotel El Cid Castilla, Av Camarón Sábalo s/n; 1-tank dive US$100, snorkeling tour US$40, paddleboard tours US$75; 9:30am-5pm; Sábalo-Centro) The place to go for all sorts of water-sports activities, including scuba diving, snorkeling rentals, jet skiing, banana-boat rides (for up to five passengers), parasailing, sailboat rentals and kayak rentals.

Sportfishing

Handily located at the confluence of the Sea of Cortez and the Pacific Ocean, Mazatlán is world-famous for sportfishing – especially for marlin, swordfish, sailfish, tuna and *dorado* (dolphin fish). It can be an expensive activity (US$455 to US$799 per boat per day, for boats ranging in size from 8m to 11m with four to 10 people fishing); fishing from a 7m *super panga* (fiberglass skiff) is less expensive (around US$349 per day with up to four people fishing).

Bibi Fleet   FISHING
(Map p512; 669-913-10-60; www.bibifleet.com; Shop 8, Marina Mazatlán, btwn docks 7 & 8; charters per day US$349-649; 9am-5pm Mon-Fri, to 1pm Sat; Sábalo-Centro) Helpful and professional fishing setup with three different boat options. Excursions last five to eight hours and this outfit honors catch-and-release practices.

Aries Fleet   FISHING
(Map p512; 669-916-34-68; www.elcidmarinas. com; Av Camarón Sábalo s/n, Marina El Cid; fishing tour per half-day/day from US$295/325; 8:30am-5pm Mon-Sat, to 2pm Sun; Sábalo-Centro) Runs highly recommended fishing tours on one of its seven boats and supports some catch-and-release practices.

🧭 Tours

⭐ **Onca Explorations**   ECOTOUR
(Map p512; 669-913-40-50; www.onca explorations.com; Av Camarón Sábalo 2100; adult/child whale- or dolphin-watching tours US$119/79, bird-watching US$99/69; 9am-5pm; Sábalo-Centro) Wildlife observation and conservation are the focus of these ecotours, led by marine ecologist Oscar Guzón. Most popular are his 'Humpback Whale Research Adventure' (8am and 1pm December to April) and 'Wild Dolphin Adventure' (8am year-round) tours, which offer excellent opportunities to observe marine mammals up close.

SINALOA'S COLONIAL GEMS

Several small, picturesque colonial towns in the Sierra Madre foothills make pleasant day trips from Mazatlán. Check safety conditions before setting out, as these villages occasionally see some trouble from local cartels.

El Quelite Taking its name from a 19th-century ranch, El Quelite lies some 43km north of Mazatlán toward Culiacán, off Hwy 15. Its charm lies in its cobbled streets, its local crafts and a mix of adobe buildings and colorful houses, clad in bougainvillea and interspersed by cacti. Local gastronomy is a draw, too, from fresh cheeses to pork dishes.

Concordia Founded in 1565, Concordia has an 18th-century church with a baroque facade and elaborately decorated columns. The village is known for manufacturing high-quality pottery and hand-carved furniture. It's about a 45-minute drive east of Mazatlán; head southeast on Hwy 15 for 20km to Villa Unión, turn inland on Hwy 40 (the highway to Durango) and go another 20km.

Copala Forty kilometers past Concordia on Hwy 40, Copala was one of Mexico's first mining towns. It still has its colonial church (1748), period houses and cobblestone streets. It's a one-hour drive from Mazatlán.

El Rosario El Rosario is another colonial mining town, 76km southeast of Mazatlán on Hwy 15. Founded in 1655, its most famous feature is the towering gold-leaf altar in its church, the Nuestra Señora del Rosario. You can also visit the home of beloved singer Lola Beltrán, whose long recording career made *ranchera* (Mexico's urban 'country music') popular in the mid-20th century.

Cosalá In the mountains north of Mazatlán, Cosalá is a beautiful colonial mining village that dates from 1550. It has an 18th-century church, a mining museum in a colonial mansion on the plaza, and the lovely hacienda-style **Hotel Quinta Minera** (☑696-965-02-22; www.hotelquintaminera.com; Hidalgo 92; d/q M$1800/2160; 🅿😊❄🛜💦). To get here, go north on Hwy 15 for 113km to the turnoff (opposite the turnoff for La Cruz de Alota on the coast) and then climb 45km into the mountains.

Buses to Cosalá, Concordia and El Rosario depart from a small station behind Mazatlán's main bus terminal (p524).

Other options include an excursion to Las Labradas (p522) beachside petroglyph site, and custom bird-watching tours to Santa María Bay, Isla Isabel National Park and the Chara Pinta Tufted Jay Preserve.

⭐ **Flavor Teller** FOOD & DRINK
(☑cell 669-1426890; www.flavorteller.com; per person US$50; ⊙Mon-Fri) Dutch expat and longtime Mazatlán resident Maaike draws on a decade's worth of street-food exploration to bring you the best of the city's typical eats. Choose the Mercado & More walking tour of Old Mazatlán, or the Barrio Bites and Night Eats tours that take you further afield by *auriga* (pickup truck). Small groups; fun atmosphere.

Blue Foot Tours OUTDOORS
(Map p512; ☑cell 669-2708212; https://blue foot.mx; Hotel Don Pelayo, Av del Mar; per person US$35-55) These outdoors enthusiasts take you on half-day cycling tours (either along

the *malecón* or on the Isla de las Piedras), or on hiking outings along the Blue Agave Trail, culminating in a visit to the Los Osuna tequila distillery, complete with samples.

Turtle Tours OUTDOORS
(☑669-160-91-66; www.turtletoursmazatlan.com; per person US$55-85; ⊙Sep-late Feb) 🌿 This respectable outfit specializes in sensitively run tours of the Verde-Camacho Turtle Sanctuary north of the city, where you can observe and help release the endangered olive ridley turtles. Depending on which package you go for, kayaking, boating and other outdoor activities may also be included.

Mazatlan Bike Tours CYCLING
(Map p512; ☑669-137-18-90; www.facebook. com/MazatlanBikeTours; Pachuca 936A; per person from US$40) Personable Rudy runs fun, moderately strenuous mountain-biking tours in the hills above the city. Two-person minimum; rides can be tailored to ability.

✱ Festivals & Events

Carnaval
CARNAVAL

(☺Feb) Mazatlán has Mexico's most flamboyant Carnaval celebrations, complete with epic fireworks displays. For the week leading up to Ash Wednesday, the town goes on a nonstop partying spree.

Festival Cultural Mazatlán
PERFORMING ARTS

(www.culturamazatlan.com; Teatro Ángela Peralta, Av Carnaval 47; ☺Oct-Dec) If you like performing arts, witness captivating theatrical and musical performances in and around the Teatro Ángela Peralta (p511).

★ Artwalk
ART

(www.facebook.com/artwalkmazatlan; ☺4-8pm 1st Fri of the month Nov-Apr) Get a taste of Mazatlán's arts scene through this self-guided walking tour of artists' studios and galleries on the first Friday of every month during November to April high season.

🛏 Sleeping

Old Mazatlán is home to atmospheric boutique hotels, while the Zona Dorada has a high concentration of beach resorts and motel-style midrange options. Inexpensive hotels of varying quality cluster around the bus station. Book well ahead for the Semana Santa (Easter) and Carnaval.

🛏 Old Mazatlán & Around

Hostal Mazatlán
HOSTEL $

(Map p517; ☎669-688-57-55; www.hostalmazatlan.com; Constitución 809; dm/d incl breakfast M$340/955; ⊛❀⊜; 🚇Sábalo-Centro) Liberally covered in scribbled messages from happy past guests, this downtown hostel has a breezy, colorful common area and a wonderful rooftop terrace, strung with hammocks. Choose between air-conditioned six-bed dorms or tidy private rooms with their own bathrooms. Bike rentals are dirt-cheap.

Hotel La Siesta
HOTEL $$

(Map p517; ☎669-981-26-40; www.lasiesta.com.mx; Paseo Olas Altas 11; r M$880-1100; ⊛❀⊜❀; 🚇Sábalo-Centro) Don't let the garish pink exterior or the tacky generic tropical art in the rooms put you off; La Siesta is a good *centro histórico* option if you can snag one of the choice sea-view rooms with floor-to-ceiling windows and balconies overlooking Playa Olas Altas. The pleasant central courtyard and attached restaurant are good places to meet other travelers.

Melville Suites
HOTEL $$

(Map p517; ☎669-982-84-74; Constitución 99; ste M$1390-2500; ⓟ⊛❀⊜; 🚇Sábalo-Centro) Inside this 1840s ex-Carmelite school, 20 high-ceilinged, fan-cooled, individually decorated suites surround a lovely, courtyard covered with creepers, and with a trickling fountain. Each suite is named after a famous writer who once passed through the city and all come with kitchenettes. The only downside: the front-facing suites may suffer from street noise on weekend nights. Car park opposite.

Villa Serena
APARTMENT $$

(Map p517; ☎cell 669-1500034; www.villa-serena.blogspot.com; Heriberto Frías 1610; 1-/2-bedroom apt from M$1340/2489; ❀⊜❀; 🚇Sábalo-Centro) This 19th-century cigar factory has been converted into a gorgeous 14-unit apartment complex, the outer walls covered with vines. The best ones are the two-story digs with high wood-beamed ceilings, tiled floors, full kitchen and private patio. A small pool in the tranquil courtyard, resident kitty, and a rooftop Jacuzzi seal the deal.

★ Casa de Leyendas
B&B $$$

(Map p517; ☎669-981-61-80; www.casadeleyendas.com; Venustiano Carranza 4; r incl breakfast M$2140-3580; ❀⊜@❀❀; 🚇Sábalo-Centro) This elegant two-story hacienda houses eight spacious, individually styled adults-only rooms, all with coffee makers, fridges, and unique art from all over Mexico. Guests may soak in the 'cocktail pool' with Jacuzzi jets, use the kitchen and library, hang out on the upstairs terrace and peruse the onsite Hecho en México tequila tasting room and cigar shop.

The attached restaurant, Macaws, is a bit of a local nightspot, known for its burgers.

★ Las 7 Maravillas
B&B $$$

(Map p512; ☎669-136-06-46; www.las7maravillas.com; Av Las Palmas 1; r incl breakfast M$2350-3340; ❀❀❀; 🚇Sábalo-Centro) A block above the waterfront, this marvelous B&B excels when it comes to personalized service (including tours of Sinaloa's historic villages), Jacuzzi with a view and a sumptuous breakfast buffet. Each of the six rooms is individually themed and decorated with artifacts from the Swiss owner's travels. Cuba and Egypt boast ocean views, while Bali accommodates three people. No children under 15.

★ Jonathon Boutique Hotel
BOUTIQUE HOTEL $$$

(Map p517; ☎55 5351 7224, 669-915-63-60; www.jonathonhotel.com; Av Carnaval 1205; d/q incl breakfast M$2259/4345; ❀❀❀❀; 🚇Sábalo-Centro)

Old Mazatlán

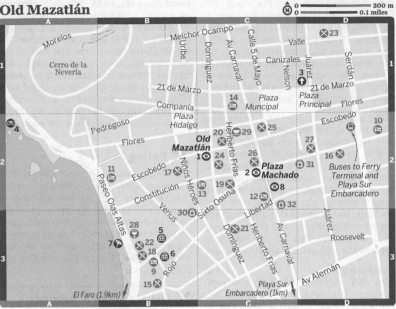

Old Mazatlán

Contemporary boutique hotel on a pedestrian street off Plaza Machado, set around a striking columnar courtyard with spiral staircase. Spacious rooms boast floating beds, hardwood floors and rain showers; the pricier setups have Jacuzzis. The location is terrific, with great old-town views from the rooftop pool.

🛏 Zona Dorada & Around

★**Funky Monkey Hostel**　HOSTEL **$**
(Map p521; ☑ cell 669-4313421; www.facebook
.com/FunkyMonkeyHostel; Cerro Boludo 112;
dm/d incl breakfast M\$341/680; 🅿😊❀@
🛜🛏; 🚌 Sábalo-Centro) In a quiet residential

suburb about 1.2km from the beach, this facility-packed hostel makes a fine place to hang out, with a kidney-shaped pool, two kitchens, hammocks and rooftop fire pit that enhances nighttime storytelling. Private rooms are en suite and come with a kitchen, while spacious fan-cooled dorms benefit from memory-foam mattresses. Surfboard rentals and free bikes.

Suitel 522
GUESTHOUSE $$

(Map p512; ☎ 669-985-41-40; www.suitel522. com; Río Presidio 522; r incl breakfast M$1218; ❄✳🖵; 🚌 Sábalo-Centro) 🏄 Three blocks from the beach, this is a good-value option offering spotless rooms with kitchenettes and either a king-size, double or twin beds along a pleasant plant-filled patio. It rents out bikes, bodyboards and fishing gear, and has an ecologically minded policy of recycling solid waste. Turn off the coast road opposite the gold statue of a *pulmonía* taxi.

Motel Marley
MOTEL $$

(Map p521; ☎ 669-913-55-33; http://travelby mexico.com/sina/marley; Av Playa Gaviotas 226; 1-/2-bedroom apt M$1500/1750; 🅿❄✳🖵; 🚌 Sábalo-Centro) The most atmospheric of the string of low-budget spots in the Zona Dorada, this two-story place offers dated but comfortable seafront apartments, set in four-unit blocks and staggered for airflow, with well-equipped kitchens, an oceanfront lawn, a pool and – best of all – privileged beach access.

Casa Contenta
APARTMENT $$

(Map p521; ☎ 669-913-49-76; www.casacontenta .com.mx; Av Playa Gaviotas 224; apt/house M$1600/3600; 🅿❄✳🖵; 🚌 Sábalo-Centro) Right on the beach in the heart of the Zona Dorada, these spacious apartments – each with cable TV, kitchenette, dining area, double bed and two twins – make a decent option for families. The rooms and beds could do with a bit of modernizing, but it's friendly and pretty fair value for this great location.

★ Inn at Mazatlán
Resort & Spa
RESORT $$$

(Map p512; ☎ 669-913-55-00; https://theinn mazatlan.com; Av Camarón Sábalo 6291; r/ste from US$118/165; 🅿❄✳🖵; 🚌 Sábalo-Centro) The pick of Mazatlán's resorts, the Inn is a wonderful choice for families, with all manner of water sports and crafts available for kids. Adults are catered for, too, with an excellent spa, Jacuzzis and pools, a great beach out front and stylish, contemporary rooms to unwind in.

Hotel Playa Mazatlán
RESORT $$$

(Map p521; ☎ 669-989-05-55; www.hotelplaya mazatlan.com; Av Playa Gaviotas 202; d/f from US$124/207; 🅿❄✳@🖵; 🚌 Sábalo-Centro) This large resort – the first built in the Zona Dorada – attracts a mix of couples and families. Splurge an extra US$30 on rooms with ocean views; all come equipped with cable TV, private terrace and other creature comforts. Manicured tropical gardens and a breezy oceanside restaurant are additional boons.

Eating

Mazatlán is famous for fresh seafood. *Pescado zarandeado* is a delicious, spiced, charcoal-grilled fish; smoked marlin is a local staple, and the shrimp is excellent. Some of the most imaginative restaurants are found in Old Mazatlán, as are excellent *taquerías* (taco stalls). *Taquerías* also line Avenida Rafael Buelna that borders the Zona Dorada.

✕ Old Mazatlán & Around

Looney Bean
CAFE $

(Map p517; ☎ 669-136-05-07; www.looneybean mzt.com; Paseo Olas Altas 166G; breakfasts M$60-99; ⏱7am-10pm Mon-Thu, to 11pm Fri-Sun; ✳🖵; 🚌 Sábalo-Centro) A terrific local coffee shop on the main seaside drag with strong coffee made from a locally roasted blend of Mexican beans, plus juices, smoothies and a choice of hearty Mexican or American breakfasts. It also makes strawberry scones bigger than your face – they're almost impossible to eat in one sitting, though you may try (they are *that* good).

Cenaduría La Copita
MEXICAN $

(Map p512; ☎ 669-123-96-89; Belisario Domínguez 2501; mains M$23-100; ⏱5:30-11:30pm Mon-Sat, from 2pm Sun) This family-run evening-only eatery that's been in business for decades is a step back in time, its walls decorated with characterful photos of Old Mazatlán. The short menu features *asado* (cubed beef, potatoes, radishes and lettuce, with a cup of flavorful beef broth to drench it with), and other beef-heavy deliciousness in the form of tacos, *gorditas, flautas* and enchiladas.

Cenaduría Chayito
MEXICAN $

(Map p512; ☎ 669-982-67-23; www.facebook. com/CenaduriaChayito; José Azueta 2407; mains M$35-180; ⏱7am-11pm) Going strong for decades, this family-run restaurant specializes in typical Sinaloan dishes. Come here in the morning for tacos with *machaca* (spicy dried Sinaloan beef), *chilorio* (stewed pork) and *chilaquiles* (salsa-drenched tortilla strips with cheese). In the afternoon the menu swings toward quesadillas, *pozole* (hominy stew) and grilled meats. *Menudo* (tripe stew) is a Sunday special and legendary hangover cure.

La Olivia
CAFE $

(Map p517; ☑ 669-985-06-42; www.facebook.com/laoliviamzt; Belisario Dominguez 1216; mains M$75-115; ⊙ 7:30am-4pm Tue-Fri, 8am-4pm Sat & Sun; ✲ 🛜 🖉) Helmed by Chihuahua chef Barbara, this cafe lives up to its motto: 'great mood, great food.' Piano music tinkles gently in the background as you order from The Lean Side (chia pudding, fancy oatmeal, eggs with spinach and avocado) or The Mean Side (berry waffles, French toast, *chilaquiles*), coupled with mugs of excellent coffee.

Homemade pesto, hummus and marmalade for sale.

★ Nao Kitchen Bar
ASIAN $$

(Map p517; ☑ 669-176-58-54; www.facebook.com/naokitchenbar; Belisario Domínguez 1502C; mains M$100-280; ⊙ 6-11pm Tue-Sat; ✲) One of Mazatlán's youngest and most innovative chefs, Andrea Lizarraga Osuna combines local ingredients with Far Eastern touches, with faultless attention to flavor and presentation. The *tiradito de pesca* is a work of art, with high notes of citrus and edible flowers, while slow-cooked Korean-style ribs simply melt off the bone. Wontons, gyozas and noodle dishes similarly shine.

Angelina's Kitchen
MEXICAN $$

(Map p517; ☑ 669-910-15-96; www.facebook.com/angelinaslatinkitchen; Venustiano Carranza 18; mains M$130-210; ⊙ noon-11pm Tue-Fri, from 8am Sat & Sun mid-Oct–Jul; 🛜 🖉 ; 🚌 Sábalo-Centro) Behind an unobtrusive facade, this surprisingly capacious restaurant is something of a local favorite and it's easy to see why. A casual menu runs from burgers and salads to ceviches and Greek pizza, plus plenty of vegetarian options. Seafood is expertly selected

---

MAZATLÁN'S STREET EATS

At any time of day, some of the city's best food is to be had at humble *taquerías* (taco stands) and other street-food stalls.

Tacos El Veneno (Map p512; ☑ 669-129-22-26; cnr Gutierrez Najera & Heroes del Cañonero Tampico; taco portion M$30; ⊙ 7-11am Tue-Sat) El Veneno (The Poisoner) and his son El Venenito do a brisk business in *tacos dorados* (crunchy tacos) topped with stewed *machaca* (dried Sinaloan beef), *chicharrón* (pork crackling) or liver and onions, served with homemade salsas and punchy shrimp broth. Get here early, as they sell out.

Taquería Playa Sur (Map p512; ☑ cell 669-9103651; cnr Av Carnaval & Playa Chametla; mains M$30-60; ⊙ 6pm-midnight) Come evening, this *taquería* becomes fragrant with smoke from the grill and fills up with hungry customers. The three specialties are: beef tacos, *chorreada* (thick tortilla fried in pork fat and topped with beef, cheese and onions) and *papa loca* (baked potato with melted cheese, beef and more).

Mercado Pino Suárez (Mercado Centro; Map p517; www.mercadopinosuarezmazatlan.com; Melchor Ocampo 7; meals M$40-60; ⊙ 6am-6pm Mon-Sat, to 2pm Sun; 🚌 Sábalo-Centro) At Old Mazatlán's central market you can fill your boots with marlin tacos and *tostadas de camarón* (deep-fried shrimp tortilla), come lunchtime. The market is filled with pungent stalls selling slabs of marlin, *machaca*, fruit, mountains of *queso fresco* (fresh cheese), dried chilies, fresh fruit and sweet *tamales*.

Nieves de Garrafa de con Medrano (Map p517; www.facebook.com/nievesdegarrafadeconmedrano; cnr Flores & Calle 5 de Mayo; ice cream M$20-30; ⊙ 11am-9pm; 🚌 Sábalo-Centro) Since 1938, this unpretentious family-run cart near Mazatlán's Plaza Principal has been dishing out delicious homemade ice cream.

Hot Dogs El Charly (Map p521; ☑ 669-158-30-97; Av Playa Gaviotas; hot dogs from M$30; ⊙ 5pm-late) As the sun goes down, hungry customers line up at El Charly for great hot dogs. Get yours slathered with a variety of sauces and topped with avocado, tomato salsa, pickles and grilled serrano chilies.

and prepared, whether it's plump, sweet crustaceans or marinated fish on your plate.

Fonda de Chalio
MEXICAN $$

(Map p517; ☑669-910-04-80; fondadechalio33@hotmail.com; Paseo Olas Altas 166; mains M$130-205; ⊙7am-11pm Sun-Fri, to midnight Sat; 🖥; 🚍Sábalo-Centro) This street-front cafe across from the *malecón* is popular with Mazatlán's middle-aged locals. Breakfasts pack out for *chilaquiles* with *machaca* and *huevos con nopales* (scrambled eggs with cactus paddles). The afternoon menu gets lively with *aguachile* (shrimp ceviche with a punchy green salsa), *sopa azteca* (avocado and cheese soup), and street-side music and dancing.

Pedro & Lola
FUSION $$

(Map p517; ☑669-982-25-89; www.restaurantpedroylola.com; Av Carnaval 1303; mains M$129-238; ⊙6pm-1am; 🖥; 🚍Sábalo-Centro) This stylish eatery overlooking Plaza Machado does outstanding small plates, including delectable shrimp and octopus dishes and slow-cooked pork tacos. The fresh fish of the day comes cooked in a variety of ways, including garlic-sautéed, and there are always interesting new takes on traditional Sinaloan recipes. Live jazz and blues acts play Thursday to Sunday.

Gaia Bistrot
INTERNATIONAL $$

(Map p517; ☑669-112-25-25; www.gaiabistrot.com.mx; Heriberto Frías 1301; mains M$130-275; ⊙noon-11pm Tue-Sat, 1:30-10pm Sun; 🖥🗡; 🚍Sábalo-Centro) Internationally taught chef Gilberto del Toro has earned praise for a menu featuring globe-trotting dishes such as rib-eye steak, coconut-braised chicken, and shrimp risotto with white wine. The strawberry panna cotta and tarte tatin are found among the sweet temptations, and the stellar location on Old Mazatlán's most popular square is a bonus for people-watchers.

★ Héctor's Bistro
FUSION $$$

(Map p517; ☑669-981-15-77; www.facebook.com/hectorsbistro; Escobedo 409, cnr Heriberto Frías; mains M$105-395; ⊙8am-11pm Mon-Sat; 🖥; 🚍Sábalo-Centro) Comfortable and with polished service, this is the praised venture of a popular local chef. Dishes such as seafood carpaccio, homemade pastrami, tasty pastas and salads bursting with fresh prawns and avocado are complemented by daily blackboard specials that might feature pork fillet or T-bone steak. The interior combines modern elegance with the high old beamed ceiling to good effect.

El Aljibe de San Pedro
MEDITERRANEAN $$$

(Map p517; ☑669-982-65-18; www.facebook.com/elaljibedesanpedro; Constitución 710; mains M$150-290; ⊙5-9pm Tue-Sat) Descend into the subterranean gloom of this 200-year-old cistern, and spot eerie mannequins, collections of forceps and other medical paraphernalia, human skulls balancing on top of goblets, and more – in this macabre cavern of wonders, the decor is the biggest draw.

The menu is Mediterranean-ish, and portions of pasta, grilled shrimp, oxtail stew and tuna tartare are hearty.

El Presidio
MEXICAN $$$

(Map p517; ☑669-910-26-15; http://elpresidio.mx; Blvd Niños Héroes 1511; mains M$169-349; ⊙1pm-midnight Sun-Wed, to 2am Thu-Sat; 🖥; 🚍Sábalo-Centro) Dining in the greenery-festooned courtyard or the pared-down, industrial-chic dining room of this beautifully restored 19th-century estate building will take you back to an other era. Standout menu items include *zarandeado* (grilled) shrimp with Mexican noodles and smoked pork shank, which is slow-cooked in a pit for 14 hours. Presidio's well-stocked cantina pours fine mezcal, tequila and local craft beer.

Topolo
MEXICAN $$$

(Map p517; ☑669-136-06-60; www.topolomaz.com; Constitución 629; mains M$230-280; ⊙3-11pm Tue-Sun, closed Sun mid-Aug–Sep; 🖥; 🚍Sábalo-Centro) For a romantic, street-minstrel-free dinner, step into this softly lit enchanted garden of a courtyard in a historic central building. Though aimed at gringos, it has plenty of charm: waiters prepare fresh salsa at your table while chefs cook specialties such as tequila shrimp or fish in cilantro butter.

✖ Zona Dorada & Around

Rico's Cafe
CAFE $

(Map p512; ☑669-913-14-44; www.ricoscafe.com; cnr Av Camarón Sábalo & Gabriel Ruíz; mains M$70-115; ⊙7am-11pm) With three branches dotted around the city and a crowd-pleasing menu of crepes, waffles, omelettes, burritos and salads, Rico's is the Zona Dorada's top cafe pick – especially since it brews its Chiapas and Oaxacan coffee 'black as night' and 'strong as sin.'

Zona Dorada & Around

Pura Vida   VEGETARIAN **$**

(Map p521; ☎669-916-10-10; Bugambilias 18; mains M$90-110; ⊙8am-10:30pm; ❄️🔁📶🅿️; 🚌Sábalo-Centro) Pura Vida serves salads, sandwiches, Mexican snacks and vegetarian fare, but it's most sought out for its juices and smoothies. The menu is packed with creative concoctions blended from all the tropical fruit you love, as well as apples, dates, prunes, wheatgrass, spirulina and strawberries.

Mi Ranchito Los Osuna   MEXICAN **$**

(Map p512; ☎669-983-06-28; www.facebook.com/MiRanchitoLosOsuna; Av Rafael Buelna 113; mains M$69-139; ⊙8am-8pm; ❄️) Hidden among the many taco joints of Avenida Rafael Buelna, this cute little restaurant is all bright tablecloths, friendly service and hearty Sinaloan dishes. Come here for breakfast of eggs with marlin or cooked *nopales* (cactus paddles) with tomatoes and chilies, pile your *chilaquiles* high with *machaca* or

chow down on slow-cooked grilled meats. People named Osuna eat for free.

LAS LABRADAS

More than 600 petroglyphs, some believed to be more than 5000 years old, are depicted on volcanic rocks known as **Las Labradas** (📱 cell 696-1041144; www.facebook.com/laslabradas; via Hwy 15D Km 51, Ejido La Chicayota; M$60; ⏱ 9am-5pm Mon-Thu, to 6pm Fri-Sun) along a sublime stretch of coast about 60km north of Mazatlán. Many of the carvings were made between 750 CE and 1250 CE and are tied to summer solstice, as evidenced by the solar and geometric engravings. You'll also see intriguing human and animal figures, such as a manta ray–shaped rock. Pack a swimsuit and lunch to enjoy some quality beach time.

Las Labradas is best reached by car. From Mazatlán take Hwy 15 to Hwy 15D and exit just past Km 51, then head coastward about 5.5km along a dirt road. Alternatively, Onca (p514) runs tours to the site.

Carlos & Lucía's CUBAN $$
(Map p512; 📞 669-913-56-77; www.facebook.com/carlosandlucias; Av Camarón Sábalo 2000; mains M$90-240; ⏱ noon-11pm Mon-Sat; 🛜; 🚌 Sábalo-Centro) What do you get when you combine the talents of a Mexican named Carlos and a Cuban-born chef named Lucía? A vibrant, colorful little restaurant serving home-style specialties from both countries. Try the *plato Carlos y Lucía,* shrimp and fish cooked in brandy, accompanied by rice, veggies and plantains. It's opposite the Palms Resort.

Los Arcos SEAFOOD $$$
(Map p512; 📞 669-914-09-99; https://restaurantlosarcos.com; Av Camarón Sábalo 1019; mains M$186-374; ⏱ 11am-10pm; 🚌 Sábalo-Centro) This venerable sea-to-fork restaurant has been around since 1977 and its reputation as a temple to seafood remains solid as a rock. Dishes are executed with flair: Pacific shrimp are served stuffed with smoked marlin and wrapped in bacon, or *enchipotlado* (baked with *chipotle*), or with *mole* (chili sauce), while sweet Teacapán oysters and catch-of-the-day are treated with equal reverence.

Pancho's Restaurant MEXICAN $$$
(Map p521; 📞 669-914-09-11; www.facebook.com/panchosrestoran; Centro Comercial Las Cabañas, Av Playa Gaviotas 408; mains M$170-290; ⏱ 7am-11pm; 🛜; 🚌 Sábalo-Centro) With two levels right on Playa Las Gaviotas, this place has a spectacular outlook and the food measures up. There's a big range, whether you want tasty *aguachile* (a local ceviche) or a huge seafood platter. Or just drop by for a drink – the army of waiting staff will snappily provide a monster margarita or ice-cold beer.

Drinking & Nightlife

In Old Mazatlán, the night scene largely revolves around strolling the *malecón* or sitting on it with a beer, or people-watching from one of several bars along Paseo Olas Altas. Zona Dorada has more of a clubbing scene around the marina area, as well as live music and wet T-shirt competitions in bars favored by spring breakers.

🍷 Old Mazatlán & Around

⭐**Cervecería Tres Islas** MICROBREWERY
(Map p512; 📞 669-688-54-57; www.facebook.com/cervezatresislas; Av Alemán 923; ⏱ 1-10:30pm Mon-Sat; 🛜; 🚌 Sábalo-Centro) The oldest and best of Mazatlán's three microbreweries, this award-winning, friendly neighborhood bar room serves four core beers, including a hoppy IPA, refreshing blonde ale and a heavy, chocolatey stout, as well as five seasonal (limited-edition) brews. There's typically live music from Tuesday to Saturday.

⭐**Tótem Cafetería de Barrio** CAFE
(Map p517; 📞 669-982-42-54; www.facebook.com/totembarriomx; cnr Heriberto Frías & Ángel Flores; ⏱ 8am-10pm Mon-Sat, 9am-10pm Sun; 🛜) Tótem is hard to pin down. It's an airy cafe with a rooftop garden, an eclectic menu of breakfast dishes and light nibbles, and a particular passion for specialty coffee. Owner David, a Barcelona-trained barista, takes his beans seriously and sources them from Chiapas and Oaxaca. Not in the mood for coffee? There are also herbal teas, wines and beers.

Bar Belmar BAR
(Map p517; 📞 669-985-11-12; www.facebook.com/barbelmardemazatlan; Paseo Olas Altas 166B; ⏱ 1pm-midnight) This simple bar only really

serves one thing: Pacífico beer, which has been a fixture of city life ever since the Germans opened the local brewery in 1900. Have it plain, or have it served *michelada*-style, with pungent chili powder on the rim, with lime and Clamato juice, kick back and settle down for a spell of people-watching, come evening.

Zona Dorada & Around

Bier Garten
BEER GARDEN

(Map p512; ☑cell 669-9131678; Av Camarón Sábalo 1520; ⊙1pm-midnight Sun-Wed, to 2am Thu-Sat) This friendly backyard, strewn with picnic tables and cushions for lounging on, is a must for beer connoisseurs. Owner Brian sources over 100 – from the US, Mexico, various parts of Europe and further afield, with five types of authentic wurst (German sausage) sizzling on the grill as a worthy accompaniment. Burgers and ribs also receive high accolades.

Veintiocho
BAR

(Map p521; ☑cell 669-6685026; www.facebook. com/VeintiochoBar; Boca del Mar 28; ⊙8:30am-11pm Sun-Thu, to 1am Fri & Sat) Trading rainy Seattle for Mazatlán sunshine, Kim and Jim run a resto-bar hugely popular with visitors – good for knocking back a Pacífico beer while tapping your foot to the local live bands, for dancing to popular tunes or for an eggs Benedict brunch and a Bloody Mary.

Joe's Oyster Bar
BAR

(Map p521; ☑669-983-53-33; http://joesoyster bar.com; Av Playa Gaviotas 100; cover charge M$70 after 9pm Fri-Sun; ⊙11am-2:30am Mon-Wed, to 4am Fri-Sun; 🛜; ☐Sábalo-Centro) Part of the Ramada resort, this popular oceanside spot with a never-ending two-for-one happy hour is a beach bar by day and morphs into a DJ-fueled disco that goes ballistic after 11pm, when it's packed with college kids dancing on tables, chairs and each other.

🛍 Shopping

Zona Dorada is replete with tourist-oriented stores that sell clothes and mass-produced jewelry and crafts. For authentic, handmade, artier offerings, explore Old Mazatlán.

★ Nidart
ARTS & CRAFTS

(Map p517; ☑669-985-59-91; www.facebook. com/nidartgallery; Libertad 45; ⊙10am-2pm Mon-Sat; ☐Sábalo-Centro) This wonderful gallery specializes in handmade leather masks by artists Rak Garcia and Loa Molina, plus sculptures and ceramics from its in-house studio. Also look out for acrylic paintings, 3D art cubes and local photography.

Casa Etnika
ARTS & CRAFTS

(Map p517; ☑669-136-01-39; www.facebook. com/casaetnika; Sixto Osuna 50; ⊙10am-7pm Mon-Sat; 🛜; ☐Sábalo-Centro) 🌿 Family-run Casa Etnika offers a tasteful inventory of unique objects made by Mexican artisans, from Huichol beadwork and psychedelic weavings and tiny, brightly painted papier-mâché skeletons to copper-wire and wool jewelry, bold contemporary art, colorful weavings, and cushions and T-shirts with original designs. There's also fair-trade coffee to hand.

Gandarva Bazar
ARTS & CRAFTS

(Map p517; ☑669-136-06-65; www.facebook. com/gandarvabazar; Constitución 616; ⊙10am-8pm Mon-Sat) Cross this creeper-choked courtyard gallery and jump from stone to stone across the little moat to check out colorful Mexican masks and dolls made from gourds. Other offerings include antique African masks, handmade Mexican journals, and some interesting reproduction Chinesco (an early-1st-millennium culture in Nayarit) ceramics too.

ℹ Information

Go Mazatlán (www.gomazatlan.com) Sleek website with extensive hotel and restaurant listings as well as ideas for day trips out of town.

Hospital Sharp (☑669-986-56-78; www. hospitalsharp.com; Jesús Kumate s/n, cnr Av Rafael Buelna; ☐Sábalo-Centro) Competent and modern private hospital.

Mazatlán Life (https://mazatlanlife.com) Fun, chatty expat website that covers everything from essential food and drink to bus routes.

Secretaría de Turismo (Map p512; ☑669-915-66-00; http://turismo.sinaloa.gob.mx; Av del Mar 882; ⊙9am-5pm Mon-Fri; ☐Sábalo-Centro) Gives out a mediocre free map.

ℹ Getting There & Away

Most US flights to Mazatlán connect through Mexico City or Phoenix, though there are a couple that fly direct from Los Angeles and Dallas.

AIR

Aeropuerto Internacional Rafael Buelna (Mazatlan International Airport; ☑669-982-23-99; www.oma.aero/es/pasajeros/mazatlan; Carretera Internacional al Sur s/n) is 26km southeast of Mazatlán's Zona Dorada. There are direct flights and seasonal charters to US and Canadian destinations.

Domestic destinations are serviced by the following airlines:

→ Cabo San Lucas – Calafia

→ La Paz – Calafia

→ Mexico City – Aeroméxico, VivaAerobús, Volaris, Interjet

→ Monterrey – VivaAerobús

→ Tijuana – Volaris

BOAT

Baja Ferries (Map p512; ☑ 800-337-74-37; www.bajaferries.com; Av Barragán s/n, Playa Sur; seat adult/child one way M$1240/620, car M$3200; ☉ ticket office 8am-6pm Mon & Wed-Sun, to 3pm Tue; ☐ Playa Sur) operates ferries from the terminal at the southern end of town between Mazatlán and the port town of Pichilingue (23km from La Paz in Baja California Sur). Boats depart at 5pm and 6:30pm (be there an hour and a half before departure) on Wednesday, Friday and Sunday and take around 12 hours (from M$1240 per passenger). They make the return journey at 6pm and 8pm Tuesday, Thursday and Saturday. Winter winds may cause delays.

BUS

The full-service **Central de Autobuses** (Main Bus Station; Map p512; ☑ 800-800-03-86, 669-982-02-87; Espinoza Ferrusquilla s/n; ☐ Sábalo-Cocos) is just off Avenida Ejército Mexicano, four blocks inland from the northern end of Playa Norte. All bus lines operate from separate halls in the main terminal.

Local buses to small towns nearby (such as Concordia, Cosalá and El Rosario) operate from a smaller station, behind the main terminal.

CAR & MOTORCYCLE

Local all-inclusive rental rates begin at around M$750 per day during the high season.

→ **Alamo** has branches at **Airport** (☑ 669-981-22-66; www.alamo.com.mx; Aeropuerto Internacional Rafael Buelna, Carretera Internacional al Sur s/n; ☉ 6am-9pm) and **Zona Dorada** (☑ 669-913-10-10; Av Camarón Sábalo 410; ☉ 7am-8pm Mon-Sat, 8am-7pm Sun; ☐ Sábalo-Centro).

→ **Budget** can be found at **Airport** (☑ 669-982-63-63; www.budget.com.mx; Aeropuerto Internacional Rafael Buelna, Carretera Internacional al Sur s/n; ☉ 7am-10pm) and **Zona Dorada** (☑ 669-913-20-00; Av Camarón Sábalo 413; ☉ 7am-8pm Mon-Sat, to 7pm Sun; ☐ Sábalo-Centro).

→ **Europcar** branches are: **Airport** (☑ 669-954-81-15; www.europcar.com.mx/en; Aeropuerto Internacional Rafael Buelna, Carretera Internacional al Sur s/n; ☉ 7am-11pm) and **Zona Dorada** (☑ 669-913-33-68; Av Camarón Sábalo 357; ☉ 8am-8pm Mon-Sat, to 6pm Sun; ☐ Sábalo-Centro).

→ **Hertz** also has branches at **Airport** (☑ 669-985-37-31; https://hertzmexico.com; Aeropuerto Internacional Rafael Buelna, Carretera Internacional al Sur s/n; ☉ 8am-8pm) and **Zona Dorada** (☑ 669-913-49-55; Av Camarón Sábalo 314; ☉ 8am-7pm Mon-Fri, to 6pm Sat & Sun; ☐ Sábalo-Centro).

❶ Getting Around

TO/FROM THE AIRPORT

Taxis and *colectivos* (shuttle buses picking up and dropping off passengers along predetermined routes) operate from the airport (p523) to four different *zonas* in town. Tickets for both can be purchased at a booth just outside the arrivals hall (*colectivo* M$115 to M$180; taxi

BUSES FROM MAZATLÁN

DESTINATION	FARE (M$)	TIME	FREQUENCY (PER DAY)
Culiacán	160-200	2¾-3hr	frequent
Durango	650-720	4-5½hr	frequent
Guadalajara	614-769	8-8½hr	frequent
Los Mochis	200-730	6-7hr	frequent
Manzanillo	929	12hr	2
Mexicali	1350	22-25hr	frequent
Mexico City (Terminal Norte)	1120-1280	13-16hr	frequent
Monterrey	1530-1780	12-14hr	8
Puerto Vallarta	700	9hr	4
Tepic	290-430	4-5hr	frequent
Tijuana	1300-1500	24-27hr	frequent

M$430 to M$510). There is no public bus running between Mazatlán and the airport.

BICYCLE

Mazatlán is an easy town to navigate by bicycle, as the *malecón* leads from the town center all the way to the Zona Dorada, complete with designated cycle lane most of the way. There are numerous **VBike** (http://vbike.mx) pickup points along the *malecón* and other points around town; download the app to make use of them.

Baikas (🖉669-910-19-99; www.facebook.com/baikasmazatlan; Paseo Olas Altas 166; city bikes per hour/day M$70/300, hybrids M$100/400; ☺8am-9pm; 🚍Sábalo-Centro) is a professional setup with city bikes and pricier hybrids. There's another **branch** (🖉669-984-01-01; Av del Mar 1111; city bikes per hour/day M$70/300, hybrids M$100/400; ☺7am-9pm; 🚍Sábalo-Centro) near the Zona Dorada.

BUS

Local buses run from 6am to 10:30pm. Regular buses cost M$8.50; those with air-con are M$11.

From the Central de Autobuses (p524) bus terminal, go to Avenida Ejército Mexicano and catch any bus going south to downtown. Alternatively, walk 400m from the bus terminal to the beach and take a Sábalo–Centro bus heading south to downtown or north to the Zona Dorada.

Main routes:

Playa Sur (Map p517; 🚍Playa Sur) Buses go south along Avenida Ejército Mexicano, near the bus terminal and through downtown, passing the Mercado Centro, then to the ferry terminal and El Faro.

Sábalo–Centro Buses go from the Mercado Centro to Playa Norte via Juárez, then north on Avenida del Mar to the Zona Dorada and further north on Avenida Camarón Sábalo.

TAXI

Mazatlán is renowned for its special *pulmonía* taxis: modified, open-air VW Beetles, similar to a golf cart. Trips within the Zona Dorada or the *centro histórico* tend to cost around M$50, whereas trips between the two zones cost M$80 to M$100, depending on the time of day and your bargaining skills. There are also *aurigas* (pickup trucks with shaded seating in the back, costing around M$50 for a trip between zones), plus regular taxis. You can also hire a *pulmonía* for tours of the city (around M$220 to M$250 per hour).

Mexcaltitán

🖉323 / POP 1100

Reachable by boat passage through a mangrove maze, this shield-shaped island village is believed by some experts to be Aztlán, the ancestral homeland that the Aztecs

left around 1091 CE to begin their generations-long migration to Tenochtitlán (modern Mexico City). Proponents point to the striking similarities between the cruciform design of Mexcaltitán's streets and the urban layout of early Tenochtitlán. A pre-Hispanic bas-relief in stone found in the area is also provided as evidence – it depicts a heron clutching a snake, an allusion to the sign the Aztecs hoped to find in the promised land.

These days, Mexcaltitán is foremost a shrimping village. Men head out into the surrounding wetlands in the early evening in small boats, to return just before dawn with their nets bulging. The 'Venice of Nayarit' is a soporific, friendly place; some of the streets turn into canals during the rainy season.

⊙ Sights & Activities

Arrange boat trips on the lagoon for bird-watching, fishing and sightseeing – every family has one or more boats. Trips start at M$60, which gets you a circuit of the island; otherwise expect to pay M$300 per hour.

Museo del Origen   MUSEUM
(🖉cell 323-1209323; Plaza s/n; M$5; ☺10am-2pm & 4-7pm Tue-Sat, 10am-1pm Sun) This small museum on the plaza focuses on pre-Hispanic civilizations that once inhabited the region, such as the Aztátlan, and there's a modest collection of ceramics and petroglyphs to peruse. There's also a reproduction of a fascinating long scroll (the *Códice Boturini*), telling the story of the Aztecs' travels, with their initial departure from an island looking very much like Mexcaltitán.

✸ Festivals & Events

Semana Santa   RELIGIOUS
(☺Mar or Apr) Holy Week is celebrated in a big way here. On Good Friday a statue of Christ is put on a cross in the church, then taken down and carried through the streets.

Fiesta de San Pedro Apóstol   RELIGIOUS
(☺late Jun) During this raucous festival, which celebrates the patron saint of fishing, statues of SS Peter and Paul are taken out into the lagoon in decorated *lanchas* (motorboats).

🛏 Sleeping & Eating

Don't leave town without trying the local specialty *albóndigas de camarón* (shrimp meatballs), shrimp *empanadas* (turnovers) or perhaps a rich *jugo de camarón* (shrimp broth). The shrimp *tamales* sold in the morning from a wheelbarrow on the streets are another culinary highlight.

Hotel La Gran Tenochtitlán
HOTEL $

(☑323-235-62-03; Hidalgo s/n; s/d/tr/q M$490/ 590/690/790; ❋) The nicer of the village's two lodgings, with austere but clean en suites and powerful air-con. Worth staying overnight if you're looking to do a dawn boat trip through the mangroves.

★La Alberca
SEAFOOD $

(☑323-235-60-27; Porfirio Díaz s/n; mains M$70-120; ⊙9am-6pm Mon-Sat) On the island's east side, this breezy restaurant has a great lagoon view and is the most reliable of the village's dining options. It's all about shrimp: try shrimp *empanadas*, shrimp ceviche and shrimp *albóndigas* in a moreish shrimp broth. There are also a couple of token fish dishes for the shrimp-shy.

❶ Getting There & Away

Catch a bus from San Blas (M$78, one hour) or Tepic (M$85, one hour) to Santiago Ixcuintla, 7km west of Hwy 15 and 52km northwest of Tepic. Once in Santiago, take a *colectivo* (M$35, 45 minutes, four daily) or taxi (M$200) to La Batanga, a small wharf 32km away where *lanchas* depart for Mexcaltitán. The boat journey takes 15 minutes and costs M$150 for up to five people.

From Mazatlán, catch a Tepic-bound bus, jump off at the junction for Santiago Ixcuintla and wait for further transportation.

If driving, ask about road conditions, as the road through the wetlands to La Batanga is prone to flooding during heavy rains.

San Blas

☑323 / POP 11,340

The tranquil fishing village of San Blas is a peaceful, drowsy backwater, and therein lies its charm. Visitors come to enjoy isolated beaches, fine surfing, abundant birdlife and tropical jungles reached by riverboats.

Founded in 1534, San Blas was an important Spanish port from the late 16th century to the 19th century and the first Pacific port of any size. The Spanish built a fortress here to protect their trading galleons from marauding British and French pirates. It was also the port from which St Junípero Serra, the 'Father' of the California missions, embarked on his northward peregrination.

While on either side of the main drag San Blas is just another soporific cobblestoned backwater, the uniform whitewashed facades on Avenida Juárez itself lend a dreamy revival quality that is immediately endearing.

◉ Sights

★Playa Las Islitas
BEACH

The best beaches are southeast of town around Bahía de Matanchén, starting with Playa Las Islitas, 7km from San Blas. To get here, take the main road toward Tepic and turn right after about 4km. This paved road goes south to Matanchén, where a dirt road leads east to Playa Las Islitas and continues on to wonderfully swimmable beaches with gentle surf.

Playa El Borrego
BEACH

The beach closest to the town is Playa El Borrego, at the end of Azueta – look for the jet aircraft. It's a long sweep of gray sand with decent waves backed by a string of casual bar-restaurants. Swimming can be treacherous – beware of rip currents – but there are flags and a lifeguard, and it's a good beach for learning to surf.

Cocodrilario Kiekari
ZOO

(☑cell 311-1456231; www.facebook.com/kiekari. cocodrilario; Ejido La Palma s/n; M$40; ⊙9am-7pm; ℗) On the river, this crocodile nursery rears toothy reptiles that later get released into the wild as part of a repopulation program. There are also some non-release crocs, felines (jaguars and lynxes) and other captive creatures. It's accessible by road (10.5km from San Blas), but can also be reached as a side trip on La Tovara boat tours (around M$200 per person).

La Contaduría
FORTRESS

(Del Panteón s/n; M$10; ⊙9am-7pm; ℗) This hill is the site of San Blas' original colonial settlement. It's worth visiting for the wonderful views of the town from the top and to stroll around the ruins of the 18th-century Spanish fort, where colonial riches were once amassed and counted before being shipped off to Mexico City or the Philippines. On the way up are the ruins of a striking vaulted church, **Templo de la Virgen del Rosario**, built in 1769.

🏃 Activities

For bird-watching, sportfishing and swimming with whale sharks, see www.sanblas rivieranayarit.com/tours to contact local tour operators.

Beginner and intermediate surfers choose to hone their skills at San Blas for its many beach and point breaks. The season starts in May, but the waves are fairly mellow until September and October when the south swell brings long rides. Surf spots include **El Borrego, La Puntilla** (by a river mouth south of Playa El Borrego), **El Mosco** (west of San Blas on Isla del Rey) and **Stoner's** point break (further south, between San Blas and Las Islitas), which is known for having one of the longest waves in the world.

Stoner's Surf Camp   SURFING
(Playa Azul; ☑cell 323-2322225; www.facebook.com/Sanblassurfcamp; Ramada 7, Playa El Borrego; classes per person M$300, board rental per hour/day from M$80/160) At Playa El Borrego, this is the nexus of the surf scene. National longboard champion 'Pompis' Cano gives lessons and holds court under the *palapa*. You can also stay at the camp.

☞ Tours

★ La Tovara   BOATING
(☑cell 323-1169997; www.latovara.com; per person to La Tovara M$200, incl cocodrilario M$400; ⊙7am-4pm; ▢San Blas-Tepic) ✦ A boat trip to the freshwater swimming hole of La Tovara allows you to spot crocodiles and assorted birdlife. Boats depart from the *embarcadero* at the eastern edge of town or the main dock 4.5km further east on the Matanchén road. The three-hour trips go up the San Cristóbal *estero* (estuary) to the spring, passing thick jungle and mangroves.

La Tovara is a designated Ramsar site, and benefits from an international treaty to conserve wetlands. Go early in the morning to maximize wildlife sightings and bring bug repellent.

The swimming hole is enclosed, so you needn't fear becoming a croc's meal. However, you can extend the trip to include the Cocodrilario Kiekari crocodile nursery.

Boats usually wait to head out with groups of six to eight people, so you're best off catching one at the main dock, where there are more frequent departures. From the *zócalo*, take a San Blas–Tepic combi to the main dock.

Boat Trips

In addition to the popular La Tovara tours (p527), more boats depart from landings on Estero El Pozo, running trips to **Piedra Blanca** (M$550 for up to six people; one hour) to visit a statue of the Virgin; to **Isla del Rey** (M$35 per person; five minutes) just across from San Blas; and to **Playa del Rey**, a 20km beach on the other side of the Isla del Rey peninsula.

At a **dock** north of Avenida Juárez you can hire boatmen to take you bird-watching (M$350 per hour), whale-watching (December through March M$300 per person) and fishing (M$3200 per boat). You can also make arrangements there to visit **Isla Isabel**, where the boatmen accompany you on an interesting overnight trip. It's a national park and protected ecological preserve three hours northwest of San Blas by boat. The island is a bird-watcher's paradise, but there are no facilities, so be prepared for self-sufficient camping. You can fish for your dinner, but tour operators will also help negotiate good prices with local fishers. Overnight trips generally go for M$9500 for up to six people.

✦✦ Festivals & Events

Festival Internacional de Aves Migratorias   BIRD-WATCHING
(www.facebook.com/fiamsanblas; ⊙Jan & Feb) Bird-watchers flock to San Blas in late January and/or early February for the week-long International Migratory Bird Festival. Highlights include tours with English-speaking ornithologists and nightly entertainment in the plaza.

⨼ Sleeping

Bungalows Conny   INN $
(☑323-285-09-86; www.bungalowsconny.com; Chiapas 26; d from M$650, bungalows M$750-950; ▣❉❀⬙⬚) On a quiet side of town, this place rests easy with just four modern rooms and bungalows. The largest bungalow is fresh and feels like a small apartment with a large kitchen. The sunny pool area provides plenty of relaxation. Owners Tom and Trini can offer great travel tips.

Stoner's Surf Camp   CABIN $
(Playa Azul; ☑cell 323-2322225; www.facebook.com/Sanblassurfcamp; Ramada 7, Playa El Borrego; cabins without bathroom d/q M$270/550; ▣) The thatched-roof *cabañas* (cabins) on stilts at this laid-back surfer joint are seriously basic but have electricity, mosquito nets (you'll need them), fans and beds so distressed they're practically inconsolable, but the sunsets from up there are priceless. You might be able to camp or sling a hammock. *Cabaña* guests get discounts at the surf center; longboards for rent here.

San Blas

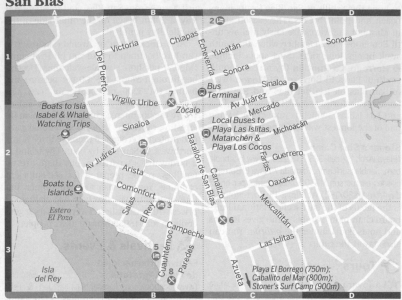

Casa Roxanna Bungalows APARTMENT **$$**
(☑ 323-285-05-73; www.casaroxanna.com; El Rey
1; d M$900-1000; P🐕❄🌐📶🏊) This peaceful
haven offers eight large apartments and two
smaller doubles; angle for one of the larg-
er upstairs units (sleeping up to five) with
full kitchen and a screened porch overlook-
ing the pool and manicured palm-treed
grounds. Owners Kurt and Luis are treasure
troves of local knowledge. Discounts offered
on monthly stays.

Hotel Marina San Blas HOTEL **$$**
(☑ 323-285-08-12; https://sanblas.com.mx/hotel
marinasanblas; Cuauhtémoc 197; d/ste M$1470/
2200; P🐕❄📶🏊) Near the estuary mouth,
within view of the harbor, is this meticu-
lously maintained three-star resort. The
grounds are lovely and guests get a free one-
hour kayak rental. Kitschy marine-themed
rooms have lighthouse lamps and a strange
amalgamation of cinder block and tile, but
they're comfy, with river views and cable TV.
There's a pool and small estuary swimming
beach.

**Hotel Hacienda
Flamingos** HISTORIC HOTEL **$$$**
(☑ 323-285-09-30; https://sanblas.com.mx/hotel
haciendaflamingos; Av Juárez 105; d from M$1740,
ste M$2450; P🐕❄@📶🏊) This 1880s haci-
enda is San Blas' most atmospheric hotel.
Elegant, spacious, high-ceilinged rooms
are arranged around a beautiful courtyard
full of greenery and a tinkling fountain, the
onsite restaurant is all soaring stone arches,
and there are evocative photos of old San
Blas in the lounge. Look out for cabinets full
of pre-Hispanic ceramics and other histori-
cal curios.

🍴 Eating

San Blas is a town of casual restaurants of-
fering Mexican standards, plus beachfront
palapas, all serving fresh, inexpensive sea-
food. Cheaper sustenance, including *tortas*
(sandwiches), *jugos* (juices) and *licuados*
(milkshakes), can be found at the local **mer-
cado** (cnr Sinaloa & Batallón de San Blas; mains
M$50-90; ⊙7am-1pm).

Restaurant McDonald MEXICAN **$**
(☑ 323-285-04-32; Av Juárez 75; mains M$45-
140; ⊙7am-10pm) Cheery tiled tables and
an equally cheery proprietor greet you at
San Blas' most popular breakfast venue.
Don't expect Big Macs, but do expect gen-
erous servings of *huevos rancheros* (fried
eggs on a corn tortilla served with refried
beans), *chilaquiles*, fruit plates and more.
The clientele is a mix of locals and gringos,
and the coffee is good and strong.

San Blas

◎ Sights
1 La Contaduría E2

🛏 Sleeping
2 Bungalows Conny C1
3 Casa Roxanna Bungalows B3
4 Hotel Hacienda Flamingos.................. B2
5 Hotel Marina San Blas B3

✦ Eating
6 Juan Bananas C3
7 Mercado B1
8 Restaurant El Delfín B3

Juan Bananas   BAKERY $

(La Tumba de Yako; ☑ 323-285-05-52; www.face book.com/panaderiajuanbananas; Batallón de San Blas 219; loaves M$65-70, snacks M$15-60; ⊙8am-7pm) For four decades this little bakery has been cranking out some of the world's best banana bread; with any luck, you'll get a loaf hot from the oven. Juan himself is a terrific source of local information.

Restaurant El Delfín   FUSION $$

(☑323-285-01-12; www.garzacanela.com/en/rest aurante-bar-el-delfin; Paredes 106 Sur; breakfast M$60-140, lunch & dinner M$180-210; ⊙8-10am & 1-8:30pm; 🅿🛜) Under the direction of internationally renowned Cordon Bleu chef Betty Vázquez, this restaurant at the Hotel Garza Canela serves French-accented dishes that make creative use of (mostly) local ingredients. Expect the likes of prune-stuffed chicken and fish baked with pistachio, and cap it off with homemade desserts and ice cream. Special diets are imaginatively accommodated.

Mysis III   SEAFOOD $$

(☑cell 323-1086405; Playa Las Islitas; mains M$80-180; ⊙9am-7pm; 🚌San Blas-Tepic) Some 2km south of the San Blas–Tepic Hwy, this *palapa* seafood restaurant is the pick of the Playa Las Islitas beach shacks. It whips up excellent shrimp dishes, including shrimp

ceviche *tostadas* and a flavorful *caldo de pescado* (fish soup). The beach scenery makes the experience all the more memorable, and the sands south of Mysis are well worth exploring.

San Blas–Tepic combis will leave you at the Playa Las Islitas entrance, from where it's a 2km stroll.

Restaurant La Isla   SEAFOOD $$

(☑cell 311-1844779; Paredes 33; mains M$140-160; ⊙2-9pm Tue-Sun; 🛜) Chef Tony really likes seashells. And fishing nets. A longtime local fave, this charismatic, kitschy, fan-cooled seafood joint has been around for more than three decades. You might try the *camarones a la diabla* (shrimp in spicy sauce) or the *platillo de mariscos* (fish, shrimp and octopus platter). Cash only.

Caballito del Mar   SEAFOOD $$

(☑323-216-92-04; Playa El Borrego; mains M$150-180; ⊙11am-7pm Thu-Tue; 🅿) A local favorite among the best of the seafood *enramadas* (thatch-covered, open-air restaurants) lined up along Playa El Borrego. Popular menu items include the *cóctel de camarón* (shrimp cocktail) and *pescado zarandeado* (grilled whole fish priced by the kilo).

🍷 Drinking & Nightlife

San Blas Social Club   BAR

(☑323-106-73-40; Batallón de San Blas 46; ⊙9am-midnight Nov-Apr) Right on the plaza, this is the beating heart of the San Blas expat community – a place to catch up on local gossip, sip an iced margarita or a bucket-sized *michelada* (beer and tomato juice), and people-watch from the outdoor tables. It does American comfort food as well, including very good burgers.

ℹ Information

Take insect repellent to San Blas: voracious mosquitoes and sandflies are often present in large squadrons.

Banamex ATM (Av Juárez s/n) One of a handful of ATMs in town.

Centro de Salud (☎323-285-12-07; cnr Azueta & Campeche; ☺24hr) This central medical center is on the road that heads down to the beach.

Tourist Office (☎cell 323-2824913; Av Juárez s/n; ☺2-8pm Mon-Fri) On the main road at the archway that marks your arrival at the center. Has maps and brochures about the area and the state of Nayarit, but keeps iffy office hours.

ℹ Getting There & Away

The little **bus terminal** (☎323-285-00-43; Sinaloa s/n; ☺6am-8pm) is served by Nayar and Estrella Blanca buses. From/to some destinations, including Mazatlán, you'll need to change in Tepic or at the junction (Crucero de San Blas; M$45) on Hwy 15.

Daily departures include Puerto Vallarta (M$273, 3½ hours, four daily), Santiago Ixcuintla (M$80, one hour, four daily) and Tepic (M$75, one hour, frequent 6am to 8pm).

Buses (cnr Canalizo & Mercado; M$15-20) depart several times a day, serving all the villages and beaches on Bahía de Matanchén.

Taxis and Tepic-bound combis congregate around the plaza's south side and will take you to nearby beaches or drop you off at the main dock for boat rides to La Tovara.

Tepic

☎311 / POP 534,000 / ELEV 920M

Founded by Nuño Beltrán de Guzmán around 1530 (the exact year is disputed), Tepic is the capital of Nayarit state, a busy town with a veritable provincial bustle playing out on its narrow streets. Indigenous Huicholes are often seen here, wearing their colorfully embroidered traditional clothing.

Across from **Plaza Principal**, the ornate **cathedral**, dedicated in 1804, casts a regal eye over the square. Opposite is the **Palacio Municipal** (city hall), where you'll often find Huicholes selling handicrafts at reasonable prices. Calle Amado Nervo, north of the city hall, and nearby streets are lined with stalls where you can try local specialties such as *tejuino* (a fermented corn drink) and *guamuchil* (a small white fruit).

◉ Sights

★**Museo Regional de Nayarit**　MUSEUM
(☎311-212-19-00; www.inah.gob.mx/es/red-de-museos/257-museo-regional-de-nayarit; Av México Norte 91; M$55; ☺9am-6pm Mon-Fri, to 3pm Sat) Inside an impressive magenta *palacio* (palace), the regional museum features Huichol and other pre-Hispanic ceramics mostly sourced from burials from around 200 BCE to 600 CE, as well as those from the Aztátlan culture (800 CE to 1350 CE). There are figures depicting pregnant women, houses, warriors, ball-players and musicians, anthropomorphic burial urns from the local Mololoa culture (late 1st millennium CE) with startled faces, and the complete contents of a recreated shaft tomb. There are also centuries-old shell adornments and information in English.

Museo de los Cinco Pueblos　MUSEUM
(Museum of the Five Peoples; ☎311-212-17-05; Av México Norte 105; ☺10am-2pm & 4-7pm Tue-Sat, 10am-2pm Sun) ✔**FREE** This museum displays contemporary popular art of Nayarit's Huichol, Cora, Tepehuano, Mexicanero and mestizo peoples, including clothing, yarn art, weaving, musical instruments, ceramics and beadwork. A shop next door practicing fair trade sells a variety of items made by indigenous artisans.

🛏 Sleeping & Eating

★**Hotel Real de Don Juan**　HISTORIC HOTEL **$$**
(☎311-216-18-88; www.facebook.com/hotelrealdedonjuan; Av México Sur 105; r/ste M$1450/1880; P❄✱@🛜🏊) This beautifully done-up hacienda overlooking Plaza Constituyentes strikes the right balance between colonial character and urban style. Upstairs rooms are decked out in appealing pastel colors, with luxurious king beds and marble-accented bathrooms. A good restaurant with alcove tables over the street, plus a classy bar and rooftop lounge and lap pool add points.

Two imposing angel-warrior statues keep watch over the tranquil lobby.

Downsides? Wi-fi comes and goes like a stray cat, and the nearby church bells are more bane than boon if you're a night owl.

★**Emiliano**　MEXICAN **$$**
(☎311-216-20-10; www.emilianorestaurant.com; Zapata Oriente 91; breakfast M$98-135, lunch & dinner M$158-305; ☺8am-midnight Mon-Sat; 🛜) Tepic's best restaurant, Emiliano serves mostly regional fare in a stylish courtyard

setting. Breakfast is very popular: fresh juices, coffee and the likes of *chilaquiles*, egg dishes and quesadillas are presented with aplomb. There are also Nayarit's regional dishes, such as slow-cooked ribs. In the evenings, let the sommelier pick the best wines to pair with chef Marco's creative dishes.

El Farallón del Pacífico   SEAFOOD **$$**
(📞311-213-11-24; www.facebook.com/elfarallondelpacificotepic; Av Insurgentes 282; mains M$140-230; ⊙11:30am-7pm; 🅿🤶) The standout dish here is the *pescado zarandeado*, but the menu features an ample offering of favorites from the sea, including *tostadas* piled high with ceviche and fresh shrimp, and shrimp baked in a pineapple half.

🛍 Shopping

Tepic is a good place to look for Huichol beadwork art, buying either directly from artisans on the main plaza or from stores, though quality varies.

Artesanías Bertha Chia   ARTS & CRAFTS
(📞311-212-12-68; www.facebook.com/ArtesaniasChia; Av Francisco Madero Pte 179; ⊙8am-8pm Mon-Sat) North of the city center, this store is well worth seeking out for its excellent selection of Huichol beadwork art, from small souvenirs to larger items: jaguars, coyotes, iguanas and skulls in full technicolor.

ℹ Information

A kiosk on the Plaza Principal (erratic hours) gives out information on Nayarit state, as does a desk at the bus terminal.

ℹ Getting There & Away

The main **bus station** (Tepic Bus Terminal; 📞311-213-23-30; Av Insurgentes 492) is on the southeastern outskirts of town; local buses (M$10) marked 'Estación' make frequent trips between the bus station and downtown. A taxi from the terminal to the center will cost M$60.

Colectivos (Durango Norte 284; M$75; ⊙5am-9pm) to San Blas depart frequently from a small terminal on Durango Norte, between Zaragoza and Amado Nervo. For Laguna Santa María del Oro, catch a **colectivo** (Av México s/n, btwn Zaragoza Poniente & Bravo Poniente; M$35; ⊙6am-9pm) from Avenida México.

ℹ Getting Around

Local buses (M$10) operate from around 6am to 9pm. Combis (M$11) operate along Avenida México from 6am to midnight. There are also plenty of street taxis and a taxi stand opposite the cathedral.

Chacala

📞327 / POP UNDER 300

Despite its ramshackle charm and the beauty of its surrounds, the tiny coastal fishing village of Chacala has managed to retain its authenticity and not be overrun by visitors. Located 96km north of Puerto Vallarta and 10km west of Las Varas on Hwy 200, it sits pretty along a beautiful little cove backed by verdant green slopes and edged by rugged black-rock formations at either end. With just one main, sandy thoroughfare and a few cobbled side streets, it's an ideal place to contemplate the horizon or to go in search of ancient cultures at a nearby petroglyph site.

👁 Sights & Activities

The sea provides most of the action here. Swimming in Chacala's long sweep of a sandy bay is safe and tranquil most of the year. You can also hike to La Caleta; it's a challenging but rewarding 3.5km walk through the jungle.

For small-boat excursions, ask at the **Chacala Fishing Cooperative** (📞cell 327-1020683; whale-watching per person M$450, fishing & surfing per boat M$850; ⊙7:30am-5:30pm), located at a dock at the northern tip of the shoreline. They run whale-watching and fishing trips as well as surfing expeditions

BUSES FROM TEPIC

DESTINATION	FARE (M$)	TIME	FREQUENCY (PER DAY)
Guadalajara	300-345	3½-4½hr	frequent
Mazatlán	312-364	4hr	7
Mexico City (Terminal Norte)	1190-1225	10-11hr	3
Puerto Vallarta	216-240	3-4¼hr	frequent
Santiago Ixcuintla	85	1¾hr	frequent

OFF THE BEATEN TRACK

LAGUNA SANTA MARÍA DEL ORO

Surrounded by forested mountains, this idyllic lake fills a volcanic crater that's over 100m deep and 2km in diameter. The clean water takes on colors ranging from turquoise to slate. It's a pleasure to walk around the lake and in the surrounding mountains, spotting birds (some 250 species) and butterflies along the way. You can also climb to an abandoned gold mine, cycle, swim, kayak or fish for black bass and perch. A number of restaurants serve fresh lake fish.

If driving, take the Santa María del Oro turnoff about 40km from Tepic along the Guadalajara road. From the turnoff it's about 9km to Santa María del Oro village, then another 8km to the lake. By bus, catch a 'Santa María del Oro' colectivo (M$35, 45 minutes) on Avenida México in Tepic, then change to a colectivo marked 'Laguna' at Santa María's town square or take a private taxi.

to La Caleta – a prime spot where a wicked left-breaking point break thrashes the rocky beach. **Xplore Chacala** (☏ cell 327-1053504; www.xplorechacala.wixsite.com/mysite; Av Chacalilla s/n; bird-watching tour per hour M$120, petroglyphs tour per person M$400, surfboard rental per hour M$120; ☺ 9am-8pm Nov-Apr, to 5pm Sat & Sun May-Oct) rents out surfboards and paddleboards.

Altavista Petroglyphs   ARCHAEOLOGICAL SITE
(Hwy 200–Altavista; M$20; ☺ 7am-4pm) At this verdant site, reachable via a picturesque, jungly walk, there are numerous well-preserved petroglyphs, some geometrical, some depicting human figures. The trail ends in a glade with cascading water and rock pools for a dip. It's a drive along a rough road off Hwy 200–Altavista, then a 1.5km walk up to this site; get good directions first, as it's not signposted.

The place is tricky to find, but you can always hook up a tour with Xplore Chacala.

★ Festivals

Chacala Music & Arts Festival   CULTURAL
(☏ 327-219-50-06; www.chacalamusicfestival.com; ☺ Mar) A four-day festival celebrating music, dance, local art and regional cuisine with events held in beachfront restaurants and open-air spaces.

🛏 Sleeping

Accommodations here range from simple guesthouses and cookie-cutter midrange hotels to luxurious boutique retreats. Although there are more than 50 choices, some need to be prebooked and cater for multiday stays only.

Techos de México   HOMESTAY, GUESTHOUSE $
(www.techosdemexico.com; r M$400-800; ☺)
🖉 Travelers interested in meeting locals

should consider this organization that helps Chacala residents build good homes with adjacent guest units. Seven local families offer comfortable budget lodging through this program, ranging from private rooms to self-contained bungalows; check the website or look for the distinctive Techos signs as you pass through town.

Casa de Tortugas   RENTAL HOUSE $$
(☏ cell 322-1464787; www.casadetortugas.com; Oceano Pacifico 4; d US$89-95, ste US$260; ☺ ❋ 🛜 ≋) This bright pink house overlooking the north end of the beach enjoys privileged views over the bay and offers three individually styled rooms, a large family suite, a roof terrace and an infinity pool. You can prepare your meals at a *palapa* outdoor kitchen and appreciate the ocean vistas over breakfast at the bar. Must be prebooked: there's no reception.

Hotel Casa Chacala   HOTEL $$
(☏ 327-219-40-57; www.hotelcasachacala.com; Golfo de Mexico 1; d/apt incl breakfast M$1000/2800; P ❋ 🛜 ≋) This friendly cheapie on the main street probably won't make your social media posts, but for all the right reasons: simple tiled rooms look out over the sea, there's a nice little plunge pool, hammocks to swing in, plus breakfast thrown in. Wi-fi is patchy.

Hotel Mar de Coral   HOTEL $$
(☏ 327-219-41-09; www.facebook.com/mardecoral chacala; Av Chacalilla s/n; d M$1100, bungalows from M$2000; ☺ ❋ 🛜 ≋) Set in the center of town across the road from the beach, this incongruous modern building offers spacious tiled rooms with wooden beds and furnishings. What it calls bungalows are much larger rooms with an attached kitchen. There's a pool in a shady courtyard lobby.

Around the corner, on Canarias, sister property Mar de Coral Elite provides slightly more upscale accommodations with a sunny pool area.

Mar de Jade RESORT $$$
(☎327-219-40-00, US 800-257-0532; www.mardejade.com; Mar de Jade 1; full board s/d from US$230/300; P⊜❋🐾🏊) Sitting amid lush vegetation, this yoga retreat at the south end of the beach curls around two sinuous pools and a Jacuzzi and offers wellness packages but welcomes independent travelers too. Crashing waves are audible everywhere, from the rooms with tiled bathtubs, and sauna and spa area, to the alfresco bar and patio where vegetarian-friendly buffet meals are served.

✖ Eating & Drinking

Mauna Kea BREAKFAST $
(☎327-219-40-67; www.casapacificachacala.com; Los Corchos 15; mains M$80-115; ⊗8-11am Mon-Sat Nov-Apr; 🐾) Watch whales over organic morning coffee, pecan pancakes, waffles, eggs cooked myriad ways and other dishes to warm the soul at this seasonal rooftop eatery on the bluffs just north of town (or get your breakfast free by staying at the attached B&B).

Chico's Restaurant SEAFOOD $$
(☎327-219-40-19; www.facebook.com/Restaurant BarChicos; Av Chacalilla s/n; mains M$70-220; ⊗8am-8:30pm) Perch in one of the plastic chairs at this pick of seaside seafood joints, dig your feet into the sand, and tuck into octopus or catch-of-the-day ceviche, grilled lobster, or *pescado zarandeado* (whole fish smoky and tender after being grilled over mangrove wood), and down an ice-cold Corona to go with it.

Majahua INTERNATIONAL $$
(☎327-219-40-53; www.majahua.com; Sur de la Bahia de Chacala s/n; mains M$110-240; ⊗breakfast 9-11am, lunch noon-4pm, dinner 5-8pm; 🐾) ✎ Perched on a jungle-covered hillside overlooking the cove, this ecolodge's terrace restaurant makes a glorious spot to greet the morning with a full breakfast, or to indulge in a sunset dinner over cocktails, fresh seafood and pasta. Reserve ahead for dinner and let the chef know what you'd like; they're adherents to the 'slow food' movement.

Onda Brewing CRAFT BEER
(☎322-116-86-17; www.facebook.com/OndaBrewing; Golfo de Mexico 10; ⊗6-10pm Fri & Sat Nov-Apr) Open only on weekend nights during season, this friendly microbrewery doubles as the village nightlife hotspot. There are five brews to choose from; particularly tasty are the crisp, hoppy Ahorita IPA and the creamy Tormenta stout. There are some clever nibbles to go with the beer, plus congenial owners to talk to.

❶ Getting There & Away

For Chacala, get off a Puerto Vallarta–Tepic bus at Las Varas and take a *colectivo* (M$18) for 11km from there: these leave every half-hour or so from directly across the road from the bus stop (look for the chairs on a corner outside a locksmith). A taxi into Chacala runs about M$140. If you're driving, the Hwy 200 turnoff is 1km south of Las Varas.

San Francisco
☎311 / POP 2940
San Francisco, aka San Pancho, is another fishing pueblo turned vacation spot, with prettier, less peopled stretches of sand and a less obvious gringo footprint than you'll find in popular Sayulita, a couple of beaches south. A reliable point break is a big draw for surfers, plus you can ride horses through the riverbed and on long, wild and driftwood-strewn white-sand beach.

Av Tercer Mundo leads from Hwy 200 a couple of kilometers through town to the beach, where sidewalk restaurants serve fish and ceviche dishes and cold beers, while taco stands take over the side streets in the evenings.

◉ Sights & Activities

Surfing is a big deal here, with a fast and powerful left- and right-hander that attracts intermediate and pro surfers. There are outlets near the beach that rent surfing gear, as does Surf House San Pancho (p534), whose owners can arrange transportation to other surf spots along the coast, as well as lessons.

Lo de Perla Jardín de Selva GARDENS
(☎322-181-19-09; https://lodeperla.org; Av Las Orquideas; adult/child M$500/250; ⊗9am-4pm) Accessible only via guided tour, this botanic garden is home to a staggering 300 types of butterflies, abundant birdlife and equally abundant insect life (bring repellent). A trail wanders amid the ferns, cacti and bromeliads, and one of the highlights for flower lovers is the orchid garden. Book ahead; the meeting point is Las Lomas,

halfway between San Francisco and Lo de Marcos, some 4km north of the former.

Tours

Lo De Marcos Horseback Rides
HORSEBACK RIDING

(☎322-728-05-44; www.facebook.com/LodeMarcos HorsebackRidesandAdventureTours; Camino a las Minitas s/n; rides from US$50 per person; ◎8am-6pm) Lenny and his team arrange rides on their placid, well-groomed steeds, both along the beach and in the hills. Riders of all abilities are catered for.

🛏 Sleeping

Refugio de Sol & Hostal San Pancho
HOSTEL, GUESTHOUSE $

(☎311-258-41-61; www.hostalsanpancho.com; Av Tercer Mundo 12; dm M$350-400, d incl breakfast M$1200-1600; ❀❋📶) Kitted out with travelers' needs in mind, this guesthouse-hostel is set around its surf shop near the highway. It offers simple yet charming rooms and snazzier 'suites' (bigger rooms with an attractive design, better bathrooms and terrace). Ground-floor dorms and their outdoor bathroom are basic but comfy.

There's free bike and skateboard use – handy to zip down to the beach, 1km away. Also offered are surfboard rental and classes, as well as various tours.

Surf House San Pancho
GUESTHOUSE $$$

(☎322-216-66-16; www.surfhousesanpancho.com; Tahiti 107; s/d US$125/140; ❋📶🏊) Surfers seeking some creature comforts during the time spent out of the sea: look no further. This hilltop duplex guesthouse has it all: pool with a view, two bright and airy rooms, a barbecue patio and two welcoming owners, Luis and Bianca, who are more than happy to arrange surfing lessons and transfers to the best surfing spots.

Bungalows Lydia
BUNGALOW $$$

(☎311-258-43-37; www.bungalowslydia.com; Clavelinas 393; bungalows US$104-235; P❀📶🏊) Overlooking two hidden beaches and surrounded by 2000 palm trees planted by the owners themselves, this restful cliffside haven appeals to those seeking solitude and communion with nature. Of the eight fan-cooled suites on offer, the Sunset and Panaroma provide the best ocean views (as does an infinity pool at the cliff's edge). It's 3km east of town along a dirt road.

It's best to have your own wheels to get out here. There's no onsite restaurant, but

the suites have full kitchens. A saltwater pool awaits on the beach below.

Hotel Cielo Rojo
BOUTIQUE HOTEL $$$

(☎311-258-41-55; www.hotelcielorojo.com; Asia 6; d/tr/f incl breakfast from US$114/156/208; ❀❋📶) The most characterful hotel in San Pancho is located a few blocks from the beach. Each of the four rooms (one a family-sized split-level suite) is individually designed, light and bright, with terra-cotta floors, objets d'art and attractive fabrics. Bicycles and beach paraphernalia are available for guests. Dinner (seasonal) in its restaurant, Bistro Orgánico, is the best in town.

🍴 Eating

Taquería Los Arbolitos
TACOS $

(☎311-258-41-39; www.facebook.com/taquerialos arbolitos; America Latina 7; tacos/quesadillas M$12/25; ◎7pm-midnight Fri-Wed) Come evening, the air fills with fragrant smoke from the grill, plastic tables are set out in the street and quickly fill up with loyal customers. Tacos come piled high with adobo, *chorizo* sausage, cheese and *nopal*, with hits of homemade salsas giving them some welcome fire.

Maria's
MEXICAN $

(☎311-258-44-39; Av Tercer Mundo 28A; breakfast & lunch M$60-115, dinner M$120-260; ◎8:30am-3:30pm & 6-10:30pm Thu-Mon, 8:30am-3:30pm Tue; 📶🌱) San Pancho's premier breakfast spot slings reliable Mexican faves such as *huevos divorciados* (fried eggs in red and green salsa) and it does North American dishes as well. The lunch and dinner menu offers plenty of vegetarian options and light fare including salads and fish tacos.

★ Bistro Orgánico
FUSION $$

(☎311-258-41-55; www.hotelcielorojo.com/bistro-organico; Asia 6; mains M$90-260; ◎8am-2pm Mon & Wed-Sat, 6-10pm Fri & Sat Nov-Apr; 📶🌱) 🌱 Tucked into a pretty plant-filled courtyard, Bistro Orgánico is San Francisco's most sophisticated dining choice. Chef Calixto adheres to the farm-to-table concept and cooks up imaginative fish and vegetarian dishes, using mostly local, organic produce (try the marlin tacos with quinoa). Breakfast stretches into the afternoon, and seasonal dinner service is best finished off with chocolate tequila truffles.

ⓘ Getting There & Away

San Francisco is 7km north of Sayulita and about 49km north of Puerto Vallarta, just west of Hwy

200. Buses (p552) (M$50, one hour) depart frequently from Nuevo Vallarta and drop you at the crossroads, about 1km from the beach. From Sayulita catch a bus (M$22, 15 minutes) from the **Compostela** (Av Revolución s/n; ⊗ 6am-10pm) station. Coming from the north, Puerto Vallarta–bound buses will drop you at the town entrance.

Sayulita

329 / POP 3210

Once upon a time – well, in the late 1990s – Sayulita really was a tranquil fishing village. Many of the town's *norteamericano* residents still describe it that way, but the truth is that in peak season the place is overrun by golf carts and cars and full of gringos drawn here by the beautiful (if not that clean) sandy beach, surfable waves for riders of mixed ability, good restaurants and tasteful B&Bs. It's a thriving hipster-surfer scene; visit out of season if you're looking for a relaxing time.

One popular destination near central Sayulita is **Playa Los Muertos**, where picnics and bodyboarding top the action. It's a 15-minute walk south along the coast road, through the Villa Amor resort and the cemetery.

✦ Activities

Surfing

Sayulita is a classic 'boarder' town. Medium-sized waves pour dependably from both the left and the right – practice your well-honed moves or take up the sport for the first time. Several surf shops offer rentals and lessons.

Oceano Adventures   SURFING, DIVING
(☑ 329-298-85-32; www.oceanoadventures.com; Av Revolución 34B; surf lesson US$45, 2-tank dive from US$147; ⊗ 9am-5pm Mon-Sat) Friendly, recommended setup that offers really good and enthusiastic surf classes at a better price than many. A 2½-hour private lesson allows for an hour's board rental free to practice afterward. It is also a PADI-certified dive operator that takes divers out to the nine dive sites offshore, and runs snorkeling excursions out to Islas Marietas (US$84).

Stand Up Sayulita   WATER SPORTS
(☑ 329-291-35-75; Marlín 59; board rental per hour/half-/full day US$12/35/50, lesson US$55; ⊗ 9am-8pm) This is the place to learn how to captain a stand-up paddleboard (SUP) and ride waves too. Lessons last 90 minutes and include a free 60-minute paddle afterward.

SURF'S UP!

This stretch of the Pacific coast is renowned among surfers. There are at least a dozen spots around Sayulita and San Francisco, though you'll need a boat transfer to reach some of them, organized via the surfing outfits in Sayulita or Surf House San Pancho (p534) in San Francisco. Here are some of the best:

Sayulita Right- and left-hander point break on the main beach, ideal for beginners and stand-up paddleboard (SUP) riders. When the swell is high, good fun for intermediate and advanced surfers.

San Pancho Powerful, fast left-hander point break off the main beach in San Francisco (p533). Higher waves in summer, intermediates and pros only.

La Lancha South of Punta de Mita (p538), this right- and left-hander point break is long and perfect for beginners. It's a 10-minute walk through jungle to reach it.

Anclote Longest right-hander point break in the area, just south of Punta de Mita. Slow and predictable, lots of beginner surfers and SUP riders.

Stinky's Near Anclote, another right-hander point break favored by beginners. Needs big swells, so summertime only.

El Faro Fast and powerful right-hander point break by the Punta de Mita lighthouse, intermediate and pro surfers only. Boat transfer.

Caleta You need a boat to reach this powerful left-hander with a fast drop and a long ride. Intermediates and pros only.

Burros Southeast along the coast from Punta de Mita, this is a long and mellow right- and left-hander point break. A bit rough for beginners.

ℹ SAYULITA'S CHANGING TIME ZONE

Sayulita and Riviera Nayarit towns as far north as Lo de Marcos are on Central Time, unlike most of Nayarit state, which is on Mountain Time. The area made the switch in 2010 in order to synchronize its clocks with neighboring Puerto Vallarta and Jalisco. Why the shift? It turns out there was an epidemic of gringos arriving at Vallarta's airport an hour late and missing their homeward-bound flights, either ignorant of the time-zone difference or too blissed out by beach life to care.

Lunazul   SURFING

(☏ 329-291-20-09; www.lunazulsurfing.com; Marlín 4; SUP/surfboard/bodyboard rent per day M$500/300/250, lesson US$60; ⊙ 9am-6pm) This well-established surf shop offer rentals and private lessons.

🛏 Sleeping

Sayulita has a vast selection of accommodations for all budgets, from excellent hostels and ho-hum midrange places to exclusive boutique hotels. A good selection of private villas can be browsed on the website **Sayulita Life** (www.sayulitalife.com). Low-season prices can drop sharply.

Hostal Tortuga   HOSTEL $

(☏ 329-298-88-91; www.facebook.com/tortuga hostal; Tortuga 10; dm/d/q US$16/54/98; ✳🛜🏊) This newcomer off the main beat is run by travelers who know what other budget travelers want. The result? Comfortable beds (and all rooms and dorms are en suite), spacious common areas, picnic tables, games room, hammocks strung by the pool – all are boons that encourage socializing. Everything is efficiently run by a friendly team eager to help their guests.

Amazing Hostel Sayulita   HOSTEL $

(☏ 329-291-36-88; www.theamazinghostelsayulita. com; Pelícanos 102; dm/d/q M$300/1100/1500; ⊖✳🛜🏊) Follow the road upriver on the plaza side of the bridge to reach this modern hostel, run by helpful, well-traveled folk and with tip-top facilities. Dark but cool en-suite dorms are downstairs; upstairs guests have use of a kitchen, climbing wall and pool. Air-con private rooms are spacious, wi-fi is reliable and bike rentals are available.

La Redonda Sayulita   HOSTEL $

(☏ 329-298-86-78; www.laredondasayulita.com; Navarrete 14; dm/d incl breakfast M$300/800; ✳🛜) Just a block from the beach, this colorful, thatch-roofed hostel is a chilled-out and sociable place without being a full-on crush-a-beer-can-against-your-forehead party place. Dorms are simple but comfy, with individual fans above the beds, though they can still get rather hot; the private room is the only one with air-con. Good breakfast included, but cleanliness could improve.

Petit Hotel Hafa   HOTEL $$

(☏ 329-291-38-06; www.hotelhafa-sayulita.com; Av Revolución 55; r US$60-105; ⊖✳🛜) The owners of this sweet small hotel near the plaza have opted for an Arabian Nights theme and run with it a few miles. Decor fuses North Africa and Mexico, with eight individually decorated rooms offering concrete floors, fans (air-con extra) and bathrooms with brass-bowl sinks. Staff are friendly though hands-off. The location means party noise can be an issue.

⭐ Siete Lunas   BOUTIQUE HOTEL $$$

(☏ cell 322-1822979; www.sietelunas.mx; Camino Playa de los Muertos 714; r/ste incl breakfast US$216/296; 🅿⊖✳🛜🏊) Perched above jungly slopes and boasting phenomenal coastal views, these seven intimate bungalows promise to help you 'return to your origins.' There is much to love about them, from the floor-to-ceiling windows to the super-comfortable beds and private decks. Around 2km from town, past Playa Los Muertos, it's a serene spot for romancing your sweetie.

Aurinko Bungalows   BUNGALOW $$$

(☏ 329-291-31-50; www.aurinkobungalows.com; Marlín 18; 1-/2-bedroom bungalows US$110/180; ⊖✳🛜🏊) An exuberant thatched roof covers this enticing complex of deconstructed houses with indoor/outdoor living rooms and kitchens, and wonderful bedrooms with river-stone floors, accented by tasteful and vibrant modern art. It feels like a secluded hideaway but is actually just steps from the plaza and the beach. A yoga center and small pool are nice extras.

Hotel Sayulita Central   HOTEL $$$

(☏ 329-291-38-45; www.hotelsayulitacentral.com; Delfines 7; r M$2600-3500; ⊖✳🛜) Perfectly located between the plaza and beach, this hotel has a variety of rooms named after classic rock bands. All are bright and creative, with nice touches such as water coolers, and share a sprawling lounge that is a great place to hang out. Prices do reflect quality: the cheapest top-floor chambers double as saunas in summer.

✗ Eating

Sayulita has a beguiling selection of small bistro-style cafes, providing an agreeable contrast to the *palapas* on the beach and the lively taco and other 'fast food' stands (try the seafood burritos) that sprout every evening on the streets surrounding the plaza.

★ Naty's Kitchen   TACOS $
(✐ 329-291-38-18; Marlín 13; tacos M$15-20; ⊙ 8:30am-4pm Mon-Sat, 9am-3pm Sun) A cute taco stand helmed by a team of no-nonsense ladies, where tortillas are stuffed with your choice of sliced poblano peppers, potatoes, green beans and mushrooms, beef, smoked marlin, chicken with *mole*, or pork and cactus paddles. Order at the counter and sit on a bench table out front. Locals descend en masse for a reason.

Mary's   MEXICAN $
(✐ cell 322-1201803; Av Revolución 36; tacos M$35-40, mains M$70-170; ⊙ 8:30am-11pm Mon-Sat, to 4pm Sun) Mary's keeps things simple, affordable and traditional with menu items such as fish tacos or grilled shrimp on handmade tortillas. The popular curbside eatery has also gained kudos for its poblano chili peppers stuffed with shrimp, chicken or cheese.

Yah-Yah Sayulita Cafe   BREAKFAST $
(✐ 329-291-36-45; www.facebook.com/CafeYahYah; Niños Heroes 3; mains M$60-95; ⊙ 7am-6pm Mon-Sat, to 4pm Sun; ⊛✐) In addition to its robust Mexican-grown coffee, this small cafe a couple of blocks from the main square prepares full breakfasts, fruit and veggie bowls, gluten-free pastries and many vegetarian options. Sit in the air-con chill or catch the sun at the outdoor tables. Makes an ideal spot to fuel up before hitting the surf.

Café El Espresso   CAFE $
(✐ 329-291-34-40; www.sayulitalife.com/elespresso; Av Revolución 51; mains M$70-140; ⊙ 7am-10pm; ⊛) This breezy spot on the plaza – where breakfast is served until 2pm – lives up to its name. The coffee is strong and sensational, and non-dairy milk options are available. The 'Tropical Heaven' smoothie blends pineapple, yogurt, honey

and papaya or strawberries with basil and coconut cream, and the Mexican breakfasts (such as *huevos divorciados*) pack authentic heat.

Yeikame   MEXICAN $$
(✐ 329-291-30-22; www.facebook.com/yeikame sayulita; Mariscal 10; mains M$95-175; ⊙ 8am-10:30pm Wed-Mon; ⊛) Welcoming and reliable, this family-run place has pleasant street-side tables and produces a range of fairly traditional Mexican fare. Enchiladas, *tostadas,* tacos and more substantial plates such as chicken in *mole* or marinated pork are priced fairly and feature tasty blue-corn tortillas. There are delicious fruit drinks on offer, and breakfast fare is equally toothsome.

▼ Drinking & Nightlife

Several bars on the plaza's west side keep fairly late hours.

Cava   BAR
(✐ cell 322-1495836; Av Revolución 54; ⊙ 1pm-1am Mon-Sat, 7pm-1am Sun) Belly up to the bar at this friendly neighborhood mezcal joint where you can sip smoky *raicilla* (tequila-like distilled agave drink), viscous *pulque* (low-alcohol brew made from the *maguey* plant), local craft beer and cocktails. After a few potent *raicillas* you'll be chatting it up in no time with the stranger sitting on the barstool next to you.

Don Pato   BAR
(✐ cell 322-1032006; www.facebook.com/bardon pato; Marlín 12; ⊙ 8pm-3am Sun-Fri, to 4am Sat) At the rubber-duck sign and up a spiral staircase, this lively bar on the main plaza pumps out live music or DJ sets most nights, with an open mike on Tuesdays. Don't expect a dress code: half the folks are in bathing suits. Table football is hotly contested, and the upstairs level is often where it's all at.

🛍 Shopping

★ Tierra Huichol   ARTS & CRAFTS
(✐ cell 322-1572725; https://tierrahuichol.com; Av Revolución 38; ⊙ 10am-9pm) ✐ This co-op shop gives an excellent introduction to the Huicholes' colorful beadwork sculptures, sold at fair prices. There are some spectacular pieces here, and you can often see an artist at work. Fair-trade crafts sold here contribute to the livelihood of artisans in Huichol communities.

Revolución del Sueno FASHION & ACCESSORIES
(☑329-291-38-50; Navarrete 55; ⊗10am-8pm)
Specializes in silk-screened T-shirts and
hipster beach bags – how about the revolutionary Emiliano Zapata holding a bouquet
of flowers/surfboard/skateboard? It also has
throw pillows, offbeat jewelry, and quirky
stickers and decorative art pieces, including
outstanding papier-mâché skeletons.

ⓘ Getting There & Away

Sayulita is about 40km north of Puerto Vallarta,
just west of Hwy 200. Buses (M$81, 50 minutes)
operate every 15 minutes or so from a stop
(p552) in front of Puerto Vallarta's Walmart,
just south of Marina Vallarta. Additionally, any
northbound 2nd-class bus from the Puerto
Vallarta bus terminal (p552) will drop you at
the Sayulita turnoff, but you'll have to walk 2km
into town.

Buses to San Francisco (M$22, 15 minutes),
Lo de Marcos (M$34, 30 minutes) and Puerto
Vallarta (M$45, 50 minutes) depart from a small
station (p535) on Avenida Revolución and
Coral.

Punta de Mita & Riviera Nayarit

Just south of Sayulita, a stunning, jungled
mountainous peninsula tumbles into the
sea. Much of it has been tamed and groomed
into gated resorts, and **Punta de Mita** village is now largely a service center for these
resorts. Nevertheless, it has a string of
beachfront restaurants popular with Vallarta families, and its little marina is a place to
jump on a boat out to sea.

The beaches that grace the coast from
here to Nuevo Vallarta – part of a larger
150km stretch known as **Riviera Nayarit** –
are some of the best on the central Pacific
coast. The water is almost always clear and
aquamarine, the sand is white and the surf
can get fun too. Laid-back fishing villages
turned beach resorts worth exploring on
this coastline include **La Cruz de Huan-
acaxtle** and **Bucerías**.

🏃 Activities

Punta de Mita's beachfront strip has several
places offering surfing classes and rentals.
Surfing outfits from Sayulita and San Francisco also run trips here. From the marina
(eastern end of the strip), boats leave for the
Islas Marietas; they also run whale-watching expeditions (December to March).

Punta Mita Charters BOATING
(☑329-291-62-98; www.puntamitacharters.com;
Av Anclote 17; fishing boat per hour US$80, Islas
Marietas M$800; ⊗office 8am-4pm) This coop-
erative can take you to the Islas Marietas,
out fishing or – from December to March –
humpback whale-watching (M$1250 for up
to eight people).

🛏 Sleeping & Eating

Villa Bella Bed & Breakfast B&B $$$
(☑329-295-51-61; www.villabella-lacruz.com;
Monte Calvario 12, La Cruz de Huanacaxtle; ste incl
breakfast from US$165; ⊗❄🛜🏊) Jaw-drop-
ping views across the Riviera Nayarit com-
bine with contemporary-bohemian decor to
make the trip up the hill to this place worth
it (a car is a must). The very private 'mas-
ter suite' has its own outdoor kitchen and
lounge, but all the suites have views and
access to the lovely garden and pool area.
Breakfast is served alfresco.

Just down the road, the small town of La
Cruz de Huanacaxtle and its marina have
plenty of eating and drinking options.

La Quinta del Sol HOTEL $$$
(☑329-291-53-15; www.laquintadelsol.com; Hidal-
go 162; d US$119-129; ⊗❄🛜) An ideal spot
for surfers and beach bums alike, the seven
tastefully appointed rooms here come with
full kitchens, slick marble sinks, excellent
beds and a sweet rooftop terrace overlooking the ocean. Right across the street awaits
a quiet beach and Stinky's, a novice-friendly
surf break. The hotel will gladly hook you up
with lessons and board rentals.

★ Tuna Blanca MEXICAN $$$
(☑329-291-54-14; www.tunablanca.com; Av An-
clote 5; mains M$425-750, tasting menu M$1200;
⊗6-10:30pm Tue-Sun; 🛜🅿) The exquisite
surf-and-turf offerings at this gorgeous-
ly designed oceanfront restaurant feature
renowned chef Thierry Blouet's tried-and-
true favorites, such as prawn-and-pumpkin
cream soup and *raicilla*-flambéed shrimp,
plus such dishes of darkness and power as
suckling pig tacos and seared tuna in ado-
bo sauce. The five-course tasting menu is a
worthy splurge that shows off Blouet's rep-
ertoire. Reserve well ahead and dress nicely.

ⓘ Getting There & Away

From Puerto Vallarta, take Hwy 200 north
through Bucerías, then veer left toward La Cruz
de Huanacaxtle to follow the coast toward the
Punta de Mita peninsula. Frequent buses depart-

ing from Puerto Vallarta (p552) can drop you at most Riviera Nayarit towns. Taxi vans shuttle between Sayulita and Punta de Mita (M$300).

Puerto Vallarta

☑ 322 / POP 245,740

Stretching around the sparkling blue Bahía de Banderas and backed by lush palm-covered mountains, Puerto Vallarta (or just 'Vallarta' to many) is one of Mexico's most enticing coastal destinations. Each year millions come to laze on the dazzling sandy beaches, browse in the quirky shops, nosh in the stylish restaurants and wander the picturesque central streets and attractive *malecón*. There are activities aplenty, including boat trips, horseback rides, diving trips and day trips to the interior. After sunset, Vallarta takes on a new identity with pumping nightlife along the cobblestone streets and numerous LGBT-friendly options in what is the gay beach capital of Mexico.

ⓘ Orientation

The 'old' town center, called **Zona Centro**, is the area north of Río Cuale. Cross the river to reach the **Zona Romántica**, a characterful, spread-out tourist district with smaller hotels, restaurants and bars, the two most central beaches and the hub of LGBT+ life. These eminently walkable downtown neighborhoods, which remain the heart and soul of Puerto Vallarta, are where most places worth visiting, staying at or eating in are located.

North of the city is a strip of giant luxury hotels, the **Zona Hotelera**, where you'll find Marina Vallarta, a large yacht marina (9km from downtown), and Nuevo Vallarta, a new area of hotel and condominium developments (18km). Just north of Marina Vallarta are the airport (p552; 10km) and the bus station (p552; 12km). To the south of the city is a string of winningly beautiful beaches, some backed by resort hotels.

◎ Sights

The heart of Zona Centro is the **Plaza Principal** (Plaza de Armas), where chain-store modernism blends with the shoeshine days of old pueblo. The wide *malecón* stretches a little south and about 10 blocks north from here, and is dotted with bars, restaurants, nightclubs and a grand collection of public sculptures.

Or you could just go to the beach. Those on the Bahía de Banderas have many personalities. Some are buzzing with cheerful activity; others are quiet and private. Two, **Playa Olas Altas** (Map p544) and **Playa de** los Muertos (Beach of the Dead; Map p541), are handy for downtown; both are south of the Río Cuale. At the southern end of Playa de los Muertos is the stretch of sand called **Blue Chairs**, one of Mexico's most famous gay beaches.

★ **Jardín Botánico de Vallarta**   GARDENS
(Vallarta Botanical Garden; ☑ 322-223-61-82; www.vbgardens.org; Hwy 200 Km 24; adult/child under 4yr M$200/free; ☺ 9am-6pm Tue-Sun Jan-Apr, 9am-6pm daily May-Dec) Orchids, bromeliads, agaves and wild palms line the paths of this gorgeous nature park, located 30km south of Puerto Vallarta. Follow hummingbirds through fern grottoes or head down to bask in a chair on the sand and swim amid huge boulders in the river below. Take the 'El Tuito' bus (M$33) from the corner of Carranza and Aguacate in Puerto Vallarta, or hop in a taxi (about M$360).

Museo del Cuale   MUSEUM
(Map p544; Paseo Isla Río Cuale s/n; ☺ 9am-2pm & 3-6pm Tue-Sat) FREE On Isla Río Cuale, this museum has a small but very well presented collection of pre-Hispanic ceramics by the Chupícuaro culture (400 BCE–200 CE), plus the more elaborate pottery of the Aztatlán people (900–1200 CE), shaft tombs typical of the region and ceramics depicting females, underlining their importance in their respective societies. It also gives a good archaeological overview of the various indigenous groups who lived in western Mexico. Most panels are well translated into English.

Isla Río Cuale   ISLAND
(Map p544) A trip to Vallarta wouldn't be complete without lingering on Isla Río Cuale, a sand island that appeared in the river mouth in the 1920s and was then consolidated. It's very pleasant for a traffic-free stroll among the trees and there's a craft market here every day.

Los Arcos   LANDMARK
(Map p544; Malecón s/n, Plaza Morelos) Public events such as gaucho parades and mariachi festivals take place on the sea side of the plaza near an outdoor amphitheater backed by Los Arcos, a row of Romanesque arches that has become a symbol of the city.

Parroquia de Nuestra Señora de Guadalupe   CATHEDRAL
(Templo de Guadalupe; Map p544; ☑ 322-222-13-26; www.parroquiadeguadalupevallarta.com; Hidalgo 370; ☺ 7am-10pm Mon-Sat, from 6:30am Sun)

The crown-topped steeple of the Parish Church of Our Lady of Guadalupe, the town's central cathedral, is a Vallarta icon, and the hand-ringing of the bells via a long rope is a local tradition.

🏃 Activities

Snorkeling, whale-watching, scuba diving, deep-sea fishing, waterskiing, windsurfing, sailing and parasailing can be arranged on the beaches in front of any of the large hotels or through the tourist office.

Cruises

Daytime, sunset and evening cruises are available in Vallarta. The most popular ones are the cruises to Yelapa and Las Ánimas beaches; others go to **Islas Marietas**. Prices are generally negotiable, starting at M$1500 for sunset cruises and beach trips; longer trips lasting four to six hours with meals and bottomless cocktails will set you back M$2500. Leaflets advertising cruises are available throughout town.

Diana's Gay & Lesbian Cruise   CRUISE
(Map p544; www.dianastours.com; Playa de los Muertos dock; cruise US$120; ⊙9am-5pm Thu/Fri Oct-May) On non-summer Thursdays or Fridays (cruise days vary by the week), Diana hosts an all-day gay and lesbian cruise, with plenty of food, an open bar and snorkeling. It leaves from the dock at Playa de los Muertos. You can book your spot via the website.

Deep-Sea Fishing

Deep-sea fishing is popular year-round, with a major international **fishing tournament** (☑322-225-54-67; www.fishvallarta.com; ⊙Nov) held mid-November every year. Prime catches are sailfish, marlin, tuna, red snapper and sea bass. Fishing trips can be arranged dockside at Marina Vallarta or through the multitude of agencies around town. Rates start at about US$300/450 for a four-/eight-hour excursion.

Diving & Snorkeling

Beneath the warm, tranquil waters of Bahía de Banderas is a world of stingrays, tropical fish and garishly colored corals. Vallarta has several diving operators. Most also offer snorkeling trips, which usually means snorkelers tag along with divers. Dives typically include transportation, gear and light meals.

Banderas Scuba Republic   DIVING
(Map p544; ☑cell 322-1357884; www.bs-republic.com; Cárdenas 230; shore/boat dives US$95/105;

⊙office 8am-1pm & 2-5pm Mon-Fri, 8am-1pm Sat) Maintains a high degree of professionalism with its small-group excursions to a dozen or so diving sites in the bay. Patient instructors and all manner of PADI dive courses on offer.

Horseback Riding

Vallarta's jungly mountains are wonderful to explore from a horseback perspective.

Rancho El Charro   HORSEBACK RIDING
(Map p541; ☑322-224-01-14; www.ranchoelcharro.com; Av Francisco Villa 1001; horseback rides US$75-135) Rancho El Charro, 12km northeast of downtown Puerto Vallarta, is recommended for its healthy horses and scenic three- to eight-hour trots into the Sierra Madre. Some rides are suitable for kids. The pickup point in Puerto Vallarta is at the Biblioteca Los Mangos, near the corners of Avenidas Francisco Villa and De Los Tules.

☞ Tours

★Ecotours de México   WILDLIFE
(Map p541; ☑322-209-21-95; www.ecotoursvallarta.com; Proa s/n, Marina Vallarta; whale-watching adult/child US$95/75, sea-kayak & snorkel combo adult/child US$76/63; ⊙9am-7pm Mon-Fri, to 5pm Sat, to 2pm Sun) 🌿 Run by enthusiastic naturalists, this outfit offers whale-watching expeditions, guided hiking and bird-watching, a dolphin-watching and snorkeling combo outing, tours to Islas Marietas and multiday trips further afield focusing on sea turtles and more. Operates tours that support local research projects and nature conservation efforts.

★Vallarta Eats   FOOD & DRINK
(Map p544; ☑322-178-82-88; www.vallartaeats.com; 2nd fl, Independencia 231; taco tour adult/child US$55/39; ⊙office 9am-5pm) Local bilingual guides run seven different terrific food- and drink-related tours about town. The mid-morning and evening taco tours take you on gastronomic journeys of discovery around the taco stands, candy shops and other venues in Zona Centro and Zona Romántica. They also run a boozy 3½-hour Mexican craft-beer tour and delve into Mexico's culinary past on the Mole Pozole tour.

Eco Ride   CYCLING
(Map p544; ☑322-222-79-12; www.ecoridemex.com; Miramar 382; tours US$50-125) Surrounded by mountains, jungle and sea, Vallarta offers truly thrilling mountain biking. This welcoming outfit runs guided one-day tours

Greater Puerto Vallarta

Greater Puerto Vallarta

◎ Sights
1	Playa Conchas Chinas	A4
2	Playa de los Muertos	A4
3	Playa Palmares	A5

◆ Activities, Courses & Tours
4	Ecotours de México	A2
5	Rancho El Charro	B3

⊟ Sleeping
6	Almar Resort	A4
7	Casa Velas	A2
8	Oasis Hostel	B4

⊗ Eating
9	Barrio Bistro	B3
10	El Carboncito	B3
11	El Taquito Hidalguense	B3
12	Icú	B2
13	La Leche	A3
14	Tintoque	A2

Canopy River   ADVENTURE
(Map p544; ☑322-223-52-57; www.canopyriver.com; Insurgentes 379; tours adult/child US$89/55; ☺office 8am-4pm) An exhilarating four-hour canopy tour up the Río Cuale, featuring 11 zip-lines ranging in height from 4m to 216m and in length from 44m to a stunning 650m run – curl up like a cannonball to reach top speed. A tequila tour and mule riding are thrown in, and you can add ATV driving or get-wet river zip-lines. Price includes transportation.

✷ Festivals & Events

Vallarta Pride   LGBT
(☑cell 322-1786787; www.facebook.com/orgullo vallartapride; ☺May) A weeklong event in May celebrating the LGBT+ community with cultural events, concerts, parades and wild beach parties in the heart of Mexico's top gay beach destination.

Festival Gourmet International FOOD & DRINK
(☑322-222-22-47; www.festivalgourmet.com; ☺Nov) Puerto Vallarta's culinary community has hosted this five-day mid-November festival since 1995. Chef masterclasses, special menus in restaurants and daily food-related events abound.

⊨ Sleeping

You're spoiled for choice here. Vallarta's cheapest lodgings lie inland, on both sides of the Río Cuale. Closer to the ocean, in the Zona Romántica, you'll find numerous

suitable for beginners and badasses alike. The all-level 20km ride takes you upriver to a lovely waterfall. The most challenging is a 48km expedition from El Tuito (a small town at 1100m) through Chacala and down to the beach in Yelapa.

Walking Tours   WALKING
(Recorridos Turísticos; Map p544; ☑322-222-09-23; www.facebook.com/turismopvoficial; cnr Juárez & Independencia; ☺9am & noon Tue & Wed, 9am Sat) **FREE** These free walking tours of Puerto Vallarta's historic center are run from the tourist office, and guides can speak Spanish, English and German. A tip is appropriate at the end.

appealing midrange options and high-end boutiques. Resorts abound, both in the Zona Romántica and in the north of the city, near the marina. Prices quoted are for the December to April high season.

🛏 Zona Romántica

Oasis Hostel
HOSTEL $

(Map p541; ☎322-222-26-36; https://oasishostel .com; Colosio 222; dm/d without bathroom M$350/700; ❋🛜) The conveniently located Oasis Downtown houses three bright dorms and one simple private room with two beds and a shared bathroom. The hostel has a policy of welcoming guests with a complimentary beer on arrival. There's also a great rooftop deck with ocean views and lockers to guard your valuables. It's a 10-minute walk to the Zona Romántica action.

Hotel Galería Belmar
HOTEL $$

(Map p544; ☎322-223-18-72; www.belmar vallarta.com; Insurgentes 161; studio/d from M$1136/1754; ❋❉@🛜) Astute use of bright colors and a plethora of original artworks enliven the tidy, comfortable rooms at this hotel in the heart of the Zona Romántica. Some have kitchenettes, others are compact studios, and many have balconies. Nicest are the top-floor chambers, which get natural light, ocean breeze and slightly less street noise.

Hotel Posada de Roger
HOTEL $$

(Map p544; ☎322-222-08-36; www.hotel posadaderoger.com; Badillo 237; s/d/tr/q US$85/92/99/105; ❋❉🛜❐) Three blocks from the beach, this agreeable travelers' hangout with a leafy courtyard and pool has long been one of Vallarta's most beloved midrange options and has a popular attached restaurant. Skip the windowless economy rooms and be aware that street-facing rooms with bougainvillea-draped balconies suffer from traffic noise during the day.

Hotel Yasmin
HOTEL $$

(Map p544; ☎322-222-00-87; www.hotelyasminpv. com; Badillo 168; s/d/tr/q M$940/1090/1160/1230; ❋🛜❐) This friendly cheapie just a block from the beach consists of simple rooms, enlivened by colorful Mexican art and rustic furnishings, and an attractive courtyard area with a small pool. Some of the rooms could be ventilated better, and traffic noise is a bane for front-facing rooms, but the location's hard to beat.

★Casa Nicole
BOUTIQUE HOTEL $$$

(Map p544; ☎322-223-24-44; https://hotelcasa nicole.com; Pino Suárez 203; r incl breakfast US$133-164; ❋❉🛜❐) Having reopened with a new name and new concept, this boutique hotel a block from the beach comprises spacious, minimalist rooms sporting slanted beamed ceilings, blond-wood furnishings, plush beds and walk-in rain showers. Honeymooners opt for the deluxe with soaking tub. American breakfast is served in the gorgeous courtyard with fountain, where Nicole's Kitchen rocks in the high season.

Rivera del Río
BOUTIQUE HOTEL $$$

(Map p544; ☎cell 322-2056093; www.riveradelrio. com; Rivera del Río 104; r incl breakfast US$79-169; ❋❉🛜❐) Along a peaceful riverside road, it's quite a surprise to come upon this place. The sumptuous interiors are eye-popping, running from Italianate frescoes and water features to 1920s plush, with not a false note. All eight rooms and suites in this vertically arranged building are strikingly different; Alejandro is our favorite, with wrought-iron bedstead, chandelier and thatched roof. Gay-friendly.

Casa Doña Susana
BOUTIQUE HOTEL $$$

(Map p544; ☎322-226-71-01; www.casadona susana.com; Diéguez 171; d US$105-123; 🅿❋❉@🛜❐) There's old-world elegance in the lobby, plenty of stone-and-brick arches, and a pretty interior courtyard at this adults-only hotel. Rooms sport antique wood furnishings and carved headboards, and the rooftop pool has mountain and sea views, plus a chapel. You get full use of the facilities at the nearby sister resort hotel (Playa Los Arcos), including beach umbrellas and a larger pool.

🛏 Zona Centro

★Casa Kraken Hostel
HOSTEL $

(Map p544; ☎322-222-92-82; https://casakraken hostel.wixsite.com/hostel; Juárez 386; dm M$275-325; ❉🛜) A lot of love has gone into Vallarta's best hostel, including meticulous attention to detail. There are good dorm beds, a great chillout area partially open to the elements, complete with climbing wall and colorful murals, a terrace overlooking the sea and, best of all, helpful staff who can arrange cooking classes, bike tours, food tours and much more.

Hostel Central
HOSTEL $

(Map p544; ☎cell 322-1341313; www.hostel centralvallarta.com; Hidalgo 224; dm/d without

DON'T MISS

THE SOUTHERN BEACHES

A string of beautiful coves and beaches graces the bay south of central Vallarta, easily accessed by bus. Further around the southern side of the bay are three more isolated beaches – from east to west, Las Ánimas, Quimixto and Yelapa – all accessible by boat but not by road, though you can walk a trail to the first two from Boca de Tomatlán.

Buses (p554) marked 'Boca' stop at both Mismaloya and Boca de Tomatlán (M$10); the 'Mismaloya' bus only goes as far as Mismaloya. Any of these buses work for Playa Conchas Chinas and Playa Palmares.

Playa Conchas Chinas (Map p541) Around 3km south of downtown is the beautiful condo enclave of Playa Conchas Chinas. It's a tiny cove favored by families for the shallow and sheltered pools created by the burly rock reef further out (that's where the snorkelers and spearfishers have fun). Although the cove is small, the beach is blond and reasonably wide, with lifeguards on duty.

Playa Palmares (Map p541) About 6km south of Zona Centro, Playa Palmares – named not for the nonexistent palms but for the condo complex of the same name – is a narrow but ample stretch of white sand. These picturesque turquoise shallows are favored by locals for swimming as the beach is far from rivers, which means clear water year-round.

Mismaloya Mismaloya, the location for the 1964 film *The Night of the Iguana*, is about 12km south of Puerto Vallarta: you can still see the dilapidated Iguana sign by the roadside. The tiny scenic cove is dominated by a gargantuan resort. Mismaloya is also the jumping-off point for snorkeling trips to the group of offshore islands known as Los Arcos, where you can swim among the reef fish; boat trips out there cost around M$450 per person.

Boca de Tomatlán Boca de Tomatlán is a seaside village that's less commercialized than Puerto Vallarta and a good place to munch ceviche *tostadas* on the beach. You can get water taxis from here to more remote beaches further along the bay. It's 16km from Puerto Vallarta, beyond Mismaloya, southwest along the coast.

Playa de las Ánimas Playa de las Ánimas is a long, sandy beach with a small fishing village and some *palapa* (thatched-roof) restaurants offering fresh seafood. It's also a great place for water sports, from parasailing to banana-boat rides.

Playa de Quimixto This beach, just beyond Las Ánimas, has a waterfall accessible by a half-hour hike or by hiring a horse (M$300) on the beach to take you up.

Yelapa Yelapa, the furthermost of the southern beaches from town, is one of Puerto Vallarta's most secluded and beloved bays, and home to a small community that still fishes off the pier. Lots of day-trippers turn up on organized tours, but this picturesque cove empties out when the boats leave in the late afternoon. There are several comfortable places to stay the night. Round-trip water taxis (p552) from Puerto Vallarta/Boca de Tomatlán cost M$340/200 per person; the trip takes 45 minutes from Vallarta.

bathroom M$300/450; ❄🛜) The little rooftop dorm here has both beds and bunks, and makes a compact central hideaway for up to eight guests. The family that runs it are helpful and can arrange snorkeling tours of Los Arcos, paddleboarding and more; there's also a cool chill-out space with hammocks for whiling away the heat of the day.

Hotel Catedral   HOTEL **$$**
(Map p544; 📞322-222-90-33; www.hotelcatedralvallarta.com; Hidalgo 166; d US$37-55, ste US$86; ❄❄🛜) A charming three-star spot, steps from the waterfront and river. The four floors of rooms surround a courtyard and

have Templo de Guadalupe views from the upper reaches. Each of the rooms is individually decorated in bold colors; you may get an inspirational quote on the wall, or quirky art, or a canopy bed and kitchenette in the suites.

★Hacienda San Angel   BOUTIQUE HOTEL **$$$**
(Map p544; 📞322-222-26-92; www.haciendasanangel.com; Miramar 336; ste incl breakfast US$435-525; ❄❄@🛜☀) The 19 suites at this characterful hacienda high above the coast are scattered across five buildings that surround a courtyard with fountains. All are exquisitely decorated with fine terra-cotta

Central Puerto Vallarta

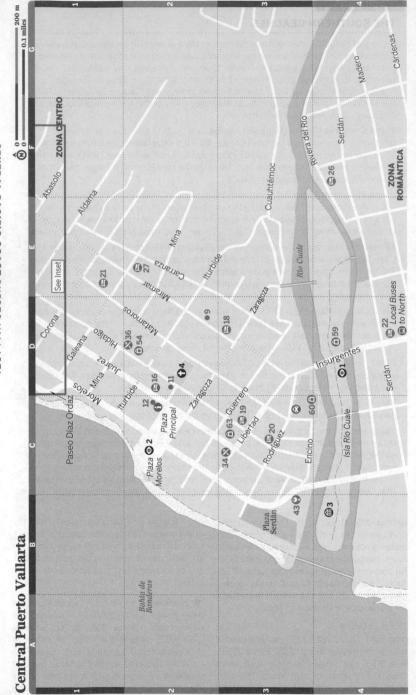

200 m
0.1 miles

ZONA CENTRO

ZONA ROMÁNTICA

Bahía de Banderas

Río Cuale

Isla Río Cuale

Local Buses to North

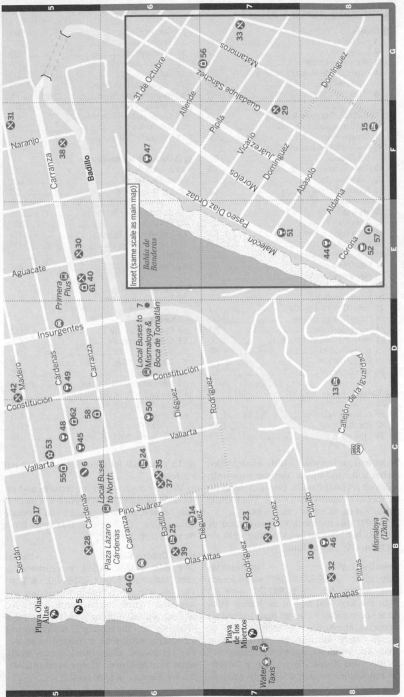

Central Puerto Vallarta

floors, antique four-poster beds, *azulejo*-tiled arches and hand-woven Mexican rugs, with religious art on the walls. Two pool decks offer special city and ocean views. The rooftop restaurant earns repeat customers.

In 1977 this hacienda was purchased by actor Richard Burton as a Valentine's gift for his then-wife, Susan Hunt.

Casa Dulce Vida APARTMENT $$$
(Map p544; ☑ 322-222-10-08; www.dulcevida .com; Aldama 295; ste US$80-170; ⊜🛇🖨) With the look and feel of an Italian villa, these six spacious suites all have individual character, emphasized by such features as contemporary Mexican art, wrought-iron doors and windows, sea-view terraces and ceramic-tiled floors. They share a beautiful red-bottom mosaic pool, leafy gardens

and a roof deck for admiring the blood-red sunsets.

Most rooms have private terraces and extra beds for groups. Even when the place is fully booked, it retains a quiet and intimate atmosphere. It's a setting that begs for a cocktail, then another.

Hotel Cuatro Vientos HOTEL $$$
(Map p544; ☑ 322-222-01-61; www.cuatrovientos .com; Matamoros 520; r US$99-110; ❄🛇🖨) This family-run hotel comprises homey and somewhat dated rooms (some with tiled ceiling), a small dipping pool, and the pièce de résistance – the rooftop El Nido bar, great for kicking back with a cocktail at sunset. The restaurant, Chez Elena, serves toothsome local favorites. Effusive hostess Gloria is a good source of local info.

🛌 Zona Hotelera & La Marina

★ Casa Velas   RESORT $$$
(Map p541; ☎322-226-86-70; www.hotelcasa
velas.com; Pelícanos 311; ste US$318-425; P ☺
❄ 🤖 🏊) The best of the resorts in Vallarta's
marina area, this adults-only property combines traditional Mexican decor with thoroughly contemporary creature comforts,
marble bathrooms, art by local sculptor
Sergio Bustamante and brightly tiled private
Jacuzzis. Lush grounds with golf course, spa,
award-winning dining, private beach club
and walking proximity to the restaurants
and nightlife around the marina are among
the many perks.

✗ Eating

There's a thriving culinary scene in Puerto
Vallarta, ranging from ubiquitous street eats
to gourmet restaurants. Taco stands are particularly prolific in the Zona Centro and Zona
Romántica, while fine dining clusters near the
marina and in the Zona Hotelera.

✗ Zona Romántica

Tacos Revolución   TACOS $
(Map p544;   ☎322-222-13-62;   http://tacos
revolucion.com.mx; Olas Altas 485; tacos M$17-
30; ⊘2-11pm Wed-Mon; 🤖🖐) Excellent *carne
asada* (marinated grilled beef), *al pastor*
(spit-cooked marinated pork), *chicharrón*
(pork crackling), fish and vegetarian tacos
are prepared on handmade tortillas and
served with kick-ass salsas at this revolu-
tionary-themed establishment, responsible
for the tongue-in-cheek 'Make Tacos Not
Walls' slogan. Unlike most *taquerías,* Revolución boasts a well-stocked bar of Mexican
craft beers, tequila and wine.

A Page in the Sun   CAFE $
(Map p544; ☎322-222-36-08; www.apageinthe
sun.com; Cárdenas 179; pastries & light meals
M$30-100; ⊘7am-11pm; 🤖) This friendly
and highly recommended cafe doubles as a
bookstore full of used books in English and
social hangout, with good espresso drinks,
delicious sweet treats, full breakfasts, sandwiches, salads, beer and regular events.

★ El Mole de Jovita   MEXICAN $$
(Map p544; ☎322-223-30-65; www.mexicanres
taurantpuertovallarta.wordpress.com; Badillo 220;
mains M$130-240; ⊘noon-10:30pm; 🤖) This
family-run restaurant specializes in chicken
with *mole* (a complex, long-simmered sauce

that includes chocolate and spices) from a
jealously guarded family recipe, but also has
a succinct menu of other well-executed Mexican standards, such as enchiladas, slow-
cooked pork ribs and crispy fish tacos.

Coco's Kitchen   INTERNATIONAL $$
(Map p544; ☎322-223-03-73; www.cocoskitchen
pv.net; Púlpito 122; mains M$99-160; ⊘8am-4pm
Jun-Nov, to 10pm Dec-May; 🤖) At this popular
brunch spot south of the river, tables are
sprinkled on a ceramic-tiled patio beneath
a stilted terra-cotta roof in a shady bar-side
garden. Dishes range from *carnitas* (braised
pulled pork) and green-chili burritos to a
range of quesadillas and salads, eggs Benedict, *chilaquiles,* French toast and pecan
waffles, executed with aplomb and served
with a smile.

Joe Jack's Fish Shack   SEAFOOD $$
(Map p544; ☎322-222-20-99; www.joe
jacks-fishshack.com; Badillo 212; mains M$150-195;
⊘noon-11pm; 🤖) With an extended happy
hour running from noon to 7pm, you can
keep the mojitos coming until day blurs into
night. The Shack's refreshing muddled-mint
cocktail goes down nicely with the fresh ceviche and *aguachile,* a house specialty, as well
as with the Baja-style fish or shrimp tacos.

Chenando's   SEAFOOD $$$
(Map p544; ☎322-222-33-28; www.facebook.
com/chenandosrestaurant; Cárdenas 520; mains
M$190-315; ⊘5:30-11pm Tue-Sun; 🤖) This de-
lightful family-run restaurant has a simple
but attractive interior with small square
tables that get very busy come sundown. It
excels in the kitchen, producing succulent
burritos bursting with shrimp and fish as
well as moreish shrimp encrusted with coconut batter, plus other dishes on its regularly
changing menu.

✗ Zona Centro

El Banquito   TACOS $
(Map p544; ☎cell 322-1412301; Libertad 189;
tacos M$15; ⊘9am-3pm Thu-Tue) For one of
Jalisco's most emblematic snacks, head to
this tiny taco joint named after the sole stool
(banquito) parked on the sidewalk. Watch
the chefs fry up tortillas and shred pork
and goat meat and *chicharrón* before deftly
heaping the latter on the former. The specialty, *taco de birria dorado,* is a hard-shell
taco with goat meat.

Orders of three tacos include a complimentary cup of rich consommé.

CENTRAL PACIFIC COAST PUERTO VALLARTA

El Taquito Hidalguense TACOS $

(Map p541; ☑ cell 322-1123740; Panamá 177; tacos M$20, consommé M$25-29; ⊘10am-3:30pm) Hailing from Mexico's *barbacoa* (lamb or mutton) capital Hidalgo, this family prepares delectable tacos on handmade tortillas with tender meat that's been slow-cooked in a pit for 12 hours. The consommé adds a little oomph to the morning grease fix.

Gaby's MEXICAN $$

(Map p544; ☑ 322-222-04-80; www.gabysrestaurant.com.mx; Mina 252; mains M$140-280, cooking class M$900; ⊘8am-11pm; 🐾) Since 1989 this brightly tiled family-run place with upstairs terrace seating and a tree-shaded back patio has specialized in stuffed poblano peppers, *tamales* and tequila-flamed enchiladas. It's especially atmospheric in the evenings when videos are cheekily projected onto a neighboring building. Fancy a five-hour Mexican cooking class? Gaby's chef Julio Castillón teaches you how to makes salsas, *mole tamales* and more.

★ Café des Artistes FUSION $$$

(Map p544; ☑ 322-226-72-00; www.cafedesartistes.com; Guadalupe Sánchez 740; mains M$290-570, tasting menu M$699; ⊘6-11pm; ❄🐾) At one of Vallarta's finest restaurants, everything impresses, from the candlelit garden with water feature and psychedelic Huichol yarn art in the subtly lit dining room to the exquisite fusion of French and Mexican influences. Expect winning combinations of ingredients, such as suckling lamb encrusted with pistachios, or broiled octopus with smoked organic beets. Great cocktails, too. Reservations recommended.

Barrio Bistro FUSION $$$

(Map p541; ☑ cell 322-3060530; www.facebook.com/barriobistromx; España 305, Colonia Versalles; mains M$210-340; ⊘6-10:30pm Tue-Sat; 🐾) Once you've been seated, chef Memo visits your table with a detailed explanation of each dish featured on a chalkboard menu that changes weekly. It may include a rack of lamb with fresh herbs plucked from the bistro's garden, or creative seafood dishes. Memo stocks a top-notch *raicilla* and quality wines and craft beers. Cash only.

El Arrayán MEXICAN $$$

(Map p544; ☑ 322-222-71-95; www.elarrayan.com.mx; Allende 344; mains M$245-385; ⊘5:30-11pm Wed-Mon; 🐾) Owner Carmen Porras takes special pleasure in rescuing old family recipes from obscurity, with an emphasis on fresh local ingredients. Specialties include crispy duck *carnitas* (deep-fried) with orange sauce, crispy cricket tacos, and *cochinita pibil* (Yucatan-style slow-cooked pork). The restaurant, with its open kitchen and impressive Huichol yarn paintings, also serves as a venue for regular cooking classes.

✖ Zona Hotelera & La Marina

★Tintoque MEXICAN $$$

(Map p541; ☑ 322-221-02-40; https://tintoque.mx; Marina Vallarta; mains M$170-300, tasting menu M$699; ⊘5-11pm Sun-Thu, to midnight Fri & Sat) If you only dine out in one fine establishment in Vallarta, make it Tintoque. Chef Joel Ornelas dazzles when it comes to creative, beautiful reimaginings of classic flavors. An amuse-bouche arrives, sitting on a sunflower. The pork-belly skin is impeccably crisp. The ceviche is embraced by a wafer-thin sliver of *nopal*. Truly a meal to remember.

★Icú MEXICAN $$$

(Map p541; ☑ 322-221-27-43; www.restauranteicu.com; Francisco Medina Ascencio 2550; mains M$205-475, tasting menu M$1500; ⊘6pm-midnight Mon-Sat; ❄🐾☑) A discreet side door leads you into a subtly lit dining room for one of Vallarta's best meals, signature cocktail in hand. Chefs Mauricio Leal and Josué Jiménez do wonderful things with local, seasonal produce. You may encounter the likes of beets with homemade *requesón* cheese, seafood risotto and *chile ancho* stuffed with roasted-garlic salsa and Chihuahua cheese. Enjoy.

La Leche MEXICAN $$$

(Map p541; ☑ 322-293-09-00; www.lalecherestaurant.com; Francisco Medina Ascencio Km 2.5; burritos M$80-100, mains M$230-390, tasting menu M$790; ⊘6pm-1am; 🐾) The restaurant owners have opted for a milk theme and have run with it a few miles. The interior is suitably Instagram-worthy, the milk gags appear throughout the meal, and the concept here is a daily changing menu with seasonal ingredients dictating the chef's dish choices. The seven-course *degustación* (tasting) menu showcases the full repertoire, including a signature duck dish.

There's an Old World–New World wine list, including a good few Mexican vintages. La Leche also runs a superlative burrito food truck outside.

VALLARTA STREET EATS

Tacos are Vallarta's essential staple. Some fillings are eaten only in the mornings, some are fuel for night owls, and some fill the gap in between. Below are some of the best taco stands across the city.

Tacos de Birria Chanfay (Map p544; 322-131-03-07; Carranza 373; tacos from M$17; 10am-4pm) This humble taco stand has been serving just four things since 1972: tacos, either *blanditos* (soft) or *dorados* (crunchy), and filled with *birria* (goat), spicy shredded beef, pork or – for connoisseurs – *chafayna* (a mix of heart, liver and lungs). Spoon one of three punchy salsas over the top and knock back a cup of rich, spicy broth.

Carnitas Lalo (Map p544; cnr Carranza & Aguacate; tacos M$12; 7am-noon) Turn up early at this taco stand, because it closes as soon as they sell out, and they sell out of pork cheek *(mejilla de cerdo)* first of all. If you miss out, just ask them to pile your tacos with their flavorsome mix of shredded pork meat and crispy pork skin, and pile on the *pico de gallo* salsa.

Taquería El Moreno (Map p544; Madero 343; tacos & quesadillas M$15-35; 9:30am-midnight Fri-Wed) Maybe you've never tasted tripe before, or maybe you didn't like it until you've rocked up at this *taquería* and they presented you with a *taco de tripa*, the meat chewy and smoky and full of flavor, pillowed against the beans and livened up with a kick of salsa. Quesadillas filled with *birria* and *carne asada* (grilled beef) also delight.

Marisma Fish Taco (Map p544; 322-222-13-95; www.marismafishtaco.com; Naranjo 320; tacos M$33-50; 9am-5pm) Delicious tacos with shrimp, smoked marlin or fried fish are served at this super-popular streetside *taquería*. Pull up a stool and watch as the cooks press fresh tortillas and fry up tasty treats from a simple, deeply satisfying menu, coupled with an assortment of fresh salsas.

Pancho's Takos (Map p544; 322-222-16-93; http://pachostakos.restaurantwebexperts. com; Badillo 162; tacos M$15-65; 6pm-2am Mon-Sat) Drawing a regular nighttime crowd, this humble *taquería* near the beach is a solid contender for the best *tacos al pastor* (spit-cooked pork with diced onions, cilantro and pineapple) in the 'hood and attracts hungry night owls after many neighborhood restaurants have closed.

El Carboncito (Map p541; 322-182-07-68; Honduras 127; tacos from M$17; 7pm-3:30am Tue-Sun) It's nighttime and the chefs are doing a brisk business at this unmarked taco stand, deftly slicing chunks of red-tinted, spit-grilled and marinated pork and dishing out what locals say are the best *tacos al pastor* in town. Their secret? Mesquite charcoal and special salsa, its recipe jealously guarded.

 Drinking & Nightlife

It's ridiculously easy to become inebriated in a town where two-for-one happy hours are as reliable as the sunset, margarita glasses look like oversized snifters and day drinking is almost an obligation. In Zona Centro, the *malecón* is a popular place to be promenading after sundown, with frequent live music performances.

Los Otros Blondies BAR
(Map p544; 322-889-60-64; www.facebook.com/losotrosblondiespv; Badillo 258; 11am-2am) What do you get if you mix pop art with slushies and add generous helpings of tequila, gin and Absolut vodka? Something like this fun bar, we imagine, where you can buy said pop art to display proudly on your belly, and while away the heat of the day, sipping a Brassy, Spicy, Classy or Platinum Blondie. Gay-friendly.

Bar Morelos BAR
(Map p544; 322-222-25-50; www.facebook.com/barmorelospuertovallarta; Morelos 589; 8pm-3am Sun-Tue, to 5am Wed-Sat;) Stylish and with professional staff, this mirror-clad bar makes for a classy drink. More than 50 mezcals are available (plus mezcal cocktails), and the staff will talk you through them. Interesting midweek DJs, a decent sound system and attractive decor make this a standout.

Los Muertos Brewing PUB
(Map p544; 322-222-03-08; www.losmuertosbrewing.com; Cárdenas 302; 11am-midnight;) An attractive brick-arched, concrete-floored

LGBTIQ+ PUERTO VALLARTA

Come on out – the rainbow flag flies high over Puerto Vallarta. Many visitors descend on the city annually for its formidable selection of gay bars, nightclubs, restaurants and hotels, as well as its busy annual calendar of gay- and lesbian-themed events. The *Gay Guide Vallarta* booklet and website (www.gayguidevallarta.com) have tons of information and a helpful map for finding gay-friendly businesses. The nine-day Vallarta Pride (p541) event in May celebrates the LGBTIQ+ community with special fervor.

Sleeping

Almar Resort (Map p541; ☑ 322-222-48-88; https://almarresort.com; Amapas 380; r US$143-295, ste US$333-409; ⓟ ⊜ ❀ ⓐ ⓡ ⋈) Puerto Vallarta's only luxury LGBT+ resort doesn't disappoint. There are great views of the Playa de los Muertos from its lofty bluff-top location and from its rooftop bar, the rooms are airy, with understated elegance, and the plushest suites let you romance your sweetie in a private hydrobath. Amenities abound, from spa and restaurant to infinity pool and affiliated beach club.

Casa Cupula (Map p544; ☑ 800-223-24-84; www.casacupula.com; Callejón de la Igualdad 129; r/ste from US$350/651; ⓟ ⊜ ❀ @ ⓡ ⋈) Sophisticated design and luxurious flourishes define this popular hotel catering to both gays and lesbians. Each room is uniquely decorated, with amenities ranging from home-theater-sized TVs to private Jacuzzis in some suites. The beach is only a few blocks downhill, although the resort's three pools, gym, onsite restaurant and bar may give you enough incentive to linger here all day.

Hotel Mercurio (Map p544; ☑ 322-222-47-93; www.hotel-mercurio.com; Rodríguez 168; r incl breakfast US$133-161; ⊜ ❀ @ ⓡ ⋈) Two blocks from Playa de los Muertos pier, some of the rooms at this three-story gay hotel could be aired out better, but are set around a pleasant courtyard with pool and bar. Rooms are modest, but have fridges, cable TV and double or king-sized beds. Generous buffet breakfast is a bonus.

Villa David (Map p544; ☑ 322-223-03-15; www.villadavidpv.com; Galeana 348; r US$126-161; ⊙ Nov-Apr; ⊜ ❀ @ ⓡ ⋈) Clothing is optional at this gay retreat in a beautiful hacienda-style mansion in the characterful streets high above the *malecón* (beach promenade), where you can wander nude among the night-blooming jasmine in the courtyard. Great views and sunsets from the roof deck, and the rooms are all individually styled.

Drinking & Nightlife

Gay Vallarta Bar-Hopping (Map p544; ☑ cell 322-1484960; https://hop.gaypv.com; Púlpito 141; per person US$60-149; ⊙ office 10am-4pm Mon-Fri) This entertaining excursion is a fun introduction to Vallarta's gay nightlife and a good way of making new friends. The most expensive outing includes dinner and drinks aplenty at six different bars. Book online.

CC Slaughters (Map p544; ☑ 322-222-34-12; www.facebook.com/CCSlaughtersPV; Cárdenas 254; ⊙ 6pm-6am) Arrive after midnight in order to share sweat with attractive strangers on the dance floor to the pulsating beats of house and techno. If you come earlier, there's a great bar for socializing adjacent to the dance floor and the drinks pack a potent punch. Admission charge varies.

La Noche (Map p544; www.lanochepv.com; Cárdenas 263; ⊙ 8pm-3am; ☎) This pre-club venue is well loved for its convivial atmosphere, buff bartenders and terrific go-go, pole and silk dancers. The soundtrack is resolutely old-school house, and you can nurse your margarita on the roof terrace.

Garbo (Map p544; ☑ 322-223-57-53; Púlpito 142; ⊙ 6pm-2am; ☎) If you enjoy jazzy stylings and like your martinis dirty or extra tart, make your way to this concrete-floor habitat. The jazz and torch singing kicks off nightly at 10:30pm and is decent to good, and there's a small dance floor to shake your moneymaker.

Antropology (Map p544; ☑ 322-117-11-31; Morelos 101; admission M$50; ⊙ 9pm-4am; ☎) It's raining men at this sizzling dance mecca and male-stripper venue; expect lots of skimpy underwear and terrific dancing. Women are unapologetically disallowed.

pub and microbrewery that draws a lively mix of old-timers and visitors. The beer comes in seven varieties including a hoppy IPA called 'Revenge,' a malty, dark 'Hop On!' that defies easy description, and a fine 'McSanchez' stout.

Puerto Cafe
COFFEE

(Map p544; ☏ 322-189-33-24; www.facebook.com/delpuertocafe; Morelos 540; ⊙7:30am-10pm Mon-Sat, to 3pm Sun; 🛜) A classic rock soundtrack, vinyl records and a giant map of the world welcome you to Vallarta's premier caffeine lab. There's seating at the back and the friendly baristas brew the specialty coffee from a Puebla roastery a number of different ways.

Mandala
CLUB

(Map p544; ☏ 322-224-38-27; www.facebook.com/mandalavallarta; Paseo Díaz Ordaz 640; cover M$150; ⊙6pm-6am) By far the best of three adjacent clubs here, this cinema-sized spot has privileged *malecón* frontage and keeps a youngish crowd happy with Latino hits until late at night under a benevolent icon's gaze. If you're determined to get blitzed, you may find yourself drifting into insolvency.

La Bodeguita del Medio
BAR

(Map p544; ☏ 322-223-15-85; www.labodeguitadelmedio.com.mx; Paseo Díaz Ordaz 858; ⊙9am-3am; 🛜) The walls are scrawled with handwritten poetics and inanities in several languages, the bar holds fine rums and tequilas, and the staff pour a mean mojito. Loud salsa music with nightly live acts is accompanied by plenty of dancing and good cheer.

☆ Entertainment

Vallarta's main forms of nighttime entertainment revolve around dancing, drinking and dining, much of which happens in establishments lining the busy *malecón*. There's often entertainment by the sea at Los Arcos (p539).

Roxy Rock House
LIVE MUSIC

(Map p544; ☏ 322-222-76-17; www.roxyrockhouse.com; Vallarta 217; ⊙10pm-6am; 🛜) In the heart of the Zona Romántica, this place draws an enthusiastic mixed crowd with its nightly rock cover bands and no admission charge. Expect tributes to the likes of Rammstein and Depeche Mode.

🔒 Shopping

In Vallarta you can find everything from exquisite Huichol beadwork and regional yarn art, locally made Talavera tiles, fine ceramics from Chihuahua and Oaxaca, and folkloric masks from all over Mexico to mass-produced tourist tat, for those whose lives simply wouldn't be complete without a 'Shut Up Liver, You're Fine' and 'Make Tacos Not Walls' T-shirts, plus Mexican wrestling masks.

Manyana
CLOTHING

(Map p544; ☏ 322-688-68-35; www.facebook.com/manyanavallarta; Carranza 263; ⊙10am-8pm Mon-Sat) The Vallarta branch of this concept store that originated in Sayulita sells mostly Mexican-made ceramics, stylish linen wear, funky glasses, Mollusc Hemp T-shirts, surfer wear by Quality People, toiletries, candles and more.

Mercado Isla Río Cuale
ARTS & CRAFTS

(Map p544; Isla Río Cuale; ⊙9:30am-6pm) Among the Mexican wrestling masks, Huichol beadwork of vastly varying quality, and T-shirts bearing slogans such as 'Puerto Vallarta Hooter Inspector,' you can also find decent woven blankets, hammocks and ponchos. Particularly worth looking out for are scratch-paper prints by Pedro Tello, responsible for sculptures on the *malecón*, and unique coffee paintings by Amado Arce Cabrera.

Mercado Municipal Río Cuale
ARTS & CRAFTS

(Map p544; Rodríguez 260; ⊙9am-6pm) If you're hankering after novelty T-shirts, boob-shaped mugs, mirror-studded ceramic skulls and other assorted tat, head to this sprawling market that provides a livelihood to many locals. If you look hard enough, you can also find quality Taxco silver, *sarapes* (blankets with a head opening) and *huaraches* (woven leather sandals).

ℹ Information

Although most businesses in Vallarta accept US dollars as readily as they accept pesos, rates are generally poor. Banks with ATMs and *casas de cambio* (currency exchange) are abundant.

Canadian Consulate (☏ 322-293-00-98; www.canadainternational.gc.ca/mexico-mexique; Francisco Medina Ascencio 2485, Plaza Peninsula; ⊙9am-1pm Mon-Fri; 🚊 Ixtapa)

Main Post Office (Map p541; ☏ 322-223-13-60; www.correosdemexico.gob.mx; Colombia 1014; ⊙8am-5:30pm Mon-Fri, 9am-1pm Sat)

Municipal Tourist Office (Map p544; ☏ 322-222-09-23; www.visitpuertovallarta.com; Juárez s/n; ⊙8am-8pm Mon-Fri, 9am-5pm Sat & Sun) Vallarta's busy office in the municipal building at the northeast corner of Plaza Principal has free maps, multilingual tourist literature and bilingual staff.

San Javier Marina Hospital (☎322-226-10-10; www.sanjavier.com.mx; Francisco Medina Ascencio 2760; ☺24hr) Vallarta's best-equipped hospital.

US Consular Agency (☎334-624-21-02; https://mx.usembassy.gov/embassy-consulates/guadalajara/vallarta-consular-agency; Paseo de los Cocoteros 85 Sur, Paradise Plaza, Nuevo Vallarta; ☺8:30am-12:30pm Mon-Thu)

ⓘ Getting There & Away

To reach downtown from the airport and bus station, it's a straight shoot southbound along Francisco Medina Ascencio (aka Hwy 200).

AIR

Aeropuerto Internacional Gustavo Díaz Ordaz (Puerto Vallarta International Airport; Map p541; ☎322-221-12-98; www.aeropuertosgap.com.mx/en/puerto-vallarta-3.html; Carretera Vallarta–Tepic Km 7.5; ☎; ⓠ Las Juntas, Ixtapa) is located 10km north of the city. There are direct flights, some seasonal, from dozens of US and Canadian cities, as well as direct charters from the UK.

Domestic destinations are serviced by the following airlines:

➡ Guadalajara – Aeromar, VivaAerobús

➡ Mexico City – Aeromar, Aeroméxico, Interjet, VivaAerobús, Volaris

➡ Monterrey – VivaAerobús

➡ Tijuana – Volaris

➡ Toluca – Interjet

BUS

Vallarta's **long-distance bus terminal** (Central Camionera; Map p541; ☎322-290-10-09; Bahía Sin Nombre 363) is off Hwy 200, about 10km north of downtown and 3km northeast of the airport. It's M$190 for a cab fare to downtown, or M$10 for a bus headed for 'Olas Altas' or 'Centro.'

Primera Plus (Map p544; ☎322-222-90-70; www.primeraplus.com.mx; Carranza 393; ☺7am-7pm Mon & Tue, to 10:30pm Wed-Sun) has a downtown office where you can buy tickets. If you're heading to Barra de Navidad, Manzanillo or other points south, you can save a trip to the bus terminal by boarding here.

Northbound **buses to Riviera Nayarit** (Map p541; Francisco Medina Ascencio s/n; ☺5am-9pm) towns depart frequently from a bus stop in front of Walmart, just south of Marina Vallarta.

CAR & MOTORCYCLE

Starting at about M$550 per day, on-the-spot car rentals can be pricey during high season; you'll often do better booking online, though extra insurance charges mean online rates aren't always what they appear to be. At other times, deep discounts are offered.

Numerous car-rental agencies maintain adjacent counters in the airport arrivals hall, with offices nearby. Below is a list of agencies with Vallarta offices.

Alamo (☎322-221-30-30; www.alamo.com.mx; Francisco Medina Ascencio 4690, Coral Plaza; ☺8am-10pm; ⓠ Ixtapa)

Avis (☎322-221-07-83; www.avis.mx; Francisco Medina Ascencio Km 7.5; ☺7am-11:30pm; ⓠ Ixtapa)

Budget (☎322-221-17-30; www.budget.com.mx; Francisco Medina Ascencio 141, Villa Las Flores; ☺7am-9pm)

Europcar (☎322-209-09-21; www.europcar.com.mx; Carretera Vallarta–Tepic Km 7.5, Aeropuerto Internacional Gustavo Díaz Ordaz; ☺7am-10pm)

Hertz (☎800-709-50-00; https://hertzmexico.com; Carretera Vallarta–Tepic Km 7.5, Aeropuerto Internacional Gustavo Díaz Ordaz; ☺7am-11pm)

National (☎322-209-03-52; www.nationalcar.com.mx; Francisco Medina Ascencio 4172; ☺7am-10pm)

Sixt (☎322-221-14-73; www.sixt.com.mx; Francisco Medina Ascencio 7930, Villa Las Flores; ☺7am-10pm; ⓠ Ixtapa)

Thrifty (☎322-221-29-84; www.thrifty.com.mx; Francisco Medina Ascencio 7926; ☺7am-10pm; ⓠ Ixtapa)

ⓘ Getting Around

TO/FROM THE AIRPORT

The cheapest way to get to/from the airport is on a local bus for M$10. 'Centro' and 'Olas Altas' buses go into town from a stop just outside the airport. Returning from town, 'Aeropuerto,' 'Juntas' and 'Ixtapa' buses stop at a pedestrian bridge near the airport entrance.

From the airport to the city, taxis charge fixed rates ranging from M$270 to M$360, depending on which neighborhood you're traveling to. Colectivo shuttle service costs M$124 to M$145. A taxi back to the airport from downtown costs around M$170.

BOAT

Vallarta's **water taxis** (Map p544; Playa de los Muertos pier; round trip M$340) serve the beautiful beaches on the southern side of the bay, some of which are accessible only by boat. Departing from the Playa de los Muertos pier, they head south around the bay, making stops at Playa de las Ánimas (25 minutes), Quimixto (40 minutes) and Yelapa (55 minutes); the round-trip fare is M$340 for any destination. Boats depart Puerto Vallarta every hour or two between 10am and 4:30pm, and leave from Yelapa (the end of the line) with the same frequency between

VALLARTA ART

You can't spell 'Vallarta' without 'art'. Appropriate, really, since the city is very rich in Mexican folk art if you know where to look. Check out www.puertovallartaartwalk.com for the weekly ArtWalk evenings (late October to mid-May, Wednesdays 6pm to 10pm), when you can do a self-guided tour of 16 of Vallarta galleries downtown, or pick up a *Vallarta ArtWalk* brochure at tourist info kiosks around town. Stores and galleries particularly worth looking out for include the following:

Galería Colectika (Map p544; ☑322-222-62-68; www.puertovallartaartwalk.com/colectika. html; Sánchez 858; ☺10am-8pm Mon-Fri, to 6pm Sat) If you only visit one art store in Vallarta, make it this one. The Huichol beadwork pieces here are mostly one of a kind, and there are some fine Huichol yarn art pieces, metalwork from Chiapas, and ceramics from Oaxaca and Chihuahua. Pieces come with authenticity stamps and owner Kevin and his assistants are happy to discuss the art in detail. They also offer Huichol beadwork classes (US$40) on request and free art tours on Wednesday nights at 6pm.

Caballito de Mar (Map p544; ☑322-129-52-09; www.puertovallartaartwalk.com/galeria-caballito-de-mar.html; Hidalgo 424; ☺10:30am-6:30pm Mon-Fri, to 4pm Sat) On display at this fantastic gallery are one-of-a-kind items acquired by owner Gloria on her road trips around Mexico, sourced directly from individual artists in the states of Oaxaca, Michoacán, Chihuahua and more. Come here for hand-woven table runners and other textiles, hand-painted folk art masks, exceptionally fine black clay ceramics from Oaxaca, silver jewelry, lithographs and much more.

Galería de Ollas (Map p544; ☑322-117-22-13; www.galeriadeollas.com; Corona 176; ☺11am-6pm Mon-Fri, to 2pm Sat) If you don't have time to travel all the way to the village of Mata Ortiz in Chihuahua, don't miss a visit to this gallery that showcases the exquisite, one-of-a-kind ceramics produced by more than 300 artisans. Each of the pots is decorated with a remarkable design, with colors obtained from natural dyes.

Peyote People (Map p544; ☑322-222-23-02; www.peyotepeople.com; Juárez 222; ☺10am-8pm Mon-Fri, to 6pm Sat) 🖉 Under the same ownership as Galería Colectika, this shop supports indigenous artisan communities and sells Huichol beadwork and yarn art of excellent quality, as well as wood carvings from the southern state of Oaxaca.

Tierra Huichol Olas Altas (Map p544; ☑322-779-77-18; https://tierrahuichol.com; Olas Altas 246; ☺9am-10pm) Come here for commercial but high-quality Huichol beadwork pieces, including some wonderful large works – toucans, parrots, jaguars. It also sells beautiful Huichol yarn art and some skeletal figures from Michoacán. There's another branch in Zona Romántica.

Galería Alpacora (Map p544; ☑322-222-41-79; Vallarta 232; ☺10am-8pm Mon-Sat) For delicate, brightly painted wooden figures of animals and mythical beasts from Oaxaca, fine ceramics from Chihuahua, skeletal figurines, hand-woven table runners and other textiles, this gallery in Zona Romántica is hard to beat.

Mundo de Azulejos (Map p544; ☑322-222-26-75; www.talavera-tile.com.mx; Carranza 374; ☺9am-7pm Mon-Fri, to 2pm Sat) This place has been making brightly colored Talavera tiles and ceramics for decades. On the walls you'll find photos of celebrities who've patronized the store, and even a letter of thanks from a British prime minister. Go upstairs to see artisans hand-paint the wares.

Olinalá (Map p544; ☑322-222-49-95, cell 322-1213576; http://brewsterbrockmann.com; Cárdenas 274; ☺11am-5pm Mon-Sat Oct-May, 11am-3pm Thu-Sat Jun-Sep) In business since 1978, this excellent little shop stocks authentic Mexican dance masks, folk art and rural antiques for genuine collectors.

7:30am and 3:45pm daily. Water taxis to the beaches also depart from Boca de Tomatlán.

Private yachts and *lanchas* can be hired from the southern side of the Playa de los Muertos pier, starting from around M$370 per hour. They'll take you to any secluded beach around the bay; most have gear aboard for snorkeling and fishing.

BUSES FROM PUERTO VALLARTA

DESTINATION	FARE (M$)	TIME	FREQUENCY (PER DAY)
Barra de Navidad/Melaque	214-345	4hr	5
Guadalajara	482-855	5½-6hr	frequent
Manzanillo	459-485	5-5½hr	4
Mazatlán	702	6½-9hr	6
Mexico City	1277-1408	11-13¼hr	7
Sayulita	81	1hr	frequent
Tepic	216-277	3-3½hr	frequent

BUS

Local buses operate every five minutes from 5am to 11pm on most routes, and cost M$10. **Plaza Lázaro Cárdenas** (Map p544; Suárez s/n) near Playa Olas Altas is a major departure hub. Northbound local buses also stop on **Insurgentes** (Map p544) near the corner of Madero. Southbound buses either pass through the center or loop round via a tunnel to Zona Romántica.

Northbound buses marked 'Aeropuerto,' 'Hotelera,' 'Mojoneras' and 'Juntas' pass through the city heading north to the airport and Marina Vallarta; the 'Mojoneras' bus also stops at Puerto Vallarta's long-distance bus terminal.

White-and-orange 'Boca de Tomatlán' buses (M$10) head south along the coastal highway through Mismaloya (20 minutes) to Boca de Tomatlán (30 minutes). They depart from the corner of **Badillo and Constitución** (Map p544) every 15 minutes.

TAXI

Cab prices are regulated by zones; the cost for a ride is determined by how many zones you cross. A typical trip from downtown to Zona Hotelera costs M$130; to the airport or the long-distance bus terminal it's M$170 to M$190; and to Mismaloya it's M$310. Always determine the price of the ride before you get in. Hailing a cab is easy in the city center along Morelos. There are several taxi stands, including one on **Insurgentes and Cárdenas** (Map p544; ☑ 322-222-24-22; cnr Insurgentes & Cárdenas), one on **Rodríguez at Matamoros** (Map p544) and one on **Olas Altas** (Map p544; ☑ 322-223-30-33; cnr Olas Altas & Carranza) at Plaza Lázaro Cárdenas.

Costalegre Beaches

South of Puerto Vallarta, the stretch of Mexico's Pacific coast from Chamela to Barra de Navidad is blessed with fine beaches and enough outdoor activities to keep nature enthusiasts thoroughly entertained; there's a sea-turtle camp, uninhabited islands providing prime bird-watching and snorkeling, and mangroves that are home to large crocs. In an effort to draw more visitors to the area, tourism promoters and developers refer to this shoreline as the 'Costalegre' (Happy Coast).

Playa Pérula
BEACH

(turnoff Hwy 200 Km 73) Playa Pérula, a sheltered beach at the northern end of the tranquil 11km-long Bahía de Chamela, is great for swimming and extended walks. There are cheap accommodations and a smattering of *palapa* restaurants. You can charter a *panga* (skiff) from here to the nine islands in the bay.

Campamento Majahuas
NATURE RESERVE

(☑ cell 322-2285806; www.facebook.com/campamentomajahuas; turnoff Hwy 200 Km 116; ☉ turtles nesting Jul-Nov) 🌿 This community-run project just north of Punta Pérula lets you camp and watch (with local guides) the turtles nest. It's become a destination for international students interested in turtles and their habitat, and offers volunteering programs. You'll need a vehicle to get here, or you can visit the camp on an overnight trip offered by MexEco Tours (p555).

You can camp here year-round, but July through November is the best time for turtle sightings.

Playa Tenacatita
BEACH

(turnoff Hwy 200 Km 28) On the palm-fringed Bahía Tenacatita, Playa Tenacatita has clear snorkeling waters and a large mangrove lagoon with good bird-watching. There is a land title in dispute here, with a development group in the process of trying to build on and partly privatize an otherwise public and relatively undeveloped beach. You can still visit, but camping is no longer allowed.

Playa El Negrito
BEACH

(turnoff Hwy 200 Km 64) At Bahía de Chamela, Playa El Negrito is an isolated, relaxing beach with a couple of restaurants but no hotels. The nine islands in the expansive bay are beautiful to see in silhouette at sunset.

❶ Getting There & Away

You'll need a car to reach most Costalegre beaches. San Patricio-Melaque and Manzanillo buses departing from Puerto Vallarta stop at the highway crossroads to Punta Pérula, where you can hopefully catch a taxi (M$60) into town.

Bahía de Navidad

The tight arc of the Bahía de Navidad is practically ringed by deep, honey-colored sand with two resort towns waving amiably at each other from either end. Situated 5km apart by road, but only a kilometer and a bit along the beach, Barra de Navidad and San Patricio-Melaque are siblings with distinct personalities. Barra is beloved by younger travelers for its attractive cobbled streets, chilled-out beach life and more active pursuits (boating, surfing), while Melaque, which is larger and more and more popular, draws snowbirds and families seeking that beachfront buzz.

San Patricio-Melaque

📞 315 / POP 11,770

Known by most as Melaque (meh-*lah*-keh), this beach resort is a popular vacation destination for Mexican families and a winter hangout that keeps on gaining in popularity. The main activities are swimming, walking in the crashing surf, watching pelicans fish at sunrise and sunset, climbing to the *mirador* (lookout) at the bay's western end, prowling the plaza and public market, and walking the beach to Barra de Navidad.

🏃 Activities & Tours

Pacific Adventures
WATER SPORTS

(📞 315-355-52-98; www.pacificadventures.mx; Gómez Farías 595; rentals per hour surfboard/paddleboard/bike M$90/150/20; ⏰ 9am-2pm & 4-7pm Mon-Sat, 10am-2pm Sun) An enthusiastic, youthful group that can rent you surfboards, paddleboards and more, and also teach you how to use them. They also rent out bikes if you're up for pedaling around town or to nearby Barra de Navidad.

★ Mex-Eco Tours
ECOTOUR

(📞 315-355-70-27; www.mex-ecotours.com; Gómez Farías 59-2; coffee plantation tour M$1300, sea-turtle camp M$2500; ⏰ 10am-2pm & 5-7pm Mon-Fri, 10am-2pm Sat) 🍃 Competent and friendly, this knowledgeable ecotourism company operates impressive day trips near Melaque and an array of multiday excursions throughout Mexico, all with a commitment to sustainable tourism. Highlights include visiting an indigenous women's cooperative coffee plantation, an overnight camping trip to a sea-turtle biological station, and boat trips. Turtle season is from August to November.

It also runs tours from Bucerías, near Puerto Vallarta.

🎉 Festivals & Events

Fiesta de San Patricio
CULTURAL

(⏰ Mar) Melaque honors its patron saint with a blowout week of festivities, including all-day parties, rodeos, a carnival, music, dances and nightly fireworks, leading up to St Patrick's Day (March 17).

🛏 Sleeping

Rates rise sharply at Christmas and Semana Santa; high season is November through April. Discounts are common for longer stays.

Hotel Bahía
HOTEL $

(📞 315-355-68-94; www.melaquehotelbahia.com; Legazpi 5; d/ste M$780/990; 🅿✳🛜🏊) Aside from being one of the cleanest budget hotels in town, the Bahía lies just one block from Melaque's most swimmable beach. Simple tiled rooms are painted in bright colors and feature cable TV, while suites include kitchenettes and refrigerators. The two-story property sits on Melaque's quiet north end, about 1km from downtown.

★ Villas El Rosario
de San Andres
APARTMENT $$

(📞 315-355-63-42; www.elrosariodesanandres.com; Hidalgo 10; d M$850-1070, bungalows M$1100-1300; 🅿🖥✳🛜🏊) This genial, family-run central complex offers bright, ceramic-tiled studios with attractive kitchenettes, high ceilings and flat-screen TVs. Sofa beds mean that children can be easily accommodated in most rooms. The rooftop deck is a wonderful common area with special mountain and sea views. There is also a small plunge pool with colorful mosaic.

Casa Misifus
SPA HOTEL $$

(☎315-355-84-47; http://casamisifus.wixsite.com/casamisifus; Av Veracruz 27; r incl breakfast M$1250; P❀❄❁✿) At the town's entrance and about five blocks from the beach, this well-run hotel exudes tranquility with its remarkably quiet pool area and rooftop terrace, full-service spa and six comfortable rooms with kitchens, balconies and snug beds.

★ La Paloma
BOUTIQUE HOTEL $$$

(☎315-355-53-45; www.lapalomamexico.com; Las Cabañas 13; r M$2250-2550, ste M$2650-2750, all incl breakfast; ◷Nov-Apr & Jun-Aug; P❀❄ ❁✿) Original art abounds at this oceanside boutique hotel hidden behind high walls. Singular, comfortable rooms have a kitchen/kitchenette plus terraces, and are vibrantly colorful, with quirky mirrors and bright ceramics. For the small price difference, consider the large penthouses with sea views – particularly Hideaway (No 15). With plush gardens and a beachside pool, it's a tranquil retreat.

Posada Pablo de Tarso
HOTEL $$$

(☎315-355-57-07; www.posadapablodetarso.com; Gómez Farías 408; d M$1800, bungalows from M$2300; P❀❄❁✿) Clustered around a courtyard bursting with greenery, this hotel with an attractive beachside pool area offers air-conditioned rooms or bungalows (with kitchenette but no air-con) that are cool and spacious, with beamed ceilings and terra-cotta floors. Some rooms have fridges too; those overlooking the road or the beach are largest. A couple of the bungalows are across the street.

✗ Eating

From 6pm to midnight, food stands serve inexpensive Mexican fare a block east of the plaza along Juárez, while daytime taco stands grace the block of Hidalgo, just south of the plaza. A row of *palapa* restaurants stretches along the beach at the western end of town.

La Flor del Café
CAFE $

(☎cell 314-1301222; www.facebook.com/laflordelcafemelaque07; Guzmán s/n, near Corona; mains M$50-140; ◷7am-1pm & 6-10pm Wed-Mon; ☎) On a plant-covered, brightly hued patio, this place eschews the hottest part of the day but opens mornings for tasty smoothies, juices, coffee, sandwiches and salads. In the evenings it adds a couple of heftier dishes to the menu, such as seafood fettuccine.

Quetzal de Laura
MEXICAN $$

(☎315-351-52-76; Guerrero 99; breakfast M$50-70, dinner M$130-260; ◷8am-1pm & 5-10pm Tue-Sun; ◿) Open to the elements, this cheerful yellow-hued restaurant is particularly good for inexpensive Mexican breakfasts, home-style *sopa azteca* or the house specialty – poblano chili stuffed with shrimp or mushrooms. Vegetarians will find plenty to choose from.

Tacos Scooby
MEXICAN $$

(☎cell 315-1075359; Obregón 34; snacks M$15-50, mains M$100-280; ◷5pm-1am; ☎) This neighborhood eatery does the tastiest *tacos al pastor* in town, and keeps expats coming back for the grilled ribs and seasonal prime rib steak on Sundays. Portions are generous and the owners couldn't be more welcoming. It does a fine *michelada* (beer with a kick of chili and lime) too.

🍷 Drinking & Nightlife

★ Taza Negra
CAFE

(☎315-355-70-80; www.latazanegra.com; Guerrero 112; coffee M$25-40; ◷8:30am-1pm Mon-Fri Oct-Apr, to noon May-Sep; ☎) This friendly neighborhood cafe has your back if you like to kick-start the day with a good strong cup of joe. Chiapas-grown beans are roasted onsite and served with efficiency and a smile, as are sticky cinnamon buns and blueberry-oatmeal-coconut muffins.

Esquina Paraíso
BAR

(☎cell 314-1624412; Obregón 13; ◷5pm-2am Dec-Mar) This curious open-air corner bar has done its decor out of driftwood, recycled

BUSES FROM SAN PATRICIO-MELAQUE

DESTINATION	FARE (M$)	TIME	FREQUENCY (PER DAY)
Guadalajara	351-495	5½-6½hr	frequent
Manzanillo	65-100	1-1½hr	frequent
Mexico City (Terminal Norte)	1257	12hr	1 (nightly)
Puerto Vallarta	338	4-5½hr	frequent

packing crates and the like; it's well worth a stop for the swing seats and nightly live music.

ℹ️ Getting There & Away

Buses stop on opposite sides of Carranza at the corner of Gómez Farías. Three companies have separate ticket offices around this intersection, with similar fares.

Local orange buses to Barra de Navidad (M$10, 15 minutes) leave every 15 minutes from the corner of López Mateos and Juárez at the southwest corner of the plaza, and do a slow circuit before hitting the main road. More direct green buses cost M$17.

Barra de Navidad

📞 315 / POP 5785

Barra de Navidad greets you with a mellow charm that's been winning visitors over for many years. It's a pueblo on a narrow isthmus between a lagoon and the beach that attracts younger gringos with surfing, SUP, bird- and crocodile-watching trips and laid-back beach life, though fewer folk come solely for the beach as it's being slowly lost to the encroaching seas.

Barra first came to prominence in 1564 when its shipyards produced the galleons used by conquistador Miguel López de Legazpi and Father André de Urdaneta to deliver the Philippines to King Felipe of Spain. By 1600, however, most of the conquests were being conducted from Acapulco, and Barra slipped into sleepy obscurity.

🏃 Activities & Tours

Barra's narrow beach is lovely to behold, but conditions are sometimes too rough for swimming. There's some decent surfing in the area, while the lagoon at the southern end of the bay is ideal for stand-up paddleboarding.

The waters near Barra are bristling with marlin, swordfish, albacore, *dorado* (dolphin fish), snapper and other, more rarefied catches.

Ecojoy Adventures ECOTOUR
(📱cell 315-1009240; www.facebook.com/ecojoyadventures; Costa Occidental 13, cnr Av Veracruz; biking & kayaking tours M$220, horseback riding per hour M$350, bike rental per day M$150; ⊘10am-2pm Mon-Fri) This tour outfit at the town's entrance offers biking and kayaking trips in and around the lagoon, and they can also hook you up with horseback riding along

the beach. If you prefer to go it alone, Ecojoy delivers bike rentals to your hotel's doorstep.

Sociedad Cooperativa de Servicios Turísticos BOATING
(📱cell 315-1077909; cnr Av Veracruz & López de Legazpi; lagoon tour M$500, fishing per hour M$800; ⊘9am-5pm) Trips into the Laguna de Navidad are a Barra highlight. This boat owner's cooperative books a variety of boat tours ranging from half-hour trips around the lagoon to half-day Playa del Coco jaunts (M$1500) and all-day jungle trips to Tenacatita (M$4500 per boat). Fishing trips on *lanchas* can also be arranged; they include gear and snorkeling stops.

🛏️ Sleeping

Barra has fewer beachfront rooms than neighboring Melaque. Book well in advance for high season (between November and May). Most options tend to be midrange, ranging from mediocre to decent.

Hotel Sarabi HOTEL $
(📱315-355-82-23; www.hotelsarabi.com; Av Veracruz 196; d with/without air-con M$650/550; ❄️✴️🛜🏊) In the heart of things in Barra, this hotel greets you with a giant Aztec calendar on the wall and three levels of basic, tiled rooms that are unlikely to make your social media posts for reasons good or bad. They are set around a gravel courtyard with a blue-tiled pool; the management is friendly and helpful.

★Hotel Delfín HOTEL $$
(📱315-355-50-68; www.hoteldelfinmx.com; Morelos 23; s/d/tr/apt M$928/978/1097/2104; 🅿️❄️✴️🛜🏊) 🅿️ The homey Delfín is one of Barra's best deals. It has large, pleasant rooms featuring shared balconies, a grassy pool area and a rooftop deck. Rooms with TV and air-con cost more but are otherwise identical; fans in the others usually do the trick as sea-facing rooms catch the breeze.

Spacious apartments with full kitchens suit families well. Repeat customers fill the place in winter. The ecofriendly Delfín composts organic waste and uses a solar hot-water system.

Hotel Bogavante RESORT $$
(📱315-355-81-09; www.bogavanteresortspa.com; López de Legazpi 259; r M$1200-1415, ste M$1850-2480; ❄️✴️🛜🏊) Right on the beach in the center of town, the Bogavante is a bit of a concrete monster from the outside, albeit with modern (if not particularly thrilling) rooms, onsite restaurant, spa and infinity pool with

an impressive view of Melaque and beyond. Worth splurging on an oceanside room or pricier suite sleeping up to five people.

Hotel Barra de Navidad HOTEL **$$**
(📞315-355-51-22; López de Legazpi 250; d M$1250-1450, ste M$1500-2150; 🅿️❄️🛜🏊) With stellar beach access, this white hotel could use a spruce-up and rooms could be cleaner, but boons include a mid-sized kidney-shaped pool. The open layout means you can hear the sea nearly throughout. Best are the seaside rooms, which are modern and nondescript but with terraces overlooking the waves and the sound of the surf as lullaby.

🍴 Eating & Drinking

Bananas BREAKFAST **$**
(📞315-355-55-54; López de Legazpi 250; breakfast M$70-95; ⏱8am-noon May-Nov, 8am-noon & 6-10pm Dec-Apr; 🛜) For breakfast with a fine ocean view, this 2nd-floor eatery above Hotel Barra de Navidad is hard to beat. Grab one of the terrace tables overlooking the beach, then peruse the menu of Mexican and North American favorites, from the trademark banana pancakes to eggs prepared every which way and *chilaquiles*.

★Barra Galería de Arte & Restaurant MEXICAN **$$**
(📞315-109-62-39; www.barragaleriadearte.com; Mazatlán 75; mains M$185-190; ⏱5-10pm) 🍴 Imagine a courtyard where secluded tables peek from behind a riot of greenery and fairy lights twinkle as evening falls. Owner Robert's photography adorns the two adjoining galleries, and old-timers sometimes make reservations weeks in advance, just to taste whatever family recipe his wife Rosy has cooked up that evening. Tequila tastings hosted on Tuesdays.

★El Manglito SEAFOOD **$$**
(📞315-355-81-09; www.facebook.com/elmanglito restaurantbar; Av Veracruz 17; mains M$170-250; ⏱noon-11pm; 🛜) With a lovely view over the lagoon and welcome breezes, this open-air restaurant with palm-thatch roofing and sand floors produces some really excellent seafood – the sweet oysters slither sensually down your tongue, the *aguachile* is punchy and tart, and you can get your fish and seafood prepared umpteen different ways.

Fortinos SEAFOOD **$$**
(📞314-337-90-75; Isla Navidad; mains M$150-170; ⏱1-8pm; 🛜) Across the lagoon, this waterfront restaurant's family-run kitchen has been winning folks over with its superb seafood dishes for more than 50 years. The *camarones costeños* (coconut shrimp with a pineapple-guayaba dipping sauce) pairs nicely with refreshing coconut water served in its shell. There's a small beach here if you're up for a swim after lunch.

To get here, **boats** (Av Veracruz) **FREE** just south of the *malecón* provide free transportation to and from restaurants on the lagoon.

★La Bruja COFFEE
(📞315-355-01-08; www.labrujacoffeebar.com; cnr Av Veracruz & Michoacán; ⏱9am-1pm Tue-Sat; 🛜) Come morning, regulars and visitors turn up, and Alison serves them excellent Oaxacan coffee from a local roastery (free refills), along with a frequently changing array of cakes (the blueberry-pecan-coffee combination is inspired). This is an informal expat community hub, where folks come for breakfast and to trade news.

Some local crafts and surfing T-shirts of Alison's own design are available for sale here.

ℹ️ Information

Banamex (Av Veracruz s/n; ⏱24hr) One of two ATMs just south of Barra's main plaza. Bring cash in case the machines dry up.

Tourist Office (📞315-355-83-83; www.costalegre.com; Av Veracruz 98; ⏱9am-5pm Mon-Fri) This regional office has maps and information about Barra and other towns of the Costalegre.

ℹ️ Getting There & Away

AIR

Barra de Navidad is served by Manzanillo's Aeropuerto Internacional Playa de Oro (p562) – it's 30km southeast of Barra on Hwy 200. The airport is served by taxis (M$550 to M$600, 30 minutes) and *colectivos* (M$200).

BOAT

Water taxis operate on demand from a dock at the southern end of Avenida Veracruz, offering service to the marina, golf course and various restaurants. Round-trip fare to any of the above is M$50; excursions along the coast are on offer from M$500.

BUS

The bus companies cluster around Avenida Veracruz just south of the marlin statue as you enter the center. There are direct **ETN** (📞315-355-84-00; www.etn.com.mx; Av Veracruz 273C) and **Primera Plus** (📞477-710-00-60; www.primeraplus.com.mx; Av Veracruz 269; ⏱6am-9pm) buses from Barra to Manzanillo (M$68 to M$80, 1½ hours), Puerto Vallarta (M$267 to M$278, five hours) and Guadalajara (M$520 to M$610, six hours). Some services (called *coordinados*) stop at both Barra and Melaque, but most only visit Melaque. You can reach Melaque by local orange buses (M$10, every 15 minutes, 6am to 9pm) that do circuits of both towns; the green buses (M$17) are more direct.

TAXI

From the taxi stand at the south end of Avenida Veracruz, fixed fares are as follows: San Patricio-Melaque (M$80 to M$90), Playa del Coco (M$220), Tanacatita (M$1200 return), Manzanillo airport (M$550) and Manzanillo (M$800).

ⓘ Getting Around

Barra de Navidad is very walkable but if you want to get to nearby Melaque on your own two wheels, you can rent a brand-new bicycle (M$150 per day) or scooter (M$650 per day) from **Barra Tours** (☏ 315-112-15-21; Av Veracruz 204; ⊙10am-6pm).

Manzanillo

☏ 314 / POP 162,310

Though it boasts miles of beaches, Manzanillo puts bread on the table by being Mexico's busiest seaport; tourism takes second place. There are some good surfing beaches here, however, though the best ones, some 20km from the old town, require a longish bus trip.

Despite that – and the fact that the beaches are backed by a busy highway where hotels and chain restaurants jostle for space with car dealerships and filling stations – there are some super places to stay here, particularly on the picturesque Península de Santiago, which offers spectacular coastal views.

The old town is atmospheric, with its attractive plaza, the people-watching on the boardwalk at sunset and its *fuentes danzarinas* (dancing fountains). The huge blue sculpture on the waterside plaza is a nod to Manzanillo's self-proclaimed status as the 'Sailfish Capital of the World.'

🐚 Beaches

★ Playa La Boquita   BEACH
Playa La Boquita is a beach with calm waters at the mouth of a lagoon where fishermen lay out their nets to dry by day, and shove off by night. The beach is lined with seafood restaurants where you can hang out for the day. A shipwreck just offshore makes this a popular snorkeling spot.

Playa Azul   BEACH
This 6km-long, curving strip of sand is rather steep and buffeted by Pacific surf, so it's better for sunbathing and walking than swimming. It stretches northwest from Playa Las Brisas to the Península de Santiago.

Playa Las Brisas   BEACH
Just across the harbor from the old town, this long stretch of sand is backed by a fast-growing zone of hotels, restaurants and bars. Buses marked 'Las Brisas' run along this stretch of the seafront.

Playa Olas Altas   BEACH
True to its name (Big Waves Beach), this attractive stretch of sand has lovely surfable breakers and is backed by a handful of simple beach restaurants.

Playa Santiago   BEACH
On the far side of the Península de Santiago from town, this is one of Manzanillo's cleaner beaches and part of the 8km-long Santiago Bay. Buses marked 'Miramar' run all the way along the bay.

Playa Miramar   BEACH
Boasting the best surfing and bodysurfing waves in the area, the long and beautiful Playa Miramar is an ideal place to take the plunge and rent a surfboard from a beach shack. Catch a bus marked 'Miramar' to get here.

🏄 Activities

Water sports are Manzanillo's big draw, from surfing to diving.

The scuba diving here is very interesting, with a highly accessible wreck, plus reefs in decent condition, tunnels, deep-water pinnacles luring pelagics (plus whales and mantas in season) at **Los Frailes**, and alluring swim-through arches at **Roca Elefante**. November to May is the best time to dive.

🛌 Sleeping

Manzanillo's cheapest hotels are located downtown, in the blocks surrounding the main plaza, and there are several decent midrange beach hotels along Playa Azul and Playa Las Brisas. Top-end places can be found on the Península de Santiago.

Greater Manzanillo

Greater Manzanillo

◎ Top Sights
1 Playa La Boquita A1

◎ Sights
2 Playa Azul...C2
3 Playa Las Brisas D2
4 Playa Miramar A1
5 Playa Olas Altas B1
6 Playa Santiago B1

⊜ Sleeping
7 Casa del Artista B1
8 Dolphin Cove Inn C1
9 Hostal Tzalahua................................C1

10 Hotel Colonial....................................D3
11 Pepe's Hideaway..............................B2

⊗ Eating
12 Blueberry Bistro Cafe........................B1
13 Chantilly D3
14 El Fogón C1
15 Legazpi C1
16 Mariscos El Aliviane B1
17 Mariscos La Huerta D2
18 Tacos de Barbacoa Ericka...................B1

◎ Drinking & Nightlife
19 Hostal Olas Altas B1

Hotel Colonial HISTORIC HOTEL **$**
(☎314-332-10-80; www.facebook.com/colonial
hotelmanzanillo; Bocanegra 28; s/d/f
M$640/790/1240; P⊖❋☎) One block
from Manzanillo's waterfront plaza, this
characterful 1940s hotel is reminiscent
of a colonial hacienda, with tiled outdoor
hallways, heavy wooden beams and central courtyard with a fountain. Spacious
rooms are set on four floors surrounding
the courtyard and have elegant drapes and
wood furnishings. Downstairs rooms are
darkish and may suffer from restaurant
noise.

Hostal Tzalahua HOSTEL **$**
(☎cell 311-1184546; www.facebook.com/hostal
tzalahua; Pájaro de Fuego 1; dm/d M$160/420;
⊖☎❋; ☐Las Brisas) Guests can rest easy
at this well-run hostel in a quiet residential
area about a block from Playa Azul. Opt to
stay in a nine-bed mixed dorm or one of
seven private rooms (five with bathrooms),
which are all cheerful and clean. A rear garden with hammocks and a swimming pool
provides a nice spot to chill.

★ Casa del Artista B&B **$$**
(☎314-334-47-04; www.casaartistamanzanillo.
com; Calle 4 No 12, Colinas de Santiago; ste incl

breakfast M$1000-1400; [P][icons]; [icon]Ruta 1) A gloriously peaceful spot up a hill on the landward side of the main road, this B&B has hummingbirds thrumming in the garden. Its four individually styled suites have kitchenettes, owner Roberto is super-helpful and there are lovely views of the bay from the hammocks in the common area.

Dolphin Cove Inn
HOTEL $$
([icon]314-334-15-15; www.dolphincoveinn.com; Av Vista Hermosa s/n; d/ste incl breakfast from M$1450/2470; [P][icons]; [icon]Ruta 8) This cliffside hotel has awe-inspiring views and huge, spacious and bright rooms on tiered floors that cascade to a pretty bayside swimming pool. Units range from basic doubles to two-room suites sleeping four, all with marble floors, kitchens or kitchenettes, vaulted ceilings and sea-view balconies. Bathrooms and fittings are rather modest for this price, but the outlook is sublime.

Pepe's Hideaway
CABAÑAS $$$
([icon]314-334-16-90, US 213-261-6821; www.pepeshideaway.com; Camino Don Diego 67, La Punta; cabins per person incl meals US$200-250; [P][icons]) This serendipitous find is set on a wild rocky point where you're lulled to sleep by the wind rustling in the coconut palms and waves lapping at your hammock deck. Seven individually styled, thatched-roof cabins with vibrant paint jobs are the ultimate in romantic seclusion.

Rates are all-inclusive. You'll need a vehicle to get here.

🍴 Eating & Drinking

The old town, within several blocks of the main plaza, is better for old-school, family restaurants that serve Mexican classics. Numerous seafood restaurants are spread out along the various beaches, taco stands dot central Manzanillo, while the town's fanciest offerings are found on the Península de Santiago.

Tacos de Barbacoa Ericka
TACOS $
([icon]314-334-22-97; www.facebook.com/tacoserickaoficial; Blvd Miguel de la Madrid 27; tacos M$15; ⊙9am-4pm Tue-Sun) This locally renowned *taquería* does one thing and does it very well: *tacos de barbacoa*, with the marinated pork meat smoky and redolent of spices, served in either soft *(blanditos)* or crunchy *(dorados)* tacos, with a generous spoon of punchy green salsa on top and fresh coconut water to wash them down with.

Blueberry Bistro Cafe
BISTRO $
([icon]314-336-79-90; www.facebook.com/blueberrybistro; Av Audiencia 37; breakfast M$55-90, dinner M$75-130; ⊙8am-2pm & 6-11pm; [icon]) Attracting a mix of hotel-dwelling gringos and locals, this contemporary cafe does many things well, from breakfast platters that include waffles and eggs prepared any way you wish to good coffee. As the day progresses, the menu moves on to fish tacos and other crowd-pleasers, with craft beer to help them on their way.

Mariscos El Aliviane
SEAFOOD $
([icon]cell 314-3536588; Playa Santiago; mains M$30-130; ⊙11am-4:30pm Mon-Sat) At this little street stall across from Hotel Playa Santiago, locals crowd wooden tables for *jaiba* (crab) *tostadas, cócteles* (seafood cocktails) and platters of shrimp, octopus, scallops and ceviche. Beers are icy and the house habanero salsa sets your lips on fire. According to residents, this is the best *cevichería* in Manzanillo, but staff won't win any congeniality awards.

Mariscos La Huerta
SEAFOOD $$
([icon]314-334-06-48; Blvd Miguel de la Madrid 873; mains M$149-275; ⊙11am-8:30pm; [icon]) A giant Neptune statue points you toward this busy seafront *palapa* restaurant. With the waves practically lapping at your table and involuntary twitching on the part of the diners to salsa music, choose between well-executed dishes such as *aguachile* and *pescado zarandeado*.

Chantilly
MEXICAN $$
([icon]314-332-01-94; www.chantillymanzanillo.com; cnr Juárez & Madero; mains M$55-240; ⊙7:30am-10pm) Right on the main plaza, this family-run restaurant is a local institution, drawing a loyal clientele for 70 years with their enchiladas, quesadillas, garlic shrimp, *carne asada* and other Mexican standards. Breakfast is a lively time to dine; go for the *huevos divorciados* and a good coffee.

El Fogón
STEAK $$
([icon]314-333-30-94; Blvd Miguel de la Madrid Km 9.5; mains M$150-240; ⊙1pm-midnight; [icons]; [icon]Ruta 1) Under a tiled roof with an open-air rustic style, this steakhouse throws prime cuts of meat on the grill just long enough to sear, while fresh tortillas are busily made in the hut opposite. Portions are large – even the tortilla chips come with a whole platter of sauces – and the pork tacos and *arrachera* (hanger steak) come highly recommended.

Legazpi
INTERNATIONAL $$$

(☎ 314-331-01-01; www.lasbrisashotels.com.mx/en/manzanillo/cuisine; Av Vista Hermosa, Las Hadas; mains M$340-470; ⊙ 7-11pm Fri-Sun) One of several restaurants that are part of the Las Hadas resort, Legazpi offers one of Manzanillo's best meals, its cuisine straddling the Mediterranean with an emphasis on Italy. Expect elegant attire (you have to dress up), live piano music, and beautifully presented fish, veal and pasta dishes put together with a light touch and a real understanding of flavors.

★ Hostal Olas Altas
BAR

(☎ 314-333-03-90; www.facebook.com/hostalolasaltas; Blvd Miguel de la Madrid 15675; ⊙ noon-2:30am; 🛜; 🚌 Ruta 1) At the center of Manzanillo's music, arts and surf scene, this hostel's beach bar hosts live bands on Saturday nights. The occasional surf tourney or art show always livens up the party atmosphere on the beach. Accommodations here are cool, appealing to night owls who like to party.

🛈 Information

Secretaría de Turismo (☎ 314-333-22-77; Blvd Miguel de la Madrid 875A; ⊙ 8:30am-4:30pm Mon-Fri) On the main waterfront boulevard, halfway between downtown and Península de Santiago. Dispenses limited information on Manzanillo and the state of Colima.

🛈 Getting There & Away

AIR

Aeropuerto Internacional Playa de Oro (☎ 314-333-11-19; www.aeropuertosgap.com.mx; Carretera Manzanillo–Barra de Navidad Km 42) lies between a long and secluded white-sand beach and tropical groves of bananas and coconuts, 35km northwest of Manzanillo's Zona Hotelera. Aeroméxico and Aeromar provide direct services to Mexico City.

BUS

Manzanillo's **Central Camionera** (☎ 314-336-80-35; Obras Marítimas s/n; 🚌 Ruta 8) is 7km northeast of downtown. It's an organized place with tourist information, phones, eateries and left-luggage facilities.

CAR & MOTORCYCLE

Renting a car is not only convenient for exploring the Costalegre beaches northwest of Manzanillo's airport, but also recommended for getting the most out of Manzanillo in general. There are several firms at the airport; some also have downtown offices.

Alamo (☎ 314-333-24-30; www.alamo.com.mx; Blvd Miguel de la Madrid 1570; ⊙ 8am-8pm; 🚌 Ruta 1)

Budget (☎ 314-333-14-45; www.budget.com.mx; Blvd Miguel de la Madrid Km 10; ⊙ 9am-2pm & 4-7pm Mon-Fri, 9am-2pm Sat; 🚌 Ruta 1)

Sixt (☎ 314-333-31-91; www.sixt.com.mx; Carretera Manzanillo–Barra de Navidad Km 42, Aeropuerto Internacional Playa de Oro; ⊙ 7am-7pm)

Thrifty (☎ 314-334-32-82; www.thrifty.com.mx; Carretera Manzanillo–Barra de Navidad Km 42, Aeropuerto Internacional Playa de Oro; ⊙ 7am-7pm; 🚌 Ruta 1)

🛈 Getting Around

BUS

Local buses marked 'Santiago,' 'Las Brisas' and 'Miramar' head around the bay to the towns of San Pedrito, Salahua, Santiago and Miramar, and to beaches along the way. Route 8 runs from Playa Las Brisas to the bus terminal and then does a circuit of the Península de Santiago. Take route 2 from the old town to reach the bus terminal or Playa Olas Altas. Fares are M$11.

There is no public transport to the airport, so you have to take a *colectivo* (M$160) or taxi (M$360 to M$460, depending on the zone).

BUSES FROM MANZANILLO

DESTINATION	FARE (M$)	TIME	FREQUENCY (PER DAY)
Barra de Navidad	267	1-1½hr	9
Colima	145-180	1½-2hr	half-hourly
Guadalajara	472-655	5-6hr	frequent
Lázaro Cárdenas	581	6-8½hr	2
Mexico City (Terminal Norte)	1169-1585	11½-12hr	5
Puerto Vallarta	455	5-5½hr	2
San Patricio-Melaque	100	1-1½hr	half-hourly
Zihuatanejo	780	8-8½hr	2 (nightly)

TAXI

Taxis are plentiful in Manzanillo, and fixed prices depend on the zone. Always agree on a price before getting into one. From the main bus terminal, a cab fare is around M$60 to the main plaza or Playa Azul, and M$80 to Península de Santiago or Playa Miramar.

Michoacán Coast

Highway 200 hugs the shoreline most of the way along the 250km coastline of Michoacán, one of Mexico's most beautiful states. This is one of the nation's most memorable drives: the serpentine road passes dozens of untouched beaches, some with wide expanses of golden sand, some tucked into tiny rocky coves, and some at river mouths where quiet estuaries harbor multitudes of birds. Several have gentle waves that are good for swimming; others have big breakers suitable for surfing. Many beaches are uninhabited, but some shelter communities, many of which are largely indigenous. Mango, coconut and banana plantations line the highway; the green peaks of the Sierra Madre del Sur form a lush backdrop inland. Signs along Hwy 200 mark the turnoffs for most beaches of interest, including **Ixtapilla** (Km 180), **La Manzanillera** (Km 174), **Motín de Oro** (Km 167), **Zapote de Tizupán** (Km 103), **Pichilinguillo** (Km 95) and **Huahua** (Km 84).

ℹ Information

SAFE TRAVEL

The 150km stretch of the Michoacán coast between Las Brisas and Caleta de Campos has traditionally been cartel-controlled, first by the notorious La Familia, then by the Knights Templar. In the wake of cartel wars and government operations, these organizations have broken down, though their main business line certainly hasn't.

Various 'self-defense groups' operate here now, and they are difficult to classify. A range of issues including poverty, indigenous rights and lack of infrastructure and jobs are enmeshed with ongoing criminal activity, drug production and transportation, and battles of loyalties. There are no police or military bases here, though heavily armed patrols run up and down the highway and you'll see temporary military checkpoints from time to time.

What does this mean for the visitor? Very little in practical terms. Roadblocks are sometimes enforced to protest against the government, so you might be delayed for a while (from hours to a couple of days), but theft or violence against tourists was never tolerated by the big cartels

ℹ MICHOACÁN'S BEACHFRONT PARADORES

Along Hwy 200 you'll see frequent signs for tourist lodgings known as *paradores turísticos* (government-run tourist lodgings). Despite mostly wearing the forlorn look of government projects paid for then not maintained, these offer reasonably priced accommodations right on or just above the beach with killer views. Some are now run privately. Also, if you have a tent, you can always ask to camp next to a beachfront *enramada* (thatch-covered, open-air restaurant) on any given beach; for the price of a meal at said *enramada*, you'll have the wild sweep of coast all to yourself.

and the region remains comparatively safe. Locals strongly recommend not driving at night along this stretch, however, and hitchhiking should be avoided.

Bear in mind that there's practically no phone signal along the coastal road, so make sure you're self-sufficient.

San Juan de Alima

☑ 313 / POP 250

Twenty kilometers into Michoacán is the cobblestoned town of San Juan de Alima (turn off Hwy 200 at Km 211). It's a pretty place with a pristine beach and is seasonally popular with surfers due to its medium-sized breakers just off the coast. There are several beachfront restaurants and modern hotels.

Hotel Hacienda Trinidad   HOTEL **$$**
(☑ 313-327-92-00; www.haciendatrinidad.com.mx; Blvd San Juan de Alima s/n; d/f/ste M$1520/2625/1950; P🖭❄🛜🌊) The village's most upscale offering has decent rooms, suite with a Jacuzzi, a lovely pool surrounded by lush vegetation, and a characterful restaurant that looks like it was decked out by some ardent gauchos. High-season prices are ridiculously steep in July, August and December, but you can get fair deals the rest of the year.

El Parador   SEAFOOD **$$**
(☑ 313-327-90-38; www.facebook.com/elhotelparador; Blvd San Juan de Alima Oriente 1; mains M$90-220; ⊙9am-9pm; P❄🛜) Don't let the casual appearance of this seafront restaurant fool you: plastic tables and chairs aside, the seafood repast placed in front of you is

PLAYA MARUATA

With clear turquoise waters and golden sandy beaches, **Playa Maruata** (turnoff Hwy 200 Km 150) is arguably the most beautiful beach in Michoacán. The Nahua fishing village has a bit of a hippie reputation, attracting beach bums from all over. It's a tranquil, friendly place to hang out with your sweetie or a large stack of paperbacks. It's also a prime nesting site for green turtles (nightly from July to December).

Maruata actually has three beaches, each with its own unique character. The left (eastern) is the longest, a 3km pristine crescent-shaped beach with creamy yellow sand and calm waves perfect for swimming and snorkeling. The small middle arc is OK for strong swimmers. It's sheltered by a climbable rocky headland riddled with caves, tunnels and blowholes, and marked by the unusual Dedo de Dios (God's Finger) formation rising from the sea. The far-right (western) beach is known as **Playa de los Muertos** (Beach of the Dead), and for good reason: it has dangerous currents and ferocious waves. During low tide you can scale the rocks on the far-right side of Muertos to reach a secluded cove where discreet nude sunbathing is tolerated. But don't get stuck here when the tide comes in. A crucifix on the rocks serves as a stark memorial to the people who have been swallowed by the sea.

Maruata is an extremely poor pueblo, though a couple of recent infrastructure projects now stand in the town center. You'll find shops and simple eateries around the semi-derelict plaza. The *enramadas* (thatch-covered, open-air restaurants) on the left beach serve fresh seafood and are also your best bet for camping: most charge from M$60 per person to pitch a tent or rent a hammock. There are rustic *cabañas* for M$350 to M$450, but the best accommodations are at the **Centro Ecoturístico Ayult-Maruata** (☑ cell 555-1505110; https://nuestrodestino.jimdo.com/ecoturismo-en-michoacán/centro-ecoturístico-ayult-maruata; hammock/d/tr/q M$100/650/820/1100; P🐶😺🌐) 🍴.

Lázaro Cárdenas–bound buses from Manzanillo will leave you at the town entrance on Hwy 200, from where it's a short walk into town.

equal to any fine-dining establishment. Try the *camarones zarandeados* (shrimp marinated and grilled in a tangy, spicy sauce).

The hotel itself offers a variety of ho-hum rooms; the best have air-con and balconies.

ⓘ Getting There & Away

Buses (M$61, one hour) departing every two hours from the Tecomán bus terminal will leave you at the town entrance on Hwy 200.

Barra de Nexpa

📞 753 / POP UNDER 100

At Km 55.6, just north of Puente Nexpa bridge, and 1km from Hwy 200 down a rough cobbled road, lies the small, unpaved, laid-back community of Nexpa, a hamlet misty with sea spray. It's long been a haven for surfers, attracted to the sandbar and long left-hand break at the river mouth, which can rise to double overhead. Rides can go 500m or more here. Wave-riding aside, there's a beautiful swimming hole you can walk to (ask the locals). There are no ATMs in town so bring cash.

Rio Nexpa Surf Resort CABAÑAS $
(☑ cell 753-1160570; www.rionexpasurfresort. com; s/d US$35/40, cabins US$40-72; P😺🌐🍴) There's a handy general store, a surf shop with board rental, and some sweet, simple digs here, including a cabin for up to five people. Expect super-clean tiled floors, rain showers and fridge; some rooms have air-con. Host Jorge also rents rooms in his large three-bedroom house.

Cabañas Alba CABAÑAS $
(☑ cell 753-1185082; www.hospedajesalba.com; d/q M$550/780; P😺) These rustic two-story cabins, some sleeping up to six people, provide a homey feel with their full kitchens, porches and balconies with ocean views, and are among the nicest accommodations in the village. The onsite restaurant opens during high season and there's also a *temascal* (steam bath) to sweat out those toxins. No air-con or wi-fi.

Chicho's INTERNATIONAL $$
(☑ cell 753-1184203; breakfast M$70-80, lunch & dinner M$90-170; ⊙9am-9pm) One of several *palapas* lining the beach, family-run

Chicho's is a great choice for meals thanks to gargantuan breakfast smoothies, pancakes, solid plates of shrimp and burgers, and inspiring views of wave-riding surfers.

ⓘ Getting There & Away

Sur de Jalisco buses (M$92, 1½ hours) depart from the Galeana bus terminal (p565) in Lázaro Cárdenas five times daily.

Caleta de Campos

☑ 753 / POP 2610

Set up on the bluffs, which taper toward an azure bay, Caleta (turn off Hwy 200 at Km 50) draws surfers in winter, its streets charmingly unpaved and folks on horseback a regular sight here.

Also known as Bahía Bufadero, Caleta de Campos is a regional service center with most of the essentials (but no ATMs in town). There's a surf shop and a protected cove suited to novice surfers, as well as several hotels in the center.

Partour Caleta (☑ cell 753-1141111; www. partourcaleta.com; Hwy 200 Km 51; d M$1100, ste M$2700-3300; ❀❄❖) has a fabulous clifftop view over the wild beach and waving palms. Its comfortable ocean-view units, with terra-cotta floors and cable TV, surround a *palapa* bar and lounge area. The best suite has a kitchenette, dining room and private terrace with Jacuzzi. Stairs lead down to a rocky beach.

It's on the highway 1km north of town.

ⓘ Getting There & Away

Sur de Jalisco buses (M$85, 1¼ hours) depart from the Galeana bus terminal in Lázaro Cárdenas five times daily. Hourly *colectivos* depart Caleta's main plaza for Lázaro Cárdenas (M$72, 1¼ hours) from 6:30am to 8pm. A taxi between Caleta de Campos and Barra de Nexpa costs M$80.

Lázaro Cárdenas

☑ 753 / POP 82,615

As an industrial port city, Lázaro has nothing of real tourist interest – but because it's a hub for buses up and down the coast, travelers regularly pass through. Lázaro is also a regional service center, but with excellent beaches and waves so near, there is no reason to spend the night.

ⓘ Getting There & Away

Lázaro has several bus terminals, all within a few blocks of each other. From the most useful **main bus terminal** (Galeana; ☑ 753-532-30-06; Av Lázaro Cárdenas 1810), operators offer services to Manzanillo, Uruapan, Morelia, Colima, Caleta de Campos, Barra de Nexpa, Guadalajara and Mexico City.

Estrella Blanca (☑ 753-532-11-71; www. estrellablanca.com.mx; Francisco Villa 65) goes to destinations including Puerto Vallarta, Mazatlán and as far north as Tijuana. The **Estrella de Oro** (☑ 753-532-02-75; www.estrellaedeoro. com.mx; Corregidora 318) terminal is one block north and two blocks west of Estrella Blanca and serves Zihuatanejo, Acapulco, Manzanillo and Mexico City.

Troncones

☑ 755 / POP 710

Years back, Troncones was a sleepy fishing and farming village. These days, expat homes and B&Bs make the long beachfront road resemble a California subdivision rather than the traditional Mexican villages at either end. The attraction is obvious: pristine beaches, a laid-back atmosphere and world-class surfing to suit all abilities. If you're looking to do more than just kick back, there's good mountain biking in the hills and trips to check out petroglyphs in a nearby cave, plus soaks in local hot springs.

BUSES FROM LÁZARO CÁRDENAS

DESTINATION	FARE (M$)	TIME	FREQUENCY (PER DAY)
Acapulco	348-433	6-7hr	frequent
Guadalajara	650-747	8-10hr	6
Manzanillo	410-581	7hr	hourly
Mexico City	805-981	8-11hr	frequent
Morelia	547-647	4-5hr	frequent
Uruapan	370-433	3-4hr	11
Zihuatanejo	128-159	1½-2hr	frequent

The village is located about 25km north-west of Ixtapa, at the end of a 4km paved road from Hwy 200. The road ends at a T-intersection, from where the beachfront road continues 4.5km northwest to neighboring **Majahua** via Troncones Point and Manzanillo Bay.

Majahua is a traditional fishing village with a few *enramadas* overlooking a pristine sweep of beach.

🏃 Activities

The swimming in the protected cove off Playa Manzanillo is glorious; the water is calmest in the middle of the bay. Mountain biking, fishing, visits to the nearby hot springs and spelunking through the limestone cave system near Majahua can be arranged through your accommodations and tour companies.

Prime Surfboards SURFING
(☑755-103-00-05, cell 755-1143504; www.prime surfboards.com.mx; Av de la Playa s/n; surf lesson US$70, board rental per day US$30; ⊙7am-8pm) Around 500m north of the T-intersection, expert surfer Bruce Grimes offers two-hour lessons (he's a hard taskmaster) and board repair. He also designs custom boards and offers surfing accommodations rentals year-round.

Tsunami Surf OUTDOORS
(☑755-103-00-18, cell 755-5589204; Av de la Playa s/n; surf lesson US$50, bicycle/surfboard/SUP rental per day US$10/20/30) This enthusiastic outfit rents surfboards and SUPs as well as bicycles and offers surfing lessons and boat trips to the best breaks. It also runs mountain-biking tours (price depends on duration and number of participants) and tours to the nearby hot springs and cave.

Inn at Manzanillo Bay WATER SPORTS
(☑755-553-28-84; www.manzanillobay.com; Av de la Playa s/n, Playa Manzanillo; surfboard & bicycle per day US$25, kayak & paddleboard per day US$40) Near the point, this hotel rents out an excellent selection of short- and longboards, bicycles, paddleboards and kayaks.

👉 Tours

Costa Nativa Ecotours ECOTOUR
(☑cell 755-1007499; www.tronconesecotours. com; Av de la Playa s/n; kayaking/hiking/snorkeling M$700/850/1250; ⊙office 9am-6pm Mon-Sat Oct-May) 🖉 This respectable outfit runs low-impact ecotours such as three-hour kayaking excursions that offer excellent

wildlife-watching, guided hiking in the Sierra Madre ending at a swimming hole, visits to the Majahua cave and snorkeling around Isla Ixtapa. Book online or inquire inside the Casa Croma boutique.

🛏 Sleeping

There are numerous places to stay; most are located along Troncones' main waterfront road. Reservations are advisable during the high season (November through April), when some places require multiple-night stays. During low season, prices can be 25% to 50% lower, but some places close during summer.

★Troncones Point Hostel HOSTEL $
(☑755-553-28-86; www.tronconespointhostel.com; Lote 49, Manzana 15, Troncones Point, off Av de la Playa; dm/tents US$19/50, r US$38-72; P😊🐕) 🖉 Handy for surfing at Troncones Point, this imaginatively designed hostel features an interesting configuration of rooms, ranging from snug dorms to 'luxury' tents and a duplex room with separate entrances. All share an alfresco shower, composting toilets and a marvelous kitchen-lounge area with sea views. Board rental is available and owners Tom and Liz are treasure troves of local knowledge.

Casa Delfín Sonriente B&B $$
(☑755-553-28-03; www.casadelfinsonriente.com; Av de la Playa s/n; r/ste incl breakfast US$85/119; 😊❄🐕❄) With welcoming caretakers and a very laid-back atmosphere, this B&B is a super place to stay. If available, grab one of the amazing upstairs suites, which have hanging beds, full kitchens, no doors (there's a lockable drawer for your valuables) and a shared rooftop patio with views of the wild Pacific. It's about a kilometer from the T-junction.

There's a guest kitchen, and staff can be brought in to cook meals for you.

Hotel Playa Troncones HOTEL $$
(☑755-103-00-79; hotelplayatroncones@hotmail. com; Av de la Playa s/n; d M$1100; P❄🐕❄) Conveniently located in the center of town and reasonably priced by Troncones' standards (especially during low season), rooms here are fairly straightforward with air-con, comfortable beds, spotless bathrooms inlaid with river rock, and ocean views from the upstairs units. Kids like the small pool.

★Lo Sereno BOUTIQUE HOTEL $$$
(☑755-103-00-73; www.losereno.com; Av de la Playa s/n; d US$290; 😊❄🐕❄) This adults-only, creeper-clad retreat is serenity itself, its 10

stylish rooms masterpieces of understatement, decked out in soothing creams. Creature comforts are taken care of: there are super-comfortable beds, alfresco rain showers, sea views from every room and bug netting that allows you to enjoy the sea breeze. Infinity pool and gourmet Mexican restaurant are bonuses.

Los Raqueros
B&B $$$

(☑ 755-553-28-02; www.raqueros.com; Av de la Playa s/n; d incl breakfast US$95-185; P ⊖ ❄ 🗕 🏊) Offering terrific value along the precious Playa Manzanillo beachfront, this well-run B&B is ideal for relaxation on its soft sands and manicured gardens. Rooms are colorful with open-plan bathrooms and some afford sweet bay views, while oceanfront family-friendly bungalows sleep four and come with open-air kitchens. The pool is wheelchair-friendly. It's 3km north of the T-intersection.

Inn at Manzanillo Bay
HOTEL $$$

(☑ 755-553-28-84; www.manzanillobay.com; Av de la Playa s/n, Playa Manzanillo; ste US$158-198; P ⊖ ❄ 🗕 🏊) In an ideal setting on Troncones' prettiest beach, this hotel has upscale thatched-roof bungalows with king-sized beds, original art, handmade marble sinks, rain showers and hammocked terraces surrounding a pool. There's also a popular restaurant and bar, a surf shop, bike rental (p566) and easy access to the Troncones Point break.

Casa Ki
B&B $$$

(☑ 755-553-28-15; www.casa-ki.com; Av de la Playa s/n; bungalow US$95-125, house US$250; ❄ 🗕 🏊) Clustered around a pool, family-friendly Casa Ki comprises colorful bungalows in all hues of the rainbow, peeking out from the verdant vegetation. There are games for kids and a well-stocked library for quiet time in the hammock, and several rescue cats in the garden, as well as visiting ones from Casa Kitty (same owners) across the street.

Tres Mujeres
BOUTIQUE HOTEL $$$

(☑ 755-553-28-89; www.tresmujeresparadise.com; Av de la Playa s/n; d/f US$185/220; ❄ 🗕 🏊) Consisting of just nine individually styled rooms in various pastel hues, this haven of tranquility is the epitome of hippie chic. There's a yoga deck overlooking the ocean, hammocks to sway in amid manicured grounds and an infinity pool. All rooms face the waves; the only quibble is that you have to choose between air-con and mosquitoes (no bug netting).

Eating

Cenaduría Cristina
TACOS $

(☑ cell 755-1030013; next to Iglesia Jesús Sacramento; tacos M$17; ⊙ 6-10pm Fri-Wed) Come evening, the open kitchen of this neighborhood *taquería* fills with fragrant smoke and the sizzle of meat on the griddle as members of the family busy themselves with dishing up their specialty: *tacos de barbacoa.* The enchiladas, drenched in piquant red or green salsa, are also good.

★ Toro del Mar
SEAFOOD $$

(☑ cell 755-1083074; Av de la Playa s/n, Playa Majahua; mains M$100-190; ⊙ 9am-9pm) On the southern end of Playa Majahua, Johny and his wife dish up some mighty fine fresh fish and seafood at this rustic oceanfront restaurant in a small fishing village. Try the grilled snapper or coconut shrimp plated with fried plantain, rice and veggies, or down a cold Tecate while watching dive-bombing pelicans.

Café Pacífico
CAFE $$

(☑ 755-101-73-72; www.facebook.com/cafepacifico troncones; Av de la Playa s/n; mains M$85-175; ⊙ 8am-4pm Nov-Aug; 🛜 🅿) At first glance, this is an international hipster cafe. Creative salads, fish tacos and hummus-smeared baguettines are all present and correct, as is 'detox' juice and good, strong coffee. But the standout dishes at this sweet brunch joint are unapologetically Mexican: poached eggs in a punchy red salsa, shrimp tacos with a dusting of chili, consumed at shaded outdoor tables.

Brisas Mexicanas
SEAFOOD $$

(☑ 755-128-34-78; Playa Majahua; mains M$140-250; ⊙ 9am-9pm) Dig your feet into the sand at this simple *marisquería* (seafood restaurant), watch the waves break on the pristine crescent of a beach and tuck into catch of the day (*al ajillo* or breaded), some *aguachile* or coconut shrimp.

Chenchos
MEXICAN $$

(☑ 755-103-00-61; Av de la Playa s/n; mains M$100-190; ⊙ 11am-9pm; 🛜) You don't get the ocean view at this mini-restaurant one block inland, so the sand floor and sea breeze will have to do. A local favorite, this family-run place does fine homestyle Mexican cooking such as shrimp enchiladas in green salsa and *chiles rellenos* (stuffed chilies).

La Mexicana
FUSION $$

(☑ 755-103-00-62; www.facebook.com/LaMexicana Troncones; Av de la Playa s/n; mains M$160-250; ⊙ 8am-11pm; 🛜 🅿) Good at any time of day, this breezy restaurant is particularly inviting at night, when it twinkles with fairy lights and the menu's creative elements come to the fore. Expect the likes of mahi-mahi on a bed of quinoa with a welcome accompaniment of green veggies or vegetarian *chile en nogada*. Tight house band livens things up on Thursdays.

Jardín del Edén　　　　　　FUSION $$
(📞 755-103-01-04; www.jardindeleden.com.mx; Av de la Playa s/n; mains M$150-230; ⊘8am-10pm Nov-Apr; 🛜) Just north of Troncones Point, the French chef's fusion menu ranges from Mediterranean (with nightly wood-fired pizzas) to traditional Mexican fare. The menu changes with the chef's whim, including nightly specials such as *cochinita pibil* cooked on the grill. Catch live salsa and *cumbia* (dance music originating from Colombia) bands on Friday nights from 7pm.

Roberto's Bistro　　　　　ARGENTINE $$$
(📞 755-103-00-19; www.robertosbistro.com; Av de la Playa s/n; mains M$260-395; ⊘8am-10pm; 🛜) Catering to the carnivorously inclined, this Argentine-style beachfront grill, 1km south of the T-intersection, is all meat and heat and smoke from the open grill, with a soundtrack of crashing waves. Come here for *chorizo* sausage starters and full-on feasts such as the *parrillada argentina* (T-bone, rib-eye and several other cuts grilled together with shrimp). Saturdays in season are salsa night.

Next to the restaurant, the owner's son runs a small turtle preserve that releases about 15,000 olive-ridley hatchlings each year (August to November).

🛈 Getting There & Around

From Zihuatanejo, take a La Unión–bound bus (M$38, 30 minutes) from the Petatlán terminal (p578) – it will drop you at the turnoff. Walk down the road a little way and you'll find a stop where vans (M$20, five minutes) shuttle into Troncones every half-hour or so until 7pm; some continue to fishing village Majahua, just north of Troncones. Some 2nd-class buses heading northwest toward Morelia or Lázaro Cárdenas will also drop you at the turnoff.

Taxis (📞755-553-28-68; Av de la Playa s/n; ⊘8am-8pm) in Troncones offer service around the area (M$100 to Playa Majahua), the hot springs (M$350), to the airport (p578; M$800) or to Zihuatanejo (M$600). A reliable air-conditioned cab is run by **Victor's Taxi Service** (📞755-553-28-08, cell 755-1110580; Av de la Playa s/n).

Ixtapa

📞 755 / POP 13,470

Ixtapa was nothing more than a coconut plantation until the late 1970s when Fonatur (the Mexican government's tourism development group) decided that the Pacific coast needed a Cancún-like resort. In came the developers and up went the high-rises. The result is a long string of huge hotels sitting cheek by jowl along a lovely beach, but little local community. Cancún took off in a big way, and Ixtapa, well...didn't. Ixtapa's appeal is best appreciated by families seeking a hassle-free, all-inclusive beach getaway, or by those who value modern chain-hotel comforts. It's close enough to Zihuatanejo that you can stay in Zihua and do a quick day trip to the beaches and island of this rather characterless place.

⊙ Sights

Playa El Palmar　　　　　　BEACH
(Blvd Paseo Ixtapa) Ixtapa's longest (2.5km) and broadest stretch of blond sand is overrun by parasailing and jet-skiing concessions. The sea takes on an aquamarine sheen in the dry season, which makes it all the more inviting. Take care while swimming, as there can be a vicious shore break and a powerful undertow when the swell comes up. Access is tricky, thanks to the mega-resorts lined up shoulder to shoulder, but you can always cut through a hotel lobby (Krystal or Hotel Emporio).

Playa Escolleras　　　　　　BEACH
(Blvd Paseo Ixtapa) Playa Escolleras, at the western end of Playa El Palmar near the entrance to the marina, has a decent break and attracts surfers.

Isla Ixtapa　　　　　　　　ISLAND
(round-trip boat M$50, snorkel rental M$150) Ixtapa's finest attraction is a popular island. The turquoise waters are crystal-clear, calm (particularly on the main **Playa Varadero**) and good for snorkeling (gear rental available). **Playa Corales** on the back side of the island is the quietest beach, with soft white sand and offshore coral reef, but more waves. Thatch-covered, open-air *enramada* seafood restaurants and massage providers dot the island. Frequent boats depart from the pier at Playa Linda. It's very busy on weekends and during high season.

Playa Linda　　　　　　　　BEACH
(Paseo de las Garzas) A long stretch of grayish sand, Playa Linda is popular with locals,

though the water toward the north end can be murky thanks to the nearby rivers and mangroves. It has some decent surf and a gaggle of *enramadas* at the south end. Banana-boat rides are offered. Local buses from central Ixtapa (M$15) can drop you here.

Playa Quieta BEACH

(Paseo de las Garzas) On the other side of Punta Ixtapa from the main resort area, Playa Quieta is popular with spring breakers staying at the Club Med, the biggest hotel on the beach. The water is good for swimming.

Cocodrilario WILDLIFE RESERVE

(Paseo de las Garzas, Playa Linda; ⊘24hr) FREE Playa Linda has a small *cocodrilario* (crocodile reserve) that is also home to fat iguanas and several bird species. You can watch the hulking crocs from the safety of the well-fenced wooden viewing platform located near the bus stop and extending toward the harbor.

🏃 Activities

Cycling is a breeze along a 15km *ciclopista* (cycle path) that stretches from Playa Linda, north of Ixtapa, practically into Zihuatanejo. You can rent bikes from Adventours (p569). Diving, snorkeling and surfing are also popular in the area and all manner of other water-based activities (parasailing, banana-boat rides) are offered by the hotels.

Mero Adventure DIVING

(☑cell 755-1019672; www.meroadventure.com; Hotel Pacífica, Blvd Paseo Ixtapa s/n; 1-/2-tank dives US$65/90; ⊘9am-5pm Mon-Sat; 🚸) Mero Adventure is highly rated by beginner divers for its patient instructors. It also runs two types of fun, child-friendly snorkeling trips; go for the four-hour jaunt to Manzanillo and Los Gatos (US$35).

Catcha L'Ola Surf SURFING

(☑755-553-13-84; www.facebook.com/catchas; Centro Comercial Kiosco 12, Plaza Zócalo; board rental per day/week US$25/100, 3hr lesson US$60; ⊘9am-7pm Mon-Sat, noon-5pm Sun) Wave riders will find everything they need – rentals, repairs, classes and surfing trips – here. It's next to the well-signed Nueva Zelanda restaurant.

👉 Tours

Ixtapa Zihuatanejo OUTDOORS

(☑cell 755-1118028; www.ixtapatoursluis.com) Long-standing guide Luis runs a variety of tours in the area, including engaging guided visits to Xihuacan historical site (US$65), kayaking in the Barra de Potosí lagoon

(US$75), horseback riding on the Barra de Potosí beach (US$69), and much more. He offers pickup from your accommodations in Ixtapa and Zihuatanejo.

Adventours ADVENTURE

(☑755-553-35-84; www.ixtapa-adventours.com; Blvd Paseo Ixtapa s/n; tours US$59-79, bike rental per hour/day M$60/250; ⊘8am-6pm) Opposite the Park Royal hotel, Adventours offers guided cycling trips, kayaking in the mangroves of El Refugio de Potosí (p579), snorkeling and kayaking off Isla Ixtapa, plus bird-watching tours.

🛌 Sleeping

The beachside hotels are mostly top-end all-inclusives and best booked through package deals or from hotel websites. A couple of cheaper, more interesting options are a few blocks inland from the main drag, but for the best variety, stay in neighboring Zihuatanejo.

Gamma Plaza Ixtapa RESORT $$

(☑755-555-05-00; www.gammahoteles.com/web/gamma-plaza-ixtapa; Av Paseo del Palmar; r from M$841; P🐶❄🛜🏊) Understated, stylish and family-friendly, this resort makes up in amenities for what it lacks in beach access (though the beach is a 10-minute walk away). Rooms are tiled, bright and spacious, there's a wading pool for kids, a pool bar for grown-ups, gym and onsite restaurants, with the added bonus of proximity to a cluster of bars and eateries.

★Casa Candiles B&B $$$

(☑cell 755-2078471; www.facebook.com/Casa CandilesInn; Paseo de las Golondrinas 65; r incl breakfast US$190-200; 🐶❄🛜🏊) Far more characterful than the hulking resort hotels is this intimate American-run hacienda on a quiet residential street about 500m from the beach. Three stylish but homey rooms are individually decorated – one with Balinese masks – and there's a lovely pool and garden. It backs onto greenery where you can spot birds and animals from a path. Hospitality is very genuine.

🍴 Eating & Drinking

There is excellent, inexpensive seafood to be had on Isla Ixtapa and in *palapa* restaurants on Playa Linda. The biggest concentration of bars, fast-food joints and other eateries is between Blvd Paseo Ixtapa and Paseo de las Gaviotas.

La Raiz de la Tierra VEGAN $

(🖉 755-553-15-03; www.laraizdelatierra.com; Plaza Zócalo s/n; mains M$65-160; ⊙8am-10pm; 🖉) A vegan cafe owned by Rodrigo Sánchez of the flamenco-metal guitar duo Rodrigo Y Gabriela, this place also sells records and books and is an activities center offering salsa and guitar classes. Menu items include cold-pressed juices, vegan *tacos al pastor* (marinated mushroom on organic corn tortilla) and many other non-meat treats.

Ruben's Hamburgers BURGERS $

(🖉 755-553-00-27; www.rubenshamburgers.com; Andador Punta San Esteban; burgers M$75-115; ⊙noon-midnight; ❋🛜🏠) The succinct menu at Ruben's revolves around several key virtues: beef patties (or chicken, if you prefer), cooked to perfection and piled high with melted Gouda cheese, grilled onions, bacon and more. For sides, choose between regular or curly fries or opt for a baked *chayote* (prickly pear) or zucchini. There are kiddie burgers too.

Lili Cipriani SEAFOOD $$

(🖉 cell 755-1200404; Playa Coral s/n, Isla Ixtapa; mains M$160-250; ⊙9am-5pm) On main Playa Varadero, on Isla Ixtapa's north side, the pick of half a dozen waterfront restaurants serve mighty fine *pescado a las brasas* (grilled fish). The whole fish comes served with handmade tortillas and a spicy habanero and *chile de arbol* (aka bird's-beak chili) salsa. Shrimp *tostadas* and pineapple stuffed with creatures of the deep are good too.

Boats to Isla Ixtapa depart from Playa Linda.

Generals Sports Bar SPORTS BAR

(🖉 755-114-99-28; Av Peralvillo 122; ⊙noon-11pm Mon-Sat, 1-11pm Sun) Popular with visitors and locals, this buzzy sports bar is good for catching the game on the big screen while downing an ice-cold Pacífico. There are standard bar nibbles as well and plenty of atmosphere, come evening.

ℹ Information

Tourist Office (🖉 755-555-07-00; www.ixtapa-zihuatanejo.com; Blvd Paseo Ixtapa s/n; ⊙8am-4pm) Provides tourist info from a little kiosk directly across from the Holiday Inn.

ℹ Getting There & Away

Overpriced private taxis (M$490) provide transportation from the airport (p578) to Ixtapa, while shuttles making multiple stops charge M$145 per person. The return journey to the airport in private taxis costs M$280. City cabs from Ixtapa to Zihuatanejo cost M$85 to M$115.

Rental cars can be hired at the airport.

There are bus-ticket offices, but very few long-distance buses actually stop here – for most destinations, go to Zihuatanejo.

Local buses run frequently between Ixtapa and Zihuatanejo from 5:30am to 11pm (M$15, 15 minutes). In Ixtapa, buses stop along the main street in front of all hotels. In Zihuatanejo, buses run along Morelos. Many Ixtapa-bound buses continue to Playa Linda (M$15).

Zihuatanejo

🖉 755 / POP 73,145

Zihuatanejo, or Zihua as it's affectionately called, is a traditional fishing village that's grown into a busy yet appealing town after the construction of Ixtapa next door in the 1970s. Considerably more characterful than its neighbor, Zihua stretches around a beautiful bay, and has retained much of its historic charm. The narrow cobblestone streets of the downtown hide some excellent *taquerías*, local restaurants, bars, boutiques and artisan studios, while the more exclusive boutique accommodations sit on the verdant slopes above the white-sand beaches further to the south, excellent for swimming and water sports. Fishers still meet every morning on the beach by Paseo del Pescador (Fisherman's Passage) to sell their catch of the day. At night, locals stroll along the waterfront sidewalk. Zihua is the best of both worlds – no wonder Andy and Red chose to live out their post-prison days here in *The Shawshank Redemption* (though that scene was shot in the Virgin Islands, in case you were wondering).

◉ Sights

Museo Arqueológico de la Costa Grande MUSEUM

(Archaeological Museum of the Costa Grande; 🖉 755-554-75-52; cnr Plaza Olof Palme & Paseo del Pescador; M$10; ⊙10am-6pm Tue-Sun) This small museum houses six rooms with exhibits on the history, archaeology and culture of the Guerrero coast. Its displays feature jewelry, stone tools, rock carvings and ceramics, with Olmec, Teotihuacana, Tarascan and Mexica elements, helping you piece together regional influences. Most displays are in Spanish.

🏊 Beaches

Waves are gentle at all of Bahía de Zihuatanejo's beaches: if you want big ocean waves, head west toward Ixtapa or south to Playa Larga. Water in the bay, particularly around the central beaches, isn't always the cleanest.

Playa Municipal (Paseo del Pescador), in the center of town, is convenient if you're staying in the neighborhood, but you can definitely find much cleaner waters elsewhere on the bay. A five-minute stroll heading east along a boardwalk leads to **Playa Madera** (🔲 Playa La Ropa), known for its shallow, swimmable beach.

Over a steep hill from Playa Madera is **Playa La Ropa** (Clothes Beach; 🔲 Playa La Ropa), about a 20-minute walk along a scenic highway with spectacular ocean views along the way. Some of the best hotels and restaurants in town are clustered in Playa La Ropa, and its sprawling beach provides fine swimming and waterskiing conditions.

Across the bay, protected beach **Playa Las Gatas** (Cat Beach; round-trip boat M$50) gets very crowded during the Mexican holiday season in July and August and the winter vacation period, but outside peak season it's Zihua's loveliest, with calm, cerulean waters and good snorkeling at the offshore reef. Boats to Las Gatas (round-trip fare M$50) depart from Zihuatanejo's main pier.

For big-wave surfing and horseback riding, hit **Playa Larga** (🔲 Coacoyul), about 12km south of the city center. Catch a 'Coacoyul' *colectivo* (p579) from the corner of Juárez and González to the Playa Larga turnoff, then take another combi to the beach.

Near Playa Larga, **Playa Manzanillo** is considered to be one of the best snorkeling spots in the area and it draws fewer visitors than the highly popular Playa Las Gatas. The secluded beach is reachable by boat (price depends on boat size and number of passengers); inquire at the main pier.

🏃 Activities

Sportfishing

Sportfishing is very popular in Zihuatanejo. Sailfish are caught here year-round; seasonal fish include blue or black marlin (March to May), roosterfish (September and October), wahoo (October), mahi-mahi (November and December) and Spanish mackerel (December). Deep-sea fishing trips start at around M$3600 for a boat holding up to four passengers. Trips run for up to seven hours and usually include equipment.

Sociedad Cooperativa José Azueta FISHING
(📞 755-554-20-56; https://sociedadcooperativa tenientejoseazueta.com; Muelle Municipal; Playa Las Gatas round trip M$50, deep-sea fishing M$4000; ⊗ office 8am-6pm) Offers full-day fishing excursions and boat transportation to Playa Las Gatas from an office at the foot of the pier.

Sociedad de Servicios Turísticos Triángulo del Sol FISHING
(📞 755-554-37-58; Paseo del Pescador 38B, near Muelle Municipal; fishing US$200-350, snorkeling per boat US$160; ⊗ office 9am-4pm) As well as fishing in small and large boats, this place offers snorkeling at Playa Manzanillo including time at Playa Las Gatas and straightforward transfers to the latter. It also runs tours of the bay.

Water Sports

Snorkeling is good at Playa Las Gatas and even better at Playa Manzanillo. Marine life is abundant here due to a convergence of currents, and the visibility can be great – up to 35m in dry months. Playa La Ropa is great for parasailing and banana-boat rides. Migrating humpback whales pass through from December to early March.

Dive Zihua DIVING
(📞 cell 755-1023738; www.divezihuatanejo.com; Ascencio 7; 1-/2-tank dive US$80/90, snorkel tour US$35; ⊗ 9:30am-6:30pm Mon-Sat) This long-standing operator offers a good variety of dives, plus snorkeling, classes in underwater photography, nitrox diving and PADI certification. It can also arrange whale-watching tours with a biologist from December to March.

Carlo Scuba DIVING
(📞 cell 755-5546003; www.carloscuba.com; Playa Las Gatas; 1-/2-tank dives US$65/90; ⊗ 8am-6pm) Carlo Scuba, run by a third-generation family operation based at Playa Las Gatas, offers all manner of dives, including night dives and discovery dives, snorkeling trips, instruction and PADI certification. Prices include pickup and drop-off at the Muelle Municipal.

🗪 Courses & Tours

⭐ **Patio Mexica Cooking School** COOKING
(📞 cell 755-1167211; www.patiomexica.com; Adelita 32, Colonia La Madera; classes M$450-500) Mónica Durán Pérez opens her home kitchen and shares her love of Mexican culinary culture in this wonderful series of classes. Start with a trip to the market (some classes only), then return to Mónica's backyard, where you grind corn, shape tortillas, make salsa in a *molcajete* (traditional mortar and pestle), and cook up ceviche, fish tacos and more.

Zihuatanejo

Estrella de Oro (1.3km);
Estrella Blanca (1.5km)

Heroico Colegio Militar

Calle La Laya

Morelos

Morelos

Palmas

Palapas

Mangos

Cocos

Altamirano

La Correa Route
Bus Stop

Juárez

Local Buses
to Ixtapa

Cuauhtémoc

Nava

Juárez

Colectivos
to Airport &
Playa Larga

Terminal for
Petatlán &
La Unión

33

Galeana

González

5 de Mayo

Ejido

Guerrero

Álvarez

Bravo

Local Buses to
Playa La Ropa

López Mateos

39

Ramírez

Naval
Base

Ascencio

35

Álvarez

Plaza
Olof
Palme

Paseo del Pescador

Marina

Muelle Municipal (Pier)

Bahía de Zihuatanejo

Hotel Villas
El Morro
(300m);
Picante
(350m)

Contramar Andador

Playa El
Almacen

Dishes might include *tamales, mole poblano* (chicken or turkey in a sauce of chilies, fruits, nuts, spices and chocolate), *tiritas* (raw fish slivers marinated with red onion, lemon or lime and chili peppers) or stuffed chilies or zucchini flowers. Check the website for details of different classes.

Picante

BOATING

(☑ 755-554-82-70; www.picantecruises.com; Muelle Puerto Mío, La Noria; sail & snorkel US$95, sunset cruise US$70) This 23m catamaran offers two enjoyable excursions. The 'Sail, Snorkel and Spinnaker Flying' trip sails south of Zihua to prime snorkeling off Pla-

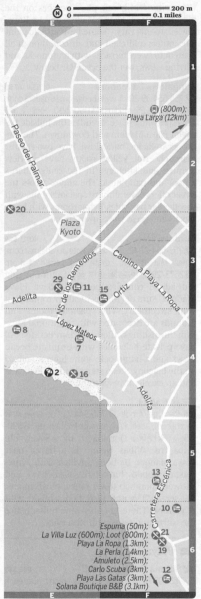

ya Manzanillo. The 'Magical Sunset Cruise' heads around the bay and along the coast of Ixtapa. Prices include food and open bar. Reservations required; see website for schedule.

🛏 Sleeping

Zihuatanejo has a huge selection for all budgets. Cheap hotels dot the center and around, hotels around Playa Madera run the gamut from cheapies to boutique hotels, while Zihua's best, most exclusive boutique accommodations are found above Playa La Ropa and around. High season is December through March. Outside high season, prices drop by up to 20%.

🛏 Central Zihuatanejo

★ Hotel Villas El Morro HOTEL $
(📲 cell 443-3191305; www.zihuatanejo-villaselmorro.com; Paseo del Morro 4, Colonia El Almacén; r M$450-600, ste M$650-1300; 🅿️ ➖ ❄ 🛜 🏊) It's all about the views at El Morro, which sits high upon a hilltop on the bay's less-visited west end. Rooms are terrific value; a M$200 upgrade gets you one with a kitchen, terrace and Jacuzzi. Going up and down all those stairs will leave you with thighs of steel; you can soak your tired muscles in the infinity pool.

Hostal ZihuAzul HOSTEL $
(📲 755-554-50-84; www.hostalzihuazul.com; Ascencio 10; dm/f/apt M$400/1200/2000; ❄ 🛜) About as central as it gets, on a quiet little pedestrian street, this is the closest Zihua has to a hostel. Branching off the plant-festooned lobby, the spartan, spotless en-suite rooms come with an assortment of beds and bunks, and there's a common kitchen and dining area. Management is a bit scatty and windows face the lobby.

Posada Citlali GUESTHOUSE $
(📲 755-554-20-43; Guerrero 4; s/d M$450/700; ➖ ❄ 🛜) Providing decent budget digs in the town center, this older, pleasant family-owned posada (inn) has simple, cozy and clean tiled rooms with queen beds and rockers on a shared patio. There's a lush garden rising through the courtyard and it's steps from the sea. It can be a bit loud on weekends with bar noise. Air-con costs an extra M$50.

🛏 Playa Madera

Hotel Villas Mercedes HOTEL $
(📲 755-544-67-81, cell 443-3191305; www.hotelvillasmercedes.com; Adelita 59; d M$750-1100; 🅿️ ➖ ❄ 🛜 🏊) Nestled in the pleasant barrio behind Playa Madera, this cheerful cheapie offers remarkably good value for clean, comfortable rooms surrounding a mosaic-tiled pool. It's a friendly place with decent security, popular with Mexican families.

Mi Casita GUESTHOUSE $
(📲 755-125-27-71, cell 755-5544510; micasita.alejandra@gmail.com; Carretera Escénica s/n; r M$650-850; ➖ ❄ 🛜; �想 Playa La Ropa) This humble and welcoming family-run place perches on the hillside between Playas Madera and La Ropa. The six rooms vary – some have artistic paint jobs, others a kitchen and air-con, though all open onto sweet terraces with hammocks and stirring views over the ocean far below.

Bungalows La Madera BUNGALOW $$
(📲 755-554-39-20; www.bungalowslamadera.com; López Mateos 25; studios M$1190-2210; ➖ ❄ 🛜 🏊) This sprawling place straddles the hillside between Playa Madera and downtown. The nicest ocean-facing bungalows have two rooms; many cheerful, yellow rooms have sea-view terraces and kitchens. In the center there's a pool and patio area. The annex across the street offers several more spacious units with spectacular balconies/living rooms with hammocks and great views over Zihua.

Aura del Mar HOTEL $$$
(📲 755-554-21-42; www.hotelauradelmar.com; López Mateos s/n; d/ste incl breakfast from M$2673/2977; 🅿️ ➖ ❄ @ 🛜 🏊) A cliff-hugging red adobe complex perched above Playa Madera, Aura del Mar is ideal for romancing your sweetheart. The spacious rooms and grounds are decorated with traditional Mexican furnishings, tiles and handicrafts. All have private balconies with exquisite ocean views and a hammock; some have a Jacuzzi on the balcony. Steep stairs lead to the beach and an excellent restaurant.

Villas Naomi HOTEL $$$
(La Casa del Árbol; 📲 755-544-73-03; www.villasnaomi.com; Adelita 114; ste with kitchenette US$90-115; ➖ ❄ 🛜 🏊) Dominated by a lovely old ceiba tree, Villas Naomi is a haven near Playa Madera. Its bougainvillea-clad, white-washed abodes have built-in shelving and showers, bamboo towel racks, plush linens, flat-screen TVs and tiled floors inlaid with river rock. There are only nine units, hence the warm and personalized service.

🛏 Playa La Ropa

★ Solana Boutique B&B B&B $$$
(📲 755-103-61-07; www.casasolana.com; Carretera Escénica s/n; studios US$150-200; 🅿️ ❄ 🛜 🏊) High above the bay in a secluded location, this welcoming B&B affords grand sea views. Six individually designed studios peek out amid lush gardens and fruit trees, and you can toast the sunset from the infinity pool, margarita in hand. Owners Melissa and Sriram are happy to share their local knowledge. It's a longish walk from Zihua and Playa La Ropa.

It requires a two-night minimum stay. No kids under 12.

★Hotel Tentaciones
BOUTIQUE HOTEL **$$$**

(📞755-544-83-83; www.hoteltentaciones.com; Camino Escénico a Playa La Ropa; r US$322; 🅿✳🛜🏊) This adults-only retreat blends earthy tones with marble and thatch, and there's plenty of natural light flooding the understated, luxurious rooms. Architect Carlos Desormaux clearly loves flowing water; there are lots of water features, including a vast infinity pool overlooking the bay. The restaurant is one of Zihua's best, with weekly changing menus (book ahead).

La Villa Luz
BOUTIQUE HOTEL **$$$**

(📞755-112-18-34; www.lavillaluz.com; Carretera Escénica 97; ste incl breakfast US$190-250; 🅿🖨✳🛜🏊; 🚍Playa La Ropa) This genuinely romantic retreat climbs the hill just above Playa La Ropa (warning: plenty of stairs). The seven suites are all sweet and characterful with artful use of inlaid wood, adobe brick and pebble mosaics; particularly nice is Suite Mar, with glorious sea vistas from the comfortable bed. A couple of them are duplexes, one with a kitchen.

La Casa Que Canta
BOUTIQUE HOTEL **$$$**

(📞755-555-70-30; www.lacasaquecanta.com; Carretera Escénica s/n; ste US$577; 🅿🖨✳🛜🏊) The 'house that sings' is perched atop cliffs between Playas Madera and La Ropa. The thatched-roof hotel features bold, striking use of interior space and shelters exquisitely decorated suites, all with sea views and the priciest with private terraces and plunge pools. But perhaps the most valuable amenity is silence: there are no TVs and kids aren't allowed.

Amuleto
BOUTIQUE HOTEL **$$$**

(📞755-544-62-22; www.amuleto.net; Carretera Escénica 9; ste incl breakfast US$285-380; 🅿🖨✳@🛜🏊) Designed by hotshot architect Enrique Zozaya, Amuleto sits high in the hills above Playa La Ropa, and consists of five individually styled suites in earthy tones, decorated in stone, ceramic and wood. Opt for Suite 1 to watch the sunset from your own infinity plunge pool. The attached fusion restaurant is a destination in itself. Three-night minimum stay; no kids.

✗ Eating

Guerrero state is famous for green *pozole*, a hearty meat-and-hominy stew that's found on most menus in town (especially on Thursdays). *Tiritas* are Zihua's specialty.

✗ Central Zihuatanejo

Many popular (if touristy) fish restaurants line Paseo del Pescador, parallel to Playa Municipal. **Mercado Municipal** (Mangos s/n; meals M$30-60; ⊘8am-6pm) has rows of *comedores* (counter eateries), and central Zihua is also peppered with excellent street-food stalls, good coffee shops and restaurants that range from Mexican home cooking to more sophisticated fare.

★La Flechita Roja
TACOS **$**

(📞cell 755-5570192; Morelos 56; tacos from M$6; ⊘24hr) You're sitting so close to the sizzling spit of *carne asada* that sweat runs down you in rivulets. You watch, transfixed, as the chefs deftly slice and dice the meat, cow eyeballs, tongue, brains and other nose-to-tail ingredients, toss them atop some freshly made tortillas and serve them with aplomb and with two types of green salsa.

★Cuattro Cycle Café & Té
CAFE **$**

(📞755-554-16-41; www.facebook.com/cuattrocafe; Altamirano 19; mains M$70-140, ⊘8am-9pm; ✳🛜) While walking around in the Zihua heat, you come to appreciate havens of arctic air-con, such as this split-level, bicycle-themed cafe – ideal for sipping a strong Guerrero coffee while clacking on your laptop, or snacking on waffles, enchiladas, sandwiches, cakes and pizza.

Fonda Doña Licha
MEXICAN **$**

(📞cell 755-1153114; Cocos 8; mains M$60-125; ⊘8am-6pm) This place near the market is renowned for its down-home Mexican cooking and casual atmosphere (complete with blaring TV). There are several *comidas corridas* (fixed-price menus) to choose from, with plates piled high with rice, beans and handmade tortillas. Breakfasts will get you through a siege and a special Sunday menu includes *tamales de elote* (sweet-corn *tamales*).

La Papa Loca
FAST FOOD **$**

(Av Heróico Colegio Militar 45; meals M$25-75; ⊘7pm-2am) These guys do wonders with the humble baked potato. Yes, there's a side show of tacos and fruit juices, but the specialty here is the 'crazy potato,' blanketed with melted cheese and piled high with *carne al pastor*, cream and other trimmings.

Carmelitas
BREAKFAST **$**

(📞755-554-38-85; www.facebook.com/holacarmelitascafe; Av Heróico Colegio Militar s/n; mains M$70-140; ⊘8am-4:30pm Mon-Sat, to 3pm Sun; 🅿🛜)

Zihua's premier breakfast spot, this open-air cafe slings a tantalizing array of Guerrero comfort food including *huevos a la pasilla* (fried eggs in tortilla bowls bathed with *guajillo* chili sauce and accompanied by fried plantain) with handmade tortillas on the side. Order from the menu or the daily blackboard specials, such as *pozole*. Cash only.

★**Restaurantes Mexicanos Any** MEXICAN **$$**
(☏755-554-73-73; www.restaurantesmexicanosany .com.mx; Ejido 18; mains M$70-220; ⊗8am-11pm; 🕾) This thatched-roofed diner with cheerful, colorful folkloric decor is an essential stop in Zihua for traditional Guerrero cuisine. Breakfast egg dishes are served with *nopal* or three kinds of salsa (including a chocolate one with a chili kick); other highlights include Guerrero-style green *pozole*, served daily, to-die-for *tamales* and sweet, corn-based hot drinks known as *atoles*.

Marisquería Yolanda SEAFOOD **$$**
(☏cell 755-1282368; cnr Morelos & Cuauhtémoc; mains M$60-200; ⊗10am-8pm) Staff here shuck oysters, and dice and drown ceviche on the street side, where boleros belly up to the sidewalk bar and sing about their unbridled, unrequited romance to one too many beers. And when the balladeers mosey along, the jukebox takes over. It's known as the Catedral del Marisco (Cathedral of Seafood) for a reason.

La Sirena Gorda SEAFOOD **$$**
(☏755-554-26-87; www.facebook.com/LaSirena GordaZihuatanejo; Paseo del Pescador 90; mains M$75-250; ⊗8:30am-10:30pm Thu-Tue; 🕾) Close to the pier, at this casual and popular open-air restaurant (The Fat Mermaid) you're met with a mural of sea maidens that Botticelli would have been proud to have painted, as well as an assortment of fish and seafood tacos and the specials: blackened snapper and blackened octopus. Service is friendly and efficient.

✖ Around the Bay

Zihua's best fine dining with panoramic views dominates the hilltop hotels (Tentaciones (p575), Amuleto (p575) and Espuma are particularly well known for theirs), while casual beachside eateries are the rule on Playa La Ropa. More affordable fare can be found in the 'gringo gastronomic ghetto' along Adelita, just inland from Playa Madera; half of the restaurants here shut down from May to November.

Patio Mexica BREAKFAST **$**
(☑cell 755-1167211; www.patiomexica.com; Adelita 32, Colonia La Madera; breakfast M$50-90; ⊗8am-2pm Mon-Sat Sep-Apr; 🕾) Squash-blossom omelette, *chilaquiles* and other Mexican delicacies get your day off to a sunny start at this informal breakfast place run by Mónica Durán Pérez of the Patio Mexica Cooking School (p571).

Las Adelitas MEXICAN **$$**
(☑cell 755-5593517; Adelita 6; breakfast M$45-65, lunch & dinner M$70-210; ⊗8am-4pm Mon-Sat May-Oct, to 10pm Nov-Apr; 🕾) This adorable breakfast and lunch cafe is on a little plaza with outdoor seating. It has a loyal local following thanks to its *chilaquiles* and omelettes in the morning and *tortas*, *chiles rellenos* and fried and grilled fish at lunch. In gringo season it opens for great-value dinners too.

La Perla SEAFOOD **$$**
(☏755-554-27-00; www.laperlarestaurant.net; Playa La Ropa; mains M$95-245; ⊗10am-10pm; 🕾; 🚍Playa La Ropa) Despite the seasonal beer-bucket NFL promos, this is a refined pavilion in dark wood right on Playa La Ropa. Best dishes include grilled octopus, tuna steaks seared as rare as you like, whole grilled fish, tacos piled with shrimp and lobster, breaded oysters... Eat here and hang on to the beach lounges for as long as you desire.

Espuma FUSION **$$**
(☏755-554-30-05; www.hoteltentaciones.com/ espuma-landing-english; Carretera Escénica s/n; mains M$140-260; ⊗8am-11pm Thu-Tue) Benefitting from stellar clifftop views of the bay, Espuma is great at any time of day. Come for the creative breakfasts (*arrachera* with cactus, frittata with squash blossoms), light seafood lunches, or romance your other half by candlelight while savoring a happy marriage of Mexican and Mediterranean flavors.

★**Restaurant El Arrayan** GRILL **$$$**
(☏755-112-11-93; www.facebook.com/restaurant elarrayan; Adelita 41, Colonia La Madera; mains M$245-385; ⊗8:30am-9pm Thu-Sat Jun-Oct, 8:30am-9pm Mon-Sat Nov-May; 🕾) From his curbside barbecue, grill master Mauricio Cancino cooks up fresh fish (usually tuna or mahi-mahi with grilled veggies) to perfection, then he finishes it off with a brush of delightful *guajillo* chili and garlic sauce. There are some gringo crowd-pleasers, such as grilled steak and key lime pie, but what you really come for is the fish.

Bistro del Mar
FUSION $$$

(☑755-554-83-33; www.bistrodelmar.com; López Mateos s/n, Playa Madera; mains M$210-320; ⊙8am-10:30pm; 🐾) With its landmark sail roof over candlelit tables and its fusion of Latin, European and Asian flavors, this beachside bistro is just meters away from the waves. Mahi-mahi, tuna, snapper and shrimp dishes are prepared with a light touch and in outstandingly inventive ways. The house wines are a cut above average too.

La Gula
FUSION $$$

(☑755-554-83-96; www.restaurantelagula.com; Adelita 8; mains M$220-270; ⊙5-10pm Mon-Sat Nov-Apr; 🐾) Playfully riffing on the idea of saintliness and sinfulness, the menu implores you to 'enjoy being sinful' with such dishes of darkness and power as mahi-mahi stuffed with crab, or tuna blackened with 10 different spices. If that weren't temptation enough, Afrodita soup and Neptune's bisque promise to give you staying power, gentlemen. Wink.

Il Mare
ITALIAN $$$

(☑755-554-90-67; www.ilmareristorante.com; Carretera Escénica 105; mains M$170-395; ⊙noon-11pm Mon-Sat, 4-11pm Sun, closed Tue May-Oct; 🐾) A romantic Italian restaurant with a fabulous bird's-eye view of the bay, Il Mare is well regarded for its Mediterranean pasta and seafood specialties, including linguini with fresh clams in a garlic-wine sauce. Pair your dish with wine from Spain, Italy, France or Argentina.

🍷 Drinking & Nightlife

Downtown has a handful of bars offering two-for-one beers and margaritas, and you can find some live music and booty-shaking bass on weekends.

Angustina
BAR

(☑755-544-85-66; www.facebook.com/angustina mezcal; Paseo del Pescador 70; ⊙1pm-2am Tue-Sun) There is much to love about this bar, from the bartenders' knowledge of mezcal and their signature cocktails (*mezcaltinis, mazcalinas,* mojitos infused with the good stuff), to the bohemian vibe and some truly unusual edibles on the menu (you'll see!).

Cafe Zihuatanejo
COFFEE

(☑cell 755-5543890; Cuauhtémoc 170; ⊙9am-5pm Mon-Sat) 🍵 This tiny cafe has been in the family since 1952. The different types of coffee are all grown on their *finca* (farm) some three hours' drive from Zihua; you can buy beans by weight here and they can grind it for you onsite while you sample the strong, aromatic brew served black as night, strong as sin.

Tasting Room por Capricho del Rey
CRAFT BEER

(☑755-102-86-52; Ascencio 9; ⊙2pm-2am Tue-Sun; 🐾) This snug little bar welcomes you with its arctic chill and Zihua's first, bona fide craft beer. It has four of its own bottled brews: a fruity IPA, a porter with notes of caramel, a nicely balanced pale ale and a hoppy lager, as well as guest craft beers from other parts of Guerrero, and some clever nibbles.

Malagua
BAR

(☑755-554-42-91; Paseo del Pescador 20; ⊙7pm-2am Wed-Sun; 🐾) A friendly neighborhood watering hole specializing in imported and Mexican craft beers. It's a nice spot to chat with locals and the fine music selection adds a touch of character to the fan-cooled bar.

☆ Entertainment

★ Loot
ARTS CENTER

(☑755-544-60-38; www.loot.mx; Playa La Ropa 55; ⊙8am-11pm Mon-Sat; 🐾; 🚌Playa La Ropa) Hipster central Loot wears many hats, and we like them all. There's the downstairs cafe and art showroom that serves Veracruz coffee and imaginative brunch dishes, art exhibits upstairs, and dinner and drinks in its open-air rooftop bar at night. It also happens to host some of the best fiestas in town, with live events such as concerts and arts festivals.

🛍 Shopping

Zihua offers abundant Mexican handicrafts and edibles, particularly masks and coffee from Guerrero, and textiles and ceramics from Oaxaca. You may also find some quality leatherwork, Taxco silver and ironwood carvings from the Sonora, as long as you're prepared to sift through mass-produced tat and slogan T-shirts at the local craft market.

★ El Jumil
ARTS & CRAFTS

(Zapotec Masks; ☑755-554-61-91; Paseo del Pescador 9; ⊙10am-8pm Mon-Sat, plus Sun Dec-Apr) Devils, angels, jaguars and other fantastic creatures peer down at you from the walls of this shop. Masks are well-known traditional handicrafts of Guerrero state, mostly used in regional fiestas, though there are also some decorative pieces carved from cattle skulls, contemporary masks that border on steampunk and antique wood carvings from Jaliaca de Campo, depicting the seven deadly sins.

Owner Magdaleno is happy to chat with you about the art of mask-making if you show a real interest.

Café Caracol
COFFEE

(☑ cell 755-5574219; www.cafecaracol.com.mx; Álvarez 15; ⊙ 8am-9pm) This shop with four branches sells three different types of delicious organic coffee from the village of Atoyac de Álvarez in Guerrero state, as well as vanilla and honey. You can also sample the brew here.

La Zapoteca
TEXTILES

(☑ 755-544-63-08; criskrebs@hotmail.com; Paseo del Pescador 9; ⊙ 10am-8pm Mon-Sat, plus Sun Dec-Apr) If you're interested in handwoven anything – *sarapes*, rugs or hammocks (it has some great ones) – find this emporium, which stands out among the handicraft huddle near the fishers' marina. The weaving is all from Teotitlán del Valle in Oaxaca.

Alberto's
JEWELRY

(☑ 755-554-21-61; Cuauhtémoc 15; ⊙ 9am-8pm Mon-Sat) A few shops along Cuauhtémoc sell silver from Taxco, a town famous for its quality craftwork. This jeweler has some of the finest and most original pieces.

Mercado de Artesanías
MARKET

(Calle 5 de Mayo s/n; ⊙ 9am-8pm) This large craft market sells mostly mass-produced tat, such as T-shirts emblazoned with 'Eat My Burrito' and other low-brow slogans, but you can also find some quality crafts, such as animal carvings made of ironwood and bags woven out of recyclable materials.

ℹ Information

You'll find several banks with 24-hour ATMs along a one-block stretch of Av Benito Juárez, including **Scotiabank** (cnr Av Benito Juárez & Las Palapas; ⊙ 24hr), **BBVA** (Av Benito Juárez s/n; ⊙ 24hr) and **Banorte** (cnr Av Benito Juárez & Ejido; ⊙ 24 hr). Banorte has the lowest withdrawal charge.

Hospital General (☑ 755-554-36-50; cnr Morelos & Mar Egeo; ⊙ 24hr) Emergency medical services halfway to the bus terminals.

Post Office (☑ 755-554-21-92; www.correosdemexico.com.mx; Carteros s/n; ⊙ 8am-4:30pm Mon-Fri, 9am-1pm Sat) Beside the big blue-and-yellow Coppel department store.

Tourist Office (☑ 755-555-07-00; www.ixtapa-zihuatanejo.com; Paseo del Pescador s/n, Muelle Municipal; ⊙ 8am-4pm) This convenient office in the Terminal Marítima at the foot of Zihua's pier stocks brochures and maps even when unstaffed.

ℹ Getting There & Away

AIR

The **Ixtapa/Zihuatanejo International Airport** (ZIH; ☑ 755-554-20-70; http://ixtapa-airport.com; Hwy 200 s/n) is 12km southeast of Zihuatanejo, several kilometers off Hwy 200 heading toward Acapulco. There are direct flights from several US cities, such as Los Angeles, and seasonal service to Canadian destinations.

The following destinations in Mexico are serviced by these airlines:

➜ Mexico City – Aeromar, Aeroméxico, Interjet, VivaAerobús, Volaris

➜ Tijuana – Volaris

➜ Toluca – Interjet

BUS

Both long-distance bus terminals are on Hwy 200 (aka Paseo de Zihuatanejo) about 2km northeast of the town center (toward the airport). The main terminal, **Estrella Blanca** (Central de Autobuses; ☑ 800-507-55-00; www.estrellablanca.com.mx; Paseo de Zihuatanejo Oriente 421; 🚍 La Correa), is adjacent to the smaller **Estrella de Oro terminal** (EDO; ☑ 755-554-21-75; www.estrelladeoro.com.mx; Paseo de Zihuatanejo s/n; 🚍 La Correa). Buses to La Unión and Petatlán (for Troncones and Barra de Potosí respectively) leave frequently from a small **terminal** (Las Palmas s/n) one block south of the municipal market.

BUSES FROM ZIHUATANEJO

DESTINATION	FARE (M$)	TIME (HR)	FREQUENCY (PER DAY)
Acapulco	232-310	4-5	15
Guadalajara	776	8	2
Lázaro Cárdenas	126-150	1½-2	frequent
Manzanillo	715	9	2
Mexico City	827-905	8-10	frequent
Morelia	534-599	5-6	7
Puerto Vallarta	1232	14-14½	2

CAR & MOTORCYCLE

There are several car-rental companies at the airport. Daily rentals including liability insurance start at about M$600.

Alamo (☑755-553-71-47; www.alamo.com.mx; Hwy 200 s/n, Ixtapa/Zihuatanejo International Airport; ◉9am-7pm Mon-Sat)

Europcar (☑755-553-71-58; www.europcar. com.mx; Hwy 200 s/n, Ixtapa/Zihuatanejo International Airport; ◉9am-6pm)

Hertz (☑755-553-73-10; https://hertzmexico. com; Hwy 200 s/n, Ixtapa/Zihuatanejo International Airport; ◉9am-6pm Mon-Thu & Sat, to 9pm Fri & Sun)

ℹ Getting Around

TO/FROM THE AIRPORT

The cheapest way to the airport is via public 'Aeropuerto' **colectivos** (Juárez s/n; M$17; ◉6:30am-8pm) departing from Juárez near González and making many stops before dropping you just outside the airport gate. Colectivo taxis are a more direct and convenient option for incoming passengers, whisking you from the arrivals area to Ixtapa or Zihua for M$150 per person. Private taxis from the airport into town cost M$420 to M$480; they're M$200 to M$250 from Zihuatanejo for the return journey.

BUS

To reach downtown Zihua or Ixtapa from Zihua's long-distance bus terminals, cross Hwy 200 using the pedestrian overpass directly opposite the Estrella Blanca bus terminal. Buses for downtown Zihua and Ixtapa stop just west of the bridge.

From downtown Zihua to the bus terminals, catch **La Correa** (cnr Nava & Juárez; ◉6am-10pm) route buses (M$10, 10 minutes). To reach Ixtapa from Zihuatanejo Centro, take a **bus** (Morelos s/n; ◉6am-10pm) from the corner of Morelos and Juárez (M$15, 15 minutes).

Playa La Ropa (Juárez s/n; ◉7am-6pm) buses go south on Juárez and out to Playa La Ropa (M$15) every half-hour.

'Coacoyul' colectivos heading toward Playa Larga and to the airport depart from Juárez, near the corner of González, every 15 minutes from 6:30am to 8pm (M$17, 15 minutes).

TAXI

Cabs are plentiful in Zihuatanejo. Fixed fares from a **taxi stand** (☑755-554-33-11; cnr Juárez & González; ◉24hr) in central Zihua cost M$80 to M$90 to Ixtapa, M$50 to M$60 to Playa La Ropa, M$100 to Playa Larga, M$200 to M$250 to the airport, and M$35 to the bus terminals. Rates run higher for air-conditioned cabs.

Barra de Potosí

☑755 / POP 410

The small fishing village of Barra de Potosí is about 26km southeast of Zihuatanejo. It's located at the far tip of Playa Larga's seemingly endless palm-fringed, white-sand beach, and at the mouth of the brackish **Laguna de Potosí**, a saltwater lagoon about 6.5km long and home to hundreds of species of birds, including herons, kingfishers, cormorants and pelicans. The village is thankfully free of any resort hotels and makes for a laid-back stay in an authentic Mexican community.

◉ Sights

El Refugio de Potosí   WILDLIFE RESERVE
(☑cell 755-5572840; www.elrefugiodepotosi. org; Colonia Playa Blanca s/n) ✿ This nature center rehabilitates injured wildlife, breeds butterflies and parrots, and contributes to environmental education in the area. The grounds are home to macaws, iguanas and an impressive 18m sperm-whale skeleton exhibit. Those interested in visiting may make arrangements by contacting the center via email. It's just inland from the beachfront, around 3.5km north of town.

☞ Tours

Nearly every *enramada* in the pueblo – all of them owned by fishing families – offers 90-minute boat tours of the lagoon, where you can glimpse crocodiles for the standard M$350 price. It's possible to rent kayaks and SUPs in the village and worth paddling around the lagoon at dawn. Luis of Ixtapa Zihuatanejo (p569) runs kayaking tours of the lagoon.

Paradise Bird Tours   OUTDOORS
(Eco Tours Cheli's Oregón; ☑cell 755-1306829; www.facebook.com/araceli.oregonsalas; Barra de Potosí–Achotes s/n; bird-watching/snorkeling/fishing M$370/2000/4500) Based at Restaurante Rosita, English-speaking guide Araceli 'Cheli' Oregón runs two-hour boat tours of the lagoon to spy a variety of birds and crocs. She also offers four-hour and six-hour snorkeling and fishing trips.

Snorkeling trips include a buzz out to the impressive Morros de Potosí, a cluster of massive guano-covered rocks about 20 minutes offshore. Boats circle the Morros, affording views of the many seabirds that nest out there, before heading to nearby Playa Manzanillo, where the snorkeling is sublime.

XIHUACAN

Known locally as 'La Chole,' the hamlet of Soledad de Maciel sits atop the largest, most important archaeological site in Guerrero state: Xihuacan. Since excavations began in earnest in 2007, archaeologists have discovered a plaza, a ball court and three pyramids – one crowned by five temples – all left behind by pre-Hispanic cultures including Tepoztecos, Cuitlatecos and Tomiles.

In Nahuatl, 'Xihuacan' (she-*wha*-cahn) means something like 'place of the people who control eternity,' with 'turquoise' being a synonym for 'time.' Dating as far back as 800 BCE, the ancient settlement of Xihuacan was at the height of its influence and power between 200 CE and 800 CE, and the largest population center between Acapulco and Zacatula at the time. It is believed that during its existence it was an important ceremonial center, used for the worship of different gods by pre-Hispanic peoples such as the Cuitlatecos, Tarascans, Mixtecas, Aztecs, Zapotecas and Totonacas. Some stone carvings found at the site suggest Olmec influence, going back even further in time, while a circular stone and various deposits of human remains suggest that human sacrifice was practiced here.

The Instituto Nacional de Antropología e Historia claims that Xihuacan ruins rival Teotihuacán or Chichén Itzá in importance, spanning the pre-Classic to post-Classic periods in Mesoamerican chronology. Ceramics and other objects recovered from the site suggest that Xihuacan had a long-standing trade relationship with Teotihuacán.

Xihuacan was all but abandoned around 850 CE after catastrophic marine flooding. This is supported by the fact that its palace, pyramids and the 55m-long ball court – the second-largest in Mexico after Chichén Itzá's – were buried under tons of sand, consistent with the damage of a tsunami wave.

Near the archaeological site, a **museum** (☑ cell 758-1043188; www.inah.gob.mx; turnoff Hwy 200 Km 214; suggested donation M$10, guided tour M$100; ⊗ 8am-4pm Tue-Sun) houses three rooms displaying clay figurines, copper axes, carved seashells, ceramics and other artifacts recovered from the site, including two granite ball hoops from the ball court. A relief map of the site excavated so far shows the locations of the temples used by various peoples for ceremonies, and a recent find on display is a stone carved with a glyph of the name of the town in the late pre-Hispanic era: Xihuacan. Another highlight is the round stone slab carved with an image of Tlaltecuhtli, a deity that devoured gods and men at the end of their life cycle.

So far, archaeologists have uncovered several major structures, including a 14m-high pyramid. A royal palace is in the process of being excavated, as is a second ball court. Visitors can access the ball court, some 500m south of the museum; other parts of the site will become accessible during the course of excavation.

Soledad de Maciel is 33km southeast of Zihuatanejo off Hwy 200. From the well-marked turnoff near Km 214, a road leads 4km coastward to the museum, then continues another kilometer to the archaeological site and village.

Any bus heading south to Petatlán or Acapulco will get you here; ask to be dropped at 'La Chole' intersection, where you can get a *camioneta* (pickup truck; M$11) into town. Alternatively, you can come here as part of a guided tour with Luis of Ixtapa Zihuatanejo (p569).

🛏 Sleeping & Eating

★ La Casa del Encanto   B&B $$
(☑ cell 755-1246122; www.lacasadelencanto.com; Rodríguez s/n; d incl breakfast US$80-90; ⊛ 🗦)

🖉 For bohemian charm and an intimate perspective on the community, nothing beats this magical space of brilliantly colored open-air rooms, hammocks, fountains and candlelit stairways. Owner Laura, a great resource for getting to know the town, has spent years organizing international volunteers to work with neighborhood children. The B&B is on a residential street about 300m inland from the beach.

Rates are flexible off-season with good deals for longer stays. Laura can help you arrange horseback-riding tours, kayak rental and more.

La Condesa   SEAFOOD $$
(☑ cell 755-1203128; Barra de Potosí–Achotes s/n; mains M$90-150; ⊗ 9am-6pm) Northernmost of the beachfront *enramada* restaurants, this

is one of the best. Try its *pescado a la talla* (grilled fish) or *tiritas*, both local specialties, while digging your feet in the sand and watching the Pacific surf batter the shore.

ℹ️ Getting There & Away

By car from Zihuatanejo, drive southeast on Hwy 200 toward Acapulco, turn off at Los Achotes and drive another 9km to Barra de Potosí.

By public transportation, catch a Petatlán-bound bus from outside Zihuatanejo's main terminals, or from the terminal (p578) near Zihua's market. Tell the driver to let you off at the Barra de Potosí *crucero* (turnoff; M$22, 30 minutes), where you can catch a *camioneta* (pickup truck; M$17, 20 minutes) the rest of the way.

Colectivos also run directly from the airport (p578) to Barra de Potosí (M$17, 30 minutes).

Acapulco

📞744 / POP 753,890

From the 1950s onwards, Acapulco, Mexico's original party town, was a household name. It was dubbed the 'Pearl of the Pacific' during its heyday as a playground for the rich and famous, including Frank Sinatra, Elvis Presley and Elizabeth Taylor. Though its reputation among international visitors has waned, to the rich and famous of Mexico City it still remains the place to see and be seen.

Acapulco's stunning topography is an additional lure: soaring cliffs curl into a series of wide bays and intimate coves, fringed with sandy beaches backed by high-rise hotels, all against a backdrop of jungle-green hills. Then there are the daredevil cliff divers, the city's most celebrated spectacle.

There are some truly unexpected surprises to discover here. Despite frightening drug wars statistics, the city's violence is largely confined to gang disputes, and you'd have to be truly unlucky to get caught up in it.

ℹ️ Orientation

Acapulco is a spread-out city, stretching from the chilled-out seaside neighborhood of Pie de la Cuesta to the north of the Bahía de Acapulco (Acapulco Bay), to Diamante, a series of beaches south of the bay where the most exclusive hotels are found, following the 11km shore en route. Old Acapulco, or the *centro histórico*, centers on the cathedral and adjacent *zócalo* in the western part of the city. Zona Dorada, with its lively mix of restaurants and hotels, heads east around the bay from Playa Hornos to Playa Icacos. Diamante ends near the airport.

Acapulco's 10km-long principal bayside avenue, Avenida Costera Miguel Alemán – often called 'La Costera' – hugs the shoreline all the way around the bay. Past the naval base, Avenida Costera becomes Carretera Escénica and climbs over the headland toward Diamante and the airport.

👁️ Sights

Most of Acapulco's hotels, restaurants, discos and points of interest are along or near Avenida Costera, especially near its midpoint at **La Diana** (Map p590; Av Costera Miguel Alemán s/n) traffic circle. From Playa Caleta on the Península de las Playas, it curves north toward the *zócalo,* then continues east along the beachfront past Parque Papagayo, all the way to Playa Icacos and the naval base at the bay's southeastern edge.

⭐**Zona Arqueológica de Palma Sola**   ARCHAEOLOGICAL SITE
(📞744-189-23-74; www.inah.gob.mx/zonas/36-zona -arqueologica-de-palma-sola; La Mona; ⊙9am-5pm) **FREE** One of Acapulco's best attractions is the least well known and also the least expected. High above the city, on the La Cuesta hill, it's a ceremonial and pilgrimage site dating back to 450 BCE to 650 CE, with some wonderfully preserved rock paintings, petroglyphs depicting the story of creation, and the best bird's-eye view of the city spread out beneath you from the site's highest point. It costs around M$350 to get here by taxi from central Acapulco, including waiting time.

Take water with you for the steep slog up between granite boulders, inscribed with human figures and odd human-anchor hybrids. Some depict the participants dancing or wearing ritual masks. The site is located at the confluence of two creeks, suggesting its importance in the worship of Tláloc, the god of rain, who is associated with running water. To reach the most important part of the site, the cave carved with petroglyphs depicting the creation myth, veer to the left. There are explanation boards in English and Spanish. Watch your step, lest you startle a snake dozing in the sun.

⭐**Museo Histórico de Acapulco**   MUSEUM
(Map p590; 📞744-482-38-28; www.facebook. com/museohistoricodeacapulcofuertedesandiego; Hornitos s/n; M$60; ⊙9am-6pm Tue-Sun; 🅿️) The Fuerte de San Diego (p582) is home to this excellent 15-room museum, an enjoyable romp through the history of the region, from its settlement by various pre-Hispanic peoples to Acapulco's days as the principal

port for the key trade route to the Philippines, responsible for Asian influence on Mexican arts and the accumulation of immense wealth that attracted pirates, corsairs and freebooters. Check out the cross-section of a galleon, and spot a Japanese katana in an exquisitely carved ivory sheath.

Other displays cover the War of Independence when the fort was taken from the Spaniards after a six-month siege under the command of the warrior-priest Morelos, and there are excellent temporary exhibitions such as the one on the importance of the jaguar in pre-Hispanic cultures.

Fuerte de San Diego
FORTRESS

(Map p590; ☑744-482-38-28; www.facebook. com/museohistoricodeacapulcofuertedesandiego; Hornitos s/n; ⊙24hr) FREE This beautifully restored pentagonal fort was built in 1616 atop a hill east of the *zócalo*. Its mission was to protect the Spanish *naos* (galleons) conducting trade between the Philippines and Mexico from marauding Dutch and English buccaneers. The fort was destroyed in a 1776 earthquake and rebuilt; it remains basically unchanged today and is home to the excellent Museo Histórico de Acapulco (p581).

Exekatlkalli
PUBLIC ART

(Casa de los Vientos; Map p587; Inalámbrica 8; ◻Caleta) A dying Diego Rivera spent the final two years of his life at this villa with his muse and lover, Mexican art collector Dolores 'Lola' Olmedo. Rivera spent over a year and a half of that time (1956–57) working on five murals, two of which fringe the entrance to the villa and are accessible to the public. Made of colored tiles and shells, the serpentine images depict Quetzalcóatl, the feathered serpent, and Tláloc, the Aztec god of rain.

Museo de la Máscara
MUSEUM

(Map p587; ☑747-484-71-68; cnr Hornitos & Morelos; ⊙10am-5pm Tue-Sun) FREE If you love masks but are unable to visit the epic museums in Zacatecas and San Miguel, swing by this new museum, where visages of devils, conquistadors, jaguars and more gaze down from the walls. Most of the masks are from Guerrero; check out the exquisite horsehair and goat's-horn ceremonial masks and the human-animal hybrids from Mexican legends that dictate that each person has a guardian animal. Watch the video on mask use in festivals and religious ceremonies.

There are also some African and Indian masks, and the curator is happy to chat about the art of mask-making.

La Capilla de la Paz
VIEWPOINT

(Chapel of Peace; ☑744-446-54-58; Vientos Cardinales s/n, Alto Las Brisas; ⊙10am-6pm) FREE Perched on a hilltop high above Acapulco is this quiet spot for reflection, an airy '70s A-frame chapel surrounded by lovely gardens and providing stunning ocean views. Despite the giant white cross that can be seen from miles away, it was built as a non-denominational chapel to welcome people of all faiths – the garden's sculpture of clasped hands perhaps better captures that spirit. Access is via a gated compound: you may have to leave ID at the gate.

Isla de la Roqueta
ISLAND

(☑744-410-97-07; www.yatesdeacapulco.com; round-trip boat M$60, glass-bottomed boat M$150) This island offers a popular (crowded) beach, and snorkeling and diving possibilities on the far side. You can rent snorkeling gear, kayaks and more. From Playa Caleta, boats make the eight-minute trip regularly. Alternatively, glass-bottomed boats (Yates Fondo de Cristal) make a circuitous trip from here or the *zócalo*, pointing out celebrity dwellings, sea life and the **Virgen de los Mares**, a submerged bronze Virgin statue. The trip takes about 45 minutes.

Pie de la Cuesta
AREA

Just 12km from central Acapulco is Pie de la Cuesta, a rustic beach suburb built on a wide sand spit that acts as a dividing line between the sea and the freshwater Laguna de Coyuca. The large freshwater lagoon contains several islands including **Isla Pájaros**, a bird sanctuary. It's a more serene place than Acapulco proper, good for enjoying dramatic sunset views from the long beach and bloody sunrises over the lagoon or for horseback riding by the crashing ocean.

Movie buffs: Laguna de Coyuca is where part of *Rambo: First Blood Part II* was filmed.

Jardín Botánico de Acapulco
GARDENS

(Map p584; ☑744-446-52-52; www.acapulco botanico.org; Av Heróico Colegio Militar s/n, Cumbres de Llano Largo; adult/child M$40/free, Sun free, guided visit per person M$60; ⊙9am-6pm) Located on the campus of a Jesuit university, these botanical gardens house an impressive collection of flora and fauna. The well-marked footpath climbs from 204m to 411m above sea level through a shaded tropical forest, with plenty of benches to stop at and smell the flowers. It's 1.2km from the main road between Acapulco and Diamante; shared cabs marked 'Base-

Cumbres' depart from the Icacos Naval Base and drop you right outside the gardens.

Zócalo
PLAZA

(Map p587; cnr Av Costera Miguel Alemán & Madero) Every night Acapulco's leafy old town *zócalo* comes alive with street performers, mariachis and sidewalk cafes; it also hosts occasional festivals. It's especially popular with multiple generations of Mexican families on Sunday nights. The **Catedral de Nuestra Señora de la Soledad** (Map p587; ☎744-483-05-63; www.facebook.com/catedral.soledad; Hidalgo s/n; ⊙7am-8pm Mon-Sat, 6:30am-9pm Sun) 【FREE】, built in 1930, dominates the square and is unusual for its blue-domed, neo-Byzantine architecture.

Sinfonía del Mar
VIEWPOINT

(Symphony of the Sea; Map p584; Av López Mateos s/n) Sinfonía del Mar is an outdoor stepped plaza that occasionally hosts concerts, but mainly serves as an amazing place to view sunsets.

Parque Papagayo
PARK

(Map p590; ☎744-486-14-14; www.facebook.com/parquepapagayoacapulcoepbs; Morín 1; ⊙6am-8pm; P) 【FREE】 This large shaded children's park, between Morín and El Cano near Playa Hornitos, is popular with Mexican families. Attractions include a lake with paddleboats, a children's train, a bar-restaurant, an aviary, a small zoo and a petting zoo. The 1.2km circuit trail is a good place for a morning jog.

Beaches

Acapulco's beaches top the list of must-dos for most visitors. The beaches heading east around the bay from the *zócalo* – **Playa Hornos** (Map p590; Av Costera Miguel Alemán), **Playa Hornitos** (Map p590; Av Costera Miguel Alemán), **Playa Condesa** (Map p590; Av Costera Miguel Alemán) and **Playa Icacos** (Map p590; Av Costera Miguel Alemán) – are the most popular, though the west end of Hornos sometimes smells of fish from the morning catch. The high-rise hotel district begins on Playa Hornitos, on the east side of Parque Papagayo, and sweeps east. City buses constantly ply Avenida Costera, making it easy to get up and down the long arc of beaches.

Playas Caleta and Caletilla (Map p584; San Martin; Caleta) are two small beaches on the south side of Península de las Playas. The calm waters make for safe swimming, but the immensely popular location draws throngs of family vacationers, especially in July and August and during the busy winter holiday season. From the city center along Avenida Costera, buses marked 'Caleta' arrive here. Boats to Isla de la Roqueta depart from a small dock.

Playa La Angosta (Map p587; Adolfo López Mateos; Caleta), a protected cove about 1.5km southwest of the *zócalo*, is reachable by walking from the main plaza; alternatively, a 'Caleta' bus will leave you one block from the beach. Locals visit La Angosta for its *palapa* seafood restaurants.

CENTRAL PACIFIC COAST ACAPULCO

CLAVADISTAS DE LA QUEBRADA

Acapulco's most famous tourist attraction, the **cliff divers of La Quebrada** (Map p587; Plazoleta La Quebrada s/n; adult/child M$40/15; ⊙shows 1pm, 7:30pm, 8:30pm, 9:30pm & 10:30pm; Caleta) have been performing daredevil dives off the La Quebrada cliffs since the 1920s, though it wasn't until 1934 that it became an organized spectacle. It's an impressive one.

Every night, as an audience gathers on the viewing platform opposite the cliff (get here early to secure a good viewing spot), a team of seven lithe young divers leaps into the churning waves of the narrow ocean cove below before scaling the vertical cliff opposite. The lights are lit at the clifftop shrine to the Virgin, asking her for protection, before the show takes place. Most dive from the lower (25m) platform – first a solo diver, then a pair simultaneously, then three divers leaping gracefully in sync. The final diver dives from the very top (35m).

The trick is the timing: they have to get it right and meet the incoming wave, otherwise there is not enough water in the churning cove to cushion their fall, and you find the audience holding their collective breaths as they watch the divers make their way out of the roiling sea without getting dashed against the rocks. The spectacle lasts for around 20 minutes. The last show, at 10:30pm, features the final diver holding two flaming torches as he dives into the darkness (they turn off the floodlights for that one). Tip the divers on your way out.

Greater Acapulco

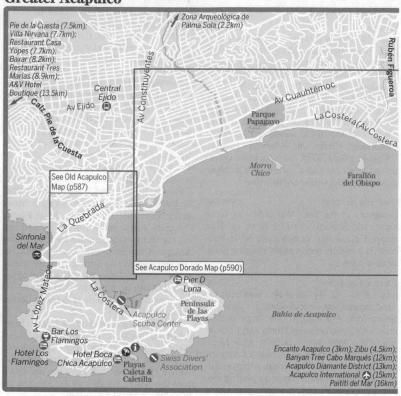

A scenic drive heading southeast of the city center along the jungle-backed Hwy 200 affords spectacular views of the Acapulco Bay before a turnoff descends to the beaches on **Bahía Puerto Marqués** (Av Costera Miguel Alemán; 🚌 Puerto Marqués), where you can get in some waterskiing and swimming on the bay's calm waters. For public transportation, take a frequent Puerto Marqués bus (p594) along Avenida Costera.

About 3km south of Puerto Marqués, rougher waters await at **Playa Revolcadero** (Costera Las Palmas), a popular surf spot but somewhat dangerous option for swimming. The long beach has seen a development boom in recent years, but it's still possible to find quiet stretches of sand.

The two beaches closest to Old Acapulco are **Playa Tlacopanocha** (Map p587; Av Costera Miguel Alemán) – not known as a swimming spot – and **Playa Manzanillo** (Map p587), a small beach where you can take a dip; note that the water quality isn't so great.

🏃 Activities

Acapulco's activities are largely beach-based.

Cruises

Various boats and yachts offer cruises around the bay. Most depart from Playa Tlacopanocha or Playa Manzanillo near the *zócalo*. Cruises are available day and night. Vessels range from glass-bottomed boats to multilevel craft (with blaring salsa music and open bars) to yachts offering quiet sunset cruises. Make reservations at the marina or through travel agencies, tour kiosks and most hotels.

Acarey   CRUISE
(Map p587; 📞744-100-36-37; www.acarey.com.
mx; Av Costera Miguel Alemán s/n; adult/child under 10yr M$350/free; ⏰cruises 4:30pm & 10:30pm daily, plus 7:30pm Sat) This popular boat cruise is sold by nearly every kiosk and agency in town, plus at the booth by the dock across from the *zócalo*. All departures have an open

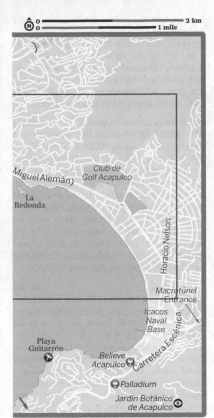

0 ━━━━━━━━ **2 km**
0 ━━━━━━━ **1 mile**

Miguel Alemán)
La Redonda
Club de Golf Acapulco
Horacio Nelson
Macrotúnel Entrance
Icacos Naval Base
Playa Guitarrón
Believe Acapulco
Carretera Escénica
Palladium
Jardín Botánico de Acapulco

bar and live music. The 4:30pm sunset outing gives a decent tour of the bay, while the night cruise is more of a fiesta. Trips last 2½ hours.

Sportfishing

Sportfishing is very popular, especially during the winter months when you can catch marlin and yellowfin tuna.

Blue Water Sportfishing   FISHING
(Map p587; ☑cell 744-4282279; www.acavio. com/aventura.html; Av Pinzona 163; fishing charters US$250-390) Fun and friendly fishing setup that will pick you up from the pier at the *zócalo*. Price varies according to boat size.

Water Sports

Just about everything that can be done on or below the water is done in Acapulco. Waterskiing, boating, banana-boating and parasailing are all popular. Outfitters, based in kiosks along the Zona Dorada beaches, charge about M$600 for a five-minute parasailing flight, and M$1500 per boat for one hour of water-

skiing or wakeboarding. The smaller Playas Caleta and Caletilla (p583) have sailboats, fishing boats, motorboats, pedal boats, canoes and snorkeling gear for rent.

Though Acapulco isn't really a scuba destination, there are some decent dive sites nearby.

The best snorkeling is off small Playa Las Palmitas on Isla de la Roqueta (p582). Unless you pony up for an organized snorkeling trip, you'll need to scramble over rocks to reach it. You can rent gear on the island or on Playas Caleta and Caletilla, which also have some decent spots.

Swiss Divers' Association   DIVING
(Map p584; ☑744-482-13-57; www.swissdivers. com; Hotel Caleta, Cerro San Martín 325; 1-/2-tank boat dive US$65/85, snorkeling US$40; ⊗9am-5pm Thu-Tue) This experienced setup offers a wide range of dives, including night dives and discovery dives, plus PADI courses. Their office is tucked above wave-lashed rocks amid the semi-ruined splendor of Hotel Caleta. Snorkeling trips also available.

Acapulco Scuba Center   DIVING
(Map p584; ☑744-482-94-74; www.acapulco scuba.com; Club Náutico La Marina Acapulco, Av Costera Miguel Alemán 215; 1-/2-tank dive M$1200/1500, snorkeling M$600; ⊗8am-4pm Wed-Mon) One of several reputable diving operators that can take you out on boat dives in the bay. Offers PADI and SSI certification. Snorkeling trips to Isla de la Roqueta (p582) are also available.

Club de Ski Cadena   WATER SPORTS
(☑cell 744-1598503; www.facebook.com/Club cadena; Av de la Fuerza Aérea Mexicana s/n, Pie de la Cuesta; tours per hour M$950) This operator in Pie de la Cuesta does waterskiing and wakeboarding outings as well as a boat tour of the lagoon, which stops at two islands. The English-speaking owner Fernando also knows a lot about the area's bird species.

🎉 Festivals & Events

Festival Francés   CULTURAL
(www.festivalfrancomexicano.com; ⊗Mar or Apr) The French Festival, usually held in March or April, celebrates French food, cinema, music and literature.

Trópico   MUSIC
(https://tropicomx.com; Forum de Mundo Imperial, Blvd de las Naciones; ⊗Dec) Taking place over the first weekend in December, this lively music festival celebrates the best that the

Guerrero state has to offer, from numerous live band performances to fashion shows, food, crafts and more. An impressive lineup of bands performs at the Forum de Mundo Imperial in Diamante.

🛏 Sleeping

Most of Acapulco's budget hotels are concentrated around the *zócalo,* and there are some in Pie de la Cuesta and along the waterfront toward the Zona Dorada. The original high-rise zone of hotels stretches from the eastern end of Parque Papagayo and curves east around the bay, while the most luxurious and exclusive options are in the hills and along the beaches of Diamante, near the airport.

🛏 Centro & Caleta

Hotel Asturias Acapulco HOTEL $
(Map p587; ☎744-483-65-48; www.facebook.com/juanaherlinda.olmedocruz; Calz La Quebrada 45; r M$370; ꔷꔷꔷ) A five-minute walk from La Quebrada, this sweet, family-run hotel may be basic, its rooms straight out of the 1980s, but the central location is good and there's a small pool as a bonus. No wi-fi.

Mirador Acapulco Hotel HISTORIC HOTEL $$
(Map p587; ☎744-271-30-75; www.miradoracapulco.com; Plazoleta La Quebrada; d/ste M$890/1190; ꔷꔷꔷ) This simple 1930s hotel has been drawing huge numbers of guests for as long as the *clavadistas* (cliff divers) have been an organized spectacle. The rooms themselves are tiled and rather bland, decor-wise, but there's a restaurant (La Perla) where you can watch Acapulco's best spectacle for free, plus three tiered swimming pools overlooking the waves.

Hotel Los Flamingos HOTEL $$
(Map p584; ☎744-482-06-91; https://hotelflamingosacapulco.com; Av López Mateos s/n; r US$46-60; ꔷꔷꔷꔷꔷ) Images of Hollywood's Golden Age adorn the walls at this retro hotel with million-dollar views, once owned by Johnny 'Tarzan' Weissmuller, John Wayne and their pals. Perched on a cliff 135m above the ocean, rooms here are modest though comfortable, with hammocks to enjoy the vistas from, and a popular bar and restaurant. Junior suite is a worthwhile upgrade.

WE Hotel Acapulco HOTEL $$
(Map p590; ☎744-485-13-12; http://wehotelacapulco.com.mx; Av Costera Miguel Alemán 248; r from M$1200; ꔷꔷꔷ) Overlooking Playa

Hornos, halfway between the historic center and the Zona Dorada, this smart new hotel probably won't make your social media posts – but for all the right reasons. Rooms are spacious, tiled and an unmemorable beige, with good beds and pool views. With a small spa, gym and poolside restaurant, it attracts a mix of businesspeople and vacationers.

Hotel Boca Chica Acapulco RESORT $$$
(Map p584; ☎744-482-78-79; www.hotel-bocachica.com; Playa Caletilla; r US$105-153, ste US$184-234; ꔷꔷꔷꔷ) With a lofty cliff-face position above one of Acapulco's favorite beaches, this stylish resort combines a 1950s interior (decorated by Mexican artist Claudia Fernández) with some thoroughly contemporary, bright rooms with iPod docks and retro showers. The pricier doubles have hammocks on balconies, and other boons include a pool terrace, spa and thatch-roofed restaurant blending Mexican and Japanese cuisines.

Pier D Luna B&B $$$
(Map p584; ☎744-480-10-18, cell 744-1792072; http://pier-d-luna-guest-house.hotelsacapulco.net; Casa No 2, Gran Vía Tropical 34; r incl breakfast US$120-155; ꔷꔷꔷꔷꔷ) This tucked-away retreat has a view so good that the enormous lounge and dining room, complete with baby grand piano, is wholly open-sided: what a marvelous space it is. Five individually designed rooms enjoy the same outlook; some have balconies to soak it all up. Hospitable hosts make this a delightful personal experience and breakfasts are abundant. Two-night minimum.

There's a pleasant pool and Jacuzzi upstairs and a great saltwater pool on the bay, to which you can descend via private stairs. Delicious chef-cooked French-Mexican meals are available by arrangement. Pay attention to the directions you'll be sent, as there are no signs. Reserve ahead.

🛏 Zona Dorada

Bali-Hai MOTEL $$
(Map p590; ☎744-485-66-22; www.balihai.com.mx; Av Costera Miguel Alemán 186; r M$1300-1800; ꔷꔷꔷꔷꔷ) This Polynesian-themed motel in the heart of Bahía de Acapulco, across the street from the beach, is ideal for the Zona Dorada exploration, with secure parking and long rows of spacious rooms flanking a pair of palm-lined pools. Upgrading to a pricier 'superior' room offers little in return.

Old Acapulco

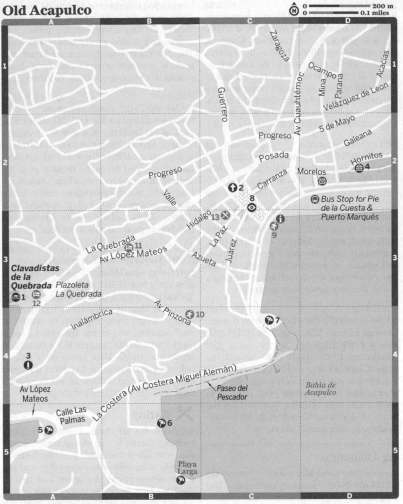

Old Acapulco

◎ Top Sights
1 Clavadistas de la Quebrada	A3

◎ Sights
2 Catedral de Nuestra Señora de la Soledad	C2
3 Exekatlkalli	A4
4 Museo de la Máscara	D2
5 Playa La Angosta	A5
6 Playa Manzanillo	B5
7 Playa Tlacopanocha	C4
8 Zócalo	C2

✪ Activities, Courses & Tours
9 Acarey	C3
10 Blue Water Sportfishing	B4

⊜ Sleeping
11 Hotel Asturias Acapulco	B3
12 Mirador Acapulco Hotel	A3

⊗ Eating
13 El Nopalito	C3

Hotel Elcano HOTEL $$
(Map p590; ☑744-435-15-00; www.hotelelcano.com.mx; Av Costera Miguel Alemán 75; d US$61-82; P❷❈@☎☀) On the Playa Condesa, this spruced-up 1950s behemoth features art-deco tiles in the breezy lobby, a maritime theme in its spacious rooms, decked out in blues and whites, and ocean views from all the rooms, plus pool area right on the beach. It's worth splurging on a room with private terrance. Low-season discounts are a steal.

★**Encanto Acapulco** DESIGN HOTEL $$$
(☑744-446-71-01; www.encantoacapulco.mx; Jacques Cousteau 51, Brisas del Marqués; r/ste/villa from US$275/474/895; P❷❈☎☀) An architectural masterpiece designed by Miguel Ángel Aragonés, aptly named Encanto (Charm) doubles as art gallery for the works of Spanish artist Fernando Bermejo. Located on the cliffs, it's all minimalist chic, with open-plan, thoroughly contemporary rooms in creams and whites, an award-winning spa and infinity pool from which to drink in the ocean vistas. You may never want to leave.

Las Brisas RESORT $$$
(☑744-469-69-00; www.lasbrisashotels.com.mx; Carretera Escénica 5255; r/ste from US$86/257; P❷☎☀) High up in the hills, this spruced-up 1950s resort once hosted the likes of Sophia Loren and Morgan Freeman. You too can stay in one of the individual casitas (villas) with a private pool, simmer in the hot tub of the master suite and hit the beach via La Concha beach club. All accommodations offer terrific sea views.

🛏 Diamante

Banyan Tree Cabo Marqués RESORT $$$
(☑744-434-01-00; www.banyantree.com; Blvd Cabo Marqués s/n, Punta Diamante; villa US$399-899; P❷❈@☎☀) Over the ocean on a gated peninsula, 20km south of downtown, this all-inclusive resort brings Asia to Acapulco. Sumptuous villas offer complete privacy to enjoy your hammock and private plunge pool, and the views of the Pacific from infinity pool are show-stopping. Highlights of the complex include a Thai restaurant, and spa with private massage rooms with a view.

🛏 Pie de la Cuesta

Villa Nirvana HOTEL $$
(☑744-460-16-31; Av de la Fuerza Aérea Mexicana 302; d US$47-68, q US$78; P❷☎☀) Villa Nirvana's American expat owners have lovingly landscaped this cheerful beachside property 500m from the main road turnoff. It has a variety of simple, comfortable rooms surrounding a central garden and sizable pool. The priciest rooms upstairs are larger and include sea-view terraces and large hammocks. A spruce-up wouldn't go amiss.

Baxar BOUTIQUE HOTEL $$
(☑744-460-25-02; www.baxar.com.mx; Av de la Fuerza Aérea Mexicana 356; r M$1583, ste M$2824-3160, all incl breakfast; P❷❈☎☀) Trimmed in pink and exuding barefoot style, this is a popular and friendly weekend getaway, though it could use some looking after. Its somewhat musty rooms include sunken sitting areas, tastefully dangling rattan lampshades, mosquito nets and other sweet little details. Rates include use of kayaks, and paddleboards are available for rent.

A&V Hotel Boutique BOUTIQUE HOTEL $$$
(☑744-444-43-29; www.avhotelboutique.com; Av de la Fuerza Aérea Mexicana Km 6.2, Colonia Luces en el Mar; r from US$115, ste US$160; ❷❈☎☀; 🖳 Playa Luces) Each of the ultra-comfortable rooms at this intimate hotel incorporates earthy design elements, such as palm-leaf wall paneling and rattan lampshades, plus quirky art and fun features like a hammock inside the room. Most come with private balconies overlooking a free-form pool and onsite restaurant, which is worth visiting even if you're not staying at the hotel.

🍴 Eating

Your best bet for cheap, if not particularly exciting, dining is the *zócalo* area. Numerous seafood restaurants line the beaches (*ceviche Acapulco* is the specialty) and get progressively pricier the nearer one gets to the Zona Dorada, where there's a mix of taco eateries and excellent restaurants serving a mix of Mexican and international cuisines. The best fine dining is found in Diamante and at exclusive hotels in the hills south of Acapulco Bay.

🍴 Centro

★**Taquería El Cheff** TACOS $
(Map p590; ☑744-247-70-44; https://taqueria-el-cheff.negocio.site; Bernal Díaz del Castillo s/n; tacos M$8; ⊙8am-midnight Mon, 24hr Tue-Sat, noon-11pm Sun) This popular neighborhood *taquería* does two things, tacos and *panuchos* (tortillas stuffed with beans) filled or topped with *cochinita pibil*, and both are fine examples of

the genre. Grab a seat at a plastic table in the street and fill your boots for a pittance.

El Nopalito
CAFE $

(Map p587; ☑ 744-294-08-58; La Paz 230; mains M$55-130, menú del día M$60; ☺ 8am-8pm) This darkish, old-school eatery attracts people for its daily menu, which includes *mole verde* (green chili sauce dish) on Thursdays and Sundays. The set-menu lunch includes fruit, juice or coffee and a main such as roast chicken, beef enchilada, *carne asada* or fried fish, served with *nopales* and tortillas.

El Amigo Miguel
SEAFOOD $$

(Map p590; ☑744-486-28-68; Av Costera Miguel Alemán s/n, Playa Hornos; mains M$80-200; ☺ 10am-8:30pm) This Acapulco mini-chain has been around since the '70s. Skip the ho-hum meat dishes and go for what these guys do best: shrimp *al ajillo* (with garlic butter) or *a la diabla* (spicy!), ceviche, grilled lobster and fish tacos. This thatch-roofed Playa Hornos branch is particularly pleasant; there are also branches in the *centro histórico* and Diamante.

✖ Zona Dorada

El Jacalito
MEXICAN $

(Map p590; ☑744-486-65-12; Gonzalo de Sandoval 26; mains M$60-120; ☺ 8am-11pm; ☜) Just off the strip and a few paces from the beach, this thatch-roofed restaurant can nevertheless have a secluded vibe. It feels very authentic, with its traditional checked tablecloths and cordial staff, and the food backs it up. Great rolled chicken tacos, delicious *frijoles* (beans), affordable fish dishes and filling breakfasts make it an oasis at any time of day.

La Casa de Tere
MEXICAN $$

(Map p590; ☑744-485-77-35; www.facebook. com/lacasadetereacapulco; Martín 1721; mains M$80-240; ☺ 8am-6pm Tue-Sun; ☜) This homespun gem near the Estrella de Oro bus terminal is the place to go for Thursday *pozole verde* (green hominy stew). Founded on doña Tere's patio in 1990 using her mother Clarita's traditional recipes, it serves a wide-ranging menu, including the sought-after Sunday special: *barbacoa de carnero* (slow-cooked lamb). All of it comes with house-made tortillas.

Chile, Maíz y Frijol
MEXICAN $$

(Map p590; ☑744-481-03-00; www.facebook.com/ chimafri; Av Costera Miguel Alemán 116, Plaza Condesa; mains M$80-160; ☺ 8am-8pm) Thimble-sized

family restaurant with an open kitchen and a very local vibe, serving generous Mexican breakfast (great *chilaquiles!*). As the day progresses, the menu moves on to enchiladas and quesadillas with homemade salsas, plus expertly executed seafood dishes.

Tacos Tumbras
TACOS $$

(Map p590; ☑721-235-73-85; www.tacos tumbras.mx; Av Costera Miguel Alemán 3124; tacos M$16, mains M$99-148; ☺ 6pm-6am Mon-Sat, to 2am Sun) A long-time favorite of the carnivorously inclined, this local *taquería* chain has been around forever and it's still the pre- or post-clubbing stop for those intent on painting the town red. Choose from filled tacos (*al pastor* are the best) or opt for *bistec* (slab of beef), with supporting cast of *pico de gallo* salsa, sweet grilled scallions and dark, piquant chili sauce.

El Cabrito
MEXICAN $$

(Map p590; ☑744-484-77-11; www.facebook.com/ elcabritoacapulco; Av Costera Miguel Alemán 1480; mains M$95-270; ☺ 2-11pm Mon-Sat, 1:30-10:30pm Sun; ☜) This beloved and brightly decorated restaurant has some of the city's finest traditional Mexican food, such as Oaxaca-style black *mole* (a dark and powerful sauce with chocolate and chilies) made from 32 ingredients. But the specialties here are *cabrito al pastor* (roast kid goat) and *cabezita de cabrito* (broiled goat's head); eat it with your fingers, say the staff.

Suntory Acapulco
JAPANESE $$$

(Map p590; ☑744-484-80-88; www.suntory. mx; Av Costera Miguel Alemán 36; mains M$200-360; ☺ 2pm-midnight; ❈☜) Step into the air-conditioned chill of this high-class establishment and prepare yourself for some theatrics and fanfare, as the chefs cook seafood and meat right in front of you on teppanyaki grills at your table. There are also numerous imaginative sushi rolls to choose from and a wine and spirits menu that's Old Testament-thick.

✖ Diamante

★ Paititi del Mar
SEAFOOD $$

(☑744-480-00-31; www.facebook.com/paititidelmar; Zaragoza 6, La Poza; mains M$160-230; ☺ 8:30am-7pm; ☐ Coloso) Set in a tropical garden under a *palapa*, this inland seafood restaurant prepares dishes that put most of Acapulco's beachside eateries to shame. The *ceviche paraiso* is a flavor explosion of fresh tuna, mango, ginger, strawberry and habanero;

Acapulco Dorado

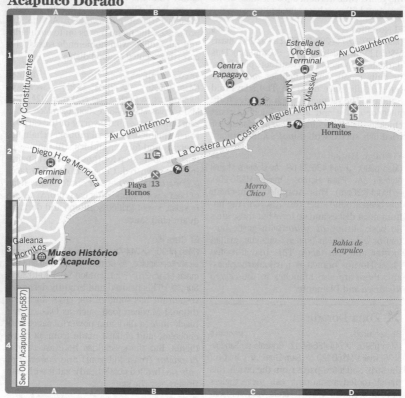

Acapulco Dorado

order it with refreshing cucumber-lime water. For the main course, the grilled or *ajillo*-style octopus draws high praise.

'Coloso' buses, which can be picked up along Avenida Costera anywhere south of

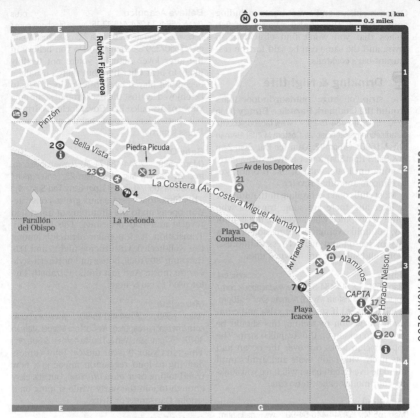

the Hwy 200 turnoff, stop about 2km north of the restaurant on Blvd de las Naciones.

Zibu
FUSION $$$

(☎744-433-30-69; www.zibu.com.mx; Carretera Escénica s/n; mains M$320-650; ☺6pm-1am; P🛜) This thatch-roofed clifftop restaurant is one of Acapulco's – and Mexico's – finest; a happy marriage of stupendous sea and sunset views and Mexican-Thai fusion. The menu is fish- and seafood-heavy, featuring the likes of *camarones sol y sombra* (shrimp with mango/ginger and tamarind/ *chipotle* sauces), pad thai with piquin chili, and Thai-style grilled fish. Impressive wine list and mango martinis.

✖ Pie de la Cuesta

Restaurant Casa Yopes
SEAFOOD $$

(☑cell 744-4605390; Playa Pie de la Cuesta; mains M$90-180; ☺8am-11pm) Come to this simple, family-run restaurant and let congenial Ricar-

da feed you Mexican standards for breakfast and catch-of-the-day and Pacific shrimp the rest of the day, cooked whichever way you like.

Restaurant Tres Marías
SEAFOOD $$

(☎744-460-00-13; www.tresmariasacapulco.com; Av de la Fuerza Aérea Mexicana 375; breakfast M$70-115, lunch & dinner M$160-260; ☺9am-6pm) In an open building by the ocean, this place has cheerfully colored tablecloths and serves fantastic *huachinango al mojo de ajo* (garlicky red snapper). You can bring your own drinks if you choose a table on the beach. Its thatched extension across the road, on the lagoon side, is popular for breakfast.

Mar de Fondo
FUSION $$$

(☎744-444-43-29; www.avhotelboutique.com; Av de la Fuerza Aérea Mexicana Km 6.2, Colonia Luces en el Mar; mains M$200-270; ☺9am-8pm Tue-Sun; P; 🚌Playa Luces) Tired of the fish and seafood routine? Hit this restaurant in A&V Hotel Boutique (p588), where you can order handmade pasta and lasagna, regional

Oaxacan cuisine and sweet treats including apple strudel. There's also a variety of fish dishes that you won't find elsewhere in town, and the same can be said for the restaurant-bar's cocktails.

Drinking & Nightlife

The strip of huge outdoor/indoor bars around the landmark **Paradise Bungy** (Map p590; ☑ 744-484-75-29; www.facebook.com/paradisebungyacaoficial; Av Costera Miguel Alemán 101; M\$600; ◷ 5pm-12:30am Tue-Thu, 3pm-2am Fri & Sat, 3-11pm Sun) tower is lively from early evening until late, with drinks promos, go-go dancers and other revelry.

Most clubs don't get rolling until midnight or later and there are some travelers who come to Acapulco who never see the light of day, not unlike vampires. Admission charges vary by season and night. Dress to impress; shorts and sneakers are frowned upon.

Mojito
COCKTAIL BAR

(Map p590; ☑ 744-484-82-74; www.facebook.com/mojitoaca; Av Costera Miguel Alemán s/n; ◷ 10pm-4am Thu-Sat; 🛜) If you prefer salsa and *cumbia* to reggaeton or techno, this should be your go-to option on the Acapulco strip. The popular club looks out over the ocean and gets lively with Latin beats and drinks until late. The live Cuban band will have you shaking your moneymaker in no time.

Palladium
CLUB

(Map p584; ☑ 744-446-54-90; www.palladium.com.mx; Carretera Escénica s/n; cover men/women M\$550/400; ◷ 11pm-6am Fri & Sat; 🛜) Still the best nightclub in town, Palladium attracts a stylish crowd in their 30s and offers fabulous bay views from floor-to-ceiling windows. An international cast of DJs pumps out hip-hop, house, trance and techno from an ultraluxe sound system. Dress up, and expect to wait in line.

Bar Los Flamingos
BAR

(Map p584; ☑ 744-483-98-06; www.hotelflamingosacapulco.com; Av López Mateos s/n; ◷ 10am-10pm; 🛜) The clifftop bar of Hotel Los Flamingos (p586) is old-school impeccable and the best sundowner spot in Acapulco, thanks to its famed menu of signature cocktails, including *Cocos Locos* (made with rum, tequila, pineapple juice and coconut crème). The restaurant offers a traditional menu, and *pozole* Thursday is a beloved local lunch tradition: reserve ahead.

Believe Acapulco
CLUB

(Map p584; ☑ 744-446-73-15; www.facebook.com/believeaca; Carretera Escénica 22; cover men/women M\$550/350; ◷ 11pm-7am) Do you believe in life after love? Actually, you're not terribly likely to hear Cher here but there's usually a decent set played by a roster of local DJs, to be enjoyed against the backdrop of some epic views of Acapulco Bay. Cover includes drinks, but bartenders expect handsome tipping. Dress smartly.

Baby'O
CLUB

(Map p590; ☑ 744-484-74-74; www.babyo.com.mx; Av Costera Miguel Alemán 22; cover men/women M\$650/400; ◷ 11pm-6am Thu-Sat; 🛜) This Flintstones-esque faux grotto construction opens up to the thumping of unbridled reverie and bad decisions. The fun kind. Translation: it's a popular nightclub among the well-heeled, with theme nights and DJs that spin '80s rock, house and northern-style *banda* music. And just think: Elizabeth Taylor used to party here.

Mezcalina
BAR

(Map p590; ☑ 744-481-15-90; www.facebook.com/mezcalinaacapulco; Av Costera Miguel Alemán 3007; ◷ 7pm-2am Wed & Thu, to 4am Fri & Sat; 🛜) This ain't your typical mezcal joint (unless dancing to loud reggaeton music is a new trend taking over *mezcalerías*), but it's easy enough to join the party while sipping on a smoky Danzantes or Bruxo.

Demás Factory
GAY

(Map p590; Av de los Deportes 10A; ◷ 10pm-7am Fri & Sat; 🛜) The city's longest-running gay club is mixed but draws a mostly male clientele. There are shows on weekend nights and M\$300 gets you all you can drink on Saturdays.

☆ Entertainment

Forum Mundo Imperial
CONCERT VENUE

(☑ 744-435-17-00; http://forummundoimperial.com; Blvd de las Naciones s/n, Acapulco Diamante; ◷ hours vary) At the airport junction in the Diamante area, this huge, striking venue attracts big-name acts for anything from dance performances to rock. It's best reached by car or taxi.

🔒 Shopping

La Europea
ALCOHOL

(Map p590; ☑ 744-484-80-43; www.laeuropea.com.mx; Av Costera Miguel Alemán 2908; ◷ 10am-8pm Mon-Thu, to 9pm Fri & Sat, 11am-

4pm Sun) Stocks a good selection of mezcals and tequilas, such as Pierde Almas and 7 Leguas.

ℹ Information

SAFE TRAVEL

At the time of writing, Acapulco ranked second in Mexico for homicides per capita, but residents rightly claim that this doesn't reflect the reality for visitors. The vast majority of violent incidents are score-settling assassinations between members of rival drug gangs. That said, while protecting the downtown areas is an absolute priority for the city, tourists have occasionally been targeted in isolated incidents or caught in the cross fire. Acapulco isn't necessarily a dangerous place to visit, but, as with most Mexican cities, caution is advised with personal possessions, exploring unfamiliar areas and taking taxis late at night.

EMERGENCY

Tourist Police (☑744-485-04-90)

MEDICAL SERVICES

Hospital Magallanes (☑744-469-02-70; https://hospitalprivadomagallanes.com.mx; Massieu 2) A well-established private hospital with English-speaking doctors and staff.

MONEY

Banks and *casas de cambio* cluster around the *zócalo* and line Avenida Costera. ATMs dot both the Zona Dorada and Diamante.

POST

Main Post Office (Map p587; ☑744-483-24-05; www.correosdemexico.com.mx; Palacio Federal, Av Costera Miguel Alemán 315; ☺8am-7pm Mon-Fri, to 2pm Sat)

TOURIST INFORMATION

CAPTA (Tourist Infomation and Assistance; Map p590; ☑744-481-18-54; www.acapulco. gob.mx/capta; Av Costera Miguel Alemán 38A; ☺office 9am-9pm) Office and 24-hour hotline for tourist information and assistance.

The city government operates several moderately helpful tourist information kiosks. They are located on the **marina** (Map p587; ☑744-481-18-54; www.acapulco.gob.mx/capta; Av Costera Miguel Alemán s/n; ☺9am-6pm) across from the *zócalo*, at **La Diana traffic circle** (Map p590; ☑744-481-18-54; www.acapulco. gob.mx/capta; Av Costera Miguel Alemán s/n; ☺9am-6pm), at **Playa Caleta** (Map p584; ☑744-481-18-54; www.acapulco.gob.mx/capta; ☺9am-6pm) and by the entrance to **Walmart** (Map p590; ☑744-481-18-54; www.acapulco. gob.mx/capta; Horacio Nelson s/n; ☺9am-6pm) near Playa Icacos.

ℹ Getting There & Away

AIR

Acapulco's **airport** (Aeropuerto Internacional General Juan N Álvarez; ☑744-435-20-60; www.oma.aero/es/aeropuertos/acapulco; Blvd de las Naciones s/n) has seen a marked decrease in international nonstop flights, although it's still easy to connect through Mexico City (a short hop from Acapulco). Airlines have offices at the airport; there are a couple of direct flights from the USA and Canada.

The following domestic destinations are serviced by these airlines:

➡ Cancún – Interjet

➡ Guadalajara – TAR, Volaris

➡ Mexico City – Aeromar, Aeroméxico, Interjet, Volaris

➡ Monterrey – VivaAerobús

➡ Queretaro – TAR

➡ Tijuana – Volaris

➡ Toluca – Interjet

BUS

Acapulco has four bus terminals. Fortunately, the two major ones are quite close together. There's also a bus station in the Acapulco Diamante resort area.

Central Ejido (Map p584; ☑744-469-20-30; Av Ejido 47) This bus terminal mostly serves departures to destinations in Guerrero and Oaxaca states, run by the AltaMar/Costeños group. Estrella de Oro services to Zihuatanejo also stop here on their way north.

Central Papagayo (Estrella Blanca Terminal; Map p590; ☑800-507-55-00; www. estrellablanca.com.mx; Av Cuauhtémoc 1605) Just north of Parque Papagayo, this modern terminal has 1st-class and luxury services all around the country run by Estrella Blanca and its affiliates. Left-luggage services available.

Estrella de Oro Bus Terminal (Central Cuauhtémoc; Map p590; ☑800-900-01-05; www. estrelladeoro.com.mx; Av Cuauhtémoc 1490) All Estrella de Oro (EDO) services leave from this modern, air-conditioned terminal, which has several ATMs and left-luggage facilities.

Terminal Centro (Map p590; ☑800-003-76-35; Av Cuauhtémoc 97) First- and 2nd-class departures to relatively nearby towns, though some services to Mexico City stop here too.

CAR & MOTORCYCLE

Several car-rental companies have offices at the airport.

Alamo (☑744-466-93-30; www.alamo.com. mx; Aeropuerto Internacional de Acapulco, Blvd de las Naciones s/n; ☺7am-10pm)

Europcar (☑744-466-93-14; www.europcar. com.mx; Aeropuerto Internacional de Acapulco, Blvd de las Naciones s/n; ☺6am-11pm)

Hertz (☑744-466-94-24; www.hertz.com; Aeropuerto Internacional de Acapulco, Blvd de las Naciones s/n; ☺6am-10pm)

❶ Getting Around

TO/FROM THE AIRPORT

Acapulco's airport (p593) is 23km southeast of the *zócalo*. You can buy a ticket for transportation into town from the desk at the end of the domestic terminal. *Colectivos* charge M$170 per person. Private taxis from the airport run constantly, ranging in price depending on the destination (M$470 to M$600 for central hotels).

Leaving Acapulco, taxis from downtown to the airport cost around M$300 to M$420, depending on the distance.

BUS

The easiest way to get around is on the 'Base–Caleta' bus route, which runs from the Icacos naval base on the southeast end of Acapulco, along Avenida Costera, past the *zócalo* to Playa Caleta. Fares are M$8 for the gussied-up former school buses from the US that turn into mobile raves in the evening, blaring salsa, and M$9.50 for buses with air-conditioning. Heading to the *centro histórico*, look for 'Zocalo'; going the other way, look for 'Condesa.'

Another option is **Acabús** (www.acabus. gob.mx), a system of red rapid-transit buses accessed via station platforms using rechargeable smart cards. The yellow RT4 line is a main route, plying Avenida Costera from Icacos to the *zócalo*. From the *zócalo* station, transfer to the complementary RA12 line to reach Playa Caleta. Rides cost M$10 including free transfers to complementary routes.

Most buses operate from 5am to 11pm. A **bus stop** (Map p587; Av Costera Miguel Alemán s/n; ☺5am-10pm) for the nearby beach towns of Pie de la Cuesta and Puerto Marqués is on Avenida Costera, about two blocks east from the *zócalo*.

To get to Pie de la Cuesta, catch a 'Pie de la Cuesta' bus on Avenida Costera across the street

from the post office. Buses depart every 15 minutes from 6am until 9pm; the trip costs M$11 and takes 30 to 90 minutes, depending on traffic.

Buses marked 'Pie de la Cuesta–San Isidro' or 'Pie de la Cuesta–Pedregoso' stop at the town's arched entryway on Hwy 200, leaving you with a short walk into town; more convenient 'Pie de la Cuesta–Playa Luces' buses turn off the main highway and follow Pie de la Cuesta's main street through town to Playa Luces.

A regular taxi from Acapulco to Pie de la Cuesta costs M$250 to M$400, depending on your negotiating skills.

CAR & MOTORCYCLE

Driving in Acapulco can be challenging, as the anarchic traffic is often horribly snarled, at least along the waterfront. A 3.3km tunnel (M$59) called Macrotúnel runs from south of the Icacos naval base to Acapulco Diamante and tends to attract little traffic, but the drive along the coast is way more scenic.

TAXI

Legions of blue-and-white 1980s Volkswagen Beetle cabs scurry around Acapulco, maneuvering with an audacity that borders on the comical. They charge according to a zone system and some have rates displayed inside, but tourists still have to bargain and it pays to agree on a price with the driver before getting in. Other blue-and-white cabs are also available. A short hop should be M$50 to M$60, while a cross-town ride will be M$100 to M$150.

Shared yellow taxis (*colectivos* or *peseros*) run along set routes and cost M$20 per journey (double if you want to sit on your own in the front and not get squashed). Their destinations are written on the windshield and they can be hailed anywhere – in fact, they'll probably hail you with their horns first.

In the Zona Dorada, fairy-light-covered Cinderella-style horse carts provide a romantic ride while breathing in exhaust fumes, if you're so inclined.

BUSES FROM ACAPULCO

DESTINATION	FARE (M$)	TIME	FREQUENCY (PER DAY)
Chilpancingo	90-140	1½-2½hr	frequent Centro, EDO, Ejido & Papagayo
Cuernavaca	434-567	4-5hr	4 EDO, 6 Papagayo
Mazatlán	1620-1900	19-21hr	2 Papagayo
Mexico City (Terminal Norte)	600-1200	6hr	frequent Centro, EDO & Papagayo
Mexico City (Terminal Sur)	600-1100	5-6hr	frequent Centro, EDO & Papagayo
Puerto Escondido	500	7-8hr	7 Centro, 7 Ejido
Taxco	240-300	4-5hr	1 Centro, 4 EDO
Zihuatanejo	250-300	4½-5½hr	frequent Centro, 6 EDO, 9 Papagayo

CENTRAL PACIFIC COAST ACAPULCO

DON'T MISS

MUSEO DE LAS CULTURAS AFROMESTIZAS

About 200km southeast of Acapulco, **Cuajinicuilapa** (Cuaji for short) is the nucleus of Afromestizo culture on the Costa Chica. If you're passing through en route between Acapulco and Puerto Escondido, it's well worth checking out this excellent **museum** (Museum of Afromestizo Cultures; ☑ cell 741-1250842; Zárate s/n; ⊙ 9am-8pm Mon-Fri, by appointment Sat & Sun) **FREE**, a tribute to the history of African slaves in Mexico and, specifically, to local Afromestizo culture. There are some interesting stories, sweet dioramas and a model slave ship, plus examples of ceremonial masks and musical instruments; all text is in Spanish. Behind the museum are three examples of *casas redondas*, the round houses typical of West Africa that were built around Cuaji until the 1960s. The museum is behind the basketball court on the main road in the town center.

Costa Chica

Guerrero's 'Small Coast,' extending southeast from Acapulco to the Oaxaca border, is much less traveled than its bigger brother (Costa Grande) to the northwest, but it has some spectacular beaches. Afromestizos (people of mixed African, indigenous and European descent) make up a portion of the population. The region was a safe haven for Africans who escaped slavery, some from the interior, others (it's believed) from a slave ship that sank just off the coast.

From Acapulco, Hwy 200 traverses inland past small villages and farmlands. **San Marcos**, about 60km east of Acapulco, and **Cruz Grande**, about 40km further east, are the only two towns of significant size before Cuajinicuilapa near the Oaxaca border. Both provide basic services including banks, gas stations and simple hotels. Playa Ventura makes a great place to spend a couple of days relaxing on a quiet beach with lovely rock formations.

Playa Ventura

☑ 741 / POP 570

Located 135km southeast of Acapulco, Playa Ventura (labeled Colonia Juan Álvarez on most maps) is a long, pristine beach with soft white-and-gold sands. Behind it is a likable Mexican village, while simple beachfront accommodations and seafood restaurants line the beaches in both directions from the center of town.

Playa Ventura is an important turtle-nesting site, and volunteers go out every night in the season (from May to January) to collect eggs and rebury them in a little beachside compound.

★ **Méson Casa de Piedra** HOTEL $
(☑ cell 741-1013129; www.playaventura.mx; Costera Ventura s/n; d M$600-1200; P ⊛ ⊗) The House of Stone features beautifully designed rustic rooms fashioned from recycled objects; some include private balconies with ocean views (the 'Cielo' room provides a sweet vista, and is studded with colorful glass). The Mesón boasts one of the best restaurants in town, serving excellent vegetarian fare, fish and seafood. It's 1.5km south of the church in the town center.

Los Norteñitos MEXICAN $
(☑ cell 745-1163957; mains M$60-160; ⊙ 7am-10pm) Totally authentic and genuinely welcoming, this *taquería* in the center of town is run by an affable local family. Delicious *cecina* (cured beef) tacos are great with freshly made tomatillo (green tomato) salsa in a *molcajete*, while fish and prawns are reliably delicious – the whole snapper cooked in foil with a mellow chili sauce is a standout.

❶ Getting There & Away

To get here by car from Acapulco, take Hwy 200 to the signposted Playa Ventura turnoff (Km 124), just east of the village of Copala, then continue 7km to the coast. Alternatively, take a southeast-bound bus to Copala (M$115 to M$145, about 3½ hours). From the Oxxo convenience store in Copala, *camionetas* (pickup trucks) and microbuses depart for the turnoff to Playa Ventura (M$12, 10 minutes). At the turnoff, shared taxis (M$20, 10 minutes) shuttle into town. Some Cuajinicuilapa-bound buses from Acapulco will drop you directly at the turnoff.

AT A GLANCE

POPULATION
6.3 million

CAPITALS
Guadalajara (Jalisco),
Morelia (Michoacán),
Colima (Colima)

**BEST NEW
MEXICAN CUISINE**
Lu Cocina
Michoacana (p641)

**BEST
TEQUILA TOUR**
Experience Agave
(p609)

BEST PIANO BAR
Cantina La Fuente
(p618)

WHEN TO GO
Dec–Feb
Probably the best
months to mingle with
the monarch butter-
flies in the Reserva
Mariposa Monarca.

Aug & Sep
Enjoy the quintessen-
tial sound of Mexico
at the Encuentro
Internacional del Mar-
iachi in Guadalajara.

Nov
Villages around Pátzc-
uaro host some of the
most colorful Día de
Muertos celebrations.

Blue agave field, Tequila (p624)
T PHOTOGRAPHY/SHUTTERSTOCK ©

Western Central Highlands

Welcome to the Mexico of your imagination! Many of the elements that define the image of Mexico worldwide originated in the western central highlands amid slumbering volcanoes, sun-drenched avocado plantations and some of the country's finest 'undiscovered' pre-Hispanic ruins. Those looking for a bit of local flavor can sip the world's best tequila in a sea of blue agave, listen to mariachi music in the region of its birth or be awed by the twin-towered magnificence of Morelia's cathedral.

Less obvious (and visited) is Lago de Pátzcuaro, where the indigenous Purépecha people display their craft-making skills and observe some of the most remarkable Day of the Dead rituals in the land.

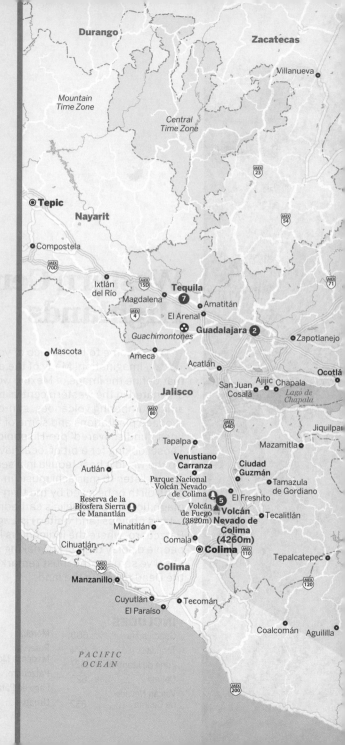

Western Central Highlands Highlights

❶ Morelia
(p635) Getting to know Michoacán's welcoming capital, with its shimmering cathedral, animated streets and delightful architecture.

❷ Guadalajara
(p600) Exploring the excellent art museums, ancient churches and superb restaurants of Mexico's second-largest city.

❸ Reserva Mariposa Monarca
(p644) Absorbing the beauty of this incredible natural phenomenon: the winter retreat of millions of butterflies.

❹ Pátzcuaro
(p646) Peering into the mystical soul of the Purépecha people in this tranquil city of art and beautiful squares.

❺ Volcán Nevado de Colima (p632) Climbing this snowy, extinct volcano that shares a national park with a more active (but off-limits) one.

❻ Tzintzuntzan
(p654) Gazing out over Lago de Pátzcuaro from the mystical and semideserted Purépechan ruins of this archaeological site.

❼ Tequila (p624) Touring and sipping your way through the distilleries in the birthplace of Mexico's most famous beverage.

History

The western central highlands were too distant from the Maya and Aztecs to fall under their influence, but from the 14th to 16th centuries the Purépacha in northern Michoacán state developed a robust pre-Hispanic civilization. When the Aztecs took notice and attacked them, the Purépacha were able to fend them off thanks to their copper blades. West of the Purépacha was their rival, the Chimalhuacán – a confederation of four indigenous kingdoms based in the present-day states of Jalisco, Colima and Nayarit. To the north were the Chichimec.

Colima, the leading Chimalhuacán kingdom, was conquered by the Spanish in 1523. The whole region, however, was not brought under Spanish control until the campaigns of the notorious Nuño de Guzmán. Between 1529 and 1536 he tortured, killed and enslaved indigenous people from Michoacán north to Sinaloa. His grisly exploits made him rich and won him governorship of his conquered lands until news of his war crimes reached home. He was sent back to Spain and imprisoned in 1538.

This fertile ranching and agricultural region developed gradually and Guadalajara, established in 1542, became the 'capital of the west.' The church, with help from Nuño de Guzmán's successor, the enlightened Bishop Vasco de Quiroga, fostered small industries and handicraft traditions around the villages of Lago de Pátzcuaro in an effort to ease the continuing poverty of the indigenous people.

In the 1920s the region's two major states, Michoacán and Jalisco, were hotbeds of the Cristero rebellion led by Catholics fighting the government's antichurch policies. As Michoacán governor (1928–32) and then federal president (1934–40), Lázaro Cárdenas instituted reforms that did much to lessen antigovernment sentiments.

Today, the states of Jalisco, Michoacán and, to a lesser extent, little Colima hold many of Mexico's natural resources – especially timber, minerals, livestock and agriculture; in addition, Jalisco has a thriving tech industry and Colima boasts one of the highest standards of living in the country. But in the past these states have seen large segments of their population head for the USA for work. Michoacán reportedly has lost almost half its population to emigration, and money sent home regularly exceeds US$3 billion. But with the economic slow-down and stricter immigration laws in place in the USA, the flow north appears to have slowed down somewhat.

GUADALAJARA REGION

Guadalajara

📱 33 / POP 1.5 MILLION / ELEV 1566M

As Mexico's second-largest city, Guadalajara delivers a less frenetic alternative to the nation's capital. And, while many of the images recognized as quintessentially Mexican have their roots here – mariachi music, wide-brimmed sombreros, the Mexican hat dance and *charreadas* (rodeos) – Guadalajara is as much a vanguard of the new Mexico as it is guardian of the old. An embarrassment of museums and theaters drive cultural life forward, fusion chefs have sharpened the edges of an already legendary culinary scene and foresighted local planners are doing their damnedest to tackle the traffic.

Guadalajara can't match the architectural homogeneity of smaller colonial cities, though its historic core, anchored by the wonderful cathedral and Instituto Cultural de Cabañas, is handsome. The hipster Colonia Americana neighborhood is sprinkled with fashionable restaurants, coffeehouses and nightclubs. The mellow suburbs of upscale Tlaquepaque and grassroots Tonalá are folk-art shoppers' dream destinations, while Zapopan has some interesting colonial architecture.

History

Guadalajara has weathered not a few false starts. In early 1531, Nuño de Guzmán and a few dozen Spanish families founded the first settlement near Nochixtlán, naming Guadalajara after Guzmán's hometown in Spain. Water was scarce, the land was dry and unyielding, and the indigenous people were understandably hostile. So in May 1533 the settlers moved to the village of Tonalá (today a part of Guadalajara). Guzmán disliked Tonalá, however, and several years later had the settlement moved to Tlacotán. In 1541 this site was attacked and decimated by a confederation of indigenous tribes led by chief Tenamaxtli. The survivors wearily picked a new site in the valley of Atemajac beside San Juan de Dios Creek, which ran where the boulevard called Calzada Independencia runs today. That's where the present Guadalajara was founded on February 14, 1550, near where the Teatro Degollado now stands.

Guadalajara finally prospered and in 1559 was declared the capital of Nueva Galicia province. The city, at the heart of a rich agricultural region, quickly grew into one of colonial Mexico's most important population centers. It also became the launch pad for Spanish expeditions and missions to western and northern Nueva España (new Spain), and others as far away as the Philippines. Miguel Hidalgo, a leader in the fight for Mexican independence, set up a revolutionary government in Guadalajara in late 1810, but was defeated near the city the following year, just months before his capture and execution in Chihuahua. The city was also the object of heavy fighting during the War of the Reform (1857–61) and between Constitutionalist and Villista armies in 1915.

Despite the violence, the 19th century was a period of economic, technological and social growth for the city, and by the close of the century Guadalajara had overtaken Puebla as Mexico's second-biggest city. Its population has mushroomed since WWII, and now the city is a huge commercial, industrial and cultural center as well as the high-tech and communications hub for the northern half of Mexico.

◉ Sights

◉ Plaza de Armas & Around

★ **Catedral de Guadalajara**   CATHEDRAL
(Catedral de la Asunción de María Santísima; Map p614; ☑ 33-3613-7168; www.facebook.com/catedral guadalajara.org; Av Alcalde 10, btwn Morelos & Av Hidalgo; ⊙ 7:30am-7:30pm Mon-Sat, to 8:30pm Sun) **FREE** Guadalajara's cathedral is the city's most conspicuous landmark with distinctive neo-Gothic towers built after an earthquake

---

COLONIAL CHURCHES

Central Guadalajara has dozens of large and small churches. The following are some of the city's most beautiful and interesting. Most are open from between 7am and 9:30am to about 1pm and then again from 4pm or 5pm to 8pm or 8:30pm.

Templo de Nuestra Señora del Carmen (Map p614; cnr Av Juárez & Calle 8 de Julio; ⊙9:30am-12:45pm & 4:30-6:45pm) Facing a small leafy plaza, this 17th-century chapel was remodeled in the 1860s with lots of gold leaf, old paintings and murals in the dome.

Templo de la Merced (Map p614; ☑ 33-3614-3412; cnr Loza & Av Hidalgo; ⊙7am-8pm), Closer to the city center, this ornate church was built between 1650 and 1721; inside are several large paintings, crystal chandeliers and lots of gold leaf.

Templo de Santa María de Gracia (Map p614; cnr Carranza & República; ⊙7am-1pm & 5-8pm) A block northeast of Plaza de la Liberación, Santa María de Gracia has a rather rough and austere interior. It was built as part of a convent in 1661, and stands in the location of the city's first cathedral (1549–1618).

Templo de San Agustín (Map p614; ☑ 33-3614-5365; Morelos; ⊙11am-1pm & 5-8pm) South of the landmark Teatro Degollado on Plaza de la Liberación, this baroque-style specimen is all gold and white. Erected in 1573, it is one of the city's oldest and loveliest churches.

Templo Santa Eduviges (Map p614; ☑ 33-3632-6156; Calle Abascal y Souza; ⊙7am-1pm & 4-8pm) Built in 1726, Santa Eduviges is usually packed with worshippers and, during services, perfumed with clouds of sandalwood smoke. It's just east of the Mercado San Juan de Dios.

Templo de Aranzazú (Map p614; ☑ 33-3614-4083; Av 16 de Septiembre 20; ⊙6am-1pm & 4-8:30pm) Compact Templo de Aranzazú is perhaps the city's most beautiful church. Built from 1749 to 1752, it has three remarkably ornate Churrigueresque (Spanish baroque) golden altars and a lovely vaulted ceiling.

Templo de San Francisco de Asís (Map p614; ☑ 33-1155-0602; cnr Sánchez & Av 16 de Septiembre; ⊙9:30am-1pm & 2-6pm) Across the road from Templo de Aranzazú, and larger but less impressive, this church which was begun in the 1660s by the Franciscans and has lovely stained glass.

WESTERN CENTRAL HIGHLANDS GUADALAJARA

Greater Guadalajara

0 — 5 km
0 — 2.5 miles

Río Verde

Río Grande de Santiago

Anillo Periférico

Av Tonaltecas

Tonalá Tourist Office

Tonalá Street Market

TONALÁ

Calz Río Nilo

Autopista Guadalajara Zapotlanejo

Av Tonalá Zapotlanejo

Nueva Central Camionera

Av Giantes

Paseo del Zoologico

Calz Obrero

San Jacinto Putárico

Elías Calles

See Tlaquepaque Map (p607)

TLAQUEPAQUE

Av de la Cruz

Calz Independencia

Domínguez

Circunvalación

Av Javier Mina

See Central Guadalajara Map (p614)

Antigua Central Camionera

Calz Revolución

Blvd Barragan

Calz Gallo

Dr Michel

Calz Curiel

Av Alcalde

Av 16 de Septiembre

Av Federalisimo

Calz Cárdenas

Aeropuerto Internacional Miguel Hidalgo (12km)

Av Camacho

Basílica de Zapopan

ZAPOPAN

Av de las Américas

Av López Mateos

Av Acueducto

Av Vallarta

See Colonia Americana Map (p612)

Av de la Patria

Av López Mateos Sur

CHAPALITA

Av Guadalupe

Av Tepeyac

Av de la Patria

Av Cruz del Sur

Av Colón

Av 8 de Julio

Av Legazpi

Av Otero

Av Vallarta

Anillo Periférico

Tequila (50km);
Tepic (215km)

Greater Guadalajara

toppled the originals in 1818. Begun in 1561 and consecrated in 1618, the building is almost as old as the city itself. Time your visit right and you'll see light filter through the stained-glass Last Supper above the altar and hear a working pipe organ rumble sweetly from the rafters.

The interior includes a Gothic **crypt** (Map p614; ☺10:30am-2pm & 4:30-7pm Mon-Sat, 9-11am & 1:30-8:30pm Sun), where three archbishops are buried, plus massive Tuscan-style gold-leaf pillars and 11 richly decorated side altars that were bequeathed to the city by King Fernando VII of Spain (1784–1833). The 18th-century glass case nearest the west entrance is an extremely popular reliquary, containing the waxed remains of the martyred Santa Inocencia. In the sacristy, which an attendant can open for you on request, is *La Asunción de la Virgen,* painted by Spanish artist Bartolomé Murillo in 1650.

Much like the city's Palacio de Gobierno, the cathedral is a bit of a stylistic hodgepodge, including baroque, Churrigueresque (late Spanish baroque) and neoclassical influences.

Palacio de Gobierno   NOTABLE BUILDING
(Map p614; ☎33-3668-1804; www.jalisco.gob. mx; Av Corona 43, btwn Morelos & Moreno; ☺9am-7pm Mon-Fri, 10am-6pm Sat, 10am-3pm Sun) FREE The golden-hued Palacio de Gobierno, which houses the Jalisco state government offices, was finished in 1774 and is well worth visiting to see two impressive murals by local artist José Clemente Orozco (1883–1949). The real head-turner is the 400-sq-metre mural of Miguel Hidalgo painted in 1937 that dominates the main interior staircase. Hidalgo brandishes a torch in one fist while the masses at his feet struggle against the twin foes of communism and fascism.

Another Orozco mural in the Ex Congreso (former Congress Hall) upstairs to the right depicts Hidalgo, Benito Juárez and other historical luminaries. On the ground floor there's an excellent multimedia **museum** about the history of Jalisco and its capital, though labeling is largely in Spanish.

Plaza Guadalajara   PLAZA
(Map p614; Av Alcalde, btwn Morelos & Av Hidalgo) Plaza Guadalajara is shaded by dozens of severely cropped laurel trees and has great views of the east of the cathedral. Boasting a few fine cafes, it's a hive of activity day and night. On its north side is the Palacio Municipal, which was built between 1949 and 1952 but looks much older. Above the main stairway inside is a dark mural by Gabriel Flores depicting the founding of Guadalajara.

Teatro Degollado   THEATER
(Map p614; ☎33-3614-4773; www.facebook. com/TeatroDegollado; Belén, btwn Morelos & Av Hidalgo; ☺box office 10am-8pm Mon-Fri, viewing 10am-2pm Tue-Sun) FREE Construction of this neoclassical theater, which is home to the Guadalajara Philharmonic, was begun in 1855 and completed four decades later. Above the Corinthian columns is a pediment with a mosaic depicting Apollo and the Nine Muses.

Museo Regional de Guadalajara   MUSEUM
(Map p614; ☎33-3613-2703; Liceo 60; adult/student & child M$60/free; ☺9am-4:30pm Tue-Sun) Guadalajara's most important museum tells the story of the city and the surrounding region, somewhat haphazardly, from prehistory to the revolution. Displays are appealing, though signage is in Spanish only. The ground floor houses a natural history collection whose unwitting star is an impressive woolly

mammoth skeleton dating from 10,000 BCE. Other crowd-pleasers include multimedia displays about indigenous life and a superb collection of pre-Hispanic ceramics and other artifacts taken from a shaft tomb in the nearby Guachimontones Archaeological Site.

The upper level of the museum is devoted to colonial paintings depicting the Spanish conquest, as well as more austere religious allegories, a revolutionary wing and exhibits showcasing the indigenous Huichol (or Wixarika) culture. The 19th-century building is worth visiting for its architecture – a gorgeous, tree-studded double courtyard with a fountain acts as its centerpiece.

Plaza de la Liberación   PLAZA
(Map p614; Av Corona, btwn Morelos & Av Hidalgo) This huge plaza due east of the cathedral was a 1980s urban planner's dream project – two whole blocks of colonial buildings to be knocked down and replaced with a concrete slab. Today, it's a popular meeting spot lined with leafy trees, benches, shoe-shining booths and the iconic 'Guadalajara' sign.

On the north side of the plaza, the **Palacio Legislativo** (Map p614; ☎33-3679-1515; www.congresojal.gob.mx; Av Hidalgo 222; ☉9am-7pm Mon-Fri) – distinguished by thick stone columns in its interior courtyard – is where the state congress meets. Just east, across Calle Belén, is the **Palacio de Justicia** (State Courthouse; Map p614; ☎33-1200-1400; https://stjjalisco.gob.mx; Av Hidalgo 190; ☉9am-3pm Mon-Fri). It was built in 1588 and began life as Guadalajara's first nunnery. Duck inside to the interior stairwell and check out the 1965 mural by Guillermo Chávez depicting legendary Mexican lawmakers, including Benito Juárez.

Rotonda de los Jaliscenses Ilustres   MONUMENT
(Rotunda of Illustrious Jaliscans; Map p614; Av Hidalgo, btwn Av Alcalde & Liceo) Jalisco's hall of fame, in the plaza on the north side of the cathedral, is ringed by 30 bronze sculptures of the state's favorite writers, architects and revolutionaries, including one woman – Rita Pérez Jiménez (1779–1861), heroine of the War of Independence.

Some of the greats depicted here are actually buried underneath the rotunda, the round, pillared gazebo-like monument in the center.

Museo de Arte Sacro de Guadalajara   MUSEUM
(Map p614; ☎33-3613-6706; Liceo 17, btwn Morelos & Av Hidalgo; adult/child M$25/15; ☉10am-5pm Tue-Sat, to 2pm Sun) This pious collection astride the eastern flank of the cathedral is filled with dark and brooding 17th- to 18th-century religious art, as well as some spectacular ecclesiastical treasures including chalices, monstrances and vestments. The view of the cathedral and the Plaza de Armas from the 2nd-floor terrace is alone worth the admission fee.

◉ East of Plaza de Armas

★Instituto Cultural de Cabañas   MUSEUM
(Map p614; ☎33-3668-1645; https://museocabanas.jalisco.gob.mx; Cabañas 8; adult/student M$70/20, Tue free; ☉10am-6pm Tue-Sun) Standing proudly at the eastern end of dramatic Plaza Tapatía is one of Guadalajara's architectural landmarks, and a Unesco World Heritage site since 1997. On the ceiling and inside the dome of the striking neoclassical Capilla Mayor (Main Chapel) is a most unexpected series of modernist murals by José Clemente Orozco, which rank among his best works and Guadalajara's top sights. The complex also houses a collection of 340 other pieces by Orozco, and works by leading lights of Mexico's contemporary art scene.

The beautiful building, which consists of a labyrinth of hidden arched courtyards and exhibition spaces, was founded by Bishop don Juan Cruz Ruiz de Cabañas and designed by Spanish architect Manuel Tolsá between 1805 and 1810. Its original purpose was as an orphanage and home for invalids, and it remained so for 150 years, housing 500 children at one time.

From 1937 to 1939, Orozco, one of the 'Big Three' of the Mexican muralist movement, channeled the archetypal struggle for freedom into 57 magnificent murals that now decorate the domed chapel at the center of the complex. Widely regarded as Orozco's finest works, they depict pre-Hispanic Jalisco and the conquest, presented through dark, unnerving and distinctly modern images of fire, armor, broken chains, blood and prayer. Given the time frame, the works almost certainly serve as a warning against fascism and any force that subverts humanity to cultivate power. Conveniently placed benches allow you to lie down and inspect the works more easily.

Free tours of the institute in a half-dozen languages (including English) depart regularly. A hands-on Orozco exhibit and a DIY art space keep kids happy and engaged.

AN EYE ON OROZCO

Long before Banksy and the rebirth of politically charged street art, Mexican muralists were making bold statements in giant public murals that expressed mostly revolutionary ideals in swirls of vivid color. Guadalajara's gift to the genre was substantial. The grandfather of Mexican *muralismo* is usually considered to be locally born artist Gerardo Murillo (1875–1964), who signed his work 'Dr Atl,' while one of his former pupils, José Clemente Orozco (1883–1949), came from the nearby city of Ciudad Guzmán.

Together with Diego Rivera and David Alfaro Siqueiros, Orozco is considered one of the 'Big Three' of Mexican mural art. Some argue he was the most original; his energetic brushstrokes depict fiery, sometimes pained, figures in vivid studies of polemic symbolism. Orozco's work decorates stairways, ceilings and public spaces everywhere from New York to Mexico City, but his most personal work can be found in Guadalajara. Don't miss the following.

Instituto Cultural de Cabañas (p604) Orozco painted 57 murals including the kaleidoscopic *Hombre del Fuego* (Man of Fire) in this Unesco-listed building between 1937 and 1939.

Palacio de Gobierno (p603) Astonishing 1937 mural of Miguel Hidalgo brandishing a torch, set on the government building's main staircase, that will literally stop you in your tracks.

Museo de las Artes (p605) Two pieces in the auditorium – *El Hombre Creador y Rebelde* (The Creator and Rebel) in the cupola and *El Pueblo y Sus Falsos Líderes* (The People and Their False Leaders) on the stage backdrop painted in 1937 – are housed in this art museum opposite the university.

Casa-Taller Orozco (p605) Contains Orozco's *La Buena Vida* (The Good Life; 1945), an uncharacteristically upbeat study of a festive scene with a chef holding up a fish surrounded by scantily clad women and food from far-off places.

Plaza Tapatía
PLAZA
(Map p614; Morelos s/n) The fabulously wide pedestrian and elevated Plaza Tapatía sprawls for more than 500m eastward from Teatro Degollado (p603) to the Instituto Cultural de Cabañas. Stroll the length of the plaza on Sunday and you'll find yourself in a sea of locals who shop at low-end crafts markets, snack (from both street vendors and cafes), watch street performers and rest on the low walls of gurgling fountains.

⊙ West of Plaza de Armas

West of the city center, where Avenidas Juárez and Federalismo meet, is the green comma of **Parque Revolución**, a haven for skaters and the focal point of Sunday's Vía RecreActiva (p621).

Museo de las Artes
MUSEUM
(MUSA; Map p614; ☑ 33-3134-1664; www.musa. udg.mx; Av Juárez 975; ⊙10am-6pm Tue-Sun) **FREE** Three blocks west of Parque Revolución is this museum of contemporary art housed in a French Renaissance–style building (1917) that once served as the administration build-

ing for the University of Guadalajara. The highlight is the **Paraninfo** (auditorium) on the 1st floor, whose stage backdrop and dome feature large, powerful murals by Orozco. The rest of the space – some 14 galleries, in fact – is given over to well-curated temporary exhibitions focusing on contemporary Mexican art. Free guided tours offered in Spanish.

Templo Expiatorio del Santísimo Sacramento
CHURCH
(Map p614; ☑ 33-3825-3410; Madero 935; ⊙7am-10pm) This dramatic neo-Gothic church, begun in 1897 but not completed until 1972, dominates the neighborhood, with enormous stone columns, 15m-high mosaic stained-glass windows, a kaleidoscopic steeple, and neon blue crosses. A carillon of 25 bells plays many religious and popular tunes. When the hour strikes, a door in the clock tower opens and the 12 Apostles march out. View it best from Parque Expiatorio to the south.

Casa-Taller Orozco
GALLERY
(Orozco House & Workshop; Map p612; ☑ 33-3616-8329; https://sc.jalisco.gob.mx; Aceves 27; ⊙10am-2pm and 4-7pm Tue-Sat, 11am-2pm and 4-6pm Sun)

FREE Orozco's former home and studio, used briefly by the celebrated muralist in the early 1940s, today hosts temporary exhibitions. On permanent display in the lobby – and worth a peek if you're in the area – is *La Buena Vida* (The Good Life), an unusually joyous Orozco mural the artist was commissioned to paint for Mexico City's Turf Club in 1945. To avoid disappointment, call before you set out; the museum does not always keep to schedule.

◎ Zapopan

The fashionable, middle-class suburb of Zapopan is just under 10km northwest of the city center. There are a few interesting sights around the main square (Plaza de las Américas), which is a fun place to hang out, with pilgrims and the faithful coming and going, and all sorts of religious items for sale. After dark, locals get the place back to themselves and the numerous bars and restaurants turn the music up and the beer flows.

To get here from the center of Guadalajara, take any bus marked 'Zapopan' (eg bus 275 or 706 TUR) heading north on Avenida 16 de Septiembre and its continuation Avenida Alcalde and get off on Avenida Hidalgo just north of the Basílica de Zapopan. The trip takes about 40 minutes. A taxi from the city center costs around M$120.

★ Basílica de Zapopan   CATHEDRAL
(Map p602; ☑33-3633-0141; Eva Briseño 152; ◎9am-8pm) One of the city's most important churches, the Basílica de Zapopan, built in 1730, is home to Nuestra Señora de Zapopan, a petite statue of the Virgin visited by pilgrims year-round. Since 1734 on October 12, thousands of kneeling faithful crawl behind as the statue is carried here from Guadalajara cathedral. The kneeling pilgrims then make the final trek up the basilica's aisle to pray for favors at the altar.

The early evening, when streams of pilgrims, nuns and monks fill the pews, is a magical time to be here.

During the rest of the year, the basilica is lit up on Friday and Saturday evenings at 9pm with a **video mapping** show – a gorgeous 3D light and sound display projected onto the facade of the church, sharing the history of Zapopan and the edifice itself. It draws crowds of locals and travelers alike (plus loads of street food vendors).

Museo de Arte Huichol (Wixarika)   MUSEUM
(Map p602; ☑33-3636-4430; Eva Briseño 152; adult/child M$10/5; ◎10am-6pm Mon-Sat, 9am-2pm Sun) This small but surprisingly informative museum has a worthwhile display of artifacts from the Huichol (or Wixarika) people, an indigenous group known for their bright-colored yarn art, beadwork and peyote rituals. (Try to look past the creepy mannequins and taxidermied creatures.) It covers all aspects of the culture, from birth to death and everything in between through everyday items and photographs. There's an excellent **shop** here too. It's just to the right of the Basílica de Zapopan, within the basilica grounds.

Museo de Arte de Zapopan   MUSEUM
(MAZ; Map p602; ☑33-3818-2575; www.maz.zapopan.gob.mx; Andador 20 de Noviembre 166; ◎10am-6pm Tue-Sun, to 10pm Thu) FREE Two blocks east of the Basílica de Zapopan, MAZ is dedicated to modern art. Four sleek minimalist galleries hold temporary exhibits, which have included works by Diego Rivera and Frida Kahlo as well as leading contemporary Mexican artists. Many of the exhibits are interactive, and the museum acts as a nexus for numerous cultural activities, including lectures, workshops and film screenings.

◎ Tlaquepaque

Though just under 8km southeast of central Guadalajara, Tlaquepaque (officially San Pedro Tlaquepaque) feels almost like a village: squint and you could well be in some small colonial town miles from anywhere. But Tlaquepaque's attractiveness is not its sole draw: artisans live behind the pastel-colored walls of the old mansions that line its narrow cobblestone streets, and their goods – such as wood carvings, sculpture, furniture, jewelry, leather items and especially ceramics – are sold on and around pedestrianized Calle Independencia. The fancy boutiques here contrast sharply with the more rough-and-ready shops and stalls of Tonalá.

The main square, **Jardín Hidalgo**, is leafy and lush with blossoms, and the benches around the fountain are always packed. The eating is very good and the strolling is even better, especially at sunset when the sky behind the gorgeous, white-domed basilica burns orange and families take to the

Tlaquepaque

0 ——— 200 m
0 ——— 0.1 miles

WESTERN CENTRAL HIGHLANDS GUADALAJARA

Tlaquepaque

◎ Top Sights
1 Museo Pantaleón Panduro C1

🛏 Sleeping
2 Casa de las Flores C4
3 Casa del Retoño C4
4 Hostal Tlaquepaque...........................C1
5 Quinta Don José C3

☒ Eating
6 Casa Fuerte..B2
Casa Luna...................................(see 14)
7 Chiles & Beer B2
8 Chimbombo's Grill C2

9 Maria Mitotes B1
TlaquePasta.................................(see 5)
10 Zaguán D3

☺ Entertainment
11 El Parián C3

🛍 Shopping
12 Antigua de México B2
13 Del Corazón de la Tierra B2
El Nahual Gallery.........................(see 2)
14 Orígenes David Luna B2
15 Taller de Cerámica Paco Padilla...........C1

streets, enjoying the last ticks of daylight. *Voladores* ('flying men' from Papantla) give spectacular performances from a special 30m-high pole in the plaza most afternoons between about 3pm and 4pm; free concerts and other events are regularly held here on weekend evenings too.

There's a handy and helpful **tourist information booth** (Map p607; www.tlaquepaque. gob.mx; cnr Av Juárez & Herrera y Cairo; ⊙9am-8pm Mon-Fri, 10am-7pm Sat & Sun) close to the junction of Juárez and Progreso, opposite El Parián (p619), that gives out pictorial neighborhood maps.

WORTH A TRIP

GUACHIMONTONES RUINS

Just 40km west of Guadalajara is the fascinating and distinctive archaeological site known as **Guachimontones** (☑ 384-109-03-88; www.inah.gob.mx/zonas/176-zona-arqueologica-teuchitlan-o-guachimontones; Juárez Norte s/n, Teuchitlán; adult/child M$30/free, free Tue; ⊙ 9am-5pm) – one of the only ancient ruins in the world whose structures were built in nearly perfect concentric circles, including a massive conical step pyramid. Easy to reach as a day trip, the site has well-preserved structures, an excellent museum, and knowledgeable (and free) guide services.

Occupied between 300 BCE and 350 CE by the Teuchitlán people, Guachimontones is believed to have been a spiritual center, used mostly for rituals honoring Ehecatl, the god of wind. There were 10 circular complexes in all, surrounding the imposing central pyramid. A hole at the top of the pyramid is thought to have been used to hold a pole that priests would suspend themselves from, simulating the flight of a bird.

The ruins are perched on a verdant hill overlooking the village of Teuchitlán and La Vega dam. Three of the 10 complexes are visible and fully excavated, while the main pyramid is a truly arresting sight: perfectly circular, with curving moss-covered steps rising some 18 meters (60 feet); you're not allowed to climb to the top, unfortunately. Two ball courts, two long plazas and several structures still to be excavated complete the site.

The site's modern museum – also circular in shape – provides an excellent overview of the ruins and the people who worshipped here. Jewelry, pottery, obsidian tools, and other artifacts are on display, as is a re-creation of the shaft tombs found under some of the structures. Several hands-on exhibits will keep young visitors engaged, and there's a surprisingly good introductory film, available in Spanish, English and French.

Tours of the ruins are offered hourly between 10am and 1pm. Guides are knowledgeable and experienced; English and French spoken. Guides also lead tours through the museum every 30 to 60 minutes, depending on numbers.

To get here from Guadalajara, take a bus to Teuchitlán (M$120, two hours, hourly from 6am to 9pm) from the Antigua Central Camionera (p623). From the village, a taxi to the ruins costs M$60.

To get to Tlaquepaque from central Guadalajara, take bus 275B, 330 or 647 (M$9.50). The turquoise 706 TUR bus marked 'Tonalá' has air-con and is more comfortable (M$15). All these buses leave central Guadalajara from Avenida 16 de Septiembre between López Cotilla and Madero; the trip takes about 20 minutes. As you near Tlaquepaque, watch for the brick arch and then a traffic circle, after which you should get off at the next stop. Up the street on the left is Independencia, which will take you to the center of Tlaquepaque.

★**Museo Pantaleón Panduro**　MUSEUM
(Museo Municipal del Premio Nacional de la Cerámica; Map p607; ☑ 33-3639-5646; www.facebook.com/museopantaleonpanduro; Sánchez 191; ⊙ 10am-6pm Tue-Sat, to 4pm Sun) **FREE** This superb collection of over 500 pieces of national folk art is housed in a converted religious mission and includes well-displayed miniature figurines, as well as enormous, lightly fired urns and other ceramic crafts from all over the country. Its focus is on winners of the prestigious National Pantaleón Panduro Ceramics Prize, first held in 1977 and named after a renowned local sculptor.

⊙ Tonalá

This dusty, bustling suburb is about 17km southeast of downtown Guadalajara and home to many artisans. You can feel Tonalá beginning to take Tlaquepaque's lead with a few airy, inviting showrooms and cafes opening around town, but it remains happily rough around the edges. It's fun to roam through the dark, dusty stores and workshops, browsing glassware, ceramics, furniture, masks, toys, jewelry, handmade soap and more. Anything you can buy in Tlaquepaque you can find here for much less, which is what attracts wholesale buyers from all over the world.

Ask staff at the **Tonalá tourist office** (Map p602; ☑ 33-3586-6062; Morelos 180; ⊙ 9am-3pm Mon-Fri) about two- to three-hour **walking tours** (by donation) of Tonalá's artisan workshops. They're given in English or

Spanish, but need to be reserved by email (recorridostonala@hotmail.com) a couple of days in advance.

To reach Tonalá, take bus 231, 275 Diagonal or 633V (M$9.50). The turquoise 707 TUR bus marked 'Tonalá' has air-con and is more comfortable (M$15). All these buses leave Guadalajara from the corner of Avenida 16 de Septiembre and Madero; the trip takes about 45 minutes. As you enter Tonalá, get off on the corner of Avenidas Tonalá and Tonaltecas. The Plaza Principal is three blocks east of Avenida Tonaltecas on Avenida Juárez. A taxi will cost about M$150.

★ **Tonalá Street Market**   MARKET
(Map p602; ⊙8am-4pm Thu & Sun) On Thursday and Sunday, Tonalá bursts into a huge street market that sprouts on Avenida Tonaltecas and crawls through dozens of streets and alleys and takes hours to explore. With *torta* (sandwich), taco and *michelada* (beer and tomato juice) stands aplenty, the whole area takes on a carnival vibe. The best pieces are usually found at the workshops and warehouses, though a little perseverance often renders one-of-a-kind finds.

Museo Nacional de la Cerámica   MUSEUM
(Map p602; ☑33-3683-2519; www.facebook.com/ museonacionaldelaceramica.tonala; Constitución 104; ⊙10am-6pm Tue-Sun) FREE Among the best of the many ceramics museums in the greater Guadalajara region, this one focuses largely on works from Tonalá, arguably the finest in central Mexico. Among the most memorable styles are *barro bruñido* and *barro canela*. Located in the one-time home of Jorge Wilmot, an artist best known for introducing high fire techniques to Mexican ceramic art.

🎒 Courses

Guadalajara is a popular place to study Spanish, with classes available to students of all ages and levels. Prices and curricula can vary considerably.

Colegio de Español
y Cultura Mexicana   LANGUAGE
(CECM; Map p612; ☑33-3616-6881; www.cecm. udg.mx; Gómez 125; 50hr tuition over 2 weeks US$500) Part of the University of Guadalajara, CECM offers several levels of tuition, including two-week intensive (50 hours) and four-week semi-intensive (50 hours) Spanish-language courses. Day trips, homestays

(from US$240 per week) and longer excursions to other parts of Mexico are available.

IMAC   LANGUAGE
(Instituto Mexico-Americano de Cultura; Map p614; ☑33-3614-1414; www.learnspanish.com.mx; Guerra 180; per 25hr week from US$230) Offers courses from one week upwards and private tutoring from US$22 per hour. Check its website for course fees and homestay options. History, culture and dance classes are also available.

👉 Tours

Bike Tours   CYCLING
(Map p614; cnr Av Juárez & Escorza; ⊙10am Sun) FREE During Guadalajara's Sunday Vía RecreActiva (p621), when the main streets are closed to traffic, an army of volunteers just west of Parque Revolución dispense free bikes (ID required), available until 1pm. Volunteer guides also offer free cycling tours to historic sites, departing at 10am and lasting three hours; sign up by 9:30am to assure a spot.

Recorridos Turísticos Guadalajara   WALKING
(Map p614; ☑33-3837-4400; www.facebook.com/ GuadalajaraGob; Plaza Guadalajara; ⊙10:30am) FREE The city runs free tours (in Spanish and English) of central Guadalajara at 10:30am daily. Tours leave across from the Palacio Municipal and last about 1½ hours; be sure to register 15 minutes beforehand. Specialty tours – traditional foods, cantinas, historic neighborhoods – also are offered once a month. Ask the tourist office (p622) for further details.

Tequila Tour by Mickey Marentes   TOURS
(Map p612; ☑33-3615-6688; www.tequilatour bymm.com; Lope de Vega 25A; adult US$105-200, child US$99-105; ⊙9am-6pm) This well-regarded agency has both private and group tours of the nearby region of Tequila, its distilleries, shops and museums. Lunch and hotel pickup/drop-off included. Prices depend on the number of people touring together and mode of transportation, be it van, jeep or on horseback. English spoken.

Experience Agave   TOURS
(☑USA 503-922-1774; www.experiencetequila.com; day trip US$135-200, 4-day package from US$1510-1675) North American tequila aficionado Clayton Szczech and his team of bilingual guides offer a variety of individualized private tours departing from Guadalajara, from basic day trips to tequila country to multiday intensive tasting seminars through the region. Book well in advance.

José Cuervo Express TOURS
(Map p602; ☑374-742-67-29; www.josecuervo
express.com; Av Circunvalación Agustín Yáñez
1009; adult/child from M$2100/1850; ☺ticket
office 9am-6pm Mon-Fri, to 1pm Sat & Sun) Ride
in elegant carriages on this high-class train
tour to the Mundo Cuervo distillery in Tequila, which departs from the Guadalajara train station at 9am on Saturdays and
at 9:30am some Sundays (check website).
Transportation in more exclusive coaches
costs M$2500 and M$2800. Prices include
transport, distillery tours, meals, a Mexican
'show' and a fair bit of tequila. Note that
train rides are one way; bus transportation
is provided on the return.

Tapatío Tour BUS
(Map p614; ☑33-3613-0887; www.tapatio
tour.com.mx; tours weekdays/weekends adult
M$140/160, senior & child M$90/110) The ubiquitous double-decker buses of Tapatío Tour
ply the city's most popular sights on four
routes: Guadalajara, Tlaquepaque, Tonalá
and Zapopan. While the narration in Spanish and English is less than riveting, the
tours allow you to hop off and on wherever you wish, making sightseeing a breeze.
Buses depart hourly from the Rotonda de
los Jaliscenses Ilustres from 9:30am to 8pm
daily.

★ Festivals & Events

★**Encuentro Internacional
del Mariachi** MUSIC
(☑33-3880-9064; www.mariachi-jalisco.com.mx;
☺Aug-Sep) In late August and early September mariachis come to Guadalajara from
everywhere in Mexico to jam, battle and
enjoy. A Campeonato Nacional Charro (National Rodeo Championship) takes place at
the same time.

Feria Internacional del Libro BOOK FAIR
(www.fil.com.mx; ☺Nov-Dec) This nine-day
book fair is one of the biggest book events in
Latin America. It's held during the last week
of November and first week of December,
headlined by major authors from around
the Spanish-speaking world.

Festival Internacional del Cine FILM
(www.ficg.mx; ☺Mar) Mexico's most important
film festival has been drawing top actors
and directors to Guadalajara for a week each
March for more than three decades, with
screenings and parties taking place across
the city.

🛏 Sleeping

During holidays (Christmas and Holy
Week/Easter) and festivals such as Día
de Muertos you must reserve ahead. Ask
about discounts if you arrive in the low
season or will be staying more than a few
days.

🛏 Centro Histórico

The Centro Histórico is full of midrange
options, many of which are housed in
charming colonial buildings. A cluster of
budget digs can be found around the Antigua Central Camionera (old bus station)
when other places are full; this part of
town is a bit rough and away from the action, but well served by buses.

Hospedarte Centro Histórico HOSTEL $
(Map p614; ☑33-3562-7520; www.hostelgua
dalajara.com; Maestranza 147; dm M$240-270, d
with/without bathroom M$650/600, ste M$750, all
incl breakfast; @🛜) This bright-yellow downtown option is popular with a young crowd
looking for a good time. The three dorms
(men, women and mixed) are spacious, with
four to eight metal bunk beds, lockers and
fans. Shared bathrooms open onto a large
communal area with a huge kitchen and
plenty of activities laid on.

Seven suites are available in a neighboring building with a great terrace. It also enjoys a recommended **second location** (Map
p612; ☑33-3615-4957; www.hospedartehostel.
com; Luna 2075; dm M$230, d with/without bath-
room M$650/550, ste M$750, all incl breakfast;
@🛜) in Colonia Americana, about 3km
west; a good option for those looking for a
more low-key stay.

Casa Vilasanta HOTEL $
(Map p614; ☑33-3124-1277; www.vilasanta.com;
Rayón 170; dm/s/d/tr M$220/550/600/700;
❋🛜) The bright, pastel-colored rooms of
this cheery guesthouse are scattered around
a spacious covered interior courtyard, decorated with pottery and flowers (and lots of
crosses). The singles can feel cramped, but
the doubles (eg room 4) are large and all
rooms have a TV. There's a shared kitchen
with a huge communal table and plenty of
chill space on both floors.

There's a sunny 2nd-floor terrace too.
But with just 17 rooms and English-speaking management, this place fills up, so book
ahead.

Dalí Plaza Hotel HOTEL $

(Map p614; ☑33-3613-0420; www.hoteldali plaza.com; Moreno 570; r M$740-840; P✳🛜) The nine-story Dalí has recently renovated rooms with mid-century modern style – natural woods, simple lines – plus sleek amenities. Be sure to ask for a room on the upper floors, which have sweeping city views (even from the bathroom!); many on the lower floors have no windows at all. Service can be brusque but the excellent nightly rate makes up for it.

★**Del Carmen**

Concept Hotel BOUTIQUE HOTEL $$

(Map p614; ☑33-3614-2640; www.delcarmen. mx; Gálvez 45; d/ste M$1350/1550; ✳🛜) This hotel in a 19th-century mansion is a great place to stop for a spell. The concept? Nine rooms individually themed around artists from Mexico's La Ruptura movement (an abstract reaction to the 20th-century muralists); hence the Tamayo room (with a curvaceous metallic bathtub), the Friedeberg room (a trippy patchwork of blinding surrealism) or the energetically blue Soriano room.

All mod cons (but no parking) are assured and the popular Café Chai chain has an outlet with patio seating on the 1st floor – handy for breakfast or a late-night beer and enchiladas.

★**Real Maestranza Hotel** HOTEL $$

(Map p614; ☑33-3109-7801; www.realmaestranza hotel.com; Madero 161; r M$1400-1540; P✳🛜) Mixing modern amenities with Mexican design, Real Maestranza offers comfort and beauty in its 76 rooms. Each is bright and spacious, integrating dark woods and Talavera tiles with deep beds and luxurious linens. Service is gracious and accommodating – a huge plus. Located just a stone's throw from the historic center's main sights too.

Hotel Morales HOTEL $$$

(Map p614; ☑33-3658-5232; www.hotelmorales. com.mx; Av Corona 243; d/ste from M$1900/2700; P✳🛜♨) The dimly lit, four-tiered colonial lobby with the stunning ceiling mural is a suitably impressive entrance to this excellent-value, central hotel. Brighter and equally brilliant is the 2nd-floor, blue-and-white-tiled, Andalucía-style courtyard. Other nooks hide fountains, bookshelves and even a rooftop pool, spa and gym. The 98 rooms are a good size, modern in style and some have Jacuzzis.

Choose one (try for room 122) facing into the courtyard in the older Virreinal section of the hotel.

Casa Pedro Loza BOUTIQUE HOTEL $$$

(Map p602; ☑33-1202-2423; www.casapedro loza.com.mx; Loza 360; r M$3200-5500; ✳🛜) Housed in an impressive colonial mansion in a charming part of the Centro Histórico, this hotel is a bit away from the action and a titch attitudy. The 12 rooms are each wildly different; some are chock-full of beautiful antiques, others are like garish love nests with plush headboards and garden setting Jacuzzis. Could be fun...

The retractable roof over the courtyard and the superb roof terrace are pluses.

🛏 Colonia Americana

Top-end accommodations are generally found in trendy Colonia Americana and points west; those in the latter are generally aimed at guests with their own transportation.

★**Villa Ganz** BOUTIQUE HOTEL $$$

(Map p612; ☑33-3120-1416; www.villaganz.com; López Cotilla 1739; ste incl breakfast M$2500-3500; P✳@🛜) Cross the threshold of Villa Ganz and behold a dazzling array of tiles, ferns, candelabras, original art and even a piano. The 10 suites are luxury personified, with bathrobes, classic furniture, rich carpets and wonderful details. Breakfast is served on the terrace with views of the lush garden with its many hidden nooks and crannies.

Master suite 17 has a balcony, while bright 13 has two outlooks and a Jacuzzi. The service is equally exemplary and there's complimentary wine and apps from 6pm to 8pm, a real fire, evening candlelight and a fine restaurant. A bargain – whatever the price!

Quinta Real Guadalajara LUXURY HOTEL $$$

(Map p612; ☑33-3669-0600; www.quintareal. com; Av México 2727; r M$2700-3400; P✳@♨) A sort of rural hacienda in a busy city, this five-star property, one of 10 in a Mexican luxury chain, is drop-dead gorgeous with its exquisite stone and ivy-covered exteriors. The lobby and bar are inviting and stylish, grounds are impeccably manicured and the service is outstanding. Choose a suite from among the 66 rooms, like garden-facing 104.

There's a lovely garden pool and fully equipped gym too. It's about 1.7km west of Avenida Chapultepec.

Colonia Americana

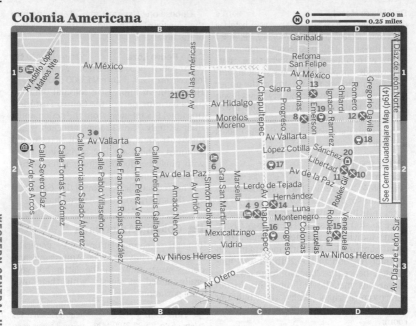

Colonia Americana

🛏 Tlaquepaque

Just 20 minutes away by bus or taxi from downtown Guadalajara, Tlaquepaque is an excellent option for those who crave small-town charm but still want to visit the sights of the big city. Added bonus: the shopping here is superb.

Hostal Tlaquepaque
HOSTEL $

(Map p607; ☎33-2696-4178; https://hostal-tlaquepaque.negocio.site; Guerra 135; dm/d incl breakfast M$417/833) Two blocks from the cen-

tral plaza, this bright and airy hostel makes a tranquil base. Set in a converted home, colorful rooms are spacious with deluxe mattresses, good linens and Mexican bedspreads; bathrooms are squeaky clean with plenty of hot water. Common areas include an open-air courtyard plus tables and chairs here and there. No guest kitchen is the only bummer.

Casa del Retoño
GUESTHOUSE $$

(Map p607; ☎33-3639-6510; www.lacasadel retono.com.mx; Matamoros 182; s/d incl breakfast M$950/1150; P@🛜) The eight rooms in this pleasant traditional house are all colorfully decorated, share an enormous garden and boast good bathrooms. It's a short walk from Tlaquepaque's main square and is run by a friendly family. It's a good idea to book ahead; reception isn't always staffed.

★ Casa de las Flores   B&B $$$

(Map p607; ☑ 33-3659-3186; www.facebook. com/pg/casadelasflorestlaquepaque; Degollado 175; r incl breakfast M$4000-4400; P❋@☞) A popular spot (and for good reason), this colorful guesthouse is positively crammed with high-end ceramics, and boasts a garden full of flowers and a decorative fireplace that defies belief. The seven rooms in an outbuilding have an engaging Mexican feel, with multicolored bedcovers, tiled sinks, haunting art, and (sometimes) skylights and balconies.

You'll spend days inspecting the details in your room and the well-stocked El Nahual Gallery (p620), its inhouse shop with wonderful ceramics, figurines and masks.

Quinta Don José   BOUTIQUE HOTEL $$$

(Map p607; ☑ 33-3635-7522; www.quintadonjose. com; Reforma 139; incl breakfast r M$1600-2200, ste M$2300-3500; P❋@☞☼) From the cozy sunken lobby to the sunny, flower-filled, kidney-shaped pool terrace complete with gurgling fountains, this charming hotel is a great place to escape while remaining in the heart of Tlaquepaque. The 18 comfortable rooms might not be as flamboyant as the gardens, but that's a minor niggle.

There's a good in-house Italian restaurant called **TlaquePasta** (Map p607; ☑ 33-3657-2483; mains M$135-360; ⊗ 5-10pm Tue-Thu, 2-10pm Fri-Sun) as well.

✖ Eating

Guadalajara is a foodie destination and many visitors find that meals here count among the highlights of their stay. A few local specialties to look out for include *birria* (a spicy goat or lamb stew), *carne en su jugo* ('meat in its juice,' a type of beef soup) and, above all, the ubiquitous *torta ahogada* (literally 'drowned sandwich'), a chili-sauce-soaked pork roll said to cure everything (but especially hangovers).

✖ Centro Histórico

The adventurous might head for **Mercado San Juan de Dios** (Mercado Libertad; Map p614; cnr Av Javier Mina & Calz Independencia

Sur; ⊗ 10am-7pm Mon-Sat, to 4pm Sun), home to endless food stalls serving the cheapest and some of the tastiest eats in town. The plaza south of the Templo Expiatorio is a good place to snag late-night tacos, *tortas ahogadas* and *elote* (grilled corn on the cob with mayonnaise and cheese).

Taco La Paz   SEAFOOD $

(Map p602; ☑ 33-1200-4647; www.tacofish-la paz.com; Av de la Paz 494; mains M$25-37; ⊗ 9am-4:30pm Mon-Sat) Guadalajara may be a fair distance from the ocean, but fish and seafood remain a passion. For prawn and fish tacos, this simple eatery can't be beat and you'll guess that as soon as you see the queues.

Dogos El Chino   HOT DOGS $

(Map p614; cnr Escorza & Moreno; mains M$20-40; ⊗ 6pm-1:30am Sun-Thu, to 4am Fri & Sat) A classic *tapatío* (local Guadalajara) experience – and must do post-bar hopping – is a two-for-one plate at El Chino, a street stand grilling up rows and rows of dogs wrapped in bacon and topped with mayo, mustard, onions, panela cheese, and the requisite grilled jalapeño. (Hold the heartburn.)

★ Birriería las Nueve Esquinas   MEXICAN $$

(Map p614; ☑ 33-3613-6260; www.las9esquinas. com; Av Colón 384; mains M$74-139; ⊗ 8am-11pm Mon-Sat, to 9pm Sun) Many restaurants in the village-like Nueve Esquinas (Nine Corners) neighborhood specialize in *birria,* meat stewed in its own juices until very tender. Birriería las Nueve Esquinas, a delightful semi-open-air restaurant covered in blue-and-white tiles, is renowned far and wide for being the king of *birria.*

The two main offerings here are *birria de chivo* (steamed goat) and *barbacoa de borrego* (baked lamb). Both cost M$140 and come with a stack of fresh tortillas, pickled onions, cilantro and two types of salsa. Wrap the meat in the tortilla, add various flavors and then dip the tortilla in the meat juice before putting it in your mouth.

La Fonda de la Noche   MEXICAN $$

(Map p614; ☑ 33-3827-0917; www.facebook. com/LaFondadelaNoche; Jesús 251; mains M$80-132; ⊗ 7:30pm-midnight Mon-Sat) Set in a rambling art nouveau house, this restaurant is a stunner in every way. The cuisine is largely from the Durango region and it would be fair to say that absolutely anything is tasty. The menu is simple and largely spoken, but

Central Guadalajara

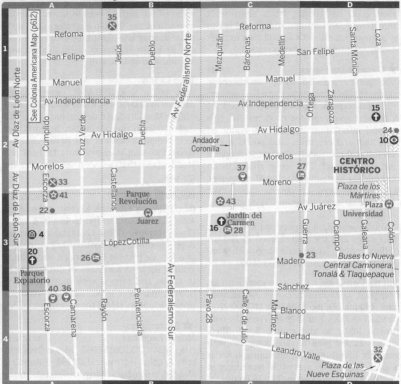

the affable owner, Carlos, does speak basic English. Try the *plato combinado* – a selection of the chef's four prize dishes.

La Chata de Guadalajara   MEXICAN $$
(Map p614; ☎33-3613-0588; www.lachata.com.mx; Av Corona 126; mains M$96-195; ☺7am-midnight) Quality *comida típica* (home-style food), affordable prices and ample portions mean this family diner always has a queue out front. Fortunately, hard-working staff keep the crowds moving quickly, plus you'll be happily distracted watching the energetic chefs spin tortillas as you wait in line. The specialty is the superb *platillo jaliscense* (fried chicken with five side dishes; M$119).

✖ Colonia Americana

★Tortas Ahogadas Migue   MEXICAN $
(Map p612; ☎33-3825-4520; www.facebook.com/TortasAhogadasMigue; Mexicaltzingo 1727;

tortas M$42-70; ☺9:30am-5:30pm) Take it from *tapatíos* in the know: this bright yellow-and-orange cafe serves the city's best *tortas ahogadas*, Guadalajara's beloved hangover cure. Baguette-like rolls called *birotes* are filled with chunks of slow-roasted pork and drenched with searing *salsa picante* – ask for yours '*media ahogada*' (half-drowned) for less burn. Only die-hard chili-heads should request '*bien ahogada*.'

La Cafetería   INTERNATIONAL $
(Map p612; ☎33-3825-7936; www.casafueradecasa.com; Libertad 1700; mains M$75-120; ☺8am-11:30pm; 🖉) A French bistro-style cafe with shabby-chic decor and a pleasant patio shaded by huge flamboyant trees. The menu consists of a creative combo of foods from around the world: Vietnamese sandwiches, lasagna, crepes, hamburgers and enchiladas. The breakfast menu is particularly inspired though the dessert offerings are tough to resist.

Tomate Taquería
TACOS $$

(Map p612; ☎33-3825-3331; www.facebook. com/pg/tomatetaqueriaoficial; Av Chapultepec 361; mains M$90-190; ⊙2pm-midnight Sun-Thu, to 2:30am Fri & Sat) A bustling, sit-down *taquería* serving up fresh tacos or, if you're really hungry, taco meat by the kilo (with unlimited corn tortillas and all the fixins). Especially well known for its heaping plates of juicy *pastor meat* (spit-grilled pork with *achiote* sauce and pineapple). Meal times bring lines but they move fast.

Pig's Pearls
BURGERS $$

(Map p612; ☎33-3825-5933; www.facebook.com/ pigspearlsgdl; Coronado 79; burgers M$100-120; ⊙1pm-midnight Mon-Sat) *Tapatíos* rave about the burgers here – there are a dozen to choose from – so who are we to argue? Sit in the industrial-chic terrace in fine weather or move behind to the small but perfectly formed bar. There's a small selection of salads (M$80 to M$90) and kebabs (from M$90) too.

Peko Peko
RAMEN $$

(Map p612; ☎33-2687-2690; www.facebook. com/PekoPekoGDL; Argentina 20; mains M$143-190; ⊙6-11:30pm Mon-Fri, 2-10:30pm Sat, 2-5pm Sun) This hopping little restaurant specializes in big, steaming bowls of ramen noodles with loads of toppings that keep vegans to meat lovers equally satisfied. Start your meal with 'pan al vapor' – a steaming pork bun served hot and quick – and don't miss the creative cocktail menu (cucumber martini, anyone?). Come mid-week to avoid the lines.

★ Alcalde
MEXICAN $$$

(Map p602; ☎33-3615-7400; www.alcalde.com. mx; Av México 2903; mains M$300-385; ⊙1:30-11pm Mon-Thu, to 11:30pm Fri & Sat, to 5pm Sun) A favorite top-end restaurant in Guadalajara, the 'Mayor' is chef Paco Ruano's local venture, after having cut his teeth at El Celler de Can Roca in Girona, Spain, and Noma in Copenhagen, Denmark. His menu changes seasonally but features creations

Central Guadalajara

like green *aguachile* (shrimp ceviche) soup with green apples, American Wagyu in rich red *mole* (chili sauce), and rice pudding with cinnamon ice cream and toasted chocolate.

The decor – colorful Perspex lights setting off a black-and-white tiled floor – is stunning.

El Sacromonte   MEXICAN **$$$**
(Map p612; ☑ 33-3825-5447; www.sacromonte.com.mx; Moreno 1398; mains M$180-320; ☺1:30-11pm Mon-Sat, to 7pm Sun) This favorite *alta cocina* (gourmet restaurant) establishment in Colonia Americana has whimsical takes on classic dishes – quesadillas sprinkled with rose petals and strawberry aioli, avocado-watermelon soup, and giant prawns in lobster sauce with fried spinach. The decor pays homage to erstwhile matadors – there are cartoons of them everywhere – and moody piano music plays in the background. Reservations recommended.

Hueso   INTERNATIONAL **$$$**
(Map p612; ☑ 33-3615-3591; www.huesorestaurant.com; Luna 2061; mains M$300-395; ☺8pm-1:30am Mon-Sat) The preserve of acclaimed chef Alfonso Cadena (it's described as his *taller*, or 'workshop'), this restaurant gets consistently rave reviews for its innovative dishes and attention to detail. Note the whitewashed walls, which are lined with some 10,000 shark, bear, deer, boar and other animal bones – a macabre nod to its name, Hueso, or 'bone.'

Allium   FUSION **$$$**
(Map p612; ☑ 33-3615-6401; www.allium.com.mx; López Cotilla 1752; mains M$295-315; ☺1:30-5pm Tue-Sun, 7-10:30pm Tue-Fri, 7-11pm Fri & Sat) ✎ This sleek fine-dining addition to Guadalajara's growing gourmet circuit directed by chef Sebastian Renner Hamdan puts emphasis on locally produced food: 90% of its ingredients come from the state of Jalisco. The minimalist interior is redolent of Michelin-star restaurants in Europe, but prices and service are down-to-earth. Try the lamb with maguey-worm salsa or the roasted octopus.

i Latina
FUSION $$$

(Map p602; ☑ 33-3647-7774; www.i-latina.mx; Av Inglaterra 3128; mains M$155-365; ⊗ 7pm-1am Tue-Sat, 1:30-6:30pm Sun) This eccentrically decorated place requires a sharp double-take with its wall of ceramic pigs, a giant swordfish and lots of kitsch, fun touches. The Asian-leaning menu is the reason to come, however, with creative and excellent dishes. It's hugely popular with a smart and fashionable crowd and can get loud. But that makes it all the more fun.

La Panadería
BAKERY

(Map p612; ☑ 33-3827-6264; www.facebook. com/lapanaderiagdl; Robles Gil 286; baked goods M$25-40, snacks M$45-60; ⊗ 9am-8pm Mon-Fri, to 3pm Sat & Sun) A self-proclaimed 'bread laboratory,' this tiny high-end bakery offers a delicious range of baked goods from around the world: buttery croissants, melt-in-your-mouth brioche, sticky cinnamon buns, artisanal breads and more. For something closer to a meal, opt for the personal pizzas, panini or *empanadas* (giant turnovers stuffed with gourmet cheeses and cured meats).

✖ Zapopan

Zapopan has its own multifarious food scene, although the places lining the main road to the basilica are generally best avoided. Head instead to the side streets to the southeast.

★ Fonda Doña Gabina Escolatica
MEXICAN $

(Map p602; ☑ 33-3833-0883; Javier Mina 237; mains M$32-62; ⊗ 2-11pm Tue-Sat, 9am-8pm Sun) This narrow, barnlike restaurant on a delightful Zapopan side street of pastel-colored houses is bedecked with sunny colored textiles and specializes in *pozole* (traditional soup or stew made with hominy, pork and chilies) and monumental *tostada de pollo*, a huge pile of chicken and cabbage on a toasted tortilla.

Café Candela
CAFE $$

(Map p602; ☑ 33-3833-4344; https://cafe-candela.negocio.site; Javier Mina 183; mains M$70-110; ⊗ 1pm-1am Tue-Fri, 6pm-1am Sat; ⊘) A boho cafe in a patio-like setting with cozy couches, repurposed tables and chilled-out tunes. Dishes use whole foods and minimal fats and sugars – healthy Mexican! The *comida corrida* includes soup, a main dish and all you can drink *aguas frescas* (fresh fruit drinks) for M$95.

✖ Tlaquepaque

Tlaquepaque's main plaza overflows with street-food vendors – look for *jericalla* (a cross between flan and crème brûlée), coconut *empanadas* and cups of lime-drenched pomegranate seeds. Just southeast of the plaza, El Parián (p619) is a block of restaurant-bars with patio tables crowding a leafy inner courtyard. This is where you can sit, drink and listen to live mariachi music (but eat elsewhere).

Maria Mitotes
MEXICAN $

(Map p607; ☑ 33-4444-0888; https://maria-mitotes.negocio.site; Guerra 242; mains M$35-99; ⊗ 8:30am-9pm Tue-Sun) This festive open-air restaurant serves up delicious Mexican *antojitos* (snacks), prepared home-style and served on traditional clay dishes. Come here for taste treats like *pozole* (hominy soup), *flautas* (fried tortilla stuffed with meat), *gorditas* (cornmeal pancake filled with meat and cheese) and much more. If you can't decide, opt for the buffet – at M$100 it's a steal.

Chimbombo's Grill
MEXICAN $$

(Map p607; ☑ 33-3954-1788; Madero 80A; tortas M$35, steaks M$80-170; ⊗ 9am-10pm) This bustling streetside grill is the place to come for steaks and spicy *tortas ahogadas*. Steaks are rubbed with olive oil, splashed with soy sauce and served with Greek salad and garlic bread. Eat in, or take your feast to the plaza and enjoy it in the sun.

Zaguán
MEXICAN $$

(Map p607; ☑ 33-3614-1814; www.facebook.com/ zaguan.restaurante.galeria; Juárez 5; mains M$90-180; ⊗ 1-9pm Tue-Sun) Touted as one of Tlaquepaque's best eateries, this restaurant and gallery places a lot of emphasis on colors, tastes and textures, and is largely successful in its endeavors. Local favorites like *crema de poblano y elote* and *carne en su jugo* take on a new taste and look; go for the *mole encacahuatado* (M$140), a *mole*-tasting treat.

Chiles & Beer
SEAFOOD $$

(Map p607; ☑ 33-1732-1342; Morelos 225; mains M$98-229; ⊗ noon-7pm Mon-Fri, to 8pm Sat & Sun) Despite its unfortunate name, this is one of the best places in Tlaquepaque for fresh seafood. It's best known for its *aguachiles* – 17 varieties in all – served up cold and in *molcajetes* (large mortar and pestles) and chili-lined mugs. Daily specials keep the crowds coming. On weekends, live music starts at 4pm; come early to get a table!

Casa Fuerte

MEXICAN $$$

(Map p607; ☑33-3639-6481; www.facebook.com/CasaFuerteTlaquepaque; Independencia 224; mains M$170-340; ☺noon-8pm; 🐾) This elegant and sprawling place leans toward fine dining, with a full cocktail bar, refreshing garden patio and a rather stately feel. It's popular with Tlaquepaque's upper crust, although you can usually get a table with no problem. Try the sizzling *queso fundido con chorizo* (melted cheese with *chorizo*) in a stone pot.

Casa Luna

MEXICAN $$$

(Map p607; ☑33-1592-2061; www.facebook.com/CasaLunaRest; Independencia 211; mains M$230-370; ☺12:30-11pm Sun-Thu, to 1am Fri & Sat) Set in the heart of Tlaquepaque, Casa Luna spreads throughout an open courtyard under the shade of a large tree and inside as well. The cuisine is Mexican with modern twists: filet mignon with gorgonzola and *chipotle* sauce or black fettuccine topped with shrimp and *huitlacoche* (corn mushrooms). The wonderfully unique lamps and other lighting fixtures come from the attached Orígenes (Map p607; ☑33-3657-2405; www.facebook.com/origenesdavidluna; ☺10am-9pm Mon-Fri, 11am-8pm Sat, to 7pm Sun) shop.

🍷 Drinking & Nightlife

The Centro Histórico gets fairly quiet at night, though there are several bright spots (if you know where to look) and a well-established gay scene; most gay clubs also welcome straight people. Colonia Americana, however, is always hopping, with both local *antros* (literally 'dens,' but meaning dives) and international-style bars and clubs. In general, *tapatíos* tend to dress up to go out, so when in Rome...

Cantina La Fuente

BAR

(La Bicicleta; Map p614; ☑33-1496-4837; www.facebook.com/cantinalafuentemx; Suárez 78; ☺noon-midnight Mon-Sat) La Fuente, set in the old Edison boiler room, is an institution in Guadalajara and a perfect example of what a proper Mexican cantina is (ie rough around the edges). It's been here since 1921 and is mostly patronized by regulars who welcome newcomers like family. A bass, piano and violin trio sets up and jams from midafternoon until last call.

Look for the rusted bicycle above the bar, left by a patron in 1957 and never reclaimed. In fact, it's been there so long, *tapatíos* often refer to the bar as *La Bicicleta*.

Centro Cultural Breton

BAR

(Map p614; ☑33-3345-2194; www.facebook.com/pg/centroculturalbreton; Manuel 175; ☺10am-8pm Mon, to 2:30am Tue-Sat) Tucked away on a side street on the eastern side of the Centro Histórico is this bohemian bar, cafe and live-music venue. One of the city's coolest hangouts, come here to enjoy craft beers from around the world plus live music every night but Monday, from 10pm (free or minimal cover). French bites (M$50 to M$90) offered too.

Grillo

CRAFT BEER

(Map p612; ☑33-3827-3090; www.facebook.com/el.grillo.cantor; Av Chapultepec 219; ☺noon-2:30am Mon-Sat, to midnight Sun) This small but mighty bar stocks over 50 (mainly bottled) Mexican craft beers. Of interest are the Guadalajara-brewed Diógenes IPA and the Loba Negra American porter. The front patio is a good starting point for a Chapultepec night out – while your taste buds are still awake to the nuances of the hoppy brews.

Romea

WINE BAR

(Map p612; ☑33-1817-0202; www.facebook.com/romea.gdl; Morelos 1349; ☺5:30pm-midnight Mon, 9am-midnight Tue-Sat, 9am-4pm Sun) This swank corner wine bar with large windows stocks a wide range of Mexican vintages as well as wine from Spain, France, Portugal and even Slovenia. Blotter is available in the form of fancy cheese plates (from M$100) and charcuterie (from M$155) boards.

Amargo

BEER HALL

(Map p614; ☑33-1075-0570; www.facebook.com/amargobar; Sánchez 807; ☺5pm-1am Tue-Fri, 4pm-1am Sat, 1-9pm Sun) A laid-back, modern beer hall pouring Mexican craft brews – sours to stouts from 14 lines – with flights offered for M$60. A full lineup of bottled labels from around the world is offered too. If you get the munchies, there's tasty pub grub to fill your belly. Popular with the university set and locals looking to chill out.

Kin Kin

CLUB

(Map p602; ☑33-1075-4528; www.facebook.com/pg/kinkinclub; Av México 2981; ☺9pm-3am Wed, to 4am Thu-Sat) Hidden in a underground setting with exposed brick walls and disco balls, the red-lit Kin Kin is *the* place to groove out to electronica and house. Local and international DJs spin tunes nightly, and the space is jam-packed by midnight with hipsters of all ages. Known for its creative cocktails incorporating top-shelf gin, vodka and mezcal too.

California's Bar   GAY
(Map p614; ☑33-3614-3221; Moreno 652; ⊙6pm-3am Wed, Thu & Sun, to 5am Fri & Sat) A two-story gay bar that's popular with a diverse 20- and 30-something crowd usually OFB (out for business). It gets packed around 10pm, and Friday and Saturday nights are a madhouse. Great DJ most nights and dancing anywhere there's a free spot.

Bar Américas   CLUB
(Map p612; ☑cell 324-1044467; http://baramericas.com.mx; Av Chapultepec 507; ⊙9pm-5am Wed-Sat) A longtime night club catering to the well-heeled, Bar Américas is best known as an after-party spot with its dance floors packed 'til dawn. The all-black entrance down the steps looks as though you're entering the gates of hell.

Pigalle   COCKTAIL BAR
(Map p612; ☑33-3825-3118; www.facebook.com/PigalleBar; Robles Gil 137; ⊙6pm-midnight Sun & Tue, to 2:30am Wed-Sat) Mexican baristas excel at making cocktails (from M$85), both the savory and sweet type, and Pigalle is yet another cut above. Come here to relax, sip some of the most inventive libations in Guadalajara and listen to music, both canned and live.

El Cardenal   BAR
(Map p614; ☑33-1520-0668; Sánchez 847; ⊙6pm-1am Tue-Sun) A dark, artsy dive bar decked out in murals of all kinds, El Cardenal is a popular spot for the 20-something crowd or those with a penchant for piercings and tats. Drinks are cheap and strong.

☆ Entertainment

Guadalajara is a musical city, and live performers can be heard most nights of the week at any of the city's many venues (which include some restaurants). Discos and bars are plentiful, but ask around for the newest hot spots – *tapatíos* love to show off their town.

Alongside the town's key cultural institutions, the Unesco World Heritage–listed Instituto Cultural de Cabañas (p604) also plays host to an array of cultural performances.

Live Music

Guadalajara is the birthplace of the mariachi tradition, and **El Parián** (Map p607; ☑33-3696-0488; www.facebook.com/ElParianDeTlaquepaque; Av Juárez 68; ⊙10am-midnight Sun-Thu, to 1am Fri & Sat), a rambling 19th-century complex in Tlaquepaque, has a score of small cantinas

---

GAY & LESBIAN GUADALAJARA

Guadalajara is one of the gayest cities in Mexico – a conservative local government and fiercely Catholic population notwithstanding. In late June everyone takes to the streets when the city hosts one of Latin America's largest gay pride parades, the *Marcha del Orgullo GDL*.

Guadalajara's so-called 'gay ghetto' radiates out a few blocks from the corner of Ocampo and Sánchez, in the city center, but Avenida Chapultepec, just west of the city center, is starting to see upscale establishments aimed at a gay clientele. Find current hot spots and gay-friendly establishments at www.gaymexicomap.com.

---

perfect for enjoying a drink and soaking in the serenades of passionate Mexican bands. From Thursday to Monday the bands battle and jockey for your ears, applause and cash in the central bandstand for about an hour from 3:30pm and then again from 9:30pm.

State and municipal bands also present free concerts of typical *música tapatía* (Guadalajaran music) in the French art nouveau (1889) bandstand in the **Plaza de Armas** at 6:30pm Tuesday, 7:30pm Wednesday and 8pm Thursday, as well as during certain holiday periods.

1er Piso Jazz Club   LIVE MUSIC
(Primer Piso Jazz Club; Map p614; ☑33-3825-7085; www.facebook.com/pg/PrimerPisoJazzBar; Moreno 947; ⊙7:30pm-3am Wed-Sat) This retro glam jazz club – tablecloths, chandeliers, martinis – on the *1er piso* (1st floor, not ground floor) of a downtown city building has sets most nights from 9pm and excellent cocktails.

Sports

Fútbol (soccer) flows strongly through *tapatío* blood. The city has two local teams in Mexico's 18-club Liga MX (formerly called the Primera División): **Las Chivas** (www.chivasdecorazon.com.mx), the second most popular team in the country and the only club in Mexico to exclusively field Mexican players, and **Atlas** (www.atlasfc.com.mx). The seasons last from July to December and from January to June, and teams play at stadiums around the city. You can get an up-to-date season schedule at **Federación Mexicana de Fútbol** (www.femexfut.org.mx).

★ **Arena Coliseo**   MEXICAN WRESTLING

(Map p614; ☑33-3617-3401; www.cmll.com; Medrano 67; tickets M$250-420; ⊙8:45pm Tue, 6pm Sun) Watching masked *luchadores* (wrestlers) with names like El Terrible and Blue Panther gut-punching each other makes for a memorable night out. Expect scantily clad women, insult-hurling crowds and screaming doughnut vendors: it's all part of the fun of this classic Mexican pastime. The neighborhood surrounding the beloved coliseum can be a bit dodgy; take the usual precautions.

Tuesday-night events are typically called '*Martes de Glamour*' (Glamour Tuesdays), a tongue-in-cheek reference to the extra raunchiness of the show and crowds.

Campo Charro Jalisco   RODEO

(Map p602; ☑33-3619-0315; www.decharros. com; Av Dr Michel 577, Rincon de Agua Azul; from M$50) *Charreadas* (or *charrerías*), which are similar to rodeos, are held at noon most Sundays in this ring just behind Parque Agua Azul south of the city center. *Charros* (cowboys) come from all over Jalisco and the rest of Mexico, and *escaramuza charra* (female stunt riding) teams perform as well.

Theater

Teatro Degollado   PERFORMING ARTS

(Map p614; ☑33-3614-4773; www.facebook.com/ TeatroDegollado; Belén, btwn Morelos & Av Hidalgo; ⊙box office 10am-8pm Mon-Fri) This historic theater is a downtown cultural center that hosts a range of drama, dance and music performances.

Teatro Diana   PERFORMING ARTS

(Map p602; ☑33-3613-8579; www.teatrodiana. com; Av 16 de Septiembre 710; ⊙box office 11am-8pm) The hippest venue in town hosting a wide range of drama, dance and music performances. It stages traveling Broadway shows, concerts with local and international artists and art installations.

Ex Convento del Carmen   PERFORMING ARTS

(Map p614; ☑33-3030-1355; www.facebook. com/ExConventoCarmen; Av Juárez 638; ⊙10am-8pm Tue-Sat, to 6pm Sun) This erstwhile 17th-century church and monastery (which mostly now dates from the 1860s) is home to a well-respected cultural center hosting a wide range of dance, music and theater performances; one wing serves as a contemporary art gallery too.

🛍 **Shopping**

For most visitors, Guadalajara's most appealing shopping trophies are the excellent handicrafts from Jalisco, Michoacán and other Mexican states available in its many markets. Tlaquepaque and Tonalá, suburbs 8km and 17km respectively from the center, are both major producers of handicrafts and furniture. You'll find the best wholesale prices in Tonalá. There's also a craft market on Avenida Chapultepec.

Chahuistle   DESIGN

(Map p612; ☑33-2304-5096; www.chahuistle mx.com; Robles Gil 274; ⊙11am-7pm Mon-Sat) A Mexican design shop in a particularly cool pocket of Colonia Americana. Come here for artisanal items with a hipster twist: hand-stitched dog collars, modern accessories with indigenous designs, organic soaps and creams, Day of the Dead jewelry, and whimsical art. The quality is tops and the prices more than fair.

Tienda Vinísfera   WINE

(Map p612; ☑33-1377-5647; www.vinisfera.com; Av Justo Sierra 2275; ⊙noon-9pm Mon-Sat) If you'd like to learn more about and/or taste Mexican wine, head for this combination shop and cafe-bar north of Chapultepec. Along with a large selection of red and white wines ranging in price from M$100 to M$4000, you'll also find a dozen craft beers from Jalisco state. Take away or sip same in the cafe or delightful back garden.

El Nahual Gallery   ARTS & CRAFTS

(Map p607; ☑33-3659-3186; www.facebook. com/elnahualgallery; Degollado 175; ⊙9am-9pm Mon-Sat) This well-stocked shop in the Casa de las Flores sells some of the finest ceramics pieces, figurines and masks in the region. Owner and collector Stan Singleton is ready and eager to explain the processes, organize workshop visits and advise on purchases.

Antigua de México   HOMEWARES

(Map p607; ☑33-3639-2997; www.antigua demexico.com; Independencia 255; ⊙10am-2pm & 4-7pm Mon-Sat, 11am-4pm Sun) A 'wow'-inducing Tlaquepaque boutique with gorgeous furniture showpieces, such as benches carved from a single tree, which are displayed in expansive, old-world courtyards. Are those ancient coaches actually for sale?

Del Corazón de la Tierra   ARTS & CRAFTS

(Map p607; ☑33-3657-5682; www.delcorazon delatierra.mx; Independencia 227; ⊙10am-8pm

Mon-Sat, to 6pm Sun) This lovely shop in central Tlaquepaque, whose name translates as 'From the Heart of the Country,' specializes in indigenous art; look for decorative items from Jalisco and Nayarit as well as textiles from Chiapas and Oaxaca. A great spot for one-of-a-kind mementos and gifts.

Taller de Cerámica
Paco Padilla   ARTS & CRAFTS
(Map p607; ☑33-3635-4838; www.facebook.com/tallerpacopadilla; Sánchez 142; ◷9:30am-3:30pm Mon-Fri) This is the workshop and showroom of noted Tlaquepaque ceramicist Paco Padilla. It's within easy walking distance of the famed Museo Pantaleón Panduro of award-winning ceramics pieces.

ℹ Information

EMERGENCY
If you are a victim of crime, you may first want to contact your embassy or consulate and/or the state tourist office.
Ambulance ☑33-3616-9616
Emergency ☑066, 080
Fire ☑33-3619-5155
Police ☑33-3668-0800

INTERNET ACCESS
A dwindling stash of internet cafes (M$10 to M$18 per hour) are scattered around the city, but tend to change location frequently. Nearly all hotels and hostels and many restaurants, cafes and bars offer free wi-fi access too.

MEDICAL SERVICES
Farmacia Guadalajara (☑33-3613-7509; Moreno 170; ◷7am-10pm) Get your first aid, sundry items and prescribed meds here.

Hospital México Americano (☑33-3648-3333, free call 01-800-462-2238; www.hma.com.mx; Colomos 2110) About 3km northwest of the city center; English-speaking physicians available.
US Consulate (☑33-3268-2100; https://mx.usembassy.gov/embassy-consulates/guadalajara; Progreso 175, Colonia Americana; ◷8am-4:30pm Mon-Fri) Keeps a regularly updated online list of local English-speaking doctors, including specialists and dentists.

MONEY
Banks are plentiful in Guadalajara and most have ATMs, known as *cajeros automáticos*.

You can change cash at competitive prices round the clock at one of the eager *casas de cambio* (money changers) on López Cotilla, between Avenida 16 de Septiembre and Maestranza. Very few change traveler's checks these days.

POST
If you go overboard stocking up on hammocks, ceramics and giant carved jaguars, **Sebastián Exportaciones** (Map p607; ☑33-3639-9297; www.facebook.com/pg/ExportacionesSebastian; Ejército 45, Tlaquepaque; ◷9am-2pm & 4-6pm Mon-Fri) has you covered. This Tlaquepaque outfit ships boxes and cartons (minimum 1 cu meter) internationally.

Main Post Office (Map p614; ☑33-3614-2482; cnr Carranza & Av Independencia 57; ◷8am-7pm Mon-Fri, to 3pm Sat)

TOURIST INFORMATION
Guadalajara Tourist Information Booth (Map p614; Plaza de la Liberación; ◷8:45am-1:30pm & 2:45-7:30pm Mon-Fri, 9:30am-2:30pm Sat & Sun) One of half a dozen generic booths scattered around the city, all with the same hours. You'll find others in Jardín San Francisco, Plaza de las Américas (Zapopan) and outside the Instituto Cultural de Cabañas.

CAR-FREE GUADALAJARA

Every Sunday since 2004, Mexico's second-largest city has celebrated the **Vía Recre Activa** (☑33-1596-2189; www.viarecreactiva.org; ◷8am-2pm Sun), when 28km of arterial streets are closed to cars and given over instead to bikes, skateboards, strollers, wheelchairs and any other form of nonmotorized forward propulsion.

Adding to the convenience is an army of enthusiastic volunteers around Parque Revolución dispensing free bikes (ID required) and offering historic bike tours (p609) departing a short distance to the west at 10am and lasting three hours (sign up by 9:30am to assure a spot).

The aim of this car-less half-day is to reduce vehicle dependence, promote health and generate social interaction. Creative artists are encouraged to take to the streets, and Parque Revolución, the nerve center of Via RecreActiva, maintains a cultural pavilion with live performances. The measure – which sees an average 220,000 *tapatíos* (Guadalajara residents) take to the streets weekly – has since been adopted by other Mexican cities, including Mexico City's DF (Distrito Federal or Federal District).

Jalisco State Tourist Office (Map p614; ☎33-3668-1601; https://secturjal.jalisco.gob.mx; Morelos 102; ◷9am-5pm Mon-Fri) Knowledgeable staff offer the nitty-gritty on Guadalajara and the state of Jalisco. Ask for a copy of the monthly events-listing 'Cartelera.' English spoken.

Tlaquepaque Tourist Office (Map p607; ☎33-1057-6212; www.tlaquepaque.gob.mx; Morelos 288; ◷9am-5pm Mon-Thu) Located on the 2nd story of a souvenir shop, Casa del Artesano. There's a much more helpful and conveniently located tourist information booth (p607) opposite El Parián.

Tonalá Tourist Office (p608) Located on the 2nd floor of Tonalá's city hall, just two blocks east of Avenida Tonaltecas.

❶ Getting There & Away

AIR

Guadalajara's **Aeropuerto Internacional Miguel Hidalgo** (GDL; ☎33-3688-5248; www.aeropuertosgap.com.mx; Carretera Guadalajara Chapala Km 17.5, Tlajomulco de Zuñiga) is 20km south of downtown, just off the Hwy 23 to Chapala. Inside are ATMs, money-exchange offices, cafes and car-rental companies.

A number of different airlines offer direct flights to major cities in Mexico.

Aeroméxico (☎800-021-40-00; www.aeromexico.com; Aeropuerto Internacional Miguel Hidalgo, Carretera Guadalajara Chapala km 17.5, Tlajomulco de Zuñiga)

Interjet (☎866-285-95-25; www.interjet.com.mx; Aeropuerto Internacional Miguel Hidalgo, Carretera Guadalajara Chapala km 17.5, Tlajomulco de Zuñiga)

VivaAerobus (☎81-8215-0150; www.vivaaerobus.com; Aeropuerto Internacional Miguel Hidalgo, Carretera Guadalajara Chapala km 17.5, Tlajomulco de Zuñiga)

Volaris (☎55-1102-8000; www.volaris.mx; Aeropuerto Internacional Miguel Hidalgo, Carretera Guadalajara Chapala km 17.5, Tlajomulco de Zuñiga)

BUSES FROM GUADALAJARA
From Nueva Central Camionera

DESTINATION	FARE (M$)	TIME (HR)	FREQUENCY (PER DAY)
Barra de Navidad	580	6	12
Colima	365	3	hourly
Guanajuato	540	4	hourly
Manzanillo	550	4½	half-hourly
Mexico City (Terminal Norte)	865	6½	half-hourly
Morelia	520	3½	hourly
Pátzcuaro	520	5½	1
Puerto Vallarta	655	5½	hourly
Querétaro	594	4½	half-hourly
San Miguel de Allende	700	5½	hourly
Tepic	480	3	9
Uruapan	505	4¾	10
Zacatecas	711	5	11
Zamora	303	2½	hourly

From Antigua Central Camionera

DESTINATION	FARE (M$)	TIME (HR)	FREQUENCY (PER DAY)
Ajijic	60	1¼	hourly
Chapala	58	1	half-hourly
Ciudad Guzmán	208	2	hourly
Tapalpa	182	3	10
Tequila	115	1¾	half-hourly
Teuchitlán (Guachimontones)	120	2	hourly

BUS

Guadalajara has two bus terminals. The long-distance bus terminal is the airport-like **Nueva Central Camionera** (New Bus Terminal; Map p602; 33-3600-0135; Av de las Torres s/n, Tlaquepaque), a large, modern, V-shaped terminal that is split into seven separate *módulos* (mini-terminals). Each *módulo* has ticket desks for a number of bus lines, plus waiting areas, restrooms and cafes. The Nueva Central Camionera is 11km southeast of Guadalajara city center, on Tlaquepaque's east side and just off the Hwy 80.

Buses go to and from just about everywhere in western, central and northern Mexico. Destinations are served by multiple companies, based in the different *módulos*, making price comparisons difficult (though prices are posted) and time-consuming. The good news is that if you're flexible, you won't have to wait long for a bus – there are departures at least once an hour for all major destinations. Fares given are for the best buses available. You can often find cheaper fares by going on slightly less plush buses.

ETN (33-3817-6618; www.etn.com.mx) and **Primera Plus** (477-710-00-60; www.primeraplus.com.mx) offer deluxe nonstop rides to many destinations. Buses have wi-fi, toilets, air-con, individual TV screens, mega-comfortable seats, and free food and drink. Prices are highly reasonable.

Guadalajara's other bus terminal is the scruffier **Antigua Central Camionera** (Old Bus Terminal; Map p602; 33-3650-0479; Los Ángeles 218), about 2km south of the cathedral near Parque Agua Azul. From here 2nd-class buses serve destinations within 100km of Guadalajara. There are two sides to it: Sala A is for destinations to the east and northeast; Sala B is for destinations northwest, southwest and south. There's a M$0.50 charge to enter the terminal. Bus services generally run between 6am and 10pm. Buses leave multiple times an hour for nearby locations, and once an hour or so for longer trips.

CAR & MOTORCYCLE

Guadalajara is 545km northwest of Mexico City and 325km east of Puerto Vallarta. Highways 15, 15D, 23, 54, 54D, 80, 80D and 90 all converge here, combining temporarily to form the Periférico Norte and Periférico Sur, the ring roads around the city.

Guadalajara has many car-rental agencies. All the large international companies are represented, but you may get a cheaper deal from a local company, so it's worth comparing prices and availability online before you travel. Prices start at around M$600 per day for a four-door sedan; it will cost you upward of M$4000 to drop off the car in any city other than the one you rented it from.

TRAIN

The only passenger **trains** (Av Circunvalación Agustín Yáñez 1009) serving Guadalajara are the two tourist 'tequila-tasting' trains to the nearby towns of Amatitán or Tequila.

ℹ Getting Around

TO/FROM THE AIRPORT

The airport is just under 20km south of central Guadalajara, just off Hwy 23 to Chapala. To get into town on public transportation, exit the airport and head to the bus stop in front of the motel-like Hotel Casa Grande, about 50m to the right. Take bus 176 (M$9.50) or the more expensive one marked 'Atasa' (M$13) – both run every 15 minutes or so from about 5am to 10pm and take 40 minutes to the Antigua Central Camionera, where you can hop on a bus to the city center.

Taxi prices are M$350 to the city center, M$310 to the Nueva Central Camionera and M$270 to Tlaquepaque. Buy fixed-price tickets inside the airport.

To get to the airport from Guadalajara's center, take bus 604 to the Antigua Central Camionera (the stop where you get off is in front of the Hotel Union) and then get on an 'Aeropuerto' shuttle bus (every 20 minutes, 6am to 9pm) at this stop. Metered taxis cost roughly M$300.

TO/FROM THE BUS TERMINALS

To reach the city center from the Nueva Central Camionera, take any bus marked 'Centro' (M$9.50). You can also catch the more comfortable, turquoise-colored TUR bus (M$15). They should be marked 'Zapopan.' Don't take the ones marked 'Tonalá' or you'll be headed away from Guadalajara's center. Taxis to the city center cost M$160 unless they let the meter tick (some don't use it). A direct taxi from the airport to the Nueva Central Camionera costs M$310.

To get to the Nueva Central Camionera from the city center, take any bus marked 'Nueva Central' such as 616 or 275B. These are frequent and leave from the **corner** (Map p614; M$9.50-15) of Avenida 16 de Septiembre and Madero.

To reach the city center from the Antigua Central Camionera, take any bus going north on Calzada Independencia. To return to the Antigua Central Camionera from the city center, take bus 604 going south on **Calzada Independencia** (Map p614). Taxis cost M$55.

Bus 616 (M$9.50) runs between the two bus terminals.

BICYCLE

Guadalajara's large-scale bike-sharing scheme **MiBici** (33-3002-2424; www.mibici.net; per day/3 days/week M$90/180/320; 6am-midnight) was introduced in 2014 and now counts some 71,600 users. Most of its users are yearly (M$404) subscribers, but you can obtain a *pase temporal* (temporary pass) by using your credit card in a machine at any of the docking stations, such as the big one on Parque Revolución. Be advised that bikes must be returned by midnight and cannot be used before 6am.

BUS

Guadalajara has a comprehensive city bus system, but be ready for crowded, rough rides. On major routes, buses run every five minutes or so from 6am to 10pm daily and cost M$9.50. Many buses pass through the city center, so for a suburban destination you'll have a few stops to choose from. The routes diverge as they get further from the city center and you'll need to know the bus number for the suburb you want. Some bus-route numbers are followed by an additional letter indicating which route they take through the suburbs.

The TUR buses, painted a distinctive turquoise color, are a more comfortable alternative. They have air-con and plush seats (M$15). If they roar past without stopping, they're full; this can happen several times in a row during rush hour and may drive you mad.

Using the website www.moovitapp.com (or downloading the app) is arguably the most effective way to navigate the complex bus routes in Guadalajara – just plug in your start and end points and it'll provide the best options, including wait times and walking instructions, if needed. Once on the bus, the site tracks your movement and even reminds you when to get off.

Notwithstanding technology, following are some common destinations, the buses that go there and a central stop from where you can catch them.

Antigua Central Camionera Bus 62 going south on Calzada Independencia or bus 320, 644A or from the center.

Colonia Americana Bus 707 TUR and metro line 3 bus replacement along Avenida Vallarta; buses 400 and 500 from Avenida Alcalde or **Colonia Americana** (Map p614; Av Alcalde, btwn Avs Manuel & Independencia; M$9.50-15).

Nueva Central Camionera Bus 616, 275B or any bus marked Nueva Central; catch them all at the corner of Avenida 16 de Septiembre and Madero.

Tlaquepaque Bus 275B, 303, 647 or 706 TUR marked Tlaquepaque (p623) at Avenida 16 de Septiembre between López Cotilla and Madero.

Tonalá Bus 231, 275D, 275 Diagonal, 633V or 707b TUR marked Tonalá at Avenida 16 de Septiembre and Madero.

Zapopan Bus 275 or 706 TUR marked Zapopan (Map p614; Av 16 de Septiembre s/n; M$9.50-15) going north on Avenida 16 de Septiembre.

METRO

At present the **Siteur** (Sistema de Tren Eléctrico Urbano; 33-3942-5700; www.siteur.gob. mx; ⊙5am-11pm) subway and light-rail system counts two lines that cross the city. Stops are marked with a 'T.' But the metro as it exists now isn't particularly tourist friendly as most stops are far from the sights. Línea 1 stretches north–south for 15.5km all the way from the Periférico Norte to the Periférico Sur. It runs below Federalismo (seven blocks west of the city center) and Avenida Colón: catch it at Parque Revolución, on the corner of Avenida Juárez. Línea 2 runs east–west for 8.5km below Avenidas Juárez and Mina. A new northwest-southeast line, Línea 3, has been under construction since 2014, with repeated delays. Once operating, it will cover 21.5km, connecting Zapopan to Tlaquepaque and passing through the interchange Juárez station; it will be particularly useful to travelers with stops near several sights and the Nueva Central Camionera (p623). The SiTren trolley-bus covers part of the route as far as Los Arcos and Centro Magno.

A single journey costs M$9.50, with a transfer at Juárez an additional M$4.75. A stored-value card (M$20) includes the first journey.

TAXI

Taxis are everywhere in the city center. They have meters, but drivers seldom use them. Most would rather quote a flat fee for a trip, especially at night. Generally it's cheaper to go by the meter – if you're quoted a flat fee and think it's inflated, try to bargain (and good luck). From 10pm to 6am fares rise by 25%. We've heard reports from both locals and visitors about endemic taxi rip-offs in Guadalajara; use Uber, which is reliable and invariably cheaper.

Tequila

📋 374 / POP 30,800 / ELEV 1180M

Surrounded by a sea of blue agave, sun-baked Tequila is a surprisingly attractive factory town despite the souvenir shops and tequila barrel–shaped shuttles that dot its cobblestone streets. The eponymous drink – the object of everyone's longing – is best observed and tasted in one of three big distilleries, all of which run tours.

The Tequila region's agave landscape and its ancient industrial facilities, both in the shadow of its namesake volcano, have been a Unesco World Heritage site since 2006.

◉ Sights

★ Centro Cultural Juan Beckman Gallardo   CULTURAL CENTER

(📋 374-742-68-40; www.facebook.com/pg/Centro CulturalJuanBeckmannGallardo; José Cuervo 124; adult/child M$70/35; ⊙10am-6pm Tue-Sat, to 3pm Sun) Opened in 2018, this gorgeous colonial-style cultural center is home to a modern museum with well-curated exhibits on the history and culture of the region, including pre-Hispanic pottery, Mexican folk art and *charrería* (Mexican horsemanship). Signage in Spanish and English. Guided tours available. Concerts and other live performances occasionally offered too.

Hacienda La Cofradia   DISTILLERY
(📞 374-742-68-00; www.tequilacofradia.com.mx; La Cofradia 1297; tour M$195, with 3 tastings M$260; ⏰ 10am-6pm) Two kilometers south of Tequila sits the beautiful Hacienda La Cofradia estate where the 100% blue agave Casa Noble tequila brand is distilled. The elegant 'factory' is set amid mango trees and uses French oak barrels to age its spirits. Aside from factory tours, La Cofradia hosts the **Museo de Sitio del Tequila** and the atmospherically cavernous **La Taberna del Cofrade** restaurant.

Casa Sauza   DISTILLERY
(📞 374-742-71-00; www.casasauza.com; Luis Navarro 70; tour M$175, with 3 tastings M$230; ⏰ 10am-6pm) The Casa Sauza estate invokes Frances Hodgson Burnett's classic fairy tale *The Secret Garden*. The colonial-style grounds are adorned with Italianate fountains, tumbling plants and even a chapel. Indeed, 'tequila factory' are the last words that spring to mind as you recline in the sun-streaked bar. Nonetheless, tequila has been made here since the 1800s and still is (if you listen hard enough, you'll hear the hum of the distillery machinery). Basic tours of Casa Sauza's **Perseverancia Distillery** (Sauza 80; tour M$170, with tasting M$230) last one hour.

Mundo Cuervo   DISTILLERY
(📞 374-742-72-00; www.mundocuervo.com; Ramón Corona, cnr José Cuervo; ⏰ 11am-5pm Sun-Fri, to 6pm Sat) Just opposite Tequila's main plaza and immediately recognizable by the enormous statue of a crow (*cuervo* in Spanish), Mundo Cuervo, which is owned by the José Cuervo distillery, is a veritable tequila theme park and the biggest game in town. Hourly tours of **La Rojeña distillery**, the oldest in the Americas, can include tastings. The hour-long tour is a bit rushed so it's worth spending a little more on one of the longer tours that takes in the agave fields (M$925).

Museo Nacional del Tequila   MUSEUM
(📞 374-742-00-12; Ramón Corona 34; adult/child M$15/7; ⏰ 9am-6pm) In an old colonial building just off the main plaza, spread over five rooms, this museum illustrates the history of tequila-making with photos and distillery apparatus; signage is in Spanish and English.

DON'T MISS

EL ARENAL

El Arenal, 43km northwest of Guadalajara and 22km southeast of Tequila, is the gateway to the Tequila region. This small settlement is the site of one of the state's best small distilleries, **Cascahuín** (📞 374-748-00-10; www.facebook.com/cascahuin; Av Ferrocarril; tour M$50, with 3 tastings M$150; ⏰ 9am-6pm Mon-Fri, to 4pm Sat & Sun). If you have time for only one distillery tour while in Tequila country, make it this one. Here you'll see the entire process, from *piña* harvesting to bottling and labeling, up close, and mostly done in the traditional way. Some of the items used, including brick ovens, *tahona* (stone mill) and charcoal firing pits, are heirlooms and the product – be it *blanco* (white), *reposado* (rested) or *añejo* (aged) – is delectable. Be sure to call in advance, as tours are offered by reservation only.

🚩 Tours

A handful of fascinating tours in and around Tequila, including by train, are offered from Guadalajara: try Tequila Tour by Mickey Marentes (p609), Experience Agave (p609) and José Cuervo Express (p610). Group size, transport type and customization determine the cost.

🍴 Eating

El Palomar   CAFE $
(📞 374-742-44-29; Av Sixto Gorjón s/n; mains M$45-80; ⏰ 8am-11pm) Overlooking a pleasant church plaza, El Palomar serves up delicious and hearty *típico* – quesadillas, *chilaquiles*, enchiladas – with a long menu of coffee drinks and milkshakes. It's especially well known for its big breakfast plates. Try to nab an outdoor table for the best people-watching.

ℹ Information

Tourist office (📞 374-742-00-12; Cuervo 33; ⏰ 9am-3:30pm Mon-Fri) This small office offers basic info about Tequila, including a calendar of events and a handy town map.

ℹ Getting There & Away

Buses to Tequila leave from Guadalajara's Antigua Central Camionera every 30 minutes (M$115, 1¾ hours).

Lago de Chapala

Lago de Chapala, Mexico's largest lake, measuring 12.5km by 80km, lies 50km south of Guadalajara. Surrounded by dramatic mountains and enjoying a mild climate (always warm during the day and pleasantly cool at night), the lake continues to lure North American retirees and, on weekends, masses of *tapatíos* out for some fresh air, a boat ride and a fish lunch. For foreign tourists, the allure is a little less compelling, although it does make for a fun escape from Guadalajara.

Sadly, the lake is not as healthy as it is beautiful. Water levels fluctuate due to Guadalajara's and Mexico City's water needs and on-again, off-again drought conditions. Commercial fertilizers washed into the lake have polluted it and nourished water hyacinth, an invasive plant that clogs the lake's surface and kills off aquatic life. You'll see very few people swimming here.

Chapala

📞 376 / POP 22,500 / ELEV 1539M

With a commanding location from the northern shore of its namesake lake, Chapala became a well-known resort destination when President Porfirio Díaz vacationed here every year from 1904 to 1909. DH Lawrence and Tennessee Williams came later, certifying the town's literary pedigree. Today Chapala is a simple but charming working-class Mexican town with lovely lakeside walks, a waterfront market and a buzzing weekend scene.

👁 Sights

Isla de Mezcala   ISLAND

The more interesting island to visit on Lago de Chapala is Isla de Mezcala. Here you'll find ruins of a fort where Mexican independence fighters held strong from 1812 to 1816, repulsing several Spanish attacks before finally earning the respect of, and a full pardon from, their enemies. A three-hour round-trip boat ride, including one hour to explore to the island, costs M$2500 for up to eight people.

Isla de los Alacranes   ISLAND

A **ticket booth** (🕘9am-7pm) at the pier's entrance sells boat tickets to Isla de los Alacranes (Scorpion Island), 6km from Chapala, which has some restaurants and souvenir stalls but is not very captivating. A round trip, with 30 minutes on the island, costs M$450 per boatload; for one hour on the island it's M$550.

Around Guadalajara

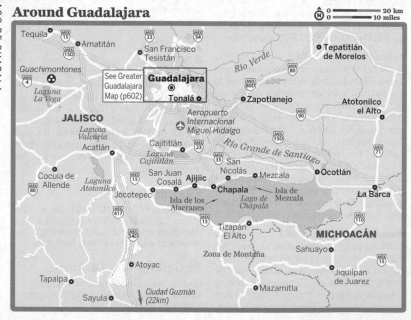

🛌 Sleeping & Eating

⭐ **Lake Chapala Inn**　　GUESTHOUSE $$$
(☎376-765-28-99; www.chapalainn.com; Paseo Ramón Corona 23; s/d incl breakfast M$1600/1800; P@🛜🏊) This very imposing white and orange building dating from 1906 right on the lakeshore is moments from the center of town and enjoys wonderful views over the waters and off to the faraway hills. The views from two of the four rooms (Rosa and Jacaranda) and the communal terrace are unbeatable. There's a wonderful library with fireplace and a garden with a lap pool.

There's a two-night minimum stay, and the traditional breakfast is the real deal. Ask to borrow one of the two bikes.

La Palapa de Don Juan　　MEXICAN $$
(☎33-1185-1771; https://la-palapa-de-don-juan.nego cio.site; Paseo Ramón Corona 32; mains M$85-140; ⏲8am-2pm) A soaring *palapa* (thatched roof) and two floors of waterfront dining make Don Juan's popular for daytime eats with locals and day-trippers alike. The menu ranges from traditional breakfast – egg dishes, *chilaquiles*, pancakes – to fresh fish and seafood plates.

ⓘ Getting There & Away

Buses from Guadalajara (M$47 to M$58, one hour, half-hourly) to Chapala leave from the Antigua Central Camionera. Buses connect Chapala to Ajijic (M$9, 20 minutes) every 20 minutes.

Ajijic

☑ 376 / POP 10,500 / ELEV 1577M
This town, with the unusual-sounding name of Ajijic (pronounced 'ah-hee-heek'), is an outpost of North American retirees and by far the most sophisticated and energetic of the towns that line the northern shore of Lago de Chapala. While the gringos may have put Ajijic on the map by opening boutiques, galleries and restaurants galore, much of the town retains its charming, colonial-era vibe, with cobblestone lanes and quiet streets of colorfully painted houses. It makes a delightful place to sit back and relax awhile, although it's far from the typical Mexico here: English is almost as commonly heard on the streets as Spanish, and prices are somewhat higher than other places on the lake.

🏃 Activities

Plus Adventure　　OUTDOORS
(☎33-1228-2617; www.facebook.com/pg/PlusAdven tureMx; Corona 7a; tours M$500-700; ⏲9am-5pm Tue-Sun) This professional and friendly outfit offers outdoor excursions in the Chapala region: kayaking on the lake, hiking to waterfalls, and rock climbing on the hills behind town. Groups are small and tours typically last three hours. All include transportation, snacks and accident insurance; guides will even snap photos and email them afterwards. Bike rentals (M$200 per day) available too.

🛌 Sleeping & Eating

La Nueva Posada　　GUESTHOUSE $$
(☎376-766-14-44; www.hotelnuevaposada.com; Guerra 9; incl breakfast s M$1300-1600, d M$1400-1800; P🛜🏊) A lovely hotel with an unspoken grandeur, this lakeside retreat offers a taste of genteel, old-world Mexico. The 19 rooms have tasteful, if occasionally dated, furnishings; almost half have expansive lake views. The garden, with resident macaw Paco and small pool, runs right down to the lake, giving you plenty of space to feel at ease with the world.

Kamellos Food Truck　　FOOD TRUCK $
(☎33-1892-7735; Blvd De Jin XI 31; mains M$45-95; ⏲noon-9pm Tue-Sat) This popular, bustling food truck sells flavorful and hearty Middle Eastern eats: falafel, kebabs, stuffed pita pockets. All meals come with a fresh, crisp Greek salad and are served on real plates with silverware (little waste here). Nab a table under the nearby shade trees – a breezy place to watch the world go by.

Ajijic Tango　　ARGENTINE $$$
(☎376-766-24-58; www.ajijictango.com; Morelos 5; steaks M$191-425; ⏲12:30-9pm Mon, Wed & Thu, to 10pm Fri & Sat, to 7pm Sun) Ajijic's most popular restaurant is never less than crammed with locals, resident expats and visitors, all here to enjoy the excellent steaks (it is an Argentinian restaurant after all). But there are other dishes too – Mexican, salads and pasta. Seating is in a colorful tented courtyard. Reservations are a must on Friday and Saturday nights.

ⓘ Getting There & Away

Buses from Guadalajara (M$60, 1¼ hour, half-hourly) to Ajijic leave from the Antigua Central Camionera and drop you on the highway at Colón, next to a small ticket office. Buses connect Chapala and Ajijic every 20 minutes (M$9, 20 minutes).

Zona de Montaña

South of Lago de Chapala, Jalisco's Zona de Montaña – the 'Mountain Zone' of seemingly endless layered peaks – is an increasingly popular weekend retreat for *tapatíos,* who come to enjoy the rangeland, pines, timeless colonial *pueblos mágicos* (magical villages), local dishes and cooler climes.

Tapalpa

📞 343 / POP 16,500 / ELEV 2068M

Tapalpa, a labyrinth of whitewashed walls, red-tiled roofs and cobblestoned streets surrounding two impressive 16th-century churches, truly deserves its designation as a *pueblo mágico* – it is one of the most beautiful mountain towns in the land. Of course, this beauty hasn't gone unnoticed – at weekends flocks of people flee Guadalajara for the hiking, trekking and generally cool and misty climate that Tapalpa offers. During the week, when visitors are few in number, Tapalpa retains a country backwater feel; horses clip-clop down the lanes and old men in cowboy hats lounge on benches in the plaza.

◉ Sights

Las Piedrotas　　　　NATURAL FEATURE

(Carretera a Chiquilistlán s/n; ♿) Las Piedrotas are a large and impressive group of rock formations set in cow pastures in what's called the Valle de las Enigmas about 6km north of town. It's a good place for walking, rock scrambling or zip-lining (M$150) between the two largest formations. Most people drive here, but it's an easy and rewarding 2½- to three-hour return walk along a quiet country lane through dark pine forests, past an abandoned old paper mill and up onto a flower-filled plateau.

To reach Las Piedrotas, take Hidalgo westward out of town, keeping to the left and following the signs for Chiquilistlán (and some signs for Las Piedrotas). Once you've cleared the edge of town, carry on straight. A taxi costs around M$150 one way.

El Salto del Nogal　　　　WATERFALL

El Salto del Nogal is a jaw-dropping, 105m-high waterfall about 18km south of town, off a dirt road. A taxi costs around M$250 one way.

⌖ Tours

Colores Tapalpa　　　　TOURS

(📞800-404-08-08, 343-432-05-52; www.colores tapalpa.mx; Matamoros 69C; ⊙10am-5pm) This upbeat and helpful travel agency on Tapalpa's main square organizes daily excursions to Las Piedrotas lasting 3½ hours and costing M$350. A five-hour trip to El Salto del No-

gal costs M$450 and typically leaves at 11am. Canyoning and mountain-biking trips also arranged. Bike rentals (M$400 per half day) offered too.

🛏 Sleeping & Eating

Las Margaritas Hotel Posada　　GUESTHOUSE **$$**

(📞343-432-07-99; www.tapalpahotelmargaritas. com; 16 de Septiembre 81; d/ste M$800/1600; 🔊) Sporting bright decorations and carved wardrobes, this seven-room inn uphill from the main plaza offers excellent value, comfort and eye-pleasing rooms; the two-bedroom suites have kitchenettes and big windows overlooking the red-roof-tile skyline.

★**Los Girasoles**　　　　MEXICAN **$$**

(📞343-432-00-86; www.facebook.com/girasoles tapalpa; Obregón 110; mains M$65-225; ⊙9am-10pm Mon-Thu, to 11pm Fri & Sat, to 7:30pm Sun) Tapalpa's classiest restaurant is just off the main plaza and offers quality dishes such as cheese- and plantain-stuffed chilies in a cilantro sauce, *tamales de acelga* (chard-filled *tamales*) and a spicy chicken dish called *cochala de polio.* There's a star-lit outdoor patio for rare warm nights or you can snuggle in front of the open log fire in the dining room.

ⓘ Information

Tourist office (📞ext 125 343-432-06-50; Portal Morelos; ⊙9am-3pm Mon-Fri, 10am-6pm Sat, to 3pm Sun) Just off the Plaza Principal; has maps and good regional info.

ⓘ Getting There & Away

Some 10 buses depart daily for Tapalpa from Guadalajara's Antigua Central Camionera (M$182, three hours); two daily also leave from the Nueva Central Camionera. There are also four buses a day to/from Ciudad Guzmán (M$126, two hours). Buses in Tapalpa stop at the **Sur de Jalisco bus office** (Juan Gil Preciado 11) down the hill from the center.

Ciudad Guzmán

📞 341 / POP 102,200 / ELEV 1535M

Large and frenetic Ciudad Guzmán is no tourist destination, but it is the closest city to Volcán Nevado de Colima, the majestic volcano about 25km to its southwest.

Guzmán's crowded main plaza is surrounded by market stalls and shopping arcades set around two churches: the 17th-century **Templo del Sagrado Corazón** and the neoclassical **Catedral de San Juan.** In the center of the adjoining Jardín Municipal (City Garden) is a stone bandstand with a copy of local boy José Clemente Orozco's mural *Hombre de Fuego* (Man of Fire) painted on its ceiling. The original is in the Instituto Cultural de Cabañas (p604) in Guadalajara.

Hotel Reforma   HOTEL **$**
(🖉341-412-44-54; www.hreforma.com; Av Reforma 77; s/d M$455/505; [P][🛜]) A spick-and-span hotel in the heart of downtown, Hotel Reforma makes for a convenient and comfortable stay. The rooms are dated – flower bedspreads, old-school TVs, no air-con – but the beds are comfy and there's wi-fi and hot water. Staff are friendly and accommodating too. A good option for a night or two.

ℹ️ Information

Tourist office (🖉 ext 102/110 341-412-25-63; Av Pedro Ramírez 2288; ⏲ 8:30am-3pm Mon-Fri) On the southern outskirts of town, about 3km from both the mammoth bus station and the central plaza. Staff can help with planning and booking an ascent of the Volcán Nevado de Colima.

ℹ️ Getting There & Away

Ciudad Guzmán's modern **bus terminal** (🖉 341-410-56-97; Av Miguel de la Madrid s/n) is about 3km west of the plaza near the entrance to (or exit from) the city from the Guadalajara–Colima highway. Hop on bus 5 (M$6.50) to get there and back or take a moto-taxi (M$25). Destinations include Guadalajara (M$208 to M$220, two hours), Colima (M$151, one to two hours), Tapalpa (M$126, two hours) and Zapotitlán, which passes 2km from El Fresnito (M$22, 20 minutes), the closest village to Volcán Nevado de Colima. An alternative way to reach El Fresnito is by taking the 1A, 1C or 1V *urbano* (urban bus) from the Los Mones crossroad in Ciudad Guzmán (M$6.50, 20 minutes).

INLAND COLIMA STATE

At just 5627 sq km and Mexico's third-smallest state, tiny but ecologically rich and diverse Colima connects lofty volcanoes in its arid northern highlands to idyllic turquoise lagoons near the hot and humid Pacific coast to the south.

Many travelers think inland Colima is poised to become Mexico's next great adventure hub. The famous volcanoes in the north – the active and constantly fuming but inaccessible Volcán de Fuego (3820m) and the extinct, snowcapped Volcán Nevado de Colima (4260m) – remain the big draws,

but the Reserva de la Biosfera Sierra de Manantlán is a jungle-and-limestone playground in waiting, with single-track mountain biking, exceptional hiking, and canyons that see a few canyoneers abseiling, leaping into crystalline streams and bathing in the magical Cascada El Salto waterfall. Tourism infrastructure hasn't caught up to the area's potential yet, so those who like virgin territory should come now.

History

Pre-Hispanic Colima was removed from the major ancient cultures of Mexico. Seaborne contacts with more distant lands might have been more important; legend says one king of Colima, Ix, had regular visitors bearing treasure from China. Eventually, though, the northern tribes began moving in. The Otomí settled here from about 250 to 750 CE, followed by the Toltecs, who flourished between 900 and 1154, and the Chichimecs from 1154 to 1428.

All of them left behind exceptional pottery, which has been found at more than 250 sites, mainly tombs, dating from about 200 BCE to 800 CE. The pottery includes a variety of comical and expressive figures. The most famous are the plump, hairless dogs known as xoloitzcuintles or, more commonly, *escuincles*.

Two Spanish expeditions were defeated and repelled by the Chichimecs before Gonzalo de Sandoval, one of Cortés' lieutenants, conquered them in 1523. That year he founded the town of Colima, the third Spanish settlement in Nueva España (after Veracruz and Mexico City). In 1527 the town moved to its present site from its original lowland location near Tecomán.

Colima

🖉 312 / POP 148.300 / ELEV 498M

Colima is a laid-back city with lush subtropical gardens, fine public plazas and the warmest weather in the western central highlands. The city's university attracts students from around the world, while its burgeoning tourism potential derived from nearby canyons, forests and mountains brings in a small but growing number of visitors.

The billowing volcano you see on clear days, Volcán de Fuego – visible 30km to the north – continues to rumble and shake, and the city has been hit by several major quakes over the centuries (the last one of 7.5

magnitude in January 2003). It's no wonder that Colima has few colonial buildings, despite having been the first city established by the Spanish in western Mexico.

◉ Sights

★ Museo Regional de Historia de Colima
MUSEUM

(📞 312-312-92-28; www.inah.gob.mx; 16 de Septiembre 29; M$60, Sun free; ⊙ 9am-6pm Tue-Sun) This excellent museum in a colonial-era *casona* (mansion) has an extensive collection of well-labeled artifacts spanning the region's history, from ancient pottery to conquistadors' armor and a 19th-century horse-drawn carriage. Don't miss the ceramic xoloitzcuintles (Colima dogs) in room 12 or the walk-through mock tomb excavation next door. There is also an interesting collection of pre-Hispanic clay figures that may depict *pelota* players or warriors. Signage in Spanish only.

La Campana Archaeological Site
ARCHAEOLOGICAL SITE

(📞 312-313-49-45; www.inah.gob.mx; Av Tecnológico s/n; M$55; ⊙ 9am-6pm Tue-Sun) The low, pyramid-like structures at this bell-shaped (thus *campana*) archaeological site date from as early as 1500 BCE. They have been excavated since the 1930s and restored, along with a small shaft tomb, with replica objects in situ and a ball court. The structures are oriented due north toward Volcán de Fuego, which makes for an impressive backdrop on clear days.

It's about 3km north of Colima city and easily accessible by bus 7 (M$8); taxis cost around M$50. A word of warning: wear good shoes and socks because there are lots of fire ants.

El Chanal Archaeological Site
ARCHAEOLOGICAL SITE

(📞 312-313-49-45; www.inah.gob.mx; Camino al Chanal; M$45; ⊙ 9am-6pm Tue-Sun) Some 4km northeast of Colima, this extensive, manicured site was settled some time around 1300 BCE, reaching its zenith between 1100 and 1400 CE. There are pyramid structures, a ball court, five patios and a small catchment to collect rainwater. Just east of Plaza del Tiempo, which contains the two most impressive structures, are several blocks with petroglyphs depicting animal figures, plants and deities. A taxi from the town center costs around M$80.

Pinacoteca Universitaria Alfonso Michel
GALLERY

(📞 312-314-33-06; www.mexicoescultura.com; Guerrero 35; M$15; ⊙ 9am-2pm & 5-7:30pm Tue-Sat, 9am-1pm Sun) FREE The modern entrance to this gallery leads into a 19th-century courtyard surrounded by seven halls filled with surrealist art. Included is a permanent collection of paintings by Colima's Alfonso Michel – whose work has been described as a cross between Picasso and Dalí – as well as works by José Luis Cuevas and Rafael Coronel. Four other *salas* are given over to temporary exhibitions.

Cathedral Basilica of Our Lady of Guadalupe
CATHEDRAL

(Reforma 21; ⊙ 7am-8:30pm) Light floods what is officially called the Basílica Menor Catedral de Colima from its circular dome windows on the northeast side of Plaza Principal. It has been rebuilt several times since the Spanish first erected a cathedral here in 1527, most recently after the 1941 earthquake, when its northern tower collapsed. Most of the current neoclassical structure dates from 1894.

🛏 Sleeping & Eating

Hotel Aldama
HOTEL $

(📞 312-330-73-06; www.facebook.com/hotelaldama colima; Aldama 134; r M$550-850; ⊛ 🛜) Four blocks northeast of the central plaza, this budget hotel punches way above its weight with 15 rooms that, though small, have some value-raising touches: flowers strewn across the bed sheets, wrought-iron and heavy wooden furnishings, and desks to work at. The 1st-floor rooms look into the courtyard; choose one on the 2nd floor, which has a lovely roof terrace.

Hotel La Casona de Don Jorge
HOTEL $$

(📞 312-330-72-89; www.hotelcasonadedonjorge. com; Juárez 88; r M$770-1060; 🅿 ⊛ 🛜) Colonial architecture meets modern Mexican style in this downtown hotel. Guests are treated to spotless rooms with soaring ceilings, all opening onto two courtyards, Talavera tiles and tasteful decor throughout. Beds are deluxe and bathrooms spacious. Ask for a room in the furthest courtyard for the quietest rooms. Service is top notch.

Llueve Café
CAFE $

(📞 312-396-64-14; www.facebook.com/lluevecafe; Santos Degollado 93; mains M$45-80; ⊙ 5:30-11:30pm Tue-Sat, to 11pm Sun) A half-block from the main plaza, this artsy two-story cafe serves up creative sandwiches, salads and des-

Colima

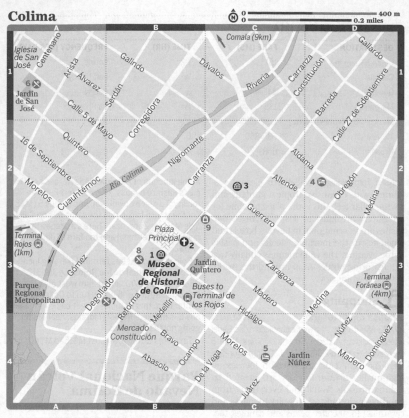

N 0 ___ 400 m
0 ___ 0.2 miles

WESTERN CENTRAL HIGHLANDS COLIMA

serts plus a mean menu of coffee drinks and shakes. Seating is at small tables and couches, or instead try the shoe-free movie room or try your luck at the ping-pong table. The rooftop has twinkling lights and great views.

★ **El Charco de la Higuera** MEXICAN $$
(☑312-313-01-92; www.facebook.com/ElCharco delaHiguera; Jardín de San José, cnr Calle 5 de Mayo; mains M$90-150; ☺8am-midnight) This salt-of-the-earth restaurant doubles as a modest museum to local mask-making and offers typical *cocina colimense* (Colima-style cuisine). The combined *antojitos* plate is a smorgasbord; the adventurous will want to try the *pepena* (cow's heart and intestines) with hot tortillas. Set in a quiet little plaza next to the San José church with live music till 8pm Thursday to Sunday.

Las Cavas de Don José INTERNATIONAL $$
(☑312-314-15-97; www.lascavasdedonjose.com; San tos Degollado 180; mains M$89-250; ☺8am-1pm

Colima

⊙ Top Sights
1 Museo Regional de Historia de Colima...B3

⊙ Sights
2 Cathedral Basilica of Our Lady of Guadalupe.....................................B3
3 Pinacoteca Universitaria Alfonso Michel...................................C2

⊜ Sleeping
4 Hotel Aldama..D2
5 Hotel La Casona de Don Jorge..........C4

⊗ Eating
6 El Charco de la Higuera.......................A1
7 Las Cavas de Don José........................B3
8 Llueve Café...B3

⊜ Shopping
9 La Casa del Artesano............................C3

BUSES FROM COLIMA

DESTINATION	FARE (M$)	TIME (HR)	FREQUENCY (PER DAY)
Ciudad Guzmán	151	1-2	hourly
Comala	10	¼	half-hourly
Guadalajara	342-440	3	hourly
Manzanillo	135	1½	half-hourly
Mexico City (Terminal Norte)	1190-1455	10	10
Morelia	685-850	6	3
Uruapan	658	6	2

Tue-Sun, 7pm-midnight Thu-Sat) An elegant restaurant with expansive tropical gardens and a wine cellar feel, this is the place to come for a leisurely breakfast or a special night out. Dishes are international in flavor – bagels and omelettes in the morning, steaks and pastas in the evening. The wine menu is equally varied, featuring bottles from around the world. Service is white glove.

🛍 Shopping

La Casa del Artesano   ARTS & CRAFTS
(☑ 312-688-48-59; www.facebook.com/lacasadel artesanocolima; Andador Constitución, cnr Calle 5 de Mayo; ◷ 10am-2:30pm & 3:30-8pm Mon-Sat, 10am-2pm Sun) This artists co-op focuses on high-quality *artesanía* (folk art) created by Colima artisans. You'll find everything from handmade clothing and jewelry to masks and ceramics.; local coffee beans and candies, too.

ℹ Information

Colima State Tourist Office (☑ 312-316-20-00; Complejo Administrativo del Gobierno del Estado, Libramiento Ejército Mexicano s/n; ◷ 8:30am-4:30pm Mon-Fri) On the outskirts of Colima, about 5km northeast of downtown.

ℹ Getting There & Away

The nearest airport, **Aeropuerto Nacional de Colima** (CLQ; ☑ 312-314-41-60; www.aeropuerto sasa.mx; Av Lic Carlos de la Madrid Bejar s/n, Cuahtémoc), is about 21km northeast of Colima's city center, off the highway to Guadalajara (taxis M$150). **Aeromar** (☑ 312-313-13-40; www.aero mar.com.mx; Aeropuerto Nacional de Colima) flies to Mexico City three times a day. It is also served by **Aeroméxico** (☑ 55-5133-4000; www. aeromexico.com; Aeropuerto Nacional de Colima) and **Volaris** (☑ 55-1102-8000; www.volaris. com; Aeropuerto Nacional de Colima).

Colima has two bus terminals. The long-distance terminal is **Terminal Foránea** (☑ 312-314-54-33; Carretera 54), 4km east of the city center

at the junction of Avenida Niños Héroes and the city's eastern bypass. There's a left-luggage facility. To reach downtown, hop on bus 5 (M$8). For the return trip, catch the same bus on Calle 5 de Mayo or Zaragoza. There's a prepay taxi booth at the terminal and the fare to downtown is M$28.

Colima's second bus terminal (serving local towns) is **Terminal de los Rojos** (☑ 312-312-03-16; Carrillo s/n), about 2km west of Plaza Principal. Ruta 4 or 6 buses run to Colima's center from this terminal. To get back here, take any bus marked **'Rojos'** (Morelos, near Medellín) going north on Morelos.

Taxi fares within town cost M$15 to M$40.

Parque Nacional Volcán Nevado de Colima

This 9.5-sq-km national park, straddling the Colima–Jalisco border, encompasses two dramatic volcanoes some 5km apart: the still-active Volcán de Fuego and the much older (and dormant) Volcán Nevado de Colima. Ciudad Guzmán is the closest city to the park, but if you have a car or hire a guide, Colima or Comala are much more pleasant bases. It can be difficult to find a guide on the fly if you only have a few days, so it's best to organize things in advance.

The national park is home to a wide range of flora and fauna, some of it endemic. Resident and/or visiting mammals include white-tailed foxes, coatimundis, coyotes, pumas and jaguars.

◉ Sights

★ **Volcán Nevado de Colima**   VOLCANO
(☑ 341-412-20-25; www.facebook.com/parque nacionalvolcannevadodecolima; M$45) Volcán Nevado de Colima (4260m) is accessible on foot from the last week of October till the first week of June. Patches of pine forest cover Ne-

vado's shoulders, while alpine desert takes over at the highest altitudes. Wildlife includes deer, wild boars, coyotes and even pumas.

The best months for climbing are generally the dry months of December through May. But temperatures from December to February often dip below 0°C (32°F) and snow can fall on the upper slopes – *nevado* means 'snow-covered.' Weather changes fast here and lightning strikes the peak in stormy weather, so make sure you keep an eye on the clouds and get an early start. The park's hours November to March are from 6am to 6pm. The summer rainy season is from July to September, when park hours are longer.

To get here on your own from Ciudad Guzmán, take the bus to El Fresnito (M$22), where you must try to hire a driver (not an easy task) to take you the remaining 20km or so up a rough road to the trailhead at La Joya/Puerto Las Cruces (3500m). You'll pass the park entrance on the way, where you'll pay a M$45 entry fee. An alternative is to walk up from El Fresnito – a much longer and tougher proposition. If you elect to walk, stay on the bus as long as you can as it covers some of the distance beyond the town.

Walkers will need camping gear and food (and some very warm clothes), because it's impossible to walk there and back in a day. Allow seven hours to get to the parking at La Joya/Puerto Las Cruces, then another three to four hours from there to the summit and about seven hours all the way back down again. You can camp at La Joya/Puerto Las Cruces a few kilometers beyond the park gates.

The hike to the summit from La Joya is around 9km and ascends 700m. Some prefer to just hike to the *micro-ondas* (radio antennae) about 90 minutes by foot from the end of the road at La Joya/Puerto Las Cruces. If you want to reach the peak, you'll need another 90 minutes, and while the peak is easy to see, you shouldn't go alone. There are many trails up and back and it's very easy to get lost or led to areas with hazardous footing. Fog can also be an impediment. You'll save a lot of time and bother going with a guide.

Driving up this volcano on the relatively good gravel road means that you'll be ascending to a high altitude very quickly. If you feel lightheaded or dizzy, you may be suffering from altitude sickness. Descend as quickly as possible, as this condition can be dangerous.

Volcán de Fuego
VOLCANO

(Volcán de Colima; ☑ 341-412-20-25; www.facebook.com/parquenacionalvolcannevadodecolima) Overlooking Comala and Colima, 23km and 30km to the north respectively, is smoking Volcán de Fuego (3820m), Mexico's most active volcano. It has erupted dozens of times in the past four centuries, with a big eruption about every 70 years. In June 2005 a large explosion sent ash almost 5km into the sky, all the way to Colima; two equally large eruptions in July 2015 and January 2017 did the same to Ciudad Guzmán.

Fuego's peak has been off-limits to visitors since 1980 and to seismologists since 2013. To hike in the vicinity of the volcano – there is an exclusion zone within 10km of the summit – it is best to organize in advance through a reputable agency.

☞ Tours

The guides we list are licensed to take visitors into the Parque Nacional Volcán Nevado de Colima. A 3½-hour tour to within 10km of the summit of Volcán de Fuego costs from M$495. Trekking to the top of Volcán Nevado de Colima with a guide will cost from M$2150. Prices include transportation and entry fees.

Admire Mexico
TREKKING

(☑ 312-314-54-54; www.admiremexicotours.com; Obregón 105, Comala) The undisputed leader of hikes and tours in the national park as well as in and around Colima and Comala is this highly regarded agency led by volcano expert Júpiter Rivera. It's based out of Casa Alvarada in Comala. English spoken.

Corazón de Colima Tours
TREKKING

(☑ 312-314-08-96; www.corazondecolimatours.com; Nayarit 1415, Colima) Runs tours to Comala, plus a hike in the skirts of Volcán de Fuego, and ascents of Volcán Nevado de Colima. Based in Colima.

✖ Eating & Drinking

★ El Jacal de San Antonio
MEXICAN $$

(☑ 312-176-99-47; www.facebook.com/eljacaldesanantonio; Carretera Comala-San Antonio Km 16.5; mains M$65-255; ⊙9am-6pm Mon-Thu, to 11pm Fri & Sat, to 8pm Sun) If you're headed toward Volcán de Fuego from Comala, don't miss this classy outdoor restaurant. Surrounded by lush tropical forest, it enjoys truly spectacular views of the volcano from it's two-story dining areas. Dishes, too, are well worth a stop: traditional Mexican fare using vegetables, fruits and herbs grown onsite. Weekends bring specials like grilled rabbit and roasted suckling pig too.

Café La Yerbabuena
CAFE

(☑312-103-17-33; La Yerbabuena; ⊙9am-6pm) While hiking up to as close as you are going to get to the summit of Volcán de Fuego, you might stop at 1500m at this rustic cafe in a working coffee plantation for a cup of homegrown and ground joe. It's in the original hamlet of La Yerbabuena, which disappeared under the lava flow of the 2005 eruption. Check it out on Facebook.

❶ Getting There & Away

The national park is not served by public transportation; the closest point you can reach from Ciudad Guzmán is El Fresnito (M$22). The best way to visit is under your own steam or in a guide's vehicle.

Comala

☑312 / POP 9450 / ELEV 600M

If you've made it as far as Colima, do not miss the gloriously idiosyncratic *pueblo mágico* of Comala, 10km to the north, famous for its *ponche* (alcoholic punch), *tuba* (fermented drink made from palm-tree sap), sweet bread and distinctive hand-carved wooden masks. Characterized by the kind of generic white colonial edifices that wouldn't look out of place in the so-called *pueblos blancos* (white towns) of Andalucía, Comala's centerpiece is its main plaza, one of the region's most beguiling, replete with *tuba* salespeople, shoe-shiners, strolling mariachis and a plethora of restaurants.

Comala's red-letter event is the **Feria de Ponche, Pan y Cafe** (Punch, Bread and Coffee Festival) held over two weeks in April.

◎ Sights

★ Ex-Hacienda Nogueras
MUSEUM

(Museo Universitario Alejandro Rangel Hidalgo; ☑312-315-60-28; https://portal.ucol.mx/ceugea; Hacienda Nogueras s/n, Nogueras; museum/hacienda M$20/10; ⊙museum 10am-6pm Tue-Sun, hacienda 10am-2:30pm Tue-Fri, to 4pm Sat & Sun) Comala's obligatory sight is this former home of Mexican artist Alejandro Rangel Hidalgo (1923–2000), which now contains a museum dedicated to the man's life and art. Here you'll see his impressive pre-Hispanic ceramics collection (including Colima dogs) and the distinctive Unicef Christmas cards for which he is largely remembered. The ha-

cienda also contains a chapel and the ruins of an old sugar factory. The grounds – including a botanical garden – are lush. Check out the shop in the former apothecary.

To get here on foot from the main square, walk 450m east along Calle Degollado, which runs to the left of Templo de San Miguel Arcángel. Turn left at Calle Saavedra, then turn left at the T-intersection, go 1km, then turn right at the next T-intersection and go another 450m. You can also take a bus (M$8) from behind the church or a taxi (M$25).

Museo Nacional de la Escultura Sebastián
GALLERY

(☑312-313-99-68; Carretera Villa de Álvarez-Comala Km 5.5; ⊙9am-7pm Mon-Fri) FREE Housed in an eye-catching steel and glass structure, the 'National Sculpture Museum Sebastián' is a two-room gallery showcasing over 70 works, the majority by one of Mexico's most celebrated artists, Sebastián. The adjoining gardens are delightful, especially the half-dozen sculptures representing one (or the other) of the two ever-dominant volcanoes by other notable sculptors. Look for the complex south of the main plaza just over the Río Suchitlán.

🛏 Sleeping & Eating

Casa Iztac
HOTEL $$

(☑312-594-56-53; www.facebook.com/CasaIztac Comala; Degollado 45; r from M$1140; ❄) A bright, airy hotel with a huge courtyard, Casa Iztac has four spacious rooms (more are in the works) just one block from the central plaza. All have 4m-high ceilings, wood floors, original artwork and elegantly sparse decor. The affable husband-wife team that runs the place is a wealth of information on area sights.

La Fregada Fonda
MEXICAN $

(☑312-310-04-87; www.facebook.com/FondaLa Fregada; Calle 5 de Mayo 46; mains $45-80; ⊙8:30am-1:30pm Thu-Sun) A small, artful eatery, La Fregada brings the outside in with tropical plants, vine-covered walls and a dining room that opens onto a lush hillside. The menu is classic Mexican: *chilaquiles, tostadas de nopal* (cactus on tortilla shells), *frijoles en caldo* (bean soup)...even coffee with cinnamon sticks. Service is friendly but uneven.

Don Comalón
MEXICAN $

(☑312-315-51-04; www.doncomalon.com; Progreso 5; drink & snack from M$63; ⊙1-7pm Mon-Thu, to 8pm Fri-Sun) One of many restaurants lining Comala's main plaza that serves a *botana* (free snack) with every drink you order. If you haven't got time to make your choice, opt for this place and pray the staff bring you a crispy *tostada* topped with ceviche.

ℹ Getting There & Away

Buses make the 15-minute trip to/from Colima (M$10) half-hourly throughout the day and will drop you near the main square. A taxi runs around M$100 each way.

INLAND MICHOACÁN

Pre-Hispanic traditions and colonial-era architecture meet in Michoacán. The state is home to three of Mexico's most fascinating under-the-radar cities: the adobe-and-cobblestone town of Pátzcuaro, where Purépecha women sell fruit and *tamales* in the shadow of 16th-century churches; the lush agricultural city of Uruapan, gateway to the mythic Paricutín volcano; and the vibrant and cultured colonial city of Morelia, with an ancient cathedral and aqueduct built from rosy pink stone.

Michoacán is also celebrated as a crafts capital: the Purépecha artisans of the state's Cordillera Neovolcánica highlands create wonderful masks, pottery, straw art and stringed instruments – all on display at the annual Tianguis Artesanal de Uruapan craft fair. Rich in natural treasures, Michoacán has one of the world's truly unmissable sights: the annual butterfly migration to the rugged Reserva Mariposa Monarca (Monarch Butterfly Reserve), where millions of mating monarchs cover the grass and trees in a shimmering carpet.

Morelia

🎵 443 / POP 597,500 / ELEV 1920M

The state capital of Michoacán and its most beautiful and dynamic city, Morelia is an increasingly popular destination and rightly so: the colonial heart of the city, with a gorgeous cathedral at its center, is so well preserved that it was declared a Unesco World Heritage site in 1991.

Elegant 16th- and 17th-century stone buildings with their baroque facades and graceful archways line the downtown streets and house museums, hotels, restaurants, *chocolaterías* (chocolate shops), sidewalk cafes, a popular university and cheap-and-inviting *taquerías* (taco stalls). There are free public concerts, frequent art installations and relatively few foreign visitors. Those who do make it here often extend their stay and enroll in classes to learn to speak Spanish. Word will almost certainly get out, but for the moment unspoiled Morelia is like an Oaxaca waiting to happen.

History

Morelia, founded in 1541, was one of the first Spanish cities in the colony of Nueva España. Its first viceroy, Antonio de Mendoza, named it Valladolid after that city in Spain and encouraged Spanish nobility to move here with their families. In 1828, four years after Nueva España had become the Republic of Mexico, the city was renamed Morelia in honor of local hero José María Morelos y Pavón, a priest who led the Mexican War of Independence movement after the execution of Miguel Hidalgo y Costilla.

◉ Sights

Morelia boasts a surfeit of high-quality museums, but many of them overlap, especially on the subject of local hero José María Morelos y Pavón. Choose carefully or prepare for Morelos information overload.

★ **Morelia Cathedral**   CATHEDRAL
(Plaza de Armas, Av Madero Poniente s/n; ⊙ 9am-9pm) Morelia's cathedral, considered by many to be the country's most beautiful, dominates the city center, where it flanks rather than faces the central plaza. It took almost a century to build (1660–1744), which explains its potpourri of styles: the twin 70m-high bell towers, for instance, have classical Herreresque bases, baroque midsections and multicolumned neoclassical tops. It's particularly impressive on Saturday evenings, when its lit up for the Encendido de Catedral (p639).

Much of the baroque reliefs inside were replaced in the 19th century with neoclassical work. Fortunately, one of the highlights was preserved: a sculpture of the crucified Christ called the **Señor de la Sacristía** in a chapel to the left of the main altar. It is made from *pasta de caña* (a paste made from the heart of the cornstalk) and is topped with a gold crown gifted to the church by the Spanish King Felipe II in the 16th century. The organ counts 4600 pipes – the second-largest pipe organ in Mexico (the first is in Zamora, Michoacán); occasional organ recitals take place here – a beautiful time to be in the cathedral.

Morelia

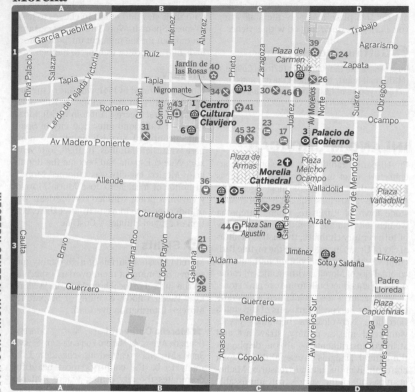

★ **Palacio de Gobierno** NOTABLE BUILDING
(☎443-312-20-32; www.facebook.com/PalacioGob
Mich; Av Madero Oriente; ☺9am-8pm Mon-Fri)
This 18th-century palace, originally a semi-
nary and now housing Michoacán state government offices, has a simple baroque facade.
Inside, its soaring historical murals (1960) in
the stairwell and 2nd-floor hallways are the
magnum opus of Pátzcuaro-born artist Alfredo Zalce (1908–2003), and arguably the city's
best. Enter from Calle Juárez.

★ **Centro Cultural Clavijero** MUSEUM
(☎443-312-04-12; www.ccclavijero.mx; Nigromante 79; ☺10am-6pm Tue-Sun) FREE From
1660 to 1767, the Palacio Clavijero, with its
magnificent minimalist main patio, imposing colonnades and pink stonework, was
home to the Jesuit school of St Francis Xavier. Today the enormous building houses a
cultural center with exhibition spaces showing off contemporary art, photography and
other creative media.

Museo Regional Michoacano MUSEUM
(Michoacán Regional Museum; ☎443-312-04-07;
www.inah.gob.mx; Allende 305; adult/child M$55/
free; ☺9am-4:45pm Tue-Sun) Housed in a doz-
en rooms of a renovated late-18th-century
baroque palace, this museum contains an
impressive array of pre-Hispanic artifacts,
including a reconstructed open tomb from
El Opeño and a carved stone coyote from
Ihuatzio, as well as colonial art and relics.
Signage in Spanish only. There are also several spectacular murals by Alfredo Zalce
on the stairway, including *Cuauhtémoc y
la Historia* (Cuauhtémoc and History) and
*Los Pueblos del Mundo contra la Guer-
ra Atómica* (Peoples of the World Against
Atomic War), both 1951.

Museo Casa de Morelos MUSEUM
(Morelos House Museum; ☎443-313-26-51; Av
Morelos Sur 323; adult/child M$45/free; ☺9am-
4:45pm Tue-Sun) This museum, arguably
Morelia's best on the subject of José María

Morelos y Pavón, resides in the former house of the independence hero, who bought the Spanish-style mansion for his sister in 1801. Well-laid-out, multimedia displays have good information panels in both Spanish and English and cover Morelos' life, military campaigns and the trajectory of the independence movement thereafter. Don't miss his study, cell-like bedroom and macabre *máscara mortuoria* (death mask).

Museo de Arte Colonial　　　　GALLERY
(MAC; ☑ 443-313-92-60; www.morelianas.com; Juárez 240; ⊙9am-8pm Mon-Fri, 10am-6pm Sat & Sun) **FREE** This ambitious museum contains five rooms chock-a-block with religious paintings and sculptures, including more than 100 depictions of the crucified Christ, some quite graphic. Highlights include a small statue of Jesus wearing a skirt in room 3 and scale models of Columbus' three ships – the *Niña*, the *Pinta* and the *Santa Maria* – in room 4. Check out the ancient streetside

windows in room 5. Signage is excellent, though in Spanish only.

**Biblioteca Pública de la
Universidad Michoacana**　　HISTORIC BUILDING
(☑ 443-312-57-25; Jardín Igangio Altamirano, cnr Av Madero Poniente & Nigromante; ⊙8am-8pm Mon-Fri) Installed inside the magnificent 17th-century **Ex-Templo de la Compañía de Jesús**, the shelves of the city's breathtaking university library rise up toward the domed and painted ceilings and are crammed from head to toe with tens of thousands (22,901 to be exact) of antique books and manuscripts, including seven incunabula dating from the 15th century. The murals date from the 1950s.

Acueducto　　　　　　　　　LANDMARK
(Av Acueducto) Morelia's impressively preserved aqueduct runs north for just over 2km along (appropriately enough) Avenida Acueducto and then curves around Plaza Villalongín. It was built between 1785 and 1788 and supplied

Morelia

the city with water until 1910. Its 253 arches – some of which are now underground – are impressive when illuminated at night.

Museo del Estado de Michoacán MUSEUM
(State Museum; ☑ 443-313-06-29; www.facebook.com/MuseoMichoacan; Prieto 176; ◎ 10am-3pm & 4-8pm Mon-Fri, 10am-6pm Sat & Sun) FREE A beautifully renovated 18th-century *casona*, this museum hosts temporary exhibits and workshops often related to the history and culture of the state of Michoacán. Occasionally, traveling exhibits from other states are showcased here too. Worth a stop to see what's on.

Museo de Arte Contemporáneo Alfredo Zalce GALLERY
(MACAZ; ☑ 443-312-45-44; http://sic.cultura.gob.mx; Bosque Cuauhtémoc, Av Acueducto 18; ◎ 10am-7:45pm Mon-Fri, to 6pm Sat & Sun) FREE Modern-art fans might find something interesting at this art museum in Morelia's city park named for the *michoacano* artist and muralist Alfredo Zalce (1908–2003). The

lovely late-19th-century building contains a dozen different spaces that host temporary exhibitions of contemporary art and photography. Outside, the sculpture garden is well worth wandering.

Plaza Morelos PLAZA
(Av Tata Vasco 1) This irregular, conspicuously vacant plaza southeast of the center surrounds the **Estatua Ecuestre al Patriota Morelos**, a majestic statue of Morelos on horseback, sculpted by Italian artist Giuseppe Inghilleri and unveiled in 1913. Running from here to the **Fuente Las Tarascas** (Plaza Villalongín, Av Acueducto 890) is the leafy and cobbled **Calzada Fray Antonio de San Miguel**, a wide pedestrian promenade framed by exquisite old buildings. Just north of its western end, narrow **Callejón del Romance** (Romance Alley) is all pink stone, trailing vines and cavorting couples.

Antiguo Palacio de Justicia NOTABLE BUILDING
(☑ 443-310-95-12; Allende 267; ◎ 10am-7pm Mon-Fri) FREE Facing the leafy expanse of Plaza

de Armas, the Antiguo Palacio de Justicia is in fact two buildings rebuilt in 1884. Its intricate facade blends French and eclectic styles, with stairwell art in the patio. An impressive mural called *Morelos y la Justicia* (Morelos and Justice) by Agustín Cárdenas (1976) was restored to its full glory by the artist 40 years later. The onsite museum has revolving exhibitions dealing with history and government, some better than others.

Museo Casa Natal de Morelos   MUSEUM
(Morelos Birthplace Museum;   ☑443-312-27-93; Corregidora 113; ☉9am-6pm Mon-Fri, from 10am Sat & Sun) FREE Independence leader José María Morelos y Pavón is king in Morelia – after all, the city is named after him. He was born on the site of this one-time *casa de salud* (health clinic); a bronze statute of Morelos marks the spot where his mother, Juana Pérez Pavón, delivered him on September 30, 1765. Now housing a museum in his honor, the collection of old photos and documents in eight rooms is poignant, but not as comprehensive as the better-curated Museo Casa de Morelos.

📷 Courses & Tours

Relatively few foreigners and plenty of culture make Morelia an exceptional place to learn how to speak Spanish or dive deeper into Mexican history, literature and culture.

The **tourist office** (☑443-317-03-35, 443-317-78-30; www.experienciamorelia.mx; Juárez 178; ☉9am-6pm Mon-Fri, 10am-6pm Sat & Sun) runs daily city tours at 10am or 4pm. For tours outside the city, ask for recommendations.

Baden-Powell Institute   LANGUAGE
(☑443-312-20-02; www.baden-powell.com; Antonio Alzate 569; per 20hr week from US$180, private lessons per hour US$18) The small, extremely well run and welcoming Baden-Powell Institute offers courses in the Spanish language, as well as Latin American history, Mexican art, literature and Spanish geared toward business and medical travelers. It can book homestays (per day US$27) for students and has a handful of well-appointed apartments (p640) available right around the corner from the school.

Yei! Tours   WALKING
(☑443-275-78-07; www.yei.tours; José Rubén Romero 62-11; tours M$320-1260) A friendly and professional outfit, Yei! offers engaging walking tours of downtown Morelia and beyond – monarch butterfly reserves, colonial villages, archaeological sites and more. All tours are led by knowledgeable and certified guide, Rodrigo Rosales. English spoken too. Trips include door-to-door service, entrance fees, a meal, and even digital photos of your tour.

Mexico Cooks!   FOOD & DRINK
(☑55-1305-7194; www.mexicocooks.typepad.com; half-day market tour per person from US$100) US-born Cristina Potters, a Mexican citizen and expert on Mexican cuisine, gives wonderful personalized culinary and cultural tours of Morelia, Pátzcuaro and the rest of Michoacán, though she is based in Mexico City. Tours include trips to markets, traditional restaurants and indigenous villages. Contact her in advance to arrange a tour.

✸✧ Festivals & Events

★ **Encendido de Catedral**   FIREWORKS
(Luces de Catedral; Plaza de Armas, Av Madero s/n; ☉9pm Sat; ⟐) FREE Every Saturday night, a festive atmosphere takes over Avenida Madero. The street is closed, street performers appear, food vendors set up shop and at 9pm, a brilliant fireworks display is held over the cathedral. The city icon is lit up in myriad colors, the lights bursting from above, music playing and the crowds cheering. Get there by 8:45pm to secure a good spot.

At the end of the fireworks, follow the crowd to nearby **Plaza Valladolid**. There, at 9:30pm, a 3D sound and light show is projected onto the facade of the Templo de San Francisco, telling the story of Morelia through animation, music and voice-over.

Expo Feria Michoacán   CULTURAL
(☑443-113-45-00; www.expofiestamichoacan.mx; Expoferia s/n, Colonia La Goleta; M$30; ☉Apr-May) Morelia's biggest fair, running for three weeks in late April through May, hosts exhibits of handicrafts, agriculture and livestock, plus regional dances, bullfights and fiestas. The city's founding date (May 18) is celebrated with a fireworks show. Held at the town's fairgrounds, about 12km east of the center of town.

Festival de Música de Morelia   MUSIC
(☑443-317-80-87; www.festivalmorelia.mx; ☉Nov) The international classical-music festival unfolds over two weeks in November with orchestras, choirs and quartets giving concerts in churches, plazas and theaters around town. Held since 1989, over 10,000 musicians have participated in the fest, accounting for over 1.3 million tickets sold.

WESTERN CENTRAL HIGHLANDS MORELIA

**Festival Internacional
de Cine de Morelia**   FILM
(www.moreliafilmfest.com; ⊘Oct) This major
international exhibition for Mexico's vibrant
film industry brings 10 days of movies, parties and star sightings in late October.

🛏 Sleeping

There are a lot of places to stay in Morelia
and not all that many tourists, so competition is fierce. Except during certain festivals,
you can be sure that all accommodations,
apart from the very cheapest hostels, will
offer discounts on rack rates.

★La Casa Azul Hostal   HOSTEL $
(📞442-312-44-75; www.lacasaazulhostal.com; Av
Morelos Norte 306; dm incl breakfast M$170; 🛜)
Facing the Casa de Cultura, this bright, shiny,
happy hostel offers a comfortable stay, especially for travelers looking to meet like-mind-
ed folks. Dorms open onto a lovely covered
courtyard with traditional tiles and exposed
stone walls. The rooms themselves have individual twin beds (no bunks here), good bedding and lockers. A breezy rooftop lounge,
TV room and guest kitchen are pluses.

Casa Baden-Powell   APARTMENT $
(📞443-312-20-02; www.furnishedapartment
morelia.com; Tagle 138; 2-/4-person apt per week
from US$275/300; 🅿🛜) The fully equipped
apartments in this delightful complex share
a courtyard and terrace. All have complete
kitchens, dining areas and one, two or three
bedrooms accommodating between two and
six people. They are at the eastern end of
Avenida Madero Oriente, an easy walk to
the sights and restaurants of Plaza de Armas
and the bars at Plaza Villalongín.

Hotel Casa del Anticuario   HOTEL $
(📞443-333-25-21; www.hotelcasadelanticuario.
com.mx; Galeana 319; s M$650, d M$770-885, ste
M$1285; 🛜) This charming 16-room guest-
house has rooms with exposed stone walls
and wooden roof beams, very helpful staff, a
nice central courtyard bedecked with vintage
radios, TVs and gramophones, and excellent
wi-fi reception. Breakfast available upon request. A very comfortable stay, though on
weekends neighboring discotheques can be
heard until the wee hours of the night.
    Ask for a room towards the back to mini-
mize the noise.

Casa Limonchelo B&B   B&B $
(📞443-232-21-14; www.limonchelomorelia.com;
Madero Oriente 742; r incl breakfast with/with-
out bathroom M$850/800; 🅿🛜) Tucked off
of busy Avenida Madero, this surprisingly
tranquil B&B is set in a beautifully renovated 18th-century *casona*. Rooms are cozy and
simple, all opening onto a sunny courtyard
with flowering plants. The affable owners
live onsite and are a wealth of information
on area sights. The only bummer: the wi-fi is
only accessible in the common spaces.

★Hotel Casa Eugenia   INN $$
(📞443-312-59-88; www.facebook.com/CasaEugenia
Hotel; 20 de Noviembre 322; d/ste incl breakfast
M$1000/1200; 🅿🛜) Soaring ceilings, exposed
wood beams, and antique furnishings pull
you into this welcoming, colonial-style inn.
Eight elegant rooms are set off a leafy courtyard. Each is slightly different from the other,
some with lofts, others with seating areas but
all with deluxe beds and updated bathrooms.
Breakfast is served on the rooftop with a spectacular view of town and nearby church bell
towers.

★Hotel de la Soledad   HISTORIC HOTEL $$$
(📞443-312-18-88; www.hsoledad.com; Zaragoza 90; r/ste incl breakfast from M$3060/4380;
🅿✳@🛜) A showstopper! Bougainvillea
frames the stone arches, fountains gurgle,
classical music wafts on the breeze and palm
trees reach for the skies – and that's all just
in the central courtyard. The 41 rooms in
this hotel all differ, but expect showers made
from ancient stone arches, translucent stone
basins, hand-carved wooden bedheads and a
general sense of class.
    The only downer here: few windows and
stone walls can make for dark rooms.

Herencia by Hosting House   HOTEL $$$
(📞443-232-02-46; www.hherencia.com; Madero Oriente 94; d M$1011-1814, ste M$1813-2595;
✳@🛜) Recently renamed and rebranded,
this hotel's 26 rooms might be small but
they are crammed with pomp and a sense of
royalty, including ornately carved bedheads,
chandeliers and bathrooms with alabaster
details. There's also a lovely courtyard bar
and restaurant. Front-facing rooms suffer
from road noise despite the soundproofing,
though the 'interior' rooms have no windows at all (pick your poison).

Cantera Diez   BOUTIQUE HOTEL $$$
(📞443-312-54-19; www.canteradiezhotel.com;
Juárez 63; r from M$2680; 🅿✳🛜) Facing the
cathedral is Morelia's slickest boutique hotel.
The 11 rooms – all suites – range from spacious to palatial, all with dark-wood floors,

stylish modern furnishings in primary colors and sumptuous bathrooms you could throw a party in. There's a popular restaurant called **Nuríte** on the 1st floor.

✖ Eating

Morelia offers some superb eating options to suit all budgets. Street food can be harder to find; seek it out in one of the city center's three *mercados* (markets): San Juan, Independencia and Nicolás Bravo.

★**La Cantera**   FOOD HALL $
(☑443-460-15-16; www.lacanteramercado.com; Tapia 153; mains from M$45; ☺10am-10pm Mon & Tue, to midnight Wed-Sat, to 6pm Sun) Self-dubbed a *mercado gastronómico* (gastronomic market), La Cantera is a sleek, modern affair in what once was a nunnery's courtyard. Inside, a dozen stalls sell all manner of eats – sushi, wood-oven pizza, crepes, tacos and more – at great prices. Weekend evenings bring live music and buckets of beer. Sit at a communal table for the best people-watching.

Mercado de San Juan   MARKET $
(Mercado Revolución; ☑443-312-03-60; cnr Revolución & Plan de Ayala; ☺8am-4pm) Also known as Mercado Revolución for its address, this is a favorite of Morelia's trinity of markets, with meat, produce, dry goods and an infinite variety of cooked foods on offer.

El Rinconcito   MEXICAN $
(☑443-292-94-12; Bartolomé de las Casas 145A; mains M$40-65; ☺9am-6pm Mon-Sat, 10am-5pm Sun) A small corner eatery with a fast-moving line, Rinconcito serves up home-style meals in a colorful dining room. Expect traditional eats like *milanesa* (chicken fried steak) with macaroni salad or steak fajitas with a stack of warm tortillas. A glass of freshly made lemonade is typically included (just like at *abuelita's* house).

Gaspachos La Cerrada   MEXICAN $
(☑443-457-22-02; Hidalgo 57; gaspachos M$35; ☺9am-9pm) Gaspacho – not a cold tomato soup in Mexico but a 'salad' of diced mango, pineapple and *jicama* (Mexican 'turnip') drowned in orange and lime juice and vinegar and dashed with salt, chili sauce, onion and grated cheese – is a Morelian favorite served all over town. The word on the street says this place is the best of them all.

Cuish Cocina   OAXACAN $$
(☑443-312-14-80; www.facebook.com/CuishCocina Boutique; Tapia 60; mains M$65-195; ☺10am-11pm

Tue-Sun) A charming restaurant with stone walls, folk art and repurposed tables, Cuish cooks up traditional dishes from Michoacán and Oaxaca: *sopa tarasca* (spicy bean soup), *taquitos de chapulines* (grasshopper tacos), *tlyuda con huitlacoche* (a large *tostada* with mushroom fungus) and more. A long menu of mezcal from both states rounds out the menu well. Service is quick and friendly too.

★**Tata**   MEXICAN $$
(☑443-312-95-14; www.tatamezcaleria.com; Bartolomé de las Casas 511; mains M$130-330; ☺1:30pm-12:30am Mon-Thu, to 2am Fri & Sat, 1:30-10pm Sun) It could very well be the 190 different mezcals from Michoacán, Jalisco and Oaxaca that keeps pulling us back to Tata, but we're more inclined to think it's the *cocina de autor* (signature cuisine) of chef Fermín Ambás, with such delectables as rabbit tartare with wasabi aioli and chili (M$85) and tuna in a tortilla crust (M$210) on offer.

Our advice? Eat here but drink at Tata's little sister Tatita (p642) two blocks to the northeast.

Lu Cocina Michoacana   NEW MEXICAN $$
(☑443-313-13-28; www.lucocinamichoacana.mx; Portal Hidalgo 229; mains M$130-210; ☺7am-10pm Sun-Thu, to 11pm Fri & Sat) This unassuming restaurant below the Hotel Casino is one of Morelia's most inventive places to dine. Talented young chef Lucero Soto Arriaga turns pre-Hispanic ingredients into exquisite gems· of beautifully presented *alta cocina*. Try the *atápakua de milpa*, a rich seasonal squash-flower soup, and the Zitácuaro trout with coconut and avocado sauce. Excellent selection of Mexican wines by the glass too.

Origo   BISTRO $$
(☑443-492-19-60; Jardín de las Rosas 121; mains M$60-155; ☺8am-11pm Mon-Fri, to midnight Sat & Sun; ☑) Opening onto the leafy Jardín de las Rosas, this charming bistro-bakery serves up a superb breakfast and lunch menu, including a handful of vegan and gluten-free options. Come here for banana pancakes, crepes stuffed with salmon and capers, egg-white omelettes and fresh baguette sandwiches. The patisserie case and Chiapanecan coffee are impossible to resist. Evenings bring thin-crust pizza and craft beer.

Fonda Marceva   MEXICAN $$
(☑443-316-90-91; www.facebook.com/Fonda Marceva; Abasolo 455; mains M$90-180; ☺9am-6pm) Specializing in the cuisine of the Tierra Caliente (Hot Land) region of Michoacán's

THE SWEET LIFE

Dulces morelianos – delicious 'Morelian sweets' made with fruit, nuts, milk and sugar – are famous throughout the region. They're showcased both at the Mercado de Dulces y Artesanías (p643) and the **Museo del Dulce** (Sweets Museum; ☑ 443-312-04-77; www.callereal.mx/#recorridos; Av Madero Oriente 440; adult/child M$30/25; ⊙10am-7:30pm Sun-Fri, to 8:30pm Sat), an old-fashioned *chocolatería* stacked with truffles, preserves, candied nuts and sugary chunks of candied peaches and pumpkin, and staffed by women in period costume.

There are up to 300 varieties, but these are some of our favorite sweets:

Ates de fruta Jewel-colored squares or strips of fruit leather, commonly made from guava, mango and quince.

Cocadas Chewy-crunchy pyramids of caramelized coconut.

Frutas cubiertas Chunks of candied fruits such as squash, fig and pineapple.

Glorias Cellophane-wrapped rolls of goat's milk caramel studded with pecans.

Jamoncillo de leche Fudge-like milk sweets sold in rectangles or molded into nut shapes.

Obleas con cajeta Gooey caramel sandwiched between two thin round wafers.

Ollitas de tamarindo Tiny clay pots filled with a sweet-salty-tangy tamarind jam-like paste.

Rompope Eggnog-like drink made with aguardiente, eggs, milk and (here) one of 16 flavorings: from pecans and walnuts to cinnamon and strawberries.

---

southeast corner, this lovely courtyard restaurant spread over three rooms and crammed with colorful handicrafts serves a mind-blowing *aporreadillo* (breakfast stew of eggs, dried beef and chili) and some of the best *frijoles de la olla* (beans slow-cooked in a pot) we've ever tasted.

★**Chango** FUSION **$$$**
(☑443-312-62-13; www.changorestaurante.com; Sor Juana Inés de la Cruz 129; mains M$150-350; ⊙1:45-11:30pm Mon-Thu, to midnight Fri & Sat, to 6pm Sun) A lovely destination restaurant south of Plaza Villalongín, Chango offers *cocina contemporánea de autor* (contemporary signature cuisine) with maestro chef Daniel Aguilar Bernal at the helm. Seating is spread around various downstairs rooms and an upstairs terrace in a house best described as 'Mexican art meets art nouveau.' The menu is international and subtly experimental (expect sous vide cooking).

Los Mirasoles MEXICAN **$$$**
(☑443-317-57-75; www.facebook.com/LosMirasoles; Av Madero Poniente 549; mains M$155-350; ⊙1-11pm Mon-Thu, to 11:30pm Fri & Sat) Morelian and Michoacán pride oozes from the kitchen at Los Mirasoles, where you'll dine in a fine Unesco-quality house bedecked (among other quirks) with a copy of Las Tarascas' fountain. The food is doused in regional flavors. Try the *chiles capones* (seedless chilies stuffed with cheese) and *atápakua de huachinango* (fish in a *mole*-like sauce).

 Drinking & Nightlife

Nightlife is more genteel than rowdy in Morelia, though a few clubs keep the music pumping into the small hours. Around the **Jardín de las Rosas** just north of the Centro Cultural Clavijero are several bars with terraces that start buzzing in the early evening. Another hot spot is the area around **Plaza Villalongin** at the eastern end of the city center.

Tatita Mezcalería BAR
(☑443-312-95-14; www.facebook.com/TatitaMezcaleria; Jardín Villalongín 42; ⊙11am-midnight Sun-Thu, to 2am Fri & Sat) A gorgeous *mezcalería* (mezcal bar) housed in a beautifully converted old villa just by the Fuente Las Tarascas, Tatita gets it all right, with superb cocktails, great DJs and friendly, attentive staff. Mezcal flights cost M$190 (Michoacán) and M$265 (Oaxaca).

El Manglar BAR
(☑443-317-61-64; Bartolomé de las Casas 600; ⊙12:30pm-midnight Mon-Thu, noon-3am Fri & Sat) A smallcantina with a great rooftop and a hipster vibe, come here for Mexican craft beers and cheap cocktails. A limited menu of finger foods – tacos, *tostadas*, fries, etc – do the trick if you get the munchies.

Con La Rojas Pop GAY & LESBIAN
(☑443-312-15-78; www.facebook.com/ConLaRojas; Allende 555; ⊙9pm-3am Thu-Sat) A hopping gay bar in a beautifully converted colonial build-

ing, Rojas Morelia Pop is one of the hottest spots in town. Cozy seating, chandeliers and a lit-up bar overlook a stage where live bands and drag queens perform nightly. If any, cover charge is minimal. All welcome.

☆ Entertainment

As a university town and the capital of one of Mexico's more dynamic states, Morelia has a thriving cultural scene. Stop by the tourist office or the Casa de la Cultura for a copy of *Cartelera Cultural,* a free weekly listing of films and cultural events.

For stage acting, visit the **Teatro Ocampo** (☑ 443-312-37-34; https://sic.cultura.gob.mx; Ocampo 256; ⊙ box office 9am-3pm & 6-10pm Mon-Fri) or **Teatro Morelos** (☑ 443-232-44-00; www.ceconexpo.com; Plaza Cantera, cnr Av Ventura Puente & Camelinas; ⊙ box office 11am-7pm Mon-Sat); the latter is part of the Centro de Convenciones complex, 3km south of the city center.

The cathedral (p635) has occasional impressive organ recitals.

Conservatorio de las Rosas   CLASSICAL MUSIC (☑ 443-312-14-69; www.facebook.com/elconser; Tapia 334) Founded in 1743, this is the oldest music conservatory in the Americas and remains something of an 'old-school' music college. In its Alhambra-esque courtyard, you can sit and seek romantic inspiration as the sound of trumpet blasts and guitar riffs emanates from the surrounding classrooms. There are free concerts at 7pm Thursdays in the Sala Niños Cantores de Morelia.

Casa de la Cultura   LIVE MUSIC (☑ 443-313-12-68; www.casaculturamorelia.gob. mx; Av Morelos Norte 485; ⊙ 8am-8pm Mon-Fri, to 7pm Sat, to 4pm Sun) With the Conservatorio de las Rosas, this is a pillar of Morelia's cultural life. Housed in an old Carmelite monastery dating from the 17th century, it's a blissful place to soak up the musical spirit of Mexico. The pleasant cafe near the entrance is a good staging post, or check the website to see what performances are coming up.

Save time for other nooks and crannies too, taking in the ancient wall paintings, enormous mirrors and cell-like monks' quarters.

🛍 Shopping

Casa de las Artesanías   ARTS & CRAFTS (☑ 443-312-12-48; www.artesanias-michoacan. com; Fray Juan de San Miguel 129, Plaza Valladolid; ⊙ 8am-7:30pm Mon-Fri, 9am-3pm & 4-8pm Sat & Sun) If you don't have time to scour the Purépecha pueblos for the perfect folk-art

piece, come to the House of Crafts inside a wing of the **Ex-Convento de San Francisco**, dating from 1541. It's a cooperative marketplace launched to benefit indigenous craftspeople; arts and handicrafts from all over Michoacán are displayed and sold here.

On the upper floor there are a few independent shops plus a free craft museum called the **Museo Michoacano de las Artesanías**.

Mercado de Dulces y Artesanías   MARKET (Sweets & Crafts Market; Gómez Farías 55; ⊙ 9am-9pm) This seductive market, on the western side of the Centro Cultural Clavijero, deals in the region's famous sweets, including a rainbow selection of *ates de fruta* (fruit leathers) in a variety of exotic flavors. Head to the 2nd floor for folk art, handcrafted toys and other artisanal crafts from around the state. Light haggling welcome.

Plaza San Agustín   ARTS & CRAFTS (cnr Corregidora & Abasolo; ⊙ 10am-10pm Sat & Sun) On weekends, a colorful outdoor *artesanía* market is set up along the arches in this square just south of the cathedral. Come here for mementos or gifts – you'll find everything from handmade clothing and jewelry to home goods and toys. In the evenings, food stalls set up to feed shoppers and passersby alike.

ℹ Information

Banks and ATMs are plentiful along Avenida Madero, especially at its western end around the plazas on either side of the cathedral.

Michoacán Tourist Office (☑ 800-450-23-00, 443-312-94-14; http://michoacan.travel/en; Hidalgo 245; ⊙ 8am-5pm Mon-Fri) Opposite the Plaza de Armas.

Morelia tourist office (p639) This helpful office can be found on Benito Juárez north of the cathedral. In addition, there are info kiosks at the northeast corner of Plaza de Armas and in Plaza Melchor Ocampo (both open 9am to 9pm daily).

Main Post Office (Av Madero Oriente 369; ⊙ 8:30am-4:30pm Mon-Fri, to noon Sat)

Sanatoria La Luz (☑ 443-315-29-66; www.sanatoriolaluz.mx; Bravo 50; ⊙ 24hr) Located just east of the center of town, near the aqueduct.

ℹ Getting There & Away

AIR

Aeropuerto Internacional General Francisco Mujica (MLM; ☑ 443-317-67-80; www.aeropuertosgap.com.mx/en/morelia-3.html; Carretera

BUSES FROM MORELIA

DESTINATION	FARE (M$)	TIME (HR)	FREQUENCY (PER DAY)
Colima	685-850	6	2 daily
Guadalajara	520-620	3½	half-hourly
Mexico City (Terminal Norte)	530	4¾	hourly
Mexico City (Terminal Poniente)	528	4½	half-hourly
Pátzcuaro	60	1	hourly
Uruapan	206	2	hourly
Zitácuaro	148-160	3	hourly

Morelia-Zinapécuaro Km 27) is 27km north of Morelia, on the Morelia–Zinapécuaro Hwy. There are no public buses; taxis to and from the airport cost about M$200. There are plenty of daily departures to cities in Mexico and limited flights serve destinations in North America.

Aeroméxico (☑ 55-5133-4000; www.aeromex ico.com; Carretera Morelia-Zinapécuaro Km 27) Flights include Cancún and Mexico City.

Viva Aerobus (☑ 443-313-19-19; www.vivaaero bus.com; Carretera Morelia-Zinapécuaro Km 27) Flights to Monterrey, Tijuana and Chicago.

Volaris (☑ 55-1102-8000; www.volaris.mx; Carretera Morelia-Zinapécuaro Km 27) Frequent flights to Mexico City, Los Angeles and Denver.

BUS

Morelia's **bus station** (Terminal de Autobuses de Morelia; ☑ 443-334-10-71; www.tam-sa. com.mx; Periférico Paseo de la República 5555) is about 4km northwest of the city center. It's separated into three *módulos,* which correspond to 1st-, 2nd- and 3rd-class buses. To get into town from here, take the Roja 1 combi (red, M$9) from under the pedestrian bridge, or catch a taxi (M$65). First-class buses depart hourly or more frequently for most destinations.

ℹ️ Getting Around

Around town, small combis and buses operate from 6am until 10pm daily (M$9). Combi routes are designated by the color of their stripe: Ruta Roja (red), Ruta Amarilla (yellow), Ruta Rosa (pink), Ruta Azul (blue), Ruta Verde (green), Ruta Cafe (brown) and so on. Ask at the tourist office for help with bus and combi routes.

Reserva Mariposa Monarca

In the eastern-most corner of Michoacán, straddling the border of México state, lies the incredible 563-sq-km **Reserva de la Biósfera Santuario Mariposa Monarca** (Monarch Butterfly Biosphere Reserve; ☑ 715-153-

38-67; http://mariposamonarca.semarnat.gob.mx; each sanctuary adult/child M$50/40; ☉ 9am-dusk Nov-Mar), a Unesco World Heritage site since 2008. Every autumn, in late October to early November, millions of monarch butterflies begin to flock to these forested highlands for their winter hibernation, having flown all the way from the Great Lakes region of the US and Canada some 4500km away. The butterflies arrive in waves, the last remaining until early to mid-March, when they begin their return journey north. It's an unforgettable sight watching clouds of the colorful insects transform the forest into a unique Technicolor world.

◉ Sights

◉ El Rosario

El Rosario is the most popular area – during the height of butterfly voyeurism (February and March) it gets as many as 8000 visitors a day. It is also the most commercial – souvenir stalls abound on the hillside and the habitat has been severely affected by illegal logging. El Rosario village and the entrance to the El Rosario reserve area are located about 12km up a good gravel road from the small village of Ocampo.

Getting to the butterflies requires a steep 2km to 4km hike (or horseback ride), a lot of it on steps, depending on the time of year. The entrance fee (adult/child M$50/40) includes a mandatory guide. Horses cost M$100 one way. There's a small, free **museum** (☉ 9am-5pm) worth perusing at the entrance gate with exhibits and a short film about the butterflies.

◉ Sierra Chincua

Sierra Chincua is some 12km northeast of Angangueo, way up in the mountains. This area has been damaged by logging, but not as badly as El Rosario. It's a less strenuous hike, so this sanctuary is for those who want an easier walk. Price-wise it's the same deal as El Rosario (adult/child M$50/40). Horses are also available. At the attractively organized entrance are souvenir shops, places to eat and a zip-line.

To get here from Angangueo, take the bus bound for Tlalpujahua or a Mexico City bus (M$10) and tell the driver you're going to Sierra Chincua. Taxis from Angangueo cost M$400 and upward, depending on the wait.

◉ Cerro Pelón

Cerro Pelón, which is actually located in México state, is by far the best choice. The mountains rise high (more than 3000m) here, the forest is in great shape and there is barely a trickle of tourism compared with the Michoacán reserves. Rangers have protected the México side of the forest for the last 45 years, reducing illegal logging considerably. Expect to see huge, cathedral fir trees, moss-covered trunks, wildflowers and incredible canyon views.

Be warned that the climb here is very steep and the relentless ascent takes a good mountain walker at least 1½ hours going at a fair pace and without stopping. People not used to mountain walking are likely to struggle; we would discourage most from attempting to do so. Most people choose to ascend the mountain on horseback (M$220).

This reserve area is about a 40-minute drive southeast of Zitácuaro, Michoacán's sixth-largest city, where you can buy necessary food, water and supplies. There are a

---

OFF THE BEATEN TRACK

MACHEROS

This quiet farming community is located close to the entrance of the Cerro Pelón sanctuary. Out of season it offers excellent birding and hiking opportunities as well as year-round scenic views.

Along with a wonderful destination B&B, **JM Butterfly** (☏715-112-54-99, WhatsApp +1-803-357-3240; www.jmbutterflybnb.com; s/d incl breakfast US$55-95; ⓟ🛜🗷), Macheros offers a campsite (from M$300) with the usual facilities, as does the village of El Capulín, a couple of kilometres to the southeast. Remember that camping is forbidden in the reserve.

---

couple of access points, including Macheros and El Capulín. Both are within 1.5km of each other and can be reached by public transportation from outside Zitácuaro's bus terminal. Combis marked 'Aputzio,' waiting to the left of the Bodega Aurrera when you exit the bus terminal, cost M$16. Get off in La Piedra and take a taxi from there to Macheros or El Capulín (from M$35). A taxi straight from Zitácuaro to either of the reserve areas costs M$300 to M$350.

◉ Piedra Herrada

The sanctuary of 'Branded Rock' is 25km outside of Valle de Bravo in México state. The road to it passes through a major monarch crossing, with thousands of monarchs fluttering across to drink before returning to their roosts every day. The entrance (adult/child M$50/40) is just past this spectacle on your left. Most of the trail up to the colony is paved. The difficulty of the hike or ride up varies by year depending on the location of the colony. Horses are available. Try to visit on a weekday to avoid the tour buses from Mexico City.

❶ Getting There & Away

At least one of the four reserves can be reached from Angangueo, Zitácuaro and Macheros, but it's easiest and most time-efficient to hire a guide with transportation.

Angangueo

☏715 / POP 4600 / ELEV 2580M

This drowsy mining town is the most popular base for butterfly-watchers, because it's close to both the Sierra Chincua and El Rosario sanctuaries. The town is layered into the hills and replete with pine forest, grazing land and cornfields. Most services can be found along a single main drag with two names (Nacional and Morelos). There are two attractive churches, including the 18th-century Templo de la Immaculada Concepción, on Plaza de la Constitución, the center of town, from which Nacional runs down the hill.

By far the best of the town's guesthouses, **Plaza Don Gabino** (☏715-156-03-22; www.facebook.com/Don.Gabino.Hotel; Morelos 147; r M$550-650, ste M$1200; ⓟ🛜) is a family-run and exceptionally welcoming place with nine sparkling-clean, if basic, rooms with hot-water showers; some have fireplaces.

There's an onsite restaurant serving excellent Michoacán specialties too. It's around a kilometer downhill from the central plaza. Transportation available to/from Mexico City. Reserve ahead in butterfly season.

During the butterfly season, from late October to mid-March, Plaza Don Gabino also organizes excursions to the Sierra Chincua and El Rosario sanctuaries.

ⓘ Information

Tourist Office (☑715-156-06-44; Nacional 1; ⊙8am-7pm daily Nov-Mar, to 4pm Mon-Fri Apr-Oct) Small office just a half-block downhill from the main plaza.

ⓘ Getting There & Away

Frequent buses from Morelia go first to Zitácuaro (M$187, three hours), where you'll catch another bus to Angangueo (M$29, 1¼ hours). From Mexico City's Terminal Poniente, you can get a Zina bus direct to Angangueo (M$233, 3½ hours, seven daily); most of the other bus lines go through Zitácuaro.

To reach the El Rosario sanctuary from Angangueo, first take a combi to Ocampo (M$20, 15 minutes, hourly), then another to El Rosario (M$25, 30 minutes, hourly), from the corner of Independencia and Ocampo. In season there are also *camionetas* (pickup trucks) that leave from the *auditorio* (auditorium) in Angangueo, or from outside hotels; these cost about M$600 for around 10 people and take 45 bumpy minutes (via a back road) to reach the sanctuary, but they go directly to the entrance. A taxi to El Rosario, including wait, costs around M$400.

For Sierra Chincua, take the Tlalpujahua or Mexico City bus (M$10) and tell the driver you're going to Sierra Chincua. Taxis from Angangueo cost M$400 and upward, depending on the wait.

Zitácuaro

☑715 / POP 84,300 / ELEV 1990M

Zitácuaro is Michoacán's sixth-largest city, but it feels like a provincial working-class town. Known primarily for its specialty breads and trout farms, it's no great looker and its layout often confuses visitors as they amble up and down the hilly streets. But Zitácuaro is a sensible base for visiting the butterflies at both the Cerro Pelón and the Piedra Herrada sanctuaries.

Hotel María Fernanda Inn   HOTEL **$$**
(☑715-153-40-40; www.mariafernanda.com.mx; Degollado Oriente 33; incl breakfast s M$940, d M$1060-1240; P✳🛜) A surprisingly sleek and modern hotel in the heart of Zitácuaro,

this low-rise offers spacious and sunny rooms with deluxe beds and gleaming bathrooms. Continental breakfast is served at its sister property across the street and valet parking is available too. Tours and/or drivers to the butterfly reserves are happily arranged.

Rancho San Cayetano   HOTEL **$$$**
(☑715-153-19-26; www.ranchosancayetano.com; Carretera a Huetamo Km 2.3; r from M$2800; P@🛜≋) This attractive but pricey property has nine rooms, three loft apartments and three separate self-catering houses spread over 5 hectares of gardens and forest with a raging creek at the bottom. Spacious rooms are rustic chic with exposed stone walls, beamed ceilings and fireplaces. The pool is a bonus. Multicourse evening meals (from M$500) available.

La Bodega Leonesa   SPANISH **$$**
(☑715-141-00-10; www.facebook.com/labodegaleonesa; Cerrada Noche Buena s/n; mains M$130-220; ⊙1-10pm Tue-Fri, 9am-10pm Sat & Sun) This tapas bar and restaurant serves specialties from León, named the 'Spanish Capital of Gastronomy 2018,' and comes highly recommended by residents. Try the *pulpo gallego* (Galician-style grilled octopus cooked with boiled potatoes and sweet paprika and drizzled with olive oil) or any of the salmon dishes. And no funny business; the owners are boxers.

ⓘ Getting There & Away

Zitácuaro's bus terminal is on General Pueblita Norte, about 1km southeast of the city center. There are frequent buses to and from Morelia (M$164, 3 hours), Angangueo (M$29, 1¼ hours) and Mexico City's Terminal Poniente (M$244 to M$297, two hours), among other destinations.

For Cerro Pelón, take a combi marked 'Aputzio' (M$16); they wait to the left of the Bodega Aurrera when you exit the bus terminal. Get off in La Piedra and catch a taxi from there to Macheros or El Capulín (from M$35). A taxi straight from Zitácuaro costs M$300 to M$350.

Pátzcuaro

☑434 / POP 57,000 / ELEV 2140M

Terracotta-tiled roofs, warped red-and-white adobe walls and narrow cobblestone streets give the city of Pátzcuaro the air of a large village. Unlike the Spanish-founded settlements of Morelia and Guadalajara, Pátzcuaro took root in the 1320s as part of the Purépecha empire, two full centuries before the conquistadors arrived, and retains its indigenous feel.

History whispers from the cobwebbed louvers that overlook the lively but hassle-free streets fanning out from the city's attractively landscaped Plaza Vasco de Quiroga (or Plaza Grande) and Plaza Gertudis Bocanegra (or Plaza Chica). Adding to the atmosphere, Pátzcuaro hosts one of the most dramatic Day of the Dead celebrations in Mexico. It's also handily placed for exploring Lago de Pátzcuaro, just 3km to the north, and the craft-making Purépecha villages that cluster around its shoreline.

Make advance reservations during holidays and bring warm clothes from November to February – you're at altitude here and it gets chilly.

History

Pátzcuaro was the capital of the Purépecha civilization from about 1325 to 1400 CE. After the death of King Tariácuri, the Purépecha state became a three-member confederation comprising Tzintzuntzan and Ihuatzio as well. The league repulsed repeated Aztec attacks, which might explain why they welcomed the Spanish when they first arrived in 1522. Bad idea. The Spanish returned in 1529 under Nuño de Guzmán, a vicious conquistador.

Guzmán's five-year reign over the indigenous people was brutal, even for those times. The colonial government recalled Guzmán to Spain, where he was arrested and jailed, and in his place dispatched Bishop Vasco de Quiroga, a respected judge and cleric from Mexico City, to clean up the mess. Quiroga was an impressively enlightened man. When he arrived in 1536, he established village cooperatives based on the humanitarian ideals described in Sir Thomas More's *Utopia*.

To avoid dependence on Spanish mining lords and landowners, Quiroga successfully encouraged education and agricultural self-sufficiency in the Purépecha villages around Lago de Pátzcuaro, with all villagers contributing equally to the community. He also helped each village develop its own craft specialty, from masks and pottery to baskets and guitars. The utopian communities declined after his death in 1565, but the crafts traditions continue to this day. Not surprisingly, Tata Vasco (Father Vasco), as the Purépecha called Quiroga, has not been forgotten: streets, plazas, restaurants and hotels all over Michoacán are named in his honor.

⊙ Sights

★ Basílica de Nuestra
Señora de la Salud   BASILICA

(☏434-342-00-55; Plaza de la Basílica, Benigno Serrato s/n; ⊗8am-9pm) Built on a hill atop a pre-Hispanic ceremonial site, this cathedral, and pilgrimage site, was intended to be the centerpiece of Vasco de Quiroga's utopia. Begun in 1540, the church was not completed until the 19th century and only the barrel-vaulted central nave is faithful to his original design. Quiroga's tomb, the **Mausoleo de Don Vasco**, is in the side chapel to the left of the main entrance. It's a massive structure and quite austere, but always full of worshippers.

Behind the altar and up some steps at the eastern end of the basilica stands a much-revered figure of the cathedral's patron, **Nuestra Señora de la Salud** (Our Lady of Health), which 16th-century Purépechans crafted with a paste made from the heart of the cornstalk and bound with *tazingue,* a natural glue. Soon after its dedication, people began to experience miraculous healings and pilgrims still arrive from all over Mexico to pray for miracles. They crawl on their knees across the plaza, into the church and along its nave. Pinned to the image and at its feet are tiny tin *votivas* (votives) of hands, feet, legs, eyes and other body parts for which the faithful seek cures.

Outside in the plaza, homeopathic cure-alls and religious items are sold at an **outdoor market**. Wandering toward the market's southern end, vendors of colorful handwoven clothing, shawls and fabrics appear too.

★ Plaza Vasco de Quiroga   PLAZA
(Plaza Grande; Morelos, btwn Hidalgo & Matamoros) Pátzcuaro's leafy main square – more commonly known as 'Plaza Grande' – is Mexico's largest plaza after the Zócalo in Mexico City and the only one in the country without a church. It is framed by the 17th-century facades of old mansions that have since been converted to hotels, shops and restaurants, and the Palacio Municipal (city hall). It is all watched over by a serene **statue of Vasco de Quiroga**, which rises from the central fountain.

The plaza's colonnaded *portales* (arcades) are full of food stalls, jewelry shops and folk-art sellers, and the atmosphere, particularly on the weekend when bands play and street performers entertain, is wonderful.

Pátzcuaro

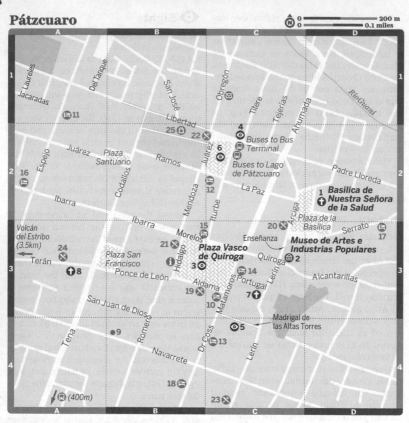

Pátzcuaro

◎ Top Sights

1 Basílica de Nuestra Señora de la
   Salud..D2
2 Museo de Artes e Industrias
   Populares...C3
3 Plaza Vasco de Quiroga B3

◎ Sights

4 Biblioteca Gertrudis Bocanegra............C2
5 Casa de los Once Patios........................C4
6 Plaza Gertrudis Bocanegra....................C2
7 Templo del Sagrario C3
8 Templo San Francisco.............................A3
Vasco de Quiroga Statue..............(see 3)

✈ Activities, Courses & Tours

9 Centro de Lenguas y Ecoturismo
   de Pátzcuaro..B4

⬡ Sleeping

10 Casa del Naranjo C3

11 Estancia de la Era A1
12 Gran Hotel Pátzcuaro.............................C2
13 Hotel Casa Encantada............................C4
14 Hotel Casa Leal C3
15 Hotel Mansión Iturbe..............................B3
16 Hotel Pueblo Mágico..............................A2
17 Mesón de San Antonio...........................D3
18 Posada Yolihuani......................................B4

◎ Eating

19 El Patio B3
20 Ivo's Pizza C3
21 La Surtidora...B3
22 Market Food Stalls...................................C2
23 Santo Huacal...C4
24 Verde Limone Ristorante-Bar...............A3

⬡ Shopping

25 Mercado Municipal...................................B2

★ Museo de Artes e Industrias Populares
MUSEUM

(☑434-342-10-29; www.inah.gob.mx; cnr Enseñanza & Alcantarillas; adult/child M$55/free; ☺9am-4:30pm Tue-Sun) Highlights among the well-curated exhibits of this impressive folk-art museum include a room set up as a typical Michoacán kitchen, cases of gorgeous jewelry, copperware, ceramics and guitars from Paracho, and an entire room filled with *votivas* and *retablos* – votives and crudely rendered devotional paintings offering thanks to God for saving the creator from illness or accident.

The museum is housed in the former Colegio de San Nicolás, founded by Quiroga in 1540 as the first university in the Americas. The building was constructed on pre-Hispanic stone foundations, some of which can be seen in the patio behind the museum. Here you'll also see an all-wood decorated *troje* (traditional granary).

Casa de los Once Patios
MARKET

(Madrigal de las Altas Torres s/n; ☺10am-7pm) This cool, rambling colonial edifice was built as a Dominican convent in the 1740s. (Before that, it was the site of the Hospital de Santa Martha, founded by Vasco de Quiroga and one of Mexico's first.) Today it houses small *artesanías* on two levels, each specializing in a particular regional craft. Renovations over the years mean there are now five patios rather than the previous 11 (as in the market's name – *once* is Spanish for 'eleven').

Templo del Sagrario
CHURCH

(cnr Lerín & Portugal; ☺8am-8pm) This creaky church is one of Pátzcuaro's oldest and was built on the site of a former hospital in the 16th century. Until the early 1900s, it housed the revered statue of Nuestra Señora de la Salud, which now takes pride of place in the basilica nearby. Note the wonderful wooden-tile floor and the majestic baroque altar.

Templo San Francisco
CHURCH

(☑434-342-00-57; Terán 11; ☺6am-2pm & 4-8pm) Built between 1526 and 1539, this pink-stone eclectic-style Franciscan church has an impressive plateresque-style doorway, an adjoining cloister and a 16th-century figure of Christ fashioned from cornstalk paste.

Plaza Gertrudis Bocanegra
PLAZA

(Plaza Chica; Juárez, btwn Padre Lloreda & La Paz) Pátzcuaro's second plaza, usually referred to as Plaza Chica, is officially named after a local heroine who was shot by firing squad in 1818 for her support of the independence movement. Her statue commands the center of the plaza. Hotels ring the plaza and on the west side is the local **market** (Ramos, btwn Juárez & Codallos; ☺7am-5pm) where you'll find everything from fruit and vegetables to herbal medicines and traditional clothing – including the region's distinctive striped shawls and *sarapes* (blankets with an opening for the head).

Biblioteca Gertrudis Bocanegra
LIBRARY

(☑434-342-54-41; http://sic.gob.mx; cnr Padre Lloreda & Títere; ☺9am-6:30pm Mon-Fri) On the northern side of Plaza Chica and occupying the cavernous 16th-century Templo de San Agustín, this stunning public library has a barrel-vaulted ceiling, oyster-shell skylights and a massive, very colorful mural (1942) by Juan O'Gorman on the rear wall that depicts the history of Michoacán from pre-Hispanic times to the 1910 Revolution. Note the remnants of original frescoes on the east and west walls.

Volcán del Estribo
VIEWPOINT

(Calle Francisco Villa s/n) This hilltop lookout on an extinct volcano 3.5km west of the city center is a quintessential morning run for Pátzcuaro's more robust residents; but don't underestimate the altitude (2175m above sea level) or the terrain – a steep, cobbled, cypress-lined road. It's all worth it in the end when you reach the viewing pavilion with killer views of Lago de Pátzcuaro and its surroundings. For those with abnormal energy reserves, 422 steps lead up to the true summit.

To reach Volcán del Estribo, take Calle Ponce de León from the southwest corner of Plaza Grande and keep walking (or running).

Courses

Centro de Lenguas y Ecoturismo de Pátzcuaro
LANGUAGE

(CELEP, ☑434-342-47-64; www.celep.com.mx; Navarrete 50; 2-week Spanish-language course US$350, language & cultural program US$540) Courses at this very enthusiastic center involve three hours of daily classes Monday to Friday. Cultural programs include seminars in Mexican literature and excursions to local villages. Homestays including meals with local families can also be arranged (from US$25 per day).

✦✦ Festivals & Events

★ Día de Muertos
RELIGIOUS

(Day of the Dead; ⊙ Nov 1 & 2) The villages around Pátzcuaro, most notably Tzintzuntzan, and the Isla Janitzio stage the most popular (and crowded!) Día de Muertos celebrations in Mexico. Parades, crafts markets, dancing, ceremonies, exhibitions and concerts are held in and around Pátzcuaro on both days, and cemeteries are packed with visitors throughout the festivities.

Pastorelas
RELIGIOUS

(Plaza Grande, Morelos, btwn Hidalgo & Matamoros; ⊙ Dec 26-Feb 2) These dramatizations of the shepherds' journey to pay homage to the infant Jesus are staged in Plaza Grande around Christmas. *Pastorelas indígenas,* on the same theme but including mask dances, enact the struggle of angels against the devils that are trying to hinder the shepherds. They're performed in eight villages around Lago de Pátzcuaro on different days between December 26 and February 2.

La Inmaculada Concepción/ Virgen de la Salud
RELIGIOUS

(⊙ Dec 8) A colorful procession to the basilica on the Feast of the Immaculate Conception honors 'Our Lady of Health' with traditional dance performances.

⌂ Sleeping

Pátzcuaro does 'pleasant colonial hotels' like Paris does refined streetside cafes. Nonetheless, it's worth reserving ahead for Friday and Saturday nights, and a year ahead for Día de Muertos, when the entire town is booked well in advance. By contrast, at all other times you need normally only raise an eyebrow at the more expensive places to see prices tumble – sometimes by as much as 40%.

Gran Hotel Pátzcuaro
HOTEL $

(☑ 434-342-04-43; www.granhotelpatzcuaro.com; Plaza Bocanegra 6; s/d from M$800; P 🕾) This squeaky clean hotel has smallish rooms, most with interior-facing windows, but is very central, perched at the southern end of Plaza Chica. Ask for a room on the 2nd floor facing the square. The restaurant behind reception serves hearty breakfasts (M$55 to M$110).

Mesón de San Antonio
GUESTHOUSE $

(☑ 434-342-25-01; Serrato 33; s/d incl breakfast M$800/965; P @ 🕾) At this great-value, old hacienda-style inn, rooms border a leafy, colonial-like courtyard. The beamed overhangs are held up by ancient timbers and the seven extremely large rooms are decorated with fine Purépecha pottery and have wood-burning fireplaces and cable TV. There's also a communal kitchen for guests' use.

★ Posada Yolihuani
B&B $$

(☑ 434-342-16-66; www.posada-yolihuani.com; Dr Coss 40; r incl breakfast M$1100-1450; 🕾) A converted colonial home with flowering gardens, this tranquil inn has 10 spacious and sunny rooms, each with tasteful decor integrating indigenous art. Tables and lounge chairs are set up throughout and music wafts through the air, inviting a sense of welcome. The owners, a friendly French–Mexican couple, are a wealth of information on area sights and activities. Yoga offered twice weekly too.

A multipurpose room at the entrance doubles as a cultural space where concerts, theater and art workshops are offered throughout the year. It is also the location of a weekly organic and gourmet farmers market.

★ Hotel Casa Encantada
B&B $$

(☑ 434-342-34-92; www.hotelcasaencantada.com; Dr Coss 15; r incl breakfast US$70-125; P @ 🕾) Enchanting is the word for this intimate American-owned B&B offering 12 elegant rooms with local rugs and beautifully tiled bathrooms in a converted 1784 mansion. Many of the rooms, like the Grand Sala at the front, are enormous and some come with kitchenettes and fireplaces. Host Virginia and her welcoming staff just can't do enough for guests.

Hotel Pueblo Mágico
HOTEL $$

(☑ 434-342-11-62; www.facebook.com/hotel. pueblomagico; Ibarra 81; r M$900-950; P 🕾) A colonial hotel in the center of town, Pueblo Magico has two floors of rooms opening onto a verdant courtyard with a gurgling fountain and countless plants. Rooms themselves are spacious and squeaky clean with good beds and decor that's pleasant if a bit sparse. Coffee and cookies served in the morning. Service is kind and accommodating, a real plus.

Hotel Mansión Iturbe
BOUTIQUE HOTEL $$

(☑ 434-342-03-68; www.mansioniturbe.com; Morelos 59; r incl breakfast M$1077; P 🕾) Right on the main plaza, the 14 rooms in this atmospheric hostelry are spacious, old-world in style, furnished in heavy dark woods, with beamed ceilings and crammed full of antiques. The wood- and stone-finished bathrooms are sumptuous. There's a wonderful terrace and patio out the back.

Estancia de la Era
B&B $$

(☑434-342-78-01; www.delaera.com; Espejo 160; r incl breakfast M$1298-1765; P🛜) Hidden on a quiet residential street, this B&B offers six surprisingly cozy rooms, spread across four levels of an updated colonial home. Rooms are simple but elegant with white-washed walls, locally carved furnishings, fireplaces and deluxe beds with thick comforters. The views from the patios are breathtaking. Above all, the feeling is relaxed and homey. A gem!

Hotel Casa Leal
BOUTIQUE HOTEL $$$

(☑434-342-11-06; www.hotelcasaleal.com; Portugal 1; d/ste from M$1950/3250; P❋@🛜) If there were a beauty contest among Pátzcuaro's boutique hotels, then this neoclassical plaza-facing stunner would win hands down. Examine the elegant sofas, the fabulous *Downton Abbey*–esque library, and the 14 grand but not grandiose rooms, which maintain a delicate balance between old-world exquisiteness and modern comfort. The icing on the sponge? The elegant roof terrace overlooking Plaza Grande.

Casa del Naranjo
BOUTIQUE HOTEL $$$

(☑434-342-08-85; www.hotelcasadelnaranjo. com; Plaza Vasco de Quiroga 29; r M$1815-2197, ste M$3080; 🛜) Set back from the main plaza, this 17th-century *casona*-turned–boutique hotel has nine elegant rooms, all on the 2nd story and opening onto a covered courtyard. Each has high vaulted ceilings and integrate stone, wood and adobe. Original art and even some fireplaces add to the ambience. Below, the hotel restaurant and a few small shops hum with customers.

✗ Eating

Pátzcuaro has some atmospheric eating options. Some of the town's best street food can be found at the **food stalls** (Juárez, cnr Lloreda; mains from $35; ⏰8am-11pm) fronting the market on Plaza Chica.

Ivo's Pizza
PIZZA $

(☑434-342-56-55; www.facebook.com/ivospizza; Plaza de la Basílica, Arciga s/n; mains from M$60; ⏰1-8pm Tue-Sat, noon-6pm Sun; ✗) Thin crispy-crust pizza loaded down with toppings ranging from pulled pork to avocado slices is what you'll find at this local fave. Seating is in a covered courtyard with copper tables, original art and fast-moving waiters. Save room for dessert – the brownies and sundaes

LOCAL KNOWLEDGE

PÁTZCUARO FOOD SPECIALTIES

Pátzcuaro has wonderful street food – look out for bright green *atole de grano* (an anise-flavored local variant of the popular corn-based drink), *nieve de pasta* (almond and cinnamon ice cream) and chunks of candied squash. Also keep your eyes open for *sopa tarasca,* a rich bean soup with cream, dried chili and bits of crisp tortilla. If it's *corundas* (triangular *tamales* served with and without fillings) you're after, head to the basilica in the morning and look for the elderly women with baskets of them.

are to die for. A good option if you're looking for a change of pace, flavor-wise.

★ La Surtidora
MEXICAN $$

(☑434-342-28-35; Hidalgo 71; mains M$45-160; ⏰7:30am-10pm) This heavenly place for refueling is living proof that no other country does atmospheric colonial cafes quite like Mexico. La Surtidora's cafe-deli has been knocking out *desayunos* (breakfasts), *comidas* (lunch) and *cenas* (suppers) on Plaza Grande since 1916. The enchiladas, cakes, balletic waitstaff and home-roasted coffee can all be recommended. And did we mention the freshly pressed juice?

El Patio
MEXICAN $$

(☑434-342-04-84; www.facebook.com/elpatio rest; Aldama 19; mains M$65-160; ⏰8am-10pm Thu-Tue) With much-coveted seating under the *portales* of the Plaza Grande, this restaurant attracts as many locals as tourists and is unquestionably a pleasant place for a meal, with decent Mexican staples and some well-prepared local dishes like *corundas*. The *Fiesta méxicana* decor is unmissable.

Verde Limone Ristorante-Bar
ITALIAN $$

(☑434-688-00-30; www.facebook.com/VerdeLim oneRistorante; Terán 22; mains M$95-280; ⏰2-11pm) A chic restaurant set in a beautifully remodeled colonial *casona*, serving gourmet Italian dishes with minimalist flair. Come for freshly made pastas, fresh local fish, wood-fired pizza and a dessert menu impossible to resist. A great spot for a special night out.

★ Santo Huacal
INTERNATIONAL $$$

(☑434-117-24-47; www.facebook.com/santohuacal; Lerin 23; tasting menu M$300-350; ⏰2-10pm Fri-Sun) This lovely garden restaurant run by

BUSES FROM PÁTZCUARO

DESTINATION	FARE (M$)	TIME	FREQUENCY (PER DAY)
Guadalajara	520	4½hr	3
Ihuatzio	15	15min	very frequent
Mexico City (Terminal Norte)	595	5½hr	2
Mexico City (Terminal Poniente)	553	5½hr	8
Morelia	60	1hr	hourly
Tzintzuntzan	25	20min	very frequent
Uruapan	84	1hr	half-hourly

a young couple from Oaxaca is a wonderful find. From the weekly-changing five-course tasting menu, choose such delectables as root vegetable salad in a honey-mustard dressing, split pea soup with Parmesan and lavender foam, and risotto with sautéed zucchini and *huitlacoche*. Desserts are to die for here. Reservations highly recommended.

❶ Information

Several banks in the city center with ATMs will also change currency.

Municipal Tourist Office (☑ 434-344-34-86; secturpatzcuaro@gmail.com; Portal Hidalgo 1; ◷ 9am-7pm)

Post Office (☑ 434-342-01-28; Obregón 13; ◷ 8am-5pm Mon-Fri, 10am-2pm Sat)

❶ Getting There & Away

Pátzcuaro's **bus terminal** (☑ 434-342-17-09; Arriaga Ochoa s/n) is a walkable 1.5km southwest of the city center. It has a cafeteria and left-luggage facilities (M$20 per item; open 7am to 7pm).

To catch a bus to the city center, walk outside the terminal, turn right and at the corner take any bus marked 'Centro' (M$9). Taxis cost M$40.

Buses back to the terminal (marked 'Central') leave from the northeast **corner** (Plaza Chica, cnr Lloreda & Iturbe) of Plaza Chica. Combis to the **boat pier** (marked 'Lago'; M$9, 10 minutes) leave from the eastern side of the square and run from about 6am to 10pm daily.

Lago de Pátzcuaro

About 3km north of central Pátzcuaro, you will come over a rise to find a lake so blue that its edges blend seamlessly with the sky. Within it are a few populated islands. It is stream-fed and natural, and though pollution is a concern, it's still beautiful.

Isla Janitzio

Isla Janitzio is a popular weekend and holiday destination. It's heavily devoted to tourism, with lots of low-end souvenir stalls, fish restaurants and drunk college kids on holiday. But it is car-free and threaded with stepped footpaths (275 at last count) that eventually wend their way to the top of the island, where you'll find a 40m-high statue of independence leader José María Morelos, erected in 1934. You can climb up inside the **Morelos Monument** (Isla Janitzio; M$10; ◷ 9am-8pm) where an ascending 56 panels painted by Ramón Alva de la Canal (between 1936 and 1940) tell Morelos' story. The last part ingeniously climbs the statue's raised arm to a lookout with panoramic lake views in the see-through wrist.

A 1200m-long zip-line links Isla Janitzio with Isla Tecuéna and costs M$350 one way for the 45-second ride; the return is by boat..

Lakeside Villages

The villages surrounding Lago de Pátzcuaro make perfect day trips from Pátzcuaro, and most can be reached by public transportation. The villages differ quite a bit from each other and many specialize in one particular type of craft, some since the 16th century.

ERONGARÍCUARO
☑ 434 / POP 2575 / ELEV 2084M

A pretty town 20km northwest from Pátzcuaro, Erongarícuaro (or 'Eronga') is one of the oldest settlements on the lake. French poet André Breton (1896–1966), who found Mexico to be 'the most surrealist country in the world,' lived here for a time in the late 1930s, where he met Leon Trotsky and was visited occasionally by Diego Rivera and Frida Kahlo. Breton designed the unusual wrought-iron cross in the forecourt of the **Templo de Nuestra Señora de la Asunción**, 50m east of Avenida Morelos. There are gorgeous gardens behind the old Franciscan monastery attached to the church. You may find the gate to them open.

ⓘ Getting There & Away

Combis run to Eronga from Pátzcuaro's bus station (M$19, one hour) every 15 minutes.

IHUATZIO
☑ 434 / POP 3550 / ELEV 2057M

Ihuatzio, 15km north of Pátzcuaro, was capital of the Purépecha kingdom after Pátzcuaro (but before Tzintzuntzan). Today it's just a slow, dusty village renowned for its weavers of animal figures –from *tule*, a reed that grows on the edge of the lake.

The Ihuatzio site contains a partially restored set of pre-Purépecha **ruins** (☑ 443-312-88-38; www.inah.gob.mx; adult/child M$45/free; ⊘ 9am-5:30pm), some of which date back as far as 900 CE. The site lies about 1.5km up a cobbled road from the village's small plaza. The ruins' best attraction is the **Plaza de Armas**, an open ceremonial space some 200m long, which doubled as a ball court and features two 15m-high squared-off pyramids at its west end. The piled stones enclosing the site are *muro-calzadas* (wall-causeways), used as paths.

Two carved stone coyotes were found at the site. One is in the National Anthropology Museum in Mexico City and the other at the Museo Regional Michoacano in Morelia. There's a copy in the museum at the Tzintzuntzan Archaeological Site.

ⓘ Getting There & Away

Combis to Ihuatzio (M$14) run directly from Pátzcuaro's Plaza Chica every 10 minutes.

Lago de Pátzcuaro

QUIROGA

📞 435 / POP 14,700 / ELEV 2080M

The bustling market town of Quiroga, 25km northeast of Pátzcuaro and 8km beyond Tzintzuntzan, is named for Vasco de Quiroga, the man responsible for many of its buildings and handicrafts. It's known for two things: *carnitas* (roasted pork) and its **mercado de artesanías** (crafts market). You'll find both on Avenida Vasco de Quiroga and the Plaza Principal, with hundreds of stalls selling brightly painted wooden, ceramic and leather goods as well as bustling taco stands lined with hungry diners getting their *carnitas* fix. The town is set at the crossroads of Hwys 15 and 120, so there is seldom a dearth of people.

On the first Sunday in July, the **Fiesta de la Preciosa Sangre de Cristo** (Feast of the Most Precious Blood of Christ) is celebrated with a long torchlight procession led by a group carrying an image of Christ crafted from a paste made of corncobs and honey.

ℹ Getting There & Away

Transportation between Quiroga and Erongarícuaro is infrequent, so head back to Pátzcuaro to travel between those two towns. Combis to Quiroga ($30, 45 minutes) leave every 15 minutes from Pátzcuaro's bus station.

TZINTZUNTZAN

📞 434 / POP 3550 / ELEV 2050M

The tiny town of Tzintzuntzan (tseen-TSOON-tsahn), some 17km northeast of Pátzcuaro, was once the Purépecha capital and served as Vasco de Quiroga's first base in the region. It has a beautiful sprawling cemetery that blooms with flowers and crepe paper during heady Día de Muertos celebrations, crumbling Purépecha ruins and some relics from the early Spanish missionary period. The town's pulse comes from its thriving Saturday and Sunday **mercado de artesanías** at the entrance to saintly Quiroga's beloved *atrio de los olivos* (olive grove), and two old churches and a former monastery now converted into a fascinating museum.

★ Antiguo Convento Franciscano de Santa Ana   MONASTERY

(Progreso 2) South of the lake and just west of Hwy 120 lies this enormous religious compound built partly with stones from the Purépecha *yácatas* (temples) taken from the site up the hill. This is where Franciscan monks began the Spanish missionary effort in Michoacán in the 16th century. The complex is composed of two churches fronted by shady olive trees in the churchyard planted by Vasco de Quiroga. Most of the monastery now houses a fascinating new **museum** (📞 434-344-30-05; www.inah.gob.mx; Progreso 2; M$20; ⊙ 10am-5pm).

The museum showcases Purépecha culture and history, and documents the arrival of the Spanish and the people's conversion to Christianity via excellent displays set up in the cloisters, refectory and two open chapels. The galleries include a number of faded murals and Mudejar-patterned wooden ceiling ornamentation, as well as a carved portal at the main entrance. A section of the 1st floor is also dedicated to rotating art exhibits. Signage is in Spanish and English. Attached is the stark **Templo de San Francisco**.

Tzintzuntzan Archaeological Site   RUINS

(📞 443-312-88-38; www.inah.gob.mx; Av Las Yácatas; adult/child M$60/free; ⊙ 9am-6pm, museum closed Mon) This site comprises an impressive group of five semicircular reconstructed temples known as *yácatas*, which are all that remain of the mighty Purépecha empire. The hillside location offers wonderful views of the town, lake and surrounding mountains and is rarely crowded. A small but well-curated **museum** showcases finds from the site, including jewelry and pottery. Don't miss the replica of the Ihuatzio coyote. English-language visitor's guide available at the entrance.

Down the hill to the east there are some boulders with carved petroglyphs of barely recognizable deities. A small info point and some flowering bushes highlight a project that's trying to entice the once-abundant hummingbird back to the area; 'Tzintzuntzan' means 'place of the hummingbird' in Purépecha.

Cerámica Tzintzuntzan   WORKSHOP

(📞 cell 434-119-06-23; moralestz@yahoo.com; Tariacuri 478; ⊙ 10am-6pm Mon-Fri) A converted missionary hospital now houses the rustic ceramics studio of Manuel Morales, a fifth-generation local potter. His colorful, intricate work is sold in galleries throughout Mexico and the USA. Inside you'll see ceramics in all stages of production and a cool, underground showroom in the back. Morales gives classes and accepts apprentices as well.

ℹ Getting There & Away

There are direct buses to Tzintzuntzan from Pátzcuaro's bus terminal (M$25).

WORTH A TRIP

TINGAMBATO RUINS

Stroll through luscious avocado groves to the beautiful ruins of this ceremonial site (☑443-312-88-38; www.inah.gob.mx; Tinganio s/n, Tingambato; M$55; ☺9am-6pm) called Tinganio in Purépecha, which predates the Purépechan empire and thrived from about 450 to 900 CE. Rarely visited and beautifully atmospheric as a result, the site is located outside the town of Tingambato, 33km northeast of Uruapan on the old road to Pátzcuaro. The ruins, which include two plazas, three altars and a ball court, have a Teotihuacán influence.

There's also an 8m-high stepped pyramid to the east and an underground tomb where 15 skeletons and 32 scattered skulls were found – hinting at beheading or trophy-skull rituals. The wooded knoll behind the fence to the west of the ball court contains an unexcavated pyramid.

Buses to Morelia and Pátzcuaro leave from Uruapan's terminal every half-hour and stop in Tingambato (M$11, 30 minutes) on the way. The ruins are 1.5km downhill on Terán, the continuation of Juárez, the sixth street on the right as you enter Tingambato.

Uruapan

☑452 / POP 279,000 / ELEV 2140M

All praise the thundering Río Cupatitzio, which brings lifeblood to Uruapan. This impressive river begins life underground, then rises to the surface, feeding a subtropical garden of palms, orchids and massive shade trees in the city's Parque Nacional Barranca del Cupatitzio. Without the river, Uruapan would not exist.

When Spanish monk Fray Juan de San Miguel arrived here in 1533, he was so taken with his surroundings that he gave the area the Purépecha name, Uruapan (oo-roo-AH-pahn), or 'Eternal Spring.' Fray Juan designed a large market square, built a hospital and chapel, and arranged streets into a grid that survives today.

Uruapan quickly grew into a productive agricultural center renowned for its macadamia nuts and high-quality aguacates (avocados); it still holds the title 'Capital Mundial del Aguacate.' Uruapan is 500m lower than Pátzcuaro and a bit warmer. It's not as enchanting a place as the latter, but is worth a stopover for a day or so.

◉ Sights

★ **Parque Nacional Barranca del Cupatitzio** PARK
(Parque Nacional Eduardo Ruíz; ☑452-523-23-09; www.uruapanvirtual.com/acerca.php?item=parque-nacional; Independencia & Culver City; adult/child M$25/10; ☺8am-6pm) This incomparable urban park is just 15 minutes west of the main plaza, but it's another world. Tropical and subtropical foliage is thick and aflutter with birds and butterflies. The Río Cupatitzio bubbles over boulders, cascades down waterfalls and spreads into wide, crystalline pools. Cobbled paths (labeled 'Recorrido Principal') follow the riverbanks to the river's source at the icy and gin-clear Rodilla del Diablo pool.

Museo Indígena Huatápera MUSEUM
(☑452-524-34-34; Portal Mercado; ☺9:30am-1:30pm & 3:30-6pm Tue-Sun) **FREE** Found in the Huatápera, an old colonial courtyard building on the northeast corner of the main plaza, this small museum showcases handsome *artesanías* from Michoacán's four main indigenous groups: Purépecha, Nahua, Mazahua and Otomí. Built in the 1530s by Fray Juan de San Miguel, the Huatápera once housed the first hospital in the Americas. The Mudejar-style decorations around the doors and windows were carved by Purépecha artisans.

Fábrica San Pedro MUSEUM
(☑452-524-06-77; www.facebook.com/FabricadeSanPedro; Treviño 57; ☺10am-2pm & 4-7pm Wed-Sun) **FREE** This 19th-century textile factory is essentially a living museum. Hand-loomed and hand-dyed bedspreads, tablecloths and curtains are still made here from pure cotton and wool, and are available for sale at the small in-house shop. The original machines are more than 150 years old and many are still used. Part of the factory also has been repurposed into an exhibition space, showcasing works by local and international artists.

✪ Festivals & Events

Semana Santa (Tianguis Artesanal de Uruapan) FAIR
(Plaza Mártires de Uruapan, Av Obregón s/n; ☺Mar/Apr) Palm Sunday is marked by a procession through the city streets and the **Tianguis Artesanal de Uruapan**, which

starts with a major crafts competition and for the next two weeks fills the main square with exhibitions and vendors of Michoacán handicrafts.

Día de Muertos
CULTURAL

(☺ Nov 1 & 2) Celebrated across Mexico but with extra enthusiasm here, the famous Day of the Dead festival brings many visitors to Uruapan for the colorful local celebrations including concerts, dance performances and competitions for the best altar.

🛏 Sleeping & Eating

Hotel Mi Solar Centro
BOUTIQUE HOTEL $$

(☎ 452-524-09-12; www.facebook.com/HotelMiSolar; Delgado 10; r M$780-1040, ste M$1000-1200; P ❄ @ 🛜) Uruapan's oldest hotel opened in the 1940s to accommodate tourists flooding in to see the newborn Volcán Paricutín. Today it's wholly remodeled, with 17 spacious rooms on three floors surrounding an atrium bar. Rooms have deluxe king beds, high ceilings and hand-carved wooden furniture.

WORTH A TRIP

VOLCÁN PARICUTÍN

The youngest volcano in the Americas, Volcán Paricutín (2800m) might be less than 80 years old, but clambering up the volcanic scree slopes to its summit and looking out across blackened, village-engulfing lava fields is sure to be a highlight of your travels in Mexico.

The story behind this volcano is as extraordinary as the views from its summit. On February 20, 1943, Dionisio Pulido, a Purépecha farmer, was plowing his cornfield when the ground began to quake and spurt steam, sparks and hot ash. The farmer struggled to cover the blast holes, but he quickly realized his futility and ran for safety. It was a good thing, because like some Hollywood B-grade movie, a growling volcano began to rise from the bowels of the earth. Within a year it had reached an elevation of 410m above the rolling farmland and lava had flooded the Purépecha villages of San Salvador Paricutín and San Juan Parangaricutiro. Thankfully, the lava flowed slowly, giving the villagers time to escape.

The volcano continued to grow until 1952. Today its large black cone spits warm steam in a few places, but otherwise it appears dormant. Near the edge of the 20-sq-km lava field, the belfry of the swamped Templo de San Juan Parangaricutiro protrudes eerily from a sea of black lava; it and the altar awash in colorful offerings of candles and flowers are the only visible traces of the two buried villages.

To climb Volcán Paricutín, start from the village of Angahuan, 40km northwest of Uruapan. Begin early, optimally before 9am. There's no shortage of guides offering their services; they meet travelers at the bus station or at the **tourist center** (Cabañas y Restaurante El Mirador Volcán Paricutín; ☎ 452-443-03-85; Av Paricutín s/n; M$10; ☺ 24hr). Don't attempt to climb the volcano on your own as trails can be hard to follow. A horse and guide costs around M$500 in total per group, a guide alone runs M$400 per person.

There are two standard routes up the volcano: a 14km round-trip short route, which starts in pine forest then switches to difficult rock-hopping across an expansive lava field, and a 24km round-trip long route, which follows a sandy track through avocado groves, agave fields and wildflowers. Horses always go via the long route to avoid the lava fields. If you ride, allow five to six hours (including at least four in an unforgiving, wooden saddle). If you prefer to hike, are fit and want variety, ask your guide to head out on the short route and return on the longer trek.

Whichever route you take, the final scramble up the volcano – a half-hour steep grunt through gravel and unstable rock – is on foot. Coming down is a different matter altogether; sliding down smooth black sand, you'll be on terra firma in two minutes. The standard route visits the San Juan church on the way back. The altar is almost always blessed with colorful offerings of candles and flowers. Close to the church are a number of food stalls serving tasty blue-corn quesadillas cooked on old, wood-burning, oil-can skillets. Bring plenty of water and wear decent shoes. And prepare for a long but rewarding day.

Buses leave Uruapan's bus station for Angahuan about every 30 minutes from 5:45am to 7pm (M$20, one hour). The last bus returns around 8pm; few cabs are available in Angahuan, so make sure you don't miss it! If you're driving, take Hwy 37 north from Uruapan to the turnoff toward Los Reyes. Angahuan is about 17.5km down the road.

BUSES FROM URUAPAN

DESTINATION	FARE (M$)	TIME	FREQUENCY (PER DAY)
Angahuan	20	1hr	half-hourly
Colima	658	6hr	2
Guadalajara	505	4¾hr	10
Mexico City (Terminal Norte)	750	6½hr	6
Morelia	206	2hr	half-hourly
Paracho	52	45min	every 15min
Pátzcuaro	84	1hr	half-hourly
Tingambato	11	30min	half-hourly

Across the road is a newer annex with larger rooms that are very comfortable but lack the character of those in the main building.

Casa Chikita Bed & Breakfast
B&B $$

(☑ 452-524-41-74; casachikita@yahoo.com.mx; Carranza 32; r incl breakfast M$900; ⓟ🛜) This 19th-century house has four lovely rooms set around a garden decorated with local pottery. The rooms vary quite a bit, but the best are extremely comfortable and decorated with lovely touches, such as granite or wooden counters in the bathroom, tiled floors and local art. Noise from nearby discotheques can be heard late on weekends – a bummer but earplugs are provided.

Cox-Hanal
MEXICAN $

(☑ 452-524-61-52; Carranza 31A; mains M$50-120; ⊙ 6-11pm Tue-Fri, 2-10:30pm Sat & Sun) The chairs are plastic, there's not much to look at decor-wise and service can be a bit slow, but so what? This place is about mix-and-match *antojitos yucatecos* (small dishes from the Yucatán) and they are well worth the wait. Try the hard *tacos de cochinita* (pulled pork) and the exquisite *sopa de lima* (lime soup with chicken).

Cocina Económica Mary
MEXICAN $

(☑ 452-519-48-69; Independencia 63; set menu M$62; ⊙ 8:30am-5pm Mon-Sat) This busy family eatery always smells delicious. The cafeteria-style open kitchen serves filling meals with your choice of main – chicken *mole,* pulled pork with squash or *chiles rellenos* (stuffed chilies with cheese or meat) – along with soup, rice, beans and freshly made tortillas. Breakfast costs M$32 to M$50.

ℹ Information

Several banks with ATMs can be found on or near the central plaza.

ℹ Getting There & Away

Uruapan's bus terminal is 2km northeast of central Uruapan on the highway to Pátzcuaro and Morelia. For Tingambato (M$45, 30 minutes), take the same bus as those heading for Pátzcuaro or Morelia.

Local buses marked 'Centro' run from just outside the bus terminal to the plaza (M$9). For taxis, prepay inside the bus terminal (M$30). For the return trip, catch a 'Central Camionera' bus from the south side of the plaza.

AT A GLANCE

POPULATION
14.7 million

LANGUAGES
Spanish, Huichol,
Náhuatl, Otomí,
Huasteco

BEST VINEYARDS
Querétaro (p660)

**BEST SCULPTURE
GARDEN**
Xilitla (p708)

BEST FESTIVAL
Festival Internacional
Cervantino (p675)

WHEN TO GO
Jul & Aug
Days are mild and
wildflowers bloom;
it's the perfect time
for do-it-yourself
explorations.

Oct–Apr
Dry season in the
Huasteca Potosina;
great for excursions
to waterfalls and
rivers.

Late Mar or Apr
Traditional religious
festivities abound
during Semana Santa
(Holy Week).

Cascada de Tamul (p706), La Huasteca Potosina
RUBI RODRIGUEZ MARTINEZ/SHUTTERSTOCK ©

Northern Central Highlands

From cobbled lanes and shaded plazas to vast deserts and cloud forest, Mexico's northern central highlands is a region as varied as its history, cuisine and cultures. Here enormous mineral wealth created rich colonial cities before revolutionary activity left ghost towns. Known as the Cuna de la Independencia (Cradle of Independence), the territory is renowned for its part in the country's fight for autonomy, spurred on by the famous Grito de Dolores, which called the Mexican people to arms against the Spanish.

Highlights include arty, gorgeous San Miguel de Allende, the waterfalls and turquoise water of the Huasteca Potosina and grand colonial silver cities of Guanajuato and Zacatecas.

History

Until the Spanish conquest, the northern central highlands were inhabited by fierce seminomadic tribes known to the Aztecs as Chichimecs. They resisted Spanish expansion longer than other Mexican peoples, but were ultimately conquered in the late 16th century. The wealth subsequently amassed by the Spanish was at the cost of many Chichimecs, who were used as slave labor in the mines.

This historically volatile region sparked the criollo fight for independence from Spain, which was plotted in Querétaro and San Miguel de Allende and launched from Dolores Hidalgo in 1810. A century later Francisco Madero released his revolutionary Plan de San Luis Potosí and the 1917 signing of Mexico's constitution in Querétaro cemented the region's leading role in Mexican political affairs.

In more recent times the region has flourished economically, due in part to the boom in the motor, aerospace, manufacturing and agricultural industries, particularly around Querétaro, while San Miguel attracts many weekenders from Mexico City and a constant stream of well-heeled creatives from the USA.

QUERÉTARO STATE

POP 1.9 MILLION

Querétaro state is full of surprises. Billed primarily as an agricultural and ranching region – with handsome and fast-developing Querétaro city as its capital – it is actually packed with diverse geography, quirky sights and historical gems. Natural phenomena, such as the world's third-largest monolith, La Peña de Bernal, pre-Hispanic ruins and the stunning Sierra Gorda Biosphere Reserve are located within its borders. The reserve protects several mission towns, from where local people run some excellent, community-owned tourism ventures – a must for the more intrepid traveler.

Querétaro

📞 442 / POP 879,000 / ELEV 1800M

The delightful colonial heart of Querétaro is jammed with museums and galleries, squares that pulsate with life, grand fountains and brightly painted low-rise buildings. Throw in a near perfect climate, some great places to eat and a wide choice of decent accommodations and you get a city tailor-made for tourism. Except that, for the moment, no-

body appears to have told the tourists. If you do come here though you'll find Querétaro to be an absorbing town in which something interesting always seems to be taking place.

You'd never guess it, but Querétaro is one of the fastest-growing cities in the northern hemisphere thanks to a booming aerospace and technologies industry.

History

The Otomí founded a settlement here in the 15th century that was soon absorbed by the Aztecs, then by the Spaniards in 1531. Franciscan monks used it as a missionary base not only to Mexico but also to what is now southwestern USA. In the early 19th century, Querétaro became a center of intrigue among disaffected criollos plotting to free Mexico from Spanish rule. Conspirators, including Miguel Hidalgo, met secretly at the house of doña Josefa Ortiz (La Corregidora), who was the wife of Querétaro's former *corregidor* (district administrator). When the conspiracy was uncovered, the story goes, doña Josefa was locked in her house (now the Palacio de Gobierno), but managed to whisper through a keyhole to a coconspirator, Ignacio Pérez, that their colleagues were in jeopardy, leading to Padre Hidalgo's call to arms. This key event is still celebrated today as part of Mexico's independence celebrations every September.

In 1917 the Mexican constitution was drawn up by the Constitutionalist faction in Querétaro. The PNR (which later became the PRI, the Institutional Revolutionary Party) was organized in Querétaro in 1929, and dominated Mexican politics for the rest of the 20th century.

◉ Sights

★ MUCAL   MUSEUM

(Museo del Calendario; www.mucal.mx; Madero 91; adult/child M$30/20; ⊙10am-6pm Tue-Sun) While a museum of calendars might not sound riveting, this extraordinary museum is unexpectedly interesting. It takes a wide-angle view of calendars and its 19 exhibition rooms start with displays relating to time itself, including a look at how the galaxy – and therefore time – works and how time is measured in other ages and cultures. The remaining galleries are devoted to calendar artwork including decades of Mexico's calendars.

The building itself is a stunningly renovated mansion, complete with beautiful gardens and courtyards. The outdoor areas and the excellent cafe on its lawns provide a perfect

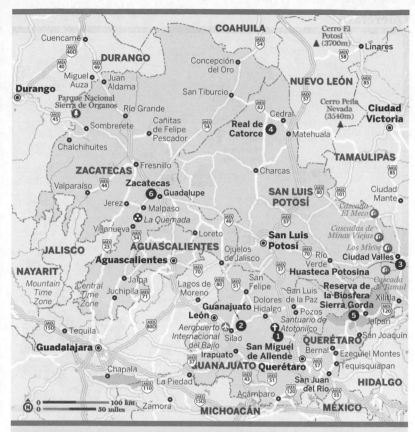

Northern Central Highlights Highlights

1 San Miguel de Allende (p682) Wandering with awe through this gorgeous colonial city, which specializes in art, food, hot springs and fiestas.

2 Guanajuato (p670) Meandering through winding cobbled alleys and discovering marvelous museums in this lively and colorful silver town.

3 La Huasteca Potosina (p705) Plunging into the remarkable turquoise rivers and surveying the extraordinary waterfalls of this incredibly scenic region.

4 Real de Catorce (p702) Sensing the glorious past in this very picturesque highland ghost town that is gradually coming back to life.

5 Reserva de la Biosfera Sierra Gorda (p669) Marveling at the mission churches and visiting communities within this wilderness jewel.

6 Zacatecas (p710) Discovering the fascinating museums that crowd this charming old silver city.

oasis from the heat, and a place to reflect on the sometimes amusing (and often titillating and politically incorrect) calendar depictions.

Templo y Convento de la Santa Cruz
CHURCH

(Independencia 148 at Felipe Luna; adult/child M$20/10; ⊙9:30am-1:30pm & 4-5:30pm Tue-Sat, 9:30am-5:30pm Sun) One of the city's most interesting sights, this convent was built between 1654 and about 1815 on the site of a battle in which a miraculous appearance of Santiago (St James) apparently led to the Otomí surrender to the conquistadors and Christianity. Emperor Maximilian had his headquarters

Querétaro

Querétaro

visiting to see the building alone: angels, gargoyles, statues and other ornamental details abound, particularly around the stunning courtyard. The gallery itself displays everything from dark and broody 16th- and 17th-century European religious paintings to the splodges of color that represents the art of today. There are frequent temporary exhibitions.

Templo de Santa Rosa de Viterbo CHURCH
(cnr Arteaga & Montes) FREE The 18th-century Templo de Santa Rosa de Viterbo is Querétaro's most splendid baroque church, with its pagoda-like bell tower, unusual exterior paintwork, curling buttresses, and lavishly gilded and marbled interior. The church also boasts what some say is the earliest four-sided clock in the New World. Opening hours are very flexible.

Templo de San Francisco CHURCH
(cnr Av Corregidora & Andador 5 de Mayo; ⊗8am-9pm) This impressive church fronts Jardín Zenea. Pretty colored tiles on the dome were brought from Spain in 1540, around the time construction of the church began. Inside are some fine religious paintings from the 17th, 18th and 19th centuries.

Museo Regional de Querétaro MUSEUM
(cnr Av Corregidora 3 & Jardín Zenea; M$60, free Sun; ⊗9am-6pm Tue-Sun) The ground floor of this museum holds interesting exhibits on pre-Hispanic Mexico, archaeological sites, the Spanish occupation and the state's various indigenous groups. The upstairs exhibits reveal Querétaro's role in the independence movement and post-independence history. The table at which the Treaty of Guadalupe Hidalgo was signed in 1848, ending the Mexican–American War, is on display, as is the desk of the tribunal that sentenced Emperor Maximilian to death.

Teatro de la República THEATER
(☑442-212-03-39; http://teatrodelarepublica. senado.gob.mx; cnr Juárez & Peralta; ⊗10am-3pm & 5-8pm) FREE This lovely old functioning theater, complete with impressive chandeliers, was where a tribunal met in 1867 to decide the fate of Emperor Maximilian. Mexico's constitution was also signed here on January 31, 1917. The stage backdrop lists the names of its signatories and the states they represented. In 1929 politicians met in the theater to organize Mexico's political party, the PNR (now called PRI). It's often possible to look inside.

here while under siege in Querétaro from March to May 1867. After his surrender and subsequent death sentence, he was jailed here while awaiting the firing squad.

Today it's used as a religious school. You must visit with a guide – you wait at the entrance until a group has formed – although tours are in Spanish. The site's main legend is the growth of the Árbol de la Cruz, an ancient tree in the convent's garden, whose thorns are in the shape of crosses. This miracle was the result of a walking stick stuck in the earth by a pious friar in 1697.

You can visit the attached church without a guide or entry fee. The entrance to the convent is to the right of the church.

Museo de Arte de Querétaro MUSEUM
(www.museodeartequeretaro.com; Allende Sur 14; by donation; ⊗10am-6pm Tue-Sun) Querétaro's art museum, adjacent to the Templo de San Agustín, occupies a splendid baroque monastery built between 1731 and 1748. It's worth

NORTHERN CENTRAL HIGHLANDS QUERÉTARO

Mirador
VIEWPOINT

From this viewpoint there's a fine view of 'Los Arcos,' Querétaro's emblematic 1.28km-long aqueduct, with 74 towering sandstone arches built between 1726 and 1738. The aqueduct runs along the center of Avenida Zaragoza.

Casa de la Zacatecana
HOUSE

(442-224-07-58; www.museolazacatecana.com; Independencia 59; adult/student M$60/45; ⏰10am-6pm) This is a finely restored 17th-century home with an impressive collection of 18th- and 19th-century furniture and decorations, which veer between the chintzy and the austere (check out the wall of gruesome crucifixes). It's a good place to get a sense of life in colonial-era Querétaro.

Cathedral
CATHEDRAL

(cnr Madero & Ocampo) FREE The 18th-century cathedral features both baroque and neoclassical styles, with an emphasis on straight lines and few curves; it's said that the first Mass in the cathedral (then known as San Felipe Neri) was led by Padre Hidalgo, of independence fame.

Templo de Santa Clara
CHURCH

(cnr Madero & Allende) The 17th-century Templo de Santa Clara has an extraordinarily ornate baroque interior. Masses are held frequently so you'll have to inquire as to the best time to enter.

Mausoleo de la Corregidora
MAUSOLEUM

(Ejército Republicano s/n; ⏰9am-6pm) The Mausoleo de la Corregidora, opposite the *mirador,* is the final resting place of local independence heroes doña Josefa Ortiz and her husband, Miguel Domínguez de Alemán.

Museo de la Ciudad
MUSEUM

(Guerrero Norte 27; M$5; ⏰11am-7pm Tue-Sun) Inside the ex-convent and old prison that held the deposed Emperor Maximilian, the 11-room Museo de la Ciudad has some good alternating contemporary art exhibits. At the time of research most of the museum was closed for extensive renovations but one or two rooms still housed art displays.

🎓 Courses

Olé Spanish Language School
LANGUAGE

(442-214-40-23; www.ole.edu.mx; Escobedo 32) Offers a range of courses with homestay options and extracurricular programs. Weeklong courses range from moderate group classes (15 hours; US$202) to 35-hour intensive courses (US$513).

🛏 Sleeping

Blue Bicycle House
HOSTEL $

(442-527-17-66, 442-455-48-13; Ejercito Republicano 15; dm M$240-260, d M$540; 🛜) Located just on the edge of the center, with a view of the aqueduct, the Blue Bicycle House (look for the bicycle hanging outside) is a highlight of Querétaro's budget sleeping scene. It's small and basic and offers dorms, including one for women only. Beds are long by Mexican standards and one-hour bike use is included in the price.

El Petate Hostel
HOSTEL $

(442-212-79-87; www.elpetatehostel.com; Matamoros 20; dm M$240, d with/without bathroom M$640/500; 🛜🍽) This hostel in a gorgeous little side street has been very attractively designed with clean and bright dorms and simple rooms, some with their own bathroom. The sunset views from the rooftop terrace are included in the price.

Hotel Quinta Allende
HOTEL $$

(442-224-10-50; www.hotelquintaallende.mx; Allende Norte 20; s/d from M$1360/1450; ⏰🍽🛜) A good-value and architecturally interesting city-center option. The front half of the hotel is housed within a tenderly restored old building made up of arches and domes, but many of the rooms are in a far less eye-pleasing modern construction. Even so, the rooms are huge, bright and spotless and most overlook a garden.

Hotel Quinta Lucca
HOTEL $$

(442-340-44-44; www.hotelquintalucca.mx; Juárez Norte 119A; r incl breakfast from M$1100; 🅿🛜) You can't fault the price of this aging hotel in the northern part of the old town, and while the rooms are plain and rather dated they're very clean and quiet and surround a little garden. Helpful staff.

Hotel Quinta Santiago
HOTEL $$

(442-251-98-00; www.hotelquintasantiago.mx; Balvanera 4; d/ste M$1474/2326; 🍽🛜) Housed inside a converted convent dating to 1750, this excellent-value place has rooms with high ceilings, colorful and richly textured walls, firm beds (too firm for some) and a huge, sunny courtyard where breakfast is served. Avoid the front-facing rooms, which can be noisy.

★ La Casa del Atrio
B&B $$$

(442-212-63-14; www.lacasadelatrio.com; Allende Sur 15; r M$1800-2750; 🛜🍽) This pretty spot has morphed from its original three-rooms-in-an-antique-store to a stunning boutique hotel, with 12 rooms built around interconnecting courtyards filled with fountains and big potted plants. The bilingual host, Antonio, will go out of his way to run a professional ship and ensure everything – from each artistic, art-filled room to the delicious breakfasts – are to your liking.

Rooms and bathrooms are spacious, though if you insist on open windows at night (all rooms feature massive doors, but not windows, that open on to courtyards), then communicate this on reservation. Otherwise it's a win-win choice. There's also an in-house spa.

✖ Eating

La Xurería DESSERTS $
(Calle 5 de Mayo; churros M$5; ⊘5-11:30pm) This hole-in-the-wall-style place sells *churros* (doughnutlike fritters) and hot chocolate and that is all. But, these are not your average greasy *churros*. These are a different creature altogether! Crispy and dusted in cinnamon, they are so good that on weekend nights the queue of people waiting can stretch out the shop, round the corner and down the street!

Tacos la Congregación MEXICAN $
(Pasteur Norte; tacos M$8; ⊘7-11:30pm Thu-Sun) Querétaro is full of taco stands that spring up most evenings, but this one, which is on a pretty little plaza, is considered one of the best and always seems to be doing a roaring trade. Choose from beef, *chorizo* or a combination of the two, lace in chili and lime and dig in.

When you're done, grab some rich chocolate from the chocolate shop right behind.

La Antojería MEXICAN $
(Calle 5 de Mayo; mains M$60-110; ⊘10am-11pm; 🖬) This fun and slightly disheveled Mexican street-food-themed place serves up every style of *antojito* (typical Mexican snacks) known in Mexico. It's busy, hot and not a place you're expected to linger over your food. In other words it's just a step up from a street-side taco stand.

La Mariposa CAFE $
(☑442-212-11-66; Peralta 7; snacks M$30-120; ⊘8am-9:30pm) Unchanged since 1940, as the photos and coffee machine testify, this Querétaro institution is more about the quaint atmosphere than the food. Don't leave without trying the mouthwatering *volteado de piña* (a version of a pineapple cake) or the *mantecado* (egg-based ice cream).

★**Alioli** SPANISH $$
(☑442-212-14-72; www.alioli.com.mx; Calle 16 de Septiembre 28; mains M$200-280, tapas M$100-120; ⊘1:30-11pm Mon-Sat, to 6pm Sun) At this classy Spanish-style tapas bar and restaurant where diners sit under a cascade of lamps, the chefs chop, sizzle, boil and fry high-end ingredients into minor works of art. The octopus is especially good and the prawns wrapped in serrano ham are a perfect warm-up for it.

Brewer Gastro Pub INTERNATIONAL $$
(☑442-212-05-22; www.facebook.com/brewer queretaro; Arteaga 55; mains M$130-235; ⊘1-11pm Wed & Thu, to midnight Fri & Sat, to 7pm Sun; 🖅)
🖉 This is what happens when a local artisanal brewer joins forces with a good chef: a casual drinking spot that serves fabulous brews, from honey IPAs *(miel de abeja)* to a mezcal beer mix (Agave Ale), to excellent dishes. The chef uses all local products of which the provenance is known. Excellent charcuterie, burgers, pizzas and salads.

Tikua MEXICAN $$
(☑442-455-33-33; www.tikua.mx; Allende Sur 13; mains M$130-280; ⊘9am-midnight Mon-Sat, to 9pm Sun; 🖅) With a giant wall mural of traditionally dressed women, this restaurant specializes in southeastern Mexican cuisine and the dishes – from the *xi'i*, a mushroom salad, to the Oaxacan *chorizo* recipes – are true to their roots. The rice with *chapulines* (grasshoppers), *tasajo* (salted beef) and chocolate *mole* (a traditional sauce) are especially good. Has a mezcal menu and cocktails too.

🍷 Drinking & Nightlife

There's a thriving bar scene in Querétaro, with bars and clubs packing the historic center and beyond. Calle 5 de Mayo is the fashionable drinking strip in the center; barflies hit these places after 10pm.

★**El Faro** BAR
(Calle 16 de Septiembre 128; ⊘5pm-2am Mon-Sat) A shining light on the local drinking scene, the Lighthouse exudes elements of old with a recent polish (it originally opened in 1927 and is believed to be the city's oldest bar). The current owners took over in early 2015 so the interior is a little hipper for it. But the swinging cantina doors and friendly vibe are standing legacies.

Guests are addressed by their first names, free bar snacks keep you standing and happy hour runs all afternoon.

BUSES FROM QUERÉTARO

DESTINATION	FARE (M$)	TIME (HR)	FREQUENCY (PER DAY)
Ciudad Valles	735	7½	3
Guadalajara	594-810	4½-5½	frequent
Guanajuato	290	2½-3	7
Mexico City (Terminal Norte)	225-410	3-4½	every 20min 4am-11:30pm
Mexico City Airport	425	3½	every 30min
Morelia	320	3-4	frequent
San Luis Potosí	225-335	2½-2¾	frequent
San Miguel de Allende	80-88	1-1½	every 40min 6am-11pm
Tequisquiapan	60	1	every 30min 6:30am-9pm
Xilitla	473	5-8	4

Gracias a Dios BAR
(Calle 5 de Mayo; snacks M$60-120; ☉2pm-1:30am Tue-Sat) One of the many bars near Calle 5 de Mayo, this place revives traditions of old: a *cantina-botanero* (bar with snacks) complete with barrels and stools and just a touch of grimy-bar syndrome. However, it also has a touch of feminine funk and attracts a young crowd out for whiskey, tequila and brandy-fueled fun.

☆ Entertainment

Querétaro is action-packed with cultural activities. For the latest on what's happening around town, look out for posters on bulletin boards, or pick up a copy of freebie listing mag *Asomarte* from the tourist office. On Sunday, free concerts usually take place in Plaza de Armas at 1pm and in the evenings in Jardín Zenea.

Teatro de la República THEATER
(☎442-212-03-39; http://teatrodelarepublica.sena do.gob.mx; cnr Juárez & Peralta; tickets M$100-250) Has regular symphony concerts most Fridays.

Casa de la Cultura CONCERT VENUE
(☎442-212-56-14; Calle 5 de Mayo 40; ☉9am-2pm & 4-8pm Mon-Fri) Sponsors concerts, dance, theater and art events; stop by to view the bulletin board.

ℹ Information

H+ Querétaro (☎442-477-22-22; www. hmasqueretaro.mx; Zaragoza 16B) This private hospital comes recommended by expats.
Hospital Angeles (☎442-192-30-00; www. hospitalesangeles.com/queretaro; Bernardo Del Razo 21, El Ensueño) Southwest of downtown, this hospital has English-speaking doctors.

Tourist Office (☎442-238-50-67, 800-715-17-42; www.queretaro.travel; Pasteur Norte 4; ☉9am-7pm) This helpful office has English-speaking staff and gives out free city maps and brochures, plus the useful publication *Asomarte* with listings of what's on.

ℹ Getting There & Away

AIR

The **Aeropuerto Intercontinental de Querétaro** (☎442-192-55-00; www.aiq.com.mx), 8km northeast of the downtown area, is around a M$300 taxi ride from the center. Primera Plus also runs from the bus terminal to Mexico City airport (M$425, three hours). As well as flights to Mexico City, there are direct services to various US cities from Querétaro.

BUS

Querétaro is a hub for buses in all directions; the modern **Central Camionera** (Parque del Cimatario) is 5km southeast of the center. There's one building for deluxe and 1st class (labeled A), one for 2nd class (B) and another for local buses (C). Facilities include luggage storage.

ℹ Getting Around

Once you have reached downtown, you can easily visit most sights on foot. City buses (M$9) run from 6am to 9pm or 10pm. They gather in an area at the end of the bus terminal; turn right from the 2nd-class terminal, or left from the 1st-class side. Several routes go to the center (the numbers change, so check). For a taxi, get a ticket first from the bus-station booth (M$60, up to four people).

To get to the bus station from the center, take city bus marked 'Central' (ie Central Camionera) from Calle Zaragoza, or any bus labeled 'TAQ' (ie Terminal de Autobuses de Querétaro) or 'Central' heading south on the east side of the Alameda Hidalgo.

Tequisquiapan

📍 414 / POP 30,000 / ELEV 1870M

This small town (teh-kees-kee-*ap*-an), 70km southeast of Querétaro, is a relaxing weekend retreat from Mexico City or Querétaro. Once known for its thermal springs – Mexican presidents came here to ease their aches and stresses – the town's natural pools may have long since dried up, but its pretty, bougainvillea-lined streets, colorful colonial buildings and excellent markets make for an enjoyable place to stroll about. The town comes alive on the weekend with couples and families wandering the streets and browsing the many *artesanías* stalls.

The town makes a good base for exploring the vineyards and cheese-producing farms that are sprinkled around the surrounding countryside.

◎ Sights

Plaza Miguel Hidalgo   PLAZA
The wide and attractive Plaza Miguel Hidalgo is surrounded by *portales* (arcades) filled with bustling cafes and handicrafts stores, and overlooked by the 19th-century neoclassical **La Parroquia de Santa María de la Asunción** (☺7:30am-8:30pm) with its pink facade and decorated tower.

Quinta Fernando Schmoll   GARDENS
(📞441-276-10-71; Pilancon 1, Cadereyta de Montes; M$40; ☺9am-5pm Tue-Sun) If you have

your own wheels, this impressive botanical garden, with over 4400 varieties of cactus, is on the east edge of the village of Cadereyta de Montes. It's 38km from Tequisquiapan.

⭐ Festivals & Events

Feria Nacional del Queso y del Vino   FOOD & DRINK
(www.feriadelquesoyvino.com.mx; Parque La Pila; ☺mid-May–early Jun) The National Wine & Cheese Fair, run by Tequisquiapan's tourist office, has been running for over four decades and includes tastings, dinners and concerts over two weeks. Most events are ticketed; buy tickets on the website.

🛏 Sleeping & Eating

The best budget accommodations are the posadas along Moctezuma. Demand is low Monday to Thursday, when you may be able to negotiate a discount.

Hotel Posada Los Arcos   HOTEL **$**
(📞414-273-05-66; adalosarcos903@hotmail.com; Moctezuma 12; s/d M$530/700; 🛜) Even by the dazzling standards of Mexico this place is eyeball-searingly colorful! The domed brick-roofed rooms, which are set around a cool courtyard containing a veritable rainforest of plant life, are also fab value and the family who owns it are superfriendly. Breakfast isn't included but there is a cafe.

DON'T MISS

THE WINE & CHEESE ROUTE

Querétaro state is famed for its vineyards and cheese production (mainly goat's cheese). The state, which is the second-biggest wine-producing region in Mexico, is best known for its sparkling wines, and much of this industry is based around the town of Tequisquiapan. It's possible to visit a number of the *bodegas* and cheese farms, and if you have your own vehicle you can visit many independently. Ask at the tourist office (p668) in Tequisquiapan for details of *bodegas* open to visitors. One of the most accommodating, and also one of the largest and most important *bodegas* in Mexico, is **Finca Sala Vivé by Freixenet México** (📞441-277-01-47; www.freixenetmexico.com.mx; Carretera San Juan del Río-Cadereyta Km 40.5, Ezequiel Montes; tours from M$120; ☺tours 11am, noon, 1pm, 3pm & 4pm Mon-Fri, 11am & 4pm Sat & Sun). Tours run regularly (English-language tours are daily at noon and 4pm) and include a look at the cellars plus the all-important wine tasting. For all tours it's wise to book ahead.

You can also take an organized tour. On a standard day tour from Tequisquiapan you will normally see a couple of *bodegas* and a cheese farm, with tastings at all. At weekends a number of tour companies set up stands in Tequisquiapan's main square. **Viajes y Enoturismo** (📞414-273-57-18; www.viajesyenoturismo.com.mx; Juárez Poniente 16, Tequisquiapan; tours from M$1150; ☺8am-8pm) is a long-established, professional agency that specializes in wine and cheese tours, and offers interesting day trips in and around Tequisquiapan..

Camino a Bremen
ITALIAN $$

(☑414-273-41-13; Prieto Norte 19; mains M$120-140; ⊗2-9pm Sun-Thu, to 10pm Fri & Sat) Simple Italian restaurant filled with character that's tucked away in a room behind a tiny, old-fashioned bakery. It serves wood-fired pizzas and good pasta dishes (the pasta with cheese and mushroom sauce is delicious). Finish with one of the homemade cakes from the bakery.

ℹ️ Information

Tourist Office (☑414-273-08-41; Plaza Miguel Hidalgo; ⊗9am-7pm) Has town maps and information on Querétaro state.

ℹ️ Getting There & Away

Tequisquiapan's **Terminal de Autobuses** (Carretera San Juan del Río-Tequisquiapan 546) is around 2km north of the center in the new part of town. Local buses (M$8) from outside the bus station run to the markets on Carrizal, one block northeast of the Plaza Principal.

Flecha Azul runs half-hourly to/from Querétaro between 6:30am and 8pm (M$60, one hour). Buses also run regularly to Ezequiel Montes (change here for Bernal; M$19, 20 minutes). ETN has deluxe buses to/from Mexico City's Terminal Norte (M$340, three hours, eight daily). Coordinados (Flecha Amarilla) and Flecha Roja have 2nd-class services to the same destination (M$221, 3½ hours, regular departures). There are also three buses a day to Xilitla (M$359, 1am, 9.25am and 11.25am; five hours).

Bernal

☑441 / POP 4000 / ELEVATION 2097M

Dominated by the impressive Peña de Bernal, a giant rock that is the third-largest monolith in the world, pretty and quaint Bernal is a likable but otherwise fairly unremarkable town known locally for its cheese, candies and street food. The town comes to life during the weekends when it's bursting with Mexican visitors; however, if you come during the week you'll avoid the crowds and find a provincial town quietly going about its business.

Bernal has several lovely churches scattered around its old town and El Castillo, a 16th-century viceregal building.

⊙ Sights

Peña de Bernal
MOUNTAIN

(M$30) This 350m-high rock spire is the third-largest monolith in the world and is considered mystical by many Mexicans.

During the vernal equinox thousands of pilgrims converge on the rock to take in its positive energy. Visitors can climb to the rock's halfway point (allow one hour both ways); only professional rock climbers can climb to its peak.

While the climb is easy it's best to come as early in the day as possible to avoid both the crowds and heat. Wear good shoes as the rock face can be slippery.

⌲ Tours

La Peña Tours
TOURS

(☑441-296-73-98, 441-101-48-21; cnr Independencia & Colon; ⊗10am-7pm Mon-Fri, 9:30am-8pm Sat & Sun) The friendly Peña Tours offers an array of tours (M$190 to M$1000), including a wine and cheese tour. It also offers climbing sessions on the Peña (half-day M$1500).

🛏️ Sleeping

Few visitors spend the night in Bernal as it's so close to Querétaro, but there are options if you want to linger and the town is much more attractive once all the day-trippers have gone home.

Hotel Casa Mateo
BOUTIQUE HOTEL $$

(☑441-296-44-72; www.hotelcasamateo.com; Calle 5 de Mayo s/n; r from M$1350; ❋❧❧) This lovely, centrally located spot is set around a grassy courtyard and pool in an 18th-century colonial stone-built mansion. The rooms are bang up to date and some even have romantic free-standing bathtubs. Just the thing if you fall under the spell of Bernal.

🛍️ Shopping

La Aurora
ARTS & CRAFTS

(☑441-296-41-62; Jardín Principal 1; ⊗10am-8pm) This interesting *artesanías* shop sells an array of rugs made on the premises; request permission to see the weavers at work at their looms in the workshop behind the shop. At one time there were a number of such traditional weaving shops in Bernal, but modern economics has taken its toll on most and now only this one remains.

ℹ️ Getting There & Away

There are regular buses to/from Querétaro (around M$50, 45 minutes). The last return bus to Querétaro departs from the main road around 5:30pm. For connections to/from Tequisquiapan, change buses at Ezequiel Montes (M$15, 30 minutes).

RESERVA DE LA BIOSFERA SIERRA GORDA

Those with a love of nature, historic churches or a hankering to get off the beaten track should not miss the scenic Reserva de la Biosfera Sierra Gorda, in northeast Querétaro, which thanks to recent ecotourism projects is becoming increasingly accessible to visitors. The landscapes here are breathtaking, with impressive mountains, thick forest and rushing rivers characterizing the terrain. The Sierra Gorda is also home to five Franciscan missions founded in the 18th century, spread out within a day's drive and now inscribed as Unesco World Heritage sites. The only limitation is transportation: while it's possible to get to some places by bus, it's much easier and less time consuming if you have your own wheels.

There are five mission churches in the region, the chief of which is in the town of Jalpan. East from Jalpan, on Hwy 120, there are missions at **Landa de Matamoros**, **Tilaco** and **Tancoyol**. The mission of **Concá** is 35km north of Jalpan on Hwy 69. To get here, you'll need your own wheels, or head out on a guided tour from Jalpan.

Several companies offer trips in the reserve, and most of them are based in Jalpan. These include **Aventúrate** (☑441-296-07-14, cell 441-1033129; www.aventurate.mx; Benito Juárez 29, Jalpan) ☑, **Sierra Gorda Eco Tours** (☑441-296-07-00, 441-296-02-42; www.sierragordaecotours.com; Av La Presa s/n, Barrio El Panteón, Jalpan) ☑ and **Arnoldo Montes Rodríguez** (☑441-101-81-31, 441-108-88-24; www.sierragordaguides.com). All can arrange trips to El Chuveje waterfall, Río Escanela, Sotano de Barro as well as day tours to the various mission churches.

Jalpan

☑441 / POP 22,000 / ELEV 760M

The attractive town of Jalpan centers on its famous mission church; the town is the gateway to the other four famous mission churches sprinkled liberally around the region. Jalpan itself is quite a charmer, with a lovely central square and church and an attractive hillside location. Not surprisingly, given its tropical climate, Jalpan specializes in artisanal – and very delicious – ice creams served in the many *heladerías* (ice-cream shops) around town.

◉ Sights

Mission Church
CHURCH

Constructed by Franciscan monks and their indigenous converts in the 1750s, the original of the five missions in the Sierra Gorda is in the middle of the town of Jalpan. It has an elaborate exterior and is devoted to the first evangelist, James the Greater. Note the carvings of plants around the main entrance to the church. The majority are species native to this region.

🛏 Sleeping & Eating

Cabaña Sierra Gorda
BUNGALOW $

(☑441-296-07-00; www.sierragordaecotours.com; Centro Tierra Sierra Gorda, Av La Presa s/n, Barrio El Panteón; d from M$700; 🕾) ☑ The best budget choice in Jalpan, these simple but charming

and comfortable rooms can be found in a pleasant garden site a 15-minute walk from the center of Jalpan, near the *presa* (reservoir). Ecologically sound construction has been carried out, all rooms have fans, and the bigger ones even have mezzanines and sleep up to five people in them.

Hotel Misión Jalpan
HOTEL $$

(☑441-296-04-45; www.hotelesmision.com.mx; Fray Junípero Serra s/n; r from M$905; ❈🕾🖭) On the west side of the Jardín Principal and right in the heart of the town, Hotel Misión Jalpan has attractive gardens and a good restaurant, plus well-cared-for rooms that enjoy comfy mattresses and high-pressure showers. Look online for cut-price rates.

El Aguaje del Moro
MEXICAN $$

(Vicente Guerrero 8; mains M$100-200; ☺7am-10:30pm Mon-Sat) Known for its exceptionally spicy enchiladas (though you'll have to request spice – gringos automatically seem to get a fairly tame order unless they insist), this pleasant place has a breezy balcony with views toward the mountains, as well as over the main road. It's a good-value and cozy place for a meal.

Restaurante Tequila
MEXICAN $$

(☑441-296-12-10; mains M$80-170; ☺10am-9pm) This large garden restaurant (complete with slides and swings to keep the kids occupied) is the most popular place to eat in Jalpan, although it's hard to know if that's because of the quality of the food (it's best known for its seafood) or because everyone gets a free shot of homemade tequila as soon as they arrive. It's around 5km south of town.

❶ Getting There & Away

Jalpan's **Terminal de Autobuses** (Heroico Colegio Militar) has hourly services to Ciudad Valles (M$266, three hours) and Xilitla (M$96, 1¾ hours), as well as four services a day to San Luis Potosí (M$370, four hours).

GUANAJUATO STATE

POP 5.8 MILLION

The rocky highland state of Guanajuato is full of riches of every kind. In colonial times, mineral resources attracted Spanish prospectors to mine for silver, gold, iron, lead, zinc and tin. For two centuries the state produced enormous wealth, extracting up to 40% of the world's silver. Silver barons in Guanajuato city enjoyed opulent lives at the expense of indigenous people who worked the mines, first as slaves and then later as wage slaves. Eventually, resenting the dominance of Spanish-born colonists, the well-heeled criollo class of Guanajuato and Querétaro states contributed to plans for rebellion.

These days, the state's treasures are the gorgeous colonial towns of Guanajuato and San Miguel de Allende. Visitors to this region can enjoy its precious legacies: stunning colonial architecture, established cultural scenes and a stream of never-ending festivals...not to mention friendly, proud locals and a lively university atmosphere.

Guanajuato

📋 473 / POP 184,000 / ELEV 2045M

The extraordinary Unesco World Heritage city of Guanajuato was founded in 1559 due to the region's rich silver and gold deposits. Opulent colonial buildings, stunning tree-filled plazas and brightly colored houses are crammed together on the steep slopes of a narrow ravine where excellent museums, handsome theaters and a fine marketplace punctuate cobblestone streets. The city's main roads twist around the hillsides and plunge into long dank subterranean tunnels, formerly rivers.

The city is best known internationally for its acclaimed annual arts event, the Festival Cervantino. Yet this colorful, lively and undeniably gritty place holds center stage all year; much of the youthful vibrancy and prolific cultural activities, from *callejoneadas* (p677), films, theater and orchestras to the bubbling street life, can be attributed to the 20,000 students of the city's own University of Guanajuato. In short, Guanajuato is the state's slightly grimy but captivating capital city and should not be missed by anyone traveling in the region.

History

One of the northern hemisphere's richest silver veins was uncovered in 1558 at La Valenciana mine; for 250 years the mine produced 20% of the world's silver. Colonial barons benefiting from this mineral treasure were infuriated when King Carlos III of Spain slashed their share of the wealth in 1765. The King's 1767 decree banishing the Jesuits from Spanish dominions further alienated both the wealthy barons and the poor miners, who held allegiance to the Jesuits.

This anger was focused in the War of Independence. In 1810 rebel leader Miguel Hidalgo set off the independence movement with his Grito de Independencia (Cry for Independence) in nearby Dolores. Guanajuato citizens joined the independence fighters and defeated the Spanish and loyalists, seizing the city in the rebellion's first military victory. When the Spaniards retook the city they retaliated by conducting the infamous 'lottery of death,' in which names of Guanajuato citizens were drawn at random and the 'winners' were tortured and hanged. Independence was eventually won, freeing the silver barons to amass further wealth. From this wealth arose many of the city's mansions, churches and theaters.

◉ Sights

★**Museo y Casa de Diego Rivera**   MUSEUM
(Positos 47; M$25; ⊙10am-6:30pm Tue-Sat, to 2:30pm Sun) Diego Rivera's birthplace is now an excellent museum honoring the famous artist, who was *persona non grata* here for years. Rivera and his twin brother were born in the house in 1886 (Carlos died at age two) and lived here until the family moved to Mexico City six years later. The museum's ground floor is a re-creation of the Rivera family home, furnished with 19th-century antiques.

The labyrinth of upper floors exhibit a permanent collection of Rivera's original works and preliminary sketches (completed for some of his famous murals in Mexico City), plus there's a nude of Frida Kahlo. Several *salas* (halls) also host temporary exhibitions of work by Mexican and international artists. An intimate theater upstairs features black-and-white photographs of Kahlo and Rivera.

★**Teatro Juárez** THEATER
(Sopeña s/n; adult/student M$35/15; ⏰10am-1:45pm & 5-7:45pm Tue-Sun) Don't leave Guanajuato without visiting the magnificent Teatro Juárez. It was built between 1873 and 1903 and inaugurated by the dictator Porfirio Díaz, whose lavish tastes are reflected in the plush red-and-gold interior. The outside features 12 columns with brass capitals, lamp posts and eight of the nine muses; inside the impression is Moorish, with the bar and lobby gleaming with carved wood, stained glass and precious metals. It's only open when no performances are scheduled.

Entertaining guided tours of the theater (in Spanish only) take place at regular intervals throughout the day.

Posters outside the theater advertise upcoming performances. Tickets normally cost between M$50 and M$100.

★**Basílica de Nuestra Señora de Guanajuato** CHURCH
(Plaza de la Paz) The attractive orange-yellow Basílica de Nuestra Señora de Guanajuato contains a jewel-covered image of the Virgin, patron of Guanajuato. The wooden statue was supposedly hidden from the Moors in a cave in Spain for 800 years. Felipe II of Spain gave it to Guanajuato in thanks for the wealth it provided to the crown. Next door, the small **Galería Mariana** is dedicated to images of Mary and other Catholic relics.

★**Templo La Valenciana** CHURCH
(Iglesia de San Cayetano) On a hill overlooking Guanajuato, 5km north of the center, is the magnificent Templo La Valenciana. Its facade is spectacular and its interior dazzles with ornate golden altars, filigree carvings and giant paintings. Ground was broken here in 1765 and the church was completed in 1788.

One legend says that the Spaniard who started the nearby San Ramón mine promised San Cayetano that if it made him rich, he would build a church to honor the saint. Another says that the silver baron of La Valenciana, Conde de Rul, tried to atone for exploiting the miners by building the ultimate in Churrigueresque churches.

Bocamina de San Ramón & Bocamina de San Cayetano MINE
(www.bocaminasanramon.com; M$45; ⏰10am-6pm) These neighboring mines are part

DON'T MISS

COLONIAL CHURCHES

Aside from the **Basílica de Nuestra Señora de Guanajuato** (p671), other fine colonial churches include **Templo de San Diego**, opposite the Jardín de la Unión; **Templo de San Francisco** (Doblado s/n); and large **Templo de la Compañía de Jesús** (Lascuraín de Retana s/n), which was completed in 1747 for the Jesuit seminary whose buildings are now occupied by the University of Guanajuato.

of the famous Valenciana mining district. Silver was discovered here in 1548. At **San Ramón** you can descend via steps into a mine shaft to a depth of 60m (note: not for the claustrophobes). **San Cayetano** has an interesting museum and former miners take you on a brief tour – including a shaft visit.

To reach the mines, take a 'Cristo Rey' or 'Valenciana' bus from the bus stop on the corner of Alhóndiga and Calle 28 de Septiembre. Get off at Templo La Valenciana and follow the signs behind the church.

Museo de las Momias MUSEUM
(Museum of the Mummies; www.momiasde guanajuato.gob.mx; Explanada del Panteón Municipal s/n; adult/student M$100/50; ⏰9am-6pm) This famous museum is one of the most bizarre (some might say distasteful) sights in Mexico. The popular attraction is a quintessential example of Mexico's acceptance of, celebration of and obsession with death; visitors come from all over to see more than 100 disinterred corpses.

While technically these are mummified remains – due to the dry atmosphere in their former crypts – the bodies are not thousands of years old. The first remains were unearthed in 1865 to make room for more bodies in the cemeteries. What the authorities uncovered were not skeletons but mummified flesh (many feature grotesque forms and facial expressions).

Some people will be horrified by this macabre collection (it's certainly not suitable for children), but many others are oddly fascinated and then leave wondering if it's normal that they found it so interesting (at least we think other people find it interesting, but perhaps that's just this writer...).

Guanajuato

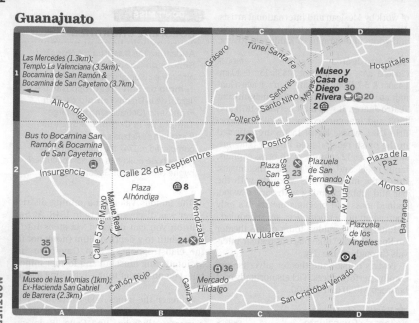

Guanajuato

The ticket also includes entry into the Museum of the Cult of the Dead though it's really just more of the same done in a more Disneyesque manner.

The complex is on the western edge of town, a 10-minute ride from Avenida Juárez on any 'Momias' bus (M$8).

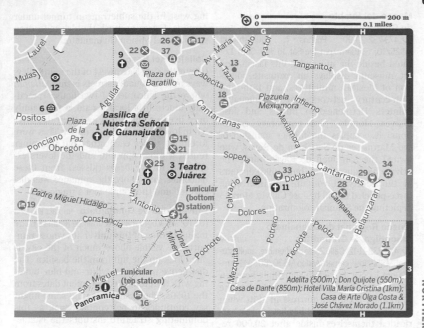

Parador Turístico
Sangre de Cristo
MUSEUM

(☑ 473-735-80-40; Carretera Silao Km 8; adult/student M$50/30; ⏱ 11am-5pm Wed-Sun) Three museums are sited in one impressively designed complex in the hills above Guanajuato. One collection explores the mining history of the region. The second has 36 mummies discovered in local churches (they look pretty gruesome so consider missing this one if you have children with you). The last looks at Day of the Dead celebrations and the *Catrina* dolls (an image/figurine of a skeleton in female clothing) that are a key part of the tradition.

To get here, take a 'Cristo Rey' bus, which depart every hour or so from near Alhóndiga (M$40 return).

Casa de Arte Olga Costa
& José Chávez Morado
MUSEUM

(Pastita 158, Torre del Arco; adult/student M$25/10; ⏱ 9:30am-5pm Tue-Sat, to 4pm Sun) In 1966 artists José Chávez Morado and Olga Costa converted a massive old well into their home and studio; before their deaths, they donated their home and its contents for public use. On display is a small, but fascinating, collection of items from the 16th to 18th centuries, including pre-Hispanic and modern ceramics, embroidery, furniture, masks and their own artworks. It's worth heading to the 'suburb' of Pastita to experience a side of Guanajuato you might otherwise miss.

The pretty approach follows the former aqueduct that ends at their house. Take any bus marked 'Pastita' from the eastern end of town.

Monumento a El Pípila
MONUMENT

(Panoramica) The monument to El Pípila honors the hero who torched the Alhóndiga gates on September 28, 1810, enabling Hidalgo's forces to win the first victory of the independence movement. The statue shows El Pípila holding his torch over the city. On the base is the inscription *Aún hay otras Alhóndigas por incendiar* (There are still other Alhóndigas to burn). The easiest way to reach it is via the funicular (p674). If you walk, go in a group and don't carry valuables.

Cristo Rey
MONUMENT

Cristo Rey (Christ the King) is a 20m bronze statue of Jesus erected in 1950 on the summit of the Cerro de Cubilete, 15km west of Guanajuato. The location of the statue at the supposed geographical center of the country holds particular significance for Mexican tourists, with impressive views an added draw. Tour agencies offer trips here, but you can also simply take a bus marked 'Cubilete' or 'Cristo Rey', departing every hour or so from near Alhóndiga (M$40 return).

Museo del Pueblo de Guanajuato
MUSEUM

(📞473-732-29-90; Positos 7; adult/student M$25/10; ⊘10am-7pm Tue-Sat, to 3pm Sun) Located beside the university, this fascinating art museum displays an exquisite collection of Mexican miniatures, and 18th- and 19th-century artworks by Guanajuatan painters Hermenegildo Bustos and José Chávez Morado, plus temporary exhibitions. It occupies the former mansion of the Marqueses de San Juan de Rayas, who owned the San Juan de Rayas mine. The private baroque chapel (built 1696) upstairs in the courtyard contains an interesting three-paneled mural by José Chávez Morado depicting the Spanish colonization.

Museo Regional de Guanajuato Alhóndiga de Granaditas
MUSEUM

(📞473-732-11-12; Calle 28 de Septiembre; adult/student M$52/free, camera/video M$30/60; ⊘10am-5:30pm Tue-Sat, to 2:30pm Sun) Built between 1798 and 1808 as a grain storehouse, the Alhóndiga became a fortress in 1810 when 300 Spanish troops and loyalist leaders barricaded themselves inside after 20,000 rebels led by Miguel Hidalgo attempted to take Guanajuato. On September 28, 1810, a young miner nicknamed El Pípila tied a stone slab to his back and, thus protected from Spanish bullets, set the entrance ablaze. The rebels moved in and killed everyone inside.

The Alhóndiga was later used as an armory, then a school, before it was a prison for 80 years (1864–1948). It became a museum in 1958, though it's arguably more interesting for its history than its display today. Don't miss José Chávez Morado's dramatic murals of Guanajuato's history on the staircases.

Ex-Hacienda San Gabriel de Barrera
MUSEUM, GARDEN

(📞473-732-06-19; Cam Antiguo a Marfil Km 2.5; adult/student M$30/20; ⊘9am-6pm) To escape Guanajuato's narrow streets, head to this magnificent colonial home that is now a museum with tranquil and attractive gardens. Built at the end of the 17th century, this was the grand hacienda of Captain Gabriel de Barrera, whose family was descended from the first Conde de Rul of the famous La Valenciana mine. Opened as a museum in 1979, the hacienda, with its opulent period European furnishings, provides an insight into noble lifestyles of the viceregal period.

The hacienda is 2.5km west of downtown. Take one of the frequent 'Marfil' buses heading west in the subterranean tunnel under Avenida Juárez and ask the driver to drop you at Hotel Misión Guanajuato.

Callejón del Beso
STREET

(Alley of the Kiss) Narrowest of the many alleyways in Guanajuato's streets is this *callejón*, where the balconies of two houses practically touch. In a local legend, a fine family once lived on this street and their daughter fell in love with a common miner. They were forbidden to see each other, but the miner rented a room opposite and the lovers exchanged furtive *besos* (kisses) from these balconies. Inevitably, the romance was discovered and the couple met a tragic end.

Universidad de Guanajuato
NOTABLE BUILDING

(UGTO; www.ugto.mx; Lascuraín de Retana 5) The main building of this university, whose ramparts are visible above much of the city, is one block up the hill from the basilica. The distinctive multistory white-and-blue building with the crenelated pediment dates from the 1950s. The design was (and some might say continues to be) controversial, as this dominating structure disrupts the characteristic, historic cityscape, but it's unusual enough to search out.

Museo Iconográfico del Quijote
MUSEUM

(📞473-732-67-21; www.museoiconografico.gua najuato.gob.mx; Manuel Doblado 1; adult/student M$30/10; ⊘9:30am-7pm Tue-Sat, from noon Sun) This surprisingly interesting museum is worth a half-hour of your time. Every exhibit relates to Spain's Don Quixote de la Mancha, Cervantes' classic literary hero, depicted in numerous different media by different artists in different styles. Paintings, statues, tapestries and even chess sets, clocks and postage stamps all feature the quixotic icon and his bumbling companion Sancho Panza.

🏃 Activities

★ Funicular
FUNICULAR

(Plaza Constancia s/n; one way/round trip M$30/60; ⊘8am-9:50pm Mon-Fri, from 9am Sat, 10am-8:50pm Sun) This incline railway inches up (and down) the slope behind the Teatro Juárez to a terminal near the El Pípila monument, from where there are stunning views of Guanajuato and the surrounding valley.

🍃 Courses

Guanajuato is a university town and has an excellent atmosphere for studying Spanish. Group classes are normally around US$120 for 20 lessons (one week's worth) and private lessons average US$20 an hour. Schools can arrange homestays with meals for around US$200 per week.

Language schools to consider include **Adelita** (☑473-732-64-55; www.learnspanishadelita.com; Agua Fuerte 56), **Don Quijote** (☑473-731-30-56; www.donquijote.org; Pastita 76, Barrio Pastita) and **Escuela Falcon** (☑473-732-65-31; www.escuelafalcon.com; Callejón de Gallitos).

**Mika Matsuishi &
Felipe Olmos Workshops** COURSE
(☑cell 473-1204299; www.felipeymika.wix.com/mojigangas) Hands-on, fun art workshops for creative souls (mask-making, clay classes etc) are run by talented artists and *mojiganga* (giant puppet) specialists. Materials are included; prices vary according to activity.

⭐ Festivals & Events

⭐ **Festival Internacional Cervantino** ART
(www.festivalcervantino.gob.mx; ⊙Oct) Beginning in the 1950s as merely *entremeses* (interludes) from Miguel Cervantes' work performed by students, the Festival Internacional Cervantino has grown to become one of Latin America's foremost arts extravaganzas. Music, dance and theater groups from around the world perform diverse works (mostly non-Cervantes related) for two weeks in October.

Tickets for single events range from M$30 to M$650 and should be booked in advance (www.ticketmaster.com.mx) along with hotels. In Guanajuato, tickets are available from a booth by Teatro Juárez (p671) two months before the festival.

Baile de las Flores RELIGIOUS
(⊙Mar or Apr) The Flower Dance takes place on the Thursday before Semana Santa. The next day, mines are open to the public for sightseeing and celebrations. Miners decorate altars to La Virgen de los Dolores, a manifestation of the Virgin Mary who looks after miners.

**Fiestas de San Juan
y Presa de la Olla** RELIGIOUS
(⊙late Jun-early Jul) The festivals of San Juan are celebrated at the Presa de la Olla park in late June. The 24th is the big bash for the saint's day itself, with dances, music, fireworks and picnics. Then on the first Monday in July, everyone comes back to the park for another big party celebrating the opening of the dam's floodgates.

🛏 Sleeping

Guanajuato has some excellent accommodations for all budgets. Particularly atmospheric are a number of midrange and top-end hotels and guesthouses in the old town. During the Festival Internacional Cervantino in October, and at Christmas, Semana Santa and, in some cases, summer vacation, prices may be hiked well above regular rates.

Corral d Comedias HOSTEL $
(☑473-732-40-54; Av María 17; dm M$245; ⊛🖎) Unusually, this hostel is run by volunteers whose presence makes it feel like more of a hangout than traditional hostel setup. There's lots of communal space and lounging room and a chilled hippy atmosphere, plus the breakfast is great. Some of the three dorms are a little on the simple side, but the location is excellent.

It's not signed at all and can be a bit hard to find. Just look for the street number.

⭐ **Mesón de los Poetas** HOTEL $$
(☑473-732-07-05; www.mesondelospoetas.com; Positos 35; s/d incl breakfast from M$1355/1773; ⊛🖎) If only all hotels were like this! This hotel's labyrinth of rooms – each named after a poet – totter up a hillside and offer spacious (though singles are small), comfortable and clean lodgings. While natural light is limited in some rooms, it's simply superb value and service is friendly. It's just a moment from the center yet quiet at night.

⭐ **Casa Zuniga** B&B $$
(☑473-732-85-46; http://casazunigabandb.com; Callejón del Pachote 38; r incl breakfast from M$1400; 🅿⊛🖎🏊) This charming B&B is run by the charismatic duo Carmen and Rick, who are famous for their warm welcome and generous breakfasts. It's located on the hill near El Pípila, to the left of the funicular (heading uphill), or by car and bus along Panoramica. Rates include a funicular pass throughout your stay. The lap pool is a plus.

Mesón Cuévano HOTEL $$
(☑473-732-60-62; www.mesoncuevano.com; Barranca 8; incl breakfast s/d from M$830/1013, f M$1797; ⊛🖎) Superbly renovated hotel with rough stone walls, exposed wooden roof beams, lots of art and all-round great insulation from the heat of the day and cold of the night. The backstreet location ensures a quiet night. A huge picture of a typewriter hangs above the breakfast tables. At these rates this place is hard to beat.

El Zopilote Mojado
HOTEL $$

(☎473-732-53-11; www.elzopilotemojado.com; De Mexiamora 51; r M$1400; ❀❖) You can't miss this summer-blue place on a quiet square. It has three traditional fan-cooled rooms in a converted colonial home, many of which feature lovely colorful tiling, wooden furniture and (from some) views onto the square. There's a cafe downstairs where breakfast can be purchased for an additional fee.

If it's full the same people have similar rooms available in two other nearby buildings.

★1850 Hotel
BOUTIQUE HOTEL $$$

(☎473-732-27-95; www.hotel1850.com/index.php/en; Jardín de la Unión 7; r incl breakfast M$2784-4423; ❀❆❖) There's nothing 18th century about this stunning hotel except perhaps the building it's housed within. One of the most memorable hotels in central Mexico, this exquisitely designed place is as much an art gallery as a hotel (it even hosts temporary exhibitions). Huge rooms are filled with high-quality furnishings and larger-than-life stencil art, and service is exemplary.

As you pass through the lobby don't forget to look up at the wonderful stained-glass ceiling.

Hotel Villa María Cristina
LUXURY HOTEL $$$

(☎473-731-21-82; www.villamariacristina.net; Paseo de la Presa de la Olla 76; ste incl breakfast from M$6127; ❀❖❅) This series of stunning converted colonial mansions, joined by a maze of patios and gardens, is one of Guanajuato's most exclusive addresses. The decor in the spacious rooms features neoclassical French designer furniture, original paintings by local artist Jesús Gallardo, and beds and bathrooms with all the fluffy trimmings. There are fountains, two swimming pools and wonderful views.

🍴 Eating

For many years Guanajuato was considered a bit of a nonevent when it came to quality food, but in the last couple of years things have started to change and there are now a small, but growing number of places in which to tuck into interesting and creative dishes as well as time-honored Mexican classics. For fresh produce and cheap lunches, head to Mercado Hidalgo (p678), a five-minute walk west of Jardín de la Unión on Avenida Juárez. Another two blocks further down on the right is **Central Comercio** (Av Juárez; ⊙8am-8pm), with a large supermarket.

Metate & Salmiana
MEXICAN $

(www.metate.mx; Positos 79; tacos M$30; ⊙3-11pm Mon-Sat) This old-school cantina-like place is a tale of two stories – literally – on the 1st floor they serve innovative tacos with weird and wonderful fillings such as duck with orange and up on the 2nd floor with its rooftop bar, they'll tempt you with quality mezcals.

El Paisa
TACOS $

(Av Juárez; tacos M$12-36; ⊙11am-11pm) This place couldn't be any different to the swanky tourist restaurants deeper in the old town. El Paisa is a sun-bleached red building right opposite the Mercado Hidalgo (p678) and it does a furious trade in cheap 'n' tasty tacos for an almost exclusively local market.

Delica Mitsu
ASIAN $

(☎473-116-64-92; Cantaritos 37; meals M$100-130; ⊙11am-6pm Wed-Mon) This tiny Japanese-run deli may not look like much (and is all but hidden in a side street off a pretty plaza), but it serves fresh, light and delicious sushi as well as salads, tofu curries and other Asian-influenced dishes. It's popular with students.

Santo Café
CAFE $

(☎473-122-23-20; www.facebook.com/santocafe; Puente de Campanero; mains M$80-180; ⊙10am-11pm Mon-Sat, noon-8pm Sun; ❖🍴) This casual but cozy spot on the quaint Venetian-style bridge is popular with students. It serves good salads and snacks; try the *queso fundido* (melted cheese) or the soy burger, both great for vegetarians. Some tables are perched on the bridge overlooking the alley below.

★Los Campos
TAPAS $$

(www.loscampos.mx; 4A de la Alameda, off Plaza Baratillo; mains M$75-185; ⊙2-10pm Tue-Sun) A Canadian-Mexican husband-and-wife team runs this small cozy, candlelit restaurant. The innovative menu, which runs from tapas plates to full dishes such as stuffed *ancho* chili on a bed of pearl barley with *huitlacoche* (corn mushrooms), *nopal* (cactus) and corn, is a cut above other Guanajuato restaurants in terms of variety and ingredients. Reserve ahead for evenings.

Costal
MEXICAN $$

(☎473-102-72-52; www.facebook.com/costalcc; Casa Cuatro, San José 4; mains M$135-210; ⊙1-10pm) Brand new at the time of research, but already causing waves of appreciation, this relaxed place with high ceilings, a jazzy soundtrack and a few window balcony seats serves wonderfully fresh and modern Mexican cuisine diffused with unexpected twists such as pork with hibiscus sauce or panna cotta with maize.

Casa Valadez MEXICAN $$
(☑ 473-732-03-11; www.casavaladez.com; Jardín de la Unión 3; mains M$170-250; ☺8:30am-11pm; ☏) This classic place enjoys an impressive perch on Jardín de la Unión and is a smart choice in every respect. As you'd expect, it attracts a loyal crowd of well-dressed locals who come for the stunning-value four-course weekday *menú del día* (set menu; M$179). Dishes are mainly international with a few Mexican favorites such as *pollo con enchiladas mineras* (chicken enchiladas).

El Trattoria ITALIAN $$
(☑ 473-732-21-58; Jardín de la Unión 1, Hotel San Diego; mains M$175-250; ☺1-11pm) With a 1st-floor view out over the comings and goings on the square below, this is an enjoyable place to tuck into some reasonable, if not mind-blowing, pasta, pizzas, steaks and fish. It also has a decent wine list.

★**Las Mercedes** MEXICAN $$$
(☑ 473-732-73-75; www.casamercedes.com.mx; Arriba 6, San Javier; mains M$200-350; ☺2-10pm Tue-Sat, to 6pm Sun; ☏) In a residential area overlooking the city is Guanajuato's best restaurant, where Mexican cuisine *como la abuela* – grandmother's cooking that takes hours to prepare – is served. Dishes include *moles* hand-ground in a *molcajete* (traditional mortar and pestle) with a contemporary twist and stylish presentation. Reservations recommended. Take a taxi to get here.

🍷 Drinking & Nightlife

Every evening, the Jardín de la Unión comes alive with people crowding the out-door tables, strolling and listening to the street musicians and mariachi bands. The city's immense student population means that there is a very busy and accessible bar scene in town. Thursday is generally their big night out, though drinking and dancing establishments in Guanajuato generally start late and go on until the students really ought to be back in class!

★**Beer Company** BAR
(www.facebook.com/tbcgto; Cantarranas 56; ☺1pm-midnight Mon-Sat) Not the place to come looking for a glass of wine...the Beer Company is a small, narrow bar with a roof terrace and the best selection of craft beers (Mexican and international) in the city. In fact, with over 50 different kinds, you could fill a whole holiday trying them all.

Cafe Conquistador CAFE
(Positos 35; ☺8am-11pm Mon-Sat, to 10pm Sun) Delightful hole-in-the-wall cafe where most of the space is taken up by a huge coffee roaster and grinder and there's only just room to squeeze in a couple of chairs around it. It offers an array of brews and unlike most Mexican coffee it's actually strong.

La Inundación de 1905 BAR
(San Fernando Plaza; ☺10am-midnight Tue-Sun) Students love this relaxed spot, named after the city's 1905 flood, for its flowing beer and, thanks to the tables out on the pretty square, the beer-garden atmosphere.

Los Lobos BAR
(Doblado 2; ☺7pm-3am Mon-Sat) This cool, gay-friendly place is decked out with images of devils and *Catrinas* (skeleton dolls) plastered on every available surface. The crowd is far less ghoulish, however, and there's a

---

CALLEJONEADOS – THE TRADITIONAL WAY TO PARTY

The *callejoneada* tradition is said to have come from Spain. A group of professional singers and musicians, dressed in traditional costumes, starts up in a central location such as a plaza, a crowd gathers, then the whole mob winds through the alleyways, streets and plazas playing, dancing and singing heartily. In Guanajuato they are also called *estudiantinas*. Stories and jokes (in Spanish) are told in between songs, often relating to the legends of the alleys. In Zacatecas there are no stories, but hired bands called *tamboras* (dressed in uniform, not traditional attire) lead dancing revelers. On special occasions a *burro* (donkey) laden with wine is brought along. Often, strangers are just expected to join the party and the crowd swells. Occasionally, the organizers foot the bill; sometimes you pay a small amount for the wine you drink (or you bring your own). In Guanajuato the groups themselves or tour companies sell tickets (around M$100 for 1¼ hours; Tuesday to Sunday) for the *callejoneadas* and juice (not alcohol) is provided. It's great fun.

great soundtrack and a pool table in the back room. They have frequent live music.

Café Tal CAFE
(☑473-111-77-17; www.cafe-tal.com.mx; Temezcuitate 4; snacks M$30-60; ☺7am-midnight Mon-Fri, from 8am Sat & Sun; ☜) Spread over two buildings on either side of a steep, narrow side street, this student favorite is always busy with modish young things who love the owners' passion for roasting coffee right on the premises. Don't miss the *beso negro* ('black kiss'), ultra-concentrated hot chocolate (M$20). If you're lucky, Tal the cat might sit on your lap.

☆ Entertainment

Teatro Cervantes THEATER
(☑473-732-11-69; Plaza Allende s/n) Has a full schedule of performances during the Cervantino festival (p675) and less regular shows at other times. Look for posters advertising shows. Statues of Don Quixote and Sancho Panza grace the small Plaza Allende, in front of the theater.

🔒 Shopping

Xocola-T FOOD
(Plazuela del Baratillo 15; ☺9am-9pm Mon-Sat, 10am-6pm Sun) This chocoholic's nirvana sells delectable rich, handmade chocolates of pure cocoa. Quirkier fillings include *chapulines*, *gusanos* (caterpillars) and *nopal*.

Mercado Hidalgo MARKET
(Av Juárez; ☺8am-9pm) Guanajuato's atmospheric and bustling market is chockablock with tourist paraphernalia, artisan products and food stalls. It's well worth a visit.

ℹ Information

Incredibly, the only formal information points in Guanajuato are two small **tourist kiosks** (Jardín de la Unión; ☺9am-6pm), located at Jardín de la

Unión and an extension of this, in Calle Allende. Note: do not confuse these with official-looking booths marked 'Information Turística' that are dotted around town. The latter are private companies touting specific hotels and other services.

Banks along Avenida Juárez change cash, offer advances on credit cards and have ATMs.

Centro Médico la Presa (☑473-102-31-00; www.centromedicolapresa.mx; Paseo de la Presa 85; ☺24hr)

Hospital General (☑473-733-15-76, 473-733-15-73; www.salud.guanajuato.gob.mx; Carretera a Silao Km 6.5)

Post Office (Ayuntamiento 25; ☺8am-4:30pm Mon-Fri, to noon Sat)

ℹ Getting There & Away

AIR
Guanajuato is served by the **Aeropuerto Internacional de Guanajuato** (Aeropuerto Internacional del Bajío; ☑472-748-21-20; www.aeropuertosgap.com.mx; Silao), which is about 30km west of the city, near the town of Silao.

BUS
Guanajuato's **Central de Autobuses** (☑473-733-28-36; Silao 450) is around 5km southwest of town (confusingly, to get there you go northwest out of town along Tepetapa). Buy deluxe and 1st-class bus tickets (ETN and Primera Plus) online direct from the bus-company websites.

Primera Plus and ETN are the main 1st-class operators, while Flecha Amarilla has cheaper services to Dolores Hidalgo, León and San Miguel de Allende.

ℹ Getting Around

A taxi to Aeropuerto Internacional de Guanajuato will cost about M$400 (there's a set rate of M$450 from the airport; you buy your ticket at a taxi counter inside the airport). A cheaper option from Guanajuato is one of the special airport buses from the bus station (M$60), which depart the station at 7:40am, 11:40am, 1pm,

BUSES FROM GUANAJUATO

DESTINATION	FARE (M$)	TIME (HR)	FREQUENCY (PER DAY)
Dolores Hidalgo	86	1½	every 30min 5:30am-10:30pm
Guadalajara	477-630	4	frequent
León	87-96	1-1¼	frequent
Mexico City (Terminal Norte)	622-795	4½	frequent
Querétaro	255-315	2½	frequent
San Miguel de Allende	164-200	1½-2	frequent
Zacatecas	532	4	1pm

5:10pm and 5:40pm. These are timed to coincide with flight check-in times.

Between the bus station and downtown, 'Central de Autobuses' buses (M$8) run round the clock. From the center, you can catch them heading west on Avenida Juárez. From the bus terminal, you will enter a tunnel running east under the *centro histórico*. Alight at one of several entry/exit points: Mercado Hidalgo, Plaza de los Ángeles, Jardín de la Unión, Plaza Baratillo/Teatro Principal, Teatro Cervantes or Embajadoras. A taxi to/from the bus station costs around M$60.

To get around town keep a look out – local buses display their destination. For the *centro histórico* the rule of thumb is as follows: all buses heading east go via the tunnels below Avenida Juárez (eg if you want to go from the market to the Teatro Principal). Those heading west go along Avenida Juárez.

City buses (M$8) run from 7am to 10pm. Taxis are plentiful in the center and charge about M$40 for short trips around town (slightly more if heading uphill to El Pípila and the like).

Buses to **Bocamina San Ramón & Bocamina de San Cayetano** (Insurgencia; M$8) leave from Calle Insurgencia near Plaza Alhóndiga.

León

📵 477 / POP 1.23 MILLION / ELEV 1815M

There's no real reason to visit industrial León, 56km west of Guanajuato, but due to its importance as a main bus hub within the state of Guanajuato you may well have to change buses here. Also, it's only 20km from Aeropuerto Internacional de Guanajuato. It's unlikely you'll need to stay here; bus connections are plentiful.

❶ Getting There & Away

Aeropuerto Internacional de Guanajuato is 20km southeast of León on the Mexico City road. Many US airlines offer flights between US cities and here. Unfortunately, no bus service operates between Aeropuerto Internacional de Guanajuato and central León. A taxi between León and the airport costs around M$300 (M$380 from the airport using the official airport taxis).

Central de Autobuses (Blvd Hilario Medina s/n), just north of Blvd López Mateos and 2.5km east of downtown, has a cafeteria, left luggage and a money exchange. There are regular 1st- and 2nd-class services to most cities in northern and central Mexico.

Dolores Hidalgo

📵 418 / POP 152,000 / ELEV 1920M

Dolores Hidalgo is a compact, working town with a pretty, tree-filled plaza, a relaxed ambience and an important history. Amazingly enough, the Mexican independence movement began in earnest in this small place when at 5am on September 16, 1810, Miguel Hidalgo, the parish priest, rang the bells to summon people to church earlier than usual and issued the Grito de Dolores (Cry of Dolores), also known as the Grito de Independencia (Cry of Independence).

Today Hidalgo is one of Mexico's most revered heroes. Dolores was renamed in his honor in 1824. Mexicans swarm here for Independence Day (September 16), during which time the price of accommodations can more than double. The town's *centro histórico* is worth a half-day visit for history buffs, not only for its interesting independence-themed museums but also for its colored Talavera ceramics workshops and famous ice cream.

It's an easy day trip from San Miguel de Allende and an absolute contrast to that town.

◎ Sights

Parroquia de Nuestra Señora de Dolores   CHURCH

(Plaza Principal) The Parroquia de Nuestra Señora de Dolores is the church where Hidalgo issued the famous *Grito* (a call to arms for the country's independence) and is the focal point for the town's independence-day celebrations each year. It has a fine 18th-century

BUSES FROM LEÓN

DESTINATION	FARE (M$)	TIME	FREQUENCY (PER DAY)
Aguascalientes	205-270	2-2½hr	frequent
Guadalajara	396-530	3hr	10
Guanajuato	87-115	45min	frequent
Mexico City (Terminal Norte)	350-750	5hr	frequent (24hr)
San Miguel de Allende	239-320	2¼hr	frequent
Zacatecas	445-555	4hr	frequent

MIGUEL HIDALGO: ¡VIVA MEXICO!

The balding head of the visionary priest Father Miguel Hidalgo y Costilla is familiar to anyone who has ogled Mexican statues or murals. A genuine rebel idealist, Hidalgo sacrificed his career and risked his life on September 16, 1810, when he launched the independence movement.

Born on May 8, 1753, son of a criollo (Mexican-born person of Spanish parentage) hacienda manager in Guanajuato, he earned a bachelor's degree and, in 1778, was ordained a priest. He returned to teach at his alma mater in Morelia and eventually became rector. But he was no orthodox cleric: Hidalgo questioned many Catholic traditions, read banned books, gambled, danced and had a mistress.

In 1800 he was brought before the Inquisition. Nothing was proven, but a few years later, in 1804, he found himself transferred as priest to the hick town of Dolores.

Hidalgo's years in Dolores show his growing interest in the economic and cultural welfare of the people. He started several new industries: silk was cultivated, olive groves were planted and vineyards established, all in defiance of the Spanish colonial authorities. Earthenware building products were the foundation of the ceramics industry that today produces fine glazed pots and tiles.

When Hidalgo met Ignacio Allende from San Miguel, they shared a criollo discontent with the Spanish stranglehold on Mexico. Hidalgo's standing among the mestizos (people of mixed European and indigenous ancestry) and indigenous people of his parish was vital in broadening the base of the rebellion that followed.

Shortly after his Grito de Independencia, Hidalgo was formally excommunicated for 'heresy, apostasy and sedition.' He defended his call for Mexican independence and stated furthermore that the Spanish were not truly Catholic in any religious sense of the word but only for political purposes, specifically to rape, pillage and exploit Mexico. A few days later, on October 19, Hidalgo dictated his first edict calling for the abolition of slavery in Mexico.

Hidalgo led his growing forces from Dolores to San Miguel, Celaya and Guanajuato, north to Zacatecas, south almost to Mexico City and west to Guadalajara. But then, pushed northward, their numbers dwindled and on July 30, 1811, having been captured by the Spanish, Hidalgo was shot by a firing squad in Chihuahua. His head was returned to the city of Guanajuato, where it hung in a cage for 10 years on an outer corner of the Alhóndiga de Granaditas, along with the heads of fellow independence leaders Allende, Aldama and Jiménez. Rather than intimidating the people, this lurid display kept the memory, the goal and the example of the heroic martyrs fresh in everyone's mind. After independence the cages were removed, and the skulls (and bodies) of the heroes are now in the Monumento a la Independencia in Mexico City.

Churrigueresque facade. Legends surround his 'cry'; some say that Hidalgo uttered his famous words from the pulpit, others claim that he spoke at the church door to the people gathered outside.

Cuna de Tierra
WINERY

(☑ 418-152-60-60; www.cunadetierra.com; Carretera Dolores Hidalgo–San Luis de la Paz Km 11; ⏲ Tue-Sun by appointment) The first and biggest winery in Guanajuato opened in 2005, heralding the reintroduction of wine production in the area 200 years after the Spanish banned it, insisting instead on Mexicans drinking only Spanish wine. A variety of tastings and tours are available every day but you need to reserve a spot in advance. The white uses Sémillon grapes; reds are a mixture. Around 80,000 bottles are produced each year.

Museo Bicentenario 1810–2010
MUSEUM

(Casa del Capitán Mariano Abasolo; adult/student M$20/10, Sun free; ⏲10am-5pm Mon-Sat, to 3pm Sun) Previously the Presidencia Municipal, this museum was inaugurated in 2010 for Mexico's bicentennial celebrations. Despite its name, the majority of its seven rooms provide a cultural and historical context of the first 100 years of independence, including mementos produced for the centenary of 1910. Quirkier items include a stunning silk scarf embroidered with hair (depicting the image of Alejandro Zavala Mangas, an architect from Guanajuato city) and the original painted poster promoting the first century of independence. Signage is in Spanish only.

Museo de la
Independencia Nacional   MUSEUM
(Zacatecas 6; adult/student M$20/10; ⊙9am-4:45pm Tue-Sun) Although this museum has few relics, it has plenty of information on the independence movement. The exhibition spans seven rooms and charts the appalling decline in Nueva España's indigenous population between 1519 (an estimated 25 million) and 1605 (one million), and identifies 23 indigenous rebellions before 1800 as well as several criollo conspiracies in the years leading up to 1810. There are vivid paintings, quotations and details on the heroic last 10 months of Hidalgo's life.

Museo Casa de Hidalgo   MUSEUM
(🖉418-182-01-71; cnr Hidalgo & Morelos; adult/student M$45/20, free Sun; ⊙9am-5:45pm Tue-Sat) Miguel Hidalgo lived in this house when he was Dolores' parish priest. It was from here, in the early hours of September 16, 1810, that Hidalgo, Ignacio Allende and Juan de Aldama set off to launch the uprising against colonial rule. The house is now something of a national shrine – think memorials, replicas of Hidalgo's furniture and independence-movement documents, including the order for Hidalgo's excommunication.

🎊 Festivals & Events

Día de la Independencia   HISTORICAL
(⊙Sep 16) As the scene of the Grito de Independencia, Dolores hosts major Día de la Independencia celebrations on September 16, which the Mexican president may officiate – according to tradition – in his fifth year of office.

🍴 Sleeping & Eating

Don't leave without sampling a hand-turned ice cream (around M$20) from an ice-cream vendor on the plaza or around town. You can test your taste buds on the flavors: *mole*,

chicharrón (fried pork skin), avocado, corn, cheese, honey, shrimp, beer, tequila and tropical fruits.

Posada Cocomacán   HOTEL $
(🖉418-182-60-86; www.posadacocomacan.com.mx; Plaza Principal 4; s/d M$450/600; 🛜) The centrally located Cocomacán is an aged but reliable option and has lots of Mexican ambience. Of the 37 rooms, those on the upper levels, with windows on to the street, are the best (but noisiest). There's also a restaurant (open 8am to 10:30pm).

★DaMónica   ITALIAN $$
(🖉418-182-45-87; Nayarit 67; mains M$150-200; ⊙10:30am-10:30pm Wed-Sun) This unexpectedly snazzy and inviting culinary marvel is hosted by Mónica, the Italian owner, whose team whips up tasty Italian delights such as lasagna, pizza and gourmet seafood treats.

🛍 Shopping

Talavera ceramics have been the signature handicraft of Dolores ever since Padre Hidalgo founded the town's first ceramics workshop in the early 19th century. Head to the Zona Artesanal; the workshops along Avenida Jiménez, five blocks west of the plaza; or (by car) to Calzada de los Héroes, the exit road to San Miguel de Allende.

ℹ Information

Tourist Office (🖉418-182-11-64; www.dolores hidalgo.com; Plaza Principal; ⊙9am-5pm Mon-Fri, 10am-2pm Sat) On Plaza Principal's southeastern side. The helpful staff provide maps and information.

ℹ Getting There & Away

The **Primera Plus/Coordinados (Flecha Amarilla) bus station** (Hidalgo) is 2½ blocks south of the plaza, near the **Herradura de Plata/Autovías bus station** (🖉418-182-29-37; cnr Chiapas & Yucatán).

BUSES FROM DOLORES HIDALGO

DESTINATION	FARE (M$)	TIME	FREQUENCY (PER DAY)
Guanajuato	82	1¼hr	frequent
León	150	2¼hr	3
Mexico City (Terminal Norte) via Querétaro	430	5-6hr	frequent
Querétaro	147	2hr	hourly
San Luis Potosí	208	2¼hr	hourly
San Miguel de Allende	55-58	45min	frequent

San Miguel de Allende

📶 415 / POP 73,000 / ELEV 1900M

With its gorgeous colonial architecture, enchanting cobblestone streets and striking light, San Miguel de Allende is pure visual poetry and easily one of the most beautiful towns in Mexico. Not surprisingly it has been popular with aesthetes and romantics for much of the past century. This includes a large population of North Americans who either live full time in the town or maintain winter homes here, bringing with them a cosmopolitan atmosphere you'll find in few other Mexican towns.

With good restaurants and high-class accommodations, numerous galleries stocked with quality Mexican *artesanías*, a fantastic spring-like climate and a surfeit of cultural activities including regular festivals, fireworks and parades, most people find San Miguel a real Mexican highlight.

However, not everyone falls under the town's spell. Maybe it's because English seems to be more commonly heard on the streets than Spanish? Perhaps it's because the town seems to have been overly gentrified for tourists? Whatever the reason, for some people the old town of San Miguel can come across as a bit soulless.

History

The town, so the story goes, owes its founding to a few overheated dogs. These hounds were loved by a Franciscan friar, Juan de San Miguel, who started a mission in 1542 near an often-dry river 5km from the present town. One day the dogs wandered off from the mission; they were found reclining at the spring called **El Chorro**. The mission was moved to this superior site.

San Miguel was then central Mexico's most northern Spanish settlement. Tarascan and Tlaxcalan allies of the Spanish were brought to help pacify the local Otomí and Chichimecs. San Miguel was barely surviving the fierce Chichimec resistance, until in 1555 a Spanish garrison was established to protect the new road from Mexico City to the silver center of Zacatecas. Spanish ranchers settled in the area and it grew into a thriving commercial center and home to some of Guanajuato's wealthy silver barons.

San Miguel's favorite son, Ignacio Allende, was born here in 1769. He became a fervent believer in the need for Mexican independence and was a leader of a Querétaro-based conspiracy that set December 8, 1810, as the date for an armed uprising. When the plan was discovered by the authorities in Querétaro on September 13, a messenger rushed to San Miguel and gave the news to Juan de Aldama, another conspirator. Aldama sped north to Dolores where, in the early hours of September 16, he found Allende at the house of the priest Miguel Hidalgo, also one of the coterie. A few hours later Hidalgo proclaimed rebellion from his church. After initial successes Allende, Hidalgo and other rebel leaders were captured in 1811 in Chihuahua. Allende was executed, but on independence in 1821 he was recognized as a martyr and in 1826 the town was renamed San Miguel de Allende.

In the early part of the 20th century a major influenza outbreak almost caused the town to be abandoned, but art came to the rescue! The Escuela de Bellas Artes was founded in 1938 and the town started to take on its current character when David Alfaro Siqueiros began mural-painting courses that attracted artists of every persuasion. The Instituto Allende opened in 1951, also attracting foreign students. Many were US war veterans (who could settle here under the GI Bill); an influx of artists has continued ever since. Today you're just as likely to hear English spoken on the streets as Spanish.

◎ Sights

★ Museo Histórico de San Miguel de Allende   MUSEUM

(Museo Casa de Allende; Cuna de Allende 1; M$50; ◎ 9am-5pm Tue-Sun) This is the house where Mexican independence hero Ignacio Allende was born in 1769, a fact that draws a steady stream of Mexican pilgrims year-round. The building is also home to the town's history museum, which relates the interesting history of the San Miguel area. Upstairs, reproductions of the Allende family's furnishings and possessions aim to give an idea of living conditions for the well to do of the period. It's well presented with signage in Spanish and English.

Oratorio de San Felipe Neri   CHURCH

(Plaza Cívica) Located near the east end of Insurgentes, this multitowered and domed church dates from the 18th century. The pale-pink main facade is baroque with an indigenous influence. A passage to the right of this facade leads to the east wall, where a doorway holds the image of Nuestra Señora de la Soledad (Our Lady of Solitude). You can see into the cloister from this side of the church.

Inside the church are 33 oil paintings showing scenes from the life of San Felipe Neri, the 16th-century Florentine who founded the Oratorio Catholic order. In the east transept is a painting of the Virgin of Guadalupe by leading colonial painter Miguel Cabrera. In the west transept is a lavishly decorated 1735 chapel, the **Santa Casa de Loreto**, a replica of a chapel in Loreto, Italy, legendary home of the Virgin Mary. Although rarely open, the *camarín* (chapel behind the main church) has six elaborately gilded baroque altars. In one is a reclining wax figure of San Columbano; it supposedly contains the saint's bones.

Jardín Botánico
El Charco del Ingenio   GARDENS
(📋 415-154-47-15; www.elcharco.org.mx; off Antiguo Camino Real a Querétaro; M$50; ☺ 9am-5pm) San Miguel's 88-hectare botanical garden is also a wildlife and bird sanctuary. Pathways head through wetlands and magnificent areas of cacti and native plants. The deep canyon at the bottom boasts the eponymous freshwater spring, El Charco del Ingenio. Don't miss the Conservatory of Mexican Plants, which houses cacti and succulent species. Two-hour tours (in English) depart every Tuesday and Thursday at 10am (M$80). Bird-watching tours take place at 9am on the first and third Wednesday of the month.

The garden is 1.5km northeast of town. A 2km vehicle track leads north from the Soriana shopping center, 2.5km southeast of the center on the Querétaro road. This can be reached on 'Soriana' buses from the bus stop from Mesones, near Plaza Cívica (10 minutes, M$5). A taxi to the gardens from the center costs from around M$80. It can be hard to find a taxi back down again after your visit so either be prepared to walk or take the driver's number. You can also walk up (very much up!) to the gardens in a little over 30 minutes.

Parroquia de San Miguel Arcángel   CHURCH
(Plaza Principal) San Miguel's most famous sight is its parish church, characterized by its pink 'wedding cake' towers that soar above the town. These strange pinnacles were designed by indigenous stonemason Zeferino Gutiérrez in the late 19th century. He reputedly based the design on a postcard of a Belgian church and instructed builders by scratching plans in the sand with a stick. The rest of the church dates from the late 17th century.

In the chapel to the left of the main altar is the much-revered image of the Cristo de la Conquista (Christ of the Conquest), made in Pátzcuaro from cornstalks and orchid bulbs, probably in the 16th century. The adjacent Iglesia de San Rafael was founded in 1742.

La Esquina: Museo del
Juguete Popular Mexicano   MUSEUM
(www.museolaesquina.org.mx; Núñez 40; adult/child M$50/20; ☺ 10am-6pm Tue-Sat, 11am-4pm Sun; 👣) This bright, modern museum is a must-visit for all kids, big or small. The toy collection of museum owner Angélica Tijerina has taken over half a century to amass and aims to preserve and continue various traditions by showcasing pieces from different regions of Mexico. The exhibits – divided into four main themed areas – are made of a range of materials, from wheat to plastic, and wood to fabric.

Escuela de Bellas Artes   GALLERY
(School of Fine Arts, Centro Cultural Nigromante; 📋 415-152-02-89; www.facebook.com/bellasartes sma; Hernández Macías 75; ☺ 10am-6pm Mon-Sat, to 2pm Sun) This former monastery was converted into a fine-arts school in 1938. Don't miss the murals of Pedro Martínez, plus the Siqueiros Room, which features the extraordinary unfinished mural by David Alfaro Siqueiros in the far corner of the complex. The rest of the gallery holds temporary exhibitions from local artists, many of whom graduated from the school.

Other Face of Mexico Gallery   MUSEUM
(📋 415-154-43-24; www.casadelacuesta.com; Casa de la Cuesta, Cuesta de San José 32; M$50) This fascinating private collection of more than 500 masks provides an excellent context to the Mexican mask tradition. It is open by appointment only. The admission fee goes to charity.

Instituto Allende   HISTORIC BUILDING
(Ancha de San Antonio 20) This large 1736 complex, originally the home of the aristocratic De La Canal family, was later used as a Carmelite convent, eventually becoming an art and language school in 1951. These days it's split into two – one area of gardens and an old chapel is used for functions, the other for courses. Above the main entrance is a carving of the Virgin of Loreto, patroness of the De La Canal family, while inside a mural depicts the history of Mexico.

Templo de la Salud   CHURCH
(Plaza Cívica) With its blue and yellow tiled dome and big shell carved above its entrance,

NORTHERN CENTRAL HIGHLANDS SAN MIGUEL DE ALLENDE

San Miguel de Allende

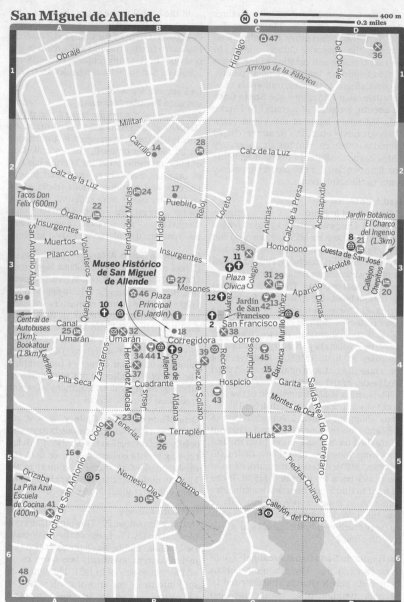

this church is just east of San Felipe Neri. The facade is early Churrigueresque. The church was once part of the Colegio de Sales, and its paintings include one of San Javier by Miguel Cabrera. San Javier (St Francis Xavier; 1506–52) was a founding member of the Jesuits. It was once part of the Colegio de Sales.

Templo de la Concepción CHURCH
(Church of the Conception; cnr Zacateros & Canal)
A splendid church with a fine altar and several magnificent old oil paintings. Painted on the interior doorway are a number of wise sayings to give pause to those entering. The church was begun in the mid-18th cen-

San Miguel de Allende

tury; its dome, added in the late 19th century, by the versatile Zeferino Gutiérrez, was possibly inspired by pictures of Les Invalides in Paris.

Capilla de la Tercera Orden   CHAPEL
(Chapel of the Third Order; cnr San Francisco & Juárez) Built in the early 18th century, this chapel, like the nearby **Templo de San Francisco** (cnr San Francisco & Juárez), was part of a Franciscan monastery complex. The main facade shows St Francis and symbols of the Franciscan order.

Activities

Balneario Xote   SWIMMING
(☏ 415-155-83-30; www.xoteparqueacuatico.com.mx; adult/child M$160/80; ☉9am-6pm;) The family-oriented Balneario Xote water park is 3.5km off the highway down a cobblestone road. It's a great place to go with kids, as it has multiple areas for children and several waterslides and pools.

La Gruta   SWIMMING
(☏ 415-185-21-62; www.spalagruta.com; Carretera Dolores Hidalogo–San Miguel de Allende Km 10; M$200; ☉7am-5pm) Upmarket La Gruta is justifiably a local and tourist favorite –it has three small pools where a thermal spring is channeled. The hottest is in a cave, which is entered through a 27m tunnel, with water gushing from the roof, lit by a single shaft of sunlight. It also offers quality spa treatments and has a good restaurant.

Escondido Place   SWIMMING
(☏ 415-185-20-22; www.escondidoplace.com; Carretera San Miguel de Allende–Dolores Hidalgo Km 10; M$150; ☉8am-5:30pm) Escondido Place has seven small outdoor pools and three connected indoor pools, with each one being progressively hotter. The picturesque grounds have plenty of picnicking space and there's a kiosk for drinks and snacks.

🎓 Courses

Several institutions offer Spanish courses, with group or private lessons and optional classes in Mexican culture and history. Most private lessons cost around US$20 an hour; group and long-term rates are much lower. Homestays with Mexican families, including a private room and three daily meals, cost around US$35 per day. Cooking courses are also very popular here.

La Piña Azul Escuela de Cocina COOKING
(🖉415-101-41-55; www.pinaazulcookingschool.com; Orizaba 39A; class per person US$85) Kirsten West, former private chef to Mick Jagger and a world expert on Mexican cuisine, opened her own Mexican cookery school in 2016. On her Market to Taco class you will buy ingredients at the market and then she'll help you chop and sizzle them up into your very own perfect taco!

Classes require a minimum of four participants and are taught in English.

El Liceo de la Lengua Española LANGUAGE
(🖉415-121-25-35; www.liceodelalengua.com; Callejón del Pueblito 5) A small, centrally located and extremely professional Spanish school, where classes never exceed five pupils. Classes start at US$55 for seven hours of tuition. To find the school, look for the big Mexican flag on top of the building.

Academia Hispano Americana LANGUAGE
(AHA! Spanish; 🖉415-152-03-49; www.academiahispanoamericana.com; Mesones 4; ☉8:30am-4:30pm Mon-Fri) Housed in a beautiful colonial building, this place has been going for 60 years; it runs quality immersion Spanish language courses incorporating history classes.

Warren Hardy Spanish LANGUAGE
(🖉415-154-40-17; www.warrenhardy.com; San Rafael 6) A North American–run school offering Spanish instruction including its own range of printed learning materials, Warren Hardy Spanish is a favorite among local expats of a mature age.

👉 Tours

★ Bici-Burro CYCLING
(🖉415-152-15-26; www.bici-burro.com; Hospicio 1; tours US$70-120) Friendly and professional, English-speaking owner Alberto conducts 10 different guided mountain-bike tours for groups of two or more and two different hiking circuits. Popular trips include six- or seven-hour excursions to Atotonilco or Min-

eral de Pozos and a wonderful 'mezcal tour' that takes in a number of haciendas. Bike rental (US$35 per day) is also available.

Albert Coffee Archaeotours TOURS
(🖉415-102-55-83; www.albertcoffeetours.com; Carrillo 5B; ☉10am-6pm Mon-Sat) Excellent guided tours (from US$50 per person) to the Cañada de la Virgen (p690) archeological site. Tours are led by an archaeologist but are in Spanish only.

Historical Walking Tour of San Miguel de Allende WALKING
(🖉415-152-77-96; www.historicalwalkingtour.org; Jardín Allende; M$300) This excellent tour takes place every Monday, Wednesday and Friday at 10am, departing from El Jardín. Tickets go on sale at 9:45am; be sure to allow good time as tours leave promptly. The English-speaking volunteer guides provide a fascinating historical, architectural and cultural commentary on the town's sights. Specialized architecture and private tours are also available.

Xotolar Ranch Adventures HORSEBACK RIDING
(🖉415-154-62-75; www.xotolarranch.com; rides from US$95) Xotolar Ranch Adventures, based on a working ranch, specializes in canyon trail rides, which can be booked as half- or full-day excursions. One tour involves riding to the pyramid of Cañada de la Virgen (p690; US$145 per person).

Bookatour TOURS
(🖉415-154-86-21; www.bookatour.mx; Estación 28; ☉10am-2pm Mon-Fri) Offers a range of walking tours with bilingual guides, including illuminating three-hour strolls around San Miguel (US$40) and hot-air-balloon rides (US$175 per person). Prices are the same for up to three people and include transportation.

🎊 Festivals & Events

San Miguel boasts a surfeit of churches (over 40) and patron saints (it has six) and enjoys a multitude of festivals, many imbued with strong spiritual themes. You'll probably be alerted to a festival event by firework bursts, while parades seem to be an almost weekly occurrence. For a full list, check with the tourist office (p692) or its website: www.visitsanmiguel.travel.

Semana Santa RELIGIOUS
(☉Mar/Apr) A week of religious activities. Two Sundays before Easter, pilgrims carry an im-

age of the Señor de la Columna from Atotonilco, 11km north, to San Miguel's church of San Juan de Dios, departing at midnight on Saturday. During Semana Santa, activities include the solemn Procesión del Santo Entierro on Good Friday and the burning or exploding of Judas effigies on Easter Day.

Fiesta de la Santa Cruz FIESTA
(☺ late May) This deeply spiritual spring festival has its roots in the 16th century. It happens at Valle del Maíz, 2km from the town center. Oxen are dressed in lime necklaces and painted tortillas, and their yokes are festooned with flowers and fruit. A mock battle between 'Indians' and 'Federales' follows. There are *mojigangas*, fireworks, dancing and musicians.

Fiesta de los Locos RELIGIOUS
(☺ mid-Jun) Part of the Festividad de San Antonio de Padua in mid-June, the 'festival of the crazies' is a colorful Carnavalesque parade through town with floats, blaring music and costumed dancers throwing out candy to – sometimes at! – the crowd. It takes place on the first Sunday after June 13.

San Miguel Arcángel RELIGIOUS
(Jardín Allende; ☺ Sep) Celebrations honoring the town's chief patron saint are held around the weekend following September 29. The party is celebrated with an *alborada,* an artificial dawn created by thousands of fireworks around the cathedral, and turns into an all-night festivity with extraordinary pre-Hispanic dances.

Guanajuato International Film Festival FILM
(GIFF; www.giff.mx; ☺ Jul) Shared with the city of Guanajuato, this short-film festival in July was founded with the intention of promoting homegrown cinema production, something it's done to great acclaim. Events include Cine entre Muertos, where horror films are screened in graveyards. Hopefully the films aren't scary enough to wake the dead!

🛌 Sleeping

Accommodations in San Miguel are generally expensive. However, thanks to a couple of fairly recent hostel additions, the city has now become somewhat more affordable for budget travelers. For those with money to burn, San Miguel has some of Mexico's best luxury B&Bs, boutique hotels and guesthouses. It's essential to book in advance for most of the B&Bs, as they can't always take walk-in guests and there might not be anyone onsite if they don't know you're coming. During festivals all accommodations book out way in advance.

Hostal Punto 79 HOSTEL $
(☎ 415-121-10-34; www.punto79.com; Mesones 79; dm M$210-250, s/d from M$920/1840, without bathroom M$600/1200; ☺ 🖥) This centrally located spot is the best hostel in town (though

---

WORTH A TRIP

SANCTUARIO DE ATOTONILCO

Known as Mexico's Sistine Chapel, this vitally important **church** (www.santuariodeatotonilco.org; Principal, Atotonilco; M$15; ☺ 10am-6pm Mon-Fri, from 1pm Sat, 10am-noon & 1:30-6pm Sun) in the hamlet of Atotonilco, 11km north of San Miguel, is defined by its connection to the independence struggle, which has made it an important icon for Mexicans. Nationalist hero Ignacio Allende married here in 1802, and eight years later he returned with Miguel Hidalgo and a band of independence rebels en route from Dolores to San Miguel to take the shrine's banner of the Virgin of Guadalupe as their flag.

A journey to Atotonilco is the goal of pilgrims and penitents from all over Mexico, and the starting point of an important and solemn procession two weekends before Easter. Participants carry the image of the Señor de la Columna to the church of San Juan de Dios in San Miguel.

Inside, the sanctuary has six chapels and is vibrant with statues, folk murals and paintings. Traditional dances are held here on the third Sunday in July. The church was named a Unesco World Heritage site in 2008.

It's free to visit the main part of the church, which has some lovely paintings, but to visit the side chapel with some truly exquisite paintings (and some far less exquisite mannequins depicting Biblical scenes!) you'll need to pay M$15. From San Miguel, taxis charge around M$200 for a one-way trip. Local buses signed 'Atotonilco' or 'Cruz del Palmar' depart from Calzada de La Luz every hour on the half-hour (M$10, 45 minutes).

that's not saying much!). The dorm rooms are segregated for male and female guests and are a decent place to bed down. Private rooms are less impressive. There are few facilities (and no breakfast), but it's a good place to meet other travelers.

Hostel Inn HOSTEL $

(☑ 415-154-67-27; www.hostelinnmx.com; Calz de La Luz 31A; incl breakfast dm from M$190, s M$580, r from M$670; ◒ ⊛) This functional converted house offers dorms and simple fan-cooled private rooms, a kitchen for guests to use, cheap laundry services and a small back garden with grassy lawns and a pleasant common area. It's on a busy main road, but most of the rooms don't look over the street.

★ Casa Maricela B&B $$

(☑ 415-152-66-31; www.casamaricela-bnb.com; Jesús 41; r incl breakfast from M$1100; ◒ ⊛) Offering perhaps the best value for money in town, this superfriendly, Mexican family-run place (great English spoken) is an absolute charmer. The homely rooms have funky wall art and bright textiles, quality mattresses and decent bathrooms. A top-notch breakfast is served at a big communal table. The roof terrace has heart-stirring city views.

Casa de la Noche GUESTHOUSE $$

(☑ 415-152-07-32; www.casadelanoche.com; Organos 19; r incl breakfast US$89-129; ⊛ ⊛) This fascinating boutique guesthouse claims to offer 'exceptional hospitality' and that seems appropriate considering that it was once a brothel! Despite its racy origins, the hotel today is a model of respectability, but even so photographs of some of the former 'hospitality experts' adorn the walls and the cheaper rooms are known as 'working girl rooms,' because yes, they were.

Rooms vary enormously in layout and size, but are all comfortable and cozy with underfloor heating. Guests can use the shared kitchen and the generous communal areas. Advance bookings essential.

★ Antigua Capilla BOUTIQUE HOTEL $$$

(☑ 415-152-40-48; www.antiguacapilla.com; Callejon Chepitos 16; r incl breakfast from US$134; P ◒ ⊛) Constructed around a tiny 17th-century chapel, this utterly stylish, spick-and-span place is hard to fault; it boasts every mod con and service imaginable plus extraordinary breakfasts and a gorgeous plant-lined courtyard. The English- and Spanish-speaking owners are delightful. Access is up a steep hill, but the rooftop terrace

affords one of the best views in San Miguel. Book in advance.

★ Hotel Amparo BOUTIQUE HOTEL $$$

(☑ 415-152-08-19; www.hotelamparo.com; Mesones 3; r incl breakfast from M$6000; ◒ ⊛ ⊛) This sublime hotel set in a painstakingly restored building pleases anyone lucky enough to snag a room, each of which is wildly different. You want classic colonial lines? They can do that. Or perhaps you prefer one with a more modern jazzy pop style? The uniting factor is all have had care and thought lavished upon them.

The rooms are set around a series of small courtyards complete with fountains and pools, and from the roof terrace there are gorgeous city views. Don't forget to have a predinner cocktail at the delightful, time-warp bar (open to nonguests). Service is friendly and efficient.

Casa Naré BOUTIQUE HOTEL $$$

(☑ 415-126-24-77; www.casanare.com.mx; Hernandez Macias 18; r incl breakfast from M$2700 Sun-Thu, M$3800 Fri & Sat; ◒ ⊛ ⊛) Friendly, good-value, family-run boutique guesthouse with huge, tastefully decorated rooms with high, domed brick ceilings. We loved the stylish, polished concrete bathrooms. It's a couple of minutes' walk from the main square.

Hacienda El Santuario BOUTIQUE HOTEL $$$

(☑ 415-152-10-42; www.haciendaelsantuario.com; Terraplén 42; r incl breakfast from M$2800; ◒ ⊛ ⊛) The communal areas of this boutique place, which is in a quiet part of town, are stuffed full of extravagant statues and other works of art (admire that Day of the Dead skeleton made from tiny carved butterflies), and there are extraordinary views from the roof terrace. The rooms are comfortable though surprisingly plain and small.

Dos Casas BOUTIQUE HOTEL $$$

(☑ 415-154-40-73; www.doscasas.com.mx; Quebrada 101; d incl breakfast from M$5490; ◒ ⊛ ⊛) This sleek sleep oozes contemporary style, with cream and black hues, fireplaces and mirrored, mosaic bathtubs. Twelve stunning rooms across two adjoining properties provide a touch of avant-garde luxury overseen by its architect owner. There's a spa, plus the restaurant Áperi (p690) in the courtyard is a culinary highlight of the region.

Rosewood San Miguel de Allende HERITAGE HOTEL $$$

(☑ 415-152-97-00; www.rosewoodhotels.com/en/san-miguel-de-allende; Nemesio Diez 11; r/ste incl breakfast from US$375/855; ⊝❄🛜🎦) The Rosewood is an over-the-top palace of a place, where seamless service, gorgeous classically decorated rooms and fairly staggering levels of opulence combine to create the ultimate weekend address. There's a great pool, beautiful manicured gardens and a rooftop bar with dizzying views over the domes and hills of San Miguel.

Casa de la Cuesta
B&B $$$

(📲415-154-43-24;　　　www.casadelacuesta.com; Cuesta de San José 32; r from M$3500; ⊝🛜) Perched on a hill behind the Mercado El Nigromante, this ornate and deeply Mexican place has spacious rooms in a decorative colonial mansion, lavish breakfasts and friendly, knowledgeable owners. Minimum stay of two nights and advance reservations are essential.

✗ Eating

San Miguel has a superb eating scene showcasing a startling variety of quality Mexican and international cuisine, and has repeatedly proven its reputation as one of Mexico's leading culinary capitals. A thriving cafe society prevails and gorgeous bakeries proliferate. As with anything to do with San Miguel, budget travelers will find their options more limited than in most other Mexican towns. However, several reliable food stands are on the corner of Ancha de San Antonio and tree-shaded Calle Nemesio Diez.

★Tostévere
TACOS $

(📲415-121-30-75; Codo 4; tacos M$50-80; ⊙1-9pm Mon, Wed & Thu, 2-10pm Fri & Sat, noon-6pm Sun) With a discreet, almost grimy exterior nothing would lead you to think that Tostévere is currently San Miguel's restaurant of the moment. Step inside though and you'll understand why. Delicious and highly inventive seafood-based tacos are served with an artistic swirl in a dimly lit, ultramodern setting. It's so popular you might have to wait for a seat.

★Baja Fish Taquito
TACOS $

(📲415-121-09-50; Mesones 11B; tacos from M$30, set meals from M$90; ⊙12:30-8pm Mon-Sat, to 7pm Sun; 🛜) You'll find extraordinarily solicitous staff here at this fabulous little joint specializing in mind-blowingly good Baja-style fish tacos and *tostadas*. While it may not look like much downstairs, where you can sit at the counter and watch the tacos being made, there's also a lovely upstairs terrace with good views of San Miguel's rooftops.

Victorias
MEXICAN $

(San Antonio 35; meals M$65-95; ⊙10am-6pm) This hazy-yellow place a short walk downhill from the old town has just four or five tables and a small selection of well-prepared and tasty enchiladas and quesadillas and is about as close as San Miguel gets to street food. It's very popular with local expats.

Tacos Don Felix
TACOS $

(📲415-154-05-05; www.tacosdonfelix.com; Fray Juan de San Miguel 15; tacos M$30-40, mains M$80-200; ⊙5-11pm Fri & Sat, 2-9:30pm Sun) An opportunity to get off the tourist trail presents itself at this pleasantly local establishment in the Colonia of San Rafael, a short way outside the center. Delicious tacos and friendly service await you either in the shady courtyard or the surprisingly large main restaurant. Take a taxi after dark.

El Manantial
BAR, CANTINA $

(Barranca 78; tacos M$85-95, tostadas M$40-60; ⊙1pm-1am Tue-Sun) Behind the swinging doors of a former saloon, 'The Spring' serves fabulously fresh ceviche in a dark and rather loud space with a cantina feel. It has a real buzz compounded by habanero salsa, the spiciest of chili sauces, and even though the staff can be somewhat surly, it's nearly always packed. Try the ginger margaritas (M$65).

San Agustín
CAFE $

(📲415-154-91-02; San Francisco 21; snacks M$30-80, mains M$70-180; ⊙8am-11pm Mon-Thu, 9am-midnight Fri-Sun) This is a 'don't leave San Miguel without...' experience. This sweet-tooth's paradise is the best place in the region for chocolate and *churros*, though you'll often have to wait in line just to get inside. Most people seem to think that it's well worth it, however.

Don Taco Tequila
TACOS $$

(📲415-154-96-08; Hernandez Macias 83; tacos around M$54; ⊙2-10pm Mon-Sat, to 8pm Sun) Trust San Miguel to turn the humble taco into hipster Instagram fodder! This stylish little restaurant serves wildly creative, fully vegan tacos that will please even a dedicated carnivore. Try the *campiramo* taco, which is filled with parboiled cactus with roasted tomatoes and cashew-nut cheese! The place also doubles as a chilled-out bar.

Lavanda
CAFE $$

(www.lavandacafe.com; Macías 87; breakfasts M$88-108; ⊙8:30am-8pm Mon-Sat, to 6pm Sun; 🛜📲) 🍴 A guitarist strums away during

WORTH A TRIP

CAÑADA DE LA VIRGEN

Cañada de la Virgen (M$50; ☺10am-4pm Tue-Sun) is an intriguing pre-Hispanic pyramid complex and former ritual and ceremonial location, dating from around 300 CE and in use until around 1050. Bones, believed to be from sacrificial ceremonies, and remnants were discovered here. The most interesting aspects include the alignment of the main temple to the planets, and the design of the site, which reflects the surrounding landscape. Although not as physically impressive as some Mexican pyramids, the site has its own special magic.

The site is around 25km southeast of San Miguel: possibly the easiest and most rewarding visit for non-Spanish speakers is to take a tour with Albert Coffee Archaeotours (p686) or **Coyote Canyon Adventures** (☎415-154-41-93; www.coyotecanyonadventures. com; rides per person half-/full day from M$1550/2450, 4-person minimum). The guides include archaeologists and anthropologists who discuss the site's fascinating cultural and historical context. Expect to pay around US$50. However, it's perfectly possible to visit completely independently. A taxi to the ticket office from San Miguel will cost around M$300. A shuttle bus is the compulsory transportation for visitors at the site. It runs between the ticket office and the ruins (several kilometers away); these depart on the hour between 10am and 4pm. At busy times you might have to queue for a seat so take a good book to read while you wait! Wear sensible shoes as you'll be walking on cobbled surfaces and steep steps. Note that larger bags are not allowed into the site due to some recent theft of relics.

popular breakfasts – get there at opening time or be prepared to queue – at this lovely place where killer coffee, superb egg dishes and delicious *cazuela* (clay cooking pot) dishes are served. The charming premises are divided into two: one high-ceilinged dining room and one garden courtyard.

Muro
MEXICAN $$

(☎415-152-63-41; www.cafemuro.com; Cerrada de San Gabriel 1; M$130-195; ☺9am-4pm Thu-Tue; 🛜) True, it's a bit of a walk from Centro, but most people are happy to make the effort. Muro serves everything from *chilaquiles con arrachera* (fried tortillas with steak) to French toast and pastries, plus fabulous freshly made juices, which combine to make it an awesome breakfast spot. Local ingredients are used where possible and the owners ensure you'll receive a warm welcome.

★Nomada
MEXICAN $$$

(☎415-121-61-65; www.facebook.com/nomadac ocinadeinterpretacion; Macias 88; mains M$170-220; ☺noon-10pm Mon-Sat, 9am-3pm Sun; 🛜🅿) This gorgeous place with friendly English-speaking staff has some of San Miguel's best contemporary Mexican and European cuisine. Try its signature dish, the delicious mushroom risotto, and afterward don't miss out on the coffee and fig flan. There's a highly recommended multicourse tasting menu served on Monday and Wednesday only. It's inside the Casa 88 Hotel.

★Áperi
INTERNATIONAL $$$

(☎415-152-09-41; www.aperi.mx; Dos Casas, Quebrada 101; 5-course tasting menu with/without wine pairing M$1300/900, mains M$360-480; ☺2-5pm & 6:30-11pm Wed-Mon; 🅿) This courtyard restaurant inside a boutique hotel (p688) is perhaps the best spot in town for fine dining. The chef here has been given the freedom to do whatever he wants and a regularly changing menu featuring the likes of duck, pork and seafood dishes, prepared with San Miguelense ingredients, is the result. Farm-to-table cuisine has never looked so glamorous.

The Chef's Table – a multicourse tasting menu for two to five people – starts at 6:30pm (by reservation). If you want to loosen the purse strings, this is the place to do it.

The Restaurant
INTERNATIONAL $$$

(☎415-154-78-62; www.therestaurantsanmiguel. com; Diez de Sollano 16; mains M$370-480; ☺noon-10pm Sun, Tue & Wed, to 11pm Thu-Sat) This fine-dining establishment set within a patio of a colonial building boasts an international menu with occasional Mexican influences, and features seasonal, organic produce inventively combined to sublime effect to leave you with a thoroughly memorable meal.

🍷 Drinking & Nightlife

In San Miguel, drinking and entertainment are often synonymous. Many bars (and restaurants) host live music; mostly on Thursday to Saturday nights, but at some places nightly. Calle Umarán has plenty of bars.

La Mezcalería
BAR

(Correo 47; ☺5-11pm) It's mezcal-mania time in San Miguel and this cool bar, where you can get your tongue around a mighty mix of mezcals from Oaxaca, plus good tapas plates (around M$120), is a local favorite. Don't miss the superb mezcal margarita.

Cantina El Tenampa
BAR

(Mesones 12; ☺10am-9pm) With taxidermied bulls heads jutting out of the walls and shelves full of dusty bottles, this is a real spit and sawdust, cowboy's kind of authentic cantina. And it's appropriate that it should feel like something from a Wild West movie because the owner's father was a true-blue cowboy. Be warned that this is not a regular tourist haunt.

La Azotea
BAR

(Umarán 6; ☺1pm-midnight) This roof-terrace cocktail lounge is a gay-friendly, laid-back place with a young and smart crowd; it's a top spot for sundowners.

El Café de la Mancha
CAFE

(www.facebook.com/elcafedelamancha; Recreo 21A; ☺8:30am-5:30pm Mon-Sat; ☏) Four people's a crowd in this tiny place that's just the spot for those who know you don't drink cappuccinos after noon! The trained owner-barista does magic with Mexican beans, and adopts every extraction method known to coffee culture (French press, Chemex, AeroPress, espresso).

☆ Entertainment

It's one big cultural party in San Miguel; check out what's on in *Atención San Miguel*. The Escuela de Bellas Artes (p683) and the Biblioteca (in the Sala Quetzal) host a variety of cultural events, many in English; check their noticeboards for schedules.

Teatro Ángela Peralta
THEATER

(☑415-152-22-00; www.teatroangelaperalta.webpin. com; cnr Mesones & Hernández Macías) Built in 1873, this elegant venue is the most impressive in town and hosts local productions, classical-music concerts and other cultural events. The ticket office is around the corner. Tickets cost between M$50 and M$500 depending on the production.

🔒 Shopping

San Miguel has a mind-boggling number of craft shops, selling folk art and handicrafts from all over the country. Anyone serious about buying should book an appointment at **Galería Atotonilco** (☑415-185-22-25; www. folkartsanmiguel.com; Camino Antiguo Ferrocarril 14, El Cortijo; ☺by appointment only). Local crafts include tinware, wrought iron, silver, brass, leather, glassware, pottery and textiles. Many shops are along Canal, San Francisco, Zacateros and Pila Seca. Price and quality varies.

Arts & Crafts
Part of the joy of wandering around San Miguel is to stumble upon the many galleries tucked away in streets around town; there are perhaps even more commercial galleries than there are cafes (and perhaps even real-estate agents) in San Miguel. The largest concentration of contemporary art galleries and design studios (mainly expatriates' work) is housed in the trendy **Fábrica La Aurora** (☑415-152-13-12; www.fabricalaaurora. com; Aurora s/n; ☺10am-6pm), a remodeled raw-cotton factory on the north end of town. It's a huge complex that's worth a visit even if you're not planning on buying. As well as the chance to browse the shops here (if you're intending to buy, be aware that this is all high-end, expensive art), there are also regular exhibitions, events and art-related workshops. The site also contains a nice cafe.

Markets
Famous **Tianguis** (Cienfuegos; ☺7am-6pm Tue), a huge outdoor affair beside the Soriana shopping center, 2.5km southeast of the center on the Querétaro road, makes an interesting excursion. Here you'll find a fantastic choice of fresh produce, and lots of lurid plastic goods; some may find the scale and crowds overwhelming. More centrally, **Mercado El Nigromante** (Colegio s/n; ☺8am-8pm) sells fruit, vegetables and other foodstuffs. An upmarket alternative to both is **TOSMA** (www.tosma.net; Ancha de San Antonio 32; ☺9am-4pm Sat), which runs all day Saturday in a lot off the Ancha de San Antonio and where you can find artisanal products, souvenirs and food stands.

ℹ️ Information

Don't even contemplate spending time in town without buying the weekly English- and Spanish-language newspaper *Atención San Miguel* (M$15). Published every Friday, it's chockablock with what's on for the coming week, including tours, concerts and gallery openings. It also lists yoga, Spanish, art and dance-class schedules. You can buy it at the public library and many cafes or from roaming vendors. The same people also publish *Que Pasa*, which gives the lowdown on things to see and do in and around the town.

Most banks have their own ATMs and are located on, or within two blocks of, El Jardín. There are also *casas de cambio* (money changers) on Correo.

BUSES FROM SAN MIGUEL DE ALLENDE

DESTINATION	FARE (M$)	TIME (HR)	FREQUENCY (PER DAY)
Celaya	64-105	1¾	every 15min
Dolores Hidalgo	55-58	1	every 30min 7am-7pm
Guadalajara	630-700	5¼-5½	6
Guanajuato	119-164	1-1½	hourly
León	265	2¼-2½	12
Mexico City (Terminal Norte)	445-520	3½-4¼	8
Querétaro	65-90	1-1½	every 40min 7am-8:30pm

The main **post office** (cnr Correo & Corregidora; ⊘8am-6pm Mon-Sat) can be found just off the Jardín, although for sending handicrafts or art home, it's better to use a delivery service such as **La Unión** (☑415-150-00-80; www.launionsan miguel.com; Umarán 25; ⊘10am-6pm Mon-Sat).

H+ San Miguel de Allende (☑415-152-59-00; www.hmassanmiguel.mx; Libramiento Jose Manuel Zavala 12) Your best bet for modern medical care and English-speaking doctors should you have a medical emergency.

Tourist Office (☑415-154-71-75, 415-152-09-00; www.visitsanmiguel.travel; Plaza Principal 8; ⊘9am-8pm Mon-Sat, to 5pm Sun) On the northern side of El Jardín. Good for town maps, promotional pamphlets and information on events.

❶ Getting There & Away

AIR

San Miguel's small airport is currently only for private planes but there has been talk in recent years of expanding the airport to allow larger commercial aircraft to land here. For the moment though, the nearest airport is the Aeropuerto Internacional de Guanajuato (p678), between León and Silao, around 1½ hours away by car. The obvious alternatives are Querétaro or Mexico City's airports.

BUS

The **Central de Autobuses** (Calz de la Estación 90) is on Canal, 3km west of the center. Second-class services (Coordinados/Flecha Amarilla and Herradura de Plata) also leave from this station. Other 1st-class buses serve Aguascalientes, Monterrey and San Luis Potosí.

CAR & MOTORCYCLE

Bajío Go offers a car-rental service. Otherwise use the agencies in Guanajuato or Bajío Airport.

❶ Getting Around

TO/FROM THE AIRPORT

Many agencies provide shuttle transportation to/from Guanajuato airport. These include **Viajes Vertiz** (☑415-152-18-56; www.facebook. com/viajesvertiz; Hidalgo 1A; ⊘9am-6:30pm Mon-Fri, 10am-2pm Sat), **Viajes San Miguel** (☑415-152-25-37; www.viajessanmiguel.com; Mesones 38, Interior 7; ⊘9am-7pm Mon-Fri, 10am-2pm Sat), **Bajío Go** (☑415-152-19-99; www.bajiogo.com; Jésus 11; ⊘8am-8pm Mon-Sat, 10am-3pm Sun) and Bookatour (p686). Alternatively, take a bus to Silao and get a taxi from there to the airport (around M$60). For Mexico City airport, get a bus to Querétaro and a bus directly to the airport from there.

If heading from the airport to San Miguel by bus, it's easiest to go to León by taxi and take a bus from there. No bus service operates between Guanajuato airport and central León. A taxi to León costs M$380 and to San Miguel M$1200 (for up to four people).

TO/FROM THE BUS STATION

Local buses (M$6) run from 7am to 9pm daily. 'Central' buses run regularly between the bus station and the town center. Coming into town, these terminate at the eastern end of Insurgentes after winding through the streets. Heading out of the center, you can pick one up on Canal. A taxi between the center and the bus station costs around M$60; trips around town cost around M$35.

Mineral de Pozos

☑442 / POP 3500 / ELEV 2217M

Not much more than a century ago, Mineral de Pozos was a flourishing silver-mining center of 70,000 people, but with the 1910 Revolution and the flooding of the mines, the population dwindled. Empty houses slowly evaporating into dust, a large and unfinished church and discarded mine shafts were the ghostly legacy of abandonment. Today this tiny place is gradually winning back its place on the map: houses have been restored and life has returned to the streets, but yet it still remains a haunting, wind-whipped village of low-rise buildings lit by rays of mountain light. Visitors can explore the crumbling buildings and tour the fascinating surrounds – including several mine ruins – by mountain bike, horse or guided tour. As well as galleries, many craft shops are dotted around town, where community members sell their work. Nowadays it can get quite busy at weekends, but during the week most places remain firmly closed and an air of silence descends.

🏃 Activities

Be sure to explore beyond the Jardín Juárez and head up the hill to Plaza Zaragoza and down the hill to Plaza Mineros. The mines are all located outside the town itself. While you can walk along the country roads and see the mines and associated buildings from afar, you can only actually access the sites by joining one of the informative and enjoyable guided tours.

Cinco Señores   TOURS
(☑ 473-756-18-44, 468-106-07-58; mineral-de pozos@outlook.com; Juárez; tours from M$150; ⏱ 11am-6pm Sat & Sun) This certified tour agency is the best in town. It offers guided tours of one (M$150) or two (M$220) mining haciendas, including transportation and a guided tour through the mine shaft. It also provides helmets for all participants. The tours usually last around two hours and the knowledgeable guides give a full historical rundown of the mining industry.

The best bit of the tours though comes when you descend into the steep, deep mine shafts. On the standard tour you walk 320m underground, but on some of the longer tours the mine shafts extend as far as 680m. Note that you have to climb down steep rock stairways or rock faces using a rope to access the mine shafts.

Tours run regularly at weekends. On weekdays they will still run tours if you let them know in advance and can form a group of at least four (ask them if they have another group coming that you can tag along with). Tours are in Spanish only.

🛏 Sleeping & Eating

★ Posada de las Minas   BOUTIQUE HOTEL **$$**
(☑ 442-293-02-13; Doblado 1; r incl breakfast from M$1200; ➌ ➐) This beautifully restored 19th-century hacienda offers charmingly old-fashioned rooms and apartments complete with Mexican ceramics and period

furnishings. The 'Santa Brígida' room has corner windows with views over town, and many others have balconies. It has a bar and restaurant, an impressive cactus garden and charming staff. They don't seem all that keen on walk-in visitors, so book ahead.

El Secreto   B&B **$$**
(☑ 442-293-02-00; www.elsecretomexico.com; Jardín Principal 4; r incl breakfast from M$1600; ➐➋) On the plaza, this small B&B run by a very friendly couple is nestled in a lovely garden featuring cacti, flowers and birds aplenty. The three elegant rooms are decorated with real artistic flair that incorporates cacti and other local plants into the look. Book in advance.

★ La Cantina Mina   MEXICAN **$$**
(Doblado 1; mains M$100-175; ⏱ 8:30am-9pm Sun-Thu, to 11pm Fri & Sat; ➐) This wonderful patio restaurant around a small fountain inside the Posada de las Minas is the best place for a leisurely meal in Mineral de Pozos. The menu is sophisticated and delicious and includes dishes such as coconut shrimp with pineapple sauce and a salmon burger, as well as Mexican classics, such as a show-stopping *queso fundido*.

🛍 Shopping

Casa del Venado Azul   MUSIC
(☑ 468-117-03-87; azulvenado@hotmail.com; Centenario 34; ⏱ 10am-6pm) Among Mexico's folk-instrument makers, shop-owner Luis Cruz stands out. The accomplished musician heads his own musical ensemble, which tours internationally. The location doubles as a chilled-out cafe. It's at the top of the village on the road to the mines.

❶ Getting There & Away

If you have your own wheels, Mineral de Pozos is a one-hour trip from San Miguel de Allende. Alternatively, the easiest way to get to Pozos is with a tour organized from San Miguel de Allende. Expect to pay around US$45 per person (minimum three). Bici-Burro (p686) offers exciting day-long bike tours to the town and mines.

Unfortunately, by bus (from San Miguel de Allende or Querétaro) it will take the best part of a day to get to this backwater: you must go first to Dolores Hidalgo, then to San Luis de la Paz (M$69; 14km north of Pozos, a detour east of Hwy 57) and then take a third bus to Pozos or a taxi (M$150), making it a real slog.

AGUASCALIENTES STATE

POP 1.3 MILLION

The state of Aguascalientes is one of Mexico's smallest and its focus is squarely on the city of the same name. According to local legend, a kiss planted on the lips of dictator Antonio López de Santa Anna by the wife of a prominent local politician brought about the creation of a separate Aguascalientes state from neighboring Zacatecas.

Beyond the museum-rich capital city formal tourist sites are few, but it's a pleasant-enough drive en route to or from Zacatecas, through fertile lands of corn, beans, chilies, fruit and grain. The state's ranches produce beef cattle as well as bulls that are sacrificed at bullfights countrywide.

Aguascalientes

✔️449 / POP 935,000 / ELEV 1880M

This prosperous industrial city is home to more than half the state's population. Despite its messy outskirts, which are defined by ring roads and the kind of urban sprawl you'll find on the periphery of almost all cities in Mexico, at its heart is a fine plaza and several blocks of handsome colonial buildings. Museums are its strong point: the absorbing Museo Nacional de la Muerte justifies a visit in itself, as do those devoted to José Guadalupe Posada and Saturnino Herrán. If you're passing through the state, its pleasant capital is worth stopping in for lunch or even overnight if you're not in a hurry.

History

Before the Spanish arrived, a labyrinth of catacombs was built here; the first Spaniards called it La Ciudad Perforada (The Perforated City). Archaeologists understand little of the tunnels and unfortunately they are off-limits to visitors.

Conquistador Pedro de Alvarado arrived in 1522, but was driven back by the Chichimecs. A small garrison was founded here in 1575 to protect Zacatecas–Mexico City silver convoys. Eventually, as the Chichimecs were pacified, the region's hot springs sparked the growth of a town (Aguascalientes means 'hot waters'); a large tank beside the Ojo Caliente springs helped irrigate local farms that fed hungry mining districts nearby.

Today the city's industries include textiles, wine, brandy, leather, preserved fruits and car manufacturing.

🔘 Sights

⭐ **Museo Nacional de la Muerte**   MUSEUM

(✔️449-910-74-00; https://museonacionaldela muerte.uaa.mx; Jardín del Estudiante s/n; adult/student M$20/10, Wed free; ⊙10am-6pm Tue-Sun) The excellent Museo Nacional de la Muerte exhibits all things relating to Mexico's favorite subject – death – from the skeleton La Catrina to historic artifacts and modern depictions. The contents – over 2500 items, drawings, literature, textiles, toys and miniatures – were donated to the Universidad Autónoma de Aguascalientes by collector and engraver, Octavio Bajonero Gil. Over 1200 are on display. They span several centuries, from Mesoamerican to contemporary artistic interpretations.

A section on the funeral rites of children is a little harrowing – not to mention pictures of a dead Frida Kahlo elsewhere – but otherwise the tone is surprisingly light. In the second to last room, look out for the (very) miniature crystal skull. It's believed to be from Aztec times and there are only two like it in the world. The upstairs gallery includes an interesting section on the different representations of death from countries around the world, and it becomes apparent that an obsession with the macabre is far from unique to Mexico. All up this wonderfully eccentric place provides a colorful, humorous and insightful encounter with the fate that awaits us all!

Palacio de Gobierno   HISTORIC BUILDING

(Plaza de la Patria; ⊙8am-8:30pm Mon-Fri, to 2pm Sat & Sun) FREE On the south side of Plaza de la Patria, the red-and-pink stone Palacio de Gobierno is Aguascalientes' most noteworthy colonial building. Once the mansion of colonial baron Marqués de Guadalupe, it dates from 1665 and has a striking courtyard with two levels of murals. Many government buildings in Mexico have wall murals but these ones really are something special.

Museo José Guadalupe Posada   MUSEUM

(✔️449-915-45-56; Jardín El Encino s/n; adult/student M$10/5, Wed free; ⊙11am-6pm Tue-Sun) Aguascalientes native José Guadalupe Posada (1852–1913) was in many ways the founder of modern Mexican art. His engravings and satirical cartoons broadened the audience for art in Mexico, highlighted social problems and were a catalyst in the later mural phase, influencing artists including Diego Rivera, José Clemente Orozco and David Alfaro Siqueiros. Posada's hallmark is the *calavera* (skull or skeleton) and many of

Aguascalientes

Aguascalientes

his *calavera* engravings have been widely reproduced. This modern and well-lit museum showcases some of his work.

Museo de Aguascalientes MUSEUM
(📞 449-916-71-42; Zaragoza 505; adult/student M$10/5, free Sun; ⊙ 11am-6pm Tue-Sun) Housed in a handsome neoclassical building dating to 1903, this museum houses a permanent collection of work by the brilliant Aguascalientes artist Saturnino Herrán (1887–1918), and there are also temporary exhibitions. His works are some of the first to honestly depict the Mexican people. The sensual sculpture *Malgretout* on the patio is a fiberglass copy of the marble original by Jesús Fructuoso Contreras.

Catedral
CATHEDRAL

(Plaza de la Patria) The well-restored 18th-century baroque cathedral, on the plaza's west side, is more magnificent inside than out. Over the altar at the east end of the south aisle is a painting of the Virgin of Guadalupe by Miguel Cabrera. There are more works by Cabrera, colonial Mexico's finest artist, in the cathedral's *pinacoteca* (picture gallery), which is open at Easter only, though if you ask a priest, he might let you in.

Museo Regional de Historia
MUSEUM

(☑449-916-52-28; Av Carranza 118; adult/child M$55/free; ⊙9am-6pm Tue-Sun) This history museum was designed by Refugio Reyes as a family home and features a small chapel. Its exhibits cover everything from the big bang and the start of time to the far more recent colonial conquest. It also has a beautiful chapel with ex-voto paintings and works attributed to Correa. Anyone interested in Mexican history will appreciate these displays. There are also temporary exhibitions.

Templo del Encino
CHURCH

(Jardín El Encino; ⊙7am-1pm & 6-9pm) This church contains a black statue of Jesus that some believe is growing. When it reaches an adjacent column, a worldwide calamity is anticipated. Fortunately, it's still some way off that height. Unbelievably, that presumably means things are only going to get worse! The huge *Way of the Cross* murals are also noteworthy. Opening hours can be flexible.

🏃 Activities

⭐ Baños Termales de Ojocaliente
THERMAL BATHS

(☑449-970-07-21; Av Tecnológico 102; private baths per hour from M$420; ⊙8am-8pm) Despite the city's name, these beautifully restored and colorful thermal baths are the only ones near the center. The brightly tiled 1808 complex truly turns back the clock; the waters are said to help all sorts of ailments. The easiest way to get there is by taxi (around M$50).

🎊 Festivals & Events

Feria de San Marcos
FAIR

(www.feriadesanmarcos.gob.mx; Expoplaza; ⊙mid-Apr) Mexico's biggest annual three- to four-week fair centers on Expoplaza and attracts thousands of visitors with exhibitions, bullfights, cockfights, rodeos, concerts and cultural events. The big parade takes place on the saint's day, April 25. As Aguascalientes' biggest event, accommodations are at a premium.

Festival de las Calaveras
CULTURAL

(⊙Nov) During the 10-day Festival de las Calaveras (the dates vary but always encompass November 1 and 2), Aguascalientes celebrates Día de Muertos (Day of the Dead) with an emphasis on the symbolism of *calavera* – the edible or decorative skull so beloved by Mexicans at this time of year.

🛏 Sleeping

Aguascalientes has a decent range of accommodations suited to most budgets, and a couple of hostels have made it cheap for backpackers to stay here too. Note that prices skyrocket during the Feria de San Marcos in April and accommodations are always completely booked for the fair's final weekend; residents run a lucrative homestay service at this time.

Hostal La Vie en Rose
HOSTEL $

(☑449-688-71-69, 437-479-24-00; lavieenrosehostal@gmail.com; Nieto 457; dm/d M$220/440; ☎) It's all about bicycles at this friendly and good-value hostel. They hang from the ceiling and are stenciled onto the walls, which gives this place a funky, memorable look. Dorms are clean and share bathrooms, while double rooms have their own facilities. There's a good kitchen, a lounge area and a roof terrace with a bar.

Art Hotel
BOUTIQUE HOTEL $$

(☑449-917-95-95, 449-269-69-95; Nieto 502; r M$1050; ❄☎) Housed in a brutalist concrete building and displaying plenty of its namesake art (including a rather striking bull in reception), this place aims to be memorable and rather neatly succeeds. Its comfortable and stylish rooms may lack natural light, but they are good value for such quality.

🍴 Eating & Drinking

There are some decent and varied eating options in Aguascalientes. Carranza is lined with restaurants. Callejón del Codo is the place to go for small cafes and coffee.

⭐ Mesa Verde
CAFE $

(☑449-688-92-08; Elizondo 113; ⊙9:30am-5pm Mon & Wed-Fri, 10:30am-6pm Sat & Sun; ☎🍴) This delightful find is fabulous for a relaxed lunch, with vegetarian-friendly *comida saludable* – health food – freshly made right in front of you and presented with an artistic touch. Artisanal beers are also on the menu, as well as great coffee. There's a roof terrace with wooden tables and a lovely vibe.

BUSES FROM AGUASCALIENTES

DESTINATION	FARE (M$)	TIME (HR)	FREQUENCY (PER DAY)
Guadalajara	342-455	2¾-3	frequent
Guanajuato	293	3	2
León	205-270	2-3½	frequent
Mexico City (Terminal Norte)	581-775	6	frequent
Querétaro	500-665	5	frequent
San Luis Potosí	204	3-3½	hourly
Zacatecas	205-270	2	frequent

★ **Restaurante La Estación**　MEXICAN $$
(☑449-918-66-64; www.restaurantlaestacion.com; 28 de Agosto 210; mains M$123-163; ☺8am-7pm Mon-Sat, 9am-5pm Sun & holidays) You can't miss this family-run, wine-red and very homely restaurant decorated in Day of the Dead skeletons and tiny cacti. The food is traditional Mexican and the portions are generous. The patriotically colored *chiles en nogada* (stuffed green chilies) is a taste triumph. It's also a good bet for a hearty breakfast.

Pulquería Posada　BAR
(La Pulque; ☑449-918-64-36; www.facebook.com/pulqueria.posada; Nieto 445; ☺10am-2:30pm, 5:30-11pm Tue-Sun) Aguascalientes used to be renowned for its pulque (a traditional Aztec tipple made from fermented agave sap), and this popular student hangout has reintroduced the tradition. It's fun and cheap, with a half-liter *jarra* (jug) of *pulque* costing M$20. There's also a good range of mezcals, flavored with everything from lime to guava.

☆ Entertainment

Aguascalientes has two theaters, **Teatro de Aguascalientes** (☑449-978-54-14; cnr Chávez & Aguascalientes) and **Teatro Morelos** (☑449-916-62-70; Nieto 113, Plaza de la Patria), which stage a variety of cultural events.

ℹ Information

Banks with ATMs are common around Plaza de la Patria and Expoplaza. *Casas de cambio* cluster on Hospitalidad, opposite the post office.
Star Médica (☑449-910-99-00; www.star-medica.com; Universidad 101) Private hospital.
State Tourist Office (☑449-910-20-88; www.aguascalientes.gob.mx; Palacio de Gobierno, Plaza de la Patria; ☺9am-8pm Mon-Sat, 10am-5pm Sun)

ℹ Getting There & Away

AIR
Aéropuerto Internacional Jesús Terán (☑449-918-28-06; www.aeropuertosgap.com.mx) is 26km south of Aguascalientes off the highway to Mexico City. There are domestic flights from here to Mexico City and Monterrey, as well as direct services to Los Angeles, Houston and Dallas/Fort Worth.

BUS
The **bus station** (Central de Autobuses Aguascalientes; Av Convención) is 2km south of the center. It has several food outlets and luggage storage. Deluxe and 1st- and 2nd-class buses operate to/from Aguascalientes. Deluxe and 1st-class companies include ETN, Primera Plus, Futura and Ómnibus de México. The main 2nd-class line is Coordinados (Flecha Amarilla).

ℹ Getting Around

Most places of interest are within easy walking distance of each other. Regular city buses (M$6) run from 6am to 10pm. From downtown, several buses head to the bus station from the corner of **Galeana** (cnr Galeana & Insurgentes).

Taxis charge as per metered fares. Between the bus station and the center the taxi fare is from around M$25 to M$30.

SAN LUIS POTOSÍ STATE

One of Mexico's most scenic and varied states, San Luis Potosí manages to charm all those who visit, whether it be with the enchanting green valleys, steep mountainsides and towering waterfalls of the Huasteca Potosina, or its eponymous historic capital, with a genteel colonial center looking more like a film set than the workaday medium-sized Mexican city it is. Elsewhere there's the fascinating 'ghost town' of Real de Catorce, the epic journey to which culminates in a long drive down a mildly terrifying tunnel through the mountain: quite an unforgettable experience that is instantly rewarded by arrival in one of the most striking *pueblos mágicos* (magical villages) in Mexico. Finally, do not miss a trip to charming Xilitla, the nearest town to Edward James' epic sculpture garden of Las Pozas, a delightful dadaist treat complete with waterfalls and rushing streams flowing down the thickly forested hillside.

San Luis Potosí

☑ 444 / POP 824,230 / ELEV 1860M

A grand old dame of a colonial city, San Luis Potosí was once a revolutionary hotbed, an important mining town and a seat of government to boot. Today the city has maintained its poise as the prosperous state capital, orderly industrial center and university seat, though it sees relatively few visitors.

A great place to wander through, the city's historic core is made up of numerous plazas and manicured parks that are linked by attractive pedestrian streets. Although not as striking as Zacatecas or Guanajuato, and definitely lacking the magic of San Miguel de Allende, this lively city's cultural elegance is reflected in its delightful colonial architecture, impressive theater and numerous excellent museums.

History

Founded in 1592, San Luis is 20km west of the silver deposits in Cerro de San Pedro, and was named Potosí after the immensely rich Bolivian silver town, which the Spanish hoped it would rival. The mines began to decline in the 1620s, but the city was established enough as a ranching center to remain the major city of northeastern Mexico until overtaken by Monterrey at the start of the 20th century.

Known in the 19th century for its lavish houses and imported luxury goods, San Luis was twice the seat of President Benito Juárez' government during the 1860s French intervention. In 1910 in San Luis, the dictatorial president Porfirio Díaz jailed Francisco Madero, his liberal opponent, during the presidential campaign. Freed after the election, Madero hatched his Plan de San Luis Potosí (a strategy to depose Díaz), announcing it in San Antonio, Texas, in October 1910; he declared the election illegal, named himself provisional president and designated November 20 as the day for Mexico to rise in revolt – the start of the Mexican Revolution.

◉ Sights

★ **Museo Nacional de la Máscara** MUSEUM
(National Mask Museum; ☑ 444-812-30-25; www. museonacionaldelamascara.com; Villerías 2; adult/ student/child M$20/10/free; ◉ 10am-6pm Tue-Fri, to 5pm Sat, to 3pm Sun & Mon) This superb museum displays a fascinating collection of ceremonial masks from across Mexico and around the world, and does a good job at explaining the evolution of pre-Columbian masks in Mexico. There are good descriptions in English of the Mexican masks, though explanations of the non-Mexican masks could definitely be improved upon.

★ **Museo Federico Silva** MUSEUM
(☑ 444-812-38-48; www.museofedericosilva.org; Obregón 80; adult/student M$30/15, free Sun; ◉ 10am-6pm Mon & Wed-Sat, to 2pm Sun) This excellent museum devoted to the work of Mexican artist Federico Silva (b 1923) should not be missed. The 17th-century building was once a hospital and later a school, but has been exquisitely transformed into a museum of sculpture, ingeniously integrating the building's previous neoclassical finish with the haunting monolithic sculptures of Silva.

Museo del Ferrocarril MUSEUM
(☑ 444-814-35-89; Av Othón; M$40; ◉ 9am-5pm Tue-Fri, from 11am Sat & Sun; 🚹) Once an important stop on two of Mexico's main train lines, San Luis Potosí has brought the past to life in this museum housed inside its glorious former train station, dating from 1936. Don't miss the two murals by Fernando Leal (completed in 1943) that grace the station interior, or a wander through the old train carriages waiting by the platforms. It's very well done and surprisingly interesting even if you've never considered yourself a train-spotter!

Museo Regional Potosino MUSEUM
(Plaza de Aranzazú s/n; M$55, Sun free; ◉ 9am-6pm Tue-Sun) This fetching museum was originally part of a Franciscan monastery founded in 1590. The ground floor – part of which is housed in the small Capilla de San Antonio de Padua – has an interesting, and well-displayed (Spanish only) collection of items from pre-Hispanic Mexico, especially the indigenous people of the Huasteca. Pottery predominates, but there are also a few skulls and skeletons, including two who were the unfortunate victims of a sacrifice.

Upstairs is a lavish, mid-18th-century private chapel constructed in Churrigueresque style. New monks were ordained here.

San Luis Potosí

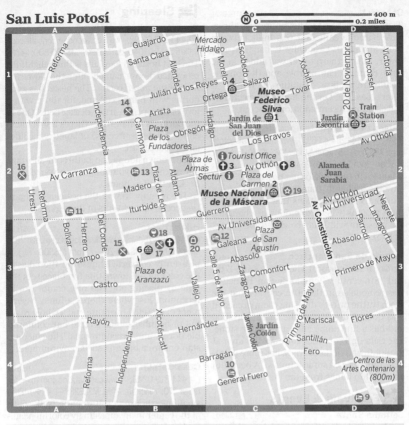

San Luis Potosí

Templo del Carmen CHURCH

(⊙8am-1pm & 5-8pm) The Churrigueresque Templo del Carmen (1749–64) is San Luis's most spectacular structure. On the vividly carved stone facade, hovering angels show the touch of indigenous artisans. The Camarín de la Virgen, with a splendid golden altar, is to the left of the main altar inside. The entrance and roof of this chapel are a riot of small plaster figures.

Catedral
CATHEDRAL

(Plaza de Armas) FREE This impressive three-nave baroque cathedral was built between 1660 and 1730. Originally it had just one tower; the northern tower was added in the 20th century. The marble apostles on the facade are replicas of statues in Rome's St Peter's Basilica. On the hour, the electronic bells, a more recent addition, ring out.

Museo de Arte Contemporáneo
MUSEUM

(MAC; 444-814-43-63; www.macsanluispotosi.com; Morelos 235; adult/student M$20/10, free Sun; 10am-6pm Tue-Sat, to 2pm Sun) This museum is housed in the city's former post office. These days the brilliantly transformed space houses temporary art exhibitions that change every three months (when exhibitions are changing, the museum will likely be closed for a week or two).

Templo de San Francisco
CHURCH

(Jardín de San Francisco) The altar of the 17th- and 18th-century Templo de San Francisco was remodeled in the 20th century, but the sacristy (the priest's dressing room), reached by a door to the right of the altar, is original and has a fine dome and carved pink stone. The Sala de Profundis, through the arch at the south end of the sacristy, has more paintings and a carved stone fountain. A beautiful crystal ship hangs from the main dome.

🎊 Festivals & Events

Semana Santa
RELIGIOUS

(Mar/Apr) Holy Week is celebrated with concerts, exhibitions and other activities; on Good Friday at 3pm, Christ's Passion is reenacted in the barrio of San Juan de Guadalupe, followed at 8pm by the Silent Procession through downtown (one of the city's most important events).

Feria Nacional Potosina
FAIR

(FENAPO; www.fenapo.mx; Aug) San Luis' National Fair, normally in the last three weeks of August, includes concerts, bullfights, rodeos, cockfights and agricultural shows.

Festival Internacional de Danza Contemporánea Lila López
DANCE

(late Jul-early Aug) A wonderful annual national festival of contemporary dance.

Día de San Luis Rey de Francia
RELIGIOUS

(Aug 25) On August 25 the city's patron saint, St Louis IX, is honored as the highlight of the Feria Nacional. Events include a parade, concerts and plays.

🛏 Sleeping

Corazón de Xoconostle
HOSTEL $

(444-243-98-98; www.corazondexoconostle.com; Calle 5 de May 1040; dm M$190, r M$430-500;) The best hostel in San Luis is this delightfully renovated house named after the flowering fruit of the *nopal* cactus. The hostel has good dorms with bunk beds and, for those with a love of high places, triple-decker beds! One of the dorms is female-only. There's also a kitchen for guest use, free use of laundry facilities and a roof terrace.

The downside is the bathroom shortage – it might keep you hopping on your feet at peak bathroom hours.

The friendly crew of the hostel also organize decent, budget tours of the region.

Hikuri Hostal
HOSTEL $

(444-814-76-01; www.hikurihostel.com.mx; Iturbide 980; dm M$160-200, r from M$500;) A pleasantly converted house on the edge of the colonial old town, this fun place sets the tone by placing one end of a combi van in reception. Elsewhere there's a funky assortment of recycled furniture and a whole room full of beanbags, plus simple but comfortable dorms and private rooms. The clued-up staff ensure a buzzing social environment.

Casa Catalina
B&B $$

(444-810-02-61; www.casacatalina.com.mx; Arteaga 270; r incl breakfast M$1622;) This small guesthouse is a 10-minute walk south of the center in an appealingly colorful neighborhood. Set around a garden and peach-pink courtyard, the small rooms gather lots of natural light and are comfortable and decorated with considerable care. The only drawback is that barking street dogs can be a pain at night.

Hotel Panorama
BUSINESS HOTEL $$

(444-812-17-77; www.hotelpanorama.com.mx; Av Carranza 315; r incl breakfast from M$1200;) It's the best of San Luis' rather average lot of midrange accommodations and has its position going for it – opposite Plaza de los Fundadores. Beyond that, it's smart(ish) and all 126 rooms have floor-to-ceiling windows; those on the south side overlook the pool and lovely garden.

⭐ Hotel Museo Palacio de San Agustín
HISTORIC HOTEL $$$

(444-144-19-00; www.hotelmuseopalaciodesanagustin.com; Galeana 240; r incl breakfast from M$4000;) Formerly a house for retired monks of the nearby San Agustín monastery, this extraordinary property has been restored to original condition, including hand-painted gold-leaf finishes, crystal chandeliers and 700 certified European antiques. Rooms are elaborately decorated in the style of the Mexican 19th-century upper classes, and feature gorgeous marble bathrooms. One to splurge on.

✗ Eating & Drinking

There's a fairly ho-hum dining scene in San Luis. One local specialty to look out for is *tacos potosinos* – red-chili-impregnated tacos stuffed with cheese or chicken and topped with chopped potato, carrot, lettuce and loads of *queso blanco* (white cheese).

★ Cafe Cortáo   MEXICAN $

(☑ 444-128-81-72; Independencia 1150; mains M$45-85; ⊙ 8:30am-1:30pm & 5-9:30pm Mon-Fri, 9:30am-1:30pm & 5-9:30pm Sat) This simple spot is a breakfast institution and at times queues of locals form outside the doors waiting for them to open in the morning. The delicious breakfasts and other meals are produced with efficient service and a warm welcome from a charismatic owner. Don't miss the heavenly *huevos abolengo* (eggs on bread with a mushroom and Manchego-cheese sauce).

Antojitos El Pozole   MEXICAN $

(☑ 444-814-99-00; cnr Carmona & Arista; mains M$50-120; ⊙ noon-11:30pm Tue-Sun) The place for the local *enchiladas potosinas* – the tortilla dough is red from chili. This place was started by a woman selling *antojitos* (Mexican snacks) in her home in the 1980s. Demand for her goods was so high she opened a restaurant specializing in what she knows best – *tacos rojos,* delicious *pozole* (hominy stew) and *quesadillas de papa* (potato quesadillas).

There are a couple of other branches out in the newer parts of the city.

Cielo Tinto   INTERNATIONAL $$

(☑ 444-814-00-40; www.facebook.com/cielotinto slp; Carranza 700; mains M$140-295; ⊙ 8am-11pm Mon-Sat, to 6pm Sun) Generally held to be San Luis Potosí's best restaurant, the 'red sky' is an attractive upscale place housed in a renovated hacienda with a beautiful courtyard. The menu is international and runs from skillfully presented grilled dishes to Mexican dishes with a creative touch. Good set breakfasts (M$90 to M$130).

La Oruga y La Cebada   INTERNATIONAL $$

(☑ 444-812-45-08; Callejón de Lozada 1; mains M$115-200; ⊙ noon-1am Tue-Sat, to 10pm Sun &

Mon; ☏) 'The caterpillar and the barley' is a large and hugely popular restaurant-bar divided between the downstairs dining room, dominated by a normally busy bar serving local craft beers, and the upstairs roof terrace complete with retractable roof. The food is assured if not spectacular, and includes Mexican favorites as well as a couple of international dishes.

Callejon 7B   CRAFT BEER

(www.7barrios.com.mx; Universidad 153; ⊙ 4:30-11pm Mon & Tue, to midnight Wed & Thu, 2pm-1am Sat, to 11pm Sun) A hip bar named after the very beer it produces, Siete Barrios, which is in turn named after the seven main regions of the city. After you've tried one of its artisanal brews, from blonde ales to robust porters, you can bar-hop your way down the laneway to surrounding drinking dens.

☆ Entertainment

San Luis has an active cultural scene. Ask in the tourist office (p702) about what's on and keep your eye out for posters and the free monthly *Guiarte* booklet. Also look on www.agendasanluis.com.

Teatro de la Paz   CONCERT VENUE

(☑ 444-814-10-75, 444-812-52-09; www.facebook.com/teatrodelapazsanluisp; Villerias 2) This exceptionally handsome neoclassical theater completed in 1894 contains a concert hall with 1500 seats where San Luis Potosí's Orquesta Sinfónica performs. There's also an exhibition gallery and a theater here. Posters announce upcoming dance, theater and music events.

🛍 Shopping

Casa Grande Esencia
Artesanal   ARTS & CRAFTS

(☑ 444-812-09-25; Universidad 220; ⊙ 10am-8pm Mon-Sat, to 5pm Sun) This cooperative of small stalls sells a great range of *artesanías potosinas* that are 100% locally made. There's also clothing and more standard souvenirs.

ℹ Information

Hospital Lomas de SLP (☑ 444-102-59-00; www.hls.com.mx; Av Palmira 600, Villas del Pedregal)

Post Office (Av Universidad 526; ⊙ 8am-6pm Mon-Fri, 9-11:45am Sat)

Sectur (State Tourist Office; ☑ 444-812-99-39; www.visitasanluispotosi.com; Av Manuel José Othón 130; ⊙ 8am-9pm Mon-Fri, 9am-3pm Sat & Sun) Has maps and good information on off-the-beaten-track attractions in San Luis Potosí state.

BUSES FROM SAN LUIS POTOSÍ

DESTINATION	FARE (M$)	TIME (HR)	FREQUENCY (PER DAY)
Aguascalientes	204-227	2½-3	hourly
Ciudad Valles	665	4½	hourly
Guadalajara	554-605	5-6	hourly
Guanajuato	355	3	1
Matehuala	308	2½	6
Mexico City (Terminal Norte)	567-805	5-6½	hourly
Monterrey	784-985	6	5
Querétaro	323-405	2½-4	frequent
San Miguel de Allende	249	4	3
Xilitla	487	6	6
Zacatecas	348	3	frequent

Tourist Office (☎444-812-27-70; Palacio Municipal; ⊙8am-8pm Mon-Sat, 10am-5pm Sun) On the east side of Plaza de Armas.

ⓘ Getting There & Away

AIR
Aeropuerto Internacional Ponciano Arriaga (☎444-478-70-00; www.oma.aero/en) is 10km north of the city off Hwy 57. There are several daily flights to Mexico City and a once- or twice-daily flight to Monterrey. There are also flights to Puerto Vallarta, Tijuana, Querétaro, Cancún and Houston.

BUS
The **Terminal Terrestre Potosina** (TTP; ☎444-816-46-02; Carretera 57), 2.5km east of the center, is a busy transportation hub that has deluxe, 1st-class and 2nd-class bus services. Its facilities include 24-hour luggage storage and fast-food outlets.

ⓘ Getting Around

Taxis charge around M$200 to M$250 for the half-hour trip to/from the airport. Coming into the city there's a fixed rate of M$260 (you'll need to line up and buy a voucher inside the terminal building).

To reach the center from the bus station, take any 'Centro' or bus 46. A convenient place to get off is on the Alameda, outside the former train station. A booth in the bus station sells taxi tickets (day/night M$41/45) to the center.

From the center to the bus station, take any 'Central TTP' or bus southbound on Avenida Constitución from the Alameda's west side.

City buses run from 6:30am to 10:30pm (M$8). For places along Avenida Carranza, catch a 'Morales' (bus 9) or 'Carranza' (bus 23) at the bus depot behind Museo de Ferrocarril.

Real de Catorce
☎488 / POP 1392 / ELEV 2730M

A wealthy silver-mining town until early last century, Real de Catorce's fortunes changed overnight when the price of silver plummeted, its mine closed and much of the population left, leaving it a 'ghost town' located an inconveniently long distance from anywhere, deep in the giant hills of the Sierra Madre Oriental. Not long ago Real was nearly deserted, with just a few hundred souls eking out a precarious existence as cold mountain winds whipped down streets lined with crumbling buildings.

But then somebody invented the weekend break and the boutique hotel, and Real de Catorce slipped into a new element, attracting outsiders who have helped with the slow (and very much ongoing) transformation of the town into a getaway destination. Although Real is no longer a ghost town, doors still creak in the breeze, cobblestone streets end abruptly and many buildings are fading away, but the fabulous scenery and slow pace of life make it a delight to visit.

History

The 14 in the town's name may have been derived from the 14 Spanish soldiers killed here by indigenous resistance fighters around 1700. The town was founded in the mid-18th century and the church built between 1790 and 1817. The town reached its peak in the late 19th century, vying to surpass the famed Valenciana mine of Guanajuato. It had opulent houses, a bullring and shops selling European luxury goods.

◉ Sights

Templo de la Purísima Concepción CHURCH
(Lanzagorta; ⊘7am-7pm) FREE This impressive neoclassical church is where thousands of Mexican pilgrims descend annually in a pilgrimage (late September to early October) to the supposedly miraculous image of St Francis of Assisi, displayed at the front of the church. A cult has grown up around the statue, whose help is sought in solving problems and cleansing sins. Walk through the door to the left of the altar to find a roomful of *retablos,* small pictures depicting threatening situations in which St Francis interceded.

**Centro Cultural de
Real de Catorce** MUSEUM
(☑488-887-50-72; www.facebook.com/culturaslp.gob; Casa de la Moneda; M$10; ⊘10am-6pm Wed-Sun) Opposite the Templo de la Purísima Concepción's facade, the Centro Cultural de Real de Catorce, the old mint, made coins for 14 months (1,489,405 pesos to be exact) in the mid-1860s. This classic monument has been exquisitely restored over the last few years and now houses a cultural center and gallery with several levels of temporary exhibitions. Check out their Facebook page for details of upcoming events. The bottom floor has a permanent exhibition depicting photos and machinery from the original mint.

Capilla de Guadalupe CHURCH
(Zaragoza; ⊘8am-5pm) This fine old 19th-century church has an interesting interior of once-glorious but now very faded and decaying frescoes. Outside, the cemetery is said to be one of the oldest structures in town. Some of the tombs date to the late 1700s. The church is around 1km north of the town center.

⚡ Activities

Hiking

The hilly and stark desert setting makes up for the lack of major sights around town. If you're into walking, there's plenty to keep you occupied for a couple of days. Be aware that at these altitudes the days can be hot and the sun burns fast (bring sun cream), but as soon as the sun drops and the winds pick up it can get icy cold. Take water.

Pueblo Fantasma HIKING
Allow at least one hour to get to this hillside ghost town, which is visible from the town. There is also a second set of ruins, not visible from Real, 100m further on. Beware that there are also two large shafts in the ruins, so take care while wandering about. From Real, head along Lanzagorta and stay left.

To extend this hike, head northwest along the ridge to the antennas and the cross over the town (make sure you note this from the town before you leave, as it becomes obscured when on the ridge). Follow the path behind the cross before you weave your way down to the cemetery. Allow three to four hours in total for the longer hike.

Socavón de Purísima HIKING
Socavón de Purísima is the large chimney of a former mine. To get here from Real, head off down Allende and veer right at its end. Follow this road until you reach the chimney (about 45 minutes one way). The road passes through a cut or split rock, the Cerro Trocado. If open, you can enter the mouth of the mine.

To return, it's a longer and harder slog back up the hill.

Horseback Riding

Numerous trails lead out into the dry, stark and fascinating desertscapes around Real. The most popular guided trail ride is the three-hour trip to El Quemado, the sacred mountain of the Huicholes. Here you'll find expansive views of the high-desert plateau and a small shrine to the sun god.

Caballerangos del Real HORSEBACK RIDING
(Plaza Hidalgo; 2hr trip M$150-200) Horse guides now belong to an association, approved by the municipality, and you'll find them hanging around Real's main square offering rides. Note that no protective hats are provided; you clomp off at your own risk.

Jeep Rides

Trips in 'Jeep Willys' can be arranged to many of the same locations as the horses go to, though mainly only on weekends. Ask any of the drivers along Lanzagorta or Allende, or at the tourist office (p704). Rates vary according to the trip and numbers; they work out cheaper if you share the cost with other visitors. In general they offer a bumpy and fairly uncomfortable ride without the clear vision and open air of the horseback riding.

Cycling

Lalo Bike CYCLING
(☑cell 488-1051981; cruz.lalo.bike@gmail.com; Lanzagorta 5; 1½hr ride per person from M$150; ⊘Fri-Sun Nov-Sep) Cyclists of all levels can head out around Real de Catorce on some great-value rides with Lalo (he speaks Spanish only, but can arrange an

English-speaking guide). Prices include mountain bike, helmet and guide. Spanish speakers can email or ring ahead or, if you are in Real, ask at Mesón de la Abundancia.

✦✦ Festivals & Events

Fiesta de San Francisco　　　　RELIGIOUS
(☉end Sep-Oct) From the end of September to the end of October, 150,000 pilgrims pay homage to the figure of St Francis of Assisi in the town's church. Many of them just come for the day, while thousands stay in the town, filling every rentable room and sleeping rough in the plazas.

The streets are lined with stalls selling religious souvenirs and food, while many of the town's more upmarket restaurants close for a month. Note: travelers who desire the tranquil 'ghost-town experience' of Real de Catorce are best to stay away during this festival period to avoid disappointment.

Festival del Desierto　　　　CULTURAL
(www.facebook.com/desiertofest; ☉Jun) This cultural festival features folkloric music and dance performances in towns all around the region. Dates vary annually; check before you come with the tourist office or on the festival's Facebook page.

🛏 Sleeping

★Mesón de Abundancia　　　HOTEL $$
(☑488-887-50-44; www.mesonabundancia.com; Lanzagorta 11; d M$850-1500; ☺☎) Easily one of Mexico's most atmospheric hotels, this 19th-century former treasury building has been wonderfully renovated with exposed stone walls and antique furnishings throughout. A massive old-fashioned key lets you into one of 11 rooms that are rich in the scent of polish on aged wood. Each is tastefully decorated with local crafts. Rates are lower outside high season.

In the evening cozy up around the open fireplace with a glass of wine in the delightful bar. There's a good in-house restaurant and staff can organize tours around the town.

Hotel Mina Real　　　　HOTEL $$
(☑488-887-51-62; www.hotelminareal.com; Corona 5B; r from M$1250; ☺☎) This stylish place is in a boldly renovated stone building whose tone is set by the modern wooden staircase leading up through its center to 11 tasteful rooms with plenty of nods to the past. Carry on up the stairs to the roof terrace with views of the church. It's a good choice for those seeking contemporary comforts.

Refugio Romano　　　　GUESTHOUSE $$
(☑488-887-50-74; www.refugioromano.com; Iturbide 38; d M$1200-1400; ☎) ✿ This true oasis at the far end of town opens up into a lovely green garden of cacti and fruit trees surrounded by four simple rooms furnished with dark-wood furniture and equipped with stylish bathrooms. The owners whip up delicious organic Italian-Mexican meals for guests, and they follow sustainable practices wherever possible.

Hotel El Real　　　　HOTEL $$
(☑488-887-50-58; Morelos 20; r M$870-1500; ☎) A historic building with plenty of atmosphere and pretty rooms on three floors around an open courtyard, some with views over the town and the hills. It's not fancy, but it's very cozy and the owners are warm and welcoming.

🍴 Eating & Drinking

Mesón de Abundancia　　MEXICAN, ITALIAN $$
(☑488-887-50-44; www.mesonabundancia.com; Lanzagorta 11; mains M$100-200; ☉7am-10pm; ☎✐) There are several cozy eating areas at the restaurant in this hugely atmospheric hotel, one with a bar and fireplace. The hearty servings of Italian and Mexican dishes are delicious and its wood-fired oven pizza is a warming evening treat. Also worth popping by for breakfast.

Amor y Paz　　　　BAR
(Juárez 10; ☉6pm-late Fri & Sat) Real's reputation as a ghost town may in part be due to the fact that its residents and visitors are often all hiding out at this funky bar, hidden behind the walls of Hotel El Real. It's decked out in antiques (note the amazing wooden bar), retro seating and quirky chandeliers, and serves a range of mezcals.

ℹ Information

There's one ATM in Real de Catorce, located in the tourist office, but on busy weekends it occasionally runs out of money and is often out of order thanks to electricity cuts and the like, so it's wise to bring cash.

There's a small but helpful **tourist office** (Palacio Municipal, Constitución s/n; ☉9am-4pm) by the church.

ℹ Getting There & Away

BUS
To get to Real de Catorce, you need to catch a bus from the town of Matehuala (M$90, 1½ hours).

Real de Catorce

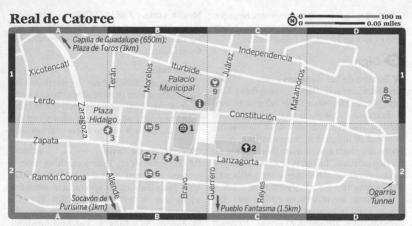

Capilla de Guadalupe (650m);
Plaza de Toros (1km)

Real de Catorce

These leave Matehuala's bus station at 8am, noon, 2pm and 6pm. Matehuala is easy to reach from elsewhere in the region, with multiple daily connections from San Luis Potosí (M$250 to M$280, three hours) and Querétaro (M$587, 5½ hours).

On arrival in Real, buses stop on the outskirts of town before the Ogarrio tunnel. There, in order to pass through the tunnel to the town proper, you change to a smaller bus that takes you the final part of the journey, dropping you on the market square.

Returning from Real to Matehuala, the small buses leave the market square in Real at 7:40am, 11:40am, 3:40pm and 5:40pm, and once again passengers pick up the bigger bus on the other side for the rest of the journey. Buy tickets on board the bus.

CAR & MOTORCYCLE

If driving from Hwy 57 north of Matehuala, turn off toward Cedral, 20km west. After Cedral, you turn south to reach Real on what must be one of the world's longest cobblestone roads. It's a slow but spectacular zigzag drive up a steep mountainside. The 2.3km-long Ogarrio tunnel (M$20 per vehicle) is only wide enough for one vehicle; workers stationed at each end with telephones control traffic flow between 7am and 11pm. If it's really busy, you'll have to leave your car at the eastern tunnel entrance and continue by pickup or cart. If you drive through, as a nonresident you are supposed to leave your car in the parking area where you exit the tunnel, rather than park in the narrow streets of the town. However you get through the tunnel, it's a memorably impressive entry to the town.

La Huasteca Potosina

The remote La Huasteca Potosina region is a hot and steamy land of iridescent tropical flowers and tangled jungles hiding a series of stunning toothpaste-blue waterfalls and swimming holes (the aquamarine hue is due to the high calcium content in the surrounding rocks). It's a landscape and climate that's worlds away from the grand colonial cities and cool ranching country that makes up so much of the rest of central Mexico. Long unknown to international visitors, this alluring region is now starting to attract a growing number of adventurous travelers who are drawn here by a beguiling combination of breathtaking scenery, the rich culture of the local Huastec people (Tének), plus extraordinary sinkholes, caves and bird-watching. The best time to visit is in the dry season, between November and March. Wet season brings heavy rains and high, less-clear waters.

◎ Sights

★ Sótano de las Huahuas   CAVE

(San Isidro Tampaxal; M$40; ⊙ dawn-dusk) This huge jungle-fringed sinkhole is home to tens of thousands of swifts as well as many green parrots, and at dawn and dusk they surge in or out of the cave in huge swirling, noisy flocks. It's much less touristy than Sótano de las Golondrinas, and so is in many ways the more appealing of the two to visit although it does require a little more effort to reach.

A favorite for rappelling enthusiasts, the chasm itself is around 478m deep and the cave mouth is around 60m across. To reach the cave from the car park you must walk 1km through remarkable jungle – but it's worth it for its beautiful cedar and local tree and bird species.

Sótano de las Golondrinas   CAVE

(Aquismón; M$40; ⊙ dawn-dusk) The extraordinary limestone sinkhole, known as Swallows' Cave, is located near Aquismón. One of the world's deepest pits at over 500m (over 370m free fall), it's known for the thousands of *vencejos* (white-collared swifts) that nest in the caves. At dawn, flocks of swifts leave the cave, spiraling their way noisily up to the opening. At dusk, on return to the cave, they circle above the cave mouth before they break off in groups and dive-bomb into the abyss.

It's popular with rappellers and base jumpers who drop from the cave's mouth (there are concerns that these activities are disturbing the birds). To get there, you must walk from the car park, down hundreds of steps (and back again), which is about a 20-minute walk.

Laguna de la Media Luna   HOT SPRINGS

(El Jabalí; adult/child M$40/20; ⊙ 9am-6pm) This surreal, mint-green-colored lagoon is fed by six thermal springs with temperatures ranging between an appealing 27°C and 30°C (80.6°F and 86°F). Its crystal-clear waters mean snorkelers and divers can view beds of water lilies, an ancient petrified forest and several fish species. Hundreds of families flock here on weekends, when it can get very busy and is worth avoiding. You can hire snorkeling gear from one of the many stalls inside the area (M$50).

Diving courses are available. The most highly recommended is **Escuela de Buceo**

Media Luna (⊡ 487-872-81-89; www.buceome-dialuna.com; diving courses from M$950), run by master scuba diver and oceanographer Ossiel Martinez.

Waterfalls

The region's main draw is its incredible waterfalls, which in most cases you can swim near or take boat trips to. A self-guided tour with your own wheels or an agency-run day trip is the perfect way to discover them all.

★ Cascada de Tamul   WATERFALL

(M$30; ⊙ 8am-6pm) Like something from a tropical postcard, Tamul is easily the Huasteca Potosina's most spectacular waterfall. Milky-blue water plunges 105m into the pristine Río Santa Maria (which becomes the Tampaón). Its setting, in a canyon surrounded on all sides with thick forest, is simply breathtaking. Best of all, you'll often have the place to yourself, due to its remote location.

To see the falls, you can drive almost all the way to the top entrance (you'll need to pay M$20 to drive along this private dirt track). When you reach the river, you'll need to park, wade across to the campsite on the other side (if the river is flowing heavily, it's best to be helped across by one of the campsite employees), from where it's an easy 1km hike to the waterfall itself. You'll emerge at its top, where there is a lovely pool to swim in, but be sure to take the rickety wooden ladder down to the bottom of the valley and see the falls from there, where they are truly a spectacular sight with thousands of butterflies flapping about in the spray.

Another way to reach the waterfall is to paddle upriver in a wooden *lancha* (boat), a return journey of around 3½ hours (M$800 to M$1000 per boat depending on your haggling skills). You can arrange trips on arrival into Tanchachín or La Morena.

If you don't have your own transportation, MS Xpediciones (p708) arranges excellent day trips from Ciudad Valles, complete with lunch at the home of a hospitable local (M$950 per person including transportation; minimum two people). It also arranges rafting trips in the area.

★ Cascadas de Minas Viejas   WATERFALL

(El Platanito; M$30; ⊙ 7am-8pm) The stunning cascades of Minas Viejas are well worth the 78km trip northwest from Ciudad Valles, if only to see the gorgeous turquoise waters here. The site comprises a principal waterfall with a drop of 55m plus a stunning water pool. From here, a series of smaller cascades and pools drop over terraces. It's a popular destination for adventure groups who jump over the terraces. Bird-watchers might find some feathered rewards hiding in the surrounding forest undergrowth.

Los Micos   WATERFALL
(M$30; ⏱8am-5pm) One of the most visited of Huasteca Potosina's falls it may be, but there's a reason for that: here seven waterfalls of different heights cascade down a riverbed, which makes for an incredible sight. You can do a quick boat tour (M$90 for 10 minutes; minimum four people) or jumping expeditions down the seven waterfalls (M$180 per person for two hours; helmet and life jacket supplied). Many operators located in the car park offer the same activity.

Puente de Dios   WATERFALL
(M$40) Around 5km northeast of Tamasopo along a rough road, Puente de Dios features a 600m-long wooden walkway with stunning rainforest views and fabulous swimming opportunities. The main feature, 'God's Bridge,' is a turquoise-colored waterhole with an adjoining cave entrance, though this is not accessible or recommended in high waters.

🏃 Activities

La Huasteca Potosina is a dream for activities enthusiasts, with swimming, hiking, rappelling, rafting and kayaking all possible on and around its rushing rivers and soaring peaks. Agencies in Xilitla, Ciudad Valles and San Luis Potosí can arrange day trips and multiday tours, though it's best to make arrangements at least several days in advance.

🛏 Sleeping

El Molino   GUESTHOUSE $$
(📞cell 444-803-73-34; www.hotelelmolino.webs.com; Porfirio Díaz 1417, Rio Verde; r from M$1000; 🅿🛜❄) Based in the rather scrappy agricultural town of Rio Verde, on the edge of the Huasteca Potosina, 'The Mill' has 15 neat and tasteful rooms (some around the central living room) and a pretty garden. Built on the ruins of an 18th-century sugarcane factory, El Molino provides sweet respite from the heat. The owners also offer meals.

Hotel Salto de Meco   BOUTIQUE HOTEL $$$
(📞477-717-28-64; www.huastecasecreta.com; El Naranjo; tent M$1500, cottage from M$2300; ❄) This small and quiet hideaway is set on a turquoise river, framed by a green lawn

and surrounded by thick forest. Chill over a pool-bar margarita, swim in the river, or hook up with the hotel's activity coordinator for waterfall visits, bird-watching outings, short walks or river-tubing fun. The **El Meco** FREE waterfall is nearby.

It offers accommodations in either attractive thatched bungalows or more rustic large, equipped tents with outdoor showers.

ⓘ Getting There & Away

You can get to the towns of Xilitla and Ciudad Valles easily by public transportation, but the nature of the region beyond these population centers means you really need your own transportation to reach the best places. Of course, you can also hire taxis or arrange trips with a local tour operator, which you'll find in both Xilitla and Ciudad Valles.

Ciudad Valles
📱481 / POP 177,000

Ciudad Valles is the chief town of La Huasteca Potosina and is useful for its adventure organizations and potentially as a transportation hub and a place to spend the night. The town itself is fairly unattractive, but it does boast two interesting museums that focus on the history of the region's Huastec and Nahuatl peoples.

👁 Sights

Museo Regional Huasteco
Joaquín Meade   MUSEUM
(📞481-381-14-48; Rotarios 623; ⏱9am-5pm Mon-Sat) FREE A small museum that showcases over 10,000 archaeological and ethnological pieces from the region, from around 600 BCE until the Spanish conquest.

Museo de Cultura de la
Huasteca Tamuantzán   MUSEUM
(📞481-381-26-75; Carretera México-Laredo y Libramiento Sur; adult/child M$10/5; ⏱9am-6pm Tue-Sat, 10am-3pm Sun) An excellent starting point to learn more about the Huasteca region and local cultures.

Tamtoc   ARCHAEOLOGICAL SITE
(Tamuín; M$70; ⏱9am-5pm) The important Huastec ceremonial center of Tamtoc flourished from 700 to 1500 CE. Today it's one of the few maintained Huastec sites. The cleared part of the expansive site is a plaza with platforms made of river stones. Look for a low bench with two conical altars decorated with faded 1000-year-old frescoes believed to represent Quetzalcóatl, the feathered serpent

DON'T MISS

LAS POZAS

Take a wealthy English eccentric, an idyllic tract of Mexican jungle and an extremely hyperactive imagination, and you'd still struggle to come up with the audacious, bizarre and – frankly – madcap experiment that is **Las Pozas** (The Pools; www.xilitla.org; adult/child M$100/50; ⊙ 9am-6pm).

Situated on the sweeping slopes of the Sierra Madre Oriental, Las Pozas is a monumental sculpture garden built in thick jungle that links a series of concrete temples, pagodas, bridges, pavilions and spiral stairways with a necklace of natural waterfalls. The surreal creation stands as a memorial to the imagination and excessive wealth of Edward James (1907–84). A drop-out English aristocrat and poet, he became a patron of Salvador Dalí in the late 1930s and subsequently went on to amass the largest private collection of surrealist art in the world. In 1945 James' adventures took him to Xilitla, where he met Plutarco Gastelum, who helped build Las Pozas. It began with 40 local workers crafting giant, colored concrete flowers beside an idyllic jungle stream. Then, for 17 years, James and Gastelum created ever larger and stranger structures – many of which were never finished – at an estimated cost of US$5 million.

James died in 1984, leaving no provision to maintain his creation, which, since 2008, has been in the hands of a Mexican-run nonprofit foundation. The magical labyrinth of surreal sculptures and edifices with swirly stairways leading nowhere and gates opening the way to dead ends covers 36 hectares and is worth a significant diversion for anyone with the vaguest creative inclinations. If you're in fairly good shape, you could spend the whole day contemplating the lovely swimming holes and mazelike trails.

Las Pozas has a good onsite **restaurant** (⊙ 10am-6pm) and there are several small campsites and posadas nearby. For the true Las Pozas experience, stay at Posada El Castillo (p709), the surrealist-inspired former Gastelum home where James himself also lived, now transformed into a verdant Pozas-esque guesthouse run by the Gastelum family.

god. It's not the most overwhelming of sites and probably of interest mainly to specialists.

It's 49km from Ciudad Valles, and you'll need to take a taxi or have your own transportation to get here.

🏃 Activities

★ **MS Xpediciones**   ADVENTURE
(☑ 481-381-18-88; www.msxpediciones.com; Blvd México-Laredo, Escontría 15B, Interior Hotel Misión; ⊙ 8:30am-8pm Mon-Sat, 9am-noon Sun) 🍃 The pick of the region's operators for its community-aware, friendly and professional approach. Its range of activities and adventures includes trips to Xilitla and Las Pozas, to the bird caves, and to many of the region's waterfalls. It also arranges excellent canoeing adventures, including to Tamul (M$950 minimum two people; including transportation and a meal with a local family), plus rafting expeditions.

🛏 Sleeping & Eating

Hotel Misión Ciudad Valles   HOTEL $$
(☑ 481-382-00-66; www.hotelesmision.com.mx; Blvd México-Laredo 15; r from M$900; ❄☎⊠) This 1930s hacienda-style building may be in need of a little love and a fresh lick of

paint, but it has good bones. There's a big pool (a plus in this climate) and spacious rooms with coffee facilities. Breakfast is not included in the price, but is available.

La Leyenda   MEXICAN $$
(☑ 481-381-92-31; Morelos 323; M$115-225; ⊙ 8am-11pm Mon-Sat, to 5pm Sun; 🅿❄) This rather dark but mercifully air-conditioned restaurant is housed in a ranch-like building where smart and attentive staff work hard for their tips. The meaty menu is pure Mexican, with tasty tacos, enchiladas and steaks.

ⓘ Getting There & Away

Ciudad Valles is well connected throughout the region, and the busy **Terminal Ciudad Valles** (Contreras s/n) can be found 3km southeast of the downtown area. To get to Real de Catorce from here, you'll need to change buses twice; first in the town of Río Verde and then in Matehuala.

Xilitla

📞 489 / POP 6500 / ELEV 489M

Surrounded by the jaw-dropping tropical scenery of the Huasteca Potosina, the remote hillside town of Xilitla (hee-*leet*-la) is an agreeable spot notable for its precariously steep streets and proximity to Las Pozas, the British eccentric Edward James' fantastical jungle sculpture garden.

The Huasteca Potosina region continues to grow in popularity as a travel destination, and Xilitla has found itself at the center of a small but quickly growing tourism bubble. It now has dozens of hotels and guesthouses as well as numerous tour operators offering rafting, rappelling, hiking and mountain-bike excursions in the surrounding countryside. There's definitely a bit of magic in the air here, as all who make it this far quickly discover.

◉ Sights

★ Museo Leonora Carrington MUSEUM
(www.leonoracarringtonmuseo.org/xilitla; Miguel Álvarez Acosta 109; adult/student M$40/20; ⊙11am-5pm Tue-Thu, to 6pm Fri-Sun) British-born but Mexican at heart, Leonora Carrington (1917–2011) was one of the last surrealist artists and a key player in the Mexican women's liberation movement. This museum showcases some of her most impressive works including beautiful tapestries and brain-bendingly bizarre paintings. Displays are well lit and labeled. Some of the creepy-looking sculptures and statues here could give you nightmares!

☞ Tours

Mundo Extreme Tours OUTDOORS
(☑489-105-30-00; www.mundoextreme.com.mx; Hidalgo 104) A highly recommended outfit specializing in extreme sports and all sorts of outdoor activities, Mundo Extreme offers a number of 'rutas' through the Huasteca Potosina, combining elements of hiking, climbing, kayaking, rafting and rappelling.

🛏 Sleeping & Eating

While things have improved noticeably in the past few years, there's still not much culinary choice. What there is can be found on and around the Jardín Principal, Xilitla's main square.

★ Hotel Camino Surreal HOTEL $$
(☑489-122-40-14; www.caminosurreal.com; Ocampo 311; r from M$1300; ❄☂❄) This is the friendliest and most comfortable place in town and makes for a very pleasant oasis of cool after a day tramping around the jungle. There are just six rooms, but they're all spacious, spotlessly clean and most have balconies overlooking a garden and a pool fringed in palm trees. There's a pleasant bar.

Grann Posada Xilitla GUESTHOUSE $$
(☑489-365-00-23; Corregidora 105; d from M$900; ❄☂) Welcoming family-run guesthouse in the heart of town. The rooms are immaculately well kept and most have attractive exposed stone walls and wooden roof beams. There's a cafe-bar right up on the roof with good views over the town. The owners will happily help you organize tours of the surrounding countryside.

Posada El Castillo GUESTHOUSE $$
(☑489-365-00-38; www.elcastilloxilitla.com; Ocampo 105; d incl breakfast M$1570; ☂❄) The former Gastelum home where Edward James stayed in Xilitla is now a verdant, Pozas-esque guesthouse run by his niece and her family. Its unique rooms are decorated with antiques and art, and some claim fantastic views. Based only on room quality, it's quite overpriced, and while the welcome is warm, they do not accept walk-ins, so reserve ahead.

NORTHERN CENTRAL HIGHLANDS LA HUASTECA POTOSINA

BUSES FROM XILITLA

Xilitla's makeshift **bus station** (Independencia s/n) is in a small lot surrounded by several ticket offices in the middle of the town.

DESTINATION	FARE (M$)	TIME (HR)	FREQUENCY (PER DAY)
Ciudad Valles	132-143	2	hourly
Jalpan	96-128	2	hourly
Mexico City (Terminal Norte)	412-534	8-9	5
Querétaro	440	5½	1
San Luis Potosí	462	5½	2
Tampico	446	5	4
Tequisquiapan	322	5	3

La Huastequita　　　　　　　　MEXICAN $$
(☑ 489-365-13-49; Miguel Álvarez Acosta 101E; mains M$100-200; ⊘ 8am-10pm Wed-Mon, to 5pm Tue) Everyone's favorite place to eat in Xilita, La Huastequita offers reassuringly simple, authentic Mexican home-style cooking that'll fill you up after a day clambering up and down forested hills. From the roof terrace there are lovely views over the main square and church. The enchiladas come with a spicy kick.

ZACATECAS STATE

The state of Zacatecas (za-ka-*te*-kas) is a sun-bleached, dry, rugged, cactus-strewn expanse on the fringe of Mexico's northern semideserts. The state is best known for the wealthy silver city of the same name, an elegant and enjoyable place full of colonial architecture and boasting an impressive cathedral. Outside the cosmopolitan city, ranchers wearing low-slung cowboy hats canter into dusty villages and the mysterious ruins of La Quemada stand in solemn testament to forgotten cultures. The state is one of Mexico's largest in area (73,252 sq km) but smallest in population (1.58 million); it is believed that as many people again, who come from the state, currently live in the USA.

Zacatecas

☑ 492 / POP 147,000 / ELEV 2430M

The most northern of Mexico's silver cities, fascinating Zacatecas – a Unesco World Heritage site – runs along a narrow valley overlooked by a steep and imposing hillside. The large historic center is jam-packed with opulent colonial buildings, a stupendous cathedral, magnificent museums and steep, winding streets and alleys that simply ooze charm.

Zacatecas was where thousands of indigenous slaves were forced by the Spanish to toil in the mines under terrible conditions. Pancho Villa enjoyed a historic victory in 1914, and he is still feted by locals today. Nowadays travelers can have their own lofty experiences in a *teleférico* (cable car) to the Cerro de la Bufa, the impressive rock outcrop that soars above the town and affords great views of the church domes and tiled rooftops below. Alternatively, visitors can drop below the surface to tour the infamous Edén mine, a sobering reminder of the city's brutal colonial past.

History

Indigenous Zacatecos – one of the Chichimec tribes – mined local mineral deposits for centuries before the Spanish arrived; it's said that the silver rush here was started when a Chichimec gave a piece of the fabled metal to a conquistador. The Spaniards founded a settlement in 1548 and started mining operations that sent caravan after caravan of silver off to Mexico City, creating fabulously wealthy silver barons in Zacatecas.

By the early 18th century, the mines of Zacatecas were producing 20% of Nueva España's silver and the city became an important base for Catholic missionaries.

In the 19th century political instability diminished the flow of silver. Although silver production later improved under Porfirio Díaz, the Revolution disrupted it. In 1914 in Zacatecas, Pancho Villa defeated a stronghold of 12,000 soldiers loyal to President Victoriano Huerta. After the Revolution, Zacatecas continued to thrive on silver until the final closure of the last mines.

⊙ Sights

★ **Museo Rafael Coronel**　　　　　MUSEUM
(☑ 492-922-81-16; cnr Abasolo & Matamoros; adult/student M$30/15; ⊘ 10am-5pm Thu-Tue) The excellent Museo Rafael Coronel is not to be missed. Imaginatively housed in the ruins of the lovely 16th-century Ex-Convento de San Francisco, it houses Mexican folk art collected by Zacatecan artist Rafael Coronel, brother of Pedro Coronel and son-in-law of Diego Rivera. Take your time to wander through the various spaces by following the arrows. The collection of masks is truly incredible, as are collections of totems, pottery, puppets and other fascinating objects. All labeling is in Spanish only.

After you've admired the treasures within, relax among the trees and (slightly disturbing!) statues and sculptures in the surrounding gardens.

★ **Museo Pedro Coronel**　　　　　MUSEUM
(☑ 492-922-80-21; Plaza de Santo Domingo s/n; adult/student M$30/15; ⊘ 10am-5pm Tue-Sun) The Museo Pedro Coronel is housed in a 17th-century former Jesuit college and is one of provincial Mexico's best art museums. Pedro Coronel (1923–85) was an affluent Zacatecan artist who bequeathed to the city his collection of art and artifacts from all over the world, as well as his own works. The collection includes 20th-century works by Picasso, Rouault, Dalí,

Goya and Miró; and pre-Hispanic Mexican artifacts, masks and other ancient pieces.

Museo del Arte Abstracto
Manuel Felguérez   MUSEUM
(☑ 492-924-37-05; www.museodearteabstracto. com; Ex-Seminario de la Purísima Concepción, Colón s/n; adult/student M$30/20; ☺ 10am-5pm Wed-Mon) This superb abstract-art museum is worth visiting for the building alone; originally a seminary, it was later used as a prison and has been renovated to create some remarkable exhibition spaces, transforming the former dark, depressing cells and steel walkways into a beautiful site. It has a stunning and varied collection of abstract painting and sculpture, particularly the work of Zacatecan artist Manuel Felguérez.

Cerro de la Bufa   LANDMARK
The most appealing of the many explanations for the name of the hill that dominates Zacatecas is that *bufa* is an old Basque word for wineskin, which is apparently what the rocky formation looks like. The views from the top are superb and there's an interesting group of monuments, a chapel and a museum. It is also the site of a zip-line, **Tirolesa 840** (☑ 492-117-15-30; www.tirolesa840.com; rides from M$250; ☺ 10am-6pm), a 1km ride across a former open-pit mine.

Once up the hill you can also visit **Capilla de la Virgen del Patrocinio**. Named after the patron saint of miners, this 18th-century chapel has a holy image of the Virgen del Patrocinio above its altar that is said to be capable of healing the sick. Standing next to the chapel are three imposing equestrian statues of the victors of the battle of Zacatecas – Villa, Ángeles and Pánfilo Natera. To the right of the statues, a paved path along the foot of the rocky hilltop leads to the **Mausoleo de los Hombres Ilustres de Zacatecas**, with the tombs of Zacatecan heroes from 1841 to the present.

A convenient way to ascend La Bufa (to the church and museum) is by **teleférico** (☑ 492-922-01-70; one way/return M$100/160; ☺ 10am-6pm). Alternatively, you can walk up, starting at Calle del Ángel from the cathedral's east end. To reach it by car, take Carretera a la Bufa, which begins at Avenida López Velarde, a couple of kilometers east of the center. A taxi costs around M$60. You can return to town by the *teleférico* or by a footpath leading downhill from the statues.

Mina El Edén   MINE
(☑ 492-922-30-02; www.minaeleden.com.mx/english; Mante s/n; tours adult/child M$100/50; ☺ tours every hour 10am-6pm) Visiting one of Mexico's

---

HUICHOL VISIONS

The remote Sierra Madre Occidental is the home of the Huichole, one of Mexico's most distinctive and enduring indigenous groups. A fiercely independent people, they were one of the few indigenous groups not subjugated by the Aztecs.

The arrival of the Spanish had little immediate effect on the Huicholes and it wasn't until the 17th century that the first Catholic missionaries reached the Huichol homelands. Rather than convert to Christianity, the Huicholes incorporated various elements of Christian teachings into their traditional animist belief systems. In Huichol mythology, gods become personalized as plants, totem animal species and natural objects, while their supernatural form is explored in religious rituals.

Every year the Huicholes leave their isolated homeland and make a pilgrimage to the Sierra de Catorce, in northern San Luis Potosí state. In this harsh desert region, they seek out the mezcal cactus (*Lophophora williamsii*), known as peyote cactus. The rounded peyote 'buttons' contain a powerful hallucinogenic drug (whose chief element is mescaline) that is central to the Huicholes' rituals and complex spiritual life.

The fact is that peyote is illegal in Mexico, though many travelers seem intent on ignoring this. Under Mexican law, the Huicholes are permitted to use it for their spiritual purposes. For the Huicholes, indiscriminate use is regarded as offensive, even sacrilegious.

Traditionally the main Huichol art forms were telling stories and making masks and detailed geometric embroidery, or 'yarn pictures.' In the last few decades, brightly colored beads have replaced the yarn. This is painstaking work, where the beads are pressed into a beeswax-covered substrate. This exquisite artwork is sold in craft markets, shops and galleries. Prices are usually fixed and the Huicholes don't like to haggle. To see the best work, visit one of the specialist museums or shops in Zapopan (Guadalajara), Tepic, Puerto Vallarta or Zacatecas.

Zacatecas

N 0 ————————— 200 m
0 ————————— 0.1 miles

Los Dorados de Villa (200m);
Museo Rafael
5 Coronel (200m)
la del Seminario

17

Museo Toma de
Zacatecas (1km)

Duranzo
Fortín
Bosque

Cerro del Grillo
Teleférico Station

Mante
Del Salto
Rojas

Capilla de la Virgen
del Patrocinio (400m);
Cerro de la Bufa (400m)

4
Bosque

Juan de Tolosa
Moral
Triste
Abasolo

Paseo Díaz Ordaz

Mante
Mercedita
López

De Los Bolos

Pankhurst

Grillo
Del Auxilio

Gómez
Serdán
Lancaster

Museo Pedro 1 10
Coronel

Plazuela
de Santo
Domingo

8
9 7

Genaro Codina
Av Hidalgo
Urizar

Mina Club
(250m)

De la Loma

Del Cobre

Villalpando

Dr Hierro
21
6
15

2

Medina

Aguascalientes

11

19

16

Plazuela
Francisco
Goitia

3
13 Callejón del Lazo
Del Estudiante
Auza

Parque
Alameda

Cadena

20
Plaza
Miguel Auza
22

12
Jardín
Morelos Jardín
Juárez

Plazuela
Genaro
Codina

Av Juárez

Amador

Arroyo de la Plata
Av Guerrero
Tenorio

Aurora

Correa

Ponce

Estrada

Parque
Enrique
Estrada

Av González Ortega
Trabajo

Jardín
Independencia

Independencia
Salazar

García de la Cadena

Salinas

Estrada

Central de
Autobuses
Zacatecas
(2.3km)

14
Rayón
Calderón
Morelos

Blvd López Mateos

Plaza del
Bicentenario
Local Buses
to Guadalupe

18

Catz de la Paz

Zacatecas

richest mines (1586–1960s) provides an insight into a source of wealth and the terrible price paid for it. Digging for hoards of silver, gold, iron, copper and zinc, enslaved indigenous people worked in horrific conditions. Up to five people a day died from accidents or tuberculosis and silicosis. These days, it's rather different: a miniature train takes you inside Cerro del Grillo, while guides lead you along floodlit walkways past shafts and over subterranean pools.

The mine has two entrances. To reach the higher one (the east entrance), walk 100m southwest from Cerro del Grillo *teleférico* (p711) station; from this entrance, tours start with an elevator descent. To reach the west entrance from the town center, walk west along Avenida Juárez and stay on it after its name changes to Avenida Torreón at the Alameda. Turn right immediately after the IMSS hospital (bus 7 from the corner of Avenida Hidalgo goes up Avenida Juárez and past the hospital) and a short walk will bring you to the mine entrance. Tours begin here with a trip on the narrow-gauge railway (540m), after which you walk another 350m or so. It's cold in the mine. Bring a jacket.

Catedral   CATHEDRAL
(Plaza de Armas) Built between 1729 and 1752, the pink-stone cathedral is an ultimate expression of Mexican baroque. The stupendous main facade is a wall of detailed carvings; this has been interpreted as a giant symbol of the tabernacle. Indeed, a tiny figure of an angel holding a tabernacle is in the middle of the design, the keystone atop the round

central window. Above this, in the third tier, is Christ and above Christ is God.

The southern facade's central sculpture is of La Virgen de los Zacatecanos, the city's patroness. The north facade shows Christ crucified, attended by the Virgin Mary and St John. Unveiled in 2010, the grand altar is the work of Javier Marín, a famous Mexican artist. It features 10 large bronze figures and the figure of Christ, arranged on a backdrop of golden blocks.

Museo Toma de Zacatecas   MUSEUM
(☑492-922-80-66; Cerro de la Bufa; adult/student M$12/6; ⊙10am-5pm; ▣) This museum memorializes the 1914 battle fought on the slopes of the Cerro de la Bufa in which the revolutionary División del Norte, led by Pancho Villa and Felipe Ángeles, defeated President Victoriano Huerta's forces. This gave the revolutionaries control of Zacatecas, which was the gateway to Mexico City. The child-friendly museum, which reopened in 2014 after a full renovation, is a technological delight, with talking ghosts, actual footage of the battle and all kinds of other interactive displays.

Plaza de Armas   PLAZA
The city's main plaza is north of the cathedral and although normally quiet in the day it buzzes at night with families promenading, children playing and occasional live music. The **Palacio de Gobierno** (⊙8am-8pm Mon-Fri) FREE on the plaza's east side was built in the 18th century for a colonial family. In the turret of its main staircase is a mural of the history of Zacatecas state, painted in 1970 by Antonio Rodríguez.

LA QUEMADA RUINS

The remote and scenic ruins of **La Quemada** (M$60; ⊙9am-6pm) stand on a hill 45km south of Zacatecas. The exact history and purpose of the site are extremely vague and many suppositions surround the area – one theory is that it was where the Aztecs halted during their legendary wanderings toward the Valle de México. What is known for sure is that the constructions were destroyed by fire – and thus they came to be called La Quemada (meaning 'burned city').

La Quemada was inhabited between about 300 and 1200 CE, and it is estimated to have peaked between 500 and 900 with as many as 3000 inhabitants. From around 400 it was part of a regional trade network linked to Teotihuacán, but fortifications suggest that La Quemada later tried to dominate trade in this region. A recent study suggests that during the settlement's peak its inhabitants engaged in cannibalism of their enemies, the remains of whom they hung up ceremonially.

Of the main structures, the nearest to the site entrance is the **Salón de las Columnas** (Hall of the Columns), probably a ceremonial hall. Slightly further up the hill are a ball court, a steep offerings pyramid and an equally steep staircase leading toward the site's upper levels. From the upper levels of the main hill, a path leads westward for about 800m to a spur hilltop (the highest point) with the remains of a cluster of buildings called **La Ciudadela** (the Citadel). There are memorable views down into the valley from here. To return, follow the defensive wall and path back around to the small **museum**, which has an interesting collection of artifacts recovered from the site and a good video summary of what is known. Relatively unknown, la Quemada receives few visitors and the ruins, which are half-covered in swaying, silver-tipped grasses, are wonderfully evocative. Note that there's very little shade. Take water and a hat and be on the lookout for rattlesnakes, which have been seen at the site.

From Zacatecas's Plaza del Bicentenario, board a combi bus for Villanueva (M$40) and ask beforehand to be let off at *las ruinas*; you'll be deposited at the turnoff, from where it's a 2.5km walk to the site entrance. Returning to Zacatecas, you may have to wait a while for a bus – don't leave the ruins too late. Alternatively, hire a taxi to take you here, which will cost around M$800 to M$900, including waiting time.

Across the road, and directly opposite the Palacio, the **Palacio de la Mala Noche** was built in the late 18th century for a mine owner and now houses state government offices.

Museo Zacatecano
MUSEUM

(☑492-922-65-80; Dr Hierro 301; adult/student M$30/15; ⊙10am-5pm Wed-Mon) Zacatecas' former mint (Mexico's second-biggest in the 19th century) now houses the wonderful Museo Zacatecano. Spread over a number of rooms, this contemporary museum exhibits a weird mix of all things *zacatecano*. Unfortunately, the first few *salas* are text-heavy information boards (in Spanish). The highlight – in the last halls – is the superb collection of Huichol art. Videos (all in Spanish) provide each hall's context.

Templo de Santo Domingo
CHURCH

(Plazuela de Santo Domingo) With a bubbly stone facade, the tarnished pink Templo de Santo Domingo, in a *plazuela* of the same name, is in a baroque style, with fine gilded altars and a graceful horseshoe staircase.

Built by the Jesuits in the 1740s, the church was taken over by Dominican monks when the Jesuits were expelled in 1767.

✷ Festivals & Events

La Morisma
RELIGIOUS

(⊙Aug) Usually held the last weekend in August, La Morisma features a spectacular mock battle commemorating the triumph of the Christians over the Muslims in old Spain. Two rival 'armies' – around 10,000 participants from the barrio of Bracho – parade through the streets in the morning, then, accompanied by bands of musicians, enact two battle sequences between Lomas de Bracho and Cerro de la Bufa.

Feria de Zacatecas
CULTURAL

(Fenaza; www.fenaza.com.mx; ⊙Sep) An annual fair with a folkloric focus, held during the first three weeks of September, featuring renowned matadors fighting famous local bulls. There are also *charreadas* (rodeos), concerts, plays, agricultural and craft shows.

On September 8 the image of La Virgen del Patrocinio is carried to the cathedral from its chapel on Cerro de la Bufa (p711).

🛏 Sleeping

★ Cielito Lindo Hostal
HOSTEL $

(☎492-921-11-32; http://cielitolindohostal.com; Aguascalientes 213; dm M$220, d with/without bathroom M$623/462; 🛜) There are few budget options in Zacatecas, but this delightful and stylish hostel, which is in the former home of a religious *padre,* has been lovingly converted into a memorable space for budget travelers. There's a big choice of rooms including dorms that come with lockers and recharging stations, as well as a (rather basic) kitchen.

La Terrasse
HOTEL $$

(☎492-925-53-15; Villalpando 209; d incl breakfast from M$900; 😊❄🛜) This small, friendly and very smart, centrally located option is run by a proud owner. It has 14 contemporary and slightly sparse rooms, but is by far the best midrange option. Back rooms have internal-facing windows: claustrophobic for some, quiet for others.

Hotel Mesón de Jobito
HOTEL $$

(☎492-924-17-22; www.mesondejobito.com; Jardín Juárez 143; r incl breakfast from M$1900; 🅿😊❄🛜) Guests come here to soak up the old-fashioned charm and sense of history that permeates pretty much every corner of this atmospheric hotel. Its 53 rooms are comfortable and spacious, if a little faded. Some have attractive exposed roof beams. There's a good restaurant and bar (plus slanting balcony, a legacy of its construction 200 years ago).

Its Sunday breakfast buffet (M$160) is a local institution. The hotel has a plumb position overlooking pretty Jardín Juárez.

Quinta Real Zacatecas
LUXURY HOTEL $$$

(☎492-922-91-04, 800-999-73-25; www.quinta real.com; Rayón 434; ste from M$2668; 🅿😊❄🛜) This luxury treat is hands down the best hotel in Zacatecas. Spectacularly situated around the country's oldest – and now retired – bullring and near El Cubo aqueduct, the 49-room hotel is one of Mexico's most contemporary and fetching. Even the least expensive rooms are spacious, comfortable master suites. An elegant restaurant, La Plaza (p716), overlooks the ring.

Santa Rita Hotel
BOUTIQUE HOTEL $$$

(☎492-925-11-94; www.hotelsantarita.com; Av Hidalgo 507A; ste from M$1500; 🅿❄🛜) A decent contemporary choice, this boutique hotel has delightful, attentive staff and some unusual decorative choices (think random Greek busts). Be aware that some of the 41 suites have internal-facing windows, an inevitability in colonial buildings but one that might surprise you at these prices.

🍴 Eating

Compared to similar-size cities in the area Zacatecas has a rather disappointing dining scene in general, though there are some notable exceptions. Local specialties feature ingredients such as *nopal* and pumpkin seeds, and the city is also known for its *asado de boda* (a citrus-orange-flavored *mole* sauce) and its *birria de chivo* (goat stew). In the morning, look around Avenida Tacuba for the *burro* (donkey) carrying pottery jugs of *aguamiel* (honey water), a nutritional drink derived from the *maguey* cactus.

Acrópolis Café
MEXICAN $

(☎492-922-12-84; www.acropoliszacatecas.wix site.com/restaurante; cnr Av Hidalgo & Plazuela Candelario Huizar; mains M$110-200; ⊘8am-10pm; 🛜) Established by a Syrian immigrant in the early 1940s, this cafe has been a city legend almost ever since. Today it retains a slightly quirky period diner feel, and is *the* breakfast place for locals and visitors alike – perhaps more for its location than its food. It offers light meals, set breakfasts and good coffee.

Rincon Tipico
MEXICAN $

(☎492-100-47-54; Av Rayón 320; mains M$60-170; ⊘8am-8pm Mon-Thu, to 10pm Fri & Sat) It's all about recipes passed down through the generations and traditional home-cooked food at this bright and boisterous little restaurant. Don't expect any decorative frills but do expect plenty of taste thrills.

Los Dorados de Villa
MEXICAN $$

(☎492-922-57-22; Plazuela de García 1314; mains M$80-240; ⊘3pm-1am Mon-Sat, to 11pm Sun; 🛜) Unless you have a reservation you're unlikely to be allowed into this revolutionary-themed restaurant – and even with a reservation you'll need to knock at the permanently locked door. Once inside though it's a blast of color, chockablock with atmosphere. Culinary highlights include an amazing selection of enchiladas and a fabulous *caldillo durangueño* (Durango beef stew).

The mezcal comes with a kick in the form of a real-life scorpion balanced atop your glass. Yes. Seriously.

Mýkonos Cocina Mediterránea
MEDITERRANEAN $$

(📋492-922-67-46; www.facebook.com/mykonos-cocinamediterranea; Juan de Tolosa 104; mains M$70-140; ⊘2:30-10pm) Hidden behind a simple exterior is this cozy and surprisingly upmarket restaurant that sells itself as being Greek, but with kofta, couscous, hummus and pasta dishes filling the menu it's more of a marriage between Italian and Lebanese cuisine. Decent wine list.

Restaurant La Plaza
INTERNATIONAL $$$

(📋492-922-91-04; Quinta Real Zacatecas, Rayón 434; mains M$200-390; 🕾) The elegant dining room at the Quinta Real Zacatecas is especially memorable for its outlook to the aqueduct and bullring, as well as for its refined ambience and good international cuisine with a few Mexican standards. Head here for Sunday brunch (M$250), a local institution. Reservations are advisable for the evening.

🍸 Drinking & Nightlife

★ Cantina las Quince Letras
BAR

(📋492-922-01-78; Mártires de Chicago 309; ⊘1pm-1am Mon-Sat) Founded in 1906, this oft-crowded classic is filled with bohemians, musicians, drunks and poets. The art showcases some well-known local and international artists, including Pedro Coronel.

Mina Club
BAR

(www.minaeleden.com.mx; Dovali s/n; cover M$70-150; ⊘4-11pm Thu & Fri, 10pm-late Sat) For a different experience, do not miss your chance to descend into the earth and party in the tunnel of the Mina El Edén (p711). On Saturday the popular attraction morphs into a club; check opening hours, as these change seasonally.

Dalí Café & Bar
BAR

(Plaza Miguel Auza 322; ⊘4pm-midnight; 🕾) This sprawling cafe-bar in front of Ex-Templo de San Agustín (⊘10am-5pm Tue-Sun) FREE offers a surreal mix of furniture, cocktails and post-drink munchies (as well as good hot-chocolate drinks).

☆ Entertainment

Teatro Calderón
THEATER

(📋492-922-86-20; Av Hidalgo s/n) This top venue hosts a variety of events including theater, dance and music performances. Check the posters or with the tourist office for current events.

🛍 Shopping

Zacatecas is known for silver and leather products and the colorful *sarape* (a blanket with an opening for a head). Try along Arroyo de la Plata (and its indoor market).

Casa de las Artesanías
ARTS & CRAFTS

(Plazuela Miguel Auza 312; ⊘9am-6pm) A not-for-profit shop that promotes and sells handmade products from Zacatecas state. These include silver jewelry, stone carvings, textiles and *talabartería* (designs handsewn into leather typical of the region).

Centro Platero
JEWELRY

(📋492-899-45-03; www.centroplaterodezacatecas. com; Ex-Hacienda de Bernardez; ⊘10am-5pm Mon-Fri, to 2pm Sat) The Zacatecas silversmith industry sells its work at its workshop a few kilometers east of town on the road to Guadalupe. Here, young artisans produce various designs, from the traditional to the contemporary. To get here, it's easiest to take a taxi.

ℹ Information

Hospital Santa Elena (📋492-922-69-70; Av Guerrero 143; ⊘24hr)

Post Office (Allende 111; ⊘8am-4pm Mon-Fri, to 2pm Sat)

Tourist Office (📋800-712-40-78; www.zaca tecastravel.com; Av Hidalgo s/n; ⊘9am-7pm Mon-Fri, to 3pm Sat & Sun) This kiosk is run by Securz, the municipal tourist organization, and offers maps and information. Ask for a copy of *Agenda Cultural*, an excellent events listing.

ℹ Getting There & Away

AIR

Aeropuerto Internacional de Zacatecas (www.oma.aero/es/pasajeros/zacatecas/ index.php) is 20km northwest of the city. There are four daily flights to Mexico City as well as direct services to Los Angeles, San Jose (California) and Dallas.

BUS

Central de Autobuses Zacatecas (📋492-922-27-74; Carretera 45) is on the southwest edge of town, around 3km from the center. Deluxe, 1st- and 2nd-class buses operate to/from here. Some buses to nearby destinations, including Villanueva (for La Quemada), leave from **Plaza del Bicentenario** (Blvd López Mateos). **Local buses to Guadalupe** leave from the other side of the road. There is no direct service to Guanajuato from Zacatecas, so take a León bus and change there. For San Miguel de Allende, change buses in San Luis Potosí or Querétaro.

GUADALUPE

About 10km east of Zacatecas, Guadalupe boasts a fascinating historic former monastery, the Convento de Guadalupe. The Convento was established by Franciscan monks in the early 18th century as an apostolic college. It developed a strong academic tradition and was a base for missionary work in northern Nueva España until the 1850s. It is now the excellent **Museo Virreinal de Guadalupe** (Jardín Juárez Oriente; adult/student M$60/free, Sun free; ⊙ 9am-6pm Tue-Sun), the reason for travelers to come here.

Visitors can enter two parts of the Convento: the impressive **church**, which attracts pilgrims to honor the country's beloved Virgin; and the museum, which features one of Mexico's best colonial-art collections with religious paintings by Miguel Cabrera, Juan Correa, Antonio Torres and Cristóbal Villalpando. Visitors can also see the library and its 9000 dusty volumes dating from as far back as 1529 – not one of which looks like it would make for light bedtime reading!

ℹ Getting Around

The easiest way to get to/from the airport is by taxi (M$350 to M$400).

Taxis from the bus station to the center of Zacatecas cost around M$50. Bus 8 from the bus station (M$6) runs directly to the cathedral. Heading out of the center, catch a 'route 8' bus heading south on Villalpando.

Jerez

📞 494 / POP 58,000 / ELEV 2000M

The delightful country town of Jerez, 30km southwest of Zacatecas, is as Mexican as can be: full of cowboys, churches and marching bands. As such, it's a great place to head for a day to soak up the traditional atmosphere. Sunday – market day – is especially fun as you'll see saddle-bound *rancheros* drinking outside the saloons, while on Saturdays you'll see wedding processions and mariachis playing around the main plaza, Jardín Páez, with its old-fashioned gazebo, trees and benches. Jerez is also known for its lively weeklong Easter fair, featuring, among other activities, *charreadas* and cockfights.

Teatro Hinojosa   HISTORIC BUILDING
(Reloj Esq Salvador Varela; ⊙ 10am-5pm Tue-Sun) Construction of this remarkable and very beautiful building is said to have taken place over two decades, thanks to the organization of a local, Don Higinio Escobedo Zauza, who got things rolling in 1867. Then Don José María Hinojos organized generous locals who

volunteered their time and donations of materials until the project was completed. It is renowned for its extraordinary shape, said to create among the best acoustics in the world. Ask the caretaker if you can look inside.

**Casa Museo Interactivo
Ramón Lopez Velarde**   HISTORIC BUILDING
(📞 494-945-59-70; Calle de la Parroquia 33; M$20; ⊙ 10am-5pm Tue-Sun) One of Mexico's favorite poets, Ramón Lopez Velarde, was born in this house on June 15, 1888, and lived here for the first eight years or so of his life. The museum is well curated and full of interactive displays, which can be interesting even if you're unfamiliar with Lopez Velarde's work.

★ **Botica del Cafe**   CAFE $
(📞 494-945-00-22; Calle del Espejo 3; sandwiches M$60-80; ⊙ 5:30-10:30pm Tue-Fri, from 10am Sat & Sun; 🛜 🍴) 🅿 This utterly delightful lime-green cafe is quite the find in a small town like Jerez. Housed in an old pharmacy, Botica del Cafe serves delicious *chapatas* (ciabatta sandwiches), salads and cakes, and does an array of coffee likely to satisfy even the most demanding customer, including Chemex and AeroPress.

ℹ Getting There & Away

There are regular services from Zacatecas' bus station to Jerez (M$83, one hour). Jerez' **bus station** (Calz La Suave Patria) is on the east side of town, 1km from the center. From here, 'Centro' buses (M$6) run to/from the center.

AT A GLANCE

POPULATION
4.6 million

CAPITALS
Mexicali (Baja California), La Paz (Baja California Sur)

BEST SEAFOOD TOSTADAS
La Guerrerense (p734)

BEST WHALE-WATCHING
Parque Marine Nacional Bahía de Loreto (p743)

BEST WINERY
Adobe Guadalupe (p730)

WHEN TO GO
Jan–Mar
Flowers bloom, things get green; whales and whale sharks play; and big waves delight surfers.

Aug & Sep
Beaches all but empty. You'll have Baja all to yourself, but it's *hot*.

Oct & Nov
The seas are crystal clear for uncrowded diving and snorkeling.

Espíritu Santo (p746)
DESIGN PICS/STUART WESTMORLAND/GETTY IMAGES ©

Baja Peninsula

Baja, the earth's second-longest peninsula, offers over 1200km of the mystical, ethereal, majestic and untamed. Those lucky enough to make the full Tijuana to Los Cabos trip will find the drive stunning at every turn. The middle of nowhere is more beautiful than you ever imagined, and people are friendly, relaxed and helpful – even in the border towns. Side roads pass through tiny villages and wind drunkenly along the sides of mountains. Condors circle in an unblemished blue sky.

Sip drinks, eat fish tacos and watch the sun disappear into the Pacific; surf that perfect wave; or walk through sherbet-colored canyons and stare up at the night's canopy of stars – whichever way you choose to experience it, Baja will not soon be forgotten.

History

Before Europeans arrived, an estimated 48,000 mobile hunter-gatherers were living in today's Baja; their mysterious murals still grace caves and canyon walls. European settlement failed to reach Baja until the Jesuit missions of the 17th and 18th centuries, and the missions soon collapsed as European-introduced diseases ravaged the indigenous people. Ranchers, miners and fishers were the next to arrive. During the US Prohibition era of the 1920s, Baja became a popular south-of-the-border destination for gamblers, drinkers and other 'sinners.' Today the region is growing in economic power, population and popularity, albeit with problematic ecological and environmental consequences.

🛈 Getting There & Away

There are six official border crossings from the US state of California to Baja.

Mexican mainland, US and international flights leave from and arrive in La Paz, Loreto, San José del Cabo and Tijuana. Ferries from Santa Rosalía and Pichilingue (near La Paz) connect the Baja Peninsula to the mainland by sea.

🛈 Getting Around

Air-conditioned, nonsmoking but relatively expensive buses operate daily between towns all along the peninsula; however, car travel is often

---

> ### BAJA SAFETY
> ●●
> The US State Department urges travelers to 'exercise increased caution' throughout the Baja Peninsula due to crime, noting particular concern over the murder rate in Tijuana, Los Cabos and La Paz due to drug cartel–related activities. In main tourist areas you'd hardly realize that violence is going on in the fringes, though, and thus far tourists have not been targeted. That said, it never hurts to use common sense, stay clear of dodgy areas and avoid driving at night. Keep valuables (including surfboards) out of sight and doors locked to minimize the risk of theft, which at present is still your greatest worry.
>
> Sanitation standards in Baja are higher than in other states, and water – even tap water – is often safe to drink.

---

the only way to reach isolated villages, mountains and beaches. You can rent cars in larger cities and major tourist destinations.

Highways are good and there are few toll roads. Drivers using the scenic (*cuota*; toll highway) route to Ensenada will need M$37; the Tijuana–Mexicali route costs M$210. Denominations larger than US$20 or M$200 are not accepted. You'll also encounter a number of harmless military checkpoints.

NORTHERN BAJA

Tijuana, Tecate and Mexicali form the northern border of an area known as La Frontera, which extends as far south as San Quintín on the west and San Felipe on the east. Increasingly, the Ruta del Vino (between Ensenada and Tecate) is gaining Napa Valley–like fame for its boutique, award-winning wines. Though northern Baja's border cities and beaches are undeniably hedonistic, Tijuana and Mexicali are also major manufacturing centers and retain a workaday feel.

Parque Nacional Constitución de 1857   NATIONAL PARK

At the end of a challenging 43km road out of Ojos Negros (east of Ensenada), Parque Nacional Constitución de 1857 has beautiful conifers, fields of wildflowers and a sometimes-dry lake, Laguna Hanson, at an altitude of 1200m. *Cabañas* (cabins; M$1100) or campsites (included with M$72 park fee) are available (686-554-44-04, 8am to 3pm Monday to Friday); the water may be contaminated so bring your own.

It's a sublime spot for mountain biking, hiking or just getting away from it all, as long as everyone else isn't getting away at the same time – in peak holiday times it can be busy, but it's a beautiful spot any time of year. The park is also accessible by a steeper road east of Km 55.2, 16km southeast of the Ojos Negros junction.

La Bufadora   LANDMARK

La Bufadora is a popular 'blowhole' (really a notch in the rock that sprays waves upward) 40km south of Ensenada. If conditions are right it sends a jet of water up to 30m into the sky, drenching cheering onlookers.

Conditions aren't always ideal, but if you're up for a gamble you can drive south on the Transpeninsular to the 'Bufadora' sign, then follow the road all the way around

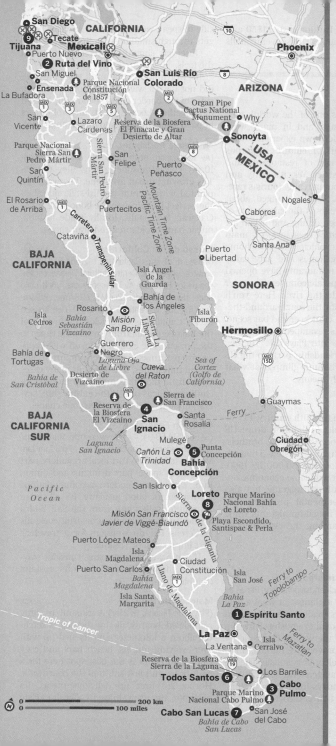

Baja Peninsula Highlights

1 **Espíritu Santo** (p746) Kayaking the blue bays, snorkeling with sea lions and beach picnicking.

2 **Ruta del Vino** (p729) Sipping and savoring the bucolic delights of northern Baja's unspoiled Valle de Guadalupe.

3 **Cabo Pulmo** (p753) Diving with a giant ball of schooling jacks and beholding the Sea of Cortez' largest coral reef.

4 **San Ignacio** (p738) Whale-watching or hiking to prehistoric petroglyphs from this authentically Mexican oasis.

5 **Bahía Concepción** (p743) Camping on the fine white sands of the peninsula's most beautiful bays.

6 **Todos Santos** (p760) Wandering cobblestone streets, dining farm-to-table and surfing till the sun goes down.

7 **Land's End** (p756) Paddling through clear waters to romantic Lovers Beach before crossing to wild Divorce Beach.

8 **Loreto** (p743) Boating and snorkeling by day; drinking and dining on the historic town square by night.

9 **Tijuana** (p722) Gorging on 'Baja Med' cuisine and downing tasty craft beers at Plaza Fiesta.

to the Pacific side. Parking costs M$50 and the approach is flanked by souvenir stalls (and touts).

Tijuana

664 / POP 2 MILLION

Tijuana (TJ) boasts one of the world's busiest border crossings, and in many ways offers the full border-town experience with its vibrant cocktail of cultures, vigorous nightlife, great range of restaurants and sleazy red-light district. Yes, it's gritty and yes, there's crime, but in reality tourists rarely become targets. What's changed about Tijuana over the years is the emergence of a dynamic craft-beer, dining and urban art scene. Several *pasajes* (passages) off main thoroughfare La Revolución are now home to contemporary galleries and arty cafes. Many hip, lauded restaurants have opened in Zona Río, the upscale commercial center that runs alongside the river. Here you'll also find Plaza Fiesta, the rough-around-the-edges center of the craft-beer and bar scene. Over at the beach, a revamped boardwalk is breathing new life into Playas de Tijuana, and a binational 'friendship' park on the US border offers a profound glimpse at what building a wall truly means.

History

At the beginning of the 20th century, TJ was literally a mud hole. Prohibition drove US tourists here for booze, gambling, brothels, boxing and cockfights, causing Tijuana's population to balloon to 180,000 by 1960. With continued growth came economic opportunity and a cultural upgrade, but also social and environmental problems. Today the drug and illegal-immigrants trade into the US are among the city's biggest concerns.

◉ Sights

★ **Parque de la Amistad** PARK
(Friendship Park; www.friendshippark.org; Playas de Tijuana; ⊙24hr) For a glimpse at what a wall between neighbors really looks like, find your way to binational Friendship Park. On the Mexico side of the wall in Playas de Tijuana, you'll find provocative murals, thriving gardens and celebratory music. The US side of the wall is austere and quiet, but on Saturdays and Sundays from 10am to 2pm, US Border Patrol guards escort visitors in-

side to speak with loved ones and touch fingers through small holes in the mesh fence.

Observers should be prepared to feel all the feels.

It's worth noting that until 1994, the park did not have a wall, and visitors from both sides of the border could spend a supervised day together. Local activists and volunteers hope to someday return to this arrangement.

★ **Pasaje Rodríguez** ARTS CENTER
(Av Revolución, btwn Calles 3a & 4a; ⊙noon-10pm) This atmospheric arty alley reflects TJ's growing urban art scene. The walls are painted with vibrant graffiti-style murals – the perfect backdrop to the boho-style cafes, Oaxacan food stalls, locally made fashion, music bars, bookstores and craft shops.

Museo de las Californias MUSEUM
(Museum of the Californias; 664-687-96-00; www.cecut.gob.mx; Centro Cultural Tijuana, cnr Paseo de los Héroes & Av Independencia; adult/child under 18yr/child under 12yr M$27/16/free; ⊙9am-7pm Tue-Sun, last entry 6:30pm; ℗) The Museo de las Californias chronicles the history of the Baja Peninsula from prehistoric times to the present. The exhibit kicks off with replica cave paintings, then covers important historical milestones, illustrated in many cases by realistic dioramas and scale models, including replicas of a 16th-century ship, several missions and even a freestone chapel.

Estación Federal AREA
(664-514-58-94; www.centroventures.com/estacion-federal; Larroque 271; ⊙6:30am-1am Mon-Sat, to 5pm Sun) Part local art gallery, part coworking space, part drinking and dining hub, with some modern accommodations thrown in for good measure. It's all just a 10-minute walk south from the San Ysidro Border, and just sayin', cactus-fruit cocktails at Cereus Bar do wonders for a traveler's first impression of Tijuana.

If you have one too many, consider staying the night in one of the lofts upstairs (doubles from US$50).

Malecón de Playas BEACH
(Playas de Tijuana; ⊙24hr) A tranquil, recently remodeled boardwalk by the sea, stretching about a kilometer and livened up with ever-evolving murals, beach bars and cozy cafes. Pub Zebra is the best spot here for a craft brew, and just south of the boardwalk, Horno 320 fires up delicious pizzas. Its neighbor, the artsy, bilevel coffeeshop Café

Aquamarino, has an amazing sunset view from a rooftop lounge.

For those interested in exploring Playas de Tijuana and visiting the nearby Parque de la Amistad, North Hostel (dorm/double from US$15/40) is a solid stay.

☞ Tours

Turista Libre   TOURS
(www.turistalibre.com; day tours from US$45) Tours to Tijuana and beyond, focusing on harder-to-find stuff like cultural events, quirky markets, craft breweries, amazing street tacos and more.

⌁ Sleeping

Hotel Nelson   HISTORIC HOTEL $
(🗷 664-685-43-02; Av Revolución 721; r from M$701; 🅿😊✳🛜) The friendly Nelson is a longtime favorite, with high ceilings and 1950s-era touches, such as a real live barbershop of old. The carpeted rooms are scuffed and some are maybe a little too authentically old (check out a few), but they come with color TV, and some have a view of bustling Avenida Revolución.

★ Hotel Caesar's   HISTORIC HOTEL $$
(🗷 664-685-16-06; www.hotelcaesars.com.mx; Av Revolución 1079; r M$990-2520; 🅿😊✳🛜) If walls could talk! Tijuana's most famous historic hotel dates from the 1920s Prohibition era when it was popular with movie stars from over the border. Today only the facade reflects this belle epoque; the rooms are large, exceptionally clean, carpeted and blandly comfortable. But it's great value, central and the adjacent restaurant holds the historic charm the hotel lacks.

One Bunk   BOUTIQUE HOTEL $$
(🗷 664-210-18-24; www.onebunk.com; Av Revolución 920; d from US$65; 🛜) A design-forward 'microhotel' recently installed on Tijuana's most happening thoroughfare, with just 14 rooms and a rooftop mezcal bar. Common spaces are adorned in bold, unique art; for instance, a lighting fixture composed of vintage tennis rackets. Rooms are small but stylish, with particularly colorful throw pillows and bathroom tiles.

Hotel Real del Río   HOTEL $$$
(🗷 664-634-31-00; www.realdelrio.com; Av Velasco 1409; r incl breakfast M$2500; 🅿😊✳🛜) The contemporary building-block-style exterior here sets the tone for a slick, modern hotel with comfortable carpeted rooms, a gym, a rooftop sundeck for catching the rays and an excellent restaurant and bar, well known among locals for its Sunday brunch. It's located in the less-gritty-than-central-Tijuana Zona Río area, near many hip restaurants and brew pubs.

✖ Eating

★ Telefónica Gastro Park   FOOD HALL $
(🗷 664-684-87-82; www.telefonicagastropark.com; Blvd Agua Caliente 8924; tacos/mains from M$35/80, parking from M$25; ⊘8am-10pm Mon-Wed, to 11pm Thu, to midnight Fri & Sat, to 9pm Sun; 🅿🛝) At the edge of the city's industrial zone perches this collection of food trucks helmed by the city's most innovative rising chefs. Each has a specialty, be it breakfast, tacos, *tostadas* (deep-fried tortillas), burgers, vegan dishes, charcuterie, ramen and the like. The strong sense of community and experimental ethos yield delicious (yet super affordable) results.

The food trucks and outside tables back up to a brick warehouse containing a coffee shop, wine bar and craft brewery, with 28 beers on tap. The look of the place is cheerful and funky, with furnishings constructed from recycled surfboards and wine bottles, and abundant piñatas and potted cacti. The children's playground makes it a great choice for families.

Tras/Horizonte   MEXICAN $
(Río Colorado 9680; dishes M$30-237; ⊘1-10pm Tue-Sat, to 7pm Sun; 🛜) With sunsets and sea creatures painted on the walls, and ferns, cacti, driftwood and fairy lights throughout, this indoor warehouse restaurant feels like a magical outdoor space. The food is even better, with generous, creative starters and tacos, from smoked marlin-stuffed *chili relleno* with serrano pepper and pumpkin-seed cream, to portobello mushroom in a goat's-cheese and red-wine reduction with spinach.

Pair them with a house-specialty mezcal cocktail.

Tacos El Gordo   TACOS $
(Av Constitución 992; tacos M$25-45; ⊘10am-3am) Locals in the know flock to this clean-cut, semi-outdoor joint decked out in white and red. Tacos include the normal suspects like *asada* (grilled beef) and *pastor* (marinated roast pork), but also include delicacies like tender *lengua* (tongue) and fatty and tasty *ojo* (cow eye). *Sopas* (soups), *tortas* (sandwiches) and *tostadas* are also on the menu.

Tijuana

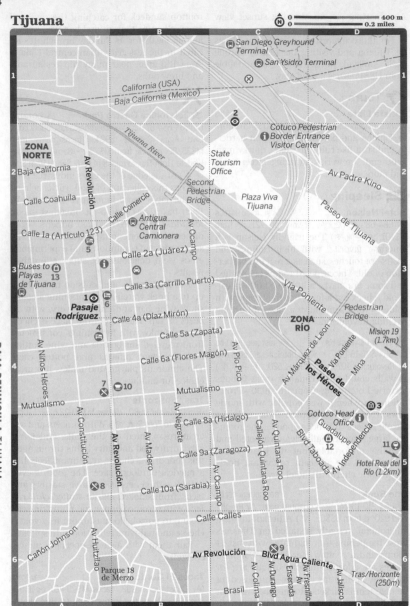

San Diego Greyhound Terminal

San Ysidro Terminal

California (USA)

Baja California (Mexico)

Tijuana River

Cotuco Pedestrian Border Entrance Visitor Center

ZONA NORTE

Baja California

Av Padre Kino

State Tourism Office

Av Revolución

Calle Coahuila

Second Pedestrian Bridge

Plaza Viva Tijuana

Paseo de Tijuana

Calle Comercio

Antigua Central Camionera

Av Ocampo

Calle 1a (Artículo 123)

5

Calle 2a (Juárez)

Buses to Playas de Tijuana

13

Calle 3a (Carrillo Puerto)

Vía Poniente

1

Pasaje Rodríguez

6

ZONA RÍO

Pedestrian Bridge

Misíon 19 (1.7km)

Calle 4a (Díaz Mirón)

4

Calle 5a (Zapata)

Av Márquez de Leon

Vía Poniente

Av Niños Héroes

Calle 6a (Flores Magón)

Av Pío Pico

Paseo de los Héroes

Mina

Mutualismo

7

10

Mutualismo

Av Constitución

Av Revolución

Av Madero

Av Negrete

Calle 8a (Hidalgo)

Callejón Quintana Roo

Av Quintana Roo

Cotuco Head Office

Guadalupe

12

3

11

Hotel Real del Río (1.2km)

Calle 9a (Zaragoza)

Av Ocampo

Blvd Taboada

Av Independencia

8

Calle 10a (Sarabia)

Calle Calles

Cañón Johnson

Av Huitzilac

Av Revolución

Blvd Agua Caliente

9

Av Colima

Av Durango

Av Ensenada

Av Fresnillo

Av Jalisco

Tras/Horizonte (250m)

Parque 18 de Merzo

Brasil

BAJA PENINSULA TIJUANA

0 400 m
0 0.2 miles

Cine Tonala   MEXICAN **$$**
(☎664-492-73-28; www.tj.cinetonala.mx; Avenida Revolución 1317; mains M$135-295, tacos M$65-110; ⊙2-10pm Mon, 1-11:45pm Tue & Wed, to 1am Thu, to 2am Fri & Sat, to 11pm Sun) Taking Av Revolución to chic new standards, this cosmopolitan rooftop bar and restaurant serves insanely good and unusual tacos like cured mackerel with cilantro and avocado or smoked tuna with prawns, garlic lime and nine chilies. Or, just go with a classic pasta dish or veggie burger with a cocktail. Definitely check out the art-house cinema downstairs.

Tijuana

Caesar's
ITALIAN $$

(📞 664-685-19-27; www.caesarstijuana.com; Av Revolución 1927; small/large Caesar salad M$95/135, mains M$185-395; ⊙ noon-10:30pm Mon-Wed, to midnight Thu-Sat, to 9pm Sun; P) Step inside and you are transported to the 1950s. Sepia pics of Hollywood movie stars line the walls, while the dark-wood decor oozes elegance. The exceptional Caesar salad, prepared with panache at your table, was apparently invented here by the restaurant's founder Caesar Cardini, an Italian immigrant who opened the place during Prohibition.

Mision 19
INTERNATIONAL $$$

(📞 664-634-24-93; www.mision19.com; Misión de San Javier 10643, Zona Río; mains M$150-395; ⊙ 1-10pm Mon-Wed, to 11pm Thu-Sat) Star Mexican chef Javier Plascencia's ode to revitalizing his hometown, Mision 19 is the city's poshest address with sparse black-and-white decor and formal service. Ingredients aim to come from a 120-mile (193km) radius to create true 'Baja cuisine.' Try the roast duck with mezcal, guava and chili or the tuna parfait with avocado meringue, Persian cucumber and pork crackling.

🍷 Drinking & Nightlife

Drinkers in TJ may feel like hounds let loose in a fire-hydrant factory. Go wild in bars or attempt refinement with craft beers, fine tequilas and local wines.

★ Plaza Fiesta
CRAFT BEER

(Erasmo Castellanos Q 9440; ⊙ 4pm-2am) Step into what seems like an aging shopping mall, to some gritty alleyways that, behold, house the heart of Tijuana's craft-beer scene as well as a slew of mezcal and sports bars

and hopping clubs. Our favorite beers come from tiny yet lauded Insurgente Tap Room, but edgy Border Psycho and fun Mamut are also worth a stop.

Evenings are mellow at the craft-beer shops, but get much, much crazier as the night rolls on at the clubs that line the back of the complex. There's no for-tourist stuff here, just full-on Mexican partying.

Norte Brewing Co
BREWERY

(www.nortebrewing.com; Diaz Miron y o cuarta 8160; beer flights M$80; ⊙ 2pm-midnight Mon-Sat, to 9pm Sun) Feel cool just finding this dark brewery hidden on a mysterious alley with windows overlooking the US–Mexico border. Try the hoppy yet easy-drinking 4 Play Session IPA or the Foreign Club Porter to go as dark as the music playing on the stereo. To get inside, go through an unmarked entrance next to the casino and take the elevator to the 5th floor.

Container Coffee
COFFEE

(Av Revolución 1348; ⊙ 8am-9pm Mon-Sat) If you seriously need a coffee and are serious about the coffee you need, make a beeline to this hip roastery, with seats made from coffee sacks and model airplanes on the ceiling, in the heart of downtown. Choose from espresso or coffee brewed as you like from drip to French press.

Playami
CRAFT BEER

(www.facebook.com/playamibyborderpsycho; Av Paseo Ensenada 795; ⊙ 8am-10pm Sun & Mon, to midnight Tue-Sat; 🐾) Channeling Miami's Wynwood art district, the latest drinking establishment from revered local brewery Border Psycho is not exactly at the beach, but the breezy beer garden offers 42 of the peninsula's best craft beers on tap, and great

FESTIVALS & EVENTS

Expo Artesanal (Centro Cultural, cnr Paseo de los Héroes & Av Independencia; ⊘Nov) A superb arts and crafts festival held at the Cultural Center, with handicrafts for sale from all over Mexico.

Expo Cerveza Artesanal (Tijuana Craft Beer Expo; Plaza Monumental, Playas de Tijuana; ⊘early Jun) This boozy festival serves some of the best beers, both new and old, sometimes featuring more than 60 craft breweries.

wine from the Valle de Guadalupe. The whole place is built from recycled shipping containers and divided into stylish terraces and lounges.

A small food menu created by Karbó includes mostly tasty breakfasts, sandwiches and burgers.

☆ Entertainment

Domo Imax CINEMA
(www.cecut.gob.mex; Centro Cultural Tijuana, cnr Paseo de los Héroes & Av Independencia; tickets M$52; ⊘1-9pm Tue-Thu, from 4pm Fri, from 11am Sat & Sun) Located in the Centro Cultural Tijuana and showing predominantly documentaries and art-house movies.

Centro Cultural Tijuana ARTS CENTER
(CECUT; ☑664-687-96-00; www.cecut.gob.mx; cnr Paseo de los Héroes & Av Independencia; ⊘9am-9pm) Tijuana's sophisticated arts and cultural center would make any comparably sized city north of the border proud. It houses several art galleries, the superb Museo de las Californias (p722), a theater and the globular cinema Domo Imax.

🛍 Shopping

Tijuana is great for souvenirs, but be cautious when buying gold and silver as much of it is fake (at those prices it would have to be, right?). You'll note the many drugstores here; they specialize in selling discounted generic pharmaceuticals to US citizens. Be sure to check out some of the local markets for another side of TJ.

Mercado Hidalgo MARKET
(Guadalupe Victoria 2; ⊘8am-6pm Mon-Sat, to 4pm Sun) Tijuana's most well-known market is also one of the biggest and most visited by tourists. It's still a great place to peruse everything from exotic fruits to fresh pastries and colorful piñatas.

Mercado El Popo MARKET
(cnr Calle 2a & Av Constitución; ⊘8am-8:30pm) El Popo is the most colorful downtown market, with stacks of fresh cheeses, sweets, wooden spoons, piles of dried chilies, kitchenware, herbs, incense, potions, candles, love soaps, stacks of bundled cinnamon sticks, bee pollen and fruit. It's like a condensed version of the bigger, better-known markets.

ℹ Information

EMERGENCY
Tourist Assistance Hotline (☑078)

MEDICAL SERVICES
Hospital General (☑664-684-00-78; Centenario 10851) Hospital with a good reputation northwest of the junction with Avenida Rodríguez.

MONEY
Use caution when changing money, especially at night. Everyone accepts US dollars and most banks have ATMs.

SAFE TRAVEL
If you're street smart and not after trouble, then it is unlikely you'll have problems.
➜ Definitely don't drink on the streets. As in any big city, being plastered late at night can invite trouble.
➜ Touts are sometimes irksome but they deserve a respectful 'no' – they are trying to make a living.

TOURIST INFORMATION
There is a small visitor center at the **border** (☑664-607-30-97; www.descubretijuana.com; ⊘9am-6pm) and a **head office** (☑664-684-05-37; www.descubretijuana.com; Suite 201, Paseo de los Héroes 9365; ⊘9am-6pm Mon-Fri) on Paseo de los Héroes.

State Tourism Office (Secretaría de Turismo del Estado; ☑664-682-33-67; www.descubrebajacalifornia.com; Av Revolución 868; ⊘8am-6pm Mon-Fri, 9am-1pm Sat) This is the main state tourism office in town. There's a small information kiosk out front.

ℹ Getting There & Away

Mexican tourist permits are available 24 hours a day at three ports of entry: San Ysidro (vehicle and pedestrian), Otay Mesa (vehicle and pedestrian) and Cross Border Xpress at the Tijuana Airport (for pedestrian airplane passengers only). At each one, an *Instituto Nacion-*

al de Migración (INM) office issues permits at a cost of M$533 for up to 180 days, or free if you're visiting Mexico for under one week.

AIR

Several airlines service Tijuana, predominantly **Aeroméxico** (☑ 664-684-92-68, 664-683-84-44; www.aeromexico.com; Plaza Rio) and **Volaris** (☑ 55-1102-8000; www.volaris.com; Aeropuerto Internacional de Tijuana), which serve many mainland Mexican and US destinations, along with Shanghai.

Aeropuerto Internacional de Tijuana (Aeropuerto Internacional General Abelardo L Rodríguez; ☑ 664-607-82-00; www.aeropuertos gap.com.mx/en/tijuana-3.html; Carretera Aeropuerto-Otay Mesa) is in Mesa de Otay, east of downtown.

BUS

The main bus terminal, about 5km southeast of downtown, is the **Central Camionera** (☑ 664-621-29-82; Chapultepec Alamar), where Elite (www.autobuseselite.com.mx) and Estrella Blanca (www.estrellablanca.com.mx) offer 1st-class buses with air-con and toilets. Destinations in mainland Mexico include Guadalajara (from M$2188, 35 hours) and Mexico City (from M$2400, 44 hours, 12 daily, hourly). ABC (www.abc.com.mx) and Auto Transporte Águila (www.autobusesaguila.com) operate mostly 2nd-class buses to mainland Mexico's Pacific coast and around the Baja Peninsula.

Local buses use the handy downtown **Antigua Central Camionera** (cnr Av Madero & Calle 1a), with buses leaving for Tecate (M$85, one hour, every 15 minutes).

Between 3am and 10pm, buses leave from the **San Diego Greyhound terminal** (☑ 800-231-22-22, US 619-515-1100; www.greyhound.com; 120 West Broadway, San Diego) and stop at the **San Ysidro terminal** (☑ 619-428-62-00; 4570 Camino de la Plaza) en route to Tijuana's Central Camionera bus terminal or the airport. Fares from San Diego/San Ysidro to the Central Camionera or airport are M$150 each way.

CAR & MOTORCYCLE

The **San Ysidro** (799 East San Ysidro Blvd) border crossing, a 10-minute walk from downtown Tijuana, is open 24 hours and offers both vehicle crossings and pedestrian crossings. Motorists can also use the Otay Mesa crossing (also open 24 hours), but it tends to be even more congested. It's 15km to the east of San Ysidro.

Rental agencies in San Diego are the cheapest option, but most of them only allow journeys as far as Ensenada. Renting a car in Tijuana or taking the bus may be your best option for heading further south, although few offer one-way rentals and those that do add a hefty surcharge.

TROLLEY

San Diego's popular and easy trolley (www.sdmts.com) runs from downtown San Diego through to the border at San Ysidro (US$2.50) every 15 minutes from about 5am to midnight. From San Diego's Lindbergh Field airport, city bus 992 (US$2.25) has a stop close to the Plaza America trolley depot in downtown San Diego, across from the Amtrak depot.

ⓘ Getting Around

For about M$14, local buses go everywhere, but the slightly pricier route taxis are much quicker. To get to the Central Camionera take any 'Buena Vista,' 'Centro' or 'Central Camionera' bus from Calle 2a, east of Avenida Constitución. Alternatively, take a gold-and-white 'Mesa de Otay' route taxi from Avenida Madero between Calles 2a and 3a (M$15). Regular taxis will charge about M$100 for rides in and around Avenida Revolucíon or the Zona Río. The airport is about M$250.

Buses to **Playas de Tijuana** (Calle 3a) leave from Calle 3a near Av Martinez in Zona Centro. Grab route taxis to **Central Camionera** (Av Madero).

Uber rideshare is popular in Tijuana and rides around town cost around M$45 – you'll need to have the app or download it on your phone. You can request an English-speaking driver on the app at no extra cost.

BAJA PENINSULA TIJUANA

BUSES FROM TIJUANA

DESTINATION	FARE (M$)	TIME (HR)	FREQUENCY (PER DAY)
Ensenada	202	1½	frequent
Guerrero Negro	1214	11	6
La Paz	2770	24	6
Loreto	2124	18	6
Mexicali	335	2¾	frequent
Santa Rosalía	1645	14	6

PARQUE NACIONAL SIERRA SAN PEDRO MÁRTIR

Bobcats, deer and bighorn sheep await visitors to San Pedro Mártir national park, but its real claim to fame isn't what's on the ground but what's in the air: this park is one of only six places in the world where the almost-extinct California condor has been successfully reintroduced into the wild.

Even if one of the world's largest birds doesn't soar over your head, there are lots of other reasons to make the detour. Conifers scrape the sky, the air is pine scented and clean, and the (tortuously winding) drive passes through boulder-studded, ethereal landscapes that seem more Martian than something here on earth.

To reach the park, turn left at the sign at approximately Km 140 on the Transpeninsular, south of Colonet. A 100km paved road climbs to the east through an ever-changing desert landscape, affording satisfying vistas all along the way. Camping is possible (no toilets; bring water) in designated areas, but there are no other facilities.

Another interesting stay not too far afield is **Adele's Ranch Bus** (☑616-104-78-58; www.facebook.com/bajacaliforniacamping; Valle de San Quentín; bus US$22, casita US$18, camping from US$10; P) 🐾. It's an off-the-grid microranch surrounded by strawberry farms, just a short walk from a near-deserted, prettier-than-postcards beach. Guests camp or sleep in a repurposed bus, share an outhouse and bucket shower, wake to bleating goats, eat farm-fresh eggs and go on clamming missions and cliffside hikes with the adventurous owners.

Playas de Rosarito

☑ 661 / POP 70,250

Once a deserted, sandy beach and then a Hollywood film location (Fox Studios Baja, built in 1996 for the filming of *Titanic*), Playas de Rosarito is finally coming into its own. Developments and condos are everywhere, but despite the construction clamor, Rosarito is a quieter place to party or just relax, and is an easy day trip (or overnight trip) from Tijuana or San Diego. There are also several excellent surf breaks nearby including the famous K28 around 15km south of town.

🛏 Sleeping

Robert's K38 Surf Motel　　MOTEL $$
(www.robertsk38.com; Carretera 1D Km 38; d US$45-85, house from US$160; P🐾🌐📶🐕) Walking distance from the famous K28 surf break, 11km south of Rosarito, this super-fun, comfortable bargain of a place is, as you'd guess, popular with surfers. You can rent gear or rack up your gear then just chill out on the beach, walk to cheap places to eat and become a beach bum.

Reservations by email only, with a deposit. Balance must be settled in cash.

Hotel del Sol Inn　　HOTEL $$
(☑661-612-25-52; www.del-sol-inn.com; Blvd Juárez 32; s/d from M$1205/1390; P🐕🌐) The Sol is a motel-style lodging right on the

main drag with clean, carpeted rooms with TV, bottled water and simple furniture. Note that prices triple during the short spring-break holiday.

🍴 Eating & Drinking

⭐**Tacos El Yaqui**　　TACOS $
(cnr Palma & Mar del Norte; tacos M$15-50; ☺9am-5pm Thu-Mon) This delicious taco stand with an outdoor grill is so popular that it often closes early when the ingredients run out. Get in line before 4pm if you don't want to risk missing out.

Susanna's　　MODERN AMERICAN $$
(☑661-613-11-87; www.susannasinrosarito.com; Blvd Juárez 4356; mains US$15-30; ☺1-9:30pm Wed, Thu, Sun & Mon, to 10:30pm Fri & Sat; 🐕) Owner Susanna dishes up delightful plates of tasty fare based on fresh seasonal produce spiked with Californian pizzazz. Light salads with innovative dressings, and pasta, meat and fish dishes can be enjoyed in a courtyard setting or homey dining room with chintzy furniture and olive-green walls. The wines are from Valle de Guadalupe.

El Nido　　STEAK $$$
(Blvd Juárez 67; mains M$150-595; ☺8am-midnight; P🐕) You can't miss the vine-covered, wagon-wheel-decorated frontage of this steakhouse in the center of town. And the atmosphere continues with exposed brick and beams, strings of garlic and a foliage-filled

back terrace, complete with aviary. Tortillas are made fresh to order and the menu includes venison, rabbit and chicken, plus the star billing: steak.

Villa Ortega's SEAFOOD $$$
(☑661-614-07-06; Barracuda 77; lobster US$15-30; ☺10am-9pm Sun-Thu, to 10pm Fri & Sat) If you insist on visiting Puerto Nuevo, a fishing village (and tourist trap) best known for its affordable lobster, at least do it right. One good option is Villa Ortega's, the big, long-standing place by the water with the brass shark out front. Views of the coastline from the outdoor patio nearly make it worthwhile to endure the crowds, traffic and pushy vendors.

For better deals, go to the smaller places on the southern edge of the village, which get less foot traffic and often outdo each other with amazing specials. Note that many are cash only.

Colectivo Surf Tasting Room CRAFT BEER
(www.colectivosurf.com; Carretera Tijuana-Ensenada Km 41; ☺noon-10pm Mon-Thu, to 11pm Fri, from 11am Sat, to 10pm Sun) An ideal après-surf hangout, this expansive, art-covered, 2nd-story beer hall and performance venue also happens to serve sushi, Mexican food and coffee. Do indulge in one of 15 craft beers on tap or some local wine or mezcal. Everything pairs well with the live music Friday or Saturday night. Consider skipping the sushi.

ℹ Getting There & Away

From downtown Tijuana, *colectivos* (shared cars) for Playas de Rosarito (M$20 to M$25) leave from Avenida Madero between Calles 3a and 4a. Tourismo Express Bus also runs a service from the border station parking in San Ysidro and downtown Tijuana (Avenida Revolución between Calles 6a and 7a) to and from Playas Rosarito (one way/round trip US$20/30).

Ruta del Vino & Valle de Guadalupe
☑646 / POP 2664

Beloved of residents of Mexico and Southern California, but a surprise to just about everyone else, Baja's wine country is an intoxicating blend of luxury lodging, wine tasting and fine dining with dirt roads, cacti amid the grapevines and a very laid-back attitude. It's actually one of the oldest wine-producing regions in the Americas,

now with over 120 wineries, and it attracts a very hip crowd of 20- to 40-somethings looking to relax and indulge in the finer things on a relatively low budget. Once people began whispering that this is the next Napa, the word spread further afield and the wines are gaining attention internationally.

◉ Sights

Museo de la Vid y El Vino MUSEUM
(www.museodelvinobc.com; Carretera Federal Tecate-Ensenada Km 81.3; M$50; ☺9am-5pm Tue-Sun) Who knew that the first wines in the Americas were produced in Baja? Follow the fascinating history of wine in the region via dioramas (in Spanish, but English speakers are given a binder with English translations) and a few artifacts. The bright, modern building (complete with cafe and gift shop) makes this even more of a worthwhile stop.

✥ Festivals & Events

Fiesta de la Vendimia WINE
(Grape Harvest Festival; ☺late Jul & early Aug) Midsummer wine harvest with galas, special tastings and elite parties around Valle de Guadalupe. Reserve far in advance with wineries for events. Cheers!

🛏 Sleeping

Glamping Ruta de Arte y Vino CARAVAN PARK $
(☑646-185-33-52; www.rutadearteyvino.wixsite.com/rutadearteyvino; Carretera Ensenada-Tecate Km 13, San Marcos; camper from US$50) A quirky place in a field with 13 vintage 1960s Airstream camper vans. Lodging is rustic and gets hot when the weather is sweltering, but otherwise expect to barbecue with your neighbors, get tips from the friendly hosts, enjoy the stars through a telescope and have a grand ole time communing with nature.

ATVs, bicycles and even *tuk tuks* are available for rent.

★Encuentro DESIGN HOTEL $$$
(☑646-155-27-75; www.grupoencuentro.com.mx; Carretera Tecate-Ensenada Km 75; r US$342-444; ☺☒) Architecturally beautiful Encuentro features 22 minimalist, glass and steel 'loft' bungalows perched on a dry grassy hill overlooking the valley. This is the type of place where people dress stylishly and take selfies. There's a photo-worthy infinity pool as well as a restaurant with one of the greatest views around.

RUTA DEL VINO – SELF-GUIDED WINERIES TOUR

Here are a few of Valle de Guadalupe's many excellent, scenic and quirky wineries that are worth adding to your itinerary (in order heading from Ensenada toward Tecate).

Cuatro Cuatros (p730) Primarily known for its swanky mountaintop bar with a bonkers ocean view. But do visit the winery, as the vineyard's unique, coastal microclimate makes for an interesting sauvignon blanc.

Clos de Tres Cantos (☑ 558-568-92-40; Carretera Ensenada-Tecate Km 89.5; tastings incl bread & cheese from US$11; ☺ 10am-5pm Wed-Sun) 🌱 From the old-seeming stone buildings and modern murals to the views, friendly staff and our favorite rosé in the valley, this is a near perfect place to sip vino with a plate of locally made bread and cheese.

El Pinar de 3 Mujeres (☑ 646-171-56-74; vinicola3mujeres@gmail.com; Carretera Tecate-Ensenada Km 83; set menu M$550, tastings M$100; ☺ winery 11am-5pm Fri-Sun, restaurant 1-6pm Sat & Sun May-Nov) Named after the three women owners and winemakers, it combines a winery, small tasting room and Mediterranean restaurant; meals are served under the trees with scenic vineyard views.

Bibayoff (☑ 646-176-10-08; www.bibayoff.mx; Carretera Francisco Zarco-El Tigre Km 9.5; ☺ 11am-5:30pm Tue-Sun) This boutique winery is set off the beaten path. Its small museum recounts the fascinating history of the Russians who immigrated here in the early 1900s (the current owner is a descendant). The wine, however, leaves something to be desired.

Adobe Guadalupe (☑ 646-155-20-94; www.adobeguadalupe.com; Parcela A-1 s/n, Ruta de Guadalupe; tastings from M$250; ☺ 10am-5pm) The most Mexican-feeling winery in the valley serves its vintages in a replica of a Spanish mission and surrounded by grapevines and a horse ranch. Its tempranillo blend is the favorite.

LA Cetto (☑ 646-155-21-79; www.lacetto.mx; Carretera Tecate-El Sauzal Km 73.5; tour & tastings from M$100; ☺ 10am-5pm) Mexico's largest producer, and often filled with the tour-bus crowd, LA Cetto is worth checking out to see how it contrasts with the smaller, boutique places. Its highlight is its cabernet sauvignon.

Cuatro Cuatros   FARMSTAY $$$
(☑ 646-174-67-89; www.cabanascuatrocuatros .com.mx; Tijuana-Ensenada Km 89, El Tigre; cabañas from M$4500; ☻ ☎) There's a lot of buzz in the valley about this swanky wine retreat and its fabulous mountaintop bar. Maximize your experience by staying in one of the cozy *cabañas* elevated with the vineyards and conveniently close to the complex's myriad activities. There's wine tasting, hiking, horseback riding, zip-lining and taking the shuttle up to the best sunset bar in Baja.

Be sure to get in line for the shuttle early on weekends, as the place becomes a madhouse. The food isn't particularly good, nor is the service. But that view, my goodness it's worth it!

La Villa del Valle   B&B $$$
(☑ 646-156-80-07; www.lavilladelvalle.com; Carretera Tecate-San Antonio de las Minas Km 88; d US$275-315; ℗ ☻ ✳ ☎) A beautiful B&B overlooking the rolling vineyards and fields in the Ruta del Vino. The owners grow their own lavender, make their own personal-care products and have fantastic meals. It feels like a modern, ultraluxe place in Tuscany. Adults only.

🍴 Eating & Drinking

La Cocina de Doña Esthela   MEXICAN $
(☑ 646-156-84-53; Ranchos San Marcos; mains M$80-210; ☺ 8am-5pm Tue-Sun) Everyone's favorite breakfast in the valley. Doña Esthela's is a welcome slice of traditional Mexico with huge egg dishes including the house specialty *machaca con huevos* (eggs with dried Sinaloan-style beef). Lunch moves on into *birria de res* (beef stew) territory. Don't miss the addictive *cafe olla* (Mexican coffee).

Troika   FOOD TRUCK $$
(☑ 646-246-41-23; Rancho San Marcos Toros Pintos; dishes M$60-250; ☺ noon-7pm Tue-Sun) Right in the middle of the vineyards and set on a little hill, this is a fabulous place

to enjoy fish, *asada* or *lechon* (roasted suckling pig) tacos or perhaps a salad or seafood *tostada* to break up a day of wine tasting.

★**Fauna**   NEW MEXICAN **$$$**
(☑646-103-64-03; www.faunarestaurante.mx/index_en.html; Carretera Ensenada-Tecate Km 73.5; set menu per person US$50; ☺1-9pm Sun-Wed, to 10pm Thu-Sat) In a region known for its superlative dining, this restaurant is our uncontested favorite. The setting is rustic-chic, with family-style seating at reclaimed wooden tables, an open kitchen and views out to a garden of herbs and cacti. The set menu, which varies based on what's available on the day and the whims of the masterful chef, is quite simply astounding.

Whatever is served, be it the tender blood clams, the abalone taco, the *chayote* (prickly pear) lasagna or any number of other experimental concoctions, the food deeply satisfies the palate while drawing artfully from the bounty and traditions of Baja, Mexico. And it's beautifully presented. The mezcal cocktails and wine pairings are also divine.

Deckman's   CALIFORNIAN **$$$**
(☑646-188-39-60; www.deckmans.com; Carretera Ensenada-Tecate Km 85.5; mains M$360-1100; ☺1-8pm Wed-Mon Mar-Sep, to 7pm Nov-Feb; 🅿) 🖉 Good luck not having some fun at this wonderful, warm-hued, adobe-walled, sand-floored restaurant, where the grill is as much aflame as the wine-drinking diners' spirits. Run by Michelin-starred chef Drew Deckman, it has hearty dishes like roast quail, rib eye and whole striped bass, with ingredients nearly entirely sourced from sustainable, local supplies. The five-course tasting menu for M$1000 is a steal.

Finca Altozano   CALIFORNIAN **$$$**
(☑646-156-80-45; www.fincaltozano.com; Carretera Tecate-Ensenada Km 83; mains M$200-700; ☺1-9:30pm Mon-Sat, noon-8pm Sun) Our favorite of celebrity-Mexican-chef Javier Placencia's restaurants, this laid-back place looking out over the vineyards has a cracking oyster bar and not-to-miss starters like chocolate clams and oak-barrel-smoked tuna. Mains include everything from risotto and confit duck in *mole* (chili sauce) to locally sourced beef brisket or wood-fired tacos.

Casa Frida   ROOFTOP BAR
(☑646-113-48-36; www.casafridavalle.com; Rancho San Marcos; ☺11am-8pm Fri-Sun) Highly incongruous with the otherwise laid-back valley, this gaudy but well-funded and Instagram-friendly project is the bane of its neighbors' existence for the raucous wine and tequila tastings in the chichi rooftop lounge. That said, on weekends the restaurant serves fresh, expertly prepared seafood in a lovely alfresco setting. Try some ceviche (seafood marinated in lime juice) to start, then take on the grilled octopus.

You can also stay the night in a bright blue cottage adorned in eye-catching art, wild patterns and whimsical furnishings. Good luck getting any sleep.

ℹ Getting There & Away

You can always skip Tijuana's long lines and treat yourself to some beautiful scenery by entering Mexico via Tecate. The border crossing (open 5am to 11pm) is far less congested, and south of Tecate lies the Ruta del Vino in the intoxicatingly beautiful Valle de Guadalupe (Hwy 3).

Ruta del Vino and Valle de Guadalupe are not reliably accessed by public transportation; you'll need your own car.

ℹ Getting Around

If you're taking your own vehicle and will be wine tasting, obviously designate a nondrinking driver first. Maps of the wine route (available at local hotels, tourist offices and wineries) will help you locate the vineyards.

You can also hire a private taxi for the day, found through hotels and word of mouth. One recommended company, **Valle Wine Life** (☑646-135-68-50, USA 602-773-1283; www.vallewinelife.com), charges US$130 for a day trip within the valley for up to four people.

Ensenada

☑646 / POP 522,768
Ensenada, 108km south of the border, is hedonistic Tijuana's only slightly more refined sister. The city has a quirky mix of just-off-the-boat cruise shippers, drive-by tourists from California, visitors from mainland Mexico and seen-it-all locals. In case you've forgotten you're in Mexico (what with all those US dollars and English menus), just look up: a Mexican flag, so large it's probably visible from space, flutters proudly over the *malecón* (waterfront promenade). Wander Avenida López Mateos (Calle 1a) and you'll find almost

everything from delicious French food to tasteless T-shirts. If you have kids, don't miss the waterfront's dancing musical fountain.

◉ Sights

★ Riviera del Pacífico   HISTORIC BUILDING
(☎646-176-42-33; Blvd Costero; **P**) **FREE**
Opened in the 1930s as Hotel Playa Ensenada, the extravagant Riviera del Pacífico, a Spanish-style former casino, is rumored to have been a haunt of Al Capone, though employees say that's a tall tale. It now houses the **Museo de Historia de Ensenada** (☎646-177-05-94; adult/child M$30/15;

⊙10am-5pm Mon-Sat, from noon Sun; 🚼) and **Bar Andaluz** (☎646-176-43-10; ⊙10am-11pm Tue & Thu-Sat, to midnight Wed, to 8pm Sun; 🕿); while the **Casa de Cultura** offers classes, film screenings and exhibitions. Just strolling around the building and grounds is a delight.

El Mirador   VIEWPOINT
Atop the Colinas de Chapultepec, El Mirador offers panoramic views of the city and Bahía de Todos Santos. Climb or drive (note: there's no off-street parking) to this highest point in town, up Avenida Alemán from the western end of Calle 2a in central Ensenada.

Ensenada

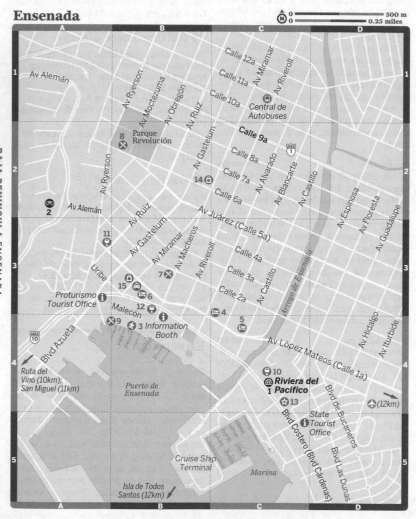

🏃 Activities

Ensenada is known the world over for its excellent sportfishing, though you must have a valid Mexican fishing license (available from sportfishing operators) if you want to reel in a live one. Most charter companies also offer whale-watching tours from mid-December to mid-April.

Sergio's Sportfishing Center   FISHING
(📲 646-178-21-85; www.sergiosfishing.com; day trips from US$70 plus fishing license; ⏰ 8am-6pm) Well-regarded Sergio's can be found on the sportfishing pier off Ensenada's *malecón*. Fishing trips include the necessary gear. Day trips are available as well as private charter trips.

✨ Festivals & Events

Ensenada hosts dozens of annual sporting, tourist and cultural happenings.

Baja 1000   RACING
(⏰ mid-Nov) Baja's biggest off-road race. See 'truggies' (truck-buggies) tear up the desert to the cheers of just about everyone. The Baja 500 is in late May or early June.

Carnaval   CARNIVAL
(⏰ Feb) A Mardi Gras–type celebration 40 days before Ash Wednesday, when the streets flood with floats and dancers.

🛏 Sleeping

Hotel demand can exceed supply at times, particularly at weekends and in summer. Many places raise their rates significantly at these times, but don't expect a lot of bang for your pesos at any time.

Hotel Santo Tomás   HOTEL $
(📲 646-178-33-11; hst@bajainn.com; Blvd Costero 609; d from M$700; 🅿️➗❄️@📶) Although the furnishing and carpets are a little tired, this vast hotel with its pea-green-and-purple exterior is still a great choice. The quirky lobby has a grand sweeping staircase, an elevator with disco mirrors and a cage of cuddly-looking chinchillas. Rates nearly double on Friday and Saturday (along with the noise levels outside).

Hotel Cortez   HOTEL $$
(📲 646-178-23-07; www.bajainn.com; Av López Mateos 1089; r from M$1942; 🅿️➗❄️@📶♨️) This is one of the best choices right in the heart of things, with facilities that include a small gym. The (heated) pool is surrounded by lofty trees. Some of the rooms are a tad dark. If you can, go for the premium rooms, with their chic and contemporary look: all earth colors and plush fabrics. It books out fast.

Best Western Hotel El Cid   HOTEL $$$
(📲 646-178-24-01; www.hotelelcid.com.mx; Av López Mateos 993; d from M$2178; 🅿️➗❄️@📶♨️) This four-star hotel has comfortable rooms with firm beds, a respected restaurant and a lively bar. The bilingual staff are particularly gracious and friendly and the situation is central, in the more upmarket part of town.

🍴 Eating

Ensenada's dining options range from outrageously delicious corner taco stands and seafood stalls around the Mercado Negro to places serving excellent Mexican and international cuisine.

Ensenada

BAJA PENINSULA ENSENADA

TOP ENSENADA SURF SPOTS

Isla de Todos Santos A pair of islands off Ensenada's coast (not to be confused with the town near Los Cabos) is home to the best big-wave surf spot in North America, rightfully dubbed Killers.

San Miguel (parking M$75) There's not much here but a few campers, a parking lot and a wonderful point break just offshore. When the waves are big it's an awesome ride.

★**La Guerrerense**   MEXICAN $
(www.laguerrerense.com; cnr Avs Alvarado & López Mateos; tostadas from M$27; ⏱10:30am-5pm Wed-Mon) Sabina Bandera's award-winning seafood stand dates from the 1960s and attracts long lines with its outstanding juicy ceviche and *tostadas*. Anthony Bourdain gave his approval in 2018, and shortly thereafter Bandera opened the equally delicious restaurant **Sabina** (⏱10am-6pm, Tue-Sun) right next door.

The food is virtually identical, though the brick-and-mortar restaurant offers tacos, soups and desserts. For a real treat, try the sea snail or sea urchin on a *tostada* (M$27).

Birreria La Guadalajara   MEXICAN $
(Av Macheros 154; tacos M$27-42; ⏱7am-8pm) A great barn of a place, rightfully famous for its *birria de chivo* (goat stew), but also serving excellent tacos and charcoal-grilled meats. Popular with families, the atmosphere is boisterous and noisy with a large open-plan kitchen, a few TVs, strolling mariachis and decor that has changed little since its opening in 1972.

Muelle 3   SEAFOOD $$
(☑646-174-03-18; Paseo del Náutico; dishes M$170-280; ⏱noon-6:30pm Tue-Sat) Right on the marina, this place looks like a hole in the wall but on closer inspection you'll see a sophisticated crowd savoring artistically presented ceviches and other Mexican classics. The flavors are balanced and subtle, and everything is fresh and prepared to perfection. It gets crowded, especially at lunchtime.

Boules   INTERNATIONAL $$$
(☑646-175-87-69; Av Moctezuma 623; mains around M$250; ⏱2-11pm Tue-Thu, to midnight Fri & Sat) Creamy risottos, pasta and fresh seafood are a draw here, but it's the setting under the trees on a deck with lights strung up above that make it taste even better. Owner Javier greets and mingles with all guests like they're regulars. Choose from a huge selection of wines at the onsite shop then bring them to your table.

🍷 Drinking & Nightlife

On weekends most bars and cantinas along Avenida Ruiz are packed from noon to early morning. If that's not your scene, head for one of the many quality hotels and fine restaurants where you're likely to find a laid-back spot to sip a margarita (said to have been invented here) or sample a top-shelf tequila.

★**Hussong's Cantina**   CANTINA
(www.cantinahussongs.com/home.html; Av Ruiz 113; ⏱11am-2am Tue-Sun) The oldest and perhaps liveliest cantina in the Californias has been serving tequila since 1892. A Friday or Saturday night will be packed with locals, a sprinkling of tourists and touting mariachis. The history is fascinating, and the revered bar once drew in the likes of Steve McQueen, John Wayne and Marilyn Monroe.

Wendlandt   BEER HALL
(www.wendlandt.com.mx; Blvd Costero 24B; ⏱6pm-midnight Tue-Sat) Enjoy craft beers made by the owners, as well as from national and international small breweries; seven samplers will cost you just 105 pesos. The surroundings have an urban-chic vibe with chunky wood furniture, exposed brick walls and clever quirky lighting incorporating beer bottles.

Aguamala   MICROBREWERY
(☑646-174-60-68; www.aguamala.com.mx; Carretera Tijuana-Ensenada Km 103; ⏱2pm-midnight Mon-Sat, 1-9pm Sun) Beloved craft microbrewery with sea-creature-themed art and an open-air, 2nd-story tasting room. Whether you're into fruity sours, frothy ales, creamy stouts or smooth IPAs, you're covered here. There's also a small food menu offering things like shrimp tacos *al pastor* (spit-grilled meat) and oysters with chimichurri.

☆ Entertainment

Centro Estatal de las Artes   ARTS CENTER
(☑646-173-43-07; www.icbc.gob.mx; cnr Av Riviera & Blvd Costero; ⏱8am-8pm Mon-Sat, noon-7pm

Sun, plus evening events) The Centro Estatal de las Artes has shows and exhibits throughout the year.

Shopping

Plaza Santo Tomás   FOOD & DRINKS
(www.santo-tomas.com; Av Miramar; ⊘10am-9pm)
A pair of old brick and stone buildings, set on a plaza and filled with delightful restaurants, cafes, shops and cozy spaces to relax. The anchor is an expansive local wine shop, Bodegas de Santo Tomás. Other vendors include a charcuterie shop, a cheese store and a hip rooftop restaurant with views of the plaza and beyond.

Plans are underway to further develop the plaza, adding outdoor seating, fountains and gardens.

Tequila Room   DRINKS
(Av López Mateos; ⊘10am-6pm Sun, Tue & Wed, from 11am Thu, to midnight Fri, from 10am Sat)
The Irish-Mexican owner is passionate about tequila, but you won't find any of the more commercial brands here; these 300-plus tequilas are sourced from all over Mexico. Even if you don't fancy a tipple (tastings are free), you can admire the bottles, many of which are works of art in themselves.

ℹ Information

Police (☑911)
Tourist assistance (☑078)
Immigration Office (☑646-174-01-64; www.gob.mx/inm; Blvd Azueta 101) Sells tourist permits for those arriving into the country by boat.
Proturismo Tourist Office (☑646-178-24-11; www.proturismoensenada.org.mx; Blvd Costero 540; ⊘8am-8pm Mon-Fri, 9am-5pm Sat & Sun) Dispenses maps, brochures and current hotel information. There's an **information**

booth (☑646-178-30-70; Plaza Cívica; ⊘Tue-Sun) in the Plaza Cívica.
Sanatorio del Carmen (☑646-178-34-77; cnr Av Obregón & Calle 11a) A small, clean, well-respected private hospital.
State Tourist Office (☑646-172-54-44; www.descubrebajacalifornia.com; Blvd Costero 1477; ⊘8am-6pm Mon-Fri, 10am-2pm Sat & Sun) Carries similar information to the Proturismo office.

ℹ Getting There & Away

Central de Autobuses (Av Riveroll 1075) Ten blocks north of Avenida López Mateos, serving far-flung destinations like Guadalajara (M$2277, 34 hours) and Mexico City (M$2087, 48 hours) as well as local Baja destinations.

The drive from Tijuana to Ensenada on the scenic *(cuota)* route has three tolls (total M$37).

ℹ Getting Around

The main **taxi stand** is at the corner of Avenidas López Mateos and Miramar. Most fares within the city cost from M$60 to M$120. Uber rideshare is also available in Ensenada, with trips in town averaging M$50.

Mexicali

☑686 / POP 689,780

The Baja Peninsula's rapidly expanding, industry-driven capital isn't exactly a must-see on international travelers' agendas. But bargain hunters like to cross the border for the shopping, and college kids tend to enjoy the rowdy bars and relatively lax drinking laws. The restaurant scene is uniquely influenced by the city's sizable population of ethnic Chinese, with tasty results.

Steer clear in summer, when Mexicali becomes one of the unpleasantly hottest places on earth.

BUSES FROM ENSENADA

DESTINATION	FARE (M$)	TIME (HR)	FREQUENCY (PER DAY)
Guerrero Negro	1040	11	5
La Paz	2140	22	5
Mexicali	463	4	12
Playas de Rosarito	176	1	frequent
Tecate	125-172	2	frequent
Tijuana	205-250	1½	frequent
Tijuana Airport	300	2	frequent

Catedral de Nuestra Señora de Guadalupe (cnr Morelos & Av Reforma) is the city's oldest and most important religious landmark.

🛏 Sleeping & Eating

Araiza
LUXURY HOTEL **$$$**

(📞 686-564-11-00; www.araizahoteles.com; Blvd Juárez 2220; d incl breakfast from US$100; 🅿❄✳@🛜🏊) An elegant hotel featuring well-appointed and spacious rooms, two excellent restaurants, a bar, tennis courts, a gym and a convention center. The playground and babysitting services make it a top choice for families.

Los Arcos
SEAFOOD **$$**

(📞 686-556-09-03; www.restaurantlosarcos.com; Calle Calafia 454; mains M$228-350; ⏱11am-10pm Mon-Wed, to 11pm Thu-Sat, to 8pm Sun) Dating from 1977, this beloved seafood chain restaurant is Mexicali's most popular dining establishment. The *culichi* shrimp (shrimp in a creamy green-chili sauce) is spectacular. Reservations are recommended.

Dragon
CHINESE **$$**

(📞 686-566-20-20; Blvd Juárez 1830; mains M$98-250; ⏱11am-11pm) A great place to try the local Chinese food with a Mexican twist.

❶ Getting There & Away

AIR

Aeropuerto Internacional General Rodolfo Sánchez Taboada (📞 686-552-23-17; www.aeropuertosgap.com.mx/es/mexicali; Carretera Mesa de Andrade Km 23.5) is 18km east of town. **Aeroméxico** (www.aeromexico.com; Aeropuerto Internacional General Rodolfo Sánchez Taboada) flies to many destinations via Mexico City, while Volaris offers direct flights to destinations around Mexico. **Calafia Airlines** (www.calafiaairlines.com; Aeropuerto Internacional General Rodolfo Sánchez Taboada) flies from Mexicali to La Paz and Tijuana.

BUS

Long-distance and mainland bus companies leave from the **Central de Autobuses** (📞 686-556-19-03; Calz Independencia 1244; ⏱24hr), near Calzada López Mateos. Autotransportes del Pacífico (www.tap.com.mx) and Elite (www.estrellablanca.com.mx) serve mainland Mexican destinations, while ABC (www.abc.com.mx) serves the Baja Peninsula.

Greyhound (📞 800-231-22-22, in USA 760-357-1895; www.greyhound.com; Calz Independencia 1244) has offices in Mexicali and directly across the border in Calexico. There are several departures daily from Mexicali to Los Angeles (one way from US$45) and a few to San Diego (one way from US$30), as well as other destinations in the USA.

CAR & MOTORCYCLE

The main Calexico–Mexicali border crossing is open 24 hours. The newer crossing east of downtown is open from 6am to midnight.

SOUTHERN BAJA

Cardón cacti, boojum trees, ocotillo, cholla and other desert marvels thrive in this beautiful desert area that sometimes doesn't receive any rain for a decade. Look out for crumbling missions, date palms, coconuts and mangrove swamps as you meander southward.

The 25,000-sq-km **Reserva de la Biosfera El Vizcaíno** is one of Latin America's largest protected areas. It sprawls from the Península Vizcaíno across to the Sea of Cortez and includes the major gray-whale calving areas of Laguna San Ignacio and Laguna Ojo de Liebre, and the Sierra de San Francisco with its stunning pre-Hispanic rock art.

The southernmost part of the peninsula contains the cosmopolitan city of La Paz, small seaside towns and villages, and the popular resorts of San José del Cabo and Cabo San Lucas, aka 'Los Cabos.' After the quiet isolation of the state's north, Los Cabos will either be a jarring shock or a pleasing respite.

BAJA PENINSULA MEXICALI

BUSES FROM MEXICALI

DESTINATION	FARE (M$)	TIME (HR)	FREQUENCY (PER DAY)
Ensenada	463	4	8
La Paz	2780	24	1
Mexico City	2401	38	3
Tijuana	335	2½	frequent

DRIVING THE TRANSPENINSULAR & HIGHWAY 5

If time permits, driving the length of the Carretera Transpeninsular (1625km) is an experience not to be missed. Most importantly, it is overall very safe; although driving at night is not recommended due to the possibility of cows wandering onto the road. The road surface is good and, in general, traffic is surprisingly light. There are several military checkpoints along the way, and tourists' vehicles are regularly stopped and searched. This is usually a friendly, quick process; just be sure to accompany the officer on the search and do not offer anything that might be interpreted as a bribe. This unnecessary gesture not only looks suspicious but also sets a bad precedent. Keep an eye on your gas gauge, fill up regularly, and be aware that from El Rosario to Guerrero Negro, a distance of some 350km, there is no gas station.

For those seeking an even less-traveled (and sometimes bumpier) route, consider spending the first leg of the trip on Hwy 5. It stretches over 400km from Mexicali south to Chapala, mainly hugging the peninsula's east coast with views of the shockingly blue Sea of Cortez. In 2018 Hurricane Rosa damaged several areas of the road over about 15km between San Felipe and Puertecitos, but viable workarounds have been created. The roughest section is a 7km stretch further south, from Gonzaga Bay to Lake Chapala, where the road has not yet been paved. Don't try this with an RV. And while you don't need 4WD, you do need to take it *very* slow.

Guerrero Negro

📞 615 / POP 14,316

After the crowds and clamor of the touristy border towns, unassuming, kind of ramshackle Guerrero Negro – a town that sprang up to service the lone salt factory – is a welcome relief. Though the main tourist draw is the proximity to the seasonal migrations of gray whales, there's also excellent bird-watching in the shallow marshes, and the salt factory's odd white crystalline plains are quite beautiful.

🛏 Sleeping & Eating

The whale-watching season can strain local accommodations; reservations are advisable from January through March.

Hotel Malarrimo HOTEL $
(📞615-157-01-00, 615-157-02-50; www.malarrimo. com; Blvd Zapata 42; s/d M$490/595; 🅿❄@🛜) Hot, strong showers and a lot more ambience than the other options in town. Whale headboards and a general whale theme make it impossible to forget why you've come here. There is also a small gift shop and an excellent **restaurant** (www.malarrimo. com; Blvd Zapata 42; mains M$125-275; ⊙7am-10:30pm; 🅿🛜), plus whale-watching and salt-mine tours can be arranged. Campsites and RV hookups available.

Halfway Inn HOTEL $
(📞615-157-13-05; Paralelo 28; d M$750-850; 🅿❄🛜🐾) North of Guerrero Negro right

off Hwy 1, this sprawling old charmer is a popular overnight stop for road-trippers. It has lovely wood floors, dramatic chandeliers, a cantina and a game room with ping-pong and pool. Rooms are dated but comfortable, and surround a somewhat bizarre courtyard.

Los Caracoles HOTEL $$
(📞615-157-10-88; www.hotelloscaracoles.com. mx; Calz de la República; d from M$800; 🅿➔ ❄@🛜) This attractive, sand-colored hotel blends well with its desert surroundings, as do the modern rooms and, come to that, the bathrooms – all are decorated in tones of yellow and gold. There's a souvenir shop and several computer terminals for the use of guests.

Santo Remedio MEXICAN $$
(📞615-157-07-50; Domingo Carballo Félix; mains M$130-380; ⊙8am-11pm; 🅿🐾) One of the fancier Guerrero Negro options, with exceptional service, soft lighting, ocher-washed walls, a pretty patio and a variety of meat and seafood dishes, ranging from T-bone steak to Galician-style octopus. There's also a kids' menu.

ℹ Information

There's an ATM at Banamex bank.
Clínica Hospital IMSS (📞615-157-03-33; Blvd Zapata) is Guerrero Negro's main medical facility.

ℹ Getting There & Away

Guerrero Negro's tiny airport is 2km north of the state border, west of the Transpeninsular.

DETOUR: BAHÍA DE LOS ANGELES

If you happen to be driving Hwy 1 in the midsection of the Baja Peninsula, consider veering off the main road a couple of hours north of Guerrero Negro. Head east for about an hour through a Seussian desertscape until the Sea of Cortéz comes into view, and finally you'll dead-end at Bahía de los Ángeles. This little fishing town (population 1000) is defined by glorious isolation and a sapphire, island-dotted bay that in 2007 was declared a biosphere reserve. Depending on the season, visitors can kayak, dive or swim with whales, whale sharks or sea lions, and these experiences feel as magical as they do personal in such an undiscovered place.

Ricardo's Diving Tours (☑200-124-92-64; www.scubadivingbaja.com; 4hr whale-shark tour for up to 4 people US$200; ☉6am-10pm Tue-Sun, to 8pm Mon) is the trusted local tour operator. **Los Vientos** (☑664-391-11-23; www.losvientoshotel.com; Carretera Bahía de los Ángeles; s/d/tr from M$1800/2200/2400; 🅿❄☎☎🏊), a fairly new beachfront hotel, also offers fishing trips and journeys to the lovingly restored and incredibly remote **Misión San Borja** (☉8am-6pm), btwn Rosarito & Bahía de los Ángeles. The mission is managed by a family descended from the area's original preconquest inhabitants, and they offer guided tours to those willing to make the long, bumpy drive. A less ambitious sightseeing option is the town's small but captivating **Museo de Naturaliza y Cultura** (☑200-124-9101; Km 530, behind the Delegación Bahía de los Ángeles; ☉9am-noon & 2-4pm Oct-Jul) FREE, which displays old mining toys, mammoth bones and a vast shell collection.

There are several hotels around town, but our favorite stay is the rustic **Campo Archelon** (www.campoarchelon.com; Carretera la Gringa; houses from US$60, palapas US$8 per person; 🅿☎) 🍴, a former turtle research center now serving as an 'ecotourist campground' with beach houses, basic huts and complimentary kayaks. There's no restaurant, so you can either head to town to sample the fish-taco stands, grab a fancier meal at Los Vientos or stock up on groceries at Mercado Isla (which accepts credit cards). Note that there's no ATM or cellphone service in Bahía de los Ángeles, but there are two gas stations.

Aéreo Calafia (☑615-157-29-99; www.aereocalafia.com.mx; Blvd Zapata; ☉8am-7pm Mon-Fri, to 4pm Sat) Runs flights to Hermosillo and Ciudad Obregón, and offers charters.

Bus Station (Blvd Marcello Rubio; ☉24hr) Offers a wide range of bus services throughout Baja.

San Ignacio

☑615 / POP 667

With its lush, leafy date palms and pretty, tranquil river, sleepy San Ignacio is a welcome oasis after the seemingly endless Desierto de Vizcaíno. Jesuits located the Misión San Ignacio de Kadakaamán here, but Dominicans supervised construction of the striking church (finished in 1786) that still dominates the picturesque, laurel-shaded plaza.

The area makes a fine base for whale-watching trips to **Laguna San Ignacio**, along with journeys to the famous cave drawings in nearby San Francisco. Less ambitious travelers can instead view the re-creations within San Ignacio's natural history museum.

⊙ Sights

Misión San Ignacio de Kadakaamán   CHURCH

With lava-block walls nearly 1.2m (4ft) thick, the former Jesuit Misión San Ignacio de Kadakaamán stands directly across from San Ignacio's small plaza and is flanked by a grove of citrus trees. Occupying the site of a former Cochimí *ranchería* (indigenous settlement), the mission has been in continuous use since its founding in 1728. It's possibly the prettiest mission in Baja.

One of the three 18th-century altarpieces inside is dedicated to San Ignacio de Loyola, the town's patron saint. The mission was initiated by the famous Jesuit Fernando Consag, and was completed in 1786 under the direction of Dominican Juan Crisóstomo Gómez. Epidemics reduced the Cochimí population from about 5000 to only 120 by the late 18th century, but the mission lasted until 1840.

Museum   MUSEUM

(Misión San Ignacio de Kadakaamán; ☉8am-5pm Mon-Sat Apr-Oct, daily Nov-Mar) FREE This small museum offers a glimpse of the area's natural history and also re-creates the famous cave drawings found in the Sierra de San Francisco.

Casa Lereé HISTORIC SITE
(📞 615-154-01-58; www.casaleree.com; Morelos 20; ⊗ 10am-1pm & 4-8pm) **FREE** Part museum and part bookstore, this beautiful old building sits around a verdant garden with magnificent trees, including a soaring (and shady) *ficus indiga*. The US owner Jane 'Juanita' Ames is a historian and author, and enjoys sharing a wealth of information about the area.

She has one of the best collections of books on the peninsula, and has created several excellent hikes near the town; ask for a copy of the map.

☞ Tours

★ Antonio's Ecotours WILDLIFE WATCHING
(www.cabanassanignacio.com; La Freidera; whale-watching day trip per adult/child US$55/40, all-inclusive overnight whale-watching per adult/child US$260/200) ✎ A long-standing, local, family-run tour business offering excellent whale-watching excursions on Laguna San Ignacio. The company also runs a beach house and 12 rustic, raised cabins right on the *laguna*, complete with a tasty restaurant, solar-heated showers, sawdust toilets and satellite wi-fi.

Excursions to the cave drawings of Sierra de San Francisco are also on offer.

Ecoturismo Kuyima ADVENTURE
(📞 615-154-00-70; www.kuyima.com; Plaza Juaréz 9; cave painting day tours per person US$75-110; ⊗ 8am-8pm) This very friendly and helpful local cooperative on the plaza arranges whale-watching trips to the beautiful Laguna San Ignacio, and can help arrange visits to the otherwise difficult-to-reach rock-art sites in the Sierra de San Francisco.

🛏 Sleeping & Eating

★ Ignacio Springs B&B $$
(📞 615-154-03-33, 615-161-52-11; www.ignacio springs.com; d US$70-130; 🅿❋🛜🐕) This Canadian-owned B&B comprises yurts and *cabañas* (cabins). Idyllically situated fronting a spring-fed river, the decor ranges from conventional US-style to Aztec ethnic, with stylish tile and ceramics. There's a full bar (on the honor system after hours), and breakfast includes homemade breads, preserves and sausages.

Kayaks and paddleboards are available free for guests, and the owners can help arrange whale-watching and cave-painting trips.

Hotel Desert Inn HOTEL $$
(📞 615-154-03-00; mcarceo@fonatur.gob.mx; Camino a San Ignacio Km 72; d M$1200; 🅿🛜🐕) While it looks like a prison from the outside, past the bleak facade you will find a modern mission-style hotel with spacious, airy rooms decorated in a soothing palette of creams, browns and ocher, plus plenty of wardrobe space and large walk-in showers. Rooms are set around a central pool area landscaped with lofty palms and dazzling bougainvillea bushes.

Taqueria Lupita TACOS $
(Plaza Juaréz; tacos M$28; ⊗ 7pm-midnight) For 29 years, the owner of this modest and wonderful stand has been serving up exactly one type of taco in San Ignacio's plaza each night. It's *carne asada* (roasted meat), and it's delicious.

❶ Getting There & Away

The **bus station** (📞 615-154-04-68) is near the San Lino junction outside town. Buses pick up passengers here at 6am, 6:30am, 8:30am, 6pm, 8:30pm and 11pm headed northbound

BUSES FROM GUERRERO NEGRO

DESTINATION	FARE (M$)	TIME (HR)	FREQUENCY (PER DAY)
Ensenada	1040	10	4
La Paz	1440	12	4
Loreto	775	6	4
Mulegé	520	5	4
San Ignacio	257	2	4
Santa Rosalía	391	3-4	4
Tijuana	1214	11	4

CALIFORNIA GRAY WHALES

The migration of gray whales from Siberian and Alaskan waters to the lagoons of Baja is an amazing animal event. In the calving grounds of Laguna Ojo de Liebre and Laguna San Ignacio, 700kg calves will draw their first breaths and begin learning the lessons of the sea from their ever-watchful mothers. The season is long but varies due to the fact that some whales arrive early in the Pacific lagoons, while others take weeks or months to round Land's End and find their favorite bays in the Sea of Cortez.

Peak months to see mothers and calves in the lagoons are February to early April, but the official whale-watching season begins December 15 and lasts until April 15.

If you have *ballena* (whale) fever, one of these destinations will provide a cure.

➡ Laguna Ojo de Liebre (Scammon's Lagoon)

➡ Laguna San Ignacio

➡ Puerto López Mateos

➡ Puerto San Carlos

and at 7am, 9am, 11am, 12:30pm, 6:30pm and 11pm headed southbound. Destinations include Tijuana (M$1755), La Paz (M$1410) and Cabo San Lucas (M$1710).

Sierra de San Francisco

The sheer quantity of beautiful petroglyphs in this region is impressive, and the ocher, red, black and white paintings remain shrouded in mystery. In recognition of its cultural importance, the Sierra de San Francisco has been declared a Unesco World Heritage site. It is also part of the Reserva de la Biosfera El Vizcaíno. Although day trips are possible, to see the region's highlights you'll need to trek for a few days with local rancher guides and donkeys to carry gear.

Cueva del Ratón ARCHAEOLOGICAL SITE
Named for an image of what inhabitants once thought was a rat (or mouse) but is more likely a cougar, this is the most easily accessible cave in the Sierra de San Francisco.

Drivers can get here on their own after registering and paying the park entry (M$75) and guide fee (M$100 for up to four people) at the office of the Instituto Nacional de Antropología e Historia (INAH; ☑ 615-154-02-22; keey_75@hotmail.com; ⊙ 8am-5pm Mon-Sat Apr-Oct, daily Nov-Mar), next to the Misión San Ignacio de Kadakaamán museum (p738) in San Ignacio, then picking up their guide in the pueblo closest to the paintings. Bringing a camera costs M$45 per day. INAH fees for guides for other trips start at M$250 per day, and each pack animal adds M$250. These are INAH fees only, and guides themselves charge additional (varying) fees.

🛈 Getting There & Away

The beautiful mule-back descent of Cañón San Pablo requires at least two days, and preferably three, and is best done through a tour operator like Ecoturismo Kuyimá (p739), which can arrange three-day trips for around US$618 per person (four-person minimum; supplies not included). Longer tours are also available.

Santa Rosalía

☑ 615 / POP 14,160

Southbound travelers will welcome their first sight of the Sea of Cortez after crossing the Desierto de Vizcaíno. Santa Rosalía's brightly painted and strangely Wild West–feeling clapboard-sided houses, Eiffel Tower–design-cousin Iglesia Santa Bárbara, French cowboy bakery, *malecón* and mining museum are prime attractions, although they're rivaled by the black-sand beaches, lazy pelicans and great views from the surrounding hills. This is no holiday haven to be sure, but it is a unique stop worth a look.

Over the last decade, the town has reclaimed its status as a prosperous mining center. As such there's a real industrial, hard-working vibe to the place.

⊙ Sights

★ **Iglesia Santa Bárbara** CHURCH
(Av Obregón 20) Designed and erected for Paris' 1889 World's Fair, then disassembled and stored in Brussels for shipping to West Africa, Gustave Eiffel's (yes, of Eiffel Tower fame) prefabricated Iglesia Santa Bárbara was, instead, shipped here when a director of the French-owned mining company Boleo signed for its delivery to the town in 1895.

🛏 Sleeping & Eating

Hotel Las Casitas
de Santa Rosalía   BOUTIQUE HOTEL $$

(📞615-152-30-23; www.facebook.com/las-casitas-santa-rosalia-164100420829302; Carretera Sur Km 195; s/d from M$900/1200; 🅿🛜) Expat-owned Las Casitas has a real five-star holiday-in-the-sun look with large rooms that have balconies, seamless Sea of Cortez views, exquisite tilework and tasteful artwork. Doubles are spacious with lovely terraces offering panoramic ocean views. The less expensive singles are considerably smaller, but they also offer sea views and a common space with a minikitchen and an exercise bike.

Hotel Francés   HISTORIC HOTEL $$

(📞615-152-20-52; Av Cousteau 15; r incl breakfast M$990; 🅿🛜❄) Overlooking the Sea of Cortez and rusting hulks of mine machinery, the historic Hotel Francés is a colonial gem. Built in 1886 and originally the dormitory for the 'working girls' of a brothel near the mine, the hotel features beautiful rooms with high ceilings, cloth-covered walls and charming stained-wood details. Cash only.

★ Panadería El Boleo   BAKERY $

(📞615-152-03-10; Av Obregón 30; baked goods M$6-15; ⏰7am-9pm Mon-Sat, 9am-2pm Sun) Since 1901 this has been an obligatory stop for those in search of Mexican pastries and, more unusually, French baguettes in a weirdly Wild West ramshackle building. While the pastries may not be world class, the setting is so unusual you have to cowboy up to the counter and order at least one. No seating.

❶ Getting There & Away

The passenger/auto ferry *Santa Rosalía* sails to Guaymas at 9am on Wednesday and Friday and 8pm on Saturday, arriving 10 hours later. It returns from Guaymas at 8pm Tuesday, Thursday and Saturday. Double-check in advance as timings may change.

The ticket office is at the **ferry terminal** (📞615-152-12-46; www.ferrysantarosalia.com; ⏰8am-1pm & 4-6pm) on the highway. Passenger fares are around M$999 (children's tickets are M$535). Vehicle rates vary with vehicle length.

Bus Terminal (📞615-152-14-08; ⏰24hr) Just south of the entrance to town, in the same building as the ferry terminal.

Mulegé

📞615 / POP 3821

The palm- and mangrove-lined Río Mulegé, with its delta, birds, wildlife and nearby snorkeling and diving opportunities, makes this town a great stop for the adventurous and the outdoorsy. And beyond the riverside setting, an 18th-century mission and town square give the place a remote, old-town feeling unique in Baja. Because it sits low in an *arroyo* (stream), Mulegé is prone to flooding during big storms (which tend to happen every two to three years).

As you wind your way south from Mulegé, you'll pass some of the peninsula's most beautiful, turquoise-hued *playas* (beaches) along Bahía Concepción. The pelican colonies, funky rock formations and milky, blue-green water make it a top stop for kayakers, although several of the beaches are becoming more built up.

◉ Sights

Museo Comunitario de Mulegé   MUSEUM

(Barrio Canenea; ⏰9am-6pm Tue-Fri, to 2pm Mon, to 1pm on alternating weekends) FREE This former territorial prison was famed for allowing prisoners to roam free in town during

BAJA PENINSULA MULEGÉ

BUSES FROM SANTA ROSALÍA

DESTINATION	FARE (M$)	TIME (HR)	FREQUENCY (PER DAY)
Ensenada	1435	13	2
Guerrero Negro	410	3	3
La Paz	1240	8	5
Loreto	380	3½	5
Mulegé	125	1	5
San Ignacio	145	1	3
San José del Cabo	1580	11	1
Tijuana	1605	14	2

the day, although the women inmates stayed to cook and clean. Now it holds a small collection of fairly mundane prison artifacts plus a mummified fox. Donations of M$20 are appreciated.

Misión Santa Rosalía de Mulegé
CHURCH

Come to the imposing, stone hilltop Misión Santa Rosalía de Mulegé (founded in 1705, completed in 1766 and abandoned in 1828) for great photos of the site and river valley.

Cañon La Trinidad
CANYON

(4hr tours per person US$50) Trinity Canyon is great for bird-watchers, with the chance to see vermilion flycatchers, gila woodpeckers and a host of raptors and buteos. The narrow, sherbet-colored canyon walls and shimmering pools of water are stunning, as are the pre-Hispanic cave paintings.

🏃 Activities & Tours

Mulegé's best diving spots can be found around the Santa Inés Islands (north of town) and just north of Punta Concepción (south of town). Diving tour operators come and go, so ask around.

The beautiful river, the estuary delta and the southern beaches make Mulegé a prime spot for kayaking.

NOLS Mexico
KAYAKING

(US 800-710-6657; www.nols.edu; kayaking/sailing courses from US$2000) Runs sea-kayaking and sailing courses and trips out of its sustainable, ecofriendly facility on Coyote Bay, south of Mulegé. The courses vary from one week to three months in length, and can also involve hiking in Parque Nacional Sierra San Pedro Mártir (p728), whale-shark encounters, staying in remote coastal communities, roasting coffee beans, farming, making tortillas and learning Spanish.

Mulegé Tours
TOURS

(615-161-49-85; mulegetours@hotmail.com; Cañon La Trinidad excursion per person US$50) Mulegé native Salvador Castro Drew of Mulegé Tours knows just about everything about the Cañón La Trinidad site you'd want to know, including how to avoid the two nasty beehives that 'guard' the paintings. He also does taxi runs to other area sites.

🛏 Sleeping & Eating

Mulegé is a very popular expat and snowbird haunt where people own their property, and short-term lodging options are pretty sparse.

Hístorico Las Casitas
HOTEL $

(615-153-00-19; javieraguiarz51@hotmail.com; Madero 50; r from M$750; P❄☀🛜) Perhaps inspired by its very pretty courtyard, fountains, statues and shady garden of tropical plants, beloved Mexican poet Alán Gorosave once inhabited this hotel. The in-house restaurant serves decent food and has an open-fire grill. The rooms are simple and somewhat threadbare, but smell delightfully like cinnamon and oranges and are decorated with traditional fabrics and artwork.

Hotel Mulegé
HOTEL $

(615-153-00-90; www.hotelmulege.wix.com; Moctezuma s/n; d M$800; P☀@🛜) Located just beyond the arch at the entrance to town, this place is an unmemorable motel on the outside, but the spotless, modern, brightly painted rooms make it the best deal in town. The staff are extra-friendly and helpful as well.

Hotel Serenidad
HOTEL $$

(615-153-05-30; www.serenidad.com.mx; d/tr M$1500/1700, cabañas M$2400; P❄☀🛜🏊) Dating to the 1960s, this hotel is a local institution. Plenty of famous folk have flown into the bumpy private airstrip here, including John Wayne. The rambling, dusty property has loads of backcountry character, with a vast restaurant, rustic and authentic-to-the-era double rooms and small *cabañas*. There's a pig roast every Saturday with live music.

Doney Mely's
MEXICAN $$

(615-153-00-95; Moctezuma s/n; mains M$90-180; 7:30am-10pm Wed-Mon Nov-Apr; 🛜) Doney Mely's is a colorfully decorated restaurant and bar with a special weekend menu for two that includes a gut-busting choice of local favorites like *chiles rellenos* (chilies stuffed with meat or cheese) and enchiladas *verdes*. Breakfasts complete with espresso beverages come recommended as well.

Los Equipales
INTERNATIONAL $$$

(615-153-03-30; Moctezuma s/n; mains M$100-415; 8am-10pm; 🛜) Just west of Zaragoza, this restaurant and bar has gargantuan meals and bright, enclosed balcony seating that's perfect for an evening margarita with friends. Lobster salad, T-bone steak and fried chicken are a sampling of the surf and turf fare.

SOUTH OF MULEGÉ: BAJA'S PRETTIEST BAYS

For its blue-green waters, white sandy coves and relative lack of construction, **Bahía Concepción** is one of the most stunningly beautiful stretches of coast in Baja, if not all of Mexico. It's great for boating, kayaking and swimming, and many smaller bays tucked into the larger bay have *palapas* (thatched-roof beach shacks) and camping areas (M$200 per night). Road-trippers often choose this region as a final destination – and stay for weeks.

Coming from the north, the first and most popular of the beaches is **Playa Santispac** (Km 117), a wide, protected cove with sparkling white sand, some *palapas* and a couple of good restaurants – **Ana's** (☑615-159-00-40; Playa Santispac; mains M$140-320; ⏱8am-9pm; P) is the go-to for delicious seafood and margaritas. In high season, local tour guides come around offering kayaking, snorkeling, hikes, clam feasts, horseback riding, fishing and more, while food vendors make the rounds selling water, *empanadas* and other snacks.

South of Santispac, a more developed cove called **Posada Concepción** has a seasonal hostel, Posada del Sol, which offers wi-fi and rents kayaks, and a new boutique hotel and several rental homes were under construction during research. Continuing down the coast, **Playa Burro** features some *palapas* on the beach as well as snorkeling excursions with **El Burro Baja Tours** (☑WhatsApp 615-155-91-14; www.facebook.com/elburrobajatours; Km 109, Playa Burro; snorkel tour for up to 6 people M$3000). Owner/guide Juan Carlos brings guests out on a pontoon boat to spot sea creatures, then prepares a seafood feast at JC's, his restaurant across from the beach (mains M$40 to M$250).

The next inlet, **Playa Buenaventura**, is another more developed beach, with a full-service **hotel & restaurant** (www.facebook.com/playabuenaventura; Playa Buenaventura; camping per person US$3, d US$40-80, rental house US$100; ❄🖧) and several rental houses. The accommodations come with wi-fi and hot-water showers (luxurious for these parts), and the restaurant is a gathering spot for sports events, holidays and raucous Taco Tuesdays (11am to 4pm, November to May).

The southernmost beaches, **Playa Requeson**, **Playa Perla** and **Playa Armenta**, are regarded as the most beautiful. Requeson offers a delightful walk along a sandbar to a cacti-and-mangrove island at low tide. Perla has some secluded camping, and Armenta's crystal-clear water is simply gorgeous.

ℹ Getting There & Away

Bus Terminal (Transpeninsular Km 132; ⏱8am-11pm) Located near the large entry arch and serving northbound destinations including Santa Rosalía (M$125, one hour) and Tijuana (M$2030, 16 hours) and stop three times daily. Southbound buses pass to destinations including Loreto (M$305, two hours) and La Paz (M$1105, seven hours) seven times daily.

Loreto

☑613 / POP 20,385

Loreto feels like somewhere between an old and new world. Linger along cobblestone streets dotted with trendy shops and a centuries-old mission, relax with a local craft beer at an outdoor cafe or stroll along the *malécon*. Out in that blue water is a water-sports paradise and the magnificent Parque Nacional Bahía de Loreto, where the shoreline, ocean and stunning offshore islands are protected from pollution and uncontrolled fishing.

◉ Sights

★Parque Marine Nacional
Bahía de Loreto   PARK

(M$33) This national marine park makes Loreto a world-class destination for all types of outdoor activities; a number of outfitters offer everything from kayaking and diving to stand-up paddleboarding (SUP) and snorkeling along the reefs around Islas del Carmen and the dormant-volcano-dominated Coronado Islands. Aside from gray whales that frequent the Sea of Cortez, this is the best place to see blue whales. Pay the entrance fee at the park's office in the marina. Staff can advise on water activities.

TOP SPOTS FOR FANTASTIC FISH TACOS

La Guerrerense (p734), Ensenada. Good enough to win an international street-food competition and Anthony Bourdain's pork-loving heart. Enough said.

La Lupita (p755), San José del Cabo. Creative new twists on the classic plus 15 mezcals to choose from as a chaser.

Tacos del Rey (p745), Loreto. Clean, simple, perfect. Pick your toppings then stuff your face on a park bench.

Sierra de la Giganta   OUTDOORS
The trails in the rugged, striated mountains that rise up behind Loreto are seldom marked, but there's great hiking for the fit and adventurous. Guides can be found at the Municipal Department of Tourism or via www.hikingloreto.com (you can also order a hiking guidebook here). Take lots of precautions out here as there's no cellphone service.

Misión San Francisco Javier de Viggé-Biaundó   CHURCH
(San Javier) FREE This wonderful mission is well worth a daytime detour. The windy road passes some beautiful *arroyos* (streams) before arriving at the mission. Be sure to wander to the back garden to see the 300-year-old olive tree with rope-like bark that looks like something out of a Tolkien fantasy. The mission itself is almost unchanged from its look of three centuries ago.

Misión Nuestra Señora de Loreto   CHURCH
Dating from 1697, this was the first permanent mission in the Californias and was the base for the expansion of Jesuit missions up and down the Baja Peninsula. Alongside the church, the **Museo de las Misiones** (☑ 613-135-04-41; Salvatierra 16; M$55; ⊙ 9am-1pm & 2-6pm Tue-Sun) chronicles the settlement of the peninsula.

☞ Tours
Loreto is awash with companies offering all manner of outdoor adventures.

Loreto Sea & Land Tours   WATER SPORTS
(☑ 613-135-06-80; www.toursloreto.com; Madero; diving/snorkeling/whale-watching from US$110/65/130) ✐ This recommended tour operator covers a wide range of activities, including horseback riding, island-hopping, diving, kayaking and snorkeling. The company's excursions to Misión San Francisco Javier de Viggé-Biaundó are especially delightful.

Blue Nation   DIVING
(☑ 613-124-06-07; www.bluenationbaja.com; Av Salvatierra; 2-tank dive from US$135, night dive US$110; ⊙ 9am-1pm & 2-6pm) A relatively new and well-regarded dive shop offering scuba trips and dive certification, as well as snorkeling, island-hopping and hiking.

⨇ Sleeping

Hostal Casas Loreto   HOTEL $
(☑ 613-116-70-14; www.hostalcasaloreto.com; Misioneros 14; s/d M$600/700; ❄ ⧵) Rooms here are set around a long covered courtyard, and are spotless and charmingly decorated with rustic furniture and stone walls. There's a well-equipped kitchen for guests and the owner, Abel, likes to bring everyone together to hang out in the common areas.

La Damiana Inn   HISTORIC HOTEL $$
(☑ 613-135-03-56; www.ladamianainn.com; Madero 8 Sur; d US$80, casitas US$90; ⊜ ❄ ⧵ ⊠) This historical posada has spacious, individually furnished rooms with decor ranging from brightly colored Baja fabrics, ceramics and artwork to mellow earth tones and Native American pieces. There's a communal kitchen and a gorgeous mature garden with fruit trees and hammocks.

Rosarito   BOUTIQUE HOTEL $$$
(☑ 613-135-27-81; www.hotelrosaritoloreto.com; Madero; s/d from US$95/115; ⊜ ❄ ⧵ ⊠) A cheerful boutique hotel built into a former two-story apartment complex, with an intimate and classy little bar just beside the pool. Rooms are immaculate but less artfully designed than the common areas, which are adorned in pop art and wacky neon furnishings.

Posada de las Flores   LUXURY HOTEL $$$
(☑ 613-135-11-62; www.posadadelasflores.com; Plaza Cívica; r incl breakfast from US$159; ⊜ ❄ ⧵ ⊠) Sitting majestically on the main plaza in town, the interior has a palatial feel due to its stone columns and arches, trickling fountains and an earthy color palette. Rooms are charming though surprisingly small, but not to worry: stunning public spaces extend to a rooftop pool, bar and

terrace that have views of the mission and beyond.

✖ Eating & Drinking

Be sure to sample the locally brewed beers at **El Zopilote Brewery & Cocina** (Davis 18; mains M$99-160; ⊘noon-10pm Tue-Sun Oct-Aug). Otherwise, any cafe in the town square is a lovely place for a tipple.

★ Asadero Super Burro   MEXICAN $

(⊘613-135-12-43; Fernández; tacos M$25-40, burritos M$95-120; ⊘6pm-midnight Thu-Tue) At this locals' favorite, watch this team of heroes press fresh tortillas, and stew and grill the beef and chicken at the open kitchen. Super Burro is known for flavorful *arrachera* (grilled skirt steak), gigantic burritos and equally huge stuffed potatoes. If you're not sharing, famished or used to eating things the size of your head, stick with the tacos.

Tacos del Rey   MEXICAN $

(cnr Juárez & Misioneros; tacos M$45; ⊘approx 9am-2pm) The best fish tacos in town are sold at this simple kiosk-restaurant, which is clinical in its cleanliness. The *carne asada* is another standout and there are plenty of toppings to custom-design your taco.

Pan Que Pan   MEXICAN, ITALIAN $

(Hidalgo s/n; breakfasts M$25-95; ⊘8am-4pm Tue-Sun) 🍴 Serving simply awesome breakfasts, this friendly, funky alfresco cafe and bakery offers big omelettes served with beans, avocado, local cheese and fresh bread, continental-style lighter breakfasts of granola or pastries and a decadent French toast with caramelized bananas. Stay for lunch for salads, pizzas, baguette sandwiches and homemade pasta.

Orlando's   MEXICAN $$

(⊘613-135-16-55; Madero Norte; mains M$100-250; ⊘7:30am-9pm Tue-Sun) Colorful tablecloths, plastic furniture, a *palapa* (dried palm leaves) roof; this place has a no-frills setting but serves superb food. Try the pineapple filled with shrimp for a real taste-bud treat. The service is gracious and efficient, the soundtrack is unobtrusive and the margaritas hit the spot.

Ask about the owner's new B&B down the street, and grab an icy treat at his ice-cream shop next door.

🛍 Shopping

Baja Books   BOOKS

(betojeannie@gmail.com; Hidalgo 19; ⊘8am-5pm Mon-Sat) Probably the most comprehensive collection of books on the Baja Peninsula to be found in the region, plus maps, art materials, pottery and a bottomless coffee pot for browsers.

Silver Desert   SILVER

(⊘613-135-06-84; Salvatierra 36; ⊘9am-4pm & 5-8pm Mon-Sat, 10am-3pm Sun) Sells good-quality Taxco sterling-silver jewelry. There's also a second **outlet** (⊘613-135-06-84; Magdalena de Kino 4; ⊘9am-2pm & 3-8pm Mon-Sat, 9am-2pm Sun).

ℹ Information

Municipal Department of Tourism (⊘613-135-04-11; Plaza Cívica; ⊘8am-3pm Mon-Fri) has a few brochures and list of guides, but not much else.

ℹ Getting There & Away

Aeropuerto Internacional de Loreto (⊘613-135-04-99; Carretera Transpeninsular Km 7) Served by several airlines, including Calafia Airlines (www.calafiaairlines.com) and Alaska Airlines (www.alaskaair.com). Alaska runs direct flights to Los Angeles. Taxis from the airport, 4km south of Loreto, cost M$260.

Bus Station (⊘613-135-11-10; ⊘24hr) Near the convergence of Salvatierra, Paseo de Ugarte and Paseo Tamaral, a 15-minute walk from the town center.

BAJA PENINSULA LORETO

BUSES FROM LORETO

DESTINATION	FARE (M$)	TIME (HR)	FREQUENCY (PER DAY)
Guerrero Negro	825	6	4
La Paz	800	5	8
San José del Cabo	1132	8-9	4
Santa Rosalía	380	3	9
Tijuana	2348	18-19	6

La Paz

☑ 612 / POP 244,219

At first glance Baja California Sur's capital is a sprawling, slightly dingy city, but after an hour or so you'll discover there's a lot more to it. The dazzling beauty of La Paz becomes apparent with a stroll along the waterfront *malecón*, and its laid-back, old-world charm can be seen in older architecture around the Plaza Constitución. Posh restaurants, cafes and bars cunningly hide in between the cracks. It's a surprisingly international town – you're as likely to hear French, Portuguese or Italian here as English or Spanish, and yet paradoxically it's the most 'Mexican' city in all of Baja. Its quirky history includes American occupation and even being temporarily declared its own republic.

All in all, it's a great place to meander, and you can shop uninterrupted by touts' invitations as you blend in to the urban vibe. The city makes a good base for day trips to Espíritu Santo, Cabo Pulmo and Todos Santos.

◉ Sights

★ Espíritu Santo   ISLAND

A treasure trove of shallow azure inlets and sorbet-pink cliffs, Espíritu Santo is one of La Paz's gems. It's part of a Unesco World Heritage site comprising 244 Sea of Cortez islands and coastal areas, and is a worthy day trip. A number of operators run activities here, including kayaking and snorkeling.

Malecón   WATERFRONT

La Paz's waterfront, with its wide sidewalk, tiny beaches, tourist pier, benches, sculptures by local artists and unimpeded sunset views, is the city's highlight. It stretches 5.5km, from the Marina de la Paz in the south to Playa Coromuel in the north. It started getting a face-lift in 2017 that will continue in stages over a few years.

Playa Balandra   BEACH

(🏖) The most beautiful in a series of beaches north of La Paz, Playa Balandra is an enclosed cove with shallow azure water that's great for toddlers. Kayaks and paddleboards are available for rent, and beachgoers can also explore tide pools, gaze upon Espíritu Santo and hike to neighboring coves.

The beach directly to the north is home to the famous mushroom rock formation, a hit on Instagram and the unofficial symbol of La Paz. Though the top part occasionally tumbles from its perch, dedicated locals always repair it.

Museo Regional de Antropología e Historia   MUSEUM

(☑ 612-122-01-62; cnr Calles 5 de Mayo & Altamirano; adult M$45; ⊗ 9am-6pm) This is a large, well-organized museum chronicling the peninsula's history (in Spanish) from prehistory to the Revolution of 1910 and its aftermath.

🏃 Activities & Tours

La Paz is an ocean-lover's dream. You can snorkel with whale sharks and sea lions, see migrating humpbacks, pods of several types of dolphin, sea turtles and maybe even get lucky to view a blue whale or orcas. Much of this action is around Espíritu Santo island, which requires a boat, but you can also rent SUPs, sea kayaks and bicycles in La Paz to cruise around the city and its waters.

★ Baja Outdoor Activities   KAYAKING

(BOA; ☑ 612-125-56-36; www.kayakinbaja.com; Pichilingue Km 1; multiday kayak trips from US$595; ⊗ 8am-1pm & 3-6pm Mon-Fri, 9am-5pm Sat, to 3:30pm Sun) Kayak and camp around Espíritu Santo or take the ultimate eight-day circumnavigation tour. This is the very best way to experience the beautiful island.

The company also runs epic kayaking trips from Loreto to La Paz, along with SUP expeditions and kayaking voyages that include yoga and more.

Mar y Aventuras   KAYAKING

(☑ 612-122-70-39; www.kayakbaja.com; Topete 564; day trips US$40-115) A well-respected company offering sea-kayaking, island-hopping, multiday camping and whale-watching excursions. Also has kayak rentals for self-guided tours, and a small hotel that caters to families (suites from US$70).

Carey Dive Center   DIVING, SNORKELING

(☑ 612-128-40-48; www.buceocarey.com; Topete 3040; snorkeling US$85, 2-tank dives US$150) A family-run and highly professional establishment that offers snorkeling, diving, whale-watching, trips to see a sea-lion colony and other tours.

Espíritu & Baja   OUTDOORS

(☑ 612-122-44-27; www.espiritubaja.com; Paseo Obregón 2130-D; full-day trips US$90) This company has knowledgable, fun guides who are passionate about the science and history of the area. Choose from Espíritu Santo day trips, shorter whale-shark tours (three-hour tour US$75) and gray-whale-watching from Bahía Magdalena on the Pacific Coast (full-day tour US$150)

🛏 Sleeping

Pension Baja Paradise
PENSION $

(☎612-128-60-97; Madero 2166; d/t from M$490/560, s without bathroom M$320) Spotless, with comfy modern beds, reliably hot showers and cold air-conditioning plus touches of art and driftwood all around, this Mexican-Japanese-run place is a lovely spot to stay. There's a kitchen and a coin laundry for guest use and it's near lots of great eating options.

Casa al Mar
BOUTIQUE HOTEL $$

(☎612-128-77-67; Paseo Obregón 220; s/ste from US$60/170; ⊕❄🅿❄) With a dreamy location on the central waterfront, this classic hacienda-style hotel was recently revamped into a classy boutique stay. Nine accommodations include everything from a small studio to multistory doubles with ocean views. The beige, sea green and white color scheme is lovely, as is the service.

★ El Ángel Azul
BOUTIQUE HOTEL $$$

(☎612-125-51-30; www.elangelazul.com; Av Independencia 518; r US$75-115; 🅿⊕❄🅿) Possibly the loveliest of La Paz' lodging options, the Blue Angel offers simply furnished, pastel-washed rooms, which surround a beautiful courtyard that is filled with palms, cacti, birdsong and bougainvillea. There is a colorfully cluttered honesty bar and sitting room, plus a kitchen for the use of guests.

Casa Kootenay
B&B $$$

(☎612-122-00-06; www.casakootenay.com; Brecha California, Playa Conchalito; d US$85-130; ❄🅿❄) An upscale B&B run by a dive master with serious baking skills (proven daily via delicious breakfasts). The four well-kept guest rooms are comfortable enough, but the amenities are unbeatable. Think pool and Jacuzzi, lush gardens, a rooftop with panoramic sea views and complimentary water toys (kayaks! paddleboards! snorkel gear!) for exploring the tranquil sea and mangroves in the backyard.

Bikes are also available for city exploration.

Baja Camp
TENTED CAMP $$$

(☎612-128-66-49; www.bajacamp.com; Espíritu Santo; all-inclusive d US$550; ⊕Jun-Sep) If you've ever wanted to live like royalty on a faraway desert beach, swimming with sea creatures by day and sleeping under the stars in a giant safari tent complete with living room, here's your big chance. It's a glamping endeavor like no other, complete with transport, boat excursions, comfy beds, bathrooms, showers, a fully stocked bar and delicious meals.

🍴 Eating

La Paz' restaurant scene has become increasingly sophisticated – you'll find most of the top culinary choices on Calles Domínguez and Madero, north of Calle 5 de Mayo.

Dulce Romero Panaderia Gourmet
BAKERY $

(Allende 167; breakfasts M$68-135; ⊕8am-10pm Mon-Sat; ❄) Come to this clean, modern, white-brick space for delicious all-organic breakfasts of perfectly poached eggs, local cheeses, veggies, salsas and more on straight-from-the-oven breads and croissants. Sandwiches and salads are served at lunch, and pizza, pasta and burgers for dinner. Then the scrumptious cakes, pastries and myriad baked goods will have you drooling for dessert.

★ Mariscos El Toro Güero
SEAFOOD $$

(☎612-122-78-92; Mariano Abasolo; mains M$100-250; ⊕10am-8pm) Often – and rightfully – packed with locals, this casual restaurant serves heaping plates of the most delicious seafood in La Paz. Try the *molcajete mariscos,* essentially a mortar (sans pestle) overflowing with fresh fish, octopus, sea snails and shrimp. Throw that on a *tostada,* add hot sauce and wash down with a Tecate. Perfection.

Maria California
MEXICAN $$

(Juárez 105; mains M$79-119; ⊕7:30am-2pm Wed-Mon) Great for breakfast with live music (on weekends) and a fabulous atmosphere throughout the cozy, cluttered dining rooms and terraces. Local artwork, photos and brilliant colored paintwork adorn the walls. Order Mexican classics, pancakes and fresh smoothies and juices.

Nim
INTERNATIONAL $$$

(☎612-122-09-08; www.nimrestaurante.com; Revolución 1110; mains M$225-370; ⊕1-10:30pm Mon-Sat; ❄) In a sumptuous historic house with art-deco floor tiles and a chic pale-gray painted interior, organic produce is used in dishes that span the continents. Think Moroccan tagines, Italian pastas, clam chowder

La Paz

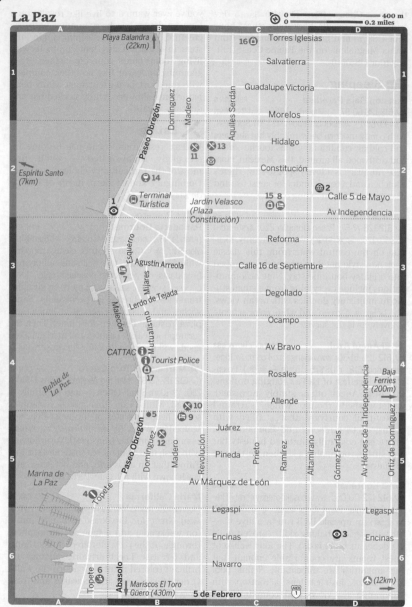

0 ——— 400 m
0 ——— 0.2 miles

Playa Balandra (22km)

Espíritu Santo (7km)

Torres Iglesias
Salvatierra
Guadalupe Victoria
Morelos
Hidalgo
Constitución
Calle 5 de Mayo
Av Independencia
Reforma
Calle 16 de Septiembre
Degollado
Ocampo
Av Bravo
Rosales
Allende
Juárez
Pineda
Av Márquez de León
Legaspi
Encinas
Navarro

16 🔲
13 🍴✉
11 🍴
14 🚌
2 🏛
1 ⚓
Terminal Turística
Jardín Velasco (Plaza Constitución)
15 8 🏛🍴
7 🏛
Agustín Arreola
Esquerro
Mijares
Lerdo de Tejada
Malecón
Mutualismo
CATTAC ℹ
Tourist Police ℹ
17 🏛
Bahía de La Paz
Marina de La Paz
5 🏛
10 🍴
9 🍴
12 🍴
Paseo Obregón
Dominguez
Madero
Revolución
Prieto
Ramírez
Altamirano
Gómez Farías
Av Héroes de la Independencia
Ortiz de Dominguez
Baja Ferries (200m) →
Baja Ferries (12km) →
3 👁
6 🏛
Topete
Abasolo
Mariscos El Toro Güero (430m)
5 de Febrero
MEX 1

Dominguez
Madero
Aquiles Serdán
Paseo Obregón

Espíritu Santo (7km) →

Legaspi
Encinas

and locally sourced sautéed oysters. Hugely popular with the resident expat population, it's La Paz at its most cosmopolitan.

Las Tres Virgenes INTERNATIONAL $$$
(📞 612-123-22-26; Madero 1130; mains M$240-1500; 🕐 1-11pm) An elegant oasis of a restaurant where you can dine in an atmospheric courtyard surrounded by leafy trees and statues. The menu includes both traditional and innovative dishes like grilled baby octopus, lots of export-quality Mexican beef cuts and a classic Caesar salad. Reservations recommended.

La Paz

♟ Drinking & Entertainment

The highest concentration of bars is between Calles 16 de Septiembre and Agustín Arreola, across from the *malecón*.

Harker Board   BAR
(cnr Constutución & Paseo Obregón; ⊙ bar 11am-1am Wed-Mon, kitchen to 11:30pm; 🛜) Head upstairs to the terrace for sweeping views over the bay and a *cerveza* (beer). Five local beers are on tap, and there about 25 bottled varieties. Pizza is also available. This great place doubles as a rental place for stand-up paddleboards and kayaks from 11am to 5pm.

Seaside   COCKTAIL BAR
(☑ 612-124-43-53; Carretera a Pichilingue Km 5, Hotel La Concha; ⊙ 1-11pm) This swanky bar and restaurant wins for its potent craft cocktails, killer sunset view and friendly service. The setting is incredibly romantic, particularly the tables set up on the pier, but do bring a sweater (and possibly a headband) to protect against strong ocean breezes. Best to stick with drinks, as the food is inconsistent.

Teatro de la Ciudad   LIVE PERFORMANCE
(☑ 612-122-91-01; Altamirano; ⊙ hours vary) Features performances by musical and theatrical groups, often by performers from mainland Mexico, as well as occasional film series. The giant theater is within the **Unidad Cultural Profesor Jesús Castro Agúndez** (☑ 612-125-02-07; ⊙ 8am-8pm Mon-Sat).

🛍 Shopping

Organic Market   FOOD
(☑ 612-124-84-07; cnr Antonio Rosales & Malecón; ⊙ 8am-noon Tue & Sat Oct-Jul) This small organic market is fun for a browse and sells all kinds of locally produced gourmet goodies, as well as local cheeses, homemade cakes and bread.

Ibarra's Pottery   CERAMICS
(Prieto 625; ⊙ 9am-3pm Mon-Fri, to 2pm Sat) See potters at work at this ceramics workshop and store that dates to 1958 – it is famed throughout Baja.

Allende Books   BOOKS
(☑ 612-125-91-14; www.allendebooks.com; Av Independencia 518; ⊙ 10am-6pm Mon-Sat; 🛜) English-language bookstore with a good selection of books on the Baja Peninsula and mainland Mexico. There's coffee, too.

❶ Information

The majority of banks (most with ATMs) and *casas de cambio* (exchange houses) are on or around Calle 16 de Septiembre.

There's an **immigration office** (☑ 612-125-49-41; Calle 5 de Febrero, Los Olivos; ⊙ 9am-1pm Mon-Fri) near the center of town.

CATTAC (Tourist Assistance Center; ☑ 612-122-59-39; cnr Paseo Obregón & Av Bravo; ⊙ 8am-8pm) Brochures and pamphlets in English, plus some maps; very helpful.

Tourist Police (☑ 612-122-04-77, 911; ⊙ 24hr) Small booth on Paseo Obregón; hours may vary.

Hospital Salvatierra (☑ 612-175-05-00; Av Paseo de los Deportistas 86; ⊙ 24hr) The largest and best hospital in southern Baja, located 4.6km southwest of the center, via Calles 5 de Febrero and Forjadores de Sudcalifornia.

Main post office (cnr Constitución & Revolución; ⊙ 8am-4pm Mon-Fri, to noon Sat)

Viva La Paz (www.vivalapaz.com) La Paz' official tourism site.

❶ Getting There & Away

AIR

Aeropuerto General Manuel Márquez de León (☑ 612-124-63-36; www.aeropuertosgap.com. mx; Transpeninsular Km 13) is about 9km southwest of the city. It has an immigration office.

Aeroméxico (☑ 612-122-00-91; www.aero mexico.com; Calle 5 de Mayo) flies to Cancún, Guadalajara and Mexico City (where it connects to many other destinations), while **Calafia Airlines** (www.calafiaairlines.com; cnr Santiago & Mulegé), Volaris and Viva Aerobus offer direct flights to additional domestic destinations including Mazatlán and Tijuana.

BOAT

Ferries to Mazatlán and Topolobampo leave the ferry terminal at Pichilingue, 23km north of La Paz. Baja Ferries has a **small office** (☑ 612-125-63-24; Port) at the port and a **larger office** (☑ 612-123-66-00; www.bajaferries.com; Allende 1025; ◷ 8am-6pm Mon-Fri, to 2pm Sat) in town.

Ferries to Mazatlán depart at midnight on Tuesday and 8pm on Thursday and Saturday, arriving 16 to 18 hours later; return ferries leave Mazatlán at 8pm Wednesday, Friday and Sunday. Passenger fares in *salón* (numbered seats) are M$1240.

Topolobampo services depart at 2:30pm Tuesday to Friday and 11pm on Saturday. The return ferry from Topolobampo to La Paz leaves at midnight from Tuesday to Friday and 11pm Sunday, arriving in Pichilingue six to seven hours later. Passenger fares in *salón* are M$1100.

Ensure that you arrive at the pier two hours before departure, and three hours before if you're shipping a car. Vehicle rates vary with vehicle length and destination.

Before shipping any vehicle to the mainland, officials require a vehicle permit. You can obtain one at **Banjército** (www.banjercito.com.mx; ◷ 7am-3pm Mon, Wed & Fri-Sun, to 6pm Tue & Thu) at the ferry terminal, or from its vehicle permit modules in Mexicali or Tijuana.

BUS

The **Terminal Turística** (☑ 612-123-00-00; cnr Malecón & Av Independencia) is centrally located on the *malecón*. Convenient local services include 10 daily buses to Playa Tecolote (M$100, 35 minutes) and 10 to Playa Pichilingue (M$100, 25 minutes) between 10am and 5pm.

CAR & MOTORCYCLE

Car-rental rates start at around M$700 per day including insurance.

Budget (☑ 612-122-60-60, 612-122-60-40; www.budget.com; cnr Paseo Obregón & Allende; ◷ 7am-7pm Mon-Sat, to 4pm Sun) has several agencies with locations both on the *malecón* and at the airport.

❶ Getting Around

There are no local buses. Uber operates in La Paz, and rides cost about M$45 around town or around M$120 from the airport to the *malecón* area.

BUSES FROM LA PAZ

DESTINATION	FARE (M$)	TIME (HR)	FREQUENCY (PER DAY)
Cabo San Lucas	300	3	frequent
Ciudad Constitución	405	3	frequent
Ensenada	2345	22	6
Guerrero Negro	1455	12-13	7
Loreto	800	5-6	11
Mulegé	1105	6-7	9
San Ignacio	1410	10	7
San José del Cabo	340	3½	frequent
SJD Airport	545	3	6
Tijuana	2505	22-24	6
Todos Santos	150	1½	frequent

CAR FERRIES FROM LA PAZ

DESTINATION	VEHICLE	FARE (M$)
Mazatlán	car 6m or less/motorcycle/motorhome	3800/2800/11,600
Topolobampo	car 6m or less/motorcycle/motorhome	2800/2400/11,100

La Ventana

🗐 612 / POP 255

Attracting kitesurfers from around the world with its consistent wind, this seaside fishing village also makes a great base for mountain biking, hiking and seeking out creatures of the sea. Depending on the season, whale sharks, sea lions, whales, sea turtles and fish can all be spotted just offshore, without ever having to battle a crowd. Diving is best in summer when the water visibility reaches 25m or 30m (80ft or 100ft).

The kitesurfing season runs from November until March with steady winds from 12 to 20 knots. A large bay with long, sandy beaches in both directions makes La Ventana an ideal place to learn.

🏃 Activities

★Palapas Ventana   OUTDOORS
(🗐612-114-01-98, in USA 310-594-3483; www .palapasventana.com; 2-tank dive US$165, kiteboarding lesson per hour US$95, snorkeling per person US$85) Organizes diving, snorkeling, windsurfing, kitesurfing, sportfishing, petroglyph hikes and more. It also organizes adventure tours to the Reserva de la Biosfera Sierra de la Laguna (p751) and elsewhere.

Its delightful *palapa*-style *cabañas* are set on a hillside just over the main beach (M$2220 to M$4800 a night). There's also a good restaurant, ideal for chilling with an ocean view post-activities.

Elevation Kiteboarding   KITESURFING
(🗐612-177-98-47; www.elevationkiteboarding.com; Baja Joe's; lessons per hour from US$210, 3-/5-day beginner package US$775/1235) Top-notch kiteboarding school with knowledgeable, experienced instructors and solid equipment. Based at Baja Joe's (p751).

🛌 Sleeping

Baja Joe's   HOTEL $$
(🗐612-114-00-01; www.bajajoe.com; Callejon 725; s US$45-115, d US$55-125; 🅿❄🛜🏊) This place is excellent value with tidy small rooms fronting a communal terrace and sharing a kitchen and common room. The property encompasses a kitesurfing school, two kitchens and Joe's Garage, a popular bar with 10 frothy ales on tap.

Casa Tara   RESORT $$$
(🗐612-100-86-16; www.casatararetreat.com; Corredor Isla Cerralvo; d from US$214; 🅿❄🛜🏊) The most upscale digs in La Ventana is a seaside

OFF THE BEATEN TRACK

RESERVA DE LA BIOSFERA SIERRA DE LA LAGUNA

Hardcore backpackers can strap on hiking boots, fill water bottles and head into the uninterrupted wilds of this lush and rugged biosphere reserve, south of the intersection of the Transpeninsular and Hwy 19. It's not a place for inexperienced hikers, or anyone unfamiliar with the unique challenges presented by desert trails, but the rewards are great: stunning vistas, close encounters with wildlife and a meadow that was once a lake bed (the feature from which the area gets its name).

Baja Sierra Adventures (🗐624-166-87-06; www.bajasierradventures.com; Belisario Dominguez; day trips from US$70; ☺7am-8pm), in a tiny ranch called El Chorro, offers a variety of day and overnight trips, biking and trekking through this unique region. Palapas Ventana (p751) is another option for tours to this region.

collection of Mediterranean-style villas and the posh restaurant, yoga shala and postcard-pretty beach club they share. Accommodations are defined by flowing white linens, teal throw pillows and natural stone and wood finishes, and the relaxing color scheme carries over into the romantic, pescatarian restaurant.

★Gran Sueño   RESORT $$$
(🗐866-202-0789; www.visitgransueno.com; Bahía de los Sueños; villas from US$300; 🅿❄🛜🏊) Thirty minutes southeast of La Ventana, this delightful surprise of a resort is perched on a glorious, hidden cove at the end of a dirt road. The beachfront villas are hopelessly posh, but a handful of day guests who take lunch at the resort are also welcomed to the property and its cascading pools, impressive model-train museum and idyllic white-sand beach.

🍴 Eating & Drinking

Playa Central   PIZZA $$
(www.facebook.com/playa.central.kiteboarding; Corredor Isla Cerralvo; pizza M$155-255; ☺9am-10pm; 🅿🛜) Located beachside in the center of town, this cavernous former shrimp factory with a rooftop patio not only serves terrific thin-crust pizza but also has regular live

RANCHO CACACHILAS

Over a decade ago, Walmart heiress Christy Walton took an interest in this remote corner of Mexico and founded Rancho Cacachilas, a large-scale, conservation-minded ranching project with a full-service **bicycle shop** (☑ 612-114-04-72; www.ranchocacachilas.com; Corredor Isla Cerralvo; mountain-bike rental US$45, guided bike tour per person US$45, hikes per person US$65; ☺ 8am-4pm) ◢ based in La Ventana. The shop handles mountain-bike rentals and repairs, and is also a tour center, offering everything from multiday hikes and wilderness camping to mule rides and cheese tastings.

The tours take place around the project's working ranches and trail systems, which are scattered across some 14,000 hectares within the Sierra Cacachilas mountains. It's an awe-inspiring backdrop for outdoor adventure, and the ranches also serve as a community training ground for agricultural best practices. Don't miss your chance to hit the trails out here, eat the best goat's cheese of your life and glamp under the stars.

music, a popular bar, plenty of bar games, and kitesurfing rental and instruction. Don't miss its margaritas.

Las Palmas
MEXICAN $$
(☑ 612-114-03-93; El Sargento; mains M$90-230; ☺ 8am-10pm) Find this great big orange restaurant in El Sargento, a couple of kilometers north of La Ventana, in a sublime spot overlooking the water and Isla Cerralvo. The Mexican dishes are definitely a notch above the norm; try the *chiles rellenos* or the fish fillet.

❶ Getting There & Away

A bus leaves La Paz at 2pm daily for La Ventana (one way M$100) and makes the return trip to La Paz at around 7am daily. Most people, however, rent a car to get here.

Los Barriles

☑ 624 / POP 1174

South of La Paz, the Transpeninsular brushes the gulf at this attractive small town. It is a spectacular spot for wind- and kitesurfing thanks to brisk winter westerlies that average 10 to 20 knots. During whale season you can see spouts close to shore and hundreds of leaping mobula rays in the waves.

Vela Windsurf
WINDSURFING
(www.velawindsurf.com; Hotel Playa del Sol; windsurfing/kitesurfing lessons from US$70/150; ☺ 9am-5pm Dec-Apr) One of the longer-established water-sports companies with centers worldwide, it caters to windsurfers, kitesurfers and stand-up paddleboarders. The winds die down considerably between April and August, so that is not a good time to take out a board.

Hotel Los Barriles
HOTEL $$
(☑ 624-141-00-24; www.losbarrileshotel.com; 20 de Noviembre s/n; s/d M$1370/1660; ℗ ❋ ❂ ☎ ❂) This hotel has a comfortable, laid-back feel. Twenty rooms are set around a pretty lagoon-style pool area. The owner prides himself on his superior German mattresses and regularly updates the rooms; most have fridges.

La Casita
SUSHI $$
(☑ 624-124-82-59; Calle 20 de Noviembre; sushi rolls M$140-170; ☺ noon-10pm) Easily the best sushi around, with top-notch service to match. Go with one of the inventive rolls made with fresh local seafood; for instance, the Derek comes with avocado, cucumber and tempura shrimp all topped with spicy tuna and a secret sauce. Also delicious: the sea scallops in an orange-liqueur reduction.

Caleb's Cafe
CAFE $$
(20 de Noviembre; mains M$65-160; ☺ 7:30am-3pm Tue-Sat; ☎) This delightful, American-run cafe is famed for its gooey, buttery, sticky buns. Other favorites include zucchini bread and carrot cake, while breakfasts are healthy and hearty (such as broccoli scrambled eggs and feta-cheese omelette).

❶ Getting There & Away

Several daily buses run between Los Barriles and San José del Cabo (M$125, two hours) and La Paz (M$160, two hours).

Cabo Pulmo

☑ 624 / POP 50

Cabo Pulmo, a tiny village and a 7110-hectare Marine Protected Area (MPA), is one of the most successful national marine parks in the world and arguably offers the best diving and snorkeling in Baja. It's also home to the largest Pacific coral reef in the Sea of Cortez. You don't necessarily need a 4WD to enjoy the drive out here along the spectacular Eastern Cape (from the south) coastal road or through the Sierra de la Laguna (to the west), but the road can get rough at times. You will escape the crowds and find a very mellow scene that can be hard to leave.

🏃 Activities

People come from all around southern Baja to dive or snorkel at Cabo Pulmo. Highlights include the coral reef, some resident bull sharks and a massive school of bigeye jacks that regularly form a giant, astonishing ball. Depending on the season, mobula rays and sea lions may also be spotted.

Snorkelers should head for the beach at **Los Arbolitos** (entry fee M$40 per person) 5km south of Cabo Pulmo, then follow the shoreline hiking trail to **Las Sirenitas**, where wind and wave erosion has made the rocks look like melting wax sculptures. Eerie and beautiful, they're accessible by boat as well.

Offshore snorkeling and diving trips can be booked via several companies that operate out of kiosks down by the water. Our favorite is **Cabo Pulmo Divers** (📞612-157-33-81; www.cabopulmodivers.com; 2-tank dives US$125, 2½hr snorkeling tours US$45), run by the Castro family. The Castros were key in creating the national park and continue to be the biggest champions in protecting it.

🛏 Sleeping & Eating

Cabo Pulmo Beach Resort   VILLA $$
(📞624-141-07-26; www.cabopulmo.com; Camino Cabo Este; villa US$80-130, all-inclusive dive package per person from US$133; ⊙8am-5pm; 🅿❄🤖🏊) For Cabo Pulmo, these five thatch-roofed villas can be considered fancy. They're set in the local village and like the rest of the community, they run on solar power; don't be surprised when the AC or wi-fi cuts off. On a brighter note, the resort's Coral Reef restaurant is fabulous and the all-inclusive (eat, sleep, dive) packages are excellent value.

Eco Adventure Bungalows   CABAÑAS $$
(📞624-157-40-72; www.cabopulmoecoadventures.com; cabañas M$1200; 🅿) 🍴 These two solar-powered *palapa*-style *cabañas* are a block from the beach, and plain but pleas-

antly furnished. The local owners organize water sports and whale-watching tours from their Eco Adventures kiosk on the waterfront.

El Caballero   MEXICAN $$
(Camino Cabo Este; mains M$90-230; ⊙7am-9pm) This place serves huge dishes of traditional Mexican cuisine, including superb fish tacos and enchiladas. Breakfast is great, too. There's a small shop here for snacks and supplies.

🛈 Getting There & Away

Many people go to Cabo Pulmo to dive on day trips from all around Baja Sur. Otherwise you'll need your own vehicle.

San José del Cabo

📞 624 / POP 93,069

San José del Cabo is like the 'mild' sister of 'wild' Cabo San Lucas, offering quiet shopping, an attractive plaza and a beautiful church in its inland, historic center. Excellent dining opportunities can be found within the city and tucked into nearby foothills, where celebrities are known to make appearances. A couple of kilometers south, the Zona Hotelera beach area has miles of white sand lining a mostly rip-tide laden ocean, built up with large hotels, condos and eyesores, er, timeshares.

The best beaches for swimming are along the road to Cabo San Lucas and include **Playa Santa María** at Km 13.

The colonial-style **Iglesia San José** (Plaza Mijares; ⊙hours vary), built in 1730 to replace the Misión San José del Cabo, faces the spacious Plaza Mijares.

🛏 Sleeping

Reserve ahead during the peak winter months.

Hotel Colli   HOTEL $$
(📞624-142-07-25; www.hotelcolli.com; Hidalgo s/n; r from M$900; 🅿➜❄🤖) Friendly and family-owned for three generations, the Colli has sunny yellow paintwork in the rooms and is in a great position, only steps away from the plaza and next to the best bakery (p755) in town. Great value.

★ Acre   FARMSTAY $$$
(📞624-129-96-07; www.acrebaja.com; Camino Real, Animas Bajas; tree house incl breakfast from US$295; 🅿❄🤖🏊) 🍴 This boutique

San José del Cabo

San José del Cabo

tree-house village perches within 25 gorgeous acres of farmland dotted with fruit trees, vegetables and flowers that define the farm-to-table restaurant's menu. Each cottage is built from ecofriendly rammed-earth and accessed via private garden path; a stay comes with morning yoga and access to a veritable menagerie, including Nigerian dwarf goats and a donkey called Burrito.

The relaxing pool and various games (think badminton, bocce, ping-pong) round out the offerings.

Casa Natalia   BOUTIQUE HOTEL $$$
(☑ 624-146-71-00; www.casanatalia.com; Blvd Mijares 4; r US$300-600; ✳🕸🛜♨) The fabulous Natalia opens onto San José's plaza and has rooms overlooking a descending series of luxurious swimming pools with hammocks and lounges all around. Arty and grand paintings on the walls, contemporary furnishings and giant bathrooms make each unique room a delight. The restaurant is superb. Standards share terraces (with woven dividers) but are the most updated.

Tropicana Inn   HOTEL $$$
(☑ 624-142-15-80; www.tropicanainn.com.mx; Blvd Mijares 30; r incl breakfast from US$105; ✳🕸♨🛜) The spacious rooms are attractively decked out with terracotta tiles and pretty floral-tiled bathrooms. The classically Mexican, hacienda-style courtyard has a huge, partially *palapa*-shaded pool, a jungle of flowers and tropical plants, and a squawking parrot named Paco. Excellent, central location.

El Ganzo   BOUTIQUE HOTEL $$$
(☑ 624-104-90-00; www.elganzo.com; Blvd Tiburon; d from US$159; 🅿✳🛜♨) A departure

from the waterfront's cookie-cutter hotels, El Ganzo makes a big to-do about independent art, music and gastronomy, identifying itself as a 'hipster hacienda.' You certainly won't find an underground recording studio at any other stay in Los Cabos, or a Thursday-night vinyl and craft cocktails event for that matter. Art-filled rooms and common spaces are super comfy.

✖ Eating & Drinking

There are some fabulous places to eat here, from cheap taco joints to upscale international cuisine.

★La Lupita   TACOS $$
(☑624-688-39-26; Morelos s/n; tacos M$35-85; ⊘2-11pm Tue & Sun, to 2am Wed-Sat) Pair flavorful, unique tacos – including Mediterranean octopus, duck *mole* or miso fish – with mezcal cocktails, amazing margaritas, live music and an all-around fun scene. Bright colors, rustic wood tables and ethnic patterns make it as hip as it is delicious. Just go.

A second location opened in Cabo San Lucas in 2018.

French Riviera   BAKERY, CAFE $$
(cnr Hidalgo & Doblado; pastries around M$40, mains M$150; ⊘7am-11pm) A French-inspired spot with tasty breads, delicious croissants and pastries, gelati that hits the spot on a hot day and excellent dinners. The Med-inspired decor is tasteful and contemporary.

El Marinero Borracho   MEXICAN $$
(Drunken Sailor; ☑624-105-64-64; Blvd Tiburon; mains M$50-290; ⊘noon-10pm Tue-Sun) Down by San José del Cabo's marina, this two-story, *palapa*-topped Mexican place serves unique fusion items (falafel tacos anyone?) along with delicious ceviche, tangy margaritas and a bangin' shrimp burger. It often fills with locals, particularly around sunset.

★Flora's Field Kitchen   INTERNATIONAL $$$
(☑624-142-14-58; www.flora-farms.com; Animas Bajas; mains M$200-520; ⊘9am-2:30pm & 5-9:30pm Tue-Sat, 10am-2:30pm Sun) Visit this farm oasis to splurge on meals finely crafted from ingredients harvested from the surrounding gardens, crusty fresh breads, locally made cheeses and refreshing cocktails, all in a rustic-chic setting right off the pages of a lifestyle magazine. Explore the relaxing, bucolic grounds, browse the adjacent Shoppes at Flora Farms or book a treatment at the Farm Spa.

Hand-built, straw-bale luxury homes and haylofts are also available for overnight stays. It's about 5km northeast of the colonial town center.

Baja Brewing Co   BREWERY
(www.bajabrewingcompany.com; Morelos 1227; ⊘noon-1am) A pub-style environment offering local microbrews. Sample 4oz measures of six different beers in a flight to find your favorite. Popular choices include the Baja Razz (raspberry ale) and the put-hair-on-your-chest Peyote Pale Ale.

There are two sister cantinas in Cabo San Lucas.

Los Barriles de Don Malaquias   BAR
(☑624-130-78-00; cnr Blvd Mijares & Juárez; ⊘10am-8pm Mon-Sat, to 6pm Sun) Los Barriles stocks over 300 varieties of tequila and keeps at least two dozen bottles open for tasting. Prices are a bit steep, but the selection is great.

🛍 Shopping

Blvd Mijares is the self-proclaimed arts district and boasts numerous galleries, studios and stores. In high season the district has an Art Walk on Thursdays from 5pm to 9pm, with open studios, wine tasting and more. For info on art galleries in the area, check out www.artcabo.com.

El Armario   ARTS & CRAFTS
(☑624-105-29-89; cnr Morelos & Obregón; ⊘9am-8pm Mon-Sat; 🛜) Grab a seat on the patio of this adorable coffee and art corner, housed in a former gas station at the heart of the Gallery District. The coffee's strong, the sandwiches are yummy and the unique handicrafts, folk art and pottery hail from around Mexico.

Mercado Orgánico   MARKET
(☑624-142-09-48; www.sanjomo.com; off Av Centenario; ⊘9am-noon Sat) The community (including plenty of gringos, mind you) gathers at this organic market every high-season Saturday (November to May) for a smorgasbord of goodness. We're talkin' local fruits and veggies, farm-raised eggs, fresh herbs, cut flowers, potted plants, local honey, Mexican folk art, yoga classes, jugglers, music, grilled meats, freshly baked bread and more.

ℹ Information

Several *casas de cambio* here keep long hours.
IMSS Hospital (☑emergency 624-142-01-80, nonemergency 624-142-00-76; www.imss.gob.

BUSES FROM SAN JOSÉ DEL CABO

DESTINATION	FARE (M$)	TIME (HR)	FREQUENCY (PER DAY)
Cabo San Lucas	40	1	frequent
Ensenada	2315-2685	24	3
La Paz	340	3½	frequent
Los Barriles	280	1½	6
Tijuana	2478-2845	26	3

mx; cnr Hidalgo & Coronado) The hospital of choice.

Secretaria Municipal de Turismo (☑ ext 150 624-142-29-60; Plaza San José, Transpeninsular; ⊘ 8am-5pm Mon-Sat) Stocks brochures and maps.

ⓘ Getting There & Away

AIR

Aeropuerto Internacional de Los Cabos (SJD; ☑ 624-146-51-11; www.aeropuertosgap.com.mx; Carretera Transpeninsular Km 43.5), north of San José del Cabo, also serves Cabo San Lucas. All airline offices are found here.

Calafia Airlines (☑ 624-143-43-02; www.calafiaairlines.com) flies direct to La Paz, Loreto, Mexicali and Tijuana, along with some mainland Mexico destinations like Los Mochis, Guadalajara and Mazatlán. **Aeroméxico** (☑ 624-146-50-98; www.aeromexico.com) has domestic and international connections via Mexico City, and daily flights to Los Angeles. **Alaska Airlines** (☑ 624-146-55-02; www.alaskaair.com) has the most flights to the US.

BUS

Buses depart from the **main bus terminal** (González Conseco s/n), east of the Transpeninsular.

CAR & MOTORCYCLE

The usual agencies rent from the airport. Rates start at about M$600 per day.

ⓘ Getting Around

The official government-run company runs bright-yellow taxis and minibuses to the airport for about M$300. The toll road from the Transpeninsular to the airport costs M$32.

Cabo San Lucas

☑ 624 / POP 81,111

Cabo San Lucas's white beaches, fecund waters and spectacular arching stone cliffs at Land's End have become the backdrop for Baja's most raucous tourism. Where else do clubs round up conga lines so that waiters can pour tequila down dancers' throats? The next morning you can be boating next to dolphins and spouting whales for a hangover cure. The activities are endless: jet-skiing, banana-boating, parasailing, snorkeling, kitesurfing, diving and horseback riding can all be found just by walking down to the beach. Outside city limits, you'll be surrounded by majestic cardón cacti, caracara birds and mystical *arroyos* that will impress you just as much as that crazy club you partied at the night before.

Unfortunately, the desert is disappearing fast. The 'Corridor,' the once-spectacular coastline between San José del Cabo and Cabo San Lucas, is being built up with cookie-cutter resorts, American chain stores, aquifer-depleting golf courses and all-inclusive hotels.

⊙ Sights

★**Land's End**　　　　　　　　LANDMARK

Land's End is the most impressive attraction in Cabo. Hop on a *panga* (skiff), kayak or SUP and head to **El Arco** (the Arch), a jagged natural feature that partially fills with the tide. Pelicans, sea lions, sea, sky – this is what brought people to Cabo in the first place, and it's still magical, despite the backdrop of cruise ships.

Beaches

For sunbathing and calm waters **Playa Médano**, on the Bahía de Cabo San Lucas, is ideal. **Playa Solmar**, on the Pacific, is pretty but has a reputation for dangerous breakers and riptides. Nearly unspoiled **Playa del Amor** (Lover's Beach; water taxi from Playa Médano or Plaza Las Glorias docks) shouldn't be missed; near Land's End, it is accessible by boat or you can paddle out on a SUP or kayak when the sea is calm. Appropriately, **Playa del Divorcio** (Divorce Beach) is nearby, across the point on the

Pacific side. **Playa Santa María**, at Km 13 toward San José del Cabo, is one of the best for swimming.

🏃 Activities & Tours

The best diving areas are **Roca Pelícano**, the sea-lion colony off Land's End, and the reef off **Playa Chileno**, at Bahía Chileno east of town.

Tio Sports (☎624-143-33-99; www. oceananddesert.com; Playa Médano; 2-tank dives with/without equipment from US$120/90; ⊙7am-5pm) is one of the largest water-sports outfitters, but there are numerous alternatives.

Surprisingly good snorkeling can be done right from Playa del Amor, swimming left, toward the marina. A mask, a snorkel and fins should run about M$200 per day. *Panga* rides cost about M$200 for a round trip if you bargain directly with a captain. Tipping is expected.

Cabo Expeditions OUTDOORS
(☎624-143-27-00; www.caboexpeditions.com. mx; Blvd Marina s/n, Plaza de la Danza Local 6; whale-watching tours from US$85; ⊙8am-5pm Mon-Sat) This well-run, eco-minded company specializes in small-group tours and is constantly seeking out new twists; eg 'whale concerts' where guests can listen to whale songs through hydrophones. Of course there are also kayaking, diving and boat trips as far as Espíritu Santo island. All are led by experienced guides offering fantastic commentary.

Ecocat BOATING
(☎624-157-46-85; www.caboecotours.com; M Dock; tours per person from US$80) Offers two-hour sunset sailing tours (open bar included), snorkeling and whale-watching trips, and also plays host to a variety of other options off its giant catamaran. The company also owns Ecobar, a *palapa*-style restaurant and sports bar where passengers convene before setting sail.

★ Mt Solmar HIKING
(Cerro del Vigía; ☎624-122-13-16; Blvd Paseo de la Marina; ⊙8:30am Mon-Sat) **FREE** A dog trainer named Enrique is the gatekeeper to the best hike in Los Cabos. Hikes start at his dog-training center and kennel across from the naval base at 8:20am, when Enrique opens a locked fence to commence the daily, guided ascent (dogs included). The 80-minute hike veers up rocky Mt Solmar, with multiple trails that are steep but doable.

The summit's 360-degree view of the Sea of Cortez, the beaches and all of Cabo is a handsome reward. Bring water, don't forget to tip and don't be late (Enrique will lock you out).

🎉 Festivals & Events

Fishing Tournaments FISHING
(⊙May-Nov) Cabo San Lucas is a popular staging ground for fishing tournaments in autumn. The main events are the **Gold Cup**, **Bisbee's Black & Blue Marlin Jackpot** and the **Cabo Tuna Jackpot**.

Sammy Hagar's Birthday Party DANCE
(Cabo Wabo; ⊙early Oct) This is a major Cabo event with lots of drinking and dancing over several nights. Tickets go fast!

🛏 Sleeping

Cabo Inn Hotel INN $
(☎624-143-08-19; www.caboinnhotel.com; 20 de Noviembre; s/d/t from US$47/65/88; 🛜🖥) This place is in town, but the *palapa* roof, colorful decor and plant-filled courtyard make you feel like you're in nature. It's close to quite a few restaurants and shops, but about 15 minutes' walk to the beach. Add a communal kitchen, rooftop hangout area and pool, and you have one of the best deals in Cabo San Lucas.

Cabo Surf Safari GUESTHOUSE $
(☎USA 541-704-5413; www.facebook.com/cabo-surfsafar; cnr Av Cárdenas & Juárez; camping US$15, d from US$45, houses US$65-140; 🅿🌸🛜🖥) Wonderful family compound stretched across a rare, quiet block in central Cabo San Lucas. Surrounded by couple of houses, an upstairs studio, a suite, a camping area and a good **pizza restaurant** (☎624-157-51-18; cnr Av Cárdenas & Cabo San Lucas; meals M$100-250; ⊙pizza 5-10:30pm Tue-Sun, breakfast 8am-12:30pm), a leafy hammock-strung courtyard serves as a relaxing sanctuary for guests and a play space for the family's children and dogs.

Accommodations are funky and comfortable, and the kind hosts have lots of local knowledge.

Hotel Los Milagros HOTEL $$
(☎624-143-45-66; www.losmilagros.com.mx; Matamoros 116; d US$85; 🅿🛜🖥) The tranquil courtyard and 12 unique rooms provide a perfect escape from Cabo's excesses. A desert garden (complete with resident iguanas),

Cabo San Lucas

Cabo San Lucas

BAJA PENINSULA CABO SAN LUCAS

beautiful deep-blue pool and friendly, courteous service make a stay here unforgettable.

★ **Bungalows Hotel**   B&B $$$
(☏ 624-143-05-85; www.thebungalowshotel.com; Miguel Angel Herrera; bungalows incl breakfast from US$165; P ❄ ⊕ 🕸 🛜 ⛑) Abundant hammocks,

tastefully furnished rooms and an expansive swimming pool set this B&B apart. Breakfasts are delicious, with fresh-fruit smoothies and excellent coffee, and the welcoming bilingual staff make the place feel like home. The beautiful handmade soaps are an added bonus.

Bahia Hotel & Beach Club
BOUTIQUE HOTEL **$$$**

(☑ 624-143-18-90; www.bahiacabo.com; Av El Pescador; r US$110-350; ❚❂❄⚟) This whitewashed grande dame is a classy choice only a few minutes' walk from the heart of Médano beach. High-ceilinged rooms with tile floors, comfy beds and all the mod cons surround a lounge-inducing pool. The onsite **Bar Esquina** means you won't have to go far for the classiest nightlife around.

✖ Eating

Cabo's culinary scene ranges from humble taco stands to gourmet restaurants.

Taqueria Las Guacamayas
TACOS **$**

(Morelos; tacos M$26-40, meals M$57-157; ⏱5:30pm-2am) The perfect mix of outrageously delicious tacos to devour at chunky wood Mexican tables in a laid-back atmosphere with stellar service. Pair with fresh juices, a beer or a margarita. All three branches of Las Guacamayas are great for families and couples alike, but our favorite is this quieter, backstreet location. For a treat order the *molcajete mixto*!

Mariscos Las Tres Islas
SEAFOOD **$$**

(☑ 624-143-32-47; cnr Revolución & Mendoza; mains M$138-300; ⏱8am-10pm) A lively thatched restaurant in the middle of town, swarming with locals who come for the best, classic Mexican seafood in the area. Prices are reasonable, the beers are cold and the circulating musicians have talent. Try the tuna medallions or the garlic octopus.

★ Sur Beach House
INTERNATIONAL **$$$**

(☑ 624-143-18-90; www.bahiacabo.com; Playa Médano; mains M$150-570; ⏱8am-11pm) With an exceptional location on the beach looking toward El Arco, this elegant yet laidback place serves ceviche and tacos using the freshest ingredients and beautifully balanced flavors. The fancier grilled fish and meat meals are just as spectacular and service is the best in town. Get lunch and drinks right on the beach or dine by candlelight for dinner.

During high season sit around the small nighttime bonfire and watch the boat lights sparkle off the sea.

Manta
FUSION **$$$**

(☑ 624-163-00-00; www.mantarestaurant.com; México 1 Km 5, The Cape; 5-course tasting menu US$90; ⏱6-11pm) Foodies will recognize Enrique Olvera as the chef behind Mexico City's world-famous Pujol, but since 2015 he's also had Manta here in Cabo. Its elegant dining room (and open kitchen) contains a floor-to-ceiling window out to the Arco, and the experimental concept fusing Mexican with the flavors of the Pacific Rim is equally attention-grabbing.

Savory ramen is paired with *espazote* (Mexican tea) and black beans. Sea urchin arrives on a *tostada* with striped bass and *salsa macha*. The tasting menu is truly an adventure, and best enjoyed with top-notch mezcal, tequila and sake.

Mi Casa
MEXICAN **$$$**

(www.micasarestaurant.com.mx; cnr Av Cárdenas & Cabo; mains M$162-468; ⏱11am-4pm & 5-10pm) This place has real wow factor. The courtyard-style interior has rooms on several levels and feels like something out of a 1950s Mexican musical – plants, statues, folksy murals, wicker lights, painted furniture, Día de Muertos figurines and wandering mariachis all set the stage. Stick with the more simple dishes. The food is good, but the atmosphere is the real draw.

◉ Drinking & Nightlife

Cabo is a proud party town, and alcoholic revelry is encouraged all day long. You have been warned.

Slim's Elbow Room
BAR

(Blvd Marina s/n; ⏱10:30am-midnight) In the shadow of Cabo Wabo, this teeny, easy-to-miss watering hole, wallpapered in dollar bills and clients' signatures, claims to be the world's smallest bar. With four seats inside and two standing spaces, it's a contender for sure.

Cabo Wabo
CLUB

(☑ 624-143-11-88; www.cabowabo.com; cnr Guerrero & Madero; ⏱9am-2am Sun-Thu, to 3am Sat & Sun; ☎) The most famous bar and club in town, established by legendary rocker Sammy Hagar of solo career and Van Halen fame. Come here for live music and the legendary margaritas made with Santo Mezquila, a combo liquor brought to you by Hagar and Maroon 5 frontman Adam Levine.

El Squid Roe
CLUB

(☑ 624-143-12-69; cnr Blvd Cárdenas & Zaragoza; ⏱10am-4am Sun-Thu, to 4:30am Fri & Sat) Crazy. Just crazy. Jello shooters, tequila conga lines. Waiters (and drunk clientele) dance on tabletops to cheering crowds. The everyday epicenter of Cabo's drunken nightlife scene.

★ **Rooftop at the Cape** COCKTAIL BAR
(☑ 624-163-00-00; México 1 Km 5; ☺ 6pm-midnight Sun-Thu, to 2am Fri & Sat) Escape the cesspool that is downtown Cabo San Lucas and regain your dignity at this classy rooftop bar, complete with trickling water features, flourishing gardens and more-than-panoramic views out to the Arco. The snazzy setting is absolutely perfect for a sunset cocktail or three.

🛍 Shopping

Mercado Marina MARKET
(Blvd Paseo de la Marina 15; ☺ 9am-5:30pm) A sprawling arts and crafts flea market with Baja souvenirs galore: skulls, ceramics, crosses, hats, clothing, you name it. Avoid this place when there's a cruise ship in port (prices go up).

ℹ Information

The tourist office **CATTAC** (Tourist Assistance Center; ☑ 624-105-15-32; Centro 23450; ☺ 8am-3pm) offers maps and brochures, as well as assistance with tourism-related difficulties.

The other 'info' booths you'll see are owned by timeshares, condos and hotels. The staff are friendly and can offer maps and info, but their only pay comes from commissions from selling timeshare visits: expect a firm, sometimes desperate, pitch for you to visit model homes. Be warned – the promised freebies are rarely worth wasting precious vacation time on.

There's an **immigration office** (☑ 624-143-01-35; cnr Blvd Cárdenas & Farías; ☺ 9am-1pm Mon-Fri) near the center.

All About Cabo (www.allaboutcabo.com) is a useful site for visitors.

Hospital General (☑ 624-146-42-62; Av Los Pinos) is the recommended hospital here.

ℹ Getting There & Away

AIR

The closest airport (p756) is at San José del Cabo. The **Transcabo Airport Shuttle** (☑ USA 1-403-5987; www.transcabo.com; per person from US$16) is one of the cheapest and best services to/from the airport and will take you directly to your hotel.

BUS

Buses depart from either the **Águila** (Hwy 19; ☺ 24hr) company, located at the Todos Santos crossroad, north of downtown, or the bus station, a 40-minute walk northwest from the tourist zone and waterfront.

CAR & MOTORCYCLE

Numerous car-rental agencies have booths along Paseo de la Marina and elsewhere in town, although booking in advance with a pickup at the airport can be cheaper.

ℹ Getting Around

Cab van fares within town are around US$10, and a taxi to the airport is around US$85. Avoid rides offered by the timeshare touts.

Todos Santos

☑ 612 / POP 6485

With a quirky mix of locals, fishers, surfers and New Age spiritualists, the town of 'All Saints' has thus far escaped the rampant tourism of the other cape towns. With its charming cobblestone streets lined with art galleries, romantic restaurants and a cactus or three, it's also, by far, the prettiest town in the far south of Baja. Long beaches and wild surf breaks mean there's a lot to do for those who want to get out of town as well. Think Taos, New Mexico, before Ansel Adams and Georgia O'Keefe brought the world there. Be prepared for high prices, however.

Like many other parts of Baja, Todos Santos is changing and local development is rampant. So come here now before it changes forever.

◉ Sights

Scattered around town are the relics of Todos Santos' prosperity in the brown-sugar indus-

BAJA PENINSULA TODOS SANTOS

BUSES FROM CABO SAN LUCAS

DESTINATION	FARE (M$)	TIME (HR)	FREQUENCY (PER DAY)
La Paz	325-355	2-3	frequent
Loreto	1100	8¾	6
San José del Cabo	40	1	frequent
Tijuana	2422	25-28	3
Todos Santos	155	1	frequent

try in the early 20th century. The restored **Teatro Cine General Manuel Márquez de León** was built with sugar profits in 1943 – it's on Legaspi, facing the plaza. There are also several former *molinos* (sugar processing plants) around, distinguished by their large brick chimneys. **Molino El Progreso**, the ruin of what was formerly El Molino restaurant, is one. On Juárez, opposite the hospital, **Molino de los Santana** is another.

Centro Cultural   MUSEUM
(☑ 612-145-06-59; Juárez; exhibition room M$20; ☺ 8am-7pm Mon-Fri, to 3pm Sat & Sun) Housed in a former schoolhouse with a lovely central courtyard, the Centro Cultural is home to some interesting nationalist and revolutionary murals dating from 1933. Also on display is a dusty collection of regional artifacts, fascinating old photos and a replica ranch house. Take note of the cradle 'cage' hanging from the ceiling.

🏃 Activities

Surfers come here for some of the nicest swells in all of Baja. **San Pedrito** offers point breaks and tubes (and gnarly rocks if you wipe out). Catch that perfect wave as eagle rays glide below you, or just hang out with the mellow crowd on **Los Cerritos** and watch the coral sun plunge into the Pacific. Boards can be rented for M$400 per day at Pescadero Surf Camp or Todos Santos Surf Shop, or from vendors on the beaches.

Mario Surf School   SURFING
(☑ 612-142-61-56; www.mariosurfschool.com; Hwy 19 Km 64; 1hr surf lesson from US$60) Offers excellent lessons and clinics for all levels in the Todos Santos and Pescadero area.

Todos Santos Surf Shop   SURFING
(☑ 612-145-11-14; www.explorabaja.com/todossurf shop; Miguel Hidalgo y Costilla; surfboard rentals US$20 per day, 2hr private lessons US$80; ☺ 10am-6pm Mon-Sat, 11am-5pm Sun) Owned by a marine biologist and an oceanographer, this recommended surf shop rents boards, offers surf lessons and sells all the requisite gear (including new and used boards). The shop's parent company Explora Baja also runs whale-watching, fishing, hiking and snorkeling trips.

Over the Edge   MOUNTAIN BIKING
(☑ 612-145-06-25; www.otebaja.com; Obregón Esquina Juárez; bike rental US$45-80; ☺ 8am-4pm Mon-Fri, 9am-3pm Sat & Sun) A full-service bicycle-rental shop and mountain-biking

tour company. Basically your one-stop-shop for access to 56km of nearby trails weaving through giant cacti along rocky cliffs and into canyons, with occasional ocean views. Inquire about tours within.

🛏 Sleeping

Most places fall in the midrange to high-end category and many of these can be rated as some of the most lovely places to stay in Baja.

Pescadero Surf Camp   CABAÑAS $
(☑ 612-130-30-32, 612-134-04-80; www.pescadero surf.com; Hwy 19 Km 64, Barrio Las Palmitas; casita M$700-900, penthouse M$1200, house M$1700, campsites per person M$200; P @ ☀) Located on a side of the highway 13km south of Todos Santos near the Pescadero surf break, this clean and surprisingly stylish place caters to wave riders with rentals, lessons and advice. Some of the thatched casitas have enough open space between the walls and ceiling that they almost feel outdoors.

There's a pool and community kitchen, and some (but not all) of the accommodations share bathrooms. Surfboards rent for M$400 per day. Wax is M$60 extra, and soft racks come with the boards.

Surf Casitas   BUNGALOW $$
(☑ 613-105-16-87; www.surfcasitas.com; Argentina, El Pescadero; d US$69-105; P �) Rustic, affordable and wonderfully secluded, these six beachfront casitas feature Mexican artwork and come with thatched roofs, mosquito nets, linens and fans. There's a communal, fully equipped outdoor kitchen and a mix of private and shared bathrooms. Hammocks abound, as do surfers.

★ Posada La Poza   HOTEL $$$
(☑ 612-145-04-00; www.lapoza.com; Camino a la Poza 282; ste incl breakfast US$165-300; P ⊝ ☀ ☎) Boasting 'Mexican hospitality combined with Swiss quality,' (meaning we found colorful surrounds and meticulous, incongruously formal service), this very private retreat is in a drop-dead gorgeous palm oasis right on the Pacific. A saltwater swimming pool, freshwater lagoon, thriving garden and superb restaurant, which is only open to hotel guests, set it apart.

Suites are large and bright, and the whole place is adorned in the magnificent work of co-owner Libusche Wiesendanger, an internationally acclaimed painter. No kids under 13 allowed.

PUNTA LOBOS

This point in Todos Santos, named for its sea-lion colony, is where local fishers launch *pangas* (skiffs). Out of town but near Hotel San Cristóbal, the quiet, sandy beach comes alive between 1pm and around 3pm, when you can come and bargain for just-off-the-boat fish to cook at home. Pelicans joust for scraps, and a hiking trail winds up the point to an unparalleled lookout spot.

For some time now, developers have been attempting to build thousands of luxury homes and a beach resort here, along with restaurants and businesses, despite concerns about an already stressed natural aquifer and other environmental issues. The efforts of fishers and Todos Santos residents to thwart the project, thus far successful, were highlighted in the award-winning bilingual documentary *Patrimonio*.

Hotel San Cristóbal　　BOUTIQUE HOTEL **$$$**
(☑612-175-15-30, USA 800-990-02-72; www.sancristobalbaja.com; Carretera Federal 19 Km 54; r from US$460; P❄🛜🏊) Style is paramount at this sleek boho resort of white walls, wood-bead chandeliers, bright throw pillows and decorative cacti. With a killer location on a long expanse of pristine beach, with crashing surf and fishing boats pulled ashore, it's too dangerous to swim in the sea but the pool is an inviting hangout with cocktails and basket-like lounge chairs.

It's about 4km south of Todos Santos.

Todos Santos Inn　　BOUTIQUE HOTEL **$$$**
(☑612-145-00-40; www.todossantosinn.com; Legaspi 33; d incl breakfast US$140-360; ♨❄🛜🏊) Fashioned from an exquisitely restored 19th-century brick hacienda, Todos Santos Inn has only eight intimate rooms, each with a four-poster bed and a luxurious, bygone-era atmosphere. Murals, palm-beam ceilings and painted ceramic sinks are just some of the touches. A tiny swimming pool sits within a verdant tropical courtyard, and the onsite bar and restaurant are truly romantic.

Hotel California　　HOTEL **$$$**
(☑612-145-05-25; www.hotelcaliforniabaja.com; Juárez s/n; r US$150-175; ❄🛜🏊) You can check out but you may never want to leave the arty-yet-homey, lively-yet-serene Hotel California. The public spaces, in particular, are lovely, especially around the pool, which is surrounded by lush foliage, blood-red hibiscus and lofty palms. There's plenty of space plus bright and tasteful artwork throughout the rooms and they're furnished with classy, traditional Mexican pieces.

There's no actual connection to the Eagles song, just FYI.

🍴 Eating & Drinking

Barracuda Cantina　　TACOS **$**
(☑612-157-53-54; Playa Los Cerritos; tacos from M$40; ☉noon-8pm Thu-Tue) After conquering the surf at Los Cerritos, slide over to this chill, open-air restaurant for delicious tacos, ceviche and a farm-to-glass cocktail. The local owner Danny Sanchez is a bonafide mixologist.

Loncheria La Garita　　MEXICAN **$**
(☑612-176-57-92; Hwy 19; dishes from M$35; ☉7am-6pm; 🚗) A great stop 19km on the way to La Paz, this family-run, always-busy, ranch-style-meal-slinging restaurant is as authentic as you'll find in this area. Try the *asada rancheros* (roast beef with beans, eggs and salsa), *empanadas* and local-style *talega* brewed coffee. It's great for kids since there are some farm animals out back amid the dust and towering cacti.

★ Hierbabuena　　MEXICAN **$$**
(☑612-149-25-68; www.hierbabuenarestaurante.com; Hwy 29 Km 62, Pescadero; mains M$170-380; ☉1-9pm Wed-Mon) Walk past growing fruit and vegetables to this farm-to-table restaurant and be greeted by a vivacious crew who will serve you one of the best meals in the area. The menu changes depending on what's fresh in the organic garden, sea and surrounds; the chef cooks it all simply, to perfection. It's around 11km south of Todos Santos.

Chicken is roasted to crispy deliciousness, salads are dressed just enough and the wood-fired pizzas are flavorful and divine.

Ristorante Tre Galline　　ITALIAN **$$**
(☑612-145-03-00; 33 Centenario; dinner mains from M$250; ☉1-10pm Tue-Sun; 🛜) This plant-laden, red-brick Italian restaurant makes its pasta fresh daily, and also serves some particularly scrumptious seafood platters. In the evening, lit candles on every table make the atmosphere even cozier.

Jazamango   NEW MEXICAN **$$$**

(☑612-688-15-01; www.facebook.com/jazaman
go; Naranjos s/n; dishes M$160-500; ◷1-9pm)
Star Mexican chef Javier Placensia brings
his signature Baja Med cuisine to Baja Sur
via this warm, open-concept place just out
of town and up a tiny hill that offers ter-
restrial views. Nearly every ingredient is
sustainably and locally produced, meaning
there's plenty of seafood, meat and vege-
table dishes on a menu that changes with
what's available.

Placensia's new, adjacent bakery (8am to
11:30am) is a great stop for freshly baked
bread, a bottle of wine or a cup of coffee.

Baja Beans   COFFEE

(☑612-130-33-91; www.facebook.com/cafebaja
beans; Pescadero; ◷7am-9pm Thu-Tue, to 6pm
Wed; ☜) Tucked into a grove of mango
trees just off the highway in Pescadero, this
pleasant coffee shop serves strong Mexi-
can-grown coffee in all the fancy ways: pour
over, Chemex, French-pressed, you name
it. On high-season Sundays (November to
May), its expansive outdoor patio hosts a
wildly popular farmers market, with fresh
produce and locally made art, clothing and
jewelry on offer.

🛍 Shopping

There are numerous galleries to wander
through, especially around the plaza.

Faces of Mexico   ARTS & CRAFTS

(Morelos; ◷11am-6pm Mon-Sat) Duck into the
warren of dark rooms here to discover an
extraordinary collection of masks, sculp-
ture, ethnic art, antique baubles and plenty
of somber Día de Muertos beaded and paint-
ed decorative skulls. This is not your usual
souvenir shop – check it out.

Nomad Chic   FASHION & ACCESSORIES

(www.nomadchic.mx; Juárez & Hidalgo; ◷11am-
5pm) A wonderful boutique fashion shop
with apparel and accessories inspired by the
owner's far-flung travels.

ℹ Information

El Tecolote (☑612-145-02-95; cnr Juárez
& Hidalgo) The town lacks an official tourist
office, but this English-language bookstore has
magazines with town maps and a sketch map of
nearby beach areas.

ℹ Getting There & Away

Hourly between 6am and 11pm, buses head to La
Paz (M$150, one hour) and to Cabo San Lucas
(M$155, one hour) from the **bus stop** (☑612-
148-02-89; Heróico Colegio Militar; ◷7am-
10pm) between Zaragoza and Morelos.

AT A GLANCE

POPULATION
4 million

LANGUAGES
Spanish, Tarahu-
mara, Yaqui, Mayo

**BEST COPPER
CANYON STOPOVER**
Creel (p778)

BEST POTTERY
Mata Ortiz (p803)

BEST SAND DUNES
Dunas de Yeso
(p813)

WHEN TO GO
Jun–Aug
Heavy rainfall, soar-
ing temperatures.
Key festivals like the
Feria de la Uva in
Parras, and Duran-
go's Feria Nacional.

Late Sep–early Nov
Milder temperatures
make it a good
time to visit the
coming-into-bloom
Copper Canyon.

Dec & Jan
Balmy, dry weather is
perfect for a Sonoran
beach escape.

Copper Canyon (p768)
KATE FISK/SHUTTERSTOCK ©

Copper Canyon & Northern Mexico

Northern Mexico is the ultimate frontier land: vast cactus-strewn deserts, craggy mountains and breathtaking canyons define this most iconic of regions, which is familiar to most from its role in countless Wild West movies. If the landscape is diverse, its people are equally so: cowboys, revolutionaries and bandits have, over the centuries, left their mark on the region, while the varied and still deeply traditional indigenous peoples remain some of Mexico's least Westernized.

Though the narco wars have impacted the north terribly, it remains a safe place to visit if you take a few sensible precautions. Highlights include Mexico's only remaining long-distance passenger train ride, colonial towns, superb beaches and diverse wildlife.

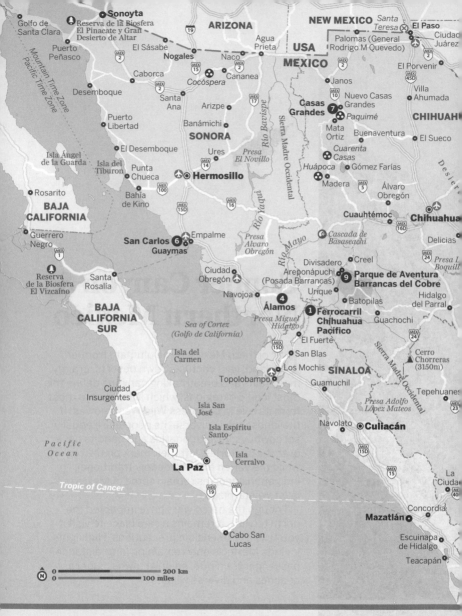

Copper Canyon & Northern Mexico Highlights

❶ Ferrocarril Chihuahua Pacífico (p770) Riding Mexico's last passenger train through mesmerizing scenery.

❷ Parras (p811) Visiting mountain-ringed wineries and

cooling off in a vast spring-fed pool.

❸ Área de Protección de Flora y Fauna Cuatrociénegas (p812) Kayaking in this protected desert oasis.

❹ Álamos (p790) Hiking through the picturesque Parque la Colorada.

❺ Monterrey (p814) Strolling the serene Paseo Sant Lucía, visiting thought-

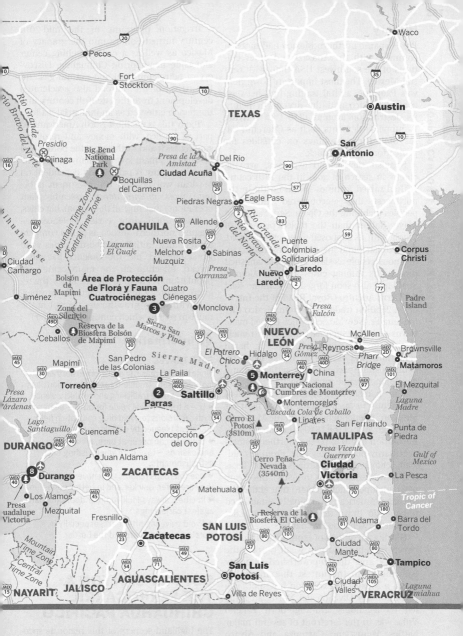

provoking MARCO, and sipping
microbrews on Calle Morelos.

6 San Carlos (p788)
Enjoying the views from
Mirador San Carlos followed by
a seafood feast on the beach.

7 Casas Grandes (p802)
Overnighting in an adobe hotel,
visiting the ruins of Paquimé
and day-tripping to Mata Ortíz.

8 Durango (p804) Soaking

up history and culture in this
charming colonial town.

9 Parque de Aventura
Barrancas del Cobre (p777)
Zip-lining over the Copper
Canyon.

History

Pre-Hispanic northern Mexico had more in common with the Anasazi and other cultures of the southwest USA than with central Mexico. The most important town here was Paquimé, a vital trading link between central Mexico and the dry north before its destruction around 1340 CE. Outlying Paquimé settlements such as Cuarenta Casas built their dwellings on cliffsides for protection against attack.

Spanish slavers and explorers, arriving chiefly in search of gold in the 16th century, had mixed fortunes in the north. In the northwest they encountered indigenous peoples including the Opata, Seri, Yaqui and Mayo. Rather than the fabled province of Cíbola with its supposed seven cities of gold, the Spanish found silver and, conscripting indigenous people as slave miners, established prosperous mining cities such as Álamos. Spaniards also soon forged the Camino Real de Tierra Adentro (Royal Road of the Interior), a 2560km trade route from Mexico City to Santa Fe, New Mexico, which helped make towns en route such as Durango extremely wealthy. In the northeast, however, harsh conditions and attacks by indigenous Chichimecs and Apaches meant settlement and development came more slowly.

The Spanish never tightened control here sufficiently to quell revolts. In the fight for Mexican Independence (1810), the Mexican–American War of the 1840s and the Mexican Revolution (1910–20), the northern states necessarily played a key role. Frontiers radically changed with Mexico's loss of Texas and New Mexico (1830s to 1850s); the Treaty of Guadalupe Hidalgo (1848) that ended the Mexican–American War finally established today's Río Bravo del Norte (Rio Grande) frontier between the two nations.

Glaring inequities of land ownership between the elite – grown wealthy from the mines – and the impoverished majority contributed to the unrest that made the north a Mexican Revolution hot spot. The revolutionary División del Norte, an army led by legendary Durango-born Pancho Villa, was in the forefront of several major battles. Venustiano Carranza and Álvaro Obregón, other main revolutionary figures, were, respectively, from the northern states of Coahuila and Sonora. All three were initially allies and subsequently enemies in the Revolution, which meant the split of allegiances in the north was acute.

Irrigation programs in the mid-20th century turned Sonora into the granary of Mexico as well as a cattle-ranching center alongside neighboring Chihuahua. Discovery of petroleum, coal and natural gas and the arrival of the railroad also accelerated development from the late 19th century, and the region emerged as an industrial leader.

Today this is the most North Americanized part of Mexico, with money and resources surging back and forth across the border and baseball the main sport in many towns. The Texan economy is particularly dependent on Mexican workers and US investment is behind most *maquiladoras* (assembly-plant operations) that ring all the region's big cities.

Since 2006 drug cartel violence has plagued northern Mexico as gangs compete for territory. Initially the border cities were worst affected, but the violence has since spread, affecting all the main centers of population. Yet despite the headlines, the region's economy remains relatively prosperous, with steady growth rates (except in the tourism sector, which continues to suffer).

ℹ Information

SAFE TRAVEL

While the vast majority of visitors to northern Mexico enjoy a safe, trouble-free trip, the region does have active drug trafficking and related violence.

➡ Use a trusted local guide for off-the-beaten-path excursions to avoid drug cultivation fields and areas plagued by cartels or gangs.

➡ Violence can occur at bars, nightclubs and casinos – take care when visiting such establishments.

➡ Use toll roads (*cuotas*) whenever possible; they are safer, quicker and in better condition.

➡ In cities, always lock your car doors to guard against carjackings.

➡ Avoid traveling after dark, especially in isolated areas and around the border.

COPPER CANYON & THE FERROCARRIL CHIHUAHUA PACÍFICO

The highland scenery of this region is spectacular. Northern Mexico does not lack for amazing attractions, but none compares to the Copper Canyon for sheer wow factor, with its astonishing cliff-top vistas, towering pine-clad mountains and the fascinating culture of the native Tarahumara (Rarámuri) people.

Copper Canyon

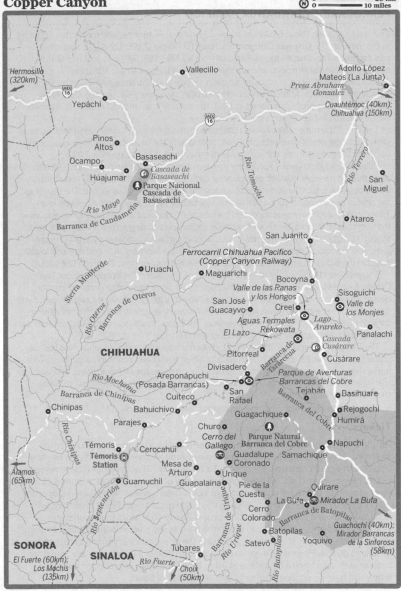

A labyrinth of six main canyons covers an area four times larger than Arizona's Grand Canyon system, and is deeper, narrower and much more verdant than its American counterpart. Tropical fruit trees grow in the canyon bottoms while the high ground is covered in alpine vegetation and, occasionally, winter snows.

A handful of towns make convenient base camps for exploring the region. Creel is the largest and home to several recommended hotels. Further into the canyon system are Divisadero, Arepo and Cerocahui, all along

DON'T MISS

FERROCARRIL CHIHUAHUA PACÍFICO

The stats say everything: 656km of track, 37 bridges, 86 tunnels and more than 60 years in the making. The **Copper Canyon Railway** (El Chepe; 800-122-43-73; www.chepe. com.mx; full journey Chepe Express/Regional from M$3743/1891;) is one of the world's most incredible rail journeys, and northern Mexico's biggest single attraction.

Nicknamed 'El Chepe' (using the Spanish initials of 'Chihuahua' and 'Pacífico'), the railway operates two different trains – the luxury Chepe Express, and the slow, bare-bones Chepe Regional. Completed in 1961, the railway is as phenomenal in its engineering prowess as in the canyon views it yields.

The line is the major link between Chihuahua and the coast, heavily used for freight as well as passengers. It connects the Pacific coast with the mountainous, arid interior of northern Mexico via tricky canyon gradients that force it to rise up over 2400m.

Between Los Mochis and El Fuerte, the train trundles through flat farmland, then begins to climb through hills speckled with dark pillars of cacti. It passes over the long Río Fuerte bridge and through the first of the 86 tunnels about four hours after leaving Los Mochis. The train hugs the sides of deepening canyons and makes a spectacular zigzag ascent into a tunnel above Témoris, after which pine trees appear on the hillsides. By the next station, Bahuichivo, you are in the Sierra Madre uplands, with flower-dotted meadows punctuating an entrancing alpine landscape. The biggest highlight of the train ride is stopping at Divisadero, where you get your only glimpse of the actual Copper Canyon. The train circles back over itself in a complete loop to gain height at the suitably named El Lazo (the Lasso), before chugging on to Creel and Chihuahua.

There's a world of difference between the Chepe Express and the Chepe Regional. The **Chepe Express**, which began running in 2018, has an attractive, vintage-inspired interior design, a lovely bar-lounge area, and a separate two-story dining car with excellent meals. If you opt for the pricier *ejecutiva* (executive) class, you'll also have access to a panoramic viewing car with huge windows affording enviable views. The Express runs only between Creel and Los Mochis, and makes just two stops (Divisadero and El Fuerte).

The **Chepe Regional**, which lumbers between Los Mochis and Chihuahua, also has two classes, though there's not much difference between *turista* and *económica* carriages – the former has a dining room, the latter a canteen. The carriages are rather showing their age (dating from the 1980s), though both classes have air-conditioning, heating and reclining seats with ample leg room.

All trains are staffed with machine-gun-toting plainclothes police.

Tickets

For the Chepe Express, you'll need to purchase tickets well in advance (four months ahead for Semana Santa, July, August and over Christmas and New Year). You can buy tickets with a credit card over the phone (1-800-122-43-73) or via email (chepe.reservaciones@ferromex.mx) with all essential details (day of travel, destination, names of travelers, etc). You'll then have to print out your tickets and travel with them. Free stopovers are allowed, though you'll have to specify this when purchasing. Ticket prices are astronomically high, and executive class tickets cost nearly 40% more than tourist class.

For the Chepe Regional, you can board the train at any station without a ticket if there are free seats, and pay the conductor. Outside the peak seasons, you will almost always be able to do this. However, it's advisable to reserve tickets a month or more ahead for peak-season travel, and a day ahead at other times, although in practice most of the time you'll have no problem buying tickets on the day of travel.

or near the famous Chepe train route, and the more remote (yet readily accessible) canyon-bottom villages of Batopilas and Urique.

🏃 Activities

All manner of natural wonders are accessible by foot, horse, bike or motor vehicle – cliffs, towering rock massifs, rivers, waterfalls, lakes and forests. For the ultimate buzz, head to the Parque de Aventura Barrancas del Cobre (p777), where you can soar over death-defying drops on a series of Mexico's most hair-raising zip-lines.

RAILWAY SCHEDULE – FERROCARRIL CHIHUAHUA PACÍFICO

The Chepe Express departs from Creel to Los Mochis at 7:30am on Tuesday, Friday and Sunday. It departs Los Mochis for Creel at 7:30am on Monday, Thursday and Saturday. The journey takes about nine hours. The train stops twice between its start/end points; you can board/disembark only at Creel, Divisadero, El Fuerte and Los Mochis.

The Chepe Regional leaves Chihuahua at 6am on Monday, Thursday and Saturday. It leaves Los Mochis on 6am on Tuesday, Friday and Sunday. The journey officially takes 15½ hours, though the slow-moving train makes many stops and often runs one to two hours late.

Eastbound – Los Mochis to Creel or Chihuahua

	CHEPE EXPRESS		CHEPE REGIONAL	
Station	Arrives (Mon, Thu, Sat)	Fare from Los Mochis Turista/ Ejecutiva (M$)	Arrives (Tue, Fri, Sun)	Fare from Los Mochis Económica/ Turista (M$)
Los Mochis	7:30am (departs Los Mochis)	-	6am (departs Los Mochis)	-
El Fuerte	9:44am	1028/1650	8:19am	348/602
Témoris	-	-	11:24am	620/1074
Bahuichivo	-	-	12:24pm	733/1269
San Rafael	-	-	1:28pm	825/1430
Posada Barrancas (Arepo)	-	-	1:46pm	854/1480
Divisadero	3:53pm	3743/6000	2:25pm	866/1500
Creel	5:14pm (final stop)	3743/6000	3:42pm	1034/1791
Cuauhtémoc	-	-	7:07pm	1506/2609
Chihuahua	-	-	9:34pm	1891/3604

Westbound – Creel or Chihuahua to Los Mochis

	CHEPE EXPRESS		CHEPE REGIONAL	
Station	Arrives (Tue, Fri, Sun)	Fare from Creel Turista/ Ejecutiva (M$)	Arrives (Mon, Thu, Sat)	Fare from Chihuahua Económica/ Turista (M$)
Chihuahua	-	-	6am (departs Chihuahua)	-
Cuauhtémoc	-	-	8:25am	385/734
Creel	7:30am (departs Creel)	-	11:47am	860/1639
Divisadero	8:47am	1000/1400	1:41pm	1028/1959
Posada Barrancas (Arepo)	-	-	1:52pm	1040/1981
San Rafael	-	-	2:16pm	1069/2037
Bahuichivo	-	-	3:12pm	1161/2213
Témoris	-	-	4:12pm	1274/2429
El Fuerte	2:29pm	3075/4920	7:19pm	1657/3157
Los Mochis	4:35pm	3743/6000	9:28pm	1891/3604

ℹ BORDER CROSSINGS

There are more than 40 official US–Mexico border crossing points, many open 24 hours. US Customs & Border Protection provides opening hours and estimated waiting times for drivers (check www.bwt.cbp.gov).

Tourists visiting Mexico must carry a passport (or passport card for US citizens) and obtain a Mexican tourist permit on arrival, unless they are staying within the border zone and not staying over 72 hours. The border zone generally extends 20km to 30km south from the border, but also stretches as far as Puerto Peñasco in Sonora, and Ensenada and San Felipe in Baja California.

Travelers taking a vehicle must purchase Mexican insurance (available at borders). If you're heading beyond the border zone deeper into Mexico (except in Baja California), you must obtain a temporary vehicle importation permit or a Sólo Sonora permit. Each costs M$1020 and can either be ordered in advance or picked up at Banjército outlets around the border (www.banjercito.com.mx).

The main border crossings (ordered west to east) are as follows:

San Diego (California)–Tijuana (Baja California) The three border crossings here include San Ysidro–El Chaparral (24 hours), the world's busiest border crossing. Others include the cross-border terminal at Tijuana's international airport (24 hours, for ticketed passengers only) and the Otay Mesa crossing (24 hours).

Calexico (California)–Mexicali (Baja California) The two border crossings here are Calexico West (24 hours) and Calexico East (6am to midnight).

Lukeville (Arizona)–Sonoyta (Sonora) Best for Puerto Peñasco (6am to midnight).

Nogales (Arizona)–Nogales (Sonora) Hwy 15/15D is the main highway south to the Deconcini crossing (24 hours).

Santa Teresa crossing Some 20km west of Juárez in Chihuahua state; good for avoiding security risks near Juárez (6am to midnight).

El Paso (Texas)–Ciudad Juárez (Chihuahua) Bridge of the Americas (24 hours); Paso del Norte (24 hours); Stanton St–Avenida Lerdo (6am to midnight); and Ysleta (24 hours). Pedestrian crossings are via the bridges of Bridge of the Americas, Paso del Norte or Ysleta. To return on foot you must use Paso del Norte. Access for vehicles is via the Bridge of the Ameri-

---

El Fuerte

🕗 698 / POP 13,200 / ELEV 90M

Clustered around a striking plaza and with a center packed full of brightly painted colonial houses, El Fuerte oozes historical character. For many centuries the most important commercial center in northwestern Mexico due to its proximity to the silver mines in the canyons, this is now a picturesque little town surrounded by one of Latin America's last-standing dry tropical forests. Far preferable to Los Mochis as a place to start or end a trip on the Ferrocarril Chihuahua Pacífico (p770), it's worth a stay of more than just a night to take a trip on the Río Fuerte and explore the unique subtropical countryside.

El Fuerte was founded in 1564 and is named for a 17th-century fort built on its distinctive high point of Cerro de las Pilas to protect settlers from indigenous attacks.

👁 Sights & Activities

★ **Bosque Secreto** FOREST
(Secret Forest) 🌿 Five hundred years ago, over 550,000 sq km of dry tropical forest stretched down the coast from northern Mexico to Panama. Today only 2% of virgin forest remains, including a breathtaking swath of greenery just outside of El Fuerte, in an area known as Bosque Secreto. The delightful Río Fuerte, which is incredibly rich in birdlife (including herons, osprey, kingfishers and flycatchers), winds through much of the forest. The area is also home to over 1800 species of native plants.

Turismo Fuerte (p772), Hotel Río Vista (p773) and Posada del Hidalgo (p774) lead sustainable boat trips along the river, taking in plenty of bird-watching and some 2000-year-old petroglyphs along the way.

Turismo Fuerte OUTDOORS
(🕗 698-889-64-50; tour per person M$150-650) This reputable outfit offers a range of reward-

cas (Puente Córdova). Tourist permits are available at the end of the Stanton St–Avenida Lerdo bridge and Bridge of the Americas. Hwy 45D from Juárez is the principal southbound route.

Presidio (Texas)–Ojinaga (Chihuahua) From Ojinaga, it's 225km along Hwy 16 direct to Chihuahua (24 hours).

Del Rio (Texas)–Ciudad Acuña (Coahuila) Open 24 hours.

Eagle Pass (Texas)–Piedras Negras (Coahuila) Two crossings: Bridge 1 (7am to 11pm) and Bridge 2 (24 hours).

Laredo (Texas)–Nuevo Laredo (Tamaulipas) Four crossings: Bridge 1 (24 hours); Bridge 2 (24 hours); Colombia Solidarity (8am to midnight); World Trade Bridge (8am to midnight). Bridge 2 bypasses the city and is the safest option, connecting with Hwy 85D from Nuevo Laredo to Monterrey, from where there are good connections to elsewhere in Mexico.

McAllen/Hidalgo/Pharr (Texas)–Reynosa (Tamaulipas) Three US towns, sitting side-by-side, serve Reynosa: Anzalduas International Bridge (6am to 10pm), Hidalgo (24 hours) and Pharr (6am to midnight).

Brownsville (Texas)–Matamoros (Tamaulipas) B&M (24 hours), Gateway (24 hours), Los Indios (6am to midnight) and Veterans International (6am to midnight).

There are plenty of cross-border bus services into the region from US cities, most involving a change of buses in a city on the US or Mexican side of the border. Given the time it can take to get through the border, it is often quicker to disembark before the border, make the crossing on foot, and pick up further transportation on the other side.

If you want to avoid staying long in Mexico's border towns, some services will take you directly deeper into Mexico, including Phoenix–Puerto Peñasco via Sonoyta with Transportes Express (p788); Chihuahua via Juárez from Dallas, Denver, Los Angeles and Las Vegas (among others) with Los Paisanos Autobuses (p801); and Tufesa (www.tufesa. com.mx), which operates many cross-border buses to California and Arizona.

Many border towns rank among Mexico's most dangerous places. The security situation can change quickly. Ciudad Juárez and Nuevo Laredo have been notorious for years and are best transited during daylight hours, but you should be careful anywhere.

ing excursions in the region. Sign up for a one-hour walking tour around the center, take an ecofriendly (motorless) boat tour along the river spotting birds and seeing petroglyphs, or visit the indigenous Mayo community on a van tour. Contact them via WhatsApp.

For something more active, book a kayaking trip down the Río Fuerte with easy, medium and advanced levels available (the latter only for highly experienced paddlers).

🛏 Sleeping

Hotel Guerrero HOTEL **$**
(☑ 698-893-05-24; www.hotelyhostelguerrero. jimdo.com; Juárez 206; r M$400-450; ☻✿🖤) This budget hotel in the center of El Fuerte has charming staff who go the extra mile to look after their guests. The rooms, set around a shady pillared patio, are comfortable, with sponge-painted walls adding color – though they're not very bright (windows are translucent).

Hotel La Choza HOTEL **$$**
(☑ 698-893-12-74; www.hotellachoza.com; Calle 5 de Mayo 101; r M$920-1600; ℗☻✳🖤✹) This deceptively large hotel has a colonial facade, but becomes rather more modern as you enter its enormous courtyard. It boasts inviting rooms, all with quaint touches such as hand-painted sinks, enormous crucifixes over the beds and high, brick-vaulted ceilings. It's excellent value, and the in-house **Diligencias** (☑ 698-893-12-74; Calle 5 de Mayo 101; mains M$120-220; ☺ 7am-10pm; 🖤) restaurant is a good bet too.

Hotel Río Vista HOTEL **$$**
(☑ 698-104-26-47; www.hotelriovista.com.mx; Progreso s/n; d/t M$800/1200; ℗✳🖤✹) This quirky place tucked behind the town's hilltop museum has been hosting travelers for years. The design is exuberant with murals, rich colors and an excess of Mexicana and other bizarre curios. The best rooms have balconies with superb views of the river.

★ **Posada del Hidalgo**   HERITAGE HOTEL $$$
(☑ 698-893-02-42, 800-552-56-45; www.hotel posadadelhidalgo.com; Hidalgo 101; s/d/ste M$1600/1800/2800; ⓟ ✳ @ 🛜 🛆) This highly atmospheric hotel inside a rusty red colonial hacienda offers bundles of classic charm with spacious, elegant rooms grouped around shady garden courtyards and attractive public areas. There's a beautiful open-air restaurant, a pool, a massage room and a bar with hummingbirds whirring nearby.

✗ Eating

The wealth of fresh water around El Fuerte produces must-have local specialties such as *cauques* or *langostinos* (freshwater crayfish) and *lobina* (black bass).

Taco Stands   TACOS $
(Juárez s/n; tacos from M$15, meal M$30-60; ⊙ 7am-3pm) A row of taco stands, set up in stand-alone concrete huts, do brisk business in all manner of grilled meats, from *al pastor* (seasoned pork) to *cabeza* (cow head; typically cheeks). Join the locals at a counter and order tacos 'til you're full. Located next to the bus stop for Los Mochis.

SU-FÓ Sushi & Cocina Bistro   BISTRO $
(☑ 698-893-50-17; www.facebook.com/pg/Sufo Sushi.Bistro; Constitución 112; dishes M$90-120; ⊙ 6-11pm Tue-Sun; 🛜) Popular SU-FÓ serves up an eclectic menu of sushi rolls (most with signature cream cheese), rice bowls, hamburgers with hand-cut fries and even fancy chicken nuggets. Seating is in an open-air lot with murals, urban-chic decor and twinkling lights. A staff member plays DJ most nights.

★ **Mansión de los Orrantía**   SEAFOOD $$
(☑ 698-893-52-84; Rosales 103; mains M$164-350; ⊙ noon-10pm; 🛜) A short hop from the main plaza, the Mansion Orrantia serves up some of El Fuerte's best cooking. Feast on beautifully prepared plates of *lobina*, *cauques* and *camarones* (shrimp) in the art-filled dining room or the more atmospheric courtyard.

Attached to the restaurant, the elegant Hotel Santa Elena has spacious colonial-style rooms overlooking the courtyard (doubles M$1000).

❶ Getting There & Away

Buses to Los Mochis (M$95, two hours) depart about every half-hour, 5am to 7:30pm, from Juárez near Calle 16 de Septiembre, right in the center of town. From Los Mochis it's easy to connect to elsewhere in northern Mexico.

The train station is 6km south of town (M$160 by taxi). Many hotels offer station pickup and drop-off for guests. If you arrive by train in the evening, waiting shared taxis charge about M$60 a person for a run into the town center.

Cerocahui

☑ 635 / POP 1310 / ELEV 1600M

The tiny, attractive village of Cerocahui, dedicated mainly to forestry, sits in the middle of a verdant, vista-laden valley, and is easily reached via the Chepe Regional (p770) stop Bahuichivo, 16km away (the Chepe Express, however, doesn't disembark here). The canyon country around here sees far fewer tourists than the region near Creel, and the enticing canyon-bottom village of Urique is within striking range.

On the central plaza, Cerocahui's pretty yellow-domed church, **San Francisco Javier de Cerocahui**, was founded in 1680.

There's good hiking around Cerocahui – with some pretty waterfalls nearby – and the excursions (offered by all accommodations) to **Cerro del Gallego**, a spectacular lookout over the Barranca de Urique, 25km along the Urique road, are well worth it.

🛏 Sleeping & Eating

All of the following hotels provide free transfers to/from the train station for overnight guests.

Hotel Jade   HOTEL $$
(☑ 635-456-52-75; www.hoteljade.com.mx; Plaza del Poblado; s/d M$550/950; ⊖ ✳ 🛜) This simple place has 15 clean and comfortable rooms, each with full beds and big windows. The warm welcome from hosts Alberto and Francia and the outstanding cooking (including homemade bread, fish dishes and veggie options; meals M$100) really make this place stand out. Area tours are also offered (from M$150 per person; minimum two people). English spoken.

★ **Hotel Paraíso del Oso**   HOTEL $$$
(☑ 635-109-01-88, Chihuahua 614-421-3372; www. mexicohorse.com; Carretera Bahuichivo-Cerocahui s/n; dm incl breakfast M$300, s/d/tr incl full board US$120/185/240; ⓟ ⊖ 🛜) This excellent, family-owned rural lodge is a great base for bird-watching, hikes and community tourism (the owners have good Tarahumara contacts). The setup includes spacious, ranch-style rooms overlooking a lush garden courtyard and a fascinating book collection to browse.

Located 4km from the center of Cerocahui, on the road to Bahuichivo.

★**Hotel Misión** HOTEL **$$$**
(☎635-456-52-94; www.hotelmision.com; Plaza del Poblado; s/d incl full board from M$4150/4605; 🅿😊🐕) This delightful former hacienda on the town's central plaza offers rustic chic accommodations with *chimeneas* (fireplaces), an evocative bar-restaurant, a games room with a pool table and lovely gardens planted with vines. It's popular with tour groups 'doing' the canyon, but also an appealing option for independent travelers.

Cabañas San Isidro CABAÑAS **$$$**
(☎635-293-75-02; Carretera a Urique Km 24; s/d/tr incl full board & transfers M$1250/1950/2800; 🅿) 🍴 High in the hills above Cerocahui, 8km along the road to Urique, this working farm makes a perfect (if isolated) base for hikes, horseback riding and trips in canyon country. Brothers and co-owners Mario and Tito have excellent connections to the Tarahumara community's runner-guides. The cozy and artful adobe-and-wood cabins have wood-burning stoves. Meals are tasty and plentiful.

❶ Getting There & Away

Cerocahui hotels will pick you up at El Chepe's (p770) Bahuichivo train stop if you have reserved a room.

Alternatively, a local bus leaves for Cerocahui (M$70, 40 minutes) and Urique (M$260, 3½ hours or more) daily at around 1:30pm; it waits for both the train from Chihuahua and the one from Los Mochis. Returning, it leaves Urique at 7am and passes through Cerocahui at around 10am and Bahuichivo at 11am. From Bahuichivo, buses depart every two hours from 6am to 2pm to Areponápuchi (M$70, one hour), Divisadero (M$70, 70 minutes), Creel (M$120, three hours) and Chihuahua (M$350, seven to eight hours).

Urique

📶 635 / POP 1150 / ELEV 550M
This starry-skied, ex-mining village lies at the bottom of the deepest of all the canyons, the spectacular Barranca de Urique, measuring 1870m from rim to river. The trip here is nothing short of spectacular. The mostly unpaved road weaves through rolling pine forest before diving suddenly into the canyon proper. Just past the rim is **Mirador Cerro del Gallego**, one of the most spectacular viewpoints in the Copper Canyon, with Urique town and river visible far below. From there, the narrow road

ULTRAMARATHONS IN URIQUE

Normally held in Urique in early March, the **Ultra Caballo Blanco** (www.facebook.com/caballoblancoultramarathon; ⊙early March) is an 82km ultramarathon on tough canyon trails and at altitude. It was established by Micah True, a legendary American runner known locally as Caballo Blanco (The White Horse) who lived for years in the Copper Canyon region, and gained international attention when featured in Christopher McDougall's book *Born to Run*.

The ultramarathon pays homage to the native Tarahumara (Rarámuri) people, who have a centuries-old tradition of long-distance running and whose very name, Rarámuri, is thought to mean 'the running people' or 'having light feet.' Tarahumara *huaraches* (sandals made from a thin strip of recycled tires) are said to have inspired the barefoot running method (which tests have shown also reduces energy use and running-related injuries) that has now gone global.

winds down the nearly sheer canyon wall, a stomach-lurching 15km descent with more hairpin bends than straight sections.

While Urique is generally a safe place, it is nevertheless known for significant marijuana and poppy cultivation. (That unusually wide street at the edge of town doubles as an airstrip, ostensibly for medical evacuations and handy for transportation of all kinds.) Stick to the main routes and don't go wandering off on your own. Tragically, a solo American traveler was murdered here in 2018.

🏃 Activities

Day hikes up the Río Urique to **Guadalupe Coronado** village (7km) or downriver to **Guapalaina** (6km) are both wonderful walks along riverside dirt roads. As ever in northern Mexico, check the safety situation carefully on the ground before setting out.

🛏 Sleeping & Eating

Entre Amigos CABAÑAS, CAMPGROUND **$**
(☎US 971-287-0593; www.amongamigos.com; Principal s/n; campsites per person US$10, dm/r US$15/50; 🅿😊🐕) 🍴 This artful place has been hosting travelers since 1975. Homey stone cabins, aging dorms and decent campsites (BYO gear) are dotted around grounds

that are dominated by fruit trees and an unbelievably gigantic cactus. No meals are offered, but there's a good guests' kitchen. Staff can hook you up with dependable local guides for hiking, camping or fishing and there's an impressive library.

Hotel El Paraíso Escondido HOTEL $$
(☎635-592-74-04; escondidodeurique@hotmail.com; Principal s/n; s/d/tr/q M$550/800/900/1000; P❄) Squeaky clean, sponge-painted and centrally located, rooms at this friendly and cheap motel are great value. All have flat-screen TVs, hot water and air-con. Units on the 1st floor have heating too. To get here, turn right when you get to the main drag as you enter the town; the hotel will be on your right-hand side.

Restaurant Plaza MEXICAN $$
(☎635-456-60-03; Principal s/n; meals M$120-180; ☺7am-9pm) This excellent, family-run restaurant offers fine food with real home-cooked flavor. The specialty is *aguachile* – a soupy, spicy shrimp cocktail full of onions and tomatoes served in a *molcajete* (traditional mortar and pestle). Don't be fooled by the tiny front dining room – there's a large shady courtyard in back and a sunny rooftop patio with views of the towering canyon walls.

❶ Getting There & Away

El Chepe (p770) stops once daily (except Wednesdays) in Bahuichivo, the closest train station to Urique. A daily bus leaves the station for Urique (M$430, 3½ hours or more) after the train arrives.

Returning, the bus circles town and leaves Urique at 7am, stopping in Cerocahui and Bahuichivo. Cerocahui hotels also offer transportation: Hotel Jade charges M$1800 for a return day trip to Urique with a guide.

Areponápuchi
☎635 / POP 250 / ELEV 2220M

Stretched along a 2km road near the lip of the canyon, the tiny settlement of Areponápuchi or 'Arepo' is just a couple of dozen houses, a church and a few hotels, the pricier of which are right on the canyon edge with mind-blowing views. This is the most touristy bit of the Copper Canyon, with its superb adventure park that allows you to take a series of seven zip-lines almost to the canyon bottom before soaring back up to the rim by cable car – a must-do half-day out.

The village itself is unremarkable, with most people just spending a night or two to visit the adventure park before continuing on El Chepe (p770). Various paths with lookouts run along the canyon edge to the left (north) of Hotel Mirador, but it's easy to get lost, so save your canyon-side strolling to the easier-to-follow path between Divisadero and the adventure park.

🏃 Activities

★Experiencias Rarámuri ECOTOUR
(☎635-110-98-72; www.experienciasraramuri.com; tour per person M$50-400) ✏ This excellent community tourism project offers one-of-a-kind Spanish-language tours led by indigenous Tarahumara guides. You can learn about native traditions and beliefs on scenic walking tours, while taking in pre-Colombian rock art, panoramic views and remote communities. Another highlight is Cooking & Weaving Stories, where you will help prepare and share a meal, and learn how to make handicrafts, while glimpsing daily life.

This two-hour experience (M$350) takes place in the Huetosachi community, a short drive from Areponápuchi.

Walking tours last 30 minutes to six hours or more and depart from the small office near the lower cable car station in the Parque de Aventura Barrancas del Cobre.

🛏 Sleeping & Eating

Cabañas Díaz Family CABAÑAS $
(☎635-578-30-08; off Principal; cabin per person M$300; P) This friendly, family-run lodge has several comfortable cabins overlooking an orchard, many with lofts, and all with fireplaces and fully equipped kitchenettes. Basic but clean hotel-type rooms (also M$300 per person) are also available. Affordable homestyle meals (around M$140) are served in a huge dining room in the main building.

Excellent guided hikes and horseback rides (two-hour outing by foot/horse per person M$300/200) are offered too. Free pick-up from the train station by advance notice.

Copper Canyon Trail Head Inn CABAÑAS $$
(☎635-294-71-11; macksplace14@hotmail.com; Principal; s/d M$600/750, cabin M$1000-1400) Set on a grassy plot in the middle of town, this place has four attractively set cabins each with fireplace, firm beds and a front porch (one has a full kitchen). Another building houses budget rooms that open onto a shared lounge and kitchen. The

> **WORTH A TRIP**
>
> ## PARQUE DE AVENTURA BARRANCAS DEL COBRE
>
> This astonishing **adventure park** (Copper Canyon Adventure Park; ☑ 635-101-0802; www.parquebarrancas.com; M$20, zip-lining M$800-1000; ☺ 9am-5pm; ⓐ) on the canyon rim between Arepo and Divisadero includes Mexico's longest series of *tirolesas* (zip-lines), suspended over some of the world's most profound canyon scenery. The park's seven lines take you from a height of 2400m to over halfway to the canyon floor, with a couple of heart-in-mouth wobbly bridges helping you to complete the cross-canyon odyssey.
>
> The separate Ziprider is an extraordinary 2.5km in length, allowing users to reach speeds of up to 135km per hour. Safety standards are excellent: you're always accompanied by a team of experienced zip-liners and all participants are decked out in full safety gear. Allow at least two hours to descend to the spectacular viewpoint of Mesón de Bacajípare, as you have to travel in a group. If zip-lining isn't your thing, you also can experience the park through the Via Ferrata, a combo rappelling–rock climbing, rope swinging excursion (M$600) to the same viewpoint; allow at least 1½ hours to complete the journey.
>
> Keep in mind there's a minimum weight requirement of 45kg for most activities, though there's a treetop walk (M$300) in the nearby forest with a 30kg minimum. This means many kids won't be able to participate.
>
> The Mesón de Bacajípare viewpoint doubles as the lower station for the *teleférico* (cable car), which you will have to take back up; it's included in the zip-lining and rappelling–rock-climbing prices. If you prefer simply to take in the spectacular views, you can head straight down from the canyon edge on the cable car (adult/child M$250/130). Experiencias Rarámuri (p776) has a post there and offers hiking with indigenous guides on trips ranging from 30 minutes (M$50) to over four hours (M$400).
>
> The main building houses the ticket office and a good restaurant.
>
> The nearest public transportation is at Divisadero, an easy 2.5km walk away via a great canyon-lip-hugging trail. Don't try to walk from Arepo; there are many trails, and it's easy to lose the path.

friendly English-speaking owners have a wealth of knowledge on the area, and can arrange tours, by car, on foot or on horseback.

Hotel Mansión Tarahumara　　HOTEL $$$
(El Castillo; ☑ 635-578-30-32, Chihuahua 614-415-47-21; www.hotelmansiontarahumara.com.mx; off Principal; s/d incl breakfast from M$1650/2100, incl full board from M$200/2400; Ⓟ☎❄) This castle-like hotel (complete with turrets and battlements) offers comfortable accommodations just a few minutes up the hill from the station. Rooms on the canyon rim (commanding the highest prices) are the show-stoppers, with plush beds and balconies. There's a huge restaurant (meals M$220) plus a pool and Jacuzzi.

Hotel Mirador　　HOTEL $$$
(☑ 635-578-30-20, 800-552-56-45; www.hotelmirador.mx; off Principal; s/d/ste incl full board M$4400/5100/5600; Ⓟ☺☎) Suspended over the canyon, this hotel's 75 rooms (each with private balcony, beamed ceilings and somewhat dated furnishings) enjoy unbeatable views, as does the restaurant where buffet meals are served at communal tables. It's

popular with tour groups and is overpriced, but you can't beat the extraordinary canyon panorama. Located on the east end of town.

★ **Restaurante Barranco**　　INTERNATIONAL $$
(☑ 664-143-23-05; www.parquebarrancas.com; Parque de Aventura Barrancas del Cobre; mains M$95-250; ☺ 9am-4pm; ⓐ) Built over a gob-smacking fissure in the canyon walls – and with floor-to-ceiling windows and plexiglass flooring to prove it – the views from this restaurant are jaw-droppingly gorgeous. Meals are generous with a good variety of steaks, salads and breakfast classics. Located in the main building of the adventure park.

❶ Getting There & Away

Most visitors arrive on El Chepe (p770) at the Posada Barrancas train station, which is within easy walking distance of the Arepo hotels.

Five daily buses operated by Autotransportes Noroeste (p781) connect Creel with Arepo (M$60, one hour) every two hours between 11:30am and 7:30pm. Buses drop off passengers either at the entrance to the adventure park or on the main highway entrance to Arepo.

Divisadero

ELEV 2240M

Divisadero, a train stop without a village, is your only chance to see into the miraculous canyon if you're just doing the train ride. Regional trains halt here for 15 minutes, giving you enough time to jump out, gawk, snap some pics at the viewpoint and hop back on. (Express trains don't always let passengers disembark). You can just discern a tiny fragment of the Río Urique at the bottom of the actual Copper Canyon. Ration your time carefully as the station is also a souvenir market and spectacular food court. All this, together with the nearby adventure park 1.5km south, means a stay of longer than 15 minutes is a great idea.

Hotel Divisadero Barrancas HOTEL $$$
(☎614-415-11-99, US 888-232-4219; www.hotel divisadero.com; Av Mirador 4516; s/d incl full board from M$2957/3526; P☻☎) Right by the canyon viewpoint, rooms are modern with a log-cabin feel, though are a bit pricey for the digs. The original units lack views (what were they thinking?), but the newer rooms have astonishing vistas. At the very least, all guests can enjoy the views from the picture windows in the attractive restaurant and lounge.

★ Mercado Divisadero MARKET $
(Av Mirador; dishes M$15-50; ☺11am-3:30pm; ☝⚐) At the foot of the train station sits the Divisadero market with stall-upon-stall of eateries selling mostly tacos, burritos and *gorditas* (stuffed thick tortillas) filled with a huge variety of homemade goodness like grilled steak, seasoned chicken, *nopales* (cactus) and even *chiles rellenos* (chilies stuffed with meat or cheese).

❶ Getting There & Away

The Chepe Regional (p770) stops at the Divisadero station as it chugs toward Los Mochis or Chihuahua. Tickets can be purchased on board as long as there are open seats, which is the case most of the year. If taking the Chepe Express, passengers are typically allowed to disembark only if they are staying in the area.

Buses serving Areponápuchi, San Rafael and ultimately Bahuichivo also run through Divisadero, stopping below the train station – which is quicker and cheaper than continuing by train.

Creel

☑635 / POP 5400 / ELEV 2345M

The Copper Canyon's main tourism center, Creel is actually no more than a low-key highland town strung out along the railway line. It's a very likable place, surrounded by pine forests and interesting rock formations, and it boasts several good hotels and restaurants. The Tarahumara, in their multihued dress, are commonly seen about town, and there's a consistent tourist presence here, mainly in the form of tour groups.

The area around Creel is rich in natural wonders, from waterfalls and hot springs to surreal rock formations and expansive parklands, all perfect for a day's hike, ride or drive. Local guides offer various tours, or you can go solo on a rented bicycle or scooter.

Creel can be very cold in winter, even snowy, and it's none too warm at night in autumn either. In summer, the alpine air is a welcome relief from Mexico's coastal lowland and desert heat.

◉ Sights

Museo de Arte Popular de Chihuahua MUSEUM
(☎635-456-00-80; casaartesanias@prodigy.net. mx; Av Vías del Ferrocarril 178; adult/child M$10/5; ☺9am-6pm; P☝) Offers excellent exhibits with text in English on local history and Tarahumara culture and crafts. Here you'll see gorgeous woven baskets, traditional clothing, photos and more. The gift shop also sells high-quality Tarahumara folk art.

🏃 Activities

Seriously consider exploring the region yourself. This is prime riding country, and many attractions near Creel can be enjoyed on horseback, bicycle or scooter. This is particularly attractive as you can cover terrain the minivans can't manage, and with significantly more peace and quiet. The whole area is a mountain-bike playground: you could just rent a bike and take in some of the area's attractions independently.

With a scooter or car, you've the chance to reach the bottom of the Copper Canyon with your own wheels. Grab a packed lunch in Creel first. The route is very simple: you follow the excellent paved highway southeast of town toward Guachochi. The scenery is staggering; the best section between Km 133 and Km 150 winds around the great

Creel

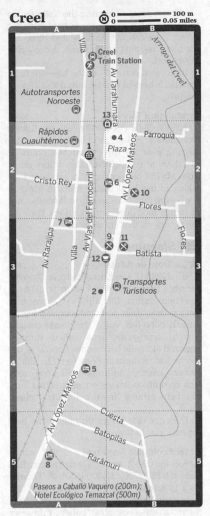

0 — 100 m
0 — 0.05 miles

Trail markers are generally every 50m, though in the fields it can be easy to lose the path, so be sure to ask locals as you go.

Another trail connects Creel train station with Divisadero, a distance of 58km. Too long to undertake in one day (unless you're a Tarahumara ultramarathoner), this trail can be hiked in segments, and since the trail travels near the highway, you can flag down a bus when you're ready to head back. A detailed trail guide provides essential info on the hike on the website.

Plans are still in the works to add more trails to the network, with the hope of creating more DIY hikes along the canyon rim and even down into the canyon.

👉 Tours

Standard minivan tours tend to be rushed, ticking off a roster of nearby sights in a short time frame (most are half-day trips), such as canyons, waterfalls, Tarahumara settlements, hot springs and other places. Themed excursions tend to be more rewarding. Most tours require a minimum number of people, typically four. One popular trip of around five hours covers Cusárare village and waterfall, Lago Arareko and the Valley of the Frogs and Mushrooms. Typical prices are M$400 per person for half-day trips and M$800 for full-day trips. Other good half- or full-day destinations include the adventure

ocher walls of the Copper Canyon itself then descends to the Humira Bridge beside the foaming waters of the Urique River. It's the same route back, via Cusárare and Lago Arareko.

Camino del Cobre HIKING
(www.caminodelcobre.org) The Camino del Cobre is a new trail system that will allow visitors to undertake hikes on their own through the stunning countryside outside of Creel. Currently, you can walk 8km to Lago Arareko, starting from the forest above Creel by following the red-and-green blazes toward San Ignacio then on to the lake.

park (p777) near Areponápuchi, Cascada de Basaseachi and Rekowata (p785) hot springs.

★ **3 Amigos**   TOURS
(☎635-456-00-36; www.amigos3.com; Av López Mateos 46; ⊙9am-6pm; ☝) A passionate and well-run English-speaking agency, 3 Amigos has built its reputation on helping you 'be your own guide in the Copper Canyon.' To do this it provides trail maps (M$20); rents out Rockhopper mountain bikes (M$400 per day), motorcycles (from US$100 per day) and scooters (from M$1200 per day); and offers personalized multiple-day guided trips, such as a three-day Batopilas adventure (US$928).

The full-day self-guided mountain-bike route to the Rekowata hot springs and full-day scooter ride to the canyon bottom by the Humira Bridge pass through simply mind-blowing scenery and are highly recommended. The agency is also the best source of information in town, and its website is a great place to start planning your Copper Canyon adventure. For something totally different, you can even arrange scenic flights over the canyons.

Paseos a Caballo Vaquero   HORSEBACK RIDING
(☎635-106-36-49; 2-/4-/8hr ride per person M$350/650/1500) Expert horseman José Luís leads memorable riding tours outside of Creel. He's very safety conscious, with helmets available for all ages, and slow-paced rides to

---

DON'T MISS

MEXICO'S HIGHEST FULL-TIME WATERFALL

Few natural sites in Mexico boast the exquisitely pristine beauty of the country's highest full-time waterfall, **Cascada de Basaseachi**, where a plume of water tumbles 246m to swimmable pools below. Basaseachi is 140km northwest of Creel, so allow a full day to visit (including three hours to walk to the falls and back). The waterfall is part of the national park of the same name, south of which is the old mining town of **Maguarachi**, where there are delightful hot springs.

Both sites are accessible via San Juanito, 35km north of Creel. To visit you'll really need your own wheels or a tour with a Creel agency.

---

scenic hot spots (including the Valle de los Hongos) for beginners. Those hankering for longer rides can opt for two- and three-day trips, overnighting at his ranch, a day's ride from Creel.

It's located across from the baseball field. Spanish is helpful, as José Luís doesn't speak English.

Tarahumara Tours   TOURS
(☎635-108-68-03; creeltour@hotmail.com; Callejón Parroquial s/n; ⊙9am-7pm) Local driver-guides offering escorted trips, from two hours to two days, at competitive rates. Prices range from M$250 per person for a two-hour tour taking in five local beauty spots to M$1200 per person for a two-day trip to Batopilas, not including food or accommodations. Look for the agency on the central plaza.

🛏 Sleeping

★ **La Troje de Adobe**   INN $
(☎635-102-10-11; www.lodgeatcreel.com; Chapultepec s/n; r M$695-895; 🛜) A short stroll from the train station, this all-wood, three-story inn has beautifully designed rooms. It has an upscale boho feel, with Tarahumara designs woven throughout, handcrafted furnishings and slate tile bathrooms. Several of the rooms have mountain views too. The affable owner – a retired anthropologist – has excellent recommendations on area sights, and can help arrange more culturally focused tours.

The cozy cafe serves up one of the best cappuccinos in town.

Hotel Ecológico Temazcal   HOTEL $
(☎635-456-09-90; www.hoteltemazcal.com; Bakusuki; d M$600-700, f M$900-1500) 🐾 Though it's a 15-minute walk to the main plaza, this welcoming hotel has earned many admirers for its green ethos (solar panels, rainwater catchment, composting). Rooms are trim and tidy with wood ceilings, colorful bedspreads and ample natural light. TVs lack cable, though guests have access to an extensive video library. There's also a full kitchen for guests.

★ **Hotel La Estación**   INN $$
(☎635-456-04-72; www.facebook.com/hotellaestacioncreel; Av López Mateos s/n; r incl breakfast M$1500; ❄🛜) An homage to El Chepe (p770), every room in this movie-house-turned-inn is dedicated to a different stop along the Ferrocarril Chihuahua Pacífico. Think murals and photos, even original train

doors. Each unit has an urban-chic feel, with creature comforts like rain shower heads and fine linens, and the balcony terrace is a great place to unwind. Breakfast includes organic and homemade regional goodies.

Quinta Mision HOTEL $$$
(☑635-456-00-21; www.quintamision.com; Av López Mateos s/n; r from M$1900; P🖘❄🐾) 🅿
An ecologically sensitive hotel, the swanky Quinta Mision recycles rainwater and uses wind and solar power. Its 25 attractive, suite-sized rooms have been created from the shell of an old furniture factory, all with fridge, microwave and coffee maker, and enough space for a small family.

Best Western The Lodge at Creel LODGE $$$
(☑635-456-07-07; www.thelodgeatcreel.com; Av López Mateos 61; r from M$2150; P🖘@🐾) Utterly fascinating in its determination to be a Wild West hotel catering to traveler fantasies, this Best Western boasts antler chandeliers and cow skins on the wall. Its 41 rooms are spacious and smart, with fireplaces, exposed stone, sitting nooks and swing seats on their verandas. There's a small fitness center and spa, plus some excellent eating and drinking options.

✗ Eating & Drinking

Simple CAFE $
(☑635-456-08-44; www.facebook.com/simple bistrocreel; Av López Mateos 17A; mains M$50-75; ❍8am-9pm; 🐾) Big sandwiches, made-to-order burgers, salads, yogurt with fruit, and a variety of crepes are offered at this tiny cafe, just steps from the central plaza. Those hitting the sights out of town can stop in early for a meal to go. On warm days, sidewalk seating is a plus.

Tío Molcas Restaurant MEXICAN $
(☑635-456-00-33; www.facebook.com/pg/tio molcasrestaurant; Av López Mateos 35; M$80-120; ❍7am-9pm) One of Creel's most reliable eateries, Tío Molcas offers solid Mexican standards in a handicraft-filled dining room. Locals and out-of-towners alike file in for juicy steaks, rich enchiladas and first-rate breakfasts – try the *chilaquiles* (fried tortilla strips with eggs, chicken and creamy salsa).

La Cabaña INTERNATIONAL $$
(☑635-456-06-64; Av López Mateos 36; mains M$120-220; ❍7:30am-10pm; 🐾) One of the fancier places in town, La Cabaña serves a good *tampiqueña* (steak accompanied by

several side orders), as well as tasty salads, grills and local specialties like trout stuffed with shrimp. Also has satisfying breakfasts.

Kino's CAFE
(Av López Mateos; 8am-1pm & 3-8pm Tue-Sat, 3-8pm Sun) On clear days, head to this outdoor-only spot for good coffees, kombucha, *tamales*, organic yogurt, carrot cake and other snacks while watching the village stroll past.

🛍 Shopping

The main drag (Avenida López Mateos) is lined with shops selling Tarahumara handicrafts.

Artesanías Misión ARTS & CRAFTS
(☑635-456-00-97; Parroquia 64; ❍9am-2pm & 3-6:30pm Mon-Fri, 9am-1pm & 3-6:30pm Sat) Facing the main plaza, this sizable shop has a traditional selection of handicrafts. All of the store's earnings go to support Creel's Catholic mission hospital, which provides free medical care for the Tarahumara.

ℹ Information

Santander (☑800-501-00-00; www. santander.com.mx; Av López Mateos 3; ❍9am-4pm Mon-Fri, 10am-2pm Sat) Has the only two ATMs in town.

Unidad Medica Santa Teresita (☑635-456-01-05; Parroquia s/n; ❍24hr) This clinic offers basic health-care services.

ℹ Getting There & Away

Construction continues on Creel's new airport, located 3km southwest of town. Assuming the project continues (funding challenges have caused lengthy setbacks since initial work in 2013), the airport is slated to open sometime in 2021.

BUS

If speed and convenience are the name of the game, then bus is actually the most efficient way to travel between Creel and Chihuahua, not to mention between Creel, Divisadero and Areponápuchi: trips are shorter, far cheaper and more frequent than the train.

Autotransportes Noroeste (☑635-456-09-45; www.turisticosnoroeste.com; Villa s/n) Runs buses to Chihuahua (M$260 to M$330, 4½ hours) eight times daily at 1½-hourly intervals from 7am until 5pm. Noroeste also offers buses to Divisadero (M$60, one hour), Areponápuchi (M$60, one hour) and Bahuichivo (M$120, three hours) every two hours between 10:30am and 6:30pm.

Rápidos Cuauhtémoc (☎635-456-07-04; Villa s/n) Has nine daily buses to Chihuahua (M$280, 4½ hours); these leave at roughly hourly intervals between 6:30am and 4:45pm. Also has four daily departures to Bahuichivo (M$120, three hours) every two hours from 10:15am to 6:15pm; they stop along the way in Divisadero (M$60, one hour) and Areponápuchi (M$60, one hour).

Transportes Turísticos (☎635-456-02-79; Av López Mateos) Runs a minibus to Batopilas (M$350, four hours) that leaves daily except Sunday from outside the handicraft store Artesanias Towi on Avenida López Mateos. The bus departs at 9:30am on Monday, Wednesday and Friday, while on Tuesday, Thursday and Saturday it departs at 7:30am. The return bus leaves Batopilas at 6am Monday to Saturday.

CAR & MOTORCYCLE

There are paved roads all the way from Chihuahua to Creel and on to Divisadero, Batopilas and Bahuichivo. Motorbikes and scooters can be rented from 3 Amigos (p780). If you want to self-drive in the region, bring a rental car from Los Mochis or Chihuahua, but proceed with caution: some areas are controlled by drug cartels, so always check your planned route with someone who has plenty of up-to-date local knowledge before setting off.

TRAIN

El Chepe (p770) regional trains pass through Creel en route toward Los Mochis or Chihuahua. For the luxury Chepe Express, Creel is the start/end point for its route to Los Mochis. Purchase Chepe Express tickets well in advance online (or over the phone). El Chepe Regional tickets can only be purchased aboard the train. No tickets are sold at the station.

Batopilas

☎649 / POP 1310 / ELEV 580M

A charming town at the bottom of the Copper Canyon, the former silver-mining village of Batopilas is a sleepy place where everybody knows everyone and whose laid-back air works a gentle magic on all who visit. The town itself sits along 2km of its winding namesake river. A paved road into the jaw-dropping Barranca de Batopilas brings you here with relative ease and it has more twists, turns and heart-in-mouth vertical drops than any amusement-park ride.

Batopilas was founded in 1708, and peaked in prominence in the late 19th century when silver mining boomed. The climate is subtropical year-round, which means scorching in the summer months and pleasantly warm the rest of the year.

Batopilas can be slightly rough around the edges, with marijuana fueling the local economy. While the odd robbery has occurred, foreign tourists aren't usually targeted, though it's important to take local advice about out-of-town excursions.

☉ Sights & Activities

Museo de Batopilas   MUSEUM
(Donato Guerra s/n; ☉9am-5pm Mon-Sat) FREE Offers a good overview of the town's history with a mock-up of a silver mine and some interesting photos and artifacts. English-speaking director Rafael Ruelas guides visitors through the exhibits, embellishing proceedings with his own anecdotes. Located on the central plaza; tourist information is available here too.

Tirolesa   ADVENTURE SPORTS
(ride from M$50; ☉9am-4pm) Batopilas' newest attraction is this two-stage zip-line that whisks you over the village and across the river. You then take a second zip-line and head back across the river, ending at the top of the pedestrian bridge. It's a fun ride that affords some fine views over the area. Reach the first zip-line by taking the stairs located a few blocks south of the main plaza.

Misión Satevó Hike   HIKING
(🚶) One of the most popular hikes from Batopilas is to the 18th-century Misión Satevó church, in a remote spot 8km down the Copper Canyon. Simply follow the Batopilas River downstream (the mission suddenly appears, framed in a forested river gorge); it's also possible to drive there. The mission itself is only occasionally open.

🛏 Sleeping & Eating

Hotel Juanita's   HOTEL $
(☎614-120-56-52; Nigromonte 7; s/d/tr M$400/500/600; ☉❋) In a great location opposite the main plaza, this familial guesthouse has basic, well-kept rooms each with their own crucifix, plus a shared river-facing courtyard with a gurgling fountain. Some rooms have air-con, but all have a fan. Ask for a room off the main street, facing the river.

Riverside Lodge   HOTEL $$$
(☎614-427-30-97; www.coppercanyonlodges.com; Juárez s/n; r incl breakfast US$195; P☉❋) For sensory overload hacienda-style, check into this labyrinthine colonial mansion, expertly and sympathetically renovated and deco-

rated with lavish murals, oil paintings, rugs and oak furniture. All 14 rooms are individually furnished and boast vast bathrooms with claw-foot tubs. Look out for its blue domes across from the church: there's no sign otherwise. Enter through the gate under an anchor.

Restaurant Carolina   MEXICAN **$$**
(☑ 649-104-81-23; Plaza de la Constitución; dishes M$100-180; ☺ 8am-8:30pm) Rifles on the walls, pickles in jars and local scenes captured in paintings sum up this family-run restaurant a block beyond Batopilas' main plaza. Choose between filling breakfasts (M$90 to M$120), delicious tacos (ask for the mango salsa) or more elaborate dishes such as freshwater trout. The whole place is inside Carolina's home, and there are always several generations at work in the kitchen.

ℹ Information

Tourist Information Center (☑ 649-123-07-77; www.visitbatopilas.com; Donato Guerra s/n; ☺ 9am-5pm Mon-Sat) This small tourist information center in the town museum – a table with brochures and maps, more than anything – is a good place to start your visit. Rafael Ruelas, the director of the museum, doubles as the director of tourism. Friendly and helpful, he often is on hand to give recommendations and tips.

THE TARAHUMARA (RARÁMURI)

A fascinating part of canyon life is the presence of one of Mexico's most distinctive indigenous groups, the Tarahumara (Rarámuri), who live in caves and small houses across the countryside here. Most easily identifiable are the women, dressed in colorful skirts and blouses and often carrying infants on their backs. They sell beautiful hand-woven baskets and carved wooden dolls and animals at ridiculously low prices at tourist sites around the sierra. Most men now wear modern clothes like jeans instead of the traditional loincloth, but both sexes still often walk in *huaraches* – sandals made from tire tread and strips of leather.

The Tarahumara remain largely an enigma. Contrary to popular belief, the Spanish incursion did not force the Tarahumara into the canyons: they were here when the first Jesuits arrived in 1608.

There are two main Tarahumara groups: the Alta (high) and the Baja (low), with whom outside contact was made by Jesuit priests from higher-altitude Parral and lower-altitude El Fuerte, respectively. Culture and language are radically different between the Altas and Bajas, and because of long-term isolation, every community has a slightly different culture and language. No one even knows how many Tarahumara exist. Estimates vary between 50,000 and 120,000.

Rarámuri means 'those who run fast' – and these people are most famous for running long distances swiftly, sometimes up to 20 hours without stopping. They used their aptitude for running to hunt deer by bow and arrow as little as a generation ago. The Copper Canyon area even has its own annual ultramarathon (p775) at Urique.

But a better cultural insight into the Tarahumara is their sense of fairness. *Korima* is a custom where someone who has a good crop is 'blessed' and obliged to share their good fortune with others. Another tradition is the *tesgüinada*, a raucous social gathering at which Tarahumara relax their natural reserve and celebrate communal work and festivals with plenty of *tesgüino*, a potent corn beer.

Even these traditionally isolated people have been influenced by incomers, and many have adopted a type of Catholicism. However, their take on Christianity and Christian festivals is often idiosyncratic – regularly accompanied by drumming and lots of *tesgüino*.

But the Tarahumara have maintained their lifestyle despite incursions of conquistadors, missionaries, railways, drug gangs and tourism. They have one word to refer to all non-Tarahumara people: *chabochi*, which means 'with spider-webbing on the face,' a reference to bearded Spanish colonists. The majority continue to live a subsistence life in the remote Sierra Madre Occidental countryside.

The Tarahumara are also generally materially poor, and their communities have some serious health problems: there are high rates of infant mortality, malnutrition and teenage pregnancy, with some of the little relief coming from Catholic missions.

OFF THE BEATEN TRACK

CANYON COUNTRY NEAR GUACHOCHI

Some 160km south of Creel, the farming town of Guachochi (population 15,000) lies near some spectacular canyon country that is rarely visited by foreign travelers. Around 18km south of Guachochi is the **Mirador Barrancas de la Sinforosa** (www.facebook.com/LasinforosaMirador; Camino de Mirador la Sinforosa), a spellbinding lookout that takes in the dramatic Sinforosa Canyon, one of the deepest in the Copper Canyon system at over 1800m. You can just discern the Río Verde threading its way along the lush canyon bottom. Those who want even more dramatic views can arrange 18-minute scenic flights over Sinforosa with Guachochi-based **Aero JoMaCha** (☑ 649-543-10-22; www.facebook.com/aerojomacha; Aeropuerto Guachochi; flight for 3/6 persons M$3600/6000).

About an hour's drive south of Guachochi is an extraordinary – but quite rustic – ecolodge. Amid waterfalls and superb canyon views, **Kokoyome** (☑ 649-101-89-49; Guachochi; d/tr/q M$1400/1800/2200) 🌿 is 100% sustainable – with solar panels, a spring-fed water source and delicious organic food (much of it grown or produced here). The stone-walled rooms have picture windows (or a skylight for stargazing), but facilities are basic, so it's not for luxury seekers. Taxis to the lodge charge about M$1000 from Guachochi. You can also arrange transport and tours with Eduardo Loera (649-105-09-77).

Rápidos Cuauhtémoc (p802) has regular bus connections to Guachochi from Chihuahua (M$490, five hours, five per day) and Creel (M$215, 4½ hours, one per day).

❶ Getting There & Away

Minibuses (M$350, four hours) run by Transportes Turisticos (p782) leave daily except Sunday from Creel (outside the handicraft store Artesanias Towi on Avenida López Mateos). The bus departs at 9:30am on Monday, Wednesday and Friday, while on Tuesday, Thursday and Saturday it departs at 7:30am. The return bus leaves Batopilas at 6am Monday to Saturday.

If you have your own wheels, it's simple to visit Batopilas independently – 4WD not required.

Cusárare

☑ 635 / POP 200

About 25km from Creel is the quiet Tarahumara village of Cusárare. Spread out along 2km of dirt road, it features an 18th-century mission church, a museum and, nearby, a set of like-named falls, perfect for a hike, swim and several selfies.

Misión Cusárare   CHURCH

(Cusárare s/n) This mission was built by Jesuits in 1741 as a religious meeting place as well as a school to teach the locals Spanish and different trades. In 1826 Franciscan friars added side altars, a choir loft and an adobe bell tower; the last collapsed in 1969, taking down a corner of the church with it. The church was repaired and restored in the early 1970s, adding striking Tarahumara patterned murals. A new stone bell tower was built too.

Museo Loyola   MUSEUM

(Cusárare s/n; M$25) Sitting alongside the Cusárare Mission church, this museum holds an exceptional collection of colonial religious paintings.

Cascada Cusárare   HIKING

(Hwy 25 Km 112; M$30; ⊙ 8am-5pm; 🚶) This lovely 30m waterfall is perfect if you're looking to take a short hike. A 3km walk from the road, the trail is shady and very beautiful, offering the chance of a dip along the way. To get here, head south on the highway 400m past the Cusárare turnoff; at Km 112, turn right at the 'Cascada de Cusárare' sign, which leads to a trail that follows a bubbling stream, then passes through a sweeping highland valley to the falls.

There are two road signs to the trailhead. If you're driving, go past the first one at Km 108 – the road is too rough unless you have a 4WD vehicle.

❶ Getting There & Away

Creel is the closest train stop if traveling on El Chepe (p770). Just north of Creel's train station, travelers can catch buses, which will drop you at Cusarare's highway entrance – take any bus with signage for 'Guachochi.' From the highway, it's a 1km walk into town. Many tours include a stop here too. Otherwise arrange for a cab driver to take you there and back, with an hour or so to visit the church and museum.

San Ignacio de Arareko

☑ 635 / POP 4000

Four kilometers southeast of Creel is the Tarahumara *ejido* (communal farming district) of San Ignacio, which spreads over some 200 sq km and is home to about 4000 people living in caves and small houses among farmlands, small canyons and pine forests. Here you'll find the photogenic 18th-century **San Ignacio Mission Church**, several spectacular rock formations and the scenic Lake Arareko. A bit further, but still within the *ejido* reach, are the popular Rekowata hot springs. Visitors to San Ignacio are charged admission (M$45). The cost includes access to most of the *ejido's* sights – be sure to keep your ticket handy!

★ **Valle de los Monjes**   NATURAL FEATURE
(Valley of the Monks; San Ignacio s/n; ⊙24hr; ⊛) Around 7km east of San Ignacio's town center, through verdant farmland, is the Valle de los Monjes. A spectacular outcrop of vertical red rock formations that inspire its Tarahumara name Bisabírachi, meaning 'Valley of the Erect Penises,' it is well worth exploring and is less visited than the **Valle de las Ranas y los Hongos** (Valley of Frogs and Mushrooms; San Ignacio s/n; ⊛).
Admission (M$15) is occasionally charged.

Lago Arareko   LAKE
(Hwy 25 Km 8) Meaning 'Horseshoe' in the Tarahumara language, the peaceful waters of this U-shaped lake reflect the surrounding pines and rock formations. Paddleboats can be rented along the lakeshore (M$100) for exploring and finding good swimming spots. Access to the lake is included in the San Ignacio admission cost (M$45); there are also viewpoints of the lake along the Creel–Cusárare highway. Located about 8km south of Creel.

A visit to Lago Arareko can be easily combined with stops at Valle de las Ranas y los Hongos as well as Valle de los Monjes – a perfect day trip.

Aguas Termales Rekowata   THERMAL BATHS
(Rekowata Hot Springs; Hwy 77 Km 7; ⊙9am-5pm; ⊛) These hot springs, averaging about 37°C (98.6°F), are channeled into modern-day pools near the bottom of the Barranca de Tarárecua. To get here, follow a signposted dirt road for 11km from the Creel–Divisadero Hwy to the parking lot. From there, it's a 3km hike down a rough cobblestone track to the blissfully warm bathing pools. Vans (M$60

one way) shuttle visitors from the parking lot; otherwise it's a beautiful walk down and a sweaty one back up. Weekends get busy.

There's also a superb mountain-bike trail to Rekowata. This route initially takes the Cusárare road, but then heads off-road down tracks to the right (south) near San Ignacio. You pass through a scenic river valley then an utterly astonishing canyon viewpoint before beginning a steep descent to Rekowata. It's a full-day return-trip ride; 3 Amigos (p780) can provide a map.

Admission to the hot springs is included in the entrance fee to San Ignacio *ejido* – be sure to save your ticket!

ℹ Getting There & Away

Most people visit here on a tour, but it's fairly easy to walk, cycle or taxi from Creel to San Ignacio's northern entrance (just outside town, past the cemetery); from there it's 1.6km to the Misión San Ignacio and Valle de las Ranas y los Hongos on a good dirt road. Buses headed to Guachochi can drop you at San Ignacio's highway entrance, but you're still 1.6km away from its main attractions.

NORTHWEST MEXICO

The dramatic beaches of the Sea of Cortez and the abundant marine life, including some 40 sea-lion colonies and 27 species of whale and dolphin, are magnets for visitors: Puerto Peñasco, Bahía de Kino and San Carlos all beckon travelers. The region, encompassing Sonora and northern Sinaloa, still bursts with homespun character. The strains of *norteña* (country) music and the inviting smell of *carne asada* (grilled beef) waft past cowboy-hatted locals on the streets.

The perfunctory towns and cities won't detain you long: Los Mochis harbors little of interest except as a jumping-off point for the spectacular train ride through Copper Canyon or the ferry to Baja. The state capital, Hermosillo, is a vast and faceless place with little cultural interest. The glorious exception is Álamos (p790), a colonial jewel surrounded by peaks of the Sierra Madre Occidental, which is replete with atmospheric hotels and restaurants and well worth a side trip.

Sonora

Mexico's second-largest state (neighboring Chihuahua is the first) has remarkable cultural and ecological diversity within its

180,000 sq km. It boasts miles and miles of gorgeous beaches, desert moonscapes in El Pinacate Reserve, near Puerto Peñasco, and everything in between. It's still undiscovered by mass tourism, but the word is definitely getting out for Mexican travelers – beach towns like San Carlos and Bahía de Kino get packed with weekend warriors from Hermosillo and beyond – and those near the US border get a steady stream of American 'snowbirds' (retired North American citizens who head south for winter). Even so, Sonora sees far fewer travelers, especially foreigners, than its myriad attractions and drop-dead beauty would suggest. But hey, who's complaining?

Puerto Peñasco

📞 638 / POP 65,800

Until the 1920s, 'Rocky Point,' as Americans affectionately call this Sea of Cortez coastal town, was just that: a landmark on military maps and no more. Its location alongside one of the driest parts of the Sonoran Desert deterred all would-be settlers bar intrepid fishers until Prohibition gave the fledgling community an unexpected boost. When the global economy nosedived in the 1930s, Peñasco enjoyed a (very) lengthy siesta, until state investment and a desalination plant kick-started the local economy in the early 1990s. The result has been a boom in both development and population, and now this beach town has become the seaside destination Arizona never had.

The historic core – El Malecón (Old Port) – hugs the rocky point itself, while just north sits the pleasant beach, Playa Hermosa. Heading west is Sandy Beach, home to a sprawling stretch of condo-hotel resorts, expensive restaurants and golf courses carved out of the desert.

◉ Sights & Activities

Fishing, snorkeling, diving, kayaking and sunset cruises are all popular. There are extensive rock pools to explore at low tide, and trips around the estuary and beyond to the remarkable Reserva El Pinacate y Gran Desierto de Altar can be set up by the likes of CEDO.

★ Isla San Jorge   ISLAND

(🚻) Also known as Bird Island, Isla San Jorge is one of the best boat excursions in northern Mexico. This rocky island 40km southeast of Peñasco is home to nesting seabirds and also a large community of sea lions (which are curious by nature and will swim alongside boats). Dolphins are often spotted en route, while whales (fin, gray, killer and pilot) are sometimes encountered between January and April. Full-day cruises are offered by **Del Mar Charters** (📞 638-383-28-02, US 520-407-6054; www.delmarcharters.com; Pelícano s/n; ⊙ 7am-6pm; 🚻).

Playa Hermosa   BEACH

(Calle 13; 🅿 🚻) Puerto Peñasco's main town beach, Playa Hermosa is an inviting swath of tawny sand with small waves and views of the rocky landscape in the distance. Vendors hawk everything from mangoes to jewelry, and beach shade, including chairs, can be had for around M$300 per day. You can arrange all manner of aquatic activities here, including hiring stand-up paddleboards (SUPs) and kayaks.

CEDO   VISITOR CENTER

(Intercultural Center for the Study of Desert & Oceans; 📞 638-382-01-13, US 520-320-5473; www.cedo.org; Blvd Las Conchas s/n; ⊙ 9am-5pm Mon-Sat, 10am-2pm Sun; 🚻) 🎟 FREE CEDO is a wonderful place to learn about Rocky Point's fascinating desert-meets-sea ecosystem. Dedicated to the conservation of the upper Gulf of California and surrounding Desierto Sonorense, CEDO has a visitor center where it hosts free natural-history talks in English at 2pm Tuesdays and 4pm Saturdays. CEDO also runs a fascinating program of nature tours, some in collaboration with local cooperatives.

Tours include tide-pool walks (US$30), kayaking on Morúa estuary (US$75), snorkeling trips to Isla San Jorge (US$150) and excursions to El Pinacate Biosphere Reserve with an English-speaking naturalist (US$80).

Cholla Bay   BEACH

(La Choya; 🚻) Located about 12km west of Puerto Peñasco, Cholla Bay is a fishing village turned expat enclave with sand roads and quiet, calm beaches. At low tide, the water recedes dramatically, revealing oysters and other shellfish. Come in the late afternoon for gorgeous sunsets.

🛏 Sleeping

El Malecón (Old Port) has agreeable down-to-earth options – though it's slim pickings for tight budgets, unless you're up for camping. All the megahotel complexes are at Sandy Beach, to the northwest. Note that

Spring Break in Peñasco is popular with US college students, so book early if coming in March or April.

Concha Del Mar
CAMPGROUND $

(📋638-113-04-67; Calle 19 No 680; campsite US$15; 🅿🛜) Sitting on a huge empty lot right on Playa Bonita, this campground offers clean bathrooms, wi-fi, laundry facilities and even 24-hour security. BYO tent or buy the basics at SAMS Club or Bodega Aurrera on your way into town. During high season, arrive midweek for an oceanfront site. Reservations not accepted.

★ Dream Weaver Inn
GUESTHOUSE $$

(📋575-613-36-52; www.facebook.com/dream weaverinn; Pescadores 3, El Malecón; apt US$65-95; ❄@🛜🐾) This welcoming and well-cared-for inn has excellent rooms, each lovingly decorated with local handicrafts in true Mexican style. Each unit has a fridge, microwave and coffee maker, and some full kitchens. It feels like a home away from home. Located near the Old Port's main plaza, with restaurants, shops and traveling oompah bands just steps away. Cash only.

Hospedaje Mulege
GUESTHOUSE $

(📋928-287-08-83; cnr Av Circunvalación & Calle 18 de Septiembre, El Malecón; r incl breakfast US$60-85; 🅿😊❄🛜) Lupita and Israel preside over guests with real pride in showing them the flip side to the town's megaresorts in this friendly and unpretentious Old Port villa. The rooms are comfortable and homey, some with spectacular ocean views.

🍴 Eating & Drinking

Kaffee Haus
CAFE $$

(📋638-388-10-65; Blvr Juárez 216B; mains M$100-180; ⊗7am-4pm Mon-Sat, 7am-2pm Sun; 🛜🐾) A long-standing favorite, this local institution draws crowds for its enormous breakfasts, served daily until 2pm. Juicy burgers, steak sandwiches, blue-cheese-topped apple-walnut salad and superb apple strudel are a few menu highlights. Portions are huge, and it's cash only.

Blue Marlin
SEAFOOD $$$

(El Marlin Azul; 📋638-383-65-64; www.facebook. com/pg/thebluemarlinrestaurant; Ignacio Zaragoza s/n, El Malecón; mains M$165-270; ⊗11am-10pm Thu-Tue) At the swankier end of the dining spectrum, Blue Marlin specializes in seafood, serving everything from simple fish tacos to hearty coconut shrimp meals. Seating is indoors in a small nautical-themed dining room or outside on a pleasant street-front patio.

La Curva
MEXICAN $$$

(📋638-383-34-70; www.facebook.com/pg/ RestaurantLaCurva.puertopenasco; Blvd Kino 100; mains M$170-300; ⊗7:45am-9:30pm; 🍴) Set in the middle of town, this low-key place serves huge plates of traditional Mexican cooking. Try the amazing *mariscada* (seafood platter) or the *carne asada*.

★ Chef Mickey's Place
INTERNATIONAL $$$

(📋638-388-95-00; Plaza del Sol 4, Blvd Freemont; mains breakfast & lunch US$8-10, dinner US$18-23; ⊗7:30am-11pm Thu-Tue, 3-11pm Wed) Eponymous

---

OFF THE BEATEN TRACK

GRAN DESIERTO DE ALTAR

About 30km from Puerto Peñasco are the lunar landscapes of **El Pinacate**, one of the driest places on earth. This remote, spectacular 7145-sq-km reserve is a Unesco World Heritage site and contains ancient eroded volcanoes, giant craters, petrified lava flows, 400-plus ash cones and the continent's largest concentration of active sand dunes. Wildlife includes pronghorn antelope (the fastest land mammal in the Americas), bighorn sheep, pumas, reptiles and bountiful birdlife. There's an excellent, highly informative, solar-powered visitor center, interpretive hiking trails and two campgrounds.

The extraordinary landscapes here are so unusual that Neil Armstrong and Buzz Aldrin used this region in the 1960s to prepare themselves for their Apollo 11 moon landing.

Today over 70km of dirt roads (4WD only in parts) penetrate the reserve. Visitors must register to climb the 1190m Cerro del Pinacate volcano.

The visitor center is about 8km west of Km 72 on Hwy 8 (27km from Puerto Peñasco). The craters are accessed by a separate turnoff further north at Km 52 on Hwy 8.

CEDO (p786) in Puerto Peñasco organizes excellent tours to the reserve: good walking shoes are recommended, and note that there's no water or electricity available anywhere in the reserve, except at the visitor center.

chef Mickey has been cooking up a storm here for years, and you'll be hard pressed to find better quality and innovation elsewhere in town. Macadamia-crusted flounder, chicken in marsala sauce, and rosemary and butter-glazed rib eye are among the many hits served in the elegant dining room. Reserve ahead.

La Casa del Capitán
BAR

(☑638-383-56-98; Av Camino del Agua; ☺10am-9pm Sun-Thu, to 10pm Fri & Sat) A short drive (or steep 10-minute walk) up above the Old Port, this place has one of the best sunset-viewing spots in town. There's a full menu of classic fare (mains US$10 to US$22), but you're better off coming for drinks (huge but pricey margaritas), best enjoyed on the breezy terrace overlooking the sea.

There's an excellent Italian restaurant next door.

🛍 Shopping

Calle 32
ARTS & CRAFTS

(Calle 32 near Pino Suárez) A fun place to browse for gift ideas is along this mural-lined street around 4km north of the Old Port. Also known as 'Rodeo Drive,' Calle 32 has numerous shops selling hammocks, woven bags, cowboy hats, T-shirts, leather goods, Mexican wrestling masks, food items and plenty of curiosities – including life-size dinosaurs, gorillas and giraffes made from repurposed scrap metal.

Galería Mercedes
ARTS & CRAFTS

(☑638-383-47-47; Alcantar 35; ☺9am-5pm) This fabulous gallery in the Old Port area sells exquisite pottery, wood carvings and textiles made by artisans from across Mexico.

Tequila Factory
FOOD & DRINKS

(☑638-388-06-06; www.facebook.com/tequila factory; cnr Blvd Juárez & Calle 12; ☺10am-6pm Wed-Mon) FREE Despite its name, this family-owned shop doesn't produce any tequila onsite, but it does offer informative and fun presentations on tequila production. Tastings of its artisanal tequilas are part of the experience (and you can always try before you buy in the shop). The flavored tequilas and oak-aged *añejo* are favorites.

ℹ Information

Convention & Visitors Bureau
(☑638-388-04-44; www.cometorockypoint.com; Av Coahuila 444; ☺9am-4pm Mon-Fri) A helpful

English-speaking tourist office located on the 2nd floor of Plaza Pelícanos.

Rocky Point 360
(www.rockypoint360.com) An excellent online resource for activities, events and other info.

ℹ Getting There & Away

A handful of shuttle-van services operate between Puerto Peñasco and Arizona, including **Transportes Express** (☑638-383-36-40, US 602-442-6670; www.transportes-express.com; cnr Lázaro Cárdenas & Sinaloa), which runs to/from Phoenix four times daily (US$50, four hours).

Albatros (☑800-624-66-18, 638-388-08-88; www.albatrosautobuses.com; Blvd Juárez, btwn Calles 29 & 30) runs 15 daily buses to Hermosillo (M$400, 5½ hours), four to Nogales (M$335, six hours), two to Guaymas (M$460, eight hours), 10 to Navojoa ($655, 12 hours) and one to Álamos ($655, 13 hours).

Autobuses de la Baja California (ABC; ☑664-104-74-00, 800-025-02-22; www.abc. com.mx; cnr Constitución & Bravo), one block north of Blvd Juárez, has six buses daily to Mexicali (M$365) and one bus to Tijuana (M$600, nine hours).

ℹ Getting Around

Travelers without a car, beware: there is no reliable local public transportation around town. **Bufalo** (☑638-388-99-99; ventas_rentacars@ hotmail.com; cnr Freemont & Chiapas; ☺8am-8pm) rents out new-ish, well-maintained cars, starting at M$1200 per day.

Taxis cost around M$40 for short rides around town. Beyond Puerto Peñasco, cabs cost M$60 from the Old Port to the Sandy Beach resorts and M$180 to Cholla Bay – and can be double that or more coming back.

San Carlos

☑622 / POP 2800

With its striking desert-and-bay landscape, the low-key beach retreat of San Carlos feels a universe apart from its gritty port neighbors. It's presided over by some dramatic hills – notably the majestic twin peaks of Cerro Tetakawi – that glow an impressive red-earthed hue as the sun descends.

San Carlos' beaches are a mix of dark sand and pebbles. Head beyond the busy and built-up central strip to remoter and quieter Playa Los Algodones (famed for its role in the movie *Catch-22*) and you'll find white sands and turquoise water on one of the best beaches in northern Mexico.

ℹ Orientation

San Carlos, spread-eagled over some 8km, is not pedestrian friendly. Most amenities are on the 2.5km stretch of Blvd Beltrones. Head right at the intersection by the Oxxo store on the north end of the Beltrones strip to get out to Playa Los Algodones (6km northwest), or straight on for Marina San Carlos (500m west).

⊙ Sights

★ Playa Los Algodones   BEACH
(Hwy 124 Km 19) Named for the cotton-ball-like dunes on the south end of the beach, Playa Los Algodones is arguably the most beautiful beach in northern Mexico. The sand is fine and white, the water blue and calm, and the view is of dramatic mountains. High season can bring crowds and traveling oompah bands – join the party or head north along the sand for a patch of peace.

There's a parking fee on Saturday and Sunday (M$30). On other days, access is free.

Isla San Pedro Nolasco   DIVE SITE
(Seal Island) A popular spot for snorkeling and dive excursions 28km west of San Carlos, Isla San Pedro Nolasco is a rocky island nature reserve that's home to a large population of sea lions. These playful creatures are active year-round. To see pups exploring their underwater surroundings, book a trip during the summer months with **Gabby's** (📞 622-125-1875; www.gabbysyachtrentalsancarlos. mx; Edificio Marina San Carlos; boat hire per hour M$1200-3500; ⊙8am-5pm) or **Gary's Dive Shop** (📞 622-226-00-49; www.garysdiveshop. com; Blvd Beltrones Km 10; ⊙8am-5pm).

Mirador San Carlos   VIEWPOINT
(off Blvd Beltrones) The magnificent views from this overlook shouldn't be missed on a visit to San Carlos. From a lofty perch 200m over the crashing waves, you can take in the dramatic sight of jagged mountains plunging into the cerulean Sea of Cortez. On lucky days, you might spy dolphins, rays and even whales. Reach the lookout by driving 4km west of San Carlos toward Playa Los Algodones, taking the first left after Cerro Tetakawi, and continuing another 2km.

🏃 Activities

Gorgeous coves, as well as the nearby sea-lion colony on Isla San Pedro Nolasco, make snorkeling and kayaking top activities. Sportfishing also is popular: April to September are best for big fish and there are several annual tournaments.

Off the water, you can also undertake hikes up iconic **Cerro Tetakawi** (off Blvd Beltrones), a two-hour (return) hike that affords magnificent 360-degree views from its 320m perch (bring water, ample sun protection and good hiking shoes). You can also go horseback riding through desert and on the beach with the recommended **El Rancho del Desierto** (📞 622-855-59-30; www. astridranch.com; Rancho el Palomar; per hour from M$300; 🅟).

Enrike's Adventures   OUTDOORS
(📞 622-130-73-38; www.facebook.com/enrikes. adventures; Blvd Beltrones s/n; tours per person from M$350, bike/kayak/snorkel rental per day $20/40/13; ⊙9am-5pm; 🅟) Personalized and bilingual service is offered on a variety of excursions, including hiking Cerro Tetakawi and paddleboarding or kayaking in the area's bays. Gear rental – bikes, SUPs, kayaks and snorkel gear – is also available.

🛏 Sleeping

Posada del Desierto   GUESTHOUSE $
(📞 622-226-04-67; Calle Bajada Comodoro 195; d/q M$700/1200; 🅟❄🛜) This friendly, family-run spot 200m south of the marina offers the best lodging deal in town. In a row of brightly painted, thick adobe-walled buildings, the seven simple rooms are nicely maintained, each with small kitchenettes (with fridge, sink and microwave) and a small sitting area in front.

Hacienda Tetakawi   HOTEL $$
(📞 622-226-02-48; www.hotelhaciendatetakawi.com .mx; Blvd Beltrones s/n; d from M$850; 🅟❄🏊) On busy Beltrones, this place offers good value for its simple but well-equipped, motel-style rooms. The palm-fringed swimming pool (with bar) is quite enticing on sunny days.

Sawari Hotel   BOUTIQUE HOTEL $$$
(📞 622-226-18-18; www.sawarihotel.com; Blvd Beltrones 1212; d from M$2100; 🅟❄🛜🏊) A stylish new hotel on bustling Beltrones, Sawari has bright, elegant rooms with quality furnishings, and the poolside is a great place to unwind during the heat of the day. There's also an outdoor bar.

🍴 Eating & Drinking

Maria's   MEXICAN $$
(Gabriel Estrada; mains M$95-180; ⊙6:30am-10pm) A great anytime spot, Maria's whips up tasty traditional fare, with an appealing menu of *sopa de tortilla* (tortilla soup),

breaded mango shrimp, and fish tacos, as well as heartier plates of barbecue ribs and chicken fajitas. Excellent breakfasts too. It's in a breezy upstairs location with a small deck near the marina.

Soggy Peso Bar & Grill   SEAFOOD $$
(☑622-125-72-38; Playa Los Algodones; mains M$125-320; ⊙11am-sunset; 🌶) With sand floors and loungers on the beach, this lively and popular seafood restaurant makes for a fun and informal seafood lunch. It's on the north end of San Carlos' best beach and also functions as a popular bar, serving up tasty margaritas, outstanding appetizers (try *tostadas de jaiba*, crab-topped crispy tortillas), and live music nightly except Monday and Wednesday. Cash only.

★Sunset Bar & Grill   SEAFOOD $$$
(☑622-109-00-03; www.sunsetsancarlos.com; Playa Los Algodones; mains M$150-270; ⊙4-11pm Thu-Mon) Overlooking a gorgeous stretch of beachfront, this open-sided gem serves up some of San Carlos' best seafood. Enjoy fantastic sunsets while tucking into mouthwatering ceviche, chargrilled fish of the day or scrumptious coconut shrimp. The cocktails are no less impressive, with a spiced hibiscus and lime Bacanoran Bay (made from Sonoran agave-derived *bacanora*) and a stellar Moscow Mule (made from fresh ginger).

There's live music Friday, Saturday and Sunday nights.

Colibrí   MEXICAN $$$
(☑622-115-34-66; www.facebook.com/ColibriSan Carlos; Blvd Beltrones 1700; mains M$185-275; ⊙5-11pm Mon, 8:30am-11pm Tue-Sun; 🍴) A wide-ranging quality menu, friendly service and an easy-going setting (and umbrella-shaded terrace) make a great combination at this popular spot on the main drag. Come for seared tuna and other seafood, brick-oven pizza and creative appetizers, with vegetarian options.

Don't miss silent movie nights on Mondays, when a talented local pianist provides live accompaniment to Charlie Chaplin and Buster Keaton films.

Meri Meri   CAFE
(☑622-132-01-70; Blvd Beltrones 715; ⊙7am-8pm Mon & Wed-Fri, from 8am Sat & Sun; 🕸) 🍃 Run by two talented sisters (one of whom contributed artwork to the walls), ecofriendly Meri Meri serves up the best coffees in town. The bright, inviting space is also perfect for a snack, with tasty sandwiches (M$92 to M$122) and desserts on hand.

ℹ Getting There & Around

Buses from Guaymas run as far as Marina San Carlos; local rides within San Carlos cost M$17. Taxis charge M$50–200 in the San Carlos area.

Long-distance buses will drop you at either the **Grupo Estrella Blanca** (☑622-222-12-71, 800-507-55-00; www.estrellablanca.com.mx; Calle 14 No 96) or **Tufesa** (☑622-222-54-53; www.tufesa.com.mx; Blvd García López 927) terminals in Guaymas. From Grupo Estrella Blanca, walk north on Calle 14 to Blvd García López and catch the white San Carlos bus (M$17, every 30 minutes). From Tufesa, cross the road to catch the same bus. A taxi from either terminal to San Carlos is M$280.

Ferry services (p796) to and from Santa Rosalía in Baja California leave Guaymas three times a week, taking passengers and vehicles across in a 10-hour overnight trip.

Álamos

☑647 / POP 9800 / ELEV 432M

One of the most architecturally rich towns in northwest Mexico, Álamos is a cultural oasis. Sheltered in the forested foothills of the Sierra Madre Occidental, its hushed cobblestone streets and imposing colonial buildings hint at a fascinating history, much of it to do with Álamos' role as Mexico's northernmost silver-mining town. The town is both a national historical monument and one of Mexico's *pueblos mágicos* (magical villages).

Álamos' charms have proven irresistible to many US retirees and creative types who, since the '50s, have snapped up decaying colonial buildings to renovate into second homes and hotels. These well-heeled expats comprise a small but influential segment of Álamos' population, and their establishments dominate the colonial center of town.

History

The area's silver mines were discovered around La Aduana (10km west of Álamos) in the 16th century. Álamos itself was founded in the 1680s, probably as a dormitory suburb for La Aduana's wealthy colonists. Despite hostilities from the indigenous Yaqui and Mayo, Álamos boomed into one of Mexico's principal 18th-century mining centers.

During Mexico's 19th-century turmoils, Álamos was attacked repeatedly: by French invaders, by factions seeking its silver wealth and by the fiercely independent Yaqui. The Mexican Revolution took a further toll, and by the 1920s most mines were abandoned and Álamos was practically a ghost town.

Álamos

In 1948 Álamos was reawakened by William Levant Alcorn, a Pennsylvania dairy farmer who bought the Almada mansion on Plaza de Armas and converted it into Hotel Los Portales. Other *norteamericanos* followed, restoring crumbling mansions to their former glory. Recently they've been joined by wealthy Mexicans, seduced by the relaxed ambience and benign winter climate, creating something of a real estate boom, which is still visible in the multiple realtor signs you see around town today.

⊙ Sights

Álamos is ideal for sauntering around and soaking up one of Mexico's most idyllic colonial centers, with perhaps a break at one of its atmospheric restaurants.

★ **Parque La Colorada**   NATURE RESERVE
(☑ 647-428-16-00;   www.parquelacolorada.org;
Barrio el Chalatón; by donation; ⊙ sunrise-sunset)
Created by an eco-minded group of residents

back in 2014, this lush reserve encompasses some 112 hectares of pristine tropical deciduous forest. Well-marked trails wind through the reserve, including a 1.5km hike up to the top of El Tecolote, which offers views over the countryside.

To find the park, follow signs to El Pedregal. Trails begin near this lodge on the outskirts of Álamos.

El Mirador   VIEWPOINT
(Camino al Mirador s/n; P♿) This magnificent lookout tops a hill on Álamos' southeastern edge, affording sweeping views of the town and its mountainous surroundings. It's accessible by steps (370 of them) from the Arroyo Agua Escondida, two blocks down Obregón from Victoria, and is best climbed first thing in the morning or late in the afternoon, when the light is better and the heat not so fierce.

**Parroquia de la
Purísima Concepción**   CHURCH
(Plaza de Armas; ☉8am-noon & 3-7pm; ♿) FREE Álamos' parish church is the tallest building in town. It was built between 1786 and 1804 and its altar rail, lamps, censers and candelabra were all originally fashioned from silver, but were melted down in 1866 on the orders of General Ángel Martínez after he booted French troops out of Álamos. Seven or so subterranean passageways between the church and Álamos mansions – probably escape routes for rich families in times of attack – were blocked off in the 1950s.

Museo Costumbrista de Sonora   MUSEUM
(☑647-428-00-53; Plaza de Armas; M$10; ☉9am-6pm Wed-Sun) This well-done museum of Sonoran customs has extensive exhibits (all in Spanish) on the history and traditions of the state. Special attention is paid to the influence of mining on Álamos and the fleeting prosperity it created for the town's well-off, including rooms filled with antiques, period furniture and even a few vintage carriages.

⛭ Tours

Emiliano Graseda   TOURS
(☑647-101-48-75; Madero s/n; tours per person from M$300; ♿) English-speaking Emiliano Graseda offers fascinating, history-packed tours that take in Álamos' landmarks and private homes and gardens. Even more rewarding are his full-day tours (M$2000 per person) that visit an indigenous community (and have lunch with members of the com-

munity), an old mission and some spectacular countryside. Contact him via phone or Whatsapp.

Solipaso   ADVENTURE
(☑647-428-15-09, US 888-383-0062; www.solipaso.com; Privada s/n, Barrio el Chalatón; half-/full-day tours for 1-4 people US$90/170) Runs expert bird-watching trips to spot some of the 300 tropical bird species living around Álamos. Groups are small – one to four people – and guides are highly knowledgeable. There are no regular office hours; call directly to book. Located at El Pedregal lodge.

⭐ Festivals & Events

★**Festival Alfonso Ortíz Tirado**   MUSIC
(☑662-213-44-11; www.festivalortiztirado.gob.mx; ☉late Jan) One of northern Mexico's premier cultural events, Álamos' nine-day late-January festival features top-class classical and chamber music, blues, *bossa nova* and *trova* (troubadour-type folk music) performed by artists from across the globe. The festival's namesake, an Álamos native, was a revered opera singer and well-respected physician (Frida Kahlo was among his patients).

Tens of thousands of people descend upon the city during this festival – be sure to book your hotel well in advance.

🛏 Sleeping

Álamos has atmospheric and attractive accommodations, many in converted colonial mansions featuring gorgeous interior design. However, peso-watchers should be aware that budget options are limited.

Such is the summer heat that the cooler months (October to April) are high season in Álamos.

Hotel Dolisa   HOTEL $$
(☑647-428-01-31; www.facebook.com/HotelDolisa; Madero 72; d/tr/q M$800/850/900; P☺❅☎) Spacious, modern rooms with a colonial-era touch – think high ceilings, stenciled walls and even adobe *chimeneas* – make this a comfortable place to stay. Some have kitchenettes. All open onto breezy arched walkways. A huge parking lot (once used for RVs) makes it a good spot for those traveling with wheels. Located two and a half long blocks northwest of Plaza Alameda.

Hotel Luz del Sol   BOUTIQUE HOTEL $$
(☑647-428-04-66; www.luzdelsolalamos.com; Obregón 3; r incl breakfast M$1400-1600; ☺❅☎❄) Set in an updated colonial home, this small

hotel has a warm ambience thanks to welcoming staff and the presence of one of the town's best cafes. The three rooms open onto a central courtyard, each simply decorated but very spacious with sultan-sized beds, high ceilings and vast bathrooms with vintage tiling. A plunge pool is a plus.

Casa Serena Vista   B&B **$$$**
(☑647-110-65-80; www.facebook.com/casaseren avista; Loma de Guadalupe 9; r incl breakfast US$95; ✳🛜🛏) Perched above the central plaza, this homey 18th-century *casona* (mansion) has just three rooms. Each is decorated with touches that make you feel at home – a set of art books, a Persian rug, a flower-printed chair. There's an airy living room where guests gather, a well-tended pool, and a sweeping patio with a pond and enviable views of downtown Álamos.

★Hacienda de los Santos   LUXURY HOTEL **$$$**
(☑647-428-02-22; www.haciendadelossantos.com; Molina 8; r/ste incl breakfast from US$200/300; P🔄✳@🛜🛏) By far Álamos' most exclusive place to stay, this hacienda encompasses five restored colonial houses and a sugar mill, four pools, two restaurants, a movie theater, spa, gym and bar (with a 520-strong tequila collection). Accommodations are luxurious and highly atmospheric, while the sheer size of the place and its lush gardens is remarkable.

Rates plummet in the hot months; bilingual M$50 tours of the property are given most days at 2pm.

★Hotel Colonial   HOTEL **$$$**
(☑647-428-13-71; www.alamoshotelcolonial.com; Obregón 4; r/ste incl breakfast from M$2500/4800; P🔄✳🛜) The attention to detail at this historic mansion is highly impressive: it feels more like you are stepping into an Edwardian period drama than a Mexican hotel. The nine units mirror the sumptuous public areas, featuring tapestries, oil paintings, antiques and stately fireplaces. Also has a spectacular rooftop terrace.

★El Pedregal   LODGE **$$$**
(☑647-428-15-09, US 888-383-0062; www.el pedregalmexico.com; Privada s/n, Barrio el Chalatón; r incl breakfast M$2000-2500; P🔄✳@ 🛜🛏) 🍃 There are just eight lovely adobe and straw-bale cabins here, all with stylish artistic furnishings and luxury bedding scattered around 8 hectares of tropical deciduous forest on the edge of Álamos, 2km from the plaza. The welcoming owners are expert birders and lead tours. A good-sized pool,

3km of trails, a yoga studio and a massage parlor complete the scene.

✖ Eating & Drinking

Mexicanadas   MEXICAN **$**
(☑647-482-76-54; Rosales s/n; mains M$50-90; ☺7:30am-9pm Mon-Sat, to 3pm Sun; 🖉🔌) You'll be greeted by high ceilings, whirring fans and watercolor paintings of the local-turned-icon Maria Felix at this locals' favorite. The menu is mostly Mexican classics – quesadillas, enchiladas, *tostadas, chilaquiles* – with a few hamburger and sandwich options thrown in. Meals are big and cheap so expect a full house most days.

Restaurant Doña Lola   MEXICAN **$**
(Koky's; ☑647-428-11-09; Volantín s/n, off Juárez; mains M$75-150; ☺7am-10pm; 🛜🔌) This fan-cooled, family-run place is both simple and welcoming, with a covered terrace at the rear. The soups are crammed with ingredients and there's a huge menu of delicious *antojitos* (typical Mexican snacks – enchiladas, tacos, *chilaquiles* etc) and breakfasts as well. It can be found on a small side street south of the Plaza de Armas.

★Teresita's   BISTRO, BAKERY **$$**
(☑647-428-01-42; www.teresitasalamos.com; Allende 46B; mains M$120-300; ☺8am-9pm Mon-Sat, 9am-6pm Sun; 🛜🖉) It's quite amazing that somewhere as small and remote as Álamos boasts this simply outstanding bakcry–bistro. There's an open kitchen and a changing menu that features mouthwatering salads, roast meat dishes and delicious breakfasts, as well as offerings less usual in rural Mexico: fettuccine alfredo, gazpacho and creative veggie burgers topped with mozzarella and avocado.

Desserts are fully catered for with sublime cakes and pastries. Excellent breakfasts too. Either eat in the fountain-flanked garden or enjoy the comfort of a royal-blue banquette inside.

Charisma Restaurant   INTERNATIONAL **$$**
(☑647-428-09-68; www.facebook.com/pg/Charisma Restaurant; Obregón 2; mains M$180-450; ☺5-10pm Wed-Sat; 🖉) The menu changes often at this artful restaurant, but typically delivers big with traditional Mexican dishes as well as lamb, steak au poivre and truffled filet mignon, all served with flair. The setting is a colonial dining room with original art and twinkling lights. The bar is a popular hangout for expats. Located inside La Mansion hotel.

Café Luz del Sol
CAFE $$

(Café Luchy; ☑647-428-04-66; Obregón 3; mains M$120-230; ⊙7:30am-6:30pm; 🛜) In a region cruelly deprived of decent coffee shops, this colonial cafe is a better find for caffeine-starved travelers than any silver mine. Devour beautifully prepared breakfasts, Mexican and North American lunches, homemade cakes and good coffee. There's a cozy interior dining room hung with locally produced art, and a small patio replete with tropical flowers.

Patagonia
COFFEE

(☑647-428-17-65; Plaza de Armas, Guadalupe Victoria 5; ⊙9am-1pm & 5-9pm Mon & Tue, 9am-9pm Wed-Sun; 🖶) This little cafe offers a full range of coffee drinks, smoothies and healthy shakes. Grab a seat in its colonial courtyard or on the front terrace and watch the village stroll past.

❶ Information

The main **tourist office** (☑647-428-00-50; Madero s/n; ⊙8am-6pm) has helpful English-speaking staff and is located near the entrance to town.

Banorte (☑800-226-67-83; www.banorte.com; Madero 37; ⊙9am-4pm Mon-Fri) ATM; currency exchange.

Hospital General de Álamos (☑647-428-02-25; Madero s/n; ⊙8am-8pm) Basic local hospital with no emergency services.

❶ Getting There & Away

Álamos is 53km east of Navojoa and 156km north of Los Mochis. Álamos' **Transportes Baldomero Corral** (☑647-428-00-96; Morelos 7) bus terminal is serviced by **Albatros** (☑647-428-00-96; www.albatrosautobuses.com; cnr Guerrero & No Reelección, Navojoa) 2nd-class buses from Navojoa (M$40, one hour) between 6:30am to 8:30pm (late bus at 10pm).

From Álamos, Albatros provides service to Navojoa from 5:30am to 7:30pm (late bus at 9pm); Hermosillo (M$310, six hours) four times daily; and Puerto Peñasco (M$650, 12 hours) at 3am.

In Navojoa, both Albatros and **Tufesa** (☑642-421-34-10; www.tufesa.com.mx; cnr Hidalgo & No Reelección, Navojoa) have onward services to Hermosillo, Puerto Peñasco, Los Mochis, Mazatlán and Guaymas.

If you're coming by car from Los Mochis, stick to the longer paved road via Navojoa, as the shorter back road is unpaved and rather wild for much of the journey.

Los Mochis
☑668 / POP 281,000

There is nothing much to detain you in Los Mochis, a giant urban sprawl mainly notable for being the first or last stop on El Chepe (p770), and within an easy hop of ferries that link the mainland to Baja California. The climate here is perpetually humid and there are no real sights worth stopping for. However, if you're venturing to Baja by boat or to the Copper Canyon by train, you may well find yourself staying overnight, and in that case you'll actually find decent eating and sleeping options available, including some top-notch seafood.

◉ Sights

Jardín Botánico
Benjamin Francis Johnston
GARDENS

(Parque Sinaloa; ☑tours 668-818-18-14; www.jbbfj.org; Blvd Rosales 750; ⊙5am-8pm Mon-Fri, to 7pm Sat & Sun; 🖶🐾) FREE This verdant park occupies part of the former estate of Benjamin Johnston, the American who founded the sugar mill around which Los Mochis grew up in the early 20th century. Beyond an array of international trees and plants, there are running trails, a small duck-filled pond, a *mariposario* (butterfly pavilion; M$20) with live specimens flitting about, and the *plantario* (greenhouse; M$20).

★Trapiche
MUSEUM

(☑668-816-71-10; www.facebook.com/TrapicheLM; Blvd Castro 711; 🖶) This fabulous hands-on museum is a must if you're traveling with kids. There are areas and activities for all ages, including virtual reality games, giant bubble-making, TV and radio broadcasting, building block stations, funhouse mirrors and a tiny train that goes around the property. There's even a bed of nails you can lie on. Enthusiastic, English-speaking docents happily guide visitors through the museum.

⛏ Sleeping

Hotel Fénix
HOTEL $

(☑668-812-26-23; hotelfenix@email.com; Flores 365 Sur; s/d M$595/705; ℗❄🛜) This is the best moderately priced hotel in town, with welcoming staff, a sparkling lobby, an excellent restaurant and renovated rooms that represent good value. Accommodations can be on the small side, and some lack natural light, but as an overnight stop it's a great choice in the center.

⭐ **Fiesta Inn** HOTEL **$$$**
(☎668-500-02-00; www.fiestainn.com; Blvd Rosales 1435 Sur; r from M$1750; P❄✳@☞✈) Fiesta Inn is a contemporary hotel with a dash of style. Rooms are mid-century modern in design with simple lines and comfort in mind: thick mattresses, high-thread-count linens, rain-shower baths and lots of natural light. There's a cozy lounge, gym and pool.

🍴 **Eating**

La Cabaña de Doña Chayo TACOS **$**
(☎668-818-54-98; Obregón 99 Poniente; mains M$35-85; ☺8am-1am) A simple, quite popular place with a warm welcome and delectable quesadillas, burritos and tacos with

carne asada or *machaca* (spiced, shredded, dried beef).

El Pecado INTERNATIONAL **$$**
(☎668-828-28-08; www.facebook.com/elpecado cafe; Independencia 528; mains M$90-130; ☺5pm-1am; ☞✈) 🌿 Los Mochis' creative set flock to this art-filled space of hanging plants, exposed bulbs, black-and-white-tile floors and eclectic furnishings. A great place for *palomas* (grapefruit and tequila) and other cocktails, along with pizzas, wings, salads and burgers (including a veggie option).

Alma Mía CAFE **$$**
(☎668-812-75-76; www.facebook.com/almamia. coffeeshop; Guerrero 401 Sur; mains M$90-160; ☺7:30am-11pm Tue-Sun; ☞) You'll find tasty coffee drinks, friendly staff and good-value bistro fare at this sunlit cafe facing the main square. Tuck into big salads, pastas, panini

Los Mochis

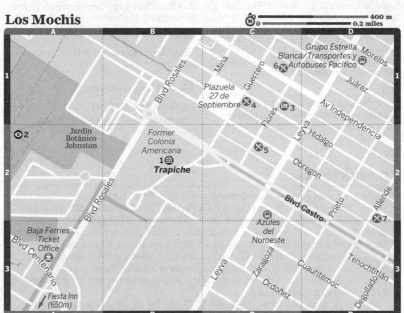

or sharing plates of ceviche – good breakfasts too.

★ El Farallón SEAFOOD $$$

(📞668-812-12-73; www.farallon.com.mx; Obregón 499 Poniente; mains around M$240; ⏰7am-11pm Sun-Thu, to midnight Fri & Sat; 🅿🛜) A handsomely designed, upmarket seafood restaurant with a delectable assortment of creative shrimp plates, seafood pastas and mouthwatering sushi. The ceviche (seafood marinated in lemon juice, garlic and seasonings) and *pescado a la plancha* (grilled fish) are particularly recommended.

❶ Getting There & Away

AIR

Aeropuerto Federal del Valle del Fuerte
(Los Mochis Airport; 📞668-818-68-70; www.aeropuertosgap.com.mx; Carretera Los Mochis–Topolobampo Km 12.5) is located 18km south of town. It has regular flights to Mexico City, Monterrey, Chihuahua, Tijuana, La Paz and Guadalajara with airlines including Aeroméxico Connect (www.aeromexico.com.mx), Aéreo Calafia (www.aereocalafia.com.mx), Viva (www.vivaaerobus.com) and Volaris (www.volaris.com).

BUS

Los Mochis lacks a central bus station, meaning that each bus company operates from its own depot in the city. Particularly useful lines are Grupo Estrella Blanca (GEB), Transportes y Autobuses Pacífico (TAP) and Tufesa.

Azules del Noroeste (📞668-812-34-91; Tenochtitlán 399 Poniente) Has 2nd-class buses to El Fuerte (M$80, 1½ hours, 5am to 8:15pm). Tickets are sold on the bus.

Grupo Estrella Blanca/Transportes y Autobuses Pacífico (GEB/TAP; 📞800-507-55-00; www.estrellablanca.com.mx; Pino Suárez 325) Deluxe and 1st-class buses to Mexico City, Guadalajara, Hermosillo and more.

Tufesa (📞668-818-22-22, 644-410-24-44; www.tufesa.com.mx; Blvd Rosales 2465) Offers 1st-class buses to Phoenix, Navojoa (for Álamos), Mazatlán and Guadalajara. The terminal is 3km northeast of the center of Los Mochis (M$50 in a taxi).

TRAIN

Los Mochis train station (📞800-122-43-73, 668-824-11-51, Chihuahua 614-439-72-11; www.chepe.com.mx; Bienestar s/n; ⏰5am-5:30pm Mon-Fri, 5-9am & 10:30am-1pm Sat & Sun) is 4km southeast of the town center at the end of Bienestar; a taxi from downtown is around M$60.

Buy Chepe Express (p770) tickets well in advance.

❶ Getting Around

TO/FROM THE AIRPORT
A cab to the airport costs around M$200.

FERRIES TO BAJA

Two ferry services link mainland northwest Mexico with Baja California.

From Topolobampo near Los Mochis, **Baja Ferries** (📞668-818-68-93, 800-337-7437; www.bajaferries.com.mx; Local 5, cnr Blvds Rosales & Centenario; ⏰10am-6pm Mon-Fri, 9am-3pm Sat) leaves at 11:59pm Monday to Friday and 11pm on Sunday to Pichilingue near La Paz in Baja; the trip takes around seven hours. On the return, the ferry leaves Pichilingue at 2:30pm Monday to Friday and 11pm on Saturday. If traveling around Semana Santa and Christmas–New Year and in June and July, reserve a month ahead. You can buy tickets in Los Mochis or, on departure day, at the Topolobampo terminal. Vehicles can also be transported on this route.

The **Ferry Santa Rosalía** (📞800-505-50-18, 622-222-02-04; www.ferrysantarosalia.com; Calz García López 1598 Bis, Guaymas; ⏰8am-2pm & 3:30-8pm Mon-Sat) sails from Guaymas for Santa Rosalía, Baja California, at 8pm Tuesday, Thursday and Saturday, arriving the next morning around 6am. All passengers and vehicles should be at the terminal by 6:30pm. From mid-November to mid-March, strong winds may cause delays, and Tuesday and Wednesday sailings are occasionally canceled in low season. The ferry departs from Santa Rosalía on Wednesday and Friday at 8:30am (arriving the same day around 6:30pm) and on Sunday at 8pm (arriving the following day at 6am). The ticket office is 2km east of Guaymas city center, though reservations are only necessary if you want a cabin or are taking a vehicle (three days in advance is sufficient).

BUSES FROM LOS MOCHIS

DESTINATION	FARE (M$)	TIME (HR)	FREQUENCY (PER DAY) & COMPANY
Guadalajara	1000-1250	13-15	16 TAP, 5 Tufesa
Guaymas	380-450	6	25 Tufesa
Hermosillo	550-650	6-7	12 GEB, 20 Tufesa
Mazatlán	250-400	6-7	frequent GEB/TAP, 11 Tufesa
Mexico City	1550-1900	23	7 GEB/TAP
Navojoa	223-291	2	12 GEB, 20 Tufesa
Phoenix	1850-2400	14-16	3 Tufesa

CHIHUAHUA & CENTRAL NORTH MEXICO

Off the tourist radar, and with an affable frontier feel, this region offers some of Mexico's most important historic sights across the colonial cities of Chihuahua and Durango. Further north is the sleepy village of Casas Grandes, gateway to the impressive ruins of Paquimé (p802), with the famed pottery settlement of Mata Ortiz (p803) nearby. The landscape itself is typified by the starkly beautiful Desierto Chihuahuense (Chihuahuan Desert), which covers most of Chihuahua, Mexico's largest state – and while it rises in the west into the fertile folds of the Sierra Madre Occidental, you'll be forgiven for thinking you've wandered into a B-grade western (Durango, incidentally, is where many famous westerns *were* filmed).

Tourism, unfortunately, has been ravaged by drug-gang violence, so don't venture off the beaten track without a guide. The 'Golden Triangle' – where Chihuahua, Durango and Sinaloa converge – is noted for its opium production and particularly high levels of violence. While there is some danger of being caught in the wrong place at the wrong time, tourists are not generally targeted.

Chihuahua

📞 614 / POP 879,000 / ELEV 1440M

Chihuahua, capital of Mexico's biggest state, is a quirky but pleasant combination of *norteño* character, revolutionary history and bohemian hangouts. Many travelers use it only as an overnight stop before or after riding the El Chepe (Ferrocarril Chihuahua Pacífico), but Chihuahua is worth more of your time. The city center combines grand colonial buildings, several beautiful plazas, pedestrianized lanes and a healthy crop of restaurants, cafes and bars. Its museums bear witness to the key episodes of Mexican history that unfolded here. In short, it's an intriguing city with a strong sense of identity.

History

Founded in 1709, Chihuahua soon became the key city of the Nueva España's Provincias Internas (stretching from California to Texas and Sinaloa to Coahuila). The Spanish brought pro-independence rebels, including Miguel Hidalgo, to be condemned and shot here in 1811. The Porfirio Díaz regime brought railways and helped consolidate the wealth of the area's huge cattle fiefdoms. Luis Terrazas, one-time Chihuahua state governor, held lands nearly the size of Belgium: 'I am not *from* Chihuahua, Chihuahua is mine', he once said.

After Pancho Villa's forces took Chihuahua in 1913 during the Mexican Revolution, Villa established his headquarters here, arranged various civic projects and soon acquired the status of local hero. Today the city has one of Mexico's highest living standards, with *maquiladora* jobs contributing significantly.

🅞 Sights

★ Casa Chihuahua   MUSEUM

(📞 614-429-33-00; www.casachihuahua.org.mx; Libertad 901; M$50; ⊙ 9am-6pm Wed-Mon; ♿) Chihuahua's former Palacio Federal (built 1908–10) has been used as a mint, a monastery, a military hospital and a post office, but is now a beautifully restored cultural center full of excellent exhibits, with most explanations in English and Spanish. Modern displays concentrate on the culture and history of Chihuahua state with features on Mormons, Mennonites and the Tarahumara people. The most famous gallery is the Calabozo de Hidalgo, the subterranean dungeon where Miguel Hidalgo was held prior to his execution.

The historic dungeon and the church towering above it were preserved within the later buildings erected on the site. A short audiovisual presentation (in Spanish) heightens the mournful atmosphere of the dungeon, which contains Hidalgo's bible and crucifix. A plaque outside recalls the verses the revolutionary priest wrote in charcoal on his cell wall in his final hours thanking his captors for their kindness.

Museo Casa Redonda
MUSEUM

(Museo Chihuahuense de Arte Contemporáneo; ☑ 614-414-90-61; www.facebook.com/museocasa redonda; Colón s/n; adult/child M$20/10, Sun free; ⊘ 10am-7pm Tue-Sun) Once a locomotive maintenance and repair shop, this renovated warehouse is home to the city's small but excellent modern art museum, with one room dedicated to the fascinating history of the building, including railroad gear and antiquities. The building itself was built curved to accommodate a huge turntable that allowed one mechanic to turn an entire railcar.

Museo Historico de la Revolución
MUSEUM

(Museo Casa de Villa; ☑ 614-416-29-58; mus_his trevol@mail.sedena.gob.mx; Calle 10 No 3010; adult/student M$10/5; ⊘ 9am-7pm Tue-Sat, 10am-4pm Sun; 🚌) Housed in Quinta Luz, Pancho Villa's 48-room former mansion, this museum is a must-see for anyone who appreciates a made-for-Hollywood story of crime, stakeouts and riches. The interior is loaded with Villa's personal effects and photographs, and in the back courtyard you'll find the bullet-riddled black Dodge that Villa was driving when he was murdered. Information is in Spanish and English.

Plaza de Armas
PLAZA

(Independencia 209; 🚌) Chihuahua's historic heart, with its mass of pigeons, shoe-shiners and cowboy-hatted characters, is a simple but pretty place. A bronze sculpture of the city's founder, Don Antonio de Deza y Ulloa, presides over the daily hubbub. The plaza also is home to the majestic baroque **cathedral** (☑ 614-416-84-10; Libertad 814; ⊘ 7am-8pm; 🚌), built between 1725 and 1826 and still containing the original organ installed in 1796.

Grutas de Nombre de Dios
CAVE

(☑ 614-432-05-18; Vialidad Sacramento s/n; adult/ child M$50/25; ⊘ 9am-3pm Tue-Fri, 10am-4pm Sat & Sun; 🚌) These caves on Chihuahua's northeast edge boast impressive stalagmites, stalactites and rock formations, making the one-hour, 17-chamber underground journey fun, espe-

cially for kids. Visitors enter with guides and typically in groups of 15 to 20 people. You can get here by taxi or ride share (around M$100). Chihuahua Bárbaro also leads group tours here (M$300 per person).

Palacio de Gobierno
HISTORIC BUILDING

(☑ 614-429-35-96; Aldama 901; ⊘ 8am-8pm Mon-Sat, 9am-7pm Sun) **FREE** The courtyard of this handsome, 19th-century, state-government building features striking 1960s murals by Aarón Piña Mora showing Chihuahua's highly eventful history.

Museo Sebastián
GALLERY

(☑ 614-200-48-00; Av Juárez 601; ⊘ 9am-7pm Mon-Sat, 11am-4pm Sun) **FREE** The main draws of this restored 1880s gallery are the small-scale models of the massive metal sculptures by renowned Chihuahuan artist Sebastián, whose work is recognized in cities worldwide. There are five real Sebastianes around Chihuahua, including one just above Parque El Palomar.

Quinta Gameros
HISTORIC BUILDING

(☑ 614-238-20-05; www.uach.mx; Paseo Bolívar 401; adult/child M$30/10; ⊘ 11am-7pm Tue-Sun) Built in an incredibly elaborate belle epoque architectural style by a wealthy mine owner, this museum is filled with a mix of period furnishings and art. Every room is unique, with quality stained glass and ornate carved wood and moldings. Upstairs, several rooms have temporary art exhibits. Definitely worth a look around, as it is one of Chihuahua's most unforgettable buildings.

👉 Tours

Chihuahua Bárbaro
TOURS

(☑ 614-425-00-06; www.chihuahuabarbaro.com; Victoria 419; ⊘ 9am-4pm Mon, to 8pm Tue-Sat, to 6pm Sun; 🚌) This trolleybus offers tours of Chihuahua's main historic sights (narrated in Spanish) and beyond. Its three-hour city tour (M$100) departs from in front of its ticket office, one block southwest of the cathedral three to six times daily, and includes the Pancho Villa museum and Quinta Gameros. Entrance fees not included.

Also offers full-day and overnight trips, with various itineraries that take in Paquimé (p802) archaeological site, historic missions, Mennonite farms and the adventure park (p777) in the Copper Canyon.

🛏 Sleeping

La Décima
GUESTHOUSE $

(☑ 614-496-07-61; Calle 10 No 1610; s/d M$282/315; ❄ 🛜) One of the best budget options in the

Chihuahua

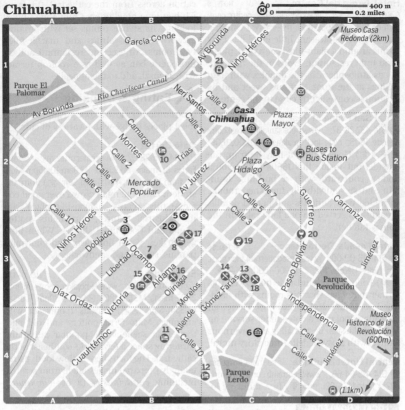

Chihuahua

center, the family-run La Décima has basic, simply furnished rooms with shared bathrooms. The friendly multilingual owner has helpful local recommendations, and you'll find good coffee and snacks at the attached cafe-bistro.

Hotel Jardín del Centro   HOTEL $
(☎614-415-18-32; www.hoteljardindelcentro.com; Victoria 818; d M$660-800; P❄@✿) Offering fine value, this pleasant little hotel has cozy rooms around a plant-filled courtyard, plus a good little restaurant. Twins in the back are not as atmospheric as the doubles with high ceilings at the front. Staff are sweet and its location is conveniently close to the center.

Hotel San Felipe El Real   GUESTHOUSE $$
(☎614-437-20-37; www.hotelsanfelipeelreal.com; Allende 1005; r/ste incl breakfast M$1300/1600; P❄✿✿) Unassuming it may be from the outside, but inside this 1880s house you'll find a courtyard with a burbling fountain and six individually furnished rooms, sprinkled with antiques and period details. Breakfast is served on one long table in the homey kitchen.

Hotel Posada Tierra Blanca   HOTEL $$
(☎614-415-00-00; www.posadatierrablanca.com.mx; Niños Héroes 102; r M$900-1500; P❄✿✿✿) Following a handsome makeover, this former motel has spacious rooms with hardwood floors and sleek furnishings. There's an appealing pool plus a dated diner serving up Mexican classics. Best of all is the cavernous lounge, with a psychedelic three-story mural.

Central Hotel Boutique   BOUTIQUE HOTEL $$$
(☎614-415-64-66; www.centralhb.com; Victoria 202; r from US$192; P✿✿) In a fantastic location across from the cathedral, this new-ish boutique hotel offers Chihuahua's finest lodging, its stylish rooms set with original artwork, luxury fabrics and marble-filled bathrooms. An excellent restaurant and atmospheric bar, as well as a rooftop terrace with Jacuzzi, add to the appeal.

✗ Eating & Drinking

Chihuahuenses love a good steak. You'll find most places oblige with a variety of cuts.

Café Cortez   CAFE $
(☎614-415-38-07; www.cafecortez.mx; Gómez Farías 8; mains M$55-80; ⊙9am-10:45pm Mon-Fri, from 10am Sat, 4-10:45pm Sun; ✿) Join the student and bohemian crowd over good coffee at this creative, hangar-like place with its industrial fixtures, fairy lights, potted plants and book-lined shelves. When hunger strikes, you'll find tasty and enormous paninis, salads and sandwiches.

El Hojaldre   MEXICAN $$
(☎614-413-43-29; www.el-hojaldre.com; Allende 200; mains M$120-180; ⊙9am-9:30pm Tue-Sat, to 3pm Sun; ✿✎) Various rooms set with antiques, Mata Ortiz pottery and old photos set the scene at this popular eating and gathering space a few blocks southeast of the cathedral. The focus here is slow food: painstakingly prepared dishes made from scratch, including *cuadripastes* (a big *empanada*

LOCAL KNOWLEDGE

SOTOL: THE DESERT SPIRIT OF CHIHUAHUA

Tequila's wild northern sibling is sotol, a fiery liquor (45% to 50% alcohol content) named after the bristly desert plant from which it is made. The spirit was popular during Prohibition in the US, but its boom days came to an end by the mid-20th century as the thirst for domestic beers and foreign liquors nearly put an end to the industry. Previously considered little more than moonshine, sotol is enjoying a renaissance spurred by a wave of young new distillers introducing artisanal brands while still remaining deeply rooted in Chihuahua's northern traditions.

One of the best places to explore the rich variety of this *chihuahuense* spirit is at the hipster-cowboy bar **La Sotoleria** (www.facebook.com/LaSotoleria; Morelos 801; ⊙1pm-2am) a few blocks from Chihuahua's Plaza de Armas. The menu has dozens of high-quality sotols, including classic varieties like *añejo* (aged), *reposado* (aged in oak) or *blanco* (pure, without any oak aging). There are fruit infusions – *piña* (pineapple), *coco* (coconut), *naranja* (orange) – and the dessert-like *crema de sotol*, which is not unlike Bailey's Irish Cream.

More adventurous drinkers should check out the offerings by the Oro de Coyome label: the *elixir* is made of 27 medicinal herbs and plants, including marijuana and peyote. Coyome's *curado de víbora*, on the other hand, is made with rattlesnake venom – check out the oversized bottle with the reptile curled inside.

For nonvenom drinkers, La Sotoleria also has craft beer and excellent food, like sirloin tacos marinated with sotol. There's live music on weekends.

filled with delicacies), creatively topped pizzas, oven-baked fish and veg-friendly portobello with goat cheese.

The cooking is slow, so help yourself to those board games and order a few drinks while you wait.

La Casa de los Milagros MEXICAN $$
(☎ 614-261-55-04; Victoria 812; mains M$150-295; ☺noon-midnight Sun & Tue-Thu, to 2am Fri & Sat; ☎) Legend has it that Pancho Villa and his pals hung out in this atmospheric 110-year-old mansion featuring tiled floors, lots of snug little rooms and an airy covered courtyard. The menu features steaks and classic Mexican dishes, and there's live music Wednesday to Saturday (from 9pm).

Taller del Chef BISTRO $$
(☎ 614-410-20-84; www.facebook.com/pg/taller delchefcuu; Independencia 1414; mains M$100-170; ☺1-9:30pm Mon-Sat, from 2pm Sun; ☎) A stylish Asian-fusion bistro restaurant, this downtown eatery serves up delicious ramen bowls overflowing with noodles, veggies and proteins. If soup isn't your thing, you'll also find salads, Asian-style stir-fries and upscale pub fare (loaded burgers, chicken wings, nachos).

Mesón de Catedral INTERNATIONAL $$$
(☎ 614-410-15-50; www.facebook.com/MesonDe Catedral; Plaza de Armas; mains M$180-290; ☺8am-midnight Mon-Wed, to 2am Thu-Sat, to 10pm Sun; ☎) Go to the 2nd floor of this modern building to find one of the best vistas in Chihuahua. With a terrace overlooking the city's cathedral, this casual place is worth spending a little extra on: try the fish fillet stuffed with shrimp and *chipotle* salsa, thick tuna steaks or a juicy T-bone.

Get there via the stairs or elevator on narrow Calle Segunda.

★La Casona MEXICAN $$$
(☎ 614-410-00-43; www.casonamx.com; cnr Aldama & Av Ocampo; mains M$290-450, steaks M$550-1100; ☺8am-11pm Mon-Sat, 1-5pm Sun; ☎) One of Chihuahua's best dining spots is set in an elaborate 19th-century mansion where well-dressed waiters serve up famed steaks and rich seafood dishes as well as delicious appetizers (try the melted Mennonite cheese with mushrooms) alongside an ample wine list. Booking is recommended.

Momposina BAR
(☎ 614-410-09-75; Coronado 508; ☺4pm-1am Tue-Sat; ☎) A brilliantly eclectic space where creative types gather during the day to lounge on mismatched seats, snack on paninis and sip espressos. Later on it morphs into a bar, and on Friday to Saturday evenings there's live music (from 9pm). Beers are inexpensive and the vibe is chilled.

🛍 Shopping

The strong cowboy culture here means there are plenty of hats, boots and belts for budding *vaqueros* (cowboys) on the prowl. Cowboy-boot shoppers should make a beeline to Libertad between Independencia and Avenida Ocampo, where boot shops line the street.

Casa de las Artesanías del Estado de Chihuahua ARTS & CRAFTS
(☎614-437-12-92; Niños Héroes 1101; ☺9am-7pm Mon-Fri, 10am-5pm Sat) Has a good selection of *chihuahuense* crafts (including Mata Ortiz pottery) and Mexican foodstuffs such as pecans, oregano oil and sotol, a local spirit made from desert spoon plants.

ℹ Information

Clínica del Centro (☎ 614-439-81-00; www.clinicadelcentro.com.mx; Ojinaga 816; ☺24hr) Has a 24-hour emergency department.

Post Office (Correos de México; ☎ 800-701-70-00; Libertad 1700; ☺9am-5pm Mon-Fri, 10am-2pm Sat)

State Tourist Office (☎614-410-10-77, 800-508-01-11; www.chihuahuamexico.com; Aldama 901, Palacio de Gobierno; ☺9am-8pm Mon-Sat) Delivers hit-or-miss service though there are plenty of maps and brochures.

ℹ Getting There & Away

AIR

Located 15km northeast of town, Chihuahua's airport has regular flights to Monterrey, Mexico City, Guadalajara and Tijuana as well as Dallas and Houston. It's serviced by **Aeroméxico** (☎614-201-96-96; www.aeromexico.com; Ortiz Mena 2807; ☺9am-7pm Mon-Fri, 9am-2pm Sat), **Interjet** (☎614-446-82-35; www.interjet.com. mx; ☺5:30am-9pm Mon-Fri, to 1:30pm Sat, 7-11am & 2-6:30pm Sun), Viva Aerobus (www. vivaaerobus.com) and Volaris (www.volaris.com).

BUS

Chihuahua's busy main **bus station** (☎614-420-53-98; Blvd Juan Pablo II No 4107) is 7km east of the center.

Los Paisanos (☎614-418-73-68, US 214-946-7777; www.lospaisanosautobuses.com; cnr Calle 78 & Degollado) offers 1st-class bus service to several US cities, including Dallas (US$69), Los Angeles ($69) and Las Vegas (US$74).

COPPER CANYON & NORTHERN MEXICO NUEVO CASAS GRANDES & CASAS GRANDES

BUSES FROM CHIHUAHUA

DESTINATION	FARE (M$)	TIME (HR)	FREQUENCY (PER DAY)
Ciudad Juárez	740	5-6	hourly
Durango	1065	10-13	10
Guadalajara	1750	16-20	4
Monterrey	1120	12	8
Nuevo Casas Grandes	500	4½-5	hourly
Parral	430	3	hourly
Saltillo	790	10	7
Zacatecas	1400	12	6

For Creel (M$260 to M$330, five hours) there are regular departures from both **Rápidos Cuauhtémoc** (☑ 614-416-48-40; Blvd Juan Pablo II No 4107) and **Autotransportes Noroeste** (☑ 614-411-57-83; www.turisticosnoroeste.com; Blvd Juan Pablo II No 4107). These companies also offer onward service from Creel to Bahuichivo (M$120, three hours), stopping in the Copper Canyon hot spots of Divisadero (M$60, one hour) and Areponápuchi (M$60, 1¼ hours) along the way.

TRAIN

Chihuahua is the northeastern terminus for the Ferrocarril Chihuahua Pacífico (p770), with departures at 6am on Monday, Thursday and Saturday. The **station** (☑ 614-439-72-12, 800-122-43-47; www.chepe.com.mx; Méndez 2205; ⊙ 5am-5:30pm Mon-Fri, 9am-12:30pm Sat) is 1.5km south of Plaza de Armas; there are no amenities – just a ticket office. You can nearly always buy tickets on the day of travel, just be sure to arrive at least one hour before departure.

❶ Getting Around

To get to the main bus station, catch a **'Circunvalación Sur'** (Av Carranza s/n) bus (M$10, 30 to 50 minutes) heading northwest on Carranza, almost opposite Plaza Hidalgo.

From the center, there are taxis to the train station (M$60), bus station (M$100) and airport (M$250). Airport taxis back to town cost around M$300.

Nuevo Casas Grandes & Casas Grandes

☑ 636 / POP 62,100 / ELEV 1457M

Nuevo Casas Grandes, 345km northwest of Chihuahua, is a prosperous but unremarkable country town, with small communities of Mormon and Mennonite settlers. Tourism-wise it's a transportation hub for those heading to the prettier village of Casas Grandes by the pre-Hispanic ruins of Paquimé (7km south) and the pottery center of Mata Ortiz (27km south).

◉ Sights

★Paquimé   ARCHAEOLOGICAL SITE
(☑ 636-692-41-40; zapaquime.museo@gmail.com; Allende s/n, Casas Grandes; adult/child under 13yr M$75/free; ⊙ 9am-5pm Tue-Sun) These ruins, in a broad valley with panoramas to distant mountains, contain the mazelike adobe remnants of northern Mexico's most important trading settlement. Paquimé was the center of the Mogollón or Casas Grandes culture, which extended north into New Mexico and Arizona and over most of Chihuahua. The site's impressive, meticulously detailed **Museo de las Culturas del Norte** has displays about Paquimé and the linked indigenous cultures of northern Mexico and the southwest USA.

The site was sacked, perhaps by Apaches, around 1340. Excavation and restoration began in the 1950s; Unesco declared it a World Heritage site in 1998. Plaques, in Spanish and English, discuss Paquimé culture while giving fascinating details on sites like the ceremonial ball court, pit ovens used to make mezcal for important festivals, the dwelling of a *curandero* (healer) and rituals performed using birds that were bred in the plaza, and a house of skulls with a mobile of skulls hanging from the ceiling of an upper floor. There was also an elaborate canal system that brought water to the community from a spring located 5km to the north.

The Paquimé people were great potters and produced striking cream-colored earthenware with red, brown or black geometric designs; some amazing original examples are on display in the museum, and modern reproductions are for sale.

🛏 Sleeping & Eating

★ Las Guacamayas B&B
B&B $$

(☑636-699-09-97; www.mataortizollas.com; Av 20 de Noviembre, Casas Grandes; s/d incl breakfast US$50/70; P😊❄🛜) 🅿 This adobe-walled place has charming rooms with beamed roofs, all built using recycled materials, and a lovely garden area. Owner Mayte Lujan has a world-class collection of Mata Ortiz pottery and is extremely knowledgeable about the region. It is located just a stone's throw from the entrance to the ruins of Paquimé.

Pueblo del Soul
B&B $$

(☑636-692-82-25; www.mihotelcasasgrandes.com.mx; 901 Juan Escutia, Casas Grandes; s/d incl breakfast M$1000/1200; P❄🛜) In an adobe-style building, this welcoming place has a row of spacious rooms set with thick wood furniture, stone fireplaces, quality mattresses and soft fluffy towels. From the walled seating area in front of each dwelling you can see the ruins framed against the fields and mountains beyond. The friendly English-speaking owner and staff have helpful advice on DIY activities in the region.

It's about a 12-minute walk west of Paquimé.

Casa del Nopal
GUESTHOUSE $$

(☑636-103-60-04; www.agavelindotours.com/casa-del-nopal; Independencia 81, Casas Grandes; r from M$850) One block south of the plaza central, several beautifully restored, century-old adobe houses have been converted into a charming guesthouse. Each of seven rooms is adorned with antiques and original artworks, and friendly English-speaking staff have excellent tips on the area. There's also a recommended **restaurant** (Independencia 81; mains around M$90; ⊘8:30am-3pm Tue-Sun) serving

COPPER CANYON & NORTHERN MEXICO NUEVO CASAS GRANDES & CASAS GRANDES

WORTH A TRIP

THE MASTERPIECES OF MATA ORTIZ

Mata Ortiz, 27km south of Casas Grandes, is a tiny town of dusty, unpaved roads, loose chickens and unfinished adobe houses. It's also home to one of Mexico's most renowned pottery traditions. Artists here use materials, techniques and decorative styles inspired by those of the ancient Paquimé culture, and their best pieces of work now sell in major galleries in the US for large sums (though you can pick up a nice small piece for M$400).

Today dozens of artists create from their home studios in Mata Ortiz, and the range of work is truly staggering. None of this though would exist without the inspiration of one man: Juan Quezada. As a young boy, Quezada discovered ancient pots in a cave hidden in the hills near his home. Through trial and error, he began making pieces using materials he found in the style of Paquimé pieces. Improbably, and despite having no formal training – and no kiln or potter's wheel – Quezada was soon creating masterpieces. His talent, however, remained largely unknown to the world.

Enter Spencer MacCallum, an American anthropologist, who in 1976 stumbled upon several of Quezada's vases in a secondhand store in New Mexico. After some sleuth work (namely driving around northern Mexico, showing photos of the pottery in hopes of finding clues), he tracked the pieces to the remote village of Mata Ortiz and discovered Juan Quezada. Over the following years, he helped introduce the artist's work to galleries in the US, creating a demand that helped transform Mata Ortiz into an artistic epicenter. Aside from producing his own art, Quezada began training a whole generation of young artists, who have since added their own unique style to the genre.

Across from the old train station, the **Galería Quezada** (☑636-661-70-32; Calle Ferrocarril 52; ⊘9am-8pm) sells works by the legendary octogenarian as well as pieces by dozens of other artists. It's easy to spot: look for the massive mural (painted by Arturo Damasco in 2018) depicting Quezada on the wall out front.

Another fine gallery is the home of **Héctor y Laura** (☑636-661-70-08; www.hectorylauramataortizpottery.com). Here you'll find jaw-dropping works created by this husband-and-wife team, plus pieces by their daughter and extended family. Prices range from US$30 to US$250. To get here, take the first left when arriving in the village; it's on the left another 300m along.

Mata Ortiz has no bus service. A taxi from Nuevo Casas Grandes, including a one-hour wait, costs about M$600. You can also book a tour here with **Agave Lindo** (☑636-692-82-67, 636-103-60-04; www.agavelindotours.com; Independencia 81).

traditional fare, and a shop that sells Mata Ortiz pottery, embroidered clothing and jewelry.

Based at Casa del Nopal, Agave Lindo (p803) offers insightful tours of the ruins of Paquimé, the pottery studios of Mata Ortiz, the petroglyphs of Cueva de la Olla and even the Copper Canyon.

El Jinete
MEXICAN $$
(☑ 636-692-43-43; Juárez 100, Casas Grandes; mains M$110-270; ☺ 12:30-10pm Tue-Sat, to 8pm Sun; ☏) Dining options are limited in Casas Grandes, but you can eat well at El Jinete, a traditional eatery serving up nicely prepared enchiladas, sizzling fajitas and grilled steaks as well as a few seafood dishes. All goes nicely with a bottle of Minerva craft beer.

It's on the main paved road in town, about six blocks west of the parque central.

ⓘ Information

Tourist Information Office (☑ ext 110 636-692-43-13; Palacio Municipal, Constitución s/n, Casas Grandes; ☺ 9am-3pm) Staff in this small office can advise on the area's attractions.

ⓘ Getting There & Away

In Nuevo Casas Grandes, **Ómnibus de México** (☑ 636-694-05-02; www.odm.com.mx; Obregón 312, Nuevo Casas Grandes) and **Estrella Blanca/Chihuahuenses** (☑ 636-694-07-80, 800-507-5500; www.estrellablanca.com.mx; Obregón 308, Nuevo Casas Grandes) offer 1st-class buses to Chihuahua (M$400 to M$490, 4½ hours, eight daily), the border at Nogales (M$690 to M$820, seven hours, six daily) and Ciudad Juárez (M$330 to M$380, four hours, six daily).

To get to Paquimé from Nuevo Casas Grandes, 'Casas Grandes' buses (M$10, 20 minutes, 8:30am to 7:30pm Monday to Saturday, to 4:30pm Sunday) depart every hour, northbound from Constitución, just north of Calle 16 de Septiembre. Get off in Casas Grandes' plaza and walk 800m south on Constitución to the ruins. A taxi from Nuevo Casas Grandes to Paquimé is around M$120.

Durango

☑ 618 / POP 655,000 / ELEV 1880M

Durango, capital of the eponymous desert state, is an immensely likable place, with an attractive, beautifully kept and laid-back city center and a friendly local populace. It is also one of Mexico's most isolated cities: you have to travel hours through the desert or the Sierra Madre mountains from here before you hit another significant settlement.

Yet isolation has fostered unique regional traits, such as the distinctive local cuisine and wry humor.

Founded in 1563, Durango's early importance was due to nearby iron-ore deposits, along with gold and silver from the Sierra Madre. Today hundreds of *maquiladoras* dominate the economy. For visitors, the city's striking colonial center commands attention, with over 70 historic buildings and several fascinating museums, while good accommodations and restaurants are plentiful.

Note: Durango state's time zone is one hour ahead of Chihuahua and Sinaloa.

⊙ Sights & Activities

Constitución, pedestrianized between Jardín Hidalgo past the Plaza de Armas to Plazuela Baca Ortiz, is among Mexico's most appealing traffic-free streets, lined with restaurants and cafes and lively day and night.

★ Museo Francisco Villa
MUSEUM
(☑ 618-811-47-93; 5 de Febrero s/n; adult/child M$20/10; ☺ 10am-6pm Tue-Fri, 11am-6pm Sat & Sun; ☕) Housed in a spectacular colonial mansion, this well-conceived museum pays deep homage to the Mexican revolutionary hero Pancho Villa. Sixteen rooms' worth of multimedia displays, films and personal effects tell the story of Durango's most famous native son. Be sure to leave some time to check out the gorgeous murals, which depict the history of the country and state. Signage is mostly in Spanish.

★ Museo de la Ciudad 450
MUSEUM
(☑ 618-137-84-90; cnr Av 20 de Noviembre & Victoria; M$26; ☺ 10am-5:30pm Tue-Sun; ☕) This impressive city museum features an interesting collection of interactive exhibits, from pre-Hispanic times through colonization to the present day, and deals with Durango's economy, mining, traditions and culture. The museum has an entire section dedicated to the film industry, highlighting the more than 130 films that have been made in and near the city, including *The Wild Bunch* (1968), *Zorro* (1997) and *Texas Rising* (2014). Don't miss the *alacraneo*, a blacklight-lit tank filled with scorpions.

Paseo del Viejo Oeste
FILM LOCATION
(☑ 618-113-12-92; www.facebook.com/paseodelviejooestedgo; Hwy 45 Km 12; M$50; ☺ 11am-7pm Tue-Sun; ☕) Many of the big-screen cowboys have swaggered through this film set. Today the set is a souvenir-drenched theme park

Durango

Durango

◎ **Top Sights**

◎ **Sights**

✈ **Activities, Courses & Tours**

🛏 **Sleeping**

✖ **Eating**

🍸 **Drinking & Nightlife**

with mock film productions on weekends (1:30pm, 3:30pm and 5:30pm Saturday and Sunday). It's located 12km north of town; a free shuttle bus leaves for here from the Plaza de Armas 30 minutes before each show and returns two hours later (though visitors are welcome to stay longer). Great fun for families.

Horseback riding and wagon rides are available too.

DON'T MISS

HIGHEST BRIDGE IN THE AMERICAS

Soaring an incredible 402m above the Río Baluarte, the **Puente Baluarte** (Autopista Durango-Mazatlán) is an incredible feat of engineering and the highest bridge in the Americas. It's one of many incredible bridges on the Durango–Mazatlán Hwy, a magnificent toll road that boasts some of Mexico's most incredible scenery, with epic tunnels through mountains, hairpin bends and jaw-dropping views all the way. If you only drive one road in Mexico, make it this one.

Plaza de Armas — PLAZA

Flower- and fountain-filled Plaza de Armas is graced by the handsome baroque **Catedral del Basílica Menor** (✏ 618-811-42-42; Plaza de Armas; ⊗ 8am-9pm). A popular meeting spot, there's a bandstand, shade trees and loads of benches. In the late afternoon and evening, vendors do brisk business in everything from corn on the cob to crepes.

The entrance to the **Túnel de Minería** (Tunnel of Mining; ✏ 618-137-53-61; Juárez 313; M$30; ⊗ 10am-9:30pm Tue-Sun), a museum devoted to the history of mining in Durango, is located on the east side of the plaza. This transforms into an evening-only, haunted-house-style 'Túnel del Terror' (M$50) from October to early November.

Museo de Arqueología de Durango Ganot-Peschard — MUSEUM

(✏ 618-813-10-47; Zaragoza 315 Sur; adult/child M$10/5; ⊗ 9am-6pm Tue-Fri, 11am-6pm Sat & Sun) This small, somewhat dated museum has fascinating displays and a collection of artifacts from the different indigenous peoples who've lived in the region since the Paleolithic era. Particularly impressive (and a little eerie) is an exhibit of deformed skulls and funerary items of the Aztlán tribe. Kids may enjoy the re-creation of an archaeological dig, complete with dim lighting, skeletons and pottery.

Museo Palacio de los Gurza — MUSEUM

(✏ 618-811-17-20; Negrete 901 Poniente; adult/child M$10/5; ⊗ 10am-6pm Tue-Fri, from 11am Sat & Sun) This small museum, housed in a gorgeous 18th-century home, has rotating exhibits of modern art by up-and-coming Mexican artists; pieces often have politicized messages about Mexico or its neighbor to the north. Oddly, there's also a permanent exhibit showcasing a collection of old Mexican coins and antique money-making machines.

Museo Regional de Durango — MUSEUM

(El Aguacate; ✏ 618-813-10-94; www.museo.ujed. mx; Victoria 100 Sur; adult/child M$10/5; ⊗ 8am-3pm Mon, 8am-6pm Tue-Fri, 11am-6pm Sat & Sun; 🏿) In a palatial French-style, 19th-century mansion, this museum has thorough displays on Durango state's geology, history and culture. Durango's main indigenous population, the Tepehuano people, and the area's impressive array of minerals get special attention; there also are paintings by Miguel Cabrera. Most explanations are in English and Spanish.

Paseo Teleférico — CABLE CAR

(Av Florida 1145; one way/return M$15/30; ⊗ 10am-9pm Tue-Sun; 🏿) This gondola takes visitors from a small hill in the center of Durango, Cerro del Calvario, to a viewpoint just 680m away, Cerro de los Remedios. A simple ride, it's all about the journey as the views from the air far outshine those at the destination. An easy, cheap outing.

🎉 Festivals & Events

Feria Nacional — FAIR

(✏ 618-137-78-76; Hwy 23 Km 3.5; from M$20; ⊗ July; 🏿) For three weeks in July, Durango's big annual party remembers its agricultural roots with *charreada*s (Mexican rodeos) plus a *duranguense* music and culture fest. Amusement-park rides and food vendors round out the festivities. Free transportation is typically offered to the fairgrounds, which are 9km from the center; check the website for pickup/drop-off spots.

🛏 Sleeping

★ **La Casa de Bruno** — HOSTEL $

(✏ 618-811-55-55; Martínez 508; d/tr M$600/750, dm/s/d with shared bathroom M$240/410/480, apt M$800; 🅿 ❄ ☎) An artsy, welcoming place, this downtown hostel has two dorms, all with tall bunks that have thick mattresses, cozy bedding and privacy curtains. Three small private rooms are set apart from the dorms, but follow suit in comfort. There's a rooftop terrace and common kitchen, with coffee and pastries offered each morning. A great place to meet other travelers.

There's also a chalet-style apartment available with a full kitchen.

Posada de María
BOUTIQUE HOTEL $$$

(☑618-189-49-18; www.facebook.com/pg/posada demariaDGO; 5 de Febrero 922; r/ste incl breakfast from M$2500/3000; P✳🛜❄) Located in the heart of downtown Durango, each room in this renovated colonial *casona* is modern and plush with Victorian-era-meets-Mexico flair (think Tiffany lamps and Oaxacan fabrics). There are loads of inviting lounge areas, including a lap pool and a rooftop with enviable views. Added bonuses include a restaurant, cafe, massage room, exercise center and private open-air Jacuzzi (reservable for guests).

Hostal de la Monja
HOTEL $$$

(☑618-837-17-19; www.hostaldelamonja.com.mx; Constitución 214 Sur; r/ste incl breakfast M$1700/2000; P😊✳🛜) This 19th-century mansion facing the cathedral has been tastefully converted into an atmospheric, 20-room hotel and is one of the best addresses in central Durango. The comfortable rooms manage to combine tradition and modern amenities well and there's a good restaurant too. Request a room at the back if you're noise sensitive, however, as sound from the restaurant carries.

Wi-fi is hit and miss in the lobby and almost nonexistent in the rooms.

✗ Eating & Drinking

Specialties in Durango include *caldillo duranguense* (Durango stew), made with *machaca*, and *ate* (pronounced 'ah-tay' – a quince paste enjoyed with cheese).

La Cosecha
VEGETARIAN $

(☑618-827-52-77; Martínez 250; mains M$50-80; 😊10am-10pm Wed-Mon; 🛜🍴) Big windows, rustic wood tables and upbeat grooves set the scene for Durango's best vegetarian eatery. Standouts include grilled ciabatta sandwiches, veggie-loaded salads with Thai-style peanut sauce, and filling Buddha bowls with mushrooms, squash and sriracha sauce.

La Tetera Bistro Cafe
CRÊPES $

(☑618-195-53-78; Callejon Florida 1135; mains M$65-100; 😊8am-10pm Sun-Thu, to 11pm Fri-Sat; 🛜) Strung with fairy lights, this cool-cat cafe specializes in crepes, which go nicely with the teas, coffee drinks and smoothies. Seating is open-air, at wood tables or any number of couches; plants and boho art fill the space.

Located on a pedestrian side street, just up an outdoor set of stairs.

Gorditas Durango
MEXICAN $

(☑618-164-44-98; Plaza IV Centenario, cnr Pino Suárez & Zaragoza; gordita M$15-20; 😊8am-4:20pm; 🚼) For good cheap eats, pop into this locals' eatery specializing in *gorditas* (a small, thick tortilla stuffed with your choice of fillings) – two or three are enough to make a hefty meal. Fillings range from *bistek* (steak) and *chicharrón* (fried pork belly) to *nopales* and *mole* (chicken in a spicy chocolate sauce). Burritos also offered.

★ Cremería Wallander
DELI $$

(☑618-811-77-05; www.wallander.com.mx; Independencia 128 Norte; mains M$95-150; 😊8am-9pm Mon-Sat, 9am-4pm Sun; ✳🛜🍴🚼) This delightful deli sells the artisanal products of the Wallander family farm as well as regional delicacies, fresh bread, preserves and pastries. Outside in the back courtyard you can enjoy healthy breakfasts, mega *tortas* (sandwiches) and creative salads.

★ Fonda de la Tía Chona
MEXICAN $$

(☑618-811-77-48; www.facebook.com/FondaTia Chona; Nogal 110; mains M$110-270; 😊5-11pm Tue-Sat, 1-5pm Sun) A Durango institution, this richly atmospheric, venerable place is dedicated to local cuisine such as *caldillos* (beef stews) and delicious *chiles en nogadas* (peppers in walnut sauce drizzled with pomegranate seeds).

Mendoza Restaurante Antiguo
MEXICAN $$

(☑618-811-56-43; www.facebook.com/pg/Mendoza RestauranteAntiguo; Hidalgo 317; mains M$85-235; 😊8:30am-5pm Sun-Wed, to 11pm Thu-Sat) *Antiques Roadshow* meets colonial Mexico in this quirky restaurant. Here, *birria* (goat stew, typical of Jalisco) gets *duranguense* twists by incorporating *guajillo* and *pasilla* chilies or substituting lamb chops and ribs. Tables themselves are set in a colonial building decorated with loads of antiques like old radios, vintage toys and grandfather clocks. A memorable stop for your belly and eyes.

★ Cafenoteca
CAFE

(☑618-204-02-25; www.facebook.com/cafenoteca; cnr Hidalgo & 5 de Febrero; 😊8am-10pm Mon-Fri, 10am-6pm Sat&Sun; 🛜) Attached to the Posada de María, this is the go-to destination for Durango's best coffee. Friendly English-speaking baristas can prepare your high-quality roasts however you prefer (Chemex, syphon, Aero-Press), or whip up an elegant cappuccino; and the setting invites lingering. Wines are also available, though only by the bottle (from M$240 to M$1650).

BUSES FROM DURANGO

DESTINATION	FARE (M$)	TIME (HR)	FREQUENCY (PER DAY)
Chihuahua	920-1070	9-11½	7
Los Mochis	1090-1300	9-12	5
Mazatlán	600-700	3-4	16
Mexico City (Terminal Norte)	1400-1600	10½-13	4
Monterrey (via Saltillo)	750-950	8-9	12
Parral	500-700	5	5
Zacatecas	370-540	4	hourly

Cervecería Durango BAR
(✆ 618-825-23-76; Av Francisco Sarabia 1005; ⏱ 4pm-2am) Although *cervecería* (brewery) is a bit of a misnomer at a place with just one craft beer on offer (the decent Mexicali-brewed Cucapá), this three-story bar makes a lively spot for an evening drink – and it tends to draw a more sophisticated crowd than the drinking dens on Constitución. Go early to score a table on the top-floor terrace.

ℹ Information

Durango State Tourist Office (✆ 618-137-43-86; http://visitdurango.mx; Florida 1106; ⏱ 9am-8pm Mon-Fri, 10am-6pm Sat & Sun) has friendly and enthusiastic staff and lots of brochures. The city also has a **kiosk** (✆ 618-137-84-30; www.durangotravel.mx; Plaza de Armas; ⏱ 9am-8pm Tue-Sun) on the Plaza de Armas, inside the bandstand.

Hospital General (✆ 618-813-00-11; cnr Av 5 de Febrero & Fuentes; ⏱ 24hr) For emergencies or walk-in medical care.

Post Office (Av 20 de Noviembre 1016 Oriente; ⏱ 8am-4pm Mon-Fri, 9am-1pm Sat) Durango's main post office.

ℹ Getting There & Away

Aeropuerto Guadalupe Victoria (✆ 618-118-70-12; www.oma.aero; Autopista Durango-Gómez Palacios Km 15.5), 20km northeast of town on Hwy 40D, is a relatively quiet regional airport. It is serviced by Aeroméxico (www.aeromexico.com), TAR Aerolíneas (www.tarmexico.com) and Volaris (www.volaris.com), plus a daily Dallas, Texas, flight with American (www.aa.com). A taxi to/from central Durango costs M$300 to M$350.

The **Central Camionera de Durango** (✆ 618-818-36-63; Blvd Villa 101), 5km east of the center, has frequent bus departures, including several 1st-class options.

ℹ Getting Around

'ISSSTE' or 'Centro' buses (M$10) from the Central de Autobuses parking lot go to Plaza de Armas. Metered taxis cost about M$45 to the center.

To reach the Central de Autobuses from downtown, catch **'Camionera' buses** (Negrete s/n) on Calle Negrete, one block south of the Museo Regional. Get off before the major intersection with the Pancho Villa equestrian monument and a McDonald's, and walk a short way northeast.

NORTHEAST MEXICO

The northeast has never been Mexico's main tourism draw, and news of cartel-related violence has turned off travelers even more. But the northeast's history, sights and people are remarkable, and it's all the more rewarding for being unexpected. Monterrey is a lively modern city, while nearby Saltillo oozes colonial charm. You can check out the idyllic wine country of Parras and the unique desert ecosystem at Cuatro Ciénegas, one of Mexico's most biologically diverse regions.

The security situation is serious but not paralyzing. Although news of the drug wars have faded considerably, border towns like Nuevo Laredo and Matamoros, and the surrounding areas can be tense. Monterrey also has neighborhoods that are best avoided. That said, virtually all the violence pits one cartel against the other, and tourists are rarely affected. Keep your wits about you and discover the myriad treasures the northeast has to offer.

Saltillo

✆ 844 / POP 810,000 / ELEV 1600M

Set high in the arid Sierra Madre Oriental, Saltillo is a large and fast-growing place with the normal endless sprawl of any big

Mexican city, but with a center that maintains a relaxed small-town feel. Founded in 1577, it's the northeast's oldest town, boasting fine colonial buildings and cracking cultural surprises (some leading art galleries and museums). Most attractions are conveniently central, and a burgeoning student population adds energy. The city is also on the main route between the northeast border and central Mexico, making it a decent spot to break a journey.

◉ Sights

Saltillo's cultural core around the expansive Plaza de Armas is replete with historic buildings and ideal for exploring on foot. Alameda Zaragoza, Saltillo's green lung, is six blocks northwest of the plaza.

★ Museo del Desierto   MUSEUM
(📷844-986-90-00; www.museodeldesierto.org; Parque Maravillas, Blvd Davila 3745; adult/child M$160/100; ⊙10am-5pm Tue-Sun; 📷) Saltillo's top attraction, this no-expense-spared natural history museum is highly enjoyable and informative (even if you don't speak Spanish). Exhibits explore the Chihuahuan Desert (the largest desert in North America), reveal why sea currents can create deserts and how sand dunes are formed. Children will love the dinosaurs, particularly the *Tyrannosaurus rex*. There's also a reptile house, prairie dogs, gray wolves and a botanical garden with more than 400 cactus species.

★ Museo de las Aves de México   MUSEUM
(Museum of Mexican Birds; 📷844-414-01-68; www.museodelasaves.org; Hidalgo 151; adult/child M$45/22; ⊙10am-6pm Tue-Sat, 11am-6pm Sun; 📷) Mexico ranks 10th in the world in terms of avian diversity, and this fascinating museum displays more than 3000 stuffed and mounted species, many in convincing dioramas of their natural habitat. Exhibits are divided by ecosystem: desert, ocean, rainforest, mangrove etc. There are special sections featuring multimedia exhibits on feathers, beaks and migration. The museum also explores the evolution of birds, with some impressive, life-size models of prehistoric ancestors. Signage in Spanish and English.

Centro Cultural
Vito Alessio Robles   HISTORIC BUILDING
(📷844-412-86-45; cnr Hidalgo & Aldama; ⊙10am-6pm Tue-Sat, 11am-6pm Sun; 📷) **FREE** Once Saltillo's city hall, this cultural center houses the most extensive mural painted by a woman in Mexico. At 500 sq meters, it is a remarkable and inspiring work of art that tells the history of Saltillo; it took almost three years for Helena Huerta Muzquiz to complete. Beyond the murals, there are several rooms exhibiting temporary exhibitions.

Museo del Sarape
y Trajes Mexicanos   MUSEUM
(📷844-481-69-00; Allende 160 Sur; ⊙10am-6pm Tue-Sun; 📷) **FREE** An excellent museum devoted to the Mexican *sarapes* (blankets with an opening for the head) that Saltillo is famous for. There's a priceless collection to admire, and lots of fascinating background information about weaving techniques, looms, natural dyes and regional variations. There's also a small section of regional dresses from around the country.

Catedral de Saltillo   CHURCH
(📷844-414-02-30; www.facebook.com/santocristosaltillo; Plaza de Armas; ⊙9am-1pm & 4-7:30pm; 📷) Built between 1745 and 1800, Saltillo's cathedral has one of Mexico's finest Churrigueresque facades, with columns of elaborately carved, pale-gray stone. The interior features dozens of paintings from the colonial era, including a work depicting the Virgin of Guadalupe by noted 18th-century artist José de Alcíbar.

🛏 Sleeping

Hotel Colonial San Miguel   HOTEL $$
(📷844-410-30-44; www.hotelcolonialsaltillo.com; Cepeda Sur 410; d/tr/q M$950/1200/1400; 🅿️❄️📶📺) This fine little hotel has a serious crush on San Miguel (St Michael) and angels in general, with statues, paintings and sculptures of angelic creatures everywhere; there's even a Sistine Chapel replica on the restaurant ceiling. Rooms themselves are modern, sleek and squeaky clean with good beds and quality linens. Some have Juliette balconies with nice city views.

Hotel Rancho el Morillo   HISTORIC HOTEL $$
(📷844-417-40-78; www.ranchoelmorillo.com; Del Morillo 264; r US$60-75; 🅿️❄️📶📺) Founded in 1934, this highly atmospheric hacienda on the edge of Saltillo is set in extensive grounds with trails that take in a pine forest, orchard and semidesert. The family owners are very welcoming and good meals are prepared – after which the homemade *licor de membrillo* (quince liquor) is the perfect digestif.

✖ Eating & Drinking

The foodie scene ranges from superb *fondas* (family-run eateries) to smart restaurants near the Plaza de Armas, plus some outstanding options within a short taxi ride of downtown.

★ **Las Delicias de Mi General** MEXICAN $$
(☑844-412-65-57; De La Fuente 218; mains M$110-220; ☺noon-midnight Mon-Fri, 9am-midnight Sat, 9am-10pm Sun; ☑🚼) Everywhere you look, this place has Mexican art and nods to those who create it. Murals of revolutionary heroes and film stars, life-sized *Catrinas* (papier-mâché skeletons), *lucha libre* (wrestling) dolls, religious art...even household items don the walls, with murals of *alebrijes* (fantastical creatures) outside. The cooking, classical Mexican, is quite good, and pairs with the inventive mezcal cocktails and craft beers.

★ **Il Mercato Gentiloni** ITALIAN $$
(www.facebook.com/MercatoGentiloni; La Gran Via 1454; mains M$160-450; ☺8am-midnight; 🛜) This shimmering new gastronomic complex houses some of Saltillo's best restaurants. Here you'll find gourmet Mexican fare, creative sharing plates, traditional Italian cuisine and pizzas fired up in a wood-burning oven. There's also a bakery, a wine bar and a sunlit cafe. More great restaurants and outdoor eateries lie just next door.

The artfully designed space, complete with terraces, a central patio and cantilevered roof, lies 5km northeast of the center (a M$70 taxi ride).

Flor y Canela CAFE $$
(☑844-414-31-43; www.facebook.com/flory canelacentro; Juárez 257; meals M$95-130; ☺8:30am-9:30pm Mon-Fri, 4:30-9:30pm Sat & Sun; 🛜☑) A welcoming cafe with a boho ambience, Flor y Canela specializes in homey breakfasts, weekday set-lunch specials (three courses for M$120), paninis and salads. There's an espresso machine for organic coffee drinks, and lots of *postre* (dessert) action on the menu. Wine and cocktails are available.

Taberna El Cerdo de Babel BAR
(☑844-135-53-60; www.facebook.com/cerdode babel; Ocampo 324; ☺4pm-1am Mon, 3pm-2am Tue-Sat) Once a 16th-century Franciscan convent, this boho-hipster tavern has live music, regular art exhibits and film showings. Seating is spread over two floors, including a leafy front patio, along a pedestrian walkway. A popular spot, this place is a go-to for university students, professors and professionals.

La Puerta al Cielo COCKTAIL BAR
(☑844-688-46-12; Allende 148; ☺5pm-1am Tue-Sat) Mixologists serve up beautiful and delicious concoctions and craft beers at this open-air bar in the heart of town. The patio setting features graffiti art, twinkling lights, and live music on weekends. A tasty menu of burgers, tacos, salads and pastas is offered too.

🛍 Shopping

El Sarape de Saltillo ARTS & CRAFTS
(☑844-414-96-34; elsarapedesaltillo@gmail.com; Hidalgo 305; ☺9:30am-1:30pm & 3:30-7:30pm Mon-Sat) With rooms upon rooms, this seemingly endless shop sells fine-quality, colorful *sarapes* and other Mexican arts and crafts; see wool being dyed and woven on looms inside.

ℹ Information

Municipal Tourist Office (☑844-439-71-95; Allende 124; ☺8am-3pm Mon-Fri) This small office is staffed by knowledgable and friendly folks. English spoken.

ℹ Getting There & Away

AIR

Saltillo's **Plan de Guadalupe Airport** (☑844-488-00-40; Carretera Saltillo–Monterrey Km 13.5, Ramos Arizpe) is 16km northeast of town and has regular flights to Mexico City. There are buses between Saltillo's bus terminal and Monterrey's airport (M$200), which has many more flights.

BUS

The **main bus station** (☑844-417-01-84; Periférico Echeverría s/n; 🛜) is on the south side of town, 2.5km from the center. Bus lines include Transportes Chihuahuenses, Futura, ETN and Omnibus de Mexico.

To reach the city center from the bus station, take bus 9 (M$13) from in front of the station; on the return, catch bus 9 on Aldama, between Zaragoza and Hidalgo.

ℹ Getting Around

TO/FROM THE AIRPORT

There are car-rental agencies at the airport. A taxi to/from the center costs around M$250.

BUSES FROM SALTILLO

DESTINATION	FARE (M$)	TIME (HR)	FREQUENCY (PER DAY)
Cuatro Ciénegas	600	5	1
Durango	820	7	7
Mexico City (Terminal Norte)	1000-1250	10-12	12
Monterrey	130-160	1¾	half-hourly
Nuevo Laredo	530	5	12
Parras	180	2½	7
San Luis Potosí	620-740	5-6	20
Torreón	450	3	hourly
Zacatecas	480-560	4½-5½	9

Parras

📞 842 / POP 45,600 / ELEV 1520M

A graceful and historic oasis town in the heart of the Coahuilan desert some 160km west of Saltillo, Parras has a beautifully cared-for center of real colonial character and a delightfully temperate climate, both of which have contributed to its reputation for being one of northern Mexico's next big things.

However, Parras is most famous for its wine: the *parras* (grapevines) that give the town its name have grown here since the late 16th century, and its most famous vineyard, Casa Madero, is the oldest winery in the Americas.

With great places to stay, gorgeous surroundings and all that vino, this is a place where you can easily linger for days.

◉ Sights & Activities

Casa Madero WINERY
(📞 842-422-01-11; www.madero.com; Carretera 102 Pila-Parras Km 18.2; winery tour adult/child under 12yr M$70/free; ⊙10am-6pm; ⊕) This, the first winery in the Americas, was established at Parras in 1597, a year before the town itself sprang up. It's now an industrial-sized operation exporting wine all over the world, although it's still housed on pleasingly old-fashioned premises. Casa Madero offers 45-minute tours through the history of winemaking. You can also just come for tastings – M$300 for three wines, served in the building next to the chapel.

On weekends, Casa Madero also offers one-hour tours through the vineyards, either on horseback (M$330) or carriage (M$600 for three people). From near the main plaza in Parras, catch one of the hourly buses (M$20) that pass the winery; just tell your driver where you want to get off. Or take a taxi (M$80); the winery is 7km north of Parras.

Viñedos Don Leo WINERY
(📞 844-698-22-00; www.vinosdonleo.com; Off Hwy 105; tour and tasting M$330-880; ⊙ by appt) In the picturesque Valle del Tunal, this mountain-backed vineyard is one of the highest in the world. The 2100m growing conditions along with technical know-how create some extraordinary wines, including an award-winning Grand Reserve cabernet sauvignon. The tasting room and terrace offer fine views over the dramatic landscape. You can opt for a 45-minute cellar tour and tasting of two wines, or make an afternoon of it with a tour and tasting followed by a meal. Reservations are essential.

It's located 40km east of Parras, with the last 8km on a dirt road off the highway.

Iglesia del Santo Madero CHURCH
(Morales Padilla s/n) This deeply striking church perched precariously on the rocky outcrop on the south edge of town has – once you've undergone the steep-but-rewarding 293-step climb up – some wonderful, expansive views over dramatic countryside beyond town. It's a 30-minute walk from the center, east along Madero then up Aguirre Benavides.

★ Estanque La Luz SWIMMING
(Aguirre Benavides 102; adult/child M$30/20, parking M$40; ⊙9am-7pm; ⊕) Fed by a natural mountain spring, the gorgeous Estanque La Luz makes a great place to be on warm days. The vast 3m-deep pool (life jackets available) draws a wide cross section of locals and out-of-towners. It's a 1km walk southwest of the Plaza de Armas.

✦ Festivals & Events

★ Feria de la Uva
FERIA

(☺early–mid-Aug; 🚶) Every August thousands of people descend upon Parras to celebrate wine, the lifeblood of the region. For two weeks there are parades featuring *vendimiadoras* (barefoot grape crushers), live dance and music performances, sporting events, religious ceremonies, a crowning of the queen of the fair, and wine, wine, wine. The entire event comes to a cacophonous climax – a dance party at Casa Madero (p811).

⌂ Sleeping

Foggara Hotel
BOUTIQUE HOTEL $$

(☎842-422-04-59; www.foggara.com.mx; Cazadores 111; r M$1050-1300; P⛾❄🛜) At this lovely hotel set in a historic home, rooms combine colonial structure with high-end, mid-century modern decor. Bathrooms are spacious with colorful tilework. Outdoor common areas include a pleasant courtyard and leafy terrace with loungers and hanging wicker chairs.

Casona del Banco
BOUTIQUE HOTEL $$$

(☎842-422-19-54; www.lacasonadelbanco.com; Ramos Arizpe 285; r/ste incl breakfast from M$3280/3810; P⛾❄🛜) For a proper splurge, opt for shabby-chic luxury on a grand and impressive scale at this wonderful but pricey conversion of a bank. The 24 plush rooms surround two grassy courtyards, and the public areas, including a lounge and stylish bar, are ideal for unwinding. Located toward the eastern entrance to town.

✕ Eating & Drinking

Las Parras de Santa Maria
INTERNATIONAL $$

(☎842-422-00-60; Cayuso 12; mains M$100-215; ☺noon-10pm Mon-Sat, to 6pm Sun; 🚶) Amid massive wood doors, 18-foot ceilings and whitewashed walls, this colonial beauty serves Mexican classics, as well as an excellent paella that comes with loads of shrimp, clams and fish plus a glass of sangria, and even tapas. Come hungry!

El Mesón de Don Evaristo
MEXICAN $$

(☎842-422-64-53; www.facebook.com/MesondeDonEvaristo; cnr Madero & Cayuso; mains M$75-150, steaks M$200-240; ☺8am-10pm; 🚶) In the middle of town, this friendly courtyard restaurant serves up meals on tables surrounding a small fountain. You'll find reliable Mexican fare, juicy steaks, and ample breakfast options.

ℹ Information

The **main tourist office** (☎842-422-31-84; Ramos Arizpe 122; ☺8am-3pm Mon-Fri) has helpful staff. Some English is spoken.

ℹ Getting There & Away

The **Parras-Saltillo bus station** (☎842-422-08-70; García 2B) is a small but modern station with seven daily buses to/from Saltillo (M$180, 2½ hours) and four daily to/from Monterrey (M$300, 3½ hours). You can also go to Cuatro Ciénegas without backtracking to Saltillo. To do so, catch a bus to San Pedro Las Colonias (M$135, 1½ hours, four daily) and then a bus from there to Cuatro Ciénegas (M$240 to M$360, two hours, eight daily).

Cuatro Ciénegas

☎869 / POP 13,500 / ELEV 747M

The serene and remote frontier town of Cuatro Ciénegas is bespeckled with adobe and colonial buildings and a handful of hotels and restaurants. It's a pleasantly out-of-the-way spot to enjoy the natural world of northern Mexico, and the perfect base for exploring the remarkable Área de Protección de Flora y Fauna Cuatrociénegas – an 843-sq-km nature reserve in the Chihuahuan Desert with turquoise rivers, strikingly white sand dunes and breathtaking mountain views – considered one of the most biologically diverse places in the world.

⊙ Sights & Activities

★ Área de Protección de Flora y Fauna Cuatrociénegas
NATURE RESERVE

(Cuatrociénegas Nature Reserve; ☎869-696-02-99; Hwy 30; M$40; ☺10am-5pm; P🚶❄) With hundreds of shimmering cerulean *pozas* (pools) and streams in the middle of the Desierto Chihuahuense (Chihuahuan Desert), this 843-sq-km nature reserve is a surreal sight. Fed by more than 500 underground springs, it's a desert habitat of extraordinary biological diversity, often compared to the Galapagos Islands. It's home to over 70 endemic species, including three kinds of turtles and 11 kinds of fish, as well as primitive organisms called *estromatolitos* (stromatolites), which are linked to the creation of Earth's oxygen-rich atmosphere.

Some pools and the nearby river have been set aside for recreational activities, including swimming. Much of the area is off-limits to the public, as it's being studied by researchers from organizations as diverse as NASA and UNAM.

The main gateway to the park is **Poza Azul** (Hwy 30). Here you'll find a **visitor center**, with displays in Spanish and English on the area's flora and fauna. The Poza Las Tortugas, a good turtle-spotting pool, is right behind here, while 1.5km further back is the aptly named Poza Azul (Blue Pond), one of the reserve's most photographed sites. Licensed guides can be hired here (there's no fee, you'll just pay admission for the individual sites). In town the tourist information office has a list of recommended guides, all of which can provide transport if you don't have a car.

Located about 9km southwest of town.

★ **Dunas de Yeso**   DUNES
(Los Arenales; Hwy 30; M$40; 🖼) Located within the Cuatrociénegas Reserve, these blinding-white gypsum sand dunes – the second largest in North America – contrast superbly with the six rocky mountain ranges that ring the valley. To visit you'll need your own transportation and a guide. (The gate to the dunes is locked and only guides have access to the key.) A licensed guide can be hired at the Poza Azul Visitors Center. The dunes are located 18km southwest of town, at the end of a sand road.

Mina de Mármol   VIEWPOINT
(Hwy 30; M$40; ⊙9:30am-5:30pm Mon-Fri; 🅿) Massive slabs of marble, some of it encrusted with fossils of fish and other marine life that swam in this valley when it was an ocean, greet you at this one-time mine.

Museo Casa Venustiano Carranza   MUSEUM
(🖉869-696-13-75; Carranza 109; ⊙10am-6pm Tue-Sun; ♿) FREE Housed in Venustiano Carranza's childhood home, this well-conceived museum relates the life story of Cuatro Ciénegas' most famous son. From mayor to senator to governor to revolutionary leader to Mexican president, Carranza was a lifelong politician who was known as savvy but stubborn. (He was assassinated in 1920.) Multimedia exhibits, personal effects and photos are displayed throughout the gorgeously restored home.

★ **Río Los Mezquites**   SWIMMING
(🖉869-696-04-08; Hwy 30; adult/child M$120/90; ⊙10am-6pm Mon-Fri, to 7pm Sat & Sun) Swimming with the fish and turtles in this sublime stretch of slow-flowing blue water amid the desert landscape of the Cuatrociénegas na-ture reserve is a surreal, revitalizing experience. There are *palapas* (thatched shelters), picnic tables and even a snack bar. Several sets of ladders and steps lead visitors into the water (or you can do as the kids do and cannonball in).

You can also hire kayaks (from M$150 per hour), for a paddle along the meandering, crystal-clear waters. Last visitors admitted at 5pm. From town, look for the turnoff just before the Poza Azul Visitor Center.

👉 Tours

One-day excursions of the spectacular Cuatrociénegas Reserve can be organized with certified guides for about M$800 per person per day. Contact them through the tourist information offices. Hotels in town can also arrange tours.

If you have your own wheels, guides also can be hired directly at the Poza Azul Visitors Center.

🛏 Sleeping & Eating

Hostal Casa Los Abuelos   HOSTEL **$**
(🖉869-696-06-01; www.facebook.com/Hostal CasaLosAbuelos; Morelos 201; dm M$250; 🛜) A great-value budget option with simple six- and eight-bed dorm rooms in a converted house a few blocks northeast of the main plaza. There's a shared kitchen, convivial English-speaking hosts and a festive outdoor restaurant (mains around M$90) down below. Also offers tours (in a blue VW bus!) from around M$650 per person to the main sites in the Cuatrociénegas Nature Reserve.

Hotel Plaza   HOTEL **$$**
(🖉869-696-00-66; www.plazahotel.com.mx; Hidalgo 202; s/d/tr/ste M$1000/1500/1700/2000; 🅿🕓❄🛜🏊) In a great location near the plaza, this good-value spot has spacious and comfortable rooms that face a shaded terrace and that all-important heat-busting pool. Rooms are cheerfully painted in a rich colonial color scheme, with tall ceilings, huge TVs and rustic wood furniture.

Hotel Misión Marielena   HOTEL **$$**
(🖉869-696-11-51; www.hotelmisionmarielena. com.mx; Hidalgo 200; r M$850-1050; 🅿🕓❄🛜🏊) Excellent value, this historic hotel on the central plaza has large, well-maintained rooms set around two leafy courtyards. The onsite restaurant is excellent. Information about the area's sites is freely given and tours are easily arranged.

Hacienda 1800 HOTEL $$$

(☑ 869-6960530; hola@hacienda1800.com; Las Parras 1007; s/d/ste from M$1600/1900/2600; ⓟ⚹⛱📶♨) Located 1.8km straight west of the Plaza Principal, Cuatro Ciénagas' poshest accommodations offers spacious, attractively set rooms overlooking an enticing, palm-fringed pool. You can relax in hammocks swaying over the water's surface or take a dip with cocktail in hand in the adults-only pool hidden behind the bar.

The restaurant serves eclectic fare (sandwiches, sushi rolls, tacos and heartier plates of grilled meats or seafood).

Prices are about 20% lower on Sunday to Thursday nights.

Cantina El 40 MEXICAN $$

(☑ 869-696-00-40; Zaragoza 204; mains M$130-295; ◷ noon-midnight Wed-Mon; 📶⛋) A swanky restaurant-bar with a colonial-meets-cowboy theme, Cantina El 40 serves up top-notch Mexican dishes with flair. Think gourmet street tacos and sizzling *molcajete* dishes (meals served in a stone mortar and pestle) paired with top-shelf cocktails and local wines. Seating is either indoors at thick wood tables with cow-patterned chairs or outdoors in a breezy courtyard.

ℹ️ Information

The tiny but helpful **municipal tourist office** (☑ 869-696-06-50; Carranza 100; ◷ 8am-3pm Mon-Fri) is inside the Presidencia Municipal (city hall) facing the Plaza Central.

ℹ️ Getting There & Away

The **bus terminal** (Blvd Juárez s/n) is opposite a paint shop, near the eastern entrance to town. First-class buses run to Torreón (M$490, 3½ hours, seven daily), Saltillo (M$600, five hours, one daily) and Monterrey (M$600, 5½ hours, one daily); a 2nd-class bus heads to the border at Piedras Negras (M$530, six hours, six daily).

Monterrey

☑ 81 / POP 1.2 MILLION / ELEV 540M

Cosmopolitan Monterrey is Mexico's third-largest city, second-largest industrial center and *número uno* in per-capita income. This economic powerhouse has a strong entrepreneurial ethos, humming cultural scene, vibrant universities and an urban hipster nightlife scene.

With sprawling suburbs of gargantuan air-conditioned malls and manicured housing estates, this is also one of Mexico's most Americanized cities. Boasting world-class museums and a jagged mountain backdrop (which offers terrific outdoor adventure sports), the city's attractions are diverse and myriad.

All of this makes Monterrey fiercely independent and very different from any other Mexican metropolis. Notably, the city experienced the drug wars up close and personal, but in recent years, cultural life was back with aplomb, especially around the Macroplaza, with thriving restaurants and bars in the newly safe Barrio Antiguo. Nevertheless, narco gangs still affect some neighborhoods, including Colonia Independencia just across the Río Santa Catarina – avoid it day or night.

History

Dating from 1596, the city did not begin to prosper until after Mexican independence – thanks to its proximity to the US, which gave it advantages in trade and smuggling.

In 1900 the first heavy industry in Latin America, a vast iron and steel works (now the site of the Parque Fundidora), rose to dominate the cityscape. Monterrey was soon dubbed the 'Pittsburgh of Mexico,' and still produces about 25% of Mexico's raw steel. The city also churns out around 60% of the nation's cement and half of its beer.

◉ Sights & Activities

Most major sights are concentrated around the extraordinary Macroplaza in the center and the atmospheric Barrio Antiguo quarter. Further east, at the far end of a beautiful river walk, is the city's other main cultural hub: the Parque Fundidora. Also adding to Monterrey's charm is the awe-inspiring nearby scenery. Just be sure to check the local security situation before embarking on a trip outside the city.

★ Paseo Santa Lucía PARK

(Plaza 400 Años; ◷ 6am-10pm; ⛋⛲) The stunning 2.3km promenade of Paseo Santa Lucía is a world-class example of urban regeneration. This (artificial) river forms a turquoise ribbon through the heart of industrial Monterrey. Take a stroll down this delightful leafy pathway, or hop in one of the regular river boats (adult/child return M$70/40; 10am to 9pm). The landscaping is amazing, with lighting illuminating the water at night plus the 24 striking bridges and 13 fountains spanning the river.

There's 24-hour security, a few bars and restaurants at its western end, and the whole

---

WORTH A TRIP

PARQUE ECOLÓGICO CHIPINQUE

Parque Ecológico Chipinque (☑81-8303-2190; www.chipinque.org.mx; Carretera a Chipinque Km. 2.5, San Pedro Garza García; pedestrian/cyclist M$20/45, vehicle M$65-125; ⊙6am-7:30pm; 🚌), a stunning mountainside reserve, is just 12km from downtown Monterrey. There's great hiking and mountain biking on over 60km of well-marked trails through dense forest and up rocky peaks, including up soaring Copete de Águilas (2200m). The tiny visitor center has snacks and permits for those heading to the summits.

Mountain-bike rentals (M$200 per hour) and three-hour bike excursions (M$650 per person, including bike) can also be arranged at the kiosk behind the visitor center.

A taxi from downtown costs about M$150 (more if you want a lift to the higher trails); ask the driver to return at an agreed-upon time to be sure you have a ride back to town. If self-driving, you'll pay M$65 if only going to the visitor center; it costs M$125 to drive further uphill to the more scenic trails and lookouts.

---

promenade has free public wi-fi. Boats leave from a dock on Plaza 400 Años (p817).

★**Horno3**   MUSEUM
(Museum of Steel; ☑81-8126-1100; www.horno3.org; Parque Fundidora; adult/child M$120/70; ⊙10am-6pm Tue-Thu, 11am-7pm Fri-Sun; Ⓜ Parque Fundidora) Blast Furnace No 3 in the former industrial site of the Parque Fundidora has been converted into Horno3, an exceptionally impressive high-tech, hands-on museum devoted to Mexico's steel industry. No expense has been spared here, from the steaming rocks at the entrance to the metal, open-air elevator that climbs to the summit for dramatic bird's-eye views of Monterrey (included in admission). The entire process of steel-making is explained (with some English translations) along with its vital relevance to Monterrey and Mexico.

Don't miss the dramatic furnace show, beamed from the bulk of Horno3 itself. On weekends, there's a combo zip-lining–rappelling tour (adult/child M$490/290) from the top of the metal tower; book ahead with Ibo Adventures (www.ibo.com.mx/tours/urban). The excellent cafe-restaurant, **El Lingote** (☑81-8126-1100, ext 3003; www.ellingoterestaurante.com; mains M$240-500; ⊙1-10:30pm Tue-Thu & Sun, to midnight Fri & Sat; 🅿🛜), serves creative fare and craft beers to views over the park. After the museum closes, you can take the open-air elevator to the summit for evening views over the city (M$60), with rides continuing until 10pm.

★**Museo de Historia Mexicana**   MUSEUM
(☑81-2033-9898; www.3museos.com; Doctor Coss 445 Sur; adult/child M$40/free; ⊙10am-8pm Tue & Sun, 10am-6pm Wed-Sat; 🚌; Ⓜ Zaragoza) This sleek modernist museum on Plaza 400 Años presents an extensive but easily manageable chronological history of Mexico. In the heart of the museum there's an Earth section, full of mounted animals and realistic-looking landscapes, representing Mexico's remarkable biodiversity. Signage is mostly in Spanish, though there are strategically placed screens with overviews in English. Free tours – in either language – can be arranged by phoning in advance. Entry is free on Tuesdays and Sundays.

Admission also covers the Museo del Noreste (p817), to which it's attached via a glass-enclosed bridge.

Macroplaza   PLAZA
(Gran Plaza; Ⓜ Zaragoza) A monument to Monterrey's late-20th-century ambition, this city-block-wide series of interconnected squares, also known as the Gran Plaza, was created in the 1980s by the demolition of a prime chunk of city-center real estate. A controversial but ultimately successful piece of redevelopment, its charm has increased over the years as the once-naked urban space – said to form the largest public square in the world – has been softened by parks, trees and fountains.

Vistas of the surrounding mountains open up between the roster of iconic edifices – classically designed municipal buildings and incongruously modern structures housing some of Mexico's finest museums – that line the Macroplaza. For visitors, it's a delight to explore on foot, as most traffic is directed away from the area by underpasses.

At the southern end of the Macroplaza, the 70m concrete tower **Faro del Comercio** (Lighthouse of Commerce; Zuazua s/n) soars above the city, its green lasers piercing the night sky. The Faro abuts the baroque form of the

Monterrey

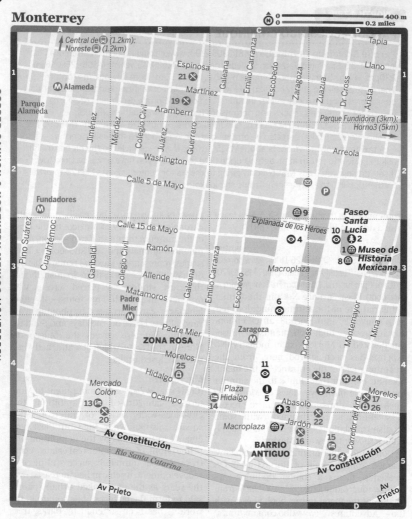

Catedral Metropolitano de Monterrey (📞81-8342-7831; Zuazua Sur 1100; ⏲7:30am-8pm Mon-Fri, 9am-8pm Sat & Sun; 🚇), capped by a neon cross. North of here is a shady park, **Plaza Zaragoza** (Zuazua s/n; 🚇🚻), popular with snacking families and smooching couples, and also the venue for open-air concerts and old-school Latin dancing every Sunday.

Continuing north, the rest of the Macroplaza is lined with a succession of concrete municipal structures. If you're a fan of brutalism, you'll love the **Teatro de la Ciudad** and its architectural cousin, the lofty **Congreso del Estado**. Then down some steps is the **Explanada de los Héroes** (Esplanade of the Heroes; cnr Zuazua & 15 de Mayo; 🚇🚻) lined with statues, and finally the 1908 neoclassical **Palacio de Gobierno** (📞81-2020-1021; Calle 5 de Mayo s/n).

Parque Fundidora PARK
(📞81-8126-8500; www.parquefundidora.org; cnr Fundidora & Adolfo Prieto; ⏲6am-10pm; 🅿🚇; Ⓜ Parque Fundidora) **FREE** Formerly a vast steel-factory complex, this once-blighted industrial zone has been transformed into a huge urban park. Designers cleverly retained the iconic smoke stacks and industrial relics to give a surreal and, at times, apocalyptic feel, but also a vibe very much in keeping

Monterrey

with Monterrey's heritage. You can jog the trails, rent bikes (from M$40 per hour), paddle a rowboat (M$50 per hour) and visit the cultural sights, of which the Horno3 museum is the undoubted star of the show.

Four other disemboweled red-brick factories comprise the **Centro de las Artes** (☏81-2140-3000; http://conarte.org.mx/centro-de-las-artes; ⊙11am-9pm Tue-Sun) **FREE**, two galleries with high-class rotating exhibitions, a theater and a movie house that screens independent and foreign films.

The metro stops within a 10-minute walk of the park, but the most enjoyable way to get here is to walk or take a boat along Paseo Santa Lucía (p814).

Plaza 400 Años   PLAZA
(Ⓜ Zaragoza) This plaza, graced with fountains and pools, forms an impressive approach to the sleek, modernist Museo de Historia Mexicana (p815) and the **Museo del Noreste** (☏81-2033-9898; www.3museos.com; Doctor Coss 445; adult/child M$40/free; ⊙10am-8pm Tue & Sun, 10am-6pm Wed-Sat; ♿). It is the terminus of the lovely Paseo Santa Lucía (p814) promenade.

Museo de Arte Contemporáneo   MUSEUM
(MARCO; ☏81-8262-4500; www.marco.org.mx; cnr Zuazua & Jardón; adult/child M$90/60; ⊙10am-6pm Tue & Thu-Sun, 10am-8pm Wed; Ⓟ; Ⓜ Zaragoza) Don't miss the outstanding Museo de Arte Contemporáneo, its entrance marked

by Juan Soriano's gigantic black dove sculpture. Inside, its idiosyncratic spaces are filled with water and light, and major exhibitions (almost all temporary; the permanent collection is quite modest) of work by renowned contemporary Mexican and Latin American artists. English-language tours (free with admission) are offered by enthusiastic university student docents. MARCO also has a fine **gift shop** (☏81-8262-4500; www.marco.org.mx; cnr Zuazua & Jardón; ⊙10am-6pm Tue & Thu-Sun, 10am-8pm Wed) and a good restaurant. Admission is free on Wednesdays.

Cooking with Juan Pablo   COOKING
(☏81-1582-5311; www.facebook.com/fonda.el.limon cito; Guillermo Prieto 938; per person US$50; Ⓜ Zaragoza) Juan Pablo, the friendly English-speaking owner of Fonda El Limoncito (p818), offers a fun and educational, all-day culinary experience. You'll have breakfast at the restaurant, then head to the market for the meal's ingredients, learning lots about Monterrey cuisine and culture along the way. You'll then return to make the meal and enjoy the fruits of your labor. Two-person minimum.

It's a fun day's outing, and Juan Pablo will make you feel like one of the family.

✦✦ Festivals & Events

Aniversario de Independencia   CULTURAL
(Explanada de los Héroes, cnr Zuazua & 15 de Mayo; ⊙Sep 15-16; ♿; Ⓜ Zaragoza) Monterrey's biggest celebrations are held on Mexico's

Independence Day, September 16, with fireworks, *musica norteña* (country ballads) and a parade. The festivities typically kick off the evening prior at the Explanada de los Héroes (p816) with the traditional cry of independence from city leaders: *¡Viva México! ¡Viva la independencia!*

Festival Internacional de Cine en Monterrey   FILM
(www.monterreyfilmfestival.com; per film M$30-40; ⊘late Aug) This impressive festival held in late August showcases Mexican and international art-house films. It's held in different venues around town, including Parque Fundidora's Centro de las Artes (p817).

🛌 Sleeping

Monterrey has some appealing accommodations in the old center, though some of the best hotels are out in the upscale district of Del Valle.

La Casa del Barrio   HOSTEL $
(📷 81-8344-1800; www.lacasadelbarrio.com.mx; Montemayor 1227 Sur; d M$750; ☕❄🎧; Ⓜ Zaragoza) A charming option in the middle of the Barrio Antiguo, this place also has a bamboo-fringed courtyard-cafe that serves tasty, waffle-centric breakfasts. The rooms are small, but bright and well maintained, and the great location puts you within a few blocks of good restaurants and bars.

Gran Hotel Ancira   HOTEL $$$
(📷 81-8345-7815; www.gammahoteles.com; cnr Hidalgo & Escobedo; d M$1300-2800; Ⓟ❄❄ @🎧❄; Ⓜ Zaragoza, Padre Mier) Dating from 1912, this grand dame was built in French art nouveau style, and has a rather extravagant, mirror-ceilinged, gingham-tiled reception and restaurant area. Rooms are spacious with classical furnishings, and sizable windows (though some have interior views). Good amenities and an excellent location.

Fiesta Americana Pabellón M   BOUTIQUE HOTEL $$$
(📷 81-1642-0600; www.fiestamericana.com; Júarez 1102; d from M$2500; Ⓟ❄🎧❄; Ⓜ Padre Mier) This stylish newcomer lies in the upper floors of the Pabellón M entertainment complex. Rooms are modern and sleek with elegant furnishings, high-quality mattresses and floor-to-ceiling windows offering grand views. Extras include a 16th-floor restaurant and bar, a fitness center, a lofty terrace, and easy access to the wealth of dining options on the building's 1st floor.

✕ Eating

Monterrey's signature dish is *cabrito al pastor* (roast kid goat). Barrio Antiguo has a good selection of places to eat (and drink). Nearby **Mercado Juárez** (Av Juárez s/n; mains M$65-120; ⊘8am-7pm Mon-Sat, to 3pm Sun; Ⓜ Alameda) has family-run eateries selling tasty, cheap grub – though be sure to keep a close eye on your belongings as the market is known as a hot spot for pickpockets.

Taqueria y Carniceria La Mexicana   TACOS $
(📷 81-8340-7175; www.taquerialamexicana.mx; Guerrero 244; taco M$11; ⊘6:45am-7:30pm Mon-Sat, to 3pm Sun; 🚻; Ⓜ Alameda) Done up like a Mexican party dress, this eatery/butcher shop is an explosion of colors – think Talavera tiles and piñatas. *Tacos de canasta* (steamed tacos) are the specialty and come filled with everything from beans or spicy potatoes to ground beef or *chicharrón*. Order at the counter and eat at one of the bustling communal tables.

Mercado Barrio Antiguo   FOOD HALL $
(www.mercadobarrioantiguo.com; Morelos 839; mains M$50-190; ⊘8am-11pm Sun-Wed, to 2am Thu-Sat; Ⓜ Zaragoza) Monterrey's new culinary destination is a photogenic food hall with communal tables ringed by over a dozen vendors selling street food and desserts. There's also a bar.

★ Fonda El Limoncito   MEXICAN $$
(📷 81-1582-5311; www.facebook.com/fonda.el.limoncito; Guillermo Prieto 938; meals M$180-200; ⊘8am-5pm; 🎧🚻; Ⓜ Zaragoza) Set in a century-old house, this atmospheric spot serves deliciously authentic, home-style Mexican cooking that would make your *abuela* (grandmother) proud. There's no menu, but the dishes change by day, and the kindly English-speaking owner can happily accommodate vegetarians; kids eat free. There's occasional live music.

★ Fonda San Francisco   MEXICAN $$
(📷 81-1957-7070; Manuel González 115; small plates M$40-80, mains M$140-200; ⊘1-11pm Mon-Sat) Knock on the metal door to gain access to this quirky and creative eatery, run by the iconoclastic master chef Adrián Herrera. It's a casual, pretension-free space, and the cooking is incredible. Opt for a delectable multicourse menu of small plates like tacos, *tamales* and the whimsically named *empalme satánico* (satanic *empalme*), a kind

of sandwich made with two corn tortillas and beans, *chorizo* and spices.

It's located in the San Pedro Garza García neighborhood, a 15-minute taxi ride from the Macroplaza. Reserve ahead.

Me Muero de Hambre   MEXICAN $$
(☑81-8340-8836; mains M$140-260; ⊘12:30-10pm Sun-Wed, to midnight Thu-Sat; Ⓜ Zaragoza) A few steps from lively Calle Morelos, this three-story building has a casual spot devoted to delectable tacos, another for *antojitos* and creative Mexican fare, and an open-sided terrace up top with fine views and popular thin-crust pizza.

Trece Lunas   INTERNATIONAL $$
(☑81-1352-1127; http://cafe13lunas.50webs.com; Abasolo 870; mains M$120-220; ⊘8am-10pm Sun-Thu, to 11:30pm Fri & Sat; ✐; Ⓜ Zaragoza) If you like your decor eclectic, your spaces multicultural and your food purposefully slow, this innovative Barrio Antiguo place may just be right for you. There's a huge menu that is focused on shared plates called *botanas*, which are piled high with food. Throw in vegetarian options, salads, sandwiches and good coffee, and you have a winner.

Madre Oaxaca   MEXICAN $$$
(☑81-8345-1459; www.facebook.com/MadreOaxaca. Mty; Jardón 814; mains M$240-420; ⊘1-10pm Mon-Sat, to 6pm Sun; ✐; Ⓜ Zaragoza) One of the Barrio Antiguo's best restaurants, this charmer is set in a historic building and decked out with an extraordinary collection of handicrafts and folk art over its several intimate dining rooms. The menu is loaded with authentic Oaxacan dishes using rich *mole* sauce – try a mixed *tlayuda oaxaqueña* (huge flatbread with toppings).

Pabellón M   FOOD HALL $$$
(☑81-2090-8800; Av Constitución; mains M$190-450; ⊘9am-11pm; ☏; Ⓜ Padre Mier) This new ultra-modern complex has a soaring atrium dotted with enticing midrange restaurants devoted to Italian fare, Asian noodle dishes, sushi, tapas and pub food (chicken wings, burgers, beers) among other options. There's also a 4200-seat concert hall, a 7th-floor cinema and a casual food court (2nd floor), plus a very prominent Starbucks.

🍺 Drinking & Nightlife

The heart of nightlife in the Barrio Antiguo is Calle Morelos, where bars, beer gardens and clubs sit side by side.

Almacén 42   CRAFT BEER
(☑81-8343-2817; www.almacen42.com; Morelos 852 Oriente; ⊘5pm-midnight Tue-Thu, 2pm-2am Fri & Sat, 2-10pm Sun; Ⓜ Zaragoza) Shipping containers and guys with bushy beards and tats greet you as you enter this urban hipster bar. Some 42 craft beers are on tap at any given time – all domestic and ranging from sours to stouts. There's a breezy stone patio in back and, when you get the munchies, a solid menu of shared plates and tacos too.

☆ Entertainment

Café Iguana   LIVE MUSIC
(☑81-8343-0822; www.cafeiguana.com.mx; Montemayor 927 Sur; ⊘7pm-1am Thu, 8pm-2am Fri & Sat; Ⓜ Zaragoza) The epicenter of alternative Monterrey, where the pierced, multi-tattooed, punk-loving tribe gathers en masse, both inside and on the street out front. Cover charge only for live bands.

🛍 Shopping

★ Corredor del Arte   ARTS & CRAFTS, MARKET
(Art Corridor; ☑81-1243-8848; www.facebook. com/CorredorDelArte; cnr Mina & Abasolo; ⊘10am-7pm Sun; ♿; Ⓜ Zaragoza) On Sundays, Calle Mina in the Barrio Antiguo becomes the Corredor del Arte, a wonderful combination of antiques, arts and crafts, and a flea market. The whole district springs to life, with festive crowds browsing for one-of-a-kind items amid piles of clothes, records, books, housewares and other objects. Bands often play too.

Carápan   ARTS & CRAFTS
(☑81-8345-4422; www.carapan.com.mx; Hidalgo 305 Oriente; ⊘10am-7pm Mon-Sat; Ⓜ Padre Mier) This shop is in a whole other class, and is Monterrey's best outlet for *artesanías* (crafts). The genial English-speaking owner, who is full of advice about what to see and do in Monterrey, stocks museum-quality work (including textiles and jewelry) from across Mexico. Don't miss exquisitely painted *alebrijes* (fantastically painted animal sculptures) or the stunningly elaborate Huichol beaded artworks.

❶ Information

SAFE TRAVEL

The Zona Rosa area on the west side of the Macroplaza and Barrio Antiguo on the east are both largely considered safe by day and night, but as in many big cities, it's advisable to avoid walking alone after dark and make sure you

BUSES FROM MONTERREY

Prices are for 1st-class buses.

DESTINATION	FARE (M$)	TIME	FREQUENCY (DAILY)
Chihuahua	1120	12hr	8
Dallas, US	1350	12hr	4
Durango	750-950	8-9hr	12
Houston, US	1150	11-12hr	5
Mazatlán	1270-1600	12hr	5
Mexico City (Terminal Norte)	1100-1300	12-14hr	half-hourly
Nuevo Laredo	350-430	3hr	every 20min
Piedras Negras	750-900	6-7hr	12
Reynosa	350-400	3hr	half-hourly
Saltillo	130-160	1¾hr	half-hourly
San Luis Potosí	650-800	7hr	half-hourly
Zacatecas	500-720	7hr	12

stick to the main roads. Across the Río Santa Catarina, the crime-plagued barrio of Colonia Independencia is still affected by narco gangs and should not be entered day or night.

TOURIST INFORMATION

The **Tourist Information Center** (☑81-2033-8414; www.nuevoleon.travel; Palacio de Gobierno, 5 de Mayo s/n; ⊗9am-5pm; Ⓜ Zaragoza) has friendly, English-speaking staff offering plentiful information about sights and events across Nuevo León.

Hospital Christus Muguerza (☑81-8399-3400; www.christusmuguerza.com.mx; Hidalgo 2525 Poniente; ⊗24hr) Monterrey's main hospital.

Post Office (☑80-0701-7000; Washington 648 Oriente; ⊗8am-5pm Mon-Fri, 10am-2pm Sat; Ⓜ Zaragoza)

❶ Getting There & Away

AIR

Monterrey's busy **airport** (☑81-8288-7700; www.oma.aero; Carretera Miguel Alemán Km 24, Apodaca) has direct flights to all of Mexico's major cities, plus direct international flights to Atlanta, Chicago, Dallas, Houston, Los Angeles, Miami and New York. The airport is located 27km from the city center, in the suburb of Apodaca.

BUS

Monterrey's colossal bus station, **Central de Autobuses** (Av Colón 855; Ⓜ Cuauhtémoc), is busy day and night with departures and arrivals from across Mexico. Use the official taxi desk inside the station; the fare is M$70 to most central locations.

❶ Getting Around

TO/FROM THE AIRPORT

Noreste (☑800-765-66-36; www.noreste.com.mx; Central de Autobuses, Av Colón 855; Ⓜ Cuauhtémoc) runs half-hourly buses around the clock (M$100, one hour) between the airport and the main bus terminal. A taxi to/from the center is around M$330.

BUS

Frequent city buses (M$14 to M$18) get you most places you can't reach by metro.

METRO

Monterrey's modern, efficient metro system **Metrorrey** (☑81-2033-5000; www.facebook.com/MetrorreyOficia; single trip M$4.50; ⊗5am-midnight) currently consists of two lines. Elevated Línea 1 runs from the northwest of the city to the eastern suburbs, passing the Parque Fundidora. Línea 2 begins underground at the Gran Plaza and runs north past Parque Niños Héroes up into the northern suburbs. The two lines cross right by the bus station at Cuauhtémoc station.

Several metro stations are connected with metrobuses (specialized buses with set stops) to outlying areas. Construction has also started on Línea 3, which will connect Zaragoza station by the Macroplaza to the northeastern suburbs. Work is expected to be completed in 2022.

TAXI

Taxis (☑81-4646-5692, 81-8372-4370; ⊗24hr) are ubiquitous in Monterrey and reasonably priced; all have meters. From the Zona Rosa to the bus terminal or Parque Fundidora is usually about M$70.

Understand
Mexico

History

Mexico's story is always extraordinary and at times barely credible. How could a 2700-year tradition of sophisticated indigenous civilization crumble in two short years at the hands of some adventurers from Spain? How could Mexico's 11-year war for independence from Spain lead to three decades of dictatorship by Porfirio Díaz? How could the people's revolution that ended that dictatorship yield 70 years of one-party rule? Mexico's past is present everywhere you go, and is key to understanding Mexico today.

The Ancient Civilizations

The political map of ancient Mexico shifted constantly as cities, towns or states sought domination over one another, and a sequence of powerful states rose and fell through invasion, internal conflict or environmental disaster. These diverse cultures had much in common. Human sacrifice, to appease ferocious gods, was practiced by many of them; they observed the heavens to predict the future and determine propitious times for important events like harvests; society was heavily stratified and dominated by priestly male ruling classes. Versions of a ritual ball game were played almost everywhere and seem to have always involved two teams trying to keep a rubber ball off the ground by flicking it with various parts of the body. The game sometimes served as an oracle, and could also involve the sacrifice of victorious players.

A common framework divides the pre-Hispanic era into three main periods: pre-Classic (before 250 CE); Classic (250–900 CE); and post-Classic (900–1521 CE). The most advanced cultures in Mexico emerged chiefly in the center, south and east of the country. Together with Maya lands in what are now Guatemala, Belize and a small part of Honduras, this zone is collectively known to historians and archaeologists as Mesoamerica.

Early Arrivals

The pre-Hispanic inhabitants of the Americas arrived from Siberia in several migrations during the last Ice Age, between perhaps 60,000 and 8000 BCE, crossing land now submerged beneath the Bering Strait. Early

TIMELINE	8000–3000 BCE	1200–400 BCE	0–150 CE
	Agriculture develops in places such as the Tehuacán valley and Yagul. Chili seeds and squashes are planted, then corn and beans are cultivated, enabling people to live semipermanently in villages.	Mexico's 'mother culture', the Olmecs, flourishes on the Gulf coast at San Lorenzo and La Venta. Jade, a favorite pre-Hispanic material, appears in a tomb at La Venta.	A huge planned city, including the 70m-high Pyramid of the Sun, is laid out in a grid arrangement at Teotihuacán in central Mexico.

Mexicans hunted big animal herds in the grasslands of the highland valleys. When temperatures rose at the end of the last Ice Age, the valleys became drier, ceasing to support such animal life and forcing the people to derive more food from plants. In central Mexico's Tehuacán Valley and at Yagul near Oaxaca, archaeologists have traced the slow beginnings of agriculture between about 8000 and 3000 BCE.

The Olmec
Mexico's 'mother culture' was the mysterious Olmec civilization, which appeared in the humid lowlands of Veracruz and Tabasco. The evidence of the masterly stone sculptures they left behind indicates that

ANCIENT RELIGION & BELIEF

The **Maya** developed a complex writing system, partly pictorial, partly phonetic, with some 500 symbols. They also refined a calendar used by other pre-Hispanic peoples into a tool for the exact recording and forecasting of earthly and heavenly events. Temples were aligned to enhance observation of the heavens, helping the Maya predict solar eclipses and movements of the moon and Venus. The Maya measured time in various interlocking cycles, ranging from 13-day 'weeks' to the 1,872,000-day 'Great Cycle.' They believed the current world to be just one of a succession of worlds, and this cyclical nature of things enabled the future to be predicted by looking at the past.

To win the gods' favor they carried out elaborate rituals involving dances, feasts, sacrifices, consumption of the alcoholic drink *balche,* and bloodletting from ears, tongues or penises. The Classic Maya seem to have practiced human sacrifice on a small scale, the post-Classic Maya on a larger scale.

The Maya universe had a center and four directions, each with a color: the center was green; east was red; north, white; west, black; and south, yellow. The heavens had 13 layers, and Xibalbá, the underworld to which the dead descended, had nine. The earth was the back of a giant reptile floating on a pond.

The later **Aztec** similarly observed the heavens for astrological purposes and also saw the world as having four directions, 13 heavens and nine hells. Those who died by drowning, leprosy, lightning, gout, dropsy or lung disease went to the paradisaical gardens of Tláloc, the rain god, who had killed them. Warriors who were sacrificed or died in battle, merchants killed while traveling far away, and women who died giving birth to their first child all went to heaven as companions of the sun. Everyone else traveled for four years under the northern deserts in the abode of the death god Mictlantecuhtli, before reaching the ninth hell, where – perhaps a blessed relief – they vanished altogether.

The Aztec believed they lived in the 'fifth world,' whose four predecessors had each been destroyed by the death of the sun and of humanity. Aztec human sacrifices were designed to keep the sun, and themselves, alive.

250–600	250–900	695	750–900
Teotihuacán's Pyramid of the Moon is built; the city grows to an estimated 125,000 people and comes to control the biggest of Mexico's pre-Hispanic empires.	The brilliant Classic Maya civilization flowers in southeast Mexico, Guatemala, Belize and parts of Honduras and El Salvador.	The great Maya city of Tikal (in modern-day Guatemala) conquers Maya rival Calakmul (in Mexico), but is unable to exert unified control over Calakmul's subjects.	Maya civilization in the central Maya heartland – Chiapas (southeast Mexico), El Petén (northern Guatemala) and Belize – collapses, probably because of prolonged severe droughts.

Olmec civilization was well organized and able to support talented artisans, and lived in thrall to fearsome deities. Its best-known artifacts are the awe-inspiring 'Olmec heads,' stone sculptures up to 3m high with grim, pug-nosed faces and wearing curious helmets. Far-flung Olmec sites in central and western Mexico may have been trading posts or garrisons to ensure the supply of jade, obsidian and other luxuries for the Olmec elite.

Olmec art, religion and society had a profound influence on later Mexican civilizations. Olmec gods, such as the feathered serpent, persisted right through the pre-Hispanic era.

Teotihuacán

The first great civilization in central Mexico arose in a valley about 50km northeast of the middle of modern Mexico City. The grid plan of the magnificent city of Teotihuacán was laid out in the 1st century CE. It was the basis for the famous Pyramids of the Sun and the Moon as well as avenues, palaces and temples that were added during the next 600 years. The city grew to a population of about 125,000 and became the center of the biggest pre-Hispanic Mexican empire, stretching as far south as modern El Salvador. It may have had some hegemony over the Zapotec of Oaxaca, whose capital, Monte Albán, grew into a magnificent city in its own right between 300 and 600 CE, with architecture displaying clear Teotihuacán influence. Teotihuacán's advanced civilization – including writing, and a calendar system with a 260-day 'sacred year' composed of 13 periods of 20 days – spread far from its original heartland.

Teotihuacán was eventually burned, plundered and abandoned in the 8th century. But many Teotihuacán gods, such as the feathered serpent Quetzalcóatl (an all-important symbol of fertility and life) and Tláloc (the rain and water deity), were still being worshipped by the Aztecs a millennium later.

The Classic Maya

Maya civilization during the Classic period (250–900 CE) flowered over a large area stretching from the Yucatán Peninsula into Belize, Guatemala, Honduras and the lowlands of Chiapas (in Mexico). The Maya attained heights of artistic and architectural expression, and of learning in fields like astronomy, mathematics and astrology, that were not surpassed by any other pre-Hispanic civilization.

Politically, the Classic Maya were divided among many independent city-states, often at war with each other. A typical Maya city functioned as the religious, political and market hub for surrounding farming hamlets. Its ceremonial center focused on plazas surrounded by tall temple

c 1000	1325	1487	1519–20
Chichén Itzá, an abandoned Maya city on the Yucatán Peninsula, is reoccupied, developing into one of Mexico's most magnificent ancient cities, in a fusion of Maya and central Mexican styles.	The Aztec settle at Tenochtitlán, on the site of present-day Mexico City. Over the next two centuries they come to rule an empire extending over nearly all of central Mexico.	Twenty thousand human captives are sacrificed in four days for the rededication of Tenochtitlán's Great Temple after a major reconstruction.	A Spanish expedition from Cuba, under Hernán Cortés, reaches Tenochtitlán. Initially well received, the Spaniards are attacked and driven out on the Noche Triste (Sad Night), June 30, 1520.

pyramids (usually the tombs of rulers, who were believed to be gods). Stone causeways called *sacbeob*, probably for ceremonial use, led out from the plazas, sometimes for many kilometers. In the first part of the Classic period most of these appear to have been grouped into two loose military alliances, centered on Tikal (Guatemala) and Calakmul (in the south of the Yucatán Peninsula).

Classic Maya Zones

Within Mexico, there were four main zones of Classic Maya concentration. Calakmul lies in a now-remote area known as the Río Bec zone, where Maya remains are typically long, low buildings decorated with serpent or monster masks and with towers at their corners. A second zone was the Chenes area in northeastern Campeche state, with similar architecture except for the towers. A third area was the Puuc zone, south of Mérida, characterized by buildings with intricate stone mosaics, often incorporating faces of the hook-nosed rain god Chaac. The most important Puuc city was Uxmal. The fourth zone was lowland Chiapas, with the cities of Palenque (for many people the most beautiful of all Maya sites), Yaxchilán and Toniná.

The Classic Maya Collapse

In the second half of the 8th century, conflict between Maya city-states started to increase, and by the early 10th century, the several million inhabitants of the flourishing central Maya heartland (Chiapas, Guatemala's Petén region and Belize) had virtually disappeared. The Classic era was at an end. A series of droughts combined with population pressure is thought to have brought about this cataclysm. Many Maya probably migrated to the Yucatán Peninsula or the highlands of Chiapas, where their descendants live on today. The jungle grew back up around the ancient lowland cities.

The Toltec

In central Mexico, for centuries after the fall of Teotihuacán, power was divided between various locally important cities, including Xochicalco, south of Mexico City; Cacaxtla and Cantona to the east; and Tula to the north. The cult of Quetzalcóatl remained widespread, society in at least some places became more militarized, and mass human sacrifice may have started here in this period. The Quetzalcóatl cult and large-scale human sacrifice were both exported to the Yucatán Peninsula, where they're most evident at the city of Chichén Itzá.

Central Mexican culture in the early post-Classic period is often given the name Toltec (Artificers), a name coined by the later Aztec, who looked back to the Toltec rulers with awe.

HISTORY THE ANCIENT CIVILIZATIONS

Mexican Heroes

Cuauhtémoc Aztec leader who resisted the Spanish invaders.

Benito Juárez Reforming indigenous president who fought off French occupiers.

Miguel Hidalgo Priest who launched the War of Independence.

Pancho Villa Larger-than-life revolutionary.

1521	1524	1534–92	1540s
The Spanish, with 100,000 native Mexican allies, capture Tenochtitlán, razing it building by building. They rename it 'México' and go on to rebuild it as the capital of Nueva España (New Spain).	Virtually all the Aztec empire, plus other Mexican regions such as Colima, the Huasteca and the Isthmus of Tehuantepec, have been brought under Spanish control.	The Spanish find huge lodes of silver at Pachuca, Zacatecas, Guanajuato and San Luis Potosí, north of Mexico City.	The Yucatán Peninsula is brought under Spanish control by three (related) conquistadors all named Francisco de Montejo. Nueva España's northern border runs roughly from modern Tampico to Guadalajara.

The Aztec

The Aztec's legends related that they were the chosen people of the hummingbird deity Huitzilopochtli. Originally nomads from somewhere in western or northern Mexico, they were led by their priests to the Valle de México, the site of modern Mexico City, where they settled on islands in the valley's lakes. By the 15th century the Aztec (also known as the Mexica, pronounced 'me-*shee*-ka') had fought their way up to become the most powerful group in the valley, with their capital at Tenochtitlán, where downtown Mexico City stands today.

The Aztec formed the Triple Alliance with two other valley states, Texcoco and Tlacopan, to wage war against Tlaxcala and Huejotzingo, east of the valley. The prisoners they took became the diet of sacrificed warriors that voracious Huitzilopochtli (no sweet hummingbird himself) demanded to keep the sun rising every day.

The Triple Alliance brought most of central Mexico, from the Gulf coast to the Pacific, under its control. This was an empire of 38 provinces and about five million people, geared to extracting tribute (tax in kind) of resources absent from the heartland – items like jade, turquoise, cotton, tobacco, rubber, fruits, vegetables, cacao and precious feathers, all needed for the glorification of the Aztec elite and to support their war-oriented state.

Legend tells that the Aztec built their capital at Tenochtitlán because there they witnessed an eagle on a cactus, devouring a snake – a sign, their prophecies told, that they should stop their wanderings. The temple they built on the spot (the Templo Mayor in Mexico City) was considered the center of the universe.

Aztec Society

Tenochtitlán and the adjoining Aztec city of Tlatelolco grew to house more than 200,000 people. The Valle de México as a whole had more than a million people. They were supported by intensive farming based on irrigation, terracing and swamp reclamation.

The Aztec emperor held absolute power. Celibate priests performed cycles of great ceremonies, typically including sacrifices and masked dances or processions enacting myths. Military leaders were usually elite professional soldiers known as *tecuhtli*. Another special group was the *pochteca* – militarized merchants who helped extend the empire, brought goods to the capital and organized large daily markets in big towns. At the bottom of society were pawns (paupers who could sell themselves for a specified period), serfs and slaves.

Other Post-Classic Civilizations

On the eve of the Spanish conquest, most Mexican civilizations shared deep similarities. Each was politically centralized and divided into classes, with many people occupied in specialist tasks, including professional priests. Agriculture was productive, despite the lack of draft animals, metal tools and the wheel. Corn tortillas, *pozole* (corn gruel) and beans were staple foods, and many other crops, such as squash,

1605	1767	1810	1811
Mexico's indigenous population has declined from an estimated 25 million at the time of the Spanish conquest to a little over a million, mainly because of new diseases from Europe.	The Jesuits, important missionaries and educators in Nueva España and many of them criollos (Mexican-born people of Spanish ancestry), are expelled from all Spanish dominions, unsettling criollos in Nueva España.	On September 16 priest Miguel Hidalgo launches Mexico's War of Independence with his Grito de Dolores (Cry of Dolores), a call to rebellion in the town of Dolores.	After initial victories, the rebels' numbers shrink and their leaders, including Hidalgo, are captured and executed in Chihuahua. José María Morelos y Pavón, another priest, assumes the rebel leadership.

tomatoes, chilies, avocados, peanuts, papayas and pineapples, were grown in various regions. Luxury foods for the elite included turkey, domesticated hairless dog, game and chocolate drinks. War was widespread, and often connected with the need for prisoners to sacrifice to a variety of gods.

Several important regional cultures arose in the post-Classic period. The Tarasco, who were skilled artisans and jewelers, ruled Michoacán from their base around the Lago de Pátzcuaro. They were one group that managed to avoid conquest by the Aztec. After 1200, the Zapotec were increasingly dominated by the Mixtec, skilled metalsmiths and potters from the uplands around the Oaxaca–Puebla border. Much of Oaxaca fell to the Aztecs in the 15th and 16th centuries.

In the Yucatán Peninsula, the abandoned Maya city of Chichén Itzá was reoccupied around 1000 CE and developed into one of ancient Mexico's most magnificent cities. The city of Mayapán dominated most of the Yucatán after Chichén Itzá declined around 1200. Mayapán's hold dissolved from about 1440, and the Yucatán became a quarreling ground for many city-states.

Books on Modern Maya

The Caste War of Yucatán by Nelson Reed

Time Among the Maya by Ronald Wright

The Modern Maya: A Culture in Transition by Macduff Everton

Enter the Spanish

Ancient Mexican civilization, nearly 3000 years old, was shattered in two short years by a tiny group of invaders who destroyed the Aztec empire, brought a new religion, and reduced the native people to second-class citizens and slaves. Rarely in history has a thriving society undergone such a transformation so fast. So alien to each other were the newcomers and the indigenous Mexicans that each doubted whether the other was human (Pope Paul III declared indigenous Mexicans to be human in 1537). From this traumatic encounter arose modern Mexico. Most Mexicans today are mestizos, of mixed indigenous and European blood, and thus descendants of both cultures.

The Spanish Background

In 1492, the year Christopher Columbus arrived in the Caribbean, Spain was an aggressively expanding state. Having establishing colonies on the islands of Hispaniola and Cuba, Spanish adventurers began seeking a passage through the land mass to the west, and soon became distracted by tales of gold, silver and a rich empire. Spain's governor on Cuba, Diego Velázquez, asked a colonist named Hernán Cortés to lead one such expedition westward. As Cortés gathered ships and men, Velázquez became uneasy about the costs and Cortés' loyalty, and tried to cancel the expedition. But Cortés, perhaps sensing a once-in-history opportunity, ignored him and set sail on February 15, 1519, with 11 ships, around 500 men and 13 horses.

1813	1821	1822	1824
Morelos' forces blockade Mexico City for several months. A congress at Chilpancingo adopts principles for the independence movement, but Morelos is captured and executed two years later.	Rebel leaders Vicente Guerrero and Agustín de Iturbide devise the Plan de Iguala, for an independent Mexico with a constitutional monarchy and Catholic religious supremacy.	Spain grants Mexico independence and Iturbide is crowned Emperor Agustín I. However, his reign lasts less than nine months and he is forced to flee the country in March 1823.	A new constitution establishes a federal Mexican republic of 19 states and four territories. Guadalupe Victoria, a former independence fighter, becomes its first president.

The Conquest

Anna Lanyon's *The New World of Martin Cortés* tells the fascinating and poignant story of the first mestizo, the son of Hernán Cortés and La Malinche, from his birth in the 1520s in Tenochtitlán to his death, forty-something years later, near Granada, Spain.

The Cortés expedition landed first at Cozumel island, then sailed around the coast to Tabasco. They defeated inhospitable locals in the Battle of Centla near modern-day Frontera, where the enemy fled in terror from Spanish horsemen, thinking horse and rider to be a single fearsome beast. Afterward the locals gave Cortés 20 young women, among them Doña Marina (La Malinche), who became his indispensable interpreter, aide and concubine.

Unhappy Aztec subject towns on the Gulf coast, such as Cempoala, welcomed the Spaniards. And as the Spaniards moved inland toward Tenochtitlán, they made allies of the Aztec's longtime enemies, the Tlaxcalans.

Aztec legends and superstitions and the indecision of Emperor Moctezuma II Xocoyotzin also worked to the Spaniards' advantage. According to the Aztec calendar, 1519 would see the legendary Toltec god-king Quetzalcóatl return from banishment in the east. Was Cortés actually Quetzalcóatl? Omens proliferated: lightning struck a temple, a comet sailed through the night skies and a bird 'with a mirror in its head' was brought to Moctezuma, who saw warriors in it.

The Taking of Tenochtitlán

The Spaniards, with 6000 indigenous allies, were invited to enter Tenochtitlán, a city bigger than any in Spain, on November 8, 1519. Aztec nobles carried Moctezuma out to meet Cortés on a litter with a canopy of feathers and gold, and the Spaniards were lodged, as befitted gods, in the palace of Moctezuma's father, Axayácatl.

Though entertained in luxury, the Spaniards were trapped. Unsure of Moctezuma's intentions, they took him hostage. Tensions rose in the city and, eventually, after six or seven months, some of the Spaniards killed about 200 Aztec nobles in an intended pre-emptive strike. Cortés persuaded Moctezuma to try to pacify his people. According to one version of events, the emperor tried to address the crowds from the roof of Axayácatl's palace, but was killed by missiles; other versions say it was the Spaniards who killed him.

The Spaniards fled, losing several hundred of their own and thousands of indigenous allies, on what's known as the Noche Triste (Sad Night). They retreated to Tlaxcala, where they built boats in sections, then carried them across the mountains to attack Tenochtitlán from its surrounding lakes. When the 900 Spaniards re-entered the Valle de México in May 1521, they were accompanied by some 100,000 native allies. The defenders resisted fiercely, but after three months the city had been razed to the ground and the new emperor, Cuauhtémoc, was captured. Cuauhtémoc asked Cortés to kill him, but he was kept alive until 1525 as

1836	1845–48	1847–48	1858–61
US settlers in the Mexican territory of Texas declare independence. Mexican forces under President Santa Anna wipe out the defenders of the Alamo mission, but are then routed on the San Jacinto River.	US Congress votes to annex Texas, sparking the Mexican–American War (1846–48). US troops occupy Mexico City. Mexico cedes Texas, California, Utah, Colorado and most of New Mexico and Arizona.	The Maya people of the Yucatán Peninsula rise up against their criollo overlords in the 'War of the Castes' and narrowly fail to drive them off the peninsula.	Liberal government laws requiring the church to sell property spark the War of the Reform: Mexico's liberals (with their 'capital' at Veracruz) defeat the conservatives (based in Mexico City).

a hostage, tortured with occasional foot-burning as the Spanish tried to make him reveal the whereabouts of Aztec treasure.

Mexico as a Colony

The Spanish crown saw Mexico and its other American conquests as a silver cow to be milked to finance its endless wars in Europe, a life of luxury for its nobility, and a deluge of new churches, palaces and monasteries that were erected around Spain. The crown was entitled to one-fifth of all bullion sent back from the New World (the *quinto real,* or royal fifth). Conquistadors and colonists, too, saw the American empire as a chance to get rich. Cortés granted his soldiers *encomiendas,* which were rights to the labor or tribute of groups of indigenous people. Spain asserted its authority through viceroys, the crown's personal representatives in Mexico.

The populations of the conquered peoples of Nueva España (New Spain), as the Spanish named their Mexican colony, declined disastrously, mainly from new diseases introduced by the invaders. Allies of sorts to the indigenous people were some of the monks who started arriving in 1523. The monks' missionary work helped extend Spanish control over Mexico – by 1560 they had 'converted' millions of people and built more than 100 monasteries – but many of them also protected local people from the invaders' worst excesses.

Northern Mexico remained beyond Spanish control until big finds of silver at Zacatecas, Guanajuato and elsewhere spurred efforts to subdue it. The northern borders were slowly extended by missionaries and a few settlers, and by the early 19th century Nueva España included (albeit loosely) most of the modern US states of Texas, New Mexico, Arizona, California, Utah and Colorado.

Colonial Society

A person's place in colonial Mexican society was determined by skin color, parentage and birthplace. At the top of the tree, however humble their origins in Spain, were Spanish-born colonists. Known as *peninsulares,* they were a minuscule part of the population, but were considered nobility in Nueva España.

Next on the ladder were the criollos, people of Spanish ancestry born in the colony. As the decades passed, the criollos began to develop a distinct identity, and some of them came to possess enormous estates (haciendas) and amass huge fortunes from mining, commerce or agriculture. Not surprisingly, criollos sought political power commensurate with their wealth and grew to resent Spanish authority.

Below the criollos were the mestizos, and at the bottom of the pile were the indigenous people and African slaves. Though the poor were

1861–63	1864–67	1876–1911	1910–11
Liberal Benito Juárez becomes Mexico's first indigenous president, but Mexico suffers the French Intervention: France invades Mexico, taking Mexico City in 1863 despite a defeat at Puebla on May 5, 1862.	Napoleon III sends Maximilian of Hapsburg over as emperor in 1864, but starts to withdraw his troops in 1866. Maximilian is executed by Juárez' forces in 1867.	The Porfiriato: Mexico is ruled by conservative Porfirio Díaz, who brings stability but curbs civil liberties and democratic rights, and concentrates wealth in the hands of a small minority.	The Mexican Revolution starts when the country rises against the Díaz regime on November 20, 1910. Díaz resigns in May 1911; reformist Francisco Madero is elected president in November.

paid for their labor by the 18th century, they were paid very little. Many were *peones* (bonded laborers tied by debt to their employers), and indigenous people still had to pay tribute to the crown.

Social stratification follows similar patterns in Mexico today with, broadly speaking, the 'pure-blood' descendants of Spaniards at the top of the tree, the mestizos in the middle and the indigenous people at the bottom.

Mexico as a Republic

Criollo discontent with Spanish rule really began to stir following the expulsion of the Jesuits (many of whom were criollos) from the Spanish empire in 1767. The catalyst for rebellion came in 1808 when Napoleon Bonaparte occupied Spain, and direct Spanish control over Nueva España evaporated. The city of Querétaro became a hotbed of intrigue among criollos plotting rebellion against Spanish rule. The rebellion was launched on September 16, 1810, by Padre Miguel Hidalgo in his parish of Dolores (now Dolores Hidalgo). The path to independence was a hard one, involving almost 11 years of fighting between rebels and loyalist forces, and the deaths of Hidalgo and several other rebel leaders. But eventually rebel general Agustín de Iturbide sat down with Spanish viceroy Juan O'Donojú in Córdoba in 1821 and agreed on terms for Mexico's independence.

Mexico's first century as a free nation started with a period of chronic political instability and wound up with a period of stability so repressive that it triggered a revolution. A consistent thread throughout was the opposition between liberals, who favored a measure of social reform, and conservatives, who didn't. Between 1821 and the mid-1860s, the young Mexican nation was invaded by three different countries (Spain, the USA and France), lost large chunks of its territory to the US and underwent nearly 50 changes of head of state.

> Santa Anna had a leg amputated after being wounded by French forces in 1838. He later had the leg buried with military honors in Mexico City. Its whereabouts are now unknown but its prosthetic replacement was captured by Americans in 1847 and now resides in the Illinois State Military Museum.

THE TRAGICOMEDY OF SANTA ANNA

Intervention in politics by ambitious soldiers plagued Mexico throughout the 19th century. Antonio López de Santa Anna first hit the limelight by deposing Emperor Agustín I in 1823. He also overthrew President Anastasio Bustamante in 1831, then was himself elected president in 1833, the first of 11 terms in 22 chaotic years. Above all, Mexicans remember Santa Anna for losing large chunks of Mexican territory to the US. After his 1836 post-Alamo defeat in Texas and his disastrous territorial losses in the Mexican–American War of 1846–48, a Santa Anna government sold Mexico's last remaining areas of New Mexico and Arizona to the US for US$10 million in 1853.

1913–14	1917	1920–24	1926
Madero is deposed and executed by conservative Victoriano Huerta. Northern revolutionary leaders unite against Huerta. Huerta's troops terrorize the countryside, but he is forced to resign in July 1914.	Reformists emerge victorious over radicals in the revolutionary conflict, and a new reformist constitution, still largely in force today, is enacted at Querétaro.	President Álvaro Obregón turns to post-Revolution reconstruction. More than a thousand rural schools are built; some land is redistributed from big landowners to peasants.	President Plutarco Elías Calles closes monasteries, outlaws religious orders and bans religious processions, precipitating the Cristero Rebellion by Catholics (until 1929).

Juárez & Díaz

It was an indigenous Zapotec from Oaxaca who played the lead role in Mexican affairs for two tumultuous decades after the midpoint of the century. Lawyer Benito Juárez was a key member of the new liberal government in 1855, which ushered in the era known as the Reform, in which the liberals set about dismantling the conservative state that had developed in Mexico. Juárez was elected president in 1861. With the French Intervention soon afterward, his government was forced into exile in provincial Mexico, eventually to regain control in 1866. Juárez set an agenda of economic and social reform. Schooling was made mandatory, a railway was built between Mexico City and Veracruz, and a rural police force, the *rurales*, was organized to secure the transportation of cargo through Mexico. Juárez died in 1872 and remains one of the few Mexican historical figures with a completely unsullied reputation.

A rather different Oaxacan, Porfirio Díaz, ruled as president for 31 of the following 39 years, a period known as the Porfiriato. Díaz brought Mexico into the industrial age, stringing telephone, telegraph and railway lines and launching public works projects. He kept Mexico free of civil wars – but political opposition, free elections and a free press were banned. Peasants were cheated out of their land by new laws, workers suffered appalling conditions, and land and wealth became concentrated in the hands of a small minority. All this led, in 1910, to the Mexican Revolution.

The Mexican Revolution

The Revolution was a tortured 10-year period of shifting conflicts and allegiances between forces and leaders of all political stripes. The conservatives were pushed aside fairly early on, but the reformers and revolutionaries who had lined up against them could not agree among themselves. Successive attempts to create stable governments were wrecked by new outbreaks of devastating fighting. All told, one in eight Mexicans lost their lives.

Francisco Madero, a wealthy liberal from Coahuila, would probably have won the presidential election in 1910 if Porfirio Díaz hadn't jailed him. On his release, Madero successfully called on the nation to revolt, which spread quickly across the country. Díaz resigned in May 1911, and Madero was elected president six months later. But Madero could not contain the diverse factions now struggling for power throughout the country. The basic divide was between liberal reformers like Madero and more radical leaders such as Emiliano Zapata, who was fighting for the transfer of hacienda land to the peasants, with the cry of '*¡Tierra y libertad!*' (Land and freedom!).

Freedom from Spain: Key Sites

Alhóndiga de Granaditas (Guanajuato)

Dolores Hidalgo (Guanajuato)

Calabozo de Hidalgo, Casa Chihuahua (Chihuahua)

Ex-Hotel Zevallos (Córdoba)

Museo Casa de Morelos (Morelia)

HISTORY THE MEXICAN REVOLUTION

The best movie about the Mexican Revolution is Elia Kazan's *Viva Zapata!* (1952), starring Marlon Brando. John Steinbeck's script is historically sound up to the 1914 meeting between Pancho Villa and Emiliano Zapata in Mexico City. Beyond that point it flounders until Zapata is assassinated.

1929	1934–40	1964–70	1980s
Elías Calles founds the Partido Nacional Revolucionario: it and its later mutations, the Partido de la Revolución Mexicana and the Partido Revolucionario Institucional (PRI), will rule Mexico until 2000.	President Lázaro Cárdenas redistributes 200,000 sq km of land and expropriates foreign oil operations, forming the state oil company Petróleos Mexicanos (Pemex). Foreign investors avoid Mexico.	President Gustavo Díaz Ordaz resists democratizing the PRI. During demonstrations against one-party rule before the 1968 Olympics, an estimated 400 protestors are massacred at Tlatelolco, Mexico City.	Oil prices plunge and Mexico suffers its worst recession in decades. Amid economic helplessness and rampant corruption, dissent and protests increase, even inside the PRI.

In 1913 Madero was deposed and executed by one of his own generals, Victoriano Huerta, who had defected to conservative rebels. The liberals and radicals united (temporarily) to defeat Huerta. Three main leaders in the north banded together under the Plan de Guadalupe: Venustiano Carranza, a Madero supporter, in Coahuila; Francisco 'Pancho' Villa in Chihuahua; and Álvaro Obregón in Sonora. Zapata also fought against Huerta.

But fighting then broke out again between the victorious factions, with Carranza and Obregón (the 'Constitutionalists,' with their capital at Veracruz) pitted against the radical Zapata and the populist Villa. Zapata and Villa never formed a serious alliance, and it was Carranza who emerged the victor. He had Zapata assassinated in 1919, only to be liquidated himself the following year on the orders of his former ally Obregón. Pancho Villa was killed in 1923.

Mexico as a One-Party State

From 1920 to 2000, Mexico was ruled by the reformists who emerged victorious from the Revolution and their successors in the political party they set up, which since the 1940s has borne the name Partido Revolucionario Institucional (Institutional Revolutionary Party), or PRI as it's universally known. Starting out with some genuinely radical social policies, these governments became steadily more conservative, corrupt, repressive and self-interested as the 20th century wore on. Mexico ended the century with a bigger middle class but still with a yawning wealth gap between the prosperous few and the many poor.

In the 1920s outstanding Mexican artists such as Diego Rivera were commissioned to decorate important public buildings with large, vivid murals on historical and social themes. Many of these can be seen in Mexico City.

Between the 1920s and '60s more than 400,000 sq km of land was redistributed from large estates to peasants and small farmers. Nearly half the population received land, mainly in the form of *ejidos* (communal landholdings). Meanwhile, Mexico developed a worrying economic dependence on its large oil reserves in the Gulf of Mexico. The 1970s and '80s saw the country veer from oil-engendered boom to oil-engendered slump as world oil prices swung rapidly up, then just as suddenly down. The huge government-owned oil company Pemex was just one face of a massive state-controlled economic behemoth that developed as the PRI sought control over all important facets of Mexican life.

Decline of the PRI

The PRI was discredited forever in the minds of many Mexicans by the Tlatelolco Massacre of 1968, in which an estimated 400 civil-liberties protesters were shot dead. The PRI came to depend increasingly on strong-arm tactics and fraud to win elections.

1985	1988–94	1994	1994–2000
On September 19 a massive earthquake, with a magnitude of 8.1 on the Richter scale, strikes Mexico City. At least 10,000 people are killed.	The PRI's Carlos Salinas de Gortari narrowly defeats left-of-center Cuauhtémoc Cárdenas in a disputed presidential election. Salinas reforms Mexico's economy toward private enterprise and free trade.	The North American Free Trade Agreement (Nafta) takes effect. The Zapatista uprising in Chiapas begins. Luis Donaldo Colosio, Salinas' chosen successor as PRI presidential candidate, is assassinated.	Under President Ernesto Zedillo, Mexico emerges from a recession triggered by a currency collapse days after he took office. Crime and migration to the US increase.

Mexicans' cynicism about their leaders reached a crescendo with the 1988–94 presidency of Carlos Salinas de Gortari, who won the presidential election only after a mysterious computer failure had halted vote-tallying at a crucial stage. During Salinas' term, drug trafficking through Mexico – on the rise since the early '80s when traffickers from Colombia began shifting their routes from the Caribbean to Mexico – grew into a huge business, and mysterious high-profile murders proliferated. Salinas did take steps to liberalize the monolithic state-dominated economy. The apex of his program, the North American Free Trade Agreement (Nafta), boosted exports and industry, but was unpopular with food growers and small businesses threatened by imports from the US. The last year of his presidency, 1994, began with the left-wing Zapatista uprising of indigenous people in Mexico's southernmost state, Chiapas, and shortly before Salinas left office he spent nearly all of Mexico's foreign-exchange reserves in a futile attempt to support the peso, engendering a slump that he left his successor, Ernesto Zedillo, to deal with.

It was also left to Zedillo to respond to the rising clamor for democratic change in Mexico. He established a new, independently supervised electoral system that opened the way for his own party to lose power when Vicente Fox of the business-oriented National Action Party (Partido Acción Nacional, PAN) won the presidential election in 2000.

Into the 21st Century

Vicente Fox's election itself – a non-PRI president after 70 years of rule by that party and its predecessors – was really the biggest news of his six-year term. He entered office backed by much goodwill but, in the end, his presidency was considered a disappointment by most. Lacking a majority in Mexico's Congress, Fox was unable to push through reforms that he believed were key to stirring Mexico's slumbering economy.

Fox was succeeded in 2006 by another PAN president, Felipe Calderón. During Calderón's term Mexico's economy sprang back surprisingly fast after the recession of 2009, and Mexico became something of a global environmental champion when it enshrined its carbon-emissions targets in law in 2012. But his presidency will be remembered far more for its war on drugs (p834).

Enrique Peña Nieto's election as president in 2012 returned the PRI to power after 12 years of PAN rule. Peña Nieto's technocrat government embraced market- and investor-friendly reforms, including ending the oil monopoly of state-owned Pemex (Petróleos Mexicanos), in order to boost both production and competition. The reforms paid off, increasing foreign investment and making Mexico's economy less vulnerable to fluctuating oil prices. However, Mexico also saw record levels of violence

Mexican Villains

Hernán Cortés *The original evil Spanish conqueror.*

Antonio López de Santa Anna *Ceded Texas, California, Arizona, Utah, Colorado and New Mexico to the US.*

Carlos Salinas de Gortari *President from 1988 to 1994, blamed for the drugs trade, corruption etc.*

HISTORY INTO THE 21ST CENTURY

2000	2006–12	2012	2014
Vicente Fox, of the right-of-center National Action Party (PAN), wins the presidential election under a new, transparent electoral system, ending seven decades of rule by the PRI and its predecessors.	In the six years of President Calderón's (elected in 2006) war on drugs, 50,000 troops are deployed around the country and some 60,000 people are killed, most of them in intergang turf wars.	The PRI returns to power as Enrique Peña Nieto wins the presidential election, promising reforms to propel the economy forward. López Obrador of the PRD again comes a close second.	Mexico's Congress passes new laws ending Pemex's monopoly in the oil industry and increasing competition in telecoms and broadcasting, intended to spark an economic takeoff.

THE DRUG WAR

Presidents Zedillo and Fox had already deployed the armed forces against the violent mobs running the multi-billion-dollar illegal-drug trade into the USA, but had failed to rein in their violence or their power to corrupt. By 2006, over 2000 people a year were already dying in violence engendered chiefly by brutal turf wars between rival gangs.

President Calderón declared war on the drug gangs and mobilized 50,000 troops plus naval and police forces against them, predominantly in cities along the US border. Some top gang leaders were killed or arrested, and drug seizures reached record levels, but so did the killings – an estimated 60,000 in the six years of Calderón's presidency. The gangs' methods grew ever more shocking, with street gun-battles, gruesome beheadings and torture. Cities such as Monterrey, Nuevo Laredo, Acapulco and Veracruz saw violence spike when local turf wars erupted.

When the numbers of killings finally started to fall at the end of Calderón's presidency, many people believed this was simply because the two strongest mobs – the Sinaloa cartel in the northwest of Mexico and Los Zetas in the northeast – had effectively wiped out their weaker rivals.

during Peña Nieto's term in offce: 28,816 homicide cases were recorded in 2018, a 15% increase over the previous year.

Such worries about increasing crime paved the way for the left-wing former mayor of Mexico City, Andrés Manuel López Obrador, to win an overwhelming victory in the July 2018 presidential election. Popularly known by his initials AMLO, the president's stated priorities are to tackle corruption – a policy on which he has taken the lead by vowing to serve only one term, cutting his salary and doing away with presidential niceties such as his official plane.

Several years into AMLO's presidency, crime rates remained high and Mexico's pandemic-hit economy was facing its worst economic downturn since the Great Depression. And yet there were some encouraging signs of economic recovery as several of the president's signature projects were moving forward, including the Tren Maya, an ambitious intercity railway project in the Yucatán Peninsula.

2015	2017	2018	2020
Drug kingpin Joaquín 'El Chapo' Guzmán escapes from Mexico's top maximum-security prison, causing major embarassment to Peña Nieto's government. He is recaptured in Los Mochis six months later.	Mexico is struck by two powerful earthquakes (8.1 and 7.1 on the Richter scale, respectively) in quick succession. The second earthquake takes place near Puebla and is more destructive, with over 230 dead.	Andrés Manuel López Obrador, now leader of the National Regeneration Movement (Morena) and head of the Juntos Haremos Historia coalition (Together We Will Make History), is elected president.	The Covid-19 pandemic claims hundreds of thousands of lives and delivers a devastating blow to Mexico's crucial tourism industry and service sector. Construction begins on an ambitious intercity railway in the Yucatán.

The Mexican Way of Life

Travels in Mexico quickly reveal how diverse the population is, from the industrial workers of Monterrey and indigenous villagers eking out subsistence in the southern mountains, to the rich sophisticates and bohemian counterculture of Mexico City. But certain common cultural threads connect almost everyone here – among them a deep vein of spirituality, the importance of family, and a simultaneous pride and frustration about Mexico itself.

Life, Death & Family

One thing you can never do with Mexicans is encapsulate them in simple formulas. They're hospitable, warm and courteous to guests, yet are most truly themselves within their family group. They will laugh at death, but have a profound spiritual awareness. They embrace modernity while remaining traditional in essence.

Many Mexicans, however contemporary and globalized they may appear, still inhabit a world in which omens, coincidences and curious resemblances take on great importance. When sick, some people still prefer to visit a traditional *curandero* – a kind of cross between a naturopath and a witch doctor – rather than resort to a modern *médico* (doctor).

While most Mexicans are chiefly concerned with earning a living for themselves and their strongly knit families, they also take their leisure time very seriously, be it partying at clubs or fiestas, or relaxing over an extended-family Sunday lunch at a restaurant. Holidays for religious festivals and patriotic anniversaries are essential to the rhythm of life, ensuring that people get a break every few weeks.

Mexicans may despair of their country ever being governed well, but at the same time they are fiercely proud of it. They naturally absorb a certain amount of US culture and consciousness, but they also strongly value what's different about Mexican life – its more humane pace, its strong sense of community and family, its unique food and drinks, and the thriving, multifaceted national culture.

Nobel Prize–winning Mexican writer Octavio Paz argued in *The Labyrinth of Solitude* (1950) that Mexicans' love of noise, music and crowds was just a temporary escape from personal isolation and gloom. Make your own judgment.

The Great Divides

The fringes of Mexico City are ringed with shacks made from a few concrete blocks or sheets of tin that 'house' the poorest. Meanwhile, in the capital's most affluent neighborhoods, imposing detached houses with well-tended gardens sit behind high walls with strong security gates.

Around 80% of Mexicans now live in an urban area. There are 14 cities with populations of more than one million, and two with over five million people. The number of urban dwellers will continue to rise as rural folk are sucked into cities.

Out in the villages and small towns, people still work the land, and members of an extended family typically live in yards with separate small buildings of adobe, wood or concrete, often with earth floors. Inside these homes are few possessions – beds, a cooking area, a table with a few chairs and a few family photos. Few villagers own cars.

Mexico's eternal wealth gap yawns as wide as ever. Entrepreneur Carlos Slim Helú is the country's richest man with a fortune worth, in 2021, US$63 billion. The poorest Mexicans live on as little as US$1 a day, with government figures showing that 40% of the population live in moderate or extreme poverty.

Land of Many Peoples

Mexico's ethnic diversity is one of its most fascinating aspects. The major distinction is between mestizos – people of mixed ancestry (mostly Spanish and indigenous) – and the *indígenas*, the indigenous descendants of Mexico's pre-Hispanic inhabitants. Mestizos are the majority that hold most positions of power and influence, but the *indígenas*, while mostly materially poor, are often culturally rich.

The secrets of physical and spiritual health of a Nahua *curandera* (literally 'curer') are revealed in *Woman Who Glows in the Dark* by Elena Ávila with Joy Parker.

According to the National Commission for the Development of Indigenous Peoples, 25.7 million people in Mexico (21.5% of the population) are indigenous, covering groups speaking 63 recognized languages. Each of these groups often have unique costumes, customs, beliefs and rituals bound up with nature. The biggest group is the Nahua, descendants of the ancient Aztec, over 2.4 million of whom are spread around central Mexico. The approximately 1.5 million Maya on the Yucatán Peninsula are direct descendants of the ancient Maya, as (probably) are the Tzotzil and Tzeltal of Chiapas. Also directly descended from well-known pre-Hispanic peoples are the Zapotec and Mixtec, mainly in Oaxaca; Totonac in Veracruz; and Purépecha (Tarasco) in Michoacán.

The Spiritual Dimension

Yoga, the temascal (pre-Hispanic steam bath) and New Age cosmic energies may mean more to some Mexicans today than traditional Roman Catholicism, but a spiritual dimension of some kind or other remains important in most Mexicans' lives.

Roman Catholicism

About 83% of Mexicans profess Roman Catholicism, making this the world's second-biggest Catholic country after Brazil. Almost half of Mexican Catholics attend church weekly and Catholicism remains very much part of the nation's established fabric. Most Mexican fiestas are built around local saints' days, and pilgrimages to important shrines are a big feature of the calendar.

The church's most binding symbol is Nuestra Señora de Guadalupe, the dark-skinned manifestation of the Virgin Mary. She appeared to an Aztec potter, Juan Diego, in 1531 on Cerro del Tepeyaca hill in what's now northern Mexico City. A crucial link between Catholic and indigenous spirituality, the Virgin of Guadalupe is now the country's religious patron, an archetypal mother whose blue-cloaked image is ubiquitous and whose name is invoked in political speeches and literature as well as religious

SANTA MUERTE

A challenge to mainstream religion comes from the cult of Santa Muerte (Saint Death) – condemned as blasphemous by the Vatican in 2013, it has, by some estimates, up to 20 million followers in Mexico. Those disillusioned with the traditional Catholic Trinity and saints pray and make offerings to a cloaked, scythe-wielding female skeleton, the goddess of death whose origins date to pre-Hispanic Mexico. Criminal gangs are notoriously among the cult's most loyal followers, and there have even been reports of alleged human sacrifices to Santa Muerte, though she is also seen as a protector of LGBTIQ+ communities and others considered outcasts from society.

ceremonies. December 12, her feast day, sees large-scale celebrations and pilgrimages all over the country, biggest of all in Mexico City.

Though some church figures have supported causes such as indigenous rights, the Mexican Catholic Church is a socially conservative body. It has alienated some sectors of the population by its strong opposition to the legalization of abortion and to gay marriages and civil unions.

Indigenous Religion

The Spanish missionaries of the 16th and 17th centuries won indigenous Mexicans over to Catholicism by grafting it onto pre-Hispanic religions. Old gods were renamed as Christian saints, old festivals were melded with Christian feast days and Christian churches were also built directly on destroyed religious centers. Indigenous Christianity is still fused with ancient beliefs today. Jalisco's Huichol people have two Christs, but Nak-awé, the fertility goddess, is a more important deity. In the church at the Tzotzil Maya village of San Juan Chamula, you may see chanting *curanderos* (healers) carrying out shamanistic rites. In the traditional indigenous world almost everything has a spiritual dimension – trees, rivers, hills, wind, rain and sun have their own gods or spirits, and illness may be seen as a 'loss of soul' resulting from wrongdoing or from the malign influence of someone with magical powers.

Sports

Fútbol

No sport ignites Mexicans' passions more than *fútbol* (soccer). Games in the 19-team Liga MX (https://ligamx.net), the national First Division, are played at weekends almost year-round before crowds averaging 25,000 and followed by millions on TV. Attending a game is fun, and rivalry between opposing fans is generally good-humored.

The two most popular teams with large followings everywhere are América, of Mexico City, nicknamed the Águilas (Eagles), and Guadalajara, commonly called Chivas (Goats). Matches between the two, known as Los Clásicos, are the biggest games of the year. Other leading clubs include Cruz Azul and UNAM (Pumas) of Mexico City, Monterrey and UANL (Los Tigres) from Monterrey, Santos Laguna from Torreón, and Toluca.

Bullfights

Bullfighting arouses strong passions in many Mexicans. While it has many fans, there is also a strong anti-bullfighting movement spearheaded by groups such as AnimaNaturalis (www.animanaturalis.org/mx). Bullfights are now banned in the states of Sonora, Guerrero and Coahuila.

Bullfights usually take place on Sunday afternoons or during local festivals, chiefly in the larger cities. In northern Mexico the season generally runs from March or April to August or September. In central and southern Mexico, including Mexico City's monumental Plaza México, one of the world's biggest bullrings, the main season is from October to February; there are moves afoot, though, to ban bullfighting in Mexico City.

Lucha Libre

The highly popular *lucha libre* (wrestling) is more showbiz than sport. Participants give themselves names like Último Guerrero (Last Warrior), Rey Escorpión (Scorpion King) and Blue Panther, then clown around in Day-Glo tights and lurid masks. Mexico City's 17,000-seat Arena México (p136) is the big temple of this activity.

THE MEXICAN WAY OF LIFE SPORTS

Around 10% of Mexicans adhere to non-Catholic varieties of Christianity. Some are members of Protestant churches set up by US missionaries in the 19th century. Millions of indigenous rural poor from southeast Mexico have been converted in recent years by a wave of American Pentecostal, Evangelical, Mormon, Seventh-Day Adventist and Jehovah's Witness missionaries.

Charreadas (rodeos) are popular events, particularly in the northern half of Mexico, during fiestas and at regular venues often called *lienzos charros* – www.decharros. com has plenty of information.

Architecture & the Arts

Mexicans are an obsessively creative people. Wherever you go in their country, you'll be impressed by the marvelous artistic expression on display. Stunning architecture, dramatic painting and beautiful crafts are everywhere; indigenous performers showcase Aztec music in the very heart of Mexico City and musicians strike up on the streets and in bars and buses. This is a country that has given the world some of its finest painting, music, movies and writing.

Architecture

Pre-Hispanic

At places like Teotihuacán, Monte Albán, Chichén Itzá, Uxmal and Palenque you can still see fairly intact, spectacular pre-Hispanic cities. Their grand ceremonial centers were designed to impress, with great stone pyramids (topped by shrines), palaces and ritual ball courts – all built without metal tools, pack animals or wheels. While the architecture of Teotihuacán, Monte Albán and the Aztec was intended to awe with its grand scale, the Maya of Chichén Itzá, Uxmal, Palenque and countless other sites paid more attention to aesthetics, with intricately patterned facades, delicate stone 'combs' on temple roofs, and sinuous carvings, producing some of the most beautiful human creations in the Americas.

The technical hallmark of Maya buildings is the corbeled vault, a version of the arch: two stone walls leaning toward one another, nearly meeting at the top and surmounted by a capstone. Teotihuacán architecture is characterized by the *talud-tablero* style of stepped buildings, in which height is achieved by alternating tablero (upright) sections with sloping *talud (sloping)*.

Colonial Period

The Spaniards destroyed indigenous temples and built churches and monasteries in their place, and laid out new towns with plazas and grids of streets lined by stone edifices – contributing much to Mexico's urban beauty today. Building was in Spanish styles, with some unique local variations. Renaissance style, based on ancient Greek and Roman ideals of harmony and proportion, with shapes such as the square and the circle, dominated in the 16th and early 17th centuries. Mérida's cathedral and Casa de Montejo are outstanding Renaissance buildings, while the Mexico City and Puebla cathedrals mingle Renaissance and baroque styles.

Baroque, which reached Mexico in the early 17th century, layered new dramatic effects – curves, color and increasingly elaborate decoration – onto a Renaissance base. Painting and sculpture were integrated with architecture, notably in ornate, enormous *retablos* (altarpieces) in churches. Mexico's finest baroque buildings include Zacatecas cathedral and the churches of Santo Domingo in Mexico City and Oaxaca. Between 1730 and 1780 Mexican baroque reached its final, spectacularly out-of-control form known as Churrigueresque, with riotous ornamentation.

Check out the latest (and the future) in Mexico City architecture and planning – from Design Week Mexico installations to plans for a Hyperloop corridor between Mexico City and Guadalajara – at www.dezeen.com/tag/mexico-city.

Indigenous artisans added profuse sculpture in stone and colored stucco to many baroque buildings, such as the Rosary Chapels in the Templos de Santo Domingo at Puebla and Oaxaca. Spanish Islamic influence showed in the popularity of *azulejos* (painted ceramic tiles) on the outside of buildings, notably on Mexico City's Casa de Azulejos and many buildings in Puebla.

Neoclassical style, another return to sober Greek and Roman ideals, dominated from about 1780 to 1830. Outstanding buildings include the Palacio de Minería in Mexico City, designed by Mexico's leading architect of the time, Manuel Tolsá.

19th to 21st Centuries

Independent Mexico in the 19th and early 20th centuries saw revivals of colonial styles and imitations of contemporary French or Italian styles. Mexico City's Palacio de Bellas Artes, mainly art nouveau on the outside and art deco on the inside, is one of the most spectacular buildings from this era.

After the 1910–20 Revolution came 'Toltecism,' an effort to return to pre-Hispanic roots in the search for a national identity. This culminated in the 1950s with the Ciudad Universitaria campus of the Universidad Nacional Autónoma de México (UNAM) in Mexico City, where many buildings are covered with colorful murals.

The great icon of more recent architecture is Luis Barragán (1902–88), who exhibited a strong Mexican strain in bringing vivid colors and plays of space and light to the typical geometric concrete shapes of the International Modern Movement. His strong influence on Mexican architecture and design is ongoing today. His oeuvre includes a set of wacky colored skyscraper sculptures in Ciudad Satélite, a Mexico City suburb, and his own house in Mexico City, which is on the Unesco World Heritage list. Another modernist, Pedro Ramírez Vázquez (1919–2013), designed three vast public buildings in Mexico City: the Estadio Azteca and Museo Nacional de Antropología in the 1960s and the Basílica de Guadalupe in the '70s.

The capital has seen its share of eye-catching, prestigious structures popping up in the last decade or so: undoubtedly the top conversation piece is the Museo Soumaya Plaza Carso, which opened in 2011 to house part of the art collection of multibillionaire Carlos Slim. Designed by Slim's son-in-law Fernando Romero, it's a love-it-or-hate-it six-story construction that resembles a giant, twisted blacksmith's anvil covered in 16,000 honeycomb-shaped aluminium plates.

Painting & Sculpture

Pre-Hispanic

Mexico's first civilization, the Olmec of the Gulf coast, produced remarkable stone sculptures depicting deities, animals and wonderfully lifelike human forms. Most awesome are the huge Olmec heads, varying in height from 1.5m to 3.5m.

The Classic Maya of southeast Mexico, which thrived between between about 250 and 800 CE, were perhaps ancient Mexico's most artistically gifted people. They left countless beautiful stone sculptures, complicated in design but possessing great delicacy of touch.

Colonial & Independence Eras

Mexican art during Spanish rule was heavily Spanish-influenced and chiefly religious in subject, though portraiture advanced under wealthy patrons. Miguel Cabrera (1695–1768), from Oaxaca, is widely considered the most talented painter of the era.

Mexico's Biggest Pyramids

Pirámide Tepanapa (Cholula)

Pirámide del Sol (Pyramid of the Sun; Teotihuacán)

Pirámide de la Luna (Pyramid of the Moon; Teotihuacán)

ARCHITECTURE & THE ARTS PAINTING & SCULPTURE

Top Art Museums

Museo Frida Kahlo (Mexico City)

Museo Jumex (Mexico City)

Museo Nacional de Arte (Mexico City)

Museo de Arte de Tlaxcala (Tlaxcala)

Museo Pedro Coronel (Zacatecas)

The years before the 1910 Revolution finally saw a break from European traditions. Mexican slums, brothels and indigenous poverty began to appear on canvases. José Guadalupe Posada (1852–1913), with his characteristic *calavera* (skull) motif, satirized the injustices of the Porfiriato period, launching a tradition of political and social subversion in Mexican art.

The Muralists

In the 1920s, immediately following the Mexican Revolution, education minister José Vasconcelos commissioned young artists to paint a series of public murals to spread a sense of Mexican history and culture and of the need for social and technological change. The trio of great muralists – all great painters in smaller scales, too – were Diego Rivera (1886–1957), José Clemente Orozco (1883–1949) and David Alfaro Siqueiros (1896–1974).

Rivera's work carried a left-wing message, emphasizing past oppression of indigenous people and peasants. His art, found in many locations in and around Mexico City, pulled Mexico's indigenous and Spanish roots together in colorful, crowded tableaux depicting historical people and events, with a simple moral message.

Siqueiros, who fought in the Revolution on the Constitutionalist (liberal) side, remained a political activist afterward and his murals convey a clear Marxist message through dramatic, symbolic depictions of the oppressed and grotesque caricatures of the oppressors. Some of his best works are at the Palacio de Bellas Artes, Castillo de Chapúltepec and Ciudad Universitaria, all in Mexico City.

Orozco, from Jalisco, focused more on the universal human condition than on historical specifics. He conveyed emotion, character and atmosphere. His work was at its peak in Guadalajara between 1936 and 1939, particularly in the 50-odd frescoes in the Instituto Cultural de Cabañas.

Other 20th-Century Artists

Frida Kahlo (1907–54), physically crippled by polio and, later, a horrific road accident, and mentally tormented in her tempestuous marriage to Diego Rivera, painted anguished self-portraits and grotesque, surreal images that expressed her left-wing views and externalized her inner tumult. Kahlo's work began to strike an international chord in the late 1970s; she's now better known worldwide than any other Mexican artist, and her Mexico City home, the Museo Frida Kahlo, is a don't-miss for any art lover.

Rufino Tamayo (1899–1991) from Oaxaca is sometimes thought of as the fourth major muralist, but he was a great artist at other scales, too, absorbed by abstract and mythological images and effects of color. After WWII, the young artists of La Ruptura (the Rupture), led by José Luis Cuevas (1934–2017), reacted against the muralist movement, which they saw as too obsessed with *mexicanidad* (Mexicanness). They opened Mexico up to world trends such as abstract expressionism and pop art. Sculptor Sebastián (b 1947), from Chihuahua, is famed for his large, mathematics-inspired sculptures that adorn cities around the world.

Contemporary Art

Today, thanks to dynamic artists, galleries and patrons and the globalization of the world art scene, contemporary Mexican art is reaching galleries the world over. Mexico City has become an international art hot spot, while other cities such as Monterrey, Oaxaca, Mazatlán and Guadalajara also have thriving creative scenes. Mexican artists attempt to interpret the uncertainties of the 21st century in diverse ways. The pendulum has swung away from abstraction to hyper-representation, photorealism, installations, video and street art. Rocío Maldonado (b 1951), Rafael Cauduro (b 1950) and Roberto Cortázar (b 1962) all paint classically depicted

Art Books

The Art of Mesoamerica by Mary Ellen Miller

Mexican Muralists by Desmond Rochfort

Mexicolor by Tony Cohan, Masako Takahashi & Melba Levick

Art and Architecture in Mexico by James Oles

Diego & Frida Books

Frida Kahlo and Diego Rivera by Isabel Alcántara and Sandra Egnolff

The Diary of Frida Kahlo with an introduction by Carlos Fuentes

Frida by Hayden Herrera

Rivera by Andrea Kettenmann

STREET ART – THE NEW MURALISTS

The contemporary art having the most public impact in Mexico – and which you are most likely to set eyes on – is street art, whose direct popular appeal provides a powerful channel for Mexicans to express themselves and reach an audience. Mexico City, Oaxaca and Guadalajara lead the way in truly accomplished street art, often with a powerful political-protest message. Check out Street Art Chilango (www.streetartchilango.com), the psychedelic images with pre-Hispanic motifs created by the Axolotl Collective (www.facebook.com/axolotlcollective); the striking, often monochrome works by internationally renowned Paola Delfin (www.urban-nation.com/artist/paola-delfin); and the kaleidoscopic portrayals of animals by Farid Rueda (www.widewalls.ch/artist/farid-rueda) in Mexico City. Find works by Lapiztola (www.facebook.com/lapiztola.stencil) and Guerilla-art.mx (www.guerilla-art.mx) in Oaxaca.

Today's street artists follow in the footsteps of the 20th-century muralists, with the difference that they tend to be independent and rebellious and do not serve governments. Some do, however, use their art for specific positive social projects – none more so than the Mexico City–based Germen Crew (www.facebook.com/muralismogermen), who in 2015 turned the entire Las Palmitas neighborhood in the city of Pachuca into one big rainbow-colored mural. It's a remarkable work, sponsored by the local city hall, which by all accounts has restored pride and smiles to a formerly sketchy area.

figures against amorphous, bleak backgrounds. Check out Cauduro's murals on state-sponsored crime in Mexico City's Suprema Corte de Justicia. Leading contemporary lights such as Minerva Cuevas (b 1975), Miguel Calderón (b 1971), Betsabeé Romero (b 1963) and Gabriel Orozco (b 1962) spread their talents across many media, always challenging the spectator's preconceptions.

Music

Music is everywhere in Mexico. Live performers range from marimba (wooden-xylophone) teams and mariachi bands (trumpeters, violinists, guitarists and a singer, all dressed in smart Wild West–style costumes) to ragged lone buskers with out-of-tune guitars. Mariachi music, perhaps the most 'typical' Mexican music, originated in the Guadalajara area but is played nationwide. Marimbas are particularly popular in the southeast and on the Gulf coast.

Rock & Hip-Hop

Mexico can claim to be the most important hub of *rock en español*. Talented Mexico City bands such as Café Tacúba and Maldita Vecindad emerged in the 1990s and took the genre to new heights and new audiences, mixing influences from rock, hip-hop and ska to traditional Mexican folk music. They're still popular and active today, as is the Monterrey rap-metal band Molotov, and El Tri, a legendary rock band active since 1968.

Mexico's 21st-century indie-rock wave threw up successful bands such as Zoé from Mexico City, which is popular throughout the Spanish-speaking world, and Monterrey's Kinky. The Mexico City five-piece Little Jesus has been winning fans with its catchy, dancey brand of pop-rock; the band's most recent album was *Disco de oro* (2019).

Mexican rap is the true sound of the streets, and top homegrown talents include Eptos One (or Eptos Uno), from Ciudad Obregón (Sonora), Bocafloja (Mexico City), C-Kan from Guadalajara, and Nuevo León Cartel de Santa.

Powerful, colorful Alejandra Guzmán is known as La Reina del Rock (Queen of Rock) and has sold over 30 million albums during a three-decade career. The Mexican rock band most famous outside Mexico is undoubtedly Guadalajara's unashamedly commercial Maná, selling 40 million albums worldwide.

Modern Art Websites

Kurimanzutto (www.kurimanzutto.com)

LatinAmerican Art (www.latinamericanart.com)

Museo Colección Andrés Blaisten (www.museoblaisten.com)

Fundación Jumex (www.fundacionjumex.org)

National Museum of Mexican Art (www.nationalmuseumofmexicanart.org)

MÚSICA TROPICAL

Although their origins lie in the Caribbean and South America, several brands of percussion-heavy, infectiously rhythmic *música tropical* are highly popular throughout the country. Mexico City, in particular, has clubs and large dance halls devoted to this scene, often hosting international bands.

Two kinds of dance music – *danzón,* originally from Cuba, and *cumbia,* from Colombia – both took deeper root in Mexico than in their original homelands. The elegant, old-fashioned *danzón* is strongly associated with the port city of Veracruz but is currently enjoying quite a revival in Mexico City and elsewhere, too. The livelier, more flirtatious *cumbia* has its adopted home in Mexico City. It rests on thumping bass lines with brass, guitars, mandolins and sometimes marimbas. *Cumbia* has spawned its own subvarieties: *cumbia sonidera* is basically electronic *cumbia* played by DJs, while 'psychedelic *cumbia*' harks back to Peruvian *cumbia* of the 1970s.

Almost every town in Mexico has some place where you can dance (and often learn) salsa, which originated in New York when jazz met *son* (folk music), cha-cha and rumba from Cuba and Puerto Rico. Musically, salsa boils down to brass (with trumpet solos), piano, percussion, singer and chorus – the dance is a hot one with a lot of exciting turns. *Merengue,* mainly from the Dominican Republic, is a blend of *cumbia* and salsa.

Pop

Paulina Rubio is Mexico's answer to Shakira, who has also starred in several Mexican films and TV series. Hot on her heels is 'Queen of Latin Pop', Thalía from Mexico City, who has sold over 25 million records worldwide. Natalia Lafourcade, a talented singer-songwriter who mixes pop and bossa nova rhythms, has won several Grammys including for her 2017 and 2018 albums *Musas, Vol. 1* and *Musas, Vol. 2.* Another versatile singer-songwriter is Julieta Venegas from Tijuana, best known for her 2006 album, *Limón y sal.*

Balladeer Luis Miguel (b 1970), known as El Sol de México (the Sun of Mexico), is incredibly popular, as was Juan Gabriel, who had sold millions of his own albums and written dozens of hit songs for others before his death in 2016.

Ranchera & Norteño: Mexico's 'Country Music'

Ranchera is Mexico's urban 'country music' – mostly melodramatic stuff with a nostalgia for rural roots, sometimes with a mariachi backing. The hugely popular Vicente Fernández and Alejandro Fernández (Vicente's son) are leading artists.

Norteño or *norteña* is country ballad and dance music, originating in northern Mexico over a century ago and now nationwide in popularity. Its roots are in *corridos,* heroic ballads with the rhythms of European dances such as waltz or polka. Originally the songs were tales of Latino-Anglo strife in the borderlands or themes from the Mexican Revolution. Modern *narcocorridos* tell of the adventures and exploits of people involved in the drugs trade. Some gangs even commission *narcocorridos* about themselves.

Norteño conjuntos (groups) go for 10-gallon hats, with instruments centered on the accordion and the *bajo sexto* (a 12-string guitar), along with bass and drums. *Norteño's* superstars are Los Tigres del Norte; the members are originally from Sinaloa but the band is now based in California. They play to huge audiences on both sides of the frontier, with some *narcocorridos* in their repertoire. Other top stars include Los Huracanes del Norte, Los Tucanes de Tijuana and accordionist/vocalist Ramón Ayala.

Also very popular, especially in the northwest and along the Pacific coast, is *banda* – Mexican big-band music, with large brass sections replacing *norteño* guitars and accordion, and playing a range of styles from

Vive Latino (www.vivelatino.com.mx), a festival held over a weekend in March at Mexico City's Foro Sol, is one of the world's major annual *rock en español* events. Big electronica events with top Mexican or international DJs are frequent in and around the big cities: www.facebook.com/kinetik.tv and www.trance-it.net/proximos-eventos have details.

ranchera and *corridos* to tropical *cumbia* and Mexican pop. Sinaloa's Banda El Recodo have been at the top of the *banda* tree for decades.

Son – Mexico's Folk Roots

Son (literally 'sound') is a broad term covering Mexican country styles that grew out of the fusion of Spanish, indigenous and African music. Guitars or similar instruments (such as the small guitar-like *jarana*) lay down a strong rhythm, with harp or violin providing the melody. *Son* is often played for a foot-stomping dance audience, with witty, sometimes improvised, lyrics. There are several regional variants. The exciting *son jarocho,* from the Veracruz area, is particularly African-influenced: Grupo Mono Blanco have led a revival of the genre with contemporary lyrics. The famous song 'La Bamba' is a *son jarocho. Son huasteco* (or *huapango*), from the Huasteca area in northeastern Mexico, features falsetto vocals between soaring violin passages. Listen out for top group Los Camperos del Valle.

> Directed by Duncan Bridgeman, the 2012 documentary *Hecho en México* is a fascinating, colorful look at contemporary Mexican life and arts, with participation from many of the country's top musicians, actors and writers.

Cinema

The historical golden age of Mexican movie-making was the 1940s, when the country was creating up to 200 – typically epic, melodramatic – films a year. Then Hollywood reasserted itself, and Mexican cinema struggled for decades, until the 1990s when the movement known as Nuevo Cine Mexicano (New Mexican Cinema) began to emerge. Three key directors rose to the fore: Alejandro González Iñárritu, whose *Amores perros* (Love's a Bitch; 2000), starred a young Gael García Bernal; Alfonso Cuarón, whose breakout movie was *Y tu mamá también* (And Your Mother, Too; 2001); and Guillermo del Toro, much of whose work has been in Hollywood. Iñárritu and Cuarón have also had much success since helming projects north of the border. Cuarón's semi-autobiographical *Roma* (2018) scooped three Oscars – for best cinematography, best director and best foreign-language film.

Other gems of recent Mexican cinema to watch out for include: Pedro González-Rubio's *Alamar* (To the Sea; 2009) a gentle, thoughtful exploration of father-son bonding between a Mexican with Mayan roots and his half-Italian son; Michel Franco's *After Lucia* (Después de Lucía; 2012), a grim, uncomfortable look at high-school bullying; Amat Escalante's *Heli* (2013), the story of a young couple caught in Mexico's violent drug wars; Gabriel Ripstein's arms-smuggling thriller *600 Miles* (600 Millas; 2015); Ernesto Contreras' *I Dream in Another Language* (Sueño en otro idioma; 2017), a meditation on the demise of indigenous languages; and *Museum* (Museo; 2018), a heist movie directed by Alonso Ruizpalacios with a plot based on a real-life robbery at Mexico City's Museo Nacional de Antropología.

> **Craft Books**
>
> *The Crafts of Mexico by Margarita de Orellana and Alberto Ruy Sánchez*
>
> *Arts and Crafts of Mexico by Chloë Sayer*
>
> *Mexican Textiles by Masako Takahashi*

Literature

Carlos Fuentes (1928–2012), a prolific novelist and commentator, is probably Mexico's best-known writer internationally. His most famous novel, *The Death of Artemio Cruz* (1962), takes a critical look at Mexico's post-revolutionary era through the eyes of a dying, corrupted press baron and landowner. Less known is the magical-realist *Aura* (1962), with a truly stunning ending.

In Mexico, Juan Rulfo (1917–86) is widely regarded as the supreme novelist, even though he only ever published one full-length novel: *Pedro Páramo* (1955), about a young man's search for his lost father among ghostlike villages in western Mexico. It's a scary, desolate work with confusing shifts of time – a kind of Mexican *Wuthering Heights* with a spooky, magical-realist twist.

Octavio Paz (1914–98), poet, essayist and winner of the 1990 Nobel Prize for Literature, wrote a probing, intellectually acrobatic analysis of Mexico's myths and the national character in *The Labyrinth of Solitude* (1950).

The 1960s-born novelists of *la generación del 'crack'* take their name from the sound of a limb falling off a tree, representing their desire to break with the past and move on from magical realism. Their work tends to adopt global themes and international settings. Best known is Jorge Volpi, whose *In Search of Klingsor* (1999) and *Season of Ash* (2009) weave complicated but exciting plots involving science, love, murder, mysteries and more, with a strong relevance to the state of the world today.

The *crack* seemed to open the way for a new generation of novelists who are right now putting Mexico back in the vanguard of world literature. These are typically superimaginative, impossible-to-classify writers whose multilayered works leap around between different times, places, voices and perspectives. US-based Valeria Luiselli's *Faces in the Crowd* (2012) and *The Story of My Teeth* (2015) are, on the surface, respectively about a woman writing a novel and a man who replaces his own teeth with (supposedly) Marilyn Monroe's. Then there's Álvaro Enrigue with *Sudden Death* (2013), a novel of vast scope set among the many world-changing events of the 16th century in Europe and the Americas. Also look out for works by prolific poet and novelist Carmen Boullosa, and Juan Pablo Villalobos, whose *Quesadillas* (2014) takes a satirical look at poverty and corruption in Mexico.

Novels Set in Mexico

The Power and the Glory by Graham Greene

Under the Volcano by Malcolm Lowry

The Lacuna by Barbara Kingsolver

The House on Mango Street by Sandra Cisneros

Folk Art

Mexicans' skill with their hands and their love of color, fun and tradition find expression everywhere in their wonderful *artesanías* (handicrafts). Crafts such as weaving, pottery, leatherwork, copperwork, hat-making and basketry still fulfill key functions in daily life as well as yielding souvenirs and collectibles. Many craft techniques and designs in use today have pre-Hispanic origins, and it's Mexico's indigenous peoples, the direct inheritors of pre-Hispanic culture, who lead the way in *artesanía* production.

Traditional Textiles

You'll be stunned by Mexico's variety of colorful, intricately decorated attire, differing from area to area and often from village to village. Traditional costume – more widely worn by women than men – serves as a mark of the community to which a person belongs. The woven or embroidered patterns of some garments can take months to complete.

Three main types of women's garments have been in use since long before the Spanish conquest:

Huipil A long, sleeveless tunic, found mainly in the southern half of the country.
Quechquémitl A shoulder cape with an opening for the head, found mainly in central and northern Mexico.
Enredo A wraparound skirt.

The 'yarn paintings' of the indigenous Huichol people – created by pressing strands of yarn onto a wax-covered board – depict scenes resembling visions experienced under the influence of the drug peyote, which is central to Huichol culture.

Spanish missionaries introduced blouses, which are now often also embroidered with great care and detail.

The primary materials of indigenous weaving are cotton and wool, though synthetic fibers are also common. Natural dyes have been revived – deep blues from the indigo plant, reds and browns from various woods, and reds and purples from the cochineal insect.

The basic indigenous weavers' tool, used only by women, is the *telar de cintura* (back-strap loom) on which the warp (long) threads are stretched between two horizontal bars, one of which is fixed to a post or tree, while the other is attached to a strap around the weaver's lower back; the weft (cross) threads are then intricately woven in, producing some amazing patterns. Backstrap-loom *huipiles* from the southern states of Oaxaca and Chiapas are among Mexico's most eye-catching garments.

Treadle looms, operated by foot pedals (usually by men) can weave wider cloth than the backstrap loom and tend to be used for rugs, *rebozos* (shawls), *sarapes* (blankets with an opening for the head) and skirt material. Mexico's most famous rug-weaving village is Teotitlán del Valle, Oaxaca.

Ceramics

Many small-scale potters' workshops turn out everything from plain cooking pots to elaborate works of art. One highly attractive pottery variety is Talavera, made chiefly in Puebla and Dolores Hidalgo and characterized by bright colors (blue and yellow are prominent) and floral designs. The Guadalajara suburbs of Tonalá and Tlaquepaque produce a wide variety of ceramics. In northern Mexico, the villagers of Mata Ortiz make a range of beautiful earthenware, drawing on the techniques and designs of pre-Hispanic Paquimé, similar to some native American pottery in the US southwest. Another distinctive Mexican ceramic form is the *árbol de la vida* (tree of life). These elaborate, candelabra-like objects are molded by hand and decorated with numerous tiny figures of people, animals, plants and so on. Some of the best are made in Metepec in the state of México, which is also the source of colorful clay suns.

Mexico City's annual contemporary art fair, Zona Maco (www.zsonamaco.com), held over five days every February, pulls in galleries, dealers and cognoscenti from around the world.

Masks & Beadwork

For millennia Mexicans have worn masks in dances, ceremonies and shamanistic rites: the wearer temporarily becomes the creature, person or deity represented by the mask. You can admire mask artistry at museums in cities such as San Luis Potosí, Zacatecas and Colima, and at shops and markets around the country. The southern state of Guerrero makes probably the broadest range of fine masks.

Wood is the basic material of most masks, but papier-mâché, clay, wax and leather are also used. Mask-makers often paint or embellish their masks with real teeth, hair, feathers or other adornments. Common masks include animals, birds, Christ, devils, and Europeans with comically pale, wide-eyed features.

The Huichol people of Jalisco, Durango, Zacatecas and Nayarit use centuries-old symbols and designs when covering masks and wooden sculptures with psychedelic patterns consisting of colorful beads, attached with wax and resin.

Lacquerware & Woodwork

Gourds, the hard shells of certain squash-type fruits, have been used in Mexico since antiquity as bowls, cups and small storage vessels. The most eye-catching decoration technique is lacquering, in which the gourd is coated with paste or paint and then varnished, producing a nonporous and, to some extent, heat-resistant vessel. Lacquering is also used to decorate wooden boxes, trays and furniture, with a lot of the most appealing ware coming from remote Olinalá in Guerrero, where artisans create patterns using the *rayado* method of scraping off part of the top coat of paint to expose a different-colored layer below.

The Seri people of Sonora work hard ironwood into dramatic human, animal and sea-creature shapes. Villagers around Oaxaca City produce brightly painted imaginary beasts carved from copal wood, known as *alebrijes*.

Landscapes & Wildlife

One of the thrills of travel in Mexico is the incredible, ever-changing scenery. From the cactus-strewn northern deserts and the snowcapped volcanoes of central Mexico to the tropical forests and wildlife-rich lagoons of the south, there's rarely a dull moment for the eye. Nature lovers will revel in this country which, thanks to its location straddling temperate and tropical regions, is one of the most biologically diverse on earth.

The Land

Nearly 2 million sq km in area, Mexico is the world's 13th-biggest country. With 10,000km of coastline and half its land above 1000m in elevation, the country has a spectacularly diverse and rugged topography. Almost anywhere you go, except the Yucatán Peninsula, there'll be a range of mountains in sight, close or distant.

Central Volcanic Belt

The Cordillera Neovolcánica, the spectacular volcanic belt running east-west across the middle of Mexico, includes the classic active cones of Popocatépetl (5452m), 70km southeast of Mexico City, and Volcán de Fuego de Colima (3820m), 30km north of Colima. Popocatépetl's eruptions (at low to intermediate intensity) have been ongoing from 2005; over 30 million people live within the area that could be directly affected should smoking 'Popo' erupt in a big way.

Also in the volcanic belt, but dormant, are Mexico's highest peak, Pico de Orizaba (5636m), and the third-highest peak, Popo's 'sister' Iztaccíhuatl (5220m). Mexico's youngest volcano, and the easiest to get to the top of, is Paricutín (2800m), which popped up in 1943 near the Michoacán village of Angahuan.

The upland valleys between the volcanoes have always been among the most habitable areas of Mexico. It's in one of these – the Valle de México (a 60km-wide basin at 2200m elevation) – that Mexico City sits ringed by volcanic ranges.

Northern Plains & Sierras

A string of broad plateaus, the Altiplano Central, runs down the middle of the northern half of Mexico, fringed by two long mountain chains – the Sierra Madre Occidental in the west and Sierra Madre Oriental in the east. The *altiplano* and the two *sierras madres* end where they run into the Cordillera Neovolcánica.

The *altiplano* is criss-crossed by minor mountain ranges, and rises from an average elevation of about 1000m in the north to more than 2000m toward the center of the country. The sparsely vegetated Desierto Chihuahuense (Chihuahuan Desert) covers most of the northern *altiplano* and extends north into the US states of Texas and New Mexico. The landscape here is one of long-distance vistas across dusty brown plains to distant mountains, with eagles and vultures circling the skies. The southern *altiplano* is mostly rolling hills and broad valleys, and includes some of the best Mexican farming and ranching land in the area known as El Bajío, between the cities of Querétaro, Guanajuato and Morelia.

Volcano Watch

....

Monitoreo volcánico Popocatépetl (http://www.cenapred.unam.mx/reportes VolcanGobMX)

Volcán de Colima Tonaltepetl y Volcanes de la Tierra (www.facebook.com/volcancolima)

....

Webcams de México (www.webcamsdemexico.com/webcam-volcan-de-colima, www.webcamsdemexico.com/webcam-popocatepetl, www.webcamsdemexico.com/webcam-popocatepetl-amecameca)

The extremely rugged Sierra Madre Occidental is fissured by many spectacularly deep canyons, including the famous Barranca del Cobre (Copper Canyon) and its 1870m-deep continuation, the Barranca de Urique. The Sierra Madre Oriental includes peaks as high as 3700m, but has semitropical zones on its lower, eastern slopes.

Baja Peninsula

Baja Peninsula, one of the world's longest peninsulas, runs down Mexico's northwest coast. It is believed to have been separated from the 'mainland' about five million years ago by tectonic forces, with the Sea of Cortez (Golfo de California) filling the gap. Baja is 1300km of starkly beautiful deserts, plains and beaches, with a mountainous spine that reaches up to 3100m in the Sierra San Pedro Mártir.

Coastal Plains

Coastal plains stretch all along Mexico's Pacific coast and as far south as the Tabasco lowlands on the Gulf coast. Both coasts are strung with hundreds of lagoons, estuaries and wetlands, making them important wildlife habitats.

On the Pacific side, a dry, wide plain stretches south from the US border almost to Tepic, in Nayarit state. As they continue south to the Guatemalan border, the lowlands narrow to a thin, increasingly tropical strip.

The Gulf coast plain, an extension of a similar plain in Texas, is crossed by many rivers flowing down from the Sierra Madre Oriental. In the northeast, the plain is wide, with good ranchland, but is semimarsh near the coast. It narrows as it nears Veracruz.

The South

Yet another rugged, complicated mountain chain, the Sierra Madre del Sur stretches across the states of Guerrero and Oaxaca, roughly paralleling the Cordillera Neovolcánica, from which it's divided by the broiling hot Río Balsas basin. The Sierra Madre del Sur ends at the low-lying, hot and humid Isthmus of Tehuantepec, Mexico's narrow 'waist', which is just 220km wide at its thinnest.

In the southernmost state of Chiapas, the Pacific lowlands are backed by the Sierra Madre de Chiapas. Dormant Volcán Tacaná, whose 4100m cone rises on the Mexico–Guatemala border, is the westernmost of a string of volcanoes that stretch across Guatemala. Behind the Chiapas highlands, the land sinks to the lowlands of the Lacandón Jungle and the flat expanses of the huge limestone shelf that is the Yucatán Peninsula. The Yucatán's soft, easily eroded limestone has led to the formation of many underground rivers and more than 6000 sinkholes, known as cenotes, many of which make fantastic swimming holes. Off the Yucatán's Caribbean coast is the world's second-largest barrier reef, known variously as the Great Maya, Mesoamerican or Belize Barrier Reef. It's home to a fantastic variety of colorful marine life that makes it one of the world's top diving and snorkeling destinations.

Wildlife

From the whales, sea lions and giant cacti of the Baja Peninsula to the big cats, howler monkeys and cloud forests of the southeast, Mexico's fauna and flora are exotic and fascinating. Getting out among it all is becoming steadily easier as growing numbers of local outfits offer trips to see birds, butterflies, whales, dolphins, sea turtles and more.

Those that Walk

The surviving tropical forests of the southeast are still home to five species of large cat (jaguar, puma, ocelot, jaguarundi and margay) in

Along its 1400km length, the Sierra Madre Occidental is crossed by only one railway and three paved roads: the Ferrocarril Chihuahua Pacífico (Copper Canyon Railway) from Los Mochis to Chihuahua, Hwy 16 (Hermosillo to Chihuahua), and Hwys 40 and 40D (Mazatlán to Durango).

LANDSCAPES & WILDLIFE WILDLIFE

isolated pockets, plus spider and howler monkeys, tapirs, anteaters and some mean reptiles, including boa constrictors. Small jaguar populations are scattered as far north as the northern Sierra Madre Occidental, just 200km from the US border, and the Sierra Gorda in the Sierra Madre Oriental. You may well see howler monkeys – or at least hear their eerie growls – near the Maya ruins at Palenque and Yaxchilán.

In the north, urban growth, ranching and agriculture have pushed the larger wild beasts – such as the puma (mountain lion), wolf, bobcat, bighorn sheep, pronghorn and coyote – into isolated, often mountainous pockets. Raccoons, armadillos and skunks are still fairly common – the last two in much of the rest of Mexico, too.

In all warm parts of Mexico you'll encounter two harmless reptiles: the iguana, a lizard that can grow a meter or so long and comes in many different colors; and the gecko, a tiny, usually green lizard that may shoot out from behind a curtain or cupboard when disturbed. Geckos might make you jump, but they're good news – they eat mosquitoes.

Those that Swim

Baja Peninsula is famous for whale-watching in the early months of the year. Gray whales swim 10,000km from the Arctic to calve in its coastal waters. Between Baja and the mainland, the Sea of Cortez hosts more than a third of all the world's marine mammal species, including sea lions, fur and elephant seals, and four types of whale. Humpback whales follow plankton-bearing currents down Mexico's Pacific coast between December and March, and, like dolphins and sea turtles, can be seen on boat trips from coastal towns.

Mexico's coasts, from Baja to Chiapas and from the northeast to the Yucatán Peninsula, are among the world's chief nesting grounds for sea turtles. Seven of the world's eight species frequent Mexican waters. Some female turtles swim unbelievable distances (right across the Pacific Ocean in the case of some loggerhead turtles) to lay eggs on the beaches where they were born. Killing sea turtles or taking their eggs is illegal in Mexico, and there are more than 100 protected nesting beaches – at many of which it's possible to observe the phenomenon known as an *arribada*, when turtles come ashore in large numbers to nest, or assist in the release of hatchlings.

Dolphins play along the Pacific and Gulf coasts, while many coastal wetlands, especially in the south of the country, harbor crocodiles. Underwater life is richest of all on the coral reefs off the Yucatán Peninsula's Caribbean coast, where there's world-class diving and snorkeling. Near Isla Contoy, off the Yucatán's northeast tip, you can snorkel with whale sharks, the world's biggest fish.

Those that Fly

All of coastal Mexico is a fantastic bird habitat, especially its estuaries, lagoons and islands. An estimated three billion migrating birds pass by or over the Yucatán Peninsula each year, and Veracruz state is a route of passage for a 'river of raptors' over 4.5 million strong every fall. Inland Mexico abounds with eagles, hawks and buzzards, and innumerable ducks and geese winter in the northern Sierra Madre Occidental. Tropical species such as trogons, hummingbirds, parrots and tanagers start to appear south of Tampico in the east of the country and from around Mazatlán in the west. The southeastern jungles and cloud forests are home to colorful macaws, toucans, guans and even a few quetzals. Yucatán has spectacular flamingo colonies at Celestún and Río Lagartos. Dozens of local operators around the country, especially along the coasts, offer bird-watching trips.

Top Turtle Conservation Projects

Cuyutlán, Colima

Isla Mujeres, Quintana Roo

Campamento Majahua, Costalegre, Jalisco

Playa Colola, Michoacán

Playa Escobilla, Oaxaca

Puerto Arista, Chiapas

Tecolutla, Veracruz

Bird Habitats

Reforma Agraria: Scarlet macaw

Reserva de la Biosfera El Triunfo: Resplendent quetzal

Parque Nacional Sierra San Pedro Mártir: California condor

Celestún & Río Lagartos: Flamingo

Mexico's most unforgettable insect marvel can be observed at Reserva de la Biosfera Santuario Mariposa Monarca (p645), where the trees and earth turn orange when millions of monarch butterflies arrive every winter.

Endangered Species

By most counts, 101 animal species are in danger of disappearing from Mexico. Eighty-one of these are endemic to the country. The endangered list includes such wonderful creatures as the jaguar, ocelot, northern tamandua (an anteater), pronghorn, Central American (Baird's) tapir, harpy eagle, resplendent quetzal, scarlet macaw, Cozumel curassow, loggerhead turtle, sea otter, Guadalupe fur seal, four types of parrot, and both spider and howler monkeys.

The beautiful little vaquita (harbor porpoise), found only in the northern Sea of Cortez, was down to between 10 and 22 individuals by 2018. The Margarita Island kangaroo rat and Hubbs freshwater snail may be less glamorous, but their disappearance too will forever affect the other plants and animals around them. Additionally, they're endemic to Mexico, so once gone from here, they're gone from the universe. A host of factors contribute to these creatures' endangered status, including deforestation, the spread of agriculture and urban areas, species trafficking and poaching.

Mexico's main tools for saving endangered species are its network of protected areas such as national parks and biosphere reserves, which cover over 11.5% of the national territory, and a range of specific schemes aimed at conserving certain habitats or species. Government programs are supplemented by the work of local and international conservation groups, but progress is slowed by large gaps in the protected areas network, patchy enforcement and limited funding.

In November 2017, Mexico announced the creation of North America's biggest marine reserve, Parque Nacional Revillagigedo (150,000 sq km), that will protect the eponymous islands which are a Unesco World Heritage site, and the marine species that inhabit the surrounding waters.

Plants

Northern Mexico's deserts, though sparsely vegetated with cacti, agaves, yucca, scrub and short grasses, are the world's most biodiverse deserts. Most of the planet's 2000 or so cactus species are found in Mexico, including more than 400 in the Desierto Chihuahuense alone, and many of them are unique to Mexico. Isolated Baja Peninsula has a rather specialized and diverse flora, from the cardón (the world's tallest cactus which can grow up to 20m) to the bizarre boojum tree, which looks like an inverted carrot with fluff at the top.

Mexico's great mountain chains have big expanses of pine (with half the world's pine species) and, at lower elevations, oak (135 types). In the southern half of the country, mountain pine forests are often covered in clouds, turning them into cloud forests with lush, damp vegetation, many colorful wildflowers, and epiphytes growing on tree branches.

The natural vegetation of the low-lying southeast is predominantly evergreen tropical forest (rainforest in parts). This is dense and diverse, with ferns, epiphytes, palms, tropical hardwoods such as mahogany, and fruit trees such as the mamey and the chicozapote (sapodilla), which yields chicle (natural chewing gum). Despite ongoing destruction, the Selva Lacandona (Lacandón Jungle) in Chiapas is North America's largest remaining montane rainforest, containing a significant number of Chiapas' 10,000 plant species.

The Yucatán Peninsula changes from rainforest in the south to tropical dry forest and savanna in the north, with thorny bushes and small trees (including many acacias).

Parks & Reserves

Mexico has spectacular national parks, biosphere reserves and other protected areas – over 910,000 sq km of its terrestrial and marine territory is under some kind of federal environmental protection. Governments have never devoted enough money for fully effective protection of these areas, but gradually, with some help from conservation organizations, more 'paper parks' are becoming real ones.

National Parks

Mexico's 67 terrestrial *parques nacionales* (national parks) cover 14,320 sq km of territory. Many are tiny (smaller than 10 sq km), and around half of them were created in the 1930s, often for their archaeological, historical or recreational value rather than for ecological reasons. Several recently created parks protect coastal areas, offshore islands or coral reefs. Despite illegal logging, hunting and grazing, terrestrial national parks have succeeded in protecting large tracts of forest, especially the high, coniferous forests of central Mexico.

Learn more about the government-protected natural areas of Mexico and the work being done around them on the website of Comisión Nacional de Áreas Naturales Protegidas (www.gob.mx/conanp).

Biosphere Reserves

Reservas de la biosfera (biosphere reserves) are based on the recognition that it is impracticable to put a complete stop to human exploitation of many ecologically important areas. Instead, these reserves encourage sustainable local economic activities within their territory. Today Mexico has over 40 Unesco-protected and/or national biosphere reserves, covering over 210,000 sq km. These include the Mexican Caribbean Biosphere Reserve (57,000 sq km) created in 2017 and covering virtually the entire coastline of Quintano Roo, and Baja's Pacific Islands Biosphere Reserve (10,926 sq km) encompassing the Coronado Islands near the US border. Biosphere reserves protect some of the country's most beautiful and biologically fascinating areas, focusing on whole ecosystems with genuine biodiversity. Sustainable, community-based tourism is an important source of support for several of them, and successful visitor programs are in place in reserves like Calakmul, Sierra Gorda, Montes Azules, Mariposa Monarca, La Encrucijada and Sian Ka'an.

Ramsar Sites

Nearly 90,000 sq km of Mexican landmass and coastal waters are protected as Wetlands of International Importance, known as Ramsar sites (www.ramsar.org). They are named for the Iranian town where the 1971 Convention on Wetlands of International Importance was signed. Mexico's 142 separate sites include whale calving grounds, turtle nesting beaches, coral reefs, and coastal lagoons and mangrove forests that are of crucial importance for birds and many marine creatures.

Mexico's largest and probably most influential environmental group is Pronatura (www.pronatura.org.mx), which has numerous programs around the country working to protect species, combat climate change, preserve ecosystems, and promote ecotourism, environmental education and sustainable development.

Environmental Issues

Mexico achieved the status of a global standard-bearer on climate change in 2012 when it became only the second country (after the UK) to enshrine carbon-emission commitments into law. The climate-change law committed Mexico, currently the world's 13th-biggest carbon emitter, to be producing 35% of its electricity from renewable and nuclear energy by 2024, and to cut its carbon emissions by 50% from previously expected levels by 2050.

In 2015 it became the first non-European country to formally submit its climate-change commitments to the United Nations, with a minimum 25% cut in greenhouse-gas emissions from previously expected levels by 2030. Mexico also set a target of zero deforestation by 2030. However, under the current government, which has been in place since December 2018, the country has taken a step backwards on achieving these targets by favoring fossil fuel over renewable-energy generation.

Air pollution and deforestation are among Mexico's own biggest environmental problems, and while the country is one of the world's major

TOP PARKS & RESERVES

PARK/RESERVE	FEATURES	ACTIVITIES	BEST TIME TO VISIT
Área de Protección de Flora y Fauna Cuatrociénegas (p812)	Desert; underground streams; extraordinary biodiversity	Swimming; wildlife-watching; hiking	year-round
Parque Nacional Archipiélago Espíritu Santo (p746)	Waters around Espíritu Santo & neighboring islands in the Sea of Cortez	Kayaking with whale sharks; snorkeling with sea lions; sailing	year-round
Parque Nacional Bahía de Loreto (p743)	Islands, shores & waters of the Sea of Cortez	Snorkeling; kayaking; diving	year-round
Parque Nacional Iztaccíhuatl-Popocatépetl (p180)	Active & dormant volcanic giants on the rim of Valle de México	Hiking; climbing	Nov-Feb
Parque Nacional Lagunas de Chacahua (p484)	Oaxacan coastal lagoons; beach	Boat trips; bird-watching; surfing	year-round
Parque Nacional Volcán Nevado de Colima (p632)	Active & dormant volcanoes; pumas; coyotes; pine forests	Volcano hiking	late Oct-early Jun
Reserva de la Biosfera Banco Chinchorro (p312)	Largest coral atoll in the northern hemisphere	Diving; snorkeling	Dec-May
Reserva de la Biosfera Calakmul (p363)	Rainforest with major Maya ruins including Calakmul, Hormiguero & Chicanná	Visiting ruins; wildlife-spotting	year-round
Reserva de la Biosfera El Pinacate y Gran Desierto de Altar (p787)	Petrified lava flows, sand dunes, giant craters; one of the driest places on earth	Hiking; wildlife-spotting	year-round
Reserva de la Biosfera El Vizcaíno (p736)	Coastal lagoons where gray whales calve; deserts	Whale-watching; hikes to ancient rock art	Dec-Apr
Reserva de la Biósfera Santuario Mariposa Monarca (p644)	Forests festooned with millions of monarch butterflies	Butterfly observation; hiking	late Oct-Mar
Reserva de la Biosfera Montes Azules (p412)	Tropical jungle; lakes; rivers	Jungle hikes; canoeing; rafting; bird-watching; boat trips; wildlife-watching	Dec-Aug
Reserva de la Biosfera Ría Celestún (p338)	Estuary & mangroves with plentiful birdlife	Bird-watching; boat trips	Nov-Mar
Reserva de la Biosfera Río Lagartos (p354)	Mangrove-lined estuary full of birdlife	Bird-, crocodile- & turtle-watching	Apr-Sep
Reserva de la Biosfera Sian Ka'an (p311)	Jungle, wetlands & islands with diverse wildlife	Bird-watching; snorkeling & nature tours, mostly by boat	year-round
Reserva de la Biosfera Sierra Gorda (p669)	Transition zone from semidesert to cloud forest	Hiking; bird-watching; colonial missions	year-round

exporters of crude oil, it has had to import half of its gasoline because it is short on refineries. Replacing costly imports with home-grown renewable energy makes a great deal of sense. Sunny Mexico has plenty of potential for solar power – already around 26% of the country's electricity is generated from renewable-energy sources including hydro, wind and geothermal.

LANDSCAPES & WILDLIFE ENVIRONMENTAL ISSUES

How the country can meet its targets is another matter. With the discovery and exploitation of up to two billion barrels in the Zama oil field 60km off the coast of Tabasco in July 2017, the prospects of reducing the country's oil dependency are slim. Wind power is the only renewable-energy source that has generated significantly increased its electricity production in recent years.

Water & Forests

Water supply is a crucial issue. Southern Mexico has 70% of the water, but the nation's north and center have 75% of the people, and around 10% of the population still lacks access to clean drinking water. The country's water supplies are often badly polluted (which is why Mexicans are the world's leading consumers of bottled water), and sewage is seriously inadequate in many areas. In 2015, the government moved to privatize the water system, or parts of it, on the theory that private companies could provide water cheaper, cleaner and more efficiently than the state. This decision was met with protests across the country, yet partial privatization went ahead regardless.

Another key issue is deforestation. The country has lost about three-quarters of the forests it had in pre-Hispanic times, as land has been cleared for grazing, logging and farming. Today about one third of Mexico is covered in forest, about half of which is primary as opposed to regenerated or replanted forest. Profepa (www.gob.mx/profepa), the federal agency that protects Mexico's natural resources, estimates that about 5260 sq km of forest is lost each year, the fifth-worst deforestation rate in the world.

Urban Problems

Mexico City is a high-altitude megalopolis surrounded by a ring of mountains that traps polluted air in the city. The capital consumes over half of Mexico's electricity and has to pump up about a quarter of its water from lowlands far below, then evacuate its waste water back to the lowlands via 11,000km of sewers. Efforts to improve air quality are intensifying. For years, private cars have been banned from the roads one day every week. The city's climate action plan for 2014–20 aims to cut CO_2 emissions by 30% through such means as energy-efficient buses, electric-powered taxis, more bicycle use, and a switch to energy-saving lightbulbs.

The capital's problems of water supply, sewage treatment, overcrowding and air pollution are mirrored on a smaller scale in most of Mexico's faster-growing cities.

Tourism, a key and growing sector of Mexico's economy, can bring its own environmental problems with large-scale development, including expanded airports. On the Caribbean coast's Riviera Maya, organizations such as Centro Ecológico Akumal (www.ceakumal.org) and Mexiconservación (www.mexiconservacion.org) work to limit damage from reckless tourism development to coral reefs, turtle nesting beaches, mangrove systems and even the water in the area's famed cenotes (limestone sinkholes). A slowly growing number of hotels and resorts in the region are adopting green policies.

The Nature Conservancy (www.nature.org), Conservation International (www.conservation.org) and WWF (wwf.panda.org; www.wwf.org.mx; www.worldwildlife.org) all provide lots of information on the Mexican environment, including their programs in the country.

Survival Guide

Directory A–Z

Accessible Travel

➡ A growing number of hotels, restaurants, public buildings and archaeological sites provide wheelchair access, but sidewalks with wheelchair ramps are still uncommon.

➡ Mobility is easiest in major tourist resorts and more expensive hotels. Bus transportation can be difficult; flying or taking a taxi is easier. The absence of formal facilities is partly compensated by Mexicans' helpful attitudes, and special arrangements are gladly improvised.

➡ In general, few provisions are made for visually and hearing-impaired travelers. **Mobility International USA** (www.miusa.org) offers useful info.

➡ Download Lonely Planet's free *Accessible Travel* guides from http://lptravel.to/accessibletravel.

Customs Regulations

As well as your personal luggage, you may bring the following into Mexico duty-free:

➡ if entering by air, up to US$300 worth of goods

➡ if entering by land, up to US$75 worth of goods

➡ medicine for personal use, with prescription or letter from the GP

See https://embamex.sre.gob.mx for further details.

Discount Cards

For reduced-price air tickets at student- and youth-oriented travel agencies, the following cards are widely recognized:

➡ ISIC student card

➡ IYTC (under 26 years) card

➡ ITIC card for teachers

Reduced prices for students and seniors on Mexican buses and at museums and archaeological sites are usually only for those with Mexican residence or education credentials, but the IYTC, ITIC and particularly the ISIC will sometimes get you a reduction.

Electricity

Type A
120V/60Hz

PRACTICALITIES

Newspapers Mexico's only English-language daily newspaper (actually, Monday to Friday) is the *News* (www.thenews.mx) available mainly in Mexico City. The best and most independent-minded Spanish-language national newspapers include *Reforma* (www.reforma.com), the left-wing *La Jornada* (www.jornada.unam.mx), and *El Universal* (www.eluniversal.com.mx/english).

Smoking Mexican law does not allow smoking in indoor public spaces, except in specially designated smoking areas. It also requires at least 75% of a hotel's rooms to be nonsmoking. Enforcement, however, is very patchy.

Weights & Measures Mexico uses the metric system.

Type B
120V/60Hz

Embassies & Consulates

The website of Mexico's foreign ministry, the **Secretaría de Relaciones Exteriores** (www.gob.mx/gobierno/mexico-en-el-mundo), has links to the websites of all Mexican diplomatic missions worldwide. If you will be traveling in Mexico for a long period of time, and particularly if you're heading to remote locations, it's wise to register with your embassy. This can be done over the phone or by email.

Australian Embassy (☑55-1101-2200; https://mexico.embassy.gov.au; Rubén Darío 55, Polanco, Mexico City)

Belizean Embassy (☑55-5520-1274; www.belizeembassy.bz/mx; Bernardo de Gálvez 215, Lomas de Chapultepec, Mexico City; ☒76-A-X)

Canadian Embassy (☑55-5724-7900; www.canada international.gc.ca/mexico-mexique; Schiller 529, Polanco, Mexico City; ⓂPolanco)

French Embassy (☑55-9171-9700; https://mx.ambafrance.org; Campos Elíseos 339, Polanco, Mexico City; ⊗9am-1pm Mon-Fri; ⓂAuditorio)

German Embassy (☑55-5283-2200; www.mexiko.diplo.de; Horacio 1506, Los Morales, Mexico City; ⊗8:30am-4pm Mon-Fri; ⓂPolanco)

Guatemalan Embassy (☑55-5540-7520; www.mexico.minex.gob.gt; Av Explanada 1025, Lomas de Chapultepec, Mexico City; ⊗9am-1pm; ☒76-A-X)

Irish Embassy (☑55-5520-5803; www.dfa.ie/irish-embassy/mexico; Cerrada Blvd Ávila Camacho 76-3, Lomas de Chapultepec, Mexico City; ⊗9:30am-1:30pm Mon-Fri; ☒76-A-X)

Netherlands Embassy (☑55-1105-6550; www.netherlands andyou.nl; 2nd fl, Qúbica Building, Volcán 150, Lomas de Chapultepec, Mexico City; ⊗8:30am-4pm Mon-Thu, until 1pm Fri)

New Zealand Embassy (☑55-5283-9460; www.mfat.govt.nz; 4th fl, Jaime Balmes 8, Polanco, Mexico City; ⊗9:30am-5pm Mon-Fri; ☒57-X)

UK Embassy (Embajada Británica; ☑55-1670-3200; www.gov.uk/world/mexico; Río Lerma 71, Colonia Cuauhtémoc, Mexico City; ⊗8am-4:30pm Mon-Thu, until 2pm Fri; ⓂInsurgentes)

US Embassy (☑55-5080-2000; https://mx.usembassy.gov; Paseo de la Reforma 305, Colonia Cuauhtémoc, Mexico City; ⊗8:30am-5:30pm Mon-Fri; ⓂInsurgentes)

Food

There is a 16% value-added tax (IVA) on restaurant prices, nearly always included in the menu prices.

Health

Travelers to Mexico need to guard chiefly against food- and mosquito-borne diseases. Besides getting the proper vaccinations, carry a good insect repellent and exercise care in what you eat and drink. Medical care in Mexico is generally of a high standard, particularly in private hospitals in big cities.

Availability & Cost of Healthcare

Private hospitals in urban areas generally provide better care than public ones and have the latest medical equipment. The best are in Mexico City and Guadalajara and many doctors speak English. Note that some private hospitals do not accept international travel insurance and you have to pay for your treatment upon being discharged.

Recommended Vaccinations

Make sure all routine vaccinations are up to date and check whether all vaccines are suitable for children and pregnant women. See the website of **Centers for Disease Control & Prevention** (wwwnc.cdc.gov/travel) for more details. There are no required vaccinations for entering Mexico, but the following are recommended:

Diphtheria Travelers visiting rural areas

Hepatitis A All travelers (except children under one year of age)

Hepatitis B Long-term travelers and trekkers

EATING PRICE RANGES

The following price ranges refer to prices of typical main dishes, including value-added tax (IVA).

$ less than M$100

$$ M$100–200

$$$ more than M$200

Rabies Trekkers and travelers who may come in contact with animals

Tetanus All travelers

Tuberculosis Travelers visiting rural areas

Typhoid All travelers

Mexico requires proof of a **yellow fever vaccination** if you're arriving from a country with risk of yellow fever.

Infectious Diseases & Parasitic Infections

Chikungunya Viral disease transmitted by infected aedes mosquitoes, causing fever and severe joint pain. Growing number of cases reported, mostly in Guerrero, Oaxaca, Chiapas and Michoacán, with isolated cases in 12 other states. There is no vaccine or treatment, but it's very rarely fatal and you can only contract it once.

Cutaneous leishmaniasis Lesions caused by sandfly bites in coastal and southern Mexico.

Dengue Fever Viral infection transmitted by aedes mosquitoes, which usually bite during the day. Usually causes flu-like symptoms. No vaccine or treatment except analgesics.

Malaria Transmitted by mosquito bites, usually between dusk and dawn. The main symptom is high spiking fevers. Present in Campeche, Chiapas, Chihuahua, Nayarit and Sinaloa. Rare cases in Durango, Jalisco, Oaxaca, Sonora, Tabasco and Quintana Roo. Consult your doctor about the best antimalarial treatment. Protecting yourself against mosquito bites is just as important as taking malaria pills.

Rickettsial Disease Tick-borne diseases include Rocky Mountain spotted fever (potentially fatal unless treated promptly with antibiotics), common in Northern Mexico, and flea-borne typhus (similar symptoms to dengue fever). Take precautions against flea and tick bites.

Zika Viral disease transmitted by infected aedes mosquitoes. It has spread across the entire country since 2015 but the majority of cases are reported in southern Mexico. Symptoms such as rash, fever and joint pain can be treated, but there's no vaccine. Infections in adults have been linked to Guillain–Barré syndrome. Pregnant women are advised against travel to Mexico as zika increases the risk of brain malformations in babies.

Environmental Hazards

Altitude Sickness May develop in travelers who ascend rapidly to altitudes greater than 2500m. Symptoms may include headache, nausea, vomiting, dizziness, malaise, insomnia and loss of appetite. Severe cases can lead to death. To lessen the chance of altitude sickness, ascend gradually to higher altitudes, avoid overexertion, eat light meals and avoid alcohol. People showing any symptoms of altitude sickness should not ascend higher until the symptoms have cleared. If the symptoms become worse, or if someone shows signs of fluid in the lungs (high-altitude pulmonary edema) or swelling of the brain (high-altitude cerebral edema), descend immediately to a lower altitude. Descent of 500m to 1000m is generally adequate except in cases of cerebral edema.

Mosquito Bites Wear long sleeves, long pants, hats and shoes. Use a good insect repellent, preferably one containing at least 50% DEET, but don't use DEET-containing compounds on children under the age of two. If sleeping outdoors or in accommodations without bug netting, use a bed net, ideally treated with permethrin.

Snake & Scorpion Bites In the event of a venomous snake or scorpion bite, keep the bitten area immobilized and move the victim immediately to the nearest medical facility. For scorpion stings, immediately apply ice or cold packs.

Sun Stay out of the midday sun, wear sunglasses and a wide-brimmed hat and apply sunscreen with SPF 30 or higher. Drink plenty of fluids and avoid strenuous exercise when the temperature is high.

Insurance

A travel-insurance policy to cover theft, loss, adventure sports and medical problems is a very good idea. Some policies specifically exclude dangerous activities such as scuba diving, motorcycling and even trekking, so check carefully to make sure you're covered for all your activities of choice.

Internet Access

Wi-fi is common in Mexican accommodations, is mostly free, and is also available in a growing number of restaurants, cafes, bars, airports and city plazas. Our wi-fi icon means that wi-fi is available on the premises. Internet cafes are very rare since it's easy and cheap to purchase a local SIM card with mobile data for your smartphone or device.

Language Courses

Mexico has many professional, experienced Spanish schools, offering everything from short courses for beginners, with emphasis on the spoken language, to longer courses for serious students. Many schools are located in Mexico's most attractive and interesting cities, such as Oaxaca, Guanajuato, Pátzcuaro, San Cristóbal de las Casas, Mérida, Cuernavaca, Morelia, Guadalajara and Xalapa, as well as Puerto Morelos and Playa del Carmen. They present a great opportunity to get an inside experience of Mexican life, with plenty of extracurricular activities such as dance, cooking, music, excursions and volunteering usually available.

Some courses are geared mainly to college students wanting credits for courses they're taking back home, while other schools focus on travelers or independent language students. Some

Mexican universities have special departments with tailor-made courses for foreigners (usually lasting between one month and one semester). Private schools typically offer shorter courses, from a few days to three months, with more flexible schedules and, often, smaller classes.

The website **123 Teach Me** (www.123teachme.com) offers listings of over 70 language schools in Mexico.

The **National Registration Center for Study Abroad** (www.nrcsa.com), **CIEE** (www.ciee.org), **AmeriSpan** (www.amerispan.com) and **Spanish Abroad** (www.spanishabroad.com) are among US-based organizations offering a range of study programs in Mexico.

Costs

➡ A typical rate for group classes in private schools is around US$15 to US$25 per hour.

➡ Most schools offer a choice of living options, including homestays, apartments and their own student accommodations. Homestays are often the cheapest option (typically around US$100 to US$170 per week for your own room in a family's home and two meals a day).

➡ All up, 25 hours of classes per week, plus homestay accommodations and meals, ranges between US$350 and US$500.

➡ Some schools charge extra for enrollment and registration and/or materials.

Legal Matters

Mexican law is based on the Roman and Napoleonic codes, presuming an accused person guilty until proven innocent.

A law passed in 2009 determined that possession of small amounts of certain drugs for personal use –

including cannabis (5g), cocaine (500mg), heroin (50mg) and methamphetamine (40mg) – would not incur legal proceedings against first-time offenders. But those found in possession of small amounts may still have to appear before a prosecutor to determine whether it is for personal use. The easiest way to avoid any drug-related problems is not to use them. As of June 2017, the medicinal use of marijuana is legal.

It's against Mexican law to take any firearm or ammunition into the country (even unintentionally).

Police corruption is a big problem in Mexico. If confronted by police soliciting bribes for bogus driving offences, you can either pretend to speak no Spanish, or else hand over photocopies of your legal documents (not the documents themselves), ask for their names and badge numbers, and call their bluff by offering to accompany them to the police station.

Useful information on Mexican law are found on the website of the **US State Department** (http://travel.state.gov).

Getting Legal Help

If a foreigner is arrested in Mexico, the Mexican authorities, according to international law, are supposed to promptly contact the person's consulate or embassy if asked to do so. They may not. If they do, consular officials can tell you your rights, provide lists of lawyers, monitor your case, try to make sure you are treated humanely and notify your relatives or friends – but they can't get you out of jail. By Mexican law, the longest a person can be detained without a specific accusation after arrest is 48 hours (though official arrest may not take place until after a period of initial questioning).

State government-run tourist offices may be able to help you with complaints and reporting crimes or lost articles, but don't count on it.

If you are the victim of a crime, your embassy or consulate, or the local tourist office are the best first stops for advice. In some cases, there may be little to gain by going to the police, unless you need a statement to present to your insurance company. If you go to the police, take your passport and tourist permit, if you still have them. If you just want to report a theft for insurance purposes, say you want to *'poner una acta de un robo'* (make a record of a robbery). This should make it clear that you merely want a piece of paper, and you should get it without too much trouble.

LGBTIQ+ Travelers

Mexico is increasingly broad-minded about sexuality but the conservative influence of the Catholic Church remains strong and the country records the second-largest number of homophobic hate crimes in Latin America after Brazil.

This said, legalization of gay marriages in Mexico City since 2009 has energized gay life in the capital. Puerto Vallarta is the gay beach capital of Mexico. There are also lively scenes in places such as Guadalajara, Cancún, Mérida and Acapulco. In June 2016, Mexico's Supreme Court gave a landmark legal ruling that concluded it was unconstitutional for Mexican states to bar gay marriages.

Useful online sources of information include www.gaymexico.com.mx and www.gaymexicomap.com, while www.gaycities.com is good for Mexico City, Guadalajara, Puerto Vallarta, Cancún, Cabo San Lucas and San Miguel de Allende.

Mexico City's **Clínica Condesa** (📞55-5515-8311; http://condesacdmx.mx; Gral Benjamín Hill 24; ⏰7am-5pm Mon-Fri; 🚇De La Salle) is a flagship health center specializing in sexual health, especially (but not only) LGBTIQ+ issues, with treatment at no charge, even for foreigners.

Free, confidential HIV rapid testing (*prueba rápida de VIH*) is available in Mexico City's Zona Rosa gay enclave by **AHF Mexico** (www.pruebadevih.com.mx).

Maps

Nelles, ITM and Michelin all produce good country maps of Mexico that are suitable for travel planning. ITM also publishes good larger-scale maps of many Mexican regions.

Local tourist offices provide free city, town and regional maps of varying quality. Bookstores and newsstands sell commercially published ones, including Guía Roji's recommended all-Mexico road atlas, *Por las carreteras de México*.

Inegi (www.inegi.org.mx) sells large-scale 1:50,000 and 1:250,000 topographical maps at its Centros de Información in every Mexican state capital (detailed on the website), subject to availability.

Maps.me is a very useful iPhone/Android app that allows you to download different regional/city maps of Mexico. The GPS function works offline.

Money

ATMs

Cajeros automáticos (ATMs) are plentiful. You can use major credit cards and Maestro, Cirrus and Plus bank cards to withdraw pesos. The exchange rate you'll get is normally better than the 'tourist rate' for currency exchange at banks and *casas de cambio* (exchange offices), though that advantage may be negated by the M$35 to M$70 fee the ATM company charges and any foreign-transaction fees levied by your card company.

For maximum security, use ATMs during daylight hours and in secure indoor locations.

Banks & Casas de Cambio

US dollars are the best currency to bring with you; Canadian dollars and euros are also widely accepted. You can exchange cash at *casas de cambio* and some banks. *Casas de cambio* exist in just about every large town and many smaller ones. They are often open evenings or weekends and usually offer similar exchange rates as banks. Banks go through more time-consuming procedures, and usually have shorter exchange hours (typically 9am to 4pm Monday to Friday and 9am to 1pm Saturday).

Cash

It's a good idea to carry cash. In tourist resorts and many Mexican cities along the US border, you can make some purchases in US dollars, though the exchange rate won't be great.

Credit Cards

Visa, MasterCard and American Express are accepted by most airlines and car-rental companies, plus many upper midrange and top-end hotels, restaurants and stores. Paying by credit card normally gives you a similar exchange rate to ATM withdrawals, but also factor in any foreign-exchange transaction fee your credit card provider may charge.

Opening Hours

Where there are significant seasonal variations in opening hours, we provide hours for high season. Some hours may be shorter in shoulder and low seasons. Hours vary widely but the following are fairly typical.

Banks 9am-4pm Monday to Friday

Restaurants 9am-11pm

Cafes 8am-10pm

Bars and clubs 1pm-midnight

Shops 9am-8pm Monday to Saturday (supermarkets and department stores 9am-10pm daily)

Photography

It's polite to ask before taking photos of people. Some indigenous people can be especially sensitive about this.

Lonely Planet's Guide to Travel Photography is a comprehensive, jargon-free guide to getting the best shots from your travels.

Special permits are required for any photography or filming with 'special or professional equipment' (which includes all tripods but not amateur video cameras) at any of the archaeological sites or museums administered by INAH, the National Archaeology and History Institute. Permits cost M$5709 per day for still photography and M$11,419 per day for movie or video filming, and must be applied for at least two weeks in advance.

Post

The Mexican postal service (www.correosdemexico.gob.mx) is slow, inexpensive and fairly reliable. Mail to the US or Canada typically takes a week to 10 days to arrive. Mail to Europe averages one to two weeks.

If you're sending a package internationally from Mexico, be prepared to open it for customs inspection at the post office; it's better to take packing materials with you, or not seal it until you get there. For assured and speedy delivery, you can use one of the more-expensive international courier services, such as **UPS** (www.ups.com),

FedEx (www.fedex.com) or Mexico's **Estafeta** (www.estafeta.com). A 1kg package typically costs around US$50 to the US or Canada, and US$100 to Europe.

Public Holidays

On official national holidays, banks, post offices, government offices and many other offices and shops close throughout Mexico.

Año Nuevo (New Year's Day) January 1

Día de la Constitución (Constitution Day) Observed on the first Monday of February.

Día de Nacimiento de Benito Juárez (anniversary of Benito Juárez' birth) Observed on the third Monday of March.

Día del Trabajo (Labor Day) May 1

Día de la Independencia (Independence Day) September 16

Día de la Revolución (Revolution Day) Observed on the third Monday of November.

Día de Navidad (Christmas Day) December 25

Día de los Santos Reyes (Three Kings' Day, Epiphany) January 6

Día de la Bandera (Day of the National Flag) February 24

Viernes Santo (Good Friday) March or April

Cinco de Mayo (anniversary of Mexico's victory over the French at Puebla) May 5

Día de la Madre (Mother's Day) May 10

Día de la Raza (commemoration of Columbus' arrival in the New World) October 12

Día de Muertos (Day of the Dead) November 2

Día de Nuestra Señora de Guadalupe (Day of Our Lady of Guadalupe) December 12

Safe Travel

Mexican authorities have been waging a war against drug-trafficking gangs for over a decade, with limited

GOVERNMENT TRAVEL ADVICE

These government websites have information on potentially dangerous areas and general safety tips:

Australian Department of Foreign Affairs (www.smartraveller.gov.au)

British Foreign Office (www.gov.uk/foreign-travel-advice)

Canadian Department of Foreign Affairs (http://travel.gc.ca)

New Zealand Ministry of Foreign Affairs (www.safetravel.govt.nz)

US State Department (http://travel.state.gov)

success. The associated violence is horrific and frightening, but almost exclusively an internal matter between the drug gangs; only very rarely tourists have been victims.

Top safety precautions throughout Mexico include:

➡ Travel by day and on toll highways where possible, and don't wander into neighborhoods unfrequented by tourists after dark.

➡ Beware of undertows and rips at ocean beaches, and don't leave your belongings unattended while you swim.

Theft & Robbery

Pickpocketing and bag snatching are risks on crowded buses and subway trains, at bus stops, bus terminals, airports, markets and in packed streets and plazas, especially in large cities. Pickpockets often work in teams, crowding their victims and trying to distract them.

Mugging is less common but more serious. These robbers may force you to remove your money belt, watch, rings etc. Do not resist, as resistance may be met with violence, and assailants may be armed. There are occasional victims of 'express kidnappings', with people forced to go to an ATM and withdraw money, but this rarely happens to foreign visitors.

The following precautions will minimize risks:

➡ Avoid semideserted places, such as empty streets and empty metro cars at night, little-used pedestrian underpasses and isolated beaches.

➡ Use official taxis and Uber instead of walking in potentially dodgy areas.

➡ Be alert to the people around you.

➡ Leave valuables in a safe at your accommodations unless you have immediate need of them. If no safe is available, divide valuables into different stashes secreted in your room or a locker.

➡ Carry just enough cash for your immediate needs in a pocket. If you have to carry valuables, use a money belt, shoulder wallet or pouch underneath your clothing.

➡ Don't keep cash, credit cards, purses, cameras and electronic gadgets in open view any longer than necessary. At ticket counters in bus terminals and airports, keep your bag between your feet.

If you are a victim of crime, report the incident to a tourist office, the police or your country's nearest consulate.

Taxes & Refunds

Mexico's *impuesto al valor agregado* (IVA; value-added tax) is 16%, included by law in the price of goods and services.

Hotel rooms are also subject to the *impuesto sobre hospedaje* (ISH; lodging tax) of 2% or 3%, depending on which Mexican state they're in.

In Cancún and along the Riviera Maya there is a tourism tax of M$20 per room, per night. Baja California Sur is charging a tourist tax of M$350 (about US$18.50) for all visitors entering the state.

Over 10,000 stores in Mexico participate in the tax reimbursement program (look for the Moneyback logo) that allows visitors to claim back 65% of the IVA, provided they spend at least M$1200 per total purchase and are leaving by air or by sea. Request a VAT-itemised invoice at the time of purchase and take it to a Moneyback office or kiosk at the airport or cruise-ship terminal to claim back tax. For more details see https://taxfree.com.mx/v1.

Telephone
Cell Phones

Mexico's main *teléfono celular* (cell-phone) companies are **Telcel** (www.telcel.com), **Movistar** (www.movistar.com.mx) and **AT&T Mexico** (www.att.com.mx). Telcel has the most widespread coverage, and both Telcel and AT&T Mexico offer both roaming and calling in Canada and the US without extra charges.

➡ Roaming in Mexico with your own phone from home is possible if you have a GSM, 3G or 4G phone, but can be expensive. **Roaming Zone** (www.roamingzone.com) is a useful source on roaming arrangements. A number of cell-phone service providers in the US now offer packages that allow customers to roam in Mexico at no (or a small) extra charge.

➡ Much cheaper is to put a Mexican SIM card ('*chip*') into your phone, but your phone needs to be unlocked for international use. Many Mexican cell-phone stores can unlock it for around M$400.

➡ SIMs are available from countless phone stores, often for around M$50.

➡ For around M$350 you can buy a new, no-frills Mexican cell phone with a *chip* and some call credit included. New smartphones start around M$1700, plus M$300 to M$500 a month for calling and data credit. Take your passport for ID when you go to buy a *chip* or phone; you may also have to provide a local address and postcode.

➡ You can buy new credit at convenience stores, newsstands, pharmacies and department stores.

PHONE CODES

Like Mexican landlines, every Mexican SIM card has an area code. The area code and the phone's number total 10 digits.

Cell phone to cell phone	10-digit number
Cell phone to landline	Area code + 10-digit number
Landline to cell phone	10-digit number
Abroad to Mexican cell phone	International access code + ☏52 + 1 + 10-digit number

Collect Calls

A *llamada por cobrar* (collect call) can cost the receiving party much more than if they call you, so you may prefer to arrange for the other party to call you. If you don't have access to a smartphone/wi-fi/Skype, you can make collect calls from public card phones without a card. Call an operator on ☏020 for domestic calls, or ☏090 for international calls.

Landlines

Mexican *teléfonos fijos* (landlines) have two- or three-digit area codes.

Landline to landline (same town)	7- or 8-digit number
Landline to landline (different town)	☏01 + area code + local number
International call from Mexican landline	☏00 + country code + area code + local number
Mexican landline from abroad	International access code + ☏52 + area code + local number

Operator & Toll-Free Numbers

Directory assistance	☏040
Domestic operator	☏020
Emergency	☏911
International operator	☏090
Mexican toll-free numbers	☏1 + 800 + 7-digit number

Public Card Phones

You'll usually find some at airports and bus terminals and around town. Most are run by **Telmex** (www.telmex.com). To use a Telmex card phone, you need a *tarjeta Ladatel* (phone card), sold at kiosks and shops everywhere.

Time
Time Zones

Hora del Centro The same as CST (US Central Time; GMT minus six hours in winter, and GMT minus five hours during daylight saving), this time zone applies to most of Mexico, including Campeche, Chiapas, Tabasco and Yucatán.

Hora de las Montañas The same as MST (US Mountain Time; GMT minus seven hours in winter, GMT minus six hours during daylight saving), this time zone applies to five northern and western states in Mexico – Chihuahua, Nayarit, Sinaloa, Sonora and Baja California Sur.

Hora del Pacifico The same as PST (US Pacific Time; GMT minus eight hours in winter, GMT minus seven hours during daylight saving), this time zone applies to Baja California Norte.

The state of Quintana Roo observes EST (US Eastern Standard Time; GMT minus five hours year-round).

Daylight Saving

Daylight saving time (*horario de verano;* summer time) in nearly all of Mexico runs from the first Sunday in April to the last Sunday in October. Clocks go forward one hour in April and back one hour in October. Exceptions to the general rule:

➡ The northwestern state of Sonora ignores daylight saving (like its US neighbor Arizona), as does Quintana Roo, so they remain on MST and EST respectively all year.

➡ Ten cities on or near the US border – Ciudad Acuña, Ciudad Anáhuac, Ciudad Juárez, Matamoros, Mexicali, Nuevo Laredo, Ojinaga, Piedras Negras, Reynosa and Tijuana – change their clocks on the second Sunday in March and the first Sunday in November to synchronize with US daylight-saving periods.

Tourist Information

Most towns of interest to tourists in Mexico have a state or municipal tourist office. These are generally helpful with maps and brochures, and some staff members usually speak English.

You can call the Mexico City office of the national tourism secretariat, **Sectur** (☑55-5278-4200; www. visitmexico.com), for information or help in English or Spanish.

Visas & Tourist Permits

Every tourist must have a Mexican-government tourist permit, easily obtained on arrival. Citizens of the US, Canada, EU countries, Argentina, Australia, Brazil, Israel, Japan, New Zealand, Norway and Switzerland are among those who do not need visas to enter Mexico as tourists. Chinese, Indians, Russians and South Africans are among those who do need a visa. But Mexican visas are not required for people of any nationality who hold a valid US, Canadian or Schengen visa.

If the purpose of your visit is to work (even as a volunteer), report, study or participate in humanitarian aid or human-rights observation, you may well need a visa whatever your nationality. Visa procedures might take a few weeks and you may be required to apply in your country of residence or citizenship.

The websites of some Mexican embassies and consulates, including those in **London** (http://consulmex. sre.gob.mx/reinounido) and **Washington** (http://consul mex.sre.gob.mx/washing ton), give useful information on visa regulations and similar matters. The rules are also summarized on the website of Mexico's **Instituto Nacional de Migración** (www.inm.gob.mx).

Non-US citizens passing (even in transit) through the USA on the way to or from Mexico should check well in advance on the US's complicated visa rules. Consult a US consulate or the **US State Department** (http://travel. state.gov) and **US Customs and Border Protection** (www.cbp.gov) websites.

Tourist Permits & Fees

You must fill out the Mexican *forma migratoria múltiple* (FMM; tourist permit), get

it stamped by Mexican immigration when you enter Mexico, and keep it till you leave. It's available at official border crossings, international airports and ports. At land borders you have to ask for the tourist permit.

The length of your permitted stay in Mexico is written on the card by the immigration officer. The maximum is 180 days, but they may sometimes put a lower number unless you tell them specifically what you need.

The fee for the tourist permit is around M$500, but it's free for people entering by land who stay less than seven days. If you enter by air, the fee is included in your airfare. If you enter Mexico by land, you must pay the fee once you arrive or at a bank in Mexico at any time before you re-enter the border zone to leave Mexico (or before you check in at an airport to fly out of Mexico). The border zone is the territory between the border itself and the INM's control points on highways leading into the Mexican interior (usually 20km to 30km from the border).

Most Mexican border posts have on-the-spot bank offices where you can pay the DNR or visitors' fee immediately on arrival in Mexico. Your tourist permit will be stamped to prove that you have paid.

Look after your tourist permit because you need to hand it in when leaving the country. Tourist permits (and fees) are not necessary for visits shorter than 72 hours within the border zones.

EXTENSIONS & LOST PERMITS

If the number of days given on your tourist permit is fewer than 180, its validity may be extended up to this maximum. To get a permit extended, apply to the INM, which has offices in many towns and cities: they're listed on the website of Mexico's **Instituto Nacional de**

Migración (www.inm.gob.mx/gobmx/word/index.php/horarios-y-oficinas). The procedure costs the same as the tourist permit and should only take half an hour or so. You'll need your passport, tourist permit, photocopies of them and, at some offices, evidence of 'sufficient funds' (a major credit card is usually OK). Most INM offices will not extend a permit until a few days before it is due to expire.

If you lose your permit, contact your nearest tourist office, which should be able to give you an official note to take to your local INM office, which will issue a replacement for about M$500.

Volunteering

A good way to engage with and contribute to Mexican communities is to do some volunteer work. Many organizations can use your services for periods from a few hours to a year or more. Work ranges from protecting sea turtles to helping out on farms. Some organizations are looking for people with relevant experience and/or Spanish-language skills, while others can use almost any willing hand.

Many language schools offer part-time local volunteering opportunities to complement the classes you take.

Volunteer Directories

Go Abroad (www.goabroad.com)

Go Overseas (www.gooverseas.com)

Idealist.org (www.idealist.org)

The Mexico Report (http://themexicoreport.com/non-profits-in-mexico)

Volunteer Oaxaca (http://volunteer-oaxaca.com)

Mexico-Based Programs
SOCIAL PROGRAMS

Casa de los Amigos (www.casadelosamigos.org) Mexico City–based, with volunteer programs to assist refugees and migrants.

Entre Amigos (www.entreamigos.org.mx) Nayarit-based project that arranges educational projects and workshops for the children of San Pancho.

Feed the Hungry (http://feedthehungrysma.org) Offers nutritious meals to several thousand disadvantaged children in San Miguel de Allende.

Fundación En Vía (www.envia.org; Instituto Cultural Oaxaca, Juárez 909; tour per person M$850; htours 1pm Thu & 9am Sat) ✈ Oaxaca-based nonprofit organization providing microfinance loans to help village women develop small businesses.

Junax (www.junax.org.mx) Offers information and lodging in San Cristóbal de las Casas for people wanting to volunteer with indigenous communities in Chiapas; Spanish-language skills needed.

Piña Palmera (www.pinapalmera.org) Work with physically and intellectually disabled people at Zipolite on the Oaxaca coast.

ENVIRONMENTAL PROGRAMS

Campamento Majahuas (www.facebook.com/campamento majahuas; hturtles nesting Jul-Nov) ✈ Excellent turtle conservation project in Costalegre (with short-term volunteering options).

Centro Ecológico Akumal (www.ceakumal.org) Environmental work, including coastal management and turtle protection.

Flora, Fauna y Cultura de México (www.florafaunaycultura.org) Conservation volunteering with turtles on the Caribbean coast.

Vida Milenaria (www.vidamilenaria.org.mx; Niños Héroes 1; donation required; ⊙7am-9am Jun-Nov) ✈ Excellent turtle project at Tecolutla.

Nomad Republic (https://nomadrepublic.org) Assisting with local cooperatives throughout Mexico in agriculture, education, tourism, health, water, energy and other fields.

Pronatura (www.pronatura-ppy.org.mx) Marine conservation and other projects in the Yucatán.

Tortugueros Las Playitas (www.todostortugueros.org) Sea-turtle hatchery in Todos Santos, Baja California Sur.

WWOOF Mexico (www.wwooflatinamerica.com) Volunteering on organic farms around Mexico. Some farms suitable for families.

Organizations Based Outside Mexico

Global Vision International (www.gviusa.com) Anything from marine conservation to teaching projects.

Los Médicos Voladores (www.flyingdocs.org) Lend your medical skills to communities throughout Mexico and Central America.

Projects Abroad (www.projects-abroad.org) Volunteer projects involving teaching, conservation, agriculture and more.

Women Travelers

Gender equality has come a fair way, and Mexicans are generally a very polite people, but machismo is still a fact of life and solo women travelers may still be subject to wolf whistles, cat-calls and attempts to chat them up.

Avoiding drinking alone in cantinas and hitchhiking can help to minimise the risk of hassle, or worse. On the streets of cities and towns and on local transportation, following the lead of local women, who don't typically display too much skin, may also help women travelers avoid unwanted attention.

Work

Mexico's economy is the 15th-largest in the world and there are work opportunities for foreigners, particularly in the service industry. A helpful website detailing how to get a work visa in Mexico is https://transferwise.com/gb/blog/mexico-work-visa, while www.mexperience.com/lifestyle/working-in-mexico and www.internations.org/mexico-expats/guide provide useful insights into working in Mexico.

Transportation

GETTING THERE & AWAY

As well as flying in, you can enter Mexico by car or bus from the USA, Guatemala or Belize and take a boat from the Belizean coast to Quintana Roo. Flights, tours and rail tickets can be booked online at www.lonelyplanet.com/bookings.

Entering the Country

US citizens traveling by land or sea can enter Mexico and return to the US with a passport card, but if traveling by air they will need a passport. Citizens of other countries need their passport to enter Mexico. Some nationalities also need a visa.

Air

More than 30 Mexican airports receive direct flights from the USA (some from several US cities, some from just a couple), and some of them also receive direct flights from Canada. **Mexico City** (☎55-2482-2424; www.aicm.com.mx; Terminal 1, Capitán Carlos León s/n, Colonia Peñón de los Baños; Ⓜ Terminal Aérea), **Cancún** (Cancún International Airport; ☎998-848-72-00; www.asur.com.mx; Hwy 307 Km 22), **Guadalajara** (GDL; ☎33-3688-5248; www.aeropuertosgap.com.mx; Carretera Guadalajara Chapala Km 17.5, Tlajomulco de Zuñiga), **Monterrey** (☎81-8288-7700; www.oma.aero; Carretera Miguel Alemán Km 24, Apodaca) and **Puerto Vallarta** (Puerto Vallarta International Airport; ☎322-221-12-98; www.aeropuertosgap.com.mx/en/puerto-vallarta-3.html; Carretera Vallarta–Tepic Km 7.5; Ⓜ Las Juntas, Ixtapa) are Mexico's busiest international airports. Only Mexico City and Cancún receive direct scheduled flights from European, Caribbean and Central and South American countries, with Cancún offering the most options from Europe.

Mexico's flagship airline is **Aeroméxico** (www.aeromexico.com); its safety record is comparable to major US and European airlines. Mexico's **Interjet** (www.interjet.com.mx) and **Volaris** (www.volaris.com) flew to several US cities. Interjet also flew to Havana and Varadero in Cuba, San José in Costa Rica, Guatemala City, and Lima, Peru. Interjet suspended operations in December 2020 due to the COVID-19 pandemic, and its future remained unclear at time of press.

Land
Border Crossings
BELIZE
Frequent buses run from Chetumal's Nuevo Mercado Lázaro Cárdenas to the Belizean towns of Corozal (M$195, one hour) and Orange Walk (M$300, 2¼ hours). Some continue on to Belize City (M$390, four hours).

CLIMATE CHANGE & TRAVEL

Every form of transport that relies on carbon-based fuel generates CO_2, the main cause of human-induced climate change. Modern travel is dependent on airplanes, which might use less fuel per kilometer per person than most cars but travel much greater distances. The altitude at which aircraft emit gases (including CO_2) and particles also contributes to their climate change impact. Many websites offer 'carbon calculators' that allow people to estimate the carbon emissions generated by their journey and, for those who wish to do so, to offset the impact of the greenhouse gases emitted with contributions to portfolios of climate-friendly initiatives throughout the world. Lonely Planet offsets the carbon footprint of all staff and author travel.

Each person leaving Belize for Mexico needs to pay a US$20 (BZ$40) exit fee in cash, in Belizean or US currency; officials usually won't have change for US currency.

GUATEMALA

The road borders at Ciudad Cuauhtémoc–La Mesilla, Ciudad Hidalgo–Ciudad Tecún Umán and Talismán–El Carmen are all linked to Guatemala City and nearby cities within Guatemala and Mexico by plentiful buses and/or combis. The Ciudad Hidalgo–Ciudad Tecún Umán border is the busiest, and famous for shakedowns on the Guatemalan side; Talismán–El Carmen is definitely the border crossing to go for.

The following companies run daily buses between Tapachula in Chiapas and Guatemala City (five to six hours):

Tica Bus (www.ticabus.com) M$850; 7am

Trans Galgos Inter (http://transgalgosintergt.com) M$500; 6am, 2.15pm and 11.15pm

For the Río Usumacinta route between Palenque (Mexico), and Flores (Guatemala), there are vans between Palenque and Frontera Corozal (M$145, 2½ to three hours), from where it's a 40-minute boat trip to Bethel (Guatemala). From Bethel, hourly buses run to Flores (4½ hours) from 8am to 4pm.

Travel agencies in Palenque and Flores offer bus-boat-bus packages between the two places for around US$33 (five hours), typically departing at 6am, but if you're traveling this route it's well worth taking the time to visit the outstanding Maya ruins at Yaxchilán, near Frontera Corozal.

Another possible route between Mexico and Flores is via the border at El Ceibo, near Tenosique in Tabasco. Vans, buses and taxis run between Tenosique and El Ceibo, and there are vans between the border and Flores.

DEPARTURE TAX

The airport departure tax Tarifa de Uso de Aeropuerto (TUA) is almost always included in your ticket cost, but if it isn't, you must pay in cash during airport check-in. It varies from airport to airport and costs between MS$460 and M$1060 for international flights and M$128 and M$540 for domestic flights. This tax is separate from the fee for your tourist permit, which is always included in airfares.

USA

There are more than 40 official US–Mexico border crossing points, many open 24 hours daily. **US Customs & Border Protection** (www.cbp.gov) provides opening hours and estimated waiting times for drivers.

Some Mexican cities on the border and elsewhere in northern Mexico are affected by drug-gang violence, so check travel warnings before you go. Ciudad Juárez and Nuevo Laredo are best avoided altogether, or at least passed through as quickly as possible.

In the Baja Peninsula, the San Ysidro border crossing is the busiest, so it's best for travelers to use another, such as Tecate, for visiting the Valle de Guadalupe.

There's a pedestrian-only crossing between the US and Mexico at Boquillas del Carmen–Big Bend National Park; see www.nps.gov/bibe/planyourvisit/visiting-boquillas.htm for details.

Cross-border bus services link many US and Mexican cities. On most trips you will transfer between a US and a Mexican bus on the US or Mexican side of the border, although you can usually buy a ticket right through to your final destination thanks to affiliations between different bus lines.

Greyhound (www.greyhound.com.mx) From California, Arizona and Texas to border cities, with onward transfers into northwest Mexico.

Ómnibus Mexicanos (www.omnibusmexicanos.com.mx)

From Texas to northeast, central north and central Mexico.

Tufesa (www.tufesa.com.mx) From many cities in the US southwest and California to northwest Mexico, Mazatlán and Guadalajara.

Turimex Internacional (www.turimex.com) From Chicago, Texas and southeastern USA to northeast, central north and central Mexico.

Most routes are covered by several buses daily. You can (often as quickly) go to the border on one bus (or train – see www.amtrak.com), cross it on foot or by local bus, then catch an onward bus on the other side.

Car & Motorcycle

The rules for taking a vehicle into Mexico change from time to time. Check with a Mexican consulate or **Sanborn's** (www.sanborns.com).

Driving into Mexico is most useful for travelers who have plenty of time, like independence, have surfboards, diving equipment or other cumbersome luggage and/or will be traveling with at least one companion. Drivers should know at least a little Spanish and have basic mechanical knowledge. A sedan with a trunk provides safer storage than a station wagon or hatchback.

Mexican mechanics are resourceful, but take as many spare parts as you can manage (spare fuel filters are very useful). Tires (including spare), shock absorbers and suspension should be in good condition. For security, have something to immobilize the steering wheel and consider getting a kill switch installed.

Motorcycling in Mexico is not for the fainthearted. Roads and traffic can be rough, and parts and mechanics hard to come by. The parts you'll most easily find will be for Kawasaki, Honda and Suzuki bikes.

Finding a gas station at or near the border crossings is not a problem.

VEHICLE PERMIT

You will need a *permiso de importación temporal de vehículo* (temporary vehicle import permit), costing around US$19.50 (not including IVA tax), if you want to take a vehicle into Mexico beyond the border zone that extends 20km to 30km into Mexico along the US frontier and up to 70km from the Guatemalan and Belizean frontiers. The only exceptions to this are the Baja Peninsula, where the permit is not needed, and Sonora state as far south as Guaymas, which offers a cheaper, simplified procedure – but you will need a permit if you embark a vehicle at Pichilingue (La Paz) in Baja California Sur, on a ferry to 'mainland' Mexico.

The vehicle permits are issued by offices at border crossings, or at posts a few kilometers into Mexico, and also at Ensenada port and Pichilingue ferry terminal in Baja California Sur. You can also apply for the permit via **Banjército** (www.banjercito. com.mx/registroVehiculos), the bank that deals with vehicle-import procedures. Online applications must be made between 60 and 11 working days in advance to allow time for the permit to reach you by mail. The online procedure also involves obtaining electronic pre-authorization for your Mexican tourist permit.

The person importing the vehicle will need to carry the original and one or two photocopies of each of the following documents, which must all be in their own name

(except that you can bring in your spouse's, parent's or child's vehicle if you can show a marriage or birth certificate proving your relationship):

➡ tourist permit (FMM); at the border go to *migración* before you process your vehicle permit

➡ certificate of title, or registration certificate, for the vehicle (you should have both of these if you plan to drive through Mexico into either Guatemala or Belize)

➡ a Visa or MasterCard credit or debit card issued outside Mexico, or a cash deposit of between US$200 and US$400 (depending on how old the car is); your card details or deposit serve as a guarantee that you'll take the car out of Mexico before your FMM expires

➡ passport or US passport card

➡ if the vehicle is not fully paid for, a credit contract, or invoice letter not more than three months old, from the financing institution

➡ for a leased or rented vehicle, the contract, in the name of the person importing the vehicle and notarized letter of permission

➡ for a company car, proof of employment by the company as well as proof of the company's ownership of the vehicle

When you leave Mexico, you must have the import permit canceled at the border to ensure that your deposit is returned to you. A permit is valid for six months (180 days), during which you may enter Mexico multiple times. You have to exit Mexico before the expiration date or else the authorities may deny you permission to bring a vehicle into the country next time.

Sea

From Chetumal, **San Pedro Belize Express** (☎983-832-16-48; www.belizewatertaxi.

com; Av Blvd Bahía s/n, Muelle Fiscal; one-way M$950-1050; ⊗8:30am-4pm) and **Water Jets International** (☎983-833-32-01; www.sanpedrowatertaxi.com; Blvd Bahía s/n, Muelle Fiscal; one-way M$1100-1200; ⊗9am-3:30pm) offer boat transport to ports in Belize.

GETTING AROUND

Air

More than 60 Mexican cities have airports with scheduled passenger services. Flying can be good value on longer journeys and the regional airlines tend to have a decent safety record.

Aeroméxico (www. aeromexico.com), including its subsidiary Aeroméxico Connect, has the biggest network, but **Aeromar** (www. aeromar.mx), **Interjet** (www. interjet.com.mx), **TAR Aerolíneas** (www.tarmexico. com), **Volaris** (www.volaris. com) and **VivaAerobus** (www.vivaaerobus.com) also serve many cities, often with lower fares. Other regional airlines are **Aéreo Servicios Guerrero** (ASG; www.asg. com.mx), **Calafia Airlines** (www.calafiaairlines.com), **Magnicharters** (www.magni charters.com) and **MAYAir** (www.mayair.com.mx).

Boat

Vehicle and passenger ferries connecting the Baja Peninsula with the Mexican mainland sail between:

➡ Santa Rosalía and Guaymas – passenger fares are around M$999 (children's tickets are M$535); vehicle rates vary with vehicle length

➡ La Paz and Mazatlán – passenger fares in *salón* (numbered seats) M$1240

➡ La Paz and Topolobampo – passenger fares in *salón* are M$1100

Bus

Mexico has a good road network and comfortable, frequent, reasonably priced bus services connect all cities. Most cities and towns have one main bus terminal from which all long-distance buses operate. It may be called the Terminal de Autobuses, Central de Autobuses, Central Camionera or La Central (not to be confused with *el centro*, the city center!).

Bus stations in major cities are generally clean, safe and highly functional.

Classes

Mexico's buses (called *camiones*, unlike in other Spanish-speaking countries) have three classes.

DELUXE & EXECUTIVE

De lujo services, *primera plus* and the even-more-comfortable *ejecutivo* (executive) buses run mainly on the busier intercity routes. They are swift and comfortable, with reclining seats, plenty of legroom, air-conditioning, movies on (individual) video screens, few or no stops, toilets on board (sometimes separate ones for men and women) and often drinks, snacks and even wi-fi. They use toll roads wherever available.

FIRST CLASS

Primera (1a) clase buses have a comfortable numbered seat for each passenger. All sizable towns are served by 1st-class buses. Standards of comfort are adequate at the very least. The buses have air-conditioning and a toilet, and they stop infrequently. They show movies on general screens and use toll roads where possible.

SECOND CLASS

Segunda (2a) clase or *económico* buses serve small towns and villages and provide cheaper, slower travel on some intercity routes. A few are almost as quick,

BUSES – PRACTICAL TIPS

➜ Buses do occasionally get held up and robbed. Traveling by day and on deluxe or 1st-class buses, which use toll highways where possible, minimizes this risk.

➜ Buying tickets several days in advance or at less busy times of day can often get you a discount fare.

➜ Baggage is safe if stowed in the baggage hold – get a receipt when you hand it over. Keep your most valuable possessions in the cabin with you.

➜ Air-conditioned buses can get cold, so wear long pants or a skirt and take a sweater or jacket and maybe a blanket on board. Eye masks and earplugs can be handy if you don't want to watch videos the entire trip!

comfortable and direct as 1st-class buses. Others are old, slow and shabby. Few have toilets. These buses tend to take non-toll roads and will stop anywhere to pick up passengers, so if you board midroute you might make some of the trip standing. In remoter areas, they are often the only buses available.

Reservations

For 1st-class, deluxe and executive buses, buy your ticket in the bus terminal before the trip; in some cities you can buy tickets from bus offices in central office locations. It is also usually possible to purchase tickets online and be sent an e-ticket or QR code for check-in.

For trips of up to four or five hours on routes with frequent service, you can usually just go to the bus terminal, buy a ticket and head out without much delay. For longer trips, or routes with infrequent service, or for any trip at busy holiday times, it's best to buy a ticket a day or more in advance. You can usually select your seat when you buy your ticket. Try to avoid the back of the bus, which is where the toilets are located and also tends to give a bumpier ride.

Many 2nd-class services have no ticket office; just pay your fare to the conductor.

Car & Motorcycle

Having a vehicle in Mexico gives you a whole lot of flexibility and freedom, and with a little adaptation to local road conditions is no more difficult than in most other countries.

Driver's License

To drive a motor vehicle in Mexico, you need a valid driver's license from your home country.

Fuel

In 2018 the monopoly Pemex (Petróleos Mexicanos) enjoyed on selling *gasolina* (gasoline) and diesel fuel in Mexico ended. There is now price competition between different stations, which are pretty common on most major roads. In remote areas, fill up whenever you can. Gasoline is all *sin plomo* (unleaded). There are two varieties:

Magna (87 octane) Roughly equivalent to US regular unleaded, costing about M$18.75 per liter (US$0.98 per US gallon).

Premium (91 octane and lower in sulfur content) Roughly equivalent to US super unleaded, costing about M$20.40 per liter.

Diesel fuel is widely available at around M$21 per liter. Regular Mexican diesel has a higher sulfur content than US diesel, but a *bajo azufre* (low sulfur) variety has started to become available in

Mexico City and some nearby areas. Gas stations all have pump attendants (whom you should tip at least M$5).

Insurance

It is essential to have Mexican liability insurance. If you are involved in an accident in Mexico, you can be jailed and have your vehicle impounded while responsibility is assessed. If you are to blame for an accident causing injury or death, you may be detained until you guarantee restitution to the victims and payment of any fines. Adequate Mexican insurance coverage is the only real protection: it is regarded as a guarantee that restitution will be paid.

Mexican law recognizes only Mexican *seguro* (auto insurance), so a US or Canadian policy, even if it provides coverage, is not acceptable to Mexican officialdom. You can buy Mexican auto insurance online through the long-established **Sanborn's** (www.sanborns.com) and other companies. Mexican insurance is also sold in border towns in the US and at some border points. At the busiest border crossings there are insurance offices open 24 hours a day.

Short-term insurance is about US$30 a day for full coverage on a car worth under US$10,000. For periods longer than two weeks, it's often cheaper to get a semi-annual or annual policy. Liability-only insurance costs around half the full coverage cost.

Rental

Auto rental in Mexico can be expensive by US or European standards, but is not difficult to organize. Many major international rental firms have offices throughout the country.

Renters must provide a valid driver's license (your home license is OK), passport and major credit card, and are usually required to be at least 21 years of age (sometimes 25, or if you're aged 21 to 24 you may have to pay a surcharge). Read the small print of the rental agreement. In addition to the basic rental rate, there will be tax and insurance costs. Comprehensive insurance can more than double the basic cost quoted in some online bookings – you'll usually have the option of liability-only insurance at a lower rate. Ask exactly what the insurance options cover: theft and damage insurance may only cover a percentage of costs, or the insurance might not be valid for travel on rough country tracks. It's best to have plenty of liability coverage.

Rental rates typically start around M$700 per day, including unlimited kilometers, basic insurance and tax. In some beach resorts you may pay as little as M$500. If you rent by the week or month, per-day costs come down. The extra charge for drop-off in another city, when available, is usually about M$10 per kilometer.

Motorbikes or scooters can be rented in a few tourist centers. You're usually required to have a driver's license and a credit card. Many renters do not offer any insurance, however.

BUS COMPANIES

Mexico has hundreds of bus companies. Many of the major ones belong to the four large groups that dominate bus transportation in different parts of the country. Their websites have schedule information.

BUS COMPANY	WEBSITE	DESTINATIONS SERVED
ETN Turistar	www.etn.com.mx	All major cities along the Pacific coast, central, northern and eastern Mexico and destinations as far south as Oaxaca. Also Tuscon, El Paso and San Diego.
Grupo ADO	www.ado.com.mx	Connects Mexico City with numerous cities in the Yucatán, Campeche, Quintana Roo, Tabasco, Chiapas, Oaxaca, Puebla, Guerrero and Veracruz.
Grupo Estrella Blanca	www.estrellablanca.com.mx	Mexico City and the center, north and west of Mexico. Major cities such as Guadalajara, Tijuana, Puebla, Monterrey, Puerto Vallarta and Ciudad Juárez.
Primera Plus	www.primeraplus.com.mx	Destinations around the center of the country include Mexico City, Guadalajara, Mazatlán, Puerto Vallarta, San Luis Potosí and San Miguel de Allende.

Road Hazards & Conditions

➜ Mexico's highways are serviceable and fairly fast when traffic is not heavy. There are more than 6000km of *autopistas* (toll highway), which are generally good, four-lane roads. Tolls cost around M$2.50 per kilometer.

➜ Driving at night is best avoided, since unlit vehicles, hard-to-see speed bumps, rocks, pedestrians and animals on the roads are common, and drunk drivers are more numerous – and general highway security is better by day.

➜ Some hijackings, holdups and illegal roadblocks connected with drug-gang activities occur, mainly in the north. The northeastern states of Tamaulipas and Nuevo León are especially notorious – particularly the Tampico–Matamoros road and Hwys 101 and 180 in Tamaulipas, which are particularly renowned for armed robberies and carjackings. In this part of the country especially, it is best to stick to toll highways, avoid driving after dark, and keep doors locked and windows closed when driving through cities. Check travel warnings and seek local advice. If you do become a victim, do not try to resist.

➜ There are also some perfectly genuine military and police roadblocks, which are generally looking for illegal weapons, drugs, migrants or contraband. They are unlikely to give tourists a hard time and are no cause for alarm.

➜ It's best to leave vehicles in secure lockup parking lots overnight. These are fairly common in cities, and hotels can tell you where they are if they don't have their own secure parking.

➜ Driving under the influence of alcohol and non-use of seat belts are more prevalent here. Traffic density, poor surfaces, speed bumps, animals, bicycles and pedestrians all help to keep speeds down.

➜ Be wary of 'Alto' (Stop) signs, *topes* (speed bumps) and potholes in the road (quite often on motorways, too). They are often not where you'd expect them and missing one can cost you in traffic fines or car damage. 'Tope' or 'Vibradores' signs warn you of many speed bumps – the deadly ones are the unmarked ones with no warning signs!

➜ There is always the chance that you will be pulled over by traffic police. If this happens, stay calm and polite. If you don't think you have committed an infraction, you don't have to pay a bribe, and acting dumb may eventually make the cop give up. You can also ask to see the officer's identification, the documentation about the law you have supposedly broken, ask to speak to a superior, and note the officer's name, badge number, vehicle number and department (federal, state or municipal). If you're told that it's cheaper to pay a ticket on the spot, make it clear that you want to pay any fines at a police station and get a receipt; bribe-seekers are likely to let you go at this point. If you then wish to make a complaint, head for a state tourist office.

Road Rules

➜ Drive on the right-hand side of the road.

➜ Speed limits range between 80km/h and 120km/h on open highways (less when highways pass through built-up areas), and between 30km/h and 50km/h in towns and cities.

➜ One-way streets are the rule in cities.

➜ Legal blood-alcohol limits for drivers range from 0.5g/L to 0.8g/L – roughly two or three small beers or tequilas.

➜ Antipollution rules in Mexico City ban most vehicles from the city's roads on one day each week.

Local Transportation

Bicycle

Cycling is not a common way to tour Mexico. The size of the country, poor road surfaces, careless motorists and other road hazards are deterrents. If you're up for the challenge, though, take the mountainous topography and hot climate into account when planning your route. All cities have bicycle stores: a decent mountain bike suitable for a few weeks' touring costs around M$5000.

Consider the bring-your-own-bike tours of southern Mexico and the central volcano country offered by the fun and friendly **¡El Tour** (www.bikemexico.com).

Bicycle culture is on the up in Mexican cities, however. Most of them are flat enough to make cycling an option and there is a growing number of designated bicycle lanes in Mexico City, Guadalajara, Puebla, Monterrey and some other large cities. Mexico City offers free bike rental. There are bicycle-sharing schemes in Guadalajara (www.mibici.net), Mexico City (www.ecobici.cdmx.gob.mx) and Puebla (www.urbanbici.mx). They work in the same way as other global bike-shares. You can hire decent road and mountain bikes in several other towns for M$300 to M$700 per day. Seek out less-traffic-infested routes and you should enjoy it.

Critical Mass bicycle rides are a growing phenomenon across the country; for a list of places where they happen see https://criticalmass.fandom.com/wiki/List_of_rides.

THE GREEN ANGELS

The Mexican tourism secretariat, Sectur, maintains a network of Ángeles Verdes (Green Angels) – bilingual mechanics in green uniforms and green trucks who patrol 60,000km of major highways and toll roads throughout the country daily from 8am to 6pm looking for tourists in trouble. They can give you directions, make minor repairs, change tires, provide fuel and oil, and arrange towing and other assistance if necessary. Service is free, and parts, gasoline and oil are provided at cost. The 24-hour toll-free number for the Green Angels is ✆01-800-987-8224. In case of an emergency, you can also dial ✆078.

Colectivo, Combi, Minibus, Pesero & Piratea

These are all names for vehicles that function as something between a taxi and a bus, running along fixed urban routes usually displayed on the windshield. They're cheaper than taxis and quicker than buses. They will pick you up or drop you off on any corner along their route – to stop one, go to the curb and wave your hand. Tell the driver where you want to go. Usually you pay at the end of the trip and the fare (a little higher than a bus fare) depends on how far you go.

Local Bus

Generally known as *camiones,* local buses are usually the cheapest way to get around cities and out to nearby towns and villages. They run frequently, and

fares in cities are just a few pesos. In many cities, fleets of small, modern *microbuses* have replaced the noisy, dirty older buses.

Buses usually halt only at fixed *paradas* (bus stops), though in some places you can hold your hand out to stop one at any street corner.

Metro

Mexico City, Guadalajara and Monterrey all have metro (subway, underground railway) systems. Mexico City's, in particular, is a quick, cheap and useful way of getting around; note, however, that in rush hours it can get very crowded.

Taxi

Taxis are common in towns and cities, and surprisingly economical. City rides cost around M$20 to M$25 per kilometer. If a taxi has a meter, you can ask the driver if it's working (*'¿Funciona el taxímetro?'*). If the taxi doesn't have a functioning meter, establish the price of the ride before getting in (this may involve a bit of haggling).

Many airports and some big bus terminals have a system of authorized ticket-taxis – you buy a fixed-price ticket to your destination from a special *taquilla* (ticket window), then hand it to the driver instead of paying cash. This saves haggling and major rip-offs, but fares are usually higher than you could get on the street.

Renting a taxi for a day-long out-of-town jaunt generally costs something similar to a cheap rental car – around M$600 to M$700.

Uber has become increasingly popular, as well as a similar app-based service, Cabify.

Train

The spectacular **Ferrocarril Chihuahua Pacífico** (El Chepe; ✆800-122-43-73; www.chepe.com.mx; full journey Chepe Express/Regional from M$3743/1891; ♿) runs through the Sierra Madre Occidental between Los Mochis and Chihuahua (the luxury *Chepe Express* travels only between Los Mochis and Creel). It's one of the highlights of travel in Mexico and the country's only remaining passenger train.

Language

Mexican Spanish pronunciation is easy, as most sounds have equivalents in English. Also, Spanish spelling is phonetically consistent, meaning that there's a clear and consistent relationship between what you see in writing and how it's pronounced. Note that kh is a throaty sound (like the 'ch' in the Scottish *loch*), v and b are like a soft English 'v' (between a 'v' and a 'b'), and r is strongly rolled. There are also some variations in spoken Spanish across Latin America, the most notable being the pronunciation of the letters *ll* and *y*. In some parts of Mexico they are pronounced like the 'll' in 'million', but in most areas they are pronounced like the 'y' in 'yes', and this is how they are represented in our pronunciation guides. In other Latin American countries you might also hear them pronounced like the 's' in 'measure', the 'sh' in 'shut' or the 'dg' in 'judge'. The stressed syllables are indicated with italics in our pronunciation guides. Bearing these few things in mind and reading our colored pronunciation guides as if they were English, you should be understood just fine.

The polite form is used in this chapter; where both polite and informal options are given, they are indicated by the abbreviations 'pol' and 'inf'. Where necessary, both masculine and feminine forms of words are included, separated by a slash and with the masculine form first, eg *perdido/a* (m/f).

BASICS

Hello.	*Hola.*	o·la
Goodbye.	*Adiós.*	a·dyos

WANT MORE?

For in-depth language information and handy phrases, check out Lonely Planet's *Mexican Spanish Phrasebook*. You'll find it at **shop.lonelyplanet.com**, or you can buy Lonely Planet's iPhone phrasebooks at the Apple App Store.

How are you?	*¿Qué tal?*	ke tal
Fine, thanks.	*Bien, gracias.*	byen gra·syas
Excuse me.	*Perdón.*	per·don
Sorry.	*Lo siento.*	lo syen·to
Please.	*Por favor.*	por fa·vor
Thank you.	*Gracias.*	gra·syas
You're welcome.	*De nada.*	de na·da
Yes.	*Sí.*	see
No.	*No.*	no

My name is ...
Me llamo ...   me ya·mo ...

What's your name?
¿Cómo se llama Usted? ko·mo se ya·ma oo·ste (pol)
¿Cómo te llamas? ko·mo te ya·mas (inf)

Do you speak English?
¿Habla inglés? a·bla een·gles (pol)
¿Hablas inglés? a·blas een·gles (inf)

I don't understand.
Yo no entiendo.   yo no en·tyen·do

ACCOMMODATIONS

I'd like a ... room.	*Quisiera una habitación ...*	kee·sye·ra oo·na a·bee·ta·syon ...
single	*individual*	een·dee·vee·dwal
double	*doble*	do·ble

How much is it per night/person?
¿Cuánto cuesta por kwan·to kwes·ta por
noche/persona? no·che/per·so·na

Does it include breakfast?
¿Incluye el een·kloo·ye el
desayuno? de·sa·yoo·no

campsite	*terreno de cámping*	te·re·no de kam·peeng
hotel	*hotel*	o·tel
guesthouse	*pensión*	pen·syon

KEY PATTERNS

To get by in Spanish, mix and match these simple patterns with words of your choice:

When's (the next flight)?
¿Cuándo sale   kwan·do sa·le
(el próximo vuelo)?   (el prok·see·mo vwe·lo)

Where's (the station)?
¿Dónde está   don·de es·ta
(la estación)?   (la es·ta·syon)

Where can I (buy a ticket)?
¿Dónde puedo   don·de pwe·do
(comprar un billete)?   (kom·prar oon bee·ye·te)

Do you have (a map)?
¿Tiene (un mapa)?   tye·ne (oon ma·pa)

Is there (a toilet)?
¿Hay (servicios)?   ai (ser·vee·syos)

I'd like (a coffee).
Quisiera (un café).   kee·sye·ra (oon ka·fe)

I'd like (to hire a car).
Quisiera (alquilar   kee·sye·ra (al·kee·lar
un coche).   oon ko·che)

Can I (enter)?
¿Se puede (entrar)?   se pwe·de (en·trar)

Could you please (help me)?
¿Puede (ayudarme),   pwe·de (a·yoo·dar·me)
por favor?   por fa·vor

Do I have to (get a visa)?
¿Necesito   ne·se·see·to
(obtener   (ob·te·ner
un visado)?   oon vee·sa·do)

youth hostel	albergue	al·ber·ge
	juvenil	khoo·ve·neel
air-con	aire acondi-	ai·re a·kon·dee·
	cionado	syo·na·do
bathroom	baño	ba·nyo
bed	cama	ka·ma
window	ventana	ven·ta·na

DIRECTIONS

Where's ...?
¿Dónde está ...?   don·de es·ta ...

What's the address?
¿Cuál es la dirección?   kwal es la dee·rek·syon

Could you please write it down?
¿Puede escribirlo,   pwe·de es·kree·beer·lo
por favor?   por fa·vor

Can you show me (on the map)?
¿Me lo puede indicar   me lo pwe·de een·dee·kar
(en el mapa)?   (en el ma·pa)

| at the corner | en la esquina | en la es·kee·na |

at the traffic lights	en el semáforo	en el se·ma·fo·ro
behind ...	detrás de ...	de·tras de ...
far	lejos	le·khos
in front of ...	enfrente de ...	en·fren·te de ...
left	izquierda	ees·kyer·da
near	cerca	ser·ka
next to ...	al lado de ...	al la·do de ...
opposite ...	frente a ...	fren·te a ...
right	derecha	de·re·cha
straight ahead	todo recto	to·do rek·to

EATING & DRINKING

Can I see the menu, please?
¿Puedo ver el menú,   pwe·do ver el me·noo
por favor?   por fa·vor

What would you recommend?
¿Qué recomienda?   ke re·ko·myen·da

Do you have vegetarian food?
¿Tienen comida   tye·nen ko·mee·da
vegetariana?   ve·khe·ta·rya·na

I don't eat (meat).
No como (carne).   no ko·mo (kar·ne)

That was delicious!
¡Estaba buenísimo!   es·ta·ba bwe·nee·see·mo

Cheers!
¡Salud!   sa·loo

The bill, please.
La cuenta, por favor.   la kwen·ta por fa·vor

I'd like a table for ...	Quisiera una mesa para ...	kee·sye·ra oo·na me·sa pa·ra ...
(eight) o'clock	las (ocho)	las (o·cho)
(two) people	(dos) personas	(dos) per·so·nas

Key Words

bottle	botella	bo·te·ya
breakfast	desayuno	de·sa·yoo·no
cold	frío	free·o
dessert	postre	pos·tre
dinner	cena	se·na
fork	tenedor	te·ne·dor
glass	vaso	va·so
hot (warm)	caliente	kal·yen·te
knife	cuchillo	koo·chee·yo
lunch	comida	ko·mee·da
plate	plato	pla·to
restaurant	restaurante	res·tow·ran·te
spoon	cuchara	koo·cha·ra

Meat & Fish

bacon	*tocino*	to·*see*·no
beef	*carne de vaca*	kar·ne de *va*·ka
chicken	*pollo*	po·yo
crab	*cangrejo*	kan·*gre*·kho
duck	*pato*	pa·to
goat	*cabra*	ka·bra
ham	*jamón*	kha·*mon*
lamb	*cordero*	kor·*de*·ro
lobster	*langosta*	lan·*gos*·ta
mutton	*carnero*	kar·*ne*·ro
octopus	*pulpo*	*pool*·po
oysters	*ostras*	os·tras
pork	*cerdo*	*ser*·do
shrimp	*camarones*	ka·ma·ro·nes
squid	*calamar*	ka·la·*mar*
turkey	*pavo*	pa·vo
veal	*ternera*	ter·*ne*·ra
venison	*venado*	ve·*na*·do

Fruit & Vegetables

apple	*manzana*	man·*sa*·na
apricot	*albaricoque*	al·ba·ree·*ko*·ke
banana	*plátano*	*pla*·ta·no
beans	*frijoles*	free·*kho*·les
cabbage	*col*	kol
cactus fruit	*tuna*	*too*·na
carrot	*zanahoria*	sa·na·o·rya
cherry	*cereza*	se·*re*·sa
corn	*maíz*	ma·*ees*
corn (fresh)	*elote*	e·*lo*·te
cucumber	*pepino*	pe·*pee*·no
grape	*uvas*	*oo*·vas
grapefruit	*toronja*	to·*ron*·kha
lentils	*lentejas*	len·*te*·khas
lettuce	*lechuga*	le·*choo*·ga

QUESTION WORDS

How?	*¿Cómo?*	*ko*·mo
What?	*¿Qué?*	ke
When?	*¿Cuándo?*	*kwan*·do
Where?	*¿Dónde?*	*don*·de
Who?	*¿Quién?*	kyen
Why?	*¿Por qué?*	por ke

mushroom	*champiñón*	cham·pee·*nyon*
nuts	*nueces*	nwe·ses
onion	*cebolla*	se·*bo*·ya
orange	*naranja*	na·*ran*·kha
peach	*melocotón*	me·lo·ko·*ton*
peas	*guisantes*	gee·*san*·tes
pepper	*pimiento*	pee·*myen*·to
pineapple	*piña*	*pee*·nya
plantain	*plátano macho*	*pla*·ta·no *ma*·cho
plum	*ciruela*	seer·*we*·la
potato	*patata*	pa·*ta*·ta
pumpkin	*calabaza*	ka·la·*ba*·sa
spinach	*espinacas*	es·pee·*na*·kas
strawberry	*fresa*	*fre*·sa
(red) tomato	*(ji)tomate*	(khee·)to·*ma*·te
watermelon	*sandía*	san·*dee*·a

Other

bread	*pan*	pan
butter	*mantequilla*	man·te·*kee*·ya
cake	*pastel*	pas·*tel*
cheese	*queso*	*ke*·so
cookie	*galleta*	ga·*ye*·ta
(fried) eggs	*huevos (fritos)*	*we*·vos (*free*·tos)
French fries	*papas fritas*	pa·pas *free*·tas
honey	*miel*	myel
ice cream	*helado*	e·*la*·do
jam	*mermelada*	mer·me·*la*·da
pepper	*pimienta*	pee·*myen*·ta
rice	*arroz*	a·*ros*
salad	*ensalada*	en·sa·*la*·da
salt	*sal*	sal
soup	*caldo/sopa*	*kal*·do/*so*·pa
sugar	*azúcar*	a·*soo*·kar

Drinks

beer	*cerveza*	ser·*ve*·sa
coffee	*café*	ka·*fe*
juice	*zumo*	*soo*·mo
milk	*leche*	*le*·che
smoothie	*licuado*	lee·*kwa*·do
sorbet	*nieve*	*nye*·ve
(black) tea	*té (negro)*	te (*ne*·gro)
(mineral) water	*agua (mineral)*	*a*·gwa (mee·ne·*ral*)
(red/white) wine	*vino (tinto/ blanco)*	*vee*·no (*teen*·to/ *blan*·ko)

EMERGENCIES

Help!	¡Socorro!	so·ko·ro
Go away!	¡Vete!	ve·te
Call ...!	¡Llame a ...!	ya·me a ...
a doctor	un médico	oon me·dee·ko
the police	la policía	la po·lee·see·a

I'm lost.
Estoy perdido/a. es·toy per·dee·do/a (m/f)

I'm ill.
Estoy enfermo/a. es·toy en·fer·mo/a (m/f)

It hurts here.
Me duele aquí. me dwe·le a·kee

I'm allergic to (antibiotics).
Soy alérgico/a a soy a·ler·khee·ko/a a
(los antibióticos). (los an·tee·byo·tee·kos) (m/f)

Where are the toilets?
¿Dónde están los don·de es·tan los
baños? ba·nyos

SHOPPING & SERVICES

I'd like to buy ...
Quisiera comprar ... kee·sye·ra kom·prar ...

I'm just looking.
Sólo estoy mirando. so·lo es·toy mee·ran·do

Can I look at it?
¿Puedo verlo? pwe·do ver·lo

I don't like it.
No me gusta. no me goos·ta

How much is it?
¿Cuánto cuesta? kwan·to kwes·ta

That's too expensive.
Es muy caro. es mooy ka·ro

Can you lower the price?
¿Podría bajar un po·dree·a ba·khar oon
poco el precio? po·ko el pre·syo

There's a mistake in the bill.
Hay un error ai oon e·ror
en la cuenta. en la kwen·ta

ATM	cajero automático	ka·khe·ro ow·to·ma·tee·ko
credit card	tarjeta de crédito	tar·khe·ta de kre·dee·to
internet cafe	cibercafé	see·ber·ka·fe
market	mercado	mer·ka·do
post office	correos	ko·re·os
tourist office	oficina de turismo	o·fee·see·na de too·rees·mo

TIME & DATES

What time is it?	¿Qué hora es?	ke o·ra es
It's (10) o'clock.	Son (las diez).	son (las dyes)
It's half past	Es (la una)	es (la oo·na)

NUMBERS

1	uno	oo·no
2	dos	dos
3	tres	tres
4	cuatro	kwa·tro
5	cinco	seen·ko
6	seis	seys
7	siete	sye·te
8	ocho	o·cho
9	nueve	nwe·ve
10	diez	dyes
20	veinte	veyn·te
30	treinta	treyn·ta
40	cuarenta	kwa·ren·ta
50	cincuenta	seen·kwen·ta
60	sesenta	se·sen·ta
70	setenta	se·ten·ta
80	ochenta	o·chen·ta
90	noventa	no·ven·ta
100	cien	syen
1000	mil	meel

(one).	y media.	ee me·dya
morning	mañana	ma·nya·na
afternoon	tarde	tar·de
evening	noche	no·che
yesterday	ayer	a·yer
today	hoy	oy
tomorrow	mañana	ma·nya·na
Monday	lunes	loo·nes
Tuesday	martes	mar·tes
Wednesday	miércoles	myer·ko·les
Thursday	jueves	khwe·ves
Friday	viernes	vyer·nes
Saturday	sábado	sa·ba·do
Sunday	domingo	do·meen·go
January	enero	e·ne·ro
February	febrero	fe·bre·ro
March	marzo	mar·so
April	abril	a·breel
May	mayo	ma·yo
June	junio	khoon·yo
July	julio	khool·yo

August	agosto	a·gos·to
September	septiembre	sep·tyem·bre
October	octubre	ok·too·bre
November	noviembre	no·vyem·bre
December	diciembre	dee·syem·bre

TRANSPORTATION

boat	barco	bar·ko
bus	autobús	ow·to·boos
plane	avión	a·vyon
train	tren	tren
first	primero	pree·me·ro
last	último	ool·tee·mo
next	próximo	prok·see·mo
A ... ticket, please.	Un billete de ..., por favor.	oon bee·ye·te de ... por fa·vor
1st-class	primera clase	pree·me·ra kla·se
2nd-class	segunda clase	se·goon·da kla·se
one-way	ida	ee·da
return	ida y vuelta	ee·da ee vwel·ta

I want to go to ...
Quisiera ir a ...   kee·sye·ra eer a ...

Does it stop at ...?
¿Para en ...?   pa·ra en ...

What stop is this?
¿Cuál es esta parada?   kwal es es·ta pa·ra·da

What time does it arrive/leave?
¿A qué hora llega/   a ke o·ra ye·ga/
sale?   sa·le

Please tell me when we get to ...
¿Puede avisarme   pwe·de a·vee·sar·me
cuando lleguemos   kwan·do ye·ge·mos
a ...?   a ...

I want to get off here.
Quiero bajarme aquí.   kye·ro ba·khar·me a·kee

airport	aeropuerto	a·e·ro·pwer·to
aisle seat	asiento de pasillo	a·syen·to de pa·see·yo
bus stop	parada de autobuses	pa·ra·da de ow·to·boo·ses
cancelled	cancelado	kan·se·la·do
delayed	retrasado	re·tra·sa·do
platform	plataforma	pla·ta·for·ma
ticket office	taquilla	ta·kee·ya
train station	estación de trenes	es·ta·syon de tre·nes

SIGNS

Abierto	Open
Cerrado	Closed
Entrada	Entrance
Hombres/Varones	Men
Mujeres/Damas	Women
Prohibido	Prohibited
Salida	Exit
Servicios/Baños	Toilets

window seat	asiento junto a la ventana	a·syen·to khoon·to a la ven·ta·na
I'd like to hire a ...	Quisiera alquilar ...	kee·sye·ra al·kee·lar ...
4WD	un todo-terreno	oon to·do-te·re·no
bicycle	una bicicleta	oo·na bee·see·kle·ta
car	un coche	oon ko·che
motorcycle	una moto	oo·na mo·to
child seat	asiento de seguridad para niños	a·syen·to de se·goo·ree·da pa·ra nee·nyos
diesel	petróleo	pet·ro·le·o
helmet	casco	kas·ko
hitchhike	hacer botella	a·ser bo·te·ya
mechanic	mecánico	me·ka·nee·ko
petrol/gas	gasolina	ga·so·lee·na
service station	gasolinera	ga·so·lee·ne·ra
truck	camion	ka·myon

Is this the road to ...?
¿Se va a ... por   se va a ... por
esta carretera?   es·ta ka·re·te·ra

(How long) Can I park here?
¿(Cuánto tiempo)   (kwan·to tyem·po)
Puedo aparcar aquí?   pwe·do a·par·kar a·kee

The car has broken down (at ...).
El coche se   el ko·che se
ha averiado (en ...).   a a·ve·rya·do (en ...)

I had an accident.
He tenido un   e te·nee·do oon
accidente.   ak·see·den·te

I've run out of petrol.
Me he quedado sin   me e ke·da·do seen
gasolina.   ga·so·lee·na

I have a flat tyre.
Tengo un pinchazo.   ten·go oon peen·cha·so

MEXICAN SLANG

Pepper your conversations with a few slang expressions! You'll hear many of the following expressions all around Mexico, but some are particular to Mexico City.

¿Qué onda?
What's up?/What's happening?

¿Qué pasión? (Mexico City)
What's up?/What's going on?

¡Qué padre!
How cool!

fregón
really good at something/way cool/ awesome

Este club está fregón.
This club is way cool.

El cantante es un fregón.
The singer is really awesome.

ser muy buena onda
to be really cool/nice

Mi novio es muy buena onda.
My boyfriend is really cool.

Eres muy buena onda.
You're really cool.

pisto (in the north)
booze

alipús
booze

echarse un alipús/trago
to go get a drink

Echamos un alipús/trago.
Let's go have a drink.

tirar la onda
try to pick someone up/flirt

ligar
to flirt

irse de reventón
go partying

¡Vámonos de reventón!
Let's go party!

reven
a 'rave' (huge party with loud music and a wild atmosphere)

un desmadre
a mess

Simón.
Yes.

Nel.
No.

No hay tos.
No problem. (literally: 'there's no cough')

¡Órale! (positive)
Sounds great! (when responding to an invitation)

¡Órale! (negative)
What the ...? (taunting exclamation)

¡Caray!
Shit!

¿Te cae?
Are you serious?

Me late.
Sounds really good to me.

Me vale.
I don't care./Whatever.

Sale y vale.
I agree./Sounds good.

¡Paso sin ver!
I can't stand it!/No, thank you!

¡Guácatelas!/¡Guácala!
How gross!/That's disgusting!

¡Bájale!
Don't exaggerate!/Come on!

¿¿Chale?! (Mexico City)
No way!?

¡Te pasas!
That's it! You've gone too far!

¡No manches!
Get outta here!/You must be kidding!

un resto
a lot

lana
money/dough

carnal
brother

cuate/cuaderno
buddy

chavo
guy/dude

chava
girl/gal

jefe
father

jefa
mother

la tira/julia
the police

la chota (Mexico City)
the police

GLOSSARY

(m) indicates masculine gender, (f) feminine gender, (sg) singular and (pl) plural

adobe – sun-dried mud brick used for building

agave – family of plants with thick, fleshy, usually pointed leaves, from which tequila, mezcal and *pulque* are produced (see also *maguey*)

Alameda – name of formal parks in some Mexican cities

alebrije – colorful wooden animal figure

Ángeles Verdes – Green Angels; government-funded mechanics who patrol Mexico's major highways in green vehicles; they help stranded motorists with fuel and spare parts

arroyo – brook, stream

artesanías – handicrafts, folk arts

atlas (sg), atlantes (pl) – sculpted male figure(s) used instead of a pillar to support a roof or frieze; a telamon

autopista – expressway, dual carriageway

azulejo – painted ceramic tile

bahía – bay

balneario – bathing place; often a natural hot spring

baluarte – bulwark, defensive wall

barrio – neighborhood of a town or city

boleto – ticket

brujo/a (m/f) – witch doctor, shaman; similar to *curandero/a*

burro – donkey

cabaña – cabin, simple shelter

cabina – Baja Californian term for a public telephone call station

cacique – regional warlord; political strongman

calle – street

callejón – alley

calzada – grand boulevard or avenue

camioneta – pickup truck

campesino/a (m/f) – country person, peasant

capilla abierta – open chapel; used in early Mexican monasteries for preaching to large crowds of indigenous people

casa de cambio – exchange house, place where currency is exchanged; faster to use than a bank

casa de huéspedes – cheap and congenial accommodations; often a home converted into simple guest lodgings

caseta de teléfono, caseta telefónica – public telephone call station

cenote – a limestone sinkhole filled with rainwater; often used in Yucatán as a reservoir

central camionera – bus terminal

cerro – hill

Chaac – Maya rain god

chac-mool – pre-Hispanic stone sculpture of a hunched-up figure; the stomach may have been used as a sacrificial altar

charreada – Mexican rodeo

charro – Mexican cowboy

chilango/a (m/f) – person from Mexico City

chinampa – Aztec garden built from lake mud and vegetation; versions still exist at Xochimilco, Mexico City

chultún – cistern found in the Chenes region, in the Puuc hills south of Mérida

Churrigueresque – Spanish late-baroque architectural style; found on many Mexican churches

clavadistas – cliff divers of Acapulco and Mazatlán

colectivo – minibus or car that picks up and drops off passengers along a predetermined route; can also refer to other types of transportation, such as boats, where passengers share the total fare

colonia – neighborhood of a city, often a wealthy residential area

combi – minibus

comedor – food stall

comida corrida – set lunch

completo – no vacancy (literally 'full up'); a sign you may see at hotel desks

conde – count (nobleman)

conquistador – early Spanish explorer-conqueror

cordillera – mountain range

criollo – Mexican-born person of Spanish parentage; in colonial times considered inferior by *peninsulares*

cuota – toll; a *vía cuota* is a toll road

curandero/a (m/f) – literally 'curer'; a medicine man or woman who uses herbal and/or magical methods and often emphasizes spiritual aspects of disease

de paso – a bus that began its route somewhere else, but stops to let passengers on or off at various points

DF – Distrito Federal (Federal District); about half of Mexico City lies in DF

edificio – building

ejido – communal landholding

embarcadero – jetty, boat landing

entremeses – hors d'oeuvres; also theatrical sketches such as those performed during the Cervantino festival in Guanajuato

escuela – school

esq – abbreviation of *esquina* (corner) in addresses

ex-convento – former convent or monastery

feria – fair or carnival, typically occurring during a religious holiday

ferrocarril – railway

fonda – inn; small, family-run eatery

fraccionamiento – subdivision, housing development; similar to a *colonia*, often modern

gringo/a (m/f) – US or Canadian (or other Western) visitor to Latin America; can be used derogatorily

grito – literally 'shout'; the Grito de Dolores was the 1810 call to independence by priest Miguel Hidalgo, sparking the struggle for independence from Spain

gruta – cave, grotto

guayabera – man's shirt with pockets and appliquéd designs up the front, over the shoulders and down the back; worn in hot regions in place of a jacket and tie

hacha – ax; in archaeological contexts, a flat, carved-stone object connected with the ritual ball game

hacienda – estate; Hacienda (capitalized) is the Treasury Department

henequén – agave fiber used to make sisal rope; grown particularly around Mérida

hostal – small hotel or budget hostel

huarache – woven leather sandal, often with tire tread as the sole

huevos – eggs; also slang for testicles

huipil (sg), huipiles (pl) – indigenous woman's sleeveless tunic(s), usually highly decorated; can be thigh-length or reach the ankles

Huizilopochtli – Aztec tribal god

iglesia – church

INAH – Instituto Nacional de Antropología e Historia; the body in charge of most ancient sites and some museums

indígena – indigenous, pertaining to the original inhabitants of Latin America; can also refer to the people themselves

isla – island

IVA – impuesto de valor agregado, or 'ee-vah'; a sales tax added to the price of many items (16% on hotel rooms)

jai alai – the Basque game pelota, brought to Mexico by the Spanish; a bit like squash, played on a long court with curved baskets attached to the arm

jardín – garden

Kukulcán – Maya name for the plumed serpent god Quetzalcóatl

lancha – fast, open, outboard boat

larga distancia – long-distance; usually refers to telephone calls

local – refers to premises, such as a numbered shop or office; a local bus is one whose route starts from the bus station you are in

maguey – agave; sometimes refers specifically to Agave americana, from which pulque is made

malecón – waterfront boulevard or promenade

maquiladora – assembly-plant operation importing equipment, raw materials and parts for assembly or processing in Mexico, then exporting the products

mariachi – small ensemble of street musicians playing traditional ballads on guitars and trumpets

marimba – wooden xylophone-like instrument popular in southeastern Mexico

mercado – market; often a building near the center of a town, with shops and open-air stalls in the surrounding streets

Mesoamerica – historical and archaeological name for central, southern, eastern and southeastern Mexico, Guatemala, Belize and the small ancient Maya area in Honduras

mestizo – person of mixed (usually indigenous and Spanish) ancestry

Mexican Revolution – 1910 revolution that ended the Porfiriato

milpa – peasant's small cornfield, often cultivated using the slash-and-burn method

mirador (sg), miradores (pl) – lookout point(s)

Mudejar – Moorish architectural style imported to Mexico by the Spanish

municipio – small local government area; Mexico is divided into 2394 of them

Nafta – North American Free Trade Agreement

Náhuatl – language of the Nahua people, descendants of the Aztecs

nao – Spanish trading galleon

norteamericano – North American; someone from north of the US–Mexican border

Nte – abbreviation for norte (north); used in street names

Ote – abbreviation for oriente (east); used in street names

palacio de gobierno – state capitol, state government headquarters

palacio municipal – town or city hall, headquarters of the municipal corporation

palapa – thatched-roof shelter, usually on a beach

PAN – Partido Acción Nacional (National Action Party); the political party of Felipe Calderón and his predecessor Vicente Fox

panga – fiberglass skiff for fishing or whale-watching in Baja California

parada – bus stop, usually for city buses

parque nacional – national park; an environmentally protected area in which human exploitation is banned or restricted

parroquia – parish church

paseo – boulevard, walkway or pedestrian street; the tradition of strolling around the plaza in the evening, men and women moving in opposite directions

Pemex – government-owned petroleum extraction, refining and retailing monopoly

peninsulares – those born in Spain and sent by the Spanish government to rule the colony in Mexico

periférico – ring road

pesero – Mexico City's word for *colectivo;* can mean 'bus' in the northeast

peyote – a hallucinogenic cactus

pinacoteca – art gallery

piñata – clay pot or papi-er-mâché mold decorated to resemble an animal, pineapple, star, etc and filled with sweets and gifts, then smashed open at fiestas

pirata – literally 'pirate'; used to describe passenger-carrying pickup trucks in some parts of Mexico

playa – beach

plaza de toros – bullring

plazuela – small plaza

poblano/a (m/f) – person from Puebla; something in the style of Puebla

Porfiriato – reign of Porfirio Díaz as president-dictator of Mexico for 30 years until the 1910 *Mexican Revolution*

portales – arcades

posada – inn

PRI – Partido Revolucionario Institucional (Institutional Rev-olutionary Party); the political party that ruled Mexico for most of the 20th century

Pte – abbreviation for *poniente* (west), used in street names

puerto – port

pulque – milky, low-alcohol brew made from the *maguey* plant

quetzal – crested bird with brilliant green, red and white plumage native to southern Mex-ico, Central America and northern South America; quetzal feathers were highly prized in pre-Hispanic Mexico

Quetzalcóatl – plumed serpent god of pre-Hispanic Mexico

rebozo – long woolen or linen shawl covering women's head or shoulders

refugio – a very basic cabin for shelter in the mountains

reserva de la biosfera – biosphere reserve; an environ-mentally protected area where human exploitation is steered toward sustainable activities

retablo – altarpiece, or small painting placed in a church as thanks for miracles, answered prayers etc

río – river

s/n – *sin número* (without number); used in addresses

sacbé (sg), sacbeob (pl) – ceremonial avenue(s) between great Maya cities

sanatorio – hospital, particularly a small private one

sarape – blanket with opening for the head; worn as a cloak

Semana Santa – Holy Week – the week from Palm Sunday to Easter Sunday; Mexico's major holiday period when accommo-dations and transportation get very busy

sierra – mountain range

sitio – taxi service

stela/stele (sg), stelae/steles (pl) – standing stone monument, usually carved

sur – south; often seen in street names

taller – shop or workshop; a *taller mecánico* is a mechanic's shop, usually for cars; a *taller de llantas* is a tire-repair shop

talud-tablero – stepped building style typical of Teotihuacán, with alternating vertical (*tablero*) and sloping (*talud*) sections

taquilla – ticket window

telamon – statue of a male figure, used instead of a pillar to hold up the roof of a temple; an *atlas*

teleférico – cable car

teléfono (celular) – (cell/mobile) telephone

temascal – pre-Hispanic–style steam bath, often used for curative purposes; sometimes spelt *temazcal*

templo – church; anything from a chapel to a cathedral

teocalli – Aztec sacred precinct

Tezcatlipoca – multifaceted pre-Hispanic god; lord of life and death and protector of warriors; as a smoking mirror he could see into hearts; as the sun god he needed the blood of sacrificed warriors to ensure he would rise again

tezontle – light red, porous vol-canic rock used for buildings by the Aztecs and *conquistadores*

tianguis – indigenous people's market

tienda – store

típico/a (m/f) – characteristic of a region; used to describe food in particular

Tláloc – pre-Hispanic rain and water god

tope – speed bump; found on the outskirts of towns and villages; they are only sometimes marked by signs

trapiche – mill; in Baja California usually a sugar mill

UNAM – Universidad Nacional Autónoma de México (National Autonomous University of Mexico)

universidad – university

voladores – literally 'fliers'; Totonac ritual in which men, suspended by their ankles, whirl around a tall pole

War of Independence – war for Mexican independence from Spain (from 1810 to 1821), ending three centuries of Spanish rule

War of the Castes – 19th-cen-tury Maya uprising in the Yucatán Peninsula

zócalo – literally 'plinth'; used in some Mexican towns for the main plaza or square

Behind the Scenes

SEND US YOUR FEEDBACK

We love to hear from travelers – your comments keep us on our toes and help make our books better. Our well-traveled team reads every word on what you loved or loathed about this book. Although we cannot reply individually to your submissions, we always guarantee that your feedback goes straight to the appropriate authors, in time for the next edition. Each person who sends us information is thanked in the next edition – the most useful submissions are rewarded with a selection of digital PDF chapters.

Visit **lonelyplanet.com/contact** to submit your updates and suggestions or to ask for help. Our award-winning website also features inspirational travel stories, news and discussions.

Note: We may edit, reproduce and incorporate your comments in Lonely Planet products such as guidebooks, websites and digital products, so let us know if you don't want your comments reproduced or your name acknowledged. For a copy of our privacy policy visit lonelyplanet.com/privacy.

OUR READERS

Many thanks to the travelers who used the last edition and wrote to us with helpful hints, useful advice and interesting anecdotes: Werner Baer, Alison Coulby, Dirk Halama, Paul Marc Leclerc, Arturo Madrigal, Sheila Miller, Eleanor Norman, Lucy Stirland

WRITER THANKS
Kate Armstrong
Muchas gracias: Sr Miguel Ángel for his advice and research, Sr Wladamir Hernández Dávila for creating a wonderful jungle-bound trip; Don Gonzalo for orienteering the extreme parts and Bruno Giesemann for his bean-scene passion. A massive thanks to Leah (Mary Poppins) Nichles whose enthusiasm, go-get-'em attitude, strong stomach, and perseverance on looonnng winding bus journeys, helped make the trip. Finally, to Martine Power for the fabulous opportunity, and Tom, Stuart and Ray, and other stalwarts of Team Mexico.

Ray Bartlett
Huge thanks to Martine Power, Tom Masters, Liza Prado, the rest of the LP staff, and to my family and friends. Met such great folks along the way: David, Ari, Eilin, Vanessa, Kimberley, Rachel, Giovanna, Vaneza, Norma, Ayiesha, Victor R, Maaike, Michelle, Stef, Marisol, and everyone else I crossed paths with. Can't wait to be back again soon.

Stuart Butler
As always a huge thanks to my wife, Heather, and children, Jake and Grace, for their patience while I

was away researching in Mexico and they were stuck at home packing up the house in time for the big move. In Mexico, thank you to all the many people I met along the way who helped out in some way or another. Thank you also to Martine back in LP HQ.

Ashley Harrell
Thanks to: my editor Martine Power for entrusting me with this fabulous assignment; my co-authors for their hard work; Vanessa Romo for being hospitable and the most fun; David Peguero Contreras and Jason Rosenburg for showing me their Tijuana; Cabo Pulmo Divers for helping to reconnect me with my passport; Juanita Ames for her wonderful company and vast book collection; and Steve Sparapani and Osa Peligrosa for being the best road-trip buddies a girl could ever ask for.

John Hecht
A heartfelt thank you to Adán Gutiérrez, Ievé López, John Dickie, Clayton Szczech, Darinel Silva and the countless *oaxaqueños* for the helpful tips, great company and free-flowing mezcal! My gratitude also goes out to Martine Power and to the past and present co-authors of this book. As always, a big hug to my wife, Lau, for all her loving support

Anna Kaminski
Thank you to Martine for entrusting me with Mexico's Pacific coast. And to everyone who helped me along the way, including Maaike in Mazatlan, John, Christina, Luis and Trilby in San Blas, Manuel, Lupita and Gloria in Puerto Vallarta, Tom and Liz in Troncones, Robert and Alison in Barra Navidad, Magdaleno in

BEHIND THE SCENES

Zihuatanejo, Jose in Sayulita, the guide at the Xihuacan archaeological site and the taxi driver who helped me find Palma Sola in Acapulco.

Tom Masters

Many thanks to various friends for advice and suggestions about researching Yucatán and Campeche States, especially to Anna Knutson Geller, Álvaro Rodríguez Martín and Alonso Dominguez. Thanks also to the tourist information offices in Mérida, Campeche and Valladolid for their comprehensive help, and for the various guides at dozens of Maya sites across the region, but especially to Abdel Adonay Padilla Ceme at Kukulkan Rising Tours for that dawn alone at Chichén Itzá.

Liza Prado

A shout out to the extraordinary LP Mexico team – I'm so proud to work with you all. *Mil gracias*: *Lalo, Carlitos y los Ramírez por su apoyo infinito*; Mom and Dad, for the love and pride in Mexico you so deeply instilled in me; Joe, Elyse and Susan for your helping hands; Eva and Leo, for your boundless curiosity about my travels (and your patience for my return!). And Gary, *mi corazón* – what can I say? Without you, none of this would be possible. Thank you, always.

Simon Richmond

Muchos gracias to the following: fellow LP writers for their advice and contributions and Martine for hiring me in the first place; Marianne Moore in Xalapa; Peter and Lidia for help in CDMX and getting me to Lago Patzcuaro; and the gorgeous Steve Boyd for his love and wonderful company in CDMX.

Regis St Louis

I'm deeply grateful to Ivan Fernandez in Creel; Juan Pablo and Porfirio in Monterrey; Norma in Saltillo; Martín at Kokoyome; Luís in Cuatro Ciénegas; Miguel León in El Fuerte; Mayté, Jack and Valeria in Casas Grandes; and Lisa, Frank and Katie in San Carlos. Special thanks to Scott Elliott and friends for the warm hospitality in Álamos. And big thanks to co-author Liza Prado for all her help. *Besos* to Cassandra, Magdalena and Genevieve, who joined me for the Copper Canyon adventure.

Phillip Tang

Thanks Martine Power for entrusting me again with CDMX. *Muchas gracias a Lalo (José Eduardo García Sánchez) por la prueba de 'Mexicanísmo' de Malinalco (Chalma no), los cerros de Taxco, los itacates de Tepoz, la espontaneidad de Cuernavaca, y vinilos y desayunos en CDMX. Gracias* Karen Villagómez Bolaños and Armando López Muñoz y Nurit Bielak for CDMX therapy! *Gracias* Daniel Belfield for *restaurantes fresas*, spontaneous taco joints and soggy parasols – '*gentle fondas*' and David always.

ACKNOWLEDGEMENTS

Climate map data adapted from Peel MC, Finlayson BL & McMahon TA (2007) 'Updated World Map of the Köppen-Geiger Climate Classification', Hydrology and Earth System Sciences, 11, 1633-44.

Cover photograph: Día de Muertos (Day of the Dead) doll, ellenkirkpatrick, Getty Images ©

THIS BOOK

This 17th edition of Lonely Planet's *Mexico* guidebook was researched and written by Kate Armstrong, Ray Bartlett, Stuart Butler, Ashley Harrell, John Hecht, Anna Kaminski, Tom Masters, Liza Prado, Simon Richmond, Regis St Louis and Phillip Tang. This guidebook was produced by the following:

Senior Product Editor Martine Power, Daniel Bolger

Product Editor Jenna Myers, Angela Tinson

Regional Senior Cartographer Corey Hutchison

Cartographer Rachel Imeson

Book Designer Wibowo Rusli, Catalina Aragón

Assisting Editors Janet Austin, Melanie Dankel, Carly Hall, Kellie Langon, Jodie Lea Martire, Brana Vladisavlijevic

Cover Researcher Naomi Parker

Thanks to Kate Chapman, Sasha Drew, Amy Lynch, Rachel Rawling, Kirsten Rawlings, James Smart, Vicky Smith, Sarah Stocking

Index

D

E

N

Map Legend

Sights
- Beach
- Bird Sanctuary
- Buddhist
- Castle/Palace
- Christian
- Confucian
- Hindu
- Islamic
- Jain
- Jewish
- Monument
- Museum/Gallery/Historic Building
- Ruin
- Shinto
- Sikh
- Taoist
- Winery/Vineyard
- Zoo/Wildlife Sanctuary
- Other Sight

Activities, Courses & Tours
- Bodysurfing
- Diving
- Canoeing/Kayaking
- Course/Tour
- Sento Hot Baths/Onsen
- Skiing
- Snorkeling
- Surfing
- Swimming/Pool
- Walking
- Windsurfing
- Other Activity

Sleeping
- Sleeping
- Camping
- Hut/Shelter

Eating
- Eating

Drinking & Nightlife
- Drinking & Nightlife
- Cafe

Entertainment
- Entertainment

Shopping
- Shopping

Information
- Bank
- Embassy/Consulate
- Hospital/Medical
- Internet
- Police
- Post Office
- Telephone
- Toilet
- Tourist Information
- Other Information

Geographic
- Beach
- Gate
- Hut/Shelter
- Lighthouse
- Lookout
- Mountain/Volcano
- Oasis
- Park
- Pass
- Picnic Area
- Waterfall

Population
- Capital (National)
- Capital (State/Province)
- City/Large Town
- Town/Village

Transport
- Airport
- Border crossing
- Bus
- Cable car/Funicular
- Cycling
- Ferry
- Metro station
- Monorail
- Parking
- Petrol station
- Subway/Subte station
- Taxi
- Train station/Railway
- Tram
- Underground station
- Other Transport

Routes
- Tollway
- Freeway
- Primary
- Secondary
- Tertiary
- Lane
- Unsealed road
- Road under construction
- Plaza/Mall
- Steps
- Tunnel
- Pedestrian overpass
- Walking Tour
- Walking Tour detour
- Path/Walking Trail

Boundaries
- International
- State/Province
- Disputed
- Regional/Suburb
- Marine Park
- Cliff
- Wall

Hydrography
- River, Creek
- Intermittent River
- Canal
- Water
- Dry/Salt/Intermittent Lake
- Reef

Areas
- Airport/Runway
- Beach/Desert
- Cemetery (Christian)
- Cemetery (Other)
- Glacier
- Mudflat
- Park/Forest
- Sight (Building)
- Sportsground
- Swamp/Mangrove

Note: Not all symbols displayed above appear on the maps in this book

John Hecht

Oaxaca John, a Los Angeles native, has contributed to more than 20 Lonely Planet guidebook and trade publication titles, many of them focused on Latin America and the USA. He is also a published food and entertainment writer. He divides his time between Mexico and California.

Anna Kaminski

Central Pacific Coast Originally from the Soviet Union, Anna grew up in Cambridge, UK. She graduated from the University of Warwick with a degree in Comparative American Studies, a background in the history, culture and literature of the Americas and the Caribbean, and an enduring love of Latin America. Her restless wanderings led her to settle briefly in Oaxaca and Bangkok, and her flirtation with criminal law saw her volunteering as a lawyer's assistant in the courts, ghettos and prisons of Kingston, Jamaica. Anna has contributed to almost 30 Lonely Planet titles. When not on the road, Anna now calls London home.

Tom Masters

Yucatán Peninsula Tom has always had a taste for the remote, the unknown and the forbidden, dating from a childhood fascination with the Soviet Union. These interests have led to a writing career that has taken him to little visited spots all over the world, including North Korea, the Arctic, Congo and Siberia. Since escaping the English countryside at 16, Tom has made London and Berlin home. He currently lives in Berlin and can be found online at www.ambiguations.com.

Liza Prado

Western Central Highlands Liza has been a travel writer since 2003, when she made a move from corporate lawyering (and never looked back). She's written over 40 guidebooks, plus related articles and blogs to destinations throughout the Americas. She takes decent photos, too. Liza is a graduate of Brown University and Stanford Law School. She lives very happily in Denver, Colorado, with her husband and fellow LP writer, Gary Chandler, and their two kids.

Simon Richmond

Veracruz A journalist and photographer, Simon has specialised as a travel writer since the early 1990s and first worked for Lonely Planet in 1999 on their *Central Asia* guide. He's long since stopped counting the number of guidebooks he's researched and written for the company, but countries covered include Australia, China, Greece, India, Indonesia, Iran, Japan, Malaysia, Mexico, Mongolia, Myanmar (Burma), Russia, Singapore, South Africa, South Korea and Turkey and the USA. Simon also wrote the Plan Your Trip, Understand Mexico and Survival Guide chapters.

Regis St Louis

Copper Canyon & Northern Mexico Regis grew up in a small town in the American Midwest – the kind of place that fuels big dreams of travel – and he developed an early fascination with foreign dialects and world cultures. He spent his formative years learning Russian and a handful of Romance languages, which served him well on journeys across much of the globe. Regis has contributed to more than 50 Lonely Planet titles, covering destinations across six continents. His travels have taken him from the mountains of Kamchatka to remote island villages in Melanesia, and to many grand urban landscapes. When not on the road, he lives in New Orleans.

Phillip Tang

Mexico City, Around Mexico City Phillip grew up on a typically Australian diet of pho and fish'n'chips before moving to Mexico City. A degree in Chinese and Latin-American cultures launched him into travel and then writing about it for Lonely Planet's *Canada*, *China*, *Japan*, *Korea*, *Mexico*, *Peru* and *Vietnam* guides. Writing at hellophillip.com, photos @mrtangtangtang, and tweets @philliptang.

OUR STORY

A beat-up old car, a few dollars in the pocket and a sense of adventure. In 1972 that's all Tony and Maureen Wheeler needed for the trip of a lifetime – across Europe and Asia overland to Australia. It took several months, and at the end – broke but inspired – they sat at their kitchen table writing and stapling together their first travel guide, *Across Asia on the Cheap*. Within a week they'd sold 1500 copies. Lonely Planet was born.

Today, Lonely Planet has offices in Franklin, Dublin and Beijing, with more than 600 staff and writers. We share Tony's belief that 'a great guidebook should do three things: inform, educate and amuse'.

OUR WRITERS

Kate Armstrong

Chiapas & Tabasco Kate has spent much of her adult life traveling and living around the world. A full-time freelance travel journalist, she has contributed to over 50 Lonely Planet guides and trade publications and is regularly published in Australian and worldwide publications. She is the author of several books and children's educational titles. Over the years, Kate has worked in Mozambique, picked grapes in France and danced in a Bolivian folkloric troupe. A keen photographer, greedy gourmand and frenetic festival goer, she enjoys exploring off-the-beaten track locations, restaurants and theatres.

You can read more about her on www.katearmstrongtravelwriter.com and @nomaditis.

Ray Bartlett

Yucatán Peninsula Ray has been travel writing for nearly two decades, bringing Japan, Korea, Mexico, Tanzania, Guatemala, Indonesia, and many parts of the United States to life in rich detail for top-industry publishers, newspapers, and magazines. His acclaimed debut novel, *Sunsets of Tulum*, set in Yucatán, was a Midwest Book Review 2016 Fiction pick. Among other pursuits, he surfs regularly and is an accomplished Argentine tango dancer. Follow him on Facebook, Twitter, Instagram, or contact him for questions or motivational speaking opportunities via www.kaisora.com, his website.

Stuart Butler

Northern Central Highlands Stuart has been writing for Lonely Planet for a decade, and during this time he's come eye to eye with gorillas in the Congolese jungles, met a man with horns on his head who could lie in fire, huffed and puffed over snowbound Himalayan mountain passes, interviewed a king who could turn into a tree, and had his fortune told by a parrot. Oh, and he's met more than his fair share of self-proclaimed Gods. When not on the road for Lonely Planet he lives on the beautiful beaches of Southwest France with his wife and two young children.

Ashley Harrell

Baja Peninsula After a brief stint selling day-spa coupons door-to-door in South Florida, Ashley decided she'd rather be a writer. She went to journalism grad school, convinced a newspaper to hire her, and started covering wildlife, crime and tourism, sometimes all in the same story. Fueling her zest for storytelling and the unknown, she traveled widely and moved often, from a tiny NYC apartment to a vast California ranch to a jungle cabin in Costa Rica, where she started writing for Lonely Planet. From there her travels became more exotic and farther flung, and she still laughs when paychecks arrive.

◀ OVER MORE
PAGE WRITERS

Published by Lonely Planet Global Limited
CRN 554153
17th edition – Nov 2021
ISBN 978 1 78701 716 0
© Lonely Planet 2021   Photographs © as indicated 2021
10 9 8 7 6 5 4 3 2 1
Printed in Singapore

Although the authors and Lonely Planet have taken all reasonable care in preparing this book, we make no warranty about the accuracy or completeness of its content and, to the maximum extent permitted, disclaim all liability arising from its use.

All rights reserved. No part of this publication may be copied, stored in a retrieval system, or transmitted in any form by any means, electronic, mechanical, recording or otherwise, except brief extracts for the purpose of review, and no part of this publication may be sold or hired, without the written permission of the publisher. Lonely Planet and the Lonely Planet logo are trademarks of Lonely Planet and are registered in the US Patent and Trademark Office and in other countries. Lonely Planet does not allow its name or logo to be appropriated by commercial establishments, such as retailers, restaurants or hotels. Please let us know of any misuses: lonelyplanet.com/ip.